NATIVE AMERICA
IN THE TWENTIETH CENTURY

Garland Reference Library of Social Science (Vol. 452)

NATIVE AMERICA
IN THE TWENTIETH CENTURY

An Encyclopedia

Edited by
Mary B. Davis

Assistant Editors
Joan Berman
Mary E. Graham
Lisa A. Mitten

Garland Publishing, Inc.
New York & London
1994

Library of Congress Cataloging–in–Publication Data

Native America in the twentieth century : an encyclopedia / edited by
Mary B. Davis.
      p. cm. — (Garland reference library of social science ; v. 452)
    Includes bibliographical references and index.
    ISBN 0-8240-4846-6 (alk. paper)
    1. Indians of North America—Encyclopedias.   I. Davis, Mary B.
II. Series.
E76.2.N36   1994
970.004'97'003—dc20   94-768
                                        CIP

Cover photograph of Bernice Roybal and Juan Cruz entitled
"Juan Cruz with his granddaughter Bernice—San Ildefonso Pueblo."

Photograph copyright © 1994 by Marcia Keegan.
Reprinted by permission of Marcia Keegan.

Cover design by Patti Hefner.

Printed on acid-free, 250-year-life paper
Manufactured in the United States of America

For my father, Maurice E. Beckett, and in memory of my mother, Margaret Henking Beckett.

CONTENTS

FOREWORD

As we look toward the twenty-first century, our understanding and appreciation of American Indian cultures are finally approaching the level they so greatly deserve. As director of the National Museum of the American Indian, I have experienced, firsthand, this desire to learn more about Indian peoples and cultures, to recognize the importance of our past and present, to understand our ways of life, and to fully appreciate the immense contributions of our ancestors to what all of us call "civilization."

As we look to the new millennium, our need to appreciate the worth of what Native cultures have to offer is paramount. *Native America in the Twentieth Century: An Encyclopedia*, which has been over six years in the making, provides valuable historical perspective in an accurate and factual manner. In addition this volume focuses on the significance of the Indians living in the Americas today and, in so doing, confirms that we remain a living, breathing, continually evolving culture that hardly deserves to be merely catalogued and placed on a museum shelf. The *Encyclopedia* represents a wonderful way for Indian America to share its remarkable history and cultural contributions, past and present, so that all of us can draw upon their values and teachings in our future together.

W. Richard West, Jr.

PREFACE

At the dawn of the twentieth century, the belief that Native Americans would vanish into the surrounding Euroamerican culture was an underlying assumption of the American public and United States government policy. In the last decade of the twentieth century the basic fallacies in this assumption are obvious: Indian people are still here; moreover, they are rapidly increasing in both power and numbers. In many ways the story of how many of America's First Peoples went from projected oblivion to their current positions of strength and cultural continuity and revitalization is the story of this encyclopedia.

Unfortunately, the stereotype of a "vanishing people" still persists, despite vigorous efforts of Native American groups and individuals to dispel the myth of "Indian as past," and recent attempts by authors and publishers to bring the people in their books into the modern era. This encyclopedia attempts to redress this stereotype by providing a reference tool devoted to Native America in the twentieth century.

The encyclopedia does not attempt to portray America's Native peoples from a particular point of view. Its signed articles are written by historians, anthropologists, and other specialists, who represent a wide range on the political spectrum. They come from professions running the gamut from tribal office to academia. In many cases this information is presented from a Native viewpoint, further enlarging the perspectives included. The diversity of the contributors ensures a diversity in styles and content for their articles. All felt it of paramount importance, however, to discuss the subjects of their articles in accurate, meaningful ways.

The encyclopedia covers important aspects of Native American life in the United States during this century. Arranged alphabetically, the encyclopedia has overview articles on such subjects as art, economic conditions, educational policy, government policy, health, languages, law, public opinion, Red Power, religion, and reservations. In many cases, the encyclopedia includes articles on specific facets of these broad subjects. A general listing of articles by subject at the beginning of the volume complements a detailed subject index at its end.

There are areas not covered by the encyclopedia. Organizational and space constraints made inclusive coverage of twentieth-century Native affairs in Canada impractical. An independent volume will be necessary to do justice to this complex area. Biographical entries were also excluded from the encyclopedia's scope. The sheer number of individuals who merit inclusion in a biographical work points to the need for a book that deals solely with this subject.

More than half of the encyclopedia's articles are devoted to twentieth-century Native nations. In the subject breakdown they are listed by geographic area. It was necessary to handle tribal entries in several ways, depending on the history of the nation(s) and the preference of the contributors writing the articles. In most cases a single article is devoted to a single Indian nation. In some cases, when a group's political units (usually reservations) are in different geographical locations, one article covers all of them. In others, separate articles discuss the parts of a group residing in a particular state or geographic area. Still others are organized by linguistic or political grouping. "See references" in the text guide the reader to appropriate articles.

The late-twentieth-century debate over correct terminology is nowhere more evident than in discussions about Native peoples. In this book the contributors speak with their own voices. Some authors use the term "American Indians" or "Indians," others discuss "Native Americans," still others employ the term "Native," and some authors use them all. There is also great variety in the use of "tribe" or "nation." Some contributors exercised their authorial privilege, usually in consultation with the tribe, to choose the name under which the group is listed. In these cases and others, "see references" are incorporated in the text to guide readers to the terminology in use. Here and elsewhere we have tried to honor the wishes of contributors and tribal officials without impairing ease of access to information.

Inevitably, errors of fact, analysis, and omission will be found in the encyclopedia, despite our efforts to eliminate them. Its articles, however, provide readers with an opportunity to begin to investigate the realities of Native American life in the twentieth century. It is a story that will continue to be told and retold, increasingly incorporating voices from the communities involved. The editors of the encyclopedia are proud to be involved with this effort.

ACKNOWLEDGMENTS

When this project began six years ago, I had no idea of its complexity, or that I would spend literally all of my free time working toward finishing it. The encyclopedia's advisors were involved almost from the beginning. I am very grateful to all of them for their assistance and for their encouragement. Bryan Johnson actively participated in developing the concept for the encyclopedia, and I acknowledge his involvement in its early stages. Joan Berman, Mary Graham, and Lisa Mitten entered the project midstream as assistant editors. They have been wonderful to work with and crucial partners in the book's completion.

In many ways, my contacts with the encyclopedia's contributors were the highlight of the project. Almost all were strangers, yet they spent their time and effort to make this book what it is. Many not only worked on their own articles but read and commented upon those of others as well. This book is theirs, for without them it would not exist.

In a book this size, organization and delineation of article topics is a major endeavor, peer review is critical, and fact-checking sometimes very illusive. Several individuals, along with advisory board members, assisted me in these tasks. For tribal assignments they include Thomas Blumer, C.B. Clark, Hiram Gregory, and Alice Kasakoff for the Southeast; Lowell Bean, Lee Davis, Allogan Slagle, and Dorothea Theodoratus for California; Stephen Beckham, Daniel Boxberger, Bruce Miller, Rudolph Ryser, Nile Thompson, and Kenneth Tollefson for the Pacific Northwest; Deward Walker for the Plateau; and Catherine Fowler for the Great Basin. Others who helped with the formulation, evaluation, and/or fact-checking sections of the encyclopedia include Eulalie Bonar, Gary Galante, Robert Grumet, Edward Morgan, Donald Parman, Anna Roosevelt, and Margaret Szasz. Armand La Potin and Marie H. Martin were generous with their advice on editing procedures. Any organizational errors that crept in despite the wise counsel of all those mentioned above are, of course, my own.

Sharon Dean of the Photography Department of the National Museum of the American Indian was generous with both time and assistance in locating photographs from that collection. I am also grateful to Christy Hoffman of the School of American Research, Arthur Olivas of the Museum of New Mexico, Geoffrey E. Stamm of the Indian Arts and Crafts Board, Julie Droke of the Oklahoma Museum of Natural History, and Susan Otto of the Milwaukee Public Museum for help in identifying and providing photographs from their respective collections. Thanks go to Gallery 10, Riva Yares Gallery, John Running, and Navajo Gallery for their generous assistance with images. I greatly appreciate the cooperation of the many artists who provided photographs and/or permissions for publication of their work.

Help also came from other areas. The board of trustees of the Huntington Free Library gave me a half-time sabbatical so work could proceed on the encyclopedia. George Cohen, Tom Klingenstein, and Richard Marks of Cohen, Davis & Marks kindly provided photocopying and faxing when I needed them most. The staff of the Huntington Free Library, especially Catherine McChesney and Catherine Sorrell, helped out in ways too numerous to mention. My thanks also to my colleagues at the National Museum of the American Indian who pitched in when needed. The people at Garland Publishing—Phyllis Korper, Gary Kuris, Helga McCue, and Chuck Bartelt—proved amazingly unflappable and very supportive. Finally, I must mention my family—Richard, Ellen, and Joe—who smiled when I said I had to work, and who are still willing to listen to me talk about "the book." Thank you.

Mary B. Davis, Bronx, NY

I feel very privileged to have discovered the network of people in Alaska who were so encouraging and supportive. David Hales, Michael Krauss, and David Maas were particularly helpful at different stages in the process. Administrative support by the Humboldt State University Library is gratefully acknowledged.

Joan Berman, Arcata, CA

I thank David Klanderman for his patience, encouragement, and good humor. My gratitude also goes to Raymond H. Thompson, director; R. Gwinn Vivian, associate director; and George Sample, former assistant director, of the Arizona State Museum for all of their support. Colleagues at the Arizona State Museum were also extremely helpful: thanks go to Madelyn Cook and Anne Laurie, Arizona State Museum Library, for their support and Diane Dittemore and Tom Kolaz for their help in filling in an important gap. James Moore, Laboratory of Anthropology, Museum of New Mexico, provided much needed help in New Mexico, and I am grateful to Irene Silentman, Ph.D. candidate, University of Arizona, for her Navajo language expertise. My thanks to Alan Ferg and Lynn Teague for their important help with some of the articles. Finally, my appreciation goes to all the contributors for their hard work, and to the various tribal authorities for their interest and support.

Mary E. Graham, Tucson, AZ

A work of this scope has a lot more input than can ever be revealed by the usual statements of responsibility. Besides the obvious debts of gratitude to all of the authors, I especially thank Brian Baker and Ted Jojola for their never-ending good humor and words of encouragement, my daughter Jessica for her ability to deal with my long confinements in front of the computer screen, and Mary Davis, who was so much fun to work with. I am grateful to the administration of the University Library System at the University of Pittsburgh for their generous support of my participation in this project.

Lisa A. Mitten, Pittsburgh, PA

Credits

A longer version of Frank Pommersheim's article on the Black Hills appeared in the spring 1988 issue of *Wicazo Sa Review*. A passage from Vine Deloria, Jr.'s *Behind the Trail of Broken Treaties* (Delta Books, 1974, p. 47–48) is quoted in Roxanne Dunbar Ortiz's article on the Trail of Broken Treaties. Other credits are acknowledged in the text. We are grateful for permission to publish from all of these sources.

ADVISORY BOARD

Michael Asch
Professor of Anthropology
University of Alberta
Edmonton, Alberta
Canada

D.C. Cole (Chiricahua Apache)
Professor of American Studies
Moorhead State University
Moorhead, MN

Frederick J. Dockstader (Oneida descent)
Adjunct Professor of Art History
Arizona State University
Tempe, AZ

Laurence M. Hauptman
Professor of History
State University of New York
College at New Paltz
New Paltz, NY

Arlene B. Hirschfelder
Author and Consultant
Native American Studies
Teaneck, NJ

Arlinda F. Locklear (Lumbee)
Attorney
Jefferson, MD

CONTRIBUTORS

The Native heritage of many contributors is listed directly beneath their names

D.K. Abbass
Newport, RI
(Ribbonwork)

George H.J. Abrams
(Seneca)
Hackensack, NJ
(Seneca)

John Active
(Yup'ik)
KYUK Radio & T.V.
Bethel, AK
(Yup'ik)

Anita Alvarez de Williams
Calexico, CA
(Cocopah)

S. James Anaya
College of Law
University of Iowa
Iowa City, IA
(Fishing and Hunting Rights; International Law; National Indian Youth Council)

Will D. Antell
(Anishinabe)
Minnesota Department of Education
Minneapolis, MN
(National Indian Education Association)

JoAllyn Archambault
(Standing Rock Sioux)
American Indian Program
National Museum of Natural History
Smithsonian Institution
Washington, DC
(Beadwork; Quillwork)

Warren L. d'Azevedo
Department of Anthropology
University of Nevada-Reno
Reno, NV
(Washoe)

W. David Baird
Department of History
Pepperdine University
Malibu, CA
(Quapaw)

Brian Baker
(Bad River Chippewa)
Department of Sociology, Anthropology, and Social Work
Central Michigan University
Mt. Pleasant, MI
(Ojibwa: Anishinabe in Wisconsin)

Dave Baldridge
(Cherokee)
National Indian Council on Aging
Albuquerque, NM
(Elders)

John W. Barry
Davis, CA
(Pottery; Pueblo of Pojoaque)

Jennifer D. Bates
(Northern Mewuk)
Bear n' Coyote Gallery
Jamestown, CA
(Miwok: Sierra Mewuk)

Lowell John Bean
Cultural Systems Research, Inc./Ballena Press
Oakland, CA
(Cahuilla; Chemehuevi; Cupeño; Gabrielino/Tongva; Serrano)

Patrick H. Beckett
COAS Publishing and Research
Las Cruces, NM
(Tortugas)

Stephen Dow Beckham
Lewis & Clark College
Portland, OR
(Chinook; Confederated Coos, Lower Umpqua and Siuslaw; Confederated Tribes of Siletz; Cow Creek Band of Umpqua; Tillamook)

Robert L. Bee
Department of Anthropology
University of Connecticut
Storrs, CT
(Quechan)

Richard Bellon
Confederated Tribes of the Chehalis
Reservation
Oakville, WA
*(Confederated Tribes of the Chehalis
Reservation)*

Marilyn G. Bentz
(Gros Ventre)
American Indian Studies
University of Washington
Seattle, WA
(Quinault)

Alison R. Bernstein
Education and Culture Program
The Ford Foundation
New York, NY
*(Military Service; National Congress
of American Indians)*

Brian Bibby
Sloughhouse, CA
(Maidu)

Martha Royce Blaine
Oklahoma City, OK
(Pawnee)

Thomas J. Blumer
Law Library of Congress
Library of Congress
Washington, DC
(Catawba; Edisto; Pamunkey; PeeDee; Santee)

John J. Bodine
Department of Anthropology
The American University
Washington, DC
(Pueblo of Picuris; Pueblo of Taos)

Loren J. Bommelyn
(Tolowa)
Crescent City, CA
(Tolowa)

Eulalie H. Bonar
National Museum of the American Indian
Smithsonian Institution
New York, NY
(Textiles: Southwest)

Peter MacMillan Booth
Purdue University
West Lafayette, IN
(Pee-Posh)

Daniel L. Boxberger
Department of Anthropology
Western Washington University
Bellingham, WA
(Duwamish; Klallam; Lummi; Sauk-Suiattle)

Paul Boyer
Tribal College: Journal of American Indian
Higher Education
Chestertown, MD
(Tribal Colleges)

Elizabeth A. Brandt
Department of Anthropology
Arizona State University
Tempe, AZ
(Pueblo of Sandia)

Donald N. Brown
Department of Sociology
Oklahoma State University
Stillwater, OK
(Ponca: Southern)

Thomas Buckley
Department of Anthropology
University of Massachusetts/Boston
Boston, MA
(Yurok)

Pamela A. Bunte
Department of Anthropology
California State University, Long Beach
Long Beach, CA
(Paiute: Southern)

Helen Chalakee Burgess
(Muscogee Creek)
Oklahoma City, OK
(Citizenship and Enfranchisement)

Larry W. Burt
Department of History
Southwest Missouri State University
Springfield, MO
*(Government Policy: Termination and
Restoration)*

Lloyd Burton
Graduate School of Public Affairs
University of Colorado at Denver
Denver, CO
(Water Rights)

Elda J. Butler
(Fort Mojave Tribe)
Needles, CA
(Mojave)

Kristie Lee Butler
Arizona State University
Tempe, AZ
(Navajo)

Naomi Caldwell-Wood
(Ramapough)
Clarion, PA
(Ramapough)

Donald G. Callaway
National Park Service
Anchorage, AK
(Ute)

Ralph Cameron
(Pee-Posh)
Laveen, AZ
(Pee-Posh)

Gregory Camp
Department of History
Minot State University
Minot, ND
(Ojibwa: Chippewa in North Dakota)

Gregory R. Campbell
Department of Anthropology
University of Montana
Missoula, MT
(Cheyenne; Cree; Indian Health Service)

Jack Campisi
Research Associates
Red Hook, NY
(Coharie; Haliwa-Saponi; Iroquois Confederacy; Lumbee; Oneida; Waccamaw-Siouan)

Leonard A. Carlson
Department of Economics
Emory University
Atlanta, GA
(Allotment; Government Policy: 1900-1933)

Cecelia Svinth Carpenter
(Nisqually)
Tahoma Research Service
Tacoma, WA
(Nisqually)

Edward D. Castillo
(Cahuilla)
Native American Studies
Sonoma State University
Rohnert Park, CA
(Mission Indian Federation)

Duane Champagne
(Turtle Mountain Chippewa)
Sociology Department
University of California, Los Angeles
Los Angeles, CA
(Bureau of Indian Affairs)

Henry H.C. Choong
Scarborough, Ontario
(Assiniboine)

Ward Churchill
(Creek-Cherokee Métis)
Center for Studies of Ethnicity
and Race in America
University of Colorado at Boulder
Boulder, CO
(American Indian Movement; Red Power; Wounded Knee II)

Blue Clark
(Muscogee Creek)
Oklahoma City University
Oklahoma City, OK
(Chickasaw)

Nicholas L. Clark, Sr.
(Adopted Miami)
Minnetrista Council for Great Lakes Native
American Studies
Minnetrista Cultural Center
Muncie, IN
(Miami)

Robert N. Clinton
College of Law
University of Iowa
Iowa City, IA
(Sovereignty and Jurisdiction)

Richmond L. Clow
Native American Studies Program
University of Montana
Missoula, MT
(Natural Resource Management)

D.C. Cole
(Chiricahua Apache)
Department of American Studies
Moorehead State University
Moorehead, MN
(Apache)

Stephen Colt
Institute of Social and Economic Research
University of Alaska, Anchorage
Anchorage, AK
(Alaska Native Regional Corporations)

Terry L. Corbett
Las Cruces, NM
(Tortugas)

Jeanette Henry Costo
(Eastern Cherokee)
American Indian Historical Society
San Francisco, CA
(American Indian Historical Society)

Thomas W. Cowger
Purdue University
Lafayette, IN
(Klamath)

Rachel Craig
(Iñupiaq [Northern Eskimo])
Northwest Arctic Borough
Kotzebue, AK
(Iñupiat)

Lorraine J. Cross
(Muckleshoot)
Muckleshoot Indian Tribe
Auburn, WA
(Muckleshoot)

Steven J. Crum
(Western Shoshone)
Native American Studies
University of California, Davis
Davis, CA
(Higher Education; Shoshone: Western)

Edmund J. Danziger, Jr.
Department of History
Bowling Green State University
Bowling Green, OH
(Government Policy: Self-Determination)

Dorothy W. Davids
(Stockbridge-Munsee)
Stockbridge-Munsee Historical Committee
Bowler, WI
(Stockbridge-Munsee)

Michael G. Davis
Department of Anthropology
Northeast Missouri State University
Kirksville, MO
(Plains Apache)

Vine Deloria, Jr.
(Standing Rock Sioux)
Center for Studies of Ethnicity and Race in
America
University of Colorado at Boulder
Boulder, CO
(Treaties)

William G. Demmert, Jr.
(Tlingit)
Department of Anthropology
Western Washington University
Bellingham, WA
(Indian Education Act, 1972; Public Schools)

Tom Diamond
El Paso, TX
(Ysleta del Sur Pueblo)

Frederick J. Dockstader
New York, NY
(Art; Silverwork and Other Jewelry)

Roxanne Dunbar Ortiz
California State University, Hayward
Hayward, CA
*(International Indian Treaty Council; Russell
Tribunal; Trail of Broken Treaties)*

N. Bruce Duthu
(Houma)
Vermont Law School
South Royalton, VT
(Houma)

Patricia A. Dyer
(Little Traverse Bay Bands of Odawa/Chahta)
Michigan State University
Lansing, MI
(Ottawa/Odawa in Michigan)

Rick Eckert
(Bad River Chippewa)
Department of Sociology, Anthropology, and
Social Work
Central Michigan University
Mt. Pleasant, MI
(Ojibwa: Anishinabe in Wisconsin)

R. David Edmunds
Department of History
Indiana University
Bloomington, IN
*(Mesquaki; Otoe-Missouria; Potawatomi in
Oklahoma)*

Janet P. Eidsness
BioSystems Analysis
Santa Cruz, CA
(Salinan)

Andrea Hawley Ellis
Florence Hawley Ellis Archives
Albuquerque, NM
(Pueblo of Santa Ana; Pueblo of Zia)

Joanna Endter-Wada
College of Natural Resources
Utah State University
Logan, UT
(Ute)

Nancy H. Evans
Newport Beach, CA
(Pit River)

Suzanne Fabricius
Office of Museum Programs
Smithsonian Institution
Washington, DC
(Tribal Museums)

Melissa Fawcett
(Mohegan)
Mohegan Tribal Office
Uncasville, CT
(Mohegan)

Catherine Feher-Elston
History Department
Northern Arizona University
Flagstaff, AZ
(Navajo-Hopi Land Controversy)

T.J. Ferguson
Southwest Program
Institute of the NorthAmerican West
Tucson, AZ
(Zuni)

Darleen A. Fitzpatrick
Everett Community College
Seattle, WA
(Tulalip)

Donald L. Fixico
(Shawnee, Sac and Fox, Muscogee Creek,
Seminole)
Department of History
Western Michigan University
Kalamazoo, MI
(Mining)

Amelia Flores
(Mohave)
Library
Colorado River Indian Tribes
Parker, AZ
(Colorado River Indian Tribes)

Jack D. Forbes
(Powhatan-Delaware)
Native American Studies Program
University of California, Davis
Davis, CA
(Powhatan/Renápe; Race Relations; Red-Black
People)

Lance M. Foster
(Iowa)
Department of Anthropology
Iowa State University
Ames, IA
(Iowa)

Catherine S. Fowler
Department of Anthropology
University of Nevada
Reno, NV
(Paiute: Northern; Paiute: Owens Valley)

Shawn Frank
American University
Washington, DC
(Gaming)

Robert J. Franklin
Department of Anthropology
California State University, Dominguez Hills
Carson, CA
(Paiute: Southern)

Rodney Frey
Division of Social Sciences
Lewis-Clark State College
Coeur d'Alene, ID
(Crow)

Nancy J. Fuller
Office of Museum Programs
Smithsonian Institution
Washington, DC
(Tribal Museums)

Walter Funmaker
(Winnebago)
Native American Institute
Mansfield University
Mansfield, PA
(Winnebago in Wisconsin)

J.T. Garrett
(Eastern Band of Cherokee Indians)
Gaithersburg, MD
(Health)

Joseph M. Giovannetti
(Tolowa)
Eureka, CA
(Indian Shaker Church)

Gerald E. Gipp
(Standing Rock Sioux)
Administration for Native Americans
Washington, DC
(Johnson-O'Malley Act)

Lynne Goldstein
Department of Anthropology
University of Wisconsin, Milwaukee
Milwaukee, WI
(Archaeology)

Victor Golla
Department of Ethnic Studies
Humboldt State University
Arcata, CA
(Languages)

Linda J. Goodman
Office of Archaeological Studies
Museum of New Mexico
Santa Fe, NM
(Pueblo of San Juan)

Lana S. Grant
(Sac and Fox and Shawnee)
School of Library and Information Studies
University of Oklahoma
Norman, OK
(Sac and Fox)

Hiram F. Gregory
Department of Anthropology
Northwestern State University of Louisiana
Natchitoches, LA
(Chitimacha; Tunica-Biloxi)

Stephen Greymorning
(Arapaho)
Arapaho Language and Culture Project
Northern Arapaho Tribe
Ethete, WY
(Arapaho)

Elizabeth S. Grobsmith
Academic Affairs, Summer Sessions
University of Nebraska-Lincoln
Lincoln, NE
(*Ponca: Northern; Prisons and Prisoners*)

George M. Guilmet
Department of Comparative Sociology
University of Puget Sound
Tacoma, WA
(*Puyallup*)

Peter R. Hacker
Department of History
Texas Christian University
Fort Worth, TX
(*Shawnee in Oklahoma*)

Betty L. Hall
(Shasta)
Fort Jones, CA
(*Shasta*)

Monica J. Hall
Fort Jones, CA
(*Shasta*)

Carol Hampton
(Caddo)
American Indian/Alaska Native Ministry
Episcopal Church
Oklahoma City, OK
(*Caddo*)

Kenneth C. Hansen
(Samish)
Shoalwater Bay Indian Tribe
Tokeland, WA
(*Shoalwater*)

Jana Harcharek
(Iñupiaq)
Commission on Iñupiat History, Language and
Culture
North Slope Borough
Barrow, AK
(*Whaling*)

Suzan Shown Harjo
(Cheyenne and Hodulgee Muscogee)
Morning Star Institute
Washington, DC
(*Senate Committee on Indian Affairs*)

Vernon Harragarra
(Otoe-Missouria)
Denver, CO
(*Housing*)

LaDonna Harris
(Comanche)
Americans for Indian Opportunity
Bernalillo, NM
(*Americans for Indian Opportunity*)

Jay Harwood
(Blackfeet)
Sacramento, CA
(*Rodeos*)

Laurence M. Hauptman
Department of History
State University of New York, New Paltz
New Paltz, NY
(*Abenaki: Western; American Indian Chicago
Conference; American Indian Federation;
Indian Reorganization Act; Iroquois
Confederacy; Seneca-Cayuga*)

Stephen Haycox
History Department
University of Alaska, Anchorage
Anchorage, AK
(*Alaska Native Brotherhood/Sisterhood*)

Russell Hayward
(Tsimshian)
Metlakatla, AK
(*Tsimshian of Metlakatla*)

Kathy Heffner-McClellan
(Wailaki)
McKinleyville, CA
(*Wailaki; Wiyot*)

Inés Hernández
(Nez Perce)
Native American Studies
University of California, Davis
Davis, CA
(*Chicanos as Indians*)

Charlotte Heth
(Cherokee Nation of Oklahoma)
Department of Ethnomusciology
University of California, Los Angeles
Los Angeles, CA
(*Music*)

Louis A. Hieb
University of Arizona Library
Tucson, AZ
(*Hopi*)

Michael J. Hill
(Blackfeet)
Salish Kootenai College
Pablo, MT
(*Blackfeet; Confederated Salish and Kootenai
Tribes*)

Norbert S. Hill, Jr.
(Oneida)
American Indian Science and
Engineering Society
Boulder, CO
(*American Indian Science and Engineering
Society*)

Arlene B. Hirschfelder
New School for Social Research
New York, NY
*(Association on American Indian Affairs;
Navajo Code Talkers)*

Carol Holmes-Wermuth
Kernville, CA
(Tubatulabal)

Herbert T. Hoover
Department of History
University of South Dakota
Vermillion, SD
*(Dakota; Sioux Federation; Yankton and
Yanktonai)*

Eugene S. Hunn
Department of Anthropology
University of Washington
Seattle, WA
*(Columbia River Indians; Confederated Tribes
of the Warm Springs Reservation)*

R. Douglas Hurt
Department of History
Iowa State University
Ames, IA
(Agriculture: 1950 to 1993)

Sally Hyer
Santa Fe, NM
(Pueblo of San Felipe)

**Staff of IKWAI Foundation of Organized
Resources in Cultural Equity**
Choctaw, OK
(Kickapoo in Oklahoma and Texas)

Gilbert C. Innis
(Pima, Tohono O'odham, Maricopa)
Tribal Education
Gila River Indian Community
Sacaton, AZ
(Pima)

M.A. Jaimes
(California Mission Band Juaneño and Yaqui)
Center for Studies of Ethnicity and Race in
America
University of Colorado at Boulder
Boulder, CO
(Indian Identity; Pan-Indianism)

Jessie James-Hawley
(Gros Ventre)
Harlem, MT
(Gros Ventre)

John R. Johnson
Santa Barbara Museum of Natural History
Santa Barbara, CA
(Chumash; Kitanemuk)

Theodore S. Jojola
(Isleta Pueblo)
Native American Studies
University of New Mexico
Albuquerque, NM
(Public Image)

Matthew L. Jones
(Kiowa and Otoe-Missouria)
Native American Public
Broadcasting Consortium
Lincoln, NE
(Radio and Television)

Vivian Juan
(Tohono O'odham)
Tohono O'odham Nation
Sells, AZ
(Tohono O'odham)

E. Barrie Kavasch
(Cherokee/Creek and Powhatan descent)
Bridgewater, CT
(Cuisine)

Joann W. Kealiinohomoku
Cross-Cultural Dance Resources
Flagstaff, AZ
(Dance)

Lawrence C. Kelly
(Nacirema)
Department of History
University of North Texas
Denton, TX
*(American Indian Defense Association;
Government Policy: Indian New Deal; Inter-
American Indian Institute)*

Harry A. Kersey, Jr.
Department of History
Florida Atlantic University
Boca Raton, FL
(Miccosukee; Seminole in Florida)

Kirke Kickingbird
(Kiowa)
Native American Legal Resource Center
Oklahoma City University Law School
Oklahoma City, OK
*(Institute for the Development of Indian Law;
Taxation; Trust Responsibilities and Trust
Funds)*

Duane H. King
National Museum of the American Indian
Smithsonian Institution
New York, NY
(Cherokee)

Carol Herselle Krinsky
Fine Arts Department
New York University
New York, NY
(Architecture)

Alysia E. LaCounte
(Turtle Mountain Chippewa)
Wisconsin State Public Defenders Office
Jefferson, WI
(Ojibwa: Chippewa in Montana)

Sylvester L. Lahren, Jr.
Department of Anthropology
Western Montana College at the University of
Montana
Dillon, MT
(Kalispel)

Julian Lang
(Karuk)
Institute of Native Knowledge
Arcata, CA
(Karuk)

Charles H. Lange
Santa Fe, NM
*(Pueblo of Cochiti; Pueblo of Santa Clara;
Pueblo of Santo Domingo)*

Patricia Fogelman Lange
Santa Fe, NM
(Pueblo of San Ildefonso)

Frank LaPena
(Wintu-Nomtipom)
Native American Studies Department
California State University, Sacramento
Sacramento, CA
(Wintun)

Armand S. LaPotin
Department of History
State University of New York, Oneonta
Oneonta, NY
*(Board of Indian Commissioners; Institute of
American Indian and Alaska Native Culture
and Arts)*

John W. Larner
Department of History
Indiana University of Pennsylvania
Indiana, PA
(Society of American Indians)

Adrian LeCornu
(Haida)
Hydaburg, AK
(Haida)

Mary Jane Lenz
National Museum of the American Indian
Smithsonian Institution
New York, NY
(Textiles: Northwest Coast and Other Areas)

Michele T. Leonard
(Shinnecock)
United American Indians of Delaware Valley
Philadelphia, PA
(Urban Indian Centers)

A. David Lester
Council of Energy Resource Tribes
Denver, CO
(Council of Energy Resource Tribes)

David Rich Lewis
Department of History
Utah State University
Logan, UT
(Environmental Issues)

Daniel F. Littlefield, Jr.
American Native Press Archives
University of Arkansas
Little Rock, AR
(Periodicals)

Carol S. Locust
(Cherokee)
Native American Research and Training Center
University of Arizona
Tucson, AZ
(Traditional Medicine)

Christopher Loether
Department of Anthropology
Idaho State University
Pocatello, ID
(Shoshone: Shoshone-Bannock)

X.L. Kugie Louis
(Colville Confederated Tribes)
National Indian Athletic Association
Salem, OR
(Sports and Games)

John R. Lovett
Western History Collections
University of Oklahoma
Norman, OK
(Ottawa/Odawa in Oklahoma)

Joseph Lubischer
Western Washington University
Bellingham, WA
(Hoh; Quileute)

David C. Maas
Department of Political Science
University of Alaska, Anchorage
Anchorage, AK
(Alaska Native Claims Settlement Act)

Helen McCarthy
Davis, CA
(Mono: Western)

James M. McClurken
Department of Anthropology
Michigan State University
Lansing, MI
(Ojibwa: Chippewa in Michigan; Potawatomi in Northern Michigan; Potawatomi in Southern Michigan)

George McCoy
(Cherokee Nation of Oklahoma)
Mental Health Programs Branch
Indian Health Service
Rockville, MD
(Mental Health)

Ann McMullen
Brown University
Providence, RI
(Nipmuc; Paugussett)

Patricia Mariella
Arizona Department of Environmental Quality
Phoenix, AZ
(Yavapai)

Cesare Marino
Handbook of North American Indians
Smithsonian Institution
Washington, DC
(Reservations)

John F. Martin
Department of Anthropology
Arizona State University
Tempe, AZ
(Havasupai)

Natasha Bonilla Martinez
Escondido, CA
(Photography)

Philip A. May
Center on Alcoholism, Substance Abuse and Addictions
University of New Mexico
Albuquerque, NM
(Alcohol Abuse)

Beatrice Medicine
(Sihasapa Band, Lakota Nation)
Royal Commission on Aboriginal Peoples
Ottawa, Ontario
(Families; Gender)

Brent W. Merrill
(Confederated Tribes of Grand Ronde)
Northwest Indian Fisheries Commission
Mount Vernon, WA
(Stillaguamish)

Ray Miles
Department of History
McNeese State University
Lake Charles, LA
(Wichita)

Bruce G. Miller
Department of Anthropology
and Sociology
University of British Columbia
Vancouver, British Columbia
(Samish; Snohomish; Swinomish; Upper Skagit)

Jay Miller
(Delaware)
Seattle, WA
(Cultural Revitalization; Delaware)

Virginia P. Miller
Department of Anthropology
Dalhousie University
Halifax, Nova Scotia
(Yuki)

Ward Alan Minge
(Acoma Pueblo)
Corrales, NM
(Pueblo of Acoma)

Violet Mitchell-Enos
(Yavapai)
Scottsdale, AZ
(Yavapai)

Paulette Fairbanks Molin
(Minnesota Chippewa Tribe, White Earth)
American Indian Educational Opportunities Program
Hampton University
Hampton, VA
(Ojibwa: Ojibway in Minnesota)

John H. Moore
Anthropology Department
University of Florida
Gainesville, FL
(Alabama-Coushatta; Creek/Mvskoke; Natchez; Yuchi)

Joann Sebastian Morris
(Sault Ste. Marie Chippewa)
Mid-Continent Regional Educational Laboratory
Aurora, CO
(Churches and Education)

Chrissandra Murphy-Reed
(Goshute)
Confederated Tribes of the Goshute Reservation
Ibapah, UT
(Shoshone: Goshute)

James D. Nason
(Comanche)
American Indian Studies Center
University of Washington
Seattle, WA
(Museums)

Tom Little Bear Nason
(Esselen)
Carmel Valley, CA
(Esselen)

Sharlotte Neely
Department of Anthropology
Northern Kentucky University
Cincinnati, OH
(Shawnee in Ohio)

Nell Jessup Newton
Washington College of Law
American University
Washington, DC
(American Indian Law Center; Gaming)

Sharon O'Brien
Department of Government and International
Relations
University of Notre Dame
Notre Dame, IN
*(Organizations and Tribal Cooperation; Tribal
Governments)*

Tracy Olson
(Confederated Tribes of Grand Ronde)
Confederated Tribes of Grand Ronde
Grand Ronde, OR
(Confederated Tribes of Grand Ronde)

Wallace Olson
Anthropology Department
University of Alaska, Southeast
Juneau, AK
(Tlingit)

Joseph B. Oxendine
(Lumbee)
Pembroke State University
Pembroke, NC
(Sports and Games)

Nancy J. Parezo
Arizona State Museum
University of Arizona
Tucson, AZ
(Drypainting)

Donald L. Parman
Department of History
Purdue University
West Lafayette, IN
*(Indian Civilian Conservation Corps; Meriam
Commission)*

Chief Kenneth Patterson
(Tuscarora)
Tuscarora Nation
Lewiston, NY
(Tuscarora)

Lotsee Patterson
(Comanche)
School of Library and Information Studies
University of Oklahoma
Norman, OK
(Comanche)

Victoria Patterson
Mendocino College
Ukiah, CA
(Miwok: Coast; Miwok: Lake; Pomo; Wappo)

Nicholas C. Peroff
Henry W. Bloch School of Business and Public
Administration
University of Missouri-Kansas City
Kansas City, MO
(Menominee)

Yvonne Peterson
(Chehalis)
The Evergreen State College
Olympia, WA
*(Confederated Tribes of the Chehalis
Reservation)*

Glenn A. Phelps
Department of Political Science
Northern Arizona University
Flagstaff, AZ
(Indian Country)

Lorrie A. Planas
(Choinumni, Mono)
Fresno, CA
(Yokuts)

Frank Pommersheim
School of Law
The University of South Dakota
Vermillion, SD
(Black Hills)

Frank W. Porter III
Chelsea Foundation for American Studies
Racine, OH
(Nanticoke; Piscataway)

J.V. (Jay) Powell
Department of Anthropology
and Sociology
University of British Columbia
Vancouver, British Columbia
(Shoalwater)

William K. Powers
Department of Anthropology
Rutgers University
New Brunswick, NJ
(Lakota; Powwow)

Harald E.L. Prins
Department of Sociology and
Anthropology
Kansas State University
Manhattan, KS
(Maliseet; Micmac; Passamaquoddy; Penobscot)

Gordon L. Pullar
(Kodiak Island Alutiiq)
Alaska Native Human Resource Development
Program
College of Rural Alaska
University of Alaska, Fairbanks
Anchorage, AK
(Alutiiq)

Jacki Thompson Rand
(Oklahoma Choctaw)
National Museum of the American Indian
Washington, DC
(Choctaw)

Ann M. Renker
Makah Cultural and Research Center
Neah Bay, WA
(Makah)

Allan Richardson
Whatcom Community College
Bellingham, WA
(Nooksack)

Trudie Lamb Richmond
(Schaghticoke)
Institute for American Indian Studies
Washington, CT
(Schaghticoke)

Robin Ridington
Department of Anthropology
University of British Columbia
Vancouver, British Columbia
(Omaha)

Lois Risling
(Hupa)
Center for Indian Community Development
Humboldt State University
Arcata, CA
(Hupa)

Beth R. Ritter
Department of Anthropology
University of Nebraska
Lincoln, NE
(Ponca: Northern)

Paul A. Robinson
Rhode Island Historical
Preservation Commission
Providence, RI
(Narragansett)

Steve Robinson
Northwest Indian Fisheries Commission
Olympia, WA
(Squaxin Island)

Mícheál D. Roe
Department of Psychology
Seattle Pacific University
Seattle, WA
(Cowlitz)

Harvey D. Rosenthal
Mount Vernon College
Alliance, OH
(Indian Claims Commission)

John Alan Ross
Department of Anthropology
Eastern Washington University
Spokane, WA
(Spokan)

Helen C. Rountree
Department of Sociology and Criminal Justice
Old Dominion University
Norfolk, VA
*(Chickahominy; Mattaponi; Monacan;
Nansemond; Rappahannock; Upper Mattaponi)*

Dan Eagle Boy Rowe
(Assiniboine)
Purdue University
West Lafayette, IN
(Indian Rights Association)

A. LaVonne Brown Ruoff
Department of English
University of Illinois at Chicago
Chicago, IL
(Literature)

Rudolph C. Rÿser
(Cowlitz)
Center for World Indigenous Studies
Olympia, WA
*(American Indian Policy Review Commission;
Quinault)*

Dalee Sambo
(Iñupiat)
International Union for Circumpolar Health
Anchorage, AK
*(Alaska Native Review Commission; Inuit
Circumpolar Conference)*

Richard A. Sattler
Newberry Library
Chicago, IL
(Seminole in Oklahoma)

Thomas F. Schilz
(Cherokee-Ottawa)
   Department of Social Sciences
   Miramar College
   San Diego, CA
   (Peoria; Tonkawa)

Mary Jane Schneider
   Department of Indian Studies
   University of North Dakota
   Grand Forks, ND
   (Three Affiliated Tribes)

Helen H. Schuster
   Poulsbo, WA
   (Yakima Nation)

Cal A. Seciwa
(Zuni)
   American Indian Institute
   Arizona State University
   Tempe, AZ
   (Zuni)

Polly Sharp
   Inter-Tribal Council of Arizona
   Phoenix, AZ
   (Child Welfare)

Demitri B. Shimkin
   (deceased)
   (Shoshone: Eastern)

Florence Connolly Shipek
   San Diego, CA
   (Kumeyaay; Luiseño)

Arthur Silberman
   Native American Painting Reference Library
   Oklahoma City, OK
   (Painting)

**Jeff Silverman, for the
Alaska Federation of Natives**
   Anchorage, AK
   (Alaska Federation of Natives)

William E. Simeone
   Stephen R. Braund and Associates
   Anchorage, AK
   (Alaskan Athabaskans)

Allogan Slagle
(Keetoowah Band Cherokee)
   Association on American Indian Affairs
   New York, NY
   *(Branch of Acknowledgment and Research;
   Cherokee: United Keetoowah Band; Federal and
   State Recognition)*

David Lee Smith
(Winnebago)
   Indian Studies Department
   Nebraska Indian Community College
   Winnebago, NE
   (Winnebago in Nebraska)

Marguerite A. Smith
(Shinnecock)
   Southampton, NY
   (Shinnecock)

C. Matthew Snipp
(Oklahoma Cherokee/Choctaw)
   Department of Rural Sociology
   University of Wisconsin-Madison
   Madison, WI
   (Economic Conditions)

Rosamond B. Spicer
   Tucson, AZ
   (Yaqui)

Squaxin Island Natural Resources Staff
   Shelton, WA
   (Squaxin Island)

Staff of Office of Community Relations
   Salt River Pima – Maricopa Indian Community
   Scottsdale, AZ
   (Pima)

Geoffrey E. Stamm
   Indian Arts and Crafts Board
   U.S. Department of the Interior
   Washington, DC
   (Indian Arts and Crafts Board)

William A. Starna
   Department of Anthropology
   State University of New York, Oneonta
   Oneonta, NY
   *(Brothertown; Cayuga; Iroquois Confederacy;
   Onondaga)*

Omer C. Stewart
   (deceased)
   (Peyote Religion)

Stockbridge – Munsee Historical Committee
   Bowler, WI
   (Stockbridge – Munsee)

Rennard J. Strickland
(Osage/Cherokee)
   University of Oklahoma College of Law
   Norman, OK
   (Sculpture)

Paul H. Stuart
   School of Social Work
   University of Alabama
   Tuscaloosa, AL
   (Government Agencies)

Donald D. Stull
Department of Anthropology
University of Kansas
Lawrence, KS
(Kickapoo in Kansas; Kickapoo in Oklahoma and Texas; Potawatomi in Kansas)

Suquamish Museum/Suquamish Tribal Archives Staff
Suquamish, WA
(Suquamish)

Imre Sutton
Geography Department
California State University, Fullerton
Fullerton, CA
(Land Claims)

Paul R. Swetzof
(Qawalangin Tribe of Unalaska)
Anchorage, AK
(Unangan)

Margaret Connell Szasz
Department of History
University of New Mexico
Albuquerque, NM
(Educational Policy)

Gladys I. Tantaquidgeon
(Mohegan)
Tantaquidgeon Indian Museum
Uncasville, CT
(Mohegan)

Nile Thompson
Puget Sound Railway Historical Society
Seattle, WA
(Skokomish; Steilacoom)

Russell Thornton
(Cherokee)
Native American Studies
Dartmouth College
Hanover, NH
(Population; Repatriation of Human Remains and Artifacts; Urbanization)

Shelby J. Tisdale
University of Arizona
Tucson, AZ
(Pueblo of Isleta; Pueblo of Nambe; Pueblo of Tesuque)

Kenneth D. Tollefson
School of Social and Behaviorial Sciences
Seattle Pacific University
Seattle, WA
(Snoqualmie)

Thomas W. Topash
(Potawatomi)
Pokagon Band of Potawatomi
Berrien Center, MI
(Potawatomi in Southern Michigan)

Debra Toya
Albuquerque, NM
(Pueblo of Laguna)

Clifford E. Trafzer
(Wyandot)
Department of Ethnic Studies
University of California-Riverside
Yucaipa, CA
(Modoc; Wyandotte)

Mary Treadwell
(Unkechaug)
Mastic, NY
(Unkechaug)

Robert A. Trennert, Jr.
Department of History
Arizona State University
Tempe, AZ
(Bureau of Indian Affairs Schools)

Jack F. Trope
Sant'Angelo & Trope
Somerville, NJ
(American Indian Religious Freedom Act; Sacred Sites)

Ronald L. Trosper
(Salish and Kootenai Tribes)
Native American Forestry Program
Northern Arizona University
Flagstaff, AZ
(Economic Development)

William E. Unrau
Department of History
Wichita State University
Wichita, KS
(Kaw)

Judith Vander
Ann Arbor, MI
(Shoshone: Eastern)

Sylvia Brakke Vane
Cultural Systems Research, Inc./Ballena Press
Menlo Park, CA
(Cahuilla; Chemehuevi; Cupeño; Gabrielino/ Tongva; Serrano)

Stefano Varesi
Native American Studies Program
University of California, Davis
Davis, CA
(Migrants and Refugees)

Christopher Vecsey
Department of Philosophy and Religion
Colgate University
Hamilton, NY
(Religion)

Deward E. Walker, Jr.
Department of Anthropology
University of Colorado
Boulder, CO
(Anthropologists and Native Americans; Coeur d'Alene; Confederated Tribes of the Colville Reservation; Confederated Tribes of the Umatilla Indian Reservation; Kutenai at Bonners Ferry; Nez Perce)

George B. Wasson, Jr.
(Coquille)
University of Oregon
Eugene, OR
(Coquille)

Lucille J. Watahomigie
(Hualapai)
Peach Springs, Arizona
(Hualapai)

Larry S. Watson
Journal of American Indian Family Research
Laguna Hills, CA
(Genealogical Research)

deanna j. harragarra waters
(Kiowa and Otoe-Missouria)
National Indian Law Library
Native American Rights Fund
Boulder, CO
(Kiowa)

Elizabeth Weatherford
National Museum of the American Indian
Smithsonian Institution
New York, NY
(Film and Video)

Jace Weaver
(Cherokee)
Union Theological Seminary
New York, NY
(Missions and Missionaries)

Laurie Weinstein
Department of Social Sciences
Western Connecticut State University
Danbury, CT
(Mohegan; Wampanoag)

Robert N. Wells, Jr.
Department of Government
St. Lawrence University
Canton, NY
(Ironworkers; Mohawk)

Thomas R. Wessel
Department of History
Montana State University
Bozeman, MT
(Agriculture: 1900 to 1950)

William J. Whatley
Pueblo of Jemez
Jemez, NM
(Pueblo of Jemez)

James D. Wherry
Groton, CT
(Pequot)

David L. Whited
Chemical Dependency Division
Metropolitan Development Council
Tacoma, WA
(Puyallup)

Andrew Hunter Whiteford
Santa Fe, NM
(Basketry)

Jeanne S. Whiteing
(Blackfeet)
Whiteing & Thompson
Boulder, CO
(Native American Rights Fund)

David Whitener
(Squaxin Island)
The Evergreen State College
Olympia, WA
(Squaxin Island)

Robert A. Williams
American Indian Studies
University of Arizona
Tucson, AZ
(Law)

Terry P. Wilson
(Potawatomi)
Native American Studies
University of California, Berkeley
Berkeley, CA
(Alcatraz Occupation; Osage)

Frederick Matthew Wiseman
(Western Abenaki)
Department of Humanities
Johnson State College
Johnson, VT
(Abenaki: Western)

Steve A. Woods
Forest County Potawatomi Community
Crandon, WI
(Potawatomi in Wisconsin)

Akira Y. Yamamoto
Department of Anthropology
University of Kansas
Lawrence, KS
(Kickapoo in Oklahoma and Texas)

Linda G. Yamane
(Costanoan/Ohlone)
Gilroy, CA
(Costanoan/Ohlone)

Yurok Transition Team
Eureka, CA
(Yurok)

Maurice L. Zigmond
Belmont, MA
(Kawaiisu)

Alvin J. Ziontz
Ziontz, Chestnut, Varnell,
Berley and Slonim
Seattle, WA
(Civil Rights)

ARTICLES BY SUBJECT

*There is no article under this title. Used for organizational purposes only.

**Article title repeated more than once.

LIST OF MAPS

ABENAKI, WESTERN

At the time of European contact, the Western Abenaki inhabited a region from Lake Champlain on the west to the White Mountains on the east, and from southern Quebec to the Vermont-Massachusetts border. The Western Abenaki are distinguished from their eastern kin, who today largely occupy Maine, by subtle differences in language rather than by distinct geographical boundaries. Today, most Western Abenakis live in Odanak (St. Francis), Quebec, and at Wolinak (Becancour), Quebec, where many of them migrated as refugees during the wars of the eighteenth century. As of 1988, two thousand Western Abenaki were also living in Vermont in and around the northern end of Lake Champlain near present day Highgate, St. Albans, and Swanton.

In the nineteenth and early twentieth centuries, the Western Abenaki kept a low profile as a strategy of survival. They lived on marginal lands, sold their splint-ash baskets to tourists, spoke French, and lived inconspicuously to avoid animosity and racism. These circumstances were to change in the last half-century.

Much of the focus of Western Abenaki nationalism and resurgence has centered on fishing and hunting rights, on their lack of state and federal recognition, or on tribal efforts to overcome miserable economic conditions. In 1941 their aboriginal hunting and fishing rights were unilaterally curtailed when the State of Vermont established a wildlife refuge at the mouth of the Missisquoi River. In recent years the Western Abenaki have staged fish-ins—fishing out of season and without state licenses—in order to assert their aboriginal rights in this area. In 1976 Governor Thomas Salmon of Vermont awarded them state recognition as an Indian tribe; however, Richard Snelling, Salmon's successor as governor, revoked the order the next year. Since that time, the Western Abenaki, under the leadership of Chiefs Leonard Lampman and Homer St. Francis, have set about to persuade the federal government and others to recognize the St. Francis-Sokoki Band of the Abenaki Nation of Vermont. Moreover, in the 1970s they created the Abenaki Self-Help Association, Inc. (ASHAI) to set about improving the community's health and housing needs.

Western Abenaki culture, driven underground by actions of the Euroamerican settlers on Abenaki land, is family band-based. Groups of families join for certain Abenaki-wide functions such as the harvest dinner in October, or the late spring and early summer powwows where traditional ceremonies, dances, stories, and political and social discussions are shared. Abenaki stories and religion have been popularized nationally by the prolific writer Joseph Bruchac. The Western Abenaki language survives in Quebec; attempts are underway to teach it in the Vermont school system. Arts are undergoing a renaissance, including traditional basketry, beadwork and graphic arts; a goal of the planned Abenaki Heritage Center is to foster traditional arts and technologies.

Frederick Matthew Wiseman
Laurence M. Hauptman

Further Reading

Bruchac, Joseph. *The Wind Eagle and Other Abenaki Stories as Told by Joseph Bruchac.* Greenfield Center, NY: Bowman Books, 1985.

Calloway, Colin C. *The Abenaki.* New York: Chelsea House Publishers, 1989.

Day, Gordon M. "Western Abenaki." *Handbook of North American Indians.* Vol. 15. *Northeast.* Ed. Bruce G. Trigger. Washington, DC: Smithsonian Institution, 1978. 148–59.

———. *The Identity of the St. Francis Indians.* Ottawa, Ontario: National Museum of Canada, National Museum of Man Mercury Series 71, 1981.

Haviland, William, and Marjory Power. *The Original Vermonters: Native Americans, Past and Present.* Hanover, NH: University Press of New England, 1981.

ABSENTEE SHAWNEE

See Shawnee in Oklahoma

ACHUMAWI

See Pit River

ACOMA

See Pueblo of Acoma

ADOPTION

See Child Welfare

AGING

See Elders

AGRICULTURE

The rural location of most Indian reservations and the necessity of developing some sort of economic base in these areas, coupled with the desire of United States policy makers to use agriculture as the vehicle for the assimilation of Indian peoples into the majority culture, made agricultural development an important aspect of United States Indian policy in the twentieth century. The history of this changing policy and its impact on the Native American population are the subjects of the following two articles.

1900 TO 1950

Indian agriculture in the first half of the twentieth century can be viewed as a virtual countermovement to the general development of agriculture in the United States. While white agriculture developed in an intensely economic climate with little regard for social consequence, Indian agriculture, through much of the first half of the century, carried a political and social imperative of acculturation and assimilation.

Successful white farmers in the twentieth century benefited from secure land title, government policies that encouraged acquisition of larger land units, access to capital, and a reasonably well-developed and supportive infrastructure. American Indian farmers had their systems of land use continuously disrupted, had little access to capital, and generally found new technological and scientific developments too expensive, inappropriate to their scale of production, and destructive to culturally bound practices.

American Indian societies at the turn of the century can be divided into three agricultural categories: societies that had little or no experience in crop production and animal husbandry, those who practiced some horticulture, and Indians with substantial agricultural experience that compared favorably with agriculture in general. By 1900, federal government policies designed to dismantle all three types of societies were already in place.

During the first two decades of the century, the government's principal vehicle of acculturation and assimilation, land allotment, fell most heavily on Indians who had no experience in agriculture and those Indians most adept at developing capitalized agriculture on relatively large units of land. The order of allotment closely followed white settlement patterns, and the pressure to open Indian lands to white occupation accelerated during periods of agricultural prosperity and diminished during periods of agricultural recession.

The General Allotment Act (Dawes Act of 1887) exempted the Five Civilized Tribes (the Cherokee, Choctaw, Chickasaw, Creek, and Seminole) from its provisions. A congressionally mandated commission, however, and the coercive Curtis Act of 1898 subjected the Five Civilized Tribes to allotment programs similar to those under the Dawes Act. Many among the Five Civilized Tribes had prospered in farming. They farmed large acreages, invested in technology, and exploited available labor in much the same manner as white farmers. Government officials insisted that some among the Five Civilized Tribes engrossed the land and left other members without subsistence. Allotment was the cure for such enterprise. In 1906, D.W.C. Duncan, a Cherokee, summarized the result. He testified that he had once farmed 300 acres, but after allotment was confined to sixty acres and was preparing to sell that, since he could not sustain a living with so little land. Allotment destroyed a successful example of Indian commercial agriculture, eliminated a potentially useful model for other reservations, and ensured that all members of the Civilized Tribes shared equally in the misery of rural poverty.

By 1900, most of the reservations in North and South Dakota and Montana had virtually abandoned crop agriculture as a viable form of economic development and had instead turned to animal husbandry, chiefly cattle raising, as the best use of reservation land. Generally, crop agriculture consisted of forage crops and gardening on relatively small acreages. While encouraging cattle raising through distribution of breeding stock and purebred bulls, the government nevertheless proceeded to break-up the reservations into small individualized units. Typically, as on the Blackfeet Reservation, individual allotments consisted of a combination of crop land and grazing land. In a country where thirty acres or more was needed to sustain one cow, the size of allotments condemned the Indian cattlemen to bare subsistence and frequent failure. The cattle industry on such reservations thrived so long as Indian cattlemen ignored allotments and grazed their herds on what amounted to a common pasture. That proved increasingly difficult as government agents insisted that allottees work their individual land and lease tribal land to white cattlemen.

Allotment and leasing seriously inhibited Indian farmers from acquiring a sufficient land base. By 1900, after several permutations, government leasing regulations basically allowed any allotment to be leased. By 1916 fully one-third of all allotments were leased to whites for either crop agriculture or grazing. In 1902 two-thirds of the Standing Rock Reservation was leased to white cattlemen. In 1907, on the Cheyenne/Arapaho Reservation, over 90 percent of the land was leased. Leased Indian land became a common source of additional crop acreage or grazing range for whites. Leased land, however, could potentially be returned to Indian use. But this was often not the case for many Indian allotments.

Inevitably, even before the allotting process was completed, some number of allottees had died leaving their allotments in heirship status. A deceased Indian's land was divided among the allottee's heirs as determined by state law until 1910, and by the secretary of the interior thereafter. It was possible for a single allotment to be divided among original heirs, the inherited land redivided on the inheritor's death, and divided again among a third set of heirs before the first trust patent was issued. By 1902, substantial land was in heirship status with some allotments divided among a large number of heirs, and some heirs holding rights in many different allotments scattered throughout the reservation.

In 1902 Congress authorized the sale of inherited land. Since heirship land was scattered throughout the reservation, its sale, generally to whites, disrupted the continuity of farming acres and grazing districts. Those allottees who did not sell their inherited land were nearly always induced to lease the land to white farmers or ranchers. By 1905 over 250,000 acres of heirship land had been sold; the number reached 3.4 million acres in 1934.

Under the Dawes Act, allotments could not be sold until the end of a twenty-five-year trust period. In 1906, however, Congress passed the Burke Act which, in part, allowed the secretary of the interior to issue fee simple patents to Indians deemed competent before the end of the trust period. Initially confined to those allottees who applied for fee simple titles, white demands for Indian land induced the government to establish a competency commission that sought out competent allottees and issued fee simple titles often without the allottee's knowledge. Inevitably, much of this land passed to white ownership. By 1934, over 23 million acres of Indian fee simple land had been sold.

Since allotments could not be encumbered during the life of the trust patent, the principal means by which white farmers raised investment funds for their farm operations was unavailable to Indian farmers and ranchers. Until 1913 Indian farmers exchanged labor for some agricultural equipment; after 1913, they had to pay cash. Government reimbursable loan funds were the principal source of Indian finance. Loans were restricted to $600 a person, a sum totally inadequate to bring the most skilled Indian farmer into a technological age. Consequently, capital investment in Indian farms lagged well behind white farms.

In the northern Plains and the Pacific Northwest, allotment generally took place on reservations occupied by tribes that had primarily subsisted from hunting. The government had the task of instructing these Indian farmers in the rudiments of agriculture. Agency farmers and boarding schools were the vehicle for such training. Agency farmers, however, engaged in little actual instruction. They presided over the issue of rations, monitored Indian activities to prevent proscribed ceremonials, occasionally tilled an agency farm to provide subsistence for agency personnel, but carried on little farming instruction among the Indians.

Boarding schools generally had an agricultural curriculum, but it usually consisted of little more than instruction in gardening and virtually no training in animal husbandry. The boarding schools at best turned out farm laborers, not farm managers. Even had government farmers been the best instructors available and devoted all their time to the task, the lack of sufficient instructors precluded reason-

able results. The number of government farmers never exceeded 320 in 1900, and was only 249 in 1913.

Many Southwest Indians had established productive farming systems over a period of several hundred years. The eastern Pueblo people constructed sophisticated ditch irrigation systems off the Rio Grande. Similar systems existed along the Gila and Colorado rivers in Arizona. The western Pueblo, Hopi, Papago, and others devised systems of flood irrigation and water distribution that concentrated seasonal rains onto numerous small fields at the mouths of arroyos. The Southwest Indians generally recognized an inheritable land use that kept land within families but was redistributed when no longer in use.

With few exceptions, the Southwest reservations were never allotted, but government programs to prepare the reservations for allotment were equally destructive. White encroachment on irrigated lands among the eastern Pueblos kept the status of their land in question throughout most of the first three decades of the century. Eventually, the matter was placed under the direction of the Pueblo Lands Board to sort out conflicting claims. The Board did not complete its work until the late 1920s, when allotment had lost most of its allure.

The western Pueblos' system of agriculture revolved around ritual and ceremony as well as actual planting, making it unacceptable to assimilationists. The government restructured Native agriculture to conform to patterns that mirrored white commercial farming, but on acreages altogether too small to make Indian farmers competitive.

With the Zuni, for example, the government embarked on a dam building program and construction of irrigation ditches intended to provide irrigated allotments to individual farmers. The government encouraged Zuni farmers to abandon their traditional flood irrigation for the irrigated allotments. Silting behind the main dam on the Zuni River soon lowered the supply of available water to virtually eliminate the irrigation project. Some have argued the abandonment of flood farming, however, left the land subject to severe erosion, making it unfit for farming under any circumstances. The Zuni were left with little crop agriculture and heavily dependent on cattle and sheepraising on limited pasture. Government policy had assured that Indian agriculture at best provided a subsistence for some and at worst destroyed systems among those who had sustained themselves in agriculture for hundreds of years.

By 1934 Indian owned land had been reduced from over 150 million acres to 52 million acres. Nearly two-thirds of the American Indians were landless, and those still engaged in farming had too few acres to sustain more than a subsistence level of agriculture and no means to enlarge their farming operations.

The New Deal years marked a fundamental change in government policy; with regard to agriculture, however, New Deal planners could not reverse the damage of the previous three decades. Consequently, government programs concentrated on making the best out of what was left of Indian land. Generally, programs were designed to rehabilitate land that suffered from erosion and establish range and forest management systems, including the reduction of livestock on overgrazed land, in some cases, and distribution of drought relief purchased cattle to Indian ranchers, in others. New Deal efforts to return land holding to more traditional systems foundered against opposition from officials still attached to assimilation and Indians who did not wish to give up allotted land. Perhaps the most constructive program of the New Deal consisted of forgiving accumulated debts from irrigation projects and reimbursable loan accounts.

Debts from irrigation charges had become particularly onerous with little tangible benefit to Indians. Like other allotments, irrigated land was subject to leasing, heirship, and fee simple patents to competent Indians. By 1934, Indians farmed only one-third of the irrigated acres on Indian reservations. At Yakima, in Washington, Indians farmed only 9 percent of the land; the rest had either been sold or was leased to white farmers.

Basically, New Deal programs provided much needed employment for Indians on the reservations, but did little to move any substantial number of Indian farmers to a level that allowed them to compete in a highly capitalized agricultural economy. World War II brought most New Deal programs to an end. Indian agriculture continued to suffer from a reduced and fragmented land base, the abandonment without adequate replacement of traditional modes of farming, and a lack of capital to exploit what remained. By 1950, few Indians had managed to establish themselves in agriculture, while the requirements necessary to compete in a market economy, large land units, capital investment, and management skills, were more imperative than ever.

Thomas R. Wessel

See also Allotment; Government Policy

Further Reading

Carlson, Leonard A. *Indians, Bureaucrats, and Land: The Dawes Act and the Decline of Indian Farming.* Westport, CT: Greenwood Press, 1981.

Hurt, R. Douglas. *Indian Agriculture in America: Prehistory to the Present.* Lawrence: University of Kansas Press, 1987.

McDonnell, Janet A. *The Dispossession of the American Indian, 1887–1934.* Bloomington: Indiana University Press, 1991.

Meriam, Lewis. *The Problem of Indian Administration.* Baltimore, MD: Johns Hopkins Press, 1928.

Parman, Donald L. *The Navajos and the New Deal.* New Haven, CT: Yale University Press, 1976.

Preston, Porter J., and Charles A. Engle. "Report of Advisors on Irrigation on Indian Reservations: Survey of Conditions of the Indians of the United States." *Hearings before the Subcommittee of the Committee on Indian Affairs.* United States Senate, 71st Cong. 2d sess. 1930. Part 6.

Prucha, Francis Paul. *The Great Father: The United States Government and the American Indians.* Vol. 2. Lincoln: University of Nebraska Press, 1984.

1950 TO 1993

The agriculture of the Native Americans has suffered from inadequate lands, credit, and science and technology since 1950. After World War II, American agriculture depended on specialized, large-scale production more than ever before. Vast acreages, expanded capital investment, intensive applications of chemical fertilizers and pesticides, and elaborate tractor-powered machinery became prerequisites for success, and Indian farmers did not have access to any of these necessities. Moreover, federal heirship policy that divided lands at the death of the owner fragmented Indian property and made farming impossible. Indeed, the heirship tangle had removed approximately 7 million acres of the best lands from cultivation by the mid-twentieth century. Many white farmers also pressured Indian landowners to purchase or rent their lands in order to expand their own agricultural operations.

In the Southwest, insufficient range land and the lingering effects of the New Deal stock-reduction program continued to limit agricultural development after 1950. Overgrazing and soil erosion prevented the Navajo from raising enough sheep for subsistence, and commercial livestock production remained insignificant. Although the United States Department of Agriculture and the Bureau of Indian Affairs (BIA) provided agricultural extension services to help farmers to raise long-staple "pima" cotton and other commercial crops, inadequate irrigation limited agricultural expansion. In the absence of ditch irrigation, some farmers, such as the Papago, practiced the ancient art of floodwater farming, while others, such as the Yuma, leased their lands to white farmers to gain at least some income from the land. The majority of the Indians in the Southwest, however, depended on raising livestock for their income. The San Carlos Apache were among the most successful cattlemen.

Environmental limitations and federal Indian policy, designed to assure assimilation and acculturation of Native Americans by forcing them to become small-scale farmers who owned their own land in the white tradition, prevented commercial agricultural development among the Native Americans. The harsh environment of the trans-Mississippi West and inadequate support by the BIA kept Indian farmers in poverty. By 1950, the average Indian farm family earned about $500 annually, compared to $2,500 for white farmers. As a result many Indian landowners sold their acreages to whites because they needed the money.

In addition to these problems, Indian farmers confronted the policy of termination at mid-point in the twentieth century, which provided for the severance of tribal bonds with the federal government. Once termination occurred, the tribes that participated in the program would no longer be wards of the federal government and subject to supervision, regulation, and support by the BIA. Theoretically and ideally free to determine their own economic destiny, in reality termination policy meant that Indian farmers would no longer have access to even minimal government credit and support. It also meant that Indian farmers would no longer have their lands protected by trust status. Those lands would now be open for taxation, liens, and foreclosure, and most Indian farmers did not have sufficient income to meet those social and economic obligations. Most important, they did not have the financial, political, or legal ability to prevent the loss of their lands. Although Congress approved the termination policy on August 1, 1953, both Indian and white opponents forced Congress to change this policy. When termination ended during the early 1960s, only 13,263 Indians (or approximately 3 percent of the Indian population) and 1.3 million acres had been withdrawn from federal protection.

The 1950s

While many tribesmen fought the termination policy during the 1950s, heirship lands so divided the reservations on the Great Plains that cattle raising proved impossible, and the lack of credit for implements and livestock prevented even subsistence agriculture. As a result, the BIA often leased reservation lands to white cattlemen, and many livestockmen used Indian lands without payment. These problems prevented the Native American from becoming agricultural or from improving their farming operations. At the same time, the old problems of overgrazing and soil erosion restricted Indian agriculturists in the Southwest. By the late 1950s, the Navajo continued to raise more sheep than their land base could support, even though most Navajo families owned fewer sheep than the 250 head needed for subsistence on an annual basis. They also continued to graze too many horses. Although horses provided social status and met cultural needs, these animals contributed to the overgrazing problem and prevented the most efficient economic use of Navajo lands. The Navajo refused to reduce the numbers of their horses because they believed that living things should not be needlessly destroyed. That belief and the absence of a market caused the goat population to increase 14 percent during the 1950s, further contributing to the overgrazing problem. Drought and overstocking of range lands also plagued Papago agriculture.

Despite these problems, the Navajo expanded their agricultural base by about 4,000 acres during the 1950s. Some Navajo also became migrant agricultural workers, who harvested sugar beets, cotton, vegetables, citrus fruits, and broom corn in Arizona, New Mexico, Colorado, Utah, and Idaho. The agricultural income of the Navajo, however, did not improve substantially. By 1958, agriculture provided about 10 percent of Navajo income. In contrast, the San Carlos Apache maintained an important cattle raising economy. By 1955, they had eleven cattlemen's associations that sold about 12,000 cattle annually for earnings of $1 million.

The 1960s

After 1950, leasing remained a serious problem on the reservations where the land had been allotted. White farmers leased extensive acres of Indian lands and the reservations were checkerboarded with non-Indian holdings. Indian farmers continued to live in poverty with little chance for success. Although they remained in rural settings, they were not an agricultural people. By 1960, less than 10 percent of the Native Americans farmed, a decrease of 35 percent since 1940. At that time, the Indians comprised less than 1 percent of the population, but nearly 70 percent lived in the countryside. Subsistence agriculture did not meet their basic economic and nutritional needs, and they simply could not compete with white farmers who had the necessary capital resources, technical skills, and managerial abilities for successful agriculture. By 1964, Indian agriculture had failed; the median income for Indians on reservations totaled only $1,800, compared to $5,710 annually for non-Indians. Moreover, few Indian cattlemen had the 100 head necessary to maintain viable operations by earning a family income of at least $3,000 each year.

During the late twentieth century, Indian farmers were caught in a vicious cycle. They could not qualify for loans to finance efficient agricultural operations, and their farming enterprises prevented them from acquiring the capital needed to make improvements. Moreover, without land reform, few Indians controlled enough acreage to become commercial farmers. Consequently, most Indians leased their lands to white farmers and cattlemen. These financial and land problems prevented the development of a viable Indian agriculture.

Heirship lands remained a problem by the late 1960s. In 1968, more than 6 million acres or about 11 percent of Indian lands were in heirship status and at least five heirs per acre claimed half of those lands. Indian farmers cultivated or grazed only 65 percent of heirship lands, while white operators used 25 percent of that acreage; 10 percent of heirship land lay idle. Rental income from the lease of those lands remained a pittance. Among the Pima, heirships had reduced the acreage per person to such a small amount that fees returned less than $1 per acre annually. Leasing, however, enabled the Indians to earn some return from their lands and freed them to seek jobs off the reservations. Culture also often prevented the Indians on the Great Plains from becoming productive farmers because agriculture had been considered women's work. Consequently, many tribesmen in the trans-Mississippi West still did not have an agricultural tradition.

The 1970s

During the 1970s, Indian agriculture continued to decline. Although 55.5 percent of the Indian population lived in rural areas, only 11.2 percent farmed the land. The problems of insufficient capital, inadequate credit, and heirship policy remained unsolved. Now, however, challenges to Indian water rights threatened the already weak agricultural economy of the Western tribesmen. During the 1970s, Indian agriculture depended on access to water. For most Indians, water was their most important natural resource and without it their lands remained unsuitable for farming. After 1970, water rights became the major issue that influenced the lives of Indian farmers.

The Western water doctrine of prior appropriation did not meet the needs of the Indians, because the tribesmen did not have the financial resources to use water in extensive irrigation systems. Although the United States Supreme Court essentially secured Indian water rights in the case of *Winters v. United States* (1908), the Western Indians then and even now have had to use the courts to maintain those rights. The courts, however, have not determined the precise quantity of water that Indian farmers can claim, nor has the judiciary decided whether the federal government or the tribes reserved the water on reservations created by treaties. Although the Indians can claim enough water for practical irrigation on the reservations, the courts have not yet decided whether the Native Americans can use water for purposes other than irrigation, or whether treaties established a special water right. Ground or subsurface water rights have not yet been resolved, although the Supreme Court held in the case of *Cappaert v. United States* (1976) that the water under reservation land belonged to the Indians, thereby making groundwater rights an extension of reserved rights to surface waters. By the late twentieth century, however, the urban needs of the western states for water continued to grow, and westerners increasingly demanded the quantification of Indian water rights to enable rational state planning. This political pressure may bring a change in Indian water rights.

The 1980s

By 1980, the Indians controlled 52 million acres of land, of which 42 million acres were under tribal ownership, while 10 million acres were under individual management. Yet without adequate capital to use water for irrigation or to finance economically viable farming operations, few Indians had any realistic hope of becoming farmers by the late twentieth century. The federal government provided only minimal economic aid programs for Indian farmers. One program called the Indian Acute Distress Donation Program, administered by the Agricultural Stabilization and Conservation Service, provided feed grains from the Commodity Credit Corporation to tribal livestockmen who could not raise sufficient feed for their cattle because of losses due to drought, flood, or other natural disasters. Another program, known as the Indian Land Acquisition Loan Program, provided federal funds to help the tribesmen purchase land

within their reservations. The Farmers Home Administration also made loans to Indian farmers to help them become owner-operators by purchasing or expanding farm land. The federal government loaned Indian livestockmen the capital needed to organize grazing associations, and it provided loans for irrigation and drainage projects.

Confronted with the frustrating and debilitating problems of insufficient land, inadequate capital, and little access to science and technology, only 7,211 Indian farmers remained by 1982. Although the Indians used 46.1 million acres for agriculture, only 4,727 farmers harvested 705,378 acres of crop land. The majority of Indian farmers were small-scale operators who held fewer than 500 acres. As a result, the majority of Indian farms in the semiarid and arid West could not support commercial agriculture. At best, these farms remained subsistence operations. Most Indian farmers remained below the poverty line in the absence of outside income, because they earned less than $10,000 annually from the sale of agricultural commodities. Only about 2,000 Indians were full-time farmers and agriculture was not attractive to young Indians. In 1982, Indian farmers averaged 50.4 years of age; only 946 farmers were below the age of thirty-five. Five years later, only 7,134 Indian farmers remained, and the acreage in farmland had decreased to 45.6 million acres. Only 2,289 farmers earned $10,000 or more from agriculture.

Consequently, by the early 1990s, most of the tribes did not have enough land or the financial means to exist independently in an agricultural economy. Although the Navajo and a few other tribes were exceptions, even these Indians struggled under difficult economic conditions. By the late twentieth century, Indian agriculture was insignificant and federal Indian agricultural policy was a failure, because it had not succeeded in providing the means for the acculturation and assimilation of the Native Americans in white society.

R. Douglas Hurt

See also **Allotment; Government Policy**

Further Reading

Burt, Larry W. *Tribalism in Crisis: Federal Indian Policy, 1953–1961*. Albuquerque: University of New Mexico Press, 1982.

DuMars, Charles T., Marilyn O'Leary, and Albert E. Utton. *Pueblo Indian Water Rights: Struggle for a Precious Resource*. Tucson: University of Arizona Press, 1984.

Hundley, Norris, Jr. "The Dark and Bloody Ground of Indian Water Rights: Confusion Elevated to Principle." *Western Historical Quarterly* 9 (1978): 455–82.

Hurt, R. Douglas. *Indian Agriculture in America: Prehistory to the Present*. Lawrence: University Press of Kansas, 1987.

McDonnell, Janet A. *The Dispossession of the American Indian, 1887–1934*. Bloomington: Indiana University Press, 1991.

Parman, Donald L. *The Navajos and the New Deal.* New Haven, CT: Yale University Press, 1976.

AHTNA

See Alaskan Athabaskans

ALABAMA-COUSHATTA

Originally living in Alabama and Mississippi in the sixteenth century, the Alabama (or Alibamu) Indians were soon caught between the major European and Indian military powers, who contested for the region during the next two centuries. Always a small nation of fewer than 3,000 persons, they frequently joined forces for protection with the Coushattas (also known as the Koasatis or Quassartes), who spoke a similar Muskogean language.

Frequently fragmented into refugee groups in these years, many Alabama and Coushatta villages and families were absorbed by intermarriage into other Indian nations, especially the Creeks, Seminoles, and Choctaws. However, three groups have survived up to the twentieth century with their language and much of their culture intact—in Louisiana, Texas, and Oklahoma.

The modern group nearest their original homeland, and numbering about 400 persons, has been known since their federal recognition in 1971 as the Coushatta Tribe of Louisiana, in Allen Parish. This group is often called Koasati by ethnographers and linguists, and this usage and spelling has been taken over by some members of the tribe. Early in the century, the Coushattas of Louisiana were not highly visible to Euroamericans, keeping gardens in the pine forest and living by wage work, supplemented by hunting and trapping. Even so, they received occasional visits from government agents and scholars and were granted supplemental funds for public education in 1930.

After World War II, the Coushattas became famous for their baskets made of native cane, and their woodcrafts, which became favorite items among tourists. Generally, however, the economy deteriorated in the 1960s until federal recognition brought an array of helpful federal programs, including a Christmas tree farm, better water and sanitation, schools, and a health clinic. A tribal bingo hall also brings in revenue and tribal members enjoy a new tribal center completed in 1984.

A second geographically distinct group is the Alabama-Coushatta Tribe of Polk County, Texas. Because they assisted Texans in the war of independence from Mexico in 1836, they were given "two leagues" of land by the Republic of Texas, which was promptly usurped by settlers. To replace this land, the revolutionary hero Sam Houston granted them a new reservation of 1,280 acres along the Trinity River in 1842. Another 3,071 acres was added by the federal government in 1928. Developing their own economy in the twentieth century, based on wage work and some farming, the Texas group applied for termination of federal control in 1954, which was granted. Dissatisfied with their status as a state reservation, they reverted to federal status in 1986.

The tribal enrollment is about 800, five hundred of whom live on the reservation. Both the Alabama and Koasati languages are still spoken on the reservation, even by younger people. The present economic basis of the reservation is the tourist industry, which sponsors Indian country and nature bus tours, as well as a train ride around the reservation. In addition, the tribe provides camping and recreation facilities for tourists in the Big Thicket area, where the reservation is located. They also maintain a museum and produce arts and crafts for sale to visitors. The tribe's annual June powwow includes dramatic entertainment, along with competition dancing and other powwow fare.

The third modern group, the Alabamas and Quassartes of Oklahoma, have a rather more complex history, but have generally been represented among the Mvskoke Creeks since removal to Indian Territory in 1832. Mostly settled around Weleetka, in Okfuskee County, many in the community have spouses or family from the Alabama-Coushatta communities in Louisiana and Texas, and there is still much visiting back and forth.

Until 1938, the group was content to be represented in the Muskogee Creek Nation as an independent tribal town, or *etvlwa*, but in that year "The Alabama-Quassarte Tribe of Oklahoma" accepted a federal charter as a separate political entity, and received several hundred acres of land under the Oklahoma Indian Welfare Act. Until now, the group has not undertaken to separate itself administratively from the Creek Nation, but discussions along this line were begun in 1990. Among the older generations of the 900 persons enrolled in this group, there are a few speakers of both languages. More so than the other two groups, these Oklahoma people are highly intermarried with other Indians, in this case the Muskogee Creeks. Because there are some economic and political advantages in maintaining a separate identity, however, many people of mixed ancestry continue their identification as Alabama-Quassartes.

John H. Moore

See also **Oklahoma Tribes**

Further Reading

Gregory, Hiram F. "The Louisiana Tribes: Entering Hard Times." *Indians of the Southeastern United States in the Late 20th Century.* Ed. J. Anthony Paredes. Tuscaloosa, AL and London, England: University of Alabama Press, 1992. 162–82.

Jacobson, Daniel. "The Origin of the Koasati Community of Louisiana." *Ethnohistory* 7 (1960): 97–120.

Jacobson, Daniel, Howard N. Martin, and Ralph Henry Marsh. *Creek Indians: Alabama-Coushatta.* New York and London, England: Garland Publishing, 1974.

Johnson, Bobby H. *The Coushatta People.* Phoenix: Indian Tribal Series, 1976.

ALASKA NATIVE PEOPLES

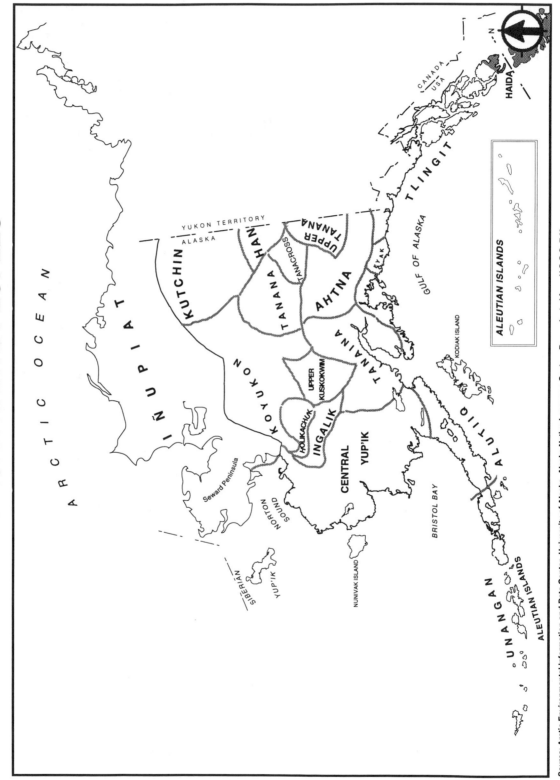

Source: Arctic Environmental Information and Data Center, University of Alaska, Alaska Native Language Center. Base adapted from U.S.G.S. E Map.

Rothe, Aline. *Kalita's People: A History of the Alabama-Coushatta Indians of Texas*. Waco: Texian Press, 1965.

Swanton, John R. "Social Organization and Social Usages of the Indians of the Creek Confederacy." *Bureau of American Ethnology 42nd Annual Report*. Washington, DC: The Bureau (1928): 23–472.

ALASKA

See Alaska Federation of Natives; Alaska Native Brotherhood/Sisterhood; Alaska Native Claims Settlement Act; Alaska Native Regional Corporations; Alaska Native Review Commission; Alaskan Athabaskans; Alutiiq; Haida; Inuit Circumpolar Conference; Iñupiat; Tlingit; Tsimshian of Metlakatla; Unangan; Whaling; Yup'ik.

ALASKA FEDERATION OF NATIVES

The Alaska Federation of Natives (AFN) was formed in October, 1966, by Alaska Natives from every region of the state. They gathered to discuss common problems and the need for a statewide organization that would work to address issues involving the settlement of Alaska Native aboriginal land claims. In the mid-1960s, many leaders felt a statewide organization of their own making was vital to solving land claims and other problems. In late 1966, more than 400 Native people gathered in Anchorage to discuss common problems, primarily the need to organize to solve land claims, and the foundation for AFN was laid.

From 1966 to 1971, AFN focused on achieving passage of a just and fair land settlement. When the Alaska Native Claims Settlement Act (ANCSA) was passed by Congress, December 18, 1971, it marked a new beginning for AFN as an organization. AFN provided technical assistance for Alaska Natives in their efforts to implement ANCSA, and eventually managed several statewide human service programs. As regional associations grew in strength and independence, the programs were transferred to these associations, thus further changing the role of AFN in Native affairs.

AFN's organizational structure evolved to respond to new challenges facing Alaska Natives. AFN became a prime negotiator in the federal legislative process to ensure that Alaska Native interests were addressed, clarified, and protected under the development and passage of the Alaska National Interest Lands Conservation Act of 1980, the 1987 Amendments to ANCSA (the "1991 Amendments"), and other federal legislation. AFN maintains an active role on the statewide level through work with the Alaska State Legislature to create policy and secure funding for new and/or existing rural programs in the areas of health, education, resource development, labor, and local government.

The Annual AFN Convention has become a traditional social and political gathering for Alaska Natives throughout the state. Held in October, the convention provides the more than 2,500 delegates an opportunity to discuss issues of concern to the community, recognize achievements and successes, greet old friends and make new ones, and set the direction for AFN for the coming year. Delegates also elect the AFN chairman of the board and the board's village representatives. Other activities corresponding with the convention include the AFN Youth Convention, the Elders Conference, workshops on a variety of issues, and AFN's popular "Quyana Alaska," including an evening of traditional Native dance with groups from all over the state performing.

Jeff Silverman (from the 1992 AFN Annual Report)

See also Alaska Native Claims Settlement Act

Further Reading

Annual Report: Alaska Native Survival—A Call for Action. Ed. Jeff Silverman. Anchorage: Alaska Federation of Natives, 1992.

Arnold, Robert D. *Alaska Native Land Claims*. Anchorage: Alaska Native Foundation, 1976, 1978.

ALASKA NATIVE BROTHERHOOD/SISTERHOOD

The Alaska Native Brotherhood, the one significant political and social intertribal organization in Alaska before it acquired statehood, was founded in 1912 as a self-help group dedicated to the betterment of Alaska Natives through service and example. Though established under the aegis of the Presbyterian mission in southeast Alaska, and at the urging of the directors of the federal school system, the ANB was a Native organization with Native officers and a nearly exclusive Native membership. A companion organization, the Alaska Native Sisterhood, was founded in 1915. Although the leadership always sought to develop the two bodies into territory-wide organizations, for all practical purposes they were limited to southeast Alaska, and membership was comprised nearly exclusively of the Tlingit and Haida Indians of that region. In the absence of another organization to articulate Native interests, however, both regional politicians and federal officials have treated the ANB (though much less so for the ANS) as the focus group for Alaska Native concerns and policies. Before statehood, Alaskan politicians routinely attended and often addressed the annual ANB conventions, and Interior Department officials often sought the testimony of ANB leaders on Alaska's policies and worked with them in implementing Alaskan programs.

In its initial period from 1912 to 1920, the ANB advocated citizenship for Natives through education and the utilization of a citizenship process adopted in 1915 by the territorial legislature at the urging of the Presbyterian mission and federal officials. In 1920 William Lewis Paul, a Tongass Tlingit who had earned a law degree, became an officer and assumed the leadership of the ANB. He gave the organization its direction for two decades and remained an important force in its history until his death in 1978. Implementing an idea he had embraced while a student at the Carlisle Indian School, Paul argued that Indians were citizens by virtue of the Fourteenth Amendment.

Paul advocated political action. In 1923 he won a court case granting the right of Alaska Natives to vote, and in the same year founded an ANB newspaper, the *Alaska Fisherman*, to publicize ANB objectives; it published until 1932. The salmon industry was the most significant economic force in Alaska in this period, and its use of fish traps threatened to destroy the Native salmon fisheries on which many families relied. Paul dedicated the ANB to the abolition of fish traps, a goal which the organization pursued unsuccessfully until statehood. In 1924 and 1926, with ANB support, Paul was elected to the territorial legislature, the first Native elected to political office in Alaska. Over the next decade he successfully fought segregated schools and the denial of widows' and orphans' benefits to Natives. In 1936, having helped draft legislation to implement the Indian Reorganization Act (IRA) in Alaska, Paul was named the first Bureau of Indian Affairs (BIA) Indian field agent in Alaska. In 1929 he won the support of the ANB in organizing a legal claim to title of ancestral Tlingit lands in southeast Alaska. Congress authorized the claim in 1935, and in 1959, the United States Court of Claims awarded title to most of southeast Alaska, nearly 18 million acres, to the Tlingit and Haida Indians. The body created to disburse settlement funds, the Central Council of the Tlingit and Haida Indian Tribes of Alaska, continues to administer social and educational funds and programs today.

After implementation of the IRA in the 1930s, Paul's leadership in the ANB was successfully challenged by Frank and Roy Peratrovich from Klawock. Roy Peratrovich served five successive terms as ANB president and Frank Peratrovich was elected to the territorial House and then to the Senate after World War II. Roy's wife Elizabeth became the principal ANB lobbyist in a campaign for legislative adoption of an antidiscrimination bill, which achieved success in 1945. In the 1940s the ANB opposed an attempt by the secretary of the interior to establish new Indian reservations in Alaska and supported the drive for Alaska statehood once statehood leaders endorsed protection of Native land title.

In the 1950s a new generation of leadership emerged, which included Cyrus Peck, Sr., and Mark Jacobs. Peck published a new ANB newspaper, the *Voice of the Brotherhood*, which helped publicize ANB policies and give tangibility to its political significance. Land claims issues became increasingly important in Alaska in the 1960s, and the ANB participated in the founding of the more broadly based Alaska Federation of Natives in 1967, to further these goals. Always important as social bodies, the ANB and the ANS continued to provide social focus for Native activities, and today they serve Tlingit and Haida social

and political objectives and are important centers of Native heritage revival.

Stephen Haycox

Further Reading

Beverly, James. "The *Alaska Fisherman* and the Paradox of Assimilation: Progress, Power and the Preservation of Culture." *Native Press Research Journal* 5 (1987): 2–25.

Drucker, Philip. *The Native Brotherhoods: Modern Intertribal Organizations on the Northwest Coast.* Bureau of American Ethnology Bulletin 168 (1958): 1–194. Brighton, MI: Native American Book Publishers, 1991.

Haycox, Stephen. "William Paul, Sr., and the Alaska Voters' Literacy Act of 1925." *Alaska History* 2 (1986): 17–38.

Metcalfe, Peter M. *The Central Council of the Tlingit and Haida Indian Tribes of Alaska: An Historical and Organizational Profile.* Juneau, AK: CCTHITA, 1981.

ALASKA NATIVE CLAIMS SETTLEMENT ACT

Historical Introduction

In the Treaty of Cession of 1867, Russia transferred the administration of what was to become Alaska to the United States. The Treaty states that "(T)he Uncivilized tribes will be subject to such laws and regulations as the United States may, from time to time, adopt in regard to aboriginal tribes in that country." Congress recognized this obligation in 1884 when it passed the Organic Act extending the civil and criminal laws of Oregon to Alaska and providing protection for Native lands: "Indians or other persons in said district shall not be disturbed in the possession of any lands actually in their use or occupation or now claimed by them but the terms under which such persons may acquire title to such lands is reserved for future legislation by Congress."

Despite this reserve clause in the Organic Act, land was always available for fish canneries, mining, townsites, schools, homesteading, railroads, and logging. With the Japanese invasion of the Aleutians in 1941 and the Cold War, the strategic importance of Alaska grew. The influx of material investment and people produced a viable effort to gain admittance into the Union. On January 3, 1959, President Eisenhower proclaimed Alaska the forty-ninth state.

Alaska Natives played a minor role in the statehood movement. Frank Peratrovich, a Tlingit from Klawock and former president of the Alaska Native Brotherhood, was the only delegate to the constitutional convention in 1955. Those who wrote the state constitution either opposed specific land grants to Native people or felt it was the federal government's responsibility to deal with the issue. Consequently, the Statehood Act contains a major contradiction. On the one hand, it requires the state to disclaim ". . . right and title to any lands or other property (including fishing rights) the right of title to which may be held by any Indians, Eskimos, or Aleuts. . . ." However, in a subsequent section, the state is given the right to select 103 million acres of public lands ". . . which are vacant, unappropriated and unreserved at the time of their selection." There were, of course, no vacant lands in Alaska.

As state officials selected valuable lands, and as different governments imposed their institutions and rules, Native opposition to this encroachment arose. Conflicts developed over a proposed nuclear explosion near Point Hope sanctioned by the Atomic Energy Commission, the prohibition of duck hunting because of an international treaty, and the plan for a hydroelectric dam in the Yukon Flats region, in north central Alaska. In March 1961, the president of the Point Hope Village Council wrote the Association on American Indian Affairs and asked for help. Soon funds were made available for intervillage meetings in which complaints were aired and solutions offered. Within six years, twelve regional associations had been formed to pursue the claims of Alaska Natives.

In 1966 the designated commissioner of the Bureau of Indian Affairs (BIA), Robert Bennett, testified before a congressional confirmation hearing by the Senate Interior and Insular Affairs Committee, and was asked about his views on Native claims in Alaska. He replied that the aboriginal claims were dubious, that state officials were frustrated because of the delays in selecting their land, and that the BIA would work to gain a settlement. Shortly thereafter Bennett, along with the assistant secretary of the interior, Harry Anderson, and the junior senator from Alaska, Ernest Gruening, met to work out an agreement to settle Native claims. They made one major mistake: they did not bother to consult with the Alaska Natives themselves.

Native reaction was swift. In October 1966 a statewide meeting was called in Anchorage by Emil Notti, president of the Cook Inlet Native Association, to join the regional groups in a statewide organization, and draft a policy statement. An agreement was soon reached and Notti was elected as the first president of the Alaska Federation of Natives (AFN). In response to Native pressure, the secretary of the interior imposed a land freeze in November 1966. The effect was to withdraw all public lands from appropriation and to stop the issuance of mineral leases and land patents. Thereafter, federal courts were required to safeguard Native land rights until Congress acted.

A bill to settle the claims of Alaska Natives was introduced in June 1967. The key to a congressional settlement was oil and the dramatic increase in the price of gas and fuel. President Nixon and powerful legislators, including Henry Jackson from Washington State and Wayne Aspinall from Colorado, wanted a domestic source of oil and gas and were committed to the construction of a trans-Alaskan pipeline from the North Slope to the port of Valdez, 800 miles south on Prince William Sound. Unresolved aboriginal claims and endless litigation were the only obstacles. As Don Wright, the newly elected president of the AFN emphasized in a 1970 letter to Len Garment, President Nixon's friend and special counsel:

> An . . . issue of vital importance to Alaska Natives is the overriding question of aboriginal title to the land which would be traversed by the pipeline. In the recent case of *Stevens Village v. Hickel* in the Washington, D.C. federal District Court, Judge Hart ruled that the federal statutes prohibited the issuance of the pipeline permit without first obtaining the consent of the Natives of the village of Stevens. . . . There are many other Native groups having similar claims and protests over which the proposed pipeline would pass.

By the fall of 1971, each party in the claims dispute saw the advantages of an agreement. Nixon and the Senate wanted an independent source of energy; the House wanted a pipeline; the state needed revenue and clear titles; environmentalists wanted more parks and wilderness areas; and Alaska Natives wanted their land. The Alaska Native Claims Settlement Act (ANCSA) was signed into law on December 18, 1971, as Public Law 92–203.

Provisions of ANCSA

ANCSA is a complex law because of the many interests, including federal, state, Native, industrial, and environmental, that it addresses. Private Native corporations will receive title to 44 million acres of land; village corporations will own 22 million acres; and 16 million acres will be owned by eleven of the twelve regional corporations that were established. The remaining 4 million acres went to Native American corporations in four cities, individual grants, allotments and reserves, and cemeteries and historic sites. The $962 million in compensation for the extinguishment of aboriginal claims was channeled through the regional corporations. The corporations are then required to distribute 10 percent of the funds to all stockholders, and 45 percent (after five years it increased to 50 percent) to village corporations and to stockholders who did not live in a village.

While some were impressed with the unusual amount of land and money that was exchanged, others were more skeptical. In the words of two leaders of the Arctic Slope Native Association, Joe Upicksoun and Charlie Edwardsen, in a letter to President Richard M. Nixon, December 18, 1971:

> Although this is a settlement of our land rights the State of Alaska comes first. The federal government . . . comes first, the third parties who have federal and state leases on our land come first. . . . We have been denied our lands, the value of our lands, the opportunity to form an economic basis and our culture is being banished to the eternal night of the Arctic Slope.

In many ways, Alaska Natives derived the fewest benefits from the passage of the Settlement Act. They lost 375 million acres of land and their rights to hunt and fish. The settlement cleared the path for the construction of the pipeline and extraordinary profits for oil and gas companies. For environmental groups and the national government, millions of acres were set aside for public use. Eventually 41 percent of Alaska will be designated as national parks, forest preserves, and scenic rivers; another 19 percent will be for recreation, petroleum reserves, and miscellaneous use. The State of Alaska was allowed to complete the selection of its entitlement under the Statehood Act and to collect over $32 billion in royalties, rents, and taxes from the development of North Slope oil fields on traditional aboriginal lands.

Problems and Difficulties with ANCSA

There are four categories of problems related to the passage of ANCSA. First are the administrative and legal entanglements involved in the implementation of the legislation. The primary issues here were the initial enrollment of Alaska Natives; which villages were eligible for funding and land selections; confusion over cultural boundaries; disputes with the federal and state governments over what lands should be subtracted from corporate entitlements; the extent of transportation and utility easements through Native lands; delays in conveyance of the lands; and revenue sharing between the regional corporations.

Second, Native leaders were also concerned with the deadlines and limitations that were part of the original settlement. After 1991 corporate shares could be sold on the open market and their lands could be taxed. Third, Natives born after December 18, 1971 were not permitted to own stock or receive dividends. To strengthen Native corporations, Congress passed the Alaska Native Claims Settlement Act Amendments of 1987, also referred to as the "1991 Amendments." This law permits the corporations to extend the original restrictions on stock ownership, to continue protecting undeveloped land, and to issue new stock to Natives who are not currently enrolled.

The last category of problems relates to the most controversial aspect of ANCSA: the subsistence lifestyle of Alaska Natives. Section Four of the Act (Public Law 92–203) states:

> All aboriginal titles, if any, and claims of aboriginal title in Alaska based on use and occupancy, including submerged land underneath all water areas, both inland and offshore, and including any aboriginal hunting or fishing rights that may exist, are hereby extinguished.

While the lands around villages could be used for hunting, gathering, and fishing, and indeed should be protected by the secretary of the interior, legislators assumed these traditional pursuits were only transitional and that Alaska Natives would eventually be integrated into the modern economic system.

These expectations have not been fulfilled. Alaska Natives have become increasingly vocal in the defense of their economies and their way of life. In 1976, 75,000 caribou from the Western Arctic Caribou Herd disappeared. Fearing the complete elimination of the herd, state officials restricted hunting to village residents only. A group of sportsmen in Fairbanks then sued, claiming the state government lacked the authority to discriminate against urban hunters. The court agreed. In response to this decision, the Alaska legislature passed a law in 1978 which gave a priority to subsistence use in rural areas. To restore some of these rights to hunt and fish and to gain the political support of Alaska Natives, Congress passed the Alaska National Interest Lands Conservation Act (ANILCA) in 1980, which established a priority for "nonwasteful subsistence use" for rural residents on federal lands. The priority is activated whenever there is a need to restrict the taking of fish and wildlife. In 1982 a number of hunting and fishing groups placed an initiative on the ballot to repeal the state's 1978 subsistence law: the initiative was subsequently defeated. Another challenge to the state law came in 1983, when Sam McDowell, an angler and conservationist, filed suit charging that the distinction that is made between urban and rural leaves out many city residents who depend on hunting and fishing subsistence and includes people in rural Alaska who do not. The Alaska Supreme Court agreed and ruled that the law unfairly discriminates against individuals and that the use of residency as a criterion for subsistence violates the constitutional prohibitions against exclusive or special privileges to hunt and fish, and the denial of equal rights between urban and rural residents.

After the *McDowell* decision, state law was no longer in compliance with the subsistence provisions of ANILCA, and the federal government had to reassume the regulation of game on all national lands in Alaska. This has resulted in a confusing system of dual management of public lands and conflicts over responsibility for migrating fish and other resources. Some Native leaders have argued for tribal control of subsistence; others have called for a constitutional amendment that would enable the state to manage fish and game within its boundaries according to federal law. Alaska's governor has expressed his opposition to a constitutional amendment and supported a suit to overturn the rural subsistence priority in ANILCA. In October 1992, the United States District Court upheld the subsistence preference in ANILCA, arguing that Congress has the right to protect alternative sources of food supply.

Ultimately, the conflict over subsistence is part of a deeper struggle over rights to self-determination and tribal self-government by the Native people of Alaska. ANCSA is silent with respect to tribal powers, though opponents claim Congress implicitly rejects tribal government in its declaration of policy:

> . . . the settlement should be accomplished rapidly, with certainty, in conformity with the real economic and social needs of Natives, without litigation, with maximum participation by

Natives in decisions affecting their rights and property, without establishing any permanent racially defined institutions, rights, privileges, or obligations, without creating a reservation system or lengthy wardship or trusteeship. . . . (Public Law 92–203, Section 2 [b]).

In a recent opinion, the solicitor of the Department of the Interior contended that the purpose of ANCSA was to develop business enterprises, an end that ". . . would be frustrated by a determination that enclaves of federal and tribal jurisdiction continue to exist." The State of Alaska has also opposed tribal initiatives. The Alaska Supreme Court ruled that villages are not immune from suits because they are ". . . not self-governing or in any meaningful sense sovereign." On August 16, 1991, the governor issued Administrative Order 125 which ". . . opposes the expansion of tribal government powers and the creation of 'Indian Country'" in Alaska.

The Alaska Federation of Natives (AFN) is deeply divided over the issue of tribal government. While AFN is funded and directed primarily by the regional corporations, it claims to speak for all Native Alaskans. However, the organization refused to support a proposal in 1987 to transfer corporate lands to what were termed "qualified transferee entities," or recognized tribal governments. During the controversy over subsistence, the AFN has consistently pressed for a state constitutional amendment establishing a rural subsistence priority and avoided the subject of tribal regulation of fish and game. In frustration, tribal advocates formed the Alaska Inter-Tribal Council in 1992 to represent their views. They point to a long history of congressional and judicial support for tribal government in Alaska. The Indian Reorganization Act (IRA), for example, encourages the organization of IRA councils, and the Indian Self-Determination Act recognizes Native villages and regional corporations as eligible for grants to strengthen tribal organizations. The Administration for Native Americans has assisted Native villages in developing tribal constitutions, codes, and courts. The Indian Child Welfare Act, the Indian Financing Act, and the Indian Tribal Governmental Tax Status Act all consider villages to be tribes.

Federal courts have consistently backed tribal governments in Alaska. The most important case involved a suit by two northern villages against the state for their share of revenue funds. State officials had denied their requests because they felt such payments would favor a particular racial class. The Ninth Circuit Court of Appeals disagreed. They first ruled that there are federally recognized tribes in Alaska and that they could find no distinction between Alaska Natives and other Native Americans. As for the racial claim by state administrators, the Court replied:

> . . . the original scheme of the bonus (revenue payments) was based on their identity as political entities. To wipe out their political status on

the ground that status had an ethnic origin is itself a violation of the constitutional command not to discriminate on the basis of race . . . and is presumptively invalid (U.S. Court of Appeals, 1990).

Many Alaska Natives realize that ANCSA and other federal actions and legal interpretations are not enough to secure their traditions and advance their interests. They have therefore acted independently to establish tribal courts, to dissolve city governments, to restrict outside interference, to claim jurisdiction over their lands and resources, to pursue relief in international forums, and to form regional and intervillage compacts. Perhaps, in their struggle for local control and self-determination, there is a lesson for all of us.

David C. Maas

See also **Alaska Native Review Commission**

Further Reading

Arnold, Robert D. *Alaska Native Land Claims.* Anchorage: Alaska Native Foundation, 1976, 1978.

Case, David S. *Alaska Natives and American Laws.* Fairbanks: University of Alaska Press, 1984.

Flanders, Nicholas E. "The ANCSA Amendments of 1987 and Land Management in Alaska." *Polar Record* 25:155 (1989): 315–22.

Morehouse, Thomas A. "Sovereignty, Tribal Government, and the Alaska Native Claims Settlement Act Amendments of 1987." *Polar Record* 25:154 (1989): 197–206.

Smith, Erik, and Mary Kancewick. "The Tribal Status of Alaska Natives." *University of Colorado Law Review* 61:3 (1990): 455–516.

ALASKA NATIVE REGIONAL CORPORATIONS

The Alaska Native Claims Settlement Act of 1971 (ANCSA) required the establishment of both regional and village business corporations to receive and manage the cash and land conveyed by the Act. Between 1972 and 1974, twelve regional and about 200 village corporations were incorporated as profit-making business corporations under the laws of the State of Alaska. The twelve regions were largely defined as the preexisting areas of twelve regional Native associations, which had been established during the 1960s (see map). Every person of at least one quarter Alaska Eskimo, Indian, or Aleut blood who was alive on December 18, 1971, was enrolled into a regional corporation and received 100 shares of stock. There were about 74,300 initial shareholders. The regional corporations were entitled to the subsurface rights to all 22 million acres of village corporation lands, plus full ownership of an additional 16 million acres. They received $440 million—about $6,000 per shareholder—as their 45 percent share of the cash settlement, paid out gradually between 1972 and 1981. The cash was distributed in proportion to the number of shareholders (see table). In 1976, a small Thir-

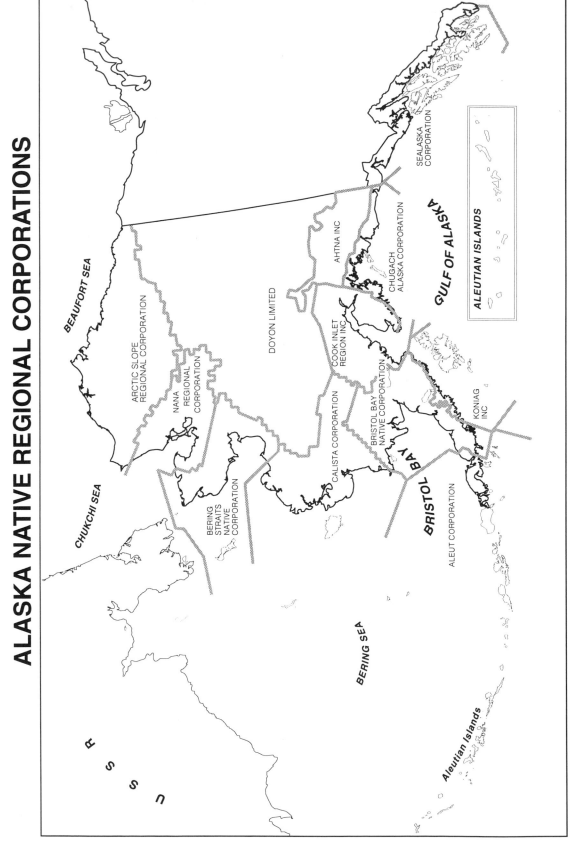

ALASKA NATIVE REGIONAL CORPORATIONS

Source: Based on maps from U.S. Department of the Interior, Bureau of Indian Affaris.

teenth Regional Corporation was established in Seattle by court order, without any land. This corporation has conducted minor business operations since then and will not be discussed further.

Operating History

During the first ten years that followed ANCSA, management struggled to secure the conveyance of promised lands from the federal bureaucracy. In many cases not enough land was available in a region to satisfy the entitlements of the Act. As a result, three corporations returned to Congress or negotiated for valuable resource lands that were not originally open for selection. Sealaska received 340 thousand acres of timberlands from the Tongass National Forest. Chugach Alaska also received national forest timber. Cook Inlet received known oil and gas deposits as well as federal surplus properties worth over $100 million. Throughout the cumbersome land selection process, however, all corporations engaged in exploration for oil, gas, and minerals, often through agreements with major resource developers.

Congress charged the corporations with the broad but elusive goal of improving shareholder well-being. Initially, senior management and boards of directors were almost exclusively Native shareholders, many of whom were political leaders. Managers had to choose how to invest their cash, and how aggressively to seek development of their land. As early as 1974, many began business operations, often entering joint ventures with established firms. In approximate order of importance, the corporations entered the oilfield service, seafood processing, construction, real estate, and marine transportation sectors throughout the state. Some also focused on local business development to provide shareholder jobs. Two of the smaller corporations, Ahtna and Nana, merged with the village corporations in their region.

During the early and middle 1980s the corporations as a group continued to move assets into active business operations. Between 1981 and 1986, their holdings of stocks and bonds dropped from 39 percent of their total asset base to 24 percent, while business capital (property, plant, and equipment) increased from 50 to 60 percent. Individual corporations made major business changes, most in response to losses in seafood, real estate, and construction. All were hurt by the 1986 collapse of world oil prices and the resulting major recession in Alaskan oil and construction. By the end of 1986, most were regrouping after significant business losses and several were near bankruptcy. Some, such as Cook Inlet, Nana, and Sealaska, were beginning large-scale resource development of oil and gas, zinc, and timber, respectively.

In 1986 Congress repealed legislation which had allowed all United States corporations to sell accumulated net operating losses (NOLs) to other corporations for cash. Through the concerted efforts of the Alaska delegation, Alaska Native corporations (both regional and village) were exempted from this repeal,

and thus became the only United States corporations which could legally sell NOLs. Between 1986 and 1988, the regional corporations sold over $1.5 billion worth of taxable losses to other United States companies for $426 million in cash. The corporations generated the losses by selling resource development rights to outside interests. Most of the claimed losses were based on declines in the value of natural resources on ANCSA lands between the time of conveyance and the time of sale. (In arguing for the exemption, Senator Ted Stevens asserted that the Natives had missed the chance to sell their resources when prices were high because of delays in land conveyance by the federal bureaucracy.) Because the corporations paid no cash for these resources and generally assigned them a value of zero on their books, almost all of the $426 million received from NOL sales was counted as corporate income. In any event, the cash infusion from NOL sales amounted to about two-thirds of the original ANCSA payments, and probably saved two corporations from liquidation. Congress stopped the NOL sales in 1988, when it became aware of how much money they were costing the treasury.

Much of the NOL cash income was locked in escrow accounts through 1991, pending IRS approval of the NOL sales. The healthier corporations will chart their course through the 1990s by the way they invest this cash after its likely release. At the start of the 1990s, the corporations seemed to cluster into three groups. The first group consists of those recovering from heavy losses and with few assets: Aleut, Bering Straits, Bristol Bay, Calista, Chugach, and Koniag. The second group—Ahtna, Doyon, Nana, and Sealaska—has consolidated operations, focused on natural resource development where possible, and established financial portfolios as major sources of ongoing income. The third group—Arctic Slope and Cook Inlet—were continuing major business expansions and active participation in oil, gas, broadcasting, and real estate.

The regional corporations were significantly less profitable than United States corporations overall during their first twenty years of operation. All made money on securities investments, and some made significant profits from resource development and sales of tax losses. However, most lost money on direct business operations. Business losses were highest in seafood processing, real estate, and construction. Oilfield services generated the bulk of direct business profits. Between 1974 and 1990, net income varied widely over time and among corporations. As a group, the corporations lost money in seven of the seventeen years. When sales of tax losses are excluded, their best performance was in 1990. After adjusting for inflation, cumulative net income earned during the period ranged from $44,000 per shareholder to a net loss of $7,000 per shareholder. Cumulative dividends paid out ranged from $10,000 to zero. At the end of 1990, book equity per shareholder varied by a factor of 100, ranging from $54,500 to $500.

Alaska Native Regional Corporations Economic Summary

	Ahtna	Aleut	Arctic Slope	Bering Straits	Bristol Bay	Calista	Chugach Alaska	Cook Inlet	Doyon	Koniag	Nana	Sealaska	Total
Initial Shareholders	1,074	3,249	3,738	6,168	5,227	13,306	1,906	6,281	9,061	3,731	4,828	15,780	74,349
Land Holdings (000 acres)													
Surface Estate	1,635	66	4,084	170	0	300	380	924	9,000	160	2,056	340	19,115
Subsurface Estate	1,750	1,572	5,102	1,300	3,037	6,500	940	1,608	12,500	733	2,243	629	37,914
Economic Snapshot													
1990 Assets ($000)	28,432	17,995	141,064	26,291	90,890	12,511	128,402	576,015	156,897	20,048	62,920	257,154	1,518,619
1990 Revenue ($000)	5,891	3,911	218,371	4,664	34,622	6,002	46,945	109,370	49,318	2,707	42,614	108,893	633,307
1990 Net Income ($000)	185	(2,299)	12,079	1,130	1,384	1,805	(25,347)	35,697	10,358	1,020	3,125	16,813	55,951
1991 Employment	375	198	2,462	15	311	NA	155	1,222	180	7	2,050	441	7,416
Shareholder Employment	55	5	827	9	7	NA	39	120	69	4	978	332	2,445
Condensed Balance Sheets (1972–1990, $000)													
Cash from ANCSA	6,429	19,504	22,540	38,086	32,525	80,147	11,471	34,363	53,423	20,031	28,594	93,162	440,275
plus Other Capital	12,819	0	0	139	170	0	12,000	128,732	357	1,563	15,179	0	170,959
plus Cumulative Net Income	8,748	(7,593)	31,564	(12,786)	19,795	(73,074)	22,906	256,595	87,128	(3,096)	19,960	79,603	429,749
less Cumulative Dividends	2,326	1,376	6,069	633	7,211	665	1,488	62,601	8,697	0	10,836	19,991	121,894
equals 1990 Equity	25,669	10,535	48,035	24,805	45,279	6,407	44,889	357,089	132,211	18,498	52,897	152,774	919,089
Cumulative Net Revenues from Natural Resources, before Sharing (1972–1990, $000)	645	56	56,180	36	348	0	0	187,110	7,220	257	11,299	134,708	397,860

Source: Alaska Native Regional Corporation Annual Reports and author estimates

Notes:1. Parentheses ( ) denote negative values.
2. Land holdings are projected full entitlements as of 1991.
3. Sealaska employment estimated from 1988 data.
4. Employment figures include joint ventures and subsidiaries.
5. Other capital comes from mergers with villages (Ahtna, Nana, Koniag); payments in lieu of land (Chugach, Cook Inlet); and partial valuation of resources on ANCSA lands.

Other Issues

Although the regional corporations were established as profit-making entities under Alaskan law, they share many special attributes: some were dictated by ANCSA; others were fostered by the common heritage and social goals of the shareholders.

Recognizing that natural resources are distributed unevenly, Congress required (Section 7[i] of ANCSA) that regional corporations share 70 percent of net revenues from developed timber and subsurface resources among themselves, with the village corporations, and with other shareholders not enrolled into village corporations. Because Congress failed to define "net revenues," the corporations engaged in years of costly litigation and negotiation before agreeing to suitable definitions in 1982. Between 1972 and 1990, the regional corporations generated $398 million in shareable net revenues (see table). Arctic Slope, Cook Inlet, and Sealaska generated 95 percent of this total by selling oil and gas leases and timber. The $139 million distributed to the village corporations has been a critical source of operating income for many. Similarly, the net transfer of $78 million from the three major resource developers to the other nine regional corporations has been an important financial boost for resource-poor shareholders. However, cash earned from sales of tax losses was determined not to be subject to revenue sharing obligations.

Several corporations have focused their efforts on shareholder employment as a corporate goal, even at the direct expense of profits. Counting direct operations, joint ventures, and subsidiaries, the regional corporations in 1991 employed about 7,500 people, or about 5 percent of Alaska's private sector work force. Both Arctic Slope and Nana employed close to 1,000 shareholders each—roughly 20 percent of their shareholders. All corporations have also invested in training programs, often in cooperation with joint venture partners. All regional corporations have contributed significant funds to scholarship, cultural preservation, and social service programs. Of equal importance, corporate leaders have skillfully exercised political power to assure that Alaska Natives received both continued funding of federal Indian programs and a fair share of the state's oil wealth. Much public spending for human services is channeled through the twelve non-profit corporations, which are directly descended from the original regional Native associations formed during the land claims battle. These nonprofit corporations exercise certain tribal authorities delegated to them by the traditional village councils within their region, such as the right to administer health and assistance programs funded by the Bureau of Indian Affairs. Finally, a continuing and critical concern for all corporations is the battle for Native subsistence rights on both corporate and public lands.

The original ANCSA contained several protective provisions which were due to expire in 1991. Native leaders lobbied Congress to extend and strengthen these provisions, and in 1988 the so-called "1991 amendments" to ANCSA became law. The 1991 amendments did three important things. First, the original ANCSA prohibited the sale of corporate stock to non-Natives only until 1991; the 1991 amendments extended sale restrictions until shareholders voted to drop them. Second, the amendments extended indefinitely the exemption of undeveloped land from property taxation, and allowed a corporation to protect land permanently from sale or adverse possession by irrevocably placing it into a "settlement trust" controlled by an independent board of directors. Third, the amendments allowed corporations to issue new stock to Natives born after December 18, 1971.

How have the 1991 amendments been used? In late 1991, before any sales became possible, Congress put a simple moratorium on stock sales until December 1993. The moratorium was largely motivated by the attempt of the Klukwan village corporation to take over Sealaska. With no mechanism for selling stock, individual shareholders lack immediate access to their corporations' wealth. This has led to vigorous debate in some corporations over cash distributions and business strategies. Management has responded with special cash distributions, especially for elders. As of 1992, no corporation had placed any lands in a settlement trust. Also as of 1992, Arctic Slope had issued new shares of stock to its youth, while Nana and Doyon shareholders had approved such an issue, and several other corporations were considering the question.

Stephen Colt

See also **Alaska Native Claims Settlement Act**

Further Reading

Alaska Native Regional Corporations. *Annual Reports.* Anchorage: University of Alaska, Anchorage, Environment and Natural Resources Institute, n.d.

Colt, Steve. "Financial Performance of Native Regional Corporations." *Alaska Review of Social and Economic Conditions* 28:2 (December 1991): 1–24.

Karpoff, Jon, and E.M. Rice. "Organizational Form, Share Transferability, and Firm Performance: Evidence from the ANCSA Corporations." *Journal of Financial Economics* 24:1 (1989): 69–105.

Wuttunee, Wanda. "Competing Goals and Policies of Alaska's Native Regional Corporations." Master's Thesis, University of Calgary, 1988.

ALASKA NATIVE REVIEW COMMISSION

The Inuit Circumpolar Conference (ICC) established the Alaska Native Review Commission (ANRC) in 1983 to review the impact of the Alaska Native Claims Settlement Act (ANCSA) on Alaska Native people. Twelve years after the act was passed by Congress, it had become increasingly apparent that Alaska Native people could lose both ancestral lands conveyed under ANCSA and also control over the Native corporations created by ANCSA. The ICC appointed the Honorable Thomas R. Berger, an internationally recognized Canadian jurist, as the sole commissioner. Berger's mandate in Alaska was to conduct a comprehensive review of the social, economic, political, and environmental impact of ANCSA, independent of the ICC or any other organization in Alaska or elsewhere. The ICC felt that it was important to provide a forum in which Alaska Native people could come forward and speak out about ANCSA and their innermost feelings since they "are their own best witnesses" as to how this congressional legislation has affected their lives. No other comprehensive review of the progress nor the impact of ANCSA had ever been done before. For these and many other reasons, the ICC established the Alaska Native Review Commission.

The backbone of the Commission's work was a village hearing process, complemented by more formal roundtable discussions. Sixty-two village hearings were held and over 1,450 Native people testified. Eight roundtable sessions were also held and both indigenous and nonindigenous representatives from throughout the world participated. All of the testimony was audio-taped and transcribed verbatim in ninety-eight volumes representing more than 800 hours of tapes. The Commission began its work in September 1983 and made its report public in September 1985.

The report of the ANRC, *Village Journey*, though authored by Justice Berger, emphasizes and quotes heavily from the testimony of Native people. The focus of the testimony in almost every community across the state was land. Every individual spoke about protection of Native lands and how it is critical to the preservation of their respective cultures. Nearly everyone discussed the importance of renewable resources, the resources that have sustained these communities through generations. The land and hunting and fishing and culture were spoken of in the same breath. The need to have direct control over the land, land use, and the fish and game was another important theme.

Commissioner Berger found that the chief concerns expressed during the hearings were the interrelated and inseparable issues of land, self-government, and subsistence, and these were thus the primary subjects he addressed in *Village Journey*. Berger's recommendations, contained in Chapter Seven, are centered around the two major themes of transferring land ownership from the corporations to tribal governments, and placing responsibility for regulation of Native lands and water with tribal governments. Berger addressed the concerns that village people raised in their testimony and attempted to provide options for every circumstance. The options outlined are based upon the testimonies of Native people in the villages of Alaska.

The village hearing process of the Commission demonstrated that ANCSA does not reflect and has never reflected the true aspirations of a majority of Alaska Native people in rural villages. Many feel that the corporate structure is not a traditional institution of the indigenous people of Alaska, nor is it one that they freely chose. The interests of the Native regional corporations are those of profit-making corporations and, in fact, many of the regional corporations did not embrace the recommendations of the Berger report.

It is safe to say that Alaska Native people in rural areas have embraced the recommendations of the report. Some have responded individually and others have tried to organize on a regional or statewide basis to gain acceptance of the Berger recommendations. Two examples are the Yupiit Nation movement in southwest Alaska and the recently formed Alaska Inter-Tribal Council. The goals of these two initiatives are to gain greater recognition of the right of self-determination and control over local and national issues relevant to tribal governments. In 1993, the conclusions and recommendations of Judge Berger are still valid and are being pursued in a variety of ways.

Dalee Sambo

See also **Alaska Native Claims Settlement Act**

Further Reading

Alaska Native Review Commission. *Transcripts.* University of Alaska Fairbanks Archives; also available from the Inuit Circumpolar Conference, Anchorage.

Berger, Thomas R. *Village Journey: The Report of the Alaska Native Review Commission.* New York, NY: Hill & Wang, 1985.

Case, Davis S. *Alaska Natives and American Laws.* Fairbanks: University of Alaska Press, 1984.

ALASKAN ATHABASKANS

There are eleven groups of Athabaskan speaking people in Alaska: the Tanaina (Dena'ina), Ingalik (Deg Het'an), Holikachuk, Koyukon, Tanana, Kutchin (Gwich'in), Han, Upper Tanana, Tanacross, Ahtna, and Upper Kuskokwim. According to 1990 United States Census figures, 13,700 Athabaskan people live in Alaska. A majority reside in 55 villages, with local Native populations ranging from less than 50 to a maximum of 500 people. Most Athabaskan villages are located along the Yukon, Koyukuk, Tanana, and Copper rivers, and only a few are accessible by road. The rest can be reached only by airplane, boat, or snowmobile.

Modern Athabaskans

Contemporary Athabaskan villages consist of a mixture of log or frame homes, usually heated by a woodstove. Most homes have running water and electricity. Public buildings include a church and a community hall used for public meetings, ceremonies such as the potlatch, and recreational activities like bingo. There is usually a store and a community office building which houses the offices of the village corporation and village council, as well as a clinic. Many villages also have a community owned laundromat. In addition to a grade school, a number of villages have their own high school which allows children to stay in the village rather than attend boarding school away from home. Modern village life continues to be regulated by the seasons. Year-round employment is rare with only a few full-time jobs available in each village. These include postmaster, community health aide, teacher's aide, and office jobs connected with either the village corporation or village council. More often people work seasonally at construction jobs or fighting forest fires, moving between these types of employment and traditional hunting, fishing, and gathering activities.

The twenty-four-hour days of light in summer bring intensive activity. Those people not involved in seasonal labor spend time fishing for salmon or whitefish which are caught with gill nets, fish wheels, or dip nets. Both kinds of fish are dried for later consumption. Late summer is the time to pick berries, which are usually frozen and eaten throughout the year. By early fall, many village residents turn their attention to hunting moose which is a staple for all Athabaskan people. Moose are often taken in the evening or early morning as they move across the land, and are hunted mainly along rivers from aluminum boats powered by outboard motors. Caribou, Dall sheep, and bears are also hunted. Commercial fur trapping begins in November and continues into early spring. Using snow machines to travel the trap lines, trappers catch lynx, marten, and fox from early to mid-winter, while beaver and muskrat are trapped in the early spring before the ice melts. As the ice leaves the lakes, trappers often finish the season by hunting muskrat with small caliber rifles. By late May or early June, people once again prepare for summer activities.

In smaller villages, government is vested in an elected council organized under the provision of the Indian Reorganization Act (IRA) of 1934. Other villages are incorporated as municipalities and a few have reservation status. Additional governing bodies include an elected school board and an elected board of directors for the village corporation which administers the assets received under the Alaska Native Claims Settlement Act (ANCSA). While formal government is usually in the hands of younger, western educated men and women, the traditional life of the village is directed by traditional chiefs or "tradition bearers." These older men and women, who were brought up under more traditional regimes, have a profound influence on village life. They provide the ties between the past and present, acting both as leaders during village ceremonies as well as advisers to younger village leaders.

Two of the most significant ceremonies are the potlatch and the stickdance. While there are a number of occasions in which the Athabaskan community draws together for the purpose of celebration, none has quite the same significance as the potlatch and stickdance, which are death related rituals. Both ceremonies involve a distribution of gifts, as well as singing, dancing, feasting, and oratory.

The stickdance, practiced by the Koyukon people, lasts from fourteen to sixteen hours and has thirteen special songs associated with it. In the beginning, a spruce pole is brought into the community hall and decorated with ribbons and furs. People then dance around the pole singing the special songs. Twice the pole is taken down and carried around the village; the second time it is not brought back but thrown over the river bank. At the end of the dance, there is a distribution of gifts in which people who actively participated in the funeral are given a new suit of clothes, representing clothing for the dead. After the ceremony is over, these new clothes are left in a sack to be picked up by the spirit of the deceased as it leaves the village for the last time.

The Tanana River potlatch lasts three days. Like the stickdance, the potlatch is hosted by people from one village who invite their relatives and friends from villages in the surrounding area. To feed their guests, which may number as many as 300 people, the hosts kill a moose. Food for the feast includes fried and boiled moose meat, moosehead soup, duck, muskrat, turkey, fish, pies, homemade donuts, and spaghetti. During the first two days there is feasting, oratory, socializing, dancing, and singing. Two kinds of dances and songs are performed at a potlatch: sorry songs which lament the dead, and dance songs which praise life. Both are accompanied by a tambourine style drum covered with moose skin. On the last night, once the dancing is finished, gifts are distributed to the guests according to status and participation in the funeral. Guests of high status, such as village elders, receive a rifle, blankets, a scarf, and a small amount of money, as do other guests directly involved in the funeral, such as pall bearers and those who dig the grave. Guests of lesser status receive blankets, cash, and beadwork. All other guests receive a blanket.

All Athabaskans in Alaska, except for those people living along the lower Yukon River, are matrilineal. This means that descent is determined through the mother and individuals are born into the clan of their mother. Athabaskan society is divided in two halves, called moieties. Each moiety consists of a number of clans. Marriage takes place between people in opposite moieties. When a person dies, members of the moiety opposite from the deceased prepare the corpse, coffin, and grave. Although this system is changing, especially where marriage is concerned, it still operates during funerals and potlatches.

Twentieth-Century History

In 1867 the United States purchased Alaska from Russia. Until then, few Athabaskans had felt the sustained presence of non-Native foreigners, although Russian traders and Orthodox missionaries had penetrated into Tanaina territory near Cook Inlet and made forays up the Copper River into Ahtna country. Additionally, both Russian and English traders had established themselves on the Yukon River. This situation changed in the late nineteenth century with the discovery of gold during the 1880s and 1890s on the upper Yukon River and its tributaries, the Stewart, Fortymile and Klondike rivers. These discoveries were followed by others on the Kuskokwim, Tanana, and Koyukuk rivers, as well as on the Kenai Peninsula. Each consecutive discovery brought hundreds, then thousands of gold seekers into Athabaskan territory. Athabaskan people were never fully involved in mining activities, in part because United States law forbade Natives to hold mining claims, but also because most of them had little interest in gold. Nevertheless, Athabaskan people played important roles by guiding prospectors and rescuing more than a few from the extremes of cold and scarcity of food. Athabaskans also became involved in peripheral activities that supported mining activities, such as supplying fresh meat and cold weather clothing, and acting as river pilots on the steam boats which plied the Yukon River. While the presence of miners was transitory, they nevertheless left a new infrastructure with forms of legal, political, economic, and social administration that continue to have far-reaching consequences for contemporary Athabaskan people.

Coinciding with the Gold Rush were the activities of Protestant and Catholic missionaries. In the mid-nineteenth century, Anglican missionaries followed English traders into the Yukon Valley. After the United States purchased Alaska in 1867, Episcopalians replaced the Anglicans, establishing missions on the Yukon, Koyukuk, and Tanana rivers, while the Catholics established themselves on the lower middle Yukon River. The missionaries struggled to maintain a balance between Native and non-Native survival skills. In addition, the missionaries fought to maintain Athabaskan rights to land and resources and to provide them with a Western education; they were, however, critical of many aspects of their life, particularly Native spirituality. Individual missionaries fought against shamanism and were highly critical of ceremonies, such as the potlatch which, because it required a large distribution of gifts, was considered wasteful and detrimental to Native economic security. Athabaskan people both acquiesced to and resisted missionization. Men like William Loola, Albert Tritt, Chief Isaac, Arthur Wright, and David Paul encouraged the Episcopal Church and participated in interpreting "The Word" to their people. On the other hand, some Athabaskan people resisted attempts by the church to abolish the potlatch, an essential part of their culture which continues to be practiced today.

To missionaries, Western education was the key to Native survival. Initially, the missions held government contracts to provide schools but the government withdrew support in 1895 when they assumed responsibility for the education of Native Americans. In most cases, the missions continued their educational activities by reassuming the government contracts. The emphasis of the missions was always on

boarding school programs which gave them greater control over the children. While boarding school, more often than day school, provided Native children with a higher level of Western educational skills, long absence from the home, however, often created conflicts between generations, especially since the schools actively discouraged the use of Native languages. In the 1930s compulsory education forced parents to send their children to school. As a consequence, families often split up, the mothers and children spending their winters in the village near the school, while the men went out on their trap lines.

The transfer of Alaska to the United States did not immediately alter the legal status of most Alaska Natives except for those, such as the Tanaina, who had been classified as Russian citizens: they lost their rights of citizenship under the treaty of purchase. In addition to having no rights of citizenship (until 1924), under American law Alaska Natives had no aboriginal claims to tribal property, as in the lower forty-eight states. The land laws passed between the Organic Act of 1884 and 1901 equated Native possession with non-Native possession of land. That is, Natives, like Euroamericans, were entitled to land they used and occupied as individuals, but not to land they utilized as a group. While the Organic Act left individual use and occupancy undisturbed, Natives had no legal recourse for getting title except through future congressional action. The Act had further repercussions, because miners were allowed to stake claims as long as they were not on land physically occupied by or improved by Native people. In the summer of 1915 the government met in Fairbanks with Athabaskan leaders from the Tanana River. The chiefs expressed concern over the steady influx of non-Natives attracted by mining and the construction of a railroad from Anchorage to Fairbanks. Federal officials offered to protect land by either establishing reservations or handing out 160-acre allotments. The chiefs declined either choice, saying that neither was appropriate to their way of life.

In 1934 the Indian Reorganization Act was passed, which gave support to the principal of self-determination and abandoned the division of reservation lands into allotments. The Act was amended in 1936 to take into account the unique situation of Alaska Natives. Because Native people already lived in isolated villages and not on reservations, the Act allowed the Department of Interior to designate lands already occupied by Natives as reservations. Yet by 1943 there were only six Athabaskan reservations in Alaska: Copper Center, Eklutna, Tetlin, Fort Yukon, Venetie, and Arctic Village.

During the early 1960s Native efforts to gain land took shape. In 1962, Athabaskans under the leadership of Al Ketzler Sr., from the village of Nenana, formed Dena Nena Henash ("Our Land Speaks") to deal with land issues. This organization was influential in the political activity which culminated in the founding of the Alaska Federation of Natives (AFN) in October 1966. The AFN was organized with financial backing provided largely by the Athabaskan village of

Tyonek, which had earned almost $13 million from oil leases on its reserve. Emil Notti, an Athabaskan from the village of Ruby, presided over the initial meetings, and became the first president of the AFN. The AFN was instrumental in the passage of the Alaska Native Claims Settlement Act (ANCSA) in December 1971. The largest of the twelve regional corporations created by ANCSA, Doyon Ltd., with its nonprofit arm, the Tanana Chiefs Conference, represents Athabaskan villages on the Yukon, upper Kuskokwim, Tanana and Koyukuk rivers. Chief Andrew Isaac of Dot Lake, another prominent figure involved in land issues, became the first traditional chief of the Tanana Chiefs Conference. Two other Athabaskan corporations were also created: Ahtna Corporation, with its nonprofit arm, the Copper River Native Association; and Cook Inlet Region Incorporated, with its nonprofit arm, Cook Inlet Native Association.

Although ANCSA has provided Athabaskan people with political and economic power, it has not been the answer to the chronic problems that face Native Americans in every part of the United States: unemployment, alcohol and drug abuse, and despair. Despite these problems, the Athabaskan people have been remarkably resilient. They continue to live on the land of their forebears, and they continue to believe in the values which tied their ancestors to the land and to one another.

William E. Simeone

See also Alaska Native Claims Settlement Act

Further Reading

Helm, June, ed. *Handbook of North American Indians.* Vol. 6. *Subarctic.* Washington, DC: Smithsonian Institution, 1981.

National Museum of Man. *The Athapaskans: Strangers of the North.* Ottawa: National Museums of Canada, 1974.

Nelson, Richard K. "Raven's People: Athabaskan Traditions in the Modern World." *Interior Alaska: A Journey Through Time.* Eds. Robert M. Thorson, et al. Anchorage: The Alaska Geographic Society (1986): 195–250.

Schneider, William S. "On the Back Slough: Ethnohistory of Interior Alaska." *Interior Alaska: A Journey Through Time.* Eds. Robert M. Thorson, et al. Anchorage: The Alaska Geographic Society (1986): 147–94.

Simeone, William E. *A History of Alaskan Athapaskans.* Anchorage: Alaska Historical Commission, 1982.

ALCATRAZ OCCUPATION

Early in the morning of November 20, 1969, between eighty and one hundred American Indians stepped off a boat onto Alcatraz Island located in the bay waters of San Francisco, California. They claimed the island, until 1963 the site of the federal prison system's toughest maximum security institution, on behalf of the nation's Native American citizenry. Although most of the original group had abandoned the

occupation within a year, as many as 300 Indians continuously controlled "the rock" until June 11, 1971, when federal marshals ousted the remaining fifteen, ending the occupation. Manifestos and demands relating to issues of Native American sovereignty and self-determination issued by the occupation failed to produce tangible results, such as the building of an Indian university on the island. Nonetheless, the drama of the confrontation between the federal government and Indians captured global media attention and a widespread support within and outside the Indian community for the occupation's goals. The Alcatraz takeover constituted one of the most powerful symbols and motivating influences of the pan-tribal Red Power movement for recognition of Native civil rights.

During the 1960s, urban Indians wrestled with feelings of alienation as they attempted to make their social and economic way in the cities. Cut off from rural and reservation tribal communities, they began to seek one another out, crossing tribal lines, and gathering together in urban Indian centers. A new "Indianness" was fostered in these local institutions and at the same time national organizations like the National Congress of American Indians and the new, more radical, National Indian Youth Council promoted Native unity for common political action. At colleges and universities, Native American studies programs were founded, the product of pressure by Indian students also eager for active roles beyond the campus. Their chance came in November 1969, when they comprised the majority of those who took part in the initial takeover of Alcatraz.

The Indian activists at Alcatraz looked to the past for historical precedents to empower Native America. They were very aware that their struggle depended less on initiating new laws establishing civil rights than in forcing acknowledgment of existing rights stemming from treaties, executive agreements, judicial decisions, and past legislation. They relied on an old law that allowed certain tribes to reclaim land appropriated from them by the federal government when the United States no longer needed it. During the next five years, Indians targeted over fifty sites for seizure and occupation as a means of protesting government and societal indifference to unfulfilled treaty rights, diminished tribal sovereignty, racial discrimination, and economic penury.

The prison on Alcatraz had been closed in 1963. The following year, a handful of Sioux occupied the island for a few hours, filing a claim for Native Americans interested in starting an all-Indian university there. They and the 1969 activists cited the 1868 Fort Laramie Treaty as the legal grounds for occupying unused federal lands that were originally Indian. The United States attorney general found this argument invalid in April 1964, but Alcatraz was still not being used by the General Services Administration in 1969. Bay Area Indian organizations had discussed asking permission to build an Indian center on Alcatraz and a conference of Native high and college students at the Santa Cruz campus of the University of California decided to make the island the scene of a demonstration for Indian educational needs. On November 11, fourteen college students occupied Alcatraz for a day and night before yielding to government officials demanding their departure.

The November 20th landing was made by a group calling themselves Indians of All Tribes. The occupation issued an invitation to all Indian tribes and bands throughout the United States, Canada, and Mexico to gather on Alcatraz for a meeting on December 23, 1969, to be tentatively called the Confederation of American Indian Nations. This public communication went on to describe the Indians of all Tribes' intent and rationale for the occupation. The occupiers believed Native Americans had relinquished too much control over their own destinies and wanted to reclaim old traditions and pass them on to their children; a task that would be aided by an Alcatraz Indian cultural center. They also hoped to build a college, a museum, a center of ecology, and a religious and spiritual center. Their invitation to all tribes emphasized the need for pan-Indian cooperation in doing something for themselves, rather than having someone else telling them what was good for them. This would require holding on to the old ways, a goal the invitation identified as the first and most important reason for the occupation.

Richard Oakes, a Mohawk student at San Francisco State University, emerged as the most prominent leader and spokesperson for the Alcatraz takeover. He consistently stressed that Indians in the 1960s were making a last stand for cultural survival, which entailed regaining a degree of self-determination from the paternalism of the federal trust relationship. Similar sentiments were expressed by other Bay Area Indian leaders, including Lehman Brightman, coordinator of the University of California's Berkeley campus' Native American Studies Program, and his student, La Nada Means, a Shoshone-Bannock and one of the first and most articulate of the early occupation. Chippewa Adam Nordwall of the United Bay Area Council of Indian Affairs carried copies of the Alcatraz proclamation to a national conference on Indian affairs in Minneapolis and distributed them after the successful landing. He utilized his extensive contacts with the national Indian community and local Bay Area non-Indian journalists and civic leaders to build support for the occupation.

Activities on the island during the first few months were carried on with tremendous optimism. Schools for the occupation's children were started, a newspaper was begun, and various committees for food and health needs were established and began operations. About ten men assumed the role of police, forming themselves as a security force named the Bureau of Caucasian Affairs. Apparently, this group took itself very seriously and later began to monitor egress and ingress in Alcatraz and searched living quarters for illicit drugs and alcohol in an overly aggressive manner.

Support for the Alcatraz occupation was heartening. Letters and petitions of sympathy and encouragement came from Indians and non-Indians across the nation and from other countries. Hundreds of letters were mailed to the White House, urging that the Alcatraz Indians' demands be met. The news media covered the takeover extensively and usually in a supportive way. Money, food, medical supplies, and other tangible support flowed to the island from non-Indian supporters crucial to the occupation's continuation.

Groups of Native Americans periodically joined the Alcatraz community for shorter or longer stays adding to the problems of organization and leadership. The Indians of All Tribes incorporated on January 15, 1970, establishing a seven-person council. The council, however, had no authority to negotiate or even speak for the occupation without the membership's approval. This evocation of traditional government by consensus was certainly Indian, but not especially effectual for dealing with the myriad complexities of maintaining the occupation and furthering its demands. The diversity of its changing and shifting island population, coupled with the formidable task of trying to represent a national Indian constituency in the face of a generally hostile federal authority, doomed the occupation to factionalism, discontent, and finally despair.

The federal government's strategy in regard to the takeover was one of watchful waiting; it proved a wise course. As disagreements over leadership, governance, and goals increasingly divided and discouraged the occupiers, media attention waned with the passage of time. Coast Guard boats patrolled the waters surrounding the island and in late May 1970, the government cut off water and electricity from Alcatraz. A fire destroyed five buildings and the local press did not buy the Indians' accusation of outsiders setting the blazes. Oakes and other early leaders departed the island and after several more months of inaction and declining numbers, the takeover ended with federal marshals taking off the last fifteen Indians.

In retrospect, the Alcatraz occupation was a symbolic victory in terms of national consciousness raising and the instillation of renewed pride among Indian people. Although specific demands were left unmet and the later occupation was clouded by disharmony and disorganization, the takeover had awakened a spirit and shown a way to combine cultural revival and radical political action. Had it not been for the passions stirred by the takeover and subsequent actions like the Wounded Knee occupation, it is doubtful that the Red Power movement would have achieved its impact on Indians and non-Indians in the 1970s.

Terry P. Wilson

See also **American Indian Movement; Pan-Indianism; Red Power**

Further Reading

Blue Cloud, Peter, ed. *Alcatraz Is Not an Island.* Berkeley, CA: Wingbow Press, 1972.

Fortunate Eagle, Adam. *Alcatraz! Alcatraz! The Indian Occupation of 1969–1971.* Berkeley, CA: Heyday Books, 1992.

Josephy, Alvin M., Jr. *Now That the Buffalo's Gone: A Study of Today's American Indians.* Norman: University of Oklahoma Press, 1984.

Sklansky, Jeff. "Rock, Reservation and Prison: The Native American Occupation of Alcatraz Island." *American Indian Culture and Research Journal* 13 (1989): 29–68.

Thompson, Erwin. *The Rock: A History of Alcatraz Island, 1847–1972.* Denver, CO: U.S. Department of the Interior, National Park Service, Historic Preservation Division, 1979.

ALCOHOL ABUSE

The literature on alcohol abuse among American Indians, at one time rather small, has grown to become a substantial body of useful documents. From approximately one thousand published works in 1977, which specifically analyzed alcohol abuse among Indians, to over twice that many today, the literature has grown in both quantity and quality.

A series of common myths and concepts regarding alcohol and Indians are presented below. These generalized myths are persistent even though more evidence has been accumulated which relates directly to them. The evidence for and against these various myths and common beliefs is presented.

Alcohol Abuse as a Major Health Problem Among Indians

That alcoholism is the leading health problem among Indians is a popular and common statement. It is frequently accepted without question by many people. Yet, it is a half truth at best.

An analysis of the 1968 to 1988 Indian Health Service (IHS) data for the thirty-three states with federally recognized reservations indicates that 17 percent of all Indian deaths are alcohol related. Similar patterns are common in other years as well. These data include an estimate of the percentage of alcohol-related deaths from motor vehicle and other accidents, suicide, homicide, and alcoholism/alcohol dependence. Therefore, alcohol consumption is involved in a very high percentage of Indian deaths; a percentage which is substantially higher than those yielded by a similar analysis for the United States' overall population (4.7 percent). But the term *alcoholism* is a very misleading term when used in the above, opening statement.

Alcoholism refers specifically to alcohol-dependent or chronic drinking behavior, which is only part of the problem. Further insight can be gained by comparing deaths from behavior which is generally the result of alcohol-abusive patterns (sporadic, binge drinking), with those that result from alcohol-specific/alcohol-dependent drinking styles (chronic alcoholic drinking). From 1966 to 1988, 2,213 or 74.9 percent of alcohol-related deaths were from alcohol abusive causes, while 742 or 25.1 percent were from alcohol-specific/alcohol-dependent causes (alcohol-dependence syndrome, alcoholic psychosis, and chronic liver disease specified as alcoholic).

Therefore, it is not fully accurate to state that alcoholism per se is the leading cause of death among American Indians. More accurately, alcohol abuse and alcoholism combine to be a leading cause of mortality. Alcohol induced morbidity (sickness) is also a great problem among Indians, but the above generalization holds true. That is, alcohol abuse produces more sickness and injury than chronic alcoholic behavior. This same pattern is also true in mainstream United States society.

Alcohol Metabolism in Indians

The most persistent myth about alcohol and Indians is that they have particular bio-physiological weaknesses to alcohol; they are "not able to hold their alcohol." In fact, not only do non-Indians believe this, but many Indians also believe that they are less able to metabolize or otherwise process alcohol. One study asked Navajo subjects if Indians have a biological weakness to alcohol that non-Indians do not, and 63 percent of the respondents agreed.

Yet, this myth has virtually no basis in fact. Only one study, done in 1971, ever reported that Indians metabolized alcohol more slowly than non-Indians; and this study has been widely criticized as using inadequate methodology. At least seven other studies of alcohol metabolism among Indians in the past fifteen years have concluded that Indians metabolize alcohol as rapidly, or more rapidly, than matched, non-Indian controls. Furthermore, liver biopsies have shown no discernible difference between Indians and non-Indians in liver structure and phenotype.

Therefore, there is no scientific basis of support for the myth of metabolic deficit. Major reviews of alcohol metabolism among all ethnic groups usually conclude that alcohol metabolism and alcohol genetics are traits of *individuals*, and that there is more variation *within* an ethnic group than there is *between* ethnic groups. Further, when investigators in the above studies attempt to explain alcohol-related behavior, they generally emphasize socio-cultural variables as the major factors.

Indian Alcohol Abuse Problems Are Not Uniquely Indian

Certainly, some of the alcohol-related behavior that Indians demonstrate seems to be quite unique in its manifestations. Indeed, this was a major theme of the early anthropology and sociology literature. Often overlooked, however, is that there are many similarities between Indians and other groups. Therefore, common explanations for both Indian and non-Indian alcohol abuse may exist.

First, the fact that Indians have high rates of alcohol-related death is influenced by *demographic traits*. The American Indian population is very *young*. The median age of Indians in reservation states is in the low twenties overall, while the median age in the United States in 1988 was 32.3. Young populations have much higher rates of alcohol abuse and death from alcohol-related causes than older populations. Therefore, the demography of many Indian communities predisposes them to higher rates of these problems than those experienced in mainstream America.

Second, *geography* plays a role in alcohol-related statistics. Because the majority of all Indians still live in rural, western states, higher death rates are to be expected from factors such as higher-risk environments, proximity to care, delayed emergency care, and availability of services. Serious alcohol-related injuries which occur in rural, western environments more frequently result in death because of the above facts.

Third, *social, political, legal,* and *local policies* create conditions which also exacerbate alcohol-related problems and rates. The low socio-economic status of many Indian families shapes behavioral patterns. Also, because most reservations are still under prohibition, drinking styles and patterns produce higher rates of alcohol-related arrest, injury, and mortality. Changes in educational attainment, social class, and policy might eventually produce very different alcohol consumption characteristics and patterns of alcohol-related problems among Indians.

Finally, tribal *culture* or social practices have in them the seeds of both problems and solutions. Elevated rates of alcohol-related accidental death may arise from dangerous cultural practices, such as not wearing seat belts and lack of concern with safety. The same can be said for other subgroups of the United States population, but common practices such as not using seat belts elevate current alcohol-related death and injury data among Indians. Recent, unpublished data from New Mexico and elsewhere indicate a variable rate of seat belt use among the youth of various tribes. Yet, the majority of Indian youth report lower use than non-Indian youth in the same schools.

In summary, the explanations of high rates of alcohol-related problems and their solutions may well be found in demographic, geographic, political, and cultural variables, which are not necessarily unique to Indians. One must not overlook these relatively simple and conventional explanations.

The Prevalence of Drinking Among Indians

It is often stated by Indians and non-Indians alike that a vast majority of all Indians drink. However, the evidence in the published literature is quite different. There is extreme variation in the prevalence of drinking from one tribal group to another. Unfortunately, however, there are only a handful of extant and published adult prevalence studies. Nevertheless, from the six published studies, one can conclude that adult drinking prevalence is lower in some tribes than the United States averages, about the same in others, and higher in others. Furthermore, drinking prevalence may vary over time in many tribal communities.

Two studies conducted among the Navajo in 1969 and 1984 indicate that in both periods, fewer Navajo adults drank at all (31 percent and 52 percent) than among adults in the general population of the United States (67 percent). The prevalence among the Navajo was increasing during the period covered. Two studies among the Standing Rock Sioux in 1960 and 1980 indicated decreasing prevalence (69 percent to 58 percent), and the overall drinking prevalence was about the same as overall United States averages. Finally, studies carried out among the southwestern Utes (80 percent in 1968) and the Brokenhead Ojibway of Canada (84 percent in 1980) found drinking prevalence rates higher than United States averages. Overall prevalence of adult drinking, therefore, varies widely from tribe to tribe and over time.

Among those who do drink in many tribes, however, there is a substantially higher prevalence (two to three times higher) of *problem drinking* indicators than among the general United States population. Experience with delirium tremens (DTs), drinking more than five drinks per episode, and experience with blackouts are much higher in Indian studies. Therefore, among those Indians who do drink, there are a substantial number of heavy and problem drinkers.

Positive findings are also presented in these studies. For example, middle-aged and older Indian males are more likely to have completely quit drinking than men of most other groups. Also, a lower proportion of the women, in virtually every tribe, drink. Therefore, the overall prevalence of drinking in Indians is not the major or most important variable in the epidemiology of drinking. More important are the *drinking styles*, some of which produce very problematic behavior and consequences.

Common Drinking Styles

Research has documented various styles of drinking among Indians. Generally, two patterns are described which cause either no or few alcohol-related problems. They are *abstinence* and *moderated social drinking*. However, at least two problem drinking patterns are common among subgroups or "peer clusters" in many tribal communities. Many authors have defined a chronic drinking pattern originally called *anxiety* drinking by Frances Ferguson. Also, a *recreational* pattern has been defined by Ferguson and others.

Recreational drinkers are predominantly young (fifteen- to thirty-five-year-old) males, who drink sporadically for special occasions, at night and on weekends, away from home, and in a celebration or party manner. Some young females also participate in this pattern, but they are less involved and generally only for shorter periods of time. This style is not unlike heavy college fraternity drinking. Indian recreational drinkers are high risk for alcohol-related injury, arrest, and death because of the emphasis on flamboyant behavior and high blood alcohol levels for a "blitzed" experience. Many people mature out of this pattern, but a disproportionate number of Indians die young first.

Anxiety drinkers, on the other hand, are more typical of the chronic alcoholic. They are downwardly mobile, unemployed, and socially marginal to both Indian and non-Indian society. They are predominantly male and tend to drink chronically whether alone or with other drinking friends. Anxiety drinkers are commonly found spending long periods of time isolated in border towns or skid-row areas of many western cities.

These two types of problem drinkers produce the alcohol-abusive and alcohol-specific problems described earlier. The recreational drinkers produce much of the accident, suicide, and homicide death, while the anxiety drinkers produce the alcoholism deaths (e.g. cirrhosis of the liver), and a preponderance of pedestrian-vehicle collision deaths.

Explanation of High Indian Alcohol-Abuse Statistics

One can see that the prevalence of drinking alone does not explain the rather extensive problems which Indians have with high rates of alcohol-related death. Recent Indian Health Service data (1986 to 1988) indicate that Indians die more frequently than United States averages from motor vehicle accidents (3 to 4 times higher); other accidents (3 to 4 times higher); suicide (1.5 to 2 times higher); homicide (2 to 2.3 times higher); and alcoholism (5.4 to 7.6 times higher). These ratios of Indian to United States averages reflect rates, not the actual numbers of deaths.

There are three explanations for these differences. One has to do with demographic, social, and political considerations previously discussed. The second is centered on drinking style. The flamboyant drinking styles which are very common in a number of Indian peer clusters (recreational drinking styles, especially) emphasize abusive drinking and high blood alcohol levels. Finally, some heavy drinking peer groups among many tribes encourage, or do not discourage, the frequent mixing of alcohol impairment, risky behavior, and risky environments. Examples are driving while intoxicated, sleeping intoxicated outside in the winter, aggressive activity, and other unsafe practices. Therefore, the mixing of high risk environments, flamboyant drinking styles, and risky after-drinking behavior combine to elevate Indian rates of alcohol-related death and injury far above those of the general United States population.

Perpetuation of the Drunken Indian Stereotype

Many authors and speakers on the topic of Indian drinking and alcohol-related problems often cite statistics which do not capture an unduplicated count of the individuals involved in abusive drinking. For example, if one looks at alcohol-related arrest data, there generally is little opportunity for knowing the true prevalence of the *individuals* causing the problems. Some studies in reservation bordertowns have found that alcohol-dependent, Indian males can account for five to twenty-five alcohol-related arrests or protective custodies in a single year. Uncritical use could therefore report this as five to twenty-five Indians with a problem, rather than a few people with chronic drinking problems and repetitive arrests.

The same can be said of morbidity data. One person with a drinking problem can generate literally dozens of visits to a clinic, inpatient admissions, and emergency incidents. Health care data indicating a large number of patient encounters should not be taken literally as indicating the prevalence of the problem. Only counts of individuals, not visits, should be used for estimating the magnitude of the problem. Even then one is only dealing with the treated prevalence.

For example, in a chart review study of Indian Health Services (IHS) records in the Southwest covering ten years, 21 percent of the individuals who were seen at six IHS general clinic facilities were seen at least once for a mental health or alcohol abuse problem. On average, each episode of mental health or alcohol-related illness accounted for 3.9 outpatient and inpatient visits, before the episode was remedied or ended. Therefore, clinic visit data might lead to the conclusion that these problems were much more prevalent than they were. Data based on individual cases are best for estimating the prevalence of these problems and are too infrequently found in the literature on Indian drinking.

Severity of Drinking

Within the drinking populations of most Indian communities, there is a substantial number of people who drink very heavily. These people are found in both the recreational and anxiety drinker populations. For example, very high levels of intoxication have been found among American Indian victims of motor vehicle crashes in New Mexico. Over 70 percent of those Indians who die in crashes in New Mexico have been drinking. In 1986, the average Blood Alcohol Concentrations (BACs) for the victims of vehicle crashes in New Mexico were: Indian .191, Hispanic .189, and Anglo .128. All ethnic groups were, therefore, averaging levels well above the legal intoxication level (.10). Indians killed in alcohol-related crashes had significantly higher BACs than the Anglos, but similar to the Hispanics. Among the decedents in these crashes who had been drinking, 85.7 percent of the Indians and 82.5 percent of the Hispanics were above the legal limit. This compared with 55.4 percent of the Anglos. Thus, the *level* or amount of drinking among the Indians and Hispanics who drink is very high, probably indicating a similar socio-cultural pattern of drinking by certain peer clusters within these groups.

A similar pattern of blood alcohol levels exists for Indian suicide victims. Among Indian suicides in New Mexico, 69 percent to 74 percent are alcohol-involved, with the alcohol level being quite bimodal. In other words, one-fourth of the victims tend to be completely sober, while three-fourths have very high BACs.

Fetal Alcohol Syndrome (FAS)

As with many alcohol abuse problems, FAS rates vary greatly from one reservation to the next. Extremely high rates have been found in two studies in northwest Canada; and the recording of FAS on Indian birth certificates has been found to be much higher than other ethnic groups. Furthermore, one other study found both high and low risk Indian communities and tribes in the southwestern region of the United States. This variance in rates was based on differing socio-cultural and drinking patterns found within the communities. The range of FAS rates in these studies is from a high of 190 per 1000 children in Canada, to 1.3 per 1,000 children. However, the study, which was based on the largest populations of Indians living in relatively stable reservation communities, documented rates of FAS which were only slightly higher than the estimated United States rate in the 1980s. The overall southwestern Indian rate in 1978–82 was 4.2 per 1000 births, compared to 2.2 for the United States overall. In general, the scientific literature points out that FAS is an "equal opportunity" birth defect and can affect any ethnic group where there are significant levels of maternal drinking. FAS, to a great degree, depends on the quantity, frequency, and timing of maternal drinking. In most tribes there are more alcohol-abstaining women than in the general United States population. This obviously protects a substantial proportion of Indian children. However, in most every Indian population ever studied, a small number of very heavy drinking women produce all of the FAS children.

Prevention Programs

In spite of the unique social and cultural nature of each tribe, prevention and intervention programs designed for one tribe can be used in others. It has often been implied that each tribal community is so unique that programs have limited or no applicability across tribal settings. But detailed knowledge of the particular history, culture, and current epidemiological features of alcohol abuse in a tribal community can provide a basis for customized adaptation of programs to other, relatively similar tribes and communities. Professionals and tribal officials can seek such data and apply them carefully and sensitively for culturally appropriate prevention programs.

Two examples of comprehensive, database-based prevention programs for Indians deserve mention here. Fetal Alcohol Syndrome (FAS) prevention was begun on a few reservations in the early 1980s in southwestern United States. Knowledge of FAS in tribal populations and among health care providers led to population-based screening to determine the prevalence of FAS in the community. The screening provided an assessment of the social, cultural, and political factors which produced maternal drinking severe enough to cause FAS. The lessons learned in the Southwest were then translated into broadly applicable prevention protocols and training curricula. These were then spread throughout the United States by the National Indian FAS Prevention Program. Indian groups now lead the nation in their knowledge of FAS and the number and quality of programs operating to prevent it.

In the future, the same sort of alcohol abuse prevention efforts could be undertaken by tribes for broad, policy-based, primary prevention initiatives. With a knowledge of a tribal community's specific patterns of alcohol abuse (and alcohol-related morbidity, mortality, and arrests), many alcohol abuse prevention techniques which were pioneered elsewhere can be applied by tribal groups for substantial gain. Most tribes have the cultural, legal, and political power to attack substance abuse of all kinds through community policy. Policy and other community-based initiatives can shape the normative practices determinant of drinking behavior and replace abusive norms with more positive ones.

Conclusion

The heavy consumption of alcohol is a problem among a certain segment of many American Indian tribal groups. Compared to United States averages, problem drinking indicators are substantially higher in many tribal groups, even though the prevalence of adult drinking is often lower. The normative pattern of drinking among these alcohol abusing subcultures combines very heavy drinking with a variety of risky behaviors, which produce high rates of morbidity, mortality, arrest, and other problems. Because Indians are similar to all other human groups in their basic biophysiologic processing of alcohol, a wide range of prevention and intervention modalities can be used to improve the extant and future problems of alcohol abuse. Cutting through the myth of the drunken Indian, however, remains a constant challenge to prevention. Tribal groups can do it, for they can draw on both their traditional culture and modern scientific and public health knowledge to implement programs of change.

Philip A. May

See also Health; Indian Health Service; Mental Health

Further Reading

Levy, Jerrold E., and S.J. Kunitz. *Indian Drinking: Navajo Practices and Anglo American Theories.* New York, NY: Wiley Interscience, 1974.

Mail, Patricia D., and David R. McDonald. *Tulapai to Tokay.* New Haven, CT: HRAF Press, 1980.

May, Philip A. "Alcohol Abuse and Alcoholism Among American Indians: An Overview." *Alcoholism in Minority Populations*. Eds. Thomas D. Watts and Roosevelt Wright. Springfield, IL: Charles C. Thomas (1989): 95–119.

———. "Fetal Alcohol Effects Among North American Indians: Evidence and Implications for Society." *Alcohol Health and Research World* 15:3 (1991): 239–48.

———. "Alcohol Policy Considerations for Indian Reservations and Bordertown Communities." *American Indian and Alaska Native Mental Health Research* 4:3 (1992): 5–59.

ALEUT

See Alutiiq; Unangan

ALIBAMU

See Alabama-Coushatta

ALLOTMENT

The allotment of Indian lands refers to the policy of the federal government of dividing Indian reservations into parcels assigned to individual families, usually under a highly restricted form of fee simple ownership (the usual form of private land ownership in the United States). The basic legislation was the General Allotment (Dawes) Act of 1887.

The humanitarian reformers who pushed for the passage of the Dawes Act believed that dividing reservations into privately owned farms would break the hold of the chiefs over individual Indians, encourage them to become farmers, and hasten their assimilation into white culture. The basis of this belief was a largely inaccurate model of Indian societies popular among social scientists in the 1880s. Some reformers also saw allotment as a way of protecting Indian lands from further loss to white settlers. The law had passed with little opposition, since it also allowed white settlers to settle and purchase unallotted lands from tribes. Allotment did not begin with the Dawes Act; the federal government had allotted some reservations by special treaty before 1887. The federal government continued to issue allotments until 1934.

At its heart, allotment was a contradictory policy. Reformers wished to make Indians into farmers by giving them private property rights in land. As the reformers did not feel that Indians could manage their own affairs, they placed numerous restrictions on the land given to protect them from unscrupulous whites or other members of their own tribe. In the end, these restrictions negated the benefits of private property without protecting Indians or allowing them to fully use their resources.

Relevant Legislation and Court Decisions

The General Allotment (Dawes) Act of 1887. This Act authorized the president to survey a reservation, prepare a tribal census, and subsequently to divide it into 160-acre holdings (or allotments), assigning each one to a head of a family. Several tribes, notably the Cherokee, Choctaw, Chickasaw, Creek, and Seminole (the Five Civilized Tribes); the Osage in Oklahoma; and the Seneca in New York were specifically not subject to the Dawes Act. These tribes had lobbied Congress to be exempt from the law, since they wished to maintain their tribal governments. Under the original terms of the Act, an Indian immediately became a citizen of the United States when granted an allotment. His or her allotment, however, was held in trust for a twenty-five-year period, during which the allottee could not lease, sell, or will his land. If an Indian died before the end of the twenty-five-year trust period, the land was divided among his heirs according to the state laws for intestate individuals. These restrictions were imposed because Congress feared that Indians would be cheated out of their land as had happened to many Indians whose land was allotted by treaty before 1887. Indians who did not live on a reservation could receive allotments from the public domain. Unallotted land on the reservation could be declared surplus and opened for sale to non-Indians, with the proceeds held in trust for the tribe.

Modifications and Amendments to the Dawes Act. Congress modified the basic provisions of the Dawes Act several times. In 1891 Congress amended it so that each adult received an allotment of 80 acres (rather than give 160 acres to the head of the household). More importantly, the amendment allowed the commissioner of Indian affairs to lease allotments to white farmers. In 1902 Congress allowed the commissioner to authorize the sale of heirship allotments (allotments of deceased Indians that had been divided among multiple heirs). This is sometimes referred to as the "Dead Indian Act."

The most important amendment to the Dawes Act was the Burke Act of 1906. The Burke Act allowed the commissioner of Indian affairs or one of his agents to declare an allottee to be competent to manage his or her own affairs before twenty-five years were up, or to extend the period of guardianship beyond the original term. If the federal agent decided an Indian was competent to manage his or her own affairs, that individual received a "patent-in-fee," indicating he or she owned the land as private property (in fee simple) without restrictions and was liable for state and local taxes. With the passage of the Burke Act, an Indian became a citizen only when he or she was recognized as competent; and he or she could be declared competent without his or her consent. In the 1920s, the courts ruled that Indians who had received patents-in-fee without their permission could return the land to trust status if they still owned the land. In 1907 Congress authorized the commissioner of Indian affairs to sell the allotments for any Indian in trust status where he deemed it appropriate. In 1910, Congress allowed Indians to make wills to avoid the problem of dividing allotments among heirs, but the problem remained.

The Curtis Act of 1898. This Act authorized the Dawes Commission to make allotments to members of the Five Civilized Tribes and abolish tribal governments without agreements with the tribes. The law was never implemented, however, as each of the tribes reached a separate agreement with the federal government. A commission headed by former Senator Henry Dawes was appointed to survey conditions in Indian Territory in 1893. This commission recommended that tribal governments be abolished and tribal lands divided among members of the tribe. Some tribes reached agreements to divide their lands in 1897; the last hold out tribe, the Creeks, ratified an agreement in 1901. These agreements divided the tribal lands among all enrolled members of the tribe. Part of each Indian's allotment, called the homestead, was held in trust and could not be sold without permission. The restrictions on sale were quickly relaxed, however. In 1908 Congress removed all restrictions on the sale of Indian land except the homesteads of Indians with half or more Indian ancestry. Remaining limits on the sale of land in Oklahoma could be removed at the discretion of the commissioner of Indian affairs. In all, 15.79 million acres were allotted to 101,506 tribal members, including 2,582 whites married to Indians and 23,405 Blacks who had been slaves prior to 1863. In 1901 Congress made all Indians in Indian Territory citizens of the United States.

Lone Wolf v. Hitchcock, 1903. A suit was brought by Lone Wolf, a Kiowa, to block the sale of surplus lands on the reservation without tribal consent. The courts ruled that the federal government did not need the tribe's consent to sell surplus land, regardless of prior treaty stipulations. This greatly weakened the position of tribes attempting to hold surplus lands as tribal property.

The Alaska Allotment Act of 1906. This Act extended the provisions of the Dawes Act to Alaska. The land in Alaska was so poor, however, that 160 acres was too small to make an efficient farm. Further, there was little pressure from the white community to purchase Indian land. As a result, no one saw any reason to allot land in Alaska and the law had no effect there.

Implementation of the Allotment Policy

The way in which the federal government allotted Indian reservations was extremely inconsistent. First, the government did not allot all reservations at once. Some were allotted shortly after the passage of the Dawes Act, but most reservations were not allotted until much later. Some reservations, however, were never allotted at all. These included reservations in New York, subject to state law, and many important and populous reservations in Arizona and New Mexico, where there was little surplus land available for non-Indians.

The government's choice of when to allot a reservation and which reservations not to allot was not by chance. The first reservations to be allotted were in areas that whites were interested in settling and developing for commercial agriculture. The allotment of reservations after 1900 followed the spread of commercial agriculture to drier areas of the West. As those lands became more valuable, settlers and their representatives in Congress placed more pressure on the commissioner of Indian affairs to allot attractive reservations. Reservations in areas where there was little pressure from outside interests to open the land, or where Indians were using most of the land, as in the Southwest, were typically not allotted.

Second, the way in which allotment was carried out also varied from reservation to reservation. On some reservations all Indians received their allotments at the same time. On other reservations, especially larger reservations in the West, allotments were issued gradually over many years. Occasionally, land was opened for sale to whites before most Indians had received allotments. The Meriam Report complained in 1928 that agents often did little to assist Indians in choosing allotments. Sometimes Indians picked less valuable farm land near water or firewood.

Once an Indian received an allotment, the federal government continued to supervise his or her property until he or she received full title to the land, called a fee patent. Thus the agent had to approve leases (after 1891) or sales (after 1901). The agent also managed individual and tribal trust funds.

The number of allotments issued varied greatly from year to year. Excluding the Five Civilized Tribes, a total of 3.72 million acres were allotted in the years from 1888 to 1899. Most of these were on reservations in western Oklahoma, the eastern Plains states (Minnesota, the Dakotas, Iowa), and the western portions of Washington and Oregon. The largest number of acres allotted was in the years from 1900 to 1916, when the federal government allotted 14.74 million acres, not including allotments from the public domain or the Five Tribes. Many of these allotments were on large reservations in the western plains states. The pace of allotment declined after 1916. A total of 5.4 million acres were allotted from 1916 to 1933. In all, roughly 25.4 million acres were allotted to Indians under the Dawes Act or by special legislation from 1887 to 1933, including 1.57 million acres of land taken from the public domain. Additionally, 15.8 million acres were allotted to members of the Five Tribes in Oklahoma between 1897 and 1902.

Outside Oklahoma, allotment did not dissolve Indian reservations. Indian reservations remained subject to special laws of the federal government concerning Indian country, although now non-Indians could own land on the reservations. In Oklahoma, reservations were abolished and many of the trusteeship functions of the federal government transferred to state courts.

The Burke Act of 1906 gave the agents the authority to remove all restrictions on allotted land. It was the policy of Commissioner Cato Sells, beginning in 1917, to end federal supervision of as many Indians as were ready. Sells also wished to put as much land as possible into production during World War I. As a result, more patents-in-fee were issued from 1917 to 1920 than in the previous ten years combined.

After 1920, the pace of allotment and the issuing of new patents-in-fee slowed, reflecting both a concern that too many Indians had sold their land, and a slowdown in the demand for Indian land by white farmers.

Consequences of the Allotment Policy

The allotment policy is almost unanimously regarded as a mistake from an Indian perspective. One consequence of the allotment policy is that the land base of Indian tribes declined from a maximum of 139 million acres (including additions to Indian reservations in the twentieth century) to 34,287,336 acres in 1934. In addition, a total of 16.4 million acres allotted to Indians under the Dawes Act or by special treaty remained under federal supervision, as were 1.43 million acres allotted to members of the Five Civilized Tribes. This total includes 6.25 million acres of heirship allotments. Allotments that were no longer in trust had either been sold by the government for individual allottees, or the owners had received title by the issuing of fee patents. There is no record of how much of the land removed from trust status was still owned by Indians, but much of it was undoubtedly sold.

Selling land was not necessarily against Indian interests; but, in many cases, the sales were without their consent and left tribes with a diminished base that was inadequate for a growing population. Often, too, reservations were checkerboarded with mixes of Indian and non-Indian lands, making it hard to form efficient sized farms or ranches.

Allotment was justified as a way of promoting Indian farming. Yet, in fact, under allotment the amount of Indian farming declined rather than grew. A number of Indians had become farmers or ranchers using modified forms of use rights in the late nineteenth century. By 1910 there were over 3.1 million acres in Indian farms in Oklahoma and the ten states in which most allotments were issued. By 1930 this had declined to less than 2.4 million acres. This decline was due in large part to allotment itself. The way in which lands were allotted discouraged Indian farmers by making it easier to sell or lease lands than before. At the same time, federal policy failed to adequately train Indians to be farmers, left them with no access to credit for improvements or machinery, and sometimes divided reservations into fragmented holdings that were hard to farm efficiently.

Evaluation

So much land was ceded by Indians or sold without their consent as a result of allotment that a natural question is whether the policy was simply a scheme to deprive them of land. The irony is that many who supported allotment were sincere in their desire to help the Indians. This includes the reformers who supported allotment and the commissioners of Indian affairs who carried out the policy. They were convinced that allotment was the best way to promote farming and the assimilation of Indians into white society. Their preconceptions were so powerful that the original reformers and those who carried out the policy failed to understand the real nature of Indian societies, the richness of their institutions, or the need to allow them to shape their own destinies. Of course, once in place, outside interests and the bureaucratic interests of the Office of Indian Affairs itself had a powerful impact on how policies were carried out.

Allotment had a number of negative consequences for American Indians, including a reduction in resources available to tribes, the checker-boarding of reservations into small parcels that has made it more difficult to use reservation resources, a discouraging of the use of reservation lands by Indians, and a legacy of heirship allotments that often have many owners and are too small to operate economically. At its heart, the policy, however paternalistic and naive, was well-intentioned. The consequences for Indian peoples, however, were largely negative, and the legacy remains today in the land tenure to be found on many reservations.

Leonard A. Carlson

See also **Agriculture; Government Policy: 1900 to 1933; Meriam Commission; Reservations**

Further Reading

Carlson, Leonard A. *Indians, Bureaucrats, and Land: The Dawes Act and the Decline of Indian Farming.* Westport, CT: Greenwood Press, 1981.

Hoxie, Frederick. *A Final Promise: The Campaign to Assimilate the Indians, 1880–1920.* Lincoln: University of Nebraska Press, 1984.

McDonnell, Janet A. *The Dispossession of the American Indian, 1887–1934.* Bloomington: Indiana University Press, 1991.

Prucha, Francis. *The Great Father: The United States Government and the American Indians.* Vol. 2. Lincoln: University of Nebraska Press, 1984.

ALUTIIQ

The Alutiiq people (plural, Alutiit) have occupied the coastal areas of southcentral Alaska, including Prince William Sound, the lower Kenai Peninsula, Kodiak Island, and the southern Alaska Peninsula, for at least 7,000 years. Alutiiq or Aleut are currently the most preferred self-designations for the indigenous people of this area. The use of the term "Aleut," however, often confuses the Alutiiq with the aboriginal people of the Aleutian Islands, who have a different culture and language. Though common today, the term Aleut was externally applied by the Russian fur traders in the eighteenth and nineteenth centuries, both to the Aleutian Island people, whose self-designation is Unangan, and to the Alutiiq people, who called themselves *Sugpiaq*. The Alutiiq people are made up of at least three major subgroups, the *Chugachmiut* (Prince William Sound), the *Unegkurmiut* (lower Kenai Peninsula), and the *Qikertarmiut* (Kodiak Island). The Kodiak Alutiit are also referred to as *Koniagmiut* or *Koniag*. Because the Alutiit are closely related to all the Inuit across the Arctic, including Alaska, Siberia, Canada, and Greenland, anthropologists have, in the past, classified the Alutiit as Pacific Eskimos. This term is falling out of favor, even among anthropologists, as Alutiiq people strenuously object to being called Eskimos.

When the Danish explorer Vitus Bering, on behalf of Russia, made the first European landing in Alaska, it was in Alutiiq territory on Kayak Island in Prince William Sound. At that time, Alutiiq culture was thriving with a population estimated at 20,000 spread among many villages, some of which were very large. The largest concentration was in the Kodiak Island area where there were sixty-five villages. Disease and natural disasters greatly reduced the population over the next two hundred years, and today there are a total of fifteen Alutiiq villages and five communities within urban settings. Currently, the total Alutiiq population is about 5,000. The villages are accessible only by water or air and severe weather conditions of wind, fog, and rain often hamper travel. As a maritime people, the Alutiit have always depended heavily on the sea for their livelihood. Into the early twentieth century, skin boats called *qayaqs* were used to pursue a variety of sea mammals including sea otters, seals, sea lions, and whales. Because of sheer abundance, the staple food was and continues to be salmon. Many Alutiiq people of today fish for salmon commercially as well as for subsistence.

From the time of the establishment of the first permanent Russian settlement in Alaska at Three Saints Bay (near present-day Old Harbor on Kodiak Island) in 1784, until Russia's sale of Alaska occupation rights to the United States in 1867, the Alutiiq people have undergone a severe assault on their culture. Enslaved by the Russians, they were forced to hunt sea otters for the valuable pelts. Introduced diseases quickly decimated the population. Despite the sad aspects of the Russian contact period, Alutiiq people of today retain considerable Russian influence. The Russian Orthodox Church remains the center of social life in Alutiiq villages, Russian surnames are common, Russian foods are still routinely eaten, and many elders still speak the Russian language.

After Alaska shifted from Russian to American control, the Alutiit were forced to acculturate for the second time in less than a century. Adapting to American ways meant learning to speak English and coming under control of the American education system that had an official policy of assimilation. Many Alutiiq adults of today are products of mission schools or Bureau of Indian Affairs boarding schools. In both cases, students were required to speak English and were punished for speaking their own language. Consequently, the Alutiiq language, also known as *Sugcestun* and *Suk*, is now considered endangered, although widespread efforts are ongoing to preserve it. Even today, however, it is not unusual to find elders who are trilingual, speaking Alutiiq, Russian, and English.

A defining twentieth-century event for Alaska Natives was the passage of the Alaska Native Claims Settlement Act of 1971 (ANCSA). The impact on the Alutiiq people may have been even more profound than in many other cases. The Alutiiq culture area fell into three of the twelve geographic regions established under the act. Thus, there are Alutiiq communities represented by three different regional ANCSA corporations, Chugach Alaska Corporation, Koniag, Inc., and the Bristol Bay Native Corporation. This added a new identity to Alutiiq people, who now often identify with an ANCSA region rather than with the Alutiiq cultural area.

Prior to European contact, the Alutiit utilized an egalitarian form of government. There was apparently no strong central government and local leaders were appointed on the basis of special skills and abilities. In the nineteenth century a form of government evolved that served the Alutiit well for a century or more. This involved an appointed chief, called a *Toyuq*, in each village who was assisted by a "second chief," called a *Sukashiq*. The appointments were done "by tongue" or consensus of a council of elders. Votes were not taken. This system worked in harmony with the Russian Orthodox Church, which was well established by this time.

With the arrival of a more visible Bureau of Indian Affairs (BIA) in the mid-twentieth century, the Alutiit, as with other Native groups in Alaska, were forced to adopt a new form of tribal government that satisfied the BIA. This new system required an elected tribal council. Following the inclusion of Alaska under the Indian Reorganization Act (IRA) by an amendment in 1936, some Alutiiq villages formed IRA governments. These remain in use today with each of the other villages having what is termed a "traditional" government. These governments also have an elected tribal council and look very much like the IRA governments, but are not sanctioned under the IRA. As the village tribal governments are the equivalent of "Indian tribes," with a government-to-government relationship with the United States government, Alutiiq villages have been very involved in federal Indian policy of self-determination. The most visible example of this has been the contracting for health, education, and social services with the federal government under the Indian Self-Determination Act. Because Alutiiq villages are so small (most in the 100 to 200 population range) this contracting has been done primarily through tribal organizations which are consortiums of village governments. Once again, because of the "regions" established under ANCSA, there are three regional tribal organizations providing services. They are the Bristol Bay Native Association (which primarily serves a Yup'ik population, but also includes the Alaska Peninsula Alutiiq villages), Chugachmiut (formerly called The North Pacific Rim), and the Kodiak Area Native Association.

Natural and human caused disasters have had a catastrophic effect on Alutiiq communities in recent decades. On March 27, 1964, the Great Alaska Earthquake unleashed a *tsunami* that devastated several Alutiiq villages. On Kodiak Island, the village of Old Harbor was nearly totally destroyed but rebuilt in its same location while the village of Kaguyak was completely wiped out and not rebuilt at all. On nearby Afognak Island, the village of Afognak was destroyed and rebuilt as Port Lions in a new location on Kodiak Island. In Prince William Sound, the village of Chenega was destroyed with twenty-three residents losing their lives. It took twenty years, but the remaining residents were able to regroup and built a new village, Chenega Bay, in a new location. On March 24, 1989, just three days short of the twenty-fifth anniversary of the Great Alaska Earthquake, the Exxon *Valdez* oil tanker ran aground in Prince William Sound four miles from the Alutiiq village of Tatitlek. By the time the nearly 11 million gallons of oil had spread, it had covered beaches at or near all of the Alutiiq villages and communities. The loss of sea life that the Alutiiq depend on for subsistence was tremendous. The total impact of that disaster may not be known for many years.

In the mid-1980s on Kodiak Island a conscious effort to preserve and revitalize Alutiiq culture was begun as a result of the realization that many aspects of Alutiiq culture, and thus of Alutiiq identity, were fading away. One visual example of this movement is the Kodiak Alutiiq Dancers, a group that now performs across Alaska. Other aspects of this revitalization effort include language preservation, wood carving, kayak building, archaeology projects, preservation of oral histories, and a "sobriety movement" that stresses pride in heritage. A significant event in 1991 was the reburial of 756 ancestral skeletons in the Kodiak Island village of Larsen Bay. They had been excavated by the Smithsonian Institution over fifty years before and were returned after a lengthy struggle. The revitalization effort has spread across the Alutiiq cultural area, and it is now clear that the Alutiiq people themselves will decide how and at what pace their culture will change.

Gordon L. Pullar

See also Alaska Native Claims Settlement Act; Yup'ik

Further Reading

Clark, Donald W. "Pacific Eskimo: Historical Ethnography." *Handbook of North American Indians*. Vol. 5. *Arctic*. Ed. David Damas. Washington, DC: Smithsonian Institution (1984): 185–97.

Crowell, Aron. "Prehistory of Alaska's Pacific Coast." *Crossroads of Continents: Cultures of Siberia and Alaska*. Eds. William W. Fitzhugh and Aron Crowell. Washington, DC: Smithsonian Institution Press (1988): 130–40.

Davis, Nancy Yaw. "Contemporary Pacific Eskimo." *Handbook of North American Indians*. Vol. 5. *Arctic*. Ed. David Damas. Washington, DC: Smithsonian Institution (1984): 198–204.

Hrdlička, Aleš. *The Anthropology of Kodiak Island*. Philadelphia: The Wistar Institute of Anatomy and Biology, 1944. New York, NY: AMS Press, 1975.

Jordan, Richard H., and Richard A. Knecht. "Archaeological Research on Kodiak Island, Alaska: The Development of Koniag Culture." *The Late Prehistoric Development of Alaska's Native People*. Eds. Robert D. Shaw, Roger K. Harritt, and Don E. Dumond. Anchorage: Alaska Anthropological Association (1988): 225–306.

AMERICAN INDIAN CHICAGO CONFERENCE

The American Indian Chicago Conference (AICC) was a major watershed in the history of contemporary Native Americans. Starting with a series of regional conferences, the AICC culminated with a week-long conference from June 13 to 20, 1961. Nearly 500 American Indians from 90 separate communities met at the University of Chicago, at a convocation organized by anthropologist Sol Tax and his assistant Nancy Lurie, to voice their opinions about a wide variety of concerns affecting Indian affairs in the United States. This convocation drafted the *Declaration of Indian Purpose*, an elaborate policy statement, which, among other things, asked for a reversal of the federal government's termination policies; for increased Indian educational opportunities; more economic development programs and better health care delivery systems; for the abolition of ten Bureau of Indian Affairs (BIA) area offices; for the protection of Indian water rights; and for presidential reevaluation of federal plans to build the Kinzua Dam.

The idea for AICC was developed in 1960. Tax, after discussions with members of the Schwartzhaupt Foundation, developed a proposal to update the Meriam Report, a comprehensive analysis of American Indian conditions and federal policies toward Indians undertaken by scholars for the Institute for Government Research and published in 1928. Tax insisted that, unlike the Meriam Report, the Indians should have the central role in producing a document assessing the current scene. Having been initially awarded $10,000 by the Schwartzhaupt Foundation, Tax then approached the leaders of the National Congress of American Indians (NCAI) for support of his idea. At a time of significant loss of Indian land as a result of federal hydroelectric and/or flood control projects, and major efforts to terminate federal treaty and trust responsibilities to Indian nations, Tax's proposal received a favorable response from the NCAI leadership. It also endorsed Tax's only stipulation, namely that any and all Indians have the opportunity to participate in the deliberations, which meant that all Native Americans, federally as well as nonfederally recognized Indians, were welcome at the AICC.

As a result of Tax's and Lurie's efforts, many nonfederally recognized Indian nations took their place in debates for the first time, thus stimulating the movement for federal recognition among these communities in the past three decades. Moreover, the AICC also stimulated the growth of American Indian activism. Since the older, more mainstream NCAI had formally endorsed the convocation, many younger, more militant delegates felt that their voices were not given full expression. After the AICC met in June 1961, these young activists proceeded to Gallup, New Mexico, where, during the late summer, they established the National Indian Youth Council.

On August 15, 1962, thirty-two Indian delegates of the AICC presented the Declaration of Indian Purpose to President Kennedy at a White House ceremony. They then met with Vice President Lyndon Johnson and other Capitol Hill leaders about a new legislative program for Native Americans. Thus, in effect, the AICC was truly a vast experiment in action anthropology, whose significance has been felt for the past three decades.

Laurence M. Hauptman

See also **National Indian Youth Council; Red Power**

Further Reading

Hauptman, Laurence M. "The Voice of Eastern Indians: The American Indian Chicago Conference of 1961 and the Movement for Federal Recognition." *Proceedings of the American Philosophical Society* 132 (1988): 316–29.
Lurie, Nancy O. "The Voice of the American Indian: Report on the American Indian Chicago Conference." *Current Anthropology* 2 (December 1961): 478–500.
Tjerandsen, Carl. *Education for Citizenship: A Foundation's Experience.* Santa Cruz, CA: Schwartzhaupt Foundation, 1980.

AMERICAN INDIAN DEFENSE ASSOCIATION

The American Indian Defense Association (AIDA), the primary vehicle for the reform of federal Indian policy during the 1920s, was incorporated under the laws of the State of New York in May 1923. The AIDA was the creation of John Collier, a former New York City community organizer who became interested in American Indians following a visit to Taos, New Mexico, in 1921. Following Collier's appointment as commissioner of Indian affairs in 1933, the AIDA floundered, although it maintained its existence until 1938, when it was absorbed into the newly created American Association on Indian Affairs.

The AIDA maintained the facade of a well-organized lobby, with offices in Washington, D.C., a board of directors composed of influential and well-known community leaders from both coasts, and fundraising chapters in New York, San Francisco, and Santa Barbara, California. But it was always a one-man organization. As executive director, Collier was the author of most of the AIDA's publicity releases, its chief fundraiser, and its spokesman in Washington. Although the AIDA conducted national fundraising campaigns and claimed over a thousand members at its peak, the bulk of its funding came from five wealthy Californians: Pearl Chase of Santa Barbara; Dr. John Randolph Haynes of Los Angeles, whose contribution was specifically designated for Collier's salary; and Charles de Young Elkus, Max L. Rosenberg, and Chauncey Goodrich, all of San Francisco. During the late 1920s, even before the onset of the Depression, all of these benefactors suffered financial reverses or declining health that resulted in reduced payments and difficult times for the AIDA at the very moment that it was approaching the height of its influence. At this point, some of the lost revenue was made up by Collier's brother-in-law, Henry Stanton, and his partner, James W. Young, the Co-Directors of the J. Walter Thompson Advertising Agency in Chicago.

The immediate cause of the AIDA's formation in 1924 was an attack upon the lands of the Pueblo Indians of New Mexico. Its successful effort to defeat a bill sponsored by United States Senator Holm O. Bursum and Interior Secretary Albert B. Fall, both of New Mexico, resulted in the creation of the Pueblo Lands Board, a quasi-judicial commission appointed to adjudicate land and water rights of Indians, Hispanics, and Anglos along the Rio Grande. Throughout the 1920s the AIDA provided legal counsel to the Pueblo Indians and represented their interests before the Pueblo Lands Board. Ironically, the AIDA's declining revenues and Collier's own growing involvement in other Indian issues resulted in a diminishment of AIDA oversight, just as the Pueblo Lands Board submitted its findings and recommendations during the late 1920s and early 1930s. The result was a further loss of Pueblo water rights and territory that resulted in litigation that continues even to the present.

The primary vehicle for dissemination of the AIDA's Indian reform program was a small periodical, irregularly issued, known as *The Bulletin of American Indian Life.* Twenty-seven issues were distributed from June 1925 to April 1936. The president of the AIDA from 1925 until 1938 was Haven Emerson, health commissioner for the city of New York, and a well-known pioneer in the public health movement. In 1933, when Collier was appointed commissioner of Indian affairs by secretary of the interior Harold Ickes (a former AIDA board member), he was succeeded as executive director by Allan G. Harper, who had previously been identified with the American Civil Liberties Union. Unable to revive the financially weakened AIDA, Harper and Haven Emerson, with Collier's blessing, agreed to the merger of the AIDA with the Eastern Association on Indian Affairs in 1938 to form the American Association on Indian Affairs.

Lawrence C. Kelly

See also **Association on American Indian Affairs;
Government Policy: 1900 to 1933**

Further Reading

Collier, John. *From Every Zenith.* Denver, CO: Sage Press,
1963.
Hertzberg, Hazel W. "Indian Rights Movements, 1887–
1973." *Handbook of North American Indians.* Vol. 4.
History of Indian White Relations. Ed. Wilcomb E.
Washburn. Washington, DC: Smithsonian Institution
(1988): 305–23.
Kelly, Lawrence C. *The Assault on Assimilation: John
Collier and the Origins of Indian Policy Reform.*
Albuquerque: University of New Mexico Press, 1983.

AMERICAN INDIAN EDUCATION ASSOCIATION

See National Indian Education Association

AMERICAN INDIAN FEDERATION

The American Indian Federation (AIF), which had
a brief existence from 1934 until its demise in the
mid-1940s, was the major voice of Native American
criticism of federal Indian policies during the New
Deal. Composed largely of individuals of diverse
opinions, the AIF was a national Indian organization whose members could agree for only a brief
time on three principal goals: that Commissioner
of Indian Affairs John Collier be removed from
office; that the Indian Reorganization Act (IRA)
be overturned; and, most importantly, that the
Bureau of Indian Affairs (BIA) be abolished.

Although the larger portion of its members
and leaders were Oklahomans, the AIF also included prominent Indians who had little in common with their Oklahoma brethren. The Oklahoma
faction, led by AIF President Joseph Bruner, a wealthy
Creek, reflected much of the uneasiness among that
state's allotted Indian populations about Commissioner Collier's emphasis on tribal communal models. Bruner and some of these Oklahoma Indians
advocated complete Indian participation in the American body politic and complete integration into white
society. This faction, which thoroughly dominated
the organization from 1939 onward, urged "emanci-
pating" Indians by pushing for a final cash settlement
through congressional legislation of all claims that
Indians had against the government. The major non-
Oklahoma members of the AIF included Alice Lee
Jemison, a Seneca Indian and the organization's major
publicist-lobbyist on Capitol Hill; Thomas Sloan,
former president of the Society of American Indians;
Adan Castillo, president of the Mission Indian Federation; Fred Bauer, vice-chief of the Eastern Band of
Cherokees; and Jacob C. Morgan, Navajo tribal chairman.

The founding of the AIF was a response by a
sizable number of Indians who feared that the IRA
would help perpetuate an agency, the BIA, that so
many Indians were bent on destroying. Through extremist right-wing rhetoric, the AIF spread its anti-
New Deal message in its two publications, *The American Indian* and *The First American,* that attracted
support from conservative congressmen bent on destroying the New Deal. Moreover, the AIF, with an
unpaid staff and few sources of financial support,
used and were used by right-wing groups, ranging
from the Daughters of the American Revolution to
William Dudley Pelley's extremist Silver Shirts of
America. Consequently by 1938, the Interior Department retaliated by infiltrating the AIF, spying on its
national conventions, making use of Indian informants, and requesting FBI surveillance of the
organization's leaders.

The AIF's failure to accomplish its three unifying
goals caused it to splinter, with the majority of the
organization advocating the so-called "Settlement Bill."
The AIF's advocacy of a final cash settlement of claims
drove many traditional supporters as well as Bauer,
Castillo, Jemison, and Sloan from the organization.
The AIF, which had served as an Indian nationalist
vehicle until 1939, soon became merely the personal
conduit of Joseph Bruner and his Oklahoma faction
until its demise in the mid-1940s.

The AIF's criticisms of the BIA contributed to a
movement after World War II to terminate the federal-Indian relationship. Hence, the irony is that
the AIF was an organization whose members
believed in Indian self-determination, but whose
actions contributed to the opposite result, namely,
termination policies.

Laurence M. Hauptman

See also **Government Policy; Indian Reorganization Act; Mission Indian Federation**

Further Reading

Hauptman, Laurence M. *The Iroquois and the New Deal.*
Syracuse, NY: Syracuse University Press, 1981.
———. "The American Indian Federation and the Indian
New Deal: A Reinterpretation." *Pacific Historical
Review* 52 (November 1983): 378–402.
Philp, Kenneth R. *John Collier's Crusade for Indian
Reform 1920–1954.* Tucson: University of Arizona
Press, 1977.

AMERICAN INDIAN HISTORICAL SOCIETY

The American Indian Historical Society, located
in San Francisco, was founded in 1964 by fifteen tribal
Indians. Rupert Costo, a full-blood Cahuilla Indian
from Southern California, was its first president, a
post he held until 1989. Its well-respected quarterly
publication, *The Indian Historian,* also began its eighteen-year run in 1964, developing a paid circulation
of 12,400 over the years.

The Society's philosophy from the start was that
Indian people could do what was needed, by their
own initiative and innovation; the Society placed

competent Indian people in control of all its activities. It also succeeded in gaining the support of outstanding non-Indian professionals who acted as consultants.

A campaign to save the Ohlone Cemetery in Fremont, which was scheduled to be made into a parking lot, was the Society's first activity. Board members met with representatives of the Catholic Church; Bishop Floyd Begin, after a meeting with Costo, agreed to deed the cemetery to the Society. The cemetery was reconsecrated in 1965. Subsequently, the Society turned over the deed to the reconstituted Ohlone Tribe.

The Society was well known for its publications. The Indian Historian Press, a for-profit arm of the Society, published its first book in 1970, *Textbooks and the American Indian*, as a response to textbook publishers' failure to make substantive changes in their materials. As of 1992 the press has issued fifty-one books, many of which have become classics: *Tsali*, by Denton Bedford, for example, sold 10,000 copies; *Give or Take a Century: An Eskimo Saga*, by Joseph Senungetuk, has been reprinted three times; *Indian Treaties*, by Rupert Costo, is still in great demand by lawyers and universities; an annual *Index to Literature on the American Indian* was published for four years, 1970 to 1973, before a malicious attack by R.R. Bowker (publishers) forced its end.

The Society published two other serial publications. *Wassaja*, a national newspaper of Indian America, began in 1972. Its circulation had reached 42,100 when it ceased publication in 1984. Recognizing that there was nothing to serve children's needs for information about Indian people, the Society began *The Weewish Tree* in 1974. Letters from Indian and non-Indian children alike bombarded the Society, which had to hire two secretaries to handle the avalanche that followed. When this popular publication ended in 1983, its circulation was 32,150.

Through the years the Society was active in supporting Indian issues across the country. It sponsored two convocations of American Indian scholars, in 1971 and 1972, and held conferences on water rights in Denver and Albuquerque. It also supported efforts of individual tribes to preserve their rights.

The Society and its press operated on slender funding through the years, usually from its own members. A number of Indian staff members, including its president, Rupert Costo, and its editor of publications, Jeannette Henry, worked without salary for many years.

The Society legally dissolved as a corporation in 1986, although it continues to function in a limited way. The press is still actively publishing books. Upon dissolution, its headquarters were sold for $500,000. The Rupert Costo Chair in American Indian History at the University of California, Riverside, was founded with these funds. Costo's library was also donated to the university, where it serves as the cornerstone for the Rupert Costo Library of the American Indian.

Jeannette Henry Costo

AMERICAN INDIAN LAW CENTER

The American Indian Law Center was founded in 1967 by the University of New Mexico Law School. In 1977, it became an independent, Indian-controlled organization under the leadership of Philip S. Deloria, who remains the director in 1993. Still located at the University of New Mexico Law School, the Law Center maintains strong ties with that institution. Staff members offer courses to UNM law students, enabling the school to broaden its offerings in Indian law to include Pueblo law, taught by staff attorney Christine Zuni, a judge at Iselta Pueblo; and courses on Indian child welfare, offered by Toby Grossman, a center staff attorney who is a national expert on Indian child welfare issues.

During the twenty-six years of its existence, the Law Center has provided policy analysis and technical assistance to tribal governments, focusing in particular on issues regarding the status of tribal governments within the federal system, and the delivery of federal domestic assistance programs to Indian tribes. The Law Center has worked with tribes on a great number of projects, including developing tribal codes and improving judicial services. For example, it currently administers the Southwest Intertribal Court of Appeals.

In 1977, the Law Center created the State-Tribal Relations Commission, the first such effort to bring together state and tribal officials occupying similar positions in their government. Although the Commission itself is no longer in existence, its efforts have sparked a movement toward increased state-tribal cooperation on a state-by-state basis.

The Center also contracts with the federal government to provide services to Indian tribes. For example, in 1992 the Center completed a congressionally mandated study describing the juvenile justice systems in operation in over 210 Indian tribes and Alaska Native villages throughout the United States.

Finally, the Law Center administers the Pre-Law Summer Institute for Native American students. This innovative summer program was designed twenty-six years ago to help prepare Native American students for law school. At the time the program began, the organizers were able to identify only twenty-five Native Americans with law degrees in the United States; consequently, the practice of Indian law was dominated by non-Indians at that time.

At present, however, over 1,000 Native Americans hold law degrees, of whom many are graduates of the Pre-Law Summer Institute. In addition to receiving eight weeks of intensive training, the students have an opportunity to meet members of their peer group who will be attending law schools throughout the country. In addition to courses on torts and property or other substantive first-year courses, the students are trained in advocacy. Because many of the schools they attend will not offer a course in Indian law, the students also take a course in Indian law. The

Institute has created a model for pre-law training that has been followed by other programs training minority students, such as the Council on Legal Education Opportunity (CLEO).

Nell Jessup Newton

See also **Tribal Governments**

AMERICAN INDIAN MOVEMENT

The American Indian Movement (AIM) emerged from the broader context of Red Power activism on the streets of Minneapolis, Minnesota, during the fall of 1968. Founded by a group of city-bred Anishinabes (Chippewas) including Dennis Banks, Mary Jane Wilson, and George Mitchell, the new organization was formed on the model of the Black Panther Party for Self-Defense, established in Oakland, California, two years earlier.

AIM's original mandate was to patrol Minneapolis's large Indian ghetto in order to monitor and thus curtail the systematic harassment, false arrest, and summary corporal punishment administered to residents at curbside by the city's mostly non-Indian police force. This "police the police" effort proved quite successful: unprosecuted arrests of Indians in Minneapolis declined by more than 50 percent during the first year of AIM's existence, and suits concerning "verbal abuse" by officers were introduced in court for the first time, giving considerable credibility to the movement and its members.

Expansion of AIM

During the 1969 to 1970 Indians of All Tribes' (IAT) occupation of Alcatraz Island, in which Banks played a role as a national spokesperson, AIM undertook a national recruitment campaign. Chapters were started in cities such as San Francisco, Los Angeles, Denver, Chicago, Cleveland, and Milwaukee. Individuals destined to be among the organization's strongest and most articulate leaders were attracted to its ranks. Among them were John Trudell, a Santee Dakota who served as AIM national chairperson from 1974 to 1979, and Russell Means, an Oglala Lakota raised in Oakland. Other key recruits included Carter Camp, a Ponca who carried a substantial Oklahoma Indian presence with him into the movement, and Larry Anderson, a Navajo who accomplished the same feat with regard to the Southwest. In Wisconsin, Herb Powless, an Oneida, took the lead; in Colorado, it was Joe Locust, a Cherokee; in Nebraska, the task was performed by John Arbuckle, an Anishinabe, and Reuben Snake, a Winnebago.

Early Demonstrations

Means' savvy in staging symbolic demonstrations was felt almost from the outset. Beginning on July 4, 1971, with a "countercelebration" atop Mount Rushmore, AIM undertook a series of spectacular actions designed to compel public acknowledgment of Indian issues. On Thanksgiving Day of the same year, a picked group took over the Mayflower Replica at Plymouth, Massachusetts, painting Plymouth Rock red for the occasion, and using the ship itself as a podium from which to air Native grievances. A grimmer event occurred in February 1972, when Means led a caravan of about 1,000 people into the small town of Gordon, Nebraska, to protest the failure of local authorities to file charges against two white men in the torture-murder of an Oglala named Raymond Yellowthunder. The two men became the first whites ever sentenced to prison in Nebraska for causing the death of an Indian, a matter which raised AIM's currency tremendously on the nearby Pine Ridge and Rosebud Sioux reservations.

During the following summer, AIM organized a caravan of Indians from across the country to go to Washington, D.C. on the eve of the 1972 United States presidential election, present a list of Native grievances, and negotiate solutions with federal officials. The caravan, called the "Trail of Broken Treaties," was composed of more than 2,000 people from perhaps a hundred reservations. They arrived in the capitol on November third bearing a twenty-point negotiating platform centered upon treaty rights and self-governance. When government officials who had earlier promised logistical support and a swift series of meetings reneged on these agreements, some 400 AIM members seized the Bureau of Indian Affairs (BIA) headquarters building and held it for six days, until the Nixon administration publicly committed itself to make a formal response to each point raised in the negotiating program. The occupiers then left peacefully, but took with them large numbers of the BIA's most confidential files. The documents revealed, among other things, a range of questionable government practices with regard to reservation land and mineral rights.

Prelude to Wounded Knee

Many AIM participants went directly from Washington to South Dakota to campaign against the pattern of anti-Indian abuse in the Rapid City area. This led, on February 6, 1973, to a major confrontation between about 200 AIM members and an equal number of police at the county courthouse in the town of Custer, in the Black Hills. At issue was a situation similar to that in Gordon the year before; a white man, Darld Schmitz, had brutally stabbed a young Oglala named Wesley Bad Heart Bull to death, and was charged only with manslaughter. AIM demanded that the charge against Schmitz be changed to murder. When local officials refused, a melee ensued. About forty AIM members were charged with serious offenses. Ultimately, several AIM leaders and the victim's mother were sent to prison. Bad Heart Bull's killer never served a day behind bars.

Wounded Knee, 1973

Meanwhile, a conflict between traditional Oglalas and the federally-sponsored tribal government of

Richard (Dick) Wilson on nearby Pine Ridge had reached crisis proportions. The traditionals requested direct support from AIM in defending themselves against both the Wilsonites and a "Special Operations Group" of sixty SWAT-trained United States marshals sent to the reservation to back them up. AIM agreed, a matter which sparked the spectacular seventy-one day armed confrontation at the tiny hamlet of Wounded Knee, beginning on February 28. By the end of the standoff on May seventh, both sides were thoroughly committed: AIM to making Pine Ridge the focal point of a campaign to reassert full-blown indigenous sovereignty in North America, and the government to destroying the movement's political effectiveness and its base of grassroots Indian support once and for all. In the end, neither side was to prove completely successful.

The Aftermath of Wounded Knee

In the aftermath of Wounded Knee, a program was undertaken to neutralize AIM by bringing a mass of criminal charges against its leadership. Eventually, Federal District Judge Fred Nichol dismissed all forty-two charges against Banks and Means in their "Wounded Knee Leadership Trial," saying that "the waters of justice [had] been polluted" by the government's use of the courts for such extralegal purposes. Although there were only fifteen minor convictions from the total of 562 Wounded Knee-related charges filed against AIM defendants, the sheer weight of the onslaught seriously eroded the movement's ability to function.

AIM responded initially in electoral fashion, advancing Means as a candidate for the Pine Ridge tribal presidency in 1974. Means outpolled Dick Wilson by a 200-vote margin during the reservation primaries, but was defeated by the incumbent during the subsequent runoff. Although the Civil Rights Commission officially recommended these results be voided, and that balloting be conducted again under close supervision, the Department of the Interior upheld the results, leaving Wilson in power.

The Oglala Firefight

By the spring of 1975, the movement was increasingly relying on armed self-defense as a means of survival. This led inexorably to the "Oglala Firefight" of June 26, 1975, when a large force of federal agents, Guardians of the Oglala Nation (armed Wilsonites known as GOONs), and BIA police attacked an AIM defensive encampment located on the Jumping Bull property, near the reservation village of Oglala. Two agents and an AIM member, Joe Stuntz Killsright (a Coeur D'Alene), were killed in the exchange. The FBI then brought a huge force of some 250 militarily equipped men onto the reservation for an extended period. This ultimately allowed the BIA to quell the Pine Ridge "uprising." The "AIM/GOON War" was finally stopped.

AIM leadership now was scattered. Carter Camp and Stan Holder (a Wichita) had gone underground to evade sentencing on Wounded Knee charges. Banks, convicted of rioting during the confrontation in Custer, had been granted political asylum in California by its governor, Jerry Brown. Russell Means was on his way to prison, convicted of "anarcho-syndicalism"; his brother Ted was incarcerated because of Custer. Herb Powless had been jailed on weapons charges, an accusation which had also sent Arbuckle into hiding. Douglass Durham, an alleged "quarter-blood Chippewa," and head of AIM security, had turned out to be a non-Indian FBI infiltrator. Only John Trudell remained at liberty and effective. Much of Trudell's time and energy, however, was consumed in the defense of the individuals accused of executing FBI agents Ronald Williams and Jack Coler during the Oglala Firefight. The accused included Bob Robideau (Anishinabe), Darrelle "Dino" Butler (Tuni) and Leonard Peltier (Anishinabe/Dakota), all from the Northwest AIM Group.

The Trials of Robideau, Butler, and Peltier

Robideau and Butler, who had been captured in the United States, were tried first in Cedar Rapids, Iowa, in 1976. Even though the two men openly acknowledged that they had fired at Coler and Williams during the firefight, they were acquitted by an all-white jury of having murdered either agent, or of having aided and abetted in their murders. The jury concluded on the evidence that the sort of tactics employed by the government against AIM had given the defendants ample reason to fear for their lives. Therefore, they had acted legitimately, in self-defense, in firing back at their attackers. Although the agents were dead, no murders had occurred.

A murder case was then brought against Peltier, who had been captured in and then extradited (many say illegally) from Canada. The 1977 trial was marked by an array of questionable evidentiary submissions by the prosecution. After judicial rulings that a self-defense presentation by the defendant would not be allowed, the government obtained murder convictions against Peltier. He was sentenced to two consecutive life terms. To date, that conviction has been upheld, despite the fact that the prosecution admitted on subsequent appeals that it has "no idea who killed the agents," and the United States Eighth Circuit Court has acknowledged that the original case presented against Peltier no longer really exists.

Dissolution of the AIM National Office

During the initial appeal process, Trudell had helped establish a national Leonard Peltier Defense Committee, for which he served as primary spokesperson. At 1:30 a.m. on the morning of February 12, 1979, his wife Tina, their three children, and his mother-in-law, were all burned to death in a mysterious fire in their house trailer on the Duck Valley Reservation in Nevada. Trudell considered the deaths a retaliation for a vociferously anti-government speech he had delivered on the steps of the FBI building on February 11. He felt that maintaining AIM as a formal national organization was accomplishing little beyond providing a list of preselected targets for government repression. He then engineered the abolition of all national titles, beginning with his own chairmanship, and dissolution of the national office in Minneapolis. Thereafter, the movement was continued solely on the basis of autonomous local initiatives.

International Indian Treaty Council

Aside from the Peltier Defense Committee, which assumed an ongoing life of its own, the major exception to Trudell's liquidation of centralization in AIM was the International Indian Treaty Council (IITC). Formed by Russell Means in 1974 at the behest of the traditional Lakota elders, IITC was originally mandated to take charges that the United States was in violation of the 1868 Fort Laramie Treaty before the United Nations. Means selected Cherokee activist Jimmie Durham to direct AIM's international diplomatic arm. Durham, in turn, broadened the agenda to include "the issues of all indigenous nations of the hemisphere with regard to the policies of the various states in which they are now encapsulated." He arranged a watershed 1977 hearing for Indian peoples from North, South, and Central America before the United Nations Economic and Social Council at the Palace of Nations in Geneva, Switzerland. As a result of this hearing, the Council created a Working Group on Indigenous Populations to conduct a comprehensive and extended investigation into the situations of Native peoples around the world, and to draft appropriate international legislation to insure their rights. IITC was designated as the first indigenous NGO (Non-Governmental Organization, Type II, Consultative) in the United Nations' history.

IITC continued to function as a viable entity throughout Durham's tenure, opening an office on U.N. Plaza in New York City and making instrumental presentations at annual Working Group meetings in Geneva during the early 1980s. By 1984, however, Durham had resigned in the face of an influx of marxian-oriented cadres eager to pursue a politics which he considered antithetical to indigenous rights. In short order, IITC's increasing sectarianism cost it most of its support among traditional Indians and the activists who had formed it. The New York office was lost, and IITC now exists only as a tiny San Francisco-based splinter group, with little or no international credibility. Fortunately, other NGOs, such as the Indian Law Resource Center, had by then emerged to pursue potentials Durham had opened up.

The Longest Walk

Probably the last unified national action undertaken by AIM was the 1978 "Longest Walk," in some ways a figurative recreation of the 1972 Trail of Broken Treaties. Organized by Dennis Banks during the

period of his California exile, the walk began in San Francisco during February. Participants spent several months hiking across the United States, holding public education events, and gathering additional numbers along the way. By the time it arrived in Washington, D.C. on July 23, the march included several hundred Indians from more than eighty nations. Several thousand people held a rally near the Washington National Monument on July 25, during which a manifesto amplifying the sentiments of the 1972 twenty-point program was read. Congressman Ron Dellums had the manifesto printed in the Congressional Record two days later.

Local AIM Groups

At the local level, AIM has demonstrated a marked resilience in some locales during the past decade. Predictably, the strongest showing has been in South Dakota, where the movement played an instrumental role in organizing the Black Hills International Survival Gathering in 1980, and was a key element in establishing the Black Hills Alliance, an entity which proved quite successful in fighting uranium development and related water draw-downs in the region. In 1981, a contingent of Dakota AIM headed by Russell and Bill Means also established Yellow Thunder Camp, a move which launched a four-year occupation of an 880-acre parcel in the hills. In litigation which attended the occupation, they secured a benchmark decision by a federal judge that the entire Black Hills area—as opposed to specific sites within it—was of bona fide spiritual significance to the Lakota Nation, and that they therefore possessed special religious rights to it. On Pine Ridge, AIM was also a vital ingredient in the founding of radio station KILI during the early 1980s.

In Arizona, Larry Anderson established a legal defense team and ongoing AIM security camp to protect the more than 10,000 traditional Diné (Navajos) faced with forced relocation from their homes. The Colorado AIM took a leadership role in supporting the Miskito Indians of Nicaragua against attempted impositions by the Sandinista government during the mid-eighties, and more recently emerged as a catalyst in opposing celebrations of the Columbian Quincentennary in the United States. In 1990, Herb Powless resuscitated the long-dormant Wisconsin AIM chapter in order to support Natives attempting to exercise their treaty-guaranteed right to maintain their traditional subsistence fishing economy. As Russell Means once summed up the situation:

> AIM never died. It only changed form. Anywhere Indians are standing up for themselves, whether they are struggling as individuals whose basic civil rights are being denied, as peoples whose human rights are being denied, as nations whose sovereign rights are being denied, or any combination of these factors, that's where you'll find the American Indian Movement. In that spirit of resistance to oppression, that's where you'll

find AIM. In other words, AIM is now in every single Indian community, and it always will be.

Ward Churchill

See also **Alcatraz Occupation; Black Hills; International Indian Treaty Council; International Law; Red Power; Russell Tribunal; Trail of Broken Treaties; Wounded Knee II**

Further Reading

Churchill, Ward, and Jim Vander Wall. *Agents of Repression: The FBI's Secret Wars Against the Black Panther Party and the American Indian Movement.* Boston: South End Press, 1988.

Deloria, Vine, Jr. *Behind the Trail of Broken Treaties.* New York, NY: Dell Books, 1974.

Johansen, Bruce, and Roberto Maestas. *Wasi'chu: The Continuing Indian Wars.* New York, NY: Monthly Review Press, 1979.

Matthiessen, Peter. *In the Spirit of Crazy Horse.* 2d ed. New York: Viking Press, 1991.

Weyler, Rex. *Blood of the Land: The Government and Corporate War Against the American Indian Movement.* New York, NY: Everest House Publishers, 1982.

AMERICAN INDIAN POLICY REVIEW COMMISSION

The American Indian Policy Review Commission was established in 1975 by the ninety-third United States Congress through passage of Public Law 93–580. The legislation authorizing the Commission was originally drafted in 1973 by Sherwin Broadhead, a staff attorney working for Senator James Abourezk ([D] South Dakota), chairman of the Senate Interior Subcommittee on Indian Affairs. The proposed bill was a direct response to a climate of confrontation between Indians and United States government officials that began in 1970. Many younger Indians had grown impatient with the United States government's treatment of Indians. They challenged the very basic assumptions of United States policy toward Indian people—challenges which eventually erupted into the violence between Indians and United States Marshals at Wounded Knee on the Pine Ridge Reservation. The Senate passed Senator Abourezk's bill to establish the Commission on December 5, 1973. The House of Representatives acted in 1974. Finally, the American Indian Policy Review Commission was established on January 2, 1975.

Fifty years after publication of the Meriam Report, which detailed United States government exploitation of Indians in the 1920s, Congress charged this new Commission to conduct a "comprehensive review of the historical and legal developments underlying the Indians' relationship with the Federal Government and to determine the nature and scope of necessary revisions in the formulation of policy and programs for the benefit of Indians." Three senators, three representatives, and five American Indians were appointed to lead the investigations. Sena-

tor James Abourezk served as the Commission's chairman. Senator Mark Hatfield ([R] Oregon) and Senator Lee Metcalf ([D] Montana) joined him as lawmakers from the Senate. Congressman Lloyd Meeds ([D] Washington) served on the Commission as its vice-chairman. Congressman Sidney R. Yates ([D] Illinois) and Congressman Sam Steiger ([R] Arizona) sat as members coming from the House of Representatives. Congressman Steiger lost his seat during Arizona's congressional elections and was replaced by Congressman Don Young ([R] Alaska). The five Indian members of the Commission were John Borbridge of the Tlingit; former Bureau of Indian Affairs Commissioner Louis Bruce, a Mohawk-Sioux; then Menominee Chairperson Ada Deer; Adolph Dial of the Lumbee; and Jake Whitecrow, a Quapaw-Seneca-Cayuga.

Commission members appointed Ernest L. Stevens of the Oneida Nation and former first vice-president of the National Congress of American Indians as director in charge of seventy-eight professional staff. To conduct the beginning inquiries into the specific topics mandated by Congress, eleven task forces with three members each were appointed. A task force was set up for each of the mandated topics to conduct a one-year study and submit findings and recommendations back to the Commission. Reflecting the areas of growing controversy concerning Indian leaders and Senator James Abourezk, the topics were:

1. Trust Responsibilities and the Federal-Indian Relationship

2. Tribal Government

3. Federal Administration and the Structure of Indian Affairs

4. Federal, State, and Tribal Jurisdiction

5. Indian Education

6. Indian Health

7. Reservation and Resource Development and Protection

8. Urban and Rural Non-reservation Indians

9. Indian Law Consolidation, Revision, and Codification

10. Terminated and Non-Federally Recognized Indians

11. Alcohol and Drug Abuse

After the task forces were created and began operating in the summer of 1975, two special task force reports were added. A special inquiry entitled "Management Study of the Bureau of Indian Affairs" was conducted by the Task Force on Federal Administration and the Structure of Indian Affairs. "Alaskan Native Issues" was the topic of a second special inquiry.

After two years of research, investigations, and public hearings, the Commission issued to Congress a 923-page final report in two volumes on May 17, 1977. Two hundred six legislative, policy, and procedural recommendations were presented to President of the Senate, Vice-President Walter F. Mondale and

Speaker of the House of Representatives Thomas P. O'Neill. The Commission contended that American Indian tribes' relationship to the United States is based on principles of international law. Furthermore, the relationship "is a political relation . . . of weak governments to a strong government . . . founded on treaties in which the Indian tribes placed themselves under the protection of the United States and the United States assumed the obligation of supplying such protection." The Commission urged Congress to adopt two basic concepts to guide future United States policy toward Indian tribes: 1. That Indian tribes are sovereign political bodies having the power to determine their own membership and power to enact laws and enforce them within the boundaries of their reservations; and 2. The relationship which exists between the tribes and the United States is premised on a special trust that must govern the conduct of the stronger toward the weaker.

Among its recommendations, the Commission urged Congress to elevate the position of the Bureau of Indian Affairs commissioner to the status of an assistant secretary of the Department of Interior for Indian Affairs. Former Senate interior committee staff member Forrest Gerard (Blackfeet tribe) was appointed by President Jimmy Carter to serve as the first assistant secretary of the Department of the Interior for Indian Affairs. Both houses of the Congress were urged to establish specific committees concerning Indian affairs. The Senate quickly formed the Senate Select Committee on Indian Affairs with Senator James Abourezk as its first chairman. The House of Representatives chose not to create a specific committee, but placed specific jurisdiction over Indian Affairs in the House Interior Committee, then chaired by Congressman Morris Udall ([D] Arizona).

During the three years remaining in the 1970s, Congress enacted several major pieces of legislation in direct response to the recommendations of the American Indian Policy Review Commission: they passed into law the American Indian Religious Freedom Act (P.L. 95–341) and the Indian Child Welfare Act (P.L. 95–608). Later, Congress adopted legislation clarifying the taxation relationship between Indian tribes and state governments. A specialized Office of Indian Education was created in the Department of Education. The Bureau of Indian Affairs established new regulations setting out a procedure for Indian tribes to petition the United States government for recognition and the reestablishment of their territories. While many of its recommendations were not acted on, the Commission's report was widely regarded as a strong statement in support of tribal autonomy. The report is often cited by United States government policy makers and federal courts as a comprehensive overview of federal Indian policy. It became an important influence on future United States and Indian relations.

Rudolph C. Rÿser

See also **Government Policy**

Further Reading

American Indian Policy Review Commission, Final Report. Washington, DC: U.S. Government Printing Office, 1977.

Batzle, Peter, and Melanie Olivero. "The Congress." *American Indian Journal* 6 (January 1980): 16–20.

Burnette, Robert, and John Koster. *The Road to Wounded Knee.* New York, NY: Bantam Books, 1974.

AMERICAN INDIAN RELIGIOUS FREEDOM ACT

For most of American history, the federal government has actively discouraged, and even outlawed, the exercise of traditional Indian religions. For more than a century, the government provided direct and indirect support to Christian missionaries who sought to "convert and civilize" the Indians. From the 1890s through the 1930s, the government moved beyond promoting voluntary abandonment of tribal religions to, in some instances, affirmatively prohibiting those religions. On those reservations where it had the authority, the Bureau of Indian Affairs outlawed the "'sun dance' and all other similar dances and so-called religious ceremonies," as well as the "usual practices of so-called 'medicine men.'" It was not until 1934 that the federal government fully recognized the right of free worship on Indian reservations.

However, many obstacles to free religious practice remained. For example, traditional Indian religious practitioners were frequently denied access to sacred sites located outside of reservations, often on federal lands. In addition, many states prohibited the possession of peyote, a sacrament used in Native American Church religious ceremonies.

Because of continuing obstacles to the free exercise of traditional Indian religions, Congress enacted the American Indian Religious Freedom Act (AIRFA) (42 U.S.C. 1996) in 1978. Congress found that "the lack of a clear, comprehensive, and consistent Federal policy has often resulted in the abridgement of religious freedom for traditional American Indians . . . [and that] such religious infringements result from the lack of knowledge or the insensitive and inflexible enforcement of federal policies and regulations." Accordingly, AIRFA established a federal policy to protect and preserve for American Indians their inherent right to freedom to believe, express, and exercise the traditional religions of the American Indian, Eskimo, Aleut, and Native Hawaiians, including but not limited to access to sites, use and possession of sacred objects, and the freedom to worship through ceremonials and traditional rites.

AIRFA required that federal agencies evaluate their policies and procedures, determine where changes are needed "to protect and preserve Native American religious cultural rights and practices," and report back to Congress with recommendations for administrative and legislative reform.

The report required by AIRFA was issued in 1979. It identified hundreds of specific examples of government-placed obstacles to the free exercise of religion, and made a number of administrative and legislative recommendations. However, except for a limited number of regulations and policies—providing for some additional opportunities for Indian input—and provisions in the Native American Graves Protection and Repatriation Act (1990), which pertain to the repatriation and illegal transport of sacred objects, the recommendations of that report have never been adopted.

Moreover, the United States Supreme Court has ruled that AIRFA is a policy statement only. In *Lyng v. Northwest Indian Cemeteries Assn.* (485 U.S. 439 [1988]), the Court, citing statements by the sponsor of AIRFA that it "has no teeth in it," held that Congress did not intend "to create a cause of action or any judicially enforceable individual rights." The *Lyng* case, and the subsequent case of *Emp Sec. Div. of Oregon v. Smith* (494 U.S. 872 [1990]), also established that the First Amendment is not available to Indian religious practitioners to protect sacred sites or the religious use of peyote. Thus, it is now clear that if agencies fail to comply with the "federal policy" established by AIRFA, Native Americans have no direct legal recourse.

For these reasons and because of a multitude of continuing disputes regarding the free exercise of religion by Indian people, a coalition of Indian tribes, national Indian organizations, environmentalists, churches, and civil rights groups is seeking in 1993 to strengthen AIRFA. Their proposal would provide a legal course of action to Indian religious practitioners when governmental actions threaten sacred sites, and require federal agencies to notify and consult with affected Indian tribes and practitioners when undertakings are planned which may impact such sites. In addition, the coalition proposal would protect the ceremonial use of peyote by Native Americans and mandate that Native American prisoners have religious rights equivalent to those of all other inmates.

Jack F. Trope

See also **Peyote Religion; Religion; Sacred Sites**

Further Reading

Association on American Indian Affairs. "Special Supplement on American Indian Religious Freedom." *Indian Affairs* 116, Summer 1988.

Echo-Hawk, Walter E. "Loopholes in Religious Liberty: The Need for a Federal Law to Protect Freedom of Worship for Native People." *NARF Legal Review* 14 (Summer 1991): 7–14.

Hirschfelder, Arlene, and Paulette Molin. *Encyclopedia of Native American Religions.* New York, NY: Facts on File, 1992.

United States Federal Agencies Task Force. *American Indian Religious Freedom Act Report.* Washington, DC: Secretary of the Interior, 1979.

Vecsey, Christopher. *Handbook of American Indian Religious Freedom.* New York, NY: Crossroad, 1991.

AMERICAN INDIAN SCIENCE AND ENGINEERING SOCIETY

The American Indian Science and Engineering Society (AISES) is a private, nonprofit organization that seeks to increase the number of Indian scientists and engineers and to develop technologically informed Indian leaders. AISES' ultimate goal is to serve as a catalyst for the advancement of Indians to become more self-determined members of society. Founded in 1977, the organization has awarded more than $1 million in scholarships and has seventy-eight student chapters across the United States and Canada. Headquartered in Boulder, Colorado, AISES is directed by Norbert S. Hill, Jr., an Oneida Indian. The eleven-member board of directors includes university, industry, and government representatives—all American Indians. Corporations, foundations, government agencies, and individuals provide financial support. In 1992 its budget was $2.2 million.

AISES' annual national conference, held each fall in a different city, has become a major event for corporations recruiting Indian students. A highlight of the conference is the presentation of scholarships to Indian youths, many of them the first in their families to attend college. In 1990, 171 students received $230,000 in scholarships; in 1991 nearly $250,000 was awarded.

College chapters have been established on campuses where there is a demonstrated interest in the advancement of Indians studying science and engineering. These include the Colorado School of Mines, Harvard, Stanford, and the Massachusetts Institute of Technology. An annual two-day leadership training conference for college chapter leaders helps students develop leadership skills and introduces them to corporate role models. It also helps prepare students to become more committed, knowledgeable Indian leaders and to serve as mentors for younger students. AISES also conducts teacher programs to improve the quality of math and science education in elementary and secondary schools, so that Indian students become better qualified to pursue math- and science-based college studies. In the summer of 1988, for example, five teacher workshops were conducted. One session, cosponsored by the National Aeronautics and Space Administration and the United States Geological Survey, brought twenty teachers to Boulder, Colorado, for an earth-science workshop.

Precollege programs introduce elementary and secondary students to science and technology and expose them to successful role models in an effort to generate interest and prepare them academically. These programs include math and science clubs, science fairs, and two- to six-week camps emphasizing mathematics and science. In the summer of 1991, more than 150 junior high school students participated in AISES' math and science camps funded by the MacArthur Foundation, JETS/UNITE, and the United States Department of Energy. Activities at the camps, which began in 1988, include culturally appropriate science and mathematics instruction, computer instruction, hands-on mathematics and science projects, field trips, guest lectures, career-preparation activities, parent seminars, and recreation.

Other AISES projects include the Science of Alcohol Curriculum for American Indians Project, which was initiated in 1988 to provide alcohol-abuse prevention, intervention, and education. It includes programs in community education, teacher training and curriculum-materials development. AISES is also developing a national educational network and clearinghouse to further promote math and science education.

AISES' four-color quarterly magazine, *Winds of Change*, provides information on educational opportunities and the society's activities and promotes the involvement of professionals in Indian concerns. The magazine won the North American Press Association award for general excellence in 1987 and in 1991, it was awarded the prestigious Ozzie Award for design excellence by *Magazine Design and Production*.

Norbert S. Hill, Jr.

See also **Higher Education**

AMERICANS FOR INDIAN OPPORTUNITY

Americans for Indian Opportunity (AIO) is a nonprofit group serving the Native American tribes and people of the United States. AIO was founded in 1970 by its current President and Executive Director, LaDonna Harris. In the 1960s, Harris founded Oklahomans for Indian Opportunity, the predecessor to AIO, to ensure that Indians from that state were afforded opportunities that would reverse the stifling socio-economic statistics which impact Indian communities.

AIO's objective is to enhance the cultural, social, political, and economic self-sufficiency of tribes. Through symposiums and information management, AIO assists Indians in investigating the dynamics of effective tribal governance. It works with key decision makers on the role and participation of tribal governments in the federal system. AIO was instrumental in establishing the Council of Energy Resource Tribes, whose forty-seven member tribes work today in concert to increase tribal control over their natural resources. One of AIO's first legislative victories was in 1971, when Harris was influential in securing the return of Taos Blue Lake to the Pueblo of Taos in New Mexico. Recently, the Taos people honored her and AIO for their role on the occasion of the twentieth anniversary of this historic feat.

AIO funding of approximately $500,000 a year is raised through public, corporate, and foundation support of its various projects. It is allocated into several areas: community and economic development, economic flows, education information and community, tribal environmental issues, leadership,

INDIANNET communications network, and governance. AIO has published several monographs, including *Messing With Mother Nature Can Be Hazardous to Your Health* (1980). Four full-time staff members and three consultants work on AIO's multiple projects.

LaDonna Harris

See also **Council of Energy Resource Tribes**

ANADARKO
See Caddo

ANISHINABE
See Ojibwa

ANTHROPOLOGISTS AND NATIVE AMERICANS

At the beginning of the twentieth century, Native Americans were largely unaware of the research and writing of the handful of anthropologists practicing at the time. In the late twentieth century, however, they are acutely aware of anthropology's role in molding public opinion about Native Americans in the United States, and increasingly in Mexico, Canada, and other regions. As anthropologists have grown in number from the handful trained by Franz Boas at Columbia University, to the thousands now practicing in hundreds of universities, colleges, museums, and private businesses, they have also become increasingly professionalized, specialized, and institutionalized with the accoutrements of the establishment. My purpose here is to briefly describe how such developments have affected relationships between Native Americans and anthropologists during the twentieth century, and the pressures for change that now confront the discipline in North America.

Although anthropology claims intellectual roots extending to the Greeks, Chinese, Arabs, and other ancients, it did not emerge as a distinct intellectual endeavor in the United States until the late nineteenth century. In 1900 the number of university-trained anthropologists working with Native Americans was fewer than fifty individuals. Thus it is not surprising that, with a few notable exceptions who became associated with anthropologists such as Boas, Alice Fletcher, and James Mooney, most Native Americans knew little of their work or influence. With the arrival of John Collier on the national scene, anthropologists began to enter government service in small numbers, particularly in the Bureau of Indian Affairs. Their influence became even more evident among the tribes after World War II as anthropologists came to play a significant role in the Indian Claims Commission cases as expert witnesses both for the tribes and for their adversaries, the federal government.

Before World War II, most anthropologists had confined themselves primarily to describing and reconstructing "disappearing" Native Americans and their cultures. While anthropologists studied Native Americans through Boas' four-field, natural science approach as a comparative study of man, tribes were being brutally decimated by federal policies of forced assimilation. Few informed Native Americans will forgive the general failure of anthropology to combat these destructive actions. For confirmation, they point to anthropology's similar failure to combat the termination legislation of the 1950s. From their perspective, anthropology fiddled while the tribes burned. Instead of joining with the tribes in common opposition to such programs of wholesale cultural extermination, most anthropologists retreated into scientism, objectivism, and a relativistic morality. Certain anthropologists, Robert Manners, for example, even advocated abandonment of the "legal-technical immunities and privileges which Indians now enjoy as a result of treaties and agreements arranged long ago. . . ."

Under a mandate in the 1930s from President Franklin Delano Roosevelt, Secretary of the Interior Harold Ickes, and Commissioner of Indian Affairs John Collier, anthropology became increasingly applied and mission oriented. This participation in government is exemplified by Philleo Nash who became commissioner of Indian affairs in 1961 during the Kennedy administration and, like John Collier, brought other anthropologists into the federal administration of Indian affairs. This entry into the federal government and into the Indian Claims Commission arena after World War II reinforced a growing division in United States anthropology between those who continued to pursue essentially academic and scholarly research in archaeology, linguistics, physical anthropology, and ethnology, and those who increasingly allied themselves with Native Americans in a pursuit of goals that reflected the contemporary needs of Native Americans. University of Chicago anthropologist Sol Tax, for example, helped focus attention on the obligation of anthropologists to deal with contemporary social, economic, and related problems of Native Americans in his "Action Anthropology" among the Fox and other groups.

The Society for Applied Anthropology, founded in 1940, was an outgrowth of the involvement of anthropologists in government, a tendency reinforced during World War II when anthropologists applied their discipline at home and abroad. Prominent figures in the emerging field of applied anthropology following 1940 included Homer Barnett, Edward Spicer, Omer Stewart, George Foster, Margaret Mead, and others. Despite efforts to become more applied and relevant, most university- and museum-based anthropologists continued to employ Euroamerican scholarly paradigms when describing and otherwise representing Native Americans, their biological characteristics, culture, history, and prehistory.

By 1960 the field of applied anthropology had become a firmly established part of the discipline. Simultaneously, a related development was emerging among Native American scholars. This growing intellectual resistance to anthropologists and their research, writing, and influence in Native American affairs quickly put those in the field on the defensive. Renowned scholar Vine Deloria, Jr., was a principal figure in articulating this critique in such works as *Custer Died for Your Sins.*

A major Native American objection to anthropology has been its elitist association with conquest and assimilationist philosophies concerning Native peoples here and abroad. Some assert that anthropologists practice their discipline primarily for the benefit, amusement, and enrichment of non-Native peoples. They suggest that anthropologists have been predatory, seeking data for their science, and "taking with no return" from the communities and tribes where they conduct research and derive their data. While recognizing that both applied and other anthropologists have made valuable contributions in the courts, classrooms, media, and legislatures, a growing number of Native American scholars are calling for a reorientation of the discipline and its traditional approaches. They stress that the historic distaste among most anthropologists for contemporary problem-solving and direct participation in the Native American struggles for survival must be abandoned in favor of research that is committed to the Native American struggle for survival and to acceptance of Native American control of the research process. Many Native American scholars and their allies assert that anthropologists must reject the Boasian notion that Native Americans are disappearing or being assimilated in either biological or cultural terms, in favor of the notion that anthropology can play a major part in Native American survival and their ongoing recovery. This requires that anthropologists abandon their primary preoccupation with defining and researching problems in favor of actually doing something about them.

A common complaint by Native Americans is that anthropologists reinforce cultural stereotypes by emphasizing the abnormal and bizarre, or the unfortunate effects of conquest and programs of forced assimilation. These ethnocentric stereotypes contribute to the perpetuation of images of Native Americans as "savage," "primitive," "preliterate," "preindustrial," "poverty-stricken," "undereducated," and otherwise "uncivilized." Ironically, Native Americans are often evaluated for their cultural authenticity as Indians by reference to these stereotypes. Some assert that anthropologists have done little to discourage the misuse and distortion of anthropological information by racists and other non-Indians who capitalize on such stereotypes. Active involvement by anthropologists in molding the public's perceptions is needed to counter the misinformation being fed to the general public by popular commentators. Omer Stewart's defense of the Native American Church is often noted as an example of how anthropologists may become engaged in the Native American struggle for survival.

Some Native American scholars suggest that anthropologists possess few conceptual tools for the study of a recovering, rapidly increasing, politically sophisticated population of educated tribal members, who are both reestablishing their sovereignty and influence among the dominant Euroamericans and retaining their tribal affiliations and identities. While abundantly qualified to describe prehistoric Native American cultures or Native American cultures of the nineteenth and early twentieth centuries, anthropologists have not often responded to the Native American challenge to develop more realistic and accurate portrayals of their contemporary culture and their recent history. In fact it appears to some that anthropologists are deliberately silent on important contemporary issues in Native American life, while expending millions of dollars in describing and interpreting remote and ancient aspects of their culture and history. This tendency reflects a common anthropological conviction that Native Americans are not so important for what they *are* as for what they *were*.

An unfortunate recent development has been the active opposition of the American Anthropological Association, to the 1990 Native American Graves Protection and Repatriation Act (NAGPRA), an opposition openly promoted by the leadership of the Society for American Archaeology (SAA). For obvious reasons, major museums such as the Smithsonian Institution, which has occupied a leadership role in anthropology during most of the twentieth century, have also been at the center of this controversy. The additional failure of most anthropologists to support the current drive to amend the American Indian Religious Freedom Act (AIRFA) is also viewed by some Native Americans as further evidence of anthropology's historic disinterest in contemporary survival issues. As yet, few anthropologists have learned that the political power of several hundred tribes and at least 1.5 million Native Americans far exceeds that of a handful of anthropologists. Clearly, tribes will influence, if not control, future anthropological research about them, their cultures, their history, and their prehistory.

Native American studies programs, which emerged in United States and Canadian universities beginning in the 1960s, advocate new curricula and new paradigms that include an increasingly strident critique of anthropology and anthropologists. This curriculum of liberation and empowerment represents a major reorientation in the study of Native Americans. While sometimes relying on the research of anthropologists, advocates of this emerging curriculum of liberation reject the antiquarian and "scientific" aspirations of anthropology in favor of a developmental, humanistic, holistic, action/applied, and tribally and community-based approach to research and teaching about their cultures. Anthropologists generally have not embraced this new curriculum, viewing it with increasing suspicion and opposition.

As anthropology approaches the end of the twentieth century, Native Americans are demanding that changes be made in the field. If made, anthropology can survive the federally mandated return of bones, burial goods, and items of cultural patrimony called for in NAGPRA, the tribal demands for religious freedom under AIRFA, the rejection of traditional anthropological stereotypes, and the increasing tribal control of research. To survive, anthropology must adopt more realistic and humane images that reflect the diversity and survival struggles of Native Americans through appropriate intellectual paradigms.

Clearly, anthropologists have made significant contributions to the well-being of Native Americans in the twentieth century. It is equally clear that anthropology has also failed Native Americans in significant ways. If it does not change, anthropology runs the very real risk of becoming an irrelevant exercise conducted by academic pedants. The increasing demands by Native Americans that anthropologists and anthropology become a part of their struggle for survival has not gone unheeded among some, especially younger anthropologists and most applied anthropologists. There is reason to hope that by the end of the twentieth century anthropology will respond to the challenge of Native Americans for change in the discipline, and emerge as a vital intellectual and political force in Native American affairs of the twenty-first century. Having been their subjects and now their adversaries, Native Americans can become full partners with anthropologists in a common endeavor.

Deward E. Walker, Jr.

See also **American Indian Religious Freedom Act; Archaeology; Government Policy; Museums; Repatriation of Human Remains and Artifacts**

Further Reading

Deloria, Vine, Jr. *Custer Died for Your Sins.* London, England and New York, NY: The Macmillan Company, 1969. Norman: University of Oklahoma Press, 1988.

Eddy, Elizabeth, and William L. Partridge, eds. *Applied Anthropology in America.* New York: Columbia University Press, 1978.

Kennard, Edward A., and Gordon Macgregor. "Applied Anthropology in Government: United States." *Anthropology Today.* Ed. A.L. Kroeber. Chicago, IL: The University of Chicago Press (1953): 832–40.

Lurie, Nancy O. "Relations Between Indians and Anthropologists." *Handbook of North American Indians.* Vol. 4. *History of Indian-White Relations.* Ed. Wilcomb E. Washburn. Washington, DC: Smithsonian Institution (1988): 548–56.

Manners, Robert. "Pluralism and the American Indian." *The Emergent Native Americans.* Ed. Deward E. Walker, Jr. Boston, MA: Little, Brown (1972): 124–43.

Rosen, Lawrence. "The Anthropologist as Expert Witness." *American Anthropologist* 79:3 (1977): 555–78.

Stewart, Omer C. "The Need to Popularize Basic Concepts." *To See Ourselves: Anthropology and Modern Social Issues.* Ed. Thomas Weaver. Glenview, IL: Scott, Foresman (1973): 55–57.

APACHE

Apaches, along with the Navajos, form the southernmost extension of the great Na-Dene language family. Historically, Apaches have been subdivided in a variety of ways; seventeenth-century Spanish records refer to Faroans, Llaneros, Palomas, and others. Later designations include the Kiowa-Apache (also Plains Apache), Lipan, Jicarilla, Pinal, Gila, Tonto, Mescalero, Arivaipa, Chiricahua, Coyotero, Mimbreno, San Carlos, Sierra Blanca, and, in addition, Mohave-Apaches and Yavapai-Apaches. Twentieth-century anthropologists and linguists categorize "Eastern" and "Western" Apaches. Western Apaches are those descended from bands holding reservations within what is now the state of Arizona. Eastern Apaches are all others; they presently occupy reservations and allotted lands in New Mexico and Oklahoma.

History

Linguistic experts have placed the Apache movement from arctic regions of western Canada to the desert southwestern United States between the late thirteenth and early sixteenth centuries. Small autonomous groups spread into the arid plains and mountains reaching from central Texas to central Arizona, and from southern Colorado in the north, to the Sierra Madre Mountains of what today are the Mexican states of Chihuahua and Sonora.

Until the arrival of Spanish colonists, Apaches subsisted by various combinations of gathering, hunting, and farming, as well as both trading with and raiding for goods from other more settled peoples, such as the Pueblo peoples of the Rio Grande drainage and the Pimans of the Gila Valley.

During centuries of conflict with Spanish, Mexican, and American authorities, Apaches earned a reputation as skilled fighters. Decades of campaigning brought them into confinement on half a dozen reservations in Arizona and New Mexico by 1872. The government, however, failed to acquire title to Apache lands by sale or treaty during this time, opening the way for a series of successful lawsuits brought by the Apaches against the United States in the 1960s and 1970s.

Shocked by the expense of maintaining a large number of reservations, the Bureau of Indian Affairs (BIA) consolidated the Apache reservations in the mid-1870s. Apaches in Arizona were concentrated at San Carlos, and those in New Mexico were sent to Mescalero. Outrage at the concentration led to renewed fighting, which lasted until 1886.

The reservation period of the late nineteenth century proved a severe trial for the Apache people. Christian denominations with the support of government authority engaged in efforts to destroy traditional religion and culture. Officials were often corrupt and incompetent. Poor housing and food were the rule and epidemics of disease were yearly events. Tuberculosis, diarrhea, pneumonia, and influenza decimated reservation Apaches as well as Apache children attending government boarding schools, such as Carlisle in Pennsylvania. Events of the twentieth century moved reservation communities along lines of separate development.

As a result of the Indian Reorganization Act (IRA) of 1934, Apache tribal governments were restructured. Elected Tribal Councils were installed, based on patterns specified in the IRA legislation. With minor changes to meet changing needs, these forms of government are still in use in the 1990s.

The IRA provided for a revolving loan fund to be used for economic development on reservations. Apaches used much of their portion to develop cattlegrazing through stock growers' associations. These were most successful at San Carlos and at Fort Apache.

During the 1960s and 1970s, various economic development programs were devised to lure industry to the Apache reservations. Most of these were only marginally successful, but did provide an infrastructure of roads and utility services to reservations. Substantial upgrading of housing and health services took place at the same time.

A major factor in the economic and social development of Apache communities is their dedication to formal education. Demographically, most Apaches are under the age of eighteen. Every community has developed a comprehensive educational plan, extending tribal support of education from preschool to college, university, and trade school. In most cases, these plans are implemented by BIA contract funds, supplemented by trust moneys obtained from Indian Claims Commission awards and money from a variety of tribally owned enterprises.

Twentieth-century Apache communities have been sustained as socio-cultural entities in large part by a distinctive worldview that is both highly spiritual and at the same time pragmatic. Cultural practices have been modified, abandoned, or under assault, but the people's concepts of reality, identity, and place remain essentially unchanged. The Apache universe is seen as an arena of conflicting forces, or *diyin*, among which the individual must strive for spiritual strength and balance. This worldview is constantly reinforced by Apache experiences with American society at large.

Fort Sill Apache

The Fort Sill Apache people were extremely affected by a decision to allow Chiricahua prisoners of war to elect removal to Mescalero, New Mexico. Of the approximately 260 Indians, 87 chose to remain in Oklahoma, where they were allotted eighty acre tracts near what is now Apache, Oklahoma. There are currently 3,568 acres of individually allotted land that serves as a base for a population of over one hundred people.

The Fort Sill Apache are recognized as a separate Apache band and are represented by an elected seven-person Business Committee established under the authorization of the IRA. Tribal headquarters are maintained in Anadarko, Oklahoma. Various members are active in tracing Apache genealogies and in pan-tribal activities such as Indian rodeo and pow-wow (contest) dancing. More and more tribal members have finished high school and begun to enter colleges and universities with the support of scholarship programs.

Efforts have been made to maintain contact with Apache communities in New Mexico and Arizona. Fort Sill Apaches participated in ceremonials and

APACHE					
Division	Reservation	Land Area (acres) Total	Allotted	Population	Economic Resources
Oklahoma Apache Tribe (Kiowa-Apache)	Anadarko, Oklahoma 73005	234,299	229,926	924	Agriculture Grazing
Ft. Sill Apache Tribe (Chiricahua)	Anadarko, Oklahoma 73005	3,568	3,568	103	Agriculture Grazing
Mescalero Apache Tribe (Mescalero, Chiricahua, Lipan)	Mescalero Reservation, New Mexico 88040	460,384	0	3,511	Recreation Grazing Lumber Government
Jicarilla Apache Tribe	Jicarilla Reservation, New Mexico 87528	742,315	0	3,100	Petroleum Grazing Recreation Lumber Government
Camp Verde (Yavapai, Apache)	Camp Verde Reservation, Middle Verde, 86322	640	80	650	Recreation
Fort McDowell (Apache, Mojave, Yavapai)	Fort McDowell Reservation, Scottsdale, Arizona 85251	24,680	0	765	Recreation Rentals Agriculture
San Carlos Apache Tribe	San Carlos Reservation, Arizona 85550	1,877,216	960	7,562	Agriculture Lumber Grazing Government
White Mountain Apache Tribe	Ft. Apache Reservation, Arizona 85941	1,664,872	0	12,503	Lumber Grazing Recreation Agriculture Government
Tonto Apache Tribe	Tonto Apache Reservation, Payson, Arizona 85541	85		92	Tourism Gambling

Sources: Population figures are from Bureau of Indian Affairs, 1992. Acreages are from *Federal and State Indian Reservations and Indian Trust Areas* (U.S. Department of Commerce, ca. 1980).

visited Skeleton Canyon, Arizona, with Chiricahua Apaches from the West during the 1986 Geronimo Centennial. Chiricahuas from both areas also visited Florida to commemorate the years of imprisonment.

Mescalero Apache

The Mescaleros were settled on nearly half-a-million acres near the sacred Sierra Blanca Mountain in south central New Mexico. They survived numerous attempts of ranchers and gold seekers to bring about their removal. Mescalero culture came under assault during the regime of Lieutenant V.E. Stottler as the government appointed agent from 1895 to 1898. Employing a policy of "repression and force," Stottler ordered forced labor for men, cutting of hair, and "civilized" dress of shirts, trousers, and boots. Houses were built and families compelled to live in them.

To destroy the influence of older women at Mescalero, Stottler jailed grandmothers whose granddaughters evaded mission schools. Men were held responsible for the actions of female relatives and children, and were punished for any offenses against government policy. Similar attacks on traditional culture and family took place on other reservations.

Agent James A. Carroll took a humanitarian approach, in the period from 1902 to 1912. During this period much attention was directed toward preserving reservation lands from encroachment by prominent New Mexicans, such as Albert B. Fall. To augment the declining Mescalero population (down to 425 from 464 a generation earlier), thirty-seven Lipan Apaches from Mexico were settled on the reservation, where they were soon absorbed into the general Mescalero population.

In 1912, arrangements were completed for the transfer of 171 Chiricahua prisoners of war from Fort Sill to Mescalero. They moved voluntarily in 1913 and settled in a sparsely populated corner of the reserve. During succeeding decades, the Chiricahuas became increasingly influential in reservation affairs.

Both the Catholic and Dutch Reformed Lutheran churches had active missions at Mescalero and managed numerous conversions from traditional beliefs. Traditional Apache religious practices also continued.

Apache religion recognized spiritual power, called *diyin,* which took many forms. White Painted Woman, the first human, bore two boys: Child of the Water, the primary culture figure; and Killer of Enemies, who struggled to make the earth safe for humanity. The training of males in previous generations commemorated the twins' ordeal. White Painted Woman's influence is celebrated in a four-day ceremony available to young women on attaining puberty. The girl's ceremony features morning and night dances by *G;an,* costumed mountain spirit dancers. At Mescalero this public ceremony now coincides with the Fourth of July celebration and tribal rodeo.

Modern tribal government at Mescalero began with meetings of the headmen of the Mescalero, Lipan, and Chiricahua bands with the government appointed agent in 1915. The tribal government was reorganized under the 1934 IRA legislation and a Tribal Council was established. This currently consists of an elected president, vice-president, and eight-member Council, all serving two-year terms with staggered elections.

Individuals such as Magoosh and Asa Daklugie were influential in reservation leadership. Since 1962, Wendell Chino has filled the tribal presidency. Chino is nationally recognized as an outstanding partisan of tribal sovereignty and economic development. Successful tribal enterprises in lumbering and tourism have been developed, and the internationally known Inn of the Mountain Gods and adjacent sports and conference facilities have proved profitable investments. In spite of such developments, unemployment and underemployment remain high. At times, as much as 70 percent of the work force is underemployed, with unemployment at above 30 percent.

Mescalero Apaches enjoy better access to health and educational services than in previous generations. However, both health and education levels remain below national averages.

Jicarilla Apache

The Jicarilla Apache Reservation in northern New Mexico was created by executive order in 1887. The 416,000-acre reservation was divided into 160-acre allotments in 1891. Incomplete surveys postponed the allotment process until 1909. Preemptions by settlers within reservation boundaries complicated the process. In efforts to create self-sufficiency through stockraising, Congress increased the size of the reservation in 1907, bringing the total acreage to 742,315 acres.

Tribal livestock development languished until 1920, when sheep from the community herd were distributed to each tribal member. Economic advancement followed but was threatened when harsh winters in 1931 to 1932 nearly destroyed reservation herds. Congress loaned money to restock, and a slow return to prosperity in the 1940s resulted.

The Jicarilla population declined from 815 persons in the period from 1900 to 1920. Tuberculosis and influenza ravaged economically depressed reservation families. Many died and some fled to nearby communities to become absorbed in northern New Mexico's predominantly Hispanic population. A sanatorium was built during the 1920s to treat tuberculosis patients and also to serve as a school. This augmented a government day school and a Dutch Reformed mission school also at the agency community.

The tribe organized a formal government in 1937 under terms of the IRA. Incorporating with a Tribal Constitution and Bylaws, they are known as the Jicarilla Apache Tribe. Using revolving loan funds, the tribe organized a cooperative store by purchase of the old Wirt Trading Post. Allotments of land were relinquished to the tribe and a profitable livestock grazing industry developed. As a result of an Indian Claims Commission case, the tribe was awarded over $9 million in 1970.

Significant deposits of oil and natural gas were developed on reservation land between 1950 and 1970; tribal royalties grew to over $1 million annually by 1960. Funds were expended by individual payments and tribal development of the Stone Lake Lodge recreation complex and a tribal education fund.

Population growth increased with accompanying centralization at Dulce. As the district system became obsolete, the Tribal Constitution was repeatedly amended. The council was reduced to ten "at-large" positions, with chairman and vice-chairman being added elective offices. Voting age was lowered to eighteen.

During the 1960s, various federally funded programs in health, education, welfare, and economic development became available to the Jicarilla. These resulted in increased health services and new housing being available at Dulce. Tribal linguistic and cultural renaissance occurred, due in part to government sponsored programs in schools, and due in part to increased income and concern of tribal members.

Traditional religious observances which are still practiced by the majority of Jicarillas include puberty ceremonials and a two-day tribal holiday, September 14 to 15, which is the occasion for a ceremonial relay race between Llanero and Ollero band runners. The relay race ceremony is a long-life celebration and harvest festival intended to insure good health and plentiful food to the participants and observers. It is based on a mythic race between the sun and the moon. Olleros represent the sun and animals; Llaneros represent the moon and plants. A second long-life ceremony, also used for curing, is the Bear Dance. This is performed over the course of four nights, during which dancers impersonating bear and snake aid shamans in curing and seeking spiritual blessings for the community.

The Vicente, TeCube, Velarde, and Vigil families have been most prominent, although not exclusively, in reservation political offices during recent years.

San Carlos Apache

The San Carlos Reservation in Arizona was established as a holding place for the multitude of Apache and allied Yavapai and Mojave bands in 1874. During the nineteenth century, the reservation suffered from a series of poor administrators whose efforts were aggravated by the harsh climate and terrain at the agency. What little arable land was available for use was flooded with the construction of Coolidge Dam in 1928, which forced the movement of the agency and town to their present location.

Poverty and divisiveness among the reservation's 3,000 people of various families and bands combined with relentless government pressure to cause the disintegration of traditional culture and religion. Complex rituals, curing ceremonies, and puberty rites became less frequently practiced through the 1940s.

A twelve-member Tribal Council was set up under the 1934 enabling legislation. Paid labor and revolving funds provided limited capital for the purchase of cattle. This led to the development of the successful San Carlos stockraisers' associations during the period from 1930 to 1960. Additional revenue was obtained from lumbering and asbestos mining on reservation lands.

Tribal government has gained increased control over social services on the reservation. Economic development has faltered. Planned recreation facilities have been slow to develop. Cattle associations have declined in influence. The tribally developed trading centers at Bylas and San Carlos and tribal farms are showing profits from crops, such as alfalfa and jojoba beans. Since the 1960s, there has been a marked revival in traditional religion, culture, and language at San Carlos.

White Mountain Apache

Like San Carlos the Fort Apache Indian Reservation in Arizona was intended as a temporary holding area for a number of Western Apache bands. These people possessed a rich and complex system of clan and band affiliations and religious traditions rivaling those of the neighboring Navajo in varied complexity.

Wage labor was introduced to the reservation's 1,900 people at the turn of the century. In 1918, the Indian Bureau issued 400 cattle to Fort Apache, where 80 families entered the cattle business; by 1931, the herds numbered over 20,000 head and were the target of forced stock reduction during the New Deal era. In 1938, the White Mountain Apache tribe was chartered under provisions of the IRA. The Constitution provided an elective Tribal Council serving two year terms. Tribal industry prospered with the expansion of lumbering among the reservation's huge stands of ponderosa pines. Tribally owned lumber mills employed over 200 people by the 1970s, and produced over 50 million board feet of lumber annually.

In 1954 the tribe began to develop recreational facilities with the construction of a number of artificial lakes and dams on the reservation. Hunting, camping, fishing, and ski facilities followed. Additional enterprises include crafts and agriculture. Tribal marketing cooperatives are based in Whiteriver, the agency center. Men and women from Fort Apache have gained wide recognition as contract fire fighters for the United States Forest Service and travel extensively during fire season. Capable tribal chairmen, such as Ronnie Lupe and others, have taken the lead in exerting tribal sovereignty and developing tribal government services.

The *Na ih es* (girl's puberty ceremony) is continued and enjoys increased popularity. After experiments with Native land syncretic religious movements, such as that of Silas John Edwards, there has been a significant return to traditional religion. Many Apaches, however, are serious practitioners in a variety of Christian denominations active on the reservation.

Conclusion

All Apache communities have experienced a considerable resurgence of self-awareness and traditional culture. The Apache language is still spoken by 75 percent of reservation dwellers, except at Jicarilla and Fort Sill. It is now taught in written form in reservation schools. There has been a growth of viable tribal governments. Conversely, there has been a severe weakening of clan and family structures, which provided the main supports and refuge for the Apache individual. Isolation, poverty, and high unemployment have resulted in increasing problems of alcohol and substance abuse on reservations. Traditional family disintegration has led to serious problems of family violence and neglect of minors and the aged. All communities are devoting their resources to programs to alleviate these problems.

With the exception of Fort Sill, the Apache communities have been fortunate in retaining large areas of land which contain useful resources and opportunities for the development of recreational industry. Apache individualism has survived and provides the human resources which will take the various communities along paths of their own choosing.

Additional Apache populations are found in Arizona and Oklahoma on lands shared with other tribes. In Arizona these include Camp Verde with a Yavapai and Apache population, and Fort McDowell with a Mojave, Yavapai, and Apache population. Oklahoma's Kiowa, Comanche, and Apache occupy jointly owned lands, which are home to 924 Kiowa-Apache.

D.C. Cole

See also **Arizona Tribes; Mojave; Oklahoma Tribes; Plains Apache; Yavapai; Ysleta del Sur Pueblo**

Further Reading

Goodwin, Grenville. *The Social Organization of the Western Apache.* Tucson: The University of Arizona Press, 1969.
Opler, Morris Edward. *An Apache Life-Way: The Economic, Social, and Religious Institutions of the Chiricahua Indians.* New York, NY: Cooper Square Publishers, 1965.
Ortiz, Alfonso, ed. *Handbook of North American Indians.* Vol. 10. *Southwest.* Washington, DC: Smithsonian Institution, 1983.
Sonnichsen, C.L. *The Mescalero Apaches.* Norman: University of Oklahoma Press, 1958, 1979.
Tiller, Veronica E. Velarde. *The Jicarilla Apache Tribe: A History, 1846–1970.* Lincoln: University of Nebraska Press, 1983.
Worcester, Donald E. *The Apaches: Eagles of the Southwest.* Norman: University of Oklahoma Press, 1979.

APACHES DEL NORTE

See Plains Apache

ARAPAHO

While some sources have mistakenly referred to the Arapaho as the Atsina or Gros Ventre, others have used such names as Caminabiches, Ca-ne-na-vich, Kananawesh, Tocaninambiches, Sta-e-tan, and Buffalo Indians. Known as "Cloud Men" by the Cheyenne, and as "Blue Clouds" by the Sioux, the Arapaho call themselves *Hinóno'éno'*, a name some translate as "Sky People," others as "Wrong Rooters," and some as "Roaming People."

History

History provides little information that accurately describes Arapaho culture prior to 1750. Linguistic study, however, offers some clues regarding the probable location of the Arapaho before they adopted a plains culture lifestyle.

Around 1000 B.C. a body of Algonquian-speaking peoples was concentrated around the Great Lakes region. Over a period of time these peoples, the Arapaho very likely among them, slowly migrated away from the area. The move out onto the plains brought about extensive change to Arapaho culture, transforming a sedentary lifestyle into one of nomadic buffalo hunting. Over time, the expanse of Arapaho territory covered southeastern Wyoming, the southwestern corner of Nebraska, all of eastern Colorado, and the upper northwestern region of Kansas. Sometime after the Arapaho had adopted a plains culture, a permanent separation occurred among them. The two groups became distinguished as the Southern and Northern Arapaho.

In 1851, the Arapahos became signatories to the Fort Laramie Treaty. In spite of the treaty, when gold was discovered in 1859 major confrontations between immigrant white settlers and the Arapaho resulted. These confrontations reached a climax in 1864. While peacefully camped at Sand Creek in Colorado, the Southern Arapaho were attacked and massacred by United States Army troops under the command of Colonel John M. Chivington. Compelled to sign the Fort Wise Treaty of 1869, the Southern Arapaho surrendered traditional land for shared reservation land with the Cheyenne in western Oklahoma. The Northern Arapaho were eventually settled with the Eastern Shoshone on the Wind River Reservation in central Wyoming in 1878.

Twentieth-Century History

After the passage of the General Allotment Act, the Southern Arapaho lost 4 million acres of reservation land. Today, finding themselves without a reservation, approximately 3,000 Southern Arapaho live dispersed throughout the northern, central, and southern parts of western Oklahoma on the last vestiges of allotted land.

Fairing more favorably than their southern counterparts, about 3,500 Northern Arapaho still reside on the 2.25 million-acre Wind River Reservation. Although about 1.75 million acres of the lands are jointly owned, the Arapaho and Shoshone tend to reside in separate areas of the reservation. In 1955, both Northern and Southern Arapaho filed grievances with the Indian Claims Commission for not being fully compensated for lands lost to white settlers. After six years, the Commission ruled in favor of the claimants; the tribes were awarded approximately 24 percent of the land's value, based upon 1865 land market figures.

From the era of the great Arapaho chiefs to the present, the ability to innovatively balance traditional and progressive approaches has enabled many aspects of Arapaho culture to persist. With the ever-increasing demands of the twentieth century, Arapaho elders realized that in order to deal more effectively with the government in Washington, D.C., a change of strategy and a new order of tribal leadership was necessary. To meet these demands, the Arapaho pushed for better educated leaders who could face the political challenges posed by an alien government without losing touch with traditional Arapaho values. Among the Northern Arapaho leaders rising to the challenge and demands of county, state, and federal governments, Henry Lee Tyler (1910 to 1936), Nell Scott (1937 to 1968), Ben Friday (1941 to 1968) and Arnold Headley (1961 to 1978) are recognized for their commitment and service. Among the Southern Arapaho, Jesse Rowlodge (1940 to 1957), Saul Birdshead (1947 to 1961), and John Sleeper (five years between 1958 and 1973) are known for their long-standing service.

Economic Development

With a 78 percent unemployment rate among the Northern Arapaho, and a combined rate of 70.6 percent for the Southern Arapaho and Cheyenne tribes of Oklahoma, economics have been a major concern. Prior to 1980, oil and gas money, in the form of per capita payments, represented a primary source of revenue for the Southern Arapahos. Since 1980, however, this revenue source has consistently diminished. Several efforts have been made toward improving economic conditions among the Southern Arapaho. One of these has been an employment and training program administered by the Southern Arapaho through the tribal agency office, a primary employer for the Southern Arapaho. Another enterprise has been a smoke-shop. The tribe remains most hopeful, however, over the prospects of a casino, which is scheduled to open sometime during 1994. Primary Northern Arapaho employers are the Wyoming Indian School District, where in 1993, 85 of 170 employees are Arapaho; the tribal government, employing 78 Arapaho; and Lower Arapaho School District, employing 48 Arapaho. Other sources of tribal economic development are a ranch, convenience store, gas station, laundromat, bingo hall and truck stop, Arapaho Sand and Gravel, and Arapaho Design Ltd., all of which have succeeded as businesses.

Water Rights

In recent years Arapaho leaders at Wind River have demonstrated their commitment to work toward the continued betterment of the tribe by opposing county and state attempts to curtail tribal control over existing water rights on the reservation. In May 1990, an unusually dry spring resulted in a decision by Arapaho and Shoshone Joint Business Council members to shut off the water flow into irrigation ditches on the reservation. This action began a struggle between county and tribal officials for the control of surface water running through the reservation. Although a Wyoming court supported the tribes authority to manage all water rights on the reservation, the Wyoming Supreme Court executed a stay of decision in May 1991.

Religion

At Wind River, where Business Council members often exhibit a strong affinity toward Arapaho tradition, reservation politics have often found guidance in time-honored cultural beliefs. In 1989, the ceremonial accessibility to a Medicine Wheel located in the Big Horn National Forest was threatened by the Forest Service's plans to develop the site as a tourist attraction. In an action that effectively combined religious and political values, tribal elders initiated and guided the formation of a multi-tribal coalition to lobby for the protection of the sacred site. Within this coalition, both Northern and Southern Arapaho leaders represented a strong voice.

The Native American Church and sweat lodge ceremonies have strong followings among the Northern and Southern Arapaho people. Northern practitioners occasionally travel to Oklahoma, and Southern Arapaho practitioners travel to Wyoming to participate in a church meeting or sweat lodge. Although both tribes actively participate in the Sun Dance Lodge, for the past several decades this ceremonial lodge has only been erected in Wyoming. The knowledge required to direct the ceremony has waned among the Southern Arapaho.

While religion has played a strong part in drawing the Southern and Northern tribes together, political, religious, social, and linguistic distinctions do exist between the two groups. Those distinctions set aside, the most crucial cultural concern for both tribes remains the loss of their language; presently, the remaining small number of Southern Arapaho speakers represent the last speakers of this dialect. Although the Northern Arapaho have been able to implement a language program in their schools from kindergarten to twelfth grade, to date this has not had a significant effect in slowing the rate of language loss.

Arapaho leaders have worked hard during the second half of the twentieth century to improve economic, educational, health, and housing standards for their people. As Arapaho leaders look ahead they recognize the need to further intensify efforts at developing innovative programs, such as Northern Arapaho efforts to establish a beef market with the Japanese, that will move them toward increased independence and a stronger voice in determining their own destiny.

Stephen Greymorning

See also **Cheyenne; Oklahoma Tribes; Shoshone: Eastern**

Further Reading

Dorsey, George. *The Arapaho Sun Dance; The Ceremony of the Offerings Lodge.* Field Columbian Museum, Publication 75, Anthropological Series, Vol. IV. Chicago: FCM, 1903.

Fowler, Loretta. *Arapaho Politics, 1851–1978: Symbols in Crises of Authority.* Lincoln: University of Nebraska Press, 1982.

Hafen, Leroy R. "Historical Development of the Arapaho-Cheyenne Land Area," *Arapaho Cheyenne Indians.* New York, NY: Garland Publishing, 1974.

Salzmann, Zdenek. *The Arapaho Indians: A Research Guide and Bibliography.* New York, NY: Greenwood Press, 1988.

Sweezy, Carl, and Althea Bass. *The Arapaho Way: A Memoir of an Indian Boyhood.* New York, NY: Clarkson N. Potter, 1966.

ARCHAEOLOGY

Approximately 95 percent or more of America's past is not written down or recorded in forms that are easily retrievable. Some of this past has been passed from generation to generation by oral tradition, but most of it remains below ground, hidden from our general view. The only way to retrieve the majority of this past is through archaeology. Archaeology focuses specifically on material culture remains, and reconstructs past cultures based on what is left behind. Modern Americans forget that this is possible, since they are trained to focus on the written word. Many think that archaeology can only tell us about that portion of the past before writing, but archaeology provides a unique perspective on all past cultures. Historically, written word was produced by an elite group of society for its own purposes. Reading historic documents and records tells us little about the dominated or unpowerful in cultures, and tells us nothing about their lives. Even for those who kept written records, we know only about a small portion of their daily lives. Archaeology is virtually the only way to learn about the everyday lives of everyday people for cultures of the past, and for some cultures, it is the *only* way to learn anything about those people and places.

On the basis of newspaper and magazine articles in the last ten years, one might easily gain the impression that the relationship between archaeologists and Native Americans is a negative one, with little in common on either side. Recent stories have focused on disputes regarding reburial and repatriation of human remains and funerary objects, with much of the Indian community attacking archaeologists for appropriating their past and violating Native American religious beliefs. While the magnitude and severity of the problem should not be underestimated, a more important and significant point has gotten lost in this debate: archaeologists and Native Americans have far more interests in common than in dispute.

Native Americans often comment that they know what they need to know about their past because they have learned it from elders and others in their tribe. As important and vital as such information is, archaeology can provide additional data to supplement what is already known and to inform about things that are no longer known. For example, the details of how houses were built or artifacts made, the specific artifacts themselves, and a range of information about cultures long forgotten can be retrieved through archaeology. While some might not see the need to learn such detail, or might argue that they know everything they need to know, most people want to learn more. The recent preponderance of Native American museums is a testament to this interest. Put simply, it is to the benefit of archaeologists and Native Americans to work together to remember, document, preserve, and protect the past for the future.

Excavation of Burial Sites

The excavation of burial sites is one of the most notorious areas of interaction between archaeologists and Native Americans. Beginning in the 1970s, Native Americans began to systematically object to the excavation of their burial sites without express permission from the group, tribe, or nation affected. These objections caused problems for archaeologists because many sites cannot be linked to a specific tribe or culture. Such sites predate the existence of modern tribes, and determination of cultural affiliation is impossible. The counterargument was that, as Native Americans, they were most closely related to these past cultures, and should have the right to determine what does or does not get excavated or analyzed or stored in museums.

There are a number of different issues that the excavation of burial sites raised:

1. Who has the right to determine who can or cannot excavate a burial site?

   a. In some instances, excavation of burial sites is unavoidable, and in these cases, what should be done? If excavation is allowed, should there be permits, and if so, who controls the permit process?

   b. Should archaeologists ever be allowed to excavate burials for research purposes alone? Must the site always be threatened by destruction?

2. What happens after a site is excavated? Where do the materials go? Who owns or controls access to them? Are they reburied, and if so, under what circumstances?

3. Who owns and/or controls the past? This is the basic question and area of dispute. Native Americans want the power of determination, and archaeologists want to continue to learn about the past through excavation and analysis of material remains. The issue is a difficult one since Native Americans believe that this past is theirs, and archaeologists are trained to believe that the past belongs to everyone, including future generations. For Native Americans, it is a religious, spiritual, and political issue. Why

excavate burial sites at all? The answer is that the way a society treats its dead is largely unaffected by what we commonly consider fundamental needs (food, shelter, etc.), and therefore reflects most clearly the organization and rituals of the society. Other sites, such as villages, hunting camps, etc., show organization and structure, but these elements are more directly determined by the aforementioned fundamental needs. For archaeologists, reburial takes away knowledge of the past from the future. As new techniques are developed to study the past, there will be nothing to study if bones are reburied. Further selective excavation of only certain kinds of sites is bound to create a biased and limited view of the past.

Not surprisingly, these issues have been the subject of major debate and emotion on all sides, and while it is not fair to say that the issues have been resolved, it is true that most states now have burial laws that attempt to address at least some of these issues. Each state has taken a somewhat different approach, but the most effective laws appear to be those that: (1) allow for the flexibility that different specific circumstances might require; (2) treat all burial sites equally, not distinguishing Native American from European or other burials; (3) involve a state-appointed board representing the different communities involved that makes ultimate decisions on specific cases; (4) provide penalties for disturbing burial sites as well as incentives for preservation of sites; and (5) require that, in the case of excavation, proper recording and analysis procedures are followed.

In most states, it is now illegal to disturb or excavate a burial site without a permit to do so, and most states also require that remains be reburied after analysis. Federal laws and regulations for federal lands follow similar procedures; on tribal lands, the permission of the tribe has long been necessary for any archaeological excavations. Once the majority of these laws came into effect, Native Americans concerned about archaeology and museums turned their attention to those human remains and funerary objects already housed in museums and scientific institutions.

The Problems of Looting

Archaeological resources are abundant—there are archaeological sites in every state and country—but these resources are non-renewable. Once an archaeological site is destroyed, the information from that site is gone forever. For both archaeologists and Native Americans, one area on which there is total agreement is the destruction caused by raiders and looters of archaeological sites. Looting and raiding of sites in most areas of the country is a real threat to the sites that remain, and in some areas, the threat from looting is far worse than the threat from development or natural processes. Looting will continue as long as people are willing and able to buy such objects for their personal collections; the prices that some are willing to pay for artifacts have increased more than ten times in the last ten years.

To the public, looting may mean taking aesthetically pleasing artifacts from sites, and keeping or selling the items. To an archaeologist, looters do more than remove artifacts from sites—they destroy the context of what is removed and what is left, and all that can be learned from the object and the site. Prosecution and active focus on the problems and consequences of looting are among the only ways that the remaining past can be protected.

Legislation to Protect Archaeological Sites

Since the 1970s, the United States has developed laws and regulations that protect archaeological sites on federal lands and on lands that will be impacted by federally funded projects. A number of states and even local governments have similarly enacted laws that protect sites on state or locally owned lands, or on lands impacted by state or local projects. While this has resulted in the protection of thousands of sites, it leaves many more thousands of sites at risk because the majority of land in the United States is in private property, and the majority of sites are on private lands. Sites on private lands are generally not protected.

Over the last one hundred years, the United States has passed a series of laws that create a comprehensive federal policy on conservation and preservation of archaeological resources. The accompanying table provides a summary of the major pieces of legislation that affect both archaeology and Native American concerns. These laws fall into one of three categories: (1) protection of specific sites or sites on federal lands; (2) consideration of archaeological and historical resources when threatened by federal action or in the planning process; and (3) reburial and repatriation, specifically in relation to Native American sites. Taken together, these laws represent national policy on archaeological and historical resources, and mandate education, as well as protection and management.

A cornerstone of federal policy is the National Register of Historic Places, created by the Historic Preservation Act of 1966. The Register is a list of historic, architectural, and archaeological sites that have been determined to have state, regional, or national significance. Federal and state laws about protection of resources come into effect only if an affected site has already been placed on the National Register, or has been determined to be eligible for inclusion on the Register. The Register is an honor and a way to recognize the significance of a site, but can also work as a way to protect that site from certain kinds of destruction. Under the Historic Preservation Act, the application of preservation laws is monitored at the state level by the State Historic Preservation Office (SHPO). When a proposed development project is on federal lands or on lands that will be impacted by federally funded projects, the following steps are taken: (1) The federal agency and SHPO determine whether or not there are historic properties in the area of the proposed activity. Next, the agency and SHPO identify all National Register properties (these may include buildings and/or archaeological sites) and properties that may be eligible for the National Register within the project area. (2) The agency and SHPO determine whether the proposed activity will affect the identified properties in any way. (3) If there is an adverse effect, an effort is made, through consultation with the relevant parties, to find acceptable ways to reduce the harm to the historic properties. (4) The agency and SHPO submit the agreed upon action to the national Advisory Council for Historic Preservation for review. (5) If all are in agreement, the proposed solution, and eventually the proposed activity, proceeds. The National Register is also used to determine whether or not properties qualify for certain tax benefits.

In preservation policy, as reflected in the laws in the accompanying chart, it is usual to have one or more review boards or panels evaluate the proposed activity. This procedure helps to insure fairness and the consideration of a variety of opinions.

International Issues

Looting and the sale of artifacts is an international problem, and in 1970 the United Nations tried to develop an international approach to the problem by having UNESCO (United Nations Educational, Scientific, and Cultural Organization) generate the Convention on the Means of Prohibiting and Preventing the Illicit Import, Export and Transfer of Ownership of Cultural Property. The purpose and content of the convention is largely self-explanatory; countries signing the convention promise to try and slow illicit trade in cultural property. Convincing nations to sign the convention proved far more difficult than generating it; looters and artifact collectors are often wealthy and powerful influences. To date, the only signatories in the major art collecting world are the United States and Canada. In the United States, the enabling legislation establishes an eleven-member committee which reviews requests from countries that wish the United States to restrict the importation of designated cultural property. Unfortunately, few countries have taken advantage of the opportunity, and the United States has not filed similar requests with other countries.

UNESCO also supported the founding of the International Council on Monuments and Sites (ICOMOS) in 1963. ICOMOS is an international nongovernmental organization. The purpose of the council is to bring together "people and institutions actively concerned with the conservation of buildings, groups of buildings, and larger units of architectural, archaeological and historical interest." One of the Council's new directions includes archaeological heritage management, focused on a Charter for the Protection and Management of the Archaeological Heritage. The thrust of the Charter is toward an integrated and systematic approach to the preservation and conservation of archaeological heritage. This approach would include

preservation of the surrounding landscape or context, as well as the specific site, and conserving and protecting what remains in the ground as well as the material that has been excavated.

Finally, UNESCO has also established the World Heritage List, a list comparable to the National Register of Historic Places, but at the international level. Sites placed on this list are considered to be of international significance. Cahokia in Illinois and Mesa Verde in the Southwest are examples of two archaeological sites in the United States that have been placed on this list.

Interactions between Archaeologists and Native American Communities

Although the press may paint a lurid picture of the relationship between archaeologists and Native Americans, the reality is different. Most states have an archaeology awareness week which targets education of the general public, school children, and Indian communities, and most also have programs which specifically work toward cooperation between Native Americans and archaeologists. A number of tribes have active preservation offices that conduct archaeological work on tribal lands and ongoing education programs (two notable examples are the Navajo Nation Historic Preservation Office and the Zuni Archaeology Program). Burial laws have resulted in discussions and negotiations over the excavation and analysis of sites, and this has resulted in compromise and settlements which try to address the concerns of both sides.

National archaeological organizations (Society for American Archaeology, Society for Historical Archaeology, and Archaeological Institute of America) have developed public education committees to educate the public more broadly about archaeology and about the problems of looting, and the Society for American Archaeology (SAA) has developed a Task Force on SAA/Native American Relations to begin discussions and programs of interest to both groups.

In general, archaeologists are spending more time talking with Native American peoples, learning about their concerns and questions, as well as trying to inform them of the benefits of archaeology—the education process is proceeding in both directions.

The Future

The future of archaeology/Native American relationships will depend upon both sides, as well as the general public, understanding that no one can own the past, and that the past and its artifacts cannot be considered "property." While we all have a responsibility to the past and to our cultural heritage, that responsibility is in the form of *stewardship*—it is up to us to protect and conserve the past for the future. In countries with a direct tie between the dominant culture and the original inhabitants, the ownership of cultural heritage is usually reserved to the state. In countries such as the United States, however, we focus

Major Federal Legislation of Concern to Archaeology and Indians[1]

TITLE OF LEGISLATION OR REGULATION	SUMMARY DESCRIPTION	COMMENT
Antiquities Act of 1906	President can establish national monuments on federal lands; authorizes permit system to investigate sites on federal lands.	The first preservation law.
Historic Sites Act of 1935	Gave National Park Service mandate to identify, protect & preserve *in situ* cultural properties of fundamental importance.	Places responsibility for protection with Park Service, & requires action.
Historic Preservation Act of 1966	Complex act requiring federal government to establish nationwide system for identification, protection, & rehabilitation of "historic places." Appropriated funds to conduct surveys & planning in each state. Created National Register of Historic Places. Required federal agencies to protect Register properties when development projects planned, & established national advisory council to oversee compliance with this requirement.	This act set up a national framework for historic preservation.
National Environmental Policy Act of 1969 (NEPA)	Comprehensive policy for government land use planning & resource management. Required federal agencies to consider environmental, historical, and cultural values to be weighed whenever federally owned land is modified or private land is modified with federal funds. Required environmental impact statements and reports.	Designed to help in planning process, but act provides no guarantees that measures to mitigate impact would be taken.
Historic Preservation Act Amendments (1980)	Made an earlier executive order into law; created national policy. Better definition of terms and regulations, requires permission of landowners before sites can be placed on the National Register, increases penalties for violations of original 1966 law.	Created a comprehensive federal policy for historic preservation.
Archaeological Recovery Act (1960, 1974) Also known as Moss-Bennett Act	Federal agencies must tell secretary of interior about any dam construction, & if archaeological resources found, must allow for recovery or salvage. Law amended in 1974 to authorize all federal agencies to provide funds for the preservation or recovery of archaeological & historic resources when these are endangered by federal or federally assisted projects; can use up to 1% of project funds.	Original bill (1960) also known as Reservoir Salvage Act. 1974 additions provided funds for analysis & publication of results for first time.
Federal Aid to Highways Acts (1956 & 1958)	Authorized use of highway funds for archaeological salvage work in federal highway rights-of-way.	Resulted in many sites excavated & salvaged; salvage eventually made way for better planning and management of resources.
Archaeological Resources Protection Act of 1979 (ARPA)	Gives more stringent protection to sites on federal lands. Provides fines & prison terms for removing archaeological materials from federal lands without a permit. Amendments made in 1988 require federal agencies to develop plans to conduct archaeological surveys of all lands, develop uniform system to report violations of law, strengthen looting provisions, and require federal land managers to develop public awareness programs.	Although it provides no protection to sites on private land, it is first law aimed at stopping commercial vandals.
National Museum of the American Indian Act	Established a separate museum of the American Indian as part of the Smithsonian Institution, & charged the Smithsonian with developing policies for the repatriation of skeletal remains held in its collections.	This was the first federal law requiring reburial of human remains.
Native American Graves Protection & Repatriation Act (1990)	Focuses on human skeletal remains housed in federal agencies, museums, and universities. In addition to skeletal remains, the law includes sacred objects and items of cultural patrimony. Each institution must conduct an inventory of its holdings and try to determine the cultural affiliation of each item. Appropriate tribes or organizations are then notified, and items transferred if the Native American group wants the remains. A review committee oversees implementation and identification process.	This represents a broad national reburial & repatriation policy. Any institution receiving federal money in any form is included.

[1] *This chart only includes legislation which has a direct effect on the archaeological and Indian communities and their relationship. Laws that more directly affect one group or another have not been included here, such as the American Indian Religious Freedom Act or the Abandoned Shipwreck Act. Legislation establishing National Park or other site-specific legislation is also omitted.*

on specific ethnic heritages, and speak of "other's" pasts. The past as a collective responsibility is not yet a matter of conscience for most of us, and we let our value of private property override our concern for the protection of cultural heritage.

Some specific ideas for future interactions might include the following: (1) the development of a national program by professional organizations to train Native American students in archaeology, physical anthropology, and museum studies, and to educate the general public about their stewardship responsibilities; (2) the inclusion of Native Americans in the development of museum and public exhibits, and the offer of a variety of different forms of assistance in creating tribal museums and displays; and (3) the commitment by individual archaeologists to make the effort to speak with Native Americans and the general public about their work, including active collaboration with Native American groups. The past will remain a foreign country if we do not try to share our knowledge and work together.

Lynne Goldstein

See also **Anthropologists and Native Americans; Museums; Repatriation of Human Remains and Artifacts; Tribal Museums**

Further Reading

Archaeological Assistance Division. *Federal Archaeology Report,* Vol. 1, No. 1–present. Washington: National Park Service, Department Consulting Archaeologist, published quarterly since 1988.

Meltzer, David J., Don D. Fowler, and Jeremy A. Sabloff, eds. *American Archaeology Past and Future: A Celebration of the Society for American Archaeology 1935–1985.* Washington, DC: Smithsonian Institution Press, 1986.

Messenger, Phyllis Mauch, ed. *The Ethics of Collecting Cultural Property: Whose Culture? Whose Property?* Albuquerque: University of New Mexico Press, 1989.

Price, H. Marcus. *Disputing the Dead: U.S. Law on Aboriginal Remains and Grave Goods.* Columbia: University of Missouri Press, 1991.

Smith, George S., and John E. Ehrenhard, eds. *Protecting the Past: Readings in Archaeological Resources Protection.* Boca Raton, FL: CRC Press, 1991.

ARCHITECTURE

Twentieth-century Native American architecture has rarely been the subject of scholarly attention, so that any discussion of it must be regarded as tentative. Nevertheless, it appears that we may divide twentieth-century architecture by and for Native Americans into three periods, one for each third of the century. The first third is characterized by a persistence of nineteenth-century patterns. This means in some cases the building of earth-sheltered houses and tipis or, increasingly, log houses in the Plains, rectilinear wooden houses in the Northwest, adobe and stone-faced buildings in Pueblos, and hogans for the Navajo. In other cases, it means the construction of Euroamerican buildings by acculturated Native Americans (or by Native Americans under pressure to erect them). The second third opens with a brief period during the New Deal and the superintendency of John Collier at the Bureau of Indian Affairs; innovative efforts were cut short by mobilization for World War II. The period concludes with an emphasis on Euroamerican building types among Native Americans. The final third of this century is marked—not widely but increasingly—by the creation of modern buildings that are responsive to Native American cultural concerns.

Early Twentieth-Century Architecture

The early twentieth-century persistence of traditional architecture was due in part to the isolation created by the remoteness of reservations or the isolation of small Native American enclaves; it was due

Navajo Nation Council Chambers, Window Rock, AZ, 1935. Mayers, Murray & Phillips, architects. Courtesy of Carol Krinsky. Copyright © 1992 Carol Herselle Krinsky.

Roundhouse, Pawnee, OK, 1971-74. Courtesy of Carol Krinsky. Copyright © 1992 Carol Herselle Krinsky.

also to poverty, which prevented many Native Americans from obtaining modern materials useful for climate control and insulation or for convenient water and energy supply; it may also have been due to the Native Americans' desire to retain meaningful parts of their past, however inconvenient a single-room dwelling or a hand-dug well may have appeared to Euroamericans. Perhaps these outsiders expected Native Americans to adopt an all-or-nothing approach, either to live in a visibly traditional way or adopt the ways of the majority culture. One does not read of efforts by the majority to create hybrid architecture that might have suited groups who, by the early twentieth century, had been affected in many ways by Euroamerican culture. In some cases, however, Native Americans themselves created buildings that maintained essential aspects of the past, while using modern and convenient materials. Ceremonial roundhouses (often, in fact, polygonal) in Oklahoma and California were covered with wooden siding of apparently standard dimensions and machine fabrication.

Frequent points of "red/white" contact were schools and churches run by Euroamericans for the supposed benefit of indigenous people. Boarding schools and mission churches used plans, forms, and styles favored by the American majority. As structures of the dominant society, these buildings were meant to reveal to Native Americans, while encompassing or controlling them, the benefits of Euroamerican and Christian culture. The architecture insured that Native American schoolchildren or churchgoers would see nothing that was familiar at home.

Mid-Twentieth-Century Architecture

The second third of the century was, overall, a period when the pressure to conform to European ways persisted. It even increased in the postwar period when many Native Americans were relocated to cities. Financial constraints and the cost of housing left no money for creative architectural solutions to suit their bicultural situation. On reservations, Bureau of Indian Affairs and federal housing officials supplied Euroamerican-styled housing and day schools, with some regional variety in style and materials. From 1934 to about 1942, however, under New Deal job creation and community development programs, efforts were made to create buildings sympathetic to the locale, tradition, and culture of various Native American groups. The Navajo Council House at Window Rock, Arizona, designed as an octagon to reflect but not copy a hogan, is one example; other examples were Navajo and Pueblo schools at Moenave, New Mexico, Taos, New Mexico, and Shonto, Arizona. Euroamerican architects under contract to the federal government erected them, but when possible, they were built by reservation residents. Hopi men, for instance, received training in construction that they used later both on and off the reservation. These buildings reveal the impact of more than job-creation programs: tribal office buildings were built because

Four Winds School, Fort Totten Reservation, ND, 1983. Denby Deegan (Sioux-Arikara), designer. Courtesy of Carol Krinsky. Copyright © 1992 Carol Herselle Krinsky.

the Indian Reorganization Act of 1934 created new forms of tribal governance, which engendered buildings to accommodate new functions.

Late Twentieth-Century Architecture

During the last third of the century, acculturation of Native Americans continued, with Euroamerican-inspired educational, social, and health facilities prominent among buildings erected by and for tribes and individuals. Although most buildings are still erected using technologically-produced materials and modern forms, increasing numbers of tribal headquarters, cultural centers, and museums (which are relatively new building types for Native Americans), social service facilities, schools, and even casinos, are being designed with reference to Native American tradition. Moreover, since the early 1960s, more Native American men and women have graduated from architecture school and have formed or worked in firms that specialize in Native American commissions. Usually without connections to wealthy corporate or residential clients, these firms may benefit from Indian preference provisions included in federal requests for bids. New laws, especially the Indian Self-Determination and Education Act of 1975, have helped to promote Native American consciousness in all aspects of culture, including architecture.

Among the ways in which traditional concerns have been incorporated into Native American architecture are the following:

1. Maintenance of traditional building types. This is easiest to achieve in Pueblo domestic architecture, but it is also seen in the construction of ceremonial roundhouses, for example, at Clearlake Oaks, California (construction leader, Delbert Thomas, Jr., Pomo), and Pawnee, Oklahoma. The traditional building type may be constructed of industrially produced materials, or lit by electricity without violating the

essentially traditional nature of the building type and function.

2. Construction using traditional processes and materials. The Hoo-hoogam Ki Museum for the Salt River Pima Maricopa Indian Community, Scottsdale, Arizona, and the Lakota Studies Building at Sinte Gleska College, Mission, South Dakota, are examples of buildings for modern purposes, but determined by the local Native Americans rather than by outsiders. The buildings were erected by reservation residents using traditional methods and communal work pro-cedures. This can be done even if the design supervisor or the person responsible for signing construction documents is a Euroamerican; when that is the case, the Euroamericans subordinate their traditions to Native American ones.

3. Use of a traditional plan. The Ned A. Hatathli Center of Navajo Community College, Tsaile, Arizona, albeit made of industrial materials and otherwise not traditional, was made eight-sided in order to recall the hogans still seen in many parts of the reservation. The education building for the Tohono O'odham people at Sells, Arizona, is designed in the shape of a simplified maze to recall a maze depicted on a significant rock and believed by the tribe to be of precontact origin (construction supervisor, Larry Garcia, Tohono O'odham).

4. Use of an innovative but symbolic plan, usually a zoomorphic one. The Cornwall Island School in Ontario was planned to recall a pheasant, and the Native American Center for the Living Arts of Niagara Falls, New York (co-designer, Dennis Sun Rhodes, Arapaho), has the plan of a turtle, an animal central to the cosmology of the thirty-eight tribes that sponsored the building. A circular plan with four major entrances leading to four major corridors along the cardinal points, recalling a medicine wheel, is seen at the Four Winds School at the Fort Totten Reservation, North Dakota (designer, Denby Deegan, Sioux/Arikara).

5. Elevation reminiscent of traditional forms, e.g., overhanging roofs, log supports, Pueblo-like shape. The Sac and Fox Nation Library at Stroud, Oklahoma, and even more so, the smoke-shop there, recall the rooflines and supports of traditional local structures. The Oke Owe'enge Cultural Center at San Juan Pueblo (collaborating architect, Andy Acoya, Laguna Pueblo), is low-lying, smooth-walled, and massive as are local traditional buildings.

6. Free invention of expressive forms. The unfinished cultural center at Pyramid Lake, Nevada (architect, Dennis Numkena, Hopi), has a vertical core, evoking laddered elements in kivas and other structures that linked people to the heavens, but the stone-faced curvilinear structure is original and bold. The Piya Wiconi Building, intended as a tribal administration building but used as the administration center for Oglala Lakota College, Pine Ridge, South

Native American Center for the Living Arts ("The Turtle"), Niagara Falls, NY, 1981. Dennis Sun Rhodes (Arapaho) and Thomas Hodne, designers. Courtesy of Carol Krinsky. Copyright © 1992 Carol Herselle Krinsky.

Dakota, incorporates projecting walls that evoke animal forms important to traditional teaching (co-designer, Sun Rhodes).

7. Emphasis on natural materials or a connection to nature. The use of a berm, as at the Independent Agencies Building for the Muscogee Nation, Okmulgee, Oklahoma, might also conserve energy and thus promote a wholesome environment as Native American tradition advocates. The tribal museum at Cherokee, North Carolina, is made of natural materials such as wood and stone, has large windows connecting the interior with the outdoors, and includes planting and a small stream of water in front of the building.

8. Use of traditional ornamental motifs on a modern building, as at the Seneca-Cayuga Tribal Office, Miami, Oklahoma (designer, Neil McCaleb, Chickasaw) or the Cultural/Tourism Building, Poplar, Montana (designer, Denby Deegan).

Current efforts to create culturally appropriate architecture complement other aspects of cultural reinforcement, e.g., music and language study. It is

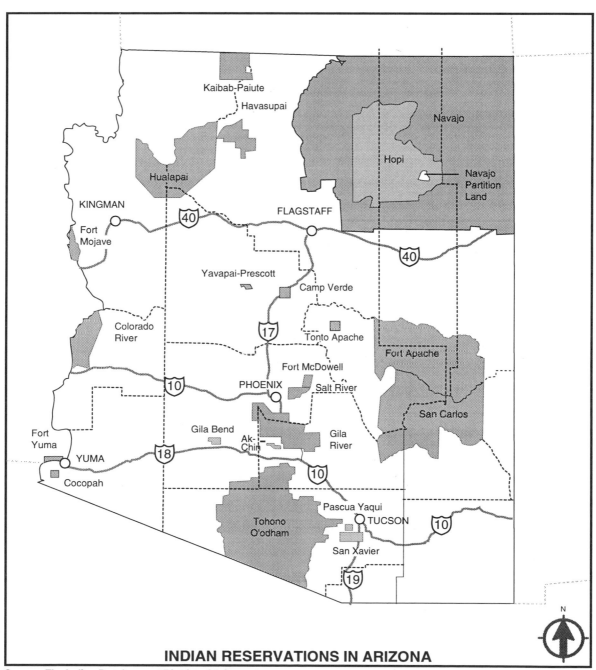

INDIAN RESERVATIONS IN ARIZONA

Source: The Indian Development District of Arizona, Inc.

hoped that these efforts will strengthen communities in their efforts to solve grave social problems.

Carol Herselle Krinsky

See also Housing

Further Reading

Jett, Stephen C., and Virginia Spencer. *Navajo Architecture: Forms, History, Distribution.* Tucson, AZ: University of Arizona Press, 1981.

Krinsky, Carol Herselle. *Native American Architecture Since 1965.* New York, NY: Architectural History Foundation and MIT Press, forthcoming.

Nabokov, Peter, and Robert Easton, *Native American Architecture.* New York, NY: Oxford University Press, 1989.

Short, C.W., and R. Stanley-Brown. *Public Buildings: A Survey of Architecture of Projects Constructed by Federal and Other Government Bodies between 1933–1939.* Washington, DC: Public Works Administration, 1939, supplemented by *Indians at Work* I 1:13 and 24 (1934): 31–33, 5–6.

ARIKARA

See Three Affiliated Tribes

ARIVAIPA

See Apache

ARIZONA TRIBES

See Apache; Cocopah; Colorado River Indian Tribes; Havasupai; Hopi; Hualapai; Mojave; Navajo; Paiute, Southern; Pee-Posh; Pima; Quechan; Tohono O'odham; Yaqui; Yavapai

See map on previous page.

ART

With the entry of the first people into the Western Hemisphere, aesthetic considerations were necessarily secondary to function, since survival was paramount. This is not to say that a sense of beauty did not exist; on the contrary, *art* was generally highly enjoyed and appreciated, but was interpreted as something very well done; the inherent beauty of the craftsmanship tended to be taken for granted, in a sense. Anything well-done was effective—functionally, emotionally, or religiously. The basic materials were those supplied by nature; colors came from plant and mineral pigments. Decorative elements were incised or painted on the surface of hides, textiles were woven of plant fibers, or related substances, decorated with appliqué designs; wood, bone, and stone were carved with various motifs usually related, but not limited, to religious needs, although social prestige often had an almost equal role. Metal was rare; only in the Great Lakes region and to a lesser extent, the Northwest Coast, did copper find any measurable use, while gold and silver were almost unknown in North America.

Out of this design development grew a visual imagery which, while universal in its use of common resources and functions, was by no means monolithic; individual creativity in form and need dictated specific differences in each region; it is these individual mannerisms which allow one to identify chronological, geographical, or tribal origins.

With the entry of the European, this world changed dramatically, and affected almost every avenue of art. Iron and steel provided more effective cutting implements, thereby giving the sculptor greater freedom in executing larger and more precise design concepts, while the carver and engraver could achieve finer detailing and control over the material. The brilliant, permanent colors of glass trade beads replaced the earlier quillwork. Aniline dyes yielded more attractive color patterns for the weaver which would not fade; and cotton or woolen trade cloth introduced a wider range of textiles than previously; these in turn were often decorated in a wider range of techniques. Gold and silver became highly prized decorative materials. Almost the only arts relatively unaffected by the more sophisticated resources were pottery and basketry—and even the latter often made use of commercial dyes. These new craft materials combined to create what some critics regard as a Golden Age in Indian art, reaching its zenith in the late eighteenth and early nineteenth centuries. Attention to detail and technique resulted in beautifully designed and decorated objects, costumery, and paraphernalia which gave the Native a brilliant, colorful palette, expressed in both sacred and secular objects.

This situation existed relatively unchanged well into the late nineteenth century, when the forced removal of many peoples out onto the Great Plains and Oklahoma, resulted in an outbreak of warfare and social demoralization in which any attention to art had to give way to simple survival. Once the Indian wars were over, the flood of explorers and settlers caused changes in crafts objects, particularly in function and size. Pieces had to be made which appealed to European taste and could be transported readily; new ideas, new designs, and new demands combined to produce pieces made largely for their visual appeal; the customer had changed from the knowledgeable indigenous resident, neighbor, or distant Native tourist, to a consumer who knew little of traditional design, and preferred more familiar motifs, or those which were possessed of certain Indian characteristics. Concomitant with this was a feeling of cultural superiority which rarely allowed the Native craftsman a financial income that would justify the time and materials invested.

In the twentieth century, the world of the Indian artist was permanently changed. Museums, which had routinely regarded Indian collections as ethnology, and displayed their most colorful, aesthetically exciting objects side-by-side with mundane craftwork, began to enter the art world via the "primitive art" rubric, and increasingly set vitrines aside for the sole purpose of dramatically exhibiting those items which would arouse the maximum public appreciation. One of the earliest was the Exposition of Indian Tribal Arts in 1931, organized by John Sloan, Oliver LaFarge, and Amelia White in New York City; another, perhaps even more influential, was the San Francisco World's Fair ten years later, designed by Frederic Douglas, Kenneth Disher, and René d'Harnoncourt, which caused a revolution in museum and art circles. Museum displays—such as at the Denver Art Museum, Museum of Northern Arizona, Philbrook Art Center, and later at the Museum of the American Indian, Museum of Primitive Art, and Brooklyn Art Museum, to name only a few—were increasingly devoted to the aesthetics of Indian culture.

As interest grew in the so-called primitive art or folk art world, dealers entered the field, and greater attention was paid by collectors to the selection of suitable pieces, accompanied by demands for greater care in technique and design; prices slowly began to increase. This in turn encouraged the artist who enjoyed greater prestige, a better income, and pride of self. The more sophisticated and skilled individuals increased their attention to new design styles and non-Indian demands, and invested the time needed to create true works of art—thereby attracting the interest of curators and collectors. Thus, a lively circle was born in which each fed the other—artist, collector, dealer, critic, and consumer.

Some of the pioneers in this movement were potters Julian and Maria Martinez, and painters Acee Blue Eagle, Harrison Begay, Oscar Howe, Fred Kabotie, and others. However, this interest did not transfer to weaving, silverwork, or basketry until later. A second generation so to speak of painters, led by Fritz Scholder and R.C. Gorman, aroused modern art critics and influenced younger painters to specialize while silversmithing can trace much of its great revival to the work of Charles Loloma, a gifted Hopi artist, and Kenneth Begay, a young Navajo. This peaked in the 1960s and 1970s, with dramatic primitive art exhibits, lively auctions, the rise of new (but often impermanent) galleries, an increasing number of collectors, and publications devoted to these interests. Never before had there been as wide a range of interest, nor had prices risen so high.

The United States Indian Arts and Crafts Board had instituted a survey to find out how vital old-time craft techniques had survived, and the results—surprising in the degree to which these had been retained, even while executed only in moderate numbers—now began to pay off; some were revived and improved upon, and many skills were refined to a remarkably sophisticated form. Weavers took pride in their skills; some, such as Daisy Taugelchee and her daughter-in-law, Priscilla, and Julia Jumbo, attained a yarn count of 140 threads per inch with commensurate beauty of design. Potters, notably Lucy Lewis, Rosa Gonzalez, Blue Corn, and Margaret Tafoya, experimented in new techniques and forms. The once-fading art of carving the great cedar totem poles and elaborate wooden masks enjoyed a resurgence of interest, highlighted by such sculptors as Mungo Martin, Lincoln and Amos Wallace, Willie Seaweed, Bill Reid, and the Hunt family, not to overlook a gifted woman sculptor, Ellen Neel.

Basketry enjoyed a remarkable focus of interest; while always a somewhat limited art form in terms of numbers, due to the amount of time required and the availability of materials, it became recognized as one of the great accomplishments of the Native artist, and commanded spectacular prices in the art market. Individuals began to enjoy personal fame, with name artists attracting widespread attention. Perhaps most striking became the importance of signing one's work— a concept totally alien to most Indian craft customs, but essential in the collecting world. It is this renaissance which gave the lie to the unfortunate practice of "collecting by the calendar"—the argument that Native American art died with the entry of the European. This near-sighted attitude denies the ongoing vitality of art, the contemporary achievements of the younger generation of artists, and the integrity of their works; and perhaps most destructively, threatens whatever stability may exist.

It is perfectly true that some of the products of this explosive output represented only mediocre quality. No craft escaped this, although silverwork was particularly a victim in the haste to produce. Part of the fault lay in a lack of knowledge on the part of the buyer—and this naïveté was also responsible for the production of indifferent copies or outright fakes. The success of some of the more innovative artists attracted rivalries, and today one sees copywork on every side; any visit to the major commercial crafts exhibits reveals an unfortunate plethora of duplication. Some of this work is of remarkably high technical achievement, to be sure; but, by and large, this tremendous replication carries the seeds of its own demise: the "production line" in effect, of almost identical objects blunts the excitement of the original.

But the general aesthetic level is better than it has been for many years; and, as had been obtained with earlier generations of artists and collectors, innovations are almost commonplace. Potters seem to be the most imaginative, with a vast range of new forms, materials, and designs. The basic clay materials have not changed as much as the forms and designs; some of the "big names" in Indian art produced work which was meretricious, and perhaps overdone, but the bulk of the work of the 1970s–1980s was a healthy expression of talented individuals who exerted far more attention to their products and certainly freely expressed imaginations. Among these latter are a host of practitioners, including Lucy Lewis, Grace Medicine Flower, Marie Z. Chino, Helen Naha, and more recently, Jody Folwell, Nancy Youngblood, Dora Tsepé, Dorothy Torivio, Rondina Huma, Dextra Nampeyo, Anna Mitchell, Cora Wahnetah, and Karita Coffey.

Another dramatic change was that of gender; while women had always been active in decorative and functional crafts, this was regarded as a necessary skill, but not with the same respect as was warfare or oratory; these were male prerogatives. With increased attention being given to the individual, particularly those blessed with creative genius, women came more

Fred Kabotie (Hopi). "The Snake Dance," ca. 1926. Casein and watercolor on paper; 12 ³/₈ by 18 ⁷/₈ inches. William and Leslie Van Ness Denman Collection. Courtesy of the U.S. Department of the Interior, Indian Arts and Crafts Board, W–68.56.27.

Al Qoyawayma (Hopi). Contemporary ceramics. Top: *"Three Corn Sikyatki," 8 by 16 inches;* bottom: *"The Voyager," 10 by 8 ¹/₂ inches.* Photo courtesy of Gallery 10, Inc., of Scottsdale, AZ, and Santa Fe, NM.

Ramona Sakiestewa (Hopi). "Morning Stars," 1985. Hand-woven textile with hand-dyed wools in indigo, cochineal, walnut, madderroot, and natural white, 48 by 73 inches. Photo courtesy of Gallery 10, Inc., of Scottsdale, AZ, and Santa Fe, NM.

R.C. Gorman (Navajo). "Natoma," 1989. Bronze; height, 6 feet. Photo courtesy of Navajo Gallery, R.C. Gorman, Taos, NM.

Fritz Scholder (Luiseño). "Dartmouth Portrait #15," 1973. Acrylic on canvas; 80 by 68 inches. Photo courtesy of Riva Yares Gallery, Santa Fe, NM.

Oscar Howe (Yanktonai). "Double Woman," 1971. Casein; 18 1/2 by 22 3/4 inches. Copyright © 1983 Adelheid Howe.

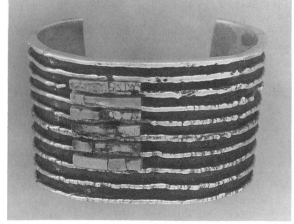

Charles Loloma (Hopi). Silver bracelet, with inlays of turquoise, 1962. Width 1 5/8 inches. Courtesy of the U.S. Department of the Interior, Indian Arts and Crafts Board, W–D63.7.

and more to the forefront, not only as major artists, but people possessed of considerable economic importance; their names were recognized equally with those of warriors of the disappearing past. They not only worked in their traditional fields of textiles, beadwork, basketry, and pottery, but took on other challenges, particularly in silverwork and sculpture. Echoing this change of pace was a group of young men who also entered new fields: traditionally, men made pottery only for a few restricted ceremonial needs, or to help create some of the tremendously large storage containers which required great strength. Today, several male artists have made great strides in the ceramic arts, led by Al Qöyawama, a Hopi whose imaginative creations are highly sought after, and including Russell Sanchez and Wallace Youvella. An increasing number of men are taking on such previously nonmasculine fields as weaving, beadwork, and quillwork.

At this same time, some artists began to ignore traditional enmities, which in the past had tended to divide and weaken their people, and sought strength in unity. The Indian Arts and Crafts Board had established craft guilds among the several tribes in the 1935–1950 era, but these had long been considered as dictated from the outside; they were helpful in improving quality and assisting craftsmen in the economic development of their work, but always met with a certain degree of resistance. The Navajo Silver Guild grew out of such an effort, as did the Artist Hopid a little later; both were essentially Indian-organized and operated. Today, there are about a dozen well-functioning cooperative guilds spread throughout the country.

Some of the most prominent Indian artists are extremely wealthy today by almost any standards and a fair number make a relatively good living. Even so, the proportion of artists who can live exclusively on their products is probably little different from those in the Euroamerican population; but the actual income level is quite different. By and large, most Native craftspeople achieve only a relatively modest income from their creativity. Part of the reason lies in the nature of Indian cultural patterns, which often deny rewards to the successful or outstanding entrepreneur in the Indian world—one must share individual success with all. This traditional outlook, vitally necessary in the early days of unity-for-survival, still holds true today and inevitably affects any productive individual effort. But it cannot be denied that there is a fair amount of white man's ignorance and prejudice involved; while this has declined considerably in the past several decades, it is still a major force in denying Indian artists the maximum return from their efforts.

Some recent innovations in the Indian art market are most obvious in the galleries which specialize in ethnic art. Perhaps the most dramatic has been the wave of reproductions of paintings or drawings. Photo offset or lithography has made this a simple practice, and the Indian artist is no different from his white counterpart in this regard. It is still subject to a certain degree of fraud, but the real problem has been the substitution of a mechanical print for an original work of art.

This healthy crafts environment began to decline in the 1980s, due to several factors: the large amount of artwork which had changed hands; replication of common motifs; a deterioration in quality versus quantity in an effort to supply this sudden large market; the presence of fakes; and, to a degree, a diversion of collector interest to other folk arts, most particularly white American folk art, African folk art, and Oriental art. Indian art has always been subject to social and political trends, and the vagaries of the always-fickle art world—even more so than by economic changes. But there remains a strong residual group of artists with new ideas, concepts, and art expressions—together with supportive collectors and patrons—which guarantee that Native American art can no longer be regarded solely as ethnology; its success has made certain that it has gained, and will continue to enjoy, a significant place as a major American aesthetic.

Frederick J. Dockstader

See also **Architecture; Basketry; Beadwork; Drypainting; Indian Arts and Crafts Board; Institute of American Indian and Alaska Native Culture and Arts; Painting; Photography; Pottery; Quillwork; Ribbonwork; Sculpture; Silverwork and Other Jewelry; Textiles**

Further Reading

Coe, Ralph T. *Lost and Found Traditions: Native American Art 1965–1985.* New York, NY: American Federation of Arts, 1986.

Dockstader, Frederick J. *Indian Art in North America: Arts and Crafts.* Greenwich, CT: New York Graphic Society, 1962.

Friedman, Martin, ed. *American Indian Art: Form and Tradition.* New York, NY: Dutton, 1972.

Furst, Peter T., and Jill L. Furst. *North American Indian Art.* New York, NY: Rizzoli, 1982.

Jacka, Jerry, and Lois Essary Jacka. *Beyond Tradition: Contemporary Indian Art and Its Evolution.* Flagstaff, AZ: Northland, 1988.

New, Lloyd, ed. *American Indian Art in the 1980s.* Niagara Falls, NY: The Native American Center for the Living Arts, 1980.

Wade, Edwin L., ed. *The Arts of the North American Indian: Native Arts in Transition.* New York, NY: Hudson Hills, 1986.

ASSIMILATION

See Allotment; Government Policy

ASSINIBOINE

The Assiniboine (Assiniboin, *Nakoda* or *Nakota*, *As'see nee poi-tuc* to the Cree meaning "those who cook with stones," *Stoneys* in Canada) are a Plains people whose original territory was around the Great Lakes. The Eastern Assiniboine are in Montana and the Stoneys are in Saskatchewan and Alberta, Canada. In Montana, most Assiniboine live on the Fort Belknap and Fort Peck reservations.

History

The Assiniboine split from the Yanktonai Sioux during the sixteenth century. In the early seventeenth century, they traded with the French in the Lake Winnipeg region, and then with the English following the establishment of the permanent trading post on Hudson's Bay in 1670. Their role in the fur trade precipitated a shift from the woodlands to the plains, where the buffalo was an important source of food and fur. Their territory included present-day Saskatchewan and Montana. In the early nineteenth century, indiscriminate hunting by whites decimated the buffalo herds; faced with poverty, the Assiniboine signed the Fort Laramie Treaty in 1851. This treaty marked the first cession of lands by the Assiniboine. The Assiniboine at this time were divided into a lower division, led by Red Stone, and an upper division, known as the Long Hair or Whirlwind bands. Separate Blackfeet, Fort Belknap, and Fort Peck reservations were established formally in 1887 by the Northwest Indian Commission. Fort Belknap was established originally as a separate reservation for the Gros Ventre, but was settled also by the upper division Assiniboine. Fort Peck was shared with the Yanktonai Sioux. The reservation period brought about a marked increase in forced dependency upon the government; by 1900, 70 percent of Assiniboine subsistence came from government rations.

Figure 1
Reservation Size and Land Distribution

Reservation	Fort Belknap	Fort Peck
Total Area	616,047.66	964,864.75
Allotted Land	427,579.93	645,114.20
Tribal-Owned*	162,932.63	233,153.17
Non-Indian	25,535.10	86,597.38

All Indian groups

In the latter part of the twentieth century the Assiniboine face the difficulty of maintaining their distinctiveness as a cultural entity in a social milieu shared with descendants of other tribes, as well as non-Indians. They maintain a solid group identity through an awareness of their history, although progressive assimilation has resulted in many younger members being enrolled as reservation "community" members, rather than identified as members of specific tribes.

Tribal Government

The fundamental difference in the tribal governments of Fort Peck and Fort Belknap stems from the tribes' reception of the Indian Reorganization Act of 1934 (IRA). The Fort Belknap Assiniboine and Gros Ventre voted overwhelmingly for the acceptance of the IRA. Eventually, the Assiniboine were disillusioned because the government considered all of Fort Belknap as one Indian community and therefore subject to the same policies. The Bureau of Indian Affairs has long dominated the affairs of the Fort Belknap reservation and discouraged Indian political enterprise.

The Fort Peck Assiniboine refused to accept the conditions imposed by the IRA, but continued to operate under a Constitution which representatives of the tribal government had written in 1927. In 1960 a system of representative government was set up. The governing body of the Fort Peck Reservation is the Tribal Executive Board.

Economic Development and Conditions

The economic situation of the Assiniboine at Fort Belknap and Fort Peck reflects the different political structures of their reservations and the economy of the region where they are located. Although not without problems, strong political leadership has allowed for greater self-determination and economic development at Fort Peck. The traditional base of the economy of northeastern Montana is agriculture. Land is leased to non-Indian farmers and ranchers. The tribal government has encouraged industrial development, creating more job opportunities. In 1983, the unemployment rate at Fort Peck was 33 percent compared to 55 percent at Fort Belknap. The Fort Peck government has invested in drilling its own oil well, which is now producing and may generate much revenue. Other mineral resources include coal, potash, and gravel. Much of this success may be attributed to the Fort Peck chairman, Norman Hollow, whose exemplary leadership has done much for tribal political and economic development.

The Assiniboine of Fort Belknap, along with the Gros Ventre, face a greater degree of underdevelopment and threat of poverty. Many Assiniboine left the reservation following the economic decline of the 1940s. The rate of unemployment at Fort Belknap was 70 percent in 1981. Farming and grazing are unpredictable sources of income, and there are no mineral resources in demand or other sources of income that could generate capital or development, aside from leasing of individually-owned land.

Population

In 1780, the Assiniboine population was esti-mated to be at 10,000. Their numbers were reduced by smallpox epidemics during the mid-nineteenth century.

Figure 2
Assiniboine Population Estimates of the Fort Peck and Fort Belknap reservations from 1885 to 1990

Year	Fort Peck	Fort Belknap	Total
1885	1,672	700	2,372
1890	721	950	1,671
1900	619	694	1,313
1921	777	657	1,434
1934	1,406	647	2,108
1970	—	—	1,108
1990	5,782*	2,338*	—

Total Indian Population

Sources: Annual Reports of the Indian Office and the United States Census.

Health Issues

A serious health problem for the Assiniboine at Fort Peck and Fort Belknap is the high prevalence of adult-onset, non-insulin-dependent diabetes mellitus (NIDDM). Fairly rare in Native American populations prior to the 1950s, this disease has reached an epidemic level. The Assiniboine at Fort Peck have the highest rate of NIDDM in Montana.

Culture

While they have maintained their cultural identity and traditions, the Assiniboine do not live as a closed group. Assiniboines have intermarried with members from other groups and are part of the larger "reservation culture." Elders see traditional values adapted to meet the demands of contemporary life, as an important resource to the younger generation growing up with the many challenges of reservation life.

Community Life

At Fort Peck, most of the Indian population is concentrated in the southern part of the reservation in the communities of Poplar, Wolf Point, Brockton, and Frazer. Poplar is the seat of tribal government and is the principal town on the reservation, next to Wolf Point. The Assiniboine live mostly on the west end of the reservation, while the Sioux live on the east end.

There are four major communities at Fort Belknap: the Fort Belknap Agency in the northwest corner of the reservation, Hays, Lodgepole, and Milk River Valley. Harlem, which lies outside the reservation boundaries north of the Fort Belknap Agency, also has a large Indian population.

Language

The Assiniboine language is part of the Dakota dialect complex, which is one of five Siouan languages spoken in historical times on the Plains. Linguists have found some differences in dialect between the Fort Peck and Fort Belknap Assiniboine. There were fewer than fifty speakers at one point, but Assiniboine is now taught to both adults and children. It is an important marker of ethnic identity and is used in public ceremonies.

Religion and Ceremonial Life

Religion is another important aspect of Assiniboine identity. Traditional religion is maintained by complex ceremonies like the handgames (which are strictly religious), spirit lodges, and the Medicine Lodge (popularly known as the sun dance). Naming ceremonies, sweat lodges, ghost feasts, wakes, and funerals are important. The calumet pipe is essential to Assiniboine religion; it is the medium through which prayer is conducted. Some members of the tribe participate in the Native American Church peyote ceremonies.

Arts and Crafts

An art form which is intertwined with the Assiniboine life is the making of star quilts. Although famous for the star motifs which represent significant aspects and events of life, the quilts are more than decorative. They are given at births and to honor friends, used to wrap those seeking visions and those who are dead. Noted makers include Josephine First Raised at Fort Belknap, and Rosaline Long Knife, Sarah Headdress, and Almira Buffalo Bone Jackson at Fort Peck. Almira's quilts have been exhibited at museums in the United States and Europe.

Henry H.C. Choong

See also **Gros Ventre; Yankton and Yanktonai**

Further Reading

Fowler, Loretta. *Shared Symbols, Contested Meanings: Gros Ventre Culture and History.* Ithaca, NY: Cornell University Press, 1987.

Lopach, James J., Margery Hunter Brown, and Richmond L. Clow. *Tribal Government Today: Politics on Montana Indian Reservations.* Boulder, CO: Westview Press, 1990.

Miller, David R. *Montana Assiniboine Identity: A Cultural Account of An American Indian Ethnicity.* Ph.D. diss. Ann Arbor, MI: University Microfilms International, 1987.

Rodnick, David. *The Fort Belknap Assiniboine of Montana.* 1938. New York, NY: AMS Press, 1978.

Sharrock, Susan R. "Crees, Cree-Assiniboines, and Assiniboines: Interethnic Social Organization on the Far Northern Plains." *Ethnohistory* 21:2 (1974): 95–122.

ASSOCIATION ON AMERICAN INDIAN AFFAIRS

The Association on American Indian Affairs (AAIA) was founded in response to the introduction of a bill in 1922 by Senator Holm Bursum of New Mexico, which would have legalized the rights of non-Indian squatters on Rio Grande Pueblo lands in northern New Mexico. The Eastern Association on Indian Affairs (EAIA), chartered in October 1922 by a sympathetic group in New York City, joined the New Mexico Association on Indian Affairs (NMAIA) and the American Indian Defense Association (AIDA) in a massive national campaign that eventually defeated the bill. The EAIA soon became involved in the battle for Pueblo Indian religious freedom. In the early 1920s, when Charles Burke, commissioner of Indian affairs, tried to forbid religious ceremonies in the Southwest and Great Plains, the EAIA, AIDA, and other allies participated in the fight to rescind Burke's edict. In 1934, when John Collier, executive secretary of AIDA, was appointed commissioner of Indian affairs, he asked Oliver LaFarge, EAIA board president since 1933, to absorb AIDA into the eastern organization. LaFarge, who merged the two organizations into the American Association on Indian Affairs (in 1946 it became the Association on American Indian Affairs, its present name) was its president from 1937 until World War II broke out. In 1942, he received a commission in the Air Transport Command.

After spending much of the next three years overseas, LaFarge returned to the AAIA and was president again until his death in 1963.

Since 1923, the AAIA, headquartered in New York City, has defended the rights of Native American people to live in communities of their inception, of their choice, in dignity, without undue outside harassment. It has a long history of defending Indian people's basic rights under the Constitution, as well as defending their lands and resources.

Association Programs

Water Rights. Since the mid-1970s, the Association has worked with a number of tribes toward negotiated settlements of their water rights, as an alternative to costly, protracted litigation. In 1978, for example, the AAIA assisted the Pima and Tohono O'odham (Papago) people of Arizona's Ak Chin Indian Community in winning a water rights settlement that allowed them to more than quadruple their irrigated land base.

Religious Freedom. Since 1943, when AAIA opposed a bill authorizing construction of dams on the Rio Grande that would have permitted drilling on sacred Indian sites, it has fought in Congress and the courts to protect and preserve sacred sites and Indian access to them. AAIA assisted the Pueblo of Zuni in its successful effort to win the return by congressional action of *Kolhu/wala:wa*, a sacred site in Arizona. It also supported the people of the Taos Pueblo in their sixty-four year, ultimately successful, struggle to regain their sacred Blue Lake in 1970. AAIA joined in a three-year effort with tribes, the National Congress of American Indians, and the Native American Rights Fund that culminated in the passage of the Native American Graves Protection and Repatriation Act, signed into law in November 1990.

Self-Determination. After a ten-year effort by AAIA and tribes, the Indian Self-Determination and Education Assistance Act was passed by Congress in 1975, mandating the right of Indian tribes to participate more directly in the conduct and administration of federal programs on their reservations. After the act's passage, AAIA assisted tribes to take over and operate programs in employment assistance, family counseling, resource management, health care, education, and law enforcement.

Federal Recognition. The AAIA helped tribal communities (Payson Band of Tonto Apaches of Arizona; the Coushattas of Louisiana; the Jamul Band of Kumeyaay Indians of California; and the Karuks of California) obtain federal recognition as Indian tribes.

Alaska. For more than a decade preceding the passage of the Alaska Native Claims Settlement Act in 1971, AAIA devoted much of its resources to the defense of Alaska Native land rights, working closely with Native leaders in their efforts to reach a settlement.

Child Welfare. AAIA placed major emphasis on halting the tragic destruction of American Indian families, focusing national attention on the unwarranted removal of Indian children from their families by non-Indian social service agencies. It drafted the initial version of the Indian Child Welfare Act of 1978, and has since helped tribes negotiate agreements with states to implement the act. AAIA has also assisted in national initiatives aimed at preventing alcohol and drug abuse among Indian teenagers.

Health. For decades, AAIA urged increased federal expenditures for construction of water and sanitation facilities to reduce the incidence of death and sickness conditioned by environmental factors. It has encouraged Native Americans in the health professions through its scholarship program, and by helping to launch the Association of American Indian Physicians, the American Indian/Alaska Native Nurses Association, and other groups.

Education. AAIA helped encourage the formation of local Indian school boards and Indian administration of local school programs; promoted the use of accurate curricular materials; and supported the creation of day schools as an alternative to federal boarding schools. It expanded its scholarship programs for Indian students at a time when other sources of financial aid were shrinking.

Legal Defense. AAIA has defended Indian constitutional and treaty rights in the courts and in the agencies of federal and state governments. It also has provided tribes with legal advice, especially in the areas of Indian land and water rights, child welfare, and religious freedom.

Cultural Preservation. AAIA played a major role in the passage of legislation that created the National Museum of the American Indian, the first federal museum dedicated to Native Americans.

Arts and Crafts. AAIA operated the New York City American Indian Arts Center from 1963 to 1977, a retail outlet and exhibition center that showcased museum-quality work of master Indian and Alaska Native artists. It stimulated the establishment of other sales outlets in department stores and specialty shops.

Economic Development. AAIA has furnished assistance and training in organizational management and financial planning, providing start-up capital and project financing, in the form of seed money consisting of small grants or loans. AAIA helped draft the Indian Tribal Governmental Tax Status Act of 1982, which permits tribes to issue tribal bonds.

Funding and Leadership

The AAIA is funded by monies generated by direct mail appeals, special events, major donors, membership dues, and foundation grants. Since May 16, 1949, AAIA has published *Indian Affairs*, a newsletter covering its various programs. In 1989, AAIA's board of directors picked its first Native American director in its history—Gary Kimble, a Gros Ventre from Montana.

Arlene B. Hirschfelder

Further Reading

"Alfonso Ortiz Retires From AAIA Presidency." *Indian Affairs* 116 (Summer 1988): 1, 5–6.

Hecht, Robert A. *Oliver LaFarge and the American Indian: A Biography.* Metuchen, NJ: The Scarecrow Press, 1991.

Indian Affairs: Newsletter of the Association on American Indian Affairs, 1949 to present.

"Oliver LaFarge." *Indian Affairs:* 52 (August 1963). Memorial issue.

ATSUGEWI

See Pit River

B

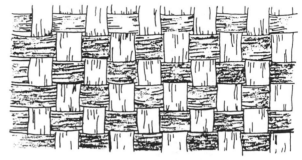

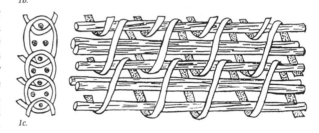

Figures 1a–1c. Three basic basketry techniques. a. Twining with stiff, spaced warps. b. Plain splint plaiting. c. Three rod coiling. Drawings by Maria del C. Gasser.

BANNOCK

See Shoshone-Bannock

BASKETRY

Native American basketmaking has continued for more than 7,000 years. From beyond the Columbia River down into the Southwest, the people of the Archaic Culture made baskets to gather and process seeds, nuts, and fruits and invented almost every basketry process used in later centuries. There are three basic basketry techniques: *twining* (figure 1a), the oldest, is done with double wefts that twist around a group of warps; *plaiting* (figure 1b) is done by weaving splints or stems over and under each other; and *coiling* (figure 1c) uses bundles of fibers or sticks bent into a spiral and wrapped and sewn together with fine splints. These techniques are still used by many Native Americans to create an endless variety of baskets from almost every kind of vegetal material: stems, roots, wood, leaves, grass, etc. Basketmakers are knowledgeable botanists.

Many Native American women still make baskets, although more are made in some areas than in others. In some tribes, the craft is alive and flourishing, but in others it has dwindled and even died. In most cases, four major reasons were responsible for its decline: (1) The need for baskets in daily life diminished as the living patterns of Native Americans changed; (2) Modern substitutes of metal and plastic replaced baskets; (3) Basketmaking is hard work, it is hard on the hands, it requires technical knowledge and training, and it cannot be done in a short time; and (4) The natural materials required to make baskets can be identified and collected only by people with experience and training, and the materials became increasingly sparse as more land was cultivated or used for grazing. Even an experienced basketmaker may have great difficulty in locating the required plants.

Considering these obstacles it is amazing that basketmaking survives and is even enjoying a revival in some areas. The most important factor in its survival is a people's pride in their cultural traditions. This never died, and an important awakening of ethnic and tribal pride in recent years has contributed to a revival of interest in traditional ways and arts. Women who make baskets feel a linkage with their past that provides them with a feeling of continuity and a sense of security through identification with their peers. These rewards have been mentioned often by Hopis, Penobscots, Cherokees and others.

In the Great Basin, where much of the basketmaking had its origins, the local Paiute, Ute, and Shoshone still make conical twined gathering baskets, hooded cradles, trays and seed-beaters, as well as a few coiled jars for seeds and water. In northern Arizona, the San Juan Paiutes now make colorful coiled baskets decorated with designs borrowed from many sources. This renaissance was shared or paralleled by the neighboring Navajos, who had practically abandoned basketry but now produce large trays with *yei* designs from sandpainting (picture 2) and original motifs. At the end of the last century, when most of the Navajos stopped producing their two-rod and bundle "wedding baskets," the Paiutes began making them to trade to the Navajos. For many years most Navajo wedding baskets were made by the San Juan Paiutes.

In the region of the Grand Canyon, the Havasupais, Walapais, Yavapais, and Chemehuevis make fine coiled baskets with three rod foundations. They are generally decorated with geometric designs with black splints of devil's claw. The Havasupais and Walapais also make twined baskets. Squat bowls with flat rims are especially typical of the Walapai. Yavapai baskets are similar to the coiled baskets of the Western Apaches, who formerly made large bowls and vase-shaped forms decorated with geometric motifs and figures of humans and animals. They also made bucket-shaped carriers with corner reinforcements and fringed buckskin strips. Modern basketmakers, like Evelyn Henry and her sisters, produce conical twined baskets that range in size from thirty-six inches to half-inch earrings.

In the Pueblo villages of Arizona and New Mexico the Hopis are the only productive basketmakers in the late twentieth century. The villages of Second Mesa make many coiled baskets for sale and for their own uses. They are sewn with yucca splints over bundles of galleta grass and decorated with colorful designs of kachinas, birds, or geometric patterns. The villages on Third Mesa make brightly colored wicker baskets

of sumac and rabbit-brush. On both mesas yucca ring-baskets are plaited, as are large flat trays to hold "piki" bread. Few baskets are made in the other Pueblos, but distinctive open-work plaited wicker baskets are still made in some of the Rio Grande villages and yucca ring-baskets are occasionally made at Jemez and San Juan.

The baskets of the Eastern Apaches of New Mexico are very different. The Mescaleros once made bowls and deep covered "boxes" with flat coils consisting of two stacked rods and a bundle of fiber. They were sewn with tan yucca leaf splints. Currently, the northern Jicarillas make stout coiled trays with designs in bright colors. The culture center hires basketmakers, and teachers such as Lydia Pesata keep the tradition alive. Many fine trays coiled with three rods and sewn with sumac splints, and a few water bottles, are produced. A few younger women are learning the craft and the future of Jacarilla basketry looks bright.

In southern Arizona, the Yuman tribes make little basketry, but the Tohono O'odham (Papagos) are among the most productive and creative tribes. They formerly made large trays and vase-shapes with narrow coils of grass sewn with willow splints and devil's claw designs. Except for one small group, they changed over to coils of bear-grass sewn with yucca splints that were often separated from each other. They were easy to make and could be sold more cheaply than

1. Yokuts bottle neck basket with geometric and human figure designs, decorated with feathers. Seven inches high. Courtesy of the National Museum of the American Indian, Smithsonian Institution 16/7097.

willow baskets. These designs have gradually been refined, with elegant stitching and complex designs. A distinctive type includes rather small baskets with many figures, which are tightly coiled with black and white horsehair, by such artists as Norma Antone, Evalena Juan, and a few others. The Pima, who are relatives of the Tohono O'odham, once made willow and devil's claw baskets, but only a few basketmakers still practice the art.

California is still one of the great basketmaking areas. In southern California, the Mission tribes have made coiled baskets with yellow mottled juncus rush splints over a bundle of fiber for a long time. Black and red figures of geometric and life forms were common. In central California, a group of tribes, the Yokuts,

Mono, and Tubatulabal, made elegant baskets with narrow coils of grass stems sewn with marsh grass and decorated with black and red bands of diamonds and triangles. They made deep bowls and "bottle neck" vases with red yarn and/or black features around the edges (picture 1). The baskets of the neighboring Panamint in Nevada were quite similar, but often coiled with one or three slender rods.

Probably the most sophisticated basketmakers were the tribes of north-central and northwestern California: the Miwok, the Pomoans, the Maidu, and the Wintu. The Pomoans coiled bowls and globular baskets with one and/or three rods stitched with sedge root and decorated with quail and woodpecker feathers or covered with feathers and beads (picture 3).

2. Large tray made by Sally Black, an innovator in Navajo basketmaking. Its yei designs are derived from Navajo sandpaintings. Twenty-four inches in diameter. Courtesy of the School of American Research, SAR 1982–5–4. Photo by Vincent Foster.

3. Pomo basket, decorated with feathers, made by William Benson. 2 3/4 by 5 1/2 inches. Courtesy of the National Museum of the American Indian, Smithsonian Institution 24/2128.

4. Coiled basket from the Puyallup at Whollochet Bay, Washington, decorated with imbrication. Courtesy of the National Museum of the American Indian, Smithsonian Institution 9/7561.

5. Seneca curlique plaited splint basket. Helen Pep Grodka Collection. Courtesy of the National Museum of the American Indian, Smithsonian Institution, 25/1251. Photo by Karen Furth.

6. *Cherokee woman demonstrating use of plaited pack basket, Cherokee Reservation, North Carolina, 1908.* M.R. Harrington Collection. Courtesy of the National Museum of the American Indian, Smithsonian Institution, 2725.

California twined fine hats and other forms with conifer roots decorated with half-twist overlay. The Chehalis and Quinault on the northwest coast of Washington used the same techniques on deep pail-shaped baskets; and the Nootka/Makah of the Olympic Peninsula used wrapped-twining with overlay for colorful decorations. Splint plaiting was also done by these people. The Salish Indians of Puget Sound, and their interior kinfolk on the Fraser and Thompson rivers, made stout and colorful baskets coiled with cedar and spruce roots and decorated with colored designs in imbrication (picture 4).

North of Puget Sound the tribes of the Northwest Coast twined finely split spruce root baskets and decorated them with designs worked in false embroidery. Cylindrical containers with lids were common and large hats were painted with totemic motifs. Many utilitarian baskets were also made by the Haida, Kwakiutl, Tlingit, and other tribes.

The nomadic tribes of the Plains made only small coiled trays for dice games, but the Mandan, Hidatsa, and Arikara village people plaited large reinforced carriers. In the Prairie area and east to the Atlantic Coast, plaiting was the predominant technique. A variety of ash splint bowls and other forms were woven by the tribes of the Great Lakes (Ottawa, Winnebago, and Chippewa, et al.), who undoubtedly acquired the craft from their Algonquian relatives further east. Throughout the St. Lawrence Valley, baskets were woven with splints and often decorated with stamped blocks, or by twisting the splints into curlicues (picture 5). The Eastern Algonquians used baskets themselves, but the fancy ones were produced for the tourist trade, and many are still being made. The Iroquois plaited stout, undecorated carrying baskets, open-work sieves, and other forms, generally for their own use, but they also twined masks and small jars with twisted corn husks.

The Cherokees of Qualla, North Carolina, plait fine baskets of oak splints and continue producing their typical southeastern style baskets of colored splints of native cane. They operate a modern demonstration center to market their products, and they sell quantities of double-woven baskets and reproductions of their large traditional storage baskets (picture 6). Cane baskets were also plaited by the Choctaws, Chickasaws, and Creeks, who created unique "elbow baskets" and also sifting trays and other utilitarian forms. Little basketry is produced by these tribes at present. In Louisiana, one or two women are still making the finest plaited cane baskets on the continent. These Chitamachas use very narrow splints dyed black and orange to create rectangular "boxes," with neatly fitting covers.

Native American basketry ranged through an infinity of forms and employed an enormous number of different techniques. Baskets are not only important for both ceremonial and utilitarian purposes to the Indians themselves, but the opening of markets to sell baskets to outsiders was a major factor in keeping basketmaking alive over the years. As the craft be-

Coiled baskets were made for ceremonial purposes, but the twined baskets were utilitarian: carriers, hoppers, cooking bowls. A variety of twining techniques were used. Pomoan artists such as Elsie Allen, Susan Billy, and Mollie Jackson are trying to teach a new generation how to make the fabulous feather and bead-covered baskets for which their people are famous. The Maidu were equally proficient, making deep bowls decorated with red bud bark, as well as tightly twined bowls and conical carriers decorated with bear grass and black bracken root in full-twist twining. Their neighbors on the Nevada state line, the Washoe, covered some small baskets with trade beads, but their fame rests upon their tightly coiled globular baskets decorated with elegant designs in black bracken root. A number of weavers achieved fame, one of the greatest of whom was Datsolalee (Louisa Kizer), whose baskets now sell for thousands of dollars.

The Maidu, Wintun technique of full-twist decoration, especially for conical carriers, extends into northeastern California and was practiced also by the Shasta and Achumawi. The Modoc twined baskets of tule and the Yurok, Hupa, and Karuk in northwestern

came a source of family income, basketry was rejuvenated and the weavers have become increasingly proficient and creative. Some of the finest Indian baskets ever made are being produced today and as collecting interest grows the financial returns for the weavers also increase. This makes it possible for women who formerly could not afford the time to make baskets to give up outside work and devote themselves creatively and profitably to a task they enjoy.

Andrew Hunter Whiteford

See also Art; Textiles

Further Reading

Adavasio, J.M. *Basketry Technology: A Guide to Identification and Analysis.* Chicago, IL: Aldine Publishing Co., 1977.

Bates, Craig D. and Martha J. Lee. *Tradition and Innovation: A Basket History of the Indians of the Yosemite-Mono Lake Area.* Yosemite National Park: The Yosemite Association, 1990.

McMullen, Ann, and Russell G. Handsman, eds. *A Key into the Language of Woodsplint Baskets.* Washington, CT: American Indian Archaeological Institute, 1987.

Mason, Otis Tufton. *Aboriginal American Basketry: Studies in a Textile Art without Machinery.* Annual Report of the Smithsonian Institution, 1902. Washington, DC: Smithsonian Institution, 1904.

Tanner, Clara Lee. *Indian Baskets of the Southwest.* Tucson: University of Arizona Press, 1983.

Turnbaugh, Sarah Peabody, and William A. Turnbaugh. *Indian Baskets.* West Chester, PA: Schiffer Publishing/Peabody Museum of Archaeology and Ethnology, Harvard University, 1986.

Whiteford, Andrew Hunter. *Southwestern Indian Baskets: Their History and Their Makers.* Studies in American Indian Art. Sante Fe, NM: School of American Research, 1988.

BEADWORK

American Indians have been making and using beads for thousands of years. Beads made from precious, semi-precious, and non-precious stones; marine and freshwater shell and pearls; horn; bird, mammal, fish and occasionally human bone, teeth, and ivory; baked clay; vegetal materials such as seeds, basketry, gum, wood and fruit pits; and gold, silver, and copper were made by members of hundreds of American Indian tribes long before the Columbian encounter. Beads are mentioned in the oral traditions of dozens of tribes in the United States where they are used as ornaments and sometimes in ceremonies. Beads found in thousands of archaeological excavations covering as many years point to the importance and ubiquity of beads in American Indian history and culture.

When Europeans first arrived, they brought with them manufactured glass beads which Indians of the Caribbean Islands found highly desirable. These sixteenth-century beads tended to be large and suitable for necklaces but not for embroidery purposes. Manufactured beads began to supplant Native-made beads in some areas, although they did not totally replace them.

The major techniques of beadwork were and continue to be strung, sewn, woven, netted, and inlay. Beads are also fastened to objects with a fixative, i.e., inlay earrings, and used as decorative elements on items like baskets. Many tribes had strong preferences for certain bead colors and in the American woodlands and plains, porcupine quillwork designs and techniques often influenced the development of beadwork aesthetics.

Glass beads were found in all Indian communities in the United States by the mid-nineteenth century. They were widely accepted and used in great quantities. Bead embroidery had replaced porcupine quillwork and some kinds of Native-made beads in the eastern states and was beginning to have the same effect in the trans-Mississippi West. However, some Native-manufactured beads continued to be made, such as the shell and turquoise beads of the Southwest and steatite beads in California.

By the twentieth century, glass bead embroidered items were ubiquitous throughout the country, and Indian artists, generally female, were extremely creative at inventing new techniques and forms. Even in areas where Native-made beads were not major traditions, i.e., the Northwest Coast, bead embroidered garments became important elements of ceremonial dress. Beaded objects were a symbol of Indian identity for both Indians and non-Indians alike. They were sold in large quantities to non-Indians, providing the makers with much needed income.

Indian artists still make beads from raw materials in some areas in the late twentieth century, particularly in the Southwest where turquoise, shell, coral, and juniper berry beads are important products. The use of modern jewelry-making equipment has enabled contemporary artists to make shell and turquoise beads (*hishe*) of a fineness unequaled anywhere else in the country. In California, a few Native beadmakers still make beads from magnetite, clam, and abalone shell. Dentalia shell, although scarce, is much sought after by northern California tribes, such as the Hupa and Karuk, where it is worn in large necklaces. In the Northeast, a few specialists make wampum from Quahog clams.

Women were generally the principal beadworkers in the past, although there were some exceptions. In the Southwest men tended to make beads, although women might assist in the process, and both created objects from the beads. Glass beadworkers, until quite recently, were overwhelmingly female, and most of the beaded objects now in museums and private collections are the product of women's labor. The only exceptions to this general rule were ceremonial objects which were often made exclusively by men.

Beginning in the 1960s, instructional programs in traditional arts, including beadwork, were established in a wide variety of settings, e.g. school systems, urban Indian centers, senior centers, recreational programs, etc. While formal instruction in traditional arts has been part of the curriculum in Bureau of Indian Affairs schools since the John Collier administration, it has been rare in other settings. With easier access to instruction, changing ideas about gender activities, and economic incentives, increasing numbers of men became active beadworkers.

By the 1990s, some men had become well known bead artists, making items principally for the marketplace. Their work is featured in art galleries and in the permanent collections of some museums. They make a wide range of objects and do not restrict themselves to making only religious or ceremonial objects; some men make objects principally for their own families.

Even with this development, the great majority of beadworkers are still women who make objects principally for the use of their families and friends. In every community, some women specialize in craft production as a means of income, and often work in collaborative groups with other women and family members. Some craft specialists, both men and women, travel to Indian events, such as powwows and conferences, to sell their wares. The income derived from the production of beadwork is hard to quantify, but is probably equivalent to the basic minimum wage for many.

Contemporary beadwork is enjoying a period of enormous creativity and invention. One of the out-

Beaded medallion by Vanessa Morgan (Kiowa). Applique beadwork in 13/0 size multi-hue cut beads. Fringe and necklace are in tile beads, faceted crystal beads, metal beads, and cowry shells. Private collection. Photo by Donald Tenoso.

standing younger beadworkers in the country, Vanessa Paukeigope Morgan of Anadarko, Oklahoma, received a National Heritage Fellowship from the National Endowment for the Arts in 1989 in recognition of her mastery of all of the traditional Kiowa art forms.

The ease of modern transportation and communication has contributed to high levels of intertribal artistic exchange among bead artists. Beaded items incorporating commercial logos, designs from popular culture and from a variety of tribal origins are common. Regional styles of beadwork have replaced specific tribal styles in most cases. Some beadworkers make unique high-style fashion items for special events, while the work of others is featured in mail order catalogues. Some beadworkers are investing tribal designs long out of fashion with new energy and creativity, so that styles once common in the nineteenth century and then replaced by others, are popular again. Beadwork has always been subject to changing fashion as bead artists developed new ideas and forms and incorporated them into local traditions. This is no less true today than in the past. There are tens of thousands of active bead artists working in the United States today, and they are making their own contributions to an ancient beadwork heritage.

JoAllyn Archambault

See also **Art; Quillwork; Silverwork and Other Jewelry**

Further Reading

Conn, Richard. *Native American Art in the Denver Art Museum.* Denver, CO: Denver Art Museum, 1979.

Heritage Center, Red Cloud Indian School. *Five Families Art Exhibition.* Pine Ridge, SD: Heritage Center, n.d.

Lyford, Carrie. *Quill and Beadwork of the Western Sioux.* Lawrence, KS: Haskell Institute, 1940.

Orchard, William C. *Beads and Beadwork of the American Indians: A Study Based on Specimens in the Museum of the American Indian, Heye Foundation.* New York, NY: The Museum, 1929, 1975.

Schneider, Mary Jane. "The Production of Indian-use and Souvenir Beadwork by Contemporary Indian Women." *Plains Anthropologist* 28 (August 1983): 235–45.

BIA

See Bureau of Indian Affairs

BIA Schools

See Bureau of Indian Affairs Schools

Big Mountain

See Navajo-Hopi Land Controversy

Bingo

See Gaming

BLACK HILLS

The starting point in tracing the legal and cultural history of the Black Hills controversy is the Fort Laramie Treaty of 1868 (15 Stat. 635, 1868). It served to end the military deadlock between the Lakota (also known as the Sioux) and the United States government in the Dakota territory and established two overarching objectives: 1) to guarantee peace between the Sioux and the United States; and 2) to establish the boundaries of the Great Sioux Nation Reservation free from white intrusion.

Article I of the treaty ended hostilities and established peace, while Article II established the geographic boundaries of the Great Sioux Reservation, which consisted of all western South Dakota including parts of present-day Wyoming, Montana, North Dakota, and Nebraska. This land was "set apart for the absolute and undisturbed use and occupation of the Indians herein named." The other key provision of the treaty is contained in Article XII, which provides that "no treaty for the cession of any portion or part of the reservation herein described which may be held in common shall be of any validity or force as against said Indians, unless executed and signed by at least three-fourths of all the adult male Indians, occupying or interested in the same." These provisions coupled with the supremacy clause of the United States Constitution recognizing treaties as the supreme law of the land should have established an unassailable and legally binding agreement between two sovereign entities. Yet history (and the law) have taken a much different course.

There are two rich benchmarks from which much of subsequent tribal history is measured. First, at the time of the Treaty of 1868, the Lakota were truly sovereign. The Sioux people not only considered themselves a nation, but they were prepared, some were even eager, to fight to the death against the United States. They had a potent military fighting force. The reach of the federal government, particularly the tentacles of its legal and political structure, had not yet penetrated Lakota society. The United States government and the Lakota saw each other vividly—proud, separate, apart.

The second point concerns the nature of the treaty itself. The Lakota did not see the treaty as the power politics of the day, subject to future accommodation to other emerging national interests. Every treaty was settled with the smoking of the pipe. As noted by Father Peter John Powell, the well-known historian and anthropologist, "[w]hites rarely, if ever, have understood the sacredness of the context in which treaties were concluded by the Lakota people. . . . Any agreement that was signed was a sacred agreement because it was sealed by the smoking of the pipe. It was not signed by the chiefs and headmen before the pipe had been passed. Then the smoking of the pipe sealed the treaty, making the agreement holy and binding. Thus, for the Lakota, the obligations sealed with the smoking of the pipe were sacred obligations." These feelings have not changed.

These elements of legal sovereignty and deep spiritual commitment make the Fort Laramie Treaty of 1868 the pinnacle from which contemporary Sioux history unfolds. Almost immediately after the signing of the treaty, General George Custer led an expedition of scientists into the area known as the Black Hills in the western part of South Dakota, clearly located within the Great Sioux Reservation boundaries as set out in the Treaty of 1868. During this expedition, gold was discovered. The expedition report excited the white community and in its wake large numbers of miners and other frontiers' people entered the Black Hills.

The federal government quickly sent the Allison Commission to the Dakota territory to negotiate a cession of the Black Hills area in accordance with the terms of the Fort Laramie Treaty of 1868. The Commission failed in its mission, but that did not deter the efforts of the federal government. In 1876, President Grant simply pulled the army out of the Black Hills and allowed miners to flood the area and file claims. The United States absolved itself of its treaty commitment which stated that "the United States now solemnly agrees that no persons except those herein designated and authorized to do so, and except such officers, agents, and employees of the Government as may be authorized to enter upon Indian reservations in discharge of duties enjoined by law, *shall ever be permitted to pass over, settle upon, or reside in the territory described in this Article.*"

The federal government then declared all Sioux that were away from the home agencies (usually for subsistence hunting) as "hostile," and subject to military engagement by the United States Army. Congress also passed a statute denying the Sioux appropriations and annuities under past treaties until they ceded the Black Hills. Another commission was sent out west, but failed to get the necessary signatures of three-fourths of the adult males as required by the treaty. Regardless of the treaty commitment, Congress simply took its proposed agreement with its pittance of signatures and enacted it into law. The result was the "confiscation" of 7.7 million acres of the Black Hills by the federal government. The federal statute which effectively annexed the Black Hills paid no recompense to the Lakota, but simply agreed to pay subsistence rations.

Two elements of this situation conspire to provide a rare historical opportunity to right a wrong and provide our nation with an opportunity to act with honor and principle. These elements are that first, most of the Black Hills are still held by the federal government (rather than the state or private landowners) and second, the Black Hills have deep spiritual and cultural significance for the Lakota people. All Lakota people and their respective tribes agree that the Black Hills are the core of their spiritual inheritance. The Black Hills hold their "Mother's heart and pulse" with sustaining myth. They are the focal point of annual pilgrimages and rich ceremonies from before the days of the white man's presence. The Black Hills represent for many Lakota the last opportunity to restore the sacred hoop and to permit a heritage to flourish.

The Legal History

These high stakes have their roots in a long and complicated legal history. In the aftermath of the Black Hills Act of 1877, there was no immediate avenue for legal redress. The federal government could not be sued by an Indian tribe without first providing its consent. The first opportunity for legal redress occurred in 1920 when Congress passed a special statute permitting the Sioux to sue. Suit was filed in 1923 in the Court of Claims alleging that the government had taken the Black Hills improperly and in violation of the Fifth Amendment to the United States Constitution. This claim was ultimately dismissed in 1942 as a moral claim not protected by the Fifth Amendment.

In 1946, Congress passed the Indian Claims Commission Act which created a new forum to hear all tribal grievances that had arisen previously. In 1950, the Sioux Nation resubmitted its original claim. Four years later, the Indian Claims Commission decided that the Sioux Nation had not proved its claim and this decision was affirmed by the Court of Claims in 1956. The Sioux Nation then filed a motion with the Court of Claims to vacate its judgment affirming the decision of the Indian Claims Commission because the record before the Commission was inadequate due to ineffective legal representation. Surprisingly, this motion was granted and in 1958 the Indian Claims Commission was ordered to reconsider its 1954 decision denying the Sioux Nation claim.

The Indian Claims Commission rendered a favorable decision in 1974, holding that the federal government had taken the land in violation of the Fifth Amendment because it had not paid just compensation. It determined that the fair market value of the land taken and the gold extracted at the time of the taking in 1877 was $17.5 million. Since this taking violated the Fifth Amendment, the tribes were also entitled to 5 percent interest, which was normally not permitted in Indian Claims Commission proceedings based on wrongdoing or treaty violations not implicating the Fifth Amendment. This decision was appealed by the United States government and one year later the Court of Claims reversed the decision of the Indian Claims Commission based on the doctrine of *res judicata*: that the issue before Indian Claims Commission had already been litigated and decided by the Court of Claims back in 1942. This meant that there was no improper taking under the Fifth Amendment and therefore the $17.5 million award plus interest was lost.

It was not, however, completely lost. The Indian Claims Commission had also found that the United States government had acquired the Black Hills through a course of unfair and dishonorable dealings for which the Sioux were entitled to damages *without interest* under S. 2 of the Indian Claims Commission Act. Interest is awarded only when there is unconstitutional taking under the Fifth Amendment. This finding against the United States government had *not* been appealed, and therefore was unaffected by the appeal to the Court of Claims. The matter of interest, however, was paramount. For example, 5 percent interest on $17.5 million from 1877 (the date of the taking) to, say, 1980, would be approximately an additional $85 million, *five times* the amount of the award itself. The Court of Claims concluded its opinion with the observation: "A more ripe and rank case of dishonorable dealings will never, in all probability, be found in our history, which is not, taken as a whole, the disgrace it now pleases some persons to believe."

On remand to the Indian Claims Commission, the Commission, with minor adjustments, made a finding for a final award of $17.5 million. It deferred the entry of final judgment, however, in view of legislation then pending before Congress. On March 13, 1978, Congress enacted legislation enabling the Court of Claims to rehear the Sioux Nation claim without regard to the potential bar of the *res judicata* doctrine.

In 1979, the Court of Claims, unshackled from the restraints of *res judicata*, found that the United States government had unconstitutionally taken the Black Hills in violation of the Fifth Amendment and it reinstated the $17.5 million award *plus* interest.

The United States government appealed this decision to the United States Supreme Court (*United States v. Sioux Nation of Indians*, 448 U.S. 371 [1980]). In 1980, fifty-seven years after the litigation began, the Supreme Court affirmed the rulings in the courts below that the federal government had taken the Black Hills unconstitutionally in violation of the Fifth Amendment. The question before the Supreme Court was never whether the federal government could take the land in question, but rather under what legal theory it acted upon, and what financial consequences, if any, flowed from its activities. As a necessary corollary, the issues before the Court never involved the question of returning the land. The return of Indian land (improperly) taken by the federal government is not generally within the province of the courts, but only within the authority of the Congress itself. For many Lakota, this limitation, which was often not fully disclosed to the Sioux Nation tribes by their lawyers, festers like an open wound; a constraint inconsistent with any notion of true justice.

The Proposed Sioux Nation Black Hills Act

The 1980 judgment of the Supreme Court for $17.5 million plus interest remains undistributed, gathering dust (plus continuing interest) in the United States Treasury. All eight participating tribes (the Rosebud, Oglala, Cheyenne River, Standing Rock, Lower Brule and Crow Creek Sioux of South Dakota, and the Santee Tribe of Nebraska and Fort Peck Sioux Tribe in Montana—the original signatories of the Fort Laramie Treaty of 1868) have passed tribal resolutions in opposition to *any* distribution of the money judgment.

The tribes want, as they always have, the land returned. And, with that continuing emphasis and commitment, the focus has shifted away from the courts to the United States Congress, which does have the clear authority to restore Indian title to lands that were improperly divested from tribal ownership. Finally in 1985, for the first time, a bill entitled the Sioux Nation Black Hills Act was submitted to Congress. The bill, which includes provision for financial compensation *and* land restoration, found no sponsors within the South Dakota congressional delegation; its lone sponsor in the Senate was Senator Bill Bradley of New Jersey.

The heart of this controversial legislation centered on two provisions. One would have been the reconveyance of all the federally held land—approximately 1.3 million acres from the federal government to the Sioux Nation (that is, the original signatories of the Fort Laramie Treaty of 1868). The other provision involves the establishment and recognition of an entity known as the Sioux National Council to govern the "reestablished area" as it is defined in the legislation. The proposed legislation did not contemplate this restoration as a static monument to commemorate some long ago historical inequity, but rather to establish a dynamic, organic entity fusing Lakota people with their past and reestablishing the sacred hoop of unity and wholeness.

Perfunctory congressional hearings were held on the Sioux Nation Black Hills Act in the summer of 1986. The Act picked up approximately a dozen additional sponsors in 1987, including Senator Daniel Inouye of Hawaii, Chairman of the Senate Select Committee on Indian Affairs, and Rep. Morris Udall of Arizona, as well as the beginnings of favorable national exposure. However, uniform opposition by the South Dakota congressional delegation and the governor and state officials based largely on political concerns remains the norm, and has effectively prevented any additional congressional hearings from being held. As of March 1993 there is no proposed Black Hills legislation pending before Congress.

Frank Pommersheim

See also **Indian Claims Commission; Land Claims**

Further Reading

Dunbar Ortiz, Roxanne. *The Great Sioux Nation: Sitting in Judgment on America: An Oral History of the Sioux Nation and Its Struggle for Sovereignty.* New York, NY: Moon Books/ Random House, 1977.

Greider, William. "The Heart of Everything That Is." *Rolling Stone* (May 7, 1987): p. 37.

Lazarus, Edward. *Black Hills, White Justice: The Sioux Nation Versus the United States, 1775 to the Present.* New York, NY: Harper Collins, 1991.

Pommersheim, Frank. "Making All the Difference: Native American Testimony and the Black Hills." *North Dakota Law Review* 69 (1993): 337–59.

BLACKFEET

The Blackfeet Indians of the United States are one of four closely related tribes of Plains Indians known generally by the name of Blackfeet. All of the tribes spoke the same Algonquian language. The Blackfeet in Montana, also known as the Southern Piegan or Pigunni, are the only group of Blackfeet Indians to have a reservation in the United States. The others, known as the Northern Piegan, the Bloods, and the Blackfeet proper, signed Treaty Number 7 with Canada in 1877; each was given a reserve in southern Alberta.

The 3,000 square-mile Blackfeet Reservation is located in northwestern Montana, abutting Canada to the north and Glacier National Park to the west. The present reservation's size represents a steady erosion of Blackfeet controlled land. In 1855, they controlled much of northern Montana west of the Rockies. Through a series of treaties, unilateral federal executive orders, and land sales, the Blackfeet land was reduced to its present size by 1897. The largest part of the reservation was established by the Sweetgrass Hills Treaty of 1887. The Piegans or Pigunni, the southernmost of the Blackfeet tribes, settled near the Indian agency in the 1880s in order to procure food. The buffalo, their chief food source, had been exterminated. By 1900, 2,000 Blackfeet lived near Badger Creek where the Blackfeet Agency was located. The earliest educational effort was a Catholic boarding school, Holy Family Mission. Soon a government boarding school and day schools were established.

Economic Conditions in the Early Twentieth Century

Although the Blackfeet were not ready to become farmers, expenditures were made for irrigation projects which employed hundreds of Blackfeet. Employment was needed since provision of rations by the Indian Bureau was curtailed after 1900. The federal government attempted to recoup irrigation costs and other expenditures by billing tribal income. In 1907, in keeping with the federal policy of investing Indians with individual land ownership, each member was given the option of receiving 320 acres of grazing land or 40 acres of irrigated land and 280 acres of grazing land. Most did not take the irrigated lands as they preferred open range or river bottoms.

By 1915 the Indian Bureau began emphasizing stockraising instead of farming. Many mixed-blood and a few full-blood Blackfeet were prosperous ranchers at this time; many, however, leased their land to whites or mixed-blood ranchers, and due to scant returns, they lived in poverty. A prolonged drought, severe winter, and low beef prices in 1919 combined to devastate cattle and horse herds. The Blackfeet were plunged into deeper poverty and rations again had to be distributed. Many of the Blackfeet sold or lost their land through nonpayment of taxes during this time; over 210,000 acres of the reservation passed out of Blackfeet hands. Presently, the tribe or individual members of the tribe hold title to 70 percent of the nearly 2 million-acre reservation. Attrition of the land base was partially due to the incompetence or malfeasance of a succession of Indian agents. The changing priorities of federal programs, one agent favoring farming and the next ranching, for example, also contributed to the loss.

Prospects improved for many Blackfeet when superintendent Frank C. Campbell began the Five Year Industrial Program in the 1920s. This successful program consisted of planting vegetable gardens and small fields of grain. This increased food supplies, especially for full-blood Indians. Many mixed-blood Indians, however, preferred a return to stockraising.

In the 1930s after Frank Campbell left, his program faltered. During these economically depressed years many Blackfeet went to work for federal relief projects such as the Works Progress Administration or the Civilian Conservation Corps. Stockraising was again considered the means to make the Blackfeet solvent.

The Indian Reorganization Act

In 1934, The Indian Reorganization Act (IRA) brought many changes to the Blackfeet. The loss of land was stemmed by putting most Indian holdings into trust status. The Blackfeet created a new Tribal Council and wrote a constitution. The IRA provided credit for sheep and cattle enterprises. A few Blackfeet were able to attend college. By 1943, average annual family income had risen to $1,320.

The Impact of World War II

World War II brought many changes to the Blackfeet. Hundreds left the reservation to work in factories in cities and many served in the armed forces. Blackfeet tribal members gained skill and confidence during this time. By 1950, a third of the tribal population was living off the reservation.

Education

The IRA and other Indian New Deal programs provided funds for college and vocational schools. As a result, education levels slowly rose. By 1950, 125 Blackfeet had college degrees and 25 percent of the adults in the tribe had high school diplomas. Overall, however, education levels for the Blackfeet remained below those of the general population. Currently, Blackfeet Community College, established in 1976, leads the efforts to improve education. By 1985, this two-year institution was fully accredited, and by 1993, over 400 students were enrolled in programs in nine fields.

Culture

During the twentieth century, the number of mixed-blood Blackfeet has increased substantially, with a corresponding decrease in the number of full-bloods. One of the major religions on the reservation is Catholicism. A recent trend has been the growth of fundamentalist Christian sects. Cultural traditions, however, continue and are highly respected. A large powwow, North American Indian Days, is held annually with tribes from all over the region joining in the dancing and singing. A small but steady percentage maintain revered religious practices of opening medicine bundles, holding an annual Sun Dance, and taking sweat baths. The Blackfeet language is becoming more widely spoken after years of neglect by education and government officials.

Blackfeet Leadership

A major political and cultural leader of the Blackfeet for the past thirty-seven years has been Earl Old Person (b. 1921). Elected to the Tribal Business Council for nineteen two-year terms, few important decisions have been made without his input. He was instrumental in obtaining two large monetary judgments for the Blackfeet: a 1972 payment for irregularities when the Blackfeet relinquished vast tracts of land in eastern Montana in 1888 (each Blackfeet member received $500); and the 1982 judgment of $29 million for unsound federal accounting practices.

George Kicking Woman (b. 1913) is another notable political and cultural leader. He maintains Blackfeet cultural traditions, opening the important Thunder Pipe Bundle each spring. He also has served on the Tribal Council for sixteen years. Other Blackfeet have had distinguished federal government careers in the field of Indian affairs. Forrest Gerard, the first Assistant Secretary of the Interior for Indian Affairs, spent a lifetime serving Indian causes in government service. Earl Barlow, who is the 1993 director of the Bureau of Indian Affairs, Minneapolis area office, was a notable Indian educator in Montana, a former superintendent of Browning Public School, and the first Indian to be appointed to the Montana State Board of Education.

Economic Development in the Latter Part of the Twentieth Century

Since the 1960s, Blackfeet became interested in economic development, venturing into business with varying degrees of success. Lumber milling has been attempted several times. The Blackfeet Writing Company has been making pencils and pens since 1971. Although this factory has not made a great deal of money for the tribe, it has provided steady employment for many Blackfeet through the years. The Blackfeet also purchased the American Calendar Company in 1988 and reconstructed the factory. Temporarily, this factory provided jobs for forty people but is now closed. Other tribal income is gained through leasing of grazing lands, oil and gas leases, and indirect cost monies for tribal sponsorship of educational programs. Although solvent, the Blackfeet tribe, which has over 13,000 members (7,000 on the reservation), is still working hard to solve a high unemployment rate, estimated in 1988 at 50 to 55 percent, and the accompanying socio-economic problems.

Michael J. Hill

Further Reading

Ewers, John C. *The Blackfeet: Raiders on the Northwestern Plains.* Norman: University of Oklahoma Press, 1959.

Johnson, Bryan R. *The Blackfeet: An Annotated Bibliography.* New York, NY: Garland Publishing, 1988.

Lancaster, Richard. *Piegan: A Look from Within at the Life, Times, and Legacy of an American Indian Tribe.* Garden City, NY: Doubleday, 1966.

McFee, Malcolm. *Modern Blackfeet: Montanans on a Reservation.* Case Studies in Anthropology. New York, NY: Holt, Rinehart and Winston, 1972.

Williams, Gary D., and Historical Research Associates. *The Blackfeet Timber Trust: A History of Forest Management on the Blackfeet Indian Reservation, Montana, 1955–1978.* Billings, MT: Bureau of Indian Affairs, 1980.

BLOOD

See Blackfeet

BOARD OF INDIAN COMMISSIONERS

The Board of Indian Commissioners was an agency consisting of private citizens appointed by the president to supervise the federal administration of Indian affairs in the Department of the Interior. It was created by President Ulysses S. Grant in 1869 as part of his so-called "peace policy" in dealing with Native American peoples. While other parts of his policy, such as the provision to appoint prominent Christian laymen as Indian agents, as well as the plan to assign Protestant missionaries to tribal reservations, were generally aborted by the 1890s, the Board survived well into the early twentieth century.

Although the Board's specific responsibilities were not spelled out in great detail by Grant, they were sufficiently defined by 1910 to make it an effective monitoring agency in the administration of Indian affairs. Board members defined their role as overseers of what they believed to be the federal government's obligation to protect reservation Natives. Consequently, they viewed federal wardship as a solemn trust and responsibility: to provide clinics and hospitals so that diseases like tuberculosis and trachoma could be eradicated; to construct and maintain schools on or near reservations so that every Indian child could have a high school education; and to appropriate funds for immediate relief in times of severe weather conditions. Board members too shared the views of many federal administrators and field personnel, *viz.* that a zealous concern for the physical condition of tribal peoples was all that was needed to facilitate their assimilation into American society.

As a result of the moral prestige and political influence of people such as Daniel Smiley, a member of a well-known Quaker family with a long interest in Indian affairs, the Board gained access to officials in the executive and legislative branches of government beyond the commissioner of Indian affairs and even the secretary of the interior. Its fact-finding authority not only included contact with these officials, but the direct inspection of tribal facilities by its members as well, with a $10,000 annual appropriation from Congress to defray expenses. It issued annual reports based on these visits that became the basis for its agenda as well as that of other traditional reform groups in improving the condition of reservation Indians.

While its sincerity and dedication on behalf of Native Americans was rarely questioned, the Board's definition of the government's role as simply guardians and protectors of Native interests became increasingly anachronistic, particularly when conditions on reservations had not markedly improved by the early twentieth century. But what triggered organized opposition to the government's Indian policy, and by implication to the Board that was empowered to monitor it, was the Pueblo Indian land dispute and the near passage of the so-called Bursum Bill (1922) in Congress.

The Pueblos of northern New Mexico who had occupied their lands even prior to the sixteenth century were granted title holdings of over 700,000 acres in 1848 by the federal government at the end of the Mexican War. Anglo and Spanish settlers in the region either squatted on these holdings or, in some cases, purchased them outright from neighboring Pueblos, believing that these Natives had the right to dispose of them. In 1910, when New Mexico submitted its enabling bill for statehood, as with all previous states, Congress required it to surrender jurisdiction of all Indian lands whose titles derived originally from the federal government. A Supreme Court decision in 1913, confirming the wardship status of the Pueblos and hence denying their legal right to dispose of their holdings, jeopardized the titles of all non-Indian settlers who lay claim to Pueblo lands after 1848. The bill proposed by New Mexico Senator Holm Bursum in 1922 sought to grant immediate title to the ancestors of both non-Indian squatters as well as legitimate purchasers who claimed ownership of tracts between 1848 and 1913.

The debate in the Senate provided many diverse groups of reformers with the opportunity to criticize not only the government's efforts in protecting the titles of reservation Indians, but the entire question of wardship as well. The Board's initial reluctance as a body to criticize the Bursum Bill and its acceptance of the government's caretaking role, made it an indirect target of increasingly vocal criticism by a growing number of newly created reform organizations. The Board's support of the stand by the Bureau of Indian Affairs (BIA) banning certain tribal dances only added to its difficulties with reformers who believed that tribal groups should be given greater autonomy in controlling their own future. The increasing debate between administrative officials and Indian reformers in the 1920s underscored the Board's declining influence in federal policy. The temporary creation of a diverse group of reformers to advise the interior secretary on policy changes in 1923, known as the "Committee of One Hundred," as well as the adoption of a plan to reorganize the BIA proposed by Lewis Meriam, a social scientist with the Brookings Institution, in 1928, failed to stifle criticism. In the minds of an increasing number of reformers, the Board was part of the old administration of Indian affairs. When twelve years of Republican control of the executive branch ended in 1933, so too did the Board, replaced by new officials in the BIA, such as John Collier, who had organized the American Indian Defense Association in opposition to federal Indian policy in the previous decade.

Armand S. La Potin

See also Government Policy

Further Reading

Fritz, Henry. *The Movement for Indian Assimilation, 1860–1890.* Philadelphia: University of Pennsylvania, 1963.

Kelly, Lawrence C. *The Assault on Assimilation: John Collier and the Origins of Indian Policy Reform.* Albuquerque: University of New Mexico Press, 1983.

Mardock, Robert W. *The Reformers and the American Indian.* Columbia: University of Missouri Press, 1971.

Philp, Kenneth R. *John Collier's Crusade for Indian Reform, 1920–1954.* Tucson: University of Arizona Press, 1971.

Prucha, Francis Paul. *The Great Father: The U.S. Government and The American Indians.* Lincoln: University of Nebraska Press, 1984.

BOARDING SCHOOLS

See Churches and Education; Bureau of Indian Affairs Schools

BRANCH OF ACKNOWLEDGMENT AND RESEARCH

Congress has created no conclusive definition of "tribe" and "Indian." While Congress has not prescribed rules governing federal recognition, law allows the president to promulgate regulations to effect provisions of any act relating to Indian affairs, and other laws charge the secretary of the interior, the assistant secretary for Indian affairs, and the commissioner of Indian affairs with responsibility for the supervision and management of Indian affairs. Until the 1970s, Bureau of Indian Affairs (BIA) recognition decisions had been made on an ad hoc basis, applying rules which the Department of the Interior had adopted to implement various statutes, particularly the Indian Reorganization Act (1934). The approach proved to be neither methodical nor equitable, and no reasonable explanation existed for the exclusion of more than one hundred tribes from the federal trust responsibility, many of whom had historical treaties or agreements, had received federal services, and remained intact as communities. The United States Supreme Court held that even "long lapse(s) in federal recognition" do not destroy the federal power to deal with recognized tribes (*United States v. John*, 437 U.S. 634, 652–653 [1979]).

By 1972, the intricate relationship between federal political developments, historical Indian factionalism over tribal status, and the federal-tribal trust responsibility had grown unmanageable. After 400 regional hearings and consultations, and a national hearing with a number of tribes, experts, and interested parties, the Department of Interior published rules and regulations governing acknowledgment determinations in order to promote equity. The procedure prescribes exact criteria Indian groups must satisfy to be acknowledged as tribes. 25 *Code of Federal Regulations* Sec. 83. 7 requires that the candidate tribe:

a. [Be i]dentified from historical times until the present on a substantially continuous basis, as "American Indian," or "Aboriginal";

b. [Prove that a substantial portion inhabits] a specific area or [lives] as a community viewed as American Indian and distinct from other populations in the area and [prove that its] members are descendants of an Indian tribe which historically inhabited a specific area;

c. [Prove that it h]as maintained tribal political influence or other authority over its members as an autonomous entity throughout history until the present;

d. [Provide] a copy of a governing document or statement describing in full the membership criteria and procedures through which the group currently governs its affairs and its members;

e. [Provide evidence of] . . . membership consisting of individuals who have established descendancy from a tribe which existed historically or from historical tribes which combined and functioned as a single autonomous entity;

f. [Demonstrate that it h]as membership composed principally of persons who are not members of any other tribe; and,

g. [Show that it i]s not expressly terminated or otherwise forbidden to participate in the federal-Indian relationship by statute.

Though deriving partly from Interior Solicitor Felix Cohen's federal acknowledgment criteria (1942), the 1978 criteria rested essentially on the secondary "ethnological criteria" of social solidarity and political authority, and demonstration of ancestry.

In 1979 the Department of the Interior established an agency branch, the Federal Acknowledgment Project (FAP, now known as the Branch of Acknowledgment and Research [BAR]) to conduct the Federal Acknowledgment Process. Congress appropriated funding to run the BAR after 1978. BAR relied on earlier case law, statutes, and administrative practices to interpret and implement the regulations and make determinations, but, in interpreting the regulations, also created new tests relying heavily on sociological, anthropological, and historical tests to determine tribal status.

Once the federal government has recognized an Indian tribe at any point in time, a presumption may arise that the tribe remains federally recognized. While certain tribes have been "recognized" historically by the federal government by such means as treaties, executive orders, or congressional orders or acts, the Department of the Interior determined in 1978 that the FAP procedure should make no special allowance for such previous recognition, since the acknowledgment process evaluates a subject tribe's ability to prove current tribal existence under the Department's present standards. The Department denies acknowledgment unless candidate tribes produce evidence which meets all the seven criteria for acknowledgment. The process, as originally proposed, did not require candidates to provide documentation on all of these points. Partly because the Department denied that previous determinations may serve as precedent, the implementation of the rule varied widely, as had been true under the Department's practices prior to the creation of the process.

The regulations required the secretary of the interior to publish an annual list in the *Federal Register* of tribes which the secretary had recognized as entities eligible to receive federal services based on a government-to-government relationship. These annual publications always were sporadic and have subsequently ceased. The original 1979 listing showed groups receiving services that year. Commissioner Louis Bruce's BIA publication, *American Indian Tribes and Their Federal Relationship* (March, 1972) listed most of them.

Generally, the FAP regulations apply only to the acknowledgment of tribes which never were recognized by any other means, but the secretary of the interior has determined that the present regulations do apply to Alaska Native villages, whose historical tribal status is uncertain, as well as to groups whose status is challenged by states, local governments, or other interested parties. As of 1991, there were one hundred and twenty-four petitioners, including four which had split off from existing petitioners, and forty whose requests for recognition or previous recognition were on file in 1978, excluding Alaska Native villages. Of the active petitioners, over twenty are California groups, thirteen are in North Carolina, and eight are in Washington State.

The Department of Interior has attempted to apply the process to previously recognized groups who were not petitioning for acknowledgment. Under the process, or has demanded that they produce similar fact showings, even where the groups were later found to be ineligible to use the process to clarify their status. Congress has found in specific instances that the present administrative recognition process is flawed. Over one hundred twenty requests for recognition sit at the BIA; in 1994, only ten tribes have been acknowledged under the 1978 process. Upon the recommendation of BAR, the secretary of the Department of the Interior has issued final acknowledgment determinations acknowledging the following tribes: the Grand Traverse Band of Ottawa and Chippewa, Minnesota (1980); the Jamestown Klallam Tribe, Washington (1981); the Tunica-Biloxi Indian Tribe, Louisiana (1981); the Death Valley Timbi-Sha Shoshone Band, California (1983); the Narragansett Indian Tribe, Rhode Island (1983); the Poarch Band of Creeks, Alabama (1984); the Wampanoag Tribal Council of Gay Head, Massachusetts (1987); the San Juan Southern Paiute Tribe,

Arizona (1990); the Snoqualmie Tribe, Washington State (1993); and The Mohegan Tribe, Connecticut (1994).

Meanwhile, since 1978, Congress has acknowledged more than twelve outside the process, and has additionally recognized a number of unrecognized or state-recognized groups, including the Pascua Yaqui near Tucson, Arizona (1978), and the Ysleta del Sur Pueblo near El Paso, Texas (1987). Congress also recognized the Texas Band of Traditional Kickapoos (1985); the Cow Creek Band of Umpqua Indians in Oregon (1982); the Western (Mashantucket) Pequot Tribe in Connecticut (1983); Confederated Tribes of Coos, Lower Umpqua and Siuslaw Indians, Oregon (1984); Lac Vieux Desert Band of Lake Superior Chippewa Indians, Minnesota (1984); and the Aroostook Micmac Tribe of Maine (1991).

On September 18, 1991, sensitized to widespread discontent over BAR's administration of the acknowledgment process, the Department of the Interior proposed new rules governing federal acknowledgment, suggesting an expedited process for petitions involving unacknowledged but "previously recognized" tribes. This proposed rule would change deadlines and otherwise adjust the process. Candidates under the expedited or regular process still would be required to show they have not abandoned tribal relations voluntarily. A successful petitioner under the expedited or regular process still will not receive services until Congress appropriates funds. Further, groups which have received federal services pending full acknowledgment would lose all these services upon acknowledgment, pending new appropriations. Successful appeals of petition denials in the Interior Department Court of Indian Appeals would be remanded to the BAR for review. No independent appeal process exists for the federal acknowledgment decisions.

John Shappard, principal author of the regulatory process, was Director of the BAR from 1978 to 1988. In 1992 and 1993, he provided written statements and testimony before congressional committees that the federal acknowledgment process has proved financially burdensome on both the government and the petitioners, and is infuriatingly slow and overly complicated. He finds this results in decisions which are by nature subjective. General congressional legislation may replace the Branch of Acknowledgment and Research with a commission independent of the Bureau of Indian Affairs, in order to resolve the difficulties with the federal acknowledgment process.

Allogan Slagle

See also **Federal and State Recognition; Government Policy**

Further Reading

Cohen, Felix S. *Handbook of Federal Indian Law.* Washington, DC: U.S. Government Printing Office, 1942.
———. *Felix S. Cohen's Handbook of Federal Indian Law.* Ed. Rennard Strickland. Charlottesville, VA: Michie/Bobbs-Merrill, 1982.

American Indian Policy Review Commission, Final Report. Washington, DC: U.S. Government Printing Office, 1977.

U.S. American Indian Policy Review Commission. *Report on Terminated and Nonfederally Recognized Indians: Final Report.* Washington, DC: U.S. Government Printing Office, 1976.

43 *Fed. Reg.* 39361, August 24, 1978. Initially 25 C.F.R. Part 54, now at 25 C.F.R. Part 83. 1, *et seq.*, 1979. *Rev.* April, 1985. (Federal regulations governing acknowledgment by the secretary of the interior of North American Indian groups as Indian tribes.)

BROTHERTOWN

The Brothertown (Brotherton) tribe was formed in the early 1770s from seven separate Indian communities representing the Narragansett-Niantic, Pequot, Mohegan, and Montauk tribes of southern New England and eastern Long Island. Soon afterwards, the tribe moved to a tract of land in upstate New York, which was granted to it by the Oneidas. By 1831, in the face of unremitting pressure from whites and the state, and after years of false starts, failed negotiations, disruptions caused by the War of 1812, and the whims of state and national policies, members of the tribe began emigrating to land in Wisconsin. The Indians' settlement here was first known as Manchester and later, Brothertown.

The fraudulent Treaty of Buffalo Creek (1838), designed to dispossess the six Iroquois tribes and the Brothertowners, Stockbridgers, and Munsees of their land and remove them to Kansas territory, put the tribe in jeopardy once again. The tribe petitioned Congress for relief, asking that its land in Wisconsin be divided in severalty and that the rights of citizenship be granted to its members. The necessary legislation was passed in 1839, which is alleged to also have terminated the Brothertowners' tribal status.

Although the actions of Congress allowed the Brothertowners to remain in Wisconsin, their tribal lands were eventually sold or otherwise lost to non-Indians. Nonetheless, the community at Brothertown remained intact. Over the years, however, many Brothertowners who had been farmers were forced to move to nearby towns and cities to find work. By the turn of the century, the now nearly landless Brothertown Indians were concentrated in Gresham, Fond du Lac, and Brothertown, Wisconsin.

Throughout the 1920s and 1930s, tribal members maintained strong social and political ties through kin networks, annual homecomings, family reunions, and visits to the Brothertown Methodist church and cemetery. During the 1920s, the Brothertowners organized Six Nations Clubs in Quinney, Fond du Lac, and Kaukauna. Although political in nature, these clubs served an important social purpose for the tribe. Family reunions, disrupted by World War II, have continued to the present.

Today tribal members can also be found in Milwaukee, Racine, and Green Bay, where individuals support themselves in a variety of occupations not unlike the surrounding non-Indian communities. Fond du Lac serves as the tribe's administrative center, and until recently, the tribe's office was here. The tribal chairman's home (Arbor Vitae, Wisconsin, in 1993) serves as current headquarters. Governance is maintained through an elected, nine member Tribal Council. Most tribal meetings are held in Fond du Lac because of its central location and the large number of tribal members living nearby.

The present tribal enrollment is 1,650, with the core community concentrated in the Fond du Lac, Fox River Valley, and Gresham areas. Gresham continues to represent the symbolic center of the tribe, since tribal members here are descended from those who moved into the area with the Stockbridgers in the latter half of the nineteenth century. Tribal members take great pride in their people's history and persistence, despite the extinction of their language. Brothertown people today are predominantly Christian. Many have travelled east to visit Brothertown, New York, and its Indian cemetery, and there are frequently told stories about important kin, political activities, and social gatherings of the tribe.

Important twentieth-century Brothertown leaders include Maynard Thompson, Mark Baldwin, Phil and Olivia Tousey, Rudi Ottery, and the present tribal chairperson, June Ezold, who is spearheading the tribe's efforts for a clarification of its federal status.

William A. Starna

See also **Stockbridge-Munsee**

Further Reading

Belknap, Jeremy, and Jedidiah Morse. *Report on the Oneida, Stockbridge and Brotherton Indians, 1796.* Indian Notes and Monographs 54. New York, NY: Museum of the American Indian, Heye Foundation, 1955.

Conkey, Laura E., Ethel Boisevain, and Ives Goddard. "Indians of Southern New England and Long Island: Late Period." *Handbook of North American Indians.* Vol.15. *Northeast.* Ed. Bruce G. Trigger. Washington, DC: Smithsonian Institution (1978): 177–89.

Ellis, Albert G. "Some Account of the Advent of the New York Indians into Wisconsin." *Annual Report and Collections State Historical Society of Wisconsin* 1855. Vol. 2. Madison: State Historical Society of Wisconsin (1856): 415–49.

Love, William De Loss. *Samson Occum, and the Christian Indians of New England.* Boston, MA: Pilgrim Press, 1899.

BUREAU OF INDIAN AFFAIRS (BIA)

During the second half of the nineteenth century, the organization of the Office of Indian Affairs, also referred to as the Indian Service, consisted of the Commissioner of Indian Affairs, who reported to the Secretary of the Interior, and several superintendents who administered directly over Indian agents. Indian agents were assigned to particular tribes and their duties consisted of distribution of treaty annuities, prohibition of trade in intoxicating beverages, supervision of education, and promotion of missionary activity. The agents were granted wide discretion and autonomy. Long distances between Washington and the Indian agencies, the difficulty of communication, the political nature of Indian agent appointments, and the absence of inspection resulted in wasteful and inefficient administration. After passage of the General Allotment Act of 1887 and the Curtis Act of 1898, the federal government initiated a campaign to actively abolish Indian government and culture. Federal policy directed the Indian Service to make Indians into self-supporting farmers on private land allotments, who would accept citizenship and integration into United States society.

The assimilation policy (1887 to 1934), and associated discouragement of Indian culture and government, left the Indian agents as the primary and dominant authority on Indian reservations. The weak supervision exercised by the Washington office enhanced the local control that Indian agents had over their reservation populations. Indian compliance to the new policies were enforced by virtue of the agent's control over food distribution, agricultural tools, access to military units, and control of the Indian police, who were on the Office of Indian Affairs' payroll. The severity of the agents administration varied with the degree of tribal opposition to the government's assimilation efforts. In order to promote assimilative goals, children were sent to school, many to boarding schools away from their parents, where they were educated and taught English. Tribal ceremonies were discouraged and political leaders and institutions undermined. The primary task of the Indian agent became the dissolution of tribal cultures, and rapid assimilation of Indian tribal members into American society. The Indian Service allotted land and issued patents to individual Indians totaling seven million acres by 1933, and, between 1887 and 1934, sold allotted lands, heirship lands, and surplus lands resulting in a reduction in Indian holdings from 138 million acres to 48 million acres.

In 1900 the Office of Indian Affairs employed 4,259 people; slightly more than half were educators or school employees. Of a budget totaling $7.75 million, the largest amount was allocated to schools, $2.9 million, while treaty obligations, the second largest item, accounted for $2.7 million. In 1908, Francis E. Leupp, commissioner of Indian affairs from 1904 to 1909, reorganized the Office and abolished regional superintendents and Indian agents. The administrative duties of the old Indian agents were taken up by bonded school teachers or government employed farmers. Leupp proposed that allotment of tribal lands required that Indians be treated as individuals rather than as tribal members. He argued that teachers and farmers working on the reservations were better capable of providing Indians with individualized assistance than were the old Indian agents. The new agency superintendents reported directly to the Washington office. In Leupp's view, the Indian Service's purpose was to "establish each Indian as a separate landholder on his own account." The Indian question could be solved by allotment and sale of Indian land, and by creating an educated and economically self-sustaining Indian population. Indians would be incorporated into United States society as taxpaying, individual landholding, and laboring citizens, with no special legal rights or consideration from the United States government. Education, farming, and practical training were the largest activities within the Office in terms of emphasis, personnel, and budget. At the same time, special agents sold Indian land, allotted land, and issued private patents to Indian allotees. For example, in the fiscal year 1908, the Indian Service issued 11,280 private land patents to Indians and approved another 5,365 allotments, which awaited issuance of patents. In addition, the Office sold surplus Indian lands, sold land of incompetent Indians, and leased Indian land. Between 1903 and 1908, the Indian Service sold slightly over 500,000 acres left by deceased Indian allotees, while in fiscal year 1908, it leased over one million acres of tribal land.

The Indian Service's mandate to assimilate Indians into United States society resulted in repressive measures against Indian dancing and other practices of Indian culture. Indian superintendents actively discouraged the practice of Indian language, customs, dress, and dancing, and in 1921 and 1923 the commissioner of Indian affairs published at least three letters instructing Indian Service employees to suppress and control Indian ceremonies, dress, and dances. Although many Indian ceremonies, dances, music, and religious practices were carried on away from Indian Service surveillance, many Indian cultural traditions and institutions were lost or changed during this period. After 1925, official repression of Indian culture eased, and some ceremonies and traditions were again tolerated in public view. In the twenties the Office employed about 5,000 people each year, and generally slightly more than half worked in education. The budget in 1928 was nearly $15 million, and educational expenditures were the largest single item at nearly $6.5 million. Sale of Indian land and the transferring of tribal lands into private allotments continued, although health and social welfare concerns gained greater significance.

Indian policy and the Office of Indian Affairs came under severe criticism during the late 1920s. The Meriam Report of 1928 underscored destitute Indian health and economic conditions, and implied that Indian policy was not effective in creating self-sufficient citizens. The report gave suggestions for improving education, health programs, and Indian Service administration. In addition, the report took issue with the forced acculturation programs of the past forty years, and recommended that the government adopt policies that conveyed respect and understanding of Indian culture and institutions. At the same time, activist Indian rights organizations, like the American Indian Defense Association, and activists like John Collier, sought Indian administrative reform that built on, rather than destroyed, Indian culture. Between 1929 and 1933, Commissioner of Indian Affairs Charles Rhoads implemented some recommendations from the Meriam Report.

During the depths of the Great Depression in 1933, John Collier was appointed commissioner of Indian affairs from 1933 to 1945 within the Roosevelt administration. Under Collier's administration, the 5,000 Indian Service employees of 1933 were augmented by an additional 7,000 employees in 1934, for a total of 12,000. In 1933 and 1934, the Indian Service enjoyed rapidly expanded budgets, $23 million and $52 million respectively, but budgets were soon cut back to an average of $12 million between 1935 and 1942, and severely slashed to an average of less than half a million during the closing years of World War II.

As commissioner of Indian affairs, Collier worked to rehabilitate Indian traditions and cultures, and provide the tribes with legal and organizational capability to promote reservation economic development while preserving cultural traditions. He convinced the members of the congressional Indian committees to repudiate the allotment acts, revive Indian governments in constitutional form, and allow them to retain and own land. As a result, in 1934, the Indian Reorganization Act (IRA) passed Congress along with a flurry of other New Deal legislation. In accordance with the IRA, or "Indian New Deal," the Indian Service administered elections among some two hundred fifty-eight tribes, although constitutional governments were adopted by only ninety-two tribes. Other tribes, who rejected the IRA, were induced to adopt electoral procedures and bylaws, often similar to IRA constitutional provisions. The IRA constitutions formally recognized the authority of the secretary of the interior to veto tribal ordinances, constitutional amendments, and issues involving federal trust responsibility over land, mineral, and water resources. The IRA, nevertheless, ended the allotment policy, provided Indian allotees with protection from further loss of land, and provided a small amount of financial support for Indian tribes to buy back land. After 1934, the Indian Service no longer has as its major task the sale and allotment of Indian land, and Indians were encouraged to develop their resources under tribal authority, rather than as individual landholders.

The IRA constitutional governments, however, were an alien political form for most Indian reservation communities, which for nearly fifty years were deprived of the right to independently manage reservation affairs. Furthermore, Indian communities and leaders had little power within and knowledge of Indian Service operations and American political culture, and were constrained by bureaucratic oversight and secretarial veto power. Consequently, the emergence of active and autonomous tribal governments was greatly hampered. The Office of Indian Affairs continued to exert considerable administrative control over reservation affairs and institutions. Furthermore, the

sentiment of Congress continued to favor assimilation of Indian people into American society, and was generally opposed to the culturally pluralistic reforms of Collier. In 1937, an originator of the IRA introduced a bill into Congress designed to neutralize the Act. Although the bill did not gain support, funds necessary for carrying out the provisions of the IRA were not available during the Depression and during World War II. To a large extent, the act went unimplemented owing to an absence of sustained congressional interest and support. The immediate impact of the IRA on restructuring Indian affairs and developing functional tribal governments was negligible. The Indian Service retained authority over most reservation government affairs, and there was little opportunity for local Indian self-government.

As early as the late 1930s and through the 1940s, Congress favored policies designed to remove Indians from special legal and institutional relations with the government. In the early 1950s, Congress moved to abolish Indian reservations, which were considered financial burdens on the government and which subjected Indians to paternalistic control. It was thought that Indians could be more efficiently integrated into society by the abolition of the Bureau of Indian Affairs (formerly the Office of Indian Affairs), the special trust-wardship relations between Indian tribes and the federal government, and the relegation of Indian lands to state jurisdiction. The "termination policy" was officially set forth in 1953 in the form of House Resolution 108 of the 83rd Congress. The resolution outlined congressional intent for the severance of direct and historical federal relations with Indian tribes. The termination period lasted until 1960, when state and Indian opposition blocked efforts to terminate more tribes.

During the termination policy period the Bureau of Indian Affairs (BIA) underwent a major reorganization. From Leupp's reorganization in 1908 until 1949, the Indian Service consisted of a central office in Washington, and seventy to eighty-two agency offices located mainly on reservations. Owing to increased volume, the Washington office experienced difficulty communicating and processing information with reservation offices, which caused long delays for obtaining routine replies to requests for direction and advice on policy and administrative decisions. In the middle 1940s a study by a private firm recommended the creation of eleven "area offices," which were delegated responsibility for administering most of the BIA's routine operations. After some delay and opposition, the reorganization plan was adopted in 1949. In the early 1950s, the BIA administered programs in education, welfare, health, law and order, training and relocating, irrigation, forestry, conservation, and others. Management and responsibility of most daily operations were delegated to the area directors, the line administrative officer in the area offices. Policy issues, legislative oversight and interpretation, and promulgation of rules and regulations became the primary focus of the central office, while the area offices progressively gained control over day-to-day program operations. A central office reorganization in 1973 delegated all daily operations to the area offices, and formalized an organizational division of labor that had already existed for some time. The reorganization of 1949 created the basic BIA structure as we know it today. While through the succeeding years there have been many internal changes, and even attempts to do away with the BIA or the area offices, none have resulted in change in the three-tiered pattern of a central Washington office, twelve area offices, and about ninety agency offices.

Two commissioners of Indian affairs, Dillon Myer (1950 to 1953), and Glenn Emmons (1953 to 1961), carried out the termination policy. Myer presented major elements of the policy to Congress in the form of reorganization of the BIA, transfer of Indian services to state and local authorities, and relocation of Indians into urban areas. In 1955, health care was transferred from the BIA to the Public Health Service, which created the Indian Health Service (IHS). Both commissioners emphasized development of Indian economic self-sufficiency and participation in United States society and market economy. There was major emphasis on providing loans and promoting economic development through the 1950s and 1960s. Despite the termination policy BIA budgets increased. In 1951, the BIA budget was $70 million and budgets continued to increase into the late 1950s.

The end of the termination policy marked a withdrawal of United States policy from direct dismantling of the reservation system and severance of Indian-federal historical and legal ties. The most significant changes came with the implementation of the "Great Society" programs of the Kennedy-Johnson administrations. The new programs in health, housing, anti-poverty, and community action delivered funds directly to Indian tribal governments. These new sources of funds allowed tribal governments to control resources that were not under the direct administrative control of BIA officials. Consequently, tribal governments became more active and created greater interest within reservation communities. A major example emerged at Zuni Pueblo, where leaders revived old and largely unused laws in order to assume administration of local institutions with the aid of federal funds and contracting of BIA services. This move toward tribal management, in part, inspired the self-determination policy, which was officially declared in a speech by President Nixon in 1970. During the later sixties and seventies, many tribes enjoyed increased funding and, increasingly, funding came from non-BIA sources. In 1968, the BIA budget was $250 million, while the IHS budget was about $100 million. Fifty-five percent of the BIA budget went to education, and 9,000 BIA employees were in education out of a total of 16,035.

The 1960s saw a major shift with the appointment of Robert Bennett, an Oneida Indian from Wisconsin, to the post of commissioner of Indian affairs (1966 to 1969). This appointment set a precedent that the BIA's chief executive have significant Indian life experience and be of Indian descent. Further changes in favor of Indian preference within the BIA occurred in the early seventies. Louis Bruce, commissioner of Indian affairs from 1969 to 1973 and a Mohawk-Sioux, was a strong advocate of BIA reorganization and promotion of Indian personnel within the BIA. In 1934, 34 percent of BIA employees were of Indian descent, and by 1941 the ratio increased to 51 percent; in 1969, 48 percent of BIA employees were of Indian descent, and most were in the lowest and least responsible positions. In 1973, a Supreme Court decision in *Morton v. Mancari et al.* ruled that Indian preference in BIA hiring and promotion did not violate equal employment practices, but was a means for Indians to exercise self government. This ruling dramatically changed the demography of the BIA. By 1980, 78 percent of BIA employees were of Indian descent, and Indian employees were consistently promoted to positions of greater responsibility and decision making. In 1977, the relative status of the BIA within the Department of the Interior was enhanced when the commissioner of Indian affairs was raised to the rank of assistant secretary of Indian affairs.

The Indian Self-Determination and Education Act of 1975 provided a procedure by which Indian tribes could contract BIA operations, and thereby gain more direct control over its functions. The Self-Determination Act created mechanisms for delegating line authority and funds from the area offices directly to tribal governments and Indian organizations. Despite the Act's attempt to reorganize the BIA, little change has occurred in BIA structure. The area offices remain firmly in administrative control of BIA operations and funds, while tribal governments and agency offices have not been able and sometimes not willing to take over more technical BIA functions. Nevertheless, the Self-Determination Act has allowed many reservation communities to regain management over some reservation institutions, especially over formerly BIA-operated reservation day schools. Since the early 1970s, several attempts have been made to restructure and decentralize the BIA in favor of tribal and agency administration, but the three-tiered system of central, area, and agency offices has survived.

In the middle 1970s, the BIA had funding of $1 billion, although non-Indian funding from non-BIA sources was twice as large. The Reagan administration saw major cutbacks in BIA and federal funding to Indian communities. In 1991, the BIA budget was again at the $1.2 billion level, but less than the 1977 sum in real terms, after taking inflation into account. In recent decades, BIA employment ranged between 15,000 and 16,000. The official goal of the BIA is to promote tribal self-determination, while retaining trust responsibility for Indian land and resources. Education, economic development, and resource management remain major BIA activities. The decline in BIA budgets in gross and real terms during the 1980s did not engender significant assertions of tribal self-determination. So far, the self-determination policy can be judged only a limited success. BIA administration, trust responsibility, and budget control continue to exert major constraints over tribal governments and Indian reservation communities. Despite continuing tribal efforts to decentralize BIA administrative and budgetary powers, the BIA most likely will remain a major force in Indian affairs and within Indian communities well into the next century.

Duane Champagne

See also Agriculture; Allotment; American Indian Policy Review Commission; Bureau of Indian Affairs Schools; Government Agencies; Government Policy; Indian Health Service; Indian Reorganization Act

Further Reading

Commissioner of Indian Affairs. *Annual Reports to the Secretary of the Interior.* Washington, DC: U.S. Government Printing Office, 1849–1967.

Kvasnicka, Robert M., and Herman J. Viola, eds. *The Commissioners of Indian Affairs, 1824–1977.* Lincoln: University of Nebraska Press, 1979.

Prucha, Francis. *The Great Father: The United States Government and the American Indians.* Vol. 2. Lincoln: University of Nebraska Press, 1984.

Schmeckebier, Laurence. *The Office of Indian Affairs: Its History, Activities, and Organization.* Baltimore, MD: Johns Hopkins Press, 1927.

Taylor, Theodore W. *The Bureau of Indian Affairs.* Boulder, CO: Westview Press, 1984.

BUREAU OF INDIAN AFFAIRS OCCUPATION

See Trail of Broken Treaties

BUREAU OF INDIAN AFFAIRS SCHOOLS

The federal government assumed responsibility for Native American education in the late nineteenth century, and has continued that obligation to the present, although reliance on schools operated directly by the Bureau of Indian Affairs (BIA) has diminished considerably since World War II. Before the federal school system began, Congress provided subsidies to religious schools through the 1819 "civilization fund." By the end of the Civil War, however, this limited program clearly needed replacement. With the western tribes being placed on reservations, it became evident to government officials that a much more centralized and comprehensive program would be necessary if Indian children were to be educated in preparation for assimilation into American society.

The repeal of civilization fund support for mission schools (1873) opened the way for a government school system. Because the transition could not be carried into effect immediately, the Indian Office contracted with existing mission schools (both Protestant and Catholic), paying them $167 per year per pupil to provide schooling. Such mission schools, called contract schools because of their governmental financial support, continued on a declining basis through the early twentieth century, with the government preferring to open officially "nondenominational" schools. As a consequence, by 1880, a number of federally operated day schools and reservation boarding schools had appeared.

Richard Henry Pratt brought federal Indian education into full bloom. In 1879 this crusty army officer opened a nonreservation Indian industrial school at Carlisle, Pennsylvania. Carlisle quickly became the nation's premier Indian school, and Pratt's educational philosophy focusing on the destruction of Indian culture and complete assimilation into American society became extremely popular. Using the slogan "To Civilize The Indian . . . Get Him Into Civilization," the school adopted military-style discipline and provided vocational training in trades such as carpentry, masonry, and blacksmithing. Since federal Indian schools were co-educational, female students learned homemaking skills in anticipation of keeping an Anglo-style home. Academic learning, while offered, took a back seat to vocational training.

With Carlisle providing an example, the federal government opened additional nonreservation schools during the 1880s, including such major institutions as Chilocco, Haskell, and Chemawa. By the end of the decade, some 153 federal Indian schools of various types were in operation. The system itself, however, lacked a uniform purpose or curriculum. These deficiencies were addressed when Thomas J. Morgan became Indian commissioner in 1889. Morgan, a Baptist minister and dedicated educator, attempted to organize the BIA schools into a replica of the American public school system. Advocating compulsory attendance, Morgan committed the government to a three-leveled educational program, with instruction beginning at a day school where students could learn a few basic skills (spelling and arithmetic), before being transferred to a reservation boarding school for intermediate work away from parental influence. Finally, after several years of preparation, the best students would be sent to an off-reservation industrial school to receive a "professional" education equivalent to eighth grade.

Although the Morgan system became institutionalized and operated pretty much unchanged until the 1930s, it was not so simple in practice. With no lower-level schools available at some locations, youngsters were often sent directly to off-reservation schools, producing the unique situation of having twenty-year-old students in classes with seven-year-olds. Superintendents, anxious to make their schools appear successful, also took in any student they could find, regardless of qualifications. Nor did many students complete the requirements for graduation. Morgan had not counted on Indian apathy, cultural differences, and an inept federal bureaucracy to frustrate the process.

Under Morgan and his immediate successors, the federal Indian school system expanded dramatically during the 1890s. By 1900, there were some 25 off-reservation boarding schools enrolling approximately 10,000 children. Major new schools included Santa Fe, Phoenix, Carson, and Sherman. In addition, the Bureau operated 81 reservation boarding schools, 147 day schools, and supported 32 contract schools. Between 1900 and 1920, Bureau schools changed little. From time to time curriculum was adjusted, but the basic program of providing for assimilation continued with little interruption under charge of an entrenched and conservative group of white administrators and teachers. Most of the Indian employees served in low-level jobs.

About the same time, federal educational efforts were slowly extended to Alaska, where mission schools had remained the norm until well into the twentieth century. In Alaska, however, schools were under the control of the United States Office of Education (Bureau of Education) until 1931, when the BIA took over. Under this system, contract schools predominated until 1900, when the government began opening day schools. Yet not until the 1920s was it possible to begin establishing Indian industrial boarding schools. These institutions were generally similar to stateside schools, although more burdened with staffing and student problems. Very few competent educators were willing to serve in remote Alaskan locations prior to the 1930s.

Before World War I, a number of significant problems began to surface as it became increasingly obvious that BIA schools were not accomplishing their primary task. Students trained at the schools could not find employment in white society and thus returned to the reservations, where there was little demand for their skills. As a consequence, many lapsed back into traditional ways. The return on the government's investment in assimilation thus seemed minimal. Additionally, Indian communities and parents disliked the schools for taking their children away, sometimes by force. By the 1910s, many school buildings were also aging and in need of repair, but Congress declined to provide the necessary funds. Finally, most schools suffered from severe overcrowding, creating significant health problems, with tuberculosis, trachoma, and other diseases running rampant. Despite a campaign to improve sanitary conditions initiated by Commissioner Francis Leupp (1905 to 1909) and the opening of several tuberculosis sanatoriums, health conditions among the students continued to be a major concern.

Student life during these years was a mixture of pain and pleasure. For many Indian children, it was a thoroughly forgettable experience. Forcibly separated from family and friends, they were placed in an unfamiliar setting, provided with strange food and clothing, and forced to speak English. Strict discipline and severe punishment for violating rules was normal. Such conditions caused emotional stress among many pupils and they reacted by being uncooperative, destructive, or attempting to run away. When their schooling ended, these individuals could hardly wait to cast off the trappings of white civilization. Other students, however, were more receptive to the schools. Imaginations were sparked by stories of the outside world and some students eagerly sought more education. At the better nonreservation schools, such as Phoenix, a large variety of extra-curricular programs offered the opportunity for social involvement.

At several schools an "outing" system provided employment for students. Under this popular program, pupils were hired out to local white families and businesses as a means of earning cash and providing youngsters with an opportunity to live in the non-Indian world. While this did provide work experience, the outing system also permitted the exploitation of students by whites who overworked and underpaid their Indian employees. Despite such drawbacks, many students fondly remember the friendships and camaraderie that developed among students, teachers, and employers.

The deterioration of BIA schools continued after World War I, as conservative government officials cut budgets and old guard administrators persisted in maintaining institutions dedicated to the assimilation philosophy of the 1890s. About the same time, a reform movement led by John Collier began a sustained attack on federal Indian policy, accusing the Indian Bureau of being corrupt, incompetent, and repressive. Labeling the government program a dismal failure, the reform organizations spawned by Collier took exception to the Indian Bureau school system, readily pointing out its flaws and abuses. Under intense pressure, old guard administrators defended their practices until overwhelmed.

The first major step in changing the educational system came with the publication of the 1928 Meriam Report. Initiated by the Secretary of the Interior in response to criticism, the massive report surveyed all fields of Indian affairs, concentrating heavily on Indian education. The education section, prepared by Dr. W. Carson Ryan, proposed a new school program for the Indian Bureau. It noted the overcrowding, health problems, harsh discipline, inadequate curriculum, and exploitation of child labor, especially at the boarding schools. In dramatic language the report pictured the schools as feudal institutions that endangered the students and destroyed Indian families. In place of the current system, Ryan suggested that the government adopt the principles of the "Progressive Education Movement," which advocated a curriculum designed to meet individual needs in a cross-cultural atmosphere. Although it was impractical to close the boarding schools as desired by some reformers, the Meriam Report gave strong backing to reservation day (community) schools where children would be closer to family. It also proposed the employment of a staff of professionally trained teachers. In all the Meriam Report made many valuable suggestions and spurred the effort to radically change the federal school system.

Stirrings of change came during the Hoover administration when W. Carson Ryan became the BIA's director of Indian education. Ryan supported an emphasis on community schools, the hiring of trained teachers and administrators, elimination of certain boarding schools, and the placement of more students in public schools. Although he managed to achieve some success, Ryan's cautious approach drew criticism from radical reformers like Collier.

With the inauguration of President Franklin D. Roosevelt in 1933, and implementation of the New Deal, the stage was set for John Collier to become commissioner of Indian affairs (Ryan stayed on as education director until 1935). Collier's "Indian New Deal" attempted to make great changes in the government school system. Always possessed with a flair for the dramatic, Collier quickly closed a number of boarding schools and activated additional community day schools in an effort to place children closer to their parents. By 1941 the number of day schools had almost doubled (to 226, with an enrollment of 15,789). At the same time, the number of boarding schools dropped to 49 (enrolling about 14,000 Indian children). Although Collier might have preferred to eliminate boarding schools entirely, the reality of the situation prevented any such action. Nonreservation schools, which now offered high school courses, continued to be necessary because of the lack of advanced facilities on reservations. Depression era budgets also hindered new construction. Nevertheless, the schools changed in many ways. The military routine was dropped, more emphasis placed on academics, and traditional cultural elements, including the use of native language, were permitted. Collier's commitment to "cultural pluralism" thus attempted to get Indian school children back into their community.

Another change in the BIA system was made possible by the Johnson-O'Malley Act of 1934, permitting the government to pay public schools to educate Indian children. Although many public schools at first resisted taking Indian students because of racial concerns, the concept of federal payment for educating Indian children eventually became a significant factor in reducing the need for Indian Bureau schools. From 1930, when public schools enrolled about 53 percent of Indian children, to 1970, by which time 65 percent of all Indian children were in public schools, the number of Indian Bureau schools proportionally declined. By the latter date, only 26 percent of Indian children remained in federal schools. Much of this was fostered by the success of the Johnson-O'Malley legislation.

Disruptions caused by World War II cost many of the gains made during the New Deal. Reduced budgets and enlistment in the military caused some innovative programs to be curtailed and many schools to shut down. In addition, a reaction to the community school philosophy set in, which, coupled with deplorable conditions at some locations, caused enrollments to fall. In all, the number of children in reservation day schools declined about 25 percent by war's end.

As a consequence, when Collier resigned as commissioner in 1945, the BIA schools were again headed for a change. A new era of "Americanizing" began, reaching its peak during the termination period of the early 1950s. With reaction to the New Deal as a driving force, the 1950s witnessed a revival of interest in boarding schools, especially the off-reservation variety. Emphasizing getting the Indian into American society, urban schools where vocational skills could be taught gained favor at the expense of day schools. With a large number of war veterans also desiring education, students flooded the schools. One noteworthy program initiated at this time was a special Navajo Education Program, directed by Hildegard Thompson, intended to train large numbers of Navajos for urban living. Schools such as Sherman Institute, Intermountain, and Phoenix were choked with Navajo students learning vocational skills. Although this program achieved some success, Indian opposition to the termination policy caused Native leaders to demand a greater voice in school policy and frown on education directed at relocation.

The 1960s thus witnessed a more accelerated shift away from the BIA school system. With no clear objectives, little financial support, and public apathy, BIA schools failed to meet changing Indian educational needs. As an increasing number of Indian students enrolled in public schools, BIA institutions degenerated, often ending up as facilities for problem children who could not be accommodated by public education. Indeed, the government itself encouraged the utilization of public schools by providing additional contract funding. Not helping were a series of investigative reports published in the early 1970s (primarily the Kennedy Report and the National Study of American Indian Education), which revealed intolerable conditions in the schools and argued in favor of community schools under parental influence. The fact that so few teachers were Indian also proved disturbing. As tribal demands for self-determination increased in the 1970s, Congress responded by letting tribes contract for educational services (Public Law 93-63B, the Indian Self-Determination and Education Assistance Act [1975]) as a method of controlling more of their own education services. This led to the creation of Rough Rock Demonstration School on the Navajo reservation, an experimental contract school that brought the community into decision-making positions, incorporated Navajo traditions into the curriculum, and became a community focal point. Although suffering from financial uncertainty, Rough Rock served as a landmark in the changing nature of Indian education.

Rough Rock epitomized the declining importance of BIA schools. As more and more community and public schools serve the reservation population, the need for boarding schools has diminished. Many of the big nonreservation schools closed in the 1980s, the latest being the 1990 closure of Phoenix Indian High School. Nevertheless, the BIA continues to run a school system. In 1988, it operated one hundred and three schools (including several off-reservation boarding schools) and funded another sixty-five under contract. BIA schools are still important to the Indian and Eskimo populations, and it seems certain that the need for them will continue for some time.

Robert A. Trennert, Jr.

See also **Churches and Education; Educational Policy; Higher Education; Johnson O'Malley Act; Meriam Commission; Public Schools**

Further Reading

Fuchs, Estelle, and Robert J. Havinghurst. *To Live on This Earth: American Indian Education.* Reprint. Albuquerque: University of New Mexico Press, 1983.

McBeth, Sally J. *Ethnic Identity and the Boarding School Experience of West-Central Oklahoma American Indians.* Washington, DC: University Press of America, 1983.

Reyhner, John, and Jeanne Eder. *A History of Indian Education.* Billings: Eastern Montana College, 1989.

Szasz, Margaret Connell. *Education and the American Indian: The Road to Self-Determination Since 1928.* 2d ed. Albuquerque: University of New Mexico Press, 1977.

Trennert, Robert A. *The Phoenix Indian School: Forced Assimilation in Arizona, 1891–1935.* Norman: University of Oklahoma Press, 1988.

CADDO

The Caddo Tribe of Oklahoma includes former tribes and villages of three allied confederacies—Kadohadacho, Hasinai, and Nachitoches—with Anadarkos and Ionies. The ancestral homeland of the Caddos was in western Louisiana and Arkansas and eastern Texas and Oklahoma. In the historical period explorers found Kadohadachos in the eastern, Hasinais in the western, and Nachitoches in the southern regions.

In 1835, the Kadohadachos signed a treaty with Louisiana ceding their land there and moved to join their kin in Texas. (In 1935, Caddo adults and children returned to Shreveport without rancor to assist that city in celebration of its centennial.) Later, they moved to the leased district of the Choctaw and Chickasaw nations in Indian Territory. Provisions of the Agreement of 1872 established a reservation which was only a portion of their former reserve for Wichitas and Affiliated Bands, including the Caddos. Less than thirty years later, the 1887 General Allotment Act divided that reservation with each enrolled Caddo receiving 160 acres and United States citizenship. Surplus lands were opened to non-Indian settlement by lottery in 1901.

Caddo leaders had fought against allotment before the fact. Caddo Jake and Whitebread were chiefs of the Caddos at the turn of the twentieth century. Henry Inkanish was tribal interpreter. Enoch Hoag, Sr., was the last Caddo chief of the south; he died in 1920. The last Caddo chief of the northern division was Francis Longhat. Their concerns finally had a hearing when, in 1924, Congress passed an act authorizing the Wichitas and Affiliated Bands (including the Caddos) to submit claims to the Court of Claims, which they did in 1925 and in 1927. In 1951, the Caddo Tribe filed a claim for land compensation for Arkansas and Louisiana lands and spent much of its collective energy throughout the 1970s in pursuit of these land claims. The Court of Claims awarded the Caddo Tribe $383,475 for the 1835 Treaty, and $1,222,800 on the accounting claim arising from the sale of unallotted and surplus lands of the Caddo Tribe on the Wichita Reservation. Part of this money funds a burial assistance program.

Each tribal resolution begins "The Caddo Tribe of Oklahoma is a federally recognized tribe, governed by a Constitution pursuant to the Oklahoma Indian Welfare Act of 1936." Caddos adopted their first Constitution and Bylaws in January, 1938, and revised them and their corporate Charter in 1976. The Constitution assigned original allottees full-blood status for purposes of enrollment and requires at least one-eighth degree Caddo blood for tribal enrollment. In the late twentieth century, Caddo tribal members are again revising their Constitution and considering a name change to become the "Caddo Nation in Oklahoma."

An elected eight-member board governs the tribe with ultimate authority resting in the tribal members as a whole. A chairman is the principal elected official, usually male. Maurice Bedoka was the first chairman of the Caddo Tribe under the 1939 Constitution. Other noted leaders following the 1939 reorganization include Andrew Dunlap, Stanley Edge, Jesse Ahdunko, and Wilbur and Melford Williams. Elmo Tewiwin Clark was elected as chairman in August 1992. The only woman to hold the office of chairman has been Mary Pat Francis, although several women have served on the Tribal Council.

The tribal complex, which includes tribal offices, a senior citizen's center, a community center, and both indoor and outdoor ceremonial dance grounds, is located on 42.5 acres near Binger, Oklahoma. The Caddo tribe also holds in trust (in conjunction with the Wichita and Delaware tribes) 2,399.5 acres comprising Riverside Indian School, the Bureau of Indian Affairs Anadarko Area Office in Anadarko, and the "Old Agency" (now the Indian Baptist Church) at Fort Cobb, Oklahoma. From a population nadir of 452 in 1910 (of which almost 57 percent were under the age of twenty), Caddos steadily increased their numbers to 3,371 by July, 1992, with approximately one-third living in Caddo County, Oklahoma. Caddos now live throughout Oklahoma, other southwestern states, and Europe.

While most Caddos work, unemployment of Caddos living on their former reservation, Caddo County, averages 40 percent. However, the Caddo tribe counts among its enrolled members lawyers, doctors, nurses and health professionals, teachers and professors, bankers, office workers, government officials, church workers, construction workers, artists, writers, barbers, athletes, ranchers, and farmers. T.C. Cannon, Caddo-Kiowa, is recognized worldwide as an outstanding artist; Dan Medrano was one of the early leaders in the National Congress of American Indians, serving as its first secretary.

Tribal economy depends almost entirely on oil, gas, and rangeland leasing. Several economic ventures with the Wichita and Delaware tribes have included agriculture, a factory, a smoke-shop, and bingo.

In the late seventies and early eighties, the Caddo tribe secured grants for two buildings, as well as funds for building and improving houses for tribal members. In the 1990s the Caddo tribe is again seeking funds for new buildings to house growing social service programs and cultural activities.

Caddos are fortunate in retaining many of their songs and dances. A Caddo ceremonial usually begins with the Turkey Dance, a serious victory dance which must be completed before sundown. Evening activities begin with the Drum Dance in which singers recount and dancers symbolically reenact their origins and emergence from within the earth. Other Caddo traditional dances follow, ending with the Morning Dance at or near dawn. In the early years of the Peyote Religion, a Caddo-Delaware named Nishkuntu (Moonhead) developed a ritual for peyote meetings based on Roman-Catholic liturgy. He is revered by Osages and others for bringing the Peyote Religion to them.

Much of the 1970s found the tribe collecting and recording songs, the Caddo language, and oral history. Recently, Caddos have initiated a culture club which meets weekly to eat together, sing Caddo songs, relearn Caddo dances, and generally keep Caddo traditions alive. Future plans for the culture club include Caddo language classes, oral history interviews, pottery classes using ancient Caddo designs, and museum development. As the Caddo Nation nears the twenty-first century, its members retain and celebrate their traditions, culture, and heritage and look confidently toward a future with a growing population, well-educated in the ways of their ancestors, as well as in the ways of their non-Indian neighbors.

Carol Hampton

See also Oklahoma Tribes

Further Reading

Doris Duke Oral History Collection. Oklahoma City: Oklahoma Historical Society; Norman, OK: University of Oklahoma, Western History Collections.

Hampton, Carol. "Caddo." *Handbook of North American Indians.* Vol. 13. *Plains.* Ed. Raymond J. DeMallie. Washington, DC: Smithsonian Institution, forthcoming.

Indian-Pioneer Papers. Oklahoma City: Oklahoma City Historical Society; Norman: University of Oklahoma, Western History Collections.

Newkumet, Vynola Beaver, and Howard L. Meredith. *Hasinai: A Traditional History of the Caddo Confederacy.* College Station: Texas A&M University Press, 1988.

Cahto Pomo

See Pomo

CAHUILLA

The Cahuilla (Caguilla, Coahuilla, or Kaweah), who speak a language belonging to the Takic branch of the Uto-Aztecan language family, are, for the most part, members of several reservations in inland southern California: Morongo, Agua Caliente, Cabazon, Augustine, Torres-Martinez, Santa Rosa, Cahuilla, Ramona, and Los Coyotes Indian Reservations. Chemehuevi, Cupeño, Luiseño, and Serrano also reside on or are members of some of these reservations; the total population of the reservation areas is approximately 2,300, but it is difficult to estimate what percentage of this is Cahuilla. Although most Cahuilla people live on or near these reservations, some live as far away as New York and Florida.

In the early years of the twentieth century, Cahuilla reservations retrieved some of the land that had been returned to the public domain by the 1891 Act for the Relief of Mission Indians. None of the Cahuilla reservations developed constitutions under the terms of the Indian Reorganization Act of 1934. Mission Creek Reservation was terminated in 1970. Cahuilla reservations joined other southern California Indian groups in the Indian Claims Commission Cases of the 1940s and 1950s (K-34 Docket 80 and 80A), and some have also sued the government for determination of damages with respect to the loss of water rights (Docket 80A-2). Bureau of Indian Affairs (BIA) policy, since the passage of Public Law 280 in 1953, is to give tribal governments much more autonomy than was the case earlier in the century, but tribal autonomy remains an issue for tribal leaders.

The General Council consisting of all members over twenty-one years of age is the governing body of most Cahuilla reservations, with elected committees or business committees carrying out day-to-day business. Ramona and Augustine are inactive; Agua Caliente Reservation is the most formally organized, with a non-Indian Reorganization Act (IRA) Constitution and Bylaws approved in 1957, and amendments approved in 1966.

During the first part of the twentieth century, Cahuilla derived their income from wage labor, farming, and stockraising on reservation lands. Reservation forests, hunting fees, sale of rights of way, and sale of such resources as peat and asbestos supplemented their incomes. Lack of water was a deterrent to farming and stockraising: although the Indian Irrigation Service, a sub-agency of the BIA, developed irrigation systems on some of the reservations, these irrigation systems were rarely dependable. The Agua Caliente Band began in the 1920s to derive significant income from the thousands of tourists who visit the Indian canyons: Palm Canyon, Andreas Canyon, and Murray Canyon.

Since 1950, Cahuillas engage in a variety of occupations in communities adjacent to their reservations. They include administrators, educators, musicians, artists, businessmen and women, craftsmen and craftswomen, museum curators, archaeological monitors, authors, and other career-oriented people among their numbers. Reservation income is derived from commercial developments, bingo parlors, advertising signs along highways, and the leasing of land for cattle raising and farming. The question of whether to lease reservation land for waste disposal, hazardous or non-hazardous, is currently a political issue. The Agua Caliente Band has formed the Agua Caliente Development Authority to handle its extensive real estate business.

The Morongo Indian Health Clinic, which is operated jointly by Morongo and Soboba reservations, opened in September 1970 and serves all Riverside County reservations. Its services now include the development of domestic water systems on reservations. Its staff includes a specialist on environmental affairs. Some of its projects, such as those having to do with domestic water systems, are funded by federal funds from the Department of Housing and Urban Development.

Schools were developed at several of the Cahuilla reservations in the 1890s. Beginning at about the same time, St. Boniface School in Banning, a Catholic institution, and Perris School in Riverside provided education for children from a number of reservations. Perris School was succeeded by Sherman Institute in the early 1900s. Children from the Agua Caliente Band in Palm Springs went to public school from the first, and by about 1914 most reservation children were attending public school. Now many go on to junior colleges and four-year institutions and a number have graduate degrees.

Katherine Siva Saubel, Edward Castillo, Richard Milanovich, and the late Jane Pablo Penn have served on the California Native American Heritage Commission, taking a lead in issues concerning cultural resource management, the treatment of Indian burials, and the question of waste disposal on Indian reservations. Anthony Largo is chairman of the California Indian Manpower Consortium and on the board of Indian Health Service; Alvino Siva serves on the Riverside County Historical Commission; and Adelaide Pressley serves as director of the Indian Services Projects and has been tribal chairman at Morongo Indian Reservation.

The Cahuilla language was spoken fluently by approximately fifty people in 1991. Traditional *nukil* (funeral) ceremonies were diminished by the late 1930s and continue in much reduced form. Although there are no priests or shamans now, the Cahuilla worldview persists in a number of respects. Traditional social structure is no longer intact, but traditional familistic structure is still significant in daily life. Some forms of traditional music, such as Bird Songs and Peon Songs, remain important and are performed regularly on social occasions. Most other traditional arts are no longer practiced, but there is some continuation of basketmaking.

Cahuillas are intensely interested in preserving the memory of their traditional culture. Malki Museum was founded on the Morongo Reservation in 1964 by Cahuillas and others. The Museum presents an annual fiesta, maintains a Cahuilla archive, and exhibits Cahuilla cultural materials. The Malki Museum Press has published a series of outstanding books on southern California Indians and copublishes the *Journal of California and Great Basin Anthropology.*

The Agua Caliente Band is establishing the Agua Caliente Cultural Museum in Palm Springs.

Lowell John Bean
Sylvia Brakke Vane

See also **California Tribes**

Further Reading

Barrows, David Prescott. *Ethno-botany of the Coahuilla Indians of Southern California.* IL: University of Chicago Press, 1900; Banning, CA: Malki Museum Press, 1967.

Bean, Lowell John. *Mukat's People: The Cahuilla Indians of Southern California.* Berkeley: University of California Press, 1972.

Bean, Lowell John, and Lisa J. Bourgeault. *The Cahuilla.* New York, NY: Chelsea House Publishers, 1989.

Bean, Lowell John, and Katherine Siva Saubel. *Temalpakh: Cahuilla Indian Knowledge and Usage of Plants.* Banning, CA: Malki Museum Press, 1972.

Strong, William Duncan. "Aboriginal Society in Southern California." *University of California Publications in American Archaeology and Ethnology* 26:1 (1929): 36–182. Banning, CA: Malki Museum Press, 1987.

CALIFORNIA TRIBES

See Cahuilla; Chemehuevi; Chumash; Costanoan/Ohlone; Cupeño; Esselen; Gabrielino/Tongva; Hupa; Karuk; Kawaiisu; Kitanemuk; Kumeyaay; Luiseño; Maidu; Miwok: Coast; Miwok: Lake; Miwok: Sierra Mewuk; Mono: Western; Paiutes: Owens Valley; Pit River; Pomo; Salinan; Serrano; Shasta; Shoshone; Tolowo; Tubatulabal; Wailaki; Wappo; Wintun; Wiyot; Yokuts; Yuki; Yurok

See map on following page.

CAMP VERDE YAVAPAI-APACHE INDIAN COMMUNITY

See Yavapai

CATAWBA

The Catawba Nation of South Carolina is centered on a 650-acre reservation on the Catawba River in eastern York County, South Carolina. In 1900, the tribe had approximately 100 members in the community; today some 1,400 people are on the tribal roll, and 69 families reside on the reservation. The majority of those living away from the community live nearby in York County or Charlotte, North Carolina. Several families migrated to Colorado in 1883, and their descendants maintain contact with the nation even though they are not on the tribal roll.

The twentieth century has been dominated by legal issues resulting from the Treaty of Pine Tree Hill (1760), the Treaty of Augusta (1763), and the unratified Treaty of 1840. Under established federal law, Catawba lands were never legally transferred and the agreement was void. Thus, the tribe claims a present right of possession to its 144,000-acre colonial treaty reservation. After spending over half a century waiting

Native California

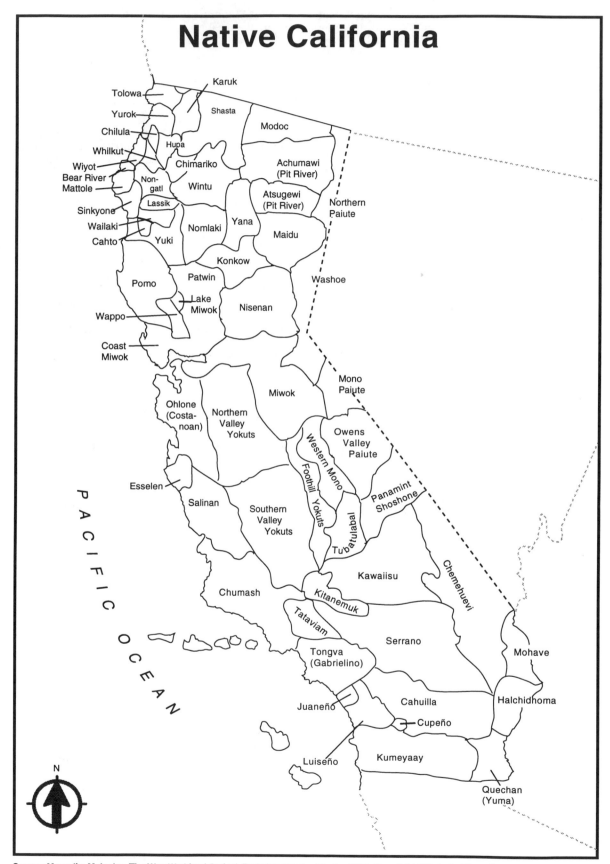

for South Carolina to honor the Treaty of 1840, the tribe first hired legal counsel in 1896 under the leadership of Chief Thomas Morrison. Although the Catawbas lacked funds to employ consistent legal assistance, efforts to obtain a resolution through the courts were pursued into the twentieth century. By the late 1930s, the Catawbas gained the attention of federal officials. In 1942, the tribe began a federal trust relationship, and in 1943 the tribe entered into a memorandum of understanding with the State of South Carolina and the federal government. The Catawbas were almost immediately swept into the termination program of the 1950s. In 1959, the Bureau of Indian Affairs and South Carolina officials succeeded in securing legislation that terminated the trust relationship begun only sixteen years earlier. As a result, federal services ended in 1962.

The Catawbas reorganized as a nonprofit corporation in 1973, and elected a new council and executive committee under the leadership of Chief Gilbert B. Blue, who continues to lead the tribe. The land issue was immediately revived, and the Native American Rights Fund agreed to pursue the Catawba land claim. After 13 years of negotiations with the State of South Carolina, a settlement bill was finally passed by the United States Congress and became effective on October 27, 1993. It includes the restoration of federal status and $50 million to be used to expand the reservation, sponsor educational and economic programs, and make per capita cash payments.

Notable Catawba twentieth-century leaders include Chiefs James and David Adam Harris, two brothers who guided the tribal government from 1897 to 1921 in several efforts to settle the land issue. Chief Robert Lee Harris (1939 to 1942) brought the nation under a formal federal trust relationship in 1942, and Chief Samuel T. Blue provided important spiritual guidance during his several terms as chief between 1930 and 1958.

The Catawbas are best known for their pottery, which is celebrated for its nearly pure aboriginal technology. Handed down within families from pre-Columbian times, its unique survival provides a clear historical connection between the late Mississippian period and the present. The Catawbas are the only eastern tribe to retain this unbroken and technically sound tradition. The Catawba potters are so conservative that they have adapted only one non-Indian technological influence, squeeze molds, in their very long period of contact with other cultures. There is evidence that the Catawba learned to make and use these molds for pipes and lugs for vessels from Moravian settlers in the middle of the eighteenth century. Molds currently in use can be dated from the 1880s to the present.

Since 1976, the Catawba Pottery Association has sponsored pottery making classes to compensate in part for a new lifestyle which makes it difficult for families to make pottery as they did in the past. At any given time, several potters are also involved in tutorials where a master potter instructs a less experienced craftsman in pottery making. Formal classes have also been held for the youth, and approximately forty children have direct knowledge of the rudiments of the tradition. A number of these youths actively sell their wares.

The Catawbas have made great economic strides in the twentieth century. This success was largely the result of the Catawba Indian School founded in 1896 and closed in 1962, a victim of the termination program. The education of the Catawbas was further strengthened by the Mormon Church. By the 1920s nearly all tribal members were of this faith, and it was not long before several young people attended college in Utah. Education was also strengthened as the men obtained work in the public sector. This trend began in the early part of the century, and was nearly completed by World War II. Its final boost was provided during the federal trust relationship from 1942 to 1962. Today work and the full range of educational opportunities are available to the Catawbas. The Catawbas have also benefited from Comprehensive Employment Training Act funds, the Job Training Partnership Act, and more recently the VISTA/ACTION Program.

The Tribal Council of eight members (chief, assistant chief, secretary/treasurer, and five council members) is active in its efforts to pursue several cultural goals. In 1990 the Cultural Preservation Program sponsored a Catawba Festival, the first since the late 1930s. There is an ongoing effort to revive the Catawba (Siouan) language. Today a number of Catawbas can boast a growing vocabulary even though the last fluent Catawban speaker died in 1959. Catawba history is being taught, and a video was produced through the assistance of the Charlotte/Mecklenburg School System in 1987. The Catawba Pottery Association also participates in the Schiele Museum's permanent Catawba Village Exhibit and the annual Indian festival (Schiele Museum of Natural History, Gastonia, North Carolina). Crafts other than pottery making are being pursued. These include the tanning of hides, beadwork, and blow-gun making. The cultural initiatives sponsored by the Council, with and without outside funding, are largely the work of E. Fred Sanders and Dr. Wenonah George Haire, both of the Cultural Preservation Program.

Thomas J. Blumer

See also Pottery

Further Reading

Blumer, Thomas J. *Bibliography of the Catawba.* Metuchen, NJ: Scarecrow Press, 1987.

Brown, Douglas S. *The Catawba Indians: People of the River.* Columbia: University of South Carolina Press, 1966.

Fewkes, Vladimir J. "Catawba Pottery-making, with Notes on Pamunkey Pottery-making, Cherokee Pottery-making, and Coiling." *Proceedings of the American Philosophical Society* 88 (1944): 69–124.

Merrell, James H. *The Indians' New World: Catawbas and Their Neighbors from European Contact through the*

Era of Removal. Chapel Hill: University of North Carolina Press, 1989.

CAYUGA

The Cayuga Tribe in New York has been without a reservation since the early nineteenth century. This situation followed from cessions to the state of its aboriginal territory, located in the Finger Lakes region, in 1789, 1795, and 1807. Today, the estimated population of this tribe is under 500. Cayugas reside on the three Seneca reservations, especially at Cattaraugus, and also on the Onondaga Reservation. While those at Cattaraugus are said to hold "life leases" on their land and homes, they remain subject to expulsion, a situation that continues to be a source of concern in Cayuga-Seneca relations. The remaining members of this tribe live elsewhere in the state, although they are concentrated primarily in western New York. Many Cayugas left the state in the years after the American Revolution and the sale of their lands. Some of their descendants eventually became founding members of the Seneca-Cayuga Tribe of Oklahoma in 1937. A large number moved into Canada, taking up residence on the Six Nations Reserve, where about 3,000 Cayugas currently live.

Despite the 200 years of its diaspora, the Cayuga Tribe has remained politically viable and culturally dynamic. Actions taken by its government in the early twentieth century are similar to those of the Seneca Nation and the Iroquois Confederacy. Nonetheless, the Cayuga chiefs remained independent, acting as effective representatives of their tribe in Confederacy councils. Accordingly political concerns of the tribe have included resistance to federal or state jurisdiction, the 1924 Indian Citizenship Act, and selective service. In the mid-1920s, the Cayugas in New York, along with those in Canada, were parties to a judgment by an international tribunal regarding the non-payment of treaty annuities by the state to the Canadian Cayugas. During the New Deal, and unlike most of the other Iroquois tribes, the landless Cayugas did not hold an official referendum on the Indian Reorganization Act.

Following the lead of the Oneidas of Wisconsin, the Oneidas of the Thames Band of Canada, and the New York Oneidas, the Cayugas brought a land claim against the state in the 1970s, maintaining that New York had violated the 1790 Nonintercourse Act in its treaty-making with the tribe. The Cayugas sought first to negotiate a settlement, and in 1980, one was reached; however, it failed to receive congressional approval. That same year, the tribe brought suit in federal district court for 64,000 acres of their aboriginal territory around Cayuga Lake. Both negotiations and litigation continued. A second settlement was announced in 1987, although this too foundered. In 1991, the federal district court issued a partial summary judgment against what was perhaps the state's last defense, although New York may seek additional legal options.

The Cayugas are governed by a council of hereditary chiefs chosen on the same basis as those of other traditional Iroquois tribes. Matrilineality determines tribal membership and clan affiliation. The tribe's seat of government is in Versailles, New York, and meetings of the Cayugas are generally held on an annual basis there and in the Buffalo area. Important contemporary leaders include Franklin Patterson, James Leaffe, Vernon Isaac, and Frank Bonamie.

A number of tribal members speak the Cayuga language; however, there are concerns regarding its preservation. Cayugas continue to participate in Longhouse ceremonies and are active in Confederacy issues. Those who choose take advantage of the health, education, and other tribal services and programs administered by the Seneca Nation.

As in other Iroquois communities, there is a high rate of unemployment. Nonetheless, Cayugas hold jobs in the trades, the service industry, construction, high-steel work, and small businesses. A number are in the teaching, health care, finance and marketing professions.

Much of the energy of the tribe's leadership and its people over the last fifteen or more years has been directed at litigating and negotiating a settlement of its land claim. Its successful resolution will provide a financial package and a land base, that is, a reservation, from which the tribe can exercise its jurisdiction and begin economic development, all toward the goal of tribal self-determination.

William A. Starna

See also **Iroquois Confederacy; Seneca**

Further Reading

Hauptman, Laurence M. *The Iroquois and the New Deal.* NY: Syracuse University Press, 1981.

———. *Iroquois Struggle for Survival.* NY: Syracuse University Press, 1986.

———. *Formulating American Indian Policy in New York State, 1970–1986.* Albany: State University of New York Press, 1988.

Vecsey, Christopher, and William A. Starna, eds. *Iroquois Land Claims.* NY: Syracuse University Press, 1988.

White, Marion E., William E. Engelbrecht, and Elisabeth Tooker. "Cayuga." *Handbook of North American Indians.* Vol. 15. *Northeast.* Ed. B.G. Trigger. Washington, DC: Smithsonian Institution (1978): 500–04.

CAYUSE

See Confederated Tribes of the Umatilla Indian Reservation

CHEHALIS

See Confederated Tribes of the Chehalis Reservation

CHEMEHUEVI

The Chemehuevi are the most southerly group of the Southern Paiutes and are very closely related to the Southern Paiutes of southern Nevada. They speak a Southern Numic language of the Uto-Aztecan family. They now not only occupy the Chemehuevi Indian

Reservation on the Colorado River, but are also represented on the Morongo Indian Reservation, the Cabazon Indian Reservation, Agua Caliente Indian Reservation, and the Colorado River Indian Tribes Reservation. In addition, many Chemehuevi live in the various cities of inland southern California.

At the turn of the century, the Chemehuevi occupied Cottonwood Island, Beaver Lake, the Needles region, and Chemehuevi Valley. A few were on the Colorado River Indian Tribes Reservation (CRIT). Some were at the Twentynine Palms Reservation, and some were in the Coachella Valley, where they intermarried with Cahuilla and Serrano. There was no organized Chemehuevi tribe at this time and, from the government's point of view, the Chemehuevi on the desert near the Colorado River were illegal occupants of government land. After the railroad reached Parker, Arizona in 1905, and irrigation was successfully introduced at CRIT, more Chemehuevi moved to CRIT. When Parker Dam was built about 1930, many Chemehuevis who had farmed in the inundated valleys were left homeless. Many Chemehuevi men had to leave home to seek wage labor elsewhere.

The Chemehuevi Business Committee, formed in 1951, was able to arrange for the Chemehuevi to join other Southern Paiute in the Indian Claims Commission Case. The Chemehuevi agreed, at a meeting in 1964 attended by all known Chemehuevi, to settle their claim with the government for $1 million. About 1,200 Chemehuevi applied for this money.

When the government awarded the Chemehuevi $82,000 from the Metropolitan Water District for the land taken from them by the dam, there were several factions who claimed it, none of them considered a legal claimant by the government. The award was not made until the formation of the Special Committee on Chemehuevi Affairs in the late 1960s. The Committee proceeded to write a constitution, approved in 1971, and to have the Chemehuevi Indian Reservation in Chemehuevi Valley set aside for the group. Three hundred and twelve Chemehuevi were enrolled there at that time and about 600 people at CRIT have some Chemehuevi blood. Georgia Laird Culp was prominent among those who worked to get land set aside for the Chemehuevi Indian Reservation. She later published the *Chemehuevi Newsletter*.

The Twentynine Palms Indian Reservation was largely Chemehuevi, but it is no longer occupied. About sixteen members of that band live in nearby areas, mostly in Palm Springs.

Lowell John Bean

Sylvia Brakke Vane

See also California Tribes

Further Reading

Kelly, Isabel T., and Catherine S. Fowler. "Southern Paiute." *Handbook of North American Indians*. Vol. 11. *Great Basin*. Ed. Warren L. d'Azevedo. Washington, DC: Smithsonian Institution (1986): 368–97.

Laird, Carobeth. *The Chemehuevis*. Morongo Indian Reservation, Banning, CA.: Malki Museum Press, 1976.

———. *Mirror and Pattern: George Laird's World of Chemehuevi Mythology*. Morongo Indian Reservation, Banning, CA.: Malki Museum Press, 1984.

Roth, George E. *Incorporation and Changes in Ethnic Structure: The Chemehuevi Indians*. Ph.D. diss., Northwestern University, 1976.

CHEROKEE

The Cherokees, originally a southeastern group, entered the twentieth century with reservations in North Carolina and Oklahoma (where most of the nation had been removed in 1838). In the 1940s a segment of the Oklahoma Cherokees formed its own political unit, the United Keetoowah Band. The Eastern Band of Cherokees (North Carolina) and the Cherokee Nation of Oklahoma are discussed in the first article in this section, while the United Keetoowah Band is the subject of the second. Other groups scattered across the United States who identify as Cherokee but are not currently federally recognized are not included in these discussions.

Today the Cherokees constitute the largest Indian tribe in the United States. In the 1990 census, 308,132 people identified themselves as Cherokees; only a fraction of these are federally recognized members of either the Eastern Band of Cherokee Indians in western North Carolina, or the Cherokee Nation of Oklahoma. The Eastern Band has approximately 9,800 members; enrollment in the band requires one-thirty-second degree of Cherokee blood through descent of an enrollee on the 1924 Baker roll. The Cherokee Nation of Oklahoma has more than 122,000 members; membership requires proof of descent from an ancestor on the 1906 Dawes commission roll and there is no blood quantum requirement. The United Keetoowah Band was organized among the western Cherokees in the 1930s as a political entity and has held federal recognition since 1946. In addition to the federally recognized groups, more than fifty other organizations in at least twelve states claim Cherokee descent.

During the early historic period the Cherokees spoke three principal dialects which corresponded roughly to the major geographical divisions of Cherokee settlements. Today, Cherokee is the seventh most populous Native language north of Mexico. Approximately 13,000 people in northeastern Oklahoma speak what was called the Overhill dialect, about 1,000 residing in western North Carolina speak the Middle (Kituhwa) dialect, and there are no remaining speakers of the Lower dialect.

Today Cherokee language is most frequently used publicly in religious services. Most Cherokees belong to one of several protestant denominations, with Southern Baptists having the largest number of members. In Oklahoma, several thousand people, commonly referred to as the Keetoowah Society or the Nighthawk Keetoowahs, adhere to the traditional religion, which is associated with several active stomp grounds.

At the time of European contact the Cherokees controlled parts of eight present states: the Carolinas, the Virginias, Kentucky, Tennessee, Georgia, and Alabama, a land mass of approximately 40,000 square miles. Through a succession of treaties between 1721 and 1819, the territory was reduced to the adjacent mountainous areas of North Carolina, Tennessee, Georgia, and Alabama. In December, 1835, the Treaty of New Echota ceded the last remaining territory east of the Mississippi. In exchange, the Cherokees received most of what is now northeastern Oklahoma.

The forced removal from their ancestral homelands, the infamous "Trail of Tears," in the winters of 1838 and 1839 adversely affected the Cherokees. Many died in camps awaiting transport for the 1,000 mile journey. Others fled to the mountains or abandoned the march in route to return to their original homes or to take up residence along the trail. Today, the Eastern Band of Cherokee Indians in North Carolina and the Cherokee Nation of Oklahoma are prosperous and vibrant communities with a deep appreciation for the past and great optimism about the future.

History of the Eastern Band of Cherokees

Members of the Eastern Band of Cherokees in North Carolina trace their ancestry to the more than 1,000 individuals who remained in the mountains after forced removal in 1838 to 1839. About 300 of these were living on non-tribal lands in 1838 and claimed United States citizenship. Others staying behind included residents of the North Carolina village of Cheoih, and refugees from such places as Turtle Town and Duck Town in Tennessee, Fighting Town in Georgia, and Shooting Creek and Hanging Dog Town in North Carolina.

For a number of years following the removal, the fate of the North Carolina Cherokees was uncertain. As late as the 1840s, the federal government was still sending agents to North Carolina in attempts to enroll Cherokees for removal. By 1848, however, the Congress of the United States recognized the rights of the North Carolina Cherokees on the condition that the state recognize their rights as permanent residents. In 1866, the state of North Carolina finally did so, and the federal government used money promised under the previous treaty to insure that the tribe would not be dispossessed.

In 1876 the first official survey of Cherokee lands was conducted and the Qualla Boundary was established. Although minor changes have taken place over the years, tribal lands today are essentially the same as defined by the Temple Survey of 1876. In 1880, 835 Cherokees lived on the Qualla Reserve; 189 in Graham; 83 in Cherokee County and 12 in Macon County. In the 1880s, many Cherokees living in the outlying areas were drawn to the Qualla Boundary by the newly established school and opportunities for community involvement.

In 1889 the Cherokees were incorporated under the laws of North Carolina and for the first time they were able to transact business as the Eastern Band of Cherokee Indians. The corporation then obtained title to tribal lands previously held by the Commissioner of Indian Affairs. By 1890, the timber industry began to develop in the mountains. The industry, which clear-cut the area and took advantage of its residents, also introduced an incipient cash economy to the reservation which lasted for several decades.

Eastern Band Cherokees in the Modern Era

In 1919 Cherokee veterans of World War I were made citizens of the United States. In 1924 the band, which had successfully resisted allotment, placed the deeds to tribal land in federal trust to ensure the land would always remain in Cherokee possession. Between 1924 and World War II, the Cherokees suffered more than other Americans from the effects of the Great Depression. However, the creation of the Great Smoky Mountains National Park in the 1930s provided considerable optimism about long-term prospects for the local economy. After the war, the scenic wilderness of the park began to draw thousands of visitors annually. In 1948, the Cherokee Historical Association was formed to preserve and perpetuate the culture and history of the Eastern Band of Cherokees. The outdoor drama, "Unto These Hills," made its debut in 1950. In 1952, the Oconaluftee Indian Village opened.

In the decades since World War II, the economy of the Cherokee community has changed from subsistence agriculture to multi-faceted wage earning. Today, tourism is the primary industry on the Qualla Boundary, providing jobs for about 65 percent of the local population. Over 180 businesses are located on the Qualla Boundary: more than two-thirds of these are owned and operated by tribal members, and the remainder are leased to non-Indians. The Qualla Boundary has developed into a prospering, vibrant community, and at the same time it has maintained its strong identity and proud heritage.

Eastern Band of Cherokee Lands

Lands presently held by the Eastern Band of Cherokee Indians include 56,572.8 acres in five counties of western North Carolina, and 76.3 acres in two counties in eastern Tennessee. In North Carolina, tribal holdings include fifty-two tracts or boundaries which are contained in thirty separate bodies of land. Most of the land is in Jackson and Swain counties. A small strip of land is in Haywood County and scattered residential tracts are in Graham and Cherokee counties. Possessory title to approximately 80 percent of tribal land is held by individuals who can transfer land only to other tribal members.

The lands in Tennessee have been returned to the tribe in recent years because of the tribe's historic connection to the properties. In July, 1976, the City of Kingsport returned 3.6 acres on the "Long Island of Holston" to the tribe because of its historic significance and sacred nature. In May, 1984, the Tennessee Valley Authority (TVA) granted permanent easement to the tribe for three tracts in the Little Tennessee Valley. The Sequoyah Birthplace Museum was built on the largest of these, a 47.5-acre tract on Fort Loudoun Island, created by the inundation of the Tellico Reservoir in 1979. The museum is now Tennessee's only Indian-owned historic attraction. Another 11.9 acres near the museum is designated for future development and a tract containing 13.3 acres at Chota is set aside for historic interpretation. This land includes the site of the Chota Townhouse, which served as the Cherokee capitol from 1753 to 1788.

Eastern Band of Cherokees' Tribal Government

Approximately 6,500 of the 9,845 members of the Eastern Band of Cherokees enrolled in 1990 live on tribal lands. The tribal government consists of executive, legislative, and judicial branches. The executive branch is comprised of the principal chief, vice-chief, and executive advisor. The former two are elected by popular vote every four years. The executive branch carries out the actions of the Tribal Council and keeps the tribal government functioning on a daily basis. The legislative branch is the Tribal Council, which is composed of two members from each of the six townships. They are elected to two-year terms and their votes are weighted on the basis of the population they represent. Although the authority of the council is basically legislative, it also has the responsibility for the management and control of tribal property and the resolution of land disputes. The judicial branch of the tribal government is charged with providing a court system for the Qualla Boundary.

The United States government as trustee of the tribal lands is represented on the Qualla Boundary by the Bureau of Indian Affairs (BIA), of the United States Department of Interior. The BIA operates the schools, maintains the roads, operates the extension programs, manages the timber resources, and generally oversees all matters relating to realty, including the records, surveys, leases, business, and possessory titles.

The major Cherokee health programs are managed by the United States Public Health Service. The present hospital facility opened in December, 1980. The Cherokee high school is also federally controlled. It was completed in 1975 and boasts numerous modern amenities. More than 70 percent of the graduating seniors go on to college.

History of the Cherokee Nation of Oklahoma

The forced removal of the Cherokees in 1838 and 1839 marked the beginning of a new era in Cherokee history. Today, it serves as a reminder of oppression but also of survival and determination. The resilient spirit borne during the removal characterizes the Cherokee Nation today.

Shortly after the majority of Cherokees arrived in the Indian Territory in 1839, they adopted a new constitution. They brought with them their concept of democratic government, their churches and schools, their newspapers and books, and their businesses. Tahlequah became the new capital and the center of business activity and Park Hill emerged as a cultural oasis in Indian Territory. The *Cherokee Advocate* and the *Cherokee Messenger*, both bilingual publications, became the first newspaper and periodical in the new territory. Soon, the Cherokees' educational system of 144 elementary schools and two higher education institutions, the Cherokee male and female seminaries, rivaled all others. The emphasis on education and the publication of religious and secular materials in the Cherokee syllabary, introduced by Sequoyah in 1821, gave the Cherokees a higher literacy level than their white neighbors.

The years between the removal and the 1860s were called their Golden Age, a period of prosperity that ended with the devastation of the American Civil War. After the war, more Cherokee land was taken to accommodate other tribes displaced by United States government policy. At the turn of the century, most of the remaining tribal land was parceled out to individual Cherokees eligible for allotments by enrolling for a census known as the Dawes Commission Rolls of 1906. The surviving original enrollees and their descendants make up today's tribal membership in the Cherokee Nation of Oklahoma.

The Cherokee Nation Today

The Cherokee Nation of today is a source of pride and identity for its more than 122,000 members. Many of the tribal members live in the original territory of the Cherokee Nation, which is located in fourteen counties of northeastern Oklahoma. The functions of the Cherokee Nation as the primary government of the area were dissolved with Oklahoma statehood in 1907. Today the land controlled by the tribe in the nineteenth century is not a reservation, but a jurisdictional service area.

The social and economic isolation experienced by the Oklahoma Cherokees after statehood was compounded by the Great Depression and dust bowl era of the 1930s. It is estimated that more than a third of the residents of eastern Oklahoma left the state during this time, including many Cherokees. The succession of principal chiefs in the sixty-five years following statehood were appointed by presidents of the United States. The chiefs during this period had little authority or responsibility, as there was no formalized Cherokee government.

Since the reorganization in the 1970s, the Cherokee Nation has become a leader in education, health care, housing, vocational training, and economic development in northeastern Oklahoma. The annual payroll currently exceeds $13 million for the 940 staff and business enterprise employees.

Assets of the Cherokee Nation includes 96 miles of the Arkansas Riverbed and more than 61,000 acres of tribal land. Over the past 15 years, the Cherokee Nation has posted dramatic and steady growth while increasing its asset base. The annual operating budget exceeds $66 million, with approximately half of the funds provided by federal programs and the remainder coming from tribally generated sources.

Tribal Government of the Cherokee Nation

In 1971, W.W. Keeler, who had served as principal chief by presidential appointment since 1949, became the first elected chief since statehood. In 1975 a new Cherokee Constitution delineating the distribution and separation of powers between three branches of government was adopted. Also in 1975, Ross Swimmer was elected to the first of three terms as principal chief. When he was appointed assistant secretary of the interior for Indian affairs in 1985, he was succeeded by the then Deputy Chief Wilma Mankiller. Mankiller, the first female chief of a major Indian tribe, along with Deputy Chief John Ketcher, decisively won the elections of 1987 and 1991.

In addition to other duties, the deputy chief presides over the fifteen-member Cherokee Nation Tribal Council. Like the principal and deputy chiefs, the Council is elected to four-year terms by a popular vote of registered adults, who are currently elected by districts. The judicial branch, a three-member Judicial Appeals Tribunal, is comprised of practicing attorneys who are tribal members. They are appointed by the principal chief to preside over jurisdictional matters related only to the Cherokee Nation.

Work of the Cherokee Nation tribal government is divided into three major areas—social programs, development and special services, and tribal operations. Among tribal business enterprises are Cherokee Nation industries, two arts and crafts outlets, a utility company, and ranching, poultry, and woodcutting operations. In November 1990 the Cherokee Nation opened its first gaming facility, called Bingo Outpost, at Roland, Oklahoma.

In addition to the decision to enter the bingo market, other recent initiatives of the Cherokee Nation tribal government include the approval of a tax code and the tribe's bid to enter the self-governance program. A Cherokee Nation tax code was approved in February, 1990, by the Tribal Council, which allows the tribe to tax businesses on tribal lands, including smoke shops. The Cherokee Nation applied for direct funding for tribal programs and services for fiscal year 1991 as part of its aggressive push for increased self-governance.

The agreement, approved by the United States Congress, authorizes the tribe to plan, conduct, consolidate, and administer programs and receive direct funding to deliver services to tribal members. Self-governance marks a shift from previous federal controls to full tribal responsibility for self-government and independence intended by the treaties with sovereign Indian nations.

The Eastern Band of Cherokees and the Cherokee Nation of Oklahoma

In 1984, the Eastern Band of Cherokee Indians and Cherokee Nation of Oklahoma met in a joint council session for the first time in nearly 150 years. The joint sessions are now regularly scheduled every two years and deal with issues which affect both groups. Both groups have celebrations in the fall; the Eastern Cherokee host a fall festival in October that features stick ball games, traditional dance demonstrations, and evening programs which include local mountain culture. The Cherokee Nation in Oklahoma celebrates the Cherokee National Holidays over Labor Day weekend, honoring the unification on September 6, 1839, of Oklahoma Cherokee groups after removal. Both groups take pride in their common history and have developed cultural attractions in North Carolina and Oklahoma which share the story of the Cherokees with the public. The re-created villages, museums, and outdoor dramas provide employment for Cherokee people, promote the continuation of traditional arts and crafts, strengthen tribal identity, and provide important educational services.

Traditional arts and crafts have survived to the present among both Cherokee groups. Basketry, pottery, woodcarving, and beadwork have all undergone some evolutionary changes in the twentieth century. Split cane and white oak basketmaking among the Eastern Band of Cherokee perhaps remains closest to ancestral forms. Today several hundred Cherokees on the Qualla Boundary and a smaller number in Oklahoma derive part of their livelihood through the production of traditional arts and crafts.

Duane H. King

See also **Oklahoma Tribes**

Further Reading

Finger, John R. *Cherokee Americans: The Eastern Band of Cherokee in the 20th Century.* Lincoln: University of Nebraska Press, 1991.

King, Duane H., ed. *The Cherokee Indian Nation: A Troubled History.* Knoxville: University of Tennessee Press, 1979.

Mooney, James. *Myths of the Cherokee and Sacred Formulas of the Cherokees.* Bureau of American Ethnology, 7th and 19th Annual Reports (1887, 1900). Nashville, TN: Charles and Randy Elder Booksellers, 1982.

Royce, Charles C. *The Cherokee Nation of Indians.* Bureau of American Ethnology, 5th Annual Report (1884). Chicago, IL: Smithsonian Institution Press, 1975.

Wardell, Morris. *A Political History of the Cherokee Nation: 1838–1907 (1938).* 2d ed. Norman: University of Oklahoma Press, 1977.

Woodward, Grace Steele. *The Cherokees.* Norman: University of Oklahoma Press, 1963.

UNITED KEETOOWAH BAND

The United Keetoowah Band of Cherokee Indians in Oklahoma (UKB) regard Keetoowah, an ancient principal town or seat of authority in western North Carolina prior to the removal of the Cherokee Nation to Indian Territory, as their source. Oklahoma and Arkansas Cherokee full-bloods united as Keetoowah Cherokees to retain traditions and oppose assimilation in the 1850s. There are at least three groups with "Keetoowah" in their name. Redbird Smith headed the religious Keetoowah Society, founded for like-minded traditional, predominantly full-blood Cherokees, under their own bylaws. The Nighthawk Keetoowah, sometimes called "Nighthawks," were formed as a conservative religious group, some of whose members were Keetoowah Cherokees. The Keetoowah Cherokees, some of whom belonged to the Keetoowah Society or the Nighthawks, eventually organized politically as the United Keetoowah Band.

During the Civil War the Keetoowah Cherokees held that deviations from Keetoowah values led Chief John Ross to tolerate slavery and to align the Cherokee Nation with the confederacy. Keetoowahs were pro-Union, Abolitionist, even "Republican."

While factions split Keetoowahs in the 1890s, all sought a Cherokee tribal identity distinct from the Cherokee Nation, which had adopted whites, Cherokee Freedmen, and others after 1839. Keetoowahs deplored the allotment of Cherokee tribal lands, abstaining from a general election of January 31, 1899, to vote on Dawes Commission terms. Congress dissolved the Cherokee Nation except for matters of administrative convenience in 1907. In 1905 the Keetoowah Society obtained its corporate Charter in United States District Court.

After 1930 most Keetoowah factions reconciled; but rancor separating the Keetoowah Society and Nighthawks from other factions increased during the reorganization of the UKB under the Oklahoma Indian Welfare Act (OIWA, 1936) and the Indian Reorganization Act (IRA, 1934). In 1937 Associate Interior-Solicitor Kirgis found the Keetoowah Society ineligible to reorganize under OIWA and IRA. Bureau of Indian Affairs field studies on the conditions and status of the Keetoowah Band in the 1940s led to the finding that Keetoowahs should be allowed to reorganize as a united, exclusively Cherokee tribal entity. In 1946, Acting Interior Secretary Abe Fortas repudiated the Kirgis Opinion and endorsed H.R. 79–341 (the Keetoowah Bill). That year the UKB had 3,687 enrolled members, 40 percent over 21 years of age, representing nearly half of Cherokees of half-degree Indian blood or more living in the geographical area of the old Cherokee Nation. Some 8,000 of the 12,000 enrollees on the 1906 Dawes Roll of Cherokee Nation remained in the area.

The Act of August 10, 1946, recognized Keetoowah Indians of the Cherokee Nation of Oklahoma (former reservation) as a Band of Indians under Section 3 of the OIWA, providing, "any recognized tribe or band of Indians residing in Oklahoma shall have the right to organize for its common welfare and to adopt a Constitution and by-laws." Keetoowah Indians organized apart from the Cherokee Nation under Section 16 of IRA, which provided that "any Indian tribe, or tribes, residing on the same reservation, shall have the right to organize for its common welfare." On May 9, 1950, Assistant Secretary William E. Warne approved submission of the Charter, Constitution and Bylaws for ratification by UKB members, adding, "All officers and employees of the Interior Department are ordered to abide by the provisions of the said Constitution and By-laws." On October 3, 1950, UKB voters ratified these documents.

The UKB determines membership, can acquire land in trust, and exercises other inherent sovereign powers through a Council composed of nine District Council members and four executive officers. Many UKB members are not Dawes enrollees or descendants, and therefore are ineligible for registration in the Cherokee Nation of Oklahoma by federal law.

The 1970 Bellmon Act allowed Cherokee Nation members to select officers. The Cherokee Nation of Oklahoma adopted a Constitution in 1978, and has attempted unsuccessfully to absorb the UKB. The UKB provides services to its 7,450 members, and conducts economic development efforts and cultural activities. Most UKB members remain in culturally identifiable settlements in the fourteen northeastern Oklahoma counties in the old Cherokee Reservation, resisting assimilation. The UKB is developing an exclusive roll, requiring one-quarter degree Cherokee Indian blood for future membership. Federal law bars UKB acquisition of a tribal land base within former Cherokee Reservation boundaries in Oklahoma, without permission of Cherokee Nation of Oklahoma (25 C.F.R. 151.8). The UKB seeks federal trust land for a reservation elsewhere.

Allogan Slagle

See also **Oklahoma Tribes**

Further Reading

Bruce, Louis. *American Indians and Their Federal Relationship, Plus a Partial Listing of Other United States Indian Groups.* Washington, DC: U.S. Department of the Interior, Bureau of Indian Affairs, 1972.

U.S. National Archives. Washington, DC Records of the BIA. Central Classified Files, Box 330, Accessions 57A-185. Records for 1948–1952. Cherokee Nation, 00–219 (010.-020.; 050.-059), Box # 12.

U.S. Congress. Senate Report 79, 2d Sess., No. 978. *See also,* U.S. Congress. House Report 79, 1st Sess., No. 444. And U.S. Congress. House Report 79, 2d Sess., No. 2705. These reports show legislative intent behind House Resolution 79–341, *P.L.* 79–715, 60 *Stat.* 976 (August 10, 1946), recognizing the UKB.

Wahrhaftig, Albert, and Jane Wahrhaftig. "New Militants or Resurrected State: The Five County Northeastern Oklahoma Cherokee Organization." *The Cherokee Nation: A Troubled History.* Ed. Duane H. King. Knoxville: University of Tennessee Press, 1979.

CHEROKEE-SHAWNEE

See Shawnee in Oklahoma

CHETCO

See Tolowa

CHEYENNE

The word Cheyenne is derived from the Lakota word *sha-hi'ye-la*, meaning "red talkers" or "people of an alien speech." The Cheyenne refer to themselves as *Tse-tsehese-staestse* or "People." Prior to the establishment of reservations, the Cheyenne occupied the Great Plains regions which extended from the Yellowstone River in Montana to the upper Arkansas River in present-day Colorado and Kansas. During the nineteenth century, Cheyenne territory was reduced drastically through a number of treaties with the United States government. On August 10, 1869, the Southern Cheyenne and Arapaho Reservation was established by executive order in Indian Territory. By 1891, the United States government decided to allot the Southern Cheyenne, eradicating their reservation. The Northern Cheyenne were placed on a reservation established by an 1884 executive order in southeastern Montana. Today many Northern Cheyenne choose to live on the reservation and many Southern Cheyenne still reside on their allotments scattered across western Oklahoma, although a substantial number of Cheyenne now reside in major urban centers.

History

Cheyenne oral tradition, in combination with early documentary sources and archaeology, confirm that the protohistoric Cheyenne occupied the woodland-prairie country of the upper Mississippi Valley region. Eventually, various Cheyenne bands migrated onto the northeastern Plains. Between 1742 and 1790, the Cheyenne acquired horses, abandoned their sedentary existence, and stabilized their geographical and political position in the Black Hills region by allying with the Arapaho and Sioux. As early as 1790, the Cheyenne began to separate into northern and southern divisions. Attracted by horses and the trade at Taos, several Cheyenne bands migrated south.

The Cheyenne signed the Treaty of 1851 in which they retained the lands between the North Platte and Arkansas Rivers. The treaty also made the division between the Northern and Southern Cheyenne permanent. The Northern and Southern Cheyenne land base stipulated in the treaty was reduced drastically by the Fort Laramie Treaty of 1868, and the 1867 Treaty of Medicine Lodge. The continued invasion of Euroamericans and the construction of forts to protect them, prompted the Cheyenne to fight. After a series of defeats, including the massacres at Sand Creek, the Washita, and the burning of several Northern Cheyenne villages, the Southern Cheyenne surrendered in 1875; Northern Cheyenne resistance ended in 1879. The Southern Cheyenne settled on their reservation in Indian Territory in 1869. The United States government attempted to consolidate the Northern and Southern Cheyenne by forcibly removing the Northern Cheyenne to the Southern Cheyenne-Arapaho Agency. Culturally alienated and faced with starvation, 257 Northern Cheyenne broke out and avoided capture until crossing the North Platte River.

After heroic attempts to preserve their freedom in which many were killed, much of those remaining were relocated to the Pine Ridge Agency in 1881. At the urging of the military, the Tongue River Reservation was established in 1884 by executive order in southeastern Montana. Fourteen years later, it was expanded to its present size.

The Southern Cheyenne-Arapaho Reservation was dissolved through allotment beginning in 1891. After 3,294 enrolled Southern Cheyenne and Arapaho were allotted 529,582 acres of land, the remaining 3,500,582 acres were opened to Euroamerican settlement. By 1901 to 1902, the Southern Cheyenne-Arapaho Reservation ceased to exist.

The Northern Cheyenne Allotment Act was signed in 1926, but the actual allotment process did not take place until 1932. Their land, however, was never opened to non-Indian homesteading, retaining the integrity of the reservation. Although the Northern Cheyenne reservation was not over-run by Euroamericans, allotment has fragmented the land base. Presently, both tribes continue to struggle to establish their legal and cultural rights that have been lost over the centuries.

Tribal Government

Traditionally, the Cheyenne have maintained the Council of Forty-Four. The Council of Forty-Four consists of forty headsmen, four selected from each of the ten Cheyenne bands. The additional four councilmen, held over from the previous Council, were known as the Old Man Chiefs, and were often the religious authorities of the tribe. To carry out their decisions, the Council relied upon the six military societies whose most prominent functions were the protection of the tribe from external threats and maintaining internal discipline. Currently, Southern and Northern Cheyenne chiefs, religious leaders, and military society members operate as the traditional tribal governmental authority. Their decisions and policies often conflict with the divisions of the officially recognized tribal governments.

In 1911 the Northern Cheyenne were organized into a fifteen-member Business Council. This Council was often under the direct control of the Northern Cheyenne superintendent, who used it to legitimize government policies and economic decisions on the reservation. The Northern Cheyenne Tribe of Montana was organized under the 1934 Indian Reorganization Act. They adopted a Constitution in 1935 and their Charter was ratified in 1936. The Constitution was amended in 1960. The tribe is governed by a Tribal Council of elected members, representing the five reservation districts. A president is elected every four years by popular vote, whereas the vice-president and sergeant-at-arms are elected by the Tribal Council. The positions of secretary and treasurer are political appointments usually made by the president. The Southern Cheyenne-Arapaho Tribes of Oklahoma, formed in 1937, are governed by a Business Council of twenty-eight members, fourteen of which are Southern Cheyenne. A tribal president and the Cheyenne-Arapaho Business Committee are elected on a regular basis.

Economic Development and Conditions

The placement of the Cheyenne on reservations during the late nineteenth century radically altered their sexual division of labor. Rations, marginal gardening, and wage labor became the mainstay of Cheyenne economy on both reservations. Cheyenne men were forced to take up agriculture and enter into an irregular, marginal wage economy; women's work was increasingly confined to the household. Today's women and men are employed in a wide range of professions.

Major employers on the Northern Cheyenne Reservation in the 1990s include the tribal and federal governments, Montana Power Company, Betchel Power Company, Western Energy Company, Morning Star Construction, Marin Financial Corporation, and the Branch of Forestry of the Bureau of Indian Affairs, which hires seasonally to fight forest fires. In the early 1980s, unemployment was 27 percent; by 1988, the unemployment rate stood at 53 percent. Throughout the 1980s and into the 1990s, employment has ranged between 48 and 89 percent annually. Northern Cheyenne tribal income is generated from grazing fees, farm and pasture leases, and timber and stumpage fees. The 1988 fiscal year funding had $4,612,382 for operation of programs and $232,086 for construction funding. Of those available funds, $2,465,008 were contracted to the tribe. The funds are administered by the Northern Cheyenne Tribal Council. Although the Northern Cheyenne Reservation has an estimated 23 billion tons of coal, since the early 1970s the tribe has opposed development of this resource, feeling that such development would threaten Northern Cheyenne cultural values.

The Southern Cheyenne are involved in wheat raising, oil exploitation, some ranching, and governmental work projects. Most recently, the Cheyenne-Arapaho Business Committee began an on-site monitoring program of all agricultural, oil, and gas leases. Despite these gains, a recent economic survey revealed that the Southern Cheyenne median annual income from all sources was approximately $3,000. Unemployment is very high. Both tribes continue to be underemployed and dependent on governmental support.

Education

Cheyenne elders and tribal leaders have encouraged their children to succeed through education. Northern Cheyenne students are served by six elementary schools, including St. Labre Indian School. All of the reservation-operated schools include Northern Cheyenne language and culture classes as part of the curriculum. High schools are located in Colstrip, Hardin, and St. Labre in Ashland. Drop-out rates, substance abuse, violence, and teenage pregnancy remain high among Northern Cheyenne youth. In order to achieve academic excellence and maintain

the Cheyenne way of life, Dull Knife Memorial College was chartered in September of 1976. The college offers an array of academic and vocational degree tracts, a library, dormitories, food services, basic health care, placement services, and an adult education program for its students. Most Southern Cheyenne children attend public schools throughout western Oklahoma, but the tribe did operate a school for some children at Concho Agency.

Priorities in the 1990s

The overriding concern for both tribes is continued economic development and providing services for their people. The Cheyenne-Arapaho Business Committee formally began a process for the ultimate recovery of the area known as the Fort Reno Military Reserve. The Northern Cheyenne have continued to be involved in the recovery of the Bear Butte and in the economic development of coal resources surrounding the reservation. Currently, some Southern and Northern Cheyenne are working together on a legal case, seeking compensation for their losses at the Sand Creek massacre. The greatest contemporary battle the Cheyenne face is their cultural survival.

Population

The Cheyenne people were never a very large nation. At contact, population estimates (circa 1780) indicate that there were approximately 3,500 Cheyenne. The 1888 Cheyenne reservation population was 3,497. Of that number, 2,096 were Southern Cheyenne living in Indian Territory (now Oklahoma), and 1,401 were Northern Cheyenne residing on the Tongue River Reservation in Montana and the Pine Ridge Reservation in South Dakota. As of 1990, the estimated total Cheyenne population was 10,838. The Northern Cheyenne population was 6,069. An exact Southern Cheyenne population figure is more difficult to attain as they are jointly enumerated with the Southern Arapaho. Currently, 9,525 Southern Cheyenne and Arapaho are enrolled at Concho Agency, Oklahoma. Of that number, at least 50 percent, or 4,762, identify themselves as Southern Cheyenne. Both populations continue to grow faster than the surrounding non-Indian population.

Figure 1
CHEYENNE POPULATION

Date	Southern Cheyenne	Northern Cheyenne
1880	3,769[1]	1,725[2]
1890	2,272	1,382
1910	1,522	1,395
1930	1,287	1,408
1970	4,515	2,357
1990	4,762	6,067

1. This figure includes some Northern Cheyenne.
2. This is an estimated figure based on historical evidence and reports from four Indian agencies where the Northern Cheyenne temporarily resided.

Health Issues

Traditional Cheyenne beliefs regarding ill-health have revolved around both natural and supernatural causes. Treatment of sickness, therefore, was designed not only to restore the patient biologically, but spiritually as well. Although Western medicine has been provided since the late nineteenth century, many Cheyenne still use traditional curing practices in combination with mainstream clinical medicine to combat ill-health.

Culture

Communities. After being placed on their reservations, the Cheyenne eventually formed communities near the government buildings or Euroamerican towns. Tipis gradually were replaced with wooden structures on both reservations at the insistence of the Bureau of Indian Affairs. In western Oklahoma, many Southern Cheyenne people congregated on allotted lands near such towns as Clinton and Canton. Although increasing numbers of Southern Cheyenne have moved to the suburban areas of El Reno, Yukon, and western Oklahoma, most reside in the 830 single-family dwellings provided by the Bureau of Indian Affairs or their own private homes near rural towns. Among the Southern Cheyenne, Concho is the administrative center, but is not a tribal community. On the Northern Cheyenne Reservation, most people reside in Lame Deer, Busby, Ashland, Birney, or along Muddy and Rosebud Creeks. Lame Deer is the seat of tribal government, the major economic center, and most populated reservation community. Most Cheyenne today live in government housing, mobile homes, or older remodeled reservation structures. Of the 939 homes on the Northern Cheyenne Reservation, many are substandard, having no running water, indoor plumbing, heat, or electricity, although continual improvements have been made since the 1960s.

Language. The Cheyenne language is one of five main Algonquian languages spoken on the Great Plains. During the pre-reservation period, there were at least two major dialects. Although Cheyenne is still used in daily intercourse, many younger Cheyenne cannot speak the Native language. To halt the loss of their language, both the Southern and Northern Cheyenne have instituted Cheyenne language and culture courses into the reservation educational curricula.

Religion and Ceremonial Life. Despite over one hundred years of religious persecution and conversion, many Cheyenne have managed to continue to practice their religion. According to contemporary Cheyenne religious leaders, the traditional Cheyenne worldview is a dynamic, operative system with interrelated components. Within the Cheyenne universe, the world is divided into seven major levels with various spirit-beings residing at each level. Their sacredness is relative to their relationship to *Ma?heo?o*, the creator of all physical and spiritual life. In Cheyenne religious expression, aspects of these spirit-beings or the spirit-beings themselves are entwined with plant and animal forms that symbolically represent the Cheyenne universe. Each year, Cheyenne religious leaders conduct ceremonies such as the renewal of the Sacred Arrows (*Mahuts*), the performance of *Hoxehe-vohomo?ehestotse* (New Life Lodge or Sun Dance), and some ceremonialism surrounding the Sacred Buffalo Hat (*Isiwun*) to renew the universe and our relationship to it. Many traditional Cheyenne today view the ecological destruction of the world as an end of the universe because of improper religious maintenance.

Since the early reservation period, many Cheyenne have become Christians or members the Native American Church. There has been Christian missionary activity among the Cheyenne for a century, especially the Mennonites, Catholics, and Southern Baptists. More recently, Pentecostalism has made significant inroads among the Northern Cheyenne. The religious fabric of contemporary Cheyenne religious life is complex. There are a variety of religious beliefs and expression, even among members of the same families.

Despite such religious complexity, *Mahuts* and *Isiwun* remain the most venerated Cheyenne sacred objects. At present, *Isiwun* is kept among the Northern Cheyenne in Montana. *Mahuts*, on the other hand, is kept by the Arrow Keeper, usually among the Southern Cheyenne of Oklahoma.

Cooperative Groups. A number of cooperative sodalities for men and women still exist. The Cheyenne military societies, both Northern and Southern, are a powerful social and political force on the reservation. They, along with Cheyenne religious leaders and chiefs, are often involved in current issues which threaten the tribe's cultural well-being. Among the women, the Quillwork Society and the War Mothers Association are quite important. The Quillwork Society is composed of women who have the greatest skill in their craft. They have sacred rights to certain quill and beadwork designs, usually used on culturally important items. The War Mothers Association was organized to honor Cheyenne veterans who are held in high esteem for the bravery and service to the United States.

Arts. Contemporary Cheyenne traditional arts include leatherworking, woodworking, quillworking, featherworking, and pipe carving. Many Cheyenne continue to make clothing, tipi covers, and dance costumes for ceremonial use, and to sell to non-Native American consumers. Presently, there are a number of prominent Cheyenne artists, including Richard West and Edgar Heap-of-Birds.

Gregory R. Campbell

See also Oklahoma Tribes

Further Reading

Ashbranner, Brent. *Morning Star, Black Sun.* New York, NY: Dodd, Mead, and Company, 1982.

Berthrong, Donald. *The Southern Cheyennes.* Norman: University of Oklahoma Press, 1972.

———. *The Cheyenne and Arapaho Ordeal.* Norman: University of Oklahoma Press, 1976.

Grinnell, George. *The Cheyenne Indians.* 2 vols. Lincoln: University of Nebraska Press, 1972.

Moore, John. *The Cheyenne Nation.* Lincoln: University of Nebraska Press, 1987.

Parlow, Anita. *A Song From Sacred Mountain.* Lakota Nation: Oglala Legal Rights Fund, 1983.

CHICANOS AS INDIANS

Chicanos are United States citizens of Mexican descent, and they are mestizos (mixed blood Spanish and "Indian"). While the exact degree of indigenous blood may vary from individual to individual, the fact that a person refers to herself or himself as Chicana or Chicano, carries with it at least a partial understanding and validation of a heritage that is indigenous to the nation of Mexico. The term Chicano is a derivative of Meshica, the tribe from which Mexico gets its name: Meshica, Meshicano, Chicano. It is the only label to describe United States citizens of Mexican descent that is not externally imposed, as are the terms Mexican American, Spanish-speaking, Latin American, and now Hispanic. Before the 1960s, Chicano was popularly known in the Mexican community of the United States as a term signifying an embedded class distinction; Chicano meant those who were at the bottom of the socio-economic scale. When the Chicano movement emerged in the 1960s, the term was employed in much the same way the "Black is beautiful" campaign worked for African-Americans. To call oneself Chicano or Chicana implied resistance to externally imposed notions of inferiority that were race or class-based. The term assumed a celebration of the predominantly working-class backgrounds of most Chicanos, and because of the origin of the word, implied a cultural pride in indigenous heritage, in particular the Aztec tradition, which had itself figured so prominently in twentieth-century Mexican revolutionary art. Greatly influenced by the pre-Columbian and Conquest periods of Mexican history, and by the way in which Mexican revolutionary intellectuals had employed Aztec images to represent resistance to foreign domination, the cultural artistic arm of the Chicano movement found inspiration (thanks also to the wealth of scholarship on both the Aztec and Maya traditions) in its recovery of Aztec (and Mayan) history and philosophy, such as the myth of Aztlan. The migration story of the Chichimecas, the Meshica-Tenochca, that is, the Aztecs, from their "homeland of Aztlan," thought by many to be the Southwest United States, down into Mexico to Tenochtitlan (today's Mexico City), has formed the basis for many Chicanos' claim to indigenous heritage. Chicano/a artists, writers, educators, cultural workers, and community organizers have employed this idea of "Aztlan" as one of the major elements in the Chicano conceptualization of community. Scholarly journals, community centers, literature festivals, and student organizations, to name a few, embraced Nahuatl terminology and Aztec philosophical concepts into their names and into their social, cultural, and political agendas.

Those Chicanos/as who have used Aztec traditions in their formulation of a distinctly Chicano/a aesthetic and worldview have been sharply criticized by some colleagues for romanticizing an indigenous past. Several Chicano/a scholars have sought to "demystify Aztlan"; a small number of Chicano/a scholars have insisted that the next logical step is oral history and archival work, the constructing of genealogies to determine the actual indigenous heritage of each member of the community, not as a nostalgic exercise, but as an affirmation of identity as Native peoples of this hemisphere.

Inés Hernández

Further Reading

Anaya, Rudolfo A., and Francisco Lomelí, eds. *Aztlan: Essays on the Chicano Homeland.* Albuquerque, NM: Academia/El Norte Publications, 1989.

Forbes, Jack D. *Aztecas del Norte: The Chicanos of Aztlan.* Greenwich, CT: Fawcett Publications, Premier Books, 1973.

Leon-Portilla, Miguel. *Aztec Thought and Culture: A Study of the Ancient Nahuatl Mind.* Trans. Jack Emory Davis. Norman: University of Oklahoma Press, 1963.

CHICKAHOMINY

The Chickahominy (or Western Chickahominy) are a state-recognized enclave (since 1983), most of whose members live south and west of Providence Forge in Charles City County, Virginia. The tribe's total enrollment is about 350, with another 200 eligible.

The Chickahominies founded their own Baptist church in the 1880s; today it is a very active congregation with its own gospel group. The tribe formally organized in 1907, then set up a school, first supported by themselves and after 1922 in part by the county. Some high school courses were added in the early 1950s. Several young people managed to finish high school and then junior college at Bacone College, Oklahoma, then returned and joined the teaching staff. The tribal school was lost in integration in 1967.

The Board of Directors (the Tribal Council) consists of a chief, assistant chief, and nine-person Council. These officers are chosen for three-tiered staggered terms by an electorate of enrolled, Chickahominy-descended adults who are sixteen or over. There are six Tribal Council meetings per year and one general meeting, all closed to non-Chickahominies. The tribe built and with their own money soon paid for a large tribal center in 1976 to 1978.

Traditional culture remains only in a few crafts (pottery, beadwork, basketry) and in the dance group which performs both pan-Indian and early twentieth-century eastern Indian programmatic dances at Indian and non-Indian festivals throughout the region. The tribe has put on a festival in late September/early October since 1951. Otherwise, the people's language and culture are those of their Anglo neighbors and have been so since before 1800.

Helen C. Rountree

Further Reading

Puglisi, Michael J. "Controversy and Revival: The Chickahominy Indians Since 1850." *Charles City County, Virginia: An Official History.* Eds. James P. Whittenburg and John M. Coski. Salem, WV: D. Mills Genealogical Publishing (1989): 97–104.

Rountree, Helen C. "The Indians of Virginia: A Third Race in a Biracial State." *Southeastern Indians Since the Removal Era.* Ed. Walter L. Williams. Athens: University of Georgia Press (1979): 27–48.

———. "Ethnicity Among the 'Citizen' Indians of Virginia, 1800–1930." *Strategies For Survival: American Indians in the Eastern United States.* Ed. Frank W. Porter. New York: Greenwood Press (1986): 173–209.

———. *Pocahontas's People: The Powhatan Indians of Virginia Through Four Centuries.* Norman: University of Oklahoma Press, 1990.

Speck, Frank G. *Chapters on the Ethnology of the Powhatan Tribes of Virginia.* Indian Notes and Monographs 1(5). New York, NY: Museum of the American Indian, Heye Foundation, 1928.

CHICKASAW

Following their 1832 removal from their western Tennessee and northern Mississippi domain, the Chickasaw eventually established a new homeland in what is now southern Oklahoma. The Chickasaw are a Muskogean-speaking people, with a language that is distinct from that of the Choctaw. Because of similarities in culture and language, however, the Chickasaw and their neighbors, the Choctaw, are often referred to as one group.

History

For the Chickasaw, as for many Indians, the ravages of allotment before 1900 has dominated the present century. The 1897 Atoka Agreement, incorporated into the Curtis Act (30 Stat. 495), launched Chickasaw and Choctaw allotment and was the first major success of the Dawes Commission to the Five Civilized Tribes heralding the official end of tribal existence. A supplemental agreement in 1902 (32 Stat. 641) made allotment a reality for 10,944 citizens entitled to them, which included 6,337 Chickasaws by blood and 4,607 freedmen. Congress successively enacted a series of measures spanning over a decade terminating tribal existence, culminating in statehood, and feeding rampant exploitation and unrivaled rapaciousness as Chickasaw land and resources rapidly passed out of Indian control. One estimate noted that by 1920 as much as 75 percent of Chickasaw landholdings, totalling 4,707,904 acres before allotment, had passed out of Indian hands into those of waiting whites, either by sale or lease, leaving only 300 acres

in tribal control. Lack of a land base thwarted tribal development through the remainder of the century, and for nearly seventy years the Chickasaw tribe struggled under the domination of federal bureaucratic imperialism.

The Chickasaw accepted white intermarriage; even before removal the tribe counted among its ranks illustrious mixed-blood families noted for their economic success, among whom are the Colbert, Adair, Love, Cheadle, and Jennings families who continue to be prominent. Intermarried whitemen William H. Murray and Lee Cruce helped shape the Oklahoma Constitution in 1906, and state politics after statehood in 1907. The federal government had rejected a last ditch attempt under the direction of Murray to achieve a separate Indian state in 1905. Cruce went on to serve as the second governor of Oklahoma, while Murray held that office from 1931 to 1935. Other state leaders proudly pointed to their Chickasaw heritage, including Oklahoma's fourteenth governor Johnston Murray and Oklahoma Supreme Court Justice Earl Welch.

Educator Douglas H. Johnston served as the last elected Chickasaw governor at the time of allotment and during the interregnum (with the exception of 1902 to 1904, when Palmer S. Moseley was governor), and he continued in that appointive role until his death in 1939. During the post-allotment period, Johnston kept the tribe together, held off through the courts nearly 4,000 white claimants to membership, averted state attempts to tax restricted lands in 1912 and 1928, and led the tribal effort to settle claims against the federal government. Although the tribe ignored the Oklahoma Indian Welfare Act during the New Deal era, some Indians did form county credit associations. In 1939, Floyd Maytubby became governor, serving to 1963, during which term he successfully concluded the sale of coal and asphalt lands, yielding per capita payments to tribal members. He also established the Chickasaw Advisory Council, forerunner of the Tribal Council. Educator and salesman Overton James became the appointive governor in 1963. Not until 1970 did Congress grant the Chickasaw the right to elect their own leadership. James's twenty-four-year administration dominated the modern rebirth of the Chickasaw Nation, seeing programs burgeon under federal and state grants, as well as Indian enterprises. The tribal budget rose from a paltry $50,000 when James's administration began, to over $10 million by 1987. In 1991 Governor Bill Anoatubby, formerly the lieutenant governor under James, foresaw even further strides toward self-sufficiency for the Chickasaw with expanded business enterprises such as theme and recreational parks, tobacco sales, bingo, and manufacturing and industrial projects. Anticipated revenue from the long-standing court battle over control of the resources underneath the Arkansas Riverbed, with the Choctaw and Cherokee nations, will add to the tribal financial base when successfully concluded. Chickasaw Nation voters approved a 1983 Constitution that provides for a governor, lieutenant governor, a three-judge judiciary, and a thirteen-member legislature.

Current Situation

Currently, there are 26,000 Chickasaw individuals scattered throughout the United States, with many more intermixed into the population. Some 9,020 Chickasaw are concentrated in a thirteen-county area of southern Oklahoma. A strong governmental infrastructure, expanding tribal business enterprises, and diverse educational, vocational, and social services mark the Chickasaw Nation. The tribe is reviving community councils for local tribal contacts. Its Ada headquarters complex in 1990 had a $15 million annual budget with nearly 300 employees handling a wide range of programs and projects.

The nation continued its path toward self-sufficiency in the 1980s when it contracted with the state and the Bureau of Indian Affairs (BIA) for Johnson-O'Malley and higher education programs. Statistics demonstrate that developmentally, Chickasaw children remain one to two years behind white students when the former enter kindergarten. An estimated 20 percent of the nation's families live below the poverty line. Early in 1990, BIA offices moved from Ardmore to the Ada tribal complex, making more efficient governmental interaction.

Culture

Although most Chickasaw Indians are Methodist or Baptist, part of the revival of interest in heritage during the 1970s included interest in the stomp dance, largely centered in the Ardmore-Mannsville region. Today, family reunions link generations with their heritage through the swapping of stories and socializing, as well as hymn singing in Chickasaw and English, and eating quantities of traditional foods like the national dish *pashofa* (cracked corn and pork), *tuchie shafut puska* (gritted corn), and *tosher* (poke greens). An estimated 550 people, mostly the elderly, speak the language today, and there is a renascent effort to teach the language. Contemporary individuals of Chickasaw heritage include storytellers Te Ata and Ataloa, poet and novelist Linda Hogan, noted artists Bert Seabourn, Mike Larsen, and Richard Anderson, as well as many others, like actor Dale Robertson and physician James W. Hampton, former president of the Association of American Indian Physicians.

Blue Clark

See also Allotment; Choctaw; Oklahoma Tribes

Further Reading

Baird, W. David. *The Chickasaw People*. Phoenix, AZ: Indian Tribal Series, 1974.

Gibson, Arrell Morgan. *The Chickasaws*. Norman: University of Oklahoma Press, 1971.

Hale, Duane K., and Arrell M. Gibson. *The Chickasaw*. New York, NY: Chelsea House, 1991.

Hoyt, Anne Kelley. *Bibliography of the Chickasaw*. Metuchen, NJ: Scarecrow Press, 1987.

Wright, Muriel. *A Guide to the Indian Tribes of Oklahoma*. Norman: University of Oklahoma Press, 1951. Reprinted 1986.

CHILD WELFARE

Historically Indian children were raised in strong extended family groups wherein adult relatives and older siblings had well-defined roles in providing instruction and nurturance. The types of roles the relatives played, from disciplinarian to teacher to advisor, varied from tribe to tribe depending on customs that were passed down for generations. For many tribes today, these extended family systems continue to be a dominant factor in Indian family organization.

It is important to note, however, that there are no typical Indian child-rearing practices, and that each tribe has its own unique tribal traditions. Some tribes, but not all, have formal ceremonies at certain points in a child's lifetime, puberty for example, at which time the various kinship roles are identified. Examples of these are the Apache and Hopi tribes in Arizona. In some tribes these traditions are still practiced while in others they are not.

Formalized child welfare services for Indian children had their antecedents in boarding school placement programs and other educational approaches to assimilate Indians into the dominant non-Indian culture of the immigrant European United States. In the early 1800s, Congress had established a "Civilization fund" for religious schools to be established to resolve the "Indian problem." These were generally small boarding schools located on reservations. Over 200 religious schools had been established by 1887 and 14,000 Indian children were enrolled.

During the late 1800s and early 1900s the federal government's policy of assimilation of the Indians had major impacts on Indian family life. The reservation system had been established and a dominant policy during this time, the Dawes Severalty Act, was a significant attempt to change Indian lifestyles by giving Indians individual ownership of lands for the purpose of agricultural pursuits as opposed to collective use of the land. It was also during this period that the federal policy toward the education of Indians shifted from support for religious schools to a federal system of schooling. Some twenty-five off-reservation federal boarding schools were established from Oregon to Pennsylvania to provide education and training to Indian children. The Indian agents who were assigned to supervise the day-to-day operations of federal programs on the reservations traveled from home to home, gathering up children as young as five to be taken from their families for long periods of educational placement. It was the belief that the only way to "civilize" the Indian population was to educate the children in settings of strict military-like discipline where the youngsters were not permitted to speak their native languages, and were trained in agricultural or industrial skills. For the non-Indian public, the boarding schools became a source of cheap labor because of their "outing" programs, which placed young people in a variety of agricultural, industrial, and domestic settings.

Federal day schools and a few boarding schools were also being established on the reservations during the early part of the twentieth century. The off-reservation boarding schools like Carlisle Indian Industrial School, Chemawa Indian School in Oregon, and Phoenix Indian School in Arizona could not accommodate the numbers of Indian children and it was costly to remove children to such great distances from their homes.

In the 1990s approximately 90 percent of the Indian student population attend public schools. Public schools were first established on reservations during the early 1900s in response to the Dawes Severalty Act when, as mentioned earlier, reservation lands were allotted and leased or sold to non-Indians whose children were in need of schools.

The destructive impact of the boarding school programs was first documented in the 1928 Meriam Report citing the effects of such schools on Indian children and their family life. The Meriam Report also cited the lack of a unified social service program for Indian families. By 1931, when the curtailment of boarding schools had begun, the first school social workers were assigned to the Bureau of Indian Affairs (BIA) Division of Education to assist children in their adjustment to returning to their own homes, and to determine which remaining children would attend the boarding schools.

The scope of the work of BIA school social workers was expanded in 1936 to include child welfare services for boarding school students. When the BIA Division of Welfare was formed in 1941, the social workers were transferred from Education to the new division, which assumed responsibility for all Indian social services, including child welfare services such as foster care.

During the 1950s, the federal government implemented another federal policy to attempt to assimilate Indian families, the BIA Relocation Program. This program, which was to assist families in locating off-reservation employment in urban settings, resulted in culture shock, loss of extended family support systems, and poverty for many Indian families. Because of their impoverishment, some families came to the attention of public and private welfare workers who had little knowledge of Indian family systems. Indian parents often did not understand their rights for maintaining custody of their children. Consequently, Indian children were placed in non-Indian foster homes, ostensibly to improve their economic circumstances.

In 1958 the Bureau of Indian Affairs and Child Welfare League of America established a project to promote the adoption of Indian children and approximately 400 children were placed in non-Indian homes between 1958 and 1967. Another 696 Indian children were placed in non-Indian adoptive homes through other public and private agencies during this time. The concepts of formal, legalized adoption and ter-

mination of parental rights is foreign to many Indian tribes. Children in need of care were traditionally tended by their extended families, and the word "adoption" does not translate into a number of Indian languages.

During the 1970s Congress took a new approach to its dealings with Indian tribes. Public Law 93–638, the Indian Self-Determination and Education Assistance Act of 1975, provided a major shift in delivery of social services, including child welfare. Indian tribes were now allowed to contract to provide social services to serve their tribal members. Tribes that control their social service departments are in the best position to determine the social and economic needs of their community because of their direct involvement with tribal members. In some areas, however, federal employees continue to provide direct services.

Additionally, during the late 1960s and 1970s tribal leaders and advocates approached members of Congress with alarming reports of the removal of Indian children from their families. After ten years of public hearings, the Congress enacted the Indian Child Welfare Act of 1978, P.L. 95–608. In passing this law, the Congress declared:

> . . . it is the policy of this Nation to protect the best interests of Indian children and to promote the stability and security of Indian tribes and families by the establishment of minimum Federal standards for the removal of Indian children from their families and the placement of such children in foster or adoptive homes which will reflect the unique values of Indian culture. . ."

The Indian Child Welfare Act offers protection to Indian parents and tribes from having their children removed. Among other things, the law requires high standards of proof for the involuntary removal of Indian children from their families, and requires that voluntary placement of children be understood in a court of law in the parents' own language, if necessary. It requires that Indian children be placed with Indian families, preferably members of their own extended family or tribe. The law applies to Indian children and families who reside both on and off the reservations.

Indian tribes, state governments, and federal agencies share a common challenge in carrying out their responsibilities under the Indian Child Welfare Act of 1978. The Act requires that the three systems of government coordinate their services to protect and care for Indian children.

Effective working relationships among tribal, federal and state governments are difficult to build even for limited or specific purposes. Federal law has, for the most part, preserved the government-to-government relationship between Indian tribes and the United States as established in the constitution, laws, and treaties. As a result, state governments are constrained by federal law from exercising jurisdiction over Indian reservations in most states. Most federal and state officials and employees have also been largely unschooled in the status of tribal governments and the manner in which they function. The majority of programs providing federal assistance to local governments have traditionally been designed to relate exclusively to state governments and their institutions.

The purpose of the Indian Child Welfare Act is to reverse the socially destructive pattern of wholesale displacement of Indian children from the Indian environment. In order to accomplish this purpose, Congress delineated the following provisions of the Act:

1. to confirm the exclusive jurisdiction of tribes over Indian children located on reservations;

2. to direct states to transfer custody proceedings involving Indian children to tribal courts, when appropriate;

3. to recognize a right of intervention in state child welfare proceedings by tribes and Indian custodians;

4. to accord full faith and credit recognition for tribal public acts and judicial proceedings applicable to Indian child custody;

5. to authorize tribal retrocession from state jurisdiction over child custody proceedings;

6. to require state compliance with tribal preferences in the placement alternatives for Indian children; and

7. to authorize states and tribes to enter into intergovernmental agreements in child welfare matters.

In 1989 the Supreme Court of the United States issued an opinion, *Mississippi Indian Band v. Holyfield*, which reaffirmed the right of Indian tribes to participate in adoptive placement decisions regarding Indian children. The case involved twins who were born in December, 1985, to non-married parents who were both members of the Mississippi Band of Choctaw Indians and who lived on the reservation.

The twins were born off the reservation and the parents signed consent to adoption forms through the State of Mississippi's legal system. A final decree of adoption of the twins by a non-Indian couple was issued in January, 1986, by the state court system. Two months later, the tribe petitioned to vacate the adoption decree on the grounds that the tribe, not the state courts, had exclusive jurisdiction over the case under the Indian Child Welfare Act.

The ruling clarified that even in cases of voluntary relinquishment of parental rights, tribal communities have a recognized interest in the welfare of tribal children and a right to retain their children, as follows:

> Congress enacted the Indian Child Welfare Act because of concerns going beyond the wishes of individual parents, finding that the removal of Indian children from their cultural setting seriously impacts on long-term tribal survival and has a damaging social and psychological impact on many individual Indian children.

The outlook for Indian children in the years to come is to some extent dependent upon the resources available to provide supportive services to families on the reservations. Tribally controlled social services under the Indian Self-Determination and Education Assistance Act of 1975 have enabled tribes to better prioritize and serve the needs of tribal members, including the welfare needs of children. The operation of programs for meeting social, educational, and economic needs is, however, in the early stages of development, when compared with the historical development of these services nationwide. The future for Indian children depends on the maintenance of strong extended family systems.

Polly Sharp

See also **Churches and Education; Educational Policy; Family; Government Policy**

Further Reading

Beane, Syd. "Indian Child Welfare Social Policy History Module." *Collaboration: The Key to Defining Entry Level Competencies for Public Child Welfare Workers Serving Indian Communities.* Eds. Edwin Gonzales-Santin and Allison Lewis. Tempe: Arizona State University, School of Social Work (1989): 29–49.

Byler, William. "The Destruction of American Indian Families." *The Destruction of American Indian Families.* Ed. Steven Unger. New York, NY: Association on American Indian Affairs (1977): 1–11.

Ryan, Robert. "Strengths of the American Indian Family: State of the Art." *The American Indian Family: Strengths and Stresses.* Ed. Fred Hoffman. Isleta, NM: American Indian School Research and Development Associates (1980): 25–44.

Szasz, Margaret. *Education and the American Indian. The Road to Self Determination.* 2d ed. Albuquerque: University of New Mexico Press, 1977.

CHINOOK

The name Chinook is widespread in the Pacific Northwest. The Chinook Salmon, the Chinook Wind, the Chinook Jargon, and Chinook, Washington, are all features of the area. The Chinook Indian tribe is also part of that vocabulary, yet its history in the twentieth century is fraught with difficulties. Although individually its members are Indians whose lands are held in trust by the federal government, the Bureau of Indian Affairs (BIA) has refused since the mid-1950s to recognize the tribe's existence. Neither recognized nor legally terminated, the Chinooks exist in a never-never land.

Early History

By the 1890s the once powerful Chinook tribe was reduced to a few hundred who resided in isolated villages in the Wahkiakum and Pacific counties of Washington State. Remaining in their old homelands, these families had endured the ravages of diseases and dislocations because of Euroamerican settlement. Speakers of a dialect of Lower Chinookan, the Chinook suffered erosion of their language with population loss and acculturation. The last fluent speakers died at the turn of the twentieth century.

The Chinook rallied to the call of Silas Smith, a grandson of Clatsop Chief Coboway, at the end of the nineteenth century to seek a modicum of justice by lobbying for the right to sue the United States. The half-Indian Smith, a graduate of Dartmouth College and an attorney, persuaded his Indian kinsmen at the mouth of the Columbia to seek a jurisdictional act to bring a land claims case before the United States Court of Claims. In 1897, Congress granted that opportunity.

The Chinooks participated twice in treaty councils with the United States. In 1851, the Lower Band of Chinooks, antecedent to the modern Chinook Indian tribe, signed a treaty at the Tansey Point Treaty Council. The agreement provided for both reservation of rights and lands within the homeland of the tribe. It was printed "in confidence" in 1852 by the Senate but never ratified. In 1855, the Lower Band of Chinooks participated in the Chehalis River Treaty Council with Governor Isaac Ingalls Stevens. The governor pressed the Chinookans and their neighbors to move to the central Washington coast to settle among their enemies, the Quinaults. The council broke up without a treaty when the tribes refused to accede to Stevens' demands.

Early Twentieth-Century History

The Chinook land claims case of 1897 to 1913 stemmed from the taking of aboriginal lands without ratified treaty or payment. The Lower Band of Chinooks joined the Clatsops, Cathlamets (or Wahkiakums), and the Nehalem Band of Tillamooks in the litigation. During the years the case was before the court, the BIA sent special enrollment agent Charles McChesney to interview the plaintiffs. McChesney's work, based upon 115 primary affidavits and numerous supporting statements, led to the "Roll of the Lower Chinook tribe of Indians of 1906." The affidavits confirmed that the vast majority of the Chinooks resided in their old homeland. Congress authorized payment in 1912 (37 Stat. 518, 535). The Lower Chinooks shared a token per capita distribution of $20,000, for the taking of an estimated 213,815 acres of their homeland.

A number of Chinooks were aware that President Ulysses S. Grant in 1873 dramatically increased the Quinault Reservation for the benefit of the "fish-eating Indians on the Pacific Coast." The BIA had commenced allotments on the Quinault Reservation in 1905, a process further defined by the Quinault Allotment Act of 1911 (36 Stat. 1345). Many Chinooks sought allotments. In 1912, the BIA called a council of the Quinault tribe "for the purpose of considering a number of people who have applied for enrollment with the tribe." The BIA plan was to seek enrollment of Quinault descendants or adoption of landless Indians seeking allotments on the reservation. Although the Quinault council approved adoption of Chinooks, the BIA deferred issuing allotments.

By 1913 members of the Chinook tribe were aware that they might not secure allotments as "fish-eating Indians" without a fight. They thus helped organize and support the Northwestern Federation of American Indians. This western Washington pan-Indian organization launched a five-point program on behalf of its members. It sought federal government compliance with treaties, protection from state infringement of treaty rights, allotments at Quinault per President Grant's order expanding the reservation, BIA enrollment of off-reservation Indians, and a forum for airing tribal concerns. Chinooks and others served on the Northwestern Federation Board and eventually compelled the BIA to send Charles E. Roblin to the state as a special enrollment agent. From 1916 to 1920, Roblin compiled hundreds of affidavits and data on tribal affiliations and enrollments. Roblin's Chinook roll of 1919 was based on more than descent: "It is necessary to show that you are now actually a member of some one of the tribes of western Washington," he wrote, "and so recognized by the tribe. . . ."

The lengthy work with Roblin, however, moved none of the Chinooks closer to adoption or allotment at Quinault. Thus in 1925 the tribe established a Business Council to seek protection of fishing rights, secure allotments, pursue a renewed land claims case, and seek basic BIA services. William Garretson became council president, the first formally elected Chinook leader.

In 1925 Congress passed the jurisdictional act (45 Stat. 886) permitting numerous western Washington tribes, including the Chinooks, to sue in Claims Court for equitable settlement for the taking of their lands. This case became known as *Dwamish et al. v. United States*. The Chinook Council hired attorney Arthur L. Griffin of Seattle, Washington. Although the Council paid Griffin's bills and supported the case for a number of years, all was lost. In 1934 the Court of Claims dismissed from litigation all "non-treaty tribes"; because the Senate had not ratified the 1851 Chinook treaty, the Court refused to consider the tribe's "occupancy rights" to the land.

Because the BIA had not allotted lands to "fish-eating Indians" from the other tribes along the coast of Washington, those tribes sued in the case *Halbert v. United States*. Ten of the eighteen plaintiffs were members of the Chinook Indian tribe. This case proved pivotal in Chinook history. The Supreme Court ruled in 1931: "it is plain, therefore, that the Quinaults are not entitled to exclusive rights in the reservation. The Quileutes, Hohs, Quits, Chehalis, Chinook, and Cowlitz tribes are also entitled to an interest therein" (283 United States 753).

As fish-eating Indians on the Pacific Coast, the Chinooks secured in 1932 full rights to lands on the Quinault Reservation. The BIA brought back Charles E. Roblin and vested him with powers as special allotting agent. The BIA reviewed Roblin's work and began allotments. By 1934 nearly 58 percent of the Quinault Reservation was held by members of the Chinook

Indian tribe. The tribe had become the largest land-holding entity on the reservation.

Passage of the Indian Reorganization Act (IRA) set the stage for a new level of Chinook participation in Indian affairs. As the major landowner on the Quinault Reservation, the Chinooks looked forward to voting on the IRA. The BIA developed a list of "Legal Voters—Quinaielt, 1935 Census." On that list appeared fifty-nine individuals listed only as "Chinook" and one hundred ten as "Quinaielt-Chinook." The voters cast their ballots in favor of the IRA. Immediately the small group of Quinaults residing on the reservation protested the majority vote. The BIA listened to their opposition and refused to organize a government under IRA pursuant to the vote in the election it had helped stage. The BIA action was ominous, for it effectively blocked the creation of a confederated tribal government representing the various tribes with lands on the Quinault Reservation. Henceforth, the BIA maintained the fiction that the Quinault tribe was the exclusive governing body on the reservation, an area where its members held less than 10 percent of the lands.

Post World War II History

Following World War II the Chinook Indians, under the leadership of Myrtle Woodcock who had served on the Council since 1925, reorganized with new governing documents. In 1951 the tribe approved the "Constitution and By-Laws of the Chinook Tribes, Incorporated" and sent copies to the Western Washington Indian Agency. Woodcock, who had worked with dozens of families to provide data for Roblin for allotments, continued to serve on the Council. That same year the tribe hired legal counsel to pursue its claims for equitable payment for taking of its aboriginal homelands. The complaint focused on the cession of the Lower Band of Chinooks in the unratified treaty of 1851 and became Docket 234.

While the case worked slowly through the Indian Claims Commission (ICC), the council experienced increasing numbers of meetings and correspondence with the BIA. While these were a prelude to anticipated actions by Congress on the Western Washington Termination Bill, they clearly documented the BIA's direct dealing with the tribe. The BIA also invited the Chinooks to participate in termination conferences on October 3 and 15, 1953, at Bay Center, Washington, and on December 1 through 3, 1954. The BIA further worked with the State of Washington in issuing Blue Cards to identify Chinook fishermen.

In 1954 Melvin E. Robertson, superintendent of the Western Washington Agency, wrote: "We are fully aware that the Chinooks are an Indian tribe." Within a year, however, the BIA returned the Chinook governing documents and roll and curtailed communication. Without statutory authority, the BIA began to act as if the Chinooks were terminated. Sporadically, the BIA wrote, addressed tribal issues, met with the membership over a possible payment in the ICC case, and in 1970 funded the study, "The Feasibility of a Charter Boat Operation for the Chinook Tribe of Washington." Slowly the tribe fell into a strange limbo. The BIA dealt with Chinooks individually as "noncompetent" Indians whose lands were in trust, but it seldom dealt directly with the tribe's elected, governing body.

In 1970 the Chinook tribe secured a judgment of $48,692 for the unpaid value of its lands taken in the 1850s. Congress appropriated the judgment and, eventually, the BIA paid attorney and expert witness fees. The remaining sum, however, the BIA refused to release to the tribe, contending that since it was not federally recognized it could not receive the award. In 1984 the Portland area office of the BIA announced a meeting to discuss its proposal to turn over the Chinook judgment fund for educational purposes at the discretion of the secretary of the interior "with any appropriate institution or agency." The Chinooks protested vehemently. Currently, in excess of $100,000 because of accumulated interest, the judgment fund continued to elude the tribe which pursued the complaint through years of litigation. The BIA held the account in its capacity as trustee for the tribe it no longer recognized.

As fishing rights issues mounted in the 1970s in federal court, the Wahkiakum Band of Chinook, Chinook Indian tribe, and Cowlitz tribe decided that they would have to litigate to protect their members' fishing interests. The State of Washington dropped them in 1976 from the Blue Card program. The tribes filed suit in 1979 in federal district court in Oregon and Washington. The United States Court of Appeals for the Ninth Circuit ruled in *Wahkiakum Band of Chinook Indians v. Bateman et al.* (1981) that Chinook tribal rights were preserved by the tribe's post-treaty affiliation with signatories of the Treaty of Olympia of July 1, 1855, and January 25, 1856. Such affiliation was affirmed by the Supreme Court in *Halbert v. United States.*

In 1978 the Chinook Indian tribe entered the Federal Acknowledgment Project and initiated a massive documentary research, affidavit, and enrollment effort. In 1987 it submitted its petition to the Branch of Acknowledgment and Research of the BIA, for initial review. Since 1988 the tribe has worked on responses to "deficiencies" in its presentation and awaits "active review" status in 1993. In addition to mounting the petition effort, the tribe has monitored and entered briefs on several occasions relating to the protection of its land interests on the Quinault Reservation.

Activities in the 1990s

The Chinooks have played an active role and assumed leadership responsibility in the Quinault Allottees Association, hundreds have participated in the case *Mitchell v. United States* over the BIA mismanagement of their allotments at Quinault, and many have joined in active leadership of the Small Tribes Organization of Western Washington. The tribe's formal enrollment project enumerated 1,203 individuals in 1982 and 1983. In 1989 to bolster tribal resources and help sustain the petition effort, they opened Chinook Indian Bingo on the Long Beach Peninsula and have sustained a thriving entertainment business since that date.

The Chinook retain an active interest in fishing. Although salmon runs have diminished in the Columbia, tribal fishermen work in the nearby Pacific Ocean and annually travel to Alaska where they participate in the commercial fishery. Chinooks also have worked in canneries and seafood freezing plants, and in logging and lumbering.

Although their tribal status and identity remained clear to the Chinooks, they await review of their petition and clarification of their federal relationship through the Federal Acknowledgment Program. Their tribal history in the twentieth century has exhibited a difficult course. They did not lose faith in the bonds of community and tribal identity which bound them from time immemorial. Their spirited defense of their land rights at Quinault, efforts to protect their fishing interests and sustain their tribal government in spite of fifty years of rebuff from the BIA, remain as proof of their tenacity and persistence.

Stephen Dow Beckham

See also Quinault; Washington State Tribes

Further Reading

Beckham, Stephen Dow. *Chinook Indian Tribe: Petition for Federal Acknowledgment.* Chinook, WA: Chinook Indian Tribe, 1987.

McChesney, Charles E. *Rolls of Certain Indian Tribes in Oregon and Washington.* Fairfield, WA: Ye Galleon Press, 1969.

Ray, Verne Frederick. "Lower Chinook Ethnographic Notes." *University of Washington Publications in Anthropology* 7(2) (1938): 29–165.

Ruby, Robert H., and John A. Brown. *The Chinook Indians: Traders of the Lower Columbia River.* Norman: University of Oklahoma Press, 1976.

Silverstein, Michael. "Chinookans of the Lower Columbia." *Handbook of North American Indians.* Vol. 7. *Northwest Coast.* Ed. Wayne Suttles. Washington, DC: Smithsonian Institution (1992): 533-46.

CHIPPEWA

See Ojibwa

CHIRICAHUA

See Apache

CHITIMACHA

The Chitimacha (Shetimasha or Chetimacha) Tribe is located on a 250-acre reservation near Charenton, Louisiana, in St. Mary Parish. Some 720 people are enrolled in the tribe; of these 290 live on the reservation. The tribe has been federally recognized since 1917, when their remaining land base was purchased by their friend Sara McIlhenny and sold to the United States. In 1919, tribal lands were placed in trust; chiefs governed the tribe, each fighting to save their diminishing tribal lands and to preserve tribal sovereignty. These have included Alexander Darden (1879), Benjamin Paul (1911), John Paul, and Ernest Darden after him. Tribal leaders then struggled with reorganization between 1935 and 1949, and in 1949, Emile Stouff was elected chairman. Stouff led the tribe in its struggle against federal termination policies, serving as chairman for most of the period between 1949 and 1969. Leroy Burgess was tribal chairman in the 1970s. Dan Darden and Larry Burgess held the tribal chairman's position in the 1980s. Ralph Darden serves as chairman in 1993.

With regard to education, the Office of Indian Education operates an elementary school on the reservation, the only Indian school in Louisiana. Business interests of the tribe include a housing authority, a processing plant, a tribal store, and a recreation-exhibit complex located on the reservation. Oil leases allow the tribe another financial base. Most tribal members work in the oil industry and local fisheries. A series of land claims to the rich Atchafalaya wetlands was filed in the 1970s and was rejected in the courts. Tribal efforts to obtain compensation for lost lands continue as a priority.

Chitimacha cane basketry, along with traditional silverwork and pan-tribal jewelry, make the tribe famous. Tribal families continue to encourage and preserve these cultural strengths. The tribe continues to develop its business and education under the leadership of its current council and chairman, Ralph Darden.

Hiram F. Gregory

Further Reading

Gregory, Hiram F. "The Louisiana Tribes: Entering Hard Time." *Indians of the Southeastern United States in the Late 20th Century.* Ed. J. Anthony Paredes. Tuscaloosa, AL and London, England: University of Alabama Press, 1992.

Hoover, Herbert. *The Chitimacha People.* Phoenix, AZ: Indian Tribal Series, 1975.

CHOCTAW

The 1830 Treaty of Dancing Rabbit Creek between the Choctaw Indians and the United States government provided for the relocation of these southeastern Indians to lands west of the Mississippi. Prior to removal, the Choctaws (Choctaw is the anglicized version of Chahta) lived principally in the area of present-day Mississippi. At the time of removal, the rolls listed 19,554 Choctaws. In the first of such removals, approximately 12,500 relocated to Indian Territory, later to become the state of Oklahoma; some 2,500 Choctaws died during the relocation.

The present-day Choctaw Tribe of Oklahoma maintains its traditional capital in Tuskahoma and tribal offices in Durant. The Mississippi Band of Choctaws, who are the descendants of many of the approximately 5,000 tribal citizens who avoided removal, is composed of seven communities located throughout Mississippi. Both are federally recognized

Indian communities; non-recognized Choctaw communities include the Clifton-Choctaws of Gardner, Jena Band of Choctaws, Jena, Louisiana; Mowa Band of Choctaws of McIntosh, Alabama; and Apache-Choctaw Tribe of Zwolle, Louisiana.

Oklahoma Choctaws

The General Allotment Act of 1887, which provided for the distribution of parcels of land to individually enrolled American Indians and the sale of remaining tribal holdings, led to the eventual establishment of the Commission to the Five Civilized Tribes, or the Dawes Commission. The Commission was responsible for negotiating an allotment agreement with the Five Civilized Tribes, as the relocated Cherokees, Choctaws, Chicawas, Creeks, and Seminoles came to be called by white society. It met with overt resistance from the Indians. Nonetheless, on April 23, 1897, the Choctaws signed the Atoka Agreement, which spelled out terms for the allotment of lands and distribution of proceeds from the sale of coal and asphalt holdings. The 1902 supplemental agreement addressed the issues of citizen rolls, status of the Chicasaw Freedmen, the rights of persons to be enrolled as Mississippi Choctaws, and special provisions concerning coal and asphalt holdings.

Although the Curtis Act of 1898 stipulated that the tribal government would be terminated as of 1906, tribal government in effect exercised limited authority after 1897 since it was able to pass legislation only with the approval of the president of the United States. Control of Choctaw educational institutions and policy passed into federal hands in 1906, and in the following year, the United States government abolished tribal courts. The United States Congress authorized a constitutional convention by the passage of the 1906 Oklahoma Enabling Act, and on November 16, 1907, Oklahoma entered into the union as the forty-sixth state.

In the following decades, the Choctaws attempted to reestablish tribal institutions in order to address the long delays in implementing the terms of the Atoka and supplemental agreements and to reassert the tribe's control over its internal affairs. Initial protests and proposals resulted from the July, 1922, Albion convention. A subsequent convention held in 1934 at the Goodland Indian School near Hugo involved the participation of delegates from the ten Choctaw counties. The convention authorized the creation of an advisory council made up of ten representatives from the counties and a representative-at-large. Although the council did not possess legislative powers, it passed a number of resolutions including endorsement of the Indian Reorganization Act of 1934 (IRA).

The IRA excluded Oklahoma from its provisions, requiring the passage of the Oklahoma Indian Welfare Act, which extended many of the provisions under the original legislation to the Five Civilized Tribes. Because of their deep mistrust of the Bureau of Indian Affairs, the Choctaws declined to recognize the measures. This resulted in the collapse of the Advisory Council by 1948. The subsequent efforts of Principal Chief Harry J.W. Belvin led to the revival of the Council, which, even in the absence of federally recognized powers, exercised influence in policy development. The 1950s and 1960s represented a period of Choctaw effort to reestablish a sovereign tribal government and to thwart the policy of termination.

The tribe has had some success in litigation concerning Choctaw lands. For example, in the case of *Choctaw Nation v. State of Oklahoma*, the tribe jointly with the Cherokees and Chicasaws filed suit in 1966 for damages stemming from the dredging and damming of the Arkansas River. Ultimately, the United States Supreme Court upheld the Choctaw argument that the tribe possessed lands exposed by the shifting course of the river, since they had neither been allotted to tribal members nor purchased by the United States government.

Since 1971 the Choctaws have been led by three prominent principal chiefs including Harry J.W. Belvin, David Gardner, and Hollis Roberts. Their energies have been directed to community improvements, particularly in the area of housing, health, and education, and attracting industry to the ten counties to promote a healthy Choctaw economy. Choctaw bingo has generated substantial revenues to support businesses including the Choctaw Nation Finishing Company, a Texas Instruments plant, and the Choctaw Travel Center. At Tuskahoma, the tribe maintains a 2,600 acre cattle ranch.

In 1984 Bureau of Indian Affairs offices in Oklahoma reported a population of 19,660 Choctaws for the state. In 1907, 7,000 full-bloods were listed for the Choctaws; in 1973, full-blood population had declined to 5,000.

Approximately 90 percent of Choctaw school-age children attend public schools. Of the Indian schools established by the Choctaws, Jones Academy remains open.

Many Oklahoma Choctaws are members of the Baptist Church, a strong holdover from the early days of the missionaries. Many elders speak and sing Baptist hymns in the Choctaw language, which is preserved in Choctaw hymnals and dictionaries and grammars. While younger Choctaws have shown an increasing interest in learning the language, more teachers and formalized instruction are needed. Increasingly, annual events such as the Choctaw Nation Labor Day Festival provide opportunities for the non-Indian public to appreciate Choctaw music, stickball, food, and traditional dance.

Mississippi Band of Choctaws

From the winter of 1831 to 1832 until 1836, 14,000 Choctaw Indians were removed from their ancestral homelands in the southeastern United States to Indian Territory. Approximately 5,000 remained behind as claimants under Article 14 of the Treaty of Dancing Rabbit Creek, which provided for the allotment of lands to individual enrollees. Until those claims were settled, the unrelocated Choctaws had no recognized tribal government or land base. After nearly two decades of commission investigations and legislation regarding the Indian claims, the Mississippi Choctaws, with few exceptions, were finally dispossessed of their lands.

Communities grew up where Choctaws congregated predominantly as squatters on poor land. The Choctaws who remained after removal tended to be the most traditional members of the tribe; they continued to live as they had before, cultivating small gardens, maintaining some domestic animals, hunting, and fishing. Following Reconstruction, the Choctaws turned to sharecropping and wage labor. Their small rural settlements, language retention, and the return of the missionaries with their churches and schools reinforced communal ties in the absence of political institutions and a stable land base.

As a result of a second attempt to remove the Mississippi Choctaws to Oklahoma in the early 1900s, the condition of the Eastern Band came to the attention of the Congress. Following a series of hearings, the Bureau of Indian Affairs (BIA) established the Choctaw Indian Agency at Philadelphia, thereby granting the Mississippi Band of Choctaws *de facto* federal recognition. During the 1920s and 1930s, some one hundred years after Choctaw removal, the BIA founded schools and an Indian hospital in Philadelphia. In December 1944 reservations were created around the existing communities. The tribe formed a Constitution and established Bylaws in 1945.

Today the Mississippi Band of Choctaws is composed of seven communities including Bogue Chitto, Bogue Homa, Conehatta, Pearl River, Redwater, Standing Pine, and Tucker; the Choctaw Indian Agency is located in Philadelphia. Phillip Martin has served as tribal chairman from 1959 to 1965 and 1971 to 1975; his current tenure began in 1979.

After the tribe obtained recognition, federal efforts focused on achieving tribal land consolidation and a transition from sharecropping to independent farming. Despite significant strides the tribe saw in the 1950s in economic development, education, health, housing, and social and human services, in 1961 a majority of the community continued to be engaged in sharecropping or farm wage labor.

The tribal government turned to industrial development to improve employment opportunities for community members. Its pursuit of improvements without compromising the tribe's role in determining the direction of its economic development has characterized the contemporary story of the Mississippi Band of Choctaws. In order to ensure that community employment opportunities accompanied new development projects, the Tribal Council in 1969 authorized the establishment of the Chata Development Company (Chata). Chata, a private stock company, is directed by a volunteer Choctaw board, and has undertaken a number of construction projects throughout the community as well as the development of an industrial park on the reservation. Chata projects provide employment to community members, and reinvests its profits in new projects, rather than distributing them to stockholders. Other Choctaw businesses include the Chahta Wire Harness Enterprise, the Choctaw Greetings Enterprise, and the Choctaw Electronics Enterprise.

The 1980 United States Bureau of the Census reported that of 6,131 Indians residing in the entire state of Mississippi, 2,756 Choctaws reside on the Mississippi Choctaw Reservation. In 1983, the Choctaw labor force totaled 1,462 with 831 employed on the reservation. The tribal government in 1986 employed 337 Choctaws. The shift from agricultural work to factory work and labor is almost total. Improvements in education continue to be made, especially in the area of retention and completion of high school.

Although the tribal government places a heavy emphasis on economic development, cultural activities are prominent in the life of the Mississippi Choctaws. Traditional stickball games are still played. The annual Choctaw Indian Fair, begun in 1949, continues to be a significant community event, and has grown into a prominent regional fair as well. The Baptist Church has a strong presence among the Mississippi Choctaws. Choctaw language continues to be spoken and, as is the case with many other Indian tribes, younger community members are attempting to learn the language.

Jacki Thompson Rand

See also **Oklahoma Tribes**

Further Reading

Baird, W. David. *The Choctaw People.* Phoenix, AZ: Indian Tribal Series, 1973.

Debo, Angie. *The Rise and Fall of the Choctaw Republic.* Norman: University of Oklahoma Press, 1961.

———. *And Still the Waters Run: The Betrayal of the Five Civilized Tribes.* NJ: Princeton University Press, 1972.

Kidwell, Clara Sue, and Charles Roberts. *The Choctaws: A Critical Bibliography.* Bloomington: Indiana University Press, 1980.

Wells, Samuel J., and Roseanna Tubby. *After Removal: The Choctaw in Mississippi.* Jackson: University of Mississippi Press, 1986.

Wright, Muriel H. *A Guide to the Indian Tribes of Oklahoma.* Norman: University of Oklahoma Press, 1951. Reprint 1976.

CHOINUMNI

See Yokuts

CHUKCHANSI

See Yokuts

CHUMASH

At the beginning of the twentieth century, Chumash Indians were living together in a community at only one location, Zanja de Cota, which officially became designated as the Santa Ynez Indian Reservation in 1901. The remaining Chumash were scattered singly and in small family groups throughout their former territory in Ventura, Santa Barbara, and San Luis Obispo Counties in southern California. Only a few individuals remained who had been raised speaking five of the original Chumash languages: Ventureño, Barbareño, Ineseño, Purisimeño, and Obispeño. By the turn of the century, Spanish had largely replaced Native speech in most Indian households. Children became conversant in English while attending public schools. The Chumash languages survived only in the memories of those born prior to the twentieth century and disappeared with the passing of the elder generation. The last known speaker, Mary J. Yee, died in 1965.

Much of our knowledge of Chumash culture, linguistics, and history comes from the extensive ethnographic research of John P. Harrington, who worked recurrently among the Chumash between 1912 and 1958. Because of publications based on Harrington's papers, his Chumash consultants have become well known. Among the most prominent were Fernando Librado, Simplicio Pico, Candelaria Valenzuela, and José Juan Olivas, Ventureño; Luisa Ygnacio, Juan de Jesús Justo, Lucrecia García, and María Joaquina Yee, Barbareño; María Solares, Ineseño; and Rosario Cooper, Obispeño.

The majority of the surviving Chumash population has resided apart from the Santa Ynez Indian Reservation. Only those families who were living at Zanja de Cota at the turn of the century were enrolled as founding members of the reservation. One Chumash family outside the reservation was the recipient of a federal land allotment. Another family enclave was still in possession of property distributed to Indians after the secularization of Mission Santa Barbara, but sold their farmstead in 1906. Most other Indian families resided in towns such as Santa Barbara or Ventura, or on ranches where they were employed as shepherds, *vaqueros*, laborers, and domestic servants.

After severe decline in the nineteenth century, the Chumash population has expanded from a relative few surviving families. Most Chumash descendants at the turn of the century were of mixed ancestry because of intermarriage with other California Indians, Mexican Americans, and Anglo-Americans. The California Indian Judgment Roll, compiled between 1968 and 1972, lists a total of 1,925 persons whose tribal ancestry was recorded as "Chumash." Only 865 of these are tabulated for the three counties which comprise the major portion of former Chumash territory.

The 1940 Santa Ynez Indian Reservation census roll, listing 85 persons, forms the basis for determining the current voting membership of 156 adults, who must possess a minimum of one-fourth "degree of blood." Housing on the reservation has increased from four households occupied in the 1930s to 81 housing units and 320 residents today. Three Housing and Urban Development grants since 1977 have been responsible for most of this expansion and have resulted in the movement of many families back to the reservation. As stated in its 1968 Articles of Incorporation, the tribe is represented by a five-member Business Council. A tribal hall was constructed in 1976. An Indian health clinic meets some of the medical needs of the reservation and manages alcohol and substance abuse programs funded through federal and county assistance. Tribal business enterprises include a campground and a high stakes bingo venture. The latter operation has at times offered expanded employment for reservation members, but has had an uneven history of remaining in business, because of difficulties between the reservation and outside management partners.

Formal organizations for nonreservation Chumash families have been in existence since about 1970. Prior to this time, family relationships provided the basis for informal group associations. Chumash identity has also been embraced by some families who lack genealogical evidence to substantiate their claims. Current efforts for federal tribal recognition by nonreservation Chumash have been hampered by unresolved questions of ancestry. Public perceptions of Chumash identity have been shaped in part by political activism by groups involved in cultural resource management concerns.

The past two decades have witnessed a resurgence of Chumash cultural pride. This revival has drawn inspiration from a number of sources, including publications based on the rich material contained in Harrington's ethnographic papers. Public performances of dances, songs, storytelling, and craft workshops are now a regular part of programming at museums, schools, and special events in a number of south central California communities.

John R. Johnson

See also **California Tribes**

Further Reading

Blackburn, Thomas C. *December's Child: A Book of Chumash Oral Narratives.* Berkeley: University of California Press, 1975.

Gardner, Louise. "The Surviving Chumash." *UCLA Archaeological Survey Annual Report* 7 (1965): 277–302.

Harrington, John P. *The Papers of John Peabody Harrington in the Smithsonian Institution.* Vol. 3. *Southern California Basin.* Eds. Elaine L. Mills and Ann J. Brickfield. Millwood, NY: Kraus International Publications, 1981.

O'Connor, Mary I. "Environmental Impact Review and the Construction of Contemporary Chumash Ethnicity." *Negotiating Ethnicity: The Impact of Anthropological Theory and Practice.* Ed. Susan E. Keefe. Washington, DC: American Anthropological Association (1989): 9–17.

CHURCHES AND EDUCATION

As the twentieth century began, the missionary movement among American Indians continued to follow the assimilationist policy and practice of the federal government. The belief that Indians had to undergo simultaneous cultural and religious conversion remained strong. A 1914 publication of the Missionary Education Movement of the United States and Canada reflected the sentiment of the day: "Give the Indian time to 'think white'—to catch the incentive and to achieve the goals which the paleface prizes —and he will make good."

In 1913 Indian students were attending a wide range of schools. In addition to 69 Indian mission boarding schools enrolling 4,804 students, there were 328 government schools (217 day schools, 76 reservation boarding schools, and 35 off-reservation boarding schools) and 45 public schools serving Indian students.

Within their own schools, the goal of the various denominations was to provide academic work (often based on the Bible); vocational training, commonly agriculture, stockraising, and domestic service; and sectarian education, including training Indian religious leaders to continue mission work among tribal members. Teaching was conducted in English only.

Federal Funding of Mission Schools

Federal funding of mission schools continued into the middle of the twentieth century in spite of arguments regarding the unconstitutionality of the practice. In the Appropriations Act of 1895, Congress declared it to be "settled" policy to make no appropriation to any religious school educating Indian students. In 1913, however, 16 of the 69 mission schools remained under contract. In that year, the government was expending $165 to $175 per pupil in all the schools it funded; mission boards were spending $125 per pupil in their schools.

Recognizing the impending loss of funding for its schools, the Catholic Church requested the release of tribal funds held in trust by the government, on the grounds that Indian parents were petitioning them to maintain the schools. President Theodore Roosevelt granted their request. Indian agents were cautioned to insure parents' signatures were valid and made voluntarily. Members of the Sioux tribe protested the transfer of tribal funds to mission schools, but in 1912 the Catholic Church still received $58,208 from the Sioux trust fund. In 1917 another law was passed that in part declared that "... no appropriation of the treasury of the United States should be used for the education of Indian children in any sectarian school."

Without government funds, some mission schools closed and others began charging tuition and fees to the Indians. As late as 1932, eight Protestant and thirteen Catholic mission boarding schools continued to receive appropriations through the Office of Indian Affairs from tribal funds at $125 per pupil in payment for tuition for 540 students in Protestant schools and 1,759 students in Catholic schools. Public concern was reawakened when it was disclosed that the churches had appropriated $146,500 for the education of Indian children in 1943. The primary recipient was the Catholic Church. The Senate Indian Commit-

tee on Appropriations called for an investigation of "all mission school contracts." In 1944, the appropriation was reduced to $94,250. By the close of that decade, no further allocations were made to church schools from tribal trust funds. Thereafter, mission schools were supported from church funds and other private sources.

Early Twentieth-Century Policies

The early policy of removing Indian children from their family and tribe led to the establishment of boarding schools. In the first quarter of the twentieth century, that practice came under question. It was considered more expedient and less expensive to bring civilization via education directly to the Indian child and community, than to send the child out. Boarding schools were also unpopular in many Indian communities. Thus, the movement to close the boarding schools or to convert them to day schools was born.

The movement received support from the Committee of One Hundred, which met in 1923 to discuss Indian affairs. Composed of wealthy non-Indians and a few Indian religious leaders of the day, it recommended improved school facilities, an increased number of day schools, and expanded enrollment of Indian children in public schools. The Meriam Report of 1928 condemned the boarding school system and urged greater use of day schools.

The mission role in Indian education continued in the 1930s, but changed in two important ways: it focused more on providing religious instruction in government schools and focused on providing Christian home facilities for Indian students. *General Regulations for Religious Worship and Instruction of Pupils in Government Indian Schools*, first issued by the Office of Indian Affairs in 1910, allowed two hours each weekday for religious instruction, encouraged on-site Sunday school classes, and established general school assembly religious exercises. A 1932 report of the Council of Women for Home Missions and Missionary Education Movement referred to eighty-four government boarding schools being "open to the ministration of Christian workers." The other adaptation in the educational work of missionaries was to provide Christian home facilities, and occasionally church-run dormitories, to those Indian students attending government day schools and public schools whose homes were at a distance and where school bus transportation was non-existent.

The Effects of the Collier Administration

From 1933 to 1945 John Collier was the commissioner of Indian affairs and greatly impacted national Indian policy. He believed in self-government and religious freedom for Indian people, and in restoring their cultures, whose destruction he blamed on the missionaries. Collier cancelled the compulsory attendance requirements at general assembly and other religious services in government schools. Aware of the monopoly many missionaries enjoyed on certain reservations, he declared Indians had the constitutional right to freedom of religion. He opened government Indian facilities to all religious groups, including traditional Indian religions, with the stipulation that Indians could attend or not the service of their choice. The ban on Indian religions by the federal government, first instituted in the 1880s, was being lifted.

Post World War II

After World War II when thousands of Indians served in the armed forces, an increasing number moved to urban areas. Churches had been slow to take notice of the urban movement, first evident in the 1930 census, but they were soon impacted by the problems faced by Indians seeking employment, housing, and acceptance in the cities. Congress spoke out against expenditures in Indian education, was especially adamant against the day school system, and sought other ways to remove itself from the Indian business. Starting in 1953, a policy of termination of services to Indians was in effect. The continued focus on eradicating expenditures on Indians impeded progress in both secular and sectarian education during this period.

Mormon Indian Student Placement Program

In 1947 Mormons informally commenced the Indian Student Placement Program of the Church of Jesus Christ of Latter-Day Saints. It was formalized in 1954 to accomplish three goals: 1) to place Indian students in Mormon foster homes; 2) to secure a public school education for them; and 3) to train them in Mormon beliefs and lifestyle.

The program is a year-round one. Indian natural parents sign a voluntary legal consent form written in English, and are discouraged from visiting, especially in the first year. Initially, children as young as six years of age were placed in Mormon homes, but that was later raised to eight years. Between 1954 and 1976, 38,260 Indian children were placed in Mormon homes. After intense lobbying by Mormons, this program was exempted from stipulations in the Indian Child Welfare Act of 1978.

Several studies have raised questions about the extent to which the placement program and its suppression of tribal identity produce psychological stress, anxiety, and alienation among Indian students. The program continues today but, due to increased criticism and Indian political awareness, is downplayed. In the late 1980s, George Patrick Lee, the first American Indian to advance within the ranks of the Mormon Church to membership on the Quorum of Seventy, was excommunicated for speaking against the Indian Student Placement Program.

Self-Determination

The destruction wrought to Indian communities during the termination era resulted in a movement uniting tribes from various parts of the country to combat government pressures and policies. The overarching educational theme emerging was for greater Indian control in education. From the 1960s on, Indian populations continued to shift from reservations to urban centers, more Indian students attended public schools, and a wide range of intertribal organizations were founded. In the 1967 to 1968 school year, the number of school-age Indian students (152,088) attending mission schools (8,544) had decreased to 6 percent, while the number in public schools (87,361) increased to 57 percent.

Churches attempted to redefine their role within Indian communities in the 1970s. Attention focused on the need for increased Indian leadership in the churches and, especially, on the education and training of Indian Christian ministers/priests.

The number of mission schools continued to decline as churches encouraged the self-determination movement, experienced financial difficulties, or both. A common pattern was for mission boarding schools to transform themselves into day schools. In the 1970s and 1980s, many mission schools elected Indian school boards for the first time, contracted with the government, and converted to tribally controlled schools. In the 1986 to 1987 school year, the Bureau of Indian Affairs (BIA) reported that 5 percent of the Indian student population attended mission schools.

Mission Schools in the 1990s

In the 1991 *Indian Nations at Risk* report of the United States Department of Education, the number in mission schools dropped to 3 percent and continues to dwindle. In the Dakotas, where substantial missionary work was done in the past, there remained in 1993 only five Catholic mission schools in South Dakota and one in North Dakota. Mission schools are more numerous in the Southwest, particularly on the Navajo Reservation. In New Mexico alone, there are sixteen mission schools run by Baptists, Catholics, and several other denominations. A continuing concern of Indian people is the cultural appropriateness of the instructional program in the mission schools. With limited funding, updated and culturally relevant teaching materials and supplies are not always available. In existing mission schools, staffs are attempting to reduce the amount of cultural discontinuity between home and school, but concerns remain.

In the last two decades, there have been several declarations of apology to the indigenous people of North America: the 1977 Statement of the United States Catholic Bishops on American Indians; the Thanksgiving Day, 1987, apology from nine Protestant and Catholic denominations in the Northwest; and a 1991 apology in Juneau citing historic wrongs done Indians and Alaska Natives. In 1992, many churches took stands against the Columbian Quincentennial activities and renewed their support of issues of importance to Indians.

The twentieth century opened with mission schools continuing a legacy of assimilationist policies and practices. The role of the churches in Indian education has since changed several times. Missionaries who served as educational agents administering hundreds of mission schools funded entirely by the government have evolved to a position of supporting self-determination among Indians by vesting final authority for education with tribes, and incorporating greater Indian involvement in the decreased number of mission schools. The churches have moved away from direct, dogmatic, and daily involvement in the education of Indian children and youth, and moved forward as participants in an ecumenical movement, working with and for Indian people, a movement driven by the need for social justice, activism, and public education.

Joann Sebastian Morris

See also **Educational Policy; Government Policy; Missions and Missionaries**

Further Reading

Bowden, Henry Warner. *American Indians and Christian Missions: Studies in Cultural Conflict.* IL: University of Chicago Press, 1981.

Fuchs, Estelle, and Robert J. Havighurst. *To Live on This Earth: American Indian Education.* Garden City, NY: Doubleday, 1972.

Meriam, Lewis, and George W. Hinman. *Facing the Future in Indian Missions.* New York, NY: Council of Women for Home Missions and Missionary Education Movement, 1932.

Moffett, Thomas C. *The American Indian on the New Trail: The Red Man of the United States and the Christian Gospel.* New York, NY: Missionary Education Movement of the United States and Canada, 1914.

Reyhner, Jon, and Jeanne Eder. *A History of Indian Education.* Billings: Eastern Montana College, 1989.

CITIZENSHIP AND ENFRANCHISEMENT

At the time of the creation of the United States, Indian tribes who were the original occupants of America were viewed as foreign nations with whom treaties were to be made. Therefore, tribal members were not considered United States citizens. From the beginning, United States citizenship for Indians through treaty-making dealt with land tenure and tribal allegiance. Early treaties containing citizenship provisions were generally tied to land cessions to accommodate the new American expansion craze. In 1830, with the passage of the Indian Removal Act, tribes were maneuvered through a harsh forced migration to Indian Territory. Indian tribes from across the country, but mainly from the East, were destined to be relocated by the federal government to Indian Territory where eventually their governments would be dissolved, their tribal communal lands would be allotted to individual tribal members, and the conveyance of United States citizenship would be bestowed upon them. Treaty-making with the tribes formally ended in 1871 with the passage of the Indian Appropriations Act (16 U S Stat. 544). The act did not invalidate or impair any previously ratified treaty. By this law, Congress could simply legislate without attempting a previous agreement with Indians.

The late nineteenth century saw all white Americans agreeing on the ideal of assimilation for Indians. In 1882, supporters of the Women's National Indian Association, an Indian reform group led by teacher and temperance organizer Amelia Stone Quinton, petitioned the United States Congress calling for a program to assimilate the Indians through education, citizenship, and allotment of tribal lands to individual Indians. The primary objective was the civilization of the tribes through education and religious instruction with full citizenship and cultural assimilation as a final goal. Quinton continued to travel, organize, write, and speak extensively to gain popular support for allotment and citizenship. She was moved by the conviction that all races were endowed with equal potential.

The United States Supreme Court, in *Elk v. Wilkins*, 1884 (112 U S 94) interpreted the Fourteenth Amendment as excluding Indians from citizenship. The Court ruled tribal members could not separate themselves from the tribes and become United States citizens. This case resulted from John Elk, an Indian voluntarily separated from his tribe and living in a civilized fashion, being denied the right to register and vote in Nebraska.

The Women's National Indian Association and the *Elk v. Wilkins* decision were among the driving forces behind Senator Henry Dawes authoring the General Allotment Act of 1887, also known as the Dawes Act, which incorporated land allotment with citizenship status. Inclusion of the citizenship section of the act resulted from the adverse ruling of the Supreme Court in *Elk v. Wilkins* and the public clamor for immediate citizenship for Indians.

The Dawes Act provided for restricted citizenship to those Indians taking allotments and to those leaving the tribe and taking up "civilized life." Many tribes had only a few years between warfare on the Plains and their submission to the new order (allotment). Previous treaties had incorporated the allotment/citizenship provision, but were largely unsuccessful as allotees often abandoned their allotments with little or no regard for their new citizenship status and rejoined their tribes.

Some tribes immediately came under the provisions of the Dawes Act; others, especially in Indian Territory, became citizens through amendments or separate statutes containing provisions similiar to those in the Dawes Act. In 1907, when Oklahoma was admitted to statehood, most tribal members in the Territory were citizens of the United States.

From 1916 to 1917, Sioux Indians deemed "competent" in North and South Dakota had their lands allotted in fee simple and were granted United States citizenship in a ritual developed with a prepared script by the secretary of the interior. In the ritual, Indians were told they had to live as white men. The men used their Indian name for the last time and shot their last arrows. They then placed their hands on a plow handle and were addressed by their white name, while being admonished about the importance of work for the white man; each was given a purse as a symbol of thrift; an oath was made while touching the American flag; and finally, badges of citizenship adorned with an eagle were pinned on their chests.

Numerous citizenship bills were proposed to Congress in the early 1900s but they were never enacted. In 1919, Representative Homer Snyder of New York authored the Indian Veteran's Citizenship Bill which granted citizenship upon application to those Indian veterans who had served in World War I. He later authored and introduced the Indian Citizenship Act, which was passed in 1924, declaring all non-citizen Indians born in the United States citizens of the United States. This affected approximately 125,000 non-citizen reservation Indians. Snyder's motive for the legislation was to end government control over the Indian. He felt the initiative would make responsible men of Indians, transform them into workers, and thus they would become good citizens.

The 1924 Act was the only citizenship legislation, aside from an 1888 act granting citizenship to Indian women marrying white men and the 1919 legislation granting citizenship to Indian veterans, that did not conjoin citizenship to land tenure and abrogation of tribal relations. Later, its provisions were incorporated into the Nationality Act of 1940, finally causing America's original occupants to become naturalized citizens.

For several decades following both the 1924 and the 1940 enactments, some states refused to enfranchise Indian citizens with the right to vote on grounds they were not taxed. Since the states possessed the power to restrict voting eligibility, citizenship had little impact on many Indian people. The literacy test and English-only practices in many state elections disenfranchised Indian citizens. Other states denied enfranchisement to Indians, seeing them as wards of the United States government. Still others said Indians living on reservations did not reside in the state. Some state election laws had property ownership as a requirement to vote.

Most of these issues have been tried and overturned in courts. It has taken the support and assistance of many committed people. One of the leaders in this cause has been the National Indian Youth Council in Albuquerque, New Mexico. For many years, its executive director, Jerry Wilkinson, now deceased, led this fight. It was under his leadership that most of the federal voting rights lawsuits on behalf of Indians to date were fought and won, resulting in profound changes in the political climate for Indians. Wilkinson was eulogized in the Congressional Record by United States Senator Jeff Bingaman, New Mexico, as ". . . a pioneer to enhance Indian's ability in the political structure affecting them in this country."

In 1993 there is no national Indian organization coordinating a united Indian voting effort, but individuals and small groups across the United States have banded to support and encourage both Indian and non-Indian candidates who show an interest in Indian affairs. Indian people have been, and still are, affected more by legislative actions than any other group of people. They realize this and are becoming more open to involvement in the political system through registering to vote, supporting candidates of choice, and running for political office. In many heavily Indian populated areas, it has been possible to elect Indian candidates to local school boards, to state legislature and state-wide offices, and to the United States Senate and Congress. After years of struggle, Indians have confirmed their rights as citizens of three sovereigns—tribal, state, and federal governments.

Helen Chalakee Burgess

See also **Government Policy**

Further Reading

Debo, Angie. *A History of the Indians in the United States*, Vol. 106. The Civilization of the American Indian Series. Norman: University of Oklahoma Press, 1989.
Gibson, Arrel Morgan. *Between Two Worlds*. The Oklahoma Series 22. Oklahoma City: The Oklahoma Historical Society, 1986.
U.S. Solicitor for the Department of the Interior. *Federal Indian Law*. Washington, DC: U.S. Government Printing Office, 1958.
Washburn, Wilcomb E. *The Indian in America*. New York, NY: Harper & Row, 1975.
———, ed. *Handbook of North American Indians*. Vol. 4. *Indian-White Relations*. Washington, DC: Smithsonian Institution, 1988.

CIVIL RIGHTS

"Civil rights" connotes *individual* freedom from governmental oppression. Since European contact, Indians have been killed, dispossessed, harassed, and oppressed by state and federal government officers. These actions have affected entire tribes as well as individual tribal members. So, it may seem somewhat incongruous to speak of the civil rights of Indians. Yet, Indians are citizens of the United States, as well as the states of their residence and their tribe. Indians continue to suffer from deprivation of rights by all three governments.

Civil Rights under State and Federal Law

Indian people have frequently been subjected to denial of their civil rights by federal and state government officials. These cases often involve off-reservation activities where Indians have tried to exercise cultural, religious, and treaty rights that collide with state and federal laws which make no allowance for such practices.

One major area of conflict has been in the area of Indian religious practices on sacred lands outside reservations. The federal government is the owner of vast tracts of lands. These lands often contain sites that are sacred to Indians. In 1988, the Supreme Court held in *Lyng v. Northwest Indian Cemetery Protective*

Association (1988) that the National Forest Service could build a road through sacred Indian lands, even where it was established that such a road would destroy the ability of the Indians to conduct their religion.

In 1978 Congress had enacted the American Indian Religious Freedom Act, which declares it to be the policy of the United States to protect and preserve freedom to exercise traditional religions. But the law is toothless and gives tribes no right to obtain a judicial remedy for any federal actions. Proposals to amend the law to provide a judicial remedy have been introduced in Congress but none have yet been enacted.

Interference with Indian religious and cultural beliefs often results from applying laws which make no exception for Indian cultural or religious practices. For example, the Supreme Court held in a 1990 decision, *Employment Division v. Smith,* that an Indian employee can be fired by a state for using peyote during religious ceremonies and can thereafter be denied state unemployment compensation benefits.

Many cases have also arisen in state prison settings, in which prison regulations have prohibited Indian religious practices, such as pipe ceremonies, sweat lodges, and wearing long hair.

Indians have had to resort to the courts to obtain protection of their right to hold state public office, to appear as witnesses in state court, to serve as jurors in state courts, to receive state public assistance, and even to attend state public schools. These issues have arisen because some states have maintained that since Indians are exempt from certain state taxes, they should not be entitled to the benefits that other state citizens enjoy.

Indeed, the claim is often made by state officials, as well as uninformed members of the general public, that to allow Indians to be exempt from some of the provisions of state law is unfair and is a denial of equal protection to others. This has been the justification offered for state refusal to recognize Indian treaty hunting and fishing rights. Yet, such officials have chosen to disregard well-established federal law holding that Indian treaties supersede state laws and do not deny equal protection to those persons not entitled to treaty benefits.

Today the law is well-established that Indians have enforceable rights to exercise such civil rights as the right to vote, to hold public office, and to be free from discrimination. Individual Indians are entitled to the entire range of rights enumerated in the United States Constitution and their respective state constitutions.

Civil Rights of Indians on the Reservation

There are some 750,000 Indians living on nearly 300 tribal Indian reservations in the United States. Members of these tribes usually share a common racial and historic ancestry. They are usually keenly aware of the history of their people and of the ties that bind them to each other. That awareness includes a sensitivity to past federal government practices, which attempted to strip Indians of their culture. It also includes a special sense of responsibility to the future survival of the tribe and its people. These unique values can be summed up in the word "tribalism."

The value system of tribalism differs from individualism, a central value in American society. In Indian society, there is often tension between those who believe in the overriding importance of the tribe, and individuals who claim violation of their rights by their own tribal governments.

The Bill of Rights and Tribal Governments

In 1896, the United States Supreme Court held in *Talton v. Mayes* that the Bill of Rights in the United States Constitution does not apply to tribal government since it only restrains the actions of federal and state governments. Indian tribes are not subordinate bodies of either the state or federal government. They derive their sovereignty from their aboriginal self-governing status. Thus, the federal Constitution simply does not apply to them.

This fact aroused little public interest until the 1960s when civil rights became a national concern. The Senate began studying the issue of civil rights on Indian reservations in 1961. Many tribal members told shocking stories of arbitrary and abusive action by tribal officials. Senators who heard such testimony were often surprised to learn that the Constitution did not apply to tribal governments.

Since the Supreme Court decision of *United States v. Kagama* in 1886, it has been established that the Congress of the United States has authority to govern the internal affairs of Indian tribes and to impose laws directly upon Indians. So it was within Congress's legal prerogative to impose restrictions on the conduct of tribal governments.

In 1968, after almost six years of hearings, Congress enacted the Indian Civil Rights Act, protecting the rights of all persons against acts of tribal governments. The Act was intended to strike a balance between individual rights of tribal members, on the one hand, and preservation of tribal autonomy, on the other. It contained many of the substantive clauses of the Bill of Rights, but omitted or revised those that would be inconsistent with the special character of Indian tribal government. For example, it prohibited Indian tribal governments from interfering with freedom of speech, religion, press, assembly, and petition for redress of grievances. It prohibited denial of equal protection or due process. It protected the right of privacy against search and seizure, using the same language as the Bill of Rights, and it extended the provisions of the Bill of Rights to those accused of crime. On the other hand, it omitted the requirement that legal counsel be provided without charge, so as to avoid burdening the tribes with the cost of providing private attorneys at tribal expense. It also was careful to allow tribal governments to establish an official tribal religion, although this was subject to the requirement that freedom of religion of individuals be protected.

One of the most noteworthy things about the 1968 Indian Civil Rights Act was what it did not include. The Act contained no reference to enforcement; only one remedy was specified: the writ of habeas corpus; no other enforcement mechanism was mentioned.

Lawsuits Against Tribes under the 1968 Indian Civil Rights Act

Before the passage of the 1968 Civil Rights Act, there had been few lawsuits against Indian tribes. Under federal common law, Indian tribes are immune from suit. In the absence of an act of Congress specifically waiving their immunity, they cannot be sued. Since the Indian Civil Rights Act contained no waiver of sovereign immunity and no remedy except for a prisoner's right to the use of habeas corpus, few thought it would lead to litigation against Indian tribes. But events soon proved them wrong.

Almost immediately after the passage of the Act in 1968, the case of *Dodge v. Nakai* arose on the Navajo Reservation. The plaintiff was a non-Indian lawyer who brought suit in federal court for an injunction against the Navajo Tribal Council, as well as money damages. The federal court upheld his suit and reasoned that the creation by Congress of a federal civil right gave the federal courts jurisdiction and thus overrode tribal sovereign immunity.

In the following ten years, many lawsuits were brought against Indian tribes under the Act. Almost every conceivable type of tribal dispute was brought to the federal courts: suits challenging election procedures, legislative apportionment, the propriety of conduct of tribal government, the constitutionality of criminal procedures and penal facilities, questions of tribal enrollment, the legality of tribal qualifications for office, for membership and for voting, property disputes, the propriety of tribal court decisions in civil matters, job discrimination, and exclusion from the reservation. Strangely enough, the kind of cases which initially aroused congressional concern, i.e., denial of due process to those accused of crime, were rare.

From 1968 to 1978, the federal courts overruled the tribes' claims of tribal sovereign immunity and challenges to the jurisdiction of the courts. The question of jurisdiction of federal courts over suits against tribes seemed settled and unchallengeable until 1978.

The Martinez Decision Closes the Doors of the Federal Courthouse

The right of federal courts to adjudicate claims against tribes under the Indian Civil Rights Act came before the United States Supreme Court in 1978 for the first time in *Santa Clara Pueblo v. Martinez*. In a surprising seven-to-one decision, the Supreme Court ruled that since the Act did not waive sovereign immunity, Indian tribes remained immune from suit under it. The position of tribal officials was also protected by the court, which found no grant in the Act of any right to sue them. Thus, the court struck down ten years of federal court decision making against tribal governments under the Indian Civil Rights Act.

The result of *Martinez* was to effectively close the doors of the federal courthouse to those who would sue Indian tribes under the Indian Civil Rights Act. While the right of habeas corpus was not affected, many civil libertarians and students of Indian government were deeply troubled. In the absence of federal court review, they asked, what would protect Indians from abuse by their tribal governments? The Supreme Court's answer was that rights under the Indian Civil Rights Act would have to be protected by the tribal court or its equivalent in the tribal government.

The Centrality of Tribal Courts after the Martinez Decision

The *Martinez* decision thrust the tribal courts into an extremely important role. While many were doubtful that the tribal courts were trustworthy guardians of civil rights, a fair assessment would seem to indicate that these doubters were wrong.

In 1970 tribal court judges had formed a national association for the purpose of providing judicial education programs to tribal judges. This organization, as well as others, has conducted training programs and seminars for tribal judges around the nation. Tribal courts have dramatically improved their capability to deal with civil rights issues. Many tribes have established courts of appeal and smaller tribes and bands have formed inter-tribal court systems. Some tribal courts are staffed by judges with law degrees, and many by lawyers who are not tribal members but are employed by the tribe.

Nevertheless, there has been continuing complaint about abuse under tribal government despite the growing sophistication of tribal courts. In 1986, the United States Civil Rights Commission conducted investigations into tribal court systems and heard complaints focusing on tribal council interference with the independence of tribal judges and tribal officials claiming sovereign immunity from actions brought against them under the Indian Civil Rights Act. Legislation has been introduced which would give the federal courts the power to review such cases. To date, none of these bills have passed. Instead, supporters of tribal government have introduced legislation to provide better funding for training and staffing of tribal courts, and to provide for national coordination of tribal court judges in order to improve tribal court procedures. At this writing, such a bill has passed both houses and awaits presidential signature.

While the tribal courts have their critics, they also have their supporters, the most important of which is the United States Supreme Court. In two recent decisions, *National Farmers Union Insurance Company v. Crow Tribe* (1985), and *Iowa Mutual Insurance Company v. LaPlante* (1987), the Supreme

Court upheld the jurisdiction of tribal courts over non-Indians to adjudicate personal injury cases. The Supreme Court made it clear that it would not approve federal courts taking jurisdiction over such cases, at least not until the tribal courts had every opportunity to hear the case first and to determine their own jurisdiction.

The tribal courts are clearly a vital institution of tribal government and, under the *Martinez* case, the only forum for relief against actions of tribal government which are claimed to violate civil rights.

Conclusion

Civil rights of Indians within the tribal community are sometimes controversial because of the tension between the values of individualism and the values of tribalism. But, Indian communities are vigorous democracies. While tribal courts are in their infancy relative to our system of jurisprudence, their achievements are remarkable considering how little formal training most tribal judges have had. There is a growing acceptance of the view that tribal courts are vital institutions of tribal government, and that they will protect the civil rights of all persons. There remain continuing struggles between Indians and surrounding state governments over recognition of those rights which Indians regard as precious: treaty rights and religious rights. It will require substantial growth in understanding and accommodation by the legal system of the dominant society to satisfy Indian demands for recognition of those rights.

Alvin J. Ziontz

See also **American Indian Religious Freedom Act; Law; Sovereignty and Jurisdiction; Tribal Governments**

Further Reading

Cohen, Felix S. *Felix S. Cohen's Handbook of Federal Indian Law.* Ed. Rennard Strickland. Charlottesville, VA: Mitchie/Bobbs-Merrill, 1982.

Pevar, Stephen L. *The Rights of Indians and Tribes.* Carbondale and Edwardsville: Southern Illinois University Press, 1992.

Ziontz, Alvin J. "After Martinez: Indian Civil Rights Under Tribal Government." *University of California, Davis, Law Review* 12:1 (1979): 1–35.

CIVILIAN CONSERVATION CORPS

See Indian Civilian Conservation Corps

CLALLAM

See Klallam

COASATI

See Alabama-Coushatta

COCHITI

See Pueblo of Cochiti

COCOPAH

The Cocopah (or Cocopa, Cucapá) people live in southwestern Arizona and northwestern Mexico. A patrilineal, exogamous, and totemic descent group, their Yuman/Hokan-speaking ancestors have lived in the lower Colorado River region for two thousand years. The Cocopah homeland was divided by the Guadalupe Hidalgo treaty in 1848, leaving some families in the United States and others in Mexico. Today, most Mexican "Cucapá" (as they are known in Mexico) families live around Pozos de Arvizu, Sonora, or on the Hardy River in Baja, California.

Through the efforts of Cocopah leader Frank Tehana, the American Cocopah received their first 446 acres of reservation lands in 1917. The acreage northeast of Somerton, Arizona, is known as West Cocopah, and the area southeast of Somerton is East Cocopah.

After this small allotment, the federal government virtually abandoned the culturally and linguistically isolated Cocopah for thirty-nine years. The Cocopah response to nonindigenous expansion in Yuma County was withdrawal.

Although things began to improve in the mid-1950s, it wasn't until 1986 that 615 acres including lots five and six, now known as the North Reservation, were secured for the Cocopah, bringing their total recognized acreage to 6,000.

Most of this is agricultural land, except for what is occupied by homes and community services. Part of the East Reservation is now utilized for a bingo hall and casino, and a tribal-managed Cocopah landfill on East Reservation serves Yuma County. On North Reservation by the Colorado River, the Cocopah Bend R.V. Park provides public recreation facilities, including an eighteen-hole golf course, a recreation building, and a swimming pool.

The Cocopah originally practiced floodplain farming along the Colorado River, but dams upriver put a stop to that. Now the Cocopah lease their farmland to nonindigenous agriculturalists. The main crops grown on Cocopah lands in 1993 are onions, cotton, lettuce, broccoli, alfalfa, and wheat.

Additional income is derived from a renaissance of traditional Cocopah crafts, such as beadwork and handmade reproductions of traditional clothing, hunting, household, and ceremonial artifacts. Cocopah craftspersons sell at Indian fairs and powwows throughout the Southwest. Now, tribal enterprises can provide employment, allowing the Cocopah to begin to share in Yuma County's relative prosperity.

In 1964 the Cocopah people formed their Constitution and a five-person Tribal Council consisting of the chairman, vice-chairman, and three councilmen selected by popular vote. The Tribal Council in 1993 consists of Chairman Dale Phillips, Vice-Chairman Sherry Cordova, and councilpersons Pauline Allen, Andrew Hayes, and Wil Ortega. The Tribal Council has improved the living conditions of the Cocopah, so that as of 1993, no one lives in substandard housing.

Many young Cocopah speak their traditional language, which is a valuable asset in maintaining their cultural identity, but a challenge for the public schools where English is to many a second language. The youth of the Cocopah also suffer cultural discrimination in an Anglo world. Although Head Start and other government programs have helped, and a number of Cocopah now hold college degrees and some teach in public schools, the tribe feels that more work needs to be done to keep the students from dropping out of secondary school. Efforts to facilitate the education of the young in an environment primarily dominated by whites include parental participation in educational activities, parent-teacher meetings, special tutoring for high school students, and encouraging awareness of Cocopah culture and pride in individual worth.

The Cocopah have a small health clinic on West Cocopah Reservation. For more serious medical problems, they go to the Public Health Service Hospital on the Fort Yuma Reservation. Alcoholism, diabetes, tuberculosis, and liver, kidney and gallbladder diseases assail the Cocopah, and they suffer nutritional deficiencies. A vigorous campaign to combat alcoholism and drug abuse has been implemented. Young Cocopah are encouraged by the tribe to seek training in various fields, including health care services.

Cocopah Traditions

The original environment of the Cocopah provided them well. Fish teemed in the river, and plenty of game was available to hunters in delta grasslands and waterways. Delta forests of mesquite, screwbean, and ironwood trees provided edible pods and seeds which were ground in stone or hardwood mortars, as were several kinds of grass seed. In May, many Cocopah rafted to the mouth of the river to collect a wild wheat that grows there even today, a remarkable plant that thrives on seawater. This halophyte, now being hybridized and grown experimentally in Namibia, Morocco, and Australia, may be an important food source to future generations around the world. The ancient Cocopah preserved topsoil by using long digging sticks to plant corn, squash, bean, and melon seeds in holes, rather than rows, in damp earth enriched by spring floods.

The first Europeans to visit the Cocopah in the sixteenth century received gifts of garden foods from them. The Cocopah, a generous, unmaterialistic people, had trouble adjusting to the ways of the Spaniards, Anglos, and Mexicans who took over their homeland.

Cocopah people did not accumulate worldly goods. Until recently, when a Cocopah died, all his or her belongings were burned in order to accompany him or her to the spirit world. A commemorative ceremony held a year or so later provided more burned offerings, assuring that the dead person wouldn't come back looking for anything—or anyone.

Some older Cocopah prefer cremation, believing that they are thus assured safe passage into the spirit world. Until well into this century even the homes, horses, and, more recently, cars of the deceased were destroyed. Then, as beliefs changed, worldly goods were either given away or traded (one made careful inquiry before buying a used car in the vicinity of Somerton). With the establishment of permanent contemporary housing, this custom has been largely abandoned.

Funeral and commemorative ceremonies are major events in the Cocopah lifestyle, with traditional male singers coming from far and near to pay their respects to the dead and relive ancient rituals with the living. In the evening of such a ceremony, the singers stand, beginning a slow, steady rhythm with their gourd rattles, and begin the long, "dreamed" song cycles that can go on for several nights, recounting Cocopah origin stories about the emerging of twin powerful-ones, and the creation of each totemic creature, plant, or object, the ancestors of Cocopah lineages. Women dressed in traditional clothing, willowbark skirts or long pioneer-type dresses, line up slowly, side-by-side, in front of the singers and, bending their knees slightly, step forwards and backwards in rhythm to the gourd rattles.

Elsewhere, a peon gambling game may be taking place, the opposing teams seated on the ground facing one another, each side trying to guess which blanket-covered hands conceal the game pieces. A referee keeps score, a singer sings traditional peon songs, and the onlookers bet like crazy on the outcome.

Other than death and puberty ceremonies, the Cocopah did not elaborately commemorate rites of passage. Warfare, on the other hand, required dreams, fasting, body painting, and a war leader. The Cocopah were allies of the Pima and Maricopa and traditional enemies of the Quechan and Mohave; they were sometimes friends and sometimes foes of the Kamia. Encouraged first by missionaries and then persuaded by national governments, the Cocopah gave up their traditional warfare.

In the summer, the Cocopah used to live under open ramadas, simple post and willow or tule-roof structures, allowing natural air conditioning. Winter houses of posts, sticks, brush, and mud had excavated floors as insulation against the cold. Wild and cultivated foods were stored in large willow baskets placed on high racks or roofs. As flood protection, the Cocopah like to live near high land.

The Cocopah were excellent potters, making cooking ware, shallow bowls for winnowing, canteens for travel, and large, small-necked storage jars. For clothing, the Cocopah wore skin blankets and cloaks. Women made and wore bark skirts and men sometimes wore deerskin breechcloths. Both men and women painted their faces and bodies for ceremony and pleasure.

When steamboats began to ply the river in the mid-nineteenth century, the Cocopah began to wear the clothing of the newcomers. Even so, there were women still wearing willowbark skirts well into this century, and even today the art of making such skirts still survives.

As river people, the Cocopah traveled the waterways on tule rafts, poling them down to the mouth of the Colorado to collect wild wheat. They made cottonwood dugouts or tule canoes to get from one side of the river to the other. The Cocopah walked well-known trails to the north into what is now California, to the east along the Gila River, or west and up into the Sierra de Juarez. After spring planting, some Cocopah families would take off for the high country and visit their PaiPai or Kumeyaay friends and relations, sometimes not returning until harvest time. Later, they traveled by horseback, and today, many adult Cocopah drive this course by automobile.

Population

In the seventeenth century, Father Francisco de Escobar estimated the "Cocopa" population as being between 5,000 and 6,000; in the nineteenth century, Father Francisco Garcés wrote that there were 3,000 "Cucapa." In May of 1993, the American Cocopah number 712, most of them living in the Yuma-Somerton area and a few near Phoenix. Several hundred of their Cucapá relatives still live in Mexico's Sonora and Baja, California.

Economic Development

Tribal Chairman Dale Phillips and the Council plan to develop the North Cocopah Reservation. Plans include:

1. Construction of a bridge near Algodones connecting the Cocopah and Quechan reservations;

2. Expansion of their casino facility and construction of a hotel;

3. Construction of an industrial park, preceded by appropriate environmental and archaeological surveys;

4. Construction of a road connecting to Eighth Street;

5. Tree planting and construction and installation of recreational facilities for the three reservations.

Development plans of the East Cocopah Reservation include:

1. Environmental and archaeological studies preliminary to land clearing and preparation, earthwork and pivot installation;

2. Installation of a medical center and double-wide dialysis facility;

3. Environmental and archaeological surveys to be followed by the construction of new tribal headquarters;

4. Construction suitable for light industry;

5. Commercial development including an anchor store and discount-house facility.

West Cocopah Reservation plans include:

1. Agricultural development of 133 acres;

2. An arts and crafts facility;

3. Construction of a levee road.

By January of 1994, the Cocopah tribe will be one of thirty tribes in the United States who will be involved in selecting those functions of the Bureau of Indian Affairs considered advantageous to the tribe.

This will include tribal budgetary control, usage to be determined by the Tribal Council.

Anita Alvarez de Williams

See also **Arizona Tribes**

Further Reading

Castetter, Edward F., and Willis H. Bell. *Yuman Indian Agriculture*. Albuquerque: University of New Mexico Press, 1951.

Crawford, James M. *Cocopa Dictionary*. Berkeley: University of California Press, 1989.

Densmore, Frances. *Yuman and Yaqui Music*. Bureau of American Ethnology Bulletin 110. Washington, DC: U.S. Government Printing Office, 1932.

Forbes, Jack D. *Warriors of the Colorado: The Yumas of the Quechan Nation and Their Neighbors*. Norman: University of Oklahoma Press, 1965.

Gifford, E.W. *The Cocopa*. University of California Publications in American Archaeology and Ethnology 31 (5). Berkeley: University of California Press (1933): 257–334.

Kelly, William H. *Cocopa Ethnography*. Anthropological Papers of the University of Arizona 39. Tucson: University of Arizona Press, 1977.

Rogers, Malcolm. "An Outline of Yuman Prehistory." *Southwestern Journal of Anthropology* 1:2 (1945): 167–98.

Williams, Anita Alvarez de. "Cocopa." *Handbook of North American Indians*, Vol. 10. *Southwest*. Ed. Alfonso Ortiz. Washington, DC: Smithsonian Institution (1983): 99–112.

COEUR d'ALENE

The Coeur d'Alene, a Salishan-speaking tribe, traditionally occupied an area of over 3 million acres, which was reduced to 598,500 acres in 1873 when the reservation was first established by executive order. It is located in the panhandle of northern Idaho, just south of the city of Coeur d'Alene near Plummer, Idaho. The tribally owned lands now consist of approximately 69,000 acres of cultivated, range, and timber lands interspersed with both individually deeded and non-Indian lands. Principal settlements on the reservation are Benewah, Desmet, Plummer, Tensed, and Worley. Spokane is approximately forty miles to the west. The topography ranges from gently sloping valleys of well-watered, agricultural land, to steeply sloping, richly timbered mountainous areas. Lands are owned as follows:

	Acres
Indian Allotments	55,814
Tribal Land	13,032
Government-Owned Land	330
Total	69,176

Range and timber land produces income for the tribe as well as for individual land owners through timber sales and farming operations. Their forest lands contain a timber resource currently valued at more than $3 million.

Most enrolled members are of Coeur d'Alene ancestry, but some are descended from Kalispel,

Spokan, and other tribes and are closely linked by language and culture to other Salishan groups of the Plateau. Approximately 800 members reside on the reservation, of a total enrollment of about 1,300. One-fourth degree Coeur d'Alene legal heredity is required for enrollment in the tribe. This is one of the most Catholic of the Northwest tribes, and the Jesuit fathers have played a significant role in recent tribal history. Many tribal members are devout and believe in Circling Raven's prophecy of the first coming of the Black Robes. Various Catholic and other ceremonies enrich tribal social life, including a summer encampment at Cataldo.

The Coeur d'Alene tribe elects a seven-member Tribal Council according to provisions of its Constitution from which a chairman, vice-chairman, and secretary are elected. Committees deal with problems related to land, law and order, education, welfare, credit, and other affairs. On November 15, 1950, the Coeur d'Alene tribe successfully filed a claim with the Indian Claims Commission and on May 6, 1958, was awarded $4,342,778. Other claims and litigation have been successfully implemented by the tribe and its attorneys. Currently, tribal claims to Lake Coeur d'Alene, a proposed gambling enterprise, and various other economic development plans occupy the attention of the tribe and its attorneys.

Agriculture has been a point of tribal interest and achievement for over a century, with tribal farmers being among the best in the Northwest. The Development Enterprise, begun in 1970, operates one of the largest farms in northern Idaho. Other businesses also operate under the Development Enterprise, especially in Plummer. The tribe is reacquiring as much land as possible and seeks to exchange lands with private owners in order to unify their land holdings for various planned enterprises. Tribal members continue to hunt, fish, and gather on and beyond the reservation boundaries, an arrangement strengthened by a recent agreement with the State of Idaho. A tribal language program has been instituted to strengthen the language, which has been severely eroded. Children attend a mission school at Desmet, as well as public schools on and near the reservation. The tribe has a health program and various natural resource programs. Many tribal members live off-reservation as successful professional and business people. The tribe has produced two outstanding political leaders in the government of the State of Idaho, Joe Garry and Jeanne Givens.

The tribe exerts influence throughout the Northwest by its membership in such organizations as the Upper Columbia United Tribes and the Affiliated Tribes of Northwest Indians. It is currently planning and participating in various federally funded projects to restore natural areas and waters that were decimated by mining activities during the nineteenth and early twentieth centuries.

Deward E. Walker, Jr.

Further Reading

Kowrach, Edward J., and Thomas E. Connolly, eds. *Saga of the Coeur d'Alene Indians: An Account of Chief Joseph Seltice.* Fairfield, WA: Ye Galleon Press, 1990.

Peltier, Jerome. *A Brief History of the Coeur d'Alene Indians, 1806–1909.* Fairfield, WA: Ye Galleon Press, 1982.

Reichard, Gladys A. *The Coeur d'Alene Reservation and Our Friends the Coeur d'Alene Indians.* Fairfield, WA: Ye Galleon Press, 1947.

Walker, Deward E., Jr. *Indians of Idaho.* Moscow: University of Idaho, 1978.

COHARIE

Coharie tribe members are located principally in Sampson and Harnett counties, North Carolina, where they have resided since at least the mid-eighteenth century. The tribe, which has approximately 1,350 members, takes its name from a principal river that runs through its territory. During the latter part of the nineteenth century and the first decades of the twentieth century, the tribe was referred to as the Croatans of Sampson County; later they were called the Indians of Sampson County; the present name came into common usage after World War II.

Little is known about the tribe during the first half of the nineteenth century. As with other tribes in North Carolina, it was adversely affected by changes made in the state constitution in 1835, which categorized all Indians as "people of color," thereby denying them many rights they had enjoyed prior to the changes. Despite the limitations on their rights, the Coharies managed to establish their own churches and schools before the Civil War. Following the Civil War, the Coharies found themselves in an ambiguous and unsatisfactory position. They were generally not accepted by whites and would not accept classification with Blacks. By 1900, the tribe had four principal settlements: the three in Sampson County were called South Clinton, New Bethel, and Shiloh, while the one in Harnett County was known as Antioch.

Initially the churches were all Baptist, but during the first decades of the twentieth century, some of the tribal members formed other denominational churches, the Methodist and Pentecostal being the most prominent. Despite doctrinal differences, the churches were closely tied to each other, primarily through kinship; the leaders of the churches were the leaders of the tribe. Among the most important of such leaders at the beginning of the twentieth century were James Simmons, Sr., Jesse Jacobs, Enoch Emanuel, and Raeford Brewington and his son, Hardy Brewington.

Along with the development of the Coharie churches was the development of tribally controlled schools in the 1870s. These "field" schools were financed from the sale of crops, generally cotton, grown on land donated for that purpose by a tribal member. By 1910, tribal leaders had formed organizations in Sampson and Harnett counties called the "Clan," to press for public support for their schools. In 1911, the state passed legislation permitting the counties to provide funding for the Coharie schools. Tribal leaders in each settlement formed school committees which determined the eligibility of individuals to attend the Indian schools. The Clan continued as the tribal government throughout the twentieth century until the end of World War II, and the tribe continued to operate a separate school system.

That system was limited to elementary education. In 1940, the Clan pressed the legislature to establish a central school for the Coharies. In 1941, the legislature acquiesced and provided funds for the Eastern Carolina Indian School (ECI). The ECI continued in operation until 1967, when it was closed and its students transferred to the county schools.

After desegregation the tribe took on the responsibility of economic development. It reorganized in the 1970s, forming two county-based councils and a combined Tribal Council. The Coharies residing in Sampson County formed the Coharie People, Inc. (CPI) and the Coharie in Harnett County formed the Harnett County Coharie Indian Association (HCCIA). Three members from each board were chosen to serve on the board of directors of the Coharie Intra-Tribal Council (CITC), along with a chairman, who was elected by the entire tribe for a three-year term.

Currently the tribe holds title to various pieces of property through the CPI and HCCIA. This includes two-day care centers, a trailer park, a catfish farm, and the former ECI building, where the tribal offices are housed. The CITC provides a number of services and administers programs including tribal enrollment and all federally funded programs. These include the pursuit of federal acknowledgment, drug and alcohol prevention, Indian singing, drumming and dance, assistance for senior citizens, rural housing, and youth recreation. Tribal representatives serve on the North Carolina Indian Affairs Council, a state organization. Every fall the tribe holds a powwow attended not only by several thousand people but by tribal representatives from across the country. The present leaders of the tribe include Tribal Chairman Tom Clark, Donald Robinson, William Groves, Jackie Brewington, Princeton Brewington, Charle Chance, and Pat Brewington.

Jack Campisi

Further Reading

Butler, George E. *The Coharie Indians of Sampson County, North Carolina: Their Origins and Racial Status*. Durham, NC: Seeman Printary, 1916.

Emanuel, Enoch. *Sketch of the Classified Indian of Sampson County, North Carolina*. Cooper, NC: n.p., 1921.

Hudson, Charles. *The Southeastern Indians*. University of Tennessee Press, 1976.

Swanton, John R. *The Indians of the Southeastern United States*. Bureau of American Ethnology Bulletin 137 (1946). Washington, DC: Smithsonian Institution Press, 1979.

Williams, Walter L., ed. *Southeastern Indians since the Removal Era*. Athens: The University of Georgia Press, 1979.

COLORADO RIVER INDIAN TRIBES

The Mohaves represent one of the largest Yuman-speaking groups along the lower Colorado River, a land they have occupied from time immemorial. The Mohave were at one time a nation undivided whose lands extended from Davis Dam to the Palo Verde Valley, but were based at what is now Mohave Valley, Arizona. Because of Chief Yara Tav's (also spelled Irataba) progressive insights, he and a portion of Mohaves moved to southern traditional lands, which centered in the lower Colorado River Valley near what is presently Parker, Arizona. The Colorado River Indian Reservation, as it is known today, was established March 3, 1865, for the "Indians of said river and its tributaries." Reservation lands are composed of approximately 270,000 acres along both sides of the Colorado River between Parker, Arizona and Blythe, California. Bisecting the reservation from north to south is the Colorado River, which forms the boundary between Arizona and California.

In the latter part of the nineteenth century, reservation life for the Mohaves was a struggle and they were faced with enormous odds. The United States government kept altering the reservation boundaries by executive orders. Traditionally these lands were Mohave, but were later shared by the Chemehuevi Tribe, who were friendly with the Mohave. The Chemehuevi are related to the Southern Paiute of Southern Nevada.

It was the government's intent to "civilize" and educate the Indians of the Colorado River Reservation, and in 1879, the first Colorado River boarding school was opened at the northern end of the reservation, adjacent to what is now Parker. Included in this campaign was the decision to introduce the Mohaves to Christianity. Consequently, the Mohave Presbyterian Church was officially organized on March 15, 1914. Manataba was chief at this time. According to his descendants, he believed Christianity was a way to keep peace among the Mohave. Presently there are eighteen denominations existing on the reservation.

The development of the irrigation system has played an important role in the history of the tribes. In 1867 Congress appropriated funds for the first time to develop a canal system. The first canal, called the Grant-Dent Canal after President Ulysses S. Grant and Superintendent of Indian Affairs George W. Dent, was built to divert river water to irrigate crops on the reservation. However, a reliable irrigation supply was not developed until the early twentieth century.

Assimilation efforts on the part of the government included teaching the Mohaves and Chemehuevis modern farming techniques, which would enable them to survive independently. The Allotment Act of April 21, 1904, brought legal allotments to the Colorado River Reservation members, beginning with five acres and changing in 1911 to ten acres per member. This process remained in effect until 1940, when the Tribal

Council adopted a land code, making it possible for the tribal members with allotments to exchange them for forty acre assignments. Five years later the Tribes passed a change in the assignment program which increased the size of the farm unit from forty to approximately eighty acres. Present-day tribal members who have land assignments may lease out their lands. Many have developed homesites upon their allotted or assigned lands.

Reform in Indian policy happened nationwide under President Franklin D. Roosevelt's administration. In 1934, Congress passed the Indian Reorganization Act (IRA), restoring the powers and sanctions of tribal governments. On August 13, 1937, the voting members of the Colorado River Tribes approved the IRA and adopted a Constitution and Bylaws for governing the tribes. Mohave leader Jay Gould was elected as the first tribal chairman on September 18, 1937.

After the outbreak of World War II, on February 19, 1942, President Franklin Roosevelt signed Executive Order 9066 establishing the War Relocating Authority, which created American internment camps for people of Japanese ancestry. Just when powers of the Tribal Council were established, the Department of Interior and the War Relocation Authority stepped in with an agreement to place a relocation center on Colorado River Indian lands. By not opposing their decision, the Tribal Council avoided condemnation (loss of land permanently to the War Department) proceedings. Compensation to the Tribes was in the form of improvements to the land and the development of irrigation facilities. The Poston Relocation Center (divided into camps I, II, and III) was one of the ten wartime camps established to house 20,000 internees. It opened on May 8, 1942, and closed November 28, 1945.

The United States government's theory of surplus Indian populations was the justification for the relocation of other tribes onto the Colorado River Indian Reservation. The theory was that "where the land base was insufficient to support the total number of tribal members, a 'surplus' of people must be moved off the reservation base onto other lands. The 'carrot' for the resettlement of the self-styled 'colonists' from the Navajo and Hopi reservations was that of farming lands and farming opportunities at Colorado River." Therefore, "progress" for the Mohaves meant the extended sharing of traditional lands with the relocated Hopi and Navajo, which took place in 1945 after World War II. Some of the lands they settled on were previously developed under the War Relocation Authority.

In 1952 tribal members voted to rescind Ordinance No. 5, which reserved a portion of the Colorado River Indian Reservation for colonization. This action was ignored by the Department of the Interior. Finally on "April 30, 1964, Congress recognized 'beneficial ownership' of reservation by the Colorado River Indian Tribes, repealing Ordinance No. 5."

During the latter half of the twentieth century, the Colorado River Indian Tribes asserted their right to protect lands that were critical to their survival. In 1963, a water rights case, *Arizona v. California*, established the extent of state and Indian water rights in favor of the Colorado River Indian Tribes and four other tribes along the Colorado River. This ruling guaranteed title to federally reserved water rights. In the last three decades, the Colorado River Indian Tribes have made several attempts before the Supreme Court to obtain additional water allocations. Currently, the justices are reserving the right to add water claims in conjunction with future boundary changes on the reservation.

The tribal government in the last four decades has exercised its sovereignty rights both economically and politically, for the benefit of the total membership. The 1937 Constitution was revised in 1961, which included modifying tribal membership, extending the powers of the Tribal Council and land use provisions. Revisions in 1975 incorporated the Indian Civil Rights Act of 1968.

The Colorado River Indian Tribes have been recognized as a progressive tribe by other tribes across the nation. In 1964, Congress granted the tribes deed to the reservation that gave the tribal government "beneficial ownership" of the reservation. With this, the Tribes took the initiative to develop resources, much of it accomplished through the granting of long-term development leases. The reservation's prime economic base is agriculture, but commercial, recreational, small business, and residential leases are also granted. These landmark leases provide income for tribal operations, with over 300 persons employed—the largest payroll in LaPaz County. The Colorado River provides the tribes with ninety miles of shoreline for recreation purposes. Riverfront property, including homesites, may be leased by nontribal members. A resort, Aha Quin Park, run by the tribes, is located on the California side of the river in Riverside County.

Eager to further develop their lands, the Tribal Council established an agricultural enterprise in 1973. Currently, the farm consists of 11,000 acres. Income from successful crops benefits the tribes annually. Currently 90,000 acres of reservation lands are under cultivation. These lands are being farmed by non-Indians, the tribes, and sixteen tribal members who have individual farms under cultivation. Cotton, alfalfa, wheat, feed grains, lettuce, and melons are the primary crops grown on fertile lands.

Today the Tribes have in place a sophisticated complex that was dedicated during the reservation's centennial in 1965. Included in the complex are a museum and library, a recreation center, and a law and order facility that includes a court house, police station, and juvenile and jail facilities. A tribal auto shop was built in 1976.

The tribal administration, which consists of the tribal chairman, vice chairman, secretary and treasurer, is under the Tribal Council's directive to carry out day-to-day governmental services, and there are currently twenty-eight departments within the tribal administration. The government also has a committee system to assist the Council in special issues. Committee members are appointed by council, with terms that vary from two to four years. They are selected from the tribal membership and the Tribal Council. Presently there are ten permanent committees, five boards and one commission.

Tribal laws in the 1990s apply to Indians and non-Indians on the reservation only and are enforced by the tribal police department. In a modern judicial system tribal judges settle disputes and punish offenders. The courts and tribal police cooperatively interact with the local county and state in jurisdiction matters. Federal courts have jurisdiction over major crimes which are committed on the reservation and those in which Indians are implicated. A major legal victory was won by the Tribes on January 17, 1989, when they challenged the legal authority of the Town of Parker regulating building activities on lands within the town that are owned by the tribes. By order of the United States District Court, the town of Parker is permanently enjoined from attempting to impose or enforce Parker town codes on tribally owned lands held in trust by the United States within the Town of Parker.

In addition to the land, the tribal people themselves are important resources. The placing of other tribes on the Colorado River Reservation has created a unique ethnic population. Intermarriage among the four tribes has produced a multicultural tribal membership. An official changeover from the Bureau of Indian Affairs in 1981 created an advanced Tribal Enrollment Department, which processes applications for tribal enrollment. This documentation is submitted to the Tribal Council for final approval of membership. See figure which follows for enrollment statistical update.

Visitors today will find modern homes rather than the traditional adobe homes that were once characteristic of the Indians. This was brought about in 1963 when the Tribal Council passed Ordinance 15, creating the Colorado River Indian Tribes Housing Authority, funded in part by the Department of Housing and Urban Development to provide low income and home ownership housing opportunities to tribal members.

As with most tribes in the United States, health care on the Colorado River Indian Reservation has been below average. To improve health care on the reservation, an Indian hospital was constructed in 1937 by the Indian Health Service and is periodically updated. The tribes oversee a segment of health services, which gives the tribal government a portion of control over the quality and quantity of services and has strengthened health services for tribal members.

Education among the Colorado River Indian Tribes continues to be an important factor. Education has helped the reservation and its people to prosper and grow. However, at one time formal education was not readily accepted, according to the late Pete Homer, Sr., who recalled how he and his brother were "lassoed, tied together and taken from our mother, who was fighting like a 'wildcat,' to the local boarding school."

Today educational opportunities are provided for all tribal members. The local public school system offers elementary and secondary education. Schooling is also offered off-reservation by local Bureau of Indian Affairs (BIA) boarding schools. Funds for higher education and adult vocational training are made available by the tribes. The Tribes have demonstrated their support of education by donating prime acreage for the use of public school facilities. An example of this is the new LePera Elementary School, which was opened in 1980, replacing an old complex that was located in one of the Japanese internment camps south of Poston. Not only is education critical, but preserving cultural heritage among the Colorado River Indians is also important in retaining their identities. This is being carried out through the tribal museum program. Tribal documents and oral histories are stored in the tribal library/archives for future generations. The Tribes recognized that providing better educational programs will help the future of the reservation so that more tribal members will be placed in key leadership positions both on the reservation as well as in the surrounding communities.

Colorado River Indian Tribal Membership January 1, 1992

Current Information

Total Membership	3,032
On-Reservation	1,783
Off-Reservation	1,249

Heads of Household

Total Heads of Household	1,799
On-Reservation	980
Off-Reservation	819
Whereabouts Unknown	8

Historical Information

Total Membership:

December 8, 1980	2,234		
December 31, 1981	2,469	Increase	235
December 31, 1982	2,651	Increase	182
December 31, 1983	2,684	Increase	33
December 31, 1984	2,790	Increase	106
December 31, 1985	2,941	Increase	151
December 31, 1986	2,979	Increase	38
December 31, 1987	2,981	Increase	2
December 31, 1988	2,992	Increase	11
December 31, 1989	3,020	Increase	28
December 31, 1990	3,028	Increase	8
December 31, 1991	3,034	Increase	6

Increase from 1980 through 1991:	800

From the Enrollment Department, Colorado River Indian Tribes

As we near the end of the twentieth century, the people of the Colorado River Indian Tribes, which consist of the Mohave, Chemehuevi, Hopi, and Navajo, continue to hold onto traditions and spiritual values. They have faced all the odds and challenges placed before them and have survived as a sovereign nation. Assured that the future of the Colorado River Indian Tribes lies in the dynamics of its people and its rich resources, the potential of the Tribes is tremendous. Demonstrating this potential and continuing to bring about optimum economic development on the reservation, the Tribal Council in 1989 opened two enterprises: a joint cotton gin venture with the Anderson Clayton Company, which utilizes the latest technology; and the Colorado River Building Materials Hardware Stores. In 1990 the Tribes signed a business lease with Weststate Carbon, a branch of Wheelabrator Technologies Company. The ten-acre recycling plant officially opened in 1992 and cleans approximatley 3.5 million pounds of activated carbon per year. The plant employs twenty people, twelve of whom are tribal members. Most recently, on April 17, 1992, the Indians signed an agreement with the McDonald's Corporation to begin construction of a $750,000 facility near the Moovalya Plaza Shopping Center, located on reservation lands. The Tribes' ultimate goal is to become self-sufficient, retaining tribal identities, and developing reservation lands for the harvest of future generations.

Amelia Flores

See also **Arizona Tribes; Chemehuevi; Mojave**

Further Reading

Bureau of Ethnic Research. *History of Colorado River Reservation.* Department of Anthropology, Social and Economic Studies, Report No. 2. Tucson: University of Arizona, 1958.

Daniel, Roger, Sandra C. Taylor, and Harry H.L. Kitano. *Japanese Americans from Relocation to Redress.* Salt Lake City: University of Utah Press, 1986.

Hinton, Leanne. *Spirit Mountain.* Sun Tracks Vol. 10. Tucson: University of Arizona Press, 1984.

LaCourse, Richard. "A Preliminary History of the Colorado River Peoples." *Manataba Messenger* 26 (September 1980): p. 6.

———. "Colorado River Reservation Chronology." *Manataba Messenger* 26 (December 1989): p. 5.

Stewart, Kenneth M. "Mohave Indian Shamanism." *The Masterkey* 44: 1 (1970): 15–24.

———. "Mohave." *Handbook of North American Indians.* Vol. 10. *Southwest.* Ed. Alfonso Ortiz. Washington, DC: Smithsonian Institution (1983): 55–70.

COLUMBIA RIVER INDIANS

The Columbia River Indians are not formally recognized by the United States. Nearly all those who identify themselves as such today (1993) are enrolled members of the Yakima, Warm Springs, Umatilla, or Colville tribes in Washington and Oregon. They trace descent from Sahaptin or Upper Chinook speaking communities based on the Columbia River at first Euroamerican contact. Their original home villages stretched from the mouth of the Little White Salmon River upstream to Priest Rapids. Two subgroups may be distinguished on the basis of dialect: the *wanahláma* (from Columbia River Sahaptin dialects, *wána* means "river," and *hláma* "people of"), who live between the Dalles in Oregon and the Umatilla River; and the *wánapam* (from Northeast Sahaptin dialects, *wána* means "river" and *pam* "people of"), which originally included Indians living at Walla Walla, lower Snake River, Palus, lower Yakima, Hanford, and Priest Rapids communities in Washington.

Substantial off-reservation communities persist at Priest Rapids, Washington, the primary Wanapam community, and at Celilo, Oregon, the main off-reservation settlement of the *wana-hláma*; smaller communities are at Cook's Landing at the mouth of the Little White Salmon River, Washington, and at Billieville and Georgeville near Goldendale, Washington. Other Columbia River Indian families live in predominantly white communities near their traditional homes. However, most Columbia River Indians live on adjacent reservations.

The Wanapam community at Priest Rapids is the direct descendant of the Indians led by the prophet Smohalla (from Sahaptin, *smúxala*) during the latter half of the nineteenth century. The Wanapams refused to participate in the treaty negotiations at the Walla Walla council grounds called in 1855 by I.I. Stevens, and they resisted efforts to relocate them onto the Yakima Reservation subsequently. Smohalla's millenarian teachings inspired Plateau-wide resistance to assimilation by Euroamerican society and culture. He and other Columbia River Indian prophets of the nineteenth century established the *Wáashat* Religion, also known as the Dreamer, Seven Drum, or Longhouse Religion. Today this is the primary form of indigenous worship in the southern Plateau region. Services are led in the Sahaptin language, providing the major social context for the continued transmission of the Sahaptin language to generations born since World War II.

The Priest Rapids community in 1992 included some ten families housed on land granted them by the Grant County Public Utility District as part of an agreement negotiated prior to the construction of Priest Rapids Dam, completed in 1962. Several members of the community work at the dam, in accordance with the negotiated agreement. Celilo Village is located near the site of Wayam, which was flooded by the Dalles Dam in 1956. There is a longhouse and a cluster of trailers housing village offices and an educational program. Five families resided here in 1992. The Council of Columbia River Indian Chiefs, an informal association, meets here. This council includes leaders selected by consensus to represent the Celilo, Rock Creek, and Klickitat communities. In 1992 the sitting chiefs were Howard Jim, Frederick Ike, and Wilbur Slokish, Sr., respectively.

Cook's Landing is located at an "in lieu" fishing site, one of five such purchased by the federal government in lieu of thirty-seven sites flooded by Bonneville Dam. The government has attempted—so far unsuccessfully—to evict the residents of Cook's Landing, who were led by David Sohappy, Sr., prior to his death in 1991. Sohappy is widely known for his challenges to state and federal regulation of Indian fishing on the Columbia River. Billieville and Georgeville were established in the 1960s and 1970s for families relocated from Rock Creek, Washington.

Columbia River individuals and families who chose not "to remove to, and settle upon" the reservations, despite the treaty provisions, have established de facto claims to an identity distinct from the established tribes. These claims are in part validated by off-reservation allotments assigned in trust to individual Columbia River Indians pursuant to the Dawes Act of 1887. These off-reservation communities fostered allegiance to traditional values and more effectively resisted Christianization. Here, much of the premodern subsistence economic system based on gathering, fishing, and hunting and the ecological knowledge on which it was based was maintained. Members of these communities continued to use the Sahaptin language and taught it to their children, although as of 1993 few fluent speakers are under fifty years of age. As inheritors of this tradition, Columbia River elders today are often consulted by tribal leaders concerning traditional cultural beliefs and practices.

There is some tension today between those who identify themselves as Columbia River Indians and their fellow Indian citizens. Treaty rights—including but not limited to the fishing rights defined by the Boldt decision in 1974—are exercised by recognized tribes only, which have the legal mandate to regulate fishing sites, seasons, and limits for their enrolled members. Though many tribal leaders are themselves of Columbia River ancestry (for example, recent Yakima Tribal Council chairmen from Columbia River families include Johnson Meninick, Levi George, and Wilferd Yallup), the authority of the tribal government to regulate fishing at traditional locations on the Columbia River is disputed by some Columbia River Indians, as is the adequacy of representation of Columbia River Indian interests by tribal governments.

Eugene S. Hunn

See also Colville; Confederated Tribes of the Umatilla Reservation; Confederated Tribes of the Warm Springs Reservation; Fishing and Hunting Rights; Yakima Nation

Further Reading

French, David. "Wasco-Wishram." *Perspectives in American Indian Culture Change.* Ed. E.H. Spicer. IL: University of Chicago Press (1961): 337–430.

Hunn, Eugene S. *Nch'i-Wa'na, "The Big River": Mid-Columbia Indians and Their Land.* Seattle: University of Washington Press, 1990.

Murdock, George P. "The Tenino Indians." *Ethnology* 19 (1980): 129–49.

Relander, Click. *Drummers and Dreamers.* Caxton Printers, 1956. Seattle, WA: Northwest Interpretive Association, 1986.

Ruby, Robert H., and John A. Brown. *Dreamer-Prophets of the Columbia Plateau: Smohalla and Skolaskin.* Norman: University of Oklahoma Press, 1989.

COLVILLE

See Confederated Tribes of the Colville Reservation

COMANCHE

The Comanche are a North American Indian tribe now living in southwestern Oklahoma. The Comanche word for themselves is "*nuumu,*" which literally translated means "the people." Originally a nomadic tribe whose territory ranged from the Rocky Mountains to the interior of Mexico, the tribe no longer has land identified as a reservation. From a population estimated at only 1,500 near the turn of the twentieth century the tribe now numbers 8,500, although many of them are of mixed blood. A tribal headquarters is located just north of Lawton, Oklahoma. Approximately 60 percent of the tribal members live nearby and in the surrounding counties. The remainder live scattered throughout the United States.

The Medicine Lodge Treaty of 1867 assigned the Comanches to a reservation in southwestern Oklahoma; however, it was not until 1876 that the last Comanche band under the leadership of Quanah Parker surrendered to the United States Army and was placed on reservation lands. The General Allotment Act of 1887 broke up the reservation where the Comanche lived. Each adult was assigned 160 acres of land, and, after placing some land in reserve for future tribal members, the remaining thousands of acres of Comanche land were sold or given away to non-Indian settlers. By 1908, all reserve land had been assigned, leaving nothing for those born after that date.

The Comanche language is of the Uto-Aztecan linguistic group, which includes Shoshone and a number of Indian languages spoken in Central America. It was extensively used throughout the southern Plains as a common language by traders and other tribespeople. In 1993, only about 250 elderly members were fluent in Comanche. An effort to preserve the language is being made by the University of Oklahoma's anthropology department and concerned tribal members in and around tribal headquarters. During World War II, seventeen young Comanche men fluent in the language were recruited by the United States Army and served in the European theater throughout the war as "Code Talkers." All seventeen of them survived and four of them are still living in 1993.

Traditionally the tribe was made up of several bands, each having its own leaders. Today the tribe is governed by a Constitution adopted in 1967 and has an elected chairperson and other officials who conduct tribal affairs. Formerly managed by the Anadarko Agency of the Bureau of Indian Affairs (BIA), the tribe exercised its right of self-determination, following passage of the Indian Self-Determination Act of 1975, and now manages many of its own programs, including education scholarships and programs for the elderly.

The Comanche are noted for their elaborate dance outfits which are highly prized by other tribes for their fine feather and bead work. Powwows and other ceremonies are held frequently in the area, often with the Kiowas, Apaches, and members of other tribes joining them. The largest of these is the Comanche Homecoming Powwow held annually in July at Walters, Oklahoma. Another favorite activity is the handgame, a traditional form of entertainment involving skillful sleight of hand, singing, and gambling.

Protestant and Catholic missionaries converted many Comanches to their religions; however, some tribal members still practice the Peyote Religion through the Native American Church, founded in 1918. Missionaries and the United States government established schools among the Comanches in the 1870s. Riverside Indian School in Anadarko, Oklahoma, operated by the BIA as a boarding school, is the only one remaining.

Among the more noted tribal members is "Doc" Tate Nevaquaya, who has brought international recognition to the traditional arts. His contributions include music, dance, art, and historical and cultural understanding. His paintings hang in museums throughout the world and audiences for his flute performances have included presidents and royalty.

Tribal members are engaged in a wide range of professions, but many of them maintain their traditions through song, dance, ceremony, language, and story. Today, this tribe that was once estimated to have numbered more than 25,000 retains its cultural heritage in a modern world.

Lotsee Patterson

See also **Oklahoma Tribes; Painting; Traditional Medicine**

Further Reading

Becker, D.N. "The Comanches: Their Philosophy and Religion." *Smoke Signals* 6, n.s. 4 (1954): 4–5.

Hagan, William T. *Quanah Parker, Comanche Chief.* Norman: University of Oklahoma Press, 1993.

Mooney, James. *Comanche.* Bureau of American Ethnology Bulletin 1, n.s. 30 (1907): 327–29.

Wallace, Ernest, and E. Adamson Hoebel. *The Comanches: Lords of the Southern Plains.* Civilization of the American Indian 34. Norman: University of Oklahoma Press, 1952.

COMMUNICATIONS

See Newspapers and Journals; Radio and Television; Film and Video

CONFEDERATED SALISH AND KOOTENAI TRIBES

The Flathead or Salish Indians, prior to the Hell Gate Treaty of 1855, ranged over a large area of the Pacific Northwest. The term Flathead is a misnomer given by early white explorers who thought they were another tribe. Classified by anthropologists as Plateau Indians, the Salish shared a similar culture with other tribes of the same area. These include the Pend d'Oreille, Kalispel, Kootenai, and some Nez Perce who hunted, fished, and gathered in similar areas.

Desire on the part of the tribes for an accommodation with the United States was evident by 1855. Moreover the United States wished to limit Native claims to western Montana and parts of surrounding states. As a result they eventually signed the Hellgate Treaty of 1855 which relinquished their rights to live permanently outside of two tracts of land set aside for them. The Bitterroot Salish were given lands in the Bitterroot Valley of Montana near present-day Missoula. Settlement by non-Indians on these lands increased, and in 1891, against the wishes of head chief, Charlo, the Bitterroot Salish were forced to move. This group of Salish then joined the other tribes on the Flathead Reservation in western Montana.

The Flathead Reservation is 1.2 million acres. It is bounded on the east by the beautiful and rugged 9,000-feet-high Mission Mountains. To the south and west are the Coeur d'Alene and Cabinet mountain ranges; on the northern end of the reservation is Flathead Lake. The lake, together with the National Bison Range, a 19,000-acre buffalo reserve, make the Flathead Reservation an increasingly popular tourist destination.

The reservation's chief populated areas are in two valleys—the Mission Valley and the Jocko Valley—and in the lake city of Polson. The Indians share these fertile areas with their non-Indian neighbors. The Confederated Salish Indians originally settled and reside primarily in the southern part of the reservation, while the Kootenai live primarily in the northern part.

The Flathead Reservation's total population is approximately 22,000 with 5,400 of Indian descent. Of that figure, 3,100 are enrolled members of the Confederated Salish and Kootenai Tribes on the reservation. In total there are over 6,000 members of the tribes, and approximately 82 percent of the reservation's total population is non-Indian.

Over 57 percent of the reservation land belongs to the tribes, the rest is deeded to non-Indians as a result of homesteading begun in 1910. The desire for Indian lands gave rise to demands by the white community to open Indian reservations. These efforts were supported by the 1887 General Allotment Act, which invested individual Indians with land ownership. Allotment of land was set in motion by the United States Congress in 1910. Over the protests of the tribes, what was termed "surplus" land was opened to homesteading. Many Indians used their personal allotments as collateral for loans and many lost their land, which greatly reduced Indian-owned lands. Around 1960, the Indian Claims Commission awarded the tribes $4,431,622 for land ceded in the Hellgate Treaty.

Cattle ranching became important soon after the reservation was founded, but dwindled in importance as free range diminished. Agriculture was not as popular as ranching among the Indians, although it was the chief livelihood of the white community. By 1944, extensive irrigation structures had been built—generally without the participation or consent of the tribes.

Under the Indian Reorganization Act of 1934 (IRA), the three tribes were chartered as the Confederated Salish and Kootenai Tribes. The tribes have a constitutional government similar to the United States government. At this time, the Bureau of Indian Affairs (BIA) became more interested in the Indians' economic development; some of the Indians interested in logging, farming, or education could obtain financial help.

Termination of the reservation was attempted by the federal government in 1954, since they believed the tribes were well integrated into the surrounding non-Indian population. This was contested by tribal leaders. Eventually the idea of termination became discredited and treaty rights are now more secure. In 1964 concurrent jurisdiction with the State of Montana was established in almost all areas of criminal law. In 1993, jurisdiction over Indians was given back to the tribes.

Kerr Dam on the lower Flathead River was built from 1934 to 1937. After attempts were made by various interests to gain control of the revenues, Indian ownership of the dam was saved through the efforts of Indian lobbying groups. In 1939 the Federal Power Commission's license to Montana Power guaranteed the tribes lease a payment of $950,000 per year; in 1985, this was raised to $10 million annually.

In the 1960s the principal employers on the reservation were the BIA and other government agencies. Lumber mills also operated on the reservation at this time. The tribal corporation employed only about eleven people. Currently, the major employer of Indian people is the Confederated Salish and Kootenai Tribe, which employs over 400 individuals, most of whom are Indian. Part of the growth is due to the revenues from Kerr Dam, timber and gravel sales, leasing income, and the tribally owned S&K Electronics enterprise. These sources provide annual per capita payments to tribal members of $1,200. The sound finances of the tribes have also allowed them to build a large resort, KwaTaqNuk, on Flathead Lake. This hotel has 112 rooms and employs over 40 tribal members.

Other Indians are self-employed in ranching or logging, and some members work in lumber mills on the reservation. Seasonal work for the Indian population can also be found in logging, fire-fighting, and road-building. Nevertheless, in 1988 the unemployment rate for tribal members was 46 percent.

Formal education for tribal members began with parochial schools subsidized in part by the federal government. The most notable was the St. Ignatius Mission School, started in 1866. Catholic clergy played a substantial part in the early lives of the Indians. Today many still practice the Catholic faith.

In the early 1900s, mission schools and government schools both on and off the reservation were attended. By the 1920s, public day schools were more favored and the Salish attended the same schools as non-Indians. Educational policy was decided by non-Indians and, partly as a result, little progress was made in the area of Indian education. There were only twenty-one college graduates by 1953. Literacy rates, numbers of high-school graduates, and holders of college degrees all lagged behind non-Indian levels.

In response to this low level of achievement, educational leaders of the tribes chartered Salish Kootenai College in 1977. A tribal high school, Two Eagle River School, was also created around this time. Salish Kootenai College offers certificates and associate degrees in ten vocational and academic programs and one baccalaureate degree program in Human Services. The college graduates an average of forty-five Indians per year.

Compared to other Indian tribes, the Confederated Salish and Kutenai Tribes are blessed with valuable assets and natural resources. They are increasing their education level. In 2015, they assume the license to operate the Kerr Dam and this will greatly improve tribal finances. These resilient people have withstood the trials imposed by the multitude of newcomers to the area. Part of their continued integrity is due to the cohesiveness brought about by practice of their Native culture. In support of their culture two large Indian powwows at Arlee and Elmo are held annually in July. The Confederated Salish and Kootenai people confidently face the challenges of the future.

Michael J. Hill

***See also* Kutenai at Bonners Ferry**

Further Reading

Fahey, John. *The Flathead Indians.* Norman: University of Oklahoma Press, 1971.

———. *The Kalispel Indians.* Norman: University of Oklahoma Press, 1986.

Fuller, E.O. "The Confederated Salish and Kutenai Tribes of the Flathead Reservation." *Interior Salish and Eastern Washington Indians* 3. New York, NY: Garland Publishing (1974): 25–168.

Smith, Burton M. "The Politics of Allotment: The Flathead Indian Reservation as a Test Case." *Pacific Northwest Quarterly* 70 (July 1979): 131–40.

Teit, James A. "The Salishan Tribes of the Western Plateaus." *Bureau of American Ethnology 45th Annual Report.* (1930): 296–396.

Turney-High, Harry Holbert. *The Flathead Indians of Montana.* Memoirs of the American Anthropological Association 48. Menasha, WI: AAA, 1937.

CONFEDERATED TRIBES OF THE CHEHALIS RESERVATION

The Chehalis Reservation is located in what is now southwestern Washington State, at the confluence of the Black and Chehalis rivers. Aboriginally, the two principal tribes in the territory between Grays Harbor and the headwaters of the Chehalis River were the Lower Chehalis and the Upper Chehalis. They spoke distinct, yet related, Salish languages, and maintained close ties through visiting, trade, and intermarriage. The Lower Chehalis relied predominantly on the resources of the sea, while the Upper Chehalis had a river-based economy.

History

While the Chehalis participated in a treaty council held by Governor Isaac Stevens in February, 1855, no treaty was signed. Although the Chehalis are not signatories to any treaty, they have ascertained that they were affiliated with the 1855 Treaty with the Quinaielt, etc. Their treaty rights as affiliates have not yet been recognized. By executive order in 1864 the secretary of the interior approved setting aside 4,214.83 acres for the Chehalis Reservation. Originally, in addition to the Lower and Upper Chehalis, the Cowlitz, Chinook, and Shoalwater Bay peoples were also to make their home there, but for the most part they declined to do so. Some Lower Chehalis families settled on the Shoalwater Reservation.

Reductions in the size of the reservation began almost immediately. An executive order of 1886, signed by President Grover Cleveland, restored 3,753.63 acres to the public domain to be used for homestead entry, and 471 acres were set aside for school purposes. Many Chehalis tribal members applied for land under homestead laws. In 1909 a third executive order further reduced the size of the reservation. In 1993 tribal trust lands totalled 1,952 acres, largely held by the descendants of the original allotees and homesteaders. The rest of the land within the reservation boundaries is alienated land, whose ownership is in non-Indian hands. Some Chehalis tribal members hold allotments on the Quinault Reservation as a result of a 1931 Supreme Court decision (*Halbert et al v. the United States*).

Land Claims

The Chehalis tribe first petitioned the United States government in 1906 for payment for the lands the government had appropriated. This effort was unsuccessful, largely because the Acting Commissioner of Indian Affairs C.F. Larrabee erroneously maintained that the Chehalis had participated in the Tansey Point (Oregon) Treaty Council in 1851. Vehement Chehalis testimony was again heard in an investigation of Native land use made in conjunction with *Dwamish et al. v. the United States* (1927), one of the first attempts of western Washington tribes to gain a settlement for the taking of their lands and resources.

In 1951 the tribe filed a joint petition with other Washington groups with the Indian Claims Commission (ICC) for a claim against the United States for appropriated lands. They appealed the 1956 decision of the ICC which had denied the claim, concluding that it was unclear who the claimant Indians or their ancestors were. When the ICC reheard the case it concluded that the Upper Chehalis had held aboriginal title to 320,500 acres and the Lower Chehalis to 517,700. The Confederated Chehalis Tribes were awarded $754,380, about $.90 an acre. Despite great dissatisfaction with the number of acres determined and the size of the payment, the descendants of the Upper and Lower Chehalis voted to accept the award in 1962. The per capita distribution amounted to about $600.

Tribal Government

While the Chehalis tribe voted to reject organization under the Indian Reorganization Act of 1934, The Confederated Tribes of the Chehalis Reservation is a self-governing, independent political unit within the United States, with a Constitution and Bylaws adopted in 1939 and approved that same year, by the commissioner of Indian affairs. The Constitution was amended in 1973. Its governing body is the Business Committee, elected every two years by the Chehalis Community Council, which is composed of all qualified voters. The Business Committee consists of a chairman, a vice-chairman, a treasurer, and a Council member. In 1993, Magdalena Medina is chairman.

Population

The Chehalis tribe has 485 enrolled members in 1993. Its service population, which includes members of other tribes who are related to Chehalis members or who have developed ties to the Chehalis community, was 742 in 1991.

Religion

The Indian Shaker Church has a strong presence and a church on the reservation. Many Chehalis attend the Little White Church, participating in Assemblies of God services.

The Reservation Today

In recent years a number of improvements have been made in the areas of housing, social, and health services. The Indian Housing Authority has built a total of seventy-five housing units since 1977. The newly expanded community center includes facilities for preschool education, classrooms, a health clinic, elders meeting room, library, and office space for tribal staff and enterprises. Its Health Clinic Enterprise, a for-profit venture, began in 1985.

In 1980 the Economic Development Administration funded the Construction, Training and Emergency Services Facility. This building was the operational base for CITE Construction Company, until recently a cornerstone of the tribes' economic development program. A Chehalis tribal bingo operation opened in 1987, bringing an increased volume of people to the reservation. Existing retail outlets are expanding to meet the need.

As subsistence and ceremonial fishing is central to Chehalis culture, the tribe's future plans include development of a fisheries industry, which will include a hatchery, a freezer-smoker operation, and a marketing enterprise to state institutions. Tourism will be another area of economic development.

Programs are underway to preserve the Chehalis language, still spoken by two family groups on the reservation, and other elements of Chehalis culture. The tribe celebrates the annual Chehalis Tribal Days on the last weekend in May. Activities include a salmon and clam bake, baseball tournament, and other events.

Yvonne Peterson

Richard Bellon

See also Washington State Tribes

Further Reading

Adamson, Thelma. *Folk-tales of the Coast Salish.* Memoirs of the American Folk-Lore Society 27. New York, NY: The Society, 1934. New York, NY: Kraus Reprint, 1969.

Are You Listening Neighbor? and *The People Speak, Will You Listen?* Olympia, WA: Governor's Committee on Indian Affairs, 1978.

The Chehalis People. Oakville, WA: Confederated Tribes of the Chehalis Reservation, 1980.

Curtis, Edward S. *The North American Indian.* Vol. 9. Norwood, MA: Plimpton Press, 1913.

Gibbs, George. *Indian Tribes of Washington Territory.* Fairfield, WA: Ye Galleon Press, 1978.

Palmer, Katherine Van Winkle. *Honne: The Spirit of the Chehalis.* Geneva, NY: WF Humphrey, 1925.

CONFEDERATED TRIBES OF THE COLVILLE RESERVATION

By 1990 the membership of the Confederated Tribes of the Colville Reservation had increased to more than 7,000. Enrolled members are descendants of the following principal Salishan and Sahaptian groups: Colville, Chelan, Entiat, Methow, Okanogan, San Poil, Lake, Nespelem, Nez Perce, Palouse, Moses, Sinkiuse, Wenatchee, and fragments of other groups such as Spokan, Coeur d'Alene, and Kalispel. About 60 percent of the current Colville population now live on or near the over 1 million acre Colville Reservation located in northeastern Washington State, while the remainder live off the reservation in the Northwest and elsewhere.

History

The Colville Reservation was initially established in 1872 by executive order of President Ulysses S. Grant, for a portion of the groups presently comprising the reservation population. Later additions of the Chief Moses and Chief Joseph bands and other groups to the reservation has helped produce a social, cultural, and political complexity rarely seen in the Northwest. This population has complex intertribal ties with both United States and Canadian bands and tribes, which are reflected in unusually complex patterns of intermarriage and intercultural borrowing.

Adding to this complexity have been various federal actions to relocate and remove portions of the original reservation; nevertheless, it remains one of the largest in the Northwest with a total area of 1,011,495 acres. Of this acreage, a relatively small amount has been allotted to individual tribal members under the federal allotment acts, with a majority remaining collectively owned and containing numerous timber resources, mineral resources, hydroelectric potential, and abundant hunting and fishing opportunities. This forms the basis of a potentially rich tribal economy.

The complex legal and social history of the Colville Reservation, absence of a common reservation-wide tribal identity, and substantial intermarriage with other tribal groups and non-Indians helped produce a movement to terminate the reservation during the 1950s and 1960s. After considerable factional infighting this movement was reversed, and in the 1970s and 1980s reservation leaders have moved toward consolidation of the tribes' resources and sovereignty through economic, legal, and political means.

The Colville leadership has successfully brought a series of claims for lands improperly taken for unconscionable prices, including reparations therefor, as well as reasserted certain of their rights to various off-reservation resources and areas. Particularly significant have been their successful claims against the federal government for mismanagement of their resources and funds, and for compensation for destruction of their fish runs by such federal hydroelectric developments as the Grand Coulee Dam.

Contemporary Life

Although the Colville were heavily converted to Catholicism in the nineteenth century, and more recently to various Protestant faiths, the religion of the prophet Kolaskin, the presence of the Chief Joseph Band of Nez Perce with their Seven Drum Religion, the Indian Shaker Church supported from the Yakima Reservation, and other traditionalists from the various bands and tribes have provided a basis for renewal of traditional religious and cultural practices witnessed on other Plateau reservations during the latter twentieth century. It is too early to determine if the recent introduction of the Native American Church (Peyote Religion) represents a move toward a pan-Indian religious life identified more with the Plains and Southwest than with the Plateau. The absence of a common tribal language has helped prevent the successful introduction of programs of language renewal. Establishment of a successful cultural resource management program and other cultural preservation programs signals a commitment of tribal leadership to revitalization of the traditional culture despite such obstacles.

In recent years, the Colville tribes have also begun to secure income from control and development of their natural resources, including especially their timber and mineral resources. As part of this, in the 1980s the tribes initiated a program of land repurchase and consolidation, which is part of an overall goal of reasserting sovereignty and control of the tribes' land base. It has been difficult to maintain a consistent program of land repurchase and consolidation, because of unpredictable national demands and prices for Colville timber and minerals, such as molybdenum. Nevertheless, the tribes' enterprises have included a successful meat-packing plant, a reforestation business, and a modern sawmill that increasingly takes advantage of their abundant timber resources in a manner similar to that seen on the Warm Springs Reservation in Oregon. As with other tribes of the Northwest, the Colville have also engaged in various fish and game rehabilitation programs and are becoming interested in developing gambling enterprises and tourism. More and more tribal members have received undergraduate and graduate degrees in natural resource management, business, law, education, health, social work, and other areas as part of an overall tribal strategy of economic and social development.

Government

The tribes are organized under an Indian Reorganization Act constitution, which was approved by the secretary of the interior in 1938. The seat of tribal government is in Nespelem. The governing body of the Confederated Tribes is the Colville Business Council, which consists of fourteen members representing four voting districts on the reservation. This Council represents all segments of the reservation. An economic development and planning committee, which also acts as the overall economic development program committee, is assisted by an advisory committee, and various other committees set policies governing tribal education, health, law and order, cultural programs, and other activities. The Colville Business Council increasingly influences state and regional political and economic life. It exercises influence over water and natural resources throughout northeastern Washington, and is rapidly becoming a full partner in managing regional federal lands and resources. The Council has taken a more active role in matters affecting the Columbia River, its various hydroelectric dams, the Columbia Basin Project, and such federal installations as the United States Department of Energy site at Hanford and Lake Roosevelt. The Colville continue to play a major role in tribal affairs in the Northwest by membership in such groups as the Affiliated Tribes of Northwest Indians, and other intertribal organizations.

Deward E. Walker, Jr.

See also **Washington State Tribes**

Further Reading

Ackerman, Lillian Alice. "Sexual Equality in the Plateau Culture Area." Ph.D. diss., Department of Anthropology, Washington State University, Pullman, 1982.

Chance, David W. "Influences of the Hudson's Bay Company on the Native Cultures of the Colville District." *Northwest Anthropological Research Notes* (Moscow, University of Idaho) Memoir No. 2, 1973.

Raufer, Maria Ilma. *Black Robes and Indians on the Last Frontier: A Story of Heroism.* Milwaukee, MN: The Bruce Publishing Co., 1963.

Ruby, Robert H., and John A. Brown. *Half-Sun on the Columbia: A Biography of Chief Moses.* Norman: University of Oklahoma Press, 1966.

Walker, Deward E., Jr., and Sylvester H. Laren, Jr. "Anthropological Guide for the Coulee Dam National Recreation Area." *Anthropological Research Manuscript* (Moscow, University of Idaho). Series No. 3, 1974.

CONFEDERATED TRIBES OF COOS, LOWER UMPQUA, AND SIUSLAW

The often desperate situation of the Coos, Lower Umpqua, and Siuslaw Indians for much of the twentieth century stemmed from turning points in their history. By unratified treaty in 1855, the Bureau of Indian Affairs (BIA) and United States Army forcibly colonized the Coos among the Lower Umpqua in 1856 at the mouth of the Umpqua River. Three years later, some 500 survivors marched northward to settle at the mouth of the Yachats River on the southern part of the Siletz Reservation. Under difficult tutelage of the "civilization" programs, more than 50 percent of the Indians perished by the time Congress opened the area in 1875 to settlement. The beleaguered survivors drifted south along the coast to settle at the Siuslaw River, along the Umpqua estuary, and particularly at Empire and on South Slough on Coos Bay.

The members of the tribes were landless in their traditional homeland. Although speaking divergent tongues of Penutian—Siuslawan and the Miluk and Hanis dialects of Coosan—they intermarried and lived as small communities surrounded by newcomers. Tribal members found work as loggers, woodcutters, washerwomen, clam diggers, and agricultural laborers. For more than forty years they constituted the primary labor force harvesting cranberries. The women manufactured cattail fiber mats for floor coverings in homes and sold their baskets to local residents and travelers. Removals and dispossession, however, so shattered their culture that by the 1870s, they observed for the last time the traditional puberty rites expected of all females. The last fluent speakers of the languages died in the 1940s.

In 1892 as an adjunct to allotment of lands on the Siletz Reservation, the BIA initiated a program of public domain allotments in southwestern Oregon. Eagerly, the Siuslaw, Lower Umpqua, and Coos selected eighty-acre parcels. Many of the tracts they selected were close to the coast and included their old subsistence areas. Forest Service officials later contested the allotments, alleging that forest and sand dune lands were unsuitable for agricultural purposes. Tribal members thus lost dozens of allotments which passed into the Siuslaw National Forest. A few used the amendment to the Homestead Act of 1862 (18 Stat. 420, Part 3) to secure Indian trust homesteads. Tribal members obtained a total of 273 allotments between 1892 and 1906 in southwestern Oregon. The bulk of these were at remote locations along the tidal estuaries or on lakes near the middens of their traditional villages.

Early Twentieth-Century History

Following the death in 1906 of Doloose, or Chief Jackson, the Coos followed the leadership of Bobbie Burns. In 1916, at the death of Chief Burns, members of the tribe organized a formal government. Having been treated collectively since their treaty councils and removals in the 1850s, the members elected a governing council of the Confederated Tribes of Coos, Lower Umpqua, and Siuslaw. The impetus for this organization developed because of the need for the tribes to deal with the Roseburg Superintendency of Indian Affairs, which opened in 1910. Commencing in 1918, the BIA through the Roseburg Superintendency and its successor offices—Greenville Indian School, Siletz-Grande Ronde Agency, and Chemawa Indian School—maintained annual statistical records on the tribes. These included individual census records giving age, blood quantum, and tribal affiliation.

In November 1916 the Confederated Tribes began working with attorney G.W. Watkins. In 1917 they entered a contract for legal assistance from the firm of Sinclair and Blatchley of Coos County, Oregon. Their efforts to find the long-misplaced treaty of 1855 with the Oregon coastal tribes and to secure a jurisdictional act to permit litigation over the taking of their lands led to H.R. 9047, introduced in 1918. Although this bill did not pass, they continued to press members of Congress for the opportunity to have their day in court. At last in 1929, they obtained a jurisdictional act (45 Stat. 1256), amended June 14, 1932 (47 Stat. 307). The law authorized the United States Court of Claims to "hear, examine, adjudicate, and render final judgment in any and all legal and equitable claims of the Coos (or Kowes) Bay, Lower Umpqua (or Kalawatset), and Siuslaw Indian tribes of the State of Oregon." At the request of the tribes, the law prohibited per capita distribution of any judgment; it called for use of any monies for educational, health, industrial, or land acquisition programs.

Between 1929 and 1938 the case was before the United States Court of Claims. In 1931, tribal members testified through the assistance of interpreter Frank Drew about their use and occupancy of their homeland of nearly 1.7 million acres of southwestern Oregon. An aged Coos, Ana-cha-har-ah, or Jim Buchanan, told of his memories of the 1855 treaty council, of removal to Fort Umpqua and Yachats, and of years of waiting for action by the federal government. In addition to the numerous tribal witnesses, a number of pioneer settlers also testified to the tribes' presence in the region. The attorneys submitted the lengthy transcripts and a copy of the unratified treaty of 1855 which explicitly defined the tribal lands. The Claims Court then considered Docket K-345. In 1938, the Court rejected the claim (87 C.Cls. 153). It observed that "an unratified treaty is not evidence of government recognition of Indian title to lands described therein." Further, it found that the seventeen Indian witnesses all had a "direct interest in the outcome of this case" and therefore their testimony was unacceptable. The Court ruled that the plaintiff tribes possessed "no right, claim, or title to any part of the coast of Oregon whatsoever." The Supreme Court declined in 1939 to consider the petition appealing the decision.

In spite of their irregular contact with the BIA, members of the tribes sent their children to Chemawa Indian School (Salem, OR), Greenville School (Fresno, CA), Riverside School (Riverside, CA), Haskell Institute (Lawrence, KS), and to Carlisle Indian School (Carlisle, PA). Such enrollments commenced as early as the 1890s and meant, for some children, years of little or no contact with their families.

The passage of the Indian Reorganization Act of 1934 (IRA), heralded a new era for the Confederated Tribes. The Siletz-Grande Ronde Agency, which had maintained little interest in Indians of the public domain, instituted a program to secure demographic and social information on the tribal members on the southwestern Oregon coast. Dorothy Cassutt, an agency employee, traveled door-to-door to collect data to help the agency plan better. These activities and the lack of tribal lands caught the attention of Louis J. Simpson and William G. Robertson. Principals in the Empire Development Company then platting a large townsite on lower Coos Bay, on May 27, 1940, they transferred to the United States 6.1 acres "in trust for such Indians of the Coos Bay and neighboring tribes, as may be designated by the Secretary of the Interior."

As part of the New Deal and improved social services for tribes, the BIA in 1941 designed and erected a tribal hall on the new reservation. The hall and reservation became both a popular meeting place as well as a symbol of hope for tribal members. On June 6, 1948, the tribes hired Everett Sanders of Washington, D.C., and John G. Mullen of North Bend, Oregon, to provide legal assistance in their suit before the Indian Claims Commission (ICC). The ICC refused to hear the complaint, alleging that the tribes had already had their day in court in the 1930s. The tribes secured H.R. 4190 and S. 1572 in 1951 to compel the Commission to hear their case. When the bills had hearings, the ICC abruptly agreed to take the complaint. The tribes' Docket 265 came before the Commission and on January 25, 1952, was summarily dismissed. The plaintiffs were unable to present any new evidence though dozens of BIA letters from the 1850s—not previously submitted in their Claims Court case—confirmed their aboriginal presence. On July 11, 1952, the ICC sustained the motion for summary judgment.

Terribly disappointed in their second futile effort to secure any settlement for the taking of their aboriginal lands in 1855, the Confederated Tribes hired James M. Green of Florence, Oregon, in 1954, as new legal counsel. Green worked with chairman Howard Barrett and the council to secure introduction of S. 3156 in 1956 to permit litigation of the claim. The bill did not pass. Similarly, S. 945 prepared by Senator Mark O. Hatfield in 1975 did not secure a hearing.

Termination and Restoration

Congress targeted the Confederated Tribes for termination in 1954. The BIA enumerated individual allotments and the 6.1 acre reservation in its summary of assets for patent or sale. The Tribal Council refused to participate in termination. Unlike other tribal governing bodies in western Oregon, it refused to endorse the BIA-drafted resolution in favor of termination. Congress nevertheless included the Coos, Lower Umpqua, and Siuslaw in Public Law 588 in 1954. As the withdrawal of programs and contacts grew more imminent, the Confederated Tribes petitioned the United Nations in August 1956. The gesture accomplished little more than gaining press attention.

The refusal of the Confederated Tribes to accede to termination posed a problem for the BIA. Without tribal consent it could not dispose of the hall and reservation in Coos Bay, Oregon. The BIA thus leased the property to the United States Navy Reserve. The Tribal Council continued to meet and use the facilities. With no maintenance, the hall deteriorated steadily, but it remained a symbol and rallying point for the tribes. On March 11, 1976, tribal members testified before Task Force Ten of the American Indian Policy Review Commission. Russell Anderson, chair, Bill Brainard, vice-chair, and Edgar Bowen, chief, told of the loss of allotments for non-payment of taxes after termination and other disabilities afflicting the tribes.

During the 1970s the Confederated Tribes reasserted their exclusive right to use their tribal hall and reservation. They tapped federal poverty programs to open a CETA Manpower Project. They solicited Indian Education Act funds to mount teacher training programs in local school districts. They commissioned the development of curricular materials, including the textbook *This Land Was Theirs: The Indians of Western Oregon* (1977). The tribes formed the Willow River Indian Benevolent Association to field grant proposals. Individual tribal members joined the American Indian Movement (AIM) and two participated in the occupation of Alcatraz Island. These commitments inspired tribal leaders to attempt to secure congressional action to overturn termination. Working with Dennis J. Whittlesey, Washington, D.C., legal counsel, the tribes obtained introduction of such legislation in 1984 by Senator Mark Hatfield and Representative James Weaver. On October 17, 1984, Public Law 84–481 restored the federal relationship of the Confederated Tribes and reconfirmed the trust status of the 6.1 acre reservation in Coos Bay, Oregon.

Recent Activities

Since restoration, the tribes have completed an enrollment project documenting family histories, adopted a Constitution and Bylaws, launched a housing improvement program, opened a health clinic, and completely restored the tribal hall. They have mounted an active program to work with federal and state agencies, especially in archaeological protection and excavation projects within their old homeland. From 1991 to 1992 the Confederated Tribes joined the Bureau of Land Management, Coos Bay District,

to plan for the Bal'diyaka Interpretive Center. Projected as a $20 million facility at the former tribal village and cemetery at the Cape Arago Lighthouse, this joint-venture project was scoped to interpret Indian culture and history and the development of the lighthouse since 1867. The tribes published the 128-page master plan in December, 1992.

The 526 enrolled members of the Confederated Tribes mostly reside in southwestern Oregon. They currently find employment in logging, lumbering, fishing, and service trades. A number still live on their former allotments or sites close to the villages their ancestors occupied from time immemorial. The tribes host an annual salmon feast in August. They take pride in the rich linguistic and cultural legacy tribal members shared with Henry Hull St. Clair, 1903; Leo J. Frachtenberg, 1909 to 1916; Melville Jacobs, 1933 to 1934; Homer G. Barnett, 1934; John Peabody Harrington, 1942; Morris Swadesh, 1953; and Dell and Virginia Hymes, 1954. From the notes and recordings of these anthropologists come the voices of the past. Through them the ancestors speak to the present generations of the Confederated Tribes.

Stephen Dow Beckham

Further Reading

Beckham, Stephen Dow. *The Indians of Western Oregon: This Land Was Theirs.* Coos Bay, OR: Arago Books, 1977.

———. *Land of the Umpqua: A History of Douglas County, Oregon.* Roseburg, OR: Douglas County Commissioners, 1987.

Beckham, Stephen Dow, and Donald Whereat. "Captured Heritage: Confederated Tribes of Coos, Lower Umpqua, and Siuslaw Indians." *The First Oregonians.* Eds. Carolyn Buan and Richard Lewis. Portland: Oregon Council for the Humanities (1992): 77–82.

Jacobs, Melville. "Coos Narrative and Ethnologic Texts." *University of Washington Publications in Anthropology* 8:1 (1939): 1–125.

Zenk, Henry. "Siuslawans and Coosans." *Handbook of North American Indians.* Vol. 7. *Northwest Coast.* Ed. Wayne Suttles. Washington, DC: Smithsonian Institution (1992): 572–79.

CONFEDERATED TRIBES OF GRAND RONDE

The Confederated Tribes of the Grand Ronde Community of Oregon are located in Grand Ronde, Oregon, in the northwestern part of the state. The tribe is comprised of five Indian groups originally located in the Willamette Valley, the Cascade Mountains, and the river valleys of southwest Oregon. They are Shasta, Kalapuya, Rogue River, Molalla, and Umpqua. There are also many tribal members whose heritage can be traced to other Indian tribes in Oregon, such as Chinook and Clackamas.

During the middle part of the nineteenth century, European settlers moved West into Oregon and began to consolidate the Indians onto reservations in the Willamette Valley, thus ensuring the availability of land for farming and other uses by the settlers. In 1857, Grand Ronde became one of the reservation areas. A school system was set up for Indian children, where English and the Christian religion, primarily Catholicism, were imposed on them in the schools and the community. Although use of their Native languages diminished with Euroamerican intrusion, the Chinook Jargon, which tribes in the Northwest had developed to communicate among themselves and with others, is still spoken by some tribal members at Grand Ronde events today.

The executive order of 1857 set aside a reservation area of 59,000 acres. As a result of the 1901 land cession, negotiated by Inspector James McLaughlin, 33,146 acres were allotted to 269 Indians, 26,551 acres were declared "surplus," of which 440 acres were reserved for government use. A majority of adult male Grand Ronde Indians formed a council in order to negotiate the price of the remaining tract of surplus land. McLaughlin assembled the men, who offered to sell for $2 per acre. McLaughlin refused, and eventually persuaded the council to agree to a price of $1.10 per acre. The final agreement was a lump sum of $28,000.

After most of their land was sold or alienated through allotment, many Indians remained in Grand Ronde. The government attempted to westernize them, stamping out the Native religion and traditional dress to force them to accept European culture. Some were moved to the Siletz Reservation, while others simply left Grand Ronde, returning only to harvest hops and visit family members. Many of the Indians who remained in Grand Ronde made their living as farmers, loggers, or by selling some type of art (like baskets and jewelry) to the whites.

In 1936, under the Indian Reorganization Act (IRA), 537 acres of land in the Grand Ronde area were purchased for the tribe. About 331 acres of the land could be used for farming; the Grand Ronde Business Committee divided it among some tribal members to provide subsistence and help the Grand Ronde economy grow. Most tribal members were in favor of the Act because it allowed them to purchase land, and it provided jobs to many people.

In 1954 the federal government declared the Grand Ronde tribe terminated. For Grand Ronde Indians, this was perhaps the most difficult stage in their existence since the arrival of the white settlers. The people were nullified by the stroke of a pen. The government quickly seized the reservation land and sold or dispersed it accordingly. Termination had several results. For many elders, it signified a loss of "home" and cultural identity, as well as loss of health and educational benefits that had been available through the Bureau of Indian Affairs (BIA) and Indian Health Services. The youth also struggled with their identity and heritage. There was no place where the children could go that symbolized the origin of their history or ancestry. All Grand Ronde Indians were denied the rights and privileges given to other recog-

nized tribes around the country. During the three decades between termination and restoration, many tribal members were forced to leave the area to look for work in Portland or Salem, or live with family members elsewhere.

With the determination and dedication of many tribal members and public officials, in 1983 Congress finally passed the Grand Ronde Restoration Act, Public Law 98–165. The Restoration Act allowed the Confederated Tribes of Grand Ronde to function as one tribal unit, with all the benefits and privileges that had applied prior to termination in 1954. The legislation restored all original rights to tribal members with the exceptions of hunting, fishing, and trapping rights.

Throughout the restoration process, there were many tribal members who chose to be on a lobbying committee for restoration. The Restoration Act would not have been possible without the persistence and effort of the members of this committee, most of whom could remember the sad effects termination had on the Grand Ronde Indians. The committee included several tribal members who serve on the Tribal Council in 1993, and whose names are synonymous with Grand Ronde tribal history: Kathryn Harrison, Mark Mercier, Margaret Provost, and Merle Holmes. They are only a few of the people who worked to restore the tribe. Senator Mark Hatfield and Congressman Les AuCoin, both from Oregon, put the Act on the national agenda, and helped orchestrate a vote for restoring the tribe.

By 1985 the tribal members had completed a Grand Ronde Reservation Plan, which was submitted to the Department of the Interior in Washington, D.C. This plan outlined tribal needs and goals for the future, and gave a brief profile of the tribe's status monetarily and demographically. In 1988, Congress transferred to the Grand Ronde tribe 9,811 acres of land to be used for the reservation, located within the confines of the original 59,000 acres. Most of the land was Bureau of Land Management timber land, and was meant to be used by the Indians to gain revenue for future development. With the timber income, the Grand Ronde tribe purchased 100 acres of land and built offices and administration headquarters. On this land, they now have programs in health care, education, economic development, social services, forestry, planning, and substance abuse control.

In 1983 a Tribal Council was formed, consisting of nine members voted into office by yearly election. The position of chairperson on the Tribal Council is a full-time job, and the chair maintains an office on the reservation. In addition to the Tribal Council, there is also a tribal court system that convenes once per month to handle legal issues and disputes existing within the jurisdiction of the tribe.

Currently there are 3,048 enrolled Grand Ronde tribal members: 40 percent live outside of Oregon, while 60 percent live in the state. Of that 60 percent, only 198 live in Grand Ronde. Currently, there is no housing on the reservation itself. However, the Confederated Tribes of Grand Ronde provide services to those members living in the six counties surrounding the reservation area. Services such as financial assistance for higher education are available for all tribal members. The tribe provides grants to students attending colleges all over the United States. This funding is provided by Grand Ronde timber revenues and by the BIA.

The tribe continues to contract certain services from the federal government and use Grand Ronde timber revenues to fund tribal operations. Of the timber revenues, 30 percent is allotted for economic development. The tribal community service center is its most recent development project. The community center is a gathering place for tribal members and the location for public hearings and general council meetings. The new dental center is also located within this building. Future development plans include a larger health clinic and private housing on the reservation.

In a recent survey mailed to tribal members, many claimed they would move back to Grand Ronde if there were housing and economic opportunity. In addition, many of the elders would like to spend their final years living on the reservation. The Confederated Tribes of Grand Ronde are currently focusing on these two projects.

Many of the tribal members who live nearby participate in tribal committees such as the elders' committee, enrollment committee, and the powwow committee. Since restoration, every year the tribe sponsors an annual powwow, which attracts visitors, tourists, and Indians from all over the United States. A record number of 7,000 attended the 1992 powwow, which was held on the Grand Ronde Reservation for the first time. Many tribal members are working to restore traditional religious practices. Others belong to the Catholic Church or other Christian denominations.

The Confederated Tribes of the Grand Ronde Community of Oregon have been on a long journey since restoration. As the tribe continues to grow and prosper, members in Oregon and elsewhere will be able to take advantage of its services and learn about the history of their people.

Tracy Olson

Further Reading

Hajda, Yvonne. "The Confederated Tribes of the Grand Ronde Community of Oregon." *The First Oregonians.* Portland: Oregon Council For the Humanities (1991): 95–100.

Lewis, John Gordon. *History of the Grand Ronde Military Bunk House.* Dayton, OR: Tribune Publishing Company, 1911.

Mackey, Harold. *The Kalapuyans: A Source Book on the Indians of the Willamette Valley.* Salem, OR: Mission Mill Publishing, 1947.

Ruby, Robert H. *The Chinook Indians.* Norman: University of Oklahoma Press, 1976.

CONFEDERATED TRIBES OF SILETZ

The Indians of the Siletz Reservation entered the twentieth century with serious disabilities. Their once expansive reservation had suffered wholesale reduction. Timbermen and politicians had participated in looting their landed estate. The allotment program had scattered and isolated families in a region with limited wagon roads and means of communication. The brightest of their young people were sent away to boarding schools—some never to return to the reservation. These realities were a terrible portent, but did not mirror the devastation which befell these people when at mid-century they became prime targets for the termination policy. The history of the Siletz is, in many ways, a reflection of the course and failures of federal Indian policy.

The Confederated Tribes of Siletz are descended from more than a dozen bands of refugees forcibly removed in 1856 by the United States Army and the Bureau of Indian Affairs (BIA) to the central coast of Oregon. Victims of the Rogue River Indian Wars, these refugees were primarily the Athabaskan-speaking survivors of the bands who resided along the southwest coast of Oregon and in the canyon of the Rogue River. Individually, they were known as the Galice Creek, Chetco, Kwaishtunnetunne, Chetleshin, Chemetunne, Yukichetunne, Tututni, Mikonotunne, Shasta Costa, Kwatami, and the Mishikwutinetunne (Upper Coquille). The federal government removed them by ship and by forced overland marches to colonize nearly 2,500 survivors along the Siletz River approximately twenty miles upstream from the Pacific Ocean.

On November 9, 1855, President Franklin Pierce created the Siletz or Coast Reservation by executive order. It extended nearly 150 miles along the central Oregon seaboard. The region was the aboriginal homeland of the Salishan-speaking Tillamook and Siletz, the Yakonan-speaking Alsea and Yaquina, and the Siuslawan-speaking Siuslaw and Lower Umpqua. In 1859 the BIA colonized the Coos and Lower Umpqua at Yachats Prairie on the southern portion of the reservation under the Alsea Subagency. By 1861 2,025 Indians resided on the reservation. Only 259 were parties to ratified treaties. This situation meant few annuities came to the agency. The Siletz Indians were compelled to mount an agricultural program in a temperate rain forest. Annually, the death toll mounted from starvation and illness. The 1900 census enumerated only 483 survivors on the Siletz rolls.

On December 21, 1865, President Andrew Johnson cut the Siletz Reservation in half, opening a twenty-mile wide section for the building of a railroad and development of Yaquina Bay. On March 3, 1875, Congress threw open the entire southern portion of the reservation to settlement and likewise redrew the northern boundary at the Salmon River, cutting off thousands of more acres. The law required Native consent. None concurred, but the legislation held. Allotment commenced in 1887, but halted temporarily in 1889. John S. Mayhugh chaired an allotment conference at Siletz and on October 31, 1892, obtained agreement from tribal leaders to renew the program. At stake was the disposition of unallotted "surplus" land, some of it covered with vast stands of old growth timber. In 1892 the reservation contained 225,280 acres; after the creation of 536 allotments approximately 43,000 acres had passed into individual trust land. The remaining tribal lands were 4.06 acres for a sawmill, 9 acres for a church and cemetery, 226 acres for the agency and school, and 5 small timber reserves.

The rush for Siletz Reservation land pitted timber speculators against each other. Ultimately, the BIA identified 175,000 "surplus" acres and provided for a payment of $.74 an acre or $142,600. The actual "surplus" acreage was 191,798. This event set the stage for the infamous plundering of both the "surplus" lands and the allotments, a tale later written in an Oregon prison by Stephen A.D. Puter. This self-proclaimed "king of the Oregon land fraud ring" entitled his book *Looters of the Public Domain* (1908). Puter observed: "What the Indians were coaxed into giving for this comparatively insignificant amount represents an area equivalent to about 1,300 homesteads of 160 acres each, or practically 200,000 acres in round numbers, and is worth today at a conservative estimate, more than $8,000,000." The allotment program scattered the Indians along the Salmon River, the coast of Lincoln County, and along nearly thirty miles of the Siletz River. Those eager for the timber on these trust lands pressed the BIA to "fee patent" the land, or to sell the allotments of those Indians who died without heirs. The scramble for these properties continued for years. In 1953 the Siletz retained only 76 allotments or 5,390 acres.

By the early twentieth century the Siletz had found a variety of forms of employment. Most engaged in subsistence farming. They raised vegetables, kept cows and other livestock, fished for salmon and eel, hunted deer, and sought seasonal employment. Men turned to logging and a number worked to fell the trees of their former reservation. Entire families became part of the agricultural labor force in the Willamette Valley. For several weeks each year, the Indians from Siletz crossed the Coast Range to pick prunes and hops and move from farm to farm in the great interior valley of western Oregon.

The Siletz children since the 1860s had attended either day schools or a boarding school at Siletz, the agency headquarters. Following the opening in 1884 of the Chemawa Indian School near Salem, Oregon, many continued their education at this regional BIA boarding school. Some students went on to Haskell Institute, Riverside School, or Carlisle Indian School. In 1905 Robert DePoe of Siletz began law study at the University of Kansas; he became a teacher. Elwood Towner of Siletz studied at Willamette University and became a lawyer. Coquille Thompson, Jr., graduated from Oregon Agricultural College in 1932. A well-known athlete, Thompson became a judge on the Warm Springs Reservation. Arthur Bensell of Siletz studied at Heidelberg College in Tiffen, Ohio, and won "All-American" honors in the 1920s as a football player. Bensell subsequently worked for the BIA and returned to Siletz after World War II where he owned the local grocery store.

The BIA worked diligently to change the lifeways, languages, and religion of the Siletz Indians. In the nineteenth century, the Methodists took control of all BIA operations at Siletz and furthered this program. The annual fourth of July parades, the encouragement of young men to serve in the military (especially in World War I and II), and the boarding school programs furthered these goals. In the 1870s a number of the Indians of the Siletz Reservation joined the Earth Lodge Cult, a short-lived messianic movement in coastal Oregon. Dozens more became active in the Indian Shaker Church in the 1890s, and subsequently erected a church in Siletz and maintained active services until the 1950s. Although the church stood until the late 1970s, the remaining Shakers held services and healings in their homes.

Several scholars worked with Siletz elders to record literary, linguistic, and cultural information. Rev. J. Owen Dorsey, who was primarily interested in kinship systems and terminologies, began this work in 1884. Harry Hull St. Clair collected literary materials in 1903 at Siletz. Between 1909 and 1914, Leo J. Frachtenbery of Columbia University carried out extensive fieldwork and published both oral literature and language monographs. Between 1928 and 1935, Melville and Elizabeth Jacobs of the University of Washington recorded data on Tillamook, Upper Coquille, and other bands of the reservation. John Peabody Harrington worked in 1942 with Siletz informants. The majority of the field notes of these scholars remain unpublished. Photographers who worked on the reservation included Edward S. Curtis in 1912, and the Rodman Wanamaker expedition in 1913.

From March 8 to 9, 1934, Siletz representatives participated in the conference at Chemawa on the Indian Reorganization Act. Most of the Siletz leaders—like Abe Logan—were highly skeptical of the law. The Siletz declined to organize under the IRA in 1934 by a vote of sixty-three to thirty-seven.

In 1935 the Siletz and Grand Ronde tribes secured a jurisdictional act to litigate over the taking of the central coast of Oregon by the United States without ratified treaty. The Claims Court ruled on April 2, 1945, in their favor. The Justice Department appealed the case to the Supreme Court, which affirmed the ruling on November 25, 1946. The settlement was made in 1947 for the value of the lands "at the date of taking" in 1855, less the value of BIA "services" since 1856, and less the value of allotted reservation lands. The Siletz Indians received $3,128,900. The Siletz also filed before the Indian Claims Commission for the unconscionable payment for the taking of their "surplus" lands subsequent to allotment in 1892. The Claims

Commission awarded $416,240 in June, 1958. Both judgments were distributed per capita.

In the 1950s the termination program fell heavily on Oregon tribes. The naming of Douglas McKay, former Oregon governor, as secretary of the interior, played an important part in the course of these events. The BIA moved rapidly to press the tribes to agree to termination of trust and federal services. The leaders of the Chetco, Coquille, Alsea, and Siletz Confederated Tribes passed resolutions in 1951 endorsing termination. On August 23, 1954, Public Law 588, effective on August 13, 1956, severed all federal relations with these Indians. The BIA issued deeds to remaining allotments, sold the Depoe Bay, Medicine Rock, and Upper timber reserves, and turned over the tribal cemetery and agency buildings to the City of Siletz.

By 1960 heirs to the allotments discovered that western Oregon counties were foreclosing for non-payment of taxes. The loss of Indian lands thus continued. These people also suffered from lack of health care, housing programs, and educational assistance. In March, 1976—twenty years after termination—the American Indian Policy Review Commission held hearings in Salem, Oregon, and gathered hours of testimony about the condition of the terminated tribes. That event coincided with a quickened effort among the Siletz to seek restoration. The documentary film, *The People Are Dancing Again*, told of tribal hopes and helped build support. On November 18, 1977, President Jimmy Carter signed the Siletz Restoration Act. Public Law 280, which transferred authority in criminal matters to the State of Oregon, remained in effect.

Working with the BIA the new Confederated Tribes of the Siletz Reservation completed in 1979 a plan for a reservation. The plan articulated a rationale based on a tribal socio-economic profile and community goals. Some of the goals were economic; others were emotional and involved acquisition of the former tribal cemetery and agency administrative headquarters on Government Hill in Siletz. Congress endorsed the concept and on September 4, 1980, created a 3,630-acre reservation (P.L. 96-340). The Act transferred trusteeship for the tribe from the Bureau of Land Management to the BIA, and included stands of timber in the Coast Range and the Government Hill tract. On August 14, 1981, Congress authorized P.L. 97-38, permitting the construction of permanent improvements on that tract. Subsequently, Congress funded a large tribal center on Government Hill.

Since 1980 the Confederated Tribes of Siletz have initiated an ambitious program of timber sales, a housing program, and secured direct funding through the BIA Self-Governance program. In 1991 the 2,000-member tribe opened a smokehouse to process salmon to sell to tourists, completed a medical clinic, and built fifty-four homes for tribal members. After operating a modest Indian bingo operation on their reservation, the Siletz announced in 1991 plans to buy land in the Willamette Valley, have it taken into trust status, and then open a casino. This initiative incurred spirited opposition from the City of Salem, the Oregon governor, Department of Justice, and other Oregon tribes. By 1993 the Siletz had purchased lands in Salem for the casino and filed suit against the State of Oregon for its opposition to its gaming plans.

Stephen Dow Beckham

Further Reading

Beckham, Stephen Dow. *Requiem For a People: The Rogue Indians and the Frontiersmen.* Norman: University of Oklahoma Press, 1971.

———. *The Indians of Western Oregon: This Land was Theirs.* Coos Bay, OR: Arago Books, 1977.

Beckham, Stephen, Kathryn Anne Toepel, and Rick Minor. *Native American Religious Practices and Uses in Western Oregon.* University of Oregon Anthropological Papers No. 31 (1984).

U.S. Department of the Interior. *Proposed Siletz Reservation Plan.* Portland, OR: Bureau of Indian Affairs, 1979.

Viles, Cynthia, and Tom Grigsby. "The Confederated Tribes of Siletz Indians of Oregon." *The First Oregonians.* Eds. Carolyn M. Buan and Richard Lewis. Portland: Oregon Council for the Humanities (1991): 106-8.

CONFEDERATED TRIBES OF THE UMATILLA INDIAN RESERVATION

The Umatilla Reservation is located in Umatilla County in northeastern Oregon, adjacent to the city of Pendleton. It is bounded on the east by the Umatilla National Forest and the Umatilla River crosses the reservation from Bringham Springs to Pendleton. The topography varies from rolling plains and river valleys to timbered, rugged mountain areas, ranging from elevations of 1,000 to 4,000 feet above sea level. Principal settlements on the reservation include Cayuse, Mission, Athena, and Thornhollow. The nearest off reservation towns are Pendleton and Hermiston, Oregon, and Walla Walla, Washington.

The Cayuse, Umatilla, and Walla Walla, along with a few Palouse and Nez Perce Indians, were brought together under the Treaty of 1855 in which they ceded over 4 million acres to the federal government. In 1993 the Confederated Tribes of the Umatilla Indian Reservation (CTUIR) has an enrollment of approximately 1,300 members, 800 of whom live in the community. Similar in culture and language to other Columbia River tribes (Cayuse is a language isolate) and closely affiliated with the Nez Perce, Yakima, and Warm Springs tribes, their recent history has been dominated by the adoption of the horse, missionization, the Cayuse destruction of the Whitman Mission, loss of lands, and pressures to adopt the culture of the whites.

Before acquiring horses early in the eighteenth century, the Cayuse, Umatilla, and Walla Walla Indians relied on salmon and game gathered seasonally with an assortment of spears, nets, traps, weirs, and other devices. They also gathered roots, berries, pine nuts, seeds, bark, and sap. Like other Plateau tribes, they lived in multifamily lodges constructed of poles and mats over shallow excavations. Their horses made them mobile, and numbers of them joined seasonally with the Nez Perce and others to hunt bison on the western Plains.

Like the Nez Perce, the CTUIR were initially provided with a large land base in the Treaty of 1855, which was later reduced drastically by various actions of the federal government to about 245,000 acres. This reservation was one of the first in the Northwest to be opened by federally sponsored allotment to white settlement. Their rich farm lands were first leased to white farmers and then quickly sold to such farmers, resulting in a sharp reduction in lands owned by tribal members. The original 245,700 acres were diminished drastically to the following:

	Acres
Tribally Owned	15,438
Allotted	79,835
Total	95,273

Both Catholic and Presbyterian missionaries have had a major impact on the Cayuse, Umatilla, and Walla Walla. Their influence has helped weaken traditional culture and language, although there is now a revitalization underway in which the Seven Drum Religion is a major force. The traditionalists of the Columbia River Sahaptins and of the Yakima Reservation are instrumental in this revitalization. In addition, an Indian Shaker Church has been occasionally active on the reservation.

The rejection of the Indian Reorganization Act in favor of another type of tribal government resembled Nez Perce reactions to John Collier and his Indian New Deal. The tribe operates under a Constitution and Bylaws adopted in December of 1949. Tribal government and business are executed by an elected Council of nine members. From this group, a chairman, vice-chairman, secretary, and treasurer are selected. Most tribal business is carried on through committees that handle issues including scholarships, credit, fishing, and approval and enrollment committees.

Like the Yakima, Nez Perce, and Warm Springs, the CTUIR benefited from the Celilo Falls settlement in which each member of the tribe was paid $3,494.61 for lost fishing sites that were inundated by the Dalles Dam. Four claims filed with the Indian Claims Commission have provided the tribes with additional income, which forms an endowment for scholarships and other purposes.

The Confederated Tribes of the Umatilla Indian Reservation now exert major economic and political influence in northeastern Oregon. They are members of the Umatilla Basin Project, the Columbia River Inter-Tribal Fish Commission, the Basalt Waste Isolation Project, the Hanford Environmental Dose Reconstruction Project, the Columbia Gorge Commission, and other planning efforts involving the United States Army Corps of Engineers and the United States Forest Service. They have an active cultural resource management program and are now developing an Oregon Trail Interpretive Center as one of their tribal enterprises.

The CTUIR have been active participants in most of the recent major cases involving reserved treaty rights to fish and hunt on the rivers and the open and unclaimed lands of the Northwest within their traditional range. Increasingly, their political and economic influence is apparent in Oregon and Northwest political life.

Most tillable Umatilla Reservation lands are leased for farming. Also leased is the McNary Dam townsite near Umatilla, Oregon, to which the Umatilla tribes obtained title under provisions of Public Law 85-186, a transaction associated with the construction of McNary Dam, which was built in 1957 on the Columbia River. On February 18, 1959, the Indians leased the townsite to S&S Steel Productions, Inc., of Los Angeles, a manufacturer of ten-by-fifty-foot mobile homes. Under the provisions of the lease, tribal members were given first preference for employment with the company; other Indians had second preference for employment. An on-the-job training contract with S&S provided training for other Indians as well as tribal members. More than 50 percent of the S&S employees were Indians in 1983.

Other indications of cultural revitalization include special tribal programs providing credit, recreation, and summer work programs. The reservation has an office for general and adult education, a day-care center, employment and health facilities, alcohol and drug treatment programs, a housing authority, and an educational program for the elderly. A forest and range enterprise is tribally owned, as are a store and a lake for camping and fishing. An arts and crafts organization teaches tribal members bead and leather working, weaving, and other skills. Cultural revitalization is evident in numerous other ways, especially in an active ceremonial life emphasizing traditional foods and practices, especially the salmon and roots ceremonies.

Deward E. Walker, Jr.

Further Reading

Anastasio, Angelo. "The Southern Plateau: An Ecological Analysis of Intergroup Relations." *Northwest Anthropological Research Notes* 6:2 (1972): 109–229.

Ruby, Robert H., and John A. Brown. *The Cayuse Indians: Imperial Tribesmen of Old Oregon.* Norman: University of Oklahoma Press, 1972.

Stern, Theodore. "White and Indian Farmers on the Umatilla Reservation." *Northwest Anthropological Research Notes* 5:1 (1971): 37–76.

Walker, Deward E., Jr. "Mutual Cross-Utilization of Economic Resources in the Plateau: An Example from Aboriginal Nez Perce Fishing Practices." *Laboratory of Anthropology, Report of Investigation* 41. Pullman: Washington State University, 1967.

CONFEDERATED TRIBES OF THE WARM SPRINGS RESERVATION

The Confederated Tribes of the Warm Springs Reservation consist of seven bands of two tribes party to the 1855 Treaty with the tribes of Middle Oregon negotiated by Joel Palmer. Bands listed in the treaty include Sahaptin-speaking groups, the Tygh or Upper De Chutes, Wyam or Lower De Chutes, Tenino (a term sometimes used collectively for all Warm Springs Sahaptin bands), and Dock-spus or John Day's River. Bands of Kiksht or Upper Chinookan speakers include the Dalles, Ki-gal-twal-la, and Dog River (i.e., Hood River). The treaty established the Warm Springs Indian Reservation, an area of 639,898 acres in north central Oregon. The reservation extends from the Cascade Mountains' crest between Mts. Hood and Jefferson east to the Deschutes River. A third tribe joined the Sahaptin-speaking Warm Springs and Upper Chinook speaking Wascos on the Warm Springs Reservation in 1879 when the first of several groups of Northern Paiute POWs were relocated there by the United States Army. The treaties imposed a tribal structure on a set of politically autonomous local villages. The "bands" and "tribes" of the treaty represent village communities and the ethnolinguistic groups to which they belonged respectively. The treaties also divided closely allied villages by drawing a boundary between villages on opposite shores of the Columbia River, assigning north shore villages to the Yakima Reservation and those opposite to the Warm Springs Reservation.

The 1855 Treaty included the key provision reserving to the Indians the right to take fish "at all . . . usual and accustomed stations, in common with the citizens of the United States . . . , also the privilege of hunting, gathering roots and berries," etc., throughout the ceded area (some 6 million acres). This passage is the basis for the decision of Judge George Boldt allocating 50 percent of returning salmon to Puget Sound treaty tribes (subsequently extended to those of the Columbia River as well). The Warm Springs Indians hold these rights today, despite an attempt to abrogate them by a fraudulent supplementary treaty of 1865.

The Dawes Severalty Act of 1887, which led to the alienation of significant fractions of the land base of many reservations, had only slight impact at Warm Springs, largely because little reservation land was readily farmed. Just over 1 percent of the Warm Spring Reservation is owned by non-Indians (about 7,500 acres in 1993) and nearly 90 percent of the reservation is tribally owned. The Warm Springs tribe's claim that a faulty survey in 1871 had deprived them of 78,000 acres known as the McQuinn Strip was resolved in 1972 when Congress returned 61,360 acres of this strip to the tribe. It supports timber valued then at $60 million.

The present tribal government was established in 1938 under provisions of the Indian Reorganization Act of 1934 (IRA). The Constitution established an eleven-member Tribal Council with authority to oversee all tribal operations. Eight Council members are elected for three-year terms from districts traditionally associated with the three tribes of the confederation, and each of the three tribal divisions is represented by a chief, who serves on the Tribal Council for life. Decisions of the Tribal Council are subject to review by a general council of all adult tribal members through a referendum process, exercised for example in 1984 when the Tribal Council's budget was rejected. Tribal membership rolls include all those individuals with one-quarter or more blood of the Confederated Tribes and who were born to a tribal member residing on the reservation. Adoption by the tribe under certain other circumstances is also allowed for. Tribal enrollment stood at 3,410 in 1993.

The tribal government oversees the management of the tribal corporation's commercial enterprises via an appointed general manager. This corporation was federally licensed in 1938, also under the IRA, but it did not assume a prominent role until the economic boom of the 1960s. This was fueled in large measure by the monetary settlement received by the Warm Springs Confederated Tribes for the flooding of Celilo Falls by the Dalles Dam in 1957. The bulk of the $4 million they received was invested in tribal economic development. However, no amount of money could replace the social and spiritual value of the Celilo fisheries, which for thousands of years were the heart of lower mid-Columbia Indian life. Fishing continues to be important to Warm Springs Reservation Indians, but is now limited to gill netting by a few fishermen along the Columbia River and dip netting at Sherars Falls on the Deschutes River, a traditional site. The tribes purchased 888 acres at this off-reservation fishery in 1980.

By 1980 tribal corporation income had reached $20 million annually, which helped support a tribal operating budget of $10 million. Successful tribal enterprises include the Warm Springs Forest Products Industries (WSFPI), which operates a mill and plywood plant to process reservation timber harvested on a sustained-yield basis; Warm Springs Power Industries, which sells electricity generated at the tribally owned Pelton Dam; the Kah-Nee-Ta resort complex; and two radio stations. WSFPI employs 300 people, mostly tribal members, and its profits contribute substantially toward the annual per capita dividends of up to $2,700 paid to each tribal member during the 1980s.

Tribal government employed 400 persons, tribal enterprises—including WSFPI—employed 600 more, and other reservation-based employers provided 400 jobs by 1980. Half of these 1,400 jobs were held by tribal members, their spouses, or other Indians. The tribal payroll in 1979 exceeded $13 million, making the tribe the largest employer in central Oregon. Clearly, Warm Springs has been unusually successful in developing a self-sufficient reservation-based economy.

Most Warm Springs Indians over the age of forty were educated at the Warm Springs Agency boarding school, which opened in 1897. Boarding school students were separated from their families except for summer vacation and holidays. Their hair was cut short and they were prohibited from speaking their Indian languages in an effort to "civilize" them. The

Warm Springs boarding school was taken over by the Jefferson County School District in 1961 and the dormitories closed in 1967. Warm Springs children now attend primary grades in a public school on the reservation. For secondary school they go to the nearby town of Madras where Indian students are in the minority. Cultural differences in styles of learning and communicating are implicated in the continuing difficulties Warm Springs children have competing in school. Nevertheless, by 1986, forty-eight tribal members had earned college degrees, assisted by a tribal-BIA scholarship program.

The tribes' first college graduate, Vernon Jackson, served as chief executive officer and secretary-treasurer for the Tribal Council until his death in 1969. His successor was Ken Smith, who continues in that capacity in 1993 following a term (1980 to 1984) as assistant secretary of the interior for Indian affairs.

The original linguistic and cultural division of the Warm Springs people among "Warm Springs Indians" (Sahaptin speakers at Simnasho to the north), Wascos (Upper Chinookan speakers once concentrated about the agency on Shitike Creek), and Paiutes (settled along Seekseequa Creek to the south) continues to be recognized today, though in attenuated form. The Northern Paiute and Upper Chinookan languages are not frequently used. In the latter case this may be attributed in part to the Wascos' reputation for entrepreneurial innovation and openness to outside influences. By contrast, Warm Springs Sahaptin survives as the linguistic bulwark of traditionalism on the reservation. Sahaptin is used regularly on ceremonial occasions and most notably in services of the *Wáashat* (or *Wáshat*) or Seven Drum Religion. *Wáashat* today is closely linked to Sahaptin-speaking communities throughout the southern Columbia plateau.

Wáashat congregations are open to all members of the community. The cultural centrality of the *Wáashat* Religion is suggested by the fact that tribal funds have been made available to renovate *Wáashat* "Longhouse" churches/community centers. *Wáashat* forms of worship are attributed in part to teachings of nineteenth-century Plateau prophets, among which Smohalla of Priest Rapids is best known. *Wáashat* worship focuses on traditional sacred foods, honored at seasonal feasts, and on rites of passage such as marriage and death.

The Feather Dance Religion was established by Jake Hunt at the turn of the century and survives primarily on the Warm Springs Reservation. The Feather Dance shares features with *Wáashat* practice, but also resembles the Indian Shaker Church, especially in emphasizing ritual healing. Andrew David was a recent Feather Dance leader, a great-grandson of the founder. He died on the Warm Springs Reservation in 1986.

Eugene S. Hunn

Further Reading

DuBois, Cora. *The Feather Cult of the Middle Columbia.* General Series in Anthropology 7. Menasha, WI: George Banta, 1938.

French, David. "Wasco-Wishram." *Perspectives in American Indian Culture Change.* Ed. Edward H. Spicer. IL: University of Chicago Press (1961): 337–430.
Murdock, George P. "The Tenino Indians." *Ethnology* 19 (1980): 129–49.
The People of Warm Springs. Warm Springs: Confederated Tribes of the Warm Springs Reservation of Oregon, 1984.
Stowell, Cynthia D. *Faces of a Reservation: A Portrait of the Warm Springs Indian Reservation.* Portland: Oregon Historical Society, 1987.

Coos

See Confederated Tribes of the Coos, Lower Umpqua, and Suislaw

COQUILLE

The Coquilles (pronounced *ko-kwel*) were first defined as a tribe when the headmen of villages/bands along the Coquille River in southwest Oregon placed their signs or marks on the Treaty of 1855 (yet unratified), which would have ceded tribal land to the United States in return for a reservation and various tribal rights. Their aboriginal territory included villages within the Coquille River drainage, and coastal villages as far south as the Sixes River.

The dominant language of the lower Coquilles (up to Coquille) was Miluk (a division of Kusan), which closely related them to the Miluk speakers at Coos Bay. The Upper Coquilles spoke Athabaskan, while Chinook Jargon, the *lingua franca* of the Pacific Northwest, was commonly used by all, which explains the bits and pieces of each remembered today.

Along with the survivors of the Rogue River Wars of 1856 (and of earlier village massacres by white miners and United States Army retaliations), the remaining Coquilles were marched overland and/or shipped by steamer to a concentration camp at Reedsport and later to Yachats. Many died or ran away, often returning home to hide out with the families of those women who were married to white men and still living in the homeland. Having no treaty, the survivors were finally moved to the Siletz Reservation.

Twentieth-Century History

In 1916 George Bundy Wasson (1880 to 1947), a graduate of Chemawa and Carlisle Indian schools and the youngest child of Susan and George R. Wasson of South Slough on Coos Bay, began investigating land claims based on the unratified treaties of 1855. By lobbying Congress he finally won permission to go to court in 1929. The Court of Claims decided favorably for the Coquilles (among other coastal groups) on April 2, 1945. Coquel Thompson (1839 to 1946), was a major informant for John P. Harrington of the Bureau of American Ethnology, on both upper and lower Coquille languages, culture, and history. It was this information in Harrington's testimony that convinced Congress of the aboriginality of the Coquille Indians.

The United States Supreme Court overruled an appeal by the Justice Department in 1946, and the case was finally closed in 1950, awarding $1.20 per acre for 722,530 acres. The Coquilles received an inheritance of $3,128,000 which, after numerous federal deductions, totaled approximately $2,000 per person.

The Coquilles were terminated, with forty-two other western Oregon tribes, in 1954 (Public Law 588). After intense lobbying by tribal leader Wilfred C. Wasson and others, the Coquille Indian tribe regained federal recognition in 1989 (Coquille Indian Restoration Act, *103 Stat. 91*).

Demographics

In 1993 there are approximately 630 tribal members, the majority of whom live in Oregon. The tribal headquarters are in Coos Bay. The tribe is governed by an elected seven-person Council, and delivers services to members living within a five-county service area in southwest Oregon. The Council meets monthly and holds biannual General Council meetings at mid-summer and mid-winter.

A 1991 survey showed that tribal members generally enjoy health and education levels on a par with others in the south coast region of Oregon. Housing and employment needs are greater than the regional averages. The tribe owns 6.2 acres of trust land in the town of Bandon at the mouth of the Coquille River. It is working with Congress to increase that land base and develop tribal economic self-sufficiency.

Culture

The culture of the Coquilles, extending into the reservation period, was a mixture of elements from the Northwest Coast (e.g., dentalium money), while their dances, ceremonial clothing, and spirituality (e.g., shamanism, reverence for flicker feathers, and pileated woodpecker scalps), were shared with their south coast neighbors. Basketry was a major industry of the Coquilles, which enhanced the fame of the basketmakers at the Siletz Reservation. Susan Adulsah Wasson (1841 to 1917) is the most frequently mentioned Coquille ancestor on the final tribal roles. She was the daughter of Kitzn-Jin-Jn (Kitchen, or Man Too Big For Elk Robe To Meet In The Middle), headman of the major south slough village on Coos Bay in 1828, and his wife, Gishgiu (Gishgewe, or Giscuae), daughter of an Upper Coquille headman. Their marriage was said to have united the Coos and Coquille tribes. Susan was an oral historian of the Coos Bay area. She was often summoned into court for evidence on Indian/white histories. She spoke several coastal languages, and taught many tribal myths, legends, and stories to her children, who carried her lessons well into the twentieth century.

Today, storytelling is practiced by only a few people, including Susan Wasson Wolgamott and her brother, George B. Wasson Jr., who learned stories and legends primarily from their father and his sisters. The last full-blood Coquille was Charles Edward "Eddy" Ned (1889 to 1956). He served in the United States Army during World War II.

In 1988, a form of the Sacred Salmon ceremony was reinstituted, along with an annual salmon bake. A Mid-Winter Gathering (aboriginally, a World Renewal ceremony) has also been revived. Today, there is virtually no knowledge or common use of the Coquille tribal languages, yet there is a strong desire among some members to relearn and revive their customs.

George B. Wasson, Jr.

Further Reading

Beckham, Stephen D. *The Indians of Western Oregon: This Land Was Theirs.* Coos Bay, OR: Arago Books, 1977.

———. "The History of Western Oregon Since 1846." *Handbook of North American Indians.* Vol. 7. *Northwest Coast.* Ed. Wayne Suttles. Washington, DC: Smithsonian Institution (1990): 180–88.

Hall, Roberta L. *The Coquille Indians: Yesterday, Today, and Tomorrow.* Lake Oswego, OR: Smith, Smith, and Smith Publishing Co., 1984.

Harrington, John P. *Alsea-Siuslaw-Coos and Southwestern Oregon Fieldnotes: John P. Harrington Papers, Alaska/ Northwest Coast.* Microfilm. Reels 021-027.Washington, DC: National Anthropological Archives, Smithsonian Institution, 1933, 1942.

Peterson, Emil R., and Alfred Powers. *A Century of Coos and Curry.* Portland, OR: Binsford and Mort, 1952.

Wasson, George B. "The Memory of a People: The Coquilles of the Southwest Coast." *The First Oregonians.* Eds. Carolyn Buan and Richard Lewis. Portland, OR: Council for the Humanities (1991): 83–87.

COSTANOAN/OHLONE

Traditional Costanoan/Ohlone territory extends along the central California coast from San Francisco Bay to Point Sur south of Monterey Bay, and eastward to the inner coast ranges and the edge of the central valley. At the time of European contact, Costanoan/ Ohlone people were not affiliated as a single political entity, but rather into fifty or more separate and politically independent nations, speaking dialects of eight or more related languages. The eight recognized Costanoan/Ohlone languages are Karkin, Chochenyo, Ramaytush, Tamyen, Awaswas, Mutsun, Rumsen, and Chalon. Modern descendants still identify with their ancestral language groups. (The terms Costanoan and Ohlone are used interchangeably today: Costanoan is from the Spanish word "Costanos" meaning "coastal people" and Ohlone is from "Olhon," a village and tribe once located in present-day San Mateo County.)

Traditional life was dramatically disrupted by the establishment of seven Spanish missions within Costanoan/Ohlone territory, later by secularization of the missions under Mexican rule, and still further by the American incursion into California. Contact with these other ethnic groups as well as with neighboring Native peoples led to extensive intermarriage. Social and physical survival in a racially biased society often required blending into other ethnic communities. However, Costanoan/Ohlone families have maintained their cultural identities even under difficult circumstances.

Because Costanoan/Ohlone people were no longer living an aboriginal lifestyle in the early twentieth century, they were declared extinct by some anthropologists. Nevertheless, people were still speaking their native languages in the 1920s and 1930s. During these years, John P. Harrington, an anthropologist and linguist working for the Smithsonian Institution's Bureau of American Ethnology, extensively interviewed Chochenyo, Mutsun, and Rumsen speakers, amassing volumes of field notes on language, ethnobotany, folklore, and other cultural information.

While no reservation lands have ever been established in Costanoan/Ohlone territory, Costanoan/Ohlone people were among other California Indians who participated in two land claims cases against the federal government; the first was initiated in the 1920s, with a compromise settlement on the second claim occurring in 1964. These cases resulted in minimal restitution for ancestral lands acquired by the government in the previous century under eighteen unratified treaties.

An unexpected result of these land claims cases, with their attendant enrollment and documentation processes, was to establish evidence of the presence of an "extinct" Costanoan/Ohlone people. Further evidence came in the 1960s when descendants of Mission San Jose successfully prevented destruction of a mission cemetery that lay in the path of a proposed freeway. These descendants incorporated as the Ohlone Indian Tribe, and now hold title to the Ohlone Indian Cemetery in Fremont, California. In 1975, a similar situation occurred in Watsonville, California, when a burial ground was discovered during construction of a warehouse. Local Native people resorted to an armed barricade in order to prevent destruction of the site, but the incident was resolved peacefully and the Pajaro Valley Ohlone Indian Council was formed to oversee future protection. In 1988 a Mutsun descendant acquired substantial acreage in the Hollister area through the General Allotment Act of 1887.

No reliable population figures are available, but there are certainly hundreds, and more likely several thousand living descendants, with many still living within traditional ancestral territory. Descendants have become increasingly active in the monitoring of construction activity on cultural sites, especially those containing Native American burials. California state law has established a process whereby "most likely descendants" are notified upon the discovery of these burials, and can then make recommendations as to their handling and disposition. In 1990 the Costanoan/Ohlone community received national attention when they completed lengthy negotiations with Stanford University for the return of ancestral skeletal remains held by the university. It was a highly controversial issue of academic freedom versus the cultural sovereignty of Native American people. The remains were reburied in ancestral ground.

There are no federally recognized Costanoan/Ohlone tribes, but as of this writing four groups are formally seeking federal acknowledgment through a process established by the Bureau of Indian Affairs. These are the Amah Band, Carmel Mission Band, Indian Canyon Band, and Muwekma Tribe.

The closing years of the twentieth century find the Costanoan/Ohlone people in a period of cultural revitalization. Language, basketry traditions, and folklore are all being revived through organizations such as the Carmel Valley Indian Cultural Center, which has been established by Rumsen Costanoan descendants. Cultural programs educate the public to the richness of the Costanoan/Ohlone experience, both past and present. We are a modern people, and although much of our aboriginal culture is gone, we are still a people with a sense of identity, a strong sense of heritage, and a spiritual connection to our cultural past.

Linda G. Yamane

See also **California Tribes**

Further Reading

Bocek, Barbara R. "Ethnobotany of Costanoan Indians, California, Based on Collections by John P. Harrington." *Economic Botany* 38:2 (1984): 240–55.

Castillo, Edward D. "Twentieth-Century Secular Movements." *Handbook of North American Indians.* Vol. 8. *California.* Ed. Robert F. Heizer. Washington, DC: Smithsonian Institution (1978): 713–17.

Harrington, John P. *The Papers of John Peabody Harrington in the Smithsonian Institution 1907–1957.* Vol. 2. *Northern and Central California.* Ed. Elaine L. Mills. Millwood, NY: Kraus International Publications, 1981.

Levy, Richard. "Costanoan." *Handbook of North American Indians.* Vol. 8. *California.* Ed. Robert F. Heizer. Washington, DC: Smithsonian Institution (1978): 485–95.

COUNCIL OF ENERGY RESOURCE TRIBES

The Council of Energy Resource Tribes (CERT) is a nonprofit organization founded in 1976 by the leaders of twenty-five American Indian tribes. CERT's founders were determined to take control of the management of the energy resources on their lands to enable their tribes to build healthy self-sufficient communities.

Because of the federal government's historic domination of resource management on Indian land, tribes have been denied opportunities to develop the professional and technical expertise necessary to competently manage their own resources. Through CERT, member tribes in 1993 have access to a primarily American Indian staff of professionals experienced in areas such as economics, energy resource management, law, engineering, enterprise development, and computer technology. Their backgrounds in tribal government, private industry, and the federal agencies governing Indian affairs bring awareness and sensitivity to the issues facing American Indians. The relationship between tribal staff and CERT fosters an invaluable sharing of technology, strengthening tribal knowledge and skill.

CERT's membership is now forty-three American Indian tribes and four Canadian Indian nations. Guided by the elected tribal officials who are CERT's board of directors, the organization is composed of three non-profit entities. In addition to CERT (the parent corporation), there are two subsidiaries—CERT Technical Services Corporation (TSC) and the CERT Education Fund, Inc.

TSC makes CERT's technical expertise available on a contractual basis to CERT member and non-member tribes as well as Indian organizations, government agencies, and private industry. The CERT Education Fund, Inc. is dedicated to providing educational opportunities for Indians.

CERT is a nonprofit corporation funded through a number of sources. These include federal funds, private foundation grants, tribal membership dues, and corporate sponsorships. The annual American Spirit Award Dinner, the country's largest Indian education fundraiser, is the cornerstone of CERT's educational fundraising efforts.

Largely through the efforts of the CERT tribes, landmark energy legislation passed during the 1980s reflects the significant role that Indian tribes play as producers of domestic energy, as well as reflecting their status as sovereign governments. A turning point in Indian resource management was the passage of two pieces of crucial legislation—the Indian Mineral Development Act of 1982 and the Federal Oil and Gas Royalty Management Act of 1982. These laws—vigorously supported by CERT—guaranteed Indian people an active role in the development of their resources.

In dozens of instances in Indian country, coal leases have been renegotiated and oil and gas agreements have taken the form of joint ventures. National environmental laws have been amended to affirm tribal primacy over their lands. Resource development agreements include provisions for tribal employment, training, and scholarship opportunities. Tribal resource development now nets millions of dollars more for tribes—funds used to address governmental responsibilities such as building reservation infrastructures, providing health care, and investing in the future.

CERT provides comprehensive services to tribes as they diversify their economies and build stable communities. It offers expertise in areas ranging from feasibility studies, to project financing, to construction supervision. It assists tribes in creating organization structures, tax codes, accounting systems, and marketing strategies.

The Tribal Resource Institute in Business, Engineering and Science (TRIBES), a pre-college program, and CERT scholarships provide academic and financial support to Indian students. CERT summer internships enable these students to work in corporate settings gaining knowledge and experience. Through a year-long CERT internship, co-sponsored with Region VIII of the Environmental Protection Agency (EPA), tribal staff learn firsthand about federal environmental regulations and procedures to be able to implement more comprehensive environmental programs on reservations. CERT also provides workshops on relevant topics providing critical information to tribal decision makers on issues such as water quality management and solid and hazardous waste disposal. The CERT-NREL (National Renewable Energy Laboratory) Teaching Fellowships offer summer training positions to Indian high school math and science teachers as well as other teachers of Indian students.

CERT is concerned with the development and utilization of renewable energy resources, as well as building diversified economic bases. Its member tribes recognize the importance of planning for the time when traditional energy resources are depleted. CERT tribes continue to explore practical applications for geothermal resources, wind energy, and solar power.

CERT's tribal leadership has adopted a dynamic three-pronged approach to achieve their goal of true self-determination: tribes must effectively govern their own lands, as well as play an important role in governing America; American Indians must master the tools of modern technology to protect and enhance their cultural heritages; and tribes must cultivate diversified economies balancing environmental and cultural concerns with economic growth.

In hundreds of instances, the CERT staff has worked with tribes as they strive to take their rightful place in the American system. CERT will continue to provide professional and technical resources tailored to the unique needs of American Indian tribes.

A. David Lester

See also **Mining; Natural Resource Management**

COURTS
See Tribal Governments

COUSHATTA
See Alabama-Coushatta

COW CREEK BAND OF UMPQUA

The specters of non-recognition and termination haunted the Cow Creek Band of Umpqua for most of the twentieth century. Residing in a mountainous region along the South Umpqua River in present-day Oregon, these people participated in the first of two treaties ratified in 1854 in the Pacific Northwest. Their treaty of 1853 (10 Stat. 1027) provided for the cession of more than 700 square miles, but called for the creation of a reservation in the lower Cow Creek Valley. The outbreak of the Rogue River Indian War of 1855 to 1856 swept the Cow Creeks into the holocaust. Numbering more than 230, they fled the reservation to hide in the mountains. For decades, they eked out an existence as refugees. Repeatedly, the Bureau of Indian Affairs (BIA) and United States Army attempted to round them up for removal; they eluded their pursuers.

Members of the Cow Creek band intermarried with Indians of other tribes and with the French-Canadian population who entered their homeland with the Hudson's Bay Company. In the twentieth century, tribal families trace their ancestries through lineages bearing the names Rondeau, Dumont, Petit, Guilbeau, LaChance, and Pariseau (Parazoo) or from trappers such as Nonta, an Algonquian who married into the tribe in the 1830s. The last known speaker of their Takelman dialect died in the 1940s.

Early Twentieth-Century History

About 1918, the Cow Creeks created a formal tribal government with elected officers, regular meetings, and programs to attempt to secure BIA services. Although a few secured public domain allotments, most remained landless or lived closely together on the property of a family member. In the 1910s a number of tribal members were enrolled as "Fourth Section/Public Domain Indians" under the jurisdiction of the Roseburg Superintendency. With the closing of that unit in 1918, they fell under the Siletz-Grande Ronde Indian Agency. Tribal children secured admission to Chemawa Indian School or Greenville Indian School near Fresno, California. The BIA, however, extended no health or other programs.

In 1921 the tribe secured legal assistance from Seneca Fouts of Portland and assistance in writing letters to lobby members of Congress through George and Jessie (Vinson) Rapp of Roseburg, Oregon. These friendships led Senator Charles McNary of Oregon to introduce S. 3254 in 1926, to permit the Cow Creeks and other tribes of western Oregon to sue in the Court of Claims over land claims. The efforts to secure a jurisdictional act led to additional House and Senate bills in 1928, 1930, and 1932. S. 826 passed both the Senate and the House and went to President Herbert Hoover, who in 1932 vetoed the legislation.

In spite of discouragement, the Cow Creeks continued to meet and seek resolution of their tenuous federal relationship. The diary of Mamie (Furlong) Archambeau, a tribal member, confirms a succession of meetings in the years 1947 to 1955. Throughout this period, tribal members corresponded with and occasionally met with BIA officials regarding enrollment and eligibility to participate in claims litigation. There is no record that the BIA ever informed the Cow Creek Band of its opportunity to file before the Indian Claims Commission. When tribal members finally learned of the Commission in 1953, they were informed that the period for filing a complaint closed on August 13, 1951. The tribe could not litigate.

Termination, Land Claims, and Restoration

Without specific assessment of their situation or any meeting with the tribe through field hearings held by the BIA, Congress included the Cow Creeks in the Western Oregon Termination Act, Public Law 588. Approved in 1954, the law severed all federal relations, including trust status of allotments. As a prelude to termination, the BIA enrolled Cow Creeks in job training programs and provided for transportation and housing to sites in Oakland, California, and St. Paul, Minnesota. For many, the work with BIA Relocation/Vocational Training Officer Leonard C. Allen was the first program activity they had encountered through the BIA. In 1956 the federal government severed all dealings with the Cow Creeks.

Termination changed little. The Cow Creeks continued to meet and plan for a better tomorrow. In the 1970s they wrote to members of Congress about Indian health issues and in 1976 adopted a wildlife plan. The tribe addressed Bureau of Land Management (BLM) and United States Forest Service management studies and became involved in Title IV, Indian Education Act programs in local schools. On February 22, 1979, S. 668 was introduced to permit the Cow Creek Band of Umpqua to file suit in the United States Court of Claims over taking of its land in the 1850s. After joint hearings chaired by Congressman James Weaver, the measure passed Congress, becoming law on May 26, 1980.

Land claims litigation deepened the political sophistication of the Cow Creeks. Tribal members traveled to and from Washington, D.C., to testify on the jurisdictional act and assist legal counsel. They also pressed Congress to overturn termination. Again, by unanimous consent and in spite of opposition testimony by the BIA, Congress passed such legislation. On December 29, 1982, President Ronald Reagan signed the recognition act. In 1984, the United States Justice Department agreed to a negotiated settlement of $1.5 million in the claims case. The tribe voted favorably to accept the award, a corrective for the $.023/acre paid under the treaty of 1853.

The Cow Creeks appointed a committee which weighed options on the judgment fund. After months of deliberation, the tribe accepted its plan to vest the entire $1.5 million in an endowment. The BIA rejected the tribal plan, called for a per capita distribution, challenged the tribal roll, and did nothing for a year to bring forward an alternative plan. With the prospect of the Cow Creek judgment falling into limbo, Congress passed P.L. 100–139 in October, 1987. It endorsed the tribal plan and provided for vesting the judgment fund in a permanent endowment.

Economic Development

Using its own resources, the Cow Creek Band purchased land in 1984 at Canyonville, Oregon. In 1986, the BIA took twenty-nine acres into trust as a reservation. Through a subsequent purchase the tribe has added twenty-eight more acres. Drawing on its endowment fund to further economic development, the tribe contracted with USA Research to prepare in 1988 a "Tribal Economic Development Strategy and Business Plan." As a result of a screen of options and assessment of its situation, in 1989 the tribe created the Umpqua Indian Development Corporation (UIDC). The UIDC board included five tribal and four non-tribal members. UIDC opened dialog with potential joint-venture partners and in May, 1992, opened with British American Bingo a full-service bingo and entertainment facility on the reservation. The Cow Creeks also secured the first gaming compact in Oregon on October 2, 1992, under the Indian Gaming Regulatory Act. Band members also find employment in logging, lumbering, and service trades.

Cultural Activities

The Cow Creeks host an annual week-long pow-wow at South Umpqua Falls each July. Many families gather in late summer at the Huckleberry Patch on the Rogue-Umpqua Divide to pick berries. While Catholicism has attracted the greatest number of Cow Creeks throughout the historic period, traditional tribal burials and reinterments have occurred at Old Tom's Prairie in the Umpqua National Forest, one of three special interest areas the Cow Creeks co-manage with the United States Forest Service.

Conclusion

Federal recognition, the impetus of the land claims judgment, and a renewed sense of well-being turned Cow Creek affairs in the late twentieth century. A tribe of 850 enrolled members, the Cow Creeks have mounted housing improvement programs, health awareness efforts, education, and economic development projects. Susan Crispen Shaffer has served as chair from 1984 to 1993. A leader in her community, she has participated in national Indian meetings, chaired the board of the local community college, served on the BLM advisory committee, and helped lead her tribe into the twenty-first century.

Stephen Dow Beckham

Further Reading

Beckham, Stephen Dow. *Requiem For a People: The Rogue Indians and the Frontiersmen.* Norman: University of Oklahoma Press, 1972.

———. *Land of the Umpqua: A History of Douglas County, Oregon.* Roseburg, OR: Douglas County Commissioners, 1987.

Beckham, Stephen Dow, and Sherri Shaffer. "Patience and Persistence: The Cow Creek Band of Umpqua Tribe of Indians." *The First Oregonians.* Eds. Carolyn M. Buan and Richard Lewis. Portland: Oregon Council for the Humanities (1992): 89–94.

Riddle, George. *Early Days in Oregon: A History of the Riddle Valley.* Myrtle Creek, OR: Myrtle Creek Mail Printers, 1953.

Young, K., and T.D. Cutsforth. "Hunting Superstitions in the Cow Creek Region." *Journal of American Folklore* 41 (1928): 293–95.

COWLITZ

Aboriginally, the Cowlitz Indians (also known as the Cawalitz, Cow-a-lidsk, Cowalitsk, Cow-e-lis-kee, Cowelits, Cowlitch, Cow-lit-sick, Kawelitsk, Kowalitsk, Kowlitch, Kowlitz) lived throughout the Cowlitz River drainage system in the interior southwest of what is now the state of Washington. They were composed of four regional divisions: the Upper, the Lower, the Mountain (to the west), and the Lewis River (to the east). The dominant divisions were the Upper and Lower Cowlitz, the latter of which was the most densely populated with an estimated 6,000 Cowlitz Indians inhabiting cedar plank longhouses, located in about thirty winter villages along the lower Cowlitz River. The Upper Cowlitz, or Taidnapam, and the Lewis River Cowlitz spoke Sahaptin, the Mountain and Lower Cowlitz spoke Salish, and all divisions utilized the Chinook Jargon as their trade language. A river and prairie people, the Cowlitz were skilled with both canoes and horses. They were described by Special United States Indian Agent Charles E. Roblin, in his 1919 enumeration of unattached Indians, as "a powerful tribe, and in the early days constituted the 'blue blood' of western Washington." Today, there are approximately 1,400 enrolled Cowlitz Indians. The vast majority continue to live in the interior of southwestern Washington between Seattle and the Columbia River, and a large portion of these remain within Cowlitz aboriginal territory.

In 1855 the Cowlitz refused the treaty offered by territorial Governor Isaac Stevens at the Chehalis River Treaty Council, since it would have required that they leave their ancestral lands to live among their traditional enemies on the Quinault Reservation. With only a small portion of its members emigrating to surrounding reserves (chiefly the Chehalis and Yakima reservations), the Cowlitz entered the twentieth century as a treaty-less, landless people, who, nonetheless, were united behind strong tribal leadership. In fact, since the beginning of this century, the Cowlitz tribe has worked with both reservation and landless tribes as a member of a variety of pan-Indian organizations, including the Northwest Federation of Indians, National Council of American Indians, Affiliated Tribes of Northwest Indians, National Congress of American Indians, and Small Tribes Organization of Western Washington.

Cowlitz-United States government interactions were numerous and varied in the first half of the twentieth century. The Cowlitz were continuously overseen by the Taholah Indian Agency for most of this period: their children were enrolled in Bureau of Indian Affairs (BIA) schools (e.g., Tulalip, WA; Chemawa, OR); they were admitted to BIA health care facilities (e.g., Cushman Indian Hospital at Tacoma, WA); and the BIA held in trust for them public domain allotments, homesteads, and allotments on the Quinault Reservation. During this same period, the Cowlitz vigorously pursued their land claims. Early letters and petitions prompted the Department of the Interior to order an investigation, from which Special United States Indian Agent Charles E. McChesney concluded in 1910 that the Cowlitz claim was just and that they should receive compensation. BIA response was inadequate; consequently, the Cowlitz obtained the introduction of twelve different bills in Congress during the period from 1915 to 1927, in pursuit of their land claims. Eventually, both houses of Congress passed a Cowlitz bill, only to have it vetoed by President Coolidge in 1928. With the Indian Claims Commission (ICC) established in 1946, the Cowlitz tribe formally submitted its petition in 1951 (Docket 218). In 1969 the ICC reached a compromise decision in favor of the tribe, and in 1973 awarded them $1,550,000. Due to disagreements between the Cowlitz tribe and the BIA regarding disbursement, the funds have not been released, and the judgment, invested by the BIA, has grown to over $7.7 million in the past two decades.

In the 1920s the State of Washington began to enforce off-reservation fishing and hunting regulations against Cowlitz Indians, arresting them and confiscating their equipment. In 1934 the Cowlitz successfully pressured the state into issuing them Washington Department of Game Indian identification cards through a petition sent to the "law-making bodies" of both the state and federal governments. The state dropped the Cowlitz from the card program in 1976; consequently, they joined with the Chinook tribe in 1979 to file suit in federal district court in Oregon and Washington. The United States Court of Appeals for the Ninth Circuit ruled in 1981 that the fishing rights of both tribes were preserved by their "affiliation" with the Treaty of Olympia (1855 and 1856); this affiliation had previously been affirmed by the Supreme Court in *Halbert et al. v. United States* (1931).

The Cowlitz were one of the landless tribes designated for federal termination in 1953; however, the Western Washington Termination Bill failed to pass Congress, and so the BIA without statutory authority began administratively to treat the tribe as if it was terminated. (In spite of continuing to administer trust lands and probate estates of individual Cowlitz Indians and to manage the Cowlitz ICC judgment funds, the BIA will not recognize the tribal organization.) In 1982 the Cowlitz tribe formally submitted a petition for initial review by the Federal Acknowledgment Project, and a revised petition in 1987. Subsequent to receiving "obvious deficiency" letters from the Branch of Acknowledgment and Research, the Cowlitz have been building a substantial case for their federal acknowledgment. In contrast to its federal standing, the Cowlitz tribe is recognized by the State of Washington and has served on the Governor's Indian Advisory Committee (later "Advisory Council") since the middle 1960s.

The Cowlitz have actively attempted to protect their ancestral lands. In 1957 they entered suit against the City of Tacoma over proposed construction of hydro-electric dams on the Cowlitz River. They lost the suit, and as a consequence fish runs were destroyed and aboriginal sites inundated. Beginning in 1978, the tribe intervened to protect archaeological sites near Cowlitz Falls from a proposed new hydro-electric dam. In contrast to the 1950s experience, throughout the 1980s, the Public Utilities District (PUD) officers, contractors, and archaeologists negotiated and worked with the Cowlitz to protect the tribe's interests; in fact, monetary compensation from the PUD permitted the Cowlitz in 1989 to purchase 17.5 acres along the Cowlitz River. For the first time in over one hundred years, the Cowlitz had a land base in their aboriginal area.

Cowlitz tribal authority and government has been continuous since aboriginal times. The tribe entered the twentieth century under the leadership of Chief Atwin Stockum, the son of Chief Scanewa, from whose daughters many of the present tribal members trace their ancestry. Precipitated by Atwin Stockum's death and the need to enter legal engagements with state and federal governments, the Cowlitz leaders elected their next chief in 1912, changed the title to president in 1921, and then to tribal chair in the 1960s. In 1950 the tribe adopted a Constitution and Bylaws in a further attempt "to obtain just recognition from the United States Government." Cowlitz leaders who followed Atwin Stockum included Baptiste Kiona (1912 to 1921), Dan Plamondon (1921 to 1922), John Ike Kinswa (Kinsawah) (1922 to circa 1930), John Sareault (circa 1930 to 1937), James Sareault (1937 to 1950), Manual Forrest (1950 to 1959), Joseph Cloquet (1959 to 1961), Clifford Wilson (1961 to 1972), Roy Wilson (1972 to 1982), and John Barnett (1982 to the present). Today tribal meetings are held semiannually, with the Tribal Council meeting much more frequently to deal with tribal business.

As the twentieth century approached, the Cowlitz could no longer subsist exclusively on hunting, fishing, and gathering, and they were forced to enter the white economy as river boatmen, longshoremen to river steamers, loggers, coal miners, and day laborers in local hops fields. Through formal and informal sanctions, white society forced the Cowlitz to cease practicing many of their traditions, to change their names, and to replace their languages with English. Although difficult to verify, it appears that no speakers of Salish Cowlitz are alive today, while a few Cowlitz descendants, who are enrolled Yakima, continue to speak some Sahaptin. A number of contemporary Cowlitz supplement their English with phrases from the Chinook Jargon.

Cowlitz means "seeker of the medicine spirit." This related to the Cowlitz use of vision quests in search of a personal spirit power and guide known as a *tomanawas*. Some Cowlitz today continue to seek *tomanawas* guidance; others recognize the presence of the spirit world through smudging ceremonies, desanctification rites at ancestral sites disturbed by modern development, and sanctification rites at sites of reburial of ancestral remains. Smoke for purification, eagle feathers, sage, sweet grass, and cedar are common sacred elements in these ceremonies. For many, this traditional spirituality exists alongside Christian beliefs and practices. In fact, the Cowlitz have had a long history with Christianity dating back to the first Catholic mission in the western Washington region, built on Cowlitz Prairie around 1840. In addition, at the turn of the twentieth century, a number of Shaker churches were established among the Cowlitz people, with some Cowlitz descendants who live on the Yakima Reservation continuing to practice the Indian Shaker religion today.

The Cowlitz experience of acculturation over the last 150 years has been one of "cultural pluralism." That is, they have been forced to live and work in white society, and yet they have not relinquished their ethnic identity or community. One dominant expression of Cowlitz ethnic identity is their intimate and personal relationship with the Cowlitz Prairie and Cowlitz River, where many continue to honor the spirits of their ancestors. As in aboriginal times, the Cowlitz Indian modern community consists substantially of extended family networks. It is within the family that they learn of their heritage, culture, and lineage. Tribal meetings and other less formal gatherings are valued as opportunities to renew family ties, and most consider Cowlitz family members to be among their closest friends.

Mícheál D. Roe

See also **Washington State Tribes**

Further Reading

Beckham, Stephen D., and Leo J. Heaney. *Petition for Federal Acknowledgment, Cowlitz Tribe, State of Washington: Criteria 54.7(a)-(g).* Supplemented by 12 volumes of exhibits, enrollment files, and oversize items. Submitted to the Branch of Acknowledgment and Research, Bureau of Indian Affairs, Washington, DC; Longview, WA: Cowlitz Indian Tribe, 1986.

Curtis, Edward. *The North American Indian.* Vol. 9. Norwood, MA: Plimpton Press, 1913.

Jacobs, Melville. *Northwest Sahaptin Texts.* Seattle: University of Washington Publications in Anthropology 2 (1929): 175–244.

———. *Northwest Sahaptin Texts.* New York: Columbia University Contributions to Anthropology 19 (1934): 1–291.

Ray, Verne F. *Handbook of Cowlitz Indians.* Seattle, WA: Northwest Copy Company, 1966.

Roe, Mícheál D. *Tribal Identity and Continuity in the Cowlitz Modern Community. Study 1: Cowlitz Tribal Leadership. Study 2: General Tribal Membership.* Technical Reports submitted to the Cowlitz Tribal Council. Longview, WA: Cowlitz Indian Tribe, 1991–1992.

COYOTERO

See Apache

CREE

The Cree, at various times called Nehethawa, Cristineaux, Southherd, and Cris, are one of the largest Native American groups in North America. Although most Cree today reside in Canada, some Plains Cree (one of four Cree divisions) eventually settled in the foothills of the Bearpaw Mountains in north central Montana on the Rocky Boy Chippewa-Cree Res-

ervation. Other Cree reside in Montana unaffiliated with a reservation or legal recognition by the federal government. One such community is called Hill 57, near Great Falls. Other Indian people of Cree descent came to be affiliated with the Little Shell people.

Throughout the nineteenth century, Cree, especially Big Bear's band, hunted on United States territory, despite United States and Canadian efforts. After the 1885 Riel Rebellion, Little Bear, son of a rebellion participant, escaped with 200 of his people to the United States. Similarly, Gabriel Dumont, after the Riel Rebellion, took a number of Indians of Cree descent into Montana where they allied themselves with Little Shell's band of Chippewa.

Little Bear, with his 200 Cree, and Little Shell with his band, were unwanted by Montana's non-Indians and Indians alike. Over the next three decades, Little Bear's Cree and Little Shell's band wandered throughout Montana searching for food. Eventually, Little Bear's Cree became associated with a band of landless Chippewa under the leadership of Stone Child or Rocky Boy. Recognizing the plight of the Cree and their Chippewa allies, a coalition of Montana citizens demanded a reservation for Montana's "homeless" Indians. In 1915, the Cree and Chippewa were granted a reservation on the westernmost portion of the former Fort Assiniboine Military Reservation. The Rocky Boy Chippewa-Cree Reservation, with approximately 451 enrollees, was established by executive order in 1916. Little Shell's band, not included at Rocky Boy, eventually settled on the fringes of Montana towns and reservations.

Since the 1920s, the Little Shell people have been fighting to gain federal recognition. In the mid-1950s, Great Falls community leaders offered to donate land to the Bureau of Indian Affairs for the band. The federal government refused the offer, stating that it was inconsistent with their present termination policy. Today, the Little Shell people are seeking formal recognition though the Branch of Acknowledgment and Research, Bureau of Indian Affairs, Department of Interior.

The Rocky Boy people have been strongly affected by federal government policies. In 1947 the reservation was expanded by 45,523 acres, bringing its total acreage to 108,015; 414 landless Indians were added to the tribal rolls, pushing the population to about 1,300, and actually worsening economic conditions. In 1992, between 40 and 50 percent of the population live off the reservation. Unemployment hovers at 74 percent. According to 1989 labor force estimates, only 10 percent of Rocky Boy's population over the age of 16 earn $7,000 or more.

The Chippewa-Cree tribe is involved in a number of economic enterprises which include cattle grazing, wheat and barley production at the Dry Fork Farms, some commercial forest interests, mineral resource development, communication leases, and a recreational-tourist industry.

According to the 1970 census, there were 2,169 Cree residing on identified reservations across the

United States. This demographic trend has continued into the 1990s. The 1990 census revealed that there were approximately 4,255 enrolled tribal members, but 54 percent of tribal members reside off-reservation. The Little Shell people, still unrecognized, had 3,300 members in 1990. Some of these people are of Cree descent.

After the passage of the Indian Community College Assistance Act of 1978, the Chippewa-Cree tribe opened Stone Child Community College. The college offers a number of programs leading to an associate of arts degree or vocational-education certificates.

The landless people of Cree descent reside across the state, but Hill 57 remains the symbol of their struggles. In 1985, a dozen families still resided there. Most children of landless Cree attend public schools, although they are not completely assimilated into a non-Indian lifeway.

The Rocky Boy Reservation has a rich and varied religious life. Aside from the Christian denominations on the reservation, many tribal members participate in the Sun Dance and sweat lodge ceremonies. One of the most active religions at Rocky Boy Reservation is the Native American Church. Cree, an Algonquian language, is still spoken on the reservation and by elders among those living off-reservation.

Gregory R. Campbell

See also Ojibwa: Chippewa in Montana

Further Reading

Bryan, William L. *Montana's Indians: Today and Yesterday.* Helena: Montana Magazine, 1985.

Lopach, James J., Margery Hunter Brown, and Richmond L. Clow. *Tribal Government Today: Politics on Montana Indian Reservations.* Boulder, CO: Westview Press, 1990.

Petersen, Jacqueline, and Jennifer S.H. Brown. *The New Peoples: Being and Becoming Metis in North America.* Lincoln: University of Nebraska Press, 1985.

CREEK/MVSKOKE

The core of the Creek Confederacy, since its founding in Georgia in the eighteenth century, has been the Muskogee-speaking towns, which have always constituted the majority. To this core of about 15,000 persons in the nineteenth century were added, at various times, remnants and refugees from other peoples speaking languages of the Muskogean family, such as the Hitchiti, Apalachee, Mikasuki, Alabama, and Koasati, and also unrelated peoples such as the Yuchis, Shawnees, Natchez, Timucua, and intermarried whites and escaped Black slaves, who became known as Freedmen. While some of these people were absorbed by intermarriage and adoption into Mvskoke towns, some remained as distinct ethnicities among the Mvskokes, such as the Yuchis, Natchez, Alabamas, and Freedmen. Also, several important new Indian ethnicities have had their roots in the Confederacy—the Seminoles of Florida and Oklahoma, and various smaller Indian groups in the Old South presently spread

from Georgia to Texas. In 1826 the core Mvskoke towns of the Confederacy were removed from Georgia to Alabama, and then in 1832 were removed much farther and with considerable hardship to Indian Territory, now Oklahoma, their present home.

Politically, the most important units of the Mvskokes have been their *etvlwas*, or tribal towns, fifty of which were the basis of the original confederacy. They were also the constituent units of the 1867 Constitution in Indian Territory and were the units solicited about reorganization under the Oklahoma Indian Welfare Act in 1937. Comprising several hundred to over a thousand persons each, these *etvlwas* have traditionally been politically sovereign, and mutual alliances among them were the basis of the confederacy. In the twentieth century, many of the tribal towns have been transformed into rural communities focused on a local Christian church, but about fourteen remain in something approaching their original condition, oriented toward a traditional stomp ground, which maintains an annual round of aboriginal ceremonies, especially including the Green Corn Dance. Even those communities which have become Christian have retained their original *etvlwa* name in their church name, such as Hutchachuppa Indian Baptist Church.

The beginnings of the twentieth century saw the Mvskoke Creeks involved in a shooting war between the two factions which have historically struggled for hegemony in Creek politics. The Lower Creeks, originally located in eastern Georgia near the white settlements and now located mostly north of Henryetta in the nine-county area of their original reservation in east-central Oklahoma, have historically been the "progressive" faction, consciously assimilating and accommodating themselves to Anglo-American society. The Upper Creeks, now located in the southern part of their original reservation, have been the militants, resisting assimilation and fighting to protect their land, language, and religious beliefs. As the twentieth century began, the Upper Creeks, under Chitto Harjo or "Crazy Snake," and also Isparhecher, who was elected principal chief in 1895, were refusing to participate in the census which was taken as preparation for allotment of reservation lands. Only a few years later, in 1917, the Upper Creeks took up arms again to join in the Green Corn Rebellion, a coalition among poor whites, Blacks, and Indians to seek an end to World War I and to allocate federal funds to relieve the conditions of rural people, especially sharecroppers.

In all cases, the Upper Creeks, although constituting a majority of the population, have lost their political struggles with the coalition of Lower Creeks and the federal government, although they remain an organized political resistance, still oriented toward the sovereignty of the tribal towns and the 1867 Constitution, which recognized the sovereignty of the tribals towns. Opposed to this orientation has been the Lower Creek faction, organized as the Creek Nation, an idea and institution first set forward by Indian Agent Benjamin Harrison in 1796 to undermine the confederacy, which had come under the influence of Upper Creek militants. The Creek Nation emerged again in Indian Territory and was the only political entity recognized by the federal government after the official Muskogee Nation government, chartered in the 1867 Constitution, was dissolved by federal edict following allotment in severalty in 1906 and statehood for Oklahoma in 1907. From then until 1970, whatever business faced the Mvskoke people was disposed of either by a business committee or a principal chief appointed by the federal government. In these years, with no tribal government to protect them and with the Bureau of Indian Affairs unwilling to do so, the Mvskokes and affiliated peoples had little defense against those who, by hook and crook, bought outright more than 2 million acres of the land allotted to individual Indians and secured mineral leases to the more than $50 billion in petroleum, which was removed from the area of the reservation in this period.

Christian missionary influence in Oklahoma had originally been primarily among the Lower Creeks, who received Presbyterian and Methodist missionaries in the late reservation period. But after allotment in 1906, the Upper Creeks also became more receptive to missionaries, although they preferred the Baptist denomination, which allowed them to remain in independent congregations, speaking their own language during services and reorganizing Christian rituals to suit themselves. About fifty rural Baptist church congregations were organized in the southern part of the Creek reservation early in the twentieth century, added to about fifteen Methodist congregations and a few Presbyterian churches among the Lower Creeks. In this period, about 1915, the government counted about 12,000 Mvskoke Creeks in the state, and about 5,000 Freedmen.

One purpose of the Indian Reorganization Act of 1934, supplemented by the Oklahoma Indian Welfare Act passed in 1936 for Oklahoma Indians, was to recognize and encourage indigenous political structures. After determining that most of the original *etvlwas* in Oklahoma were still intact, federal charters were offered them in 1937. Only three of the tribal towns accepted charters, and these were not necessarily the strongest or largest of the towns. The Alabama-Quassartes applied for a charter, in part because of their continuing linguistic and ethnic differences from the Mvskoke Creeks, and their desire to remain distinctive. The Kialegee and Thlopthlocco towns also applied, mostly because both towns contained progressive leaders who wanted access to the land and loans offered by the government to improve the economic condition of chartered groups. However, the Yuchis, who were even more distinct from the Mvskokes than the Alabama-Quassartes, refused to seek a separate charter because of their deep distrust for the federal government, which had, by allotment in severalty, laid the groundwork for the loss of their land and minerals in the period after 1906. They joined the balance of Upper Creek towns in keeping the confederacy alive.

World War II saw the increasing migration of Mvskoke people to the cities, and to the armed forces. This urbanization of the population continued after the war so that the population of the rural communities has become progressively smaller and older. Many of the churches and stomp grounds found it difficult to function, and so the number of churches has diminished to about thirty-five, and the number of stomp grounds to about eleven, all mostly composed of older members. In the twentieth century, the total population of Mvskoke Creeks has expanded enormously and become, on average, much younger, because of high fertility. While the total population at allotment was about 10,000, excluding Freedmen, in 1980 the total number of self-reported Creeks in the United States was 28,278, of whom 8,766 lived in their traditional rural area in Oklahoma. The enrollment office of the Creek Nation reports that in 1990 there were about 30,000 documented and enrolled Creeks in the United States (as opposed to "self-reported"), of whom 16,000 lived in Oklahoma.

Until 1970, the Creek Nation government was mostly appointed and mostly symbolic, and did little or nothing to help the rural communities and the Creek citizens living in the larger cities of Okmulgee, Tulsa, and Oklahoma City. But in 1970 Public Law 91-495 was passed, setting in motion a chain of events which led to the creation of the modern multi-million dollar institution called "The Creek Nation of Oklahoma." Public Law 91-495 allowed the free election of the principal chief, and there soon followed grants and programs which allowed the chief to collect a staff, build a tribal headquarters, and create health, education, and economic development programs for Creek citizens. For legal and programmatic purposes, a Creek citizen was anyone who could prove descent from a person on the 1906 allotment roster.

Not surprisingly, the Lower Creeks were more precocious in recognizing the possibilities of the new arrangements, and a leader soon emerged who has been the dominant figure in Creek politics until now. Claude Cox, a retired postal official and Methodist church leader, was first elected principal chief in 1971, and soon organized a "spoils system" for managing Creek Nation affairs that was modelled after the two-party political system of the dominant society. Personable and politically astute, Cox created a political party which dominated Creek elections and which was increasingly oriented at the state level toward the Republican party, thereby flying in the face of traditional rural politics in eastern Oklahoma, which has been populist and Democratic.

The opposition, consisting mostly of Upper Creeks, both Baptists and traditionalists, rallied around a man named Allen Harjo, whose name is permanently preserved in Indian Law as a participant in the 1978 landmark case called *Harjo v. Kleppe*. After losing the election to Cox, Harjo argued in federal court that the newly created Creek Nation was illegal and that the legal government was the tribal towns as organized under the 1867 Constitution. The court agreed, but the Cox faction persisted and soon retaliated by pressing for a new constitution, which was soon written, discussed, and upheld in the general tribal election of 1979, by a vote of 1896 to 1694. Many of the Upper Creeks boycotted the election, and the descendants of the Harjo faction continue to struggle against the Creek Nation. One group, the Redstick Party, organized themselves as official Democrats in 1980, while the heirs of the confederacy, the Mvskokullke Etvlwa Etelaketa, received a state charter as a nonprofit organization in 1984. Members of both groups have elected representatives to the National Council, under provisions of the new constitution, where they occasionally force a budget stalemate on the Cox administration, although they have not successfully challenged his hegemony over tribal administration and the judicial system.

In the last decade, the Cox administration has created a tribal complex and a set of social services which officials of the Bureau of Indian Affairs describe as "the best in the nation." It consists of a system of health care including a hospital and three clinics, and traveling community health representatives. Funds for education, funerals, heating oil, and food are also provided on application, although the out-faction maintains that this is treated as part of the spoils system. The housing authority has built over a thousand homes for Creek citizens in the last two decades, and jobs are provided by employment in the tribal government and in tribal enterprises such as a farm and bingo halls.

Besides the Mvskoke Creeks of Oklahoma, the only other group of Mvskoke Creeks in the United States to maintain their communities into modern times and, consequently, to receive official recognition from the federal government, is the Poarch Band located near the town of Atmore in Escambia County, Alabama. The descendants of certain "friendly Creeks" who escaped removal to Indian Territory, the Poarch Band now numbers about 1,875 persons and has received continuous informal recognition from state and federal authorities since removal, until they finally received federal recognition in 1984.

Although the very oldest members of the Poarch community can remember hearing the Muskogee language spoken in their youth, the language is now gone, along with the rest of aboriginal Mvskoke culture. In contrast with the Oklahoma Mvskokes, there is no stomp grounds in Alabama, and people can no longer recollect their town or clan affiliations. But they are phenotypically or "visibly" Indian in appearance.

Between 1947 and his death in 1970, the leader of the Poarch community was Calvin W. McGhee. Before he assumed leadership, the community had been content to hide in the interstices of rural Alabama, happy that they did not have the same debilitating legal status as Negroes. But under McGhee's leadership, the community began its quest for federal rec-

ognition and now has qualified for most of the United States grants and programs which have assisted in education, health care, and economic development. The band maintains a tribal office building and senior citizen building and, most recently, has developed plans for a museum and community center. At Thanksgiving, the Poarch Band holds its traditional pow-wow, which is largely based on the traditions of Plains Indians rather than those of their Mvskoke ancestors.

Other Creek descendants east of the Mississippi are dispersed, rather than being located in discrete communities. Most of these groups, numbering from a handful to several hundred persons each, are now organizing to seek federal acknowledgment. They include the Principal Creek Indian Nation East of the Mississippi, Florala, Alabama; the Lower Muskogee Creek Tribe East of the Mississippi, Inc., Cairo, Georgia; Creeks East Mississippi, Molino, Florida; MaChis Lower Alabama Creek Indian Tribe, New Brocton, Alabama; and the Florida Tribe of Eastern Creek Indians, Bruce, Florida.

John H. Moore

See also **Oklahoma Tribes**

Further Reading

Green, Michael D. *The Creeks: A Critical Bibliography.* Bibliographical Series, the Newberry Library, Chicago. Bloomington: Indiana University Press, 1979.

Moore, John H. "The Mvskoke National Question in Oklahoma." *Science and Society* 52:2 (1988): 163–90.

Swanton, John R. "Social Organization and Social Usages of the Indians of the Creek Confederacy." *Bureau of American Ethnology 42nd Annual Report.* Washington, DC: The Bureau, 1928. 23–472.

CROW

The Crow call themselves Absaroka or Apsaalooke, often translated "children of the large-beaked bird." Linguistically part of the Siouan family, the Crow are historically associated with the Hidatsa. Today, the Crow are located on their reservation in south central Montana and number 8,491 enrolled members (Bureau of Indian Affairs, June 1991). Despite Euroamerican acculturation, the cultural institutions of the Crow remain vibrant and expressive of their Plains Indian orientation.

While among the ancestral Hidatsa-Crow tribe, No Vitals received a vision instructing him to lead his people into the western mountains where they would find a sacred tobacco plant. The harvesting of the tobacco seeds would safeguard the people, becoming a source for their identity. Eventually the vision of No Vitals was fulfilled as two groups, the River Crow and Mountain Crow, separated from the Hidatsa. As early as the 1600s, the Crow had made their way into the Powder, Yellowstone, and Mussellshell river drainages of what would become southern Montana and northern Wyoming.

By the 1750s, the Crow were introduced to the horse, and the tipi and hunting had replaced the earthen lodge and farming. A man's status was measured in terms of gifts given and achieved skills—coups counted and buffalo hunted. The Tobacco Society planted and harvested the seeds of the sacred plant. Young men sought visions on distant hilltops and in the Sun Dance Lodge. During these buffalo-days, the Crow were estimated to number between eight to ten thousand individuals.

While early relations with Euroamericans were characterized as "friendly," the consequences of that relationship for the Crow were anything but beneficial. Throughout the early 1800s, a series of smallpox epidemics decimated the population by as much as 50 percent. Under pressure first by gold seekers, then cattleranchers, and finally homesteaders, and as a result of treaties, acts of Congress, and other land cessions to the United States government, the 38,531,147-acre territory set aside under the provisions of the 1851 Fort Laramie Treaty was by 1905 reduced to approximately 2,285,000 acres. The overall boundaries of the Crow Reservation have remained constant since the 1937 Hardin cession, though almost half of the land base is currently owned by Euroamericans. By the 1880s, the great herds of buffalo had vanished, and government and Catholic boarding schools had been established. The 1884 regulations of the Indian department "outlawed" and made it an "Indian offense" to hold a giveaway, a feast, a Sun Dance, to have more than one wife, to be a medicine man, to sell a horse to another Indian, or to leave the reservation without permission. The Crow had an estimated thirty to forty thousand head of horses in 1914; by 1921, those numbers were reduced to less than a thousand.

In the 1950s, under the threat of a government condemnation suit, the Crow were coerced to sell rights to much of the Bighorn Canyon so that the multipurpose Yellowtail Dam could be built. In 1981, the ownership of the Bighorn River was transferred to the State of Montana by a ruling of the United States Supreme Court.

The Crow response to Euroamericans has always been rather pragmatic, guided Euroamericans in part by the visions of their great chiefs. In 1857, a nine-year-old Plenty Coups had a vision that foretold drastic changes and offered advice—learn from the mistakes of others and establish peaceful relations with the Euroamericans. Plenty Coups saw education as the Crow's greatest defense. Plenty Coups, along with others such as Pretty Eagle and Medicine Crow, provided leadership into the early part of the twentieth century.

Retaining their unique vision of themselves, the Crow today remain a culturally distinct people. The Crow language is spoken by a majority of both youth and adults. A matrilineal clan system helps organize inter-family and kinship relations as exemplified in the *aassahke* relation. *Aassahke* are males and females of an individual's father's clan. They are to be respected and acknowledged through gifts of food and blankets at giveaways. In return, *aassahke* be-

stow Indian names, sing "praise songs" for good deeds, and offer prayer before a meal or during a sweat bath ritual.

Each August, social and kinship ties are renewed at Crow Fair, involving a week of parades, giveaways, powwow dancing, feasting, and rodeo. While choosing not to commercialize their traditional arts, the Crow nevertheless take tremendous pride in the beadwork with which they adorn dance costumes and horse-riding gear. The vivid colors and geometric and flower designs can be seen on those who dance at the various powwows throughout the year, and on the horses ridden during the dance parades at Crow Fair.

Along with the high school basketball season, excitement runs high during the handgame and arrow-throw tournaments. Education remains a priority as expressed in the success of the tribally controlled Little Big Horn College, a two-year community college. While healing is sought at the Indian Health Service hospital, medicine bundles are still opened and prayers given for the family's health. Medicine men still perform healing ceremonies. Interspersed throughout the reservation are Catholic, Baptist, Pentecostal, and other Christian churches along with sweat lodges, peyote tipis, and vision quest sites. New members continue to be adopted into the Tobacco Society.

In 1941 the Crow again held a Sun Dance. Sponsored by William Big Day, who had sun danced with the Wind River Shoshoni and received several visions, the Crow adopted the Shoshoni form of Sun Dance. In 1991, at the fiftieth anniversary, Heywood Big Day sponsored the Sun Dance in honor of his father. Crow sun dancing continues each summer with as many as two and three dances being held, and from 80 to 120 men and women fasting from food and water for the three and occasionally four days of each dance.

Electing not to adopt most of the specific provisions of the Indian Reorganization Act of 1934, the Crow wrote their own Constitution in 1948 and codified the general-council government they had developed over the preceding years. All Crow women over the age of eighteen and all men over the age of twenty-one are members of the Council, who in turn elect four officers—a chairman, vice-chairman, secretary and vice-secretary—and establish various governing committees. Along with the tribal court, the Council governs over the internal affairs of the tribe.

Among those most influential during this time of cultural renewal was Robert Yellowtail (1887 to 1988). He served as tribal chairman and for twelve years as the Bureau of Indian Affairs (BIA) superintendent for the reservation. Yellowtail had supported Big Day's Sun Dance efforts and the Constitution adoption, as well as the preservation of the tribe's natural resource base in order to secure economic self-sufficiency. While Yellowtail had fervently opposed the government's Bighorn Canyon Dam project, ironically, the government named the dam in his honor.

The reservation is rich in natural resources—virtually all the land is classified as either irrigated, dry-land, or grazing land, and billions of tons of sub-bituminous coal reserves are to be found in the 1.1 million acres of ceded land to the north and east of the reservation boundaries. The Crow retain mineral rights under the ceded areas. But with most of the agricultural lands leased to large Euroamerican interests and with powerful resource and mining corporations to negotiate with for the coal, channeling Crow resources to the Crow people remains a challenge.

Employment opportunities include work for the tribal government as resource and program managers, social workers, and reservation policemen. Teachers and educational support staff are employed in the local public schools and the Little Bighorn College. Coal-mining companies employ equipment operators and clerks. Several Crow have successfully developed their artistic abilities, as exemplified in Kevin Red Star, a painter, Hank Real Bird, a poet; and T.R. Glenn, a jeweler. Despite these opportunities, periods of unemployment as high as 50 percent still plague the Crow.

The desire for quality education for all and economic self-sufficiency, and the problems associated with alcohol and drug abuse, unemployment, and Euroamerican prejudice, will continue to challenge the Crow into the twenty-first century. But with the vitality of Crow culture and with emerging leaders such as Janine Pease Windy Boy, president of Little Big Horn College, Angela Russell, Montana state representative; and Bill Yellowtail, Montana state senator, the challenges will be faced.

Rodney Frey

Further Reading

Fitzgerald, Michael. *Yellowtail: Crow Medicine Man and Sun Dance Chief (An Autobiography)*. Norman, OK and London, England: University of Oklahoma Press, 1991.

Frey, Rodney. *The World of the Crow Indians: As Driftwood Lodges*. Norman, OK and London, England: University of Oklahoma Press, 1987.

Hoxie, Frederick. *The Crow*. New York, NY and Philadelphia, PA: Chelsea House Publishers, 1989.

Lowie, Robert. *The Crow Indians*. New York, NY: Holt, Rinehart and Winston, 1956.

Voget, Fred. *The Shoshoni-Crow Sun Dance*. Norman, OK and London, England: University of Oklahoma Press, 1984.

CUISINE

American Indian foods provide a rich legacy for contemporary Americans; 75 percent of the foods we eat today originated in the Western Hemisphere. Wild and cultivated, hunted, fished, and gathered, they form the base for our modern civilization. Food is a common denominator for all people; it transcends ethnic differences, language barriers, and political or religious misunderstandings. We are nurtured by a vast array of modern foods largely developed from American Indian origins. Centuries of cultural cross-fertilization in the Western Hemisphere enliven our modern diets, forming the basis of twentieth-century American Indian cuisine.

Many complex regional cuisines comprise the dynamic field of Native American foods. Blended with multi-ethnic food influences from around the world, modern American Indian cuisine is as diverse as the cultures from which it stems. These foods continue to be the mainstay of their own, plus many other unique ethnic cuisines. Examples of modern Native cuisine include roast turkey with oyster-cornbread stuffing, cranberry-black walnut relish, regional clam chowders, variations on succotash, and Indian pudding, to name a few.

Regional specialties abound, even in this era where transportation, genetics, and sophisticated farm, ranch, and horticultural techniques extend and often blur most regional and seasonal restrictions. Alder-smoked chinook salmon, abalone chowder, planked halibut steaks, goeduck clams, and caribou rib roasts from the Northwest Coast and Alaska, for example, just scratch the surface of regional cuisine.

Respect for life was the key to much of Native thought and survival. Corn was the life sustainer to many horticultural tribes, yet not all tribes were agricultural. The buffalo was central to most of the Plains Indians, as were salmon and halibut to the people of the Northwest Coast. Eastern Woodland groups thrived on deer, beaver, and game birds, while alligator, crayfish, and shrimp were central to many southern tribes. People of the Great Lakes area were nourished by deer, wild rice, and maple sugar. The Native seasonal cycle was punctuated with periodic celebrations of thanksgiving. Harvest ceremonies recognized the abundance of various tree saps, syrups, and sugars, while other hunting and gathering sequences were observed and honored throughout the year. During Green Corn ceremonies, eastern Native Americans celebrated the earliest sweet corn from their fields. Maple sugaring time was a rich late winter celebration. These traditions provided the indigenous foundations for our annual Thanksgiving Day observances.

Early Background

Algonquian Indian tribes in the Powhatan Confederacy encountered the earliest English colonists on Roanoke Island off the southeast coast in 1584. Pictured and detailed in *A Brief & True Report of the New Found Land of Virginia*, written in 1590 by Thomas Harriot, we gain early glimpses of Native foods and fields. John White's watercolors (1585) illustrated a rich Native lifestyle. The sixteenth century engravings by Theodore de Bry, based upon White's works, of Powhatan food quests, fields, and preservation methods show diverse animals, and fields of corn, beans, sunflowers, and tobacco. Early eastern settlers encountered thriving Indian villages and gardens. Captain John Smith, writing in 1607, noted that the settlers of Jamestown, Virginia, would have starved if the Indians of that region had not brought corn, squash, and beans to them. This famous Indian triad, "the Three Sisters," soon became the most important foods in pioneer America.

Corn, first called maize, originally grew wild in Central America, and was domesticated, archaeological evidence reveals, more than 7,000 years ago by horticultural peoples in what is now highland Mexico. During the following millennia, corn planting, hybridization, and trading spread along pre-Columbian trade routes throughout much of the Americas, often accompanied by diverse varieties of beans, squashes, melons, gourds, pumpkins, and sunflowers.

Gourds, squash, and pumpkins (of the great Cucurbit family of plants) are believed to be the earliest plants cultivated in the Americas, starting over 8,000 years ago. Earliest evidence for the domestication of beans dates to 7500 before present, probably originating in the Andean highlands of northern South America along with hundreds of varieties of potatoes, tomatoes, peppers, and peanuts. Eventually, many of these foods became early economic trade items internationally. They are common in our gardens and on our tables today.

Native Wild Foods

Most American Indian tribes are strikingly different from each other, as to some extent are their foods. Still, many common bonds exist. Much of traditional life is influenced by the local ecology. Indians have used hundreds of different native fruits and berries to flavor, color, and cure foods, including wild strawberries, blueberries, cranberries, blackberries, huckleberries, elderberries, and raspberries, along with bear, buffalo, goose, snow, june, juniper, sumac, spicebush, salal, sarsaparilla, sasskatoon, and solomon seal berries. These were used extensively, either whole, mashed into pastes, pemmicans, butters, or dried like raisins. Sometimes they were added to seasonal harvests of may apples, wild currants, grapes, persimmons, and wild plums to create various high-energy foods, which hikers today consider fine trail foods.

Varieties of carbohydrate-rich nuts growing throughout the country include acorns, butternuts, black walnuts, beechnuts, chinkapins, chestnuts, hazelnuts, hickory nuts, pecans, and pinyons, which are easily ground into flours, butters, and oils as energy-filled foods and food accents. Regionally, Indians gather and use various kinds of pollen, wild mushrooms, ferns, wild herbs, and roots.

Regional Feasts

Various American Indian celebrations and feasts dominate tribal traditions, and change to incorporate current food choices. Indian families in different regions host special occasions in which certain foods, their abundance, and manner of preparations make personal statements. These include relieving sadness at funerals, rejoicing in generous harvests and hunts, honoring family wealth, puberty rites, marriage ceremonials, and a panoply of rituals in the ceremonial year.

Potlatch. Although outlawed for a time by missionaries and governments, the ceremonial distribution of wealth and food in potlatching and feasting continues on the Northwest Coast. A Tlingit or Haida potlatch might include alder-smoked salmon, grilled halibut steaks, pork roasts, turkey, pilot bread, cranberry sauce, salmonberry, soapberry, or cloudberry puddings, cookies and tarts, peach and pumpkin pies, pink frosted layer cakes, fruit juices, coffee, tea, and soda.

Pueblo Foods. Pueblo Indian festival foods in the Southwest might embrace Hopi blue-corn marbles (tiny dumplings), pink piki bread, *posole, guacamole,* juniper-lamb stew, *atole,* San Ildefonso salsa, Navajo kneel-down bread (in cornhusk packets), *sopapillas* with honey, wild sage bread, sweet pumpkin pudding, pinon cookies, and fresh melons.

Festival Foods in the Southeast. From Oklahoma to Tennessee and Georgia, you will enjoy the unique native corn dish *soffkee* in private homes and at special events. Festival foods from the Southeast might include, seasonally, sauteed froglegs, alligator and crawfish gumbo, batter-fried catfish, corn and peanut salad, jicama-sunchoke salad with wild greens, hush puppies and okra patties, pecan pie, fresh persimmons and melons, along with rootbeer, birch beer, sarsaparilla, sassafras tea, and other conventional beverages.

Festivities on the Plains. Festival foods among Plains Indians can be drawn from a variety of wild game: jerked-buffalo or venison pounded into traditional *wasna,* grilled rack of antelope, buffalo, wild ducks, or rabbit, corn soup, diverse frybreads with honey or wild-berry jams or *wojapi,* wild-plum cakes, with wild-raspberry butter, roast camas bulbs, boiled prairie turnips with wild onions, fatback, and honey, along with fruit drinks, colas, and strong coffee.

Iroquois Celebrations. In an Iroquois longhouse wedding celebration, strawberry kool-aid, jello, jelly, jam, shortcake, and ice cream could enhance the traditional medleys of Iroquois corn and eel soup, Three Sisters succotash, stuffed squash, beef or venison stew with corn and red-bean dumplings, smoked trout, roast turkey with all the trimmings, cornbreads, frybreads, pumpkin pudding, various pies, tarts, cookies, puddings, and cobblers, ginseng root tea, and chilled sumac-ade, and other coffees, teas, cocoas, and colas. From shad roe in early spring, to the delicious roe and milt of native sturgeon, trout, salmon, and bluefish, to succulent lamprey eels and winter muskrat stew, foods in the tribal Northeast embraced the seasonal cycles.

Powwow Foods. The respect for the bounties in nature is continually reflected in the ubiquitous powwow foods that flavor these intertribal gatherings all over North America. You may find every variation of frybread, and Navajo tacos, roast ears of sweet corn, chili-stuffed baked potatoes, smoked trout, baked bluefish, fried froglegs, snapping turtle subs, Rocky Mountain salads, and sweet-berry breads and cakes, along with lemonade, sumac-ade, blackbirch and sassafras teas, plus every variety of regional corn soups, chowders, and stews, depending upon seasonal meats and beans. Buffalo burgers, crab cakes, roast turkey, and Indian puddings can turn up almost anywhere in the country. Modern powwow visitors eat their way around the broad circle of powwow booths, going from food stand to food stand, sampling contemporary, regional favorites, some of which may mirror ancient Native festival or ceremonial foods.

Frybread

Most contemporary cultures existing from Italy to Tibet, from the American Plains to Patagonia, have their own frybread, which is remarkably similar: basically flour, water (or milk), baking powder, salt, and oil or fat for frying. This modern pan-Indian bread is served at countless American Indian gatherings, from powwows to university, family, and tribal functions. Almost every cook or chef has his or her own version of the standard recipe, varied according to quantity, altitude, regional preferences, and inspiration. Tacos, tortilla salad, chili, cheese, honey, or powdered sugar toppings are just a few of the possible embellishments, which can also include wild mushrooms, spicy herbs, vegetables, wild rice, and healing herbs worked into the batter or stuffed into pockets in the dough before frying.

Popular Mainstream Foods

It is impossible to consider native foods and American Indian cuisine without thinking of medleys of colorful chili peppers, tomatoes, and corn creations. Many popular snack foods evolved from early American Indian origins, seasoned and intermingled with complements from other cuisines. From colas, rootbeers, and bottled spring waters to chocolate drinks, Native contributions are exceedingly widespread.

Many of today's high-energy health foods were inspired by early Indian trail foods, such as regional pemmicans, maple sugar-parched corn, journey cakes, hoe cakes (*yokegs*), popcorn, bannocks, raw or roasted seeds mixed with dried fruits, thick peanut and other nut butters, wild rice, quinoa cakes, and chips. Modern health food stores develop active, lucrative businesses in many native herbal teas, edible roots, high-fiber wild greens, and organic vegetables. Ubiquitous cranberry, bearberry, jojoba, and aloe products, along with sassafras, blackbirch, and ginseng teas and sodas are part of the growing multi-billion dollar business based upon early dietary uses of native plants that boost the human immune system. Echinacea, evening primrose, hawthorne, and a unique spectrum of other Native foods lead this growing market. A diversity of native wild mushrooms from many regions and some reservations enlivens American Indian cuisine. These delicacies, still harvested and dried by Indians in many regions, include wild truffles, morels, corals, chanterelles, agarics, and puffballs.

American Indian cuisine comes full circle in restaurant treatments of classic native foods, often without acknowledging their Native American origins. Fine recipes for quail, venison, elk, alligator, buffalo, and rabbit, as well as rattlesnake, froglegs, turtle, and armadillo, are often smoked over mesquite, hickory, alder, or corncobs. The shrimp, crab, octopus, squid, snails, lobsters, crayfish, and catfish in today's meals were common in Indian diets as well. Many of these valuable food resources are commercially ranched and farmed; some of these operations on Indian reservations and in their coastal waters are remarkable successes.

America's dining tables are piled high with the diversity of Native foods. American Indian cuisine also incorporates elements of many immigrant cultures whose culinary gifts are well-integrated into contemporary recipes. On the threshold of the twenty-first century, Native cuisine reaches around the world, yet remains common around our own campfires, at powwows, church dinners, and in corporate boardrooms. Native foods are truly one of the great gifts of the Americas.

E. Barrie Kavasch

See also Powwows

Further Reading

Cox, Beverly, and Martin Jacobs. *Spirit of the Harvest: North American Indian Cooking*. New York, NY: Stewart, Tabori & Chang, 1991.

Frank, Lois Ellen. *Native American Cooking*. New York, NY: Clarkson N. Potter, 1991.

Hays, Wilma P., and R. Vernon Hays. *Foods the Indians Gave Us*. New York, NY: Ives Washburn, 1973.

Kavasch, E. Barrie. *Native Harvests: Recipes and Botanicals of the American Indians*. New York, NY: Random House, 1979.

Williamson, Darcy, and Lisa Railsback. *Cooking with Spirit: Native American Indian Food and Fact*. Bend, OR: Maverick Publications, 1988.

CULTURAL REVITALIZATION

A recurrent process among the Native peoples of the Americas, cultural revitalization involves a public mobilization that makes an appeal to the past while focusing community attention on the improvement of contemporary social, moral, or ritual conditions. Usually, in response to a perceived loss or a threat to a sense of identity, community sentiment is focused by a family or individual who formulates a plan to return to the past in some satisfying way.

During this century, some efforts have been motivated by world events, such as the revival of various warrior sects or rituals after the World Wars. Thus, several Pueblos revived warrior priesthoods to safeguard their towns from the dangers brought back by soldiers who had fought and killed the enemy. As in the past, these acquired powers were channeled by initiation into rain-making abilities. During the 1950s, the Plains Apache reconstituted the Black Leggings sect for their own returned soldiers.

The intertribal camaraderie fostered by World War I led to the growth of pan-Indianism and the spread of the powwow, which continues to offer an obvious sign of Native identity. As recently as the

1990s, tribes in Virginia were beginning their own annual sponsorship of powwows.

After World War II, the availability of cars and pickup trucks aided the spread of the Native American Church, political efforts with a religious theme like the Iroquois White Roots of Peace, and various Christian Protestant denominations with a growing appeal to Native communities because they were spread by Native missionaries. During the 1980s, the message of sobriety and rejection of alcohol was similarly being spread by members of the Shuswap community at Alkali Lake, British Columbia.

Some revitalizations began out of a sense of threat that some resource, talent, or cohesion was about to be lost or taken away. In the Pacific Northwest, depleting salmon resources sparked legal challenges to commercial enterprise by insisting on the Native right to take fish "in common," according to their treaties of 1855. Natives had been increasingly shut out of their usual and accustomed fisheries, when the "treaty tribes" went to court. They revived the First Salmon ceremony to empower their efforts, and won the stunning 1974 Boldt Decision which entitled them to half of the harvestable salmon.

At the same time, other traditions were rekindled in the region. The aboriginal weaving of goat wool blankets among the Fraser River Salishans had lapsed, but one woman was weaving rugs from cloth remnants. With the support of Oliver Wells, Salish weaving was revived and an active women's cooperative continues to sell their manufactures from Coqualitsa.

More dramatic was the revival of winter spirit dancing among many tribes of British Columbia and Washington State. Before mid-century, only a few dancers required the singing and drumming that cured them from personal distress, when the spirit helper of each one returned to its human partner during the winter. With an increase in the number of youngsters and a decision to accept inherited spirits in lieu of those who had been personally quested, many communities built smoke houses and began initiating younger members.

Actively associated with this ritual renewal were attempts to encourage the use of Salishan languages through the development of teaching materials that included depictions of a cartoon character called Super Stalo, a personification of the traditions of Fraser River communities. The Quileute of coastal Washington briefly experimented in their high school classes with a jargon that blended Native words with English grammar. Around Puget Sound, Violet Anderson Hilbert, a Skagit elder better known as Taqwsheblu, is committed to assuring that Lushootseed Salish are the best recorded of all the languages in the region. As a scholar, teacher, and storyteller, she has done much to support the rebirth of Native arts and literature.

When the Samish tribe of northern Puget Sound was denied federal recognition, they responded by commissioning a huge wooden sculpture of the "Maiden of Deception Pass," a figure important in their mythology. They dedicated it with an elaborate potlatch that welcomed other tribes and showed the strength of their community continuity.

During the 1980s, treaty fishing rights also became subject to a showdown in Michigan, Wisconsin, and other Great Lakes states. In particular, the right to spear walleyes in Wisconsin became embroiled in a racist backlash that included violent confrontations and attempts by white men to sell a brand of beer to finance a movement to abrogate treaties. Ojibwa and other tribes responded with passivist fish-ins and a strengthening of earlier spiritual traditions about their role as stewards of the environment.

A threat to drill for oil off the shores of Santa Barbara mobilized the Chumash at Santa Ynez mission to reaffirm their tribal identity and fight for their rights. The recovery of the fieldnotes of J.P. Harrington with Fernando Librado, a Chumash elder, did much to bolster this identity.

Other Californian crafts and traditions have similarly been revived by remarkable individuals. Among the Pomo at Kashia, Essie Parish led a return to healing and ritual patterns and cooperated in the filming of these rituals by professionals from the University of California at Berkeley. During the 1980s, Lauren Brown was also active in ritual changes at Kashia.

The roundhouse rituals of central California have benefited from the enthusiasm of Frank LaPena, a Native artist who has encouraged the return of Maidu dances.

The Mashpee of Massachusetts went through a law suit, stacked against them by the way it was legally contrived, to lay claim to land that had been theirs since the mid-1600s. Abused by wealthy white homeowners and the media, the Mashpee experienced a revitalization in which their culture became defined as secret information that was passed down through their leaders, and, thus, was not subject to outside review. This enabled the Mashpee to retrench, despite losing in court.

Among the Oklahoma Delaware, the Big House ceremony lapsed after 1924 until it was briefly revived for three simplified occasions during World War II. Fearful of the fate of their enlisted members and of the world generally, this revival was occasioned by a sense of doom. Since then, many of the same sentiments have been expressed by Delawares through the Native American Church.

Among Inuit (Eskimo), the endangered status of sea mammals has led to other outlets to make a living in the north. They formed printmaking and sculpture guilds to perpetuate or revive events of the past in saleable forms. Similarly, the founding of their own CBC broadcast affiliate television station has helped to revive dances, songs, and rites to be shown in Inuit homes.

Recognizing both Christian and Native symbols, the Native American Church has been a potent force in various cultural revitalization movements, such as that among the Winnebago. During the 1990s however, an adverse federal ruling forbidding the use of peyote by Native drug councilors in Oregon has renewed feelings of repression among members.

Many of the strides in the upholding of cultural traditions were made possible by legal efforts. In particular, the Native American Rights Fund, closely associated with the Pawnee Echohawk family, has been in the forefront of the protection of sacred sites and the repatriation of human remains.

The passage of the 1978 American Indian Religious Freedom Act by Congress, although only advisory and not legally binding, is regarded by Native communities as a long overdue endorsement of their aboriginal beliefs and rituals. Similarly, formal apologies by the churches of Seattle and Alaska for the pain caused by zealous missionization have encouraged many Native communities to appreciate the worth of their aboriginal faiths.

Combining such legal sanctions with moral stands, some Native peoples have repatriated the bones of their ancestors and significant religious articles from museum collections. The Omaha of Nebraska were particularly successful in pursuing the return of their Sacred Pole and other tribal symbols from the Peabody Museum at Harvard. Stanford University, the Chicago Field Museum, and the Smithsonian have returned burials to tribes in California, Montana, and Alaska. Moreover, the liberal repatriation policy of the new National Museum of the American Indian suggests a ray of hope for future tribal efforts at revitalization.

Jay Miller

Further Reading

Amoss, Pamela T. "The Fish God Gave Us: The First Salmon Ceremony Revived." *Arctic Anthropology* 24:1 (1987): 56–66.

Campisi, Jack. *The Mashpee Indians: Tribe on Trial.* NY: Syracuse University Press, 1991.

Churchill, Ward. *Critical Issues in Native North America.* Document 62. Copenhagen: International Work Group for Indigenous Affairs, 1989.

Kehoe, Alice. *North American Indians: A Comprehensive Account.* 2d ed. Englewood Cliffs, NJ: Prentice Hall, 1992.

Miller, Jay. *Shamanic Odyssey: The Lushootseed Salish Journey to the Land of the Dead.* Ballena Press Anthropological Papers 32. Menlo Park, CA: Ballena Press, 1988.

Wells, Oliver N. *The Chilliwacks and Their Neighbors.* Vancouver, BC: Talonbooks, 1987.

CUPEÑO

The Cupeño spoke a Takic language closely related to that of the Cahuilla, and have traditionally occupied two villages near Warner Springs, California. In 1903, they were forcibly moved from their traditional territory to Pala Indian Reservation in Luiseño territory. To accommodate the Cupeño, the government purchased additional land that was added to the reservation. The Cupeño share that reservation with Luiseños to the present day, although a signifi-

cant number of them moved early in the century to Morongo Indian Reservation, where they have intermarried with Cahuillas, Serranos, and others. The present Pala population is approximately 700, but because of intermarriage patterns it is not possible to say how much of the population is Cupeño.

Pala was the site of an *asistencia*, a subsidiary of Mission San Luis Rey established in 1815. This is now the Pala Mission, a Catholic church that serves the Catholic community at Pala as it has since its founding. It maintains a museum that deals to some extent with Cupeño and Luiseño culture and history, as well as the history of the church. Another prominent institution, the Cupa Cultural Center, maintains a museum that deals with Cupeño culture and history, and sponsors an annual event celebrating Cupeño culture and history.

Pala's present-day governing body is the General Council, which consists of all members of the tribe over twenty-one years of age. A five-member Executive Committee acts for the General Council on a day-to-day level. Of major interest to tribal members today are concerns for economic development, issues of tribal sovereignty, health, housing development, and sewer line development. The reservation has its own fire station. Tribal members are also concerned about off-reservation environmental conditions, waste disposal issues, and the protection of sacred sites. Agricultural land and mineral resources, mainly sand and gravel, are the reservation's principal economic resources.

Robert Lovato was a prominent political leader at Pala for many years. Juliana Calac was politically active, both regionally and locally. The late Rosinda Nolasquez served for many years as an interpreter of Cupeño language and culture to anthropologists and linguists. She co-authored a book on the Cupeño language and was instrumental in establishing language classes for Cupeño children. Robert Smith, current tribal chairperson, has a long history of service to the band, contributing significantly to the maintenance of tribal culture. William Pink was the second executive director of the California Native American Heritage Commission.

Cultural traditions that have continued to the present day include rituals for the dead, the playing of the gambling game called peon, and the singing of Bird Songs. People at Pala still live in a central village, a settlement pattern brought from the Cupeño homeland at Warner Springs.

Lowell John Bean
Sylvia Brakke Vane

See also **California Tribes**

Further Reading

Bean, Lowell John, and Charles R. Smith. "Cupeno." *Handbook of North American Indians.* Vol. 8. *California.* Ed. Robert F. Heizer. Washington, DC: Smithsonian Institution (1978): 588–91.

Hill, Jane H., and Rosinda Nolasquez. *Mulu'wetam, The First People: Cupeno Oral History and Language.* Banning, CA: Malki Museum Press, 1973.

Strong, William Duncan. "Aboriginal Society in Southern California." *University of California Publications in American Archaeology and Ethnology* 26:1 (1929):183–273. Banning, CA: Malki Museum Press, 1987.

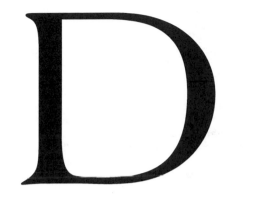

DAKOTA

For approximately a century after non-Indians appeared, all the Sioux Indians occupied village sites near Mille Lacs in order to hunt, fish, and plant along the Minnesota-Wisconsin border, and several times a year they traveled to hunt or gather resources. En masse, they scattered across nearly 100 million acres they had long claimed through seasonal use. Many of these groups were Dakota-speaking and were known generally as Dakotas or by their individual group names. Dakotas settled in band communities from the Mississippi to an area surrounding the headwaters of the Red and Minnesota rivers.

Throughout the fur trade era, Dakotas dealt mainly with operatives from Mendota Post in a network between Fort Snelling and the James River Basin. A census in 1839 reported 1,658 Mdewakantons; 325 Wahpekutes; 980 north and 276 south Sissetons; and 425 west plus 325 east Wahpetons—a total of 3,989 Dakota Indians in this area.

When non-Indian settlers appeared, Mdewakantons and Wahpekutes (Santees) accepted terms of the 1851 Mendota Treaty, and Sissetons and Wahpetons accepted those of the 1851 Traverse des Sioux Treaty. By 1854, Dakotas exchanged use rights on some 21 million acres for a narrow strip along the upper Minnesota River plus annuities and agency services: Santees were situated around Lower Agency (Morton), and the Sissetons and Wahpetons were around Upper Agency (Granite Falls) in Minnesota.

The agonizing Minnesota Sioux War of 1862 represented understandable resentment toward intrusion by white settlers plus annuity mismanagement during the Civil War. It ended in the conviction of approximately 300 Dakota men by military tribunal, the hanging of 38 at Mankato, incarceration of others accused at Fort Davenport (Iowa), and expulsion of the remainder. With the Forfeiture Act of February 16, 1863, Congress negated treaty rights, confiscated land, and ordered Dakotas' exile from Minnesota.

Through a complex odyssey, some 2,500 Dakotas moved to Canada, where several hundred remained to establish seven tiny reserves—Portage la Prairie, Sioux Valley, Pipestone, and Bird Tail in Manitoba; and Fort Qu'Appelle, Moose Wood, and Round Plain in Saskatchewan. Others made their way to Fort Peck Reservation (Montana), where in 1909 officials found fifty-eight Sissetons and Wahpetons living among Assiniboines and Yanktonais.

Federal officials placed subdivisions of Sissetons and Wahpetons on both Lake Traverse and Devil's Lake reservations; moved Santees to Crow Creek; and, after nearly 300 Santees fled or perished, in 1866 relocated a residue of about 1,000 in Nebraska on the Santee Reservation for unification with prisoners and families from Davenport.

From Santee Reservation small groups emigrated eastward. In 1869, fifty families homesteaded around Flandreau in South Dakota. Others (including some Yanktons, Sissetons, and Wahpetons) drifted into Minnesota. During the 1880s, Congress set aside small areas in trust for those "peaceably" disposed during the 1862 War. Eventually, they scattered into five Minnesota communities.

Throughout the twentieth century Dakotas have shared common circumstances, mainly in claims against the United States for losses by the Forfeiture Act, and in movements onto reservations of choice. Sissetons and Wahpetons wandered with no federally recognized place of occupancy until February 19, 1867, when the Treaty of Fort Wadsworth (Fort Sisseton) assigned them a 12-million-acre province. During 1873 Congress created Lake Traverse and Devil's Lake reservations within it, and offered the remaining acreage to non-Indians.

Groups from both tribes gathered on both reservations: at Lake Traverse approximately half mixed and half full-blood; at Devil's Lake, mainly full-blood. The latter welcomed some "Cuthead Yanktonai."

The Dakota Reservations in the Twentieth Century

Lake Traverse Reservation. Residents of the Lake Traverse Reservation, located on the border of North and South Dakota and officially called the Sisseton-Wahpeton Sioux Reservation, endured land loss, financial distress, and federal paternalism. From 918,779.32 acres, officials allotted 309,913.16 to 2,697 members, purchased 608,866 for non-Indian settlement, and assigned a residue to miscellaneous functions. For survival, Dakotas sold allotments, and by 1952 retained only 117,119 acres (92 percent in heirship entanglements).

In return for 608,866 acres they received $1,699,000, to which Congress added compensation for losses under the Forfeiture Act. From the aggregate came occasional per capita payments: as small as $4.86 in 1910; as great as $292.35 in 1917. Mainly, these Dakotas relied on personal earnings deposited with payments in Individual Indian Money (IIM) accounts, whose aggregate grew to $206,536.08 in 1913, then shrank to $9,000 by 1950. By then they had little money or benefit from the land, except hunting, fishing, and gathering privileges.

Tribal governance came through the constitutional Renville Republic until its president, Gabriel Renville, died in the 1890s. A Business Committee dealt with enrollment, land, and per capita payments until 1933, when members adopted their Constitution and Bylaws. A decade later they revised it according to terms in the 1934 Indian Reorganization Act (IRA).

Since then, voters have elected district representatives to a Tribal Council, with a chairperson. The Council's greatest challenge has been establishing economic opportunity in a cultural environment suitable to a growing population. From 1,677 in 1875, enrollment increased to 3,648 in 1952, to 10,073 in 1992. By 1980, federal relocation efforts pared resident population to only 2,750 on 102,597 acres in South and 2,592 acres in North Dakota. By 1992, enrolled population on-reservation or nearby increased to 5,306.

To accommodate an increase came tribal activities in "cluster housing" at Old Agency site, plus "scatter housing" across the reservation. Elders Jenny Thompson, Blossom Keeble, Henry Red Star, and Elijah Blackthunder supplied substance for a reservation history with language instruction, and brought the Sacred Pipe Religion into open use.

Cultural renewal inspired change in education and governance. To federal, ecclesiastical, and public schools, Congress added a grade school in Peever and a high school in Sisseton for integrated instruction during the 1960s. In the 1980s, a federal judge ordered "cumulative" balloting so every voter could "aggregate votes" to elect Dakotas to Roberts County school boards. In 1975, at Old Agency grounds, councilors chartered the Sisseton-Wahpeton Community College, then opened Tiospa Zina High School, to emphasize tribal values.

Dakotas supplemented subsistence farming with trust-fund payments, wages, trapping, hunting, and fishing until New Deal programs appeared. Especially valuable were Civilian Conservation Corps-Indian Department jobs; Indian Relief and Rehabilitation employment and home repairs; Indian Department Roads Division wage-labor; Works Progress Administration activities; and Department of Agriculture Surplus Commodities. Wartime employment and field work sustained them to mid-century, when Dakotas farmed only 12,500 acres. Federal support for housing and tribal facilities came in the 1960s and tribal programs through the 1980s, when Sisseton-Wahpetons opened a bingo hall, then the Dakota Sioux Casino near Watertown. Steady income encouraged a burgeoning roll and reservation population that blends tribal values with practical objectives.

Devil's Lake Reservation. Similar themes have been evident among other Dakotas. Devil's Lake Reservation in North Dakota accommodates Sissetons and Wahpetons "who had not surrendered to the United States government previous to 1867," wrote Gabriel Renville. Original boundaries contained 220,834.24 acres, of which 136,299.74 went into allotments for 1,205 members, 88,000 to sale as surplus for white settlers, and 2,350 for missions and schools. By 1937, allottees sold 84,682 acres and retained 51,618. By 1955, Indian land grew through federal purchases to 59,665 acres, mainly leased for returns distributed among many Dakotas.

A census of 732 in 1871 grew to 1,240 by 1950, and to 4,420 by 1992 (two-thirds in residence). Largely full-blood at the outset, Devil's Lake Dakotas retained tribal ways that manifested in powwows, Native American Church (peyote) meetings, Sacred Pipe ceremonies, and the Dakota dialect. They suffered from the consolidation with Turtle Mountain Agency in 1947, after which the Belcourt agent admitted to giving Dakotas the "left-over services."

Tribal government was irregular until its IRA organization on April 14, 1944. Since then, elected councilors have searched for viable industries. In 1974, Devil's Lake Sioux Manufacturing Company opened to produce camouflage materials for the United States military forces, and remains in operation. Recently, a bingo hall and gambling casino have provided employment. A resident population of nearly 3,000 (of 4,420 enrolled) lives under economic constraint but flourishes with cultural guidance from a committee headed by tribal elder Paul Little.

Santee Reservation. The Santee reunited in 1866 on four inhospitable townships of Nebraska sand-hill country, under hereditary Chiefs Wapasha, Wakoota, and Hooshowhaw. In 1875, a constitutional government replaced them. In 1885 came allotment on eighty-acre farms. Missionaries were influential; Congregationalists Alfred and Frederick Riggs operated Santee Normal Institute from 1869 to 1936; Episcopalians Samuel Hinman and William Hare provided instruction until Santees enrolled in Knox County district schools.

Without surplus land to sell, they relied on farming, hunting, fishing, and gathering plus treaty claims payments. New Deal programs helped, but an initial land base of 72,468 acres shrank to 5,811.37 by 1950—2,864 as tribal, 2,947 as allotment—on which to support residents from a tribal roll of 1,210. Since then, many have shuttled between reservation homes and such urban centers as Sioux City, Yankton, Omaha, and Lincoln for employment.

Federal grants, business loans, and housing brought renewal. Yet aside from tribal or federal employment, in 1992 the only wage-producing industry was Becton and Dickinson Pharmaceuticals, employing some twenty-five people for the production of medical equipment. A majority resisted a casino and focused on cultural revival through a tribal community college and high school.

Flandreau Santees. The Flandreau Santees in South Dakota trace descent from fifty families that arrived in 1869 to homestead, and renounced tribal membership in 1870. There, in seventy-five families 312 "citizen" Indians gathered by 1873. Through the Depression years, Presbyterian missionary John Williamson arranged federal aid. After 1878, Flandreau Santees were on their own except for access to a federal day school and identity on Santee rolls. As citizens, they took fee patents and paid taxes without benefits from the Indian Field Service.

Again plagued by depression and drought in the 1890s, they appealed to the superintendent of the new federal boarding school founded in 1892 at Flandreau City. In 1901, he accepted their roll from Santee Reservation, and thereafter provided meager benefits through an "overseer," for a population that grew to 282 by 1915, scattered in 154 houses and a tipi. Children attended the boarding school, some drew rations and coal, and all had part-time services from a physician. Otherwise, all lived without benefits as Indians.

Tribalization came in 1929, when 312 individuals formed a Provisional Council, which approved a Constitution and Bylaws in 1931 that were changed to accommodate the terms of the IRA in 1936. New Deal programs featured a garment factory that produced 30 different items for use at 156 federal schools and hospitals until it closed in 1952.

An enrolled population (366 by 1941) saw federal assistance wither and tribal government languish until the 1960s, when Flandreau Santees received Great Society funds to construct 50 homes, irrigate drylands on 2,300 acres, and provide community health care. Marginal conditions remained until October, 1990, when leaders founded the Royal River Casino. By fall, many in a resident population of about 230 worked here for wages, and all 611 enrolled members applied for benefits.

Minnesota Sioux Reservations. The Minnesota Sioux reservations accommodated Indians who were friendly to non-Indians during the Minnesota Sioux War of 1862. Into federal trust went 1,151 acres at five locations for family heads to occupy by "assignment," if productively employed without lapses in excess of two years.

Pipestone Indian School was their agency until 1952, after which time the Minnesota Dakotas attached themselves to Cass Lake Agency (of Ojibwas) for approximately two decades, then to the director of reservation programs at the area office in Minneapolis. From the outset, they traveled great distances to Pipestone seeking help: 100 miles from the Upper Sioux community, 107 from Lower Sioux, 200 from Prior Lake, 274 from Prairie Island, and more than 300 miles from Wabasha. Because they were "citizens amenable to the laws of Minnesota," their privileges as Indians included only land assignments; education at Pipestone or tuition support at some public schools; health and dental care; occasional reimbursable loans; and Santee claims payments due them because of the 1863 Forfeiture Act. Mainly they gardened, worked for wages, and applied for county benefits when in need.

Federal officials grappled with classification. In 1923 Indian Commissioner Charles Burke called them "nonallottees" to be treated "as if they were whites." In 1935 New Deal spokesman Felix Cohen said "residence on reservation land" was the only basis for tribal organization, and wondered whether their assignments comprised one or many reservations. Commissioner John Collier doubted that restricted land without funds made them eligible for recognition, and if so, wondered whether they comprised one group in "five or six localities" or "five or six groups" in "one community." Indecision led to recognition for five groups under Pipestone jurisdiction, on acreages expanded with IRA funds by 1939 for 556 enrolled (with other Indians elevating the population to approximately 900):

Figure 1
Dakota Land in Minnesota

Community	Original acreage	IRA purchase	Total acreage
Lower Sioux	623.17	1,119.76	1,742.93
Upper Sioux	none	743.57	743.57
Prairie Island	120.00	413.98	533.98
Prior Lake	258.43	none	258.43
Wabasha	110.24	none	110.24

Because none of the Indians used the Wabasha Reservation for permanent residence, on June 13, 1944, Public Law 335 allocated $1,261.20 for its purchase as an addition to the Upper Mississippi Wild Life and Fish Refuge, and Santee claimants were restricted to residence at other sites.

In 1940, the Pipestone superintendent issued a revealing census. At Lower Sioux were one Sisseton, twenty Mdewakanton, and eighteen Flandreau Santee families; at Prairie Island one Sisseton, twenty Mdewakanton, two Flandreau Santee, and two Nebraska Santee families; at Prior Lake forty-one Mdewakanton, two Flandreau Santee, and forty Nebraska Santee families; at Upper Sioux one Mdewakanton, three Yankton mixed with Santee, three Flandreau Santee, and seventeen Sisseton-Wahpeton families; and at Wabasha were no resident families.

A profile for 1929 portrayed a meager livelihood on assignments containing seventeen to twenty acres per family. Minnesota Dakotas since have had characteristic tribal experiences, with one exception. All received Indian New Deal assistance together with tribal recognition at Prairie Island, Prior Lake, and Lower Agency, but Upper Agency Sisseton-Wahpetons declined to surrender rights on Lake Traverse Reservation. To render Upper Sioux members eligible for New Deal benefits, the Pipestone superintendent established a board of trustees, which since has remained a unique agency of government for peoples enrolled at Lake Traverse, Devil's Lake, Yankton, Flandreau, and Santee agencies.

In 1981 Minneapolis Area Office Reservation Programs Director Bernard Granum observed that the creation of recognized governments transformed a "federal obligation" into a "trust responsibility." As tribes under the IRA, Lower Sioux and Prairie Island have been classified as "communities"; and as those otherwise established, Prior Lake and Upper Sioux as "groups." All four were exposed to relocation, and eligible for Great Society supports of the 1960s, including grants for such industries as a gravel pit and pottery manufacture at Lower Agency.

On the reservations leaders emerged to encourage cultural integrity and self-reliance. Hereditary Chief Ernie Wabasha retired from a career in Minneapolis to Lower Sioux community, where his decorum in leadership became obvious at the annual Mankato Dakota Powwow. At Prairie Island Lena Campbell preserved ethnohistory; Amos Owen became a medicine man; his son succeeded him to maintain the Sacred Pipe Religion; and Noah White, a Winnebago, bequeathed a Minnesota chapter of the Native American (Peyote) Church.

Norman Crooks of Prior Lake led a search for viable industries. From a burning site for diseased elm trees and a rubbish disposal area, he turned to gaming. From bingo halls evolved gambling casinos on all four reserves, where by 1992 Tribal Councils distributed payments as great as $3,000 a month per capita.

That year, spokespersons reported approximate statistics for Lower Sioux, Prairie Island, Prior Lake, and Upper Sioux, respectively. On or near-reservation residents numbered some 300, 200, 175, and 180. Enrollments for Lower Sioux, Prairie Island, and Prior Lake were about 750, 440, and 227 respectively. All those living at Upper Sioux were enrolled elsewhere.

Fifteen reservations survive for descendants of four Dakota tribes expelled from Minnesota in 1863. On small tracts they have endured greater exposure than have middle Sioux or Lakota tribes, yet remain distinctively Dakota through tribal integrity.

Herbert T. Hoover

See also **Lakota; Sioux Federation for map of reservations; Yankton and Yanktonai**

Further Reading

Allen, Clifford, et. al. *History of the Flandreau Santee Sioux Tribe*. Flandreau, SD: Flandreau Santee Sioux Tribe, 1971.

Blackthunder, Elijah, et. al. *History of the Sisseton-Wahpeton Sioux Tribe*. Sisseton, SD: Sisseton-Wahpeton Sioux Tribe, 1972.

Meyer, Roy W. "The Prairie Island Community: A Remnant of Minnesota Sioux." *Minnesota History* 37:7 (1961): 271–82.

———. *History of the Santee Sioux: United States Indian Policy on Trial*. Lincoln: University of Nebraska Press, 1967.

Tape-recorded oral history collections are available for all Dakota Tribes at the Oral History Center at the University of South Dakota in Vermillion.

DANCE

Dance is a specially patterned extension of ordinary bodily movement, just as singing or chanting is

FIGURE 2 DAKOTA RESERVATION GROUPS

RESERVATION	TRIBES	ENROLLED	IN RESIDENCE	PRINCIPAL INDUSTRIES
Lake Traverse	Sisseton, Wahpeton	10,073	5,306	Dakota Sioux Casino; Dakota Western Corp. (plastic bag mfg.)
Devil's Lake	Sisseton, Wahpeton, Cuthead Yanktonai	4,420	2,900	Fort Totten Casino; Devil's Lake Sioux Manufacturing Co. (military camouflage)
Santee	Mdewakanton, Wahpekute	3,000	748	Becton and Dickinson Pharmaceuticals
Flandreau Santee	Mdewakanton, Wahpekute	611	230	Royal River Casino
Upper Sioux	Sisseton, Wahpeton, Flandreau Santee, Santee, Yankton	none	181	Fire Fly Casino
Lower Sioux	Mdewakanton, Wahpekute	750	300	Lower Sioux Casino
Prior Lake	Mdewakanton, Wahpekute	227	174	Mystic Lake Casino
Prairie Island	Mdewakanton, Wahpekute	440	200	Prairie Island Casino
Fort Peck	Upper Yanktonai, Assiniboine, Sisseton-Wahpeton	10,500	6,700	Wolf Point Community Bingo Hall

enhanced, embellished speech. For Native Americans, dance, in partnership with appropriate oral and other acoustic expressions, codifies prayer, celebration, commemoration, mysteries, identity, values, and canons of excellence.

Although there are as many variations in Native American dances as there are dance groups, certain stylistic characteristics are pan-Indian. For example, there are more group than solo dances. And, except for some social dances, women and men dance differently and often separately. Dancers flex forward toward the ground, from slight to acute angles, and the upper and lower torso parts are not articulated separately. Movements tend to be contained, with arms held close to the body, while the feet are kept close to the ground. The spatial level of dancing is upright, with no tradition of reclining dances or dances elevated above normal body height. Clothing conceals body contours, and silhouettes are transformed by paraphernalia such as feathers and fringes. Dancers frequently hold artifacts, such as rattles or the edges of shawls. The feet are bare or in moccasins but they are not encased in foot restricting or sound producing shoes. Dance rhythms match those of the drum or other sound accompaniments. Dancing spaces may be specially constructed enclosures or areas that are used for ordinary activities that become dedicated during a dance performance. And traditionally the time and length of performances are not calculated by the clock.

In all Native American tribes dance is considered to be inherent to the proper functioning of the culture. Dance provides a means by which religion is made tangible. Traditional dances are treasures. They must be carefully managed. This serves to maintain ancestral dances, to breathe new vitality into dance cultures with fresh new versions, and to discover new opportunities to dance.

Ritual dances are integral to tribal ceremonies. These include the False Face dances of the Iroquois of the northeast United States and Canada; the seasonal summer and winter dances of the Pueblos of New Mexico; the annual rites of intensification of the Hopi; the timely rites of passage of the Apache; the healing dances of the Pomo of California; the status validating potlatch festivities of the Northwest Coast; and the shamanic dances of the Inuit of the far north. Indeed, without dance, Native American ceremonials would not occur, because dance provides personal and group experiences that are spiritually empowering. Dance is pleasurable, but it is also considered to be ritual "work."

Tribal dances are not exclusive to weighty events, however. Many tribes have groups that provide music for popular recreational dancing. For example, the Tohono O'odham (Papago) of southern Arizona dance and play *waila* (also known as "chicken scratch"), first noted at San Xavier, Arizona, in the 1860s. The word *waila* is derived from the Spanish word *baile*, meaning "dance," and is a version of country-western dance and music. It is said to have come across the

Mexico border in the middle of the last century when popular Mexican music was influenced by the polka imported by German settlers from the Rio Grande Valley in Texas.

Outside of exclusive tribal contexts, pan-Indian dances have blossomed in this century, most especially powwow dances. At powwows people from differing tribes follow a mutually accepted protocol that allows all to take part in a dance celebration of "Indianness." Powwow dances signify to participants and observers alike that Indianness is more than a state of mind, more than indigenous ancestry, but also an identity that is intensified and expressed when Native Americans dance together without regard for the tribes they belong to.

Over the years, commencing in the last century with the world's fairs in the United States and abroad, Native Americans were encouraged by non-Natives to use dance for cultural outreach. During the same era touring extravaganzas featured Native American dances and dancers. The most famous touring show was Buffalo Bill's Wild West Show, established in 1883.

In the first half of the twentieth century, numerous annual events were organized by non-Natives in which the special attractions were Native American dances. Such events include the former Chicago Railroad Fairs, the Gallup, New Mexico, "Ceremonial" that has been ongoing for three-quarters of a century, and the Flagstaff, Arizona, "All-Indian Powwow" that endured for fifty years until 1980. In 1990 it was revived on a limited scale by Native Americans in north-

The Naa Kahidi Theater, established by the Sealaska Heritage Foundation, performs at the National Museum of the American Indian, New York, January 1993. Its artists are Native people from southeastern Alaska. Courtesy of the National Museum of the American Indian, Smithsonian Institution. Photo by Pamela Dewey.

ern Arizona who are determined that it will continue and expand.

Adaptations are necessary when Native American dances move from an indigenous context to a public venue. While maintaining the traditional flavor, dances must be abbreviated and edited adroitly for an alien context and audience, tasks that can be performed by knowledgeable participants only. The challenge must be pleasing, because many Native Americans choose to pursue these sensitive adjustments.

On the other hand, some non-Indians have poorly understood and usurped elements of Native American dances. Countless numbers of preschool and kindergarten children, taught by their teachers to pretend to be Indians, wear paper feather bonnets, and toe-heel around classrooms while they tap their fingers over their open mouths to produce waa-waa-waa noises. Other outsider groups claim ownership of their interpretations of Indian dances. For example, the Boy Scout dance group that calls itself "Koshare" was

Corn Dancers with Koshare, San Ildefonso Pueblo, 1974. Photo by John Running.

Impressions of a Chicken Scratch Dance (Waila) *by Matt Tashquinth, Pima-Tohono Oodham artist from the Salt River Pima-Maricopa Reservation. From the record album* Chicken Scratch *(CR-6093). Courtesy of Canyon Records Productions, Phoenix, AZ.*

established in 1933, and is still going strong in the 1990s. Native American dances have been parodied in theatrical productions, such as the hit Broadway show *Annie Get Your Gun* (1946, book and music by Dorothy and Herbert Fields with Irving Berlin).

Some Native Americans discovered that their dances can provide a source of income. Performance groups earn money at concessions such as the Fred Harvey enterprises at the Grand Canyon, and in shopping malls. These performance groups, often families, organized and directed by an entrepreneurial parent, often set aside many traditional restrictions on, say, who dances when and with whom. In order to satisfy tourists' expectations, performers of whatever tribe include elements of Plains clothing, for example, a feathered war bonnet worn by the male group leader. The inevitable climax of the show is the hoop dance (some say the hoop dance was invented by Tony Whitecloud in Taos, New Mexico, in the 1920s). This spectacular dance continues to thrill audiences and is the favorite showstopper.

Parlaying the Indian mystique to serve several purposes, some tribes have developed elaborate pag-

Choctaw Stomp Dance, Philadelphia, Mississippi, 1990. Photo by John Running.

Dancers from the American Indian Dance Theatre perform a Fancy Shawl Dance, Nashville, Tennessee, 1990. Photo by John Running.

eants to appeal to a non-Native-American public. An effective pageant projects a selected positive image to audiences, while it confirms a viewpoint towards history reinforced by repetitive participation in the pageant. A successful pageant brings revenue to the tribe, the performers, and associated concessionaires. Foremost among Native American pageants is *Unto These Hills*, written a generation ago by Kermit Hunter, a professional pageant writer who was commissioned by the eastern Cherokees. It is presented annually in an outdoor amphitheater during summer weekends. It seems at the outset the dancers were Cherokees; soon dance students from nearby North Carolina universities auditioned for summer jobs, and because they were trained dancers they were hired. Although currently there are few, if any, Cherokees who dance in their pageant, the tribe benefits by its ongoing success.

Selected Pueblo individuals earn fees by performing at the Indian Pueblo Cultural Center in Albuquerque, New Mexico, where performances are scheduled regularly for tourists. Likewise, in the 1970s, the Tigua of El Paso, Texas, developed a museum and cultural center at which there are daily demonstrations of Tigua dances. Wages help keep young dancers within the community. There are several other Native American cultural centers around the United States that use dance for similar purposes.

Income from dancing is also available to winners at competitive powwow events. Some powwow dancers support themselves with prize monies during the annual powwow circuit from Memorial Day to Labor Day.

That dance has been a means by which Native Americans earn income is not an anomaly because it was customary among many tribes to use dances and songs as trade items. Perhaps it is a logical step to go from trade to the market.

A Native American dance phenomenon in this century is a revival movement among some groups who aim to recover diminished or even extinct dances. The Tigua, mentioned above, is one such group. Of interest is the ever-increasing number of "Aztec" dance groups from Mexico. This is noteworthy because even though Aztec culture is extinct, many Mexican people apparently wish to be associated with that prestigious culture. Miraculously the catalogue of Aztecan dances keeps growing as well. With their lively dances, colorful outfits, and dramatic presentations, the Aztecan dances are a great hit in the United States with both Native Americans and non-Native American observers. Both Aztecan dances and a highly romanticized version of the Yaqui deer dance have been incorporated in the repertories of various Mexican Ballet Folklorico groups that are regularly invited to perform in the United States. Folklorico performances are not well attended by Native Americans. The impact of Mexican Indian dances on Native Americans in the United States is keenest at mutually shared events, where a new awareness of the diversity of Native American dances and a new sense of kinship with their neighbors to the south have taken place.

Until recently Native American dances were not traditionally considered to be "art," and the dancers were not "artists," as those terms are most commonly used by Western Europeans and Euroamericans. But many outsiders, engaged by Native American dance and dancers and unaware of traditional aesthetic systems, have used the terms "art" and "artists" to describe Native American dance and dancers. In traditional Native American societies, dances do not occur for their own sake, and there is no role for a professional dancer. Traditionally Native Americans take part in dances according to criteria beyond artistic considerations. Performers are selected for each dance genre because of appropriate age, gender, kinship ties, ritual obligations, and commitment. Dances are inherited, dreamed, borrowed, or traded from other tribes and adapted and rearranged for specific events. These processes often require creative ingenuity by special persons who are authorized to lead and arrange dance activities, but there is no traditional equivalent of a "choreographer" as known in the Western context.

The latest development in Native American dance is that of choreographed works presented in a concert format by professional dance companies. Dancers are chosen from several tribes for their talents and stage presence. Dances, selected for variety and theatrical effect, are performed on a proscenium stage and targeted at audiences who buy tickets and sit in darkened theaters. With the new arena and with the move towards "Art for Art's sake," Native American dance concerts are now subject to media reviews by dance critics. So far the critics have tread lightly because they are uncertain about evaluative criteria. But, as increasing numbers of Native American concert groups are seen and compared, critics will develop a connoisseurship, and they will sharpen their judgmental skills to critique Native American dances and dancers who present art as artists.

One of the first and most prominent of these groups is the American Indian Dance Theatre, which has toured in the United States and abroad, and was the subject of two PBS television programs. Another is the Great American Indian Dance Company from Oklahoma City, whose title of "Native American Ambassadors" took them in 1991 to eastern Europe to launch a program called "500 Years Since Columbus' Arrival in the New World." Although traveling abroad by Native American dancers began a century ago and has continued intermittently ever since, the booking of Native American dance companies as concert artists is new.

History set the stage for the phenomenon of Native American dances as a concert art. Native Americans who danced for others at fairs and the like established the precedent of adapting dances to non-Native contexts. In the present era adults aspire to specialized professional skills. That, and a response to outsiders' high esteem for artists, combined with both the positive insistence that Native American dance is art, and the need to make a living in a world where old subsistence patterns are no longer viable, all contribute to Native American dances on the concert stage.

Some Native Amerians have forged individual dance careers. There are those who, as choreographers and performers, have used Native American themes and movement patterns in their choreography. Rosalie Jones ("Day Star") studied at Juilliard and earned a master's degree in dance from the University of Utah, and is director of the performing arts department at the Institute of American Indian Arts in Santa Fe, New Mexico. Her choreography is based largely, but not exclusively, on Native American themes. Mary Jane Bird, another Native American, earned a master's degree in dance from Arizona State University. Today, she incorporates Native American motifs in her performances and classes at various schools in the Southwest. Still others are dancers who are Indians but do not perform Indian dances. Rosella Hightower, and sisters Maria and Marjorie Tallchief, are retired, renowned ballerinas, and Jock Soto is a member of the New York City Ballet Company. For concert performers, dance is a way of life; for more traditional Native American dancers, dance is part of the way of life.

Whether Native Americans are traditional tribal dancers, recreational dancers, pan-Indian dancers, show people, or professional artists, they continue to cherish dance as an affirmation of life. No description of Native Americans is complete without full attention on dance and its context.

Joann W. Kealiinohomoku

***See also* Music; Powwows**

Further Reading

Heth, Charlotte, ed. *Native American Dance: Ceremonies and Social Traditions*. Washington, DC: National Museum of the American Indian, Smithsonian Institution with Starwood Publishing, 1992.

Highwater, Jamake. *Ritual of the Wind: North American Indian Ceremonies, Music and Dances*. New York, NY: The Viking Press, 1977.

Kealiinohomoku, Joann W. "The Would-Be Indian." *Explorations in Ethnomusicology: Essays in Honor of David McAllester*. Ed. Charlotte J. Frisbie. Detroit Monographs in Musicology 9. MI: Information Coordinators in Detroit (1986): 111–26.

Kurath, Gertrude Prokosch. *Half a Century of Dance Research: Essays by Gertrude Prokosch Kurath*. Flagstaff, AZ: Cross-Cultural Dance Resources, 1986.

Laubin, Reginald, and Gladys Laubin. *Indian Dances of North America*. New York, NY: The Viking Press, 1977.

Dawes Act

See Allotment

DELAWARE

The Delaware, who call themselves Lenape, now reside in widely scattered communities, primarily in Ontario and Oklahoma. Forced by 1700 from their homeland along the shores of the Atlantic and the Delaware River, where they were divided into northern or Munsi-speaking and southern or Unami-speaking communities, their ancestors briefly settled in Pennsylvania, Ohio, Indiana, Missouri, or Kansas.

Today, aside from Munsis living in the Stockbridge-Munsee of Wisconsin and a tiny Chippewa community in Kansas, most Munsi live in Ontario, where Delaware share the Six Nations or Grand River reserve under the sponsorship of the Cayuga, who loaned them the use of their longhouse when the Big House was abandoned. Along the nearby Thames River, Delaware converts founded Moraviantown in 1792, while further upriver most Munsis settled at Munceytown and converted to Methodism in the 1830s. In 1900, over 600 people identified as Munsi, while by 1950, there were about 1,000.

The majority of Unami Delaware are in eastern Oklahoma, where they purchased rights in the Cherokee Nation in 1867, but had to fight in federal court for full Cherokee citizenship in 1890. By 1900, the government of the tribe had shifted from elected chiefs to a Business Council. Cherokee and others suffered allotment, due to the 1898 Curtis Act, after 1902. Delaware allotments ended in 1907, and remaining land was sold, except for cemeteries held in trust. Poverty was common. The Dust Bowl and Depression drove many Christian Delaware to California where the language was used for hymns and sermons until mid-century. In 1900 about 1,000 people identified as Delawares, but by 1980 the tribal roll, which recognizes only descendancy, not blood quantum, included almost 10,000 recruited by land claim settlements in 1963, 1969, and 1971 that were finally released by court order in 1977.

Delaware in western Oklahoma, who moved from Missouri into Texas and lived with the Caddo until forced to Anadarko in 1859, are the only federally recognized Delaware community in the United States, although for much of this century they were submerged under the official designation of Wichita and Affiliated Bands. Just before 1900, only a few dozen tribal members were recorded, but, by 1990, enrollment included about a thousand people defined as one-quarter or more Delaware.

Traditionally, villages were dominated by one of three clans: Turkey, Wolf, or Turtle. While the Unami definitely had all three clans, the Munsi seem to have had only the first two. By this century, clans were no longer firmly matrilineal nor socially important except among the traditionalists around Dewey, Oklahoma, who continued to celebrate the Big House Rite until 1924, with three attenuated revivals during World War II to safeguard soldiers in combat.

The twentieth century marked the end of several other cultural features. The Munsi and Unami languages had become moribund (and near extinction), men gave up wearing earloops, and women gave up puberty observances. Most Delaware became Christians, either Baptist or Methodist, while a few families became Catholic. Simultaneously, many Delaware became active in the Peyote Religion, particularly after John Wilson (Moonhead), whose father was Delaware, began composing songs and conducting meetings of the Big Moon Way. Over time, however, Delaware adopted the forms of the Little Moon Way of Quanah Parker and the Comanche, Caddo, and Kiowa. Little Moon is now the preferred practice of the Delawares.

During the summer, each community hosts a tribal powwow, when ceremonial outfits in Woodland style are still worn. Naming ceremonies continue to be held, but without the ancient supernatural sanction of a personal vision to enhance the seniority of the name giver.

Until her death in 1983, Nora Thompson Dean, who was the last to perform many of the rituals, dedicated her life to correcting the available materials on traditional Delaware culture, working with various students and scholars. Lucy Parks Blalock continues these efforts, teaching the language to tribal members and others. In Anadarko, Linda Poolaw has directed cultural maintenance programs. During the 1980s Unami elders banded together to prevent the exploitation of the old Big House site when the Army Corps of Engineers built Lake Copan.

Most Delaware have been unskilled laborers, but increasing numbers are becoming professionals. Those near urban centers have been better paid and employed, particularly in the oil or cattle industry. Payment for land claims provided each enrolled member with a modest sum, with 10 percent of the total reserved for various tribal enterprises. A tribal or band Business Council now governs each community. Oklahoma groups have also generated tribal income from bingo and the sale of tobacco products.

For Delaware, the highlights of recent decades have been events when leaders and others from many communities have come together. In March of 1983, Delaware leaders attended an exhibit in Katonah, New York. In June of 1987, they gathered again to rebury the bones of an ancestor found during the renovation of Ellis Island. Civic leaders of New Philadelphia, Ohio, hosted academic and social gatherings concerned with the Delaware in 1988, 1990, and 1992, fostering renewed contacts among all Delawares under the auspices of the Delaware Nation Grand Council of North America, incorporated in Ohio in August of 1992.

Jay Miller

See also Oklahoma Tribes

Further Reading

Goddard, Ives. "Delaware." *Handbook of North American Indians.* Vol. 15 *Northeast.* Ed. Bruce G. Trigger. Washington, DC: Smithsonian Institution (1978): 213–39.

Hale, Duane. *Peacemakers on the Frontier: A History of the Delaware Tribe of Western Oklahoma.* Anadarko: Delaware Tribe of Western Oklahoma Press, 1987.

Miller, Jay. "A 'Struckon' Model of Delaware Culture and the Positioning of Mediators." *American Ethnologist* 6:4 (1979): 791–802.

———. "A Structuralist Analysis of the Delaware Big House Rite." *Papers in Anthropology* 21 (Fall 1980): 107–33.

Miller, Jay, and Nora Thompson Dean. "A Personal Account of the Delaware Big House Rite." *Pennsylvania Archaeologist* 48:1, 2 (1978): 39–43.

Roark-Calnek, Susan. "Indian Way in Oklahoma: Transactions in Honor and Legitimacy." Ph.D. diss., Bryn Mawr College, 1977.

Weslager, C.A. *The Delaware Indians. A History.* New Brunswick, NJ: Rutgers University Press, 1972.

DIEGUEÑO

See Kumeyaay

DINÉ

See Navajo

DRAMA

See Literature

DRYPAINTING

Drypaintings are ephemeral paintings made of dry pulverized materials strewn onto a level surface primarily for religious ceremonies of divination and curing or for teaching. They are made by many groups throughout the world, including India, Australia, Africa, Central America, and North America. They are most developed, however, in the American Southwest, where they have been used by the various Puebloan, Apachean, Piman, and Cahitan groups since before European contact. Drypaintings appear to have been developed as a sacred form by Uto-Aztecan speakers and from this base spread from Guatemala to California, Arizona, and New Mexico. Drypaintings are also referred to as sandpaintings, sand altars, sand mosaics, groundpaintings, earth pictures, and sand pictures.

The group that has developed and elaborated drypaintings the most, as both a religious act and a secular artform, are the Navajo. Drypaintings, or *iikáah*, which means "the place where the gods come and go," are symbolic representations of powerful supernaturals used in curing ceremonies. They serve as a temporary altar and a means of attracting the Holy People who are invoked to cure and bless. Each of the approximately 1,200 paintings used in 56 different ceremonies is a visual mythical statement and mnemonic device. The paintings are specific to a song ceremonial that in turn is related to a particular set of etiological factors and supernatural powers. Figures in the paintings symbolize human-like portrayals of protagonists of the origin myths that accompany each ceremonial, figures of the Holy People, and various personified beings, animals, and plants from the Navajo religious pantheon. The drypainting serves as a membrane through which the holiness and goodness of the Holy People can be transferred with the illness in a patient. Drypaintings, because of this ability to take on supernatural power, are considered living

"Talking Gods, Calling Gods, and Female Gods with Corn," Nightway ceremony. *Sandpainting demonstration, Gallup Ceremonial, 1930.* Courtesy of the Arizona State Museum, PIX 1316-X-1. Photo by W.T. Mullarky.

"Four Cloud People," Windway ceremony. *Sandpainting demonstration with singer measuring headdress, Arizona State Museum, late 1950s.* Courtesy of the Arizona State Museum, 25903. Photo by Helga Teiwes.

entities when consecrated and hence are revered as beautiful. They are not, however, considered "art" in the Euroamerican sense.

Gifts of the Holy People, drypaintings are to be used only under the direction of highly trained religious specialists and treated with respect because they are dangerous. They must be made perfectly in order to be effective; they are destroyed at the end of the ceremony because they are full of the transferred sickness. However, during the twentieth century, permanent forms of sandpaintings have been developed to both preserve Navajo sacred designs and as a form of secular art. Based on technological changes in the backing and adhesive, artistic sandpaintings have been made for the regional and international ethnic art market since the 1960s. Founded by Fred Stevens, Jr., a Navajo singer, and Luther A. Douglas, an Anglo artist, Navajo secular sandpaintings—which are permanent paintings made of pulverized dry materials glued onto a sand-covered wood backing—have become a minor art tradition. While not as large an industry as weaving or silversmithing, several million dollars worth of sandpaintings were being sold each year in the 1980s, and over 600 Navajos, both men and women, were or have been painters. While sacred drypaintings are made primarily by men, Navajo artistic sandpaintings are one of the few Navajo artcraft forms that are produced in equal numbers by both sexes.

Artistic sandpaintings, while developing out of sacred drypaintings, are not conceptualized as the same thing. They are felt to be art in the Western sense and are made intentionally for sale to non-Navajos. A process of secularization has resulted in this new category. This transformation has been accomplished by the singers and artists themselves intentionally making the saleable paintings "imperfect," by changing symbolism through simplification, elaboration, transportation, and several other symbolic and artistic devices. The design symbolism is changed to such an extent that the resulting compositions do not call the Holy People, yet they retain enough symbolism to be readily recognized as Navajo-made and conceptualized drypaintings.

Thus the designs in sacred and artistic drypaintings differ. Artistic drypaintings also vary among themselves because they are made for different markets: some are produced as large and expensive fine art with full reproductions of sacred designs, while others are made as medium-priced and medium-sized compositions, designed to be sold as gifts and home decorations and still others are designed as small, inexpensive souvenirs that evoke images of the Native American Southwest. Sandpaintings designed for each market differ by size, composition, complexity, and price range. Painters have also expanded the repertoire of appropriate subject matter to include non-drypainting motifs, such as landscapes, *yeibichai* dancers, portraits, and still lifes. As a result, drypainting has become an art form similar in technique and purpose to easel art.

Nancy J. Parezo

***See also** Art; Navajo; Religion*

Further Reading

Parezo, Nancy J. *Navajo Sandpainting: From Religious Act to Commercial Art.* Tucson: University of Arizona Press, 1983. Albuquerque: University of New Mexico Press, 1991.

Reichard, Gladys A. *Navajo Religion: A Study of Symbolism.* Bollingen Series 17. NJ: Princeton University Press, 1950, 1963, 1970. Tucson: University of Arizona Press, 1989.

Wyman, Leland C. *Southwest Indian Drypainting.* Albuquerque and Santa Fe: School of American Research and University of New Mexico Press, 1983.

DUWAMISH

Prior to the signing of the Treaty of Point Elliott on January 22, 1855, the Duwamish inhabited several villages along the Black and Duwamish rivers in Washington State. The Duwamish utilized an area extending along the east side of Puget Sound from the mouth of the Duwamish River north to the present site of Edmonds, and inland from the Duwamish River upstream including the Black, Green, Cedar, and Sammamish rivers and Lakes Washington and Sammamish. From their winter villages the Duwamish traveled seasonally to fishing, shellfishing, and plant gathering sites. The traditional homeland of the Duwamish is the general area of the city of Seattle, named after one of the Duwamish signators to the treaty.

History

Contact with Euroamericans was sporadic prior to the 1850s. After the ratification of the treaty in

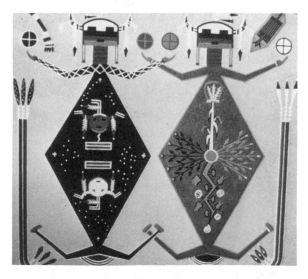

"Mother Earth, Father Sky," from Female Shootingway, by Juanita Stevens, Chinle, AZ, 1978. Photo by Nancy J. Parezo.

1859, the Duwamish were to remove to the Port Madison Reservation on the west side of Puget Sound. Although a number of Duwamish did go there, some also moved to the Tulalip and Muckleshoot reservations and a significant number stayed in the area of their traditional villages, eventually being engulfed by the expanding non-Indian population. The Duwamish were party to land claims cases against the United States federal government in the 1930s (*Dwamish et al. v. United States*, 79 Ct. Cl., No. F-275 [1934]) and in the 1950s (*Duwamish v. United States*, Indian Claims Commission, Docket 109). The latter resulted in a $62,000 award in 1962. In 1977, the nonreservation Duwamish filed a petition for federal recognition which is presently under consideration.

Recent History

The Duwamish have been organized since 1925 when they adopted a Constitution and Tribal Council form of governance. As a nonrecognized tribe they do not receive benefits from federal agencies and programs as do the nearby reservation communities, nor do they have a tribal land base. After the Boldt Decision of 1974 (*United States v. State of Washington*, Civil No. 9213, 384 F. Supp. [1974]) allocated 50 percent of the commercial harvest of salmon in western Washington to treaty Indians, the Duwamish sought inclusion as a treaty fishing tribe but were denied on the basis of lack of federal recognition. The recent history of the Duwamish is characterized by their struggle to become acknowledged as a federally recognized tribe and obtain the rights and privileges that entails. The 1991 population of the nonreservation Duwamish is approximately 400 enrolled members.

Culture

As a nonreservation community, the Duwamish are scattered throughout the Puget Sound area, but periodically participate in community gatherings and tribal meetings. They are of the Coast Salish language family, originally speaking a dialect of Lushootseed, although there are few speakers of Duwamish today. In the literature, the Duwamish have been particularly noted for a ceremony known as the "spirit canoe" in which a journey to the land of the dead was acted out for the purpose of lost soul recovery. It appears that this ceremony has not been practiced for over sixty years. Many Duwamish converted to the Indian Shaker Church in the early 1900s, and many are now members of one of various Christian denominations. Although today they may seem indistinguishable from their non-Indian neighbors, the Duwamish still constitute a functioning entity that maintains the traditions and culture of the tribe.

Daniel L. Boxberger

See also **Washington State Tribes**

Further Reading

Haeberlin, Hermann, and Erna Gunther. "The Indians of Puget Sound." *University of Washington Publications in Anthropology* 4:1 Seattle: (1930): 1–83.

Suttles, Wayne, and Barbara Lane. "Southern Coast Salish." *Handbook of North American Indians.* Vol. 7. *Northwest Coast.* Ed. Wayne Suttles. Washington, DC: Smithsonian Institution (1990): 485–502.

Tollefson, Kenneth D. "Political Organization of the Duwamish." *Ethnology* 29 (1989): 135–49.

Waterman, T.T. *Notes on the Ethnology of the Indians of Puget Sound.* Indian Notes and Monographs Miscellaneous Series 59. New York, NY: Museum of the American Indian, Heye Foundation, 1973.

Eastern Shawnee

See Shawnee in Oklahoma

ECONOMIC CONDITIONS

Historical Background

Throughout this century, American Indians have been the poorest of the poor in American society. The seriously disadvantaged economic position of American Indians has many causes. In the early years of this century, American Indians were concentrated in remote regions of the nation, distant from urban centers of economic growth. From about 1890 to 1930, the federal government's so-called "allotment" programs vigorously promoted farming as a means for American Indians to become self-sufficient. Allotment programs typically gave an American Indian family 160 acres for farming or cattlegrazing. However, the farm land allotted to Indian families was often arid and of poor quality. In the Plains, many tribes were former nomadic hunters and had neither the knowledge nor the desire to become farmers. In other places, Indian farming declined because allotment privatized communal agricultural systems, such as irrigation ditches, and this disrupted traditional farming practices.

After forty years, the allotment programs completely failed to help American Indians become self-sufficient. In retrospect, encouraging American Indians to become farmers was a poorly conceived idea at best. Since 1890, agriculture has been a declining industry in the United States, and small-scale family farms have been dwindling rapidly. It should be no surprise that American Indians could not make a living as small farmers during an era when many other Americans were giving up farming as a livelihood.

After allotment failed, the Indian New Deal was created by the Roosevelt administration in the 1930s to help reservations deal with the economic hardships created by the Great Depression. The Indian New Deal helped tribal governments reorganize, as well as put American Indians to work on projects such as dams, roads, and irrigation systems. However, the Indian New Deal was cut short by the outbreak of World War II. After the war, the federal government adopted a new set of policies known as "termination" and "relocation," which were designed to dissolve reservations and resettle American Indians in urban areas.

The legislation for termination and relocation was enacted in the late 1940s and early 1950s. One especially important congressional resolution was enacted in 1953 (HCR 108) and mandated the abolition of reservations across the country. At the same time, the Bureau of Indian Affairs implemented programs to relocate American Indians living on reservations to urban areas such as Los Angeles and Chicago. Between 1952 and 1972, more than 100,000 American Indians were relocated to cities. It was believed that by moving American Indians to urban labor markets, they would be able to find jobs and improve their standard of living. However, American Indians often lacked the education, skills, and experience they needed to find employment, and benefited little from relocation.

Opposition from American Indians kept all but a few reservations from being terminated. Furthermore, the failure of relocation programs to significantly improve the standard of living for American Indians caused the federal government to reconsider its termination and relocation policies. Since the early 1970s, the federal government has adopted a policy of "self-determination" that has allowed American Indians to be more involved in issues affecting their reservations. In economic terms, this has meant that American Indians have had a larger role in efforts to improve reservation conditions.

American Indian leaders have taken a variety of steps to increase economic activity on reservations. Many reservations are endowed with natural resources such as timber, minerals, water, and pristine recreational areas. Tribes with such resources have developed them with varying degrees of success. The Crow Tribe in Montana has encouraged coal mining, the Menominee in Wisconsin have a lumber mill, and the White Mountain Apache have a successful resort. Other reservations have few natural resources, so they have pursued manufacturing. The recent decline of United States manufacturing has made this type of enterprise as risky as farming, but some tribes such as the Mississippi Choctaw have been highly successful.

During the 1980s, many tribes established gambling operations. Gaming revenues have been a lucrative source of income for a number of reservations. However, it has also been highly controversial. State governments complain that reservation gambling violates state laws, but, in fact, tribal sovereignty makes reservations exempt from state jurisdiction. Congress has tried to address these disputes by passing legislation regulating reservation gambling, but this is likely to remain a contentious issue for the foreseeable future.

Urban American Indians typically have not participated in many of these initiatives because they do not live on reservations and are outside the jurisdiction of tribal governments. In most cities, there are few activities or programs designated for specific tribes. However, urban Indians, like other ethnic minorities, qualify for special assistance from agencies such as the Small Business Administration. This has helped individual urban American Indians start their own businesses. Other urban American Indians can participate in programs such as those funded by the Job Training Partnership Act (JTPA) to obtain employment skills and work experience.

A Statistical Profile

Statistical data clearly show how American Indians have been deeply affected by federal policies and by changes in the United States economy. At the turn of the century, only about 60 percent of American Indian males age ten and older were designated by the United States Census Bureau as being "gainfully employed" (figure 1). In this period of United States history, few American Indian women worked outside their home. Thirty years later, more American Indians, men and women, were gainfully employed but this increase was small. That is, the number of American Indian men with gainful employment increased only from 59 percent to 65 percent between 1900 and 1930. For American Indian women, there was almost no change during these decades.

One reason that American Indians have not fared well in the United States economy is that they have been concentrated in rural areas where agriculture represented the only livelihood available. Federal allotment policies also caused American Indians to depend heavily on agriculture. In 1930, for example, about one-half of the United States population resided in urban areas, while the homes of 90 percent of American Indians were in rural places. Although farmwork was once one of the few livelihoods in rural areas, by depending on agriculture, American Indians, like many other rural Americans, have been adversely affected by long-term declines in small-scale farming.

As figure 2 shows, nearly three-fourths of American Indian men who were employed in 1910 were either farmers or farm workers. However, this number shrank in later years, and in 1930, there were fewer Indian males in agriculture and more in other kinds of occupations, mostly unskilled labor. Compared to American Indian men, fewer American Indian women worked, but among those who were employed, they were less likely to be doing physically demanding farm work. Nonetheless, as figure 3 shows, about 20 percent of working American Indian women were employed as farm laborers and about an equal number as domestic servants. However, the majority of employed American Indian women held semiskilled factory jobs. Notably, there was a sharp increase in the percent of American Indian women employed in so-called professional and clerical occupations between 1910 and 1930, from 3.5 to 9.4 percent, respectively. Most likely, this represented a growing number of American Indian women trained as teachers, nurses, and clericals.

The outbreak of World War II in 1941 was a significant event in the economic lives of American Indians. About 25,000 American Indians served in the military, while nearly twice as many were employed in civilian war industries. This experience helped acquaint American Indians with Euroamerican culture and urban life. After the war, the GI Bill helped many Indian servicemen obtain higher education and this often led to jobs in urban areas. Relocation programs in the 1950s and 1960s also resettled American Indians in a handful of large cities. These developments have had a major impact on American Indians, rural and urban alike.

Unfortunately, one characteristic that has not changed much is the rate of labor force participation for American Indians. As figure 4 illustrates, the percentage of American Indians not in the labor force is not much lower in the second half of this century than

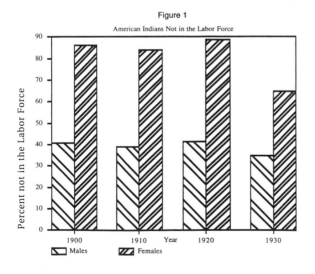

Figure 1

American Indians Not in the Labor Force

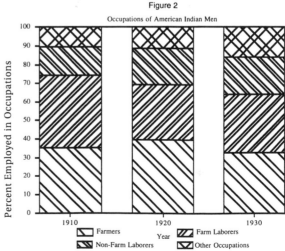

Figure 2

Occupations of American Indian Men

it was in the first half. The percentage of American Indian men in the labor force has increased modestly from about 63 percent in 1970 to 69 percent in 1990. In relative terms, this is about a 19 percent increase in twenty years. However, like other women in the United States, American Indian women have entered the labor force in great numbers. From 1970 to 1990, the percent of American Indian women in the labor force rose from 35 to 55 percent. This represents a relative increase of 44 percent in twenty years.

Higher rates of labor force participation do not necessarily mean that there is less joblessness among American Indians. Higher rates of labor force participation means that there are more American Indians working or seeking employment. When the number of persons seeking employment exceeds the number of jobs available, the result is higher unemployment. Since 1970 American Indian men have been consistently more prone to spells of unemployment than either white or African-American men (figure 5). However, despite this pattern of unemployment, the unemployment rate for American Indian men is slightly lower in 1990 than in 1980. Coupled with higher rates of labor force participation (figure 5), these unemployment figures suggest a modest improvement in the employment status of American Indian men. In contrast, while labor force participation rates for American Indian women have been steadily increasing for the past twenty years, this trend has been matched by steadily rising unemployment rates (figure 6). American Indian women have higher rates of unemployment than either African-American or white women.

American Indians have been affected by trends in the United States economy in ways similar to the non-Indian workforce. For example, changes in agricultural production have meant that fewer Indians are employed in this industry. In the latter half of this century, relatively few American Indians have worked in agriculture and related industries. In 1980, only about 6 percent of American Indian men and 1 percent of American Indian women were employed in agriculture, forestry, and fishing occupations. Most

American Indian men, about 53 percent, are employed in manual occupations as skilled workers, semiskilled manufacturing operations, or unskilled laborers. In comparison, about 54 percent of American Indian women are employed in technical, service, and administrative support occupations, working in jobs such as retail sales clerks, nurses, teachers, and teacher and nurse aides.

However, there are relatively few American Indians in high paying white collar jobs such as doctors, lawyers, or business executives. This, along with high rates of unemployment and relatively low levels of labor force participation, keeps the incomes of American Indian households at low levels, especially compared to whites. The economic disadvantages of American Indians are evident in table 1. Without doubt, American Indians did not prosper during the 1980s. Unlike Blacks and whites whose incomes increased by 8 to 12 percent respectively, the household income of American Indians was virtually unchanged between 1979 and 1989.

Furthermore, the income gap between white households and American Indian households grew substantially during the 1980s. In 1979, white household incomes were 37 percent higher than American Indian household incomes, an absolute difference of $9,829. Ten years later, this gap has grown to an absolute difference of $14,102, making white household incomes about 54 percent higher than American Indian households. This represents a 46 percent increase in the income gap between white and American Indian households. The economic hardships reflected by these numbers are more stark considering that American Indian households are typically larger (3.1 persons) than either African-American (2.9 persons) or white (2.5 persons) households. Dividing average household income by these numbers yields per capita income estimates of $16,123 for whites, $8,921 for African-Americans, and $8,453 for American Indians. Despite the considerable changes in labor force participation, American Indians continue to be the poorest of the poor.

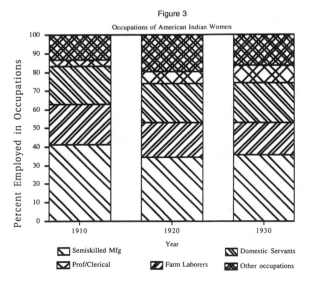

Figure 3

Occupations of American Indian Women

Figure 4

American Indians Not in the Labor Force

Table 1
Average Household Income by Race
of Householder in 1979 and 1989
(In Constant 1989 Dollars)

Householder's Race	1979	1989
American Indian	26,334	26,206
African-American	23,999	25,872
Whites	36,163	40,308

Source: United States Bureau of the Census, STF 3; General Social and Economic Characteristics, United States Summary, PC80–1–C1.

The economic hardships facing American Indians are also reflected in poverty statistics. The federal government computes a dollar figure based on what it considers to be the minimum expenditure required to have adequate food, shelter, and clothing. In 1989, it was estimated that a family of four needed at least $12,675 to meet basic needs and stay out of impoverishment. As Table 2 shows, there were slightly more American Indians living in poverty in 1989 than 1979. In 1989, about 31 percent of American Indians were impoverished, compared with 30 percent of African-Americans and 10 percent of whites. The lack of growth in real income for American Indians caused them to slip further into poverty while African-Americans and whites stayed at the same levels in 1989 as they were ten years earlier.

Table 2
Percent of Persons Living
in Poverty, by Race, 1979 and 1989

Race	1979	1989
American Indians	27.5	30.9
African-Americans	29.9	29.5
Whites	19.4	19.8

Source: United States Bureau of the Census, STF 3; General Social and Economic Characteristics, United States Summary, PC80–1–C1.

An even more alarming view of poverty exists in data for families with children. About 30 percent of married American Indian couples with children were living in poverty in 1989. This rate of poverty is higher than the rates for either the African-American or the white population. However, the economic circumstances of married couples are considerably better than those of single parent households, especially the households of single mothers.

Married couples have higher incomes because both spouses may be able to work outside the home, and most importantly, married couples have a male worker in the household. There is no question that American Indian women have been adversely affected by the so-called "feminization" of poverty. Over 70 percent of families headed by single American Indian mothers have incomes below the official poverty threshold. This rate is higher than the rate for African-American families headed by single mothers (68 percent), and noticeably higher than families headed by white women (57 percent). Families headed by single fathers are disadvantaged by having only one income. But the benefits of being a male worker means that these households have poverty rates substantially below the rates experienced by the families of single mothers.

Table 3
Percent of families with children under
age 18 living in poverty, by family type
and race of householder

Family Type	American Indian	African-American	White
Married Couple	29.9	17.4	19.1
Male Householder, No Spouse	54.6	37.6	25.2
Female Householder, No Spouse	70.5	68.0	56.8

Source: United States Bureau of the Census, STF 3.

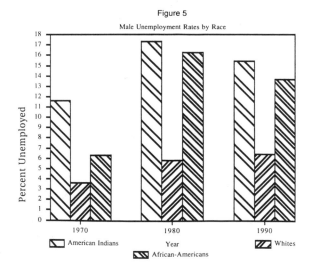

Figure 5

Male Unemployment Rates by Race

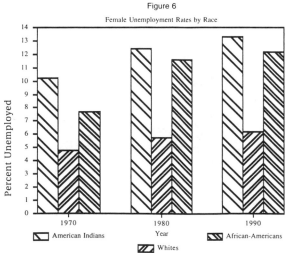

Figure 6

Female Unemployment Rates by Race

Conclusion

Although American Indians are considerably more urbanized and less dependent on agriculture than they were at the beginning of this century, they are still one of the poorest groups in American society. Throughout this century, more American Indians have become employed members of the labor force. For women in particular, this increase has been striking. However, the economic position of American Indians slipped during the 1980s. In most respects, they are now more disadvantaged than the African-American population. An especially alarming statistic is the large percentage of American Indian families with single mothers that are living in poverty.

To significantly improve the economic position of American Indians, it will be necessary to revitalize reservation economies and to provide opportunities for urban American Indians. Revitalizing reservation economies requires efforts to nurture various kinds of economic development projects that will provide jobs and income to reservation residents. Reservation and urban American Indians need job opportunities, as well as the experience, education, and skills necessary to compete in the labor market. The federal government has a large role to play in these efforts. During the 1980s, the federal government virtually abandoned all efforts to help American Indians improve their standard of living. Until the federal government acknowledges its trust responsibilities and obligations to American Indians and takes positive steps to improve economic conditions, past experience suggests that the economic circumstances of American Indians are unlikely to improve for the foreseeable future.

C. Matthew Snipp

See also Economic Development

Further Reading

Carlson, Leonard A. *Indians, Bureaucrats, and Land: The Dawes Act and the Decline of Indian Farming.* Westport, CT: Greenwood Press, 1981.

Fixico, Donald L. *Termination and Relocation: Federal Indian Policy, 1945–1960.* Albuquerque: University of New Mexico Press, 1986.

Prucha, Francis Paul. *The Great Father: The United States Government and the American Indians.* Lincoln: University of Nebraska Press, 1984.

Snipp, C. Matthew. *American Indians: The First of this Land.* New York, NY: Russell Sage, 1989.

Snipp, C. Matthew, and Gene F. Summers. "American Indians and Economic Poverty." *Rural Poverty in America.*. Ed. C.M. Duncan.Westport, CT: Auburn House (1992): 155–76.

ECONOMIC DEVELOPMENT

Tribal economies were shrinking at the start of the twentieth century as the dominant society used the General Allotment Act to move the best land on reservations out of Indian control. Indian land ownership fell from 138 million acres to 55 million between 1887 and 1934. Although the 1934 Indian Reorganization Act (IRA) stopped the massive transfer of land, its support for paternalism by federal officials prevented the recreated tribal governments from pursuing economic development. Efforts to terminate the existence of reservations in the 1950s forced Indian leadership to use their energies to prevent another disaster such as the General Allotment Act. Finally, in the late 1960s, programs initiated under Great Society legislation began to provide needed resources. The principles of local empowerment fostered by the Office of Economic Opportunity provided a way for tribes to start economic development programs they wanted.

Reservation governments struggle with many difficulties when attempting to develop their economies. External barriers to successful economic development consist of restricted access to Indian-owned property, regulation of property by the Bureau of Indian Affairs (BIA), conflict with state governments over economic activities, and obtaining access to capital and product markets. Internal obstacles include political difficulties, which are often a result of the structure of a reservation's government; cultural difficulties in dealing with the modern economy; and the need of the Indian population for additional skills. Because reservations vary greatly in their combination of obstacles, generalizations about economic development on reservations are difficult to establish.

Effective governmental leadership seems to be essential to the success of any economic development strategy. Often the internal and external barriers to development are so great that a tribal government needs to address its internal governmental processes in order to begin to resolve the many problems.

The self-determination movement of the 1970s and 1980s has greatly aided economic development by returning power to reservation leadership. In 1970 President Richard Nixon announced his support for tribal self-determination. His proposal, weakened to protect BIA prerogatives, became the Indian Self-Determination and Education Assistance Act of 1975 (PL 93–638). Through the use of "638 contracts," in which a tribe contracts with the BIA or Indian Health Service (IHS) to carry out services those bureaus normally provide, a tribal government can administer federal programs on its reservation. By asserting their own powers of inherent sovereignty, the powers recognized by the Indian Reorganization Act, and the steps allowed by 638 contracts, tribal governments can greatly expand their own powers, selecting and implementing appropriate economic development strategies. When a tribal government has succeeded in implementing an appropriate strategy, considerable progress can be made in developing a reservation economy.

One background condition is shared by most reservations: there is a shortage of jobs for Indians. Reported unemployment rates are high, and often understated because a number of people have given up looking for work. One commonly used definition of economic development on reservations is the generation of jobs. Because many tribes wish to preserve the quality of their environment and their ability to govern themselves, however, jobs are not pursued at any cost. Even in the face of what appears to be considerable poverty as perceived by a non-Indian observer, economic development in the form of job creation may not be the number one priority of a community.

Cutting across the internal and external dimensions of struggle is the selection of possible niches for economic development activity. Tribes need to find a place in the economy where they can fill a need. Given the complexity and size of the American economy, many niches are available. Reservations that successfully identify such niches have considerable success in economic development. Niches are defined by the natural resources a tribe controls, the skills of the tribal members, the location of the reservation, and characteristics of the neighboring economy.

External Struggles

Limited access to resources. The first of the externally generated obstacles is difficulty using property owned by Indians. In their treaties, the salmon-fishing tribes of the Pacific Northwest, for example, specifically reserved the right to fish at "all usual and accustomed places." This right, which referred to the optimal fishing sites near the mouths of rivers, turned out to be elusive as non-Indians could catch the fish in the open ocean or in Puget Sound, prior to the arrival of the salmon at the mouths of rivers. In addition, state fishing regulators began to prohibit Indians from using even the usual fishing places which they had been promised, and hydroelectric dams inundated other sites. The consequence was loss of access to the resource.

Other tribes found that water was diverted from streams before they could use it to water their fields. The federal government coerced tribal governments into signing long-term leases, often at very low rates of return, for land and for mineral resources, removing the land or resources from availability to Indians. These methods are not-so-subtle ways to take property without formal confiscation.

Indian lands were also taken formally. The allotment policy, which assigned allotments to individual Indians and opened the rest of the land to homesteading, effectively removed much land from Indian ownership. Although not all reservations were homesteaded, sale of allotments by individual Indians to non-Indians created checker-boarded land ownership situations on all allotted reservations, making concerted economic development in these areas extremely complex.

The struggle for Indians today is to regain control of resources that are still technically theirs. The salmon-fishing tribes went to court and finally obtained a clear right to take half of the fish. With the right to fish restored, Indians could earn substantial incomes from a traditional activity, upgraded by modern technol-

ogy. Even after obtaining rights to half the fish, however, struggles continued to define and enforce the right. Tribes had to settle among themselves which runs belonged to which reservations. They had to set up commissions and negotiate with states in order to enforce the division of harvest with non-Indians.

The Passamaquoddy and Penobscot tribes began successful economic development by obtaining control of land taken illegally in the late eighteenth century. Although they claimed most of the State of Maine, they settled for 300,000 acres and $81.6 million. By investing the capital, the Passamaquoddies have developed a diversified collection of businesses in Maine.

Control of resources. In the area of water rights, one also has to distinguish between a court victory which awards water in theory, and enforcement of the decision, which means delivery of water in fact. The tribes along the southern Colorado River successfully obtained control of their water and established prosperous farming activities which they now manage. They also lease the irrigated lands at excellent rental rates. When federal policies prevent control of land and water, an Indian tribe first must struggle to get the land back from non-Indian lessors before developing tribal or individual enterprises. Some tribes, however, have not been able to control water which should be theirs under the reserved water rights doctrine. As administered by the Bureau of Indian Affairs, many Indian irrigation projects do not deliver enough water to Indian lands. Indians must struggle with bureaucratic and legal systems in order to obtain water.

Oil and gas leasing is another area where the struggle for control is important. Several different aspects are significant. The first is obtaining a good rental rate, or royalty, for minerals taken from Indian lands. Indians traditionally have been in poor bargaining positions, and only in recent years have they been able to drive hard bargains for their oil, gas, and mineral resources. Once agreements are written, enforcement often depends upon the BIA; tribes have found they must watch their resources themselves if they want adequate enforcement.

Exclusion of state jurisdiction. In recent years, many Indian tribes have taken advantage of the unique status of reservations as federally protected enclaves within states to engage in business enterprises that would otherwise be heavily regulated or taxed by the state. The sale of tobacco and the development of gambling on reservations are lucrative because of state taxation of cigarettes and regulation of gambling. Because profits can be substantial in these areas, there is an ongoing struggle with the states to preserve tribal jurisdiction.

Internal Struggles

To further complicate the process of economic development, tribes must confront internal barriers to successful organization for economic development. The difficulties arise from a complex combination of causes. Governments on reservations were often imposed by the federal government. These imposed structures sometimes fit the situation of a tribe; usually some sort of dysfunction has been created.

The Choctaw Band of Mississippi, for instance, was able to pursue economic development when a strong tribal chief was in place. They reformed their Constitution, separating legislative from executive functions. Once the office of the tribal chief had been reinstated—the idea had historical roots among the Choctaw—the new chief could undertake economic development. The creation of labor-intensive assembly plants on the Choctaw Reservation is one of the important success stories. The foundation of this success was constitutional reform.

Several of the Plains tribes provide examples in which some kind of political reform is needed before economic development strategies can succeed. Tribal enterprises typically fail among Plains tribes, because individuals operating the enterprises are unable to withstand political pressures from tribal councils. Traditionally, these tribes have operated as bands, with family units as the most important entities. Economic development in the form of small enterprises is more likely to succeed in situations where there is little loyalty to a tribal government.

In contrast to the Plains situation is that of the Apache in the Southwest. On reservations such as White Mountain and Mescalero, tribal enterprise is very successful when coordinated by an honest tribal chairman.

Once a tribe has obtained effective rights to self-government, it appears that the tribe needs to develop institutions needed for economic development. The tribal government needs to provide stability, which is aided by setting up professional record-keeping and personnel systems. Plans need to be carried out consistently, which is helped when a judicial system that is independent of the electoral political system exists. Indian private enterprise succeeds on the Flathead Indian Reservation in Montana, for example, because the tribal court system can be counted on to enforce agreements impartially.

Another separation that aids tribal enterprise is to insulate day-to-day management of enterprise activities from interference by elected politicians. Tribes set up independent boards to serve as buffers between tribal councils and enterprise managers. This is successful if the tribal councils, or elected tribal chairmen, do indeed let the enterprises retain a certain amount of autonomy. Only 50 percent of enterprises directly controlled by tribal councils are profitable, while almost 75 percent of indirectly controlled enterprises show a profit. The White Mountain Apache lumber mill, for example, prospered when its manager was able to make day-to-day decisions without interference.

Although certainty and stability are important, the exact form of the structure of internal political systems can vary substantially. A traditional Pueblo can continue to use its old methods of selecting political leaders as long as these leaders retain the ability to run day-to-day operations without continuous interference. A powerful political leader can even work as a laborer in one of the firms, if he is willing to abide by traditional limits on his powers. At Cochiti Pueblo, for instance, a leader has the power of appointment and dismissal, but no ability to control other details.

Conclusion

The development of reservation economies is often difficult and frustrating. Faced with tremendous needs for jobs and income, tribes struggle with both external and internal obstacles to economic development. The external struggle involves substantial expense in hiring lawyers to pursue tribal rights in court. When a tribe cannot afford legal help, it is caught in an underdevelopment trap. The poor fishing tribes in the Northwest had to fight for years, with underpaid lawyers, before obtaining control of sufficient salmon to pursue their development plans.

After having struggled for decades to obtain *control* of land and resources, economic development often requires that political leadership appear to "let go" of a certain amount of control in order to let business managers run business affairs, either in tribal enterprises or in individual enterprises that use tribally owned resources. This requires a difficult balancing act in which the tribal government tries to set up the legal and policy framework which will assist entrepreneurs, while also ensuring that some of the negative aspects of economic development do not occur.

Ronald L. Trosper

See also Allotment; Economic Conditions; Government Agencies; Government Policy; Reservations

Further Reading

American Indian Policy Review Commission. *Report on Reservation and Resource Development and Protection.* Washington, DC: U.S. Government Printing Office, 1976.

Anderson, Terry L. *Property Rights, Constitutions and Indian Economies.* Lanham, MD: Rowman and Littlefield, 1992.

Cornell, Stephen, and Joseph Kalt, eds. *What Can Tribes Do? Strategies and Institutions in American Indian Economic Development.* Los Angeles: American Indian Studies Center, University of California, 1992.

Stanley, Sam, ed. *American Indian Economic Development.* The Hague, The Netherlands: Mouton Publishers, 1978.

U.S. Congress. Senate. Select Committee on Indian Affairs. *An American Indian Development Finance Institution.* 99th Cong. 2d sess. S. Print 99-142. 1986.

White, Robert H. *Tribal Assets: The Rebirth of Native America.* New York, NY: Henry Holt and Company, 1991.

EDISTO

The Edisto Tribe of South Carolina traces its origins to a Natchez Indian splinter group and settlement Indian communities including the Kuzzo, who gathered together in the latter half of the eighteenth century. The tribe has two primary population centers in Colleton and Dorchester counties: the Four Hole community of Edisto reside adjacent to the Givehan State Park; and Creeltown is the home of the other community, approximately eight miles away. Both are centered around churches: the Pentecostal Holiness of Givehans and the Edisto Indian Church of God at Creeltown. A total of about 455 people listed on the tribal roll live in 47 households. A number of Edistos also live in Charleston, South Carolina, mainly in the Brentwood area. The tribe is also known as Creeltown Indians, Four Hole Indians, Natchez, and Kuzzo Indians.

The Edistos reorganized in 1969 after over a century of inactivity. Major contributions to this effort were made by the late Georgia Davidson. The tribal government has been led by Chiefs Robert Davidson (1973 to 1982), Eddie Leroy Martin (1982 to 1986), and Johnny Creel (1986 to 1988). Current Chief Matthew Creel was elected in 1988, and he is assisted by a nine-member Tribal Council. The Edistos received a charter from the State of South Carolina in 1970. The Edisto Tribal Council submitted a letter of intent to the Bureau of Indian Affairs in December 1976 concerning their desire to obtain federal recognition. The tribe is currently number twenty-four on the BIA priority list.

Today most Edisto cultural affairs continue to be centered around their two churches. In 1989, the state returned the land on which their former Indian school was located. The building serves as a community center, and the surrounding plot is maintained for the tribe's benefit.

Basketmaking was discontinued in the late 1930s. The only craft currently practiced by the Edisto is beadwork, and an occasional boat paddle is carved. The tribe sponsors an annual powwow every May. Several years ago, classes in welding and pottery making were held under a state grant for adult education and the Comprehensive Employment and Training Act. As a result of these efforts, seven tribal members received their GED and several men were trained in welding and continue to practice that trade. The tribe also participated in the Job Training Partnership Act and is currently active in the VISTA/ACTION program. The two communities support five small Indian-owned businesses.

Thomas J. Blumer

Further Reading

Taukchiray, Wesley DuRant. *Edisto Tribe*. Series II, *Wesley D. White Papers*. Charleston: South Carolina Historical Society.
Taukchiray, Wesley DuRant, and Alice Bee Kasakoff. "Contemporary Native Americans in South Carolina: An Overview." *Indians of the Southeastern United States in the Late Twentieth Century*. Ed. J. Anthony Parades. Tuscaloosa, AL and London, England: University of Alabama Press (1992): 72–101.

EDUCATIONAL POLICY

Education for American Indians and Alaska Natives has undergone more changes in the twentieth century than at any other time in the five centuries since contact. The major thrust of this metamorphosis has been a movement toward Indian involvement and control over schooling, whether in public schools, schools funded by the Bureau or Indian Affairs (BIA), or tribally controlled community colleges. Increasing availability of schooling has led to virtually universal enrollment; simultaneously, the vast majority of students have moved from federal to public schools, although education directed by church groups has continued to play a small role.

In 1900 only half of all Native American children or about 21,500 were enrolled in school; 15 percent were in schools operated by church groups; and over 80 percent were in BIA schools. At the end of the 1980s, the number of children not enrolled in school was statistically insignificant. By 1990, most Indian children were in public schools: about 5 percent were in church-run or private schools; almost 10 percent were in BIA-funded schools; and the remaining 85 percent were in public schools. The majority of BIA-funded schools in 1990 were located in four states: Arizona, New Mexico, South Dakota, and North Dakota. Remaining BIA-funded schools were scattered throughout the country. By 1985, all of the BIA-funded schools in Alaska had been closed down in accordance with an agreement between the BIA and the State of Alaska, which transferred jurisdiction of these institutions to the state.

When the twentieth century opened, many Native American families continued to rely on traditional forms of childrearing rooted in their enduring cultural heritage. Although several hundred different groups speaking over two hundred different languages reveal the wide diversity of cultures, some common themes have characterized traditional childrearing among Native peoples. A sense of identity and a sense of community have permeated most Native groups. Networks of family, clan, or lineage groupings shared responsibility for educating the young. Youth were deemed mature when they had demonstrated some mastery of economic skills, had gained knowledge of their cultural heritage, and had become spiritually aware. Storytelling played an important role in teaching the young, yet stories were often told in winter, when people gathered around the fire in the long evenings. As increasing numbers of children attended BIA boarding schools at the turn of the century, so, too, did they begin to lose this dimension of their Native educational heritage.

Within the BIA educational system, the first quarter of the century saw a subtle shift in policy. In the late nineteenth century, when the federal government had moved aggressively into Indian schooling, it had followed the lead of Richard Henry Pratt, the influential founder of Carlisle Indian School (1879). Pratt had urged total assimilation of Indian youth through the expansion of an off-reservation industrial boarding school system. Around 1900, BIA leaders such as Estelle Reel, superintendent of Indian schools (1898 to 1909), and Commissioner of Indian Affairs Francis E. Leupp (1901 to 1909), began to shift to reservation schools that would train Native youth for life among their own people. However, Reel's introduction of a uniform curriculum for all BIA schools and a continued disregard for all aspects of Native cultures, including language, meant that these English-only schools maintained ambivalent goals: cultural assimilation and physical separation. At the same time, BIA leaders also urged public school enrollment, a policy begun in 1891 when the federal government began to reimburse public schools for each Indian pupil enrolled, a process gauged to offset tax losses. Thus from the 1880s through the 1920s, education became the twin partner of the allotment policy introduced in the Dawes Act of 1887: both aimed toward the reformers' dream of detribalization and independent citizenship for Native Americans.

Not until the decade of the 1920s did these policies come under the scrutiny of a new generation of reformers who attacked both Congress and the BIA for the deplorable results of allotment and assimilation schooling. Although most of the reform leadership was non-Indian, exceptions included Henry Roe Cloud, a Winnebago educator. In 1915, Roe Cloud had founded the American Indian Institute, a prep school for Indian students located in Wichita, Kansas; and in the 1930s, he headed Haskell Institute. The 1920s reformers, under the leadership of John Collier, launched a campaign to improve economic conditions, health, and education for American Indians. The target for their most severe criticism was the BIA boarding school. In the previous two decades, these institutions had degenerated. Even before World War I, financial restrictions had forced the schools to shift from institutions that provided basic academic training and vocational skills to those that provided only minimum reading, writing, and arithmetic for children who were forced to spend much of their day engaged in tedious chores that maintained the school itself. Thus, Indian pupils sewed the school uniforms, cooked the meals and washed the dishes, and constructed and repaired the buildings. Marched to class, to meals, and to chapel; underfed and often ill due to the rapid spread of contagious diseases in overcrowded dormitories, many children ran away. Nonetheless, tribes began to view "their" schools possessively, and to derive from them whatever positive attributes they offered.

When the reformers' attacks on the BIA schools began to alarm the American public, the federal government was forced to take action. The net result was the government-sponsored study that led to the Meriam Report. One of the most important assessments of federal Indian policy in the century, the Meriam Report was a severe chastisement of the BIA, but its strongest censure fell on the BIA boarding schools themselves. Perceiving the primary mission of the Indian Bureau as one of education, the report argued that the BIA must provide both Indian children and their parents with the tools to adapt to two worlds: both Indian and white. It recommended increased day schools and dramatic changes in the boarding schools, including provision for adequate food and health care, a curriculum sensitive to Native cultural heritage, fewer students, and the removal of pre-adolescent children to day schools.

Will Carson Ryan, Jr., well-known progressive educator, was largely responsible for the educational section of the report, and was one of two directors of education for the Indian Bureau during the 1930s. A transitional figure, Ryan served through the last years of the BIA reform administration of the late twenties, and into the early years of Collier's commissionership, the Indian New Deal (1933 to 1945). Aware of increased enrollment of Indian children in public schools, who, by 1928, outnumbered those in BIA schools, Ryan recognized the need to simplify the procedure of federal reimbursement to public schools. One of his strongest achievements was the passage of the Johnson-O'Malley Act of 1934, dubbed J-O'M by Indian educators. J-O'M provided that states, rather than individual school districts, sign contracts with the BIA, the agency responsible for this funding. Initially a sound plan, J-O'M eventually disintegrated into a program used by state school systems as a funding source for general needs. Not until reforms in the 1970s would this misuse of funds intended for Indian pupils begin to change. In addition to public school legislation, Ryan also introduced changes in BIA schools. He closed some boarding schools, changed the curriculum in others, and strengthened community schools on the reservations.

Ryan's successor, Willard Walcott Beatty, also came from a progressive education background. Beatty provided the strongest leadership in BIA education until the rise of Indian self-determination. He directed Indian Bureau education from 1935 to 1953 and was moving into his stride when the war began. In the half a dozen years before the war, he expanded programs begun by Ryan. He also introduced teacher training, acquainting the BIA teachers with progressive educational concepts and with the unique characteristics of Indian cultures. In 1931, schools for Alaska Natives were transferred from the United States Office of Education, which had been responsible since 1887, to the BIA; consequently the Alaska schools fell under the jurisdiction of Ryan and Beatty. Beatty also developed bilingual texts for Sioux, Navajo, and Pueblo children and introduced one of the earliest programs in this country for training teachers in bilingual education. In early 1942 these programs came to a halt with the nation's involvement in the war.

For many Native Americans World War II underlined the importance of education. Indians enlisted directly from BIA boarding schools and from remote reservation locations, and the thousands who served in Europe and the Pacific encountered worlds vastly different from places like Chinle, Arizona; Wapato,

Washington; and Muskogee, Oklahoma. Those who worked in wartime industry also brushed with the outside world of urban America, where knowledge of English and the "3 R's" was crucial to survival. Reaction to these experiences enhanced the role of education in Indian lives. Veterans turned to assistance through the GI Bill of Rights and other legislation; tribal governments introduced compulsory education laws and set aside tribal funds for scholarship; and the BIA, under Beatty's guidance, created schooling for post-war Indian needs. Some BIA schools developed curricula directed toward urban life; others introduced the Navajo Special Education Program, which offered basic schooling for overaged Navajo youth at Intermountain Indian School (Utah) and other locations. In the 1940s and 1950s BIA schools, which in 1953 came under the direction of Hildegard Thompson, overflowed with students, including thousands of Navajo, Alaska Natives, and Mississippi Choctaw, who had never had any schooling; simultaneously, urban schools saw an increase in Indian enrollment through families who emigrated to cities during the war or under the relocation program of the termination era. By the mid-1960s, when pressures mounted for Indian control in education, almost all Native American children were enrolled in school.

The movement for Indian self-determination in education was born in the John F. Kennedy and Lyndon B. Johnson administrations, but the groundwork for this change was laid during earlier decades. The impact of urbanization, the increasing sophistication of Indian leadership, the rise of pan-Indian organizations, and the growing numbers of Indian parents who had attended school were all present when the political yeast of Johnson's Great Society began to ferment.

Like their counterparts during the Indian New Deal, federal Indian programs in the 1960s relied on funding outside the BIA. The Office of Economic Opportunity (OEO) provided funding for several programs affecting Indian schooling: Head Start preschools; Navajo Community College, the first Indian-controlled and Indian-directed college in the nation, founded in 1969; and Rough Rock Demonstration School, the first Indian community school, founded in 1966 and also located on Navajo land. These innovations marked the beginning of change, but the pace did not accelerate until the publication of *Indian Education: A National Tragedy—A National Challenge* (1969), a Senate report that was soon known as the Kennedy Report. Like the Meriam Report, the Kennedy Report severely censured Indian schooling and recommended changes. It urged that native cultures be stressed in curricula and that Indian parents be involved in BIA schooling. Other studies added fuel to the national debate, and legislation soon followed.

The 1970s saw the passage of more legislation on Indian education than any other time in American history. The major measures included: the Indian Education Act of 1972; the Indian Self-Determination and Education Assistance Act of 1975; Title XI of the Education Amendments of 1978; and the Tribally Controlled Community College Assistance Act, also of 1978. Collectively, this legislation provided for Indian participation in and direction of the federally funded programs for Indians in public schools; for contracting of BIA-funded schools by Indian tribes or groups; for local control of BIA schools by Indian school boards; and for federal funding of tribally controlled community colleges. The Indian Education Act mandated parental and community participation in programs engendered by the Impact Aid Laws of the 1950s and the Elementary and Secondary Education Act of 1965; it authorized programs stressing culturally relevant and bilingual curricula; and it established the Office of Indian Education under the United States Office of Education and directed by a deputy commissioner of education, a position first held by William G. Demmert, a Tlingit educator from Alaska. It also created the National Advisory Council on Indian Education to review applications for grants. The Indian Self-Determination Act also addressed public school issues by shifting the control of J-O'M programs from public school districts to Indians by direct contracting with Indian groups. In addition, this legislation provided for BIA-funded contract schools, such as the Santa Fe Indian School.

The 1970s, therefore, held much promise for Indian self-determination in education, but as the decade drew to a close, Indian parents, communities, and tribes asked the old question: would the federal government stand by its word when the mood for reform had dissipated? During the two-term Ronald Reagan administration the answer became increasingly clear: the victories of the seventies could be held only with persistent struggle. In both the BIA and Department of Education programs, the Reagan policymakers curbed budgets; made temporary appointments to replace effective Indian leadership; and introduced arbitrary unilateral policy changes, such as the controversial plan rejected by the tribes to transfer responsibility for BIA schooling to the tribes and then, by default, to the states, that was introduced by Assistant Secretary of the Interior for Indian Affairs Ross Swimmer (Cherokee). Early indicators of the George Bush administration suggested that cooperation, rather than confrontation, might be resumed but as of this writing, it was too early to draw conclusions.

As the last decade of the twentieth century opened, the promise for self-determination remained, and the lessons learned in earlier decades suggested that Indians would gain increasing control over their children's schooling. By the end of the 1980s, almost one-third of the BIA-funded schools were contract schools, run by Indian groups or tribes, and in programs for Indian children in public schools, there was Indian involvement at all levels. Chemawa and Riverside were among the few remaining boarding schools that had survived attrition. The BIA had added or changed other schools, such as Haskell Indian Junior College, the Institute of American Indian Arts in Santa

Fe, and Southwestern Indian Polytechnic Institute in Albuquerque. With the exception of these flagship institutions, and the twenty-four tribally controlled community colleges, most schools that Indian youth have attended have been public schools, but even some of these are operated through direct contracts with Indian groups, such as the Zuni public school district in New Mexico. The face of Indian education has changed dramatically in the twentieth century, and it is likely to become increasingly a Native American face in the twenty-first century.

Margaret Connell Szasz

See also Bureau of Indian Affairs Schools; Churches and Education; Higher Education; Indian Education Act, 1972; Johnson-O'Malley Act; Meriam Commission; National Indian Education Association; Public Schools; Tribal Colleges

Further Reading

Demmert, William G., Jr. "Native Education: The Alaskan Perspective." *Indigenous Peoples and Education in the Circumpolar North.* Ed. William G. Demmert, Jr. Godthab, Greenland: Gronlands Seminarium, 1986.

Fuchs, Estelle, and Robert J. Havighurst. *To Live on This Earth: American Indian Education.* 2d ed. Albuquerque: University of New Mexico Press, 1983.

Hyer, Sally. *One House, One Voice, One Heart: Native American Education at the Santa Fe Indian School.* Santa Fe: The Museum of New Mexico Press, 1990.

Indian Nations at Risk: Listening to the People. Charleston, WV: Eric/Cress, 1992.

Szasz, Margaret Connell. *Education and the American Indian: The Road to Self-Determination Since 1928.* 2d ed. Albuquerque: The University of New Mexico Press, 1977.

———. "Listening to the Native Voice: American Indian Schooling in the Twentieth Century." *Montana, The Magazine of Western History* 39 (Summer 1989): 42–53.

United States Department of the Interior. Bureau of Indian Affairs. Office of Indian Education Programs. *Report on BIA Education: Excellence in Indian Education Through the Effective School Process. Final Draft Review.* Washington, DC: March, 1988.

ELDERS

Although Congress describes them as "a vital resource," they are America's forgotten elderly. Aged 65 and over and 165,000 strong, they comprise more than 8 percent of the nation's American Indian/Alaska Native population. Representing more than 50 percent of tribal groups nationwide, they speak about 150 different languages. Eighty percent live west of the Mississippi, divided more or less evenly between reservation and urban residences. They live diversely—in Arizona they live in hogans miles from the nearest paved roads; and in Oklahoma they reside in HUD housing projects. More than 5,000 of them live in Los Angeles. They live on treaty-based reservations, executive order reservations, state-created reservations, or with the large number of bands of Indians who do not have federal recognition. They belong to termi-

nated tribes; a high percentage of them, both rural and urban, are not served by the reservation system.

Elders in the Past

The roles of Indian elders in traditional societies reflected their full integration into family, clan, and tribal activities. In every aspect of Indian life, elders were acknowledged as a stabilizing influence—a constant source of reaffirmation for religious, cultural, and social values. Their influence bore no relationship to formal education. Accumulated years of experience, memory, and wisdom brought elders to the forefront of tribal religious life. To become a traditional religious leader was a calling, not a profession that could be learned at any school, or relayed by a book.

In Indian extended families, which often included uncles, aunts, grandchildren, and other relatives and clan members, elders served as mentors and counselors, reinforcing a wide range of mores and folkways.

> "Our grandparents taught us that every visitor to our home should be fed," reports a Laguna Pueblo Indian woman. "My grandmother always said, 'Even if you have nothing, offer them a drink of water.' Years later, a stranger knocked on our door and I left him on the porch for a few minutes. My grandmother was upset with me: 'What's the matter,' she said, 'have you forgotten everything?'"

Although not expected to work, many elders reportedly tended communal fields and gardens, performed light housekeeping chores, and assisted with day care for the young children of their extended families. At the end of the 1800s, however, federal initiatives to assimilate Indians into the larger society began in earnest. Given their formerly high status and prominent place in traditional Indian society, elders have subsequently experienced an evolution into unclear and less meaningful roles.

Traditional medical practitioners were replaced by contemporary health care workers. Traditional leadership patterns were replaced by appointed or elected tribal officials. Extended family-based, long-term care was replaced by distant nursing homes. Reservation economics required elders to seek full or part-time employment. Elders whose predecessors had been healthy began to experience medical problems associated with diabetes and alcoholism. The elder population, once carefully nurtured by their extended families, became instead primary care givers and, frequently, sole financial providers.

Educational patterns changed entirely. Indian children, once raised by extended families, instructed by elders, and honored for their heritage were now, under Bureau of Indian Affairs (BIA) regulations, removed from their homes to be placed in repressive boarding schools. At best, BIA boarding schools offered inferior educations; at their worst, they succeeded in dampening any pride these young students felt for their culture or hopes they carried of obtaining a better life. The failure of America's Indian educational system was accompanied by the absence or breakdown of reservation economic and health provision systems. Frequently located on arid wastelands with few natural resources, Indian reservations quickly became rural ghettos.

Unemployment resulted from lack of reservation industry; poverty from lack of education and opportunity; disease from lack of health care, sanitation, and immunization. Alcoholism—the bane of Indian communities everywhere—sprang, at least in part, from idleness and despair.

Reservation economics, poor health, and educational deprivation all played roles in Indian elders' separation from society. Having quickly discovered white perceptions of them as second-class citizens, a whole Indian generation found themselves uneducated (nearly 12 percent have no formal education, only 22 percent have graduated from high school), and frequently unemployable, even if reservation jobs were available (and most often, there were none). Consequently, many elders chose, early in their lives, to not participate in the larger society. Remaining on the reservation meant a guaranteed life of poverty. It also offered comfort, in the familiar faces of family and friends, traditional ceremonies and language, and unquestioned acceptance.

By their standards, reservation life was clearly superior to the failure-laden probabilities of the outside world. Additionally, the frenetic, achievement-driven pace of the larger society was, if not laughable, totally alien to their values. What good is a life without respect for all, tradition, community love, and honor?

Elders in the Present

Mistrustful of non-Indian services, dependent on the federal government for subsistence, and isolated by huge cultural and social barriers, reservation Indian elders are insistent that they are not welfare recipients. They have paid with their land and often with their ancestors' blood. The treaties and federal law both say that they are entitled to decent lives, and that the United States of America will provide the means.

That the government of the United States has failed to honor its trust responsibilities to these elders is without question. In 1987, Congress found Indian elders to be:

- Unemployed at levels exceeding 80 percent, with unemployment reaching 95 percent on some reservations;
- Living in poverty on reservations at a rate of 61 percent;
- Living eight years less than the general population;
- Living in substandard, over-crowded reservation housing, 40 percent of which has been deemed unfit for occupancy;
- Receiving less-than-adequate health care;

- Served by Title VI nutrition programs at a rate of less than 19 percent;
- Served by area agencies on aging at a rate of less than 1 percent of total participants;
- Physically and mentally abused at an estimated rate of 30 percent; and
- Excluded from Social Security benefits at a rate of 57 percent.

The lives of many Indian elders are most accurately reflected by findings of the 1980 census about their homes: sixteen percent lacked electricity, 17 percent had no refrigerators, 21 percent had no indoor toilets, and 50 percent had no telephones. A 1981 White House Conference on Aging report added that 26 percent of their homes were built prior to 1939, 26.3 percent had no indoor plumbing at all, and only 50 percent had complete bathrooms indoors. And a 1986 National Indian Council on Aging (NICOA) study revealed that 68.8 percent had more than three persons co-resident; 49.4 percent had areas with no floor covering; 42.1 percent had broken windows; 35 percent had broken doors; 47.4 percent had no heat other than wood stoves or fireplaces; and 75 percent had no telephones.

Despite provisions of the 1921 Snyder Act that United States trust responsibility to American Indians includes health care, Indian elders suffer poorer health than any comparable population in America. With a life expectancy of sixty-five years, eight years less than whites, Indian elders are more likely than whites to die of alcoholism by 459 percent; tuberculosis by 233 percent; diabetes by 107 percent; and pneumonia by 66 percent.

With their health care managed by the Indian Health Service (IHS) and, to a lesser extent their own tribes, Indians are served by more than 51 hospitals and 400 outpatient clinics. Despite its staff of more than 11,000, the IHS is hard-pressed to meet the needs of a burgeoning Indian population which, with an average age of 24, is the youngest of any American minority. According to the National Institutes of Health, Indian diabetes rates are four times the national average, with some Arizona reservations exhibiting the highest known rates in the world.

For Indian elders, the health care crisis is extreme—the IHS offers no individual case management, does not consider long-term care its responsibility, and provides no geriatric focus or staff training whatsoever. In order to re-focus IHS priorities, advocacy to change the Indian Health Care Improvement Act appears to have limited value. In the final analysis, the issue is one of trust responsibility versus budget considerations.

Elders requiring nursing home care must either pay for private care or find admission at one of the nation's eleven tribally operated nursing homes. With only 644 available beds in the entire nation, America's 200,000 Indian elders are understandably distressed at the IHS's refusal to fund community-based or in-home care.

Elders in the Future

The picture is not a bright one. Economically, the average income of a male Indian elder is $6,253, compared to $11,203 for comparable white males. Socially, the problems of neglect and abuse are growing as reservation extended families break down. While younger family members succumb to alcohol or leave the reservation to find work, Indian youngsters, educated at public schools, learn fewer and fewer traditional values.

Spiritually, however, Indian elders remain secure in beliefs and values that have sustained their tribes for hundreds of years. They are, almost without exception, convinced that Indian people will endure well beyond the present white-dominated society. The mission for their advocates, the federal government, and its agencies, remains to bring some semblance of the American Dream to them before they become another resource that is lost forever. Time is running out.

Dave Baldridge

See also **Alcohol Abuse; Family; Government Policy; Health; Indian Health Service**

Further Reading

American Indian Elderly: A National Profile. Albuquerque, NM: National Indian Council on Aging, 1981.

Indian Elderly and Entitlement Programs: An Accessing Demonstration Project. Albuquerque, NM: National Indian Council on Aging, 1981.

John, Robert. *Health Research, Service, and Policy Priorities of American Indian Elders.* Lawrence, KS: American Indian Research Institute, 1993.

A Survey to Determine the Housing, Health, and Safety Status of Indian Elderly. Albuquerque, NM: National Indian Council on Aging, 1986–1987.

White House Conference on Aging. *The American Indian and Alaska Native Elderly.* Technical Report, 1981.

ENVIRONMENTAL ISSUES

Traditionally Native Americans have had an immediate and reciprocal relationship with their natural environments. At contact, they lived in relatively small groups close to the earth. They defined themselves by the land and sacred places, and recognized a unity in their physical and spiritual universe. Their cosmologies connected them with all animate and inanimate beings. Indians moved in a sentient world, managing its bounty and diversity carefully lest they upset the spirit "bosses," who balanced and endowed that world. They acknowledged the power of Mother Earth and the mutual obligation between hunter and hunted as coequals. Indians celebrated the earth's annual rebirth and offered thanks for her first fruits. They ritually addressed and prepared the animals they killed, the agricultural fields they tended,

---

MEMORIES OF 1934

The little knot of crew-cut Indian boys stood uneasily in the center of the Bureau of Indian Affairs (BIA) Chemewa Boarding School gymnasium. They were going to be punished. It seemed that someone was always getting punished.

Today, a special assembly had been called to embarrass them for their secret ceremony. They had been caught sneaking down to a little clearing in a nearby forest to dance. They often did this—partly in play, partly serious—wearing their homemade cardboard feathers and singing traditional songs when they danced, using a stick and a discarded wash tub for a makeshift drum.

Now they were going to have to dance again and look foolish, embarrass themselves in front of the several hundred other Indian kids who, like them, had been taken from their reservation homes and forced to attend Chemewa. The school superintendent told them, "If you want to be Indian so much, you can do your little dance in front of us all."

R.S., age six and the tallest of the five boys, was scared. This was going to be embarrassing. Ever since he came to this school last year, taken against his grandparents' wishes, his life had been miserable.

More than anything, he wanted to go home. When he spoke the only language he knew, Tututni, teachers had whipped him with canes, leaving red welts on his back and legs. But they hadn't made him white . . . and they hadn't made him quit.

In his coveralls, cardboard feather sticking up behind his right ear, he looked up from the floor with an anger that would follow him for much of his life. He began to sing, in a quavering, adolescent falsetto: "Wi hi yiii . . . " Every eye in the gym was on him. Silence.

Then, from just behind him, the voice of another young boy. "Wi hi yo, yah . . ." And then another, and another, until five hundred Indian kids were singing the ancient prayer song. Heads high, defiant, eyes shining. They knew they would pay for their insubordination—but for that one afternoon, they didn't care. Nor did they care that fifty years later, theater audiences across the country would cheer Will Sampson and Jack Nicholson enacting similar acts of defiance in *One Flew Over the Cuckoo's Nest.*

If we could script their story, typical of a whole generation of American Indian elders, it would end with that afternoon of moral victory. But the reality, unfortunately, does not have R.S. graduated from Chemewa, overcoming a drinking problem, and soon earning two Purple Hearts and a Silver Star as a Marine in Korea. He is now a spiritual leader for his tribe. His classmates weren't so fortunate; 80 percent of them have died, almost all from alcohol-related causes.

and the vegital and mineral materials they processed. They used song and ritual speech to modify their world, while physically transforming that landscape with fire and water, brawn and brain. They did not passively adapt, but responded in diverse ways to adjust environments to meet their cultural as well as material desires.

The pace of change in Indian environments increased dramatically with Euroamerican contact. Old World pathogens and epidemic diseases, domesticated plants and livestock, the disappearance of native flora and fauna, and changing resource use patterns altered the physical and cultural landscape of the New World. Nineteenth-century removal and reservation policies reduced the continental scope of Indian lands to mere islands in the stream of American settlement. Reservations themselves were largely unwanted or remote environments of little perceived economic value. Indian peoples lost even that land as the General Allotment Act of 1887 divided reservations into individual holdings. By 1930, this policy contributed to the alienation of over 80 percent of Indian lands—a diminishment of land, resources, and biotic diversity that relegated Indians to the periphery of American society.

By the beginning of the twentieth century, Native Americans controlled mere remnants of their former estates, most in the trans-Mississippi West. Relatively valueless by nineteenth-century standards, their lands contained unseen resources of immense worth. This single fact informs nearly all Native American environmental issues in the twentieth century. Land, its loss, location, and resource wealth or poverty, the exploitation and development of that land, and changing Indian needs and religious attitudes all define the modern environmental debates.

By the beginning of the twentieth century, agriculture and grazing had fundamentally changed the face of Indian lands. In Oklahoma and on the high plains, Indians and agents cleared, plowed, and planted large areas in a succession of monoculture crops. Overcropping marginal lands, drought, the Dust Bowl, the Great Depression, isolation, and the vagaries of the American market economy led to the wide-scale abandonment of Indian agriculture after World War II. Likewise, the adoption of domestic animals radically changed the landscape and biotic diversity of reservations. In the 1930s, the government instituted drastic livestock reduction and reseeding programs on southwestern reservations. Range scientists introduced new plant and animal species into fragile ecosystems, but were unable to solve problems of overgrazing on the drought-ravaged Navajo and Papago reservations. On a cultural level, the programs backfired by ignoring Native explanations and ecological methods, resulting in increased Indian economic dependence. Since then, tribes have had to deal with overgrazing and erosion, invasive noxious plants, reclamation, and improper land use. Given past experience, tribes are beginning to weigh the relative utility of leasing lands to non-Indians against developing their own operations which might be more sensitive to sustainable agricultural alternatives.

In the early twentieth century, some reservations contained extensive forests that made them attractive targets for exploitation. To protect these forests government officials outlawed Indian burning as a means of environmental management—clearing forest underbrush to reduce the potential for destructive crown fires while improving game animal habitat and useful vegetal materials. Government-managed timber sales brought some economic development and prosperity to the Yurok, Karuk, Hupa, and Klamath of California and Oregon; to Western Apaches in Arizona; and to Chippewas and Menominees in Minnesota and Wisconsin. But gross mismanagement of sustained yield programs led to reckless clear-cutting, erosion, and the loss of forest habitats on all these reservations. In the Black Hills of South Dakota and near Taos Pueblo's sacred Blue Lake, lumbering operations in national forests threatened sacred sites. The process continues today as the Bureau of Land Management chain-clears piñon-juniper forests in Nevada to improve the grazing potential of the land for white permit holders, destroying traditional Western Shoshone resources and gathering areas without Indian consent.

Modern hunting, gathering, and fishing rights based on nineteenth-century treaties have created a number of problems between Indians, sportsmen, and state and federal governments. In the early twentieth century, under pressure from commercial and sports fishermen, state and federal officials limited Indian off-reservation hunting and fishing. These regulations hit Native fishermen in the Northwest particularly hard. They were competing with a growing number of commercial operations and losing Native fishing sites to dams. In the 1960s, Indian activists staged "fish-ins" to publicize the situation, and tribes took their case to court. In *United States v. State of Washington* (1974), Judge George Boldt reaffirmed the rights of Northwest tribes to harvest fish under provisions of the 1854 Treaty of Medicine Creek, without interference by the State of Washington. The Boldt Decision restored a measure of Indian control over their environment and natural resource use. Today, these tribes have built a world-class fishery management system, allowing them a sizable subsistence and small commercial catch. Likewise, the Mescalero Apaches, Pyramid Lake Paiutes, Wind River Shoshones, and Arapahos have developed scientific and culturally sensitive programs for managing their faunal resources.

Across the country, hunting and fishing rights continue to stir public debate. In Wisconsin, ugly confrontations between whites and Chippewas over off-reservation hunting and spearfishing continue even after court decisions quantified Indian treaty rights at 50 percent of the annual harvest—a level Indians have never approached. On the Uintah-Ouray Reservation in Utah, Northern Utes and terminated mixed-blooded people fight over reservation hunting, fishing, and use privileges. White sportsmen and environmentalists question Native rights to kill bald eagles, bowhead whales, Florida panthers, or other endangered species guaranteed under the National Environmental Policy Act of 1969 and the American Indian Religious Freedom Act of 1978—both of which have environmental consequences by protecting Native cultural and religious practices. The acts have safeguarded and allowed Indian access to sacred non-reservation areas and resources, and injected a level of legal tolerance to Native religious practices that revolve around resource use.

Since the majority of Indian reservations are in the arid West, it is understandable that water has been a central environmental issue. By 1900, whites actively competed with Indians for this scarce resource. At Fort Belknap Indian Reservation in Montana, white settlers diverted water from the Milk River. When ordered to stop, they argued that the Indians had not made prior appropriation use. In 1908 the Supreme Court ruled in *Winters v. United States* that in establishing reservations, Congress implied and reserved the priority water rights necessary for present and future use. Encouraged by the *Winters* decision, the Indian Bureau used Indian funds to construct elaborate irrigation systems to protect Indian water and improve the agricultural potential of tribal and allotted holdings. Irrigation promised to change the landscape and increase Indian self-sufficiency, but the systems suffered from poor construction, improper use and maintenance, and often ended up in the hands of white settlers who bought up the best Indian lands.

Twentieth-century reclamation, irrigation, and big dam projects have had unforeseen consequences for Indians and their lands. As part of the Newlands Project in 1905, the government dammed and diverted the Truckee River for white irrigation. The Lahontan trout, the Pyramid Paiutes' chief source of subsistence, became extinct, and the diversion of water nearly killed Pyramid Lake. During the New Deal, the Civilian Conservation Corps and Indian Emergency Conservation Works program completed numerous, if not always successful, water and erosion control projects on western reservations. Since the 1930s, dams on the Columbia River and its tributaries have impeded the migration of salmon and other anadromous species, flooded sacred sites and Indian fisheries like Celilo Falls, and ruined upstream spawning grounds. On the Missouri River, the Pick-Sloan Plan for damming and flood control proved disastrous for Indians of the Standing Rock, Cheyenne River, Crow Creek, and Fort Berthold reservations. They watched the waters cover rich agricultural lands, villages, and sacred sites in the name of progress. Similar things happened in the 1960s and 1970s with Senecas and the Kinzua Dam, and Eastern Cherokees and the Tellico Dam.

Today, these dams raise important environmental issues of water flow through places like the Hualapai and Havasupai reservations in the Grand Canyon, of aquatic species preservation and Indian fishing rights, and the ownership and sale of water. While the *Winters* Doctrine assured Indian water rights, it never quantified those rights. The issue of how much water tribes can legitimately use and sell has become critical in the arid West, especially for tribes in states member to the Colorado River Compact. The pending completion of the Central Utah and Central Arizona projects promises a massive redistribution of water in the arid West and a test of Indian water rights. Future water marketing by Shoshones, Utes, Paiutes, Navajos, Tohono O'odhams, and other groups raises critical economic and environmental issues for Indian peoples and the entire region.

In addition to water, the mineral wealth of some modern western Indian reservations has proved both a blessing and a curse. Beginning as early as 1900 with the discovery of oil on Osage land, non-renewable resource development to ease reservation economic dependency has unleashed the most environmentally destructive forms of exploitation, threatening tribal land, water, air, and health. Government mismanagement has compounded these problems. Coal and uranium mining on the Navajo Reservation has destroyed large areas of land, polluted water and air, and caused untold long-term health problems. The 273-mile-long Black Mesa coal-slurry pipeline sucks 1.4 billion gallons of water every year out of the arid region, lowering the water table and literally undermining Hopi water sources. Coal from Black Mesa fires the Navajo Generating Station near Page, Arizona, casting a haze over the Grand Canyon and Four Corners region. Despite the efforts of the Council of Energy Resource Tribes to balance use and protection of Native resources, mining, oil, and gas exploration scars thousands of acres of Indian land. In Alaska, the Alaska Native Claims Settlement Act (1971) and the subsequent North Slope energy boom with its drilling sites, pipelines, and access roads has transformed the landscape, threatening migratory mammals and waterfowl and contributing to changes in Native Alaskan land use and ownership patterns.

Off-site pollution is a major problem for Native Americans. When tankers like the Exxon *Valdez* spill their cargoes of crude oil, they pollute thousands of miles of coastline destroying both Native and white resources. Pollutants from mining and processing plants migrate into reservation air and water. Cyanide heap-leach mining in Montana is polluting water on the Fort Belknap Reservation. Radioactive pollution and toxic waste from the Hanford nuclear weapons plant threatens all tribes who depend on the Columbia River salmon for their livelihood. The Mdewakanton Sioux of Prairie Island, Minnesota, fear the health impacts of a nuclear power plant built on the edge of their small reservation, while Western Shoshones protest the use of their land as a nuclear test site. Industrial waste dumps surround the St. Regis Indian Reservation, fouling the St. Lawrence River. Poorly treated urban waste and agricultural effluent threatens nearby reservation environments. Today, groups like the Standing Rock Sioux and Northern Cheyenne are beginning to enforce federal laws protecting their land, water, and air from such pollution.

Recently, governments and industries are looking at reservations as potential disposal sites for solid, hazardous, and nuclear wastes. In 1990 the Pine Ridge Sioux rejected proposals by subsidiaries of O&G Industries to build a landfill, but the neighboring Rosebud Sioux council approved a 5,700-acre facility, "big enough to take care of all the waste in the United States." Under the proposal, they would receive one dollar per ton of trash, an economic bonanza for the depressed reservation unless, as some Sioux and environmental critics warn, the dump becomes a toxic nightmare. The pressure for some type of economic development and employment on underdeveloped and resource-poor reservations has led the Campo of California to agree to a 600-acre landfill, and the Kaibab-Paiutes of Arizona and Kaw of Oklahoma to accept hazardous waste incinerators. Presently, the Mescalero Apaches, Skull Valley Goshutes, and others are debating the location of nuclear waste storage facilities on their lands. Their decisions may pose long-term environmental problems that could outweigh the short-term benefits.

In recent years, tribal development and land use has put some Indians at odds with environmentalists. This fascinating turn of events emerges as modern Indians begin placing needs over older cultural regulatory patterns, shattering white stereotypes of Indians as "the original conservationists." Early environmentalists found inspiration in Native American actions and attitudes. Those who followed perpetuated many of the grosser stereotypes of Indians as beings who left no mark on the land, essentially denying them their humanity, culture, history, and modernity. In the 1960s and 1970s, Indians became symbols for the counterculture and conservation movements—Iron Eyes Cody shedding a tear in television ads as he looked over a polluted landscape; an apocryphal speech attributed to Chief Seattle became the litany of true believers. The issue continues to be hotly debated. Indians were never ecologists—something that refers to a highly abstract and systematic science—but they were careful students of their functional environments, bound by material and cultural needs and constraints, striving for maximum sustained yield, not maximum production. They possessed an elaborate land ethic based on use, reciprocity, and balance. Those attitudes persist today and contribute to the debate within and between Indian communities, corporations, environmentalists, and governments about the future of Indian peoples and environments.

David Rich Lewis

See also Economic Development; Fishing and Hunting Rights; Mining; Natural Resource Management

Further Reading

Callicott, J. Baird. "American Indian Land Wisdom." *The Struggle for the Land: Indigenous Insight and Industrial Empire in the Semiarid World.* Ed. by Paul A. Olson. Lincoln: University of Nebraska Press (1990): 255–72.

Schwartz, O. Douglas. "Indian Rights and Environmental Ethics: Changing Perspectives, and a Modest Proposal." *Environmental Ethics* 9 (Winter 1987): 291–302.

Vecsey, Christopher. "American Indian Environmental Religions." *American Indian Environments: Ecological Issues in Native American History.* Ed. Christopher Vecsey and Robert W. Venables. NY: Syracuse University Press (1980): 1–37.

White, Richard. "Native Americans and the Environment." *Scholars and the Indian Experience: Critical Reviews of Recent Writing in the Social Sciences.* Ed. W.R. Swagerty. D'Arcy McNickle Center of the History of the American Indian, Newberry Library, Chicago. Bloomington: Indiana University Press (1984): 179–204.

White, Richard, and William Cronon. "Ecological Change and Indian-White Relations." *Handbook of North American Indians.* Vol. 4. *History of Indian-White Relations.* Ed. Wilcomb E. Washburn. Washington, DC: Smithsonian Institution (1988): 417–29.

ESKIMO

See Alutiiq; Iñupiat; Yup'ik

ESSELEN

The Esselen Tribe is located in the Santa Lucia Mountain range of Big Sur in Monterey County, California. Although pronounced extinct by the end of the eighteenth century following Spanish occupation, this tribe, one of the smallest in the state, never numbering more than 750 to 1,000 members, is once again alive and thriving with over 80 members. In 1960, a young Esselen boy named Tom Little Bear was born in a remote pocket of the Esselen territory where a small group of Esselens had been keeping the tradition alive for many generations. Little Bear started having visions at the age of eight, visions which revealed to him that he was chosen to resurrect the Esselen tribe. This was an incredible responsibility for a growing boy, but with the guidance of his elders he succeeded in the task.

Since contact with Europeans, a number of researchers had recorded Esselen word lists. In 1981 a graduate student in linguistics collected the known data and began language reconstruction efforts. This work continues; recently, new data was recovered from the Naval Archives in Madrid, filling in gaps in the language and adding many new words to the dictionary in progress. Songs, recorded on wax cylinders in 1904, were located and are now sung in ceremony. In addition, extensive ethnographic, archaeological, and genealogical research efforts have shown that the present district of Cachagua is indeed the boundary of an ancient Esselen district whose descendants still live in the ancestral homeland.

In 1992, while conducting extensive research, the Esselen Tribe filed for federal recognition. They are currently involved in a battle to stop construction of a huge new dam on the Carmel River, a project which would destroy a large portion of the most sacred tribal lands and burial grounds and seriously impair the tribe's efforts to reestablish basketry and other sacred uses of native plants gathered along the river.

The tribe has reconstructed a traditional village and ceremonial grounds which now features a round-house, built in the sacred way, in which the old dances and songs are performed in ceremony. Tribal events are held regularly and are occasionally opened to guests. With the assistance of a local nonprofit organization, Window to the West, the tribe is building a camp for people of all ages and religions, and plans to offer programs in Native California tribal culture. The tribe also offers wilderness horseback trips that take people into the Esselen ancestral homelands.

Tom Little Bear Nason

See also **California Tribes**

Further Reading

Beeler, Madison S. "Esselen." *Journal of California Anthropology Papers in Linguistics* 1 (1978): 3–38.

Breschini, Gary, Anna Runnings, and Trudy Haversat. *Cultural Resource Reconnaissance of the New Los Padres Dam and Reservoir Project, Carmel Valley, Monterey County, California.* Salinas, CA: Archaeological Consulting, 1992.

Hester, Thomas Roy. "Esselen." *Handbook of North American Indians.* Vol. 8. *California.* Ed. Robert F. Heizer. Washington, DC: Smithsonian Institution (1978): 496–99.

Milliken, Randall. *Ethnogeography and Ethnohistory of the Big Sur District, California State Park System.* Berkeley: University of California, Department of Anthropology, 1990.

Shaul, David. *The Huelel (Esselen) Language.* Tucson: University of Arizona, Bureau of Applied Research in Anthropology, 1992.

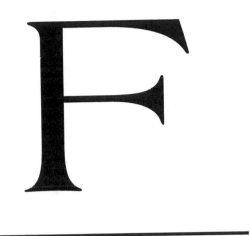

FAMILIES

The term "family" is an English gloss which has been superimposed upon Native societies of North America as part of the colonization process. Although the term has meaning as a nuclear family composed of mother, father, and their off-spring or issue, there are other connotations which should be recognized as underlying premises in Native family dynamics. In traditional societies, there was often a delicate equilibrium between males and females in social, economic, and ritual roles. This seems apparent whether the family structure was patrilineal, matrilineal, or bilateral in kinship reckoning. At present, however, individuals of Native societies are controlled by legal definitions of the dominant society's justice systems. In many cases, it is the social welfare system which determines family structure and function.

Traditional Lakota Families

It is appropriate to chart some of the enduring family structures of various groups to provide a baseline for the great diversity of contemporary societies. The Lakota, a Siouan-speaking group in the Plains culture area, shows one variation. Their traditional extended family structure conforms to a bilateral descent model. Lakota nuclear families were embedded within a larger kinship unit called a *tiospaye* (*ospaye*, "part of" and *ti*, "a dwelling unit"). Thus, a family unit is placed within a larger context which extends the socialization or enculturation mechanisms. Because the Lakota ideal marriage pattern was sororal polygyny, a man who was fully able to provide for two wives was expected to marry the younger sister (or a younger female cousin, who fit the kinship category of younger sister) of his first wife. The cowife was called "mother" by all the issue. This guaranteed dual socialization into Lakota cultural norms and values. Because sexual continence was mandated by the supernatural belief systems while either mother was lactating, and because the lactation period was four to five years, spacing of children

was ensured. The normative practice also placed women in a protected position. Life was difficult among Plains Indian societies and a woman's pregnancies were culturally controlled. Perhaps the sororal marriage pattern also dealt with a possible excess of females in a warrior society. Interestingly, children were referred to as *wakan-yesha* —"like the Sacred." This Native term also indicates a great valuation of children, who were seen as autonomous individuals capable of decision making at an early age. The *tiospaye*, or extended family, also served as a protective device in case of a marriage dissolution or if the child became an orphan. Caretaking of children (and elders, or grandparents) was absorbed by the larger kin unit. Grandparents played an important role in the transmission of cultural norms; the parents of the child provided food, lodging, and other needs of the grandparents.

A decided dynamic of reciprocity allowed a smooth functioning of the *tiospaye*. The cardinal virtues of bravery, generosity, fortitude, and wisdom were constantly evoked within the extended family as a means of maintaining cultural balance and continuity to ensure individual and group survival.

Demoralizing Patterns of Euroamerican Acculturation

When the Lakota and other Plains nations were encapsulated on barren reservations as a result of their fight to maintain their lifeways, many changes occurred. Their very livelihood, the dependence on the buffalo, was destroyed. Governmental policies legally suppressed the Native belief systems. The Sun Dance was outlawed. Native language was forbidden. Traditional kinship units were forced to conform to Euroamerican concepts of the nuclear family. Christian churches came into the reservations and cross-cut *tiospaye* affiliations. In many cases, they forbade Christian converts to interact with their traditional kin who were converted to another Christian faith. These patterns of demoralization of peoples of all tribes struck at the very roots of Indian families and hence, traditional cutlural beliefs.

Coterminous with governmental edicts and intense Christianization processes was the introduction of an educational system which removed children from the natal family structures and sent them to boarding schools. In most cases, various Christian denominations operated the schools. This new religion emphasized a patriarchal, punishing God, an emphasis of sin, monogamous marriages, and an ethos of physical punishment of children.

Perhaps the most devastating and lasting effect on Native families was the forced removal of children from their homes. In a new social environment, every manifestation of their Native culture was systematically assaulted. Native language, beliefs, kinship terms, and interaction with siblings of the opposite sex were forbidden. But in damaging effects, the lack of parental role models seems most pervasive. Parental surro-

193

gates—the Caucasian matron and her male disciplinarian counterpart—were cold, punishing models which possibly account for many of the family dysfunctions in contemporary Native life. In the summer, the children did not go home but often worked as laborers on surrounding farms and as maids in rural and urban homes. Educational excellence in the classrooms was superceded by Christianization and the establishment of a foreign work ethic. When these captives of "civilization" returned home (many succumbed to introduced diseases in their captivity), marginality prevailed. They were unable to effectively "return to the blanket" (as their return to Native cultures was called by school personnel). They often were social outcasts as they had forgotten their language, culture, and expected behavior patterns. Most importantly, traditional parenting skills were extinguished and new modes were lacking.

One lasting legacy, however, is the intertribal marriages which resulted from the interaction of members of various tribes in these off-reservation boarding schools. Today, there are many instances of these marriages, or consensual marriages, which often contribute to uncertainty in the cultural transmission of Native values and child socialization patterns. This does not say that all persons who went to boarding schools are ineffective parents, but as a result of these experiences, the core values of family structure and strengths were often eroded.

Because of the so-called "outing" system in the student work force, some students remained in the larger society, beginning an off-reservation or urban contingent of Native peoples. The trend toward urbanization escalated during the 1950s when the government's policy was to transport families and young people into the cities. Today, 55 percent of the Native population lives in urban areas. There appears to be a movement back and forth from reservation to city on the part of some of the indigenous population. Some families return for ritual events; others may opt to send their children home for the summer, thus maintaining a semblance of cultural continuity.

The Status of Native Families in the Late Twentieth Century

The status of Native families is highly divergent in the last part of the twentieth century because of education, urbanization, and in some cases, rejection of an Indian identity. Despite all efforts to destroy the aboriginal family, this social structural unit in its diverse forms—patrilineal, matrilineal, and bilateral—has persisted, adjusting to the form imposed upon it. The nuclear family with neo-local residence and patrilineal names of all the family members is the overt model imposed by the colonizers.

Covertly, however, various indigenous family forms persist to meet the various needs of the different tribal groups. The Navajos, for example, who are the largest culturally intact nation numerically, have maintained a functional clan system in their matrilineally oriented society. Traditionally, descent

was recognized as passing from the female line. Women owned the dwellings, men marrying into the clan and moving into the matrilineage in matrilocal residence. Clans, which were named entities, Salt or Water, for example, regulated marriage. When the Indian Reorganization Act of 1934 imbued the Navajo Tribal Council with male predominance in the election process, the governance aspects of the female role were eroded. This patriarchal mode is still evident among the Navajo. However, the decision-making power of women in the "outfit," or matrilineally oriented kin group, is still operative. One often hears "I am from the Salt clan, born for Water clan." This individual identification clearly shows one's embeddedness in a clan with an affiliation with another one. Among the Navajo, the outfit is a functional extension of a nuclear family in the present day.

Clan identity is also important to other matrilineal groups, such as the Pueblo and Iroquois. Because of the long and continuous period of occupancy in the Pueblo societies, clan organizations are still important in their educational, social, and ritual structures. Clan affiliation is still operative among the Iroquois, especially in Native rituals and marriage regulation.

As the data regarding the extended family among the Lakota indicate, the *tiospaye* currently operates as the family of procreation and as orientation. The caring and sharing aspects which are basic to this family structure have allowed Lakota families to function in dire conditions of poverty in both reservation and urban settings.

As the *tiospaye* and clans functioned in traditional societies and, to some extent, in the present social situation, child training and care of the elderly were part of the extended social unit. Social changes in the twentieth century have greatly impacted the family unit—of whatever description—in contemporary Native societies throughout North America. Families have been altered, not only by legal and religious actions on the part of the institutions of the larger society, but by the external forces that policies put into play. Removal of children from Indian homes by social welfare regulations (two or three children sleeping in one bed, a grandmother as care-taker, or a child in the care of extended family members) has often led to fosterage and adoption. These capricious actions have done much to destroy Indian families. The Indian Child Welfare Act of 1978 was enacted with the support of Native communities to prevent such abuses, recognizing the validity of indigenous childrearing practices. Ongoing court cases attest to the continued assault on Indian life via attacks upon family structures.

One outstanding cause of dysfunctionality in Indian families derives from the use and abuse of alcohol. Introduced by Europeans, liquor has had devastating effects upon families. Much spousal and child physical abuse, as well as sexual abuse, seems to stem from alcohol. Divorce decisions are often traced to this addiction. Many of the dismal statistics—car accidents, shootings, in-group violence, and aggressive behavior which eventually impacts upon family stability—is attributable to the excessive use of alcohol and other drugs. Studies on teenage pregnancies, suicides of young Indian males, and dropout rates from high school seem to correlate with the reliance upon alcohol or drugs. Lack of parenting skills and the disorienting conditions which often result from generations of culture change, poverty, racism, and a powerless position in the dominant society are also factors which have been detrimental to family functioning. Conversely, the sharing mechanisms of extended family and clan systems may have been instrumental in allowing disenfranchised and poverty-stricken family units to persist into the present.

Among most aboriginal societies in North America, the importance of families is paramount in the late twentieth century. A common metaphorical statement that "Women are the carriers of Indian cultures" is a constantly heard axiom. The strength of the aboriginal family as a persistent mechanism for the transmission of Native culture and identity to its members is remarkable. Certainly, many of the social ills which are attributed to Indian life, both on reservations and in urban centers, seem to be based on introduced items such as alcohol, drugs, and federal government policies. The persistence of Indian cultures and Native identity, founded upon socialization in an Indian family milieu, is significant and reflects the wide diversity of the Native nations in America.

Presently, there appears to be a diversification of Indian family structures and a reconceptualization of family life. This seems a result of various historic and legal factors. These salient differences may be suggested. There are different norms about childbearing and childrearing. There is an increase in the number of teenage pregnancies which mirrors the statistics of the dominant society. This may be an adaptive strategy in poverty situations, which prevail in Native communities. This fact may also indicate the breakdown of sex education, which was part of the puberty rites in many aboriginal societies. In some communities, there is a normative acceptance of this fact.

One notes a rise in male superiority and sexist attitudes toward females. There is, however, an increase in educational and economic achievement in Indian females. Physical and sexual abuse of spouses and children is increasing. It is possible that the structure of the Indian family reflects that of the larger society, as well as generations of coerced social change and cultural domination. Female-headed single parent families are becoming the norm. In sum, the colonization process seems to have altered the basic unit and the kinship nexus in Native societies.

Native American Families in the Twenty-First Century

A noted aspect of contemporary Native life, and a power for the future, is the enhancement of traditional belief systems which have been recently activated in various ways in remote reservation areas. Emerging self-help systems which confront alcohol abuse and encourage sobriety often are employed along with the treatment programs adapted from the larger society to culturally-specific effectiveness. Indigenous models of alcohol control, the beginnings of examining traditional parenting models with the hope of utilizing these in educational systems, the emphasis of community control of educational systems, and the increasing growth of tribally controlled community colleges all seem to bode well for self-determination in Native communities. Thus, traditional belief systems become the vehicle for changing the dysfunctional aspects of family life and re-orienting the basic human unit—the family.

Beatrice Medicine

See also Alcohol Abuse; Child Welfare: Gender; Mental Health

Further Reading

Attneave, Carolyn. "American Indians and Alaska Native Families: Emigrants in Their Own Homelands." *Ethnicity and Family Therapy*. Eds. Monica McGoldrick, John K. Pearce, and Joseph Giordo. New York, NY: Guilford Press, 1982.

Medicine, Beatrice. "American Indian Family: Cultural Change and Adaptive Strategies." *Journal of Ethnic Studies* 8:4 (1982): 14–23.

FEDERAL ACKNOWLEDGMENT PROJECT

See Branch of Acknowledgment and Research

FEDERAL AND STATE RECOGNITION

While the United States of America has recognized its governmental relationship with certain North American Indian tribes by making treaties, through statutes, or establishing other contractual relationships with them including appropriations for services, the United States Congress never has defined the term "tribe," or prescribed rules governing federal recognition. The federal government did not assert jurisdiction over or responsibility for all existing Indian groups by making treaties or agreements with them, or by extending federal services to them. The Indian Commerce Clause and the Treaty Clause in the United States Constitution and the Indian Non-Intercourse Acts establish the exclusive federal power to deal with Indian tribes, without defining "Indian" or "tribe." Language in the Indian Appropriations Act of 1871 barred the president and the Senate from making new treaties with tribes thereafter, while expressly reaffirming the obligation to uphold previously ratified treaties recognizing named Indian tribes. Presidents issued executive orders establishing reservations for certain groups, acknowledging them as tribes, until Congress barred such measures by statute in 1919. Congress now relies heavily on the secretary of the interior's recommendations supporting acknowledgment of certain groups, primarily basing determinations upon forms of previous recognition of petitioning groups, and sociological tests.

Tribal Organization Under the Indian Reorganization Act

Federal authorities have considered extensively whether particular North American Indian groups constitute tribes or bands in connection with the process of tribal organization under the Indian Reorganization Act (1934). The commissioner of Indian affairs formerly determined whether a particular tribe met the Act's definition of "tribe" (and was therefore eligible to organize under the Act by holding a referendum on a proposed tribal Constitution), by stating such finding in a letter to the secretary of interior, and recommending the submission of a tribal constitution to a referendum vote. The commissioner relied upon the solicitor for the Department of the Interior to assess the tribal status of the group seeking to organize in difficult cases. The solicitor's finding that a group constituted a "tribe" or "band" relied on one or more of the following tests, regardless of whether the group had a land base: (1) the group had treaty relations with the United States; or, (2) the group had been named as a tribe by an act of Congress or executive order; or, (3) it had held collective rights in tribal lands or funds; or (4) it had been treated as a tribe or band by other Indian tribes; or, (5) it had exercised political authority over its members, through a tribal council or other governmental form. Secondary factors included proof that Congress had appropriated any funds for the group; or, that the group showed social solidarity; or, that ethnological and historical considerations supported the claim of tribal existence.

The first three factors gave weight to previous congressional and executive recognition. These and the fourth criterion indicated federal action or other identification of the group as distinct from any other. The fifth criterion concerned the group's exercising of political authority. Other factors concerned the question of tribal character. Common American Indian ancestry among tribal members, common community and political leadership, and historical association of the group with a particular territory are essential to positive determinations of tribal recognition, or of continuous tribal existence. Even North American Indian tribes which may have originated in or had ties with Canada or Mexico have been recognized, including the Metlakatla (Tsimshian) tribe in Alaska (1891), the Pasqua Yaqui near Tucson, Arizona (1978), the Texas Band of Traditional Kickapoos (1985), and the Aroostook Micmac Tribe of Maine (1991).

Presumption of Federal Recognition

The United States Supreme Court has ruled that the federal government has a trust responsibility toward Indian tribes regardless of whether specific federal actions had been taken which recognized that responsibility. Once it is shown that the federal government historically recognized a tribe by treating it as sovereign, a presumption arises that federal recognition continues which must be rebutted by the party denying present-day recognition or continued existence. Mere internal changes in form, even assimilation of tribal members into the surrounding society, are not sufficient to declare a recognized tribe to have abandoned tribal relations, and hence, tribal existence. It is for Congress to decide when changes warrant removal of Indian tribes from their special status. Tribal political or social deterioration, or even periodic or noncontinuous exercising of federal jurisdiction, cannot abrogate federal supervision after it has commenced. The Bureau of Indian Affairs (BIA) cannot terminate or redetermine a previously acknowledged federal-tribal relationship unless it can show by "clear, cogent and convincing evidence" that either: (1) Congress expressly intended to abrogate the relationship with the tribe; or (2) the tribe voluntarily and knowingly abandoned its status as a tribe.

Lumbee Recognition Act

In the Lumbee Recognition Act (June 7, 1956), Congress renamed the Lumbee tribe the "Lumbee Indians of North Carolina," but the act denied federal services to the tribe. The Lumbee tribe petitioned for federal acknowledgment between 1979 and 1989. The associate solicitor of Indian affairs, Department of the Interior, determined (October 23, 1989) that the Lumbee Act of 1956 precludes the Lumbee tribe of Cheraw Indians and eight other North Carolina groups from petitioning for acknowledgment under the federal acknowledgment process prescribed under 25 C. F. R. 83. Federal legislation is required to reverse the effect of congressional action in such cases.

State Recognition

Certain states have recognized certain tribes within their territorial boundaries, or recognized them based on predecessor governments' official actions. For example, some states are required to honor the actions of the colony or state which formerly included the named state's territories within its boundaries. Maine honors treaties Massachusetts adopted with certain tribes prior to the separation of Maine from Massachusetts in 1841. State standards for acknowledgment vary widely, and alone do not determine cases for federal acknowledgment. North Carolina, for example, adopted a tribal acknowledgment process similar to the federal model in 1980, having recognized the Lumbee tribe in 1885 by statute.

Allogan Slagle

See also **Branch of Acknowledgment and Research; Government Policy**

Further Reading

Berry, Brewton. *Almost White*. New York, NY: Macmillan Co., 1963.

Blu, Karen I. *The Lumbee Problem: The Making of an American Indian People*. Cambridge, England: Cambridge University Press, 1980.

Cohen, Felix S. *Handbook of Federal Indian Law.* Washington, DC: U.S. Government Printing Office, 1942.

———. *Felix S. Cohen's Handbook of Federal Indian Law.* Ed. Rennard Strickland. Charlottesville, VA: Mitchie/ Bobbs-Merrill, 1982.

Weatherhead, L.R. "'What is an Indian Tribe'?—The Question of Tribal Existence." *American Indian Law Journal* 8 (1980): 1, 7.

FEDERAL POLICY

See Government Policy

FICTION

See Literature

FILM AND VIDEO

The history of Native Americans in film and video begins approximately one hundred years ago when moving images were added to the representational media already in use—drawings, paintings, engravings, and photographs. Early on, camera and sound recording equipment were used to document Native events and activities, a forecast of the documentary videos generated since the 1970s. The motion picture tools also enabled the development of an entertainment industry, its productions grounded in plots and character types already familiar to Euroamerican audiences. Late nineteenth-century dime novels, plays, and Wild West shows had fixed the image of Indians as feathered savages in people's minds.

Early Stereotypes

A significant aspect of visual media, vis-à-vis American Indians, lies in the power of images to misrepresent, an especially critical issue when images are the sole source of information about a people. Because these stereotypes are generated and perpetuated by the majority society, they simply reflect popular premises of white culture.

The mass distribution of stereotypes through film and video affects how Native Americans see themselves, distorts their cultural life, and affects the way generations to come will perceive Native values and historical actions. Therefore, the involvement of Native Americans in media, and ultimately their access to creative control, can be seen as part of a set of historical developments underscoring the acceptance of Native assertions of their right to self-determination.

Indian stereotypes in early films were constructed from some factual information and a great attachment to previous ways of representing Indians. Movie images conformed to those developed centuries before in art, literature, and drama. Indians were portrayed as violent enemies—"the savage reactionary"—which permitted movie directors to show exciting outdoor battle scenes and use villainous Indians to rouse the audience. The "Pocahontas image" created a sentimental version of Indians, portraying women who sacrificed themselves to aid beleaguered whites. The "noble anachronism" was a portrayal of Indian protagonists whose attempts at education and participation in white society led to tragedy as well as alienation from their own background.

The earliest films were pieces which included views of many "exotic" subjects and were intended as entertainment for audiences at urban vaudeville theaters. The earliest known documentaries were Thomas Alva Edison's kinetoscopic views of Native American dances, such as the Hopi Snake Dance, shown at the 1893 World's Columbian Exposition in Chicago.

The beginnings of the film industry came on the heels of the struggles of Indians in many parts of North America to remain autonomous and to survive as peoples. The late nineteenth-century encounters on the northern Plains had been widely published in the popular press. Undoubtedly, the vast American expansion onto tribal lands and federal policies to assimilate Indians played a key role in early entertainment with Indian themes, from Wild West shows to films.

Early Films

The success of early film shorts with Indian imagery quickly led to the production of one and two-reel films. Out of thousands of films produced in the first twenty years of motion pictures, hundreds had Native American plots. Many films presented the Indians as vicious, but some showed that their actions were provoked by white skullduggery. Others focused on the tragic clash of cultures. Jay Hunt's "The Last of His Line" (1914) showed the tragedy facing an Indian father, who promised to honor a peace agreement, when his son returns from boarding school an alcoholic and outlaw.

As movies became popular, plots were standardized. Early films pointed out the unresolved questions in America of cultural and racial differences and mixed heritage. For example, love between Natives and whites was portrayed as inevitably tragic. This idea started early and continued, from Cecil B. DeMille's "The Squaw Man" (1913) through Arthur Penn's "Little Big Man" (1971). In George Seitz's "The Vanishing American" (1925), the Navajo veteran Nophaie, who returned from World War I to find his reservation controlled by greedy whites, was loved by the white school teacher, but died before a relationship develops.

Indian clothing and outdoor locations were rarely accurate in early films and Indians were rarely recruited to play major roles. By 1911, criticisms of the treatment of Indians in films were printed in the popular press. In that year, a group of Indian delegates visited Washington, D.C., denouncing films for their inaccurate depictions of Indians.

Some early cameramen made documentary films to preserve a picture of Indian customs for posterity. In 1915, the Rodman Wanamaker Expedition employed an able filmmaker, Rollyn S. Dixon, who shot thirteen reels of ceremonials, battle reenactments, reservation life, and Indian ranching. By 1918, documentaries captured Yuman, Alaskan Eskimo, Winnebago,

Blackfeet, Crow, and many Pueblo peoples (Hopi, San Felipe, Santo Domingo, Isleta, and Laguna). Some tribes were split in their reactions, however, and many refused to pose for the camera. In some communities, documentation was not permitted because it violated standards of privacy. In 1923 at Zuni Pueblo, for example, ceremonial leaders forbade the continuation of a film project.

A few filmmakers sought to create a more authentic type of commercial film by locating their projects in Native locations. Edward S. Curtis' "In the Land of the Head Hunters" (1917), Robert J. Flaherty's "Nanook of the North" (1922), and H.P. Carver's "The Silent Enemy" (1930) employed all-Native casts to reenact the culture of their people and pursue activities as they had been performed "before the white man came." However, these filmmakers took liberties with the plots and characters to conform to what was considered entertaining at the time. With the exception of "Nanook," these films achieved no real popular success.

In the years between World War I and II, poverty on reservations and outright corruption of govern-

ment agents and others prompted a reform of national policy. Indian tribal reorganization became a federal goal. A few films produced with Indian plots, such as "Massacre" (1934) and "The Vanishing American," focused on Indian characters who had tried living in the white world, but were forced back to reservation communities to confront white greed and villainy.

Films After World War II

It was not until after World War II that authenticity in film would become a goal, and even then it was clouded by other Hollywood concerns, including the necessity of using recognizable stars. Hollywood did not simply view film as a vehicle for telling Native American history as it happened. Through its films, it reinterpreted the history of the West, frequently framing plots to illuminate the problems and values of American society of the time of film production. In the late 1940s, the importance of the nation's military strength to national identity is reflected in John Ford's westerns and during the Vietnam era, films like "Little Big Man" and Ralph Nelson's "Soldier Blue" (1970) posed

"Nanook of the North," directed by Robert Flaherty, 1922. Photo courtesy of the Museum of Modern Art.

questions about the costs of military actions. Between 1950 and 1970, some directors humanized plots, portraying stronger Indian characters and sometimes sympathetic encounters between whites and Natives. These films were enormously popular and had considerable impact. In John Ford's "She Wore a Yellow Ribbon" (1949), the Indian fighter and the old chief sit together under a tree, their characters trading anecdotes on aging and the younger generation. Delmar Daves' "Broken Arrow" (1950) portrayed the leader Cochise, played by Jeff Chandler, as fully dimensional, and the film ends with the implication that a peace agreement between the Apaches and whites will work. It also sympathetically views the love between Cochise's daughter and the white man who has come to make an agreement, but in typical Hollywood fashion, the daughter's death makes a positive outcome impossible.

Following the war, mobility characterized American culture. The federal government developed policies to persuade Indians to leave reservation communities. Following the success of "Broken Arrow," many pro-Indian movies came out, and they often dealt with the difficulties of assimilation in white society.

Plots also included contemporary settings. "Tell Them Willie Boy Is Here" (1968) created an Indian anti-hero who confronted authorities trying to control his actions—a new kind of hero for a new countercultural audience. Plots offered new interpretations and a deeper appreciation of Native cultures, and by implication, a critique of white values. By the 1970s, films also tackled issues of how Indian history gets told. It may be a tale of resistance to American militarism, its brutality and bureaucracy. In "Ulzana's Raid" (1972), an "incorrigible savage" led a group of Apache from the reservation in desperation, expressed in a brief reign of terror.

To heighten the sense of authentic alternatives, other films have experimented with the narrative form. In "Little Big Man" the documentary-like setting of an oral historian who recorded the central character's accounts provided an intimate view of Native history. Keith Merrill's "Windwalker" (1980) experimented with

strictly Native American settings by employing only Native languages, with subtitles in English. Other films attempted to show that Native Americans have an alternative worldview, both historically, as in "White Dawn" (1974), a story of sailors shipwrecked among an Inuit community in the nineteenth century; and in contemporary times, as in the mystical characterizations of Indians in New York City in thriller "Wolfen" (1981). After more than a decade-long hiatus in the production of Indian films, ideas like these were skillfully used in Kevin Costner's immensely successful "Dances with Wolves."

Until the 1970s, there were few Native American stars, and the studios were convinced that only stars could attract audiences to their films. Therefore major Indian roles were played by Jeff Chandler, Natalie Wood, Burt Lancaster, Tony Curtis, Robert Blake, Dame Judith Anderson, Anthony Quinn, Jack Palance, and Trevor Howard. Pressure for more accurate portrayals and a deeper interest in nonstereotyped plots and characterizations created opportunities for the growing number of American Indian actors to find work in films.

Such actors as Chief Dan George (Salish) and Will Sampson (Creek) created memorable film characters, secure in their own Native identities, and often symbols of successful resistance to white systems and values. By the 1990s, a new generation of actors— including Graham Greene (Oneida), Rodney Grant (Winnebago), Tantoo Cardinal (Cree), Floyd Westerman (Dakota), and Wes Studi (Cherokee)—were portraying contemporary as well as historical Indian figures and creating a greater feeling of authenticity in Hollywood films.

Indians have demanded that the film industry present accurate images almost since the beginning of film making. Hollywood's concerns for attracting audiences has led its directors to use authentic locations and Native actors, both as extras and sometimes as stars. Hollywood has also used Indian plots to reflect on the confrontation of white and Native societies, through various time periods.

"Harold of Orange," directed by Richard Weise, script by Gerald Vizenor, 1983. Photo courtesy of Film in the Cities.

"Broken Arrow," directed by Delmar Daves, 1950. Twentieth Century Fox. Photo courtesy of the Museum of Modern Art.

Documentary Filmmaking

In the past two decades, however, it is documentary media that has been most forceful in creating an arena for both authentic coverage and for greater participation by Native Americans in expressing their own viewpoints. Perhaps most important to many Native Americans, documentaries have served to communicate both the long history of Native peoples and the message, "we are still here." As Makah videomaker Sandra Osawa has noted about society's perceptions of Indians, "The problem is not that we are stereotyped, although indeed we are. It is that we are not seen as living in the present."

After the late 1960s, many documentary filmmakers turned their attention to Native tribes and nations, producing nearly 1,400 works concerned with both interpretating Native culture and presentating contemporary Native lifeways and concerns. Many tribal people have agreed to be in documentaries in which tribal members speak about their cultures.

Documentary filmmaking can be seen as an antidote to the excessive romanticization and distortion of Indian history by Hollywood. It also has created an alternative to other forms of reporting, like journalism, in which stories about Native people rarely appear. A continuing interest in Native American ways of life and concern with the social conditions facing them has fueled the production of independent films and videos, including documentaries and also short features, animations, and experimental art works.

Between 1968 and 1990, productions about tribal history, Native cultures, current concerns, and struggles for the recognition of Indian rights have been produced in approximately three hundred Native communities throughout the Americas. During this period, government funding has supported some of these efforts in North America. New films and videos have gained wider audiences through public television and festivals showcasing independent works—the American Indian Film Festival in San Francisco, the Native American Film and Video Festival in New York City, and the Two Rivers Native Film and Video Festival in Minneapolis.

These works mainly focus on individual tribal groups and emphasize the variety of Native cultures. By featuring many Native people on-camera they develop a sense of authority for their presentations of a Native viewpoint. For the participants, the film presents an opportunity to tell their own stories. For others, the films or videos become a way to share with the public their insights into tribal ways. Many Native filmmakers view films or videos as ways to communicate with the younger generation in their own communities.

"Wiping the Tears of Seven Generations," directed by Fidel Moreno and Gary Rhine, 1992. Photo courtesy of the filmmakers.

Video documentaries both clarify and inform the public about important battles tribes are fighting. For example, in "In the Heart of Big Mountain" (1988), Makah filmmaker Sandy Osawa explored the problems of Navajos inhabiting the joint Navajo-Hopi lands following the congressional order to oust them from their centuries-old homelands. In "The Great Spirit Within the Hole" (1983), Chris Spotted Eagle (Houma) investigated the issue of religious freedom and the impact on Native prisoners of observing Native American spiritual practices. Similarly concerned with the ongoing struggle of Native Americans for the recognition of their religious rights, partners Fidel Moreno (Yaqui/Huichol) and Gary Rhine documented the current struggle of the Native American Church for recognition in "The Peyote Road" (1992). Michael Zaccheo's "River People" (1990) documented the struggle of Wanapam elder David Sohappy, who refused to give up his traditional fishing rights and was jailed for his resistance. Repatriation of sacred objects has concerned many tribes, and independent productions have documented successful struggles pursued by the Kwakiutl in British Columbia, the Omaha in Nebraska, and the Aymara of Coroma, Bolivia.

Native directors have explored United States history as well as contemporary struggles. In "Surviving Columbus" (1992), director Diane Reyna (Taos Pueblo)

"Little Big Man," starring Dustin Hoffman and Chief Dan George, directed by Arthur Penn, 1971. National General. Photo courtesy of the Museum of Modern Art.

reexamined the history of contacts of the Pueblo peoples with Spanish and American culture through versions told by traditional elders, Pueblo scholars, journalists, and community members. Using an innovative visual style, the filmmaker, and executive producer George Burdeau (Blackfeet), are responsible for the first major production by Native Americans to be nationally broadcast, as well as widely seen in festivals.

Video artist Victor Masayesva, Jr. (Hopi) has produced a body of works that demonstrate how the white world has misunderstood and devalued the Hopi people's experience. In his recent "Imagining Indians" (1992), he viewed the history of Hollywood film through Indian eyes in communities where the films have been shot and where community members have been hired to play roles. The sense of inescapable white control is reflected in a fictional scene set in a dentist's office which threads through the film's interviews and selections from Hollywood movies. Both of these projects were funded by the Corporation for Public Broadcasting (CPB), which plans to have more works by Native American producers on the air.

Works have been made throughout the Americas. Canadian directors Alanis Obomsawin (Abenaki) and Gil Cardinal (Metis) each produced films examining the impact of the social services system on Native foster children. In "Foster Child" (1986), Cardinal created a moving autobiographical journey in search of his own Native parents. Staffen and Yiva Julen's "Inughuit: People at the Navel of the World" (1985) is beautifully filmed with scenes in which many residents of Greenland's most northern community recount their traditions and the impact of outsiders on their lives. Jed Riffe and Pamela Roberts' "Ishi: The Last of His Tribe" (1992) looks at the history of the single survivor of the Yahi tribe in California, and the intervention in his life of the anthropologists who befriended him.

A growing number of Native Americans are now working as independent film and video producers. In 1992, Native independents in both the United States and Canada organized a national Native producers organization to promote their work. In 1980, an experiment to utilize satellite communications in the Canadian North resulted in the formation of the Inuit Broadcasting Corporation, which produces original programs in seven Arctic communities. Now Northern Native Broadcasting-Yukon, located in the Northwest Territories, has joined with IBC and the Canadian Broadcasting Corporation-North in a programming consortium. Also in Canada, training and production access for Native independents is provided by the National Film Board, which founded Studio One to serve aboriginal production needs. Television series are being initiated by Native independent directors with the cooperation of CBC. In the United States, training initiatives have been regional. The Native Voices Public Television Workshop in Montana receives production proposals from Native producers in several northwestern states, and provides production assistance at all stages. As part of a broad initiative, several production, media distribution, and funding agencies, including the Rockefeller Foundation and the National Endowment for the Arts, have been increasingly active in locating and assisting Native American independent producers. Throughout the Americas, members of tribal communities are also obtaining video cameras to document their own ways of life.

The growing numbers of production opportunities promise there will be expanding and lively Indian and Eskimo productions. Making media is a complex and often costly enterprise. It is grounded in intense communication between media maker and participants in film and video, and between them both and the audience. For Native Americans, the promise of media is in its ability to communicate both over great distances and within Native communities. For audiences film and video programs serve to bring a better sense of Native realities to those who live remote from Indian communities. And in their effect, they potentially convey to the entire American culture the presence of our nation's first people, those who originally understood how to inhabit these lands.

Elizabeth Weatherford

See also **Public Image; Radio and Television**

Further Reading

Bataille, Gretchen M., and Charles L.P. Silet, eds. *The Pretend Indians: Images of Native Americans in the Movies*. Ames: Iowa State University Press, 1980.

Berkhofer, Robert F., Jr. *The White Man's Indian*. New York, NY: Alfred Knopf, 1979.

Brownlow, Kevin. *The War, the West, and the Wilderness*. New York, NY: Alfred Knopf, 1978.

French, Philip. "The Indian in the Western Movie." *Art in America* 60 (July-August 1972): 32–39. Reprinted in *The Pretend Indians*.

Marsden, Michael T., and Jack Nachbar. "The Indian in the Movies." *Handbook of North American Indians*. Vol. 4. *Indian-White Relations*. Ed. Wilcomb E. Washburn. Washington, DC: Smithsonian Institution (1988): 607–16.

Weatherford, Elizabeth. "Starting Fire with Gunpowder." *Film Comment* 28 (May-June 1992): 64–67.

Weatherford, Elizabeth, and Emilia Seubert. *Native Americans on Film and Video* and "Supplement." New York, NY: Museum of the American Indian, Heye Foundation, 1981, 1988.

FISHING AND HUNTING RIGHTS

Since before Europeans arrived on the shores of the continents of the Western Hemisphere, hunting and fishing have been an important part of Native American life. In pre-Columbian times, abundant wildlife was an essential source of food, clothing, shelter, and tools for Native Americans. Additionally, religious beliefs and spirituality were intertwined with hunting and fishing patterns, within a worldview highly cognizant of the natural environment. In particular, the close link between Native Americans and wildlife is evident in the animal names frequently given individuals, clans, and places, and in the various art forms depicting animal life.

Contact with Europeans spawned significant changes for Native American peoples and their hunter-gatherer societies. European trading and settlement patterns, intermarriage, and missionary activity altered the course of the development of Indian cultures, political institutions, and economies. After the American Revolution, the United States embraced the ideology of manifest destiny, and pursued a series of initiatives to accelerate the taking and settling of Indian lands. By the end of the nineteenth century, the process of limiting Native land holdings to relatively small reservations was nearly complete, and the United States adopted and pursued a policy of defeating what was left of tribal cultures and institutions. Assimilation of Indians into the Euroamerican society was the goal of a series of congressional enactments and executive initiatives that continued up to the middle of this century.

Despite such forces of change, Indian nations and their cultures have proved resilient. The defense of hunting and fishing rights represents in many ways the defense of Native American cultural identity, communal property, and tribal sovereignty.

The United States, like the European powers before it, negotiated treaties with Indian tribes as the primary means of taking Indian lands and establishing reservations for tribes. Although the United States clearly was the dominant party in the treaty negotiations, the tribes were real participants and insisted on certain guarantees. When tribes in the Pacific Northwest entered into treaties with the United States in the nineteenth century and ceded vast areas of their aboriginal lands, they were not about to give up their main source of livelihood: fishing the salmon and steelhead trout that were plentiful in the streams, rivers, and ocean inlets, and hunting the abundant game. A number of the treaties involving tribes in the Pacific Northwest, therefore, included express provisions guaranteeing hunting and fishing rights in the ceded lands. Typical of these provisions is Article 3 of the Treaty with the Nisqually, Puyallup, and other tribes of 1855:

> The right to take fish, at all usual and accustomed grounds and stations, is further secured to said Indians in common with all citizens of the Territory, and of erecting temporary houses for the purpose of curing, together with the privilege of hunting, gathering roots and berries, and pasturing their horses on open and unclaimed lands . . .

Treaties involving tribes in other parts of the country similarly included provisions securing off-reservation hunting and fishing rights. The 1837 and 1842 treaties with the Lake Superior Chippewa, for example, provided: "The privilege of hunting, fishing, and gathering the wild rice, upon the lands, the rivers and the lakes included in the territory ceded, is guarantied [sic] to the Indians, during the pleasure of the

President of the United States." The importance of this guarantee to the survival of the Chippewa was emphasized during the treaty negotiations in a speech by Aish-ke-bo-gi-ko-she, or Flat Mouth, one of the fifty-one Chippewa chiefs and warriors who signed the 1837 treaty.

After an act of Congress in 1871 prohibited subsequent treaties with Indian tribes, the United States dealt with tribes through statute, executive order, or agreement later approved by Congress. Thus, such instruments were additional means of establishing reservations for Indian tribes and, in some instances, of securing off-reservation hunting and fishing rights. For example, an 1891 executive agreement ceded portions of the Colville Reservation while providing that "the right to hunt and fish in common with all other persons on [the ceded lands] shall not be taken away or in anywise abridged."

The design of the United States was that Native Americans would ultimately abandon their hunting, fishing, and gathering as tribal cultures and institutions disintegrated under the pressures of assimilation; nineteenth-century treaty and statutory guarantees were to be merely transitory. Native people had a different vision. Native cultures have persisted, and hunting and fishing practices—although undeniably altered by time and events—have continued as an important component of the economic, political, and spiritual life of Native communities. Native peoples, therefore, have vigorously defended hunting and fishing practices within reservation lands as well as in off-reservation areas pursuant to historical usufruct, treaty entitlement, executive agreement, or statutory guaranty.

In modern times, the courts have been critical battlegrounds on which tribes have fought for and in many cases secured legal confirmation of hunting and fishing rights. Federal court decisions have established that, in general, tribes have hunting and fishing rights on reservation lands, even in the absence of express treaty or statutory provision. The existence and scope of *off*-reservation rights depends more on a case by case assessment of the relevant historical circumstances and treaty provisions or other federal enactments. Under prevailing doctrine established by early Supreme Court cases, courts are to read the language in federal instruments liberally and to resolve conflicting inferences in favor of the tribe concerned. Typically, however, the courts have required express treaty or statutory language confirming off-reservation hunting or fishing rights, in order to find that the rights exist.

Whereas treaties or other federal enactments may reserve or create Indian hunting and fishing rights, subseqent congressional action may be held to limit or abrogate the rights. In *United States v. Dion*, for example, the United States Supreme Court held that the 1962 amendments to the Bald and Golden Eagle Protection Act abrogated treaty rights to hunt eagles. The taking of eagles under the amended act is limited to what is permitted by the United States secretary of the interior. The act specifies that the secretary may permit Indians to take eagles for religious purposes, independently of any reserved hunting right. The permit scheme developed by federal officials, however, has been criticized by Indian activists and at least one lower federal court (*United States v. Abeyta* [1986]) as not sufficiently accommodating to Native American religious practices.

A major issue faced by Native peoples regarding unabrogated hunting and fishing rights is the question of the extent to which the states of the Union can restrict or regulate the exercising of rights. The issue has become acute as wildlife resources have become increasingly scarce and as states consequently have more aggressively sought to regulate the resources. Tribal members in the Pacific Northwest forced the issue by organizing and participating in "fish-ins" in defiance of restrictions imposed by the State of Washington. Washington attempted to restrict both the manner in which Indians harvested anadromous fish and the size of their take, despite nineteenth-century treaties expressly affirming the right of tribes of the Pacific Northwest to fish "at all usual and accustomed" places.

Conflicts among the Indians, the State, and nontreaty fishers led to a series of court decisions, including the now famous 1974 ruling by federal district court Judge George Boldt. Judge Boldt held that the treaties entitled the tribes up to a 50 percent share of the harvestable run, a holding affirmed by the United States Supreme Court in collateral proceedings in *Washington v. Washington State Commercial Passenger Fishing Vessel Association* (1979). Similar controversies in other parts of the United States have also given way to protracted litigation, including litigation concerning the off-reservation treaty and aboriginal fishing rights of the Chippewa in the Great Lakes region.

The court rulings in these cases reflect the complexity in determining the scope and character of Indian hunting and fishing rights in the face of competing demands upon the resource and attempted state regulation. While it is beyond the scope of this writing to explore fully the intricacies and confusing elements of these rulings, some general principles from the case law can be identified. An effective presumption exists against state regulation of Indian hunting and fishing pursuant to federally reserved rights. State regulation of Indian hunting and fishing is constrained by the sovereign powers of Indian tribes, as well as by the preemptive supremacy of applicable federal treaties and statutes. Whether the state can apply its laws to Indians in a particular case is determined by reference to the applicable federal instruments and by a balancing of the state, federal, and tribal sovereignty interests at stake. A state's potential for exercising regulatory authority is lowest where on-reservation Indian hunting and fishing is concerned. Where a tribe enjoys hunting or fishing rights off-reservation, tribal members are entitled to a moderate standard of living from the wildlife resource.

States may tip the balance in favor of their regulatory authority where a sufficient conservation or safety interest is demonstrated, particularly as to off-reservation rights held "in common" with the general population. In order to justify a regulation of Indian hunting or fishing on conservation or safety grounds, the state must show that a substantial hazard exists, that the state cannot meet its safety or conservation objective by regulating non-Indians alone, and that the regulation is the least restrictive alternative available.

These principles are manifested in the court rulings exempting from generally applicable state regulation members of Pacific Northwest tribes that signed treaties securing off-reservation fishing rights. In order to set seasonal harvesting allocations and meet conservation objectives within the framework of the judicial determination that treaty fishers in the state of Washington are entitled to as much as a 50 percent share of the harvestable run, tribal and state officials have established cooperative management and regulatory schemes. Similar court rulings have benefited the Chippewa of the Great Lakes region and other Native peoples whose ancestors refused to give up hunting and fishing as an integral part of life and who, in modest exchange for vast areas of land and wealth, sought to guarantee hunting and fishing for successive generations.

S. James Anaya

See also Environmental Issues; Natural Resource Management

Further Reading

Cohen, Felix S. *Felix S. Cohen's Handbook of Federal Indian Law.* Ed. Rennard Strickland. Charlottesville, VA: Mitchie/Bobbs-Merrill, 1982.

Meyers, Gary D. "Different Sides of the Same Coin: A Comparative View of Indian Hunting and Fishing Rights in the United States and Canada." *Journal of Environmental Law* 10 (1991): 67–121.

Turner, Shelly D. "The Native American's Right to Hunt and Fish: An Overview of the Aboriginal Spiritual and Mystical Belief System, the Effect of European Contact and the Continuing Fight to Observe a Way of Life." *New Mexico Law Review* 19 (1989): 377–423.

Vessels, R. "Fishing Rights in the Pacific Northwest: The Supreme Court 'Legislates' a Solution." *American Indian Law Review* 8 (1982): 117–37.

Wilkinson, Charles F. "To Feel the Summer in the Spring: The Treaty Fishing Rights of the Wisconsin Chippewa." *Wisconsin Law Review* (1991): 375–414.

FIVE CIVILIZED TRIBES

See Cherokee; Choctaw; Chickasaw; Creek/Mvskoke; Seminole

FLATHEAD

See Confederated Salish and Kootenai Tribes

FORESTRY

See Natural Resource Management

FORT MCDOWELL MOHAVE-APACHE INDIAN COMMUNITY

See Yavapai

FOX

See Mesquaki; Sac and Fox

GABRIELINO/TONGVA

The Gabrielino, a name which here also includes the Fernandeño of the Los Angeles, California, area, spoke a Takic language of the Uto-Aztecan language family and had the most elaborate cultural patterns of any of the Takic-speaking groups. Early ethnographers Alfred L. Kroeber, John Peabody Harrington, and J. Hudson found a few remaining individuals to interview in the early years of the twentieth century. At mid-century, they were considered to be extinct. Many had married non-Indians and their children chose alternate identities in public contexts. People sometimes found it advantageous to be known as Mexican to avoid social and economic discrimination, to avoid being placed on reservations, or having children sent to Indian boarding schools.

The Indian Claims Commission cases of the 1950s and mandates for cultural resource management studies have encouraged Indian identity in the late twentieth century. A number of Gabrielino have come forth. Three hundred and fifty people are actively involved in Gabrielino/Tongva affairs, but there are possibly 1,000 to 2,000 descendants, most of whom live in the Los Angeles area. Three separate Gabrielino groups are now active. They are the Gabrielino-Tongva Tribal Council, the Intertribal Council of Tongva, and the Gabrielino Band of Mission Indians.

No reservation or rancheria has been set aside for the Gabrielino. A number of Gabrielino did appear on the claims case rolls, however. The three known groups are active to varying degrees in protecting sites of special significance to their people from development. To varying degrees, they retain aspects of traditional worldview. None are known to speak the Gabrielino language. Fred Morales stands out as a significant person, who has been active as a civic and political leader since 1947.

Lowell John Bean
Sylvia Brakke Vane

See also California Tribes

Further Reading
Bean, Lowell John, and Charles R. Smith. "Gabrielino." *Handbook of North American Indians.* Vol. 8. *California.* Ed. Robert F. Heizer. Washington, DC: Smithsonian Institution (1978): 538–49.
Johnston, Bernice Eastman. *California's Gabrielino Indians.* Los Angeles, CA: Southwest Museum, 1962.

GAMBLING

See Gaming

GAMING

Federal funding of Indian governmental programs during the 1980s diminished; consequently, tribal governments pursued alternative means of generating the revenue needed to finance important tribal programs. Many tribes lacking considerable natural resources or a sizable tax base turned to gaming to provide the needed revenue. Concerns surrounding competition with off-reservation gaming enterprises, state lotteries, and the possibility of organized crime infiltration threatened tribal gaming ventures. Federal, state, and tribal governments have addressed many of these concerns through federal statute and tribal-state agreements, permitting tribes to continue to rely on gaming for economic development.

At present, Indian tribes operate over 100 high-stakes bingo operations and over 60 casino facilities in 24 states. Since 1980, the extent of Indian gaming has literally exploded; by 1983, approximately 180 tribes were conducting bingo operations with 20 to 25 tribes managing high-stakes bingo operations producing $100,000 to $1 million in monthly revenue. Consequently, Indian gaming has grown into a $6 billion a year business. By mid-1993, over 63 tribes had entered into gaming agreements with individual states to establish high-stakes casino facilities. With the success of tribal gaming enterprises, increasing numbers of tribes are exploring gaming as a means of economic development and several tribes are actively negotiating with states to establish gaming facilities.

Although casino-style gambling is relatively new to Indian tribes, Indian gaming is not a new concept. The roots of various forms of gambling run deep into the spiritual and cultural core of many tribes. For example, the Navajo creation myth describes two types of animals inhabiting the earth: night animals seeking total darkness and day animals yearning for light. To settle the dispute, the creatures devised the "shoe game," betting on who would be the first to find a disc hidden in a moccasin. Because neither side won, the night and day animals agreed to divide the day into periods of daylight and darkness. Other tribes played similar moccasin games in which three similar and one distinct stone were distributed under four moccasins. The player must then try to identify the moccasin hiding the distinct object. In addition to tribal social games, many tribes play games directly linked to spiritual and cultural well-being. While these traditional games manifest cultural and religious concepts, modern Indian gaming has become by necessity a major source of funds for tribal treasuries.

Although states can regulate gaming within their boundaries, gaming on Indian lands generally is exempt from state regulation under basic principles of Indian law. In the absence of any express delegation by Congress, states continue to lack jurisdiction over Indian tribes themselves or over property the United States holds in trust for tribes and tribal members. In short, state jurisdiction over Indians in Indian country remains extremely limited. An important federal statute, Public Law No. 83–280 ("P.L. 280"), granted specific states limited jurisdiction over Indian country. Several of these so-called P.L. 280 states argued that P.L. 280 granted jurisdiction to enforce their gambling laws. In *California v. Cabazon Band of Mission Indians*, 480 United States 202 (1987), the Supreme Court ruled that P.L. 280 permits enforcement of criminal laws but not civil regulatory laws. In other words, if a P.L. 280 state regulates an activity, those regulatory laws do not extend over Indian lands. In contrast, if a P.L. 280 state prohibits an activity, this strict prohibition applies to all lands within the state, including Indian lands. Since California regulated but did not bar gambling in the state, California could not regulate Indian gaming. Since most states permit certain kinds of gambling, this case clarified the law and thus permitted many tribes to begin gaming operations.

As tribes moved toward more economically oriented gaming, the federal government enacted a comprehensive scheme to regulate Indian gaming. The Indian Gaming Regulatory Act of 1988 (IGRA), 25 U.S. C. §§ 2701–2721, separates gaming into three classes and allocates regulatory jurisdiction over each class among tribal, federal, and state sovereigns. Class I consists of social games of minimal value, as well as traditional Indian gaming played as part of or in connection with ceremonies. The IGRA subjects all Class I gaming to exclusive tribal regulation. Class II gaming includes bingo, lotto, pull-tabs, and other similar games, and is subject to tribal regulatory jurisdiction with extensive oversight by the National Indian Gaming Commission. Class III encompasses all other forms of gaming, including casino-style gaming. Class III gaming activities require authorization by a tribal ordinance and approval by the chairperson of the Gaming Commission. The state must permit the Class III gaming activity for any purpose by any person, but the tribe must conduct the activity in conformance with a tribal-state compact. A compact serves as a contract between the tribe and the state, setting forth the parameters of permissible gaming and establishing the extent of state regulation of Class III gaming. In sum, the compacting process is designed to balance the protective goals of the state and the economic interests of the tribe, by establishing a system of Indian gaming beneficial to both the state and the tribe.

The IGRA requires that both tribal bingo parlors and casino halls be tribally owned. Additionally, trib-ally run gaming enterprises must use their gaming revenue for specified tribal activities. By restricting the scope of Indian gaming to tribal governments, the IGRA ensures that Indian gaming remains a governmental function and not a personal endeavor.

The IGRA also provides for a three-member National Indian Gaming Commission with a chairperson appointed by the president and the other two members appointed by the secretary of the interior. The Gaming Commission is empowered to approve all tribal ordinances and resolutions affecting Class II and Class III gaming, to close gaming activities, and to levy and collect fines. The Gaming Commission also has extensive authority over management contractors dealing with Indian tribes for both Class II and Class III gaming. For example, the Commission may impose limitations on the length of management contracts, set the proportion of fees allowed, and specify the general background and character of those who may operate gaming in Indian country.

In sum, the IGRA provides a comprehensive scheme that tribes must follow in establishing tribal gaming enterprises. The Act separates gaming activities into three classes and appropriates regulatory control among federal, state, and tribal governments. The Act also requires tribal governments to satisfy certain conditions before high-stakes gaming activities will be authorized. Nevertheless, even if tribal governments are able to satisfy these conditions, other obstacles may inhibit gaming development.

A major obstacle in establishing gaming operations is securing adequate financing to begin these programs. The Bureau of Indian Affairs administers a loan program for tribes; under this program, a tribe with a valid tribal-state compact can apply for funding to develop, plan, and construct gaming facilities. In addition, other tribes have formed joint ventures with outside financing companies to construct their casinos. The Mashantucket Pequot tribe's casino in Connecticut, for example, was financed by investors from foreign countries. The growth of Indian gaming has also attracted private business firms interested in backing Indian gaming operations.

The development of gaming on the reservation has been an economic salvation for tribes throughout the United States. Consequently, Indian gaming has generated income enabling tribes to supplement tribal programs that were either underfinanced or had been discontinued by the federal government, to provide loans to other tribal businesses, to fund legal services and tribal land acquisition projects, to provide comprehensive medical and dental coverage to members, and to establish scholarship and educational funds.

The success of the gaming operation has led to significant benefits for individual tribal members also. The Cabazon Band of Mission Indians, for example, uses gaming revenues to provide tribal members with employment opportunities, health and dental benefits, housing, and educational assistance. Specifically, gaming revenue has allowed the Cabazon to construct a biomass-fueled electric power plant, a 950–unit housing development, a child development center, and a tribally owned and operated restaurant. Gaming has also enabled the Saginaw Chippewa Indian Tribe of Michigan to significantly reduce its unemployment, which had approached 50 percent in 1980. In addition to the direct tribal impact, gaming has had an overflow effect on outside communities by providing job opportunities to non-Indians and bolstering tourism and local economies.

While gaming provides a means towards tribal economic independence, it also presents problems within tribes and among neighboring communities. In 1990, violence erupted on the St. Regis Akwesasne Indian Reservation in upstate New York over the appropriate role gaming should play in the Mohawk tribal government. The Warrior Society supported tribal casinos as a way to economic independence and sovereignty from white society, while other traditionalists and elected officials opposed gaming. On the Oneida Reservation, also in New York, a dispute between tribal factions over the role of gaming on their reservation culminated in the destruction of their bingo hall.

Indian gaming has also sparked intense controversy between tribal and state governments. Many states operate lotteries for the same reasons that Indian tribes operate gaming facilities—to raise revenue for social programs. These states fear that an increase in Indian gaming could represent a decrease in state revenues. Some states have raised public policy arguments based on the perceived social ills that accompany gambling. When these states ban all gambling within the state, they are most reluctant to enter into tribal-state compacts to permit Indian gaming. For example, Rhode Island adamantly opposes any Indian gaming within its boundaries. States also raise concerns about public safety and the welfare of their citizens and visitors. These states question whether tribal law enforcement is adequate to protect the large numbers of patrons who flock to reservation gaming facilities. State governments continue to voice concerns surrounding organized crime's attraction to Indian gaming. They maintain that the possibility of criminal infiltration is real and substantial, because the high stakes that attract non-Indian patrons also attract organized crime. On the other hand, the United States Department of Justice has concluded that there has not been a widespread or successful effort by organized crime to infiltrate Indian gaming to date. (*Statement of Paul L. Maloney, Senior Counsel for Policy, Criminal Division, before the Senate Committee on Indian Affairs, March 18, 1992*).

For these reasons, some states have refused to negotiate with tribes, despite the fact that the IGRA requires states to do so. As a result of states' refusal to negotiate and enter into gaming compacts with tribes, tribes have filed suit in federal court seeking to enforce compact negotiations. These issues have not been resolved, however, because states contend that the Eleventh Amendment sovereign immunity provisions bars tribes from suing them despite the language in the IGRA.

Widespread Indian gaming and the concomitant legal and political issues only began in the early 1980s. The rapid development of Indian gaming has sparked enormous debate and many efforts to curb the prevalence of Indian gaming. For example, several amendments to the IGRA have been proposed that would limit the scope of the gaming permitted, place a moratorium on new Indian gaming facilities, and refine the state-tribal negotiation process. Additionally, several cases pending in federal court address issues affecting the future of Indian gaming, such as whether tribes may sue uncooperative states to compel them to negotiate in good faith to achieve agreements on tribal-state compacts. Nevertheless, the revenues generated from gaming enable tribal governments to finance many important governmental programs adversely affected by federal funding cutbacks. Moreover, Indian gaming continues to be a powerful means towards stimulating economic growth in many tribal communities, and enabling some tribes to become increasingly self-sufficient financially.

Nell Jessup Newton

Shawn Frank

Further Reading

Clinton, Robert N., Nell Jessup Newton, and Monroe E. Price. *American Indian Law: Cases and Materials.* Charlottesville, VA: Mitchie/Bobbs-Merrill, 1991.

Culin, Stewart. "Games of the North American Indians." *Bureau of American Ethnology 24th Annual Report 1902–1903.* Washington, DC: U.S. Government Printing Office, 1907. New York, NY: Dover, 1975

MacFarlan, Allan A. *Book of American Indian Games.* New York, NY: Associated Press, 1958.

Pommersheim, Frank. "Economic Development in Indian Country: What Are the Questions?" *American Indian Law Review* 12 (1987): 195–217.

Santoni, Roland J. "The Indian Gaming Regulatory Act: How Did We Get Here? Where Are We Going?" *Creighton Law Review* 26 (1993): 387–447.

GAY HEAD

See Wampanoag

GENDER

Gender and role variations reflecting the differentiated social structures and cultural diversity of aboriginal peoples is often clouded by the widely held rubric of the American Indian or Alaska Native. In the cultural construction of gender categories, one must be especially careful to contextualize the society under discussion.

In many societies, there were strict segregations of rights and duties which were sexually specific. That is, women's and men's roles were defined and the occupiers of these roles were expected to fulfill these categories efficiently and to perform the activities outlined so as to promote the smooth functioning and continuity of the social group. For example, among members of the Iroquois Confederacy, composed of such nations as the Onondaga, Seneca, Mohawk, and others, the matrilineal principle reigned. Women owned the fields. However, men cleared the land of trees and readied the fields for planting which was done by the women, who cultivated the sustaining crops of corn, beans, and squash. Moreover, the men hunted and upon return presented the animal to the women for distribution as they then owned it. There are other instances in which strict role categories for males and females prevailed. In other arenas, as in belief systems and ritual structures, gender roles were also designated and followed fastidiously.

Proper and expected behaviors for these roles were carefully inculcated into both males and females in their enculturational processes. Careful indoctrination into proper behavioral norms of males and females was often buttressed by the ideals of the society and transmitted by the significant others in the socialization of children. Ideal behaviors were part of learning to be a "good" man or a "good" woman of, for instance, the Zuni Pueblo in New Mexico. Much of the molding of male and female children to these role expectancies was done through informal education and precept of good behavior of the adults. Thus the children were effectively socialized to proper gender behavior.

However, among many aboriginal societies in North America, not all individuals followed normative roles and behavior of their gender. Gender enactment seen as gender-crossing as either male or female points to a certain flexibility and institutionalization of certain gender behaviors which did not stem from biological sex-typing. This nonjudgmental characterization is better comprehended by using case studies of this phenomenon. The term *berdache* has been used extensively in courses in anthropology, where it often has been equated with male homosexuality. It has also included the category of male transvestites. These terms of definition have often piqued the imagination of students who are often intolerant of gender variation. However, the emic (or Native) definitions have not been considered in the explanation of this cultural construct.

In general, the Siouan term *winkte* means simply that men assumed some aspects of the feminine role—nurturing children and being skilled in feminine endeavors such as tanning skins and other domestic arts. It may also include homsexuality. Pottery making, weaving, or other artistic skills were often highly developed among men in southwestern tribes. The most widely published individual known for these skills was a Zuni and interacted effectively in his own Pueblo culture and in society circles in Washington, D.C. His name was We'wha, the Zuni man-woman. Recent studies have exalted this role into one of sacredness (i.e. Williams).

The term *winkte* derives from the Siouan language spoken by the Lakota/Dakota Native peoples. In examining Native categories, one gets a more adequate definition of this term. It is commonly trans-

lated in the English gloss to mean "like a woman." A more linguistically bound term with deeper structural meaning can be interpreted as "kills women." Thus, when dealing with gender and Native categories, one must be careful in the translation process. In Lakota language, for example, there is no word which would equate with the English term "lesbian." Although Paula Gunn Allen states that *koskalaka* means "dyke" in the Lakota language, it actually means male youth, or post-pubescent male. As in many Native societies where there is equilibrium in kinship terminology and descriptors of gender, there is an equivalent term *wikoskalaka*, which means maiden or young woman. The most striking role for lesbians was among the Mohave in the American Southwest, where they were known as *hwame* and assumed the male role of marriage to other women; they hunted and participated in other male occupations.

Essentially, the mandate of individual autonomy or the strong notion of personhood which seems pervasive in many Native societies allowed the assumption of cross-gender roles without major disruption to the fabric of society. The separation of gender from biological sex was not seen as debilitating or shameful.

Women in cultures of the Plains Indians, often referred to as "male dominant" or "warrior societies," also had sex role alternatives. A woman sometimes went on a warring expedition, mainly to avenge the death of a male in her family. There were also instances of "manly-hearted women" (especially among the Piegan of the Blackfoot Confederacy), who were economically self-sufficient and aggressive in sexual demeanor. Their use of domestic skills such as tanning skins led to self-actualization during the fur trade era. In the Southeast "beloved women" among the Cherokee often functioned in a chiefly role. At present, many contemporary Native women are chairpersons of their tribal councils.

In sum, it is apparent that aboriginal peoples in North America were more tolerant than many other cultures of gender variation. Androgynous males and lesbians in contemporary societies often refer to themselves as "two-spirited" people. However, in many Native communities, there seems to be an emerging intolerance which may mirror that of Anglo society. Still a tolerance is also evident. There is a strong respect for persons and their individual autonomy, despite any cross-gender orientation.

Beatrice Medicine

Further Reading

Allen, Paula Gunn. *The Sacred Hoop*. Boston, MA: Beacon Press, 1986.

Medicine, Beatrice. "Warrior Women: Sex Role Alternatives for Plains Indian Women." *The Hidden Half: Studies of Plains Indian Women*. Eds. Patricia Albers and Beatrice Medicine. Langam, MD: University Press of America (1983): 267–80.

Roscoe, Will. *The Zuni Man-Woman*. Albuquerque: University of New Mexico Press, 1991.

Williams, Walter L. *The Spirit and the Flesh.* Boston, MA: Beacon Press, 1986.

GENEALOGICAL RESEARCH

Genealogical research into one's family background has proved invaluable in many cases for documenting an individual's Native American heritage or for demonstrating family relationships within an Indian group. The major purposes for carrying out this research are: to provide tribal ancestry for the purposes of enrollment in a particular tribe, or other legal purposes; to demonstrate connections to a Native American group for one's personal satisfaction, or to complete one's family tree; and to document family connections within a Native American group.

Enrollment

Most tribes have requirements for enrollment as a member of that tribe. In all cases, an individual must demonstrate descent from someone on the tribal rolls, often at a particular point in time. Many have minimum blood quantum requirements, often one-quarter, of ancestry from their group. These requirements differ from group to group. The Cherokee of Oklahoma, for example, require proof of decent from the Dawes Commission roll, but have no blood quantum; the Eastern Band of Cherokee require at least one-thirty-second degree of Cherokee blood through descent from an enrollee on the Baker roll. Membership rolls of the Confederated Tribes of the Warm Springs Reservation include individuals with one-fourth or more blood, who were born to a member living on the reservation.

Enrollment in a federally recognized tribe can be beneficial. Enrollees are often eligible for health and educational benefits, and sometimes participate in monetary distributions from land and other claims awards or from tribal enterprises. In some parts of the country, fishing and hunting rights are accorded to members of the tribe.

Research for Personal Satisfaction

Often individuals are simply curious about their Indian ancestry, or want to fill in the blanks on the family tree. In some cases, very little is known about the Native American ancestor. Researchers find themselves piecing together small bits of information from a variety of sources to uncover their ancestors' tribal affiliation. A good understanding of the history of Native Americans, particularly the tribe in question, will be helpful in locating the required genealogical information.

Tribal Research

Members of existing Indian groups may want to document their family relationships for a variety of reasons. In some cases, important oral records have been forgotten and need to be reestablished. In other cases, the degree of "Indian blood" is important for gaining federal or state recognition. In yet other cases, proving blood relations are paramount to determining the right of individuals to share in monetary awards from claims cases. In some instances, additional research helps determine the individuals who are entitled to be included in a given group. The Old Settler Cherokee are an example of this type of group. All of those classed as "Old Settlers" are Cherokee, but not all were entitled to be included on the Dawes Commission roll.

Conducting Genealogical Research

An individual who is trying to establish Native American ancestry will need to identify the Indian person from whom he or she is descended, that person's tribe, and when and where that individual lived. Genealogical research always begins at home. Researchers should consult birth, marriage, Bible records, and other personal papers that document the family's history. Family members can often provide leads. Oral information, however, must be substantiated elsewhere.

It is a good idea to verify the tribe of one's ancestor. It seems everyone believes there is an Indian princess in the family, usually Cherokee. These "noble" ancestors often turn out to be from another tribe, male, or not Indian at all.

Government Records. The records of the federal government are crucial sources of information once the tribe of one's ancestor has been established. These records document the government's day-to-day relations with the tribe. They also include enrollment records, allotment records, annuity payroll records, court records, estate files, and Indian hospital and health records. One may need to contact the National Archives or the Branch Archives to examine nonactive tribal records. Where federal government contact with the tribe has been limited, various state and local records may be helpful. Individuals may appear on federal census records, or the census rolls of the tribes.

Tribal Records. Contact with the tribe can speed up research in cases where the family members are already recognized by the tribe. In most cases, the tribe can advise one on how to add family members to the tribal rolls. Tribal offices are sometimes understaffed, and responses to inquiries may be delayed. Some tribes have people who will assist a person once it has been established that an individual has family ties to the respective tribe.

Other Information Sources. Churches and schools which were located on or near Indian reservations often have useful records in their archives. Indian boarding schools have maintained records on their students. Many museums, historical societies, universities, and local history collections in public libraries also have pertinent archival records. Some of the major manuscript collections are located at the Newberry Library in Chicago, the Western History Collection at the University of Oklahoma, Yale University, Harvard University, and the Oklahoma

Historical Society. Oral history collections, such as the Indian-Pioneer Papers at the University of Oklahoma and the Doris Duke Collection, housed at the Universities of Arizona, Illinois, Oklahoma, Utah, Florida, New Mexico, and South Dakota, can also yield much needed information. Genealogical collections, such as that of the Church of Jesus Christ of Latter-Day Saints, are another potential source of information.

Native Americans, because of their unique relationship with the federal government, are among the world's most documented peoples. Difficulties in locating information about an individual can be due to the voluminous sources which must be consulted, or inaccurate information at the start of the search. Intermarriage with non-Indians, loss of contact with the tribal group, and the reluctance of some individuals to reveal their Native American ancestry are other obstacles to research. Perseverance and luck are important elements in one's search for a Native American ancestry.

Larry S. Watson

Further Reading

Carpenter, Cecelia Svinth. *How to Research American Indian Blood Lines: A Manual on Genealogical Research.* Orting, WA: Heritage Quest, 1987.

Carter, Kent. "Wantabees & Outalucks: Searching for Indian Ancestors in Federal Records." *Chronicles of Oklahoma* 56 (1988): 94–104.

Hill, Edward E. *Guide to Records in the National Archives Relating to American Indians.* Washington, DC: National Archives, 1982.

Parker, Jimmy B. "American Indian Records and Research." *Ethnic Genealogy: A Research Guide.* Ed. Jessie Carney Smith. Westport, CT: Greenwood Press (1983): 209–38.

Watson, Larry S., ed. *Journal of American Indian Family Research.* Laguna Hills, CA: Histree, 1979–ongoing.

GILA

See Apache

GOSHUTE

See Shoshone: Goshute

GOVERNMENT AGENCIES

A number of government agencies are involved in Indian affairs. Some provide funds to tribes and other Indian organizations, others provide direct services to American Indian people, while others gather information. In addition to federal and state government agencies, interest groups and other associations, missionary societies and other religious organizations, foundations and service clubs, and associations of tribes and Native American people, are important participants in Indian affairs. During the twentieth century, changes in the organizational and policy-making environment have been significant for the content and outcome of federal Indian policy and programs.

At the turn of the century, the organizational environment of Indian affairs was relatively simple. One federal agency, the Office of Indian Affairs, dominated official Indian affairs and daily life on most reservations. The Indian Office, never a very smooth-running bureaucracy, regulated many aspects of reservation life and provided a variety of services to Indian people. While a number of missionary organizations educated Indian children and proselytized their parents, the Indian Office funded many of the missionary societies by contracting for the educational services provided to Indian children and by providing rations to students in church-run boarding schools.

Some private membership organizations, including the Lake Mohonk Conference of Friends of the Indian, the Indian Rights Association, and the Women's National Indian Association, were interested in Indian affairs. Often operating through the United States Board of Indian Commissioners, an unpaid board of leading Indian reformers which exercised a nominal oversight over the Indian Service, these organizations advanced a reformist, pro-Protestant approach to Indian affairs. The Bureau of Catholic Indian Missions represented the interests of Roman Catholic missions, and the views of other denominations were represented by denominational Indian organizations.

Most reform activities during the first decades of the twentieth century were oriented toward achieving the goal of "civilization," or forced assimilation of the Indians. The elements of "civilization," reformers believed, included conversion to the Christian religion, adoption of the English language, literacy, land ownership, and the abandonment of tribal relations or at least the adoption of a "progressive" stance in tribal affairs. The General Allotment Act of 1887 (24 Stat. 388) provided the basis for United States Indian policy between its enactment and the 1920s.

A crisis in Indian affairs in the 1920s resulted in the involvement of more organizations in Indian affairs. Prior to 1920, the services provided to Indian people by the Office of Indian Affairs had their legislative authorization in treaties and agreements entered into with the various tribes by the United States. However, many treaties and agreements provided that services would be offered for a limited term of years, and, by the 1910s, an increasing number of Indian people were no longer technically eligible for federal social, health, and educational services. The Snyder Act of 1921 (42 Stat. 208) granted legislative authorization for the Indian Office to provide social, health, and educational services to Indians, including those for whom the United States had no treaty obligation to provide such services. The act also gave Indian Service officials on or near the reservations local governmental powers.

Problems of landlessness, poverty, and ill-health became increasingly apparent during the 1920s. In addition, attempts by government officials in the Harding administration to exploit Indian resources for personal gain presented sympathetic whites with an agenda for reform. Organizations such as the American Indian Defense Association, founded by John Collier, a community organizer turned Indian reformer, and the General Federation of Women's Clubs, pressed for Indian reform. In 1923, Secretary of the Interior Hubert Work organized the Committee of One Hundred, a voluntary fact-finding panel, which recommended reforms in Indian affairs.

The Meriam Report of 1928, an independent survey of Indian administration, recommended increased appropriations for health and education, improvements in personnel standards and the Indian Office's planning capacity, and increased attention to reservation economic development. The report, prepared by the Brookings Institution at the request of Secretary Work, influenced the administrations of the next two commissioners of Indian Affairs, Charles J. Rhoads, appointed by President Herbert Hoover in 1929, and John Collier, appointed by President Franklin D. Roosevelt in 1933. Both commissioners viewed the Indian Office as an organization in need of renewal; both looked outside the organization for resources and expertise to provide that renewal.

Rhoads sought the assistance of the United States Public Health Service to provide health care to Indian people. The Indian Office also began to contract with some states which were willing to provide social, health, and educational services authorized by the Snyder Act on the reservations. The Johnson-O'Malley Act of 1934 (48 Stat. 596) provided legislative authorization for this activity. Most widely used in education, Johnson-O'Malley contracts provided funds to school districts in states with reservation Indian pupils. Since the funds were funnelled through state education agencies, the legislation resulted in the creation of Indian education offices within the governments of states with large numbers of Indian public school students.

Roosevelt's commissioner, Indian reformer John Collier, was astute at involving various New Deal agencies in the Indian Office's work; these agencies made significant monetary contributions to the agency's Indian Office's activities during the 1930s. Collier funneled the New Deal appropriations through the Indian Office, maintaining central control. His crowning legislative achievement, the Indian Reorganization Act of 1934 (IRA) (48 Stat. 984), provided the legislative basis for the modern tribal government. The act authorized the creation of tribal governments with limited powers; tribes could also organize tribal business corporations to pursue economic development activities. Tribal government decisions and the actions of the business corporations were subject to review by the secretary of the interior.

The adequacy of reservation resources to maintain Indian populations caused increasing concern during the 1930s. On many reservations, resources were inadequate to support the resident Indian population. During World War II, the Indian Office sponsored the migration of Indian people to urban areas to work in defense industries. After the war, this experience provided the basis for an expanded assisted migration effort, known as the Relocation Program.

Congress cut funds for Collier's community development programs during the war, while increasing funding for education and health programs aimed at individual Indians. Congressional interest in tribal reorganization appeared to be flagging; during the war years, Collier was less and less successful in getting his legislative program approved. In 1944, representatives of IRA tribal governments, together with some American Indian employees of the Indian Office, organized the National Congress of American Indians (NCAI), "the United Nations of the tribes," which became a leading Indian advocacy organization during the post-war years.

After the war, Congress created the Indian Claims Commission (ICC) to provide expedited handling of tribal claims against the United States. Prior to the creation of the ICC in 1946, tribes with claims had to pursue them in the United States Court of Claims. While the Court of Claims had decided only 175 dockets between 1881 and 1946 (137 of them by dismissals), the ICC decided 546 dockets (204 by dismissals) between 1947, its first year of operation, and 1978, its last. (Sixty-eight dockets not completed by September 30, 1978, were turned over to the Court of Claims.) The existence of the ICC stimulated many tribes to pursue claims. Attorneys, as well, became interested in Indian law; during the post-war years the tribal attorney became a fixture in many tribal governments.

Collier, who had favored creation of the ICC, left office in 1945. Following his departure, many in Congress began to push for a termination of the trust relationship and of special federal services for Indian people. In 1949, the Hoover Commission recommended transfer of the service programs of the Bureau of Indian Affairs (BIA), as the Indian office had come to be known, to the states or to federal agencies, such as the Public Health Service (PHS), which were concerned with the population at large.

The decade of the 1950s was the high-water mark of the termination movement. In 1953, Congress passed a resolution declaring that termination was national policy, repealed legislation prohibiting the sale of alcoholic beverages to Indians, and transferred civil and criminal jurisdiction over local Indian reservations to five states. The legislation which transferred jurisdiction, Public Law 280 (67 Stat. 588), provided that other states could assume civil and criminal jurisdiction over reservations without consultation with the tribes involved. On reservations in states which had not assumed jurisdiction, the Federal Bureau of Investigation, an agency of the Department of Justice, investigated major crimes, while BIA and tribal police were responsible for ordinary police functions.

In 1954, Congress transferred responsibility for Indian health from the BIA to the PHS. The Transfer Act (68 Stat. 674) encouraged the PHS to contract with state and local governments and with other health care providers for the provision of health services to Indian people. The PHS established a Division of Indian Health, later known as the Indian Health Service (IHS), to discharge its new Indian health responsibilities. The transfer made Indian health more visible to legislators; in addition, PHS officials proved to be skillful lobbyists; expenditures for Indian health increased rapidly after PHS assumed responsibility for Indian health in 1955.

During the 1950s, a number of water projects undertaken by the United States Army Corps of Engineers and the Bureau of Reclamation, an Interior Department agency involved in irrigation projects on Indian lands, threatened to inundate Indian lands. The Pick-Sloan Plan in North and South Dakota, which led to the construction of a number of dams on the Missouri River, was intended to control flooding on the Missouri, generate electric power, and provide water for irrigation of white and Indian farms. The Corps of Engineers' Kinzua Dam Plan in western New York State flooded Seneca lands; other water projects threatened Indian lands in Arizona, California, Montana, Nebraska, and Wyoming. Although the projects were supposed to benefit Indian as well as white area residents, few of the projected benefits materialized, and the projects left a heritage of suspicion of the agencies on the part of many Indian people. The Bureau of Reclamation has continued to be involved in irrigation projects on a number of reservations.

While the policy was not to be rejected until the Nixon administration, by the 1960s termination was dead. John F. Kennedy promised a more vigorous domestic policy; his election to the presidency in 1960 was followed by a cautious expansion in domestic programs, including social services and housing. Some tribal governments created tribal housing authorities to take advantage of Public Housing Administration (PHA) programs. Otherwise, Indian affairs were little affected until President Lyndon Johnson, Kennedy's successor, declared a "War on Poverty." The Economic Opportunity Act of 1964 (78 Stat. 508) established local Community Action Agencies (CAAs) to spearhead anti-poverty efforts on the local level. Funded by the new federal Office of Economic Opportunity (OEO), the CAAs would develop innovative local solutions to the vexing poverty problem. The Economic Opportunity Act empowered tribal governments to declare themselves CAAs. Promoting itself as a fresh alternative to an exhausted and ineffective BIA, OEO stimulated the development of tribal anti-poverty programs, including Head Start, youth employment, community development, and health programs. Soon, the Economic Development Administration (EDA) and other federal agencies began funding tribal programs; with the creation of the Department of Housing and Urban Development (HUD) in 1965, a much broader variety of housing programs became available to the tribes.

As OEO programs were broken up and allocated to more traditional federal agencies during the administration of President Richard M. Nixon, these agencies established "Indian desks" to oversee tribal contracts. Citing successful tribal experience in administering OEO and other federal grants, President Nixon called for a new policy of tribal self-determination. In 1975, Congress approved Nixon's self-determination proposal by passing Public Law 93–638, the Indian Self-Determination and Education Assistance Act (88 Stat. 2203). The act called on the BIA to contract with Indian tribes to provide the services which the respective federal agencies had provided. Despite defects in the self-determination policy, the act resulted in the strengthening of tribal governments and the transfer of a variety of services to tribes.

The self-determination ideology was reflected in other Indian reform legislation enacted during the decade. The Indian Education Act of 1972 (86 Stat., 334) provided financial assistance to educational agencies in communities with Indian students in their schools. In 1973, the OEO Indian programs were merged with a small Office of Indian Affairs in the Department of Health, Education, and Welfare to create the Office of Native American Programs, now the Administration for Native Americans (ANA). The Native American Programs Act of 1974 expanded the program and included Native Hawaiian groups as eligible beneficiaries. The Indian Health Care Improvement Act of 1976 (90 Stat., 1400) extended the application of P.L. 93–638 to the IHS.

As important as the changes in the way in which the BIA and IHS operated were changes in the relationship of the tribes with other federal agencies. Beginning with the OEO programs of the 1960s, Indian tribes were eligible to apply directly for program grants provided by many federal domestic assistance programs, with the applications often routed through special Indian divisions or desks within the headquarters of the agency administering the program. By the 1970s, significant providers of grant-in-aid programs to Indian tribes included the Departments of Commerce; Labor; Health, Education and Welfare (HEW); and Housing and Urban Development, as well as the Office of Education, then an educational assistance agency in HEW, now the cabinet-level Department of Education.

Transfers of funds from the federal government to state and local governments became a significant element in financing state and local government services during the 1970s. Tribes, along with states, counties, cities, and other local governments, received federal funds with relatively few strings attached under the General Revenue Sharing program, initiated in 1972. Frequently, tribes were designated as eligible grantees for new grant-in-aid programs. For example, the Comprehensive Employment and Training Act (CETA) of 1973, a program which provided jobs for the unemployed, included Indian tribes, Alaska Native villages, Native Hawaiians, and non-reservation Indian groups as eligible grantees. The Department of Labor, which administered CETA, created a Division of Indian and Native American Programs, to fund Indian employment and training programs. In 1977, the American Indian Policy Review Commission (AIPRC), which had been created by Congress to review federal Indian policy, recommended "guaranteeing the permanency of tribal governments within the Federal domestic assistance program delivery system." The AIPRC viewed access to funds from federal agencies other than the BIA and the PHS as a key to strengthening the autonomy of tribal governments.

A number of Indian communities lacked federal recognition. Some were recognized by their states, while others were not recognized by any official body. Members of these groups were not eligible for the services and protection provided to Indian people by the federal government. In 1977, the AIPRC recommended that Congress establish an independent agency to extend federal recognition to unrecognized Indian communities. However, in 1978, Congress authorized the BIA to develop a Federal Acknowledgment Project (FAP) to determine whether to recognize Indian communities seeking federal recognition. The FAP prescribed specific procedures for unrecognized Indian communities seeking recognition to follow. By 1988, petitions had been submitted from over one hundred Indian communities seeking federal recognition.

By the 1980s, the intergovernmental system of funding Indian programs seemed well-established. Several new federal grant-in-aid programs became available to Indian tribes during the decade. For a variety of reasons, elderly Native Americans were not being helped by Area Agencies on Aging, regional organizations created by the Older Americans Act of 1965 to provide health and social services to older Americans. In response, Congress added Title VI, Grants to Indian Tribes, to the Older Americans Act in 1980. Title VI provided funds for tribal governments and Alaskan Native villages to provide a variety of special services to older Native Americans. In 1982, Congress replaced CETA with the Job Training Partnership Act (JTPA), a scaled-down employment program with increased participation by private business and industry. Under JTPA, tribal grants were continued, although at a lower level than under CETA.

In 1983, President Ronald Reagan transferred White House management of Indian affairs from the Office of Liaison, which managed presidential relations with a variety of interest groups, to the Office of Intergovernmental Affairs, the White House office for relating to states, counties, and cities. In doing so, he explicitly defined the relationship between the Indian tribes and the federal government as a "government-to-government" relationship. This government-to-government relationship appeared to enhance the status of tribal governments, which now dealt with a variety of federal, state, and local government agencies.

As certain kinds of grants acquired stability, national interest groups composed of tribal employees in a specific functional area, such as aging or employment programs, emerged. Frequently, these organizations sought and obtained funding. Groups like the National Indian Council on Aging, composed of tribal Title VI program personnel, were able to secure federal funding for studies and special projects. Combined with interest groups like the Indian Rights Association and the Association on American Indian Affairs, and intertribal Indian organizations, like the NCAI and the National Tribal Chairmen's Association, established in 1971, these organizations had a significant influence on congressional committees, and on the federal and emerging tribal bureaucracies.

Domestic spending was cut during the Reagan administration, resulting in funding cuts in all federal domestic programs, including tribal programs. General revenue sharing, the federal program which provided funds with the fewest strings attached, was eliminated in 1986 as a result of a growing federal budget deficit. BIA expenditures were cut by over 5 percent during the Reagan administration, Indian Education Act grants by nearly 35 percent, ANA expenditures by 32 percent, and JTPA expenditures by 28 percent. Only PHS expenditures increased during the Reagan administration, by nearly 25 percent.

The new "government-to-government" relationship implies that tribes will have relationships with state government agencies as well as federal agencies. In addition to the state Indian education offices, organized in response to the availability of Johnson-O'Malley Act contracts, thirty-nine states have offices or commissions on Indian affairs. These vary from formal commissions with paid staffs to an individual in the governor's office or in a legislative staff position. Many of the state Indian offices were created in the 1960s or 1970s to serve as a conduit for federal funds flowing through government to Indian groups within the state, to assist with economic development programs, to assist non-recognized Indian groups negotiate the federal recognition process, and to maintain liaison with tribes and other Indian groups within the state.

Efforts at coordinating the increasingly complex organizational environment of Indian affairs have been sporadic at best. Prior to the 1950s, such coordination as was needed was provided by the BIA. During the Johnson and Nixon administrations, a National Council on Indian Opportunity, chaired by the vice-president and composed of representatives from the relevant cabinet departments, attempted to mediate the competing claims of government agencies and Indian people. In the 1980s, President Reagan appointed a National Commission on Reservation Economies to promote economic development on the reservations.

Paul H. Stuart

See also **Bureau of Indian Affairs; Government Policy; Indian Health Service; Johnson-O'Malley Act; Organizations and Tribal Cooperation**

Figure 1
Agencies and Expenditures
1991 Fiscal Year

Agency	$ Outlays
Department of Education Office of Elementary and Secondary Education Indian Education	66 million
Office of Vocational and Adult Education Indian Programs	15 million
Department of Health and Human Services Indian Health Service Direct Program and Contract Care	1,250 million
Indian Health Facilities	166 million
Department of Labor Training and Employment Services Native American Programs	59 million
Department of the Interior Bureau of Indian Affairs Federal Funds	1,481 million
Trust Funds	364 million

Source: Budget of the United States, 1991.

Figure 2
Agencies Involved in Indian Affairs

Agency	Date Established
Department of Commerce Economic Development Administration	1961[1]
Department of Defense Army Corps of Engineers	1802
Department of Education Office of Indian Education Programs	1972
Office of Vocational and Adult Education	1979
Department of Health and Human Services Administration for Native Americans	1973
Administration on Aging	1965
Indian Health Service	1955
Department of Housing and Urban Development Indian Housing Programs	1965
Department of the Interior Bureau of Indian Affairs	1824
Bureau of Reclamation	1902
Department of Justice Federal Bureau of Investigation	1908
Department of Labor Division of Indian and Native American Programs	1978
Department of the Treasury General Revenue Sharing	1972[2]

[1]Established as the Area Redevelopment Administration.
[2]Program terminated in 1986.

Further Reading

Dobyns, Henry F. "Therapeutic Experience of Responsible Democracy." *The American Indian Today*. Eds. Stuart Levine and Nancy Oestreich Lurie. Baltimore, MD: Penguin (1968): 268–91.

Gross, Emma R. *Contemporary Federal Policy Toward American Indians*. Westport, CT: Greenwood Press, 1989.

Stuart, Paul H. "Financing Self-Determination: Federal Indian Expenditures, 1975–1988." *American Indian Culture and Research Journal* 14:2 (1990): 1–18.

———. "Organizing for Self-Determination: Federal and Tribal Bureaucracies in an Era of Social and Policy Change." *American Indians: Social Justice and Public Policy*. Eds. Donald E. Green and Thomas V. Tonnesen. Milwaukee: The University of Wisconsin System Institute on Race and Ethnicity (1991): 83–108.

Taylor, Theodore W. *American Indian Policy*. Mt. Airy, MD: Lomond Publications, 1983.

GOVERNMENT POLICY

The policy of the United States government toward American Indians has been a controversial subject throughout the twentieth century. The history of this policy and its impact upon the Native American populations are the subjects of the following four articles, which are arranged chronologically.

1900 TO 1933

In the early twentieth century, the federal government, through the Office of Indian Affairs, touched virtually every aspect of the lives of reservation Indians. The federal government's main concerns were: 1) to control and regulate the use of tribal and allotted Indian land; 2) to provide health care for Indians; and 3) to provide education for Indian children, most of whom were under federal (not state), supervision.

Federal policy was shaped by legislation, court decisions and the day-to-day decisions made by officials of the Office of Indian Affairs, a part of the Department of the Interior. Congress passed the basic legislation that defined the role of the federal government in supervising Indian affairs. The federal courts were important in specifying the rights of Indians. The Office of Indian Affairs had the responsibility for the day-to-day administration of federal programs for Indians, and its agents had great power over the lives and property of Indians. Notable by its absence was a direct role for Native Americans, either individually or through tribal governments. Indians were given so little input into the policies shaping their own lives because the federal government was committed to a policy of assimilation of Indians into white society, and policy makers were not ready to allow Indians to choose to resist these changes.

Policy Making, 1900 to 1933

During the 1880s and 1890s Indian reform groups meeting annually at Lake Mohonk, New York, had considerable moral authority over federal policy and influenced the legislation passed by Congress and the policies of successive commissioners of Indian affairs. The Dawes Act of 1887 marked the height of the influence of these groups. Members of these reform organizations were largely Protestants who wished to promote the assimilation of Indians into Anglo-American society. After 1900 Congress and the commissioner of Indian affairs became increasingly willing to ignore the wishes of the reformers, many of whom remained committed to a policy of removing Indians from federal supervision. Commissioner Francis Leupp (1905 to 1909), himself a former participant in the Lake Mohonk Conferences, defied the wishes of the reformers in pressing for the passage of the Burke Act in 1906. To his credit, Leupp also showed greater respect for Indian traditions than had many of his predecessors.

The 1920s saw a distinct shift in attitudes towards Indians. New groups of reformers, including the General Federation of Women's Clubs and its representative, John Collier, attacked the Bureau for failing to respect Indian traditions or to safeguard Indian interests. Controversies in these years focused the attention of the public at large on Indian issues. In particular, concern over the possible loss of land by the Pueblos attracted national attention in the 1920s. Collier rallied opposition to the Bursum Bill, which would have settled land claims in New Mexico in a way that was unfavorable to Pueblo interests. These efforts led to the passage of the Pueblo Lands Act in 1924. Collier also opposed Commissioner Charles Burke's attempts to restrict those traditional Indian dances which Burke saw as immoral or interfering with the education of Indian children. Collier and the American Indian Defense Association, another group active in publicizing Indian reform issues, also publicly criticized other aspects of Indian policy, including the state of health care, the loss of Indian lands after allotment, and the failure to protect the interests of Indians, such as members of the Osage Tribe in Oklahoma, who had received large payments from the discovery of oil on tribal lands. One result of widespread complaints about the plight of Indians in the United States were a number of investigations in the 1920s into the quality of Indian programs. The most influential and well known of these investigations was the Meriam Report, published in 1928.

Activities of the Federal Government

Allotment and Land Administration. Allotment was the policy of dividing Indian reservations into one hundred sixty-acre farms, with the land held in trust for a twenty-five-year period. Unallotted lands could be opened for sale to non-Indians. Most lands were allotted under terms of the Dawes Act of 1887, but some tribes, especially in Oklahoma, were allotted under special legislation. Tribes in New York were under special state laws and some important reservations in the Southwest and elsewhere were never allotted. Beginning in 1902, federal agents could sell inherited land for an allottee whose land was still in trust. The Burke Act of 1906 empowered the president

to either extend the twenty-five-year trust period of the original Dawes Act, or to remove all restrictions on the lease or sale of land before the twenty-five-year period had ended. Citizenship was not granted until restrictions on property were removed.

The policy of removing Indians from federal supervision reached its peak during the term of Cato Sells (1913–1920). Sells in 1917 instituted a policy of removing from trust status the allotments of a large number of Indians. This policy ended in 1920, as a number of observers complained that too many Indians were selling their land and ending up without a means of support. During the 1920s, the federal government moved more cautiously in removing restrictions from Indian lands, and many fewer Indians received trust patents in those years. Additionally, the number of allotments issued declined sharply.

Federal agents also controlled the use of land and other assets owned by tribes, rather than individuals. A number of issues arose as to how to develop or lease tribal forests and mineral rights in these years, and a number of the assessments of Indian policy in the 1920s concluded that the Office of Indian Affairs had done a relatively poor job of managing tribal resources. In Oklahoma, many Indians were turned over to state rather than federal supervision and a number of cases of abuse of Indians by state courts were reported in the press in the 1920s.

A number of Indian reservations in the West were relatively dry and made ideal sites for large dams and irrigation projects. A number of major irrigation projects were built on Indian reservations in the twentieth century. The Preston-Engle Report in 1928 concluded that very often Indians leased or sold irrigated lands to whites and that some projects, paid for in part with Indian funds, did not really benefit Indians.

The Office of Indian Affairs supervised a vast amount of Indian land in these years. In 1900, there were roughly 77.8 million unallotted acres of tribal land and supervised allotments in the United States. Twenty million acres were allotted after 1900, not including acreage in Oklahoma. In 1933, roughly 17.8 million acres of allotted land were still in trust status, and 34 million acres of tribal land remained under federal supervision.

The stated goal of Indian policy in these years was to make Indians self-sufficient through the development of Indian agriculture. By this standard, federal policies clearly failed. The number of Indian farmers and ranchers declined from 1900 to 1930, as did the amount of land farmed by Indians. Yet Indians continued to live in rural areas where agriculture was the primary opportunity for employment. Farming was becoming an increasingly difficult endeavor, as farms became larger and more mechanized in the twentieth century, but federal policies clearly were also a factor in the decline of Indian agriculture. Indeed, an unintended consequence of the allotment policy was that the way it was administered often encouraged Indians to sell or lease land, rather than to farm it themselves.

Health Care. Reservation Indians in the early twentieth century had dismal health statistics. A number of infectious diseases, including tuberculosis and trachoma, an eye disease, were far more common among Indians than the general population. Indians also suffered from a high rate of infant mortality. This reflected poverty, a lack of sanitation, and the poor quality of medical care provided to Indians by Indian doctors. Sanitary conditions were often very bad at Indian boarding schools. Problems with Indian health only gradually attracted the attention of either the commissioners of Indian affairs or Congress. Federal appropriations for Indian health care increased after 1910, but declined with budget cutbacks during World War I and the early 1920s. Critics of the Indian Office, especially John Collier and the American Indian Defense Association, remained critical of Indian health care throughout the 1920s. The Meriam Report was especially critical of Indian health care. Overall in these years, there was some improvement in health care and sanitation services on Indian reservations, but Indians continued to endure poorer health and sanitation conditions than did the average United States citizen.

Education. In the 1890s, the fastest growing activity of the Office of Indian Affairs was education. It was charged with providing education to Indians. Indian children were sent to four types of schools: off-reservation boarding schools; on-reservation boarding schools; day schools (for Indians); and local public schools. The emphasis in the 1890s was on off-reservation boarding schools, the most famous of which were the Carlisle Indian Industrial School in Pennsylvania, headed by Richard Pratt, and the Hampton Institute in Virginia. Beginning in 1900, Commissioner William A. Jones and, later, Commissioner Leupp, began to reduce the role of off-reservation schools, despite congressional support for such schools. Instead, more Indian children were sent to on-reservation day schools or on-reservation boarding schools. This movement reflected the influence of Superintendent of Indian Schools Estelle Reel (1898 to 1909).

After 1910, it was argued that Indian children would assimilate faster and learn more if they attended local public schools. Since Indians were often not subject to state taxes, the federal government paid the tuition of Indian students in state schools. In the 1920s, the board of Indian commissioners persuasively argued that regular public schools did not meet the needs of Indian students, in part because Indian children often lacked language skills needed to compete with non-Indian children, and in part because of discrimination on the part of students and teachers. The 1920s saw the Office of Indian Affairs shift resources towards more exclusively Indian schools.

Commissioners Sells and Burke were articulate in pointing out the successes of Indian schools. The Meriam Report, however, presented a detailed criticism of Indian education and concluded that most Indian schools lacked sufficient resources to properly educate Indians.

Growth of the Office of Indian Affairs

In the years from 1900 to 1920, years known as the progressive era in politics, the federal government took on increased powers to regulate the economy. Many federal agencies evolved into modern bureaucracies with a hierarchical structure staffed by professional bureaucrats. Indian policy saw a parallel development. Guided by commissioners who enjoyed relatively long terms in office and who were able administrators, the Office of Indian Affairs also became a more formal, professional bureaucracy. Officially, the policy of the federal government was one of promoting assimilation of Indians and ending federal control over Indian lives and property. Indeed, commissioners in the 1890s and first decade of the twentieth century predicted that the assimilation of Indians would result in a gradual fading way of the Office of Indian Affairs. In practice, however, the policy of allotting lands to Indians meant that while in trust, each Indian's property and funds were under federal supervision. Further, the Office of Indian Affairs took on an expanded role in providing education and health care for reservation Indians. This required a growth in federal personnel in Washington, D.C. and in the field to handle the increased paper work. For example, the number of employees in Washington, D.C. rose from 115 in 1900, to 262 in 1920, and the number of communications from the field increased from 63,000 to 261,000. Overall, the number of employees in the Office of Indian Affairs grew from roughly 2,900 in 1891, to 3,900 in 1897, and 6,000 in 1918. During the Burke administration in the early 1920s, there was a decline in health and other services provided to Indians as part of a general cut in federal spending.

Newly elected President Herbert Hoover selected Ray Lyman Wilbur to be secretary of the interior in 1929. Wilbur in turn appointed two respected Quaker businessmen who were active in the Indian Rights Association, Charles Rhoads and J. Henry Scattergood, to be commissioner and associate commissioner of Indian affairs. In office, Rhoads and Scattergood began to implement many of the proposals put forth in the Meriam Report. These reforms, however, did not satisfy critics of Indian programs. Rhoads and Scattergood were committed to working within the existing system and their attempts at reform were hampered by problems with Congress and resistance to change by the bureaucracy. Critics such as John Collier pointed out that they had failed to change the allotment system or to move toward the incorporation of tribal governments. Nor had they succeeded in getting Congress to establish an Indian Claims Commission, an arts and crafts board, or to get state cooperation with federal Indian programs.

Commissioners

From 1897 to 1933, only six men were commissioners of the Office of Indian Affairs. They were: William A. Jones (1897 to 1904); Francis Leupp (1905 to 1909); Robert G. Valentine (1909 to 1912); Cato Sells (1913 to 1920); Charles H. Burke (1920 to 1929);

and Charles J. Rhoads (1929 to 1933). It was in the administration of these men that the Office of Indian Affairs took on the shape of a modern bureaucracy.

Issues of This Period

Alcohol. In the twentieth century, alcohol abuse was seen as a major health and social problem among Indians. Beginning with Commissioner Jones in 1901, the Office of Indian Affairs sought to limit alcohol use by Indians. The Supreme Court held in *Matter of Heff,* 1905, that the Office of Indian Affairs could not restrict the sale of liquor to Indians who were citizens. The Burke Act met this challenge by withholding citizenship until an allottee was issued a patent-in-fee. The Office of Indian Affairs interpreted this to mean that they could restrict the sale of alcohol to Indians whose land they held in trust. The Supreme Court in *United States v. Nice*, 1916, overturned Heff and allowed Congress to act as a guardian for Indians, even if they were citizens. National prohibition in 1919 limited liquor sales still further, but the remote nature of Indian reservations and the proximity of some to Mexico and Canada made bootlegging a continuing problem.

Peyote. The use of peyote, a narcotic drug obtained from a cactus, became common among some Indians, especially in the Southwest. It attracted the condemnation of reformers and the Office of Indian Affairs as a harmful narcotic. Beginning in 1914, some in Congress introduced legislation to outlaw the drug. Indians who used peyote in religious ceremonials organized as the Native American Church in order to have their use of the drug protected by the Constitution. The Office of Indian Affairs, however, rejected religion as a protection for using the drug. Yet, even so, Congress did not pass legislation to limit the use of peyote in these years.

Citizenship and Enfranchisement. Before 1887, most Indians living on reservations were members of "domestic dependent nations," but not citizens of the United States. Under the Dawes Act, Indians who received allotments automatically became citizens of the United States. The Burke Act of 1906 changed the law to delay citizenship until a fee-patent was granted to an individual. As late as 1924, as many as one-third of the Indians in the United States were still not citizens. This fact did not sit well with members of Congress and their constituents who were aware that Indians had served bravely in the army during World War I. The Act of June 2, 1924, made all Indians citizens of the United States, although many were still denied the right to vote in state elections. In particular, Arizona and New Mexico restricted the voting rights of Indians until after World War II.

Pueblo Issues. A Supreme Court decision in 1913, *United States v. Sandoval,* upheld the principle that Pueblo Indians in New Mexico were under federal rather than state supervision. This called into question the land titles of whites living on land claimed by the Pueblos. Senator Holm Bursum of New Mexico in 1922 introduced a bill, known as the Bursum Bill, to quiet title to lands held by non-Indians in areas claimed by the Pueblos and to clarify the issues raised in *United States v. Sandoval.* The bill passed the Senate, but was the subject of heated criticism in the press for failing to protect the interests of the Pueblos or to compensate them for lost property. The opposition was organized in part by John Collier. As a compromise, Congress passed the Pueblo Lands Act in 1924. It provided for a commission to establish the borders of the Pueblo land grants and the status of non-Indian land holders in the Pueblo territory. The United States was to compensate the Pueblos for any land and water rights lost.

Declaration of Policy, 1917. During World War I, there was a sharp rise in agricultural prices and a demand for agricultural land. In addition, Commissioner Cato Sells was determined to "bring about the speedy individualizing of the Indians." Sells, with the backing of reform groups such as the Indian Rights Association, concluded that one way to do this was to remove the restrictions on Indian allotments. He also wished to place as much land in production as possible to satisfy the war-time demand for agricultural products. In April 1917, Sells announced a policy of issuing more Indians patents-in-fee, which allowed allotted Indians to sell or lease their land without the approval of the Indian agent. It also made Indians liable for state and local taxes. All Indians of less than one-half Indian blood were to be issued patents-in-fee immediately, as well as other Indians if they were found competent. So-called competency commissions traveled from reservation to reservation issuing fee patents to allotted Indians. This policy was ended in 1920, when the fall in agricultural prices reduced the demand for farm land and the rapid increase in land sales by Indians raised concern that a number of Indians who were not competent to manage their own affairs were losing their land.

Religious Freedom. The Office of Indian Affairs had a long tradition of trying to "civilize" Indians, which typically meant to convert them to Protestant Christianity. This took many forms. Commissioner Burke in the 1920s sought to limit the practice of Indian dances that he considered immoral, as well as the practice of having Indian children miss school to learn traditional dances.

Collier's Early Years

John Collier was a one-time social worker in New York City who came to greatly admire the culture of the Pueblos while living in New Mexico. He was hired as a field representative of the General Federation of Women's Clubs. In that position, he wrote articles in magazines and newspapers and rallied opposition to the Bursum Bill in the early 1920s. He remained an active critic throughout the 1920s, continually challenging the policies of Commissioner Burke, Secretary of the Interior Hubert Work, and their successors, Commissioner Charles J. Rhoads and Assistant Commissioner J. Henry Scattergood. In general, Collier advocated a greater respect for Indian cultures and a greatly increased role for tribal leaders, such as those he knew among the Pueblos.

Evaluation of the Period

The years from 1900 to 1930 are often neglected in the study of Indian history. This is unfortunate, for these were the years in which all tribes were forced to come to terms with the loss of land and the need to adjust to a new way of life. There were a number of important changes. Illiteracy among Indians over ten declined from 56.2 percent to 25.7 percent. The number who could not speak English declined to 17 percent of the population. These bright spots were offset by the dismal record of Indian farmers and the poor state of Indian health care. Most Indians in 1930 lived in rural areas where farming or ranching were the primary means of employment, and yet Indian farmers and ranchers were further behind white farmers in 1930 than they had been in 1900.

In 1900, reformers were optimistic that Indians would assimilate into white society and succeed economically, and that the Office of Indian Affairs would fade out of existence. By 1930, there was widespread agreement that Indian policy had failed. This failure was discussed both in the press and in serious government studies, such as the Meriam Report. From a modern perspective, part of the failure can be blamed on the unwillingness of policy makers to respect Indian traditions or allow Indians to shape their own destiny, as well as bureaucratic opposition to change. But the problems of Indians in the 1920s also reflected the difficulty of finding a set of policies that promoted economic development.

There were a variety of possible solutions. The Meriam Commission called for reform of programs and services within the existing structure. Some then and later called for less federal regulation. These were very real possibilities, but the Great Depression of 1929 to 1933 and the election of Franklin Roosevelt meant that more radical change was possible. Roosevelt and Congress, especially in the so-called first one hundred days, were willing to try a variety of new approaches to government, some of them inconsistent with one another. Roosevelt named John Collier commissioner of Indian affairs, and he was ready and willing to propose legislation to create a different governmental approach to Indian policy.

Leonard A. Carlson

See also **Allotment; Citizenship and Enfranchisement; Educational Policy; Meriam Commission**

Further Reading

Hoxie, Frederick. *A Final Promise: The Campaign to Assimilate The Indians, 1880–1920*. Lincoln: The University of Nebraska Press, 1984.

Kelly, Lawrence C. *The Assault on Assimilation: John Collier and the Origins of Indian Policy Reform*. Albuquerque: University of New Mexico Press, 1983.

Meriam, Lewis. *The Problem of Indian Administration*. Baltimore, MD: Johns Hopkins Press, 1928.

Prucha, Francis. *The Great Father: The United States Government and the American Indians*. Vol. 2. Lincoln: The University of Nebraska Press, 1984.

Schmeckebier, Laurence F. *The Office of Indian Affairs: Its History, Activities and Organization*. Baltimore, MD: Johns Hopkins Press, 1927.

INDIAN NEW DEAL

The reform programs that collectively constitute the Indian New Deal were almost solely the products of Indian Commissioner John Collier (1933 to 1945) and Secretary of the Interior Harold Ickes. During the 1920s, Collier founded the American Indian Defense Association (AIDA) as a vehicle for attacking the assimilationist policies of the federal government. Ickes was a charter member of the AIDA and after his surprise appointment as secretary of the interior, he nominated Collier for the position of Indian commissioner. President Franklin D. Roosevelt was totally ignorant on the subject of Indians, but he was supportive of his appointees, at least during the early years of the New Deal.

Although many of the reforms achieved during the Indian New Deal had been identified during the administration of President Herbert Hoover, his Indian commissioner, Charles J. Rhoads, was unwilling to press the Congress on the topic of reform. The most important of these reforms involved halting the loss of Indian tribal lands through the division of reservations into individually owned allotments and the sale of the "surplus" to whites, a procedure adopted in 1887 in the Dawes Severalty Act. By 1933, much of the landed estate of American tribes had already passed into private ownership as a result of the Dawes Act and companion statutes. Collier, whose knowledge of Indians centered mainly on the Indians of the Southwest whose tribal lands were still largely intact, and his staff spent most of 1933 drafting legislation (the Indian Reorganization Act) to reverse the Dawes Act. They submitted their draft to Congress in the spring of 1934.

During the period of preparing the Indian Reorganization Act (IRA), Collier launched the Indian New Deal through a series of administrative orders. He issued regulations guaranteeing Indians full expression of their religious and cultural traditions and prohibiting compulsory attendance by Indian students in government schools at Christian religious services, cancelled most of the debt charged against tribal funds as a result of earlier federal loan programs, persuaded President Roosevelt to abolish the assimilationist-minded Board of Indian Commissioners, and worked closely with Secretary of Agriculture Henry C. Wallace to obtain agricultural and reclamation relief funds for Indians. During his first year in office, Collier also steered through Congress the Pueblo Relief Act, which increased monetary awards to the Pueblo Indians of New Mexico for losses of their land and water determined under a 1924 statute; a bill that repealed twelve objectionable nineteenth-century statutes limiting Indians' right to exercise basic civil liberties; and in the Johnson-O'Malley Act, obtained authority to contract with the states for the educational, medical, and social welfare needs of Indians.

The focal point of the Indian New Deal, however, was passage of the IRA or, as it was popularly known, the Wheeler-Howard Act (after its congressional sponsors, Senator Burton K. Wheeler of Montana and Congressman Edgar Howard of Nebraska). As originally conceived by Collier, this major piece of legislative reform was composed of four titles that sought to replace "several thousand pages of Indian law."

Title I proposed that Indians be granted "freedom to organize for purposes of local self-government and economic enterprise, to the end that civil liberty, political responsibility and economic independence shall be achieved." Under this provision, tribal governments were to be created, empowered to adopt ordinances for their reservations, including the right to tax, and Indian courts to enforce the ordinances were authorized. Title II declared it to be "the purpose and policy of Congress to promote the study of Indian civilization, including Indian arts, crafts, skills, and traditions," and provided modest appropriations for Indian education. Title III abolished the land allotment provisions of the Dawes Severalty Act, and provided for the restoration to tribal ownership of previously allotted lands and lands withdrawn from Indian reservations but never patented to non-Indians. Title III also declared that the policy of the United States would henceforth be to "undertake a constructive program of Indian land use and economic development," in order to make Indians self-supporting. To this end, it called for the annual appropriation of $2 million for land acquisition and authorized the secretary of the interior to issue regulations that would restrict the number of livestock grazed on Indian lands, and the amount of timber cut on Indian forest lands. Title IV proposed the creation of a court of Indian affairs having original jurisdiction in all cases involving Indians organized under Title I. The rules and procedures in the proposed court were to be designed to "be consonant with Indian traditions."

The reforms proposed in Collier's bill proved too radical for Congress, which immediately rejected most of Title II and all of title IV. In the face of growing congressional hostility, only a personal appeal by the president for an end to allotment and the extension of self-government salvaged its remaining provisions. The final bill retained the provision for the creation of tribal governments, although the self-governing powers of the tribes were severely limited, and permitted the tribes to vote for acceptance or rejection of the IRA in a referendum. The land allotment provisions of the Dawes Severalty Act were abolished, but the Indians of Oklahoma were specifically exempted from the act, and the Indians of Alaska were denied access to the credit loan funds. The provision in Title III requiring the restoration of previously allotted lands to tribal ownership was also removed when many Plains Indians successfully protested the

loss of their allotments. The final bill also greatly increased appropriations for Indian education and loans to tribal corporations for economic development, although these provisions have been interpreted more as measures to draw Indians into white society than to preserve Indian societies. The bill that emerged was, therefore, a compromise between Collier's dream of a new policy encouraging the growth of Indian society and culture, and the traditional forces of assimilation.

Following the passage of the IRA, Indians first had to vote to accept or reject its applicability to their reservations. In the referenda that followed, 174 Indian tribes and bands representing approximately 129,750 Indians voted to accept the IRA, while 78 tribes representing approximately 86,365 Indians voted against its application. Close examination of the voting returns reveals that of the approximately 97,000 Indians who were declared eligible to case ballots in the referenda, only 38,000 voted in favor of the IRA, while 24,000 voted against it, and 35,000 failed to vote. Major tribes like the Navajos, the Crows, the Assiniboine and Sioux of Fort Peck, the Klamath, Crow Creek Sioux, and the Shoshone-Arapaho of Wyoming voted against the IRA. Their negative votes deprived them of both the right to adopt tribal constitutions under the protective guarantees of the IRA, and to qualify for the land purchase and economic development loans. Subsequently, some of the tribes that approved the IRA failed to adopt constitutions, while others failed to incorporate themselves for business purposes; they too became ineligible for the land purchase and economic development loans. It is estimated that of the approximately 216,115 Indians recognized as potentially eligible for IRA benefits, only 69,922 later qualified for full benefits: tribal organization, business incorporation, land purchases, and credit loans.

Collier's New Deal program was obviously weakened by Congress's refusal to enact all the reforms proposed in his initial draft of the IRA, by its failure to include the Indians of Oklahoma in the IRA and the limitations it placed upon the Indians of Alaska, and by the opposition and distrust subsequently exhibited by the many tribes that failed to avail themselves of the IRA's protective and economic provisions. However, he persisted and in 1936 he succeeded in securing passage of the Alaska Reorganization Act, which extended the most important provisions of the IRA to Alaska Natives, and the Oklahoma Indian Welfare Act, which salvaged some of the IRA benefits for the Indians of Oklahoma. The previous year, he had also obtained passage of the Indian Arts and Crafts Act to promote and enlarge the market for traditional Indian handicrafts. Under the direction of Rene d'Harnoncourt, an Austrian émigré, standards for Indian crafts were adopted and production and marketing mechanisms created that enhanced both the quality of Indian crafts and contributed to the creation of a small, but influential, group of Indian artisans.

The Indian New Deal was not, however, limited only to statutory reform. Having insured the preservation of a land base for those tribes that still retained tribal lands, Collier implemented a variety of administrative actions designed to strengthen tribal cohesion and to encourage the revival of Indian cultures and society. The financing for these programs came from various federal emergency agencies created by the New Deal.

From the Civilian Conservation Corps and the Public Works Administration, two New Deal work relief programs, Collier eventually secured more than $100 million for soil conservation, irrigation, and road-building programs on reservations. From the Resettlement Administration and the Farm Security Administration, he obtained over 1 million acres of "sub-marginal" lands for addition to tribal land bases. From the Federal Emergency Relief Administration, the Civil Works Administration, and the Works Progress Administration, he obtained relief funds that employed thousands of Indians on reservation projects and stimulated their involvement in industries devoted to traditional arts and crafts. Community centers, tribal government offices, and day schools on the reservations (rather than off-reservation boarding schools) were constructed. Where Indian children were educated in federal schools, he introduced a new curriculum that encouraged the teaching of Indian languages, Indian history and culture, and Indian religious beliefs.

Collier's efforts to implement reforms deleted by Congress from the IRA resulted in appropriations battles with congressional committees, battles which he eventually lost. The Indian New Deal also encountered opposition from Indians, most notably from members of the Five Civilized Tribes of Oklahoma, many of whom favored integration with white society, and the Navajos of Arizona and New Mexico, who bitterly protested New Deal soil conservation programs that forced them to reduce the size of their sheep herds. The government's sheep reduction program on the Navajo Reservation was hastily improvised and poorly implemented, leading to economic destitution among Navajos with small flocks and undying hatred for Collier and the New Deal on the part of most Navajos, despite the comparatively large sums of money and the number of New Deal programs that were focused on the Navajo Reservation.

By 1939 Indian opposition to the New Deal was skillfully manipulated by conservative congressmen and senators who twice attempted to repeal the IRA. These efforts failed, but Indian Office budgets were severely cut and in 1941, when the United States entered World War II, most of the New Deal relief programs that Collier depended upon were ended, and the Indian New Deal essentially ended. Collier remained in office until 1945, protecting the reforms that had been begun earlier, but increasingly his interest turned to the promotion of the Inter-American Indian Insti-

tute, a hemispheric pan-Indian organization for which he obtained initial funding.

Although the reforms that the Indian New Deal hoped to achieve were weakened both in the formulation of statutory authority and in the execution of various programs, the passage of fifty years provides sufficient perspective to see those reforms as essentially sound and far more than a temporary detour in the twisted path of federal Indian policy. With only a few exceptions during the termination period of the 1950s, the Indian tribal land base, so crucial to the preservation of Indian cultures, has been maintained and, in some cases, enlarged. Tribal governments have become a major source for the assertion of tribal and individual Indian rights and for the protection of Indian natural resources. Throughout Indian country, Indian tribes are successfully exerting their authority against encroachments from state and federal authorities, and they have managed to sustain their claim to being a third force in the governmental structure of the United States. The assimilationist goal of prior Indian policy, while not extinct, is definitely subordinated to a policy that permits, and sometimes encourages, Indian tribes and smaller groups to preserve their religious and cultural heritage in ways determined by the Indians themselves.

Economic survival on tribal lands remains the greatest challenge to Indians today. On most reservations, unemployment greatly exceeds the national average. Agriculture and animal husbandry, the New Deal's answers to Indian poverty, are clearly insufficient to employ all the reservations' peoples or to provide them with a standard of living equal to that of the nation's white majority. Federal subsidies to tribal groups, the negotiated price for taking the Indian's lands in the eighteenth and nineteenth centuries, are still required, although most non-Indian Americans fail to comprehend the contractual nature of this obligation. The hope of the Indian New Deal, to make Indians self-sufficient, was not achieved.

Lawrence C. Kelly

See also **Indian Arts and Crafts Board; Indian Civilian Conservation Corps; Indian Reorganization Act; Inter-American Indian Institute**

Further Reading

Deloria, Vine, Jr., and Clifford Lytle. *The Nations Within: The Past and Future of American Indian Sovereignty.* New York, NY: Pantheon Books, 1984.

Hauptman, Laurence M. *The Iroquois and the New Deal.* NY: Syracuse University Press, 1981.

Kelly, Lawrence C. "United States Indian Policy, 1900–1980." *Handbook of North American Indians.* Vol. 4. *Indian–White Relations.* Ed. Wilcomb E. Washburn. Washington, DC: Smithsonian Institution (1988): 66–80.

Philp, Kenneth R. *John Collier's Crusade for Indian Reform, 1920–1954.* Tucson: University of Arizona Press, 1977.

Taylor, Graham D. *The New Deal and the American Indian Tribalism*. Lincoln: University of Nebraska Press, 1981.

TERMINATION AND RESTORATION

After World War II, the government returned to goals of rapidly assimilating Indians in a policy known as termination. It attempted to extinguish the special federal-tribal relationship and thus bring an end to tribal government and sovereignty, treaty rights, federally supplied services, and the nontaxable status of reservation lands. But termination quickly became controversial and was largely discredited and rejected by the early 1960s. In fact, some of those groups terminated by Congress later launched efforts to regain federal recognition of tribal status in actions referred to as restoration.

There were many reasons for the increasing popularity of termination, beginning in the 1940s. The Indian New Deal of the previous decade had been promoted largely by liberals in the Franklin Roosevelt administration, and politics were becoming more conservative. The war experience generated a spirit of nationalism and a more narrowly defined notion of Americanism that made Indian culture and sovereignty seem to many to be out of step with the times. In the atmosphere of the subsequent Cold War, Indian communal traditions appeared to be too similar to the dreaded communist systems that the United States pitted itself against in foreign policy.

Many individual Indians, especially those who had served in the military, got caught up in the era's nationalism as well. They were eager to join the consumer culture and began to identify more as Americans and less as members of sovereign tribes. In the years after the war, some began agitating for civil rights based on United States citizenship, seeking an end to aspects of Indian special status, such as trust restrictions on allotted reservation lands and prohibitions on the purchase of alcohol.

Private economic interests in the West often promoted termination as well. They saw it as a way of easing access to Indian trust lands that contained some of the nation's last remaining untapped natural resources. The economic boom after World War II intensified pressure for the development of those resources. It also stimulated population growth in the region. State and local governments searched for new sources of revenue to fulfill escalating demands for public services, and the prospect of taxing Indian land made termination seem appealing.

Some liberals in Congress supported termination as an extension of the emerging post-war civil rights movement, identifying its assimilationist goals as similar to the integration sought by African-Americans. But conservatives were generally the most vigorous promoters of termination. Expressing a more extreme version of the era's nationalism, they were more likely to believe that a separate Indian sovereignty was incompatible with American sovereignty.

They saw termination as "liberating" Indians from obstacles, like the Bureau of Indian Affairs (BIA), the trust status of land, and tribalism, that prevented their competing individually within a political and economic system based on personal property rights and private enterprise.

The momentum for termination was soon reflected in Congress, where legislative action began shortly after the war. In 1946 Congress passed the Indian Claims Commission Act, allowing tribes to sue the government in a special court for inadequate compensation in past land transactions. It was intended in part to be a final settlement between old antagonists as a prelude to termination. In 1947, the Indian Affairs Subcommittee of the House Committee on Public Lands held hearings on bills to "emancipate" Indians from the BIA. That same year, the Senate Civil Service Committee directed the acting Commissioner of Indian Affairs (CIA), William Zimmerman, to identify and classify tribes on the basis of their readiness for termination. In 1949, a special body studying government efficiency known as the Hoover Commission recommended complete Indian integration and phasing out of all federal Indian programs.

President Harry Truman's CIA, Dillon Myer, was the first BIA head to actively push termination. He did as much as he could administratively within existing legislation to achieve terminationist goals. But it was the 1952 election that gave the essential boost to termination, because the victory of Dwight Eisenhower and Republican congressional majorities brought more conservatives into positions of influence in Indian affairs. Eisenhower selected a terminationist from New Mexico, Glenn Emmons, as his CIA. Conservative Republicans now chaired both Indian affairs subcommittees, with E.Y. Berry of South Dakota in the House and Arthur Watkins of Utah in the Senate. In 1953, they helped push Public Law 280 through Congress. It directed the states of California, Minnesota, Nebraska, Oregon, and Wisconsin to assume law and order jurisdiction on most reservations within their boundaries. In the most controversial provision, it also authorized any other state to similarly take over legal jurisdiction without Indian consent. That same year, Congress committed itself to goals of phasing out the BIA and ending separate Indian status in House Concurrent Resolution 108. This document not only stood as an important expression of congressional sentiment, but also became a sort of blueprint by specifying certain tribes to target first for specific termination legislation.

Eager to act quickly while support was strong, Senator Watkins arranged joint hearings with both Indian affairs subcommittees to consider the first group of thirteen termination bills, shortly after the opening of the 1954 congressional session. The tribes in most cases objected, but six of the proposals were enacted at this time and several more succeeded a few years later. By 1962, Congress had passed fourteen bills terminating 109 tribes and bands, but this represented only 3 percent of all federally-recognized Indians and 3.2 percent of trust lands. Most of the groups affected, like the thirty-eight rancherias in California and the sixty-one bands in western Oregon, were very small with minor assets and little tribal cohesiveness. Others such as the Peorias, Wyandots, and Ottawas of Oklahoma were not much larger and had a number of assimilated members who had requested the move.

For the few larger groups affected, termination stirred major controversies, pitting off-reservation members who were attracted to the per capital distribution that would follow reservation liquidation, against on-reservation members who usually opposed the change. Among the Klamaths of Oregon, for example, Wade Crawford, who lived off the reservation, led a movement in favor of termination, while Tribal Councilman and reservation resident Boyd Jackson lobbied against it.

In addition to legislation ending the tribal status of individual groups, termination policy also included a number of moves designed to withdraw the federal government from Indian affairs and assimilate Native Americans into the mainstream. Educational policies, for example, emphasized enrolling Indian students in public schools and transferring many functions to states. Other BIA services such as agricultural extension work were also turned over to the states. BIA health service responsibilities were taken over by the Public Health Service in 1955. Indian lands were made more readily available for purchase or leasing by non-Indians, and the BIA promoted a relocation program to encourage Native Americans to move to large urban areas in pursuit of industrial employment.

Already by the late 1950s termination came under heavy criticism and support faded. Tribes, led by the National Congress of American Indians, mounted an increasingly effective opposition. Church groups protested what they saw as a social injustice. State and local governments' interest in termination dropped off as it became clear that the costs of taking over the financial burden of social services on reservations outweighed the benefits of taxing Indian land. Republicans lost their congressional majorities and key subcommittee positions. Many of the Democrats who replaced them became vocal critics, coming increasingly to view termination as a violation of Native tribal and sovereign rights rather than as an extension of United States citizenship rights. More and more, the specter of abandoning indigent people and unwanted responsibilities replaced that of "liberation." In 1958, Secretary of the Interior Fred Seaton became the first administration official to acknowledge the controversy and back away from a faltering policy by announcing that no additional tribes would be terminated unless they fully supported the change.

As individual termination bills were implemented throughout the 1960s, it became clear that the transition would be difficult and the impact would be devastating. Many of the people and tribes affected sunk deeper into poverty. Some were unable to pay taxes and lost their land. In the case of the Menominees of Wisconsin, disagreement among tribal members over termination made it harder for the group to coalesce and successfully make the adjustment. From the beginning, the new county created within Wisconsin out of the old reservation faced enormous problems, since it suffered from the state's worst statistics in most economic and social categories. Its primary source of tax revenue, the former tribal lumber industry renamed Menominee Enterprises Incorporated, provided nearly the only base for the area's economy. In the new arrangement, it came more under the control of non-Indian outsiders and struggled for survival in the unfamiliar world of private enterprise.

As the dismal results of termination legislation unfolded, anger and opposition grew. The Red Power movement that emerged in the late 1960s emphasized themes like pride in Indian culture, tribal sovereignty, and Indian self-determination and led to demands that the policy be changed. Some tribes initiated action to reverse termination and restore tribal status. In 1970, President Richard Nixon gave the movement a big boost when he rejected termination and stated policy goals of self-determination very similar to those championed by Red Power Indian activists. In a striking policy reversal, the restoration drive finally achieved a major victory with the Menominee Restoration Act of 1973.

Congress later went on to restore many more of the tribes affected by termination legislation, although in some cases not all terminated rights were returned. Federal recognition and a trust relationship were returned to the Modocs, Wyandottes, and Peorias in 1978, and to the Paiutes of Utah in 1980. In 1983, the Confederated Tribes of Grand Ronde in western Oregon were restored, although hunting and fishing rights were not included. Congress brought back tribal status for the Klamaths in 1986, but law and order jurisdiction remained with the State of Oregon. The following year, Congress restored the Alabama-Coushatta Tribe of Texas, but gaming or gambling activities that violated state law were prohibited. And in 1990, the Poncas of Nebraska regained federal recognition, but the trust lands set up for them were designated not to have reservation status.

Termination stood as the last in a long history of policies to extinguish tribalism and force the rapid assimilation of individual Native Americans. It stalled not only because of problems in implementing termination bills, but also because the social and political atmosphere after the late 1950s became more accepting of cultural diversity and more sympathetic toward racial minorities. Americans recognized increasingly the historic injustices Indians had suffered. While this change derived in part from the national civil rights movement and an international movement asserting the rights of indigenous peoples, restoration and the opposition to termination had, in fact, played a role as well. As Indian culture, land, and sovereignty seemed threatened by termination, reservation leaders rose up in resistance. Many would later expand their efforts into the Red Power movement in defense of a broad array of tribal rights. Termination had become a symbol of historic mistreatment, while restoration had become identified with Red Power activism and the new national conscience.

Larry W. Burt

See also **Indian Claims Commission; Military Service; Red Power; Senate Committee on Indian Affairs**

Further Reading

Burt, Larry W. *Tribalism in Crisis: Federal Indian Policy, 1953–1961*. Albuquerque: University of New Mexico Press, 1982.

Fixico, Donald L. *Termination and Relocation: Federal Indian Policy, 1945–1960*. Albuquerque: University of New Mexico Press, 1986.

Peroff, Nicholas C. *Menominee Drums: Tribal Termination and Restoration, 1954–1974*. Norman: University of Oklahoma Press, 1982.

Stefon, Frederick J. "The Irony of Termination: 1943–1958." *The Indian Historian* 11 (Summer 1978): 3–14.

Wilkinson, Charles, and Eric R. Biggs. "The Evolution of the Termination Policy." *American Indian Law Review* 5:1 (1977): 139–284.

SELF-DETERMINATION

The federal government's self-determination policy has dominated Indian affairs since the 1960s. Its keystone was the 1975 Indian Self-Determination and Education Assistance Act, which confessed that "prolonged Federal domination of Indian service programs has served to retard rather than enhance the progress of Indian people." To assure maximum Indian participation in the future, Congress directed the secretaries of the Departments of the Interior and Health, Education, and Welfare, upon the request of any Indian tribe, to enter into contracts to design, carry out, and evaluate programs and services previously provided by the federal government. Responding to Washington's encouragement that they take greater responsibility for their communities, Native Americans have operated hospitals and health clinics through contractual arrangements with the Indian Health Service (IHS), sponsored millions of dollars in economic development programs, and working through parent committees have asserted greater control over their children's education. "There are still a lot of problems," admitted Cecil D. Williams, chairman of Arizona's Papago tribe in 1978, but "self-determination is the best thing that has come along yet, and it should mean a brighter future for Indians."

Disrespect for tribal sovereignty characterized United States political leaders since the early 1800s. Three sets of historical factors triggered self-determination reform legislation. First, several national task forces, commissions, and congressional committees investigated reservation living conditions in the 1960s

and uncovered grave problems. Some involved government administration of Indian affairs; others stemmed from low levels of health, education, and family income. What could Washington do to reduce reservation poverty and improve Indian education? Amidst a multitude of recommendations, one theme predominated. The "objective which should undergird all Indian policy," reported the Commission on the Rights, Liberties, and Responsibilities of the American Indian in 1966, was that "the Indian individual, the Indian family, and the Indian community be motivated to participate in solving their own problems."

Second, Congress was also spurred to action by Native agitation during the 1960s and early 1970s as exemplified by the founding of the American Indian Movement, fish-ins, the occupation of Alcatraz Island as well as several Bureau of Indian Affairs [BIA] offices, the Trail of Broken Treaties Caravan to Washington, and the dramatic confrontation at Wounded Knee. White House encouragement was the third factor that triggered self-determination reform. The Kennedy administration began the subtle shift away from the termination policy and toward self-determination for Indian communities. President Lyndon B. Johnson gave major attention to Indian matters. The Office of Economic Opportunity and other federal grant-in-aid programs benefited rural and urban Natives. They also gained experience planning and managing Indian programs. Richard Nixon maintained the pressure on Congress, and in a Special Message of July 8, 1970, underscored that the time had come to "break decisively with the past and to create the conditions for a new era in which the Indian future is determined by Indian acts and Indian decisions."

Indian leaders had long been calling for "more rain and less thunder" from Washington. During the 1970s, the heavens opened as national support for aboriginal peoples followed Nixon's lead. Between 1968 and 1976, for example, Congress increased the BIA budget from $262 to $777 million. Federal monies devoted to Native health expanded nearly fourfold. Congress also wanted Indians to control and operate their own federal programs. In January, 1975, Gerald Ford signed what he called "a magna carta for Indian people." The Indian Self-Determination and Education Assistance Act, described in the opening paragraph of this essay, made Nixon's 1970 promise the law of the land. Henceforth, Native people were to have "an effective voice in the planning and implementation" of education, health, economic development, housing, law enforcement, and other programs "for the benefit of Indians which are responsive to the true needs of Indian communities." Congress and the president formally renounced the bankrupt policies of the past, which had swung between the extremes of suffocating paternalism and the threat of terminating federal responsibilities.

New federal legislation embodying the self-determination philosophy and contracting process touched every facet of Indian life—on and off the reservations. Tribal communities quickly seized these new opportunities. By 1980, they had signed 370 agreements with Washington to provide $200 million in services to their people.

Congress expanded its commitment to Native American self-determination in three education acts. The Indian Education Act of 1972 promised to "provide financial assistance to local educational agencies to develop and carry out elementary and secondary school programs specially designed" to meet the unique educational needs of Indian people. The act also provided aid for adult education and gave Indian parents greater control over federally funded public school programs. Noteworthy successors—the Indian Education Assistance Act (1975) and the Education Amendments Act (1978)—supplemented the funding for Indian students and schools. Increased, too, was the responsibility of Native parent committees for planning local educational programs.

The most conspicuous feature of Indian response to these educational programs was the high level of community participation. During fiscal year 1973, the start of operations under the Indian Education Act, Washington granted $17 million to 507 Native organizations and school districts on and outside the reservations. Six years later, $43.6 million went to 1,148 school districts in 42 states to benefit approximately 332,000 Indian and Alaska Native elementary and secondary students—80 percent of those eligible. Under terms of the Tribally Controlled Community College Assistance Act of 1978, the BIA subsidized 19 such institutions that enrolled over 3,300 Indian students by 1984.

Indian self-determination legislation of the 1970s was Washington's response to growing public anxiety over the human problems afflicting Native communities. In September, 1976, Congress passed the Indian Health Care Improvement Act because it found that, despite previous federal efforts, "the unmet health needs of the American Indian people are severe and the health status of the Indians is far below that of the general population of the United States." The act explicitly set forth the national goal of "providing the highest possible health status to Indians"; then it authorized government funds to eliminate specific backlogs in Indian health care services. The Indian Health Care Improvement law, like the Self-Determination Act of the year before, encouraged maximum Indian participation in the planning and management of these reservation services. Indian response to the act's provisions was dramatic. By 1982, Native organizations operated 4 hospitals and 272 health clinics through contractual arrangements with the IHS.

Other federal legislation touched every aspect of Indian life. The Alaska Native Claims Settlement Act of 1971 and the Menominee Restoration Act two years later, for example, increased the material resources available to aboriginal people, whereas the 1979 Archaeological Resources Protection Act secured endangered sites on Indian lands that were considered an irreplaceable part of the nation's legacy. The Indian Child Welfare Act of 1978 committed Washington to oversee any removal of these youngsters from their families, and to encourage their placement in foster or adoptive homes that taught unique Indian cultural values. Also supportive of tribal cultural rights was a 1978 Senate and House resolution (also known as the American Indian Religious Freedom Act) that stated it was United States policy to protect and preserve American Indian religious freedom, including "worship through ceremonials and traditional rites."

Washington worked to make Native people more prosperous and independent. With the Indian Financing Act, Congress pledged loans to help develop and utilize tribal resources. Section 302 of the Comprehensive Employment and Training Act of 1973 (CETA) cited the pressing need for these programs among Indian and Alaska Native communities. Congress directed the secretary of labor to contract with Indian governing bodies whenever possible in order to provide the new manpower services created by this legislation. CETA quickly became the prime source of funding for the day-to-day operations of tribal governments and urban Indian organizations. In fiscal year 1978, the Department of Labor made 160 employment and training grants to Indian and Native sponsors in 43 states. The cost was $200 million and over 100,000 persons participated. In line with the Reagan administration's strategy of shifting more power from Washington to the state governments, Congress supplanted CETA in 1982 with the Job Training Partnership Act. Title IV, Part A, of this legislation focused on Native American training and employment programs.

Native leaders clearly grasped the significance of economic development acts and other self-determination opportunities. We must act decisively now to develop Native communities "in a manner beneficial to our people," urged one tribal chairman, because self-determination opportunities could mean "a new beginning or our last hurrah." Act they did: sponsoring millions of dollars in CETA programs across the United States; operating hospitals and health clinics through contractual arrangements with the Indian Health Service (IHS)—420 in September, 1987; working through parent committees to reaffirm a traditional role in Indian education and to better meet the needs of their children. During the first 14 years of the Indian Education Act, Congress appropriated more than $850 million to an average of 1,000 school districts. Alaska Native communities alone administered $62.7 million in self-determination contracts with the BIA and IHS by the late 1980s. Applying for and administering federal programs preoccupied Native communities nationally. Washington had become "the Indian's new buffalo."

Grantsmanship yielded mixed results. For numerous Native leaders, the 1970s and 1980s were a time of significant reform in Washington's Indian policy and a consequent improvement in the status of their people. On Cecil D. Williams' Connecticut-size reservation, tribesmen were enthusiastic about the accomplishments of Indian assertiveness when coupled with government receptivity to local input: improved roads, a new Papago headquarters building, a children's center, and an upgraded school system. The unemployment rate then declined from 70 to 38 percent between 1973 and 1978. Speaking before the United States Senate Select Committee on Indian Affairs in 1987, an official from the Department of Education reported that between 1970 and 1980, "the percentage of Indian adults 25 and over who are high school graduates increased from 33 percent to 56 percent . . . [and] the median years of school completed for the Indian population aged 25 and older increased from 9.8 years to 12.2 years."

Judgments were not unanimous. For some Indians the 1970s and 1980s were an era of frustration and dashed hopes. Staunch critics vilified Congress for reneging on its financial commitments and Executive Branch agencies—the BIA, IHS, Office of Indian Education—for throwing up every conceivable roadblock in order to protect themselves and thwart grass roots Indian program control. "Excessive regulation and self-perpetuating bureaucracy have stifled local decisionmaking," admitted President Reagan in 1983, "thwarted Indian control of Indian resources, and promoted dependence rather than self-sufficiency . . . Despite the Indian Self-Determination Act, major tribal government functions . . . are frequently still carried out by Federal employees." (Congress' 1988 amendments to the Indian Self-Determination Act gave Indian groups greater authority over the contracting process.) The United States Senate Select Committee on Indian Affairs and several scholars have echoed Reagan's assessment. Federal budget cuts in the 1980s also hurt Native programs. Indian Education Act grants declined 34.6 percent between 1981 and 1988, for example.

Disagreements about self-determination were of course predictable. Native American community leaders and concerned federal officials faced deep-rooted Indian cultural, social, and economic problems not amenable to easy remedy. Although attacked for moving too quickly or not moving fast enough, Congress continued to support self-determination for Native peoples. And well it should, reported Ross O. Swimmer, assistant Secretary of the Interior for Indian affairs in 1988: "We have seen some tremendous benefits. Nearly one-third of our budget of $1 billion is now contracted by tribes[,] and programs are being operated directly by tribal governments that formerly were operated by the Bureau of Indian Affairs . . . [N]ow tribal government is capable of doing planning and development work from the reservation's perspective, and we do not need the Bureau of Indian Affairs to be the overseer."

Native leaders, strengthened by the surge of Indian nationalism and federal money, boldly asserted tribal sovereignty in dealing with federal and state overseers during the 1970s and 1980s. Without control of Native land, water, and wildlife, how could their communities determine the future and strive for economic self-sufficiency? United States Indian groups fought in the courts for land claims, jurisdiction within reservation boundaries, hunting and fishing rights, and for fair access to crucial water resources. Supreme Court decisions generally affirmed sovereign tribal powers. Less controversial, but also illustrative of self-determination activity, were Native claims to their historic artifacts held by non-Natives. In the 1990 Native American Graves Protection and Repatriation Act, Congress established a policy and process for the repatriation of aboriginal human remains, associated funerary objects, and other items of cultural importance.

The future of self-determination for America's aboriginal peoples, who numbered 1,959,234 according to the 1990 census, remains obscure. Flourishing tribal governments are determined to control their communities, and Congress annually appropriates over $3 billion for Indian programs. Difficulties nevertheless remain. In 1989, United States Senate investigators reported that Washington still retains "a stifling bureaucratic presence in Indian country, and fails to deal with tribal governments as responsible partners in our federalist system." Senators called for the tribes to assume the "full responsibilities of self-government"; federal "assets and annual appropriations must be transferred *in toto* to the tribes." Yet, how are poverty-stricken Indian communities to become financially independent of the federal government and truly self-determining? History suggests that the answer must come from Indian country rather than from Uncle Sam. At a meeting with President Ronald Reagan, Hopi Tribal Chairman Ivan Sydney remarked: "We have the best answers to our problems. We need a helping hand, not a handout." Tribal leaders like Sydney, if they are to break the cycle of federal dependency, must continue to rouse their people to the challenges of self-determination.

Edmund J. Danziger, Jr.

See also **American Indian Policy Review Commission; Economic Development; Government Agencies; Indian Education Act, 1972**

Further Reading

Hagan, William T. "Tribalism Rejuvenated: The Native American Since the Era of Termination." *Western Historical Quarterly* 12 (January 1981): 5–16.

O'Brien, Sharon. *American Indian Tribal Governments.* Chap. 5. Norman: University of Oklahoma Press, 1989.

Prucha, Francis Paul. *The Great Father: The United States Government and the American Indians.* Vol. 2. Chaps. 43–47. Lincoln: University of Nebraska Press, 1984.

Stuart, Paul H. "Financing Self-Determination: Federal Indian Expenditures, 1975–1988." *American Indian Culture and Research Journal* 14 (1990): 1–18.

United States Congress. Senate. Special Committee on Investigations of the Select Committee on Indian Affairs. *Final Report and Legislative Recommendations.* 101st Cong., 1st. sess. 1989. S. Rep. 101–216. Washington, DC: U.S. Government Printing Office, 1989.

GRAND RONDE

See Confederated Tribes of Grand Ronde

GROS VENTRE

The home of the Gros Ventre tribe is Fort Belknap, in north central Montana, which encompasses 652,593 acres. Called Atsina by the Blackfeet, their former allies, they call themselves Ah-ah-nee-nin, or "White Clay People."

When the Gros Ventre tribe agreed in 1888 to give up their larger territorial rights and settle for a reservation land base, the federal government wrote, "This reservation to be set apart for the Gros Ventre tribe . . . and such other Indians as the President might, from time to time, see fit to locate thereon . . ." Therefore, the reservation is shared with the Assiniboine tribe, once considered by many to be mortal enemies to the Gros Ventre. Differences between the two tribes continue to exist, yet they have managed to work amazingly well together during the twentieth century. So-called "landless" Indians of the Little Shell and Pembina bands, although not at Fort Belknap by federal mandate, are a past and present part of Gros Ventre communities and many families. While other reservations are pockmarked with non-Indian ownership of land within reservation boundaries, Fort Belknap lands are primarily owned by Indian individuals or the tribes.

The Gros Ventre are a small tribe whose population was decimated by small pox and influenza epidemics. The 1888 enrollment records included 964 Gros Ventres; by the turn of the century this number was reduced to 576. From this low point, Bureau of Indian Affairs records show the population grew to 2,900 in 1992.

Land Loss and Land Claims

The Gros Ventre started legal action first in 1891 to get compensation for lands alienated in an 1855 treaty. They received the first monetary award in 1935. Awards were also made in 1972 for lands ceded by the Gros Ventres and Assiniboines for an unconscionable amount in 1888, and in 1983 for interest from 1874 to 1981 on lands taken by the government for which they were not compensated until 1935. In 1993, interest from treaty fund investments is used by the Gros Ventre Treaty Committee for its burial assistance program and annual family interest payment distributed during the Christmas Holidays.

The Gros Ventre and the Assiniboine vehemently opposed the "sale of the mountains," advocated by federal Commissioners W.C. Pollock, W.M. Clements, and George Bird Grinnell, who were assigned to negotiate the sale of the gold-mining country in 1896. Advising the impoverished Indians that they would starve in two years if they did not make an agreement with the government, Grinnell and Pollock convinced tribal representatives to sell a strip of land, seven miles long and four miles wide, for $360,000. Pegasus Gold Company now mines this site, with heavy opposition from tribal members, such as Joe Azure. This historic theft of land and gold is compounded by the current reality of contaminated land, water, and the accompanying health risks to the reservation people.

Government

The Fort Belknap Community Council was organized under the 1934 Indian Reorganization Act. Its Constitution and Bylaws were approved in 1935, and a corporate Charter was ratified in 1937. The Council has twelve members, six Gros Ventre and six Assiniboine elected by the community at large, with three officers elected by the Council. In 1935, the Gros Ventre opposed the community concept of government, wanting the tribes to retain their individual identities. They were overruled. In 1993, William Main, Gros Ventre, serves as Council chairman, and John Capture is Gros Ventre's eldest active Council member.

A Constitution Review Committee was established in 1992, with three representatives each from the Gros Ventre and Assiniboine tribes, to study, update, and propose changes to the Constitution. Under consideration is the change of tribal names from Gros Ventre to Ah-ah-nee-nin ("White Clay People") and Nakota for the Assiniboine. They are also investigating a confederation form of government to solidify individual tribal identity.

Education

The Gros Ventre realized early in the twentieth century that progress for them entailed developing an educated leadership and striving for political self-determination. Organized education at Fort Belknap began with the Industrial Boarding School, which served the people from 1891 until it closed in 1934. St. Paul's Mission School opened in 1887 and is still operating. In 1993, most Gros Ventre children attend public schools in Lodgepole, Hays, Harlem, and Dodson; some go to off-reservation boarding schools. The Fort Belknap Education Department was established in 1977. Loren "Bum" Stiffarm, past president of the National Indian Education Association, serves as its director.

The Fort Belknap Community College opened in 1984. Its curriculum blends culture with academic subjects. A library and tribal archives were added in 1988, and the college is presently seeking funding to construct a museum, with the assistance of George P. Horse Capture, a well-known Gros Ventre historian and museum curator.

Culture

Indian culture is so integrated into daily living and thinking that it is difficult to discuss separately. Annual Gros Ventre activities include the Hays Community Powwow and the Hays Christmas Powwow.

While approximately ten tribal members speak the Gros Ventre language fluently, revival and retention of both language and culture are of top priority to Gros Ventre people. The Gros Ventre language is currently taught in the elementary grades and at the Community College.

The traditional Gros Ventre religion centers around the two sacred pipes, the Feathered Pipe and the Flat Pipe, given to the Gros Ventre people by the Great Spirit. The largest Christian denomination is Catholicism.

The Economy

Fort Belknap has an agriculturally based economy, that includes farming, ranching, and leasing lands. The federal and tribal governments, however, are the major employers. The unemployment rate is 54 percent, and 40 percent of those employed have an income of less than $7,000 annually. From an average take-home salary of $583 monthly, families living in Housing and Urban Development homes pay 25 percent of this income for housing, leaving a consumable spending amount of $438 per month.

The tribe has developed businesses such as stores and a bingo hall, but the growth of business does not equal the need for jobs. Gaming machines also add money to the tribal coffers, usually at the expense of tribal members who can ill afford it.

Health

Only 10 percent of the reservation population lived free of tuberculosis in 1912. Mrs. Julia Ereaux Schultz, a Gros Ventre, was chairman of the Montana Tuberculosis Association during this time. Influenza epidemics, trachoma, and tuberculosis continued to plague the reservation, whose primitive infirmary served as a death house for terminal cases. A small hospital was finally completed in 1931. While health on the reservation has improved since that time, this sixty-two-year-old structure with a capacity of fewer than ten beds continues to house most of the Indian Health Service's activities.

The Gros Ventre in the Twentieth Century

The most outstanding feature of the Gros Ventre is our ability to survive—not so much as a "tribe," but as a people, alive and well. There have been tremendous changes, losses in "quantity," including reductions in blood degree, language, and cultural practices. But being Gros Ventre is not about numbers or quantity; it is about quality of the spirit, the soul, and the inner being. It is a willingness to place being Gros Ventre over "self," to know the deep debt owed to our grandparents and to our ancestors. It is better for us to be one drop Gros Ventre than to be 100 percent of anything else. Lonesome is the human being who does not know or care what his history is, or who he really is. Coming together in the twenty-first century, the White Clay People will find the comfort that has remained just out of their reach, knowing that it will be good.

Jessie James-Hawley

See also Assiniboine

Further Reading

Bull Lodge. *The Seven Visions of Bull Lodge; as Told by His Daughter, Garter Snake.* Comp. Fred P. Gone. Ed. George P. Horse Capture. Ann Arbor, MI: Bear Claw, 1980. Lincoln: University of Nebraska Press, 1992.

Cooper, John M. *The Gros Ventres of Montana.* Part 2. *Religion and Ritual.* Ed. Regina Flannery. The Catholic University of America Anthropological Series 16. Washington, DC: 1957, 1975.

Flannery, Regina. *The Gros Ventre of Montana.* Part 1. *Social Life.* The Catholic University of America Anthropological Series 15. Washington, DC: 1953, 1975.

Fowler, Loretta. *Shared Symbols, Contested Meanings: Gros Ventre Culture and History, 1778–1984.* Ithaca, NY: Cornell University Press, 1987.

Penney, David W. *Art of the American Indian Frontier: The Chandler-Pohrt Collection.* Seattle: University of Washington Press, 1992.

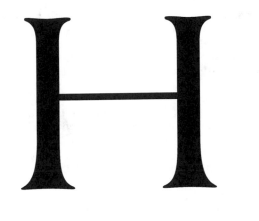

HAIDA

The Haida are an international tribe. In the United States, the Alaska Haida were located in the traditional villages of Howkan, Koinglas, Klinquan, Sukkwan, and Kasaan; most of the people of these villages relocated to the villages of Hydaburg and Craig as well as Ketchikan, Seattle and other urban centers. Today, Hydaburg is the last organized Haida community in Alaska; Kasaan still remains but has a sparse Haida population. The 1990 census gives a total United States Haida population of 1,805, with 342 Haidas in Hydaburg. In Canada, the principal villages are Skidegate and Massett, with Haidas also located at Prince Rupert and Vancouver.

During the latter half of the nineteenth century, the United States government sought a peaceful solution to the "Indian Problem" in the United States by initiating a long-term partnership with the major religious societies in the nation to educate and civilize Native Americans. It was hoped that by incorporating the individual Indians into the larger body politic as individuals, rather than as tribal members, bloodshed between the tribes and the federal government could be averted. In furthering this philosophy, two Presbyterian ministers, S. Hall Young and G. W. Lyon, made a visit to Cordova Bay in the spring of 1880 and located a site for a new mission town adjacent to existing Haida villages to be established on what was described as the "Metlakatlah plan": " . . . first a sawmill, which would soon pay for itself—the Indians readily buying the lumber—the church and school house built by native workmen properly directed, then a town of neat commodious houses, built and filled by a population which subscribes to the laws, and conforms to the plans of the settlement." This plan was adopted by the Presbyterian Board of Home Missions and was discussed at various times in the period from 1890 to 1910, but was not implemented until the fall of 1911. Hydaburg was established with the assistance and encouragement of the Bureau of Education and the Presbyterian Church. Howkan,

Klinquan, and Sukkwan were eventually abandoned due to the withdrawal of the government-funded school and appurtenant services and support.

Moving to Hydaburg was not a unanimous decision. Some Haidas wanted to continue life in the old towns according to the customs and traditions of their ancestors, whereas others believed that the move to Hydaburg was their only way to participate in the civilized progress of mankind. These differences continue to this day.

In 1912 President William H. Taft created a 7,833.6 acre (12.24 square mile) executive order reservation for the Haida; however, in 1926, President Calvin Coolidge revoked the reservation created by President Taft and made instead a two-acre school reserve. With the passage of the Indian Reorganization Act in 1934 and its amendment to include the Natives of Alaska in 1936, Hydaburg became the first Native group in Alaska to adopt a Constitution under its authority. Once organized, the Haida petitioned the federal government for a 905,000-acre reservation. Over the next eleven years, the Haida experienced a confusing and divisive legal exercise that left them bereft of their reservation and uncertain of their political and economic future. There was general non-Native opposition to the reservation policy of the Department of the Interior, which was organized and coordinated by the Alaska Salmon Industry, Inc., an organization which lobbied federally to protect their extensive commercial fishery activities, which had by this time severely impacted Native fishing in southeast Alaska.

In September of 1944 the Department of the Interior began a series of hearings on the claims of the Natives of the villages of Hydaburg, Klawock, and Kake. In July 1945 the secretary of the interior issued his findings of fact and conclusions of law. On November 30, 1949, Secretary of the Interior Julius Krug proclaimed the Hydaburg Indian Reservation and called for an election of the Natives of Hydaburg. On April 24, 1950, an election was held at which the reservation was accepted by a vote of ninety-five for, to twenty-nine against. Shortly after the Hydaburg Reservation was proclaimed, the Alaska Salmon Industry issued a memorandum objecting to its establishment. In 1951, Hydaburg filed suit in federal court to compel Libby, McNeill, and Libby to pay a fee for locating a fish trap off the shores of the reservation. The federal judge, in his inflammatory decision denying trespass, also ruled that the Hydaburg Indian Reservation was not validly created.

Congress had passed the Tlingit and Haida Jurisdictional Act in 1935, which authorized the Tlingit and Haida tribes to bring suit against the United States for the loss of their tribal territories and in 1959 the Tlingit and Haida Indian tribes of Alaska were awarded a $7.5 million judgment by the Court of Claims for their aboriginal claims to southeast Alaska. The terms of this settlement were not implemented until 1970. In December, 1971, the United States Congress passed the Alaska Native Claims Settlement Act (ANCSA). Under the terms of this act, the Haida established the Haida Corporation in Hydaburg; Kavilco in Kasaan; and Shaan Seet, Inc., in Craig. In May 1985 Haida Corporation filed bankruptcy and pursuant to an act of Congress passed in 1986, it had to sell a portion of its land to settle past debts and to reorganize.

Hydaburg is incorporated as a first class city under the laws of Alaska. Although the municipal government is presently predominantly Haida, there are no guarantees to assure that it remains Haida or that it will remain sympathetic to the needs and desires of the Haida people. The people recognize that it is in their best interest to maintain a close relationship with the State of Alaska, but at the same time they know that the state is not an advocate for tribal rights and entitlements. The Haida continue to seek self-determination for their people. The Hydaburg City School District is a municipal organization governed by a five-member school board who are also predominantly Haida. The school board has sought to incorporate the Haida cultural knowledge and traditions into the curriculum. The economy for the Alaska Haida in recent years has been focused on logging with the hope of utilizing the money gained from logging to develop sustainable enterprises.

The twentieth century has been a difficult period of transition for the Haida. A general history of the Haida is made difficult by the diverse responses of the various Haida villages to the problems and opportunities presented by the encroaching Canadian and United States societies. The traditional values of the people are being reassessed in light of these responses. The Haida continue to cherish and maintain their cultural heritage and to assert their rights as aboriginal people.

Adrian LeCornu

Further Reading

Blackman, Margaret B. "Haida: Traditional Culture." *Handbook of North American Indians*. Vol. 7. *Northwest Coast*. Ed. Wayne Suttles. Washington, DC: Smithsonian Institution (1990): 240–60.

Stearns, Mary Lee. "Haida Since 1960." *Handbook of North American Indians*. Vol. 7. *Northwest Coast*. Ed. Wayne Suttles. Washington, DC: Smithsonian Institution (1990): 261–66.

Worl, Rosita. "History of Southeastern Alaska Since 1867." *Handbook of North American Indians*. Vol. 7. *Northwest Coast*. Ed. Wayne Suttles. Washington, DC: Smithsonian Institution (1990): 149–58.

HALIWA-SAPONI

The Haliwa-Saponi tribe resides on the border of Halifax and Warren counties, North Carolina. The first part of the tribe's name—Haliwa—derives from a combination of the names of the two counties; the second part—Saponi—refers to a tribe that for a period of time resided in nearby Nash County. Many tribal members are actually descended from a Nansemond family of the seventeenth century. The original name of the community, which dates back to the eighteenth century, was the Meadows. The family names of the original Indian settlers included Richardson, Bass, and Weaver, supplemented in the nineteenth century by Lynch, Silver, Mills, and Hedgepeth. All but Bass and Weaver survive as tribal names today.

Throughout the nineteenth century the Haliwa-Saponi community remained isolated from other non-Indian groups. It developed its own schools and churches. In the 1880s lumber companies began exploiting the pine forests of the area, and soon there was an influx of Black workers and white managers. Due to segregation, a two-tiered school system developed with the Indian children forced to attend the schools for Blacks. Many Indian parents refused to send their children, and some attempted to operate private schools. The state took steps to enforce its segregated rules, and, as a result, many parents moved away while their children were growing up, particularly to Washington, Baltimore, and Philadelphia, where schools were better and jobs more abundant. The settlement of non-Indians in the vicinity of the Meadows resulted in the establishment of a number of Indian churches. These, and the Indian private schools, became the principal vehicle for the expression of Indian identity. Important tribal leaders at the turn of the twentieth century were Tilman Lynch, Cofield Richardson, Bill Silver, and Gordon Hedgepeth.

Following World War II, the tribe more formally organized, first under the name of the Essex Indian Club and later as the Haliwa Indian Club. Finally, in the 1970s it adopted its present name. The tribe organized with two principal concerns in mind: establishing an Indian high school and correcting the birth certificates of members to reflect their Indian ancestry. In the 1950s, the community built and operated its own high school; in 1964, it successfully prosecuted a case to force the state to change the birth certificates of all of its members to show that they are Indian. In 1967, the tribe sponsored the first Haliwa-Saponi Powwow, which continues to this day as one of the largest events of its type in the Southeast. The individual who was primarily instrumental in achieving these goals was William R. (W.R.) Richardson, who has served as chief for over thirty years.

Presently the tribe is governed by an elected chief and a Tribal Council. Besides Chief Richardson, other present-day tribal leaders include the Reverend C.H. Richardson, who although in his nineties continues to preach every Sunday; and Linda Mills, the tribe's executive director. The tribe is presently seeking federal acknowledgment from the Department of the Interior. It owns a tribal building, a tribal center, a day-care center, and has invested in a number of small businesses. The tribe presently numbers 2,700.

Jack Campisi

Further Reading

Bell, Albert D. *Bass Families of the South*. Rocky Mount, NC: Privately published, 1961.

Brewington, C.D. *The Five Civilized Tribes of Eastern North Carolina.* Clinton, NC: Bass Publishing Co., 1959.

Feest, Christian F. "Notes on Saponi Settlements in Virginia Prior to 1714." *Quarterly Bulletin, Archaeological Society of Virginia* 28 (1974): 152–55.

Swanton, John R. *The Indians of the Southeastern United States.* Bureau of American Ethnology Bulletin 137 (1946). Washington, DC: Smithsonian Institution Press, 1979.

Williams, Walter L., ed. *Southeastern Indians Since the Removal Era.* Athens: The University of Georgia Press, 1979.

HAN

See Alaskan Athabaskans

HANNAHVILLE POTAWATOMI

See Potawatomi in Northern Michigan

HASINAI

See Caddo

HAVASUPAI

The Havasupai are the descendants of the easternmost of thirteen regional bands of the upland Yuman-speaking Pai. Separated from the other Pai bands by the Hualapai War (1866 to 1869), and the government's perception of them as a separate people, in 1880 the Havasupai received a reservation of 518 acres at the bottom of Havasu Canyon. This canyon carves into the Coconino Plateau, draining northward into the Grand Canyon. At Supai, the present site of the tribal population, the canyon floor is at 3,300 feet above sea level. Springs feed a permanent stream which cascades over a series of waterfalls on its way to the Colorado River, some ten miles to the north. The waters of the stream have been and continue to be used to irrigate 200 acres of alluvial silt within the boundaries of the reservation.

Through the fall, winter, and spring, the Havasupai lived by hunting and gathering. Only in the summer did some of their number go to Havasu Canyon to make gardens. Prior to the establishment of the reservation, the Havasupai were organized into ten local groups, with a mean size of twenty-eight. These local groups were composed of patrilocal extended families that served as domestic groups. The regional band really represented a network of personal, marital, kinship, and friendship ties which linked individuals in the ten local groups. In the summer, perhaps 200 of these people might live near each other in Havasu Canyon, and the men of the regional band occasionally joined to fight the Yavapai. In short, the enduring cooperative groups were the local groups and families. The Havasupai had no tradition or developed institutions to facilitate bandwide, corporate action.

Havasupai religion was shamanistic. While there were weather shamans, most practitioners focused on diagnosing and curing illness in individuals, and everyone had access to the supernatural through dreams. Group activities were restricted to an annual harvest dance in Havasu Canyon and occasional social dances and funerals.

With the creation of the reservation, all this began to change. Miners, ranchers, the United States Forest Service and, eventually, Grand Canyon National Park increasingly forced them off their traditional hunting-gathering range. Initially, this led to an increase in gardening on the reservation in Havasu Canyon. However, the Havasupai rapidly began to substitute wage work with the Bureau of Indian Affairs (BIA) on the reservation, the Park Service at the Grand Canyon, and ranchers on Forest Service and private lands for gardening and gathering. They also developed a small cattle herd which was run on lands leased from the government and which substituted for hunting. By the 1920s, cash income from wages and cattle exceeded the value of garden produce, and by 1939 the tribe had been effectively transformed into wage workers dependent on the BIA and the Park Service for jobs. They supplemented their wages with meat and cash from cattle, and with garden produce.

Havasupai economic dependence was paralleled by political dependence. With their concentration on the reservation, winter local groups lost their functions and disappeared. As tribal members became increasingly dependent on federal wages and as the BIA increasingly managed reservation economic development, transportation and communication, education, health, and social control, the leaders or chiefs lost their significance. As this occurred, fewer young males earned the title and the number of chiefs dwindled.

The decline in the power of indigenous leaders did not end with the creation of a Tribal Council in 1939. The Council included four elected members and three chiefs. The latter were to be replaced by election from among the surviving sub-chiefs as they died or retired, thus institutionalizing a role which had been dying. However, for the first twenty-five years of the Council's existence (1939 to 1964), it had few financial resources, no technical expertise, little to manage, and virtually no prestige among tribal members. Two of the three hereditary chiefs married out of the tribe and left the reservation, leaving Council to be run by the four elected members and the third chief.

If the economic and political transformation of the period from 1880 to 1939 destroyed Havasupai economic independence and the few political roles and processes they had brought to the reservation system, the years 1940 to 1964 threatened to destroy the patrilocal extended family. In the early reservation years (1880 to 1920) and before the reservation, a marriage and new family began to emerge when a man moved into a woman's family's camp, to work and live there for several years or until the birth of a child. At this point, couples generally moved to the camp of the male and, when he was young, to live with his parents. As they matured and begot children, the extended family cut new gardens from free and fallow lands to feed the growing household. If the family shrank due to death or girls moving off with husbands, gardens were abandoned and, as the improvements disappeared, these lands became free and open to other families.

Eventually, when the family head became incompetent or died, the son would succeed him as head of the household, managing things until his sisters left and his younger brothers matured, married, and began their own families. As the family cycled joint activities fragmented; maturing younger couples established separate houses for sleeping, separate tables and, eventually, separate gardens. The extended family finally dissolved when the brothers and any resident females divided the improved lands.

The cycle became increasingly difficult as the population recovered from the epidemics which had reduced it to 166 by 1906. As it grew, growing families could no longer find free cultivatable land, which had disappeared by 1936. Wages dampened the potential for conflict in this, as senior brothers tended to use their position as successors to the family head to keep control of family land for their children, while their brothers relied on wages on the reservation and elsewhere. However, with the onset of World War II and following the war, when federal Indian policy aimed at terminating the trust relationship, reservation wages declined.

The decline culminated in 1955 when the local day school, open more or less continuously since 1892 and a major source of reservation wages, was closed. At that point, wage income was less than it was in 1930 and the Havasupai were trying to live by purchasing food in the tribal store at prices 140 percent of retail prices in neighboring towns. In response, gardening expanded but so too did conflicts over land. Maturing extended families were strained by suppressed, and sometimes open, violent competition among brothers. This competition and its impact on extended families were exacerbated after 1960 when new economic developments began to ameliorate the loss of wages.

Tourists discovered Havasu Canyon after 1960. In 1963 and 1964, 4,000 visited the roadless but beautiful canyon, and many rented pack or saddle horses from tribal members to travel the eight-mile trail into the canyon. Income from horse rentals and other sales to tourists raised per capita income to $315 per year by 1963 and 1964, but it also increased the competition for land. Packing tourists was the largest source of cash income, but it required horses and horses required pasture. The result was fraternal strife in families with multiple sons and increasing difficulties in family life. As Havasupai culture—origin accounts, religion, folktales, and other cultural knowledge—was transmitted mainly in the family, family strife and the removal of children at age six to go to boarding schools led to considerable cultural loss. The years 1940 to 1964 were thus ones of economic deprivation, political impotence, and deculturation.

Fortunately, changes in federal policies after 1960 and the continued growth of tourism began to alter these trends. As federal policy shifted to reservation development and stronger self-government, and especially after tribal governments were allowed to contract with federal agencies to provide these agencies' services on the reservations, wage labor began to expand. The school was reopened and the growth of training and other educational programs, as well as the provision of new housing and other physical facilities, added to the wage work. Tourism also grew to roughly 30,000 visitors a year; today it generates 60 percent of the $2,800 annual per capita income.

A significant portion of the tourist-generated income is earned in a new lodge and restaurant, and at the tribal store. The result, besides an increase in wages and a decrease in land conflicts and intrafamilial strife, has been a tremendous growth in the prestige and importance of the Tribal Council, which directly or indirectly controls the wage work. In addition, with overhead funds and interest from Indian claims money, the Council hires its own advisors, bypassing the BIA and empowering itself in the process. Such advisors and the tribe's growing financial resources were instrumental in the success of their struggle to have the reservation expanded, a struggle which culminated in the addition of 185,000 acres in 1975. Their success in turn fueled the Council's prestige and the tribe's feeling of having some control over its destiny.

The Council is now a rallying point for another struggle which pits the Havasupai as a people against outsiders. Recent advances in technology have led to the discovery of uranium deposits along the southern and eastern boundaries of the reservation. All are in the drainage area which goes right through the center of Supai. The first of a series of proposed mines has been the focus of a continuing but unsuccessful struggle by the tribe to stop exploration of the deposits through regulatory and court actions. To date, they have fought the mine on the basis of the American Indian Religious Freedom Act, claiming that the mine site at Red Butte, Arizona is on or near a sacred site. In part due to the absence of references to Red Butte in the anthropological and historical literature, they have lost at every level, most recently in the Supreme Court.

While their struggle has yet to achieve its manifest end, it has reinforced the tribe's growing sense of political community, something which did not really exist until recently. And, as the fight has been waged on religious grounds, this growth in communal political consciousness has taken a religious cast. While dimensions of the traditional religion which focused on individuals (curing and individual dreaming) have declined, the communal dimensions have grown and new ones have been elaborated.

Whether or not Red Butte was sacred in the past, it is now, and the tribe holds an annual politico-religious gathering there, maintaining it is the locus of an "earth navel" through which ancestors climbed to the present world and where "Grandmother" and "Grandson," figures in a traditional world renewal story, stage their periodic, life-sustaining reunions. The annual peach festival, while still highly social, has come to be infused with strong religious and nationalistic activity, and teenagers may be heard in the tribal cafe discussing traditional religious concepts. For guidance in these discussions, they turn to a semi-official religious leader, a member of the Tribal Council whose family came from the Red Butte area. This sincerely religious man is striving to preserve and spread what he takes to be the traditional religion. In short, the traditional religion is resurgent but is also being transformed.

At the same time, many young people, in particular young males, have embraced Rastafarianism. The image of Bob Marley graces many house walls, the tribe has its own, commercially successful reggae band, dreadlocks are in evidence, and there are now reggae songs about Red Butte. Balancing off against these two politico-religious developments is a small, Christian community led by a white pastor who married into the tribe and who emphasizes the salvation of souls.

In summary, since 1880 the Havasupai have experienced tremendous economic, political, social, and religious change. Transformed from a loosely related collection of families and winter camp groups, the population is growing into a small (565 people) corporate, politically aggressive community, with a resurgent and creative religious and cultural life.

John F. Martin

Further Reading

Dobyns, Henry F., and Robert C. Euler. *The Havasupai People*. Phoenix, AZ: Indian Tribal Series, 1971.

Hirst, Stephen. *Havasuw' Baaja: People of the Blue Green Water*. Supai, AZ: Havasupai Tribe, 1985.

Martin, John F. "The Havasupai." *Plateau* 56:4 (1986): 1–32.

Schwartz, Douglas. "Havasupai." *Handbook of North American Indians*. Vol. 10. *Southwest*. Ed. Alfonso Ortiz. Washington, DC: Smithsonian Institution (1983): 13–24.

Smithson, Carma Lee, and Robert C. Euler. *Havasupai Religion and Mythology*. University of Utah Anthropological Papers 68. 1964. New York, NY: Johnson Reprint, 1971.

Spier, Leslie. *Havasupai Ethnography*. Anthropological Papers of the American Museum of Natural History 29, Pt. 3. New York, NY: American Museum Press (1928): 81–329.

HEALTH

The health of American Indian people has improved since the 1900s; however, the health of American Indians is still worse than the United States population by almost every indicator. There is a tremendous challenge regarding health today because the Indian population continues to increase, and because it is younger than the United States population by almost eight years. The unique and diverse cultures of American Indian people—who also have an extraordinary relationship with the federal government—add an additional challenge, which can best be met by better understanding the people and their rich cultural heritages that have impacted on almost every aspect of American life.

Since the arrival of Europeans on these shores, Indian people have lost almost everything—from original lands to personal dignity and self-worth. Indian sacred customs and traditional ways of life have changed forever. The introduction of disease with viruses and bacteria that were not familiar to the medicine men and women of that time caused the annihilation of Indian people at a devastating rate. The changing way of life eroded the health of Indian people, with the introduction of alcohol, sugar, and very different social and religious customs. Today, many tribes face the potential devastation of their tribal existence due to the high incidence of alcoholism, diabetes, chronic disease, and inordinate social and cultural stresses.

The Native American Population

American Indians and Alaska Natives today are composed of more than 500 federally recognized tribes, tribal groups, and Alaska Native villages. The federal Indian policy reaffirms the government-to-government relationship that exists between today's tribal nations and the United States government. There are over 150 different languages spoken among Indians today. American Indian people are a very diverse group that presents a geographic picture of tribal people from Barrow, Alaska to the Everglades in Florida. The American Indian and Alaska Native population is growing and changing rapidly. Indian people numbered fewer than 240,000 in 1900, and only 260,000 by 1950, according to the census. By 1980, the population had grown to nearly 1.4 million. According to the 1990 census, there were 1,959,234 identified as American Indian and Alaska Natives. The Indian population is younger than the United States population by almost eight years (twenty-two versus thirty). On the average, an Indian nuclear family consists of five people in comparison with the four-member family of the general population. These differences require models of health services and disease prevention approaches unlike those used for the general population. In addition, cultural heritage and language become barriers to effective and efficient health delivery and disease prevention.

Early Health Services

The earliest services to Indians began in 1803 to curb smallpox and other contagious diseases in the vicinity of military posts. The primary intent was to protect the military from disease. Congress authorized the secretary of war to provide vaccinations to Indians to prevent smallpox in 1832. By 1890, the Indian Office hired physicians, who often gave pills rather than medical care, for reservation Indians. An early example was a doctor at Pine Ridge agency, who dispensed medicine to the Sioux and Cheyennes through a hole in his office wall.

The early focus was on control of communicable diseases and prevention associated with the spread of

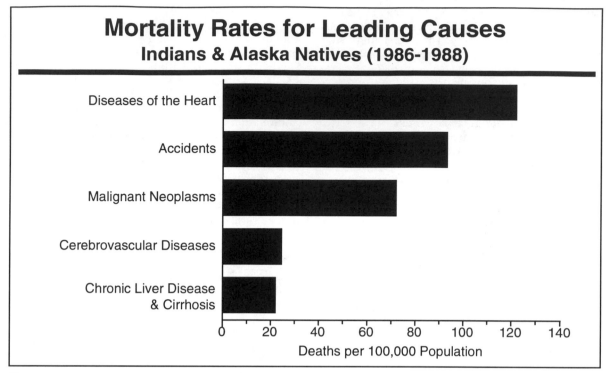

Figure 1

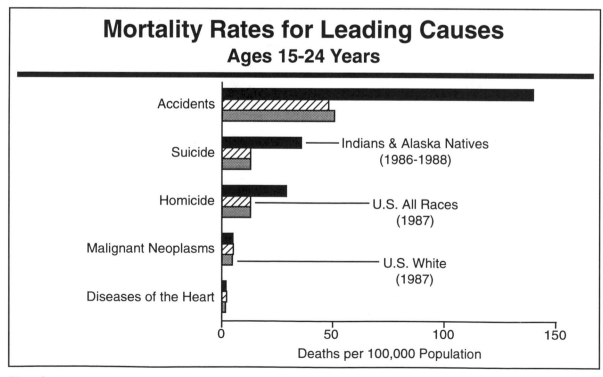

Figure 2

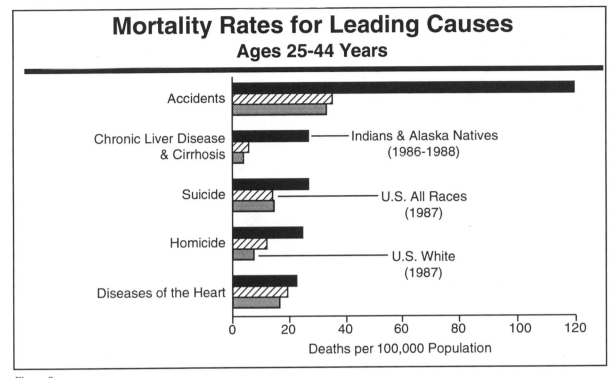

Figure 3

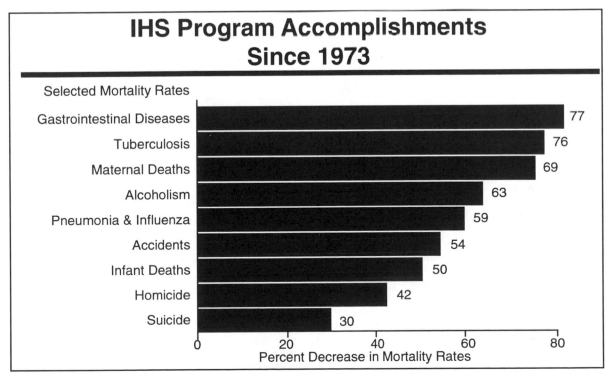

Figure 4

such diseases, particularly tuberculosis and trachoma. The discovery of sulfanilamide around 1938 rapidly cured or arrested trachoma. Institutional and school sanatoria for tuberculosis prevention and treatment were started in 1911 for children excluded from boarding schools. The period between the early 1900s and 1955 resulted in heightened interest in defining responsibility for Indian health and establishing more vigorous preventive programs.

Indian Health Since 1955

Diseases of the heart are the leading cause of death today for American Indians and for the United States population in general. This indicates a transition from acute disease to chronic diseases emerging as the primary health concern (figure 1). Today, accidents rank as the second leading cause of death among the Indian population. Malignant neoplasms rank third and cerebrovascular diseases rank fourth as causes of death. About 33 percent of the Indian population dies before age 45, compared to 11 percent for the overall United States population. Rather disturbing are the mortality rates for children age 15 to 24 (figure 2) with very high accident rates, as well as suicide and homicide rates. Causes of death for the ages from 25 to 44 indicate the involvement of alcohol, with chronic liver disease and cirrhosis as well as accidents being unusually high in prevalence (figure 3).

There is a lower prevalence of cancer among American Indians; however, breast cancer is increasing. The prevalence of diabetes and gallbladder disease are higher than the general population. Diabetes Mellitus death rate is 2.6 times higher than the United States population. The loss of limbs due to diabetes and diabetic retinopathy are of critical concern in the treatment and management of diabetic cases. Diabetes does not hit all Indian populations equally. The Pima Indians in Arizona, for example, are near epidemic proportions, while the incidence is very low among Eskimos. There are several model diabetes health care programs that serve as excellent examples of programs focusing on the prevention and treatment needed to control diabetes among American Indians. Tribes operating diabetes education programs work with both the Indian Health Service (IHS) and the American Diabetes Association. They represent the future of health programs to Indians. Multidisciplinary teams with upgraded preventive services provide routine screening for complications, patient education, nutrition counseling, foot care, and related conditions. These programs are culturally sensitive in working with the Indian tribes. While the results are still being evaluated, there is hope that these and other programs will reduce the complications of diabetes and provide innovative and needed health direction for the prevention of diseases and related conditions for American Indians.

Another disease suffered disproportionally by Native Americans is gastrointestinal disease. The rate for American Indians has decreased by 86 percent since 1955. However, the rate is still 62 percent higher than the United States population. Sanitation and environmental programs with facilities, solid waste disposal systems, and technical assistance to tribes for sanitation facilities have been provided by the IHS. This includes sanitation services that have been provided to over 176,000 Indian homes since 1960. Unfortunately, many water and sewer facilities on reservations are inadequate, requiring an inordinate amount of maintenance for outdated equipment. This is a very important concern in looking at the health status of Indian people, particularly since acute infectious diseases can occur again as they did in the early 1900s without these facilities and controls.

The Indian Health Service Successes

The IHS of the United States Public Health Service is charged with administering the principal health program for American Indians and Alaska Natives. The drastic reduction in infant mortality has served as an example of what can be done to improve the Indian health status. Since 1955, the infant mortality rate has decreased by 80 percent. The IHS has been very successful in programs associated with gastroenteritis, diabetes, fetal alcohol syndrome, maternal and child care, community health representative programs, community injury control, and alcoholism (figure 4). Key to these special initiatives and approaches is tribal involvement and respect for cultural traditions and environment. The goal of the IHS is to raise the health status of the American Indian and Alaska Natives to the highest possible level. The cooperation between the Congress and the IHS has meant improved programs and health for Indian people. Of course, funding through appropriation never seems to be enough to curb the high prevalence of disease and historical abuse done to our Indian population.

In summary, diversity and disparity are very real concerns in regard to the status of the health of our Indian population. It is a story of too little, too late. The government-to-government relationship does not provide entitlement programs to some Indian people who too often get caught in the squeeze between federal regulations, congressional intent, and the basis on which this relationship was based, namely treaties, executive orders, and judicial decisions.

The answer on how to improve the health status of Indian people depends on increased appropriations and resources focused on programs that have demonstrated success. The involvement of tribes, local universities, private service organizations, and a renewed involvement of the states can make the difference. Greater emphasis on self-governance in program management by tribes and tribal organizations, with technical assistance provided by the federal government, will turn the corner in the future on resolving the health problems of the Indian population.

An Indian elder once said that the heart of any program serving Indian people must be in the heart of the people themselves. As is the practice in Indian tradition, there must continue to be a coming together into the circle in a sacred way to begin to solve the problems and concerns.

J.T. Garrett

Further Reading

Garrett, J.T. "Indian Health: Values, Beliefs, and Practices." Publication No. HRSA-DV90–4. Rockville, MD: Public Health Service, Health, Resources, and Services Administration. 179–91.

Todd, John G. "Implication of Policy and Management Decisions for Native Americans." *International Journal of Health Planning and Management* 2 (1987): 259–68.

U.S. Department of Health and Human Services. *Prevalence of Chronic Diseases: A Summary of Data from the Survey of American Indians and Alaska Natives.* Data Summary 3. *APHCPR Publication* 91–0031. Rockville, MD: Agency for Health Care Policy and Research, Center for General Health Service Intramural Research, 1991.

U.S. Indian Health Service. *Trends in Indian Health.* Rockville, MD: 1991.

HIDATSA

See Three Affiliated Tribes

HIGHER EDUCATION

From 1900 to 1930 there was limited activity in the domain of higher education for Native Americans. This was largely the result of the federal sector neither encouraging nor supporting advanced education for tribal people. The government's position of nonsupport was best expressed by Theodore Roosevelt who wrote in his presidential report of 1901: "In the [Indian] schools the education should be elementary and largely industrial" since "the need of higher education among the Indians is very, very limited." Thus, before 1921, the Bureau of Indian Affairs' (BIA) large, off-reservation boarding schools ended at the eighth or tenth grades. None offered all twelve grades. As a result, it was difficult if not impossible for Indian students to pursue a college or university education in the opening decades of the twentieth century.

It was the Native Americans themselves who wanted more education at the outset of this century. Certainly this was the case with the Society of American Indians (SAI), the intertribal organization founded in 1911 by a few college-educated Indians. The most vocal SAI advocate for higher education was Henry Roe Cloud, a full-blood Winnebago Indian who graduated from Yale University. Roe Cloud believed that Indians needed a full high school education in order to enter college. He therefore established the American Indian Institute (1915 to 1939) for this purpose. Located in Wichita, Kansas, and funded by private donors and other sources, his institute was one of the first all-Indian high schools emphasizing college preparation. Roe Cloud was later a member of the Meriam Report staff, which produced the well-known Meriam Report of 1928. This lengthy reform document stated that the federal government should provide educational loans and grants for Indians accepted into college. Several Meriam Report recommendations, including the ones for Indian education, were carried out in the following decade.

The development of higher education therefore blossomed in the 1930s. In this decade, the federal sector committed itself to providing funds for the postsecondary education of Native students. In 1930 Congress authorized an annual $15,000 for an educational loan fund for those admitted into colleges, universities, and other postsecondary institutions. In 1932 it authorized $10,000 annually for grants to defray tuition. These two sources allowed many students to pursue a higher education, and some became notable public figures. One of the early loan recipients was Benjamin Reifel, a Lakota who graduated from the South Dakota College of Agriculture and Mechanic Arts in 1932. He later became a United States congressman representing his home state of South Dakota.

The major source of funding for Native American higher education came from the Indian Reorganization Act (IRA) of 1934. One of its provisions allowed Congress to appropriate $50,000 annually for another higher education loan fund. From 1935 to 1944, 1,933 Native students received IRA loans to pursue postsecondary education: 458 of them graduated from four-year colleges and universities; 159 from postsecondary vocational schools; and 126 from nursing schools. Like the earlier 1930 loan fund, the IRA loans had to be repaid within eight years after graduation.

By the 1940s the BIA recognized that many Indian college students had become indebted under the IRA loan program. They simply could not generate enough capital to repay their loans. To prevent further indebtedness, the Branch of Education of the BIA no longer issued loans in the post-World War II period. Replacing the loan program was the Indian Bureau's Higher Education Grant Program (HEGP), established in 1948 when Congress amended the language of the IRA appropriations bill to include non-reimbursable educational grants for higher education. Administered by the BIA's area offices, the HEGP has grown over the years. In 1950 the grant fund totaled only $9,390 and benefited only forty-nine Native students. By 1972 the appropriation was $15 million and was shared by 12,438 students. The HEGP still exists in the early 1990s and continues to be the main source of federal assistance for Native American college students.

One of the more important historic developments in twentieth-century Native American higher education was the establishment of the Navajo Community College (NCC). Founded and chartered by the Navajo Nation in 1968, this unique two-year Native college was the first reservation-based postsecondary institution to be run by a Native government. Much of NCC's financial support comes from the Navajo Community College Act, enacted by Congress in 1971. Under this law, NCC has received up to $5.5 million for the "construction, maintenance, and operation" of the college. NCC now has a permanent campus located in Tsaile, Arizona. The college was fully accredited by the North Central Association of Colleges and Schools in 1976.

Besides the Navajo, other tribes have also recognized the importance of and the need for community-based higher education. As a result, since 1970, twenty-seven other tribal colleges have emerged.

In 1973 the existing Indian colleges created the American Indian Higher Education Consortium (AIHEC) to deal with mutual concerns and problems. The biggest concern was funding for institutional development. As a result, AIHEC became a lobbying group to persuade Congress to appropriate funds for college development. Its efforts paid off in 1978 when Congress passed the Tribally Controlled Community College Assistance Act (TCCCAA). This act provides grants for the "operation and improvement" of the existent Native postsecondary institutions run and chartered by tribal governments. TCCCAA was amended twice, in 1983 and again in 1986, allocating more funds for the Indian colleges.

Besides the TCCCAA, Congress has passed other legislation to benefit Native American higher education. The Indian Education Act of 1972 was one of these laws. In part it authorizes federal funds for university-based teacher training programs. This higher education provision was included because of the limited number of Native teachers serving tribal students in elementary and secondary schools. Several university-based programs became the recipients of these 1972 act funds, including the Center for Indian Education at Arizona State University and the Native American Program at Pennsylvania State University.

In 1974 Congress amended the Indian Education Act of 1972 to include a special graduate-level fellowship program. Around two hundred fellowships were awarded each year under the "Indian Fellowship Program" for graduates majoring in medicine, law, education, business administration, engineering, and natural resources. Although current information is not available, figures do exist for the Indian students funded during the academic years 1977 to 1978: two hundred seven received fellowships; fifty-seven of these graduated in the spring of 1978; one hundred forty-one were continuing their education after the spring term of 1978; four had withdrawn from the program after receiving monies from other sources; nine withdrew completely; and one did not reapply for the academic year 1978 to 1979.

In addition to the 1972 Indian Education Act and its 1974 amendment, the Indian Health Care Improvement Act of 1976 also impacted Native American higher education. Title I, as it was referred to, created the "Indian Health Scholarships." This program was established because of the limited number of professionally-trained Natives serving their people in the health professions. Qualified students now receive scholarships to pursue "study in schools of medicine, osteopathy, dentistry . . . nursing, or allied health professions." This higher education provision has done much to increase the number of Indian health professionals. Before the passage of the act, there were only fifty-two Indian physicians, eight optometrists, and four hundred nurses; by 1983, there were two hundred thirty-seven physicians; fourteen optometrists, and six hundred forty-four nurses.

Although Native American students have received much of their twentieth-century financial support from the federal government, they have also received support from other sources, including tribal assistance. In 1947 the Menominee Tribe in Wisconsin became the first to establish a tribal scholarship program. This was done at the urging of the BIA since it had already inaugurated its termination policy (1945 to 1960), characterized in part by reduced funds for Indian education. Other tribes followed suit, including the Southern Ute Tribe in Colorado in 1951, the Yakima tribe in Washington in 1954, and the Navajo Nation, also in 1954. By 1959 twenty-nine tribes had created postsecondary scholarship programs. Combined, this tribal assistance totaled $286,000 in 1959, surpassing BIA support which totaled only $170,000 in the same year.

In addition to tribal and federal governments, Native American students have also received some support from various state governments. In response to BIA termination, seven states passed legislation to create Indian scholarship programs: South Dakota in 1949, Montana in 1951, New York in 1953, Arizona in 1954, Alaska in 1955, Minnesota in 1955, and Wisconsin in 1957. All these states have identifiable Native populations and did not provide financial assistance to Native college students before World War II. Montana provided tuition waivers whereas the other states awarded scholarships to in-state residents admitted into college. The funds were administered by newly created Indian divisions under state departments of education. State assistance, however, was not substantial. New York provided only $350 annually, which was shared by twenty-four Native collegians in the mid-1950s.

Still another source Indian students depended upon for financial assistance was from several colleges and universities. The University of Michigan was the first in the twentieth century to create a scholarship program for Indians. It was established in 1932 in recognition of the Treaty of Fort Meigs of 1817, which the university interpreted as having a higher education provision. Thus, five students were awarded tuition waivers annually. Dartmouth College and Dickinson College in Pennsylvania also offered support before World War II. In the postwar period they were joined by seventeen other postsecondary institutions, including the University of Arizona, Brigham Young University, the University of Oklahoma, and the University of New Mexico. All these universities are located in states having sizable Native populations.

Some individual Native Americans who earned their degrees had a marked impact on their respective Native communities. One such person was Ada Deer of the Menominee tribe in Wisconsin. She earned her bachelor's degree from the University of Wisconsin, Madison, in 1957, and then a master of Social Work from Columbia University School of Social Work in 1961. Her tribe was one of several terminated by the BIA in the late 1950s and early 1960s. Deer opposed this policy because she maintained the BIA had a legal obligation to look after the affairs of tribal people. Along with other concerned Menominee, she formed DRUMS in 1970 to repeal Menominee termination. They won a victory in December 1973 when the Menominee Restoration Act returned the tribe's federal recognition.

Another college-educated Native American who impacted his community was Lionel Bordeaux, a member of the Lakota tribe of the Rosebud Sioux Reservation in South Dakota. He earned his bachelor's degree from Black Hills State College in 1964, a master's degree from the University of South Dakota in 1971, and in 1992 is a doctoral candidate at the University of Minnesota, Minneapolis campus. Since 1973, Bordeaux has been president of Sinte Gleska College, established in 1971 and chartered and operated by the Rosebud Reservation. Under his leadership, the college has flourished. It is now accredited by the North Central Association of Colleges and Schools. Besides associates degrees, Sinte Gleska also awards bachelor's degrees in particular areas, thus making it the only Indian-controlled college to offer this kind of advanced degree. From 1980 to 1986, twenty students earned bachelor's degrees in elementary education, nine in mental health, and two in criminal justice. This development is the work of Lionel Bordeaux and his associates.

Although more Native Americans have entered the higher education domain, they have also faced new and unique problems. In some instances, academic survival was a major concern. Some struggled because of an inadequate pre-collegiate education in BIA and other secondary schools. Others dealt with financial problems—even though the BIA grants had increased, they could not cover the rising costs of education. Still others had difficulty because of their upbringing in rural cooperative Native environments. They therefore dealt with "culture shock," since the university system was large and impersonal, or the antithesis of reservation life. Some felt guilty about abandoning their tribal way of life in favor of a modern education, something that symbolized white America. Still others became disillusioned with the universities' emphasis on Euroamerican studies as few, if any, programs existed in the area of minority studies before 1970. All these factors led to an increased dropout rate in the 1970s and 1980s.

Nevertheless, many Native American students survived the rigor and competitiveness of higher education for various reasons: the encouragement coming from family and other tribal members; retention programs created at some postsecondary institutions; and precollege orientation programs to ensure student success at a later date. More importantly, some universities created courses in Native American history and culture, primarily after 1970. In several instances, these new courses were taught in newly established Native American studies programs. Thus, Indian students were able to identify with the new subject matter and felt more comfortable in mainstream higher education.

Despite the increased enrollments of the twentieth century, Native Americans still lag behind the general population with respect to representation in American higher education. Dean Chavers (Lumbee), a Stanford Ph.D., argued that instead of the actual enrollment of 35,000 Native students in 1980, Native America needed at least 85,000 in order to reach parity with the larger Anglo population. Perhaps more Native Americans will pursue a higher education in the years to come.

Steven J. Crum

Further Reading

American Indian Issues in Higher Education. Los Angeles, CA: American Indian Studies Center, UCLA, 1980.

Boyer, Ernest L. *Tribal Colleges: Shaping the Future of Native America.* Princeton, NJ: The Carnegie Foundation for the Advancement of Teaching, 1989.

Crum, Steven. "Henry Roe Cloud, A Winnebago Indian Reformer: His Quest for American Indian Higher Education." *Kansas History* 11 (Autumn 1988): 171–84.

Forbes, Jack D. *Native American Higher Education: The Struggle for the Creation of D-Q University, 1960–1971.* Davis, CA: D-Q University Press, 1985.

Haymond, Jack Harrison. "The American Indian and Higher Education: From the College for the Children of the Infidels (1619) to Navajo Community College." Ph.D. diss., Washington State University, 1982.

Szasz, Margaret. *Education and the American Indian.* 2d ed. Albuquerque: University of New Mexico Press, 1977.

HOH

The Hoh tribe inhabited and utilized the drainage of the Hoh River system on the Pacific Coast side of the Olympic Peninsula of Washington State. The Hohs, also *chà·lá·i̧,* historically spoke Quileute and are therefore part of the linguistically isolated Chimakuan family. Due to the small size of the tribe and lack of accessibility, very little ethnographic information was collected. Therefore, presumptions of traditional lifeways are based on observations of the neighboring Quileute with whom they are closely related.

History

Despite contacts with the seafaring vessels *Imperial Eagle* in 1787 and the *Sv. Nikolai* in 1808, lack of an anchorage minimized interaction with Europeans. The Hoh were signatories of the Treaty with the Quinaielt, etc., 1855 negotiated by M.T. Simmons. Although the written treaty called for removal to the Quinault Reservation (set aside in 1873), Simmons evidently gave assurances that the Hoh would not have to relocate. In 1893, the small 443 acre Lower Hoh Reservation was created at the mouth of the Hoh

River mouth by executive order. Because of the treaty stipulation of movement to Quinault, Hohs may choose membership at either reservation. After 1910, some Hohs acquired eighty acre timber allotments on the Quinault Reservation without a change of residence.

The town site at the mouth of the Hoh River was accessible only by foot and canoe until 1953, when logging on the reservation provided road access. In 1966, a power line was extended to Lower Hoh. Tribal incorporation occurred in 1969 and the four members of the Hoh Tribal Business Committee are elected biannually. Members in 1993 were Vivian Lee (chair), Jerry Horejsi, Yvonne Soeneke, and Marietta Obi.

Current Situation

Population was estimated to be 71 in 1893. This number, however, would not include upriver Hohs who had moved to the Quinault or other reservations. Current tribal enrollment, requiring 25 percent blood quantum, was 156 in 1990. Nearly three-fourths of the Hoh—114—live at Lower Hoh, which has a total population of about 135.

The tribe's economy has been totally reliant on fishing, but salmon runs continue to decrease and catches have decreased despite allocation of 50 percent of the harvestable catch to treaty fishermen by the 1974 Boldt Decision. In recent years, the tribal fisheries department has encouraged spawning habitat restoration, but is faced with the difficulty of improving logging practices as well as continued pressure for cutting by an industry suffering from the effects of nonsustainable cutting rates in past years. Although logging has dominated the region's economy, Native American participation has been limited. Timber sales on Quinault allotments have provided unpredictable windfalls to some families. A few jobs are provided by the tribal government and the tribal fisheries and hatchery program. Long-term economics represent a major challenge and current tribal policy focuses on the creation of new, on-reservation jobs.

Current land issues include treaty protected off-reservation resource utilization rights as well as protection of those resources. Additionally, questions remain concerning the northern reservation boundary and areas of former residence that were adversely homesteaded or otherwise taken.

Culture

Despite the losses since contact, the Hoh are heir to a rich cultural tradition. Potlatches and naming ceremonies are still conducted with traditional songs and dances. Language use, however, is minimal and only two native speakers remain. The gathering of many of the natural resources and their utilization for subsistence and crafts, especially basketmaking, is still a vital part of the culture. Protestant, Indian Shaker, and traditional practices co-exist, but there are no churches at Lower Hoh. Schooling has generally been at the nearest town of Forks, although some children are now bused to the more distant Quileute Tribal School in La Push. The Hoh are active in the current

revival of canoe voyaging and participated in the 1989 "Paddle to Seattle" and the 1993 voyage to meet with canoe tribes at Bella Bella, British Columbia. It is of interest to note that while in 1988 only motorized race canoes were in active use at Hoh River, the oldest canoe in the "Paddle to Seattle" was paddled by the Hoh tribe.

The Hoh have had to make major political and economic changes in a relatively short time. A very different tribal government structure supplanted a hereditary leadership system which viewed the chiefs not as decision makers, but as workers for the people. The salmon runs which were the tribe's economic base have dwindled precipitously. During this period, the older members of the tribe have consistently met their traditional obligations. Now there is renewed interest in cultural activities and younger generations are challenged to pick up the traditional responsibilities.

Joseph Lubischer

Further Reading

Owens, Kenneth N., and Alton S. Donnelly. *The Wreck of the Sv. Nikolai.* Portland, OR: Western Imprints, 1985.
Powell, James V. "Quileute." *Handbook of North American Indians.* Vol. 7 *Northwest Coast.* Ed. Wayne Suttles. Washington, DC: Smithsonian Institution (1990): 431–37.

HOLIKACHUK

See Alaskan Athabaskans

HOOPA

See Hupa

HOPI

The Hopi people live on or near the southern escarpment of Black Mesa in northeastern Arizona on a reservation which is surrounded by the reservation of their neighbors, the Navajo. The Hopi language is a member of the Uto-Aztecan family; today most Hopis speak English and Hopi. Traditionally Hopis were farmers who supplemented their diet with small game. Today Hopis farm, raise cattle, and engage in a variety of occupations both on and off the reservation. As the westernmost Puebloan people, the Hopis live in thirteen villages on three finger-like projections south from Black Mesa and to the west along Moencopi Wash. There are three villages on First Mesa: Walpi, Sichomovi, and the Tewa-speaking village of Hano; the modern community Polacca has spread at the base of the narrow mesa. Second Mesa includes the villages of Shipaulovi and Mishongnovi, which occupy small, isolated promontories, and the large village of Shungopavi. Prior to the twentieth century, there was only one Third Mesa village, Oraibi. But a factional split in 1906 and further dissension over the next several years led to the development of Hotevilla, Bacabi, and New Oraibi (now Kyakotsmovi). Forty miles to the west, a summer farming village expanded and divided to form Lower and Upper Moencopi.

Twentieth-Century History

Although there have been efforts at resistance, areas of compartmentalization (especially with regard to religion), and a conscious effort to "preserve the good things of Hopi life," nevertheless, this century has been one of rapid cultural change for the Hopi people. One of the most dramatic events in Hopi history, the "Oraibi split," occurred on September 6, 1906, when the "friendlies" forced the "hostiles" over a line drawn in the sandstone and out of the village. From 1910 to 1911, the federal government attempted to allot Hopi lands but succeeded only at Moencopi before the effort was abandoned. Between 1894 and 1912 schools were established near the Hopi villages, and a government hospital was opened at Keams Canyon in 1913. Several hundred Hopis served in World War I and contact with the outside world increased significantly during the next decade. Following the passage of the Indian Reorganization Act in 1934, the Hopi Tribal Council was established in 1935 and a Tribal Constitution was written by Oliver LaFarge in 1936. Hopi economic development in the 1930s was affected by an increase in federally funded employment and, at the same time, by stock reduction programs. In 1939, the Oraibi High School was opened. During World War II, Hopis served in the military; some registered as conscientious objectors, and many others left the reservation for work in neighboring cities.

Experience away from the reservation during World War II increased Hopis' demand for cash. Jobs were scarce, unemployment high. In 1950 Congress passed the Navajo-Hopi Long Range Rehabilitation Act, and between 1951 and 1962 approximately $90 million was spent to improve the reservations' infrastructure (roads, schools, hospitals, water, electricity, and sewers). The Hopi Tribal Council, which had been disbanded in 1943, was reconstituted in 1950 and given federal recognition in 1955. Two years earlier, in 1948, the first meeting of the Hopi traditionalists took place in Shungopavi. Contemporary Hopi factionalism is expressed in terms of this "progressive"/"traditionalist" dichotomy. In 1961 the secretary of the interior authorized the Tribal Council to lease Hopi lands. In 1966 the Council signed a lease with the Peabody Coal Company allowing for strip mining of 25,000 acres in the Joint Use Area, and mining operations began on Black Mesa in 1970. Traditionalist efforts to block strip mining in 1971 (*Lomayaktewa v. Morton*) failed. There was a noticeable decrease in farming in the 1960s and 1970s. The conflicts between the traditionalists and Tribal Council escalated as environmental and political activists found common concerns expressed in traditionalist prophecies. Throughout this period the Hopi and Navajo tribes confronted each other in the courts over issues relating to land.

Hopi population has grown from about 2,200 in 1900 to 7,360 in 1990. At the same time, an increasing number of Hopis live off-reservation for education and employment. In 1970 the Hopi Cultural Center was opened in an effort to create on-reservation employment. An undergarment factory established by the B.V.D. Company in Winslow in 1971 failed by 1975. Overall, however, there has been a shift from an economy based on subsistence agriculture to a cash economy centered on wage labor. The 1980s show an increasing interest by the Tribal Council in solving not only the land dispute with the Navajos, but also a whole series of internal problems such as alcoholism, drug abuse, suicide, and child abuse. Four Hopi mental health conferences held 1981 to 1984 sought to relate Hopi prophecy to contemporary issues and crises. In a document entitled *Hopi-Tunat'ya/Hopi Comprehensive Plan*, published in 1987, the Tribal Council spoke to the issue of cultural resources by noting that "The Hopi way is a living tradition that shapes every aspect of the lives of the Hopi people," and included among its goals the preservation of the Hopi way of life and the protection of sacred places and subsistence-gathering areas.

The Hopi-Navajo Land Dispute

For the Hopi people, a key issue in the twentieth century has been land. As the century began Hopis were protesting the intrusion of Navajos onto the 2.5 million acre, 1882 executive order Moqui (Hopi) Reservation. So extensive was Navajo occupancy of the area that in 1936, as part of a stock reduction plan which divided the Hopi and Navajo reservations into eighteen grazing units, Hopis were given exclusive use only of Grazing District 6, which included 499,248 acres (expanded in 1943 to 631,717 acres by the revised W.R. Centerwall recommendation). In 1958, Congress passed legislation formally allowing the Hopi and Navajo tribes to sue each other. In 1962 the United States Supreme Court found in *Healing v. Jones* that the Hopi and Navajo tribes had joint undivided and equal rights to the reservation (excepting District 6, which was reserved exclusively for the Hopis), and that the courts had no authority to partition this Joint Use Area. The Navajo-Hopi Indian Land Settlement Act of 1974 led to the partition of the 1.8 million acre Joint Use Area with the United States District Court of Arizona providing a plan for partition in 1977. Litigation followed regarding Hopi claims to the Moencopi area of the Navajo Reservation assigned in 1934. In 1992 a United States District Court of Arizona decision in *Masayesva v. Zah* awarded 22,675 acres as the 1934 Hopi Exclusive Use Area, and 37,843 acres of the 1934 Navajo-Hopi Joint Use Area was partitioned to the Hopi tribe. Various suits and appeals regarding the 1977 and 1992 decisions are still pending.

Present Situation

A number of issues concern the Hopi people today. While much of the Hopi-Navajo land dispute has been resolved, Hopis plan to appeal the partitioning of the 1934 Navajo-Hopi Joint Use Area. The economic development of an isolated reservation with few natural resources has become increasingly critical as federal employment opportunities have lessened. The question of Hopi identity—from legally defining a Hopi tribal member to maintenance of the Hopi language and religion—is not easily resolved. The theft of sacred objects as well as the improper possession and display of sacred objects in museums is an ongoing concern. While the Hopis have had many dedicated tribal chairmen, the Tribal Council has struggled with the lack of representation from traditionalist villages, on the one hand, and complex legal and economic problems in dealing with the federal government and modern corporations, on the other.

Culture

Architecture. At the beginning of the twentieth century, a Hopi village consisted of a series of multi-storied, terraced structures, each containing a number of living units, which were arranged in long rows or irregularly around a central plaza, the *kisoni.* The *kihu*, the individual matrilineal/matrilocal residence, was a rectangular structure constructed of sandstone and adobe mortar, with a roof built up of layers of timbers, cedar bark, and adobe mud. The kiva, a semi-subterranean religious structure constructed of similar materials and built in the form of a rectangular keyhole, was located in the plaza, in the broad streets and/or at the ends of the house-blocks. Other functionally specific structures included a small building for the preparation of *piki* bread, shelters for various materials near the fields and orchards, and stacked stone corrals for sheep, horses, and cattle.

After World War II rapid culture change affected all aspects of Hopi life, although the rate of change was more marked in some villages than others. Especially in Polacca and Kyakotsmovi, larger homes with hipped roofs, concrete block walls, large windows, and indoor plumbing appeared. More importantly, the settlement pattern of the villages changed. Hotevilla and Bacabi followed the traditional pattern of house blocks forming a central plaza, but in some areas of these and other villages there is a pattern of newer homes being built at greater distances from the village center with no overall coordination of arrangement. At the beginning of the twentieth century the Hopi landscape included trading posts and mission churches. Today, gasoline stations, laundromats, arts and crafts shops, the Hopi Cultural Center (Second Mesa), schools, and an airport are reflective of Hopi involvement in a growing number of cultural and economic developments.

Architecture and Worldview. At the turn of the century the metaphors by which Hopis perceived, experienced, and described their architecture derived largely from their worldview. Hopi cosmology includes the notion of the evolution of mankind through four worlds, with final emergence of the Hopi in the Grand Canyon, by way of the *sipapu*, or opening from the underworld below. In Hopi thought the architecture of the kiva—through the *sipapu*, an opening in the floor, and the levels of the floors—replicated this account. The ladders, which stood against the doorless first floor exterior of the traditional *kihu*, or extended above the entrance into the kiva, reminded Hopis of the trees they climbed at the emergence. For Hopis, the *sipapu* is the first component of a village to be constructed, and around it the houses are built which form the plaza. The *sipapu* is a symbolic medium of exchange and communication between the upper world of the living and the lower world of the spirits—between life and life after this life. From this conception, the levels of the kiva, the tall ladders, the architecture of this world, and the architecture of their cosmology correspond and compliment each other. Today Hopis know the names and functions of these structures, but few recall the metaphoric connections to their emergence.

The central plaza remains the focal point for a complex ritual calendar and the center of a series of roughly concentric circles of men's and women's space. A tendency towards bilateral inheritance and neolocal residence has altered this view of the *kihu* as women's space. The kiva, however, continues to serve predominantly as men's space. Nearby gardens are tended by women, while men care for corn fields and livestock at some distance from the villages. Beyond these categories of space, priests collect snakes and eagles (messengers to sacred space), make offerings at shrines, and go on expeditions for salt.

At the turn of the century ten-mile-long trails connected the three mesas. Today highways link the mesas to surrounding communities. Burros, horses, and wagons have been replaced by trucks (1930s) and cars (1950s). Telephones and television have been present for the past twenty-five years, further connecting Hopis to the world beyond the mesas.

Arts and Crafts. Hopi material culture at the beginning of the twentieth century included a wide variety of ceramics, basketry, textiles, silverwork, religious objects (including kachina dolls, *tithu*), and implements relating to agriculture and hunting. Today Hopis make wide use of modern technology. At the same time a number of traditional material objects have been transformed from utilitarian purposes to art forms and religious objects have become secularized art. It was not until the 1940s that Hopi art was viewed as art rather than "ethnographic art." By the turn of the century a woman from Hano, Nampeyo, was creating pottery which was marketed as art to non-Hopis, a pottery which was to make her and Hopi pottery world renowned. Today, many Hopi women excel in pottery. The kachina doll, an early object of interest to collectors, has evolved into a secularized art form in the kachina sculptures of the 1980s. Fred Kabotie was one of the first Hopi painters to be successful commercially. Kabotie, too, was an important figure in the development of silver overlay jewelry. The Hopi Arts and Crafts Guild and, later, Hopicrafts developed as cooperative marketing efforts, and today a number of independently owned arts and crafts enterprises exist. Charles Loloma was one of the most successful Hopi artists at having his jewelry recognized as art at an international level. Traditional ceremonial textiles continue to be made for Hopi use, for trade or sale to other Puebloan peoples, and for the arts market. Hopi artists continue to explore various forms of creative expression which reflect the richness of Hopi culture, and to this end, Artist Hopid was formed in 1973. More recently several Hopis have explored poetry and photography as a means of presenting the Hopi way to non-Hopis.

Religion. Hopi religion has its foundations in the emergence myth and clan traditions. This sacred knowledge (*wiimi*) is given expression in prayer offerings and ritual. Only those who have been initiated into various societies or are proper members of the clan may have access to this knowledge and the sacred objects which embody it. No greater conflict exists between the Hopi people and non-Hopis than in this area. In 1984, the Hopi attempted to put together an ordinance to not only control the documentation of Hopi traditions and culture, but to protect artifacts, especially religious artifacts, as well. This ordinance was not implemented but all plans for study or publication should be cleared by the Hopi Tribal Council's Office of Cultural Preservation.

The Hopi ritual calendar may be portrayed as having two halves, turning on the summer and winter solstices, with priestly ceremonies involving the Snake, Antelope, *Wuwtsim* (the ceremonies of the four men's societies), and women's societies in the summer and fall, and kachina (*katsina*) ceremonies in the winter and spring. The so-called "social dances," the Buffalo (winter; hunting) and Butterfly (summer; agriculture) appear immediately following the solstices. Hopi rituals involve communications and exchanges, prayers and offerings, between the world of the living and the world of the spirits for the mutual benefit of both. Much of Hopi religion is concerned with sustaining life, and corn is the most important symbol and substance of this concern. Just as the path of an individual moves from birth to death, the Hopi emergence myth and prophecies make clear the Hopi Path of Life (*Hopivötskwani*). Thus, the Oraibi split mentioned earlier was not so much a consequence of acculturation, but a deliberate act carried out within this sacred plan.

Baptists, Catholics, Mennonites, Mormons, and others have established missions among the Hopi, several with sustained presence throughout this century. While there are Hopi converts, on the whole the Hopi people have not found the redemptive metaphors of Christianity meaningful to their lives.

Louis A. Hieb

Further Reading
Loftin, John D. *Religion and Hopi Life in the Twentieth Century.* Bloomington: Indiana University Press, 1991.

Ortiz, Alfonso, ed. *Handbook of North American Indians.* Vol. 9. *Southwest.* Washington, DC: Smithsonian Institution, 1979.

Rushforth, Scott, and Steadman Upham. *A Hopi Social History.* Austin: University of Texas Press, 1992.

Talayesva, Don. *Sun Chief: The Autobiography of a Hopi Indian.* Ed. Leo W. Simmons. New Haven, CT: Yale University Press, 1942.

Teiwes, Helga. *Kachina Dolls: The Art of Hopi Carvers.* Tucson: University of Arizona Press, 1991.

Whiteley, Peter. *Bacavi: Journey to Reed Springs.* Flagstaff, AZ: Northland Press, 1988.

HOPI-NAVAJO LAND CONTROVERSY

See Navajo-Hopi Land Controversy

HOUMA

The Houma (also historically, Ouma) are the largest tribe in Louisiana and inhabit the lower southeastern marshlands of the state. Most of the 11,000 members reside in seven communities in Terrebonne and Lafourche Parishes, with Dulac-Grand Caillou and Golden Meadow having the largest concentrations.

Fishing, trapping, and hunting remain the primary occupations with some tribal members now working in the oil fields of the marsh and the gulf. Interaction with the non-Indian community, until recently, was quite limited and was usually conducted by the local leadership in each Houma community. David Billiot of Golden Meadow, Jean Victor Naquin of Isle de Jean Charles, and Jean Baptist Parfait of Dulac-Grand Caillou were among the more influential leaders during the century.

The discovery of oil during the 1930s led to the loss of much family-owned Indian land. Oil speculators frequently took advantage of Houma landowners who were illiterate and predominantly non-English speakers. Local Houma leaders began an aggressive campaign during this period to bring formal education to their people. Most Houma members did not enter public schools until the 1950s. Even then, the schools were segregated; the last Indian elementary school was not integrated with other parish schools until 1969.

The Houma have retained distinctly Native cultural elements as demonstrated in their crafts, folklore, folk medicine, and kinship patterns. The native palmetto plant is still used by Houma weavers to make baskets, fans, mats, and dolls. Folk stories of false lights, tricksters, and the supernatural are passed on through the oral tradition. Traditional healers or *traiteurs* provide treatments for illnesses using both native plants and Christian prayers. Family kinship patterns remain strong in identifying the individual's family and community. A long history of intermarriage between Houma and the French resulted in a strong influence of the French language and Catholic religion. French was the primary language of the Houma throughout this century, with only a few Houma words known by the oldest members of the tribe.

Contemporary tribal government is through an elective body, the United Houma Nation, Inc., formed in 1979. Kirby Verret, chair, and Helen Dardar Gindrat, vice-chair, are in 1991 among the key leaders of the modern era. Since the Houma never formally entered into treaties or other agreements with the United

States, they are pursuing a process of recognition through the federal government which would accord them the governmental status enjoyed by other tribes.

The tribe's major initiatives at the local level have been on education and economic development. More Houma youth are completing high school, and a few have attained college and post-graduate degrees. The decline in oil production combined with extensive damage due to erosion of the marshlands pose the most serious threats to the Houma's economic health.

N. Bruce Duthu

Further Reading

Bowman, Greg, and Janel Curry-Roper. *The Houma People of Louisiana: A Study of Indian Survival.* Houma: The United Houma Nation, 1982.

Downs, Ernest C., and Jenna Whitehead. "The Houma Indians: Two Decades in a History of Struggle." *American Indian Journal* 2:3 (1976): 2–18.

Duthu, N. Bruce, and Hilde Z. Ojibway. "Future Light or Feu-Follet." *Southern Exposure* 13:6 (1985): 24–32.

Gregory, Hiram F. "The Louisiana Tribes: Entering Hard Times." *Indians of the Southeastern United States in the Late 20th Century.* Ed. J. Anthony Paredes. Tuscaloosa, AL and London, England: University of Alabama Press (1992): 162–82.

U.S. Congress. Senate. *Hearing before the Committee on Indian Affairs. Houma Recognition Act.* (August 7, 1990): S.2423.

HOUSING

Indian country covers a wide expanse of geography in which there are many diverse Indian/Alaska Native cultures. There are differences in housing and housing conditions from one reservation or community to another, due to cultural variations and vast differences in economic conditions. Approximately 35 percent of the current American Indian/Alaska Native population live on reservations, trust lands, tribal jurisdiction lands, and in Alaskan villages. The majority, 65 percent, live in other areas in the United States. The 1990 United States census data indicates that for the American Indian/Alaska Native population of 1,959,234 living in Indian country and elsewhere in the United States, there were 318,001 owner-occupied dwellings and 273,371 renter-occupied dwellings.

The Face of an Indian Community

Indian reservations and Alaska Native communities have a wide variety of housing types and styles, ranging from traditional shelters and buildings particular to individual tribes, to modern-day residential structures. These include mobile homes, cabins, wood frame and masonry construction, and various forms of manufactured housing construction. The same types of residential construction are found in a Native community as in the non-Native communities around it.

Individuals who are financially able solve their housing needs in a variety of ways. Some construct homes using their own labor and resources. Their homes may follow the traditional style of residential construction of their tribe or band. Conversely, some choose to build contemporary-style homes, including various amenities and all utility services. In some cases, their houses blend traditional design and materials with contemporary building technology. For others, purchasing a mobile home and moving it onto their land meets their housing need. For those who are financially able, options such as these are available. But for many others, the choices are much more limited.

Privately financed speculative development of housing is not known in Indian country as it is in the larger urban areas or even in smaller non-Indian rural communities. One simply does not see realty company "for sale" signs in Indian communities. The lack of real estate development is sometimes due to restricted land status in Indian country, lack of marketability due to cost, lack of interested developers, or reluctance on the part of financiers. There are not the kinds of housing entrepreneurship and housing market conditions in Indian country that exist in mainstream America.

Constraining Factors in Housing

An individual family's ability to build its own home within its own community depends upon several major factors. The family's financial situation plays a large role, particularly if the family decides to build a contemporary style house. Even if the house is of modest design, the family must have enough money to purchase building materials. The task of borrowing money for housing construction may be further complicated if the house is to be constructed on tribal/trust land or individually allotted trust land.

A second factor involves the availability of a buildable home site. Does the family currently own an interest in land or can the family acquire land for a home site? Is there an accessible, buildable parcel of land which can be served by electrical power, water, sanitary sewer, and natural gas? Economics again may be a factor, if there is a cost to acquiring land and bringing utility services to the site. Finally, the success of the individual family in carrying out this endeavor depends upon its own initiative and perseverance, skills, capabilities, and desire. To the degree that the family can cope with and achieve success in dealing with these factors, it will be able to realize home ownership. Some families have achieved home ownership on their own; many others rely on subsidized housing.

Subsidized Housing Programs

Economic conditions range from bad to very bad on most Indian reservations, communities, and Alaska Native villages. Unemployment rates are as high as 80 percent in some areas. Even on reservations near large metropolitan areas, where the rate should be much lower, unemployment figures are still many times the national rate. Therefore, it is very difficult, if not impossible, for many individual Native families to achieve adequate affordable housing on their own.

They simply do not have the personal financial resources to do it. They may or may not have land on which to build, by ownership or assignment. If acquiring a home site is not possible, this further compounds the problem and stands as a major hurdle. And for many, the multitude of tasks involved and the time associated with planning the construction of a home is far too complicated and cumbersome.

To overcome the major housing problem confronting many economically disadvantaged Native families, tribal governments and village leadership have worked with the federal government to create federally subsidized housing programs addressing growing housing needs. These programs are administered by the United States Department of Housing and Urban Development (HUD) and the Bureau of Indian Affairs (BIA) of the Department of Interior. Many of the houses seen in Indian communities and Alaska Native villages across the country are federally assisted houses built through the HUD/BIA programs.

There were no major national programs addressing the housing needs of Indians and Alaska Natives before 1960. The Housing Act of 1937, which is the basis for HUD's Indian Housing Program, was in force for twenty-four years before the federal government determined that the law was also applicable to Indian/Alaska Native areas. HUD's program came into being in 1961, and the BIA's program started in 1965. Local tribal housing agencies, known as Indian Housing Authorities (IHA), administer the HUD-assisted housing programs for their respective communities. IHAs are established pursuant to tribal law or in some cases pursuant to state enabling legislation.

The BIA's Housing Improvement Program, initially funded in 1965 pursuant to Snyder Act (1921) provisions, is administered by the BIA or by tribal governments through contracts with the BIA. This program is intended to assist those with the very lowest incomes. It is a grant program that primarily addresses the needs for rehabilitation of existing housing, in order to benefit more of those in need. Other eligible costs include enlargements and funding for new construction, and assistance to eligible applicants needing help with down payments for housing purchases. The BIA program does not require the repayment of financial assistance. In comparison to the HUD Indian Housing Program, funding suballocations are smaller at all levels.

HUD's Indian Housing Program was structured after the Public Housing Program in the beginning. Financial assistance for both home ownership and rental housing was provided via contracts between housing authorities and the federal government, and through the sale of bonds and notes to provide capital for the development of new housing. Over the last twenty-five years that has changed. The program has been transformed to a grant program, which differs from the BIA's program. Congress, in the housing law, set forth provisions for the structure and financial management of the program, which places the burden of responsibility upon the shoulders of HUD and the 183 Indian housing authorities nationwide. HUD continues to be the only major source of program funding for new housing developments. The responsibility for long-term management and financial solvency rests with the IHA. Monthly individual home buyer payments (or rental payments in the case of rental housing) remain requirements of the program. The BIA and the Indian Health Service also participate in the development of infrastructure for housing sites. Their responsibilities include access roads and community water and sewage facilities. By 1988, over 65,000 houses had been built under the HUD Indian Housing Program.

Other Housing Programs

Tribes and individual tribal members have also sought out other housing alternatives. In some cases, tribal governments have funded housing for their members. Through the Farmers Home Administration, programs such as rural housing, home ownership loans, rural rental housing, and housing preservation are available and have been utilized to a small degree. In the past, HUD's mortgage insurance program was used by a number of Indian tribes to develop housing pursuant to Section 221(d)(3) and Section 236. Currently, there is a newer HUD program known as Section 248, which allows for single-family mortgage insurance on Indian reservations. Under this program, private lenders provide the mortgage financing. HUD insures the mortgage in the event of default by the mortgage holder. Few Indian families have utilized the program to date, but the capacity for full usage is there. The program is virtually the same one utilized in non-Indian areas all across the country, except that it takes into account the unique nature of land ownership on Indian reservations. Other HUD housing programs, such as HOPE (Housing for People Everywhere) and HOME (HOME Investment Partnership Program) are also available to IHAs and Indian tribes. As the first funding year for these programs was 1992, their success is yet unproven.

Summary

While housing conditions are adequate for most Indian people, a significant number of Indian families currently live in overcrowded conditions, in substandard unsanitary housing, or in structurally unsound buildings. This is acknowledged by Indian and Alaska Native groups, by Indian housing advocacy groups, and by agencies of the federal government. All agree that there is a need for more and better Indian housing. Programmatically, those involved are concerned with the workability of the various programs and the effectiveness of their delivery. The constraints and limitations imposed by law, and the procedures and criteria mandated by regulation, are continually reevaluated with the hope of improving the delivery of these programs. While they are successful in providing housing to some, not everyone agrees that enough is being done.

Vernon Harragarra

See also **Architecture; Bureau of Indian Affairs (BIA); Economic Conditions; Government Agencies**

Figure 1

Fiscal Year	Number of Dwellings
1965	300
1970	4,609
1975	20,286
1980	38,342
1985	54,979
1988	65,660

Source: HUD

Figure 2

Fiscal Year	Appropriation
1965	$ 500
1970	7,774
1975	13,203
1980	19,380
1985	22,736
1990	22,463

Source: **Final Report of the National Commission on American Indian, Alaska Native, and Native Hawaiian Housing, 1992.**

Further Reading

Building the Future: A Blueprint for Change. Final Report. Washington, DC: National Commission on American Indian, Alaska Native, and Native Hawaiian Housing, 1992.

Nabokov, Peter, and Robert Easton. *Native American Architecture*. New York, NY: Oxford University Press, 1989.

Stea, David. "Indian Reservation Housing: Progress Since the Stanton Report." *American Indian Culture and Research Journal* 6:3 (1982): 1–14.

U.S. Congress. Senate. Committee on Interior and Insular Affairs. Henry M. Jackson, Chrmn. *Indian Housing in the United States*. Staff Report, 1975.

U.S. Department of Housing and Urban Development. *Indian Housing*. Revised Consolidated Program Regulations; Final Rule. Code of Federal Regulations, Title 24, Pts. 905, 965.

U.S. Department of the Interior. Bureau of Indian Affairs. Housing Improvement Program. Code of Federal Regulations, Title 25, Pt. 256.

HUALAPAI

The Hualapai Indians (also spelled Walapai), together with the Havasupai and the Yavapai, form the Upland Yuman language group of the Pai branch of the Yuman language family. The Hualapai and Havasupai Indians, commonly referred to as the Northeastern Pai, have inhabited northwest central Arizona for well over a millennium. They occupied lands at the western edge of the Colorado Plateau, and their lifestyle was classified as the "basin plateau" type. They have engaged primarily in hunting wild game and gathering seeds, roots, berries, nuts, and fruits, while cultivating gardens with relatively scant water resources. They apparently had close contacts with the Puebloan peoples and the Mohave Indians and traded peacefully especially with Hopis for manufactured goods and garden produce. On their southern border, however, the Yavapais remained hostile toward the Hualapais.

History

In the 1820s white fur trappers and prospectors entered the northeastern Pai territory. Their number was small and at first they were sometimes ignored or sometimes attacked by the Indians. Beginning in the late 1840s, a large number of white miners and settlers started to move into the territory. The Hualapai Indians and other Northeastern Pai worked in the white-owned mines; these Indians became a reliable, cheap labor force for the mine owners. Hualapais were not always happy with the exploitative practices of the white newcomers, and they fought a number of wars with them. By 1896 these wars had destroyed the traditional Hualapai patterns of living, and they eventually surrendered to the whites. They were permitted to continue to live in their territory for the time being, and many of them consequently returned to jobs in the white-owned mines. However, in 1874, the Office of Indian Affairs demanded that the army forcefully move the Hualapais to La Paz, the Colorado River Indian Reservation, 2009 miles to the south of Hualapai territory. Two years later they moved back to their homeland with an agreement that they would make peace with the white settlers as long as they stayed there. The white cattlemen opposed the Hualapais' return, but the mine owners supported them since the Indians were the only source of dependable labor in the area. On January 4, 1883, by a decree of President Chester A. Arthur, their present reservation was established—some 997,045 acres of deep canyons and high plateaus.

With the Indian Reorganization Act of 1934, the Hualapai people voted to organize the tribe and, in 1938, a new Constitution and Bylaws were adopted. The tribal membership was established, an elective nine-member council was created, and the Peach Springs settlement was designated as the tribal capital. In June 1970, a new tribal Constitution was ratified, which was adapted to the changing and progressively educated Hualapai tribe. The new Constitution had input from all tribal members during a period of two years.

Social Organization

What is notable for the Hualapai is the relative absence of intertribal factionalism. The bands have been described as follows: 1. Middle Mountain; 2. Red Rock (*Wi gahwaða Ba:*'); 3. Cerbat Mountain (*Ha'emðe" ba:*'); 4. Plateau People; 5. Clay Springs (*Haduva Ba:*',); 6. Grass Springs (*ðanayka Ba:*'); 7. Hackberry (*Qwaq We' Ba:*'); 8. Milkweed Springs (*He:l' ba:*'); 9. Peach Springs (*l'qað Ba:*'); 10. Pine Springs (*Hak saha Ba:*'); 11. Cataract Canyon (*Hav'suwa Ba:*'); 12. Hualapai Mountain (*Mað hwa:la Ba:*'); 13. Big Sandy River (*Haksigaela Ba:*'); 14. Mahone Mountain (*Ha gi a:ja Ba:*'); and 15. Juniper Mountain (*Hwalgijapa Ba:*'). These bands inhabited the four directions and were known to roam in the territories of their bands: North

(*Mata'v g'bay*); West (*Guwev g'bay*); East (*Nyav g'bay*); and South (*S'ʔul g'bay*).

Individuals were not subjected to centralized control or authority beyond the limits of their immediate families, extended families, and local group or band, and they were involved with other Hualapais only if they chose to do so. It seems unlikely that these subgroups of the Hualapai congregated with any regularity except during such religious occasions as the mourning ceremony, which usually included Havasupai and Mohave Indians as well. It is only after the coming of the whites that these seven bands were grouped together and designated as "Hualapai." An important note is that in spite of this lack of a centralized political institution, they did not suffer from any serious factionalism amongst themselves.

Environment

Currently the Hualapai occupy 991,680 acres of range and forest lands in the eastern portion of Mohave County, the western part of Coconino County, and the northwestern corner of Yavapai County—all in the northwestern section of Arizona. The territory ranges from 2,000 to 7,000 feet in elevation and from densely wooded areas to barren desert areas with rainfall ranging from five to fifteen inches annually. The tribal headquarters is located in the community of Peach Springs, 4,830 feet above sea level, where it is cool in winter with occasional snowfalls that rarely accumulate, and hot and dry during summer months. The temperature in Peach Springs averages sixty degrees Fahrenheit, with an average annual rainfall of eight inches.

The Hualapai Reservation in the 1990s

Peach Springs lies along the mainline of the Santa Fe Railroad and along the United States Highway 66, about one hundred twenty miles west of Flagstaff and fifty miles east of Kingman. Peach Springs has one public school with a teaching staff of thirty-two, and two hundred four kindergarten through eighth grade students. Lucille J. Watahomigie, superintendent and principal, has headed the Hualapai Bilingual and Bicultural Education program since its inception in 1973. Students travel forty to fifty miles to attend high school either at a BIA boarding school or Kingman High School. There is a post office, a small general store with limited supplies, a gas station, the tribal office complex, and a United States Indian Health Service clinic, which may be utilized by non-Indians in emergency cases.

On both sides of the Santa Fe Railroad tracks lay clusters of homes—a number of modern houses with all the modern conveniences along with a few one- or two-room huts with outdoor plumbing. Approximately two hundred forty modern houses were built under the Housing and Urban Development project since the 1970s, and the tribe is planning to build another sixty-five modern houses on the reservation area west of Peach Springs. The suburban-style houses have contributed to the breakdown of the transmittal of traditional culture and language, since modern living does not include a grandparent or "culture bearer" in the home. Television and radio entertainment are the prominent activities.

The population of the tribe in 1993 is 1,872. The unemployment rate averages above 80 percent with most jobs related to government services. The main revenue for the Hualapai tribe comes from forestry, cattle ranching, wildlife, and Colorado River rafts operations. There are four churches: the Hualapai Bible Mission, a Latter-Day Saints church, Foursquare Church, and an Episcopal church. All have active congregations.

The Hualapai language and culture are very much a part of the older Hualapai people's everyday life. Among the young the traditional lifestyle has lost its primary role but the young still consider the knowledge of the traditional lifestyle to be crucial for their identity as Hualapai. The school has played an important role in the maintenance of the language and culture among the young by implementing a nationally recognized bilingual/bicultural program, incorporating modern technologies into educational processes, and involving the community in the education of the Hualapai youth. Social and ceremonial gatherings such as powwows, meetings, funerals, festivals, and holidays are vital parts of the community life. At such social and ceremonial occasions, the Hualapai language is extensively used, and is, therefore, an inseparable part of the traditional and contemporary life of the Hualapai people.

Lucille J. Watahomigie

Further Reading

Dobyns, Henry F., and Robert Eule. *The Walapai People.* Phoenix, AZ: Indian Tribal Series, 1976.

Kniffen, Fred. *Walapai Ethnography.* Memoirs of the American Anthropological Association 42. Menasha, WI: AAA, 1935.

McGuire, Thomas R. "Walapai." *Handbook of North American Indians.* Vol. 10. *Southwest.* Ed. Alfonso Ortiz. Washington, DC: Smithsonian Institution (1983): 25–37.

Manners, Robert A. "An Ethnological Report on the Hualapai (Walapai) Indians of Arizona." *American Indian Ethnohistory: Indians of the Southwest.* New York, NY: Garland Publishing, 1974.

Spicer, Edward H. *Cycles of Conquest: The Impact of Spain, Mexico, and the United States on the Indians of the Southwest 1533–1960.* Tucson: University of Arizona Press, 1962.

Watahomigie, Lucille J., and Akira Y. Yamamoto. "Linguists in Action: The Hualapai Bilingual/Bicultural Education Program." *Collaborative Research and Social Change: Applied Anthropology in Action.* Eds. Donald D. Stull and Jean J. Schensul. Boulder, CO: Westview Press (1987): 77–98.

Weaver, Thomas, ed. *Indians of Arizona: A Contemporary Perspective.* Tucson: University of Arizona Press, 1974.

HUMAN REMAINS

See Archaeology; Repatriation of Human Remains and Artifacts

HUPA

The Hoopa Valley Indian Tribe is indigenous to the lower Trinity River area of northwestern California. Prior to contact with Euroamericans, the people of the Hoopa Valley referred to themselves in their Athabaskan language as *Natinook-wa* and called the valley they lived in *Natinook*, "Where the Trails Return." Today the tribe is known as the Hoopa Valley Tribe and the people are called Hupa.

On May 7, 1828, an American trapping party led by Jedediah Smith entered the Hoopa Valley. In the next decade several non-Indian groups came to the area and more Euroamericans came to Hoopa following the 1849 Gold Rush. A treaty was negotiated by Special Indian Agent Redick McKee in 1851, but this treaty was never ratified. A second treaty was negotiated on August 12, 1864, by Austin Wiley, newly appointed superintendent of California Indian affairs, which established "peace and friendship" with the Hupa (Hoopa Valley, South Fork, Redwood, and Grouse Creek) and established the reservation's boundaries, which were later approved by a series of executive orders beginning in 1876.

The Hoopa Valley Indian Reservation, the largest reservation in California, was established pursuant to a congressional act of April 8, 1864. The site for the reservation was reaffirmed on June 23, 1876, by executive order issued by President U.S. Grant. Its boundaries were expanded by President Benjamin Harrison in an executive order issued on October 16, 1891. This order added a connective strip of land joining the old Klamath River Reservation (Yurok) to the Hoopa Valley Reservation. In 1963 the *Jessie Short v. United States* case was filed in the United States Court of Claims and was decided in the plaintiffs' favor in 1974. In the same year the United States seized 70 percent of the Hoopa revenues to be placed in the United States Treasury under federal control. In 1978 the federal government took over all control of the Hoopa Tribe's resources. In 1988 the Bureau of Indian Affairs assumed control of tribal funds for use according to United States government priorities but without tribal approval. On October 31, 1988, President Ronald Reagan signed the Hoopa-Yurok Settlement Act (PL 100–580), reaffirming the Hoopa Valley Tribe's jurisdiction to the original Hoopa Valley Reservation.

The reservation is located within the aboriginal homeland of the Hupa. Geographically, it is a square, twelve miles on a side, and it is rich in natural resources. The reservation, which consists of only a portion of the Hoopa Valley Tribe's aboriginal territory, comprises 88,601 acres, of which 73,592 are classified as commercial timberlands. The reservation has a level valley floor two miles wide. The climate is moderate, with rain of more than forty inches falling annually in the winter months. Dense vegetation, predominately evergreen forests of pines, cedars, and douglas firs, covers most of the reservation. Salmon, steelhead, and lamprey eels inhabit the Trinity River

which flows through the reservation. The six-mile-long valley that runs along the Trinity River has always been and still remains the center of the Hupa world and homeland. Salmon and acorns provided the bulk of the local Native diet and remain very important as ceremonial foods today. During the spring and fall of each year there are two major salmon runs. Acorns are harvested from the tan oak trees during the fall of the year.

For ceremonial purposes Hoopa is divided into a southern and a northern district, each forming a unit in the dances and ceremonies. In the heart of the valley lies the ancient village of *Takimildin*, the spiritual center for the people of the valley. In late summer and spring the Hoopa give their major ceremonials, the White Deerskin Dance and the Jump Dance. The Deerskin Dance is given to renew and revitalize the world and to stop famine, disease, and other disasters. The Jump Dance is a thanksgiving dance. Tribal historian Byron Nelson wrote, and it is still true today:

> These elaborate dances required extensive preparations. The people who inherited the right to sponsor them had many responsibilities. They had to maintain the dance grounds, care for the regalia, prepare camps for all of the visitors who would come to the valley to watch and participate, and provide food for the feasts which accompanied the dances. . . . The ceremonies, the beliefs, and the land where the people had come into being were the Hupa's greatest treasures, and each new generation learned to honor and care for them.

The population of the Hoopa Valley Indian Reservation is estimated at 4,300. Of the 4,300 people residing on the reservation, 75.3 percent are classified as American Indian. The general membership of the Hoopa Tribe elects a governing body of seven council persons and one chairperson. The Tribal Council has taken an increasing responsibility in recent years for governing the affairs of the Hoopa Valley Reservation. The Council wishes to address the critical economic and social problems of the reservation by improving employment opportunities and retaining a larger share of the tribe's resources.

The Hoopa Valley Tribe, a federally recognized and organized Indian tribe, adopted a Constitution and Bylaws on May 5, 1950, which was approved by the commissioner of Indian affairs on September 4, 1952, and amended on August 18, 1972. Currently the tribe is participating in developing and implementing self-governance. For the past 135 years the tribe has been dependent on and dominated by the Bureau of Indian Affairs but now is working toward taking control of its future as Hupa people.

The Hupa people desire to maintain their extended family ties and their tribal culture without sacrificing a decent standard of living. The management practices of the tribe reflect an ongoing commitment to the perpetuation of both forest and wildlife resources, as an integral component of the tribe's cultural, social, and economic development strategies. The Hoopa Tribe is actively engaged in clarifying how the United States government and a sovereign tribe relate to one another, deciding their own tribal priorities, and helping the tribe to do more for itself in terms of cultural, social, and economic conditions, as well as building political strength.

The Hupa people from the South Fork of the Trinity and New River areas were relocated to the Hoopa Valley Reservation during the early years of conflict. These people call themselves Tsnungwe. When it was first safe during the 1880s, many Tsnungwe returned to their homeland, *yinah-chin*, up the Trinity River. The Tsnungwe, an organized and unacknowledged tribe, have maintained tribal relations since then. Their federal acknowledgment application is in process; current enrollment is approximately 150, with an expected enrollment of 300 to 400.

Lois Risling

Further Reading

Berman, Joan. *Ethnography and Folklore of the Indians of Northwestern California: A Literature Review and Annotated Bibliography.* Salinas, CA: Coyote Press, 1986.

Goddard, Pliny Earle. "Life and Culture of the Hupa." *University of California Publications in American Archaeology and Ethnology* 1:1 (1903–1904): 1–88.
———. "Hupa Texts." *University of California Publications in American Archaeology and Ethnology* 1:2 (1904): 89–368.
Nelson, Byron, Jr. *Our Home Forever: A Hupa Tribal History.* Hoopa, CA: Hupa Tribe, 1978.
Wallace, William J. "Hupa, Chilula, and Whilkut." *Handbook of North American Indians.* Vol. 8. *California.* Ed. Robert F. Heizer. Washington, DC: Smithsonian Institution (1978): 164–79.

HURON

See Wyandotte

HURON POTAWATOMI

See Potawatomi in Southern Michigan

INDIAN ARTS AND CRAFTS ACT

See Indian Arts and Crafts Board

INDIAN ARTS AND CRAFTS BOARD

The Indian Arts and Crafts Board was established by Congress in 1935 by P.L. 74-355, as an independent federal agency, under the United States Department of the Interior. Five commissioners, appointed by the secretary of the interior, direct its policies. Since 1971, most of the appointees have been Indian. The commissioners, who serve without pay, choose a chairman from their members. They employ a general manager to administer the agency's activities and programs, assisted by a small professional staff.

The agency's legislative mandate is "to promote the development of Indian arts and crafts" of the United States, and thus the economic welfare of Indian people. The legislation permits the Board to consider a broad spectrum of informational, advisory, and promotional activities in its work with Indian artists and craftsmen, and with other public and private agencies. It does not authorize the agency to make grants or loans, nor may the agency deal in Indian arts and crafts. It does permit the Board to participate in the market by creating and registering government trademarks, and it provides criminal penalties for willful misrepresentation of imitation Indian arts and crafts. The Board refers such complaints to the United States Department of Justice or local district attorneys, as it does not have powers of investigation or prosecution.

The Board has responsibility for administering three federal museums: the Museum of the Plains Indian in Browning, Montana; the Sioux Indian Museum, in Rapid City, South Dakota; and the Southern Plains Indian Museum in Anadarko, Oklahoma. Each of these is locally supervised by a curatorial staff hired by the Board. These museums maintain exhibition and promotional facilities, specializing in the arts and crafts of their local areas, and have proven to be particularly helpful to artists in the sale and exhibition of their work.

In the 1930s the Board set out to determine the state of Indian arts, to find out what crafts were still being produced by Indian people, and to locate the outstanding artists and craftsmen of the time. This work led to two seminal exhibitions at the 1939 World's Fair in San Francisco, and at the Museum of Modern Art in New York in 1941, that presented Indian creative work as art rather than ethnographic curiosities. The public reacted enthusiastically.

The Board then concentrated in the 1940s and 1950s on setting up tribally owned crafts marketing enterprises as well as marketing cooperatives owned by the craftsmen themselves to capitalize on the demand for their work. This emphasis evolved into helping especially creative individuals to develop their skills and visions, and led the Board in 1960 to recommend the founding of the Institute of American Indian Arts to provide heritage-centered instruction to artistically talented Indian youth.

Responding to the success of the Institute and related concepts, the Board placed special emphasis throughout the 1970s and 1980s on helping Indian cultural leaders to establish the varied institutional framework they feel is necessary to support the preservation and evolution of Indian culture in the years ahead.

The Board's work has been strongly influenced by two individuals, although others have played important roles as well. Rene d'Harnoncourt, first as general manager and subsequently as chairman of the board until 1961, firmly established its reputation for professional quality and pioneering exhibitions that put twentieth-century Indian art in a new light. Lloyd Kiva New (Cherokee), who was first appointed to the Board in 1961 and has served as chairman since 1972, expanded on that foundation and has been the conceptual thinker behind its broad-based support for developing Indian-controlled cultural institutions.

During most of its existence, the Board has been notable as one of the few sustained advocates for Indian cultural vitality, especially within the federal government. The broad scope of its activities, ranging from curating international exhibitions seen by millions to assisting rural craftsmen to locate materials for their work, has given it a greater influence on contemporary Indian life than is readily apparent. Throughout, the dominant characteristic of the Board has been its dedication to economic growth for Indian, Eskimo, and Aleut artists and craftsmen.

Geoffrey E. Stamm

See also **Institute of American Indian and Alaska Native Culture and Arts**

Further Reading

Libhart, Myles. "The Indian Arts and Crafts Board and Leslie Van Ness Denman." In Tryntje Van Ness Seymour's *When the Rainbow Touches Down*. Phoenix, AZ: The Heard Museum (1988): 340–45.

Schrader, Robert Fay. *The Indian Arts and Crafts Board: An Aspect of New Deal Indian Policy*. Albuquerque: University of New Mexico Press, 1983.

INDIAN CENTERS

See Urban Indian Centers

INDIAN CIVILIAN CONSERVATION CORPS

Regarded as the most successful emergency work program of the New Deal era, the Indian Civilian Conservation Corps (CCC) played an important role in Commissioner John Collier's reform of Indian administration.

During the organization of the national CCC in 1933, interior department officials insisted on a separate organization for Indians, and President Roosevelt authorized the Indian Emergency Conservation Work (IECW) program in April. IECW had several unique features, including the enlistment of both married and unmarried enrollees, camps which varied according to local conditions, and the supervision of project work and camp life by the Bureau of Indian Affairs.

Diversity characterized the IECW's attempts to conserve and upgrade Indian land and resources. In the Great Lakes and Pacific Northwest, enrollees concentrated on conservation of timber resources. Projects in the northern Plains, the Great Basin, and the Southwest usually involved improving rangelands. In farming areas, enrollees typically worked on erosion control. In all, the Indian CCC carried out 126 types of work, spent $72 million, and employed some 85,000 Indians.

In education and rehabilitation, the Indian CCC showed little progress in its early years. After Congress passed the CCC Act of 1937, IECW was renamed the Civilian Conservation Corps-Indian Division, and, more importantly, the legislation required that all enrollees receive ten hours of instruction per week. The "enrollee program" afterward offered more on-the-job training and general educational instruction on many reservations. Numerous enrollees took defense vocational classes after 1940, and this (plus their CCC experience) qualified several thousand for wartime jobs. In July 1942 Congress ended the CCC program.

Donald L. Parman

See also **Government Policy: Indian New Deal**

Further Reading

Gower, Calvin W. "The CCC Indian Division: Aid for Depressed Americans." *Minnesota History* 43 (1972): 3–13.

Indians at Work. Frederick, MD: University Publications of America. Microfilm.

Parman, Donald L. "The Indian Civilian Conservation Corps." Ph.D. diss., University of Oklahoma, 1967.

———. "The Indian and the Civilian Conservation Corps." *Pacific Historical Review* 40 (1971): 39–56.

Shunk, Harold W. [Mato Ska]. "Reminiscing about the Dakota." *Kansas Quarterly* 3 (1971): 116–23.

INDIAN CLAIMS COMMISSION

Congress created the Indian Claims Commission in 1946 to hear and resolve the hundreds of Indian tribal claims, accumulated from the nineteenth century, that were clogging the docket of the United States Court of Claims. Working as a quasi-judicial branch of Congress, it awarded over $800 million on nearly 300 claims ruled valid before it ceased operation in 1978. Its twin goals were to relieve Congress from the press of tribal claimants and to satisfy Indian desires for justice. Neither of these goals was fully realized.

Between 1784 and 1871, in 370 treaties, Indian tribes negotiated away almost 2 billion acres of North America. The treaties, usually coerced, embodied 720 land cessions in return for nearly $800 million from the United States government. In fact, payment was always unconscionably small or made only in part. The tribes went to court.

The Indian legal wars began in 1831 when the Cherokees sought to protect their lands from encroachment. The Supreme Court was sympathetic (*Worcester v. Georgia*, 6 Pet. 515, 1832), the nation was not, and enforced removal dominated the next quarter century. Indian access to the new federal Court of Claims (est. 1855) was barred in 1863, and the treaty-making process ended in 1871. The treaties, however, were not invalidated; in 1881 the Choctaws gained entry to the Court of Claims through an act of Congress. This act waived the sovereign immunity of the United States from suit, and this immunity necessitated a separate act for each claim. By World War I, thirty-one Indian claims against the federal government had reached the Court, all in spite of the assimilationist General Allotment Act of 1887, which was relentlessly moving toward making any Indian tribal claim a moot point by individualizing Indian lands. The tribes persevered. Honorable war service, the grant of citizenship (1924), and an increase in reservation population gave the Indians new life. The number of tribal claims filed rose rapidly, putting increased pressure on the courts and Congress for some form of resolution. The courts balked at settling most of these claims and sought dismissal on a jurisdictional technicality ruling that such claims were best resolved by legislation rather than adjudication. Thus, from 1881 to 1946, only 35 of the 219 claims filed with the Court of Claims won awards totaling some $77 million. The result was the Indian Claims Commission (ICC), a forum to finally settle the dogged persistence of the tribes for their day in court.

The ICC was the product of government awareness of past moral wrongs, a movement for the reform of Indian administration and congressional legislation, and a resolve to remove any lingering clouds from the title to the lands of America. In 1928, with the backing of the influential Meriam Report, the idea of a commission format gained acceptance. Commission legislation was debated in Congress throughout the 1930s amid intergovernmental wrangling and pressure from interested parties. The Depression years and World War II sidetracked legislators from the issue until 1945, when Congress held extensive hearings and, under the leadership of Henry M. Jackson, passed the commission act.

The ICC, granted a ten-year lifespan, began its first full year of operation in July 1947. The three commissioners and a staff of twelve adopted rules of procedure, notified one hundred seventy-six Indian groups of their intent, and prepared to hear and resolve the hundreds of claims anticipated by the end of the five-year filing period given the tribes. Although designated as a commission by statute, the ICC quickly, in practice, became a court. The Court of Claims was an inescapable precedent, and all parties involved conceded their preference for an adversarial proceeding.

Ninety percent of the claims concerned issues of land; the rest were labeled "accounting cases." The former were heard in three complex stages: title, value-liability, and offsets. The adversaries, tribal attorneys, and Justice Department lawyers had to define "territory the Indians occupied exclusively," then establish the value of the land at "the time of taking," and finally, assuming liability, offset any proper government payment against that value before a final payment would be ordered. The latter cases required a government accounting of tribal funds. The government, as legal guardians for the tribes, was accountable for tribal assets and their management. As with the land cases, the massive record revealed an abundance of evidence of mishandling and misfeasance, and involved a lengthy process for presentation.

The age and complexity of these claims was not the only barrier to Indian recovery. A subtle but strong anti-Indian bias existed within the government and the public. The tribes had to overcome an early attempt by the Justice Department and the ICC to allow the defense of *res judicata*, which would have effectively barred most cases because of prior judgment in the Court of Claims. Many tribes had to prove their very existence as tribes to be recognized by the ICC. The recognition of Indian title as valid for compensation, left unresolved by the Supreme Court, was only settled by the Court of Claims, as appellate to the ICC, in the landmark *Otoe and Missouria* (United States 131 Ct. Cls. 593) case of 1955. In each of these challenges, the Court of Claims, now unhindered by the jurisdictional question, was a friend to the tribes, balancing a conservative ICC with its experience and a sense of responsibility for carrying out the mandate of Congress.

By 1956 it was obvious that the ten-year lifespan granted by the ICC's enabling act was insufficient. Only 80 cases had been completed out of a docket of 600 claims. Congress voted renewal in 1956 and again in 1961. By 1960, 125 claims had been disposed and, though this total would double by 1967, Congress had become alarmed at the prolongation in the life of its temporary creation.

In 1967 the ICC received its most extensive hearings and scrutiny since the 1940s, but another five-year renewal was passed. The ICC was also expanded to five members and the incumbent members removed. Another renewal was voted in 1972. In 1975, with only 176 cases remaining, Chief Commissioner Jerome Kuykendall notified Congress that the ICC would not seek extension, even though the work could not be completed by 1977. Proponents of the ICC, though, did press for its continuance and secured an eighteen-month *final* renewal, whereupon all remaining cases would be transferred to the Court of Claims. The ICC formally ceased operation on September 30, 1978, leaving a legacy of sixty-eight cases (mostly accounting) to the Court of Claims.

The legislative history of the ICC reveals that Congress wanted finality to the claims, tribal termination, and Indian assimilation, reduced expenses, settled title, and to "get out of the Indian business." It got little of this. The Indians wanted a major involvement in the claims process, land, and justice. They got money. Technically, the tribes did get their day in court, but, of equal importance, the claims resolution process also provided needed development capital to some tribes, raised their legal consciousness, broadened public awareness of an iniquitous period in American history, and amassed a huge record for future scholarly study of Indian-white relations.

Harvey D. Rosenthal

See also Government Policy; Land Claims

Further Reading
Barsh, Russel L. "Indian Land Claims Policy in the United States." *North Dakota Law Review*, 58 (1982): 7–82.
Federal Indian Law. New York, NY: Association on American Indian Affairs, 1966.
Lurie, Nancy O. "The Indian Claims Commission." *Annals of the American Academy*, 436 (March 1978): 97–110.
Records of the United States Indian Claims Commission. New York, NY: Clearwater Publishing Company, 1973–1985. Microfiche.
Rosenthal, Harvey D. *Their Day in Court: A History of the Indian Claims Commission*. New York, NY: Garland Publishing, 1990.
U.S. Indian Claims Commission. *Final Report*. Washington, DC: The Commission, 1979.
Washburn, Wilcomb E. *Red Man's Land—White Man's Law: A Study of the Past and Present of the American Indian*. New York, NY: Scribner, 1971.

INDIAN COUNTRY

"Indian country" is a phrase whose meaning remains elusive. Its most common usage, as expressed in Felix Cohen's seminal treatise on Indian law, is that "Indian country" may be "most usefully defined as country within which Indian laws and customs and federal laws relating to Indians are generally applicable." As a matter of geography, Indian country includes the land within the boundaries of any Indian reservation or within the boundaries of any "dependent Indian communities" who reside on lands set aside for them by the federal government. Indian country includes not only reservation lands held in trust by the tribes, but also 1) privately held lands, whether owned by Indians *or non-Indians*, within the boundaries of reservations; 2) rights-of-way (most commonly federal and state highways) through Indian country; and 3) any additional lands legally acquired by the tribes.

This geopolitical conception of Indian country is significant because it defines the reach of tribal jurisdiction. Within Indian country, tribes may exercise control over their internal affairs and may assert jurisdiction over criminal and civil matters subject only to any limitations set forth in treaties or congressional statutes.

But there are many who perceive Indian country in ways very different from this legalistic conception. For example, many Indians believe that Indian country must transcend the political boundaries of reservations, especially since such boundaries usually were established arbitrarily under the threat of military force. They argue that "Indian country" must include those territories integral to the economic sustenance of the tribes (for example, lands for hunting and grazing or waters for fishing), whether they lie within the reservations or not.

Others insist that lands invested with cultural or religious significance to the tribes be included in Indian country. For example, there are lands long-since severed from the legal control of tribes (e.g. the Black Hills of South Dakota or the San Francisco Peaks of Arizona) that remain central to their religious heritage. In addition, some tribes were forcibly displaced from lands they had occupied for many generations, onto reservations whose lands were alien to them. To a relocated Creek or Cherokee, would Indian country be the land in the Oklahoma territory to which he had been assigned by governmental fiat, or the Georgia ancestral lands from which he had been removed?

Prior to European settlement Indian country included all of the North American continent. As European settlements became more numerous in the seventeenth and eighteenth centuries, Indian country was contrasted with the "civilized" areas under control of the colonists. In this sense, the frontier was not so much a separation between east and west as it was a rough and movable demarcation, between "white man's country" and Indian country. In an attempt to formalize these lines of demarcation, the European powers in North America (principally England and France) negotiated directly with many Indian tribes. In nearly every sense the Indian tribes were recognized as sovereign entities and the resulting treaties vested the tribes with complete jurisdiction over their own "country." European powers and their colonial administrations could (and did) lay political claim to much of this Indian country, but such claims were intended to exclude other Europeans, not the indigenous Indians.

This sovereign status of Indian country became compromised under the federal Constitution of 1787. On the one hand, the Constitution authorized the national government to "regulate commerce with foreign nations, and among the several states, and with the Indian tribes," suggesting that Indian tribes still retained sovereign status. Yet the Constitution in almost every other way acknowledged the existence of only two sovereign entities within the territorial boundaries of the United States—the states and the federal government. As the territorial claims of the United States expanded in the nineteenth century, the shrinking islands of Indian country—neither states nor fully autonomous foreign nations—lay in a constitutional limbo.

This constitutional tension came to a head in a series of cases pitting the State of Georgia against the Cherokee Nation. Georgia insisted that all lands within its territorial boundaries, whether Indian country or not, were subject to its jurisdiction. If Georgia were to prevail, Indian country would cease to exist; Indian land (and sovereignty over it) would dissolve into the general mix of lands subject to the jurisdiction of the states. In the most famous of these cases, *Worcester v. Georgia* (1832), Chief Justice of the United States Supreme Court John Marshall, denied Georgia's claims. Marshall argued that the state laws were "in direct hostility with treaties . . . which mark out the boundary that separates the Cherokee country from Georgia [and] guaranty to them all the land within their boundary."

But *Worcester v. Georgia* was a hollow victory for the Cherokees, for the Court's decision did not establish the inviolability of Indian country. Instead, it renounced Georgia's claims because the state was trespassing into an area of *federal* supremacy. Rather than autonomous sovereign powers, the tribes were deemed to be "domestic dependent nations," whose treaties with the federal government only accentuated their status as wards under the special guardianship of Congress, a doctrine made more clear in *United States v. Kagama* (1886). The federal government was free to permit a substantial degree of tribal autonomy over territory within Indian country, but it was not constitutionally obligated to do so. Indian country was (and to a large extent still is) whatever Congress says it is.

For the most part, Congress and the federal courts have insulated Indian country from the reach of state taxing authority and state criminal and civil jurisdiction. But important exceptions abound. For example, Public Law 280, enacted in 1953, permitted some states (originally California, Minnesota, Nebraska, Oregon, and Wisconsin—with certain named tribes exempted from the law's provisions) to assume jurisdiction over Indian country within their borders. Several additional states have accepted Congress's invitation to assume jurisdiction under P.L. 280, but many have declined because of an unwillingness to take over the fiscal responsibilities previously exercised by the federal government.

While the notion of Indian country remains a formidable barrier against unwanted state intrusions into Indian life, the same cannot be said with regard to the federal government. Two recent Supreme Court decisions have substantially eroded the principle that tribal governments are sovereign within Indian country. In *Oliphant v. Susquamish Indian Tribe* (1979), the Court held that even *within* Indian country tribal courts had no criminal jurisdiction over non-Indians. The Court reiterated the doctrine that tribes were dependent, rather than wholly sovereign, entities and that they therefore could exercise control only over internal (tribal) affairs. *Duro v. Reina* (1990) recently extended the *Oliphant* principle to exclude tribal control over the actions of nonmember Indians within Indian country. Felix Cohen's fifty-year-old notion of Indian country as land governed by Indian laws and customs and federal law seems to be giving way to one in which federal law alone prevails.

Glenn A. Phelps

See also Law; Sovereignty and Jurisdiction

Further Reading

Cohen, Felix S. *Handbook of Federal Indian Law* (1942). Buffalo, NY: William S. Hein Co., 1988.

Deloria, Vine, Jr., and Clifford M. Lytle. *American Indians, American Justice.* Austin: University of Texas Press, 1983.

"Special Edition: The Political Geography of Indian Country." *American Indian Culture and Research Journal* 15:2 (1991): 1–169.

Wilkinson, Charles. *American Indians, Time and the Law: Native Societies in a Modern Constitutional Democracy.* New Haven. CT: Yale University Press, 1987.

INDIAN EDUCATION ACT, 1972

The roots of the Indian Education Act of 1972 started in 1967 with the formation of the Senate Special Subcommittee on Indian Education, chaired by Senator Robert Kennedy. After his tragic death, Senators Edward Kennedy (Massachusetts) and Walter F. Mondale (Minnesota) cochaired the committee which spent the next two years conducting hearings and reviewing reports, studies, and evaluations of Indian educational programs. The committee's final report, *Indian Education: A National Tragedy—A National Challenge*, also known as the "Kennedy Report," called for major changes in the way the United States Office of Education served Indian and Alaska Native students. Its recommendations advocated extending federal educational services to Indians who were not

members of federally recognized tribes. They also focused on parental involvement and local control as important to improving academic performance among Native students. Draft legislation was prepared.

Senators Kennedy and Mondale, recognizing the importance of involving the Indian community in developing this new legislation, invited representatives of the newly created National Indian Education Association to suggest ways the proposed legislation could be improved. Will Antell of the Association and Harvard University graduate student William Demmert were hired to consult with Indian communities and Native graduate students. Their efforts resulted in recommendations which strengthened the bill, and they were able to gain Indian support for its passage.

The Act as passed had four major parts. Part A provided formula funding for public schools serving Indian children; it included a 10 percent set-aside for Indian controlled schools. Part B provided direct grants to Indian tribes and organizations, colleges and universities, state departments of education, and other private nonprofit groups. With a funding priority for Indian tribes and organizations, grants could be used for demonstration sites, planning and evaluation, and a variety of projects that were designed to meet the special educational needs of American Indian and Alaska Native students. Part C provided monies for adult education that were tied to job training activity. And Part D was primarily administrative and called for an Office of Indian Education in the United States Office of Education, a deputy commissioner of Indian education, and a National Advisory Council for Indian Education, with responsibility for recommending a deputy commissioner, advising the United States commissioner of education, the Congress, and the president on Indian educational issues. Part D of the law was only fully implemented when a lawsuit by the Minnesota Chippewa tribes forced the Nixon administration to appoint the National Advisory Council required by the new legislation.

Funding for the legislation was forced through by the United States Senate, starting in 1973 at $18 million. It grew steadily through 1981 to $81.68 million. There were annual decreases from 1981 to 1987, with a low of $64.187 million in 1986. It has since grown to $75.364 million (1991).

The first amendment to Title V (as the Act is now known) was a special appropriation to Part B for Indian professional development at the graduate level. Substantive changes from the original act include a change from a deputy commissioner to a director; the addition of a gifted and talented program; Indian preference for employees in the program; eligibility of Bureau of Indian Affairs (BIA) schools for formula grants originally limited to public schools; and for the director to recommend policy on all programs for Indians funded by the Department of Education.

The Indian Education Act of 1972 (orginally Title IV of PL 92–318, as amended) has made a major contribution to improving the quality of Indian education in the United States. Since its passage, Indians have benefited from an increase in the number of Indian professionals educating Native students; an increased involvement of parents in the education of their children; the development of curriculum materials that are positive about Indians and present an Indian perspective; an extension of responsibility to other federal departments for providing education programs; an increase in Indian students attending and graduating from college; a significant increase in the development of parent-based early childhood programs; and the development of positive attitudes among a majority of American Indian and Alaska Native students.

William G. Demmert, Jr.

See also Educational Policy; Johnson-O'Malley Act

Further Reading

Building From Yesterday to Tomorrow: The Continuing Federal Role in Indian Education. The National Advisory Council on Indian Education, 15th Annual Report to the United States Congress, 1988.

Demmert, William G., Jr. "Critical Issues in Indian Education." Ed.D. diss., Harvard University, 1974.

U.S. Congress. Senate. Committee on Labor and Public Welfare. Hearings before the Subcommittee on Education. *Education Amendments of 1971.* 92d Cong., S.659, Pt. 4. Washington, DC: U.S. Government Printing Office, 1971.

U.S. Congress. Senate. Committee on Labor and Public Welfare. Special Subcommittee on Indian Education Report. *Indian Education: A National Tragedy—A National Challenge.* 91st Cong., 1st sess. Washington, DC: U.S. Government Printing Office, 1969.

U.S. Department of Education. The Indian at Risk Task Force. *Indians at Risk: An Educational Strategy for Action.* Washington, DC: 1991.

INDIAN EDUCATION ASSOCIATION

See National Indian Education Association

INDIAN HEALTH SERVICE

The Indian Health Service (IHS) is one of eight agencies in the United States Public Health Service. The primary responsibility of the IHS is to provide comprehensive health care for eligible Native Americans and Alaska Natives. The current mission of the IHS is to achieve the highest attainable level of health for American Indian and Alaska Native people. Its broad goals are to ensure equity in health care delivery, assist Native people in defining their health needs, establish local health care priorities, and provide management for health programs. Despite IHS efforts, American Indian and Alaska Native health in many areas remains below the national average.

Early History of the Indian Health Service

From the first contact with Europeans, the health status of Native Americans changed dramatically. Infectious diseases, especially smallpox brought to America by Europeans, ravaged Native American nations. Despite the heavy loss of Indian lives, it was not until the early 1800s that federal health services for American Indians began under the auspices of the War Department, who administered Indian affairs, providing sporadic medical care and emergency health measures to Indian people in the vicinity of military posts in order to protect the soldiers from infection.

The first legal commitment to provide an Indian nation with health services was in 1832. The federal government negotiated a treaty with the Winnebago which stipulated that a physician would be provided as partial payment for ceded lands. By 1871, when Congress terminated treaty-making, at least twenty-four ratified treaties promised some form of medical services. Health care, however, remained sporadic and reactionary.

With the transfer of the Bureau of Indian Affairs (BIA) to the newly created Department of Interior in 1849, a bureaucratic structure emerged to serve the growing health needs of Indian people. By the 1880s, the permanent settlement of Native Americans on reservations allowed the Indian administration to construct a system of hospital-based care, establish a nursing staff, and a field matron corps in the 1890s. Although the availability of health care improved, the delivery of services was plagued by inadequate facilities, a lack of medical supplies, transportation problems, and incompetent personnel as well as a general resistance by many Indian people toward Western medicine.

The period between 1900 and 1955 saw revolutionary changes in the administration and the practice of curative and preventive medicine. Centralized medical supervision began in 1908 with the creation of the position of chief medical supervisor. The supervisor position was strengthened in 1924 with the creation of the Health Division of the Bureau. Two years later, the Indian Medical Service underwent a general reorganization. The country was divided into four medical districts, each with a district medical director and a chief medical director. The reorganization of the Indian Medical Service was a response to the 1921 Snyder Act, which designated that routine health care be provided to Indian people by the federal government. As these bureaucratic changes took place, the practice of medicine among Native Americans also changed. These changes largely were prompted by major health surveys conducted by the Public Health Service in 1913 and the 1928 Meriam Report. The quality of hospital facilities improved greatly. At the turn of the century, for example, Indian hospitals had fewer than 150 beds to serve Indian people. This number grew to more than 4,000 beds just before World War II. After World War II, a lack of qualified medical personnel, combined with a lack of funds, prompted the BIA in 1952 to adopt a policy of closing Indian health facilities and contracting health services to state or local non-Indian hospitals. By

1955, the Bureau had contracted with sixty-five community hospitals, sixteen tuberculosis sanitoria, and five mental institutions. It was argued that contract care was less expensive and allowed Indian patients to stay closer to home, but closings of Indian health facilities paralleled the termination of Indian reservations. By the mid-1950s only sixteen Indian hospitals and sanatoria met accreditation requirements of the Joint Commission on Accreditation of Hospitals.

As the bureaucratic structure of health care delivery was undergoing changes, so too were the personnel who staffed the facilities. Health personnel employed by the Bureau of Indian Affairs increased both in number, qualifications, and occupation. Beginning in 1926, physician-officers in the Public Health Service (PHS) Commissioned Corps were detailed to hold health positions in the Indian Medical Service. Positions held by PHS commissioned health officers grew slowly until the 1950 Doctor-Dentist Draft Law, which permitted members to serve required duty in the Public Health Service. Under the law, by 1955 over fifty physicians, twelve public health nurses, and a few dentists, pharmacists (organized in 1953), and sanitary engineers were working for the Indian Medical Service.

Dental services were instituted in 1913, with the assignment of five traveling dentists to visit Indian boarding schools and reservations. Dental services expanded to twenty-eight full-time and seventeen part-time dentists by 1939. After 1950, dental needs were met by the assignment of Public Health Service dentists to the Indian Medical Service, but dental health care delivery lagged far behind other health services.

Motivated by a 1922 American Red Cross report, public health nurses were added to the medical staff in 1924. These nurses reached a peak number of one hundred ten in 1939, but declined to seventy in 1955. Indian participation in the Indian Medical Service began in 1935, with the establishment of the Kiowa School of Practical Nursing. Through a nine-month course of study, Indian women were trained in practical nursing skills.

During this same period, BIA health officials instituted a number of specific disease control programs, especially for tuberculosis and trachoma, and health education programs on reservations. In 1911 the Indian Medical Service declared tuberculosis, trachoma, and infant mortality a national health tragedy. In response, between 1911 and 1940 the BIA created a system of boarding school tuberculosis sanatoria as well as a sanatoria system for nonschool-aged Indian people. Concomitant with the expansion of sanatoria, as early as 1909, the Indian Bureau launched a medical education program and by 1935 began a BCG tuberculosis vaccination program. Similarly, trachoma campaigns were carried out by medical doctors, especially at the boarding schools. The discovery of sulfanilamide rapidly arrested the trachoma epidemic. Other disease control programs included smallpox vaccination in 1901, and a 1935 venereal disease program in cooperation with the American Social Hygiene Association.

Throughout this period, the Indian Medical Service attempted to improve reservation sanitation, promote health education, improve nutrition, seek state and local cooperation on Indian health issues, begin medical social work, and hire more qualified personnel. These changes were reflected in the federal appropriations for Indian health services (figure 1). In 1911 appropriations for general health care was $40,000; by 1955, $17,754,555 were allocated for health services among Indian people. Although the annual appropriations increased dramatically during this period, the success of the IHS was marred by a lack of efforts to identify Indian health needs, a lack of qualified personnel, and underfunding. Many of these problems continue to plague the IHS today. For Indian people, the inadequate delivery of health care during this period meant continued ill-health and suffering.

Figure 1
Federal Appropriations for American Indian and Alaska Native Health Services, 1911 to 1955

Fiscal Year	Appropriation
1911	$ 40,000
1920	$ 375,000
1930	$ 1,514,000
1940	$ 5,088,170
1950	$ 10,016,615
1955	$ 17,754,555

Source: U.S. Department of Health, Education, and Welfare 1959:31

Recent History and Developments

As early as 1919, the House Committee on Indian Affairs recommended that Indian health care be taken out of the BIA and transferred to the United States Public Health Service (USPHS). Indeed, many prominent health organizations lobbied heavily for the transfer of Indian health care to the USPHS. Transfer of federal responsibility of Indian health care delivery from the BIA to the USPHS was accomplished July 1, 1955 (42 U.S.C. 2004a). The USPHS Division of Indian Health, it was argued, would provide a firm bureaucratic foundation for direct and contract medical care to Indian people. In reality, federal termination policy was behind the transfer. Thousands of Indian people were denied their rights, including the right to health services, as a result of termination.

During the 1960s and into the early 1970s, the USPHS assumed full jurisdiction over Indian health (Public Law 151; Public Law 121). Under USPHS management, Congress increased health appropriation monies dramatically (figure 2). The goal was to achieve a level of health and well-being comparable to the general non-Indian population. Despite the increase in appropriations, a 1961 report by the Commission on the Rights, Liberties, and Responsibilities of the American Indian stated that a large disparity remained between the health status of American Indians and the general population. Most importantly, the report concluded that the health status of American Indians would improve only when their economic conditions are raised.

Figure 2
Federal Appropriations for American Indian and Alaska Native Health Services, 1972 to 1986

Fiscal Year	Appropriation
1972	$ 156,673,492
1973	$ 176,804,073
1974	$ 202,048,191
1975	$ 237,296,900
1976	$ 285,151,500
1977	$ 347,715,600
1978	$ 440,455,700
1979	$ 495,912,100
1980	$ 551,016,900
1981	$ 613,244,100
1982	$ 627,644,500
1983	$ 690,971,900
1984	$ 785,600,300
1985	$ 807,147,900

Source: Office of Technology Assessment 1986:345–349

The watershed for American Indian health legislation came in the mid-1970s. In 1975, the Indian Self-Determination and Education Assistance Act (Public Law 93–638) permitted Indian nations to directly administer programs managed by the BIA or the IHS. The following year, Congress passed the Indian Health Care Improvement Act (Public Law 94–437). The act clarified and reiterated federal health care responsibilities outlined in the 1921 Snyder Act. An amendment, Public Law 96–537, was passed in 1980 to clarify further federal responsibility in elevating the health status of American Indians and Alaskan Natives.

The 1980s, especially during the Reagan administration, saw declines in funding social services. With declining resources, new issues arose in health care delivery. The first issue was eligibility for health care services. The Snyder Act has no express statutory language on who is eligible for IHS services. Since the 1974 decision of *Morton v. Ruiz*, the IHS has attempted to limit eligibility of Indians by residence, blood quantum, or other criteria. A second related issue is whether the IHS is a primary or residual health care provider for Indian people. In 1986, in *McNabb v. Heckler, et al.*, the United States District Court for the District of Montana ruled that the federal government was primarily responsible for health care services. Since that ruling, the IHS has had to assure reasonable health care for eligible American Indians and Alaskan Natives.

Current Issues in Federal Indian Health Care and Policy

Despite legislative reinforcement of Public Law 94–437 through Public Law 101–630 surrounding federal responsibility for Native American health care, eligibility and entitlement to services remain in the forefront in health policy in the 1990s. Other issues include availability and adequacy of health resources, self-determination and tribal assumption of health services, the extent of congressional control of health care policies for American Indians and Alaska Natives, and especially the future of urban Indian health programs. Census data indicate that over 50 percent of the Native American population now reside in urban areas. Despite this profound shift in population geography, the appropriations for urban Indian health care have eroded steadily since 1980. To date, urban Indian health programs emphasize increasing access to existing services funded by private and public sources, rather than the IHS paying for those services directly. Underlying all of these questions are concerns over increasing health care quality, accessibility, and economics.

Indian Health Service Organization and Service Population

On January 4, 1988, the IHS was elevated to agency status, becoming the seventh agency of the Public Health Service. IHS health delivery is composed of two major systems: (1) a federal health care delivery system, administered by federal personnel and; (2) a tribally based health care system, administered by Indian nations. Both systems utilize contract health care services from over 2,000 private providers. In addition, there are thirty-four urban Indian health projects located in major urban areas with concentrated Indian populations.

The IHS is composed of twelve regional administrative area offices (figure 3, map). IHS headquarters are in Rockville, Maryland, although some head office functions are conducted in Phoenix, Tucson, and Albuquerque. As of 1991, the area offices consisted of 136 service units, of which 58 were operated by Indian nations. Tribal nations operated 7 hospitals, 89 health centers, 3 school health centers, 64 health stations, and 173 Alaska village clinics; while the IHS operated 43 hospitals, 66 health centers, 4 school health centers, and 51 health stations. The IHS has approximately 14,000 employees; the medical staff is comprised of 1,200 physicians and dentists, 100 physician assistants, and 2,400 nurses; and the remaining staff includes pharmacists, nutritionists, engineers, health administrators, medical records staff, support staff, and numerous other allied health personnel.

As the Native American and Alaska Native population grew, so too did the service responsibility of the Indian Health Service. Today the IHS serves over one million eligible Native American and Alaska Native people. The service population is composed of over 500 federally recognized Native nations, groups, and

INDIAN HEALTH SERVICE HOSPITALS AND AREA OFFICES

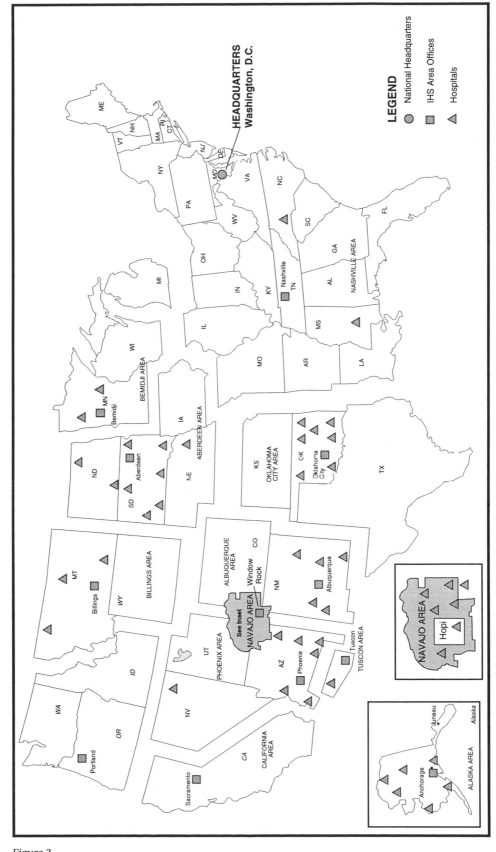

Source: U.S. Department of Health and Human Services, Indian Health Service. 1992

Figure 3

villages in all or parts of 33 states. In 1989, the IHS user population was approximately 1,012,000. Demographically, the Indian population is younger, less educated, and poorer than the general United States population. Although there is considerable variation between service areas, the data indicates a growing population with a wide range of health needs, and a population that has not achieved health parity with the general United States population.

Current Demographics and Health Status

In 1890, there were approximately 273,607 American Indian and Alaska Natives in the United States. For Indians and Alaska Native peoples, this represented a population nadir. From this demographic nadir, their populations have made a remarkable recovery. To some degree, their health has also improved, but they have not as yet achieved the same level of health enjoyed by the majority of the non-Indian population.

The birth rate for American Indians and Alaska Natives residing in the IHS service area was 30.3 per 1,000 (figure 4), nearly double the 1987 birth rate for the United States "All Races" population. In short, Native American populations are growing at least two times faster than other segments of our society.

Figure 4

Native American and Alaska Native Birth Rates (per 1,000), Birth Rates for All U.S. Races and U.S. Other than White, 1955 to 1980 (per 1,000)

Year	1955	1960	1970	1980	1986–88
Indian and Alaska Native Birth Rate	37.5	42.1	32.0	27.0	30.3
U.S. All Races Rate	24.6	23.7	18.4	15.9	15.7[1]
U.S. Other than White Rate	33.1	32.1	25.1	22.5	NA

[1]*U.S. All Races Rate, 1987*

Sources: Stuart 1987:103; U.S. Department of Health and Human Services 1991:21

Although the birth rate is exceeding the rate of the general population, from 1986 to 1988 the age-adjusted mortality rate (all causes) for the IHS service area was 665.8 per 100,000. This is 50 percent higher than the 1987 United States All Races rate of 535.5 per 100,000. As the IHS controlled infectious diseases that plagued Indians well into the twentieth century, sanitation improved, dietary patterns changed, and minimal economic gains were made, and thus the causes of death shifted radically (figure 5). From 1951 to 1953, for example, tuberculosis was the fourth leading cause of death. By 1972 to 1974, the chronic infectious disease had no appreciable impact on American Indian mortality. Currently, the two leading causes of death are diseases of the heart and accidents and adverse effects. These causes indicate that changes in the lifestyle and behavior are impacting mortality.

Figure 5

Leading Causes of Death, American Indians and Alaska Natives, Ranked Change by Years, 1951 to 1988

All Causes	Changes in Ranking by Years			
	1951–53	1972–74	1980–82	1986–88
Heart Diseases	1	2	1	1
Accidents	2	1	2	2
Influenza and Pneumonia	3	5	6	NA
Tuberculosis	4	—	—	NA
Certain Diseases of Early Infancy	5	7	10	NA
Malignant Neoplasms	6	3	3	3
Gastritis, Duodentis, Enteritis, and Colitis	7	—	—	NA
Vascular Lesions Affecting the Central Nervous System	8	—	—	NA
Congenital Malformations	9	—	—	NA
Homicide (including Legal Execution)	10	8	8	NA
Cirrhosis of the Liver	—	4	4	5
Cerebrovascular Lesions (Diseases)	—	6	5	4
Diabetes Mellitus	—	9	7	NA
Suicide	—	10	9	NA

Sources: Stuart 1987:108;110; U.S. Department of Health and Human Services 1991:36

A sensitive indicator of the health status of any population is infant mortality rates and life expectancy. Since 1955, the infant mortality has dropped considerably, but remains higher than the rate for the general United States population. The infant mortality rate for American Indians and Alaska Natives was 11.1 per 1,000. This is greater than the 10.1 1987 rate for the United States All Races population (figure 6). However, when the rate is adjusted for underreporting, the infant mortality rate is 12.7, 26 times greater than the United States rate. Clearly, Native American infants are dying in greater proportion than the general non-Indian population.

Figure 6

Infant Mortality Rates (per 1,000), Native American, Alaska Native, and U.S. All Races, 1955 to 1988

Year	1955	1960	1970	1980	1986–88
American Indian and Alaska Native	62.7	48.0	24.6	13.8	11.1
American Indian	60.9	45.5	24.3	13.4	——
Alaska Native	79.5	72.1	28.1	20.4	——
U.S. All Races	26.4	26.0	20.0	12.6	10.1[1]

[1]*U.S. All Races Rate, 1987*

Sources: Stuart 1987:105; U.S. Department of Health and Human Services 1991:24

Since 1940, the life expectancy of Indians and Alaska Native people has steadily risen, although it remains below the national rate (figure 7). In short, Native people experience a far greater loss and remain a population at risk.

Figure 7
Life Expectancy at Birth, Native Americans and Alaska Natives, U.S. White Population, 1940 to 1988

Year	American Indian and Alaska Natives	U.S. White Population
1940	51.0	64.9
1950	60.0	69.0
1960	61.7	70.7
1970	65.1	71.6
1980	71.1	74.4
1986–88	72.0	75.0[1]

[1]*U.S. All Races Rate, 1987*
Sources: Stuart 1987:105; U.S. Department of Health and Human Services 1991:53

Conclusions

The role and goals of the Indian Health Service have changed dramatically since its beginning in the early 1870s. During its bureaucratic development, the IHS evolved from an organization devoted to missionizing Indian and Alaska Native people in the "ways of civilization," through the introduction of Western medicine, to a reactionary organization trying to control infectious diseases, and finally, a service devoted to providing comprehensive health care and promoting health equity among Indian and Alaska Native people.

During the twentieth century, the health status of Native Americans has improved dramatically, especially after 1955. Despite the tremendous gains in the level of health, they have not achieved an equitable level of health parallel to the general population. In a nine-IHS service area comparison of rates to the 1987 United States rates, American Indians and Alaska Natives experienced a 400 percent greater rate of tuberculosis, a 663 percent greater rate for alcoholism, and a 295 percent greater rate for accidents than did the United States general population. In addition, American Indians and Alaska Natives suffer a 268 percent greater rate for diabetes mellitus, a 134 percent greater rate for homicide, and a 95 percent greater rate for suicide. Such statistics reveal how large the gap is in health equity between the non-Indian population and our nation's indigenous peoples.

Gregory R. Campbell

See also **Government Policy; Health; Mental Health**

Further Reading

Brophy, William A., and Sophie D. Aberle. *The Indian, America's Unfinished Business: Report of the Commission on the Rights, Liberties, and Responsibilities of the American Indian.* Norman: University of Oklahoma Press, 1966.

Campbell, Gregory R., ed. "Contemporary Issues in Native American Health." Special Issue of *American Indian Culture and Research Journal* 13:3, 4 (1989).

Indian Health Care. Office of Technology Assessment. Washington, DC: U.S. Government Printing Office, 1986.

Putney, Diane T. "Fighting the Scourge: American Indian Morbidity and Federal Indian Policy, 1897–1928." Ph.D. diss., Marquette University, 1980.

Stuart, Paul. *Nations Within a Nation: Historical Statistics of American Indians.* Westport, CT: Greenwood Press, 1987.

U.S. Department of Health and Human Services. *Indian Health Service: Regional Differences in Indian Health.* Washington, DC: U.S. Government Printing Office, 1991.

INDIAN IDENTITY

One of the more perplexing issues confronting the indigenous peoples of North America during the late twentieth century is the question of how to go about defining who is and who is not "Indian." At base, the problem devolves from confusion as to whether Native peoples are to be understood as distinct nationalities, as their several hundred ratified treaties with the United States and other powers clearly entitles them to be, or to be classified merely as a "racial group." In the first instance, American Indian identity would be determined not only by birth into one or another nation—Mohawk, Ute, Bannock, etc.—but by exercise of such sovereign group prerogatives as naturalization by marriage, adoption, and application. In the latter case, considerations of genealogy predominate to the exclusion of all other factors. For reasons of its own, the United States has chosen to impose both mutually contradictory standards of identification, often simultaneously.

Traditionally, most Native peoples employed concepts of group membership which much more closely resemble the time-honored ideals of citizenship than notions of race or "blood." In precontact times, intertribal marriage was common, with either husband or wife assuming membership in the group of his/her spouse, depending upon the matrilocality or patrilocality of the cultures involved. Even more pervasive was the practice of adopting children, and sometimes adults, taken as captives in intergroup warfare. After contact, such inclusive procedures were expanded to accommodate the desire for membership expressed by both a steady stream of European frontiersmen and a rather larger number of escaped African chattel slaves. Hence, whatever "genetic purity" might ever have existed within indigenous North American societies had been willingly and thoroughly diluted through a sustained process of intermixing long before the pedigrees of individual Indians began to be catalogued by anthropologists and bureaucrats employed by the federal government.

During the early period of United States-Indian relations, Native criteria regarding membership in their various societies continued to prevail. In none of the many treaties the United States negotiated with indigenous nations prior to 1871, did the government attempt to limit by blood or any other measure the constituency embodied by the other parties to such agreements. It was not until Indians were militarily subdued that the United States felt free to undertake such unilateral presumption. This new federal policy was first evidenced in coherent fashion in the General Allotment or Dawes Act of 1887, through which the government set out to assign each Indian it chose to recognize as such an individual deed to a parcel of land within existing reservation boundaries. Once all recognized Indians had received their 160-acre tracts, all remaining reservation property was declared surplus and opened to non-Indian utilization. The standard for the federal recognition of "Indianness" entitling applicants to receive deeds was that they be, not members/citizens of their respective nations, but "of one-half or more Indian blood."

Needless to say, there were far more 160-acre parcels available within the reservations than there were individuals meeting federal criteria to claim them. Consequently, of the approximately 150 million acres of reservation land inside the United States in 1890, nearly 100 million had passed from Native ownership by the time allotment had run its course in the early 1930s. By then, the government had come to appreciate the extent to which the "blood quantum" method of Indian identification could be utilized to its advantage, not only in controlling Native land and resources, but in constraining its financial obligations in areas such as education. Moreover, the method could be employed—by the simple expedient of raising or lowering quantum requirements—as a mechanism to manipulate indigenous polities and demographies, virtually at will. Thus, blood quantum identification standards have been maintained, despite recent official adoption of a rhetoric of sovereignty and self-determination for Indians, as an integral aspect of federal Indian policy through the present day.

There have been numerous ill effects of this for Native people. The nature of these effects is exemplified by the fact that, while the 1990 United States Census formally acknowledges the presence of fewer than 2 million Indians in the country, more realistic appraisals indicate an additional 14 million who are unrecognized as being who they are, categorized instead as "white," "hispanic," or "Black." Such circumstances fuel a sharp and ever-increasing divisiveness within Native communities as to "who's Indian." In the arena of art, this has been exacerbated by the passage of the Indian Arts and Crafts Act of 1990 (PL 101–644), which makes it a crime for individuals lacking enrollment certification to publicly identify as American Indians when selling art, or for a gallery to exhibit their art as "Indian."

The system in place also lends credence to contentions that the blood quantum system—which has been described as a "eugenics code comparable to those deployed by such blatantly racist countries as nazi Germany and South Africa"—adds up to a form of "statistical extermination" of Native Americans. As the noted Western historian Patricia Nelson Limerick has observed, "Set the blood quantum [standard], hold to it as a rigid definition of Indians, let intermarriage proceed as it had for centuries, and eventually Indians will be defined out of existence. When that happens, the federal government will be freed of its persistent 'Indian problem.'"

M.A. Jaimes

See also **Allotment; Chicanos as Indians; Government Policy; Migrants and Refugees; Race Relations; Red-Black Indians**

Further Reading

Forbes, Jack D. *Black Africans and Native Americans: Color, Evolution and Class in the Evolution of Red-Black Peoples.* Oxford, England: Basil Blackwell Publishers, 1988.

Franklin, John Hope. *Color and Race.* Boston, MA: Beacon Press, 1968.

Jaimes, M. Annette. "Federal Indian Identification Policy: A Usurpation of Indigenous Sovereignty in North America." *The State of Native America: Genocide, Colonization, and Resistance.* Ed. M. Annette Jaimes. Boston, MA: South End Press, 1992. 123–38.

Limerick, Patricia Nelson. *The Legacy of Conquest: The Unbroken Past of the American West.* New York, NY: W.W. Norton, 1987.

Reuter, Edward B. *Race Mixture: Studies in Intermarriage and Miscegenation.* New York, NY: McGraw-Hill, 1931.

Thornton, Russell. *American Indian Holocaust and Survival: A Population History Since 1492.* Norman: University of Oklahoma Press, 1987.

INDIAN MUSEUMS

See Tribal Museums

INDIAN OFFICE

See Bureau of Indian Affairs

INDIAN REORGANIZATION ACT

The Indian Reorganization Act (IRA), signed into law by President Franklin D. Roosevelt on June 18, 1934, is the most important and far-reaching piece of legislation affecting Native Americans in the twentieth century. It is also one of the most controversial. To some Native Americans, such as the Oneida Nation of Indians of Wisconsin, who had been dispossessed of almost all of their 65,000-acre reservation under the allotment provisions of the Dawes Act of 1887 (also known as the General Allotment Act), the IRA provided hope for the future as well as the mechanism for beginning tribal economic restoration, political reform, and meaningful self-government. For others, such as many Lakota, the act contributed to increased discord between traditional tribal leadership and leaders under the new systems of tribal government created under the IRA; in some ways, this added tension is viewed as leading to the take-over at Wounded Knee in February of 1973.

Much of the commentary on the IRA has ignored a central fact: that it was largely an administrative reorganization following a century of mismanagement and mistaken policies that had seriously depleted Indian resources and reduced the Indian population to subsistence. Much of the reorganization was an in-house effort that involved changes in attitudes and perceptions, reallocations of administrative powers and responsibilities, and revision of ad-hoc rules and regulations that had accumulated over the preceding century. It was clearly time to clean house, but it is ironic that the government bureau responsible for the situation both sponsored the remedial legislation and was charged with carrying out the reforms. This dual role of the Bureau of Indian Affairs (BIA) is a major reason why many Indians look at the IRA with both admiration and suspicion.

Between the passage of the Dawes Act and the IRA, the Indian land base had shrunk by over 90 million acres. Even worse, some reservations were still being allotted, although almost every policy-maker knew that allotment was a discredited policy. In 1933, Indians retained approximately 48 million acres of land, much of it arid, unusable, and nonproductive. The Great Dust Bowl conditions made substantially more land unliveable. Moreover, 49 percent of the Indians on allotted reservations were landless. Even before the onset of the Great Depression, 96 percent of all Indians earned less than $200 per year. Much of this income was derived from leasing their allotments to whites, who could afford to invest in the necessary equipment to farm. When these farmers went broke, the leases were cancelled, and the Indians were returned their badly eroded lands without any income to make the land productive.

With the election of Franklin Delano Roosevelt and his appointment of Harold Ickes as secretary of the interior, the New Deal became a reality for Indians. Ickes recommended John Collier as commissioner of Indian affairs, a well-known critic of the Indian Bureau. Along with Collier came two attorneys who made significant contributions to reform: Felix S. Cohen and Nathan Margold. Together, they provided the legal talent needed to orient the massive bureaucracy toward reform. When the second year of Congress during the New Deal began in 1934, this interior team submitted a massive forty-eight-page bill, originally introduced into Congress by Senator Burton K. Wheeler of Montana and Representative Edgar Howard of Nebraska.

Collier's originally drafted bill proposed to stop allotments, form tribal governments, create a court of Indian Affairs, and establish radical changes in land tenure. Congress substantially altered Collier's proposal, eliminating the four-title bill and substituting a new bill which contained several provisions not germane to self-government, but vital for congressional passage. The final version provided for the establishment of tribal elections to accept or reject the provisions of the legislation and of tribal constitutions and corporations. It established a revolving loan fund to assist organized tribes in community development, and by waiving civil service requirements, it offered preference to Indians who sought employment in the BIA. The act also created an educational loan program for Indian students seeking a vocational, high school, or college education. Perhaps most important, the act ended the land allotment policies of the Dawes Act for those tribes accepting the new provisions, and provided for the purchase of new lands for Indians. Unallotted surplus lands were authorized to be returned to tribal governments. Conservation efforts were encouraged by the establishment of Indian forestry units and by herd reduction on arid land to protect range deterioration. This later program cost Collier the support of the Navajo, because it meant a radical reduction of their sheep herds.

A total of 258 tribal referenda were held on whether to accept or reject the act. Native Americans in Oklahoma and Alaska were excluded from the IRA; special enabling legislation—the Oklahoma Indian Welfare Act (1936) and the Alaska Reorganization Act (1936)—later brought the Native Americans of these two areas into the fold. More than two-thirds of eligible Indian nations voted to accept the IRA, although only 40 percent of votes cast in all the referenda held was favorable to the legislation. Under the provisions of the IRA, 36 percent of all Indian nations, 92 in number, wrote new tribal constitutions; 28 percent of all Indian nations, 72 in number, drafted charters of incorporation for business purposes.

The IRA achieved some noteworthy initial successes. It helped some tribes increase their tribal land base, and, especially when contrasted with the allotment period, helped some gain better control of tribal property. Yet even in these areas it was limited. According to the American Indian Policy Review Commission (1977), in the first forty years after passage of the IRA, only 595,157 acres were purchased for tribal use, while government agencies condemned 1,811,010 acres of Indian land for other purposes. The blame, of course, rests with subsequent Congresses and administrations which failed to provide funds for land purchase, not with the originators of the land purchase program. Yet it is noteworthy that both Indians and policy-makers alike look back to the Indian Reorganization Act of 1934 as the foundation upon which to make these judgments—as if the mere passage of the act guaranteed the actions and attitudes of subsequent generations of Indians and congressmen. Moreover, even those American Indian nations who benefited from the IRA have been burdened because the structures created under the act are virtually impossible to change since the amendment process is so rigid.

The act itself and the way it was "sold" explain in part why many Indian nations and individual Indians voted it down. Instead of true self-rule, the act actually increased the secretary of the interior's supervisory authority. Moreover, Section 18, which provided for the tribal referenda, proclaimed that a majority of adult Indians had to vote *against* the act, to prevent its going into effect; this provision was seen by many Indians as another Indian Bureau scheme, since many Indians show their displeasure by boycotting elections.

Nor did the Indian Bureau build trust in winning tribal approval. It attempted to manipulate congressional hearings, looking more favorably on requests for travel funds from supporters than from opponents of the IRA. Moreover, as early as 1938, the FBI was directed to trail dissidents. In addition, despite the major structural changes that the act achieved, it failed to correct a sore point in Indian-federal relations: the everyday abuses of authority and the corruption of BIA reservation superintendents.

Tribal business committees and councils fared little better than individual Indian leaders under the IRA. Despite a sincere commitment by some of these new organizations for economic, educational, and political development, many Indians labeled these committees as tools of the BIA. It is little wonder that by the 1970s, these "IRA councils" became the focus of Red Power militancy that sought to "restore" traditional government to some reservations.

The road to Wounded Knee in 1973 was blazed by the paradoxes and inconsistencies of the Indian Reorganization Act. Although today's critics of the act should remember that self-government was a radical policy for the 1930s, there is no question that the IRA was and is a seriously flawed piece of legislation.

Laurence M. Hauptman

> See also **American Indian Policy Review Commission; Government Policy: Indian New Deal; Wounded Knee II**

Further Reading

Deloria, Vine, Jr., and Clifford Lytle. *The Nation Within: The Past and Future of American Indian Sovereignty.* New York, NY: Pantheon Books, 1984.

Hauptman, Laurence M. "The Indian Reorganization Act." *The Aggressions of Civilization: Federal Indian Policy Since the 1880s.* Eds. Sandra L. Cadwalader and Vine Deloria, Jr. Philadelphia, PA: Temple University Press, 1984. 131–48.

Kelly, Lawrence C. "The Indian Reorganization Act: The Dream and the Reality." *Pacific Historical Review* 44 (August 1975): 291–312.

Philp, Kenneth R., ed. *Indian Self-Rule: First-Hand Accounts of Indian-White Relations from Roosevelt to Reagan.* Salt Lake City, UT: Howe Brothers, 1986.

Washburn, Wilcomb E. "Fifty-Year Perspectives on the Indian Reorganization Act." *American Anthropologist* 86 (June 1984): 279–89.

INDIAN RIGHTS ASSOCIATION

The Indian Rights Association, now inactive, entered the twentieth century as the most respected organization to champion the rights of American Indians. Herbert Welsh founded the Association in December, 1882, after visiting Sioux reservations in Dakota territory earlier that year. He visited at the invitation of Episcopalian Bishop William Hare, and maintained close ties to the Episcopal Church. The organization he founded, however, had an inter-denominational membership of influential philanthropists. The central offices remained in Philadelphia, although Welsh established numerous branches in other Eastern cities. Welsh aligned the Association with Amelia S. Quinton and her Women's National Indian Association, as well as the Board of Indian Commissioners. He also sought counsel from assimilationist Richard H. Pratt of the Carlisle Indian School and Hampton Institute's General S.C. Armstrong. The Assocation reflected the views of many reform groups of the 1870s and 1880s who sought to protect Indians until they assimilated into mainstream American society. It called for land allotments in severalty, education, a legal system, and Christianity.

The Indian Rights Association differed from other reform groups in several features. It employed a full-time agent in Washington to represent its interests. The agent testified at hearings, kept the leadership informed on the progress of important legislation, and, as in the case of the Indian Citizenship Act of 1924, actually drafted legislation. Secondly, the Association benefited from a remarkable continuity in its leadership. Welsh served as executive secretary for forty-five years until 1927 (although he was less active after 1904). Matthew K. Sniffen held key positions for fifty-five years until 1939. Samuel M. Brosius filled the post of Washington agent for thirty-five years until 1933. Finally, the leadership routinely traveled widely on fact-finding tours. These unique features made the Association a powerful and credible voice in Indian affairs until the 1950s.

Early in the twentieth century, the slow pace of assimilation disappointed reformers. They recognized that Indians needed longer than one or two generations to be assimilated. During the first two decades, the Association position shifted somewhat to include protecting Indian rights to property held in common, such as Indian water rights, and called for more Indian participation in decision making in such matters as the leasing of tribal lands. Breaking down tribalism remained a goal, however. The Association believed that Indians should be citizens of states and subject to state laws. It made full citizenship for Indians a top priority, asserting that uncertainty about their legal and tax status, and the status of their allotments, hindered assimilation. It consistently opposed the use of peyote by Indians in religious ceremonies.

Welsh clung to the increasingly anachronistic philosophy of assimilation amid a growing belief in cultural pluralism espoused by reformers led by John Collier and his American Indian Defense Association. Financing and membership from the liberal Eastern establishment dwindled as older members died. In 1922 income did not cover expenses for the first time in Association history. Renewed interest in Indian affairs, mostly as a result of the Pueblo lands fight, provided fresh support. In 1924, a Rockefeller grant allowed the Association to hire more staff and to begin publication of its monthly, *Indian Truth*. Still a powerful organization, it scored an important victory in 1927 when Congress passed legislation guaranteeing Indian title to 22 million acres of executive order reservations.

John Collier's appointment as commissioner of Indian affairs in 1933 and passage of the Indian Reorganization Act in 1934 dealt blows to Association power in Indian affairs. Though Sniffen maintained a good working relationship with Collier, he feuded openly with him in 1935 over Bureau of Indian Affairs' treatment of the Navajos. This disagreement pointed out the extent to which Association policy changed to embrace protection of Indian tribal rights. The Association did not support a bill to repeal the Indian Reorganization Act in 1937, and in 1944, openly opposed its repeal.

Association activity and influence declined appreciably in the 1940s and never regained its former levels. Efforts on behalf of Alaska Natives and Navajos dominated its agendas. In the 1950s the Association fought against House Concurrent Resolution 108, the termination legislation, claiming that Indians needed more time to prepare for full participation in society. The Association's weakness revealed itself in this fight. In 1956, it began a ten-year losing campaign on behalf of the Seneca Nation of New York against the Kinzua Dam project. Increasingly inactive in the 1960s and 1970s, the Association filed its last financial report in 1986 and held its last annual election of officers in 1987.

Dan Eagle Boy Rowe

See also **American Indian Defense Association; Government Policy**

Further Reading

Cadwalader, Sandra A., and Vine Deloria, Jr., eds. *The Aggressions of Civilization: Federal Indian Policy Since the 1880s*. Philadelphia, PA: Temple University Press, 1984.

Dorcy, Michael Morgan. "Friends of the American Indians, 1922–1934: Patterns of Patronage and Philanthropy." Ph.D. diss., University of Pennsylvania, 1978.

Hagan, William T. *The Indian Rights Association: The Herbert Welsh Years, 1882–1904*. Tucson: University of Arizona Press, 1985.

Indian Rights Association. *Papers, 1882–1965: Indian Rights Association*. Glen Rock, NJ: Microfilming Corporation of America, 1975.

Prucha, Francis Paul. *The Great Father: The United States Government and the American Indians*. Lincoln: University of Nebraska Press, 1986.

INDIAN SELF-DETERMINATION AND EDUCATION ASSISTANCE ACT

See Government Policy: Self-Determination

INDIAN SHAKER CHURCH

The Indian Shaker Church, which is unrelated to the American Shakers, the United Society of Believers, was initially formed following an 1882 death-conversion experience by Southern Coastal Salish Indian John Slocum. It continues in the 1990s as a viable movement of Christian churches providing the fellowship of a worshipping community to Indians, principally in British Columbia, Washington, Oregon, and northern California. This area encompasses about 21 churches and estimates of membership range from 1,000 to 3,000. While the movement has been seen by some as stagnant since the 1950s, some evidence exists of successful Shaker evangelism as far away as the Navajo in 1992. The church operates with two major groups: l) followers of the tradition given in the original "Shake" (i.e., those who depend on direct revelation from the Spirit and do not read the Bible for revelation from God); and 2) "Independent" Shakers (i.e., those who have incorporated an acceptance of the Bible and its use during services, along with direct revelation). While doctrinal and dogma differences exist, these do not typically hinder the groups coming together to perform the work of the church.

During 1882, John Slocum, a Southern Coast Salish Indian, became sick and died. According to Shaker tradition, as people went to seek a coffin, Slocum awoke and shared a revelation from an angel of God that would spawn an indigenous American Indian religious movement now over 110 years old. Slocum reportedly told witnesses that God had told him to go back and take this religion back. Slocum, energized by this gripping encounter with God, informed his people that God would give salvation to those who would turn away from drinking, gambling, smoking, and the still numerous shamans or Indian doctors. Slocum also informed them that God had promised a medicine for followers which would surpass the efficacy of the Indian healers. About a year later, Slocum was again taken ill. His father summoned a shaman, to the dismay of Slocum's wife Mary. She exited the house where her sick husband lay and proceeded to pray and weep. Mary Slocum became overcome by an uncontrollable shaking. She reentered the house and prayed over her husband, who was quickly restored. The event of Mary Slocum receiving the "Shake" was acclaimed as the promised medicine from God. Word of Slocum's miraculous restoration quickly spread throughout the southern Puget Sound area.

Early leaders of the church were Slocum, his wife Mary, Skokomish prophet "Big Bill," Mud Bay Louis, and Mud Bay Sam. The first Shaker church was built at Shaker Point (opposite Squaxin Island) according to Slocum's request. Between 1883 and 1932, the movement spread through Washington, into British Columbia, and then through Oregon and into northern California in the late 1920s. The movement formed after the Indians of the northwest had experienced two generations of genocide, disease, removal to reservations, and extinguishment of aboriginal rights. Indian religions were outlawed by United States government memoranda in the 1920s. The Shakers encountered interference from certain missionary groups and religious oppression from Indian agents in the early days.

In 1892 the Shakers organized themselves as a church, incorporating under Washington State law in 1910. At that time, the church adopted a hierarchical organizational scheme similar to other Protestant churches of the era. In 1927 differences about whether to use the Bible in services crystallized in the most serious split in Shaker history. When pro-Bible leader William Kitsap of Tulalip was elected bishop, incumbent Peter Heck refused to leave office. To resolve the ensuing dispute, the Snohomish County superior court created two separate churches: the Indian Shaker Church, whose name was kept by Bishop Heck's supporters; and Bishop Kitsap's group, which became the Indian Full Gospel Church. This original schism has continued to plague the movement into the 1990s.

The Shaker church is a path of love and action with a strong respect for the metaphysical realm. Principal tenets of the Shaker faith include an abiding respect for the experience of direct revelation, or guidance from Christ for one's life, along with obedience to the Gospel of Jesus Christ. Shaker ritual simultaneously creates sacred space and provides communication from this world to the spirit world. The experience of "the Shake," or trembling, has also integrated the experience of individuals receiving the Holy Spirit, as manifested by the experience of persons "speaking in tongues." California elder George Blake relates a story told by a Shaker leader, Harris Teo, where Teo's father heard an Indian speak of the praises of God in many different Indian languages simultaneously, echoing the testimony of Luke recorded in Acts 2:1-12 of the Bible. When Shakers say that they don't believe in the Bible, they're stating that the experience of Gospel is written in the unconscious. Shaker dancing is always symbolic of inner transformation, which serves as a cosmic trigger to the collective unconscious, in the terminology of Carl Jung. Singing and dancing both assist the believer with transcendent experiences, where individuals experience that they are connected to something greater than themselves, but that they are simultaneously part of this greater force. In the process of singing and dancing at Shaker services, believers are hallowing or making sacred the moment. As Shakers enter the church, they symbolically turn away from the world of the profane, or unconscious, to the world of the Holy.

Shaker ritual protects believers from ego inflation, or being overcome by evil. Without the container of the church, a person could be overcome by chaos. One contemporary depth psychologist, who calls the Shakers "post-modern healers," feels the Shake has survived and spread largely due to its reliance on oral tradition and direct revelation. The Shaker movement believes that man can have a dialogue, rather than just a monologue, with God. The Shakers draw from traditional Indian belief to say that everything is enveloped by God, is influenced by God, and influences God. This belief also states that there are absolute parts of God that are not influenced, but that there are parts that are open and expressible in the world. This idea embraces the belief that God is influenced by one's behavior.

The Shaker church is a community religion, with community support, which does not rely on the authority of the church. The largest gatherings of the church are the Mud Bay, Washington, Fourth of July gathering and the Smith River, California, gathering in late August.

Joseph M. Giovannetti

See also Religion

Further Reading

Amoss, Pamela T. "The Indian Shaker Church." *Handbook of North American Indians*. Vol. 7. *Northwest Coast*. Ed. Wayne Suttles. Washington, DC: Smithsonian Institution (1990): 633-39.

Barnett, Homer G. *Indian Shakers: A Messianic Cult of the Pacific Northwest*. Carbondale: Southern Illinois University Press, 1957.

INDIAN TREATY COUNCIL

See International Indian Treaty Council

INDIGENOUS RIGHTS

See International Law

INGALIK

See Alaskan Athabaskans

INSTITUTE FOR THE DEVELOPMENT OF INDIAN LAW

The Institute for the Development of Indian Law is a nonprofit legal research organization originally located in Washington, D.C. It was founded in 1971 by three Indian attorneys, Vine Deloria, Jr., Franklin D. Ducheneaux, and Kirke Kickingbird. The primary goal of the Institute is to strengthen the rights of Indian people, their governments, and societal institutions, in order to assure their capability to govern themselves in an effective manner, and secure their future through the exercise of tribal sovereignty.

The strategy to achieve these goals has called for research, education, publication, and litigation. Two of the Institute's first efforts focused on expanding the written materials available on Indian law. The Institute published *Taxing Those They Found Here*, by Jay White, which addresses tax issues affecting American Indians. A second early research effort focused on American Indian land problems, and the result was published by Macmillan as *100 Million Acres*, by Kirke Kickingbird and Karen Ducheneaux in 1973.

Litigation efforts to protect Indian rights were reflected in *Red Man v. Ottina*, one of two suits seeking to stop the impoundment of $18 million appropriated to fund the Indian Education Act. The suit was successful and release of the funds began the implementation of the Indian Education Act. *Harjo v. Kleppe* (1976) was a second case in which the Institute participated. This case focused on treaties that guaranteed the Muskogee Creek Nation self-government. The guarantees of self-government were upheld. The Court characterized the extralegal usurpation of tribal authority by the Bureau of Indian Affairs over a period of seventy years as "bureaucratic imperialism."

The Institute was asked by the Native American Rights Fund to organize an Eastern Indian Conference, which was instrumental in the creation of the Coalition of Eastern Native Americans (CENA) organization. The Institute provided office facilities and technical assistance during CENA's formative period. The activities of CENA launched a number of tribes towards federal recognition.

With the implementation of the Indian Education Act, the Institute began publication of the *Indian Education Journal*, which evolved into the *American Indian Journal*. Educational efforts increased with financial assistance from the Administration for Native Americans, and the Institute began to develop and implement a nationwide training program on federal Indian law for tribal government, administrative staff, and tribal members. The training materials evolved into the books *Indian Sovereignty, Indian Jurisdiction, Indian Treaties, Indians and the U.S. Government*; and the *Federal Indian Trust Relationship*. The training programs would add introductory films and instructional filmstrips on these same topics, and convert these materials to videotape in the 1980s.

The publications grew to include treaties broken down on a regional basis, specialized manuscripts on treaty negotiations in various parts of the country, community education tools, research on the status of Indians in Latin America, tribal constitutions, and economic development. *Indians and the Constitution: A Forgotten Legacy* by Kirke and Lynn Kickingbird, won an award from the United States Bicentennial Commission on the Constitution in 1987.

The Institute for the Development of Indian Law can be contacted through the Native American Legal Resource Center, at the Oklahoma City University School of Law, 2501 N. Blackwelder, Oklahoma City, OK, 73106.

Kirke Kickingbird

See also Civil Rights; Indian Education Act, 1972; Law; Treaties

INSTITUTE OF AMERICAN INDIAN AND ALASKA NATIVE CULTURE AND ARTS

The Institute of American Indian and Alaska Native Culture and Arts (IAIA) began in 1962 to promote the development and appreciation of Native culture through the arts. An act of Congress in 1968 separated the organization from the executive branch of government and awarded it a federal charter with a nineteen-member independent board of trustees consisting of prominent representatives of the Native American community from throughout the nation.

The Institute, currently a fully accredited college offering associate of fine arts degrees, is the only higher education institution of its kind to focus exclusively on the artistic and cultural traditions of all American Indian and Native Alaskan peoples. Over two hundred twenty students representing seventy-six tribes are enrolled in courses in painting, ceramics, film-making, sculpture, and jewelry, to learn both artistic techniques and to acquire an appreciation for artistic expression within their own individual culture.

The Institute of American Indian Arts museum is an integral part of the IAIA. The National Collection of Contemporary Indian Art is home to a unique collection of contemporary Native American art and some historical material—over 8,000 paintings, sculpture, ceramics, jewelry, graphics, costumes, beadwork, textiles, photographs, and written sources. This collection traces the thirty-year history of the Institute. Works of alumni as well as nationally recognized Indian artists from across the country are held for display.

The collections and museum exhibitions serve all the Institute's students as inspiration for their creativity. They also provide students in the museum studies program with hands-on experience. The museum serves the general public by enhancing their awareness of an appreciation for the richness and diversity of Native artistic expression.

The Institute is on the threshold of dynamic growth and expansion in the early 1990s. A recent grant from the MacArthur Foundation and the gift of a 140-acre tract near Santa Fe Community College will enable the Institute to have its first permanent campus, with an anticipated increase in the student body and the possibility of growth into a four-year college. As of the summer of 1992, the museum collection is permanently located in an historic renovated Pueblo revival building in downtown Santa Fe, with plans for an outdoor amphitheater and exhibition area where the public can view Native artists at work. Consequently, the IAIA will be in an even stronger position to meet its goals in serving Native peoples and the general public in training and education.

Armand S. La Potin

See also Art; Higher Education

Further Reading

The Future Institute of American Indian Arts and Culture: A Major Multi-Phased National Cultural Advancement Center. n.p.: Native American Council of Regents, 1979.
Garmhausen, Winona. *History of Indian Arts Education in Santa Fe: The Institute of American Indian Arts, with Historical Background, 1890–1962.* Santa Fe, NM: Sunstone Press, 1988.

Fritz Scholder (Luiseño). "Staff of the Institute of American Indian Arts at 4:15 p.m." Oil. Courtesy of the Museum of New Mexico, 46224.

INTER-AMERICAN INDIAN INSTITUTE

During the 1930s, students of indigenous peoples in the Western Hemisphere, "Indianistas," formed a fraternity to promote the study and preservation of Native cultures and to improve the economic well-being of the hemisphere's estimated 249 million Indians. The United States, in the person of Commissioner of Indian Affairs John Collier (1933 to 1945); and Mexico, represented by the social scientists Luis Chavez Orozco and Moises Saenz, provided the leadership for the convening of the first Inter-American Conference on Indian Life under the sponsorship of the Pan American Union in April 1941 at Patzcuaro, Mexico. As a result of this meeting, the Inter-American Indian Institute (IAII), with permanent headquarters in Mexico City, was created.

The purpose of the Institute was to institutionalize the interests of the Indianistas through formal treaties signed by member states of the Pan American Union, and to obtain governmental support for the research and publications of the IAII. Under the umbrella of the IAII, each signatory nation was obli-

gated to create a National Indian Institute to promote the well-being of Indians within its borders. The United States, Mexico, Honduras, and El Salvador immediately ratified treaties approving the creation of the IAII and other Central and South American nations followed later. The first director of the IAII was Moises Saenz who died shortly after his appointment; he was succeeded by the eminent Mexican anthropologist, Manuel Gamio.

There is good evidence to indicate that the United States was primarily interested in the IAII as a means to improve relations with Latin America and to insure that the Indians of the hemisphere were not swayed by Nazi propaganda during World War II. Financing for American participation in the IAII and for the United States National Indian Institute was initially provided by the Office of the Coordinator of Inter-American Affairs, created in 1940 to improve relations with Latin America. Efforts to obtain permanent funding for the United States National Indian Institute met resistance in Congress and it ceased to exist as a viable entity once the Office of the Coordinator was abolished at the end of World War II. United States participation in the IAII continued through minimal financing by the State Department after 1946.

The IAII publishes a quarterly, bilingual journal of research, *América Indígena,* and occasional monographs. From 1941 to 1961 it also published the informative *Boletín Indigenista,* a newsletter reporting on the work of the IAII and its National Indian Institute affiliates. Since 1962 the *Boletín* has been replaced by the *Anuario Indigenista.* During the 1940s, it published a number of monographs written by United States Indian office officials on the reforms then being implemented by the Indian New Deal. During these years, the IAII also supervised the work of American anthropologists working in Mexico, primarily that of Bronislaw Malinowski in the Valle de Oaxaca, and Oscar Lewis in Tepoztlan.

Current members of the IAII are Mexico, El Salvador, Argentina, Bolivia, Brazil, Chile, Colombia, Costa Rica, Ecuador, Guatemala, Honduras, Nicaragua, Panama, Paraguay, Peru, the United States, and Venezuela.

Lawrence C. Kelly

See also **Government Policy: Indian New Deal**

Further Reading

Collier, John. *From Every Zenith.* Denver, CO: Sage Press, 1963.

"The Final Act." *The First Inter-American Conference on Indian Life.* Washington, DC: Office of Indian Affairs, U.S. Government Printing Office, 1940.

INTER-TRIBAL COOPERATION

See Organizations and Tribal Cooperation

INTERNATIONAL INDIAN TREATY COUNCIL

The International Indian Treaty Council (IITC) was founded in June 1974 at the First International Indian Treaty Conference, which was held on the Standing Rock Sioux Reservation in South Dakota. The meeting was organized by the American Indian Movement (AIM) in cooperation with traditional Indian leaders and elders from all over North America.

The conference produced a document from the several thousand Indian participants who represented ninety-seven indigenous peoples from all parts of the Western Hemisphere. "The Declaration of Continuing Independence," as the founding document was titled, outlined the philosophy and responsibilities of the newly created IITC, including a mandate to open offices in New York and elsewhere in order to facilitate access to international political forces. The Declaration states:

> Might does not make right. Sovereign people of varying cultures have the absolute right to live in harmony with Mother Earth so long as they do not infringe upon this same right of other peoples. The denial of this right to any sovereign people, such as the Native American Indian Nations, must be challenged by truth and action. World concern must focus on all colonial governments to the end that sovereign people everywhere shall live as they choose, in peace with dignity and freedom.

The Declaration cited specifically the illegal seizure of the Black Hills from the Great Sioux Nation in 1877, sacred land that belonged to the Sioux under the Fort Laramie Treaty of 1868. It also specified the forced march of the Cherokee from their ancestral lands in the Southeast to "Indian Territory," in contradiction to the United States Supreme Court decision that Cherokee treaty rights were inviolate. The Declaration points to Article VI of the United States Constitution, which recognizes the treaties as part of the supreme law of the land.

The gathered Indians vowed in the founding document to seek the support of "all world communities in the struggle for the continuing independence of native Nations." they also allied themselves with "the colonized Puerto Rican People in their struggle for Independence from the same United States of America." The Declaration concludes:

> We recognize that there is only one color of Mankind in the world who are not represented in the United Nations; that is the indigenous Redman of the Western Hemisphere. We recognize this lack of representation in the United Nations comes from the genocidal policies of the colonial power of the United States . . .

> We, the People of the International Indian Treaty Council, following the guidance of our elders through instructions from the Great Spirit, and out of our respect for our sacred Mother Earth, all her children, and those yet unborn, offer our lives for our International Treaty Rights.

In 1977 the International Indian Treaty Council received consultative status as a nongovernmental organization in the Economic and Social Council of the United Nations. From its founding in 1974 to the acquisition of United Nations (UN) status in 1977, the IITC organized numerous activities in preparation for its international role. In 1975, it sponsored a seminar on international law for traditional Indian leaders, bringing them together with several well-known international lawyers. The IITC also sent representatives to international conferences including: the UN International Women's Year Conference in Mexico City (1975); the Conference on Solidarity with Puerto Rican Independence in Havana (1975); the Conference of the Movement of Non-Aligned Countries in Peru (1976); the Second Congress of the Puerto Rican Socialist Party (1976); the UN Habitat Conference in Vancouver (1976); the UN Conference on Decertification in Buenos Aires; and the "Builders of Peace" World Peace Council conference in Warsaw (1977). By means of participation in such conferences, the IITC was able to make important contacts and inform governmental and nongovernmental representatives about the situations of Indians of the Americas.

The IITC early decided to focus on human rights violations by governments against Indian peoples, including their denial of self-determination. In its third International Indian Treaty conference in 1977, a study was made of the International Convention on the Prevention and Punishment of the Crime of Genocide, which covers violations experienced by Indians: killing members of a group; causing serious bodily or mental harm to the group; deliberately inflicting on the group conditions of life calculated to bring about its physical destruction in whole or in part; imposing measures intended to prevent births within the group; and forcibly transferring children of the group to another group. The third conference also cited the international human rights covenants of the United Nations and the final act of the Conference on Security and Cooperation in Europe (CSCE) which was signed by thirty-five European states, the USSR, Canada, and the United States.

The key event initiated by the International Indian Treaty Council, and which marked the beginning of Indian direct activity in the international context, was the 1977 International Non-Governmental Organizations' Conference on Indigenous Peoples of the Americas, held at the United Nations offices in Geneva, Switzerland. The more than a hundred Indian representatives from all over the Americas reflected organized forces of much larger dimensions.

The conference formulated a program of action for all international organizations with recommendations to submit the conference documents to all divisions of the United Nations. It called on the United Nations to declare October 12, Columbus Day, as the International Day of Solidarity and Mourning with Indigenous Peoples of the Americas. The conference documentation was formally submitted to the UN Secretary-General and the President of the UN General Assembly in November 1977.

Among the recommendations from the conference was the establishment of a UN Working Group on Indigenous Populations (WGIP). That recommendation was taken up by the UN in 1981, and the WGIP began meeting in August 1982. In the decade that followed, the Working Group developed a draft declaration of the rights of indigenous peoples worldwide, and an international treaty is expected before the turn of the century. On recommendation from the Working Group, 1993 was declared the UN Year of the World's Indigenous Peoples.

The Working Group is regularly attended by hundred of representatives of indigenous peoples. The International Indian Treaty Council continues to play a central role in the WGIP and other United Nations and international activities. Surely the greatest single vindication of the International Indian Treaty Council was the establishment in the UN Working Group of a study of treaties made between states and indigenous peoples.

Roxanne Dunbar Ortiz

See also **International Law; Red Power**

Further Reading

Deloria, Vine, Jr. *The Nations Within: The Past and Future of American Indian Sovereignty*. New York, NY: Pantheon, 1984.

Dunbar Ortiz, Roxanne. *The Great Sioux National Sitting in Judgment on America: An Oral History of the Sioux Nation and Its Struggle for Sovereignty*. New York, NY: Moon Books/Random House, 1977.

———. *Indians of the Americas: Human Rights and Self-Determination*. London, England: Zed Press, 1984.

Treaty Council News. San Francisco, CA: International Indian Treaty Council, 1977–1990.

INTERNATIONAL LAW

Half a millennium ago the peoples indigenous to the continents now called North and South America began to experience change, a kind of change they had not experienced before. Europeans arrived and began to lay claim to their lands, frequently slaughtering the Native children, women, and men who stood in the way. For many of those who survived, the Europeans brought disease and slavery.

Not long after the genocidal patterns began, concerned European theologians and jurists questioned the legality and morality of the onslaught. What emerged from their lectures and writings were prescriptions designed to shape encounters with the peoples of the "New World." The dominant sixteenth-century juridical view was expressed by the Spanish Dominican cleric Francisco de Vitoria who, applying natural law precepts, challenged the Spanish claims to Native lands. Vitoria argued that the Indians of the Americas were the true owners of their lands, with "dominion in both public and private matters," and upon this premise he set forth the rules by which the Europeans could validly acquire Indian lands or assert authority over them. Vitoria's work, grounded in the European theocratic world view of the sixteenth century, was filled with cultural biases, and he provided conceptual support for colonial patterns by his theory of just war. Nonetheless, within the limitations of that world view, Vitoria essentially treated the Indians as having the same rights and duties as all of humanity. Like all others, Indians could have war waged against them for "just" cause; but in the absence of conquest following a just war, Indians could not unilaterally be dispossessed of their lands or their autonomous existence.

Vitoria's lectures on the Indians established him among the oft-cited founders of modern international law. His prescriptions for the European encounters with the aboriginal peoples of the Western Hemisphere were building blocks for a system of principles and rules governing encounters among all peoples of the world. Subsequent theorists continued through the nineteenth century to include non-European aboriginal peoples as among the subjects of what came to be known as the "law of nations," and later, "international law." Accordingly, the law of nations was the grounding for the first pronouncements of the United States Supreme Court on the status and rights of Native Americans. In *Johnson v. M'Intosh* (1823), *Cherokee Nation v. Georgia* (1831), and *Worcester v. Georgia* (1832), cases authored by Chief Justice John Marshall, the Supreme Court invoked international law to uphold the "original rights" of Native peoples as well as to signal the means by which those rights could be limited or abrogated.

Whatever protection the early law of nations afforded the non-European aboriginal peoples, it was not enough to stop the forces of colonization and empire as they extended throughout the globe. Theorists eventually modified the law of nations to reflect, and hence legitimize, a state of affairs that subjugated indigenous peoples. Forgetting the origins of the discipline, theorists described the law of nations, or international law, as concerning itself only with the rights and duties of European and similarly "civilized" states, and as having its source entirely in the positive, consensual acts of those states. Vitoria's admonishments concerning the rights of American Indians were recast as statements of morality as opposed to law; international law moved to embrace what the "civilized" states had done, regardless of justification, and what they had done was to invade foreign lands and peoples and assert sovereignty over them.

Since the human suffering of World Wars I and II, international law again has shifted, but this time in retreat from the orientation in which theorists divorced law from morality and denied international rights to all but states. International law now contains among its constitutional elements precepts based on visions of a peaceful world order and the concept of human rights. The United Nations, other modern international organizations, and enhanced communications media provide institutional support for the promotion of peace and human rights. The modern human rights program focuses directly on the welfare of individuals and, increasingly, of groups, and hence extends the competency of international law beyond concern for relations among states only.

Within the last several years, concern for groups identified as indigenous has assumed a prominent place on the international human rights agenda. The category of indigenous peoples is generally understood to include not only the Native tribes of the American continents, but also other culturally distinctive non-state groupings, such as the Australian aboriginal communities and tribal peoples of southern Asia, that are similarly threatened by the legacies of colonialism.

Indigenous peoples are themselves largely responsible for the mobilization of the international human rights program in their favor. During the 1970s, indigenous groups organized and extended their efforts internationally to secure legal protection for their continued survival as distinct communities with historically based cultures, political institutions, and entitlements to land. In appeals to the international community, indigenous groups and supportive international nongovernmental organizations (NGOs) linked their concerns with general human rights principles such as self-determination and nondiscrimination. Among the major developments were several international conferences attended by indigenous peoples' representatives, including the 1977 International Non-Governmental Organizations Conference on Indigenous Peoples of the Americas, held in Geneva, Switzerland. Indigenous peoples' efforts coalesced into a veritable international campaign, aided by an increase of supportive scholarly writings from moral and sociological, as well as juridical, perspectives.

A series of processes promoted through international organizations have translated indigenous peoples' demands into a new and still developing body of international human rights law. A watershed in United Nations (UN) activity concerning indigenous peoples was the 1971 resolution by the UN Economic and Social Council authorizing a study on the conditions of indigenous populations. The study was entrusted to Ambassador Martinez Cobo, and was prepared largely by the UN Center for Human Rights. The fifth and final volume of the study was completed in 1983. One of the most comprehensive surveys of the status of indigenous communities worldwide at the time of its writing, the study includes extensive recommendations and conclusions generally supportive of indigenous peoples' demands. The study, which makes a strong case for special protections to safeguard indigenous cultures, has become a standard reference for normative deliberations concerning indigenous peoples within the UN system.

The case for the protection of indigenous rights and the conceptualization of those rights was further advanced by the 1981 Conference of Specialists on Ethnocide and Ethnodevelopment in Latin America, sponsored by the UN Educational, Scientific, and Cultural Organization. The Conference, held in San Jose, Costa Rica, adopted a declaration affirming the "inalienable right of Indian groups" to consolidate their cultural identity and to "exercise . . . self determination."

Shortly after the 1981 Conference, and upon the recommendation of the Martinez Cobo study, the UN Human Rights Commission and the Economic and Social Council approved the establishment of the UN Working Group on Indigenous Populations. An organ of the Sub-Commission on Prevention of Discrimination and Protection of Minorities, the Working Group has met annually since 1982 in one- or two-week sessions. The original mandate of the Working Group was to review developments concerning indigenous peoples' rights and to work toward the evolution of corresponding international standards. The Working Group's standard-setting mandate was refined in 1985 when the Sub-Commission approved its decision to draft a declaration on the rights of indigenous peoples for consideration by the UN General Assembly. In 1988 the Working Group chair produced a draft of the declaration and, after comments by government and indigenous peoples' representatives, revised the draft in 1989. Discussion on the revised draft has continued throughout the Working Group's subsequent sessions.

The Working Group itself is composed of five rotating members of the Sub-Commission, who act in the capacity of experts rather than government representatives. Yet, through its activities, the Working Group has engaged states, indigenous peoples, and others in an extended multilateral dialogue on the conditions of indigenous peoples around the world, and on the standards that should govern behavior towards them. The Working Group has provided a forum for indigenous representatives to articulate concerns and assert rights, which they have done in part by promoting their own written declarations of rights, and government representatives have joined in the discussion. Virtually every state of the American continents has participated in the Working Group's activity. Canada, with its large indigenous population, has taken a leading role. States of other regions with significant indigenous populations also have been active, especially Australia and New Zealand. The Philippines, Bangladesh, and India are just a few of the other numerous states that have made regular oral or written submissions to the Working Group.

Although the Working Group's activity has yet to result in a declaration of rights approved by the UN General Assembly, these years of work have vastly contributed to the articulation and affirmation of indigenous rights precepts. A broad consensus of opinion about a certain minimum set of standards favorable to indigenous peoples' demands is now evident in the multitude of government and other authoritative statements to the Working Group.

Following the lead of the UN Working Group, the International Labour Organization (ILO), a specialized agency within the UN system, set about in the middle 1980s to revise its convention on indigenous peoples. The original 1957 ILO Convention Concerning the Protection and Integration of Indigenous and Other Tribal and Semi-tribal Populations in Independent Countries (No. 107) had been widely criticized for being out of step with current thinking on indigenous peoples. Adopted during a period in history when the dominant political elements in domestic and international circles placed little or no value on indigenous cultures, the 1957 Convention, as its title suggests, presumed a norm of assimilation.

In 1986, the ILO convened a "Meeting of Experts," which recommended that the Convention be revised. The meeting unanimously concluded that the "integrationist language" of Convention No. 107 is "outdated" and "destructive in the modern world." Discussion on the revision proceeded at the 1988 and 1989 sessions of the International Labour Conference, the highest decision-making body of the ILO. Thirty-nine government representatives participated in the conference committee for the revision, in addition to the worker and employee delegates that are part of the "tripartite" system of governance in the ILO. All of the states that have been active in the UN Working Group meetings took on highly visible roles in the Conference Committee. The United States, which thus far has participated minimally in the Working Group's activity, played a major part in the ILO process.

The Conference Committee approved a new text by consensus, and at the close of the 1989 session, the full Labour Conference adopted the new Convention on Indigenous and Tribal Peoples (No. 169) by an overwhelming majority of the voting delegates. The new Convention No. 169 carries the basic theme of the right of indigenous peoples to live and develop by their own designs as distinct communities. The Convention has extensive provisions advancing indigenous cultural integrity, land and resource rights, and non-discrimination in social welfare spheres; and it generally enjoins states to respect indigenous peoples' aspirations in all decisions affecting them. Some indigenous rights advocates have expressed dissatisfaction with language in Convention No. 169, viewing it as not sufficiently constraining government conduct in relation to indigenous peoples' concerns. But whatever its shortcomings, the Convention succeeds in affirming the value of indigenous communities and cultures, and in setting forth a series of basic standards in that regard. As of February 1992 four states had already ratified the Convention (Bolivia, Colombia, Mexico, and Norway), and ILO officials reported that several other ratifications were expected in the immediate future.

The Organization of American States (OAS) is another international venue that has promoted international norms concerning indigenous peoples. In 1973 the OAS Inter-American Commission on Human Rights adopted a set of policy guidelines which affirm respect for the integrity and well-being of indigenous communities. Outside the Commission, the OAS maintains a permanent interest in indigenous peoples through its Inter-American Indian Institute, which provides advisory services and convenes periodic conferences.

In November 1989, the OAS General Assembly resolved to "request the Inter-American Commission on Human Rights to prepare a juridical instrument relative to the rights of indigenous peoples . . ." To that end, the Commission convened a meeting of indigenous peoples' representatives in Mexico City in January of 1991 to discuss the project. It appears that the first OAS instrument on indigenous rights will take the form of a resolution, which would lay the groundwork for a subsequent OAS-sponsored convention.

Through these multiple international processes, indigenous peoples and their supporters have been successful in moving the international community to an ever greater accommodation of their demands.

While the movement can be expected to continue as indigenous peoples continue to press their cause, a new body of international law specifically concerned with indigenous peoples has emerged already. The recently adopted ILO Convention No. 169 on Indigenous and Tribal Peoples stands as an express affirmation of the burgeoning commitment by the world community to secure a future in which indigenous communities may retain their unique characteristics and develop freely in co-existence with all of humankind.

In addition to creating treaty obligations among ratifying countries, Convention No. 169 reflects emergent customary international law. The existence of customary law concerning indigenous peoples is significant in that customary norms are generally binding upon states regardless of any formal act of assent to the norms. It is evident that states and other relevant actors have reached a certain common ground about minimum standards that should generally govern behavior toward indigenous peoples, and it is further evident that the standards already are in fact guiding behavior. Under modern conceptions of international law, such a controlling consensus which follows from widely shared values of human dignity is constitutive of customary law.

The new international norms upholding indigenous rights are grounds upon which Native Americans may appeal to decision makers in international forums, although international procedures for the enforcement of human rights law are limited. Relevant procedures within the UN, the OAS, and specialized international agencies such as the ILO, rest mostly on the threat of placing a human rights violator in a shameful light in the eyes of world public opinion, rather than on formal sanctioning mechanisms. Nonetheless, the mobilization of shame can wield significant influence.

Contemporary international indigenous rights norms may also be invoked in purely domestic settings. The norms are appropriately invoked in direct appeals to the political branches of government. Additionally, in the United States, as in many countries, domestic tribunals may consider international treaty and customary norms as rules of decision; or international norms may be used to guide judicial interpretation of domestic rules. Indeed, the genesis of United States legal doctrine concerning Native peoples is in the international law of the colonial period. The United States doctrine is likely again to cross paths with the relevant international law.

S. James Anaya

See also **Inter-American Indian Institute; International Indian Treaty Council; Law; Russell Tribunal**

Further Reading

Anaya, S. James. "Indigenous Rights Norms in Contemporary International Law." *Arizona Journal of International and Comparative Law* 8 (no. 2) (February 1991): 1–39.

Barsh, Russell. "Indigenous Peoples: An Emerging Object in International Law." *American Journal of International Law* 80 (1986): 269–85.

Hannum, Hurst. "New Developments in Indigenous Rights." *Virginia Journal of International Law* 28 (1989): 649–78.

Swepston, Lee. "A New Step in the International Law on Indigenous and Tribal Peoples: ILO Convention No. 169 of 1989." *Oklahoma City University Law Review* 15 (1990): 677–714.

United National Subcommission on Prevention of Discrimination, and Protection of Minorities. *Study of the Problem of Discrimination Against Indigenous Populations.* Jose R. Martinez Cobo, Special Rapporteur. U.N. Doc. E/CN.4/Sub.2/1986/ 7 & adds. 1–4. (1986).

Williams, Robert A., Jr. "Encounters on the Frontiers of International Human Rights Law: Redefining the Terms of Indigenous Peoples' Survival in the World." *Duke Law Journal* (1990): 660–704.

Inuit

See Alutiiq; Iñupiat; Yup'ik

INUIT CIRCUMPOLAR CONFERENCE

The Inuit Circumpolar Conference (ICC) was organized in 1977 under the leadership of Eben Hopson, the late mayor of the North Slope Borough of Alaska. Following Hopson's unsuccessful attempts to convince United States policy makers of the need for direct Inuit involvement in decisions that affected their lives, he chose to establish an international Inuit organization, the ICC, to advance Inuit rights and interests. This effort was prompted in part by the mounting threat of off-shore oil and gas development along Alaska's Arctic coast, and the need to mobilize opposition to such a threat.

The first organizing meeting of the ICC took place in June 1977 and was hosted by the North Slope Borough and its Environmental Protection Office. For the first time, Inuit of Alaska, Canada, and Greenland gathered to create a united voice. Russian Inuit were invited; however, due to Soviet government policy and a fear that Inuit would "nationalize" the Arctic, they were unable to participate at that time. Since the founding meeting in 1977, general assemblies and elders conferences have been held in Nuuk, Greenland (1980); Iqaluit, NWT, Canada (1983); Kotzebue, Alaska (1986); Sisimiut, Greenland (1989); and Inuvik, NWT, Canada (1992). The 1995 General Assembly will be hosted by Alaska. In 1989, the Russian Inuit were able to send a small delegation as observers and they selected two ex officio representatives to the ICC Executive Council. At the 1992 Assembly, Russian Inuit became full members of the ICC, seated a full delegation and elected two executive council members.

The objectives of the ICC are:

... to strengthen unity among the Inuit of the region; to promote Inuit rights and interests at the international level; to seek full and active partnership in the political, economic, and social development of circumpolar regions in order to promote greater self-sufficiency among Inuit and to ensure the growth of their culture; and, to develop and encourage long-term policies which safeguard the Arctic environment.

In 1983, the ICC gained nongovernmental organization status, providing Inuit with a formal voice within the United Nations. Most recently, the ICC has concerned itself with the development of a comprehensive Arctic policy document, which will serve as a "blueprint" to guide policies and actions affecting Arctic regions. Environmental activities with which the ICC has been involved include the development of an Inuit Regional Conservation Strategy; participation in the Arctic Monitoring and Assessment Program initiated by the Finnish government in 1989; the promotion of traditional knowledge of Inuit peoples; and protection of traditional Inuit economies based on whaling, sealing, fishing, and other hunting activities.

The ICC has become a leading international organization in the promotion of indigenous human rights. It has participated in the work of the United Nations Working Group on Indigenous Peoples, whose charge is to monitor the status and conditions of indigenous peoples worldwide and to draft a Universal Declaration on Indigenous Rights. In addition, the ICC played a major role in the 1989 revision of the International Labour Organization Indigenous and Tribal Peoples Convention. The ICC has also participated in and supported a variety of international cooperative efforts, and, in fact, has become a vital force in the international networking of indigenous peoples in the North and elsewhere.

Dalee Sambo

Further Reading

Hannum, Hurst. *Autonomy, Self-determination and Sovereignty: The Accommodation of Conflicting Rights.* Philadelphia: Pennsylvania University Press, 1990.

Inuit Regional Conservation Strategy Framework Document. Anchorage, AK: Inuit Circumpolar Conference, 1986.

Principles for a Comprehensive Arctic Policy. Anchorage, AK: Inuit Circumpolar Conference, 1989.

Publications. Copenhagen, Denmark: International Work Group for Indigenous Affairs, ongoing.

IÑUPIAT

The Iñupiat (Eskimo) of Alaska inhabit all of northwest and northern Alaska, beginning at Unalakleet on the west coast, up through the Bering Straits (Nome area), Northwest Arctic Borough (Kotzebue area), and the North Slope Borough (Barrow area). There are today approximately 12,000 Iñupiat in Alaska. In spite of political boundaries, the Iñupiat population continues across northern Canada and into Greenland. Our Canadian relatives are generally known as the Inuit, and Greenlandic groups are called Kalaallit. Other Eskimo groups include the Yup'ik of southwest Alaska, as well as the Russian Eskimos in Chukotka in Far East Russia. After two centuries of isolation, we are now beginning to come together through organizations like the Inuit Circumpolar Conference.

Traditionally, the population of northern Alaska was located in small extended family settlements. In addition to permanent winter settlements, there were other strategically located sites used during certain times of the year either for hunting or fishing. Most of the settlements were located near the mouths of rivers for access to fresh water and for catching fish. Since all travel was by dog team, permanent settlements were small so as not to discourage the migration of animals near the settlement. Hunting then, as it is today, was an important part of Native life.

The advent of explorers in the early 1800s in search of the Northwest Passage was the beginning of change for the Iñupiat. Whalers came, some of them marrying local women. Churches sent their missionaries and teachers: Presbyterians to Barrow, Congregationalists to Cape Prince of Wales, and Episcopalians to Point Hope in 1890. By 1897, the Society of Friends sent teachers to Kotzebue. These were people who came to stay and teach a new life of literacy and Christian ethics to the Native people. The gold miners came in 1898 and traveled all over the region in search of gold. They established a few new villages. The fur buyers were not far behind and established trading posts in some of the existing villages.

As the responsibility for schools passed from the churches to the federal government after the turn of the century, the Native students, who were the first generation of Eskimos being taught this foreign English language, were punished every time they spoke their native Iñupiaq language. They had to stand with their faces to the corner, have their hands hit with a ruler, had their mouths washed out with soap, and had to write one hundred lines of "I will not speak Eskimo." Needless to say, that generation of Iñupiat tried to make the educational system easier for their children, and so they spoke nothing but English to them. What really impacted the Iñupiaq language, too, was that there were no high schools in the villages and those students whom the Bureau of Indian Affairs (BIA) recommended for high school education had to travel away from home to boarding schools and stay for four years. When they came home, they didn't know their own language well enough to use it when they began to raise their children.

As for alcohol, the whalers and explorers introduced this to the local Natives and because they drank straight from the bottle, that is the way most of our people drink alcohol today. Of course, the whites who introduced alcohol to the Iñupiat didn't warn us of the social ills that would befall us. Because the consumption of alcohol became epidemic in recent times, the ten villages in the Northwest Arctic Borough have gone "dry" (no importation to or sale of alcohol in their villages) and Kotzebue has gone "damp" (no sale of alcohol in the village, but people can order alcohol for their own consumption). In its wake, there are hundreds of children with varying degrees of fetal alcohol syndrome (FAS), and it is now just beginning to be recognized. In the meantime, many young people are in jail for various crimes and others are being shifted through social service programs without accurate diagnoses because FAS symptoms are largely unknown by service providers. The larger question then becomes: if they are FAS, what then? Alcohol has not done one bit of good for us, and it will take much community education and commitment from parents to repair the damage.

World War II and the Cold War brought immense changes to northern Alaska in the form of military preparedness. National Petroleum Reserve No. 4, first set aside in 1932 by executive order, was developed, first by the Navy and then by a private contractor, providing employment for Iñupiat through 1953. Beginning in 1954, Distant Early Warning (DEW-line) stations began to be constructed by the Air Force; seventeen of these stations were built across the North Slope, providing unprecedented wage opportunities for Iñupiat, especially in the rapidly growing town of Barrow.

In 1958 the Atomic Energy Commission (AEC) actively sought Alaskan support for Project Chariot, which would create a deep-water port near Cape Thompson by detonating atomic bombs many times more powerful than Hiroshima. When the Native people found out about it, they held meetings and wrote letters of protest to President Kennedy. In 1961 the Native people of Barrow had a "duck-in" to protest enforcement of the Migratory Bird Act of 1916, which banned waterfowl hunting between March and September—the only time these birds are in northern Alaska. Finally, in November 1961, Iñupiat village leaders came together to talk about these problems at a conference in Barrow. Out of this came Iñupiat Paitot, a political organization concerned with land and subsistence issues.

Shortly after this, the AEC scratched Project Chariot, but thirty years later we found out that the AEC had dumped 15,000 pounds of radioactive material from Nevada at the site. In the meantime, several members of a family whose campground is the Cape Thompson site died of cancer. There were no cautionary signs or indication that deadly radioactive material was dumped in the area. Now the North Slope Borough and the Northwest Arctic Borough are involved in meetings with federal agencies, trying to figure out ways to remove that material without hurting anyone, and there is no way to tell how much of it has seeped into the ground. The waste was not put in any kind of container; holes were dug and the radioactive waste dumped into the ground and cov-

ered with gravel. Now we are finding out that the government was carrying on experiments on flora and fauna, to see what radioactive material would do to them. Any thinking person knows that wild game eats the vegetation and small game, and we in turn eat the wild game. Reports of fish with sores and sickly whales also bespeak the contamination that has affected them. However, it is unknown how much of it is from Project Chariot and how much of it is from waters polluted by the Russian nuclear waste-dumping practices.

The land and subsistence issues of the 1960s, and the discovery of oil on the North Slope in 1968, resulted in the passage of the Alaska Native Claims Settlement Act (ANCSA) in 1971, with major roles played by the Arctic Slope Native Association, formed in 1966, its leaders Joe Upicksoun and Charlie Edwardsen, and the Northwest Alaska Native Association, formed in 1963 by Willie Hensley who later became state representative and then state senator. ANCSA has had a great impact on our lives, and will continue to do so for generations to come. The Iñupiat had no voice until the land claims were enacted by Congress; now, as landholders of millions of acres and shareholders of millions of dollars of assets, people in places of responsibility and positions of trust are seeking our opinions.

Also, as a result of litigation in the 1970s, high schools were built in villages which never had them before and Native students were then able to stay home in their Native environment until they were ready for college. In what became the Northwest Arctic Borough, the educational system broke away from the BIA in 1976 and the policies of education began to change with decisions made by the local board of education. The teaching of Native language and culture in our schools was mandated for the first time. Appropriate curricula had to be developed locally for language and cultural instruction because they were nonexistent. In 1986, with the creation and establishment of the Northwest Arctic Borough, the school system became part of the borough government and local involvement continues to enrich it. The North Slope Borough, which was established in 1972, took responsibility for education from the BIA in 1975, and proceeded to construct new schools in every village. Language and cultural preservation are the mission of the borough's Commission on Iñupiat History, Language and Culture. Elders' conferences and the recording of oral history are major activities in both boroughs.

Two major gatherings were part of the Iñupiat annual cycle: the trading fairs which took place in the summer and the Messenger Feast in the winter. In Kotzebue, the Native Trade Fair has been reinstituted and it now occurs immediately after the Fourth of July celebration. In the summer of 1991, Russian Eskimos came over from Chukotka to celebrate with us for the first time in about a century. Six boats full of Russian Eskimos came and were greeted with Eskimo dancing on the beach by the Northern Lights Dancers. It was an exciting event and was broadcast live on the radio. The Messenger Feast is held during January in Barrow; it is a time of gift giving, dancing, and social communication.

The only regional industry in the Northwest Arctic Borough is the Red Dog Mine near Kivalina. A major employer is the school system. Other employers are mostly government, such as the Indian Health Service, the Federal Aeronautics Administration, the Weather Bureau, and communications systems. Major employers in the North Slope Borough are the borough itself and various oil-related activities. Working in the oil fields does not, however, do away with the need for subsistence activities. Wage economy opportunities are concentrated in the two towns of Kotzebue and Barrow, where the borough governments, the regional corporations (Nana and Arctic Slope), and the nonprofit corporations (Maniilaq and Iñupiat Community of the Arctic Slope) are located. Since the villages have no industry, hunting, fishing, and food gathering are still an important part of life. Without subsistence activities, many Iñupiat would go hungry.

Alaskan Iñupiat are caught up in life in the twentieth century. We are distant descendants of our forefathers, concerned with the retention of our language and culture, fighting to keep our subsistence activities intact, yet also sending our children to college to prepare for twentieth-century technological life. Our culture is built around hunting, fishing, and food gathering; these subsistence activities are still a big part of our life as we lack industry in our villages to support a cash economy lifestyle. We work with federal, state, regional, and local governments to exercise our voice in matters important to us. We are no longer isolated; the price of crude oil affects our lives; we see what's going on in the world on television. We communicate instantly through CBs, telephones, and faxes. In addition to daily jet service which connects us with the urban areas, we also have scheduled air taxis taking us to our villages in a short time. We are resisting building roads connecting our villages because the influx of people would have an adverse impact on our subsistence activities. We are dependent on each other. We are working together to try to keep in balance the varying needs and demands of both our subsistence and wage economies.

Rachel Craig

See also Alaska Native Claims Settlement Act; Inuit Circumpolar Conference; Whaling

Further Reading

Bodfish, Waldo. *Kusiq: An Eskimo Life History From the Arctic Coast of Alaska*. Eds. William Schneider, Leona Kisautaq Okakok, and James Mumigana Nageak. Fairbanks: University of Alaska Press, 1991.

Burch, Ernest S. *The Eskimos*. Norman: University of Oklahoma Press, 1988.

Chance, Norman. *The Iñupiat and Arctic Alaska: An Ethnography of Development*. Fort Worth, TX: Holt, Rinehart and Winston, 1990.

Fitzhugh, William W., and Aron Crowell. *Crossroads of Continents: Cultures of Siberia and Alaska*. Washington, DC: Smithsonian Institution Press, 1988.

Ray, Dorothy Jean. "Bering Strait Eskimo." *Handbook of North American Indians*. Vol. 5. *Arctic*. Ed. David Damas. Washington, DC: Smithsonian Institution (1984): 285–302.

Spencer, Robert F. *The North Alaskan Eskimo; A Study in Ecology and Society*. Bureau of American Ethnology Bulletin 171. New York, NY: Dover Publications, 1976.

IONIE

See Caddo

IOWA

The Iowa call themselves "Ioway," or, in their own language, *Paxoje* ("Dusty Noses"). The preferred usage is "Iowa" for the legal tribal entities (the Iowa Tribe of Kansas and Nebraska, and the Iowa Tribe of Oklahoma), and "Ioway" for the people themselves. The Ioway people are divided into two independent groups: the Southern Ioway, in Oklahoma, and the Northern Ioway, in Kansas and Nebraska. This split occurred soon after the Civil War, with one group accepting individual allotment of lands near the Missouri River along the Kansas-Nebraska border. The other group left for Indian Territory (now Oklahoma) in the 1870s, in order to continue to live in the traditional way on lands held in common.

The Iowa Tribe of Kansas and Nebraska (R.R. 1, Box 58A, White Cloud, Kansas) is located on a 1,500-acre reservation in the extreme northeastern corner of Kansas (Brown and Doniphan Counties) and the extreme southeastern corner of Nebraska (Richardson County). The Iowa Tribe of Oklahoma (P.O. Box 190, Perkins, Oklahoma) does not have a federally recognized reservation. After their move to Indian Territory in the 1870s, they were eventually assigned a reservation there in 1883. After the Dawes Act of 1887, this reservation, which bordered unassigned lands, was opened to white settlers as part of the 1889 Oklahoma Land Run.

The Iowa Tribe of Kansas and Nebraska is administered by its Executive Committee and is located on a reservation near White Cloud, Kansas. It is served by the Horton Indian Agency in Horton, Kansas, which provides health and other services. The Iowa Tribe owns a tribal farm operation, a dairy herd, a gas station, a fire station, a bingo operation, and a grain processing business operating out of a leased mill in Craig, Missouri. The approximately 1,500-acre reservation is checkerboarded with Indian and non-Indian ownership, and reacquisition of the land base is seen as a primary goal, as well as developing an infrastructure attractive to potential employers. About 588 Ioway were reported to be living on or near the reservation in 1993; many live in nearby towns in Kansas and Nebraska. The total enrollment for the Iowa Tribe of Kansas and Nebraska is reported at 2,089, although blood quantum is often quite low.

Directed to accept a form of tribal government based on a model provided by the federal government as part of the Indian Reorganization Act of 1934, the Oklahoma Iowa finally ratified a Tribal Constitution delimited by that model. The Iowa Tribe of Oklahoma is administered by its Business Committee, located near Perkins, Oklahoma. It is served by the Shawnee Indian Agency, in Shawnee, Oklahoma, but the tribe contracts with the Potawatomi for health and food programs. The Iowa Tribe owns about 200 acres of scattered land in trust as well as a bingo operation. Of 366 individuals on the tribal roll, nine are listed as full-bloods. Blood quantum tends to be higher than among the Kansas group, but the requirement was lowered to $1/16$ around 1991. The Oklahoma Ioway live on about 1,300 acres of individually owned land, much of which is surface-leased to non-Indians for grazing or farming. Leasing provides some income, but most of the Ioway have jobs in nearby towns. Fifty-two land owners gain some income from oil and gas leases. As a member of the United Indian Nations of Oklahoma, the Iowa Tribe of Oklahoma is currently fighting a toxic dump proposed by a subsidiary of Amoco, which is to be located on burial grounds in Mercer County, Missouri.

The Iowa of Oklahoma shared in the almost $8 million land claims judgment awarded to both groups of Ioway by the Indian Claims Commission in the 1970s. Notable leaders of this century have included Marvin Franklin of the Kansas Ioway, who was appointed as acting commissioner of Indian affairs in 1973, and Chief David Tohee, Blaine Nawanoway Kent and Solomon Nawanoway Kent of the Oklahoma Ioway.

Alanson Skinner visited the Oklahoma Ioway in 1914, and both groups in 1922 and 1923. He collected for the Milwaukee Public Museum and the Museum of the American Indian in New York; these two museums have the best collections of Ioway material culture. Skinner's ethnographic work provides the most complete data on traditional Ioway culture. It includes *Societies of the Iowa, Kansa, and Ponca Indians* (1915), *Medicine Ceremony of the Menomini, Iowa, and Wahpeton Dakota* (1920), "Traditions of the Iowa Indians" (1925), and *Ethnology of the Ioway Indians* (1926).

Community life in both tribes is based on extended kinship groups, with some use of the traditional clan system among the Oklahoma Ioway, notably during funerals. Factionalism is present in both groups, and limited interaction occurs between the Oklahoma and Kansas Ioway, except for mutual visits in a few families. Each group sponsors an annual powwow, and the Kansas Ioway also have a rodeo. Artwork tends to be individualized and produced for in-group use, such as ribbonwork and beadwork used in dance regalia.

The Ioway language is grouped with Otoe and Missouria as Chiwere, a Siouan language, and is closely related to Winnebago. It is difficult to say how many speakers of the language are left; a few Northern Ioway know mostly isolated words and phrases, and some Southern Ioway families attempt to keep some limited use, especially if there are older members in the family, or if they are trying to strengthen their identity as Ioway. William Whitman described the language in "Descriptive Grammar of the Ioway-Oto" (1947). A two volume primer, *Iowa and Otoe Indian Language* (1977, 1978), was developed by Lila-Wistrand Robinson and Jimm Garrett-Good Tracks as part of the Christian Children's Fund American Indian Project. Garrett-Good Tracks has also edited a lexicon, *Iowas-Otoe-Missouria Language to English* (1992), distributed by the Department of Linguistics at the University of Colorado at Boulder.

Almost all of the Ioway in Kansas and Oklahoma identify themselves as Christians of various Catholic and Protestant denominations. Some, even self-identified Christians, attend ceremonies such as funerals, namings, Native American Church meetings (more popular earlier in the century), sweats, and inter-tribal dances. Some Ioway, especially those living away from their home communities, make friendships with members of other tribes and join in their ceremonies. Several individuals and families are attempting to redefine their identities as Ioway through the retention of the Ioway language, the reinterpretation of remembered cultural elements, and the borrowing of missing cultural elements from appropriate, similar models in other tribes.

Lance M. Foster

See also Allotment; Cultural Revitalization; Environmental Issues; Indian Identity; Land Claims; Natural Resource Management; Religion

Further Reading

Anderson, Duane. "Ioway Ethnohistory: A Review, Part II." *Annals of Iowa*, 3rd ser. 42 (1973): 41–59.

Blaine, Martha Royce. *The Ioway Indians.* Civilization of the American Indian 151. Norman: University of Oklahoma Press, 1979.

Herring, Joseph B. *The Enduring Indians of Kansas.* Lawrence: University Press of Kansas, 1990.

Wedel, Mildred Mott. "Iowa." *Handbook of North American Indians.* Vol. 13. *Plains.* Washington, DC: Smithsonian Institution, forthcoming.

Wright, Muriel H. *A Guide to the Indian Tribes of Oklahoma.* Civilization of the American Indian 33. 1951. Norman: University of Oklahoma, 1986.

IPAI

See Kumeyaay

IRONWORKERS

Native American ironworkers have enjoyed a prominent place in high steel construction for over a century. They have been involved in the construction of almost every major North American bridge and skyscraper in the twentieth century. Currently there are over 7,500 Native American ironworkers in Canada and the United States. Prominent among this group are the Akwesasne Mohawks from the St. Regis Reservation in upstate New York, and the Caughnawaga Mohawks from the Kahnawake Reserve near Montreal, Canada. Ironwork is an immense source of cultural pride within the Indian world and the tools of the trade, belt, bolt pin, and bag, are passed from father to son in a ritualistic manner, not unlike ceremonial rituals of the past. Recently, Native women have entered the profession. Ironwork is a dangerous occupation, and many Native Americans have died or become disabled for life from injuries suffered on the job. Despite this danger, generations of Native Americans have entered the profession and earned recognition as premier tradesmen in a prestigious construction field. Ironwork has also provided a steady infusion of money into Native communities, where local employment opportunities are scarce.

It all began in 1886, just over a century ago, when the Dominion Bridge Company began construction of a railroad bridge over the St. Lawrence River near Montreal, Canada. The site of the bridge was near the Kahnawake Reserve, and Mohawks were hired on as day laborers. To the astonishment of the supervisors and foremen, untrained Mohawks mingled with ironworkers on the elevated steel beams and navigated the heights with the confidence of veteran ironworkers. Henceforth no major bridge or steel construction project in Canada was undertaken without Mohawk crews.

It was the construction of major bridges and skyscrapers in large cities in Canada and the United States that drew large numbers of Native Americans into the high steel industry. Even today, over half the men in Kahnawake and Akwesasne continue to be enrolled ironworker union members. Local 440 in Utica, New York, has a heavy concentration of Native American ironworkers. In addition, large numbers of Onondagas, Senecas, and Tuscaroras are engaged in high steelwork. Individuals from other tribes are also ironworkers today. This high concentration in ironwork has not always been an occupational blessing. On August 29, 1907, ninety-six ironworkers were killed when the Quebec Bridge, a cantilever bridge under construction, collapsed into the St. Lawrence River. Thirty-five Caughnawaga Mohawks were killed in this accident, which came to be known as the worst bridge construction disaster in history.

After World War I, Native American ironworkers began moving into the cities with their families. The largest populations were in Brooklyn, New York City, Buffalo, Cleveland, and Detroit. As late as the 1950s, over five hundred Native Americans, predominantly Mohawks, lived in the Canarsee section of Brooklyn. Each community had its ironworkers' bar, community hall, and church.

Native American ironworkers have worked predominantly as "Indian gangs." Each gang has three distinct sections: raisers, fitters, and riveters, although today the use of rivets has been replaced by specialized structural steel bolts. Native American ironworkers develop a special bond as a result of traveling, working, living, and socializing together. In the literature of Indian humor, ironworker stories and exploits are legendary. "Boomers," ironworkers who travel to and from a job, think nothing of commuting on the weekend from Chicago to Upstate New York or Montreal, Canada.

Ironwork has brought Native Americans prestige, self-esteem, international recognition, and compensation, far beyond what other Native peoples can earn. The "Indian Skywalkers," as they are referred to, are the modern-day successors of the Native guides, trappers, voyageurs, river pilots, and loggers who excelled at their professions in earlier times. The CN Tower in Toronto; George Washington Bridge and World Trade Center in New York; and the Golden Gate Bridge in San Francisco are but a few of the modern edifices that bear the imprint of the Native American ironworker.

Robert N. Wells, Jr.

See also **Mohawk**

Further Reading

Blanchard, David. "High Steel! The Kahnawake Mohawk and the High Construction Trade." *Journal of Ethnic Studies* 11:2 (1983): 41–60.

Dupont, John. "Mohawks in High Steel." *Naho*. Vol. 6, pt. 3. Albany: New York State Museum and Science Service, 1973.

Hill, Richard. *Skywalkers: A History of Indian Ironworkers.* Brantford, Ontario, Canada: Woodland Indian Cultural Educational Center, 1987.

Katzer, Bruce. "The Caughnawaga Mohawks: The Other Side of Iron Work." *Journal of Ethnic Studies* 15:4 (1988): 39–55.

Mitchell, Joseph. "The Mohawks in High Steel." *Apologies to the Iroquois.* Ed. Edmund Wilson. New York, NY: Farrar, Straus and Cudahy, 1960.

IROQUOIS

See Cayuga; Mohawk; Oneida; Onondaga; Seneca; Seneca-Cayuga; Tuscarora

IROQUOIS CONFEDERACY

In the early historic period there was a loosely organized ceremonial system shared by the five Iroquoian-speaking tribes (Mohawks, Oneidas, Onondagas, Cayugas, Senecas) in what is now New York State. At its core was an elaborate funeral rite known as the Condolence. Through time, the Condolence became a vehicle for political meetings as it functioned to bring together leaders from the various Iroquois tribes and villages. By the eighteenth century, while some of these leaders were identified as peace chiefs (sachems), the real political power resided with the war chiefs.

The underlying myth of the present-day Six Nations Confederacy (the Tuscaroras were added in the 1700s) is concerned with the journey of a culture-hero named Deganawidah who brought a plan of harmony and peace to the five warring Iroquois tribes. Out of this reformation came a confederacy that called for the establishment of a hereditary council of fifty sachems from the five tribes appointed by clan matrons, a decision-making process based on consensus, and a political and ceremonial protocol rooted in the kinship structure and worldview of the people.

The council fire of the Confederacy was extinguished in 1777, when the five tribes could not agree on which side to support in the American Revolution. After the war, a large number of Iroquois left New York, settled on the Six Nations Reserve near Brantford, Ontario, and established a confederacy council. Most of those who remained in New York moved to the Buffalo Creek Reservation, founding a second confederacy council that today sits at Onondaga.

At Tonawanda (Seneca) and Onondaga, and with the Cayugas and Tuscaroras, a "nonvoting" member, the system of hereditary chiefs has been maintained. It was replaced by an elective council at Allegany and Cattaraugus (Seneca reservations) in 1848. New York State acknowledged an elective system for the Mohawks at St. Regis (American side) in the 1800s. After a long absence, the hereditary system was reinstated among the New York Oneidas in the 1980s. In 1924, the Canadian government ousted the hereditary council at Six Nations, installing an elective form of government.

In 1799 the Seneca sachem Handsome Lake had a series of visions that called upon the Iroquois to return to their former ways, modified somewhat by the influence of Christian beliefs that followed from 200 years of contact. His message was formalized as the Code of Handsome Lake, which became the controlling belief system at the three Seneca reservations and Onondaga. Handsome Lake supporters also established longhouses at the Six Nations Reserve, and later appeared among the Tuscaroras, Mohawks, and Oneidas. Currently, most of the members of the hereditary councils are followers of the Code of Handsome Lake, thus providing an ideological and also political link to all of the reservation communities.

Today there is less than a full complement of sachems in both confederacies, and there is considerable "borrowing" of chiefs and titles. Neither Confederacy is officially recognized by its respective state/province or federal government; nonetheless, they both exert considerable political influence. In New York, an express purpose of the confederacy is to extend its authority over all of the Iroquois communities, replacing the remaining elective systems with hereditary councils.

Elements that sustain and strengthen the Confederacy in New York include its nativistic beliefs, its assertions and expressions of sovereignty, and a small corps of activist leaders who are skilled politicians and information managers. Its activities are directed primarily at the state and federal governments. For example, the Confederacy resisted the 1924 Indian Citizenship Act, the Indian Reorganization Act of 1934, and the Selective Service Act. It also opposed federal legislation that conferred criminal and civil jurisdiction on New York in 1948 and 1950. Recently, the Confederacy has intervened, not without opposition from other Iroquois, in the Seneca lease issue and the land claims. It fought both the construction of Route 17 in western New York and the expansion of Interstate 81 on the Onondaga Reservation. In 1989, after years of demands and negotiations, the State of New York returned twelve wampum belts to the Onondagas who are holding them in their traditional role as wampum keepers of the Confederacy.

Legislative efforts by the Confederacy have resulted in the introduction of an Indian burial protection bill and passage of a measure exempting Indians from the oath of allegiance to New York and its constitution required of state employees. Over the past several years the Confederacy has concerned itself primarily with preventing gambling casinos from operating on reservations and controlling lands claims.

William A. Starna

Jack Campisi

Laurence M. Hauptman

See also **Organizations and Inter-Tribal Cooperation**

Further Reading

Hauptman, Laurence M. *The Iroquois and the New Deal.* Syracuse, NY: Syracuse University Press, 1981.

———. *The Iroquois Struggle for Survival.* Syracuse, NY: Syracuse University Press, 1986.

———. *Formulating American Indian Policy in New York State, 1970–1986.* Albany: State University of New York Press, 1988.

Tooker, Elisabeth. "The League of the Iroquois: Its History, Politics, and Ritual." *Handbook of North American Indians.* Vol. 15. *Northeast.* Ed. Bruce G. Trigger. Washington, DC: Smithsonian Institution (1978): 418–41.

———. "Iroquois Since 1820." *Handbook of North American Indians.* Vol. 15. *Northeast.* Ed. Bruce G. Trigger. Washington, DC: Smithsonian Institution (1978): 449–65.

Wallace, Anthony F.C. "Origins of the Longhouse Religion." *Handbook of North American Indians.* Vol. 15. *Northeast.* Ed. Bruce G. Trigger. Washington, DC: Smithsonian Institution (1978): 442–48.

ISLETA

See Pueblo of Isleta

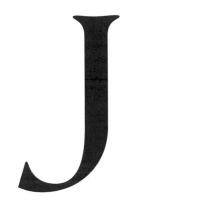

JEMEZ

See Pueblo of Jemez

JEWELRY

See Beadwork, Quillwork, Silverwork and Other Jewelry

JICARILLA

See Apache

JOHNSON-O'MALLEY ACT

The Johnson-O'Malley Act (J-OM) was enacted on April 16, 1934, authorizing the secretary of the interior to enter into contracts with any state or territory for the purpose of funding education for Indian children in public schools and other purposes. The original act authorized the funding of activities far beyond the J-OM educational programs as they are known today. At the secretary's discretion, he was authorized:

> ... to enter into a contract or contracts with any State or territory having legal authority so to do, for the education, medical attention, agricultural assistance, and social welfare, including relief of distress, of Indians in such State or territory, and to expend under such contract or contracts moneys appropriated by Congress for the education, medical attention, agricultural assistance, and social welfare, including relief of distress, of Indians in such State. (J-OM Act, 1934)

On June 4, 1936 a significant amendment was made to the Act which authorized parties other than the state to contract with the Department of the Interior; theoretically, this would allow Indian tribes or organizations to incorporate under state law and contract directly with the Department of the Interior. The original purposes were left intact and the act

remained relatively unchanged until amended by Public Law 93-638, the Indian Self-Determination and Education Assistance Act of 1975. The new legislation essentially reformed the Johnson-O'Malley Act by providing new contracting arrangements by Indians for Indian education in the public sector.

Throughout the history of administering the program, numerous issues have been encountered. Some of the major issues include: service to nonreservation versus reservation people; equitable distribution of funds; parental involvement; supplemental programs versus basic support for schools; and the definition of eligibility for services.

Nonreservation versus Reservation Indians

One of the major concerns when the legislation was passed was the need to deal with the rural or scattered Indian population mixed in with the general population. The Bureau of Indian Affairs (BIA) changed the intent of Congress by promulgating regulations establishing blood quantum requirements for eligibility of individuals, and later rules requiring the presence of large tracts of nontaxable land for school districts. Thus service was limited to reservation Indians. Today the majority of eligible Indian students live off of the reservations, in many small towns and cities and in virtually every major city in the nation. The land requirement is no longer an issue, but the BIA continues the policy of limiting J-OM funding to those schools serving Indian students on or near reservations.

Eventually the needs of nonreservation Indian students, coupled with the concern for services for nonfederally recognized tribes, contributed to passage of the Indian Education Act of 1972. Because of programmatic similarities, the two programs continue to face questions regarding coordination and duplication of services among their common service population.

Parental Involvement

New regulations under the Indian Self-Determination and Education Assistance Act (1975) clarified and strengthened the role of Indian parents in public school J-OM programs. These regulations require maximum participation and control by Indian parents, including full veto power over supplemental J-OM programs and related expenditures. Great strides have been made to empower Indian people with their participatory rights. Yet, parents often find it difficult to exercise their obligations to the fullest extent possible, and some school districts are still unwilling to share the power of decision making resulting in some J-OM programs now being contracted and operated outside the public school system.

Distribution of Funds

The distribution of J-OM funds is problematic. The wide variance of J-OM funding levels among states, based upon average per pupil expenditures, has led to a weighted formula to be phased in over three years, effective in fiscal year 1990. While the new formula did not satisfy all parties, it did reduce the disparity of funding levels between states.

Basic Support versus Supplemental Programs

Contracting with states through the J-OM program grew out of an earlier tuition payment program, which addressed basic support concerns, covering the per capita costs of educating Indian students in public schools. J-OM basic support funds were part of the general fund of the school. They did not directly benefit Indian students and were not accountable for that purpose. The supplemental J-OM programs were considered experimental and for enrichment purposes for Indian students. Today, authority for the J-OM basic support program still remains, but funding was gradually phased out in the 1970s in favor of the supplemental programs with greater accountability.

Eligibility for Services

With the passage of time, the issue of eligibility for federal services has become increasingly complex. The question is often driven by attempts to define who is an Indian and for what purposes. The definition as of 1991 encompasses those students recognized as "a member of or at least a one-quarter degree Indian blood descendent of a member of a tribe which is eligible for the special programs and services provided by the United States through the Bureau of Indian Affairs to Indians because of their status as Indians, and resides on or near an Indian reservation or meets the criteria for attendance at a Bureau off-reservation boarding school." This change will result in more students being eligible for the J-OM program, and could significantly increase the demands for services.

Summary

The J-OM program has taken many twists and turns over the course of almost sixty years. The act remains a powerful piece of legislation with the authority to fund a wide array of activities beyond supplemental education. From the outset, it was primarily viewed as a means to offset the costs of public education for Indian students. As the program evolved, embracing the supplemental and enrichment perspectives, coupled with the strengthening of Indian parental control, the J-OM program slowly garnered the support of the Indian community. The reality of this phenomenon was fully realized much to the dismay of the BIA, who unsuccessfully sought to defund the program in 1986. Congress responded to the overwhelming support of Indian people by restoring funding.

Historically, the BIA has held the J-OM program in low priority, and funding levels continue to be problematic. Average awards remain low at slightly over $100 per student, while participation increased to over 225,000 students in 1991. A review of recent BIA budget requests reveals that the agency continues to recommend to Congress reductions in budgets or, no growth budgets, at best. This is based on the BIA's perspective that J-OM eligible students are in the public sector and are not the BIA's primary responsibility. Further, BIA budget personnel rationalize that the Indian community will seek the support of Congress to restore their recommended cuts, thus giving the BIA license to show overall reductions in the annual budget requests. This convoluted philosophy has resulted in minimal budget requests and deterred program growth and development.

The stated policy of the BIA is "to serve as an advocate and carry out responsibilities for Indian and Alaska Native students in public and other non-Bureau operated schools consistent with the wishes of the appropriate Indian tribes and Alaska Native entities, particularly in regard to Impact Aid, Johnson-O'Malley and all Elementary and Secondary Education Act programs."

The BIA gives little time, energy, or resources to this policy. Despite the nonaggressive implementation of the policy, the Johnson-O'Malley Act has played and continues to play a significant role in supporting change in Indian education. It provides the impetus for a grassroots movement to legitimize the role of Indian parents who best represent the needs of their children in public schools. Yet, the future of the J-OM program, as in the past, remains an enigma.

Gerald E. Gipp

See also Educational Policy; Indian Education Act; Public Schools

Further Reading

A Study of Title II of PL 93-638: A Report. Minneapolis, MN: National Indian Education Association, 1975.

Szasz, Margaret Connell. *Education and the American Indian: The Road to Self-Determination Since 1928.* 2d ed. Albuquerque: The University of New Mexico Press, 1977.

JOURNALS

See Periodicals

JUANEÑO

See Luiseño

JUDGES

See Tribal Government

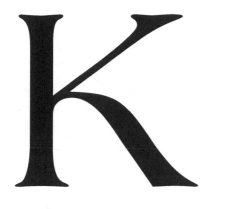

KADOHADACHO

See Caddo

KALISPEL

Historically there has been a confusing use of the names Kalispel and Pend d'Oreille. An analysis of the literature leads to the conclusion that the names Kalispel and Pend d'Oreille are synonyms with a spatial distinction between Upper Kalispel/Upper Pend d'Oreille and Lower Kalispel/Lower Pend d'Oreille. Each division had a name, occupied a specific geographical area, had a separate political structure, and were not considered a tribe in terms of socio-political organization. Both divisions spoke the Interior Salish language.

The Lower Kalispel occupied the territory along the Pend Oreille River below Lake Pend Oreille in Idaho to the confluence of the Salmo River in British Columbia. The Upper Kalispel occupied the area around Lake Pend Oreille and up the Pend Oreille River to the confluence of the Clark Fork and Flathead Rivers near Plains, Montana. After the introduction of the horse, the territorial limit of the Upper Kalispel was extended eastward to the Mission Valley and Flathead Lake in Montana, and south to include the Bitterroot Valley. It was in this area that they congregated with other Plateau groups to form "Bison-hunting task groups" for mutual protection to hunt on the Great Plains.

On July 16, 1855, Isaac Stevens concluded the Hell Gate Treaty of 1855 in the Bitter Root Valley of Montana, with the Flathead, Kootenai, and Upper Kalispel/Pend d'Oreille. Alexander signed for the Upper Kalispel, but Stevens would not let him speak for the Lower Kalispel. This treaty created the Flathead Reservation located in western Montana, which is occupied by the Confederated Salish (which includes the Kalispel) and Kootenai tribes.

In 1887 the United States wanted the remaining Lower Kalispel moved to the Flathead Reservation. At this time the Lower Kalispel consisted of two major bands: one was under Victor and his son Marcella, and the other under Michael. Michael signed the agreement and moved his band to the Flathead Reservation; Marcella did not sign the agreement and remained in the Pend Oreille Valley. In 1914 President Woodrow Wilson issued an executive order for this band, which created the Kalispel Reservation on the east side of the Pend Oreille River in the vicinity of Cusick/Usk, Washington. It consisted of 4,629 acres. In 1924, it was allotted but the allotments were only for 40 acres, in contrast to the 160-acre allotments on other reservations. Sixty acres are held in tribal trust, and only one 40-acre allotment has been lost to non-Indian ownership. The tribe ratified a Constitution in 1938, and in 1989 their enrolled population was 246. They were awarded $3 million in about 1960 by the Indian Claims Commission for the loss of their aboriginal lands.

The Kalispel Indian Development Enterprise has been considering economic development activities in the areas of recreation, livestock, forage production, fish and wildlife management, and commercial and industrial development. As of 1989, specific economic development projects consisted of Kalispel Caseline, Kalispel Agricultural Enterprise, and Kalispel Tribal Bingo. They are in the process of planning a tribal store and a fish and game enterprise. In 1977 they began an important land acquisition program seeking 8,321 acres of federal and state forest lands. Because of the small size of the reservation, additional land is essential to its various development efforts.

Sylvester L. Lahren, Jr.

***See also* Confederated Salish and Kootenai Tribes**

Further Reading

Chalfant, Stuart A. "Aboriginal Territory of the Kalispel Indians." *Interior Salish and Eastern Washington Indians 3.* New York, NY: Garland Publishing, 1974.

Fahey, John. *The Kalispel Indians.* Norman: University of Oklahoma Press, 1986.

Lahren, Sylvester L., Jr. "Kalispel." *Handbook of North American Indians.* Vol. 12. *Plateau.* Ed. Deward E. Walker, Jr. Washington, DC: Smithsonian Institution, forthcoming.

Ray, Verne F. "Culture Element Distribution: Plateau 22." *Anthropological Records*, 8:2. Berkeley, CA: University Publications (1942): 99–262.

Smith, Alan. *Kalispel Ethnography.* Smith Manuscript. Exhibit 65, Docket 94. Indian Claims Commission, 1950.

Teit, James A. "The Salishan Tribes of the Western Plateaus." *Bureau of American Ethnology 45th Annual Report* (1930): 295–396.

KANSA

See Kaw

KARANKAWA

See Tonkawa

KARUK

The Karuk Tribe of California was constituted on April 6, 1985. The resulting tribal government is a consolidation of the autonomous political organizations that had represented the interests of Karuk individuals since the 1970s. The organizations represented four geographic areas: the Orleans (Panamniik) district located in Humboldt County; the Happy Camp (Athithufvuunupma) district; the Yreka (Kahtishram) district; and the Forks of the Salmon region, located in Siskiyou County.

Karuk (also Karok) aboriginal territory is located in northwestern California along the midstretch of the Klamath River. The turn of the century found many families leaving the river in search of wage-earning employment in the agricultural valleys and shipping centers on the coast. Many Karuk children were removed for long periods from their homes to be educated in the government boarding schools in Oregon, Nevada, southern California, and the Midwest. They often received vocational training in occupations more suited to job opportunities found in urban areas. Many tribal members remained at home, however, and continued to speak the language, a member of the Hokan language family, and to live a subsistence lifestyle. Seasonal employment opportunities were combined with salmon fishing, deer hunting, and gathering, resulting in a relatively stable "traditional" lifestyle. Tribal ceremonies to "fix the earth" (known as *Irahiv*) were conducted continuously until World War II at the three religious centers located at the present towns of Orleans, Somes Bar and Clear Creek. With the return of the young after the war, the ceremonies were held intermittently. During the 1970s the younger generation, working with the traditional elders, initiated a renaissance of traditional culture that has continued to the present. This activity mirrors similar cultural rejuvenation among the Karuk's neighbors: the Hupa, Yurok, Shasta, and Tolowa.

During the 1960s and 1970s the interests of the Karuk people were represented by nonprofit corporations chartered by the State of California. These groups provided the political representation which ordinarily is the provenance of a tribal government. The Karuk organizations administered programs, purchased land, and operated under democratically elected boards of directors. Through the persistent efforts of such tribal members as Jack Sanderson, Charlie Thom, Bessie Tripp, Shan Davis, and others, the Karuk people were recognized as a tribe by the United States Congress on January 15, 1979. Since adoption of the 1985 Constitution, the tribal government has established and expanded a number of public services for tribal members in the areas of housing, education, health and related areas. Although one of the largest tribes in the state of California, the Karuk

have a small land base. Federal recognition occurred because a 6.6-acre parcel, which was first purchased by a group of elders and then placed in trust status, qualified the tribe as eligible for establishment under the Indian Reorganization Act of 1934. Today's tribal land base is 300 acres.

An official report published in 1905 cites a total population figure of 576, and the 1910 census estimated 775 persons: both are considered significant undercounts. Today's population figures exceed the estimated 1,500 people at the time of first contact as the official enrollment in 1992 is 1,900. The Tribal Council officially asserts the figure to be 4,800, a number currently used by the Bureau of Indian Affairs and other governmental agencies. In recent years population growth has been coupled with moderate increases in average income and educational level. Health statistics, however, reveal increased rates of hypertension, heart disease, and diabetes, and a special emphasis is being placed on preventive medicine and health education. Economic development is occurring primarily within the human services area, retail sales, and forest management and logging. Entrepreneurship is on the rise.

The sacred practices and ceremonial sites continue to be vital aspects of the contemporary cultural identity of the tribe. Ceremonies to "fix the world" are still performed at Ka'tim'iin (the Center of the World) and Inaam (Clear Creek). Many aboriginal village sites have been continually inhabited since precontact times at Panamniik (Orleans), Asanaamkarak (Ike's), Vuunxarak (Oak Bottom), Tithuuf (Tea Bar), Ishvirip (Cottage Grove), and other sites along the Klamath River.

The traditional Karuk worldview is firmly rooted within the natural environment. Many of the issues facing us today are related to disputes over the land, natural resource management, water rights, regulation of the salmon fishery, and religious use of public lands. Most important is the need to acquire land to meet the needs of a growing population.

Julian Lang

See also **California Tribes**

Further Reading

Arnold, Mary Ellicott, and Mabel Reed. *In the Land of the Grasshopper Song; A Story of Two Girls in Indian Country in 1908–09.* New York, NY: Vantage Press, 1957. Eureka, CA: Schooner Features, 1975.

Bright, William. "The Karok Language." *University of California Publications in Linguistics* 13 (1957): 1–457.

———. "Karok." *Handbook of North American Indians.* Vol. 8. *California.* Ed. Robert F. Heizer. Washington, DC: Smithsonian Institution (1978): 180–89.

Harrington, John P. *Tobacco Among the Karuk Indians of California.* Bureau of American Ethnology Bulletin 94. Washington, DC: U.S. Government Printing Office, 1932.

———. *The Papers of John Peabody Harrington in the Smithsonian Institution, 1907–1957.* Vol 2. *Northern and Central California.* Ed. Elaine L. Mills. Millwood, NY: Kraus International Publications, 1981.

KASHAYA POMO

See Pomo

KASKASKIA

See Miami; Peoria

KAW

Formerly known as the Kansa (or Konza) people, the Kaws are a Dhegiha-Siouan linguistic group who arrived in present northeastern Kansas from the lower Ohio Valley sometime prior to the mid-seventeenth century. With the establishment of Kansas Territory in 1854 and Kansas statehood seven years later, the Kaws were exploited by white squatters and missionaries, town and railroad jobbers, and the federal government's policy of land seizure prior to and after the American Civil War. Despite passionate efforts by the highly venerated Chief Al-le-go-wa-ho to prevent the tribe's removal from Kansas in the 1860s, the Kaws were removed to a small reservation in future Oklahoma in 1873. Three decades later, in 1902, they fell under the hammer of allotment.

The Kaw Allotment Act of 1902 was largely the work of Charles Curtis, a one-eighth blood member of the tribe who eventually served as vice-president of the United States under Herbert Hoover, and who in 1902 was a Kansas congressman and member of the House Committee on Indian Affairs. Listed on the allotment rolls were 249 persons, of which nearly 50 percent were mixed bloods. A significant minority of full-bloods opposed allotment, and until the tribe was reconstituted under authority of the Department of Interior in 1959, factionalism and legal struggles over political control of the tribe were commonplace.

Until their land was inundated by the Kaw Reservoir constructed by the United States Army Corps of Engineers on the Arkansas River just northeast of Ponca City in the mid-1960s, the tribe retained 260 acres near the Beaver Creek confluence with the Arkansas. Here were located the old councilhouse, the abandoned Washungah townsite, and the tribal cemetery. Eventually the cemetery was removed to Newkirk, Oklahoma, and the councilhouse to a fifteen acre tract a few miles northwest of the former Beaver Creek trust lands. Subsequently, by action of Congress, the new councilhouse tract was enlarged to include 135.5 acres, which presently are administered by the Kaw as official trust lands.

The Kaw Nation of Oklahoma is a federally recognized tribe with headquarters at Kaw City, Oklahoma. Having been reduced from a 1700 population of nearly 5,000 to less than 700 a century and a half later, the official membership in 1993 is 1,678, including five full-bloods. The present Constitution was adopted by the Kaw Nation General Council (enrolled members over the age of eighteen) on August 14, 1990. The seven-member Kaw Nation Executive Committee, elected by a majority of the General Council, is the governing body.

There are presently less than a dozen Kaws who are fluent in their traditional Siouan language, although efforts are underway to remedy this regrettable circumstance. The Kaw people prefer to keep their religious preferences to themselves. An increasingly popular cultural event is the annual Kaw pow-wow, held each year the first weekend of August on tribal grounds in northern Oklahoma.

The Kaw Nation of Oklahoma owns and operates four businesses: (1) Kaw Nation Bingo Enterprise, located near Newkirk, Oklahoma; (2) the Kanza Nursery; (3) the Braman Properties/Oklahoma Truck Stop at the intersection of Interstate 35 and Oklahoma State Highway 177; and (4) the Kaw Nation discount tobacco shops at Newkirk and Braman. There is also a successful Kaw Housing Authority project near Newkirk, Oklahoma. The Kaw Nation maintains membership (with the Pawnee, Tonkawa, Ponca, and Otoe-Missouria tribes) in the Chilocco Development Authority, and more recently has organized the Kaw Enterprise Development Authority, with the objective of increasing the Kaw land base and related economic enterprises, particularly on former Kaw land in the Kansas City, Kansas, metropolitan area.

With funds generated by its very successful bingo and other economic enterprises, the Kaw Nation provides academic scholarships for tribal members, social service programs, and emergency assistance. On April 9, 1992, the Kaw Nation Tribal District and Supreme Courts were dedicated at an elaborate ceremony at tribal headquarters in Kaw City, Oklahoma.

William E. Unrau

See also **Oklahoma Tribes**

Further Reading

Unrau, William E. *The Kaw People.* Phoenix, AZ: Indian Tribal Series, 1975.
——. *The Kansa Indians: A History of the Wind People, 1673–1873.* Civilization of the American Indian 114. Norman: University of Oklahoma Press, 1986.
——. *Mixed-bloods and Tribal Dissolution: Charles Curtis and the Quest for Indian Identity.* Lawrence: University Press of Kansas, 1989.
——. *Indians of Kansas: The Euro-American Invasion and Conquest of Indian Kansas.* Topeka: Kansas State Historical Society, 1991.

KAWAIISU

The Kawaiisu are located in Kern County, California, between the Mohave Desert and the San Joaquin Valley. Their language is a Southern Numic dialect of the Uto-Aztecan language. The aboriginal population of perhaps 500 had been diminished to about 100 in 1936; the present population is about 35.

The infiltration of the non-Indians received a powerful stimulus when gold was discovered in California in 1849, and was actually found in Kawaiisu territory in the 1850s. There followed "a rush of prospectors" and soon the very center of Kawaiisu habitation around Havilah, Piute, Claraville, and Sageland was dotted with mining claims. There were occasional clashes between the Natives and the newcomers, but the territorial penetration was not, at least at the beginning, the usual basis for the disputes. Of more concern was the alleged thievery of the Indians, especially of cattle and horses (for food) and the stealing of women by the non-Indians. The intermixing and intermarriage between the Indians and the Caucasians became a rather common phenomenon. The Indians also became involved in well-established commercial activities, such as cattle raising, farming, and government projects. Some found jobs in the large cement plant in Monolith, near Tehachapi.

Despite their small numbers, there is reason to believe that the Kawaiisu have been in their present core habitat for at least 2,000 years. There are vivid reminders of ancient activity of the Kawaiisu. Scattered throughout the area are hundreds of bedrock mortar holes made for grinding and pounding acorns, seeds, and tobacco leaves. As use gradually enlarged the holes, they were abandoned and new ones started; as many as 300 holes can be counted in one area. Further evidence of the long presence of Indians are the pictographs to be found on smooth rock surfaces and natural stone walls. The Indians, however, firmly believe that neither the mortar holes nor the pictographs are the work of human beings. The mortar holes, they say, are the natural contours of the rock. As for the pictographs, they are the work of the malevolent Rock Baby, who dwells in the rock and paints according to his mood. To see the Baby is to bring death and even to touch the paintings or to photograph them can be disastrous. The Rock Baby continues to draw and paint so one is likely to note some new figures from time to time.

An ethnobotanical study in the 1930s and again in the early 1970s resulted in the listing of one hundred twenty plants, which have provided food and beverage, over one hundred medicines, ninety miscellaneous uses, while forty plants had ritualistic, mythological, and supernatural associations.

The Kawaiisu have never been consigned to an Indian reservation. Today the young Kawaiisu are seeking federal recognition in order to achieve basic economic stability. They are conscious of their position as descendants of an ancient tradition. They want to preserve their culture and language and to this end they ask for federal support.

Maurice L. Zigmond

See also California Tribes

Further Reading

Zigmond, Maurice L. *Kawaiisu Mythology*. Socorro, NM: Ballena Press, 1980.

———. *Kawaiisu Ethnobotany*. Salt Lake City: University of Utah Press, 1981.

———. "Kawaiisu." *Handbook of North American Indians*. Vol. 11. *Great Basin*. Ed. Warren L. d'Azevedo. Washington, DC: Smithsonian Institution (1986): 398–411.

KICKAPOO

The Kickapoo were originally a Woodland people, first mentioned by Europeans in 1667 as living in southern Wisconsin. A series of treaties and conflicts with the United States government between 1795 and 1862 resulted in several removals that placed the Kickapoo in two separate political and cultural communities by the turn of the twentieth century—one spread across Oklahoma, Texas, and Mexico; and another in Kansas.

KICKAPOO IN KANSAS

The Kickapoo Tribe in Kansas is one of three federally recognized Kickapoo groups; others are the Kickapoo Tribe of Oklahoma and the Texas Band of Kickapoo (Mexican Kickapoo). The Kansas Kickapoo are descended from the followers of Kenekuk, the Kickapoo prophet. They were removed from Illinois in 1832 following the Treaty of Castor Hill. This treaty provided 768,000 acres in northeast Kansas, but these lands were steadily reduced. The reservation presently measures six by five miles and is located in rural Brown County, some forty miles north of Topeka. A classic case of "checkerboarding," only 37 percent of the 19,200-acre reservation is under Indian ownership. Indian lands are divided about equally between acreage held communally by the tribe (about 3,500 acres), and that held by individual allottees (about 3,700 acres). There are no significant mineral resources, and much of the allotted land is leased to non-Indian farmers.

Twentieth-Century History

In 1900, 255 Kickapoos lived on the reservation. They resisted allotment, but by 1908 the entire area had been broken up into individual parcels of land. On January 23, 1937, the tribe approved a Constitution and Bylaws under provisions of the Indian Reorganization Act; they also chartered a corporation for business purposes. By the mid-1940s, the council form of government had gained wide acceptance.

At a Tribal Council meeting on June 25, 1951, William Ben Sacquat, speaking in Kickapoo, addressed the problems then facing the tribe. Reservation day schools had been closed and budget reductions led to layoffs at the Bureau of Indian Affairs' (BIA) agency office in nearby Horton. Sacquat, a respected elder, felt that reductions in government support would further erode the already precarious economic, medical, and educational conditions on the reservation. And the following year, the reservation population reached its lowest point—162.

The House and Senate Subcommittees on Indian Affairs held joint hearings on termination of the Kansas tribes in February 1954. Tribal Council members Vestana Cadue, Oliver Kahbeah, and Ralph Simon traveled to Washington, D.C. at their own expense to testify against termination. Because of strong opposition from the Kickapoo and Prairie Band Potawatomi representatives at these hearings, the Kansas tribes avoided the devastation of termination.

In the 1970s, the Kansas Kickapoo took full advantage of legislation and funding opportunities ushered in by the new era of Indian self-determination. Between 1976 and 1981, federal grants enabled the tribe to construct a gymnasium, a quick shop/gas station, centers for senior citizens and day care, and homes for the elderly and single families. With money from Indian Claims Commission settlements, the tribe repurchased more than 2,400 acres within the boundaries of their reservation, and established a farm and ranch. Following closure of the public school that served the reservation, the tribe moved aggressively to obtain it. Overcoming obstacles at the local, state, and federal levels, the Kickapoo Nation School—an Indian contract school serving grades kindergarden through twelve—opened in 1981.

The Kickapoos' success proved to be a mixed blessing. Federal funds created rapid infrastructural development and jobs for a growing number of tribal members, but they also increased dependency on the federal government. Beginning in the fall of 1981, reductions in funding and delays in passage of the federal budget led to serious loss of programs, services, and jobs. Between August 1980 and January 1982, reservation unemployment soared from 34 percent to 93 percent.

Current Situation

According to the 1990 census, 478 people, occupying 143 households, live on the Kansas Kickapoo Reservation; of these, 368, or 77 percent, are American Indian. Another 178 Indians live in the surrounding county. The reservation population is young; 37 percent are under 18 years of age, while only 15 percent are 60 or over. It is also poor; per capita income for Indians living on the reservation is $4,831; 37 percent of the Indians have incomes below federal poverty levels. Almost half the Indians 25 and over living on the reservation have graduated from high school, and 25 percent have some college, but none hold bachelor's degrees. Unemployment remains high; tribal officials estimate it to be around 40 percent. Most tribal members work for the tribe, their school, or the local BIA agency office. Economic development efforts in the 1990s have focused on gaming. The tribe has held bingo games in its gymnasium for several years. In 1992, the Kickapoo signed a compact with the governor of Kansas to allow them to build a casino in the nearby town of Hiawatha, but the state legislature opposed the agreement and a federal suit is pending.

Like their ancestors who moved to Kansas more than 150 years ago, today's Kansas Kickapoo struggle to preserve their traditions even as they seek access to the social and economic benefits of the larger society. Tribal members no longer speak the Kickapoo language, though some speak the language of their neighbors, the Prairie Band Potawatomi, with whom many have intermarried. Still, most tribal members participate in one or more of three surviving traditional religions. The smallest is the Kenekuk Religion, whose numbers have steadily dwindled since the death of the prophet in about 1858. The Drum Religion, or Dream Dance, reached the Kansas Kickapoo in the 1880s from Wisconsin. In 1910, a Prairie Band Potawatomi brought the Peyote Religion, or the Native American Church, to Kansas from Oklahoma. Both religions remain strong, and their leaders continue to provide spiritual guidance for the Kansas Kickapoo.

Donald D. Stull

***See also* Potawatomi in Kansas**

Further Reading

Herring, Joseph B. *The Enduring Indians of Kansas: A Century and a Half of Acculturation.* Lawrence: University Press of Kansas, 1990.

Return to Sovereignty: Self-Determination and the Kansas Kickapoo. Prod. Donald D. Stull. University of California Extension Media Center, 1982. Videocassette. 46 min.

Stull, Donald D. *Kiikaapoa: The Kansas Kickapoo.* 1984, Horton, KS: Kickapoo Tribal Press, 1994.

Stull, Donald D., Jerry A. Schultz, and Ken Cadue, Sr. "Rights Without Resources: The Rise and Fall of the Kansas Kickapoo." *American Indian Culture and Research Journal* 10.2 (1986): 41–59.

KICKAPOO IN OKLAHOMA AND TEXAS

Although administratively distinct, the Oklahoma and Texas Kickapoos view themselves as one people. Cultural and historical differences distinguish them from the Kickapoo Tribe in Kansas, with whom they have had only sporadic contacts for the past 150 years.

The French first encountered the Kickapoo around the lower Great Lakes in the late 1600s. Subsequent European expansion and intertribal conflicts led to migrations and dispersal as Kickapoo bands scattered widely throughout Indiana, Illinois, Missouri, and Texas. In 1839, one group migrated to Mexico, where others later joined them, and by 1865 the only large concentration of Kickapoos in the United States was in Kansas.

In 1873 the United States Cavalry crossed into Mexico in retaliation for Kickapoo raids in Texas and captured about forty women and children. The cavalry held them hostage at Fort Gibson, Oklahoma, hoping to entice those in Mexico to Oklahoma. Eventually some three hundred of the captives' relatives relocated and were given a reservation in central Oklahoma, but about half the group chose to remain in Mexico. Many Kickapoos became dissatisfied with the federal government's allotment of their reservation in 1891, and by 1905 many had returned to Mexico. In that year, 247 Kickapoos lived in Oklahoma, while some four hundred were in Mexico.

Today the Oklahoma and Texas Kickapoos (sometimes called the Mexican Kickapoos) constitute two separate and distinct tribes. Each maintains its own government and membership. The Oklahoma Kickapoos live in Lincoln, Potawatomie, and Oklahoma counties in central Oklahoma, concentrated in eight communities: Choctaw, Jones, Harrah, McLoud, Shawnee, Dale, Tecumseh, and Oklahoma City. Since 1937, the Kickapoo Tribe of Oklahoma has been governed by a five-person Business Committee. Tribal offices are located near McCloud on one of the few tracts of land the tribe holds in common. Individual members hold some 6,000 acres of the 22,000 originally allotted to them, but much is leased to non-Indian farmers. In 1975, there were 1,184 enrolled members of the Kickapoo Tribe of Oklahoma, but only about 500 continued to live in the area of the original allotments. In 1992, tribal officials estimated the Kickapoo Tribe in Oklahoma had 1,900 members of one-quarter or more blood quantum.

Since the 1860s, some Kickapoos have lived in a village (El Nacimiento Rancheria) of traditional houses made of reed mats on 7,000 hectares (17,290 acres), granted them by the Mexican government. The village is located in the state of Coahuila, 25 miles northwest of Muzquiz and 125 miles southwest of Eagle Pass, Texas. For the past century, these Kickapoos, holding fast to their central Algonquian heritage, have lived by hunting, gathering, farming, and migrant farm labor. In the 1940s fencing of nearby lands by Mexican ranchers, overhunting, and drought led them to migrate annually to the United States to work as farm laborers.

Each March, members of this group begin their annual farmwork "tour" of the United States, picking cucumbers and onions in south Texas, then following the harvest through the midwestern and western states. They return to Mexico for the winter, their ceremonial season, when Nacimiento is the site of religious ceremonies and the main base for economic activities. These Kickapoos have long used Eagle Pass, Texas, as their base of operations when in the United States. They live in a village of traditional houses made of cane and cardboard under the international bridge over the Rio Grande, between Eagle Pass and Piedras Negras, Mexico. A small group of Kickapoos presently live in the Mexican State of Sonora.

Until recently, Kickapoos who chose dual residency did not have clear legal status in either the United States or Mexico, and they received only limited assistance and government services from either country. In 1979 they asked the United States government to clarify their American citizenship status; these Kickapoos wished to continue to move freely between the United States and Mexico and be granted trust land and government services in the Eagle Pass area. With legal assistance from the Native American Rights Fund, and support from Kickapoos in Oklahoma and Kansas, they entered into negotiations with the United States Departments of the Interior and State, the

Mexican government, and the Inter-American Indian Institute, resulting in the passage of Public Law 97–429, the Texas Band of Kickapoo Act, in January 1983. This act recognized the "Texas Band of Kickapoo" as a distinct, self-governing subgroup of the Kickapoo Tribe of Oklahoma. With federal recognition, the Texas Band became eligible for federal programs and assistance without having to travel to Oklahoma.

The Kickapoo Trust Land Acquisition Committee raised more than $300,000 and in 1984 purchased 125 acres along the Rio Grande in Maverick County, Texas, about 8 miles south of Eagle Pass. But the Kickapoo have been slow to move to their new land, called Nuevo Nacimiento, preferring instead to remain in their village under the international bridge. Public Law 97–429 gave members of the Texas Band the option of citizenship in either Mexico or the United States, and on November 21, 1985, 145 members of the 650–member band became American citizens.

In 1989, the Texas Band of Kickapoo developed a Constitution and submitted it to the secretary of the interior, requesting federal recognition as a separate and distinct tribe. The request was granted and the Kickapoo Traditional Tribe in Texas was established.

The Kickapoo aboriginal religion remains largely intact. Life revolves around a seasonal ceremonial cycle, which opens in the early spring with a series of major ceremonies lasting several weeks. Many ceremonies take place in Nacimiento, and a large number of Oklahoma Kickapoo travel to Mexico to join with their kin in a traditional Kickapoo environment.

The Kickapoo in Oklahoma and Texas continue to preserve and promote their native language and culture. Approximately 45 percent of tribal members in Oklahoma are monolingual in Kickapoo, half are of limited English proficiency, and only about 5 percent, mostly youth, are fluent in English. Their commitment to their language and culture has cost them in socio-economic development and status. For example, their level of formal education is low; unemployment is extremely high. Nevertheless, the Kickapoo Tribe of Oklahoma and the Kickapoo Traditional Tribe in Texas remain dedicated to the well-being of their members, recognizing the need to balance their traditions with the challenges of the twenty-first century.

Donald D. Stull

Akira Y. Yamamoto

Staff, IKWAI Foundation of Organized Resources in Cultural Equity, Choctaw, Oklahoma

See also Migrants and Refugees; Oklahoma Tribes

Further Reading

Callendar, Charles, Richard K. Pope, and Susan H. Pope. "Kickapoo." *Handbook of North American Indians.* Vol. 15. *Northeast.* Ed. Bruce G. Trigger. Washington, DC: Smithsonian Institution (1978): 656–67.

Gibson, Arrell Morgan. *The Kickapoos: Lords of the Middle Border.* Civilization of the American Indian 70. Norman: University of Oklahoma Press, 1963.

Latorre, Felipe A., and Delores L. Latorre. *The Mexican Kickapoo Indians.* Austin: University of Texas Press, 1976.

Ritzenthaler, Robert E., and Frederick A. Peterson. *The Mexican Kickapoo Indians.* Milwaukee Public Museum Publications in Anthropology 2. Milwaukee, WI: 1956.

KIOWA

Kiowa is a corruption of the word *Ga'igwu* or *Ka'i-gwu*, meaning "Principal People," the name they call themselves. The Kiowa tribal land base is in southwest Oklahoma.

The beginning of the twentieth century was disheartening for the Kiowa. In 1903, the United States Supreme Court declared in *Lone Wolf v. Hitchcock*, 187 United States 553 (1903), that Congress had a plenary power as guardian to manage Kiowa property, and could abrogate a treaty provision unilaterally without the consent of the Kiowa. On June 6, 1900, Congress ratified the Jerome Agreement, which authorized individual allotments. A total of 443,338 acres of the Kiowa-Comanche-Apache Reservation was allotted to 2,759 tribal members, and the remaining 2,033,583 acres, purchased by the United States for $2 million, was open to white homesteaders on August 6, 1901.

In the transition which followed, Kiowas accepted the educational opportunities offered to them and established the framework for their future. In Oklahoma in 1906, there were two boarding schools serving the 1,195 member tribe: Riverside near Anadarko (still in operation in the 1990s), and Kiowa near Fort Sill (later known as Fort Sill and closed in the 1970s). There were also five mission schools: Rainy Mountain, operated by the American Baptists near Gotebo; St. Patrick, operated by the Roman Catholics near Anadarko; Methvin, operated by the Methodists in Anadarko; Mary Gregory Memorial, operated by the Presbyterians east of Anadarko; and Cache Creek, operated by the Dutch Reformed Church near Anadarko. Kiowa scholars have also attended Carlisle Indian School in Carlisle, Pennsylvania, and Haskell Institute in Lawrence, Kansas.

Kiowa leaders have included Ahpeahtone, chosen by his people as the last Kiowa chief, and Delos K. Lone Wolf, a graduate of Carlisle Indian School. Louis Toyebo, Robert Goombi, Jasper Saunkeah, Guy Queotone, Gus Bosin, Frank Kauahquo, and Scott Tonemah were the Kiowa representatives to the Kiowa-Comanche-Apache Intertribal Business Committee in the early 1990s.

The Kiowa Tribal Council was organized in 1968 to govern tribal affairs. The Constitution and Bylaws of the Kiowa Tribe of Oklahoma were approved by a vote of 484 for and 253 against on May 23, 1970. With its adoption, power was divided between the Kiowa Indian Council (the governing body comprised of tribal members), and the Kiowa Business Committee, an eight-member elected body. Kiowas serving as tribal chairmen have included Bob Cannon (1973 to 1976), Presley Ware (1976 to 1977), Jacob Ahtone (1978 to 1981), Billy Evans Horse (1982 to 1986), Glen Hamilton (1987 to 1988), Hershal Sahmaunt (1988 to 1989; 1992 to present), and J.T. Goombi (1989 to 1992).

The seat of Kiowa government is the Kiowa Tribal Complex located in Carnegie, Oklahoma. In 1992, the tribally owned Kiowa land base in southwest Oklahoma was 150,000 acres within Caddo, Kiowa, Comanche, Tillman, and Cotton counties. The Kiowas enrolled their 10,000th member in January 1992. The tribe dispenses its own funds along with federal government grant and contract funds through a variety of programs designed to serve its members in the realms of social services, health, education, housing, employment, transportation, and tribal government.

Since the beginning of the twentieth century Kiowas have valued education. They have more college educated tribal members than any other tribe in western Oklahoma, including a significant number of members in the legal and medical professions. A unique honor for the Kiowa occurred in 1969, when the Pulitzer Prize for fiction was awarded to tribal member N. Scott Momaday for his novel *House Made of Dawn* (1968).

The Kiowa can be considered a rural people. The largest settlement of Kiowas is near Carnegie, Oklahoma, where the total population in 1986 was 9,050. The majority of Kiowa are Christians, with the Baptist and Methodist denominations claiming the largest membership. Many tribal members also belong to the Native American Church. The Kiowa language is spoken by fewer than four hundred people. There are very few fluent speakers under the age of fifty.

The preservation of Kiowa art has been manifested by many tribal members. In 1927, a group of young Kiowa artists became internationally known. Spencer Asah, Jack Hokeah, Stephen Mopope, Monroe Tsatoke, and James Auchiah—known as the "Kiowa Five"—and Lois Smoky fell under the tutelage of Oscar B. Jacobson, the University of Oklahoma's director of the school of art. The world was introduced to their style of painting in November 1927, at the American Federation of Arts convention, and in Europe in 1928 at an international art festival. An enthusiasm for Indian art was kindled that has continued throughout the century. The legendary Kiowa artist T.C. Cannon was part of an exhibition entitled "Two American Painters," at the National Collection of Fine Arts in Washington, D.C. in 1972 when he was only twenty-two years old. In 1984, the Kiowa tribe commissioned three of its artists—Parker Boyiddle, Mirac Creepingbear, and Sherman Chaddleson—to record Kiowa history in ten massive murals. Today, these murals are housed in the Kiowa Nation Culture Museum. Numerous other Kiowa artists and sculptors have received recognition. With the quantity and quality of work being done in a variety of media, including buckskin, beads, and German silver, Kiowas are solidly in the forefront of Indian fine arts and crafts.

Kiowas have preserved their customs, traditions, stories, dances, and songs. Much of late twentieth-century Indian dress, songs, and dances originated with the Kiowa. For example, the Forty-Nine Dance evolved from the Kiowa war journey songs. The Oho-mah Lodge, the Kiowa Gourd Clan, and the Kiowa Blacklegs are traditional men's warrior societies that still practice their particular songs and dances. Even Kiowa children have their own Rabbit Society, with its unique songs and dances.

Kiowa men and women have served in the armed forces of all wars beginning with World War I and have commemorated Armistice Day since 1917. The Kiowa were the first tribe to have a flag song, containing words about the United States flag set to a Kiowa victory dance song.

deanna j. harragarra waters

See also Cultural Revitalization; Oklahoma Tribes; Painting

Further Reading

Marriott, Alice Lee. *The Ten Grandmothers*. Civilization of the American Indian 26. Norman: University of Oklahoma Press, 1945.

Mayhall, Mildred P. *The Kiowas*. Civilization of the American Indian 63. 2d ed. Norman: University of Oklahoma Press, 1984.

Momaday, N. Scott. *The Way to Rainy Mountain*. Albuquerque: University of New Mexico Press, 1969.

Watkins, Laurel J. *A Grammar of Kiowa*. Lincoln: University of Nebraska Press, 1984.

Wright, Muriel Hazel. *A Guide to the Indian Tribes of Oklahoma*. Civilization of the American Indian 33. 1951. Norman: University of Oklahoma, 1986.

KIOWA APACHE

See Plains Apache

KITANEMUK

The history of the Kitanemuk Indians is closely interwoven with that of the Tejon Ranch Indian community southeast of Bakersfield, California. By the mid-nineteenth century, the Kitanemuk had been joined in their tribal homeland by refugees from the secularized Spanish missions and from neighboring California Indian groups. A mixed tribal community of independent rancherias formed the basis for the San Sebastian Indian Reserve, established in 1853. This reservation was short-lived because its lands had already been claimed, and later were patented, as the Rancho El Tejon grant. The Indian community at the Tejon Ranch persisted for more than a century. Indian residents worked as vaqueros or general laborers for the ranch, while maintaining their own farmsteads. Home-grown produce was supplemented by acorns, chia, and wild game. For much of the nineteenth century, the principal Kitanemuk rancheria had been located at the Monte, an area of oak and sycamore woodland on lower Tejon Creek. In 1876, the last remaining families at the Monte were relocated to the Tejon Canyon rancheria. The surname "Montes," still carried by their descendants, denotes their Kitanemuk ancestry.

Intertribal marriage had occurred since aboriginal times, but was accentuated as population declined during the latter half of the nineteenth century. By the turn of the century, only a few children learned the Kitanemuk language from birth, being raised by a mother or grandmother who was a Native speaker. Spanish became the lingua franca of the mixed Indian community, which numbered about ninety persons in a dozen households by 1915.

The Tejon Canyon rancheria was visited by several ethnologists and linguists who worked with elderly residents to record aspects of their culture, history, and language. Principal among these were C.H. Merriam, A.L. Kroeber, and J.P. Harrington, who lived at the Tejon community for an extended period in 1916 to 1917, and returned for shorter visits in 1922 and 1933. It is especially through Harrington's research that most of what is known about the Kitanemuk language and culture has been preserved. His principal consultants were Eugenia Méndez, Magdalena Olivas, Angela Montes, and Juan José Fustero.

By the second decade of the twentieth century, the Bureau of Indian Affairs sought to establish the Tejon Canyon rancheria as a reservation under federal auspices. A survey was undertaken in 1917 to establish boundaries of the proposed reservation. A lawsuit was then brought by the government against the Title Insurance and Trust Company to prove rights of occupancy and possession for the Tejon Indians. In 1924, the case was unsuccessfully argued before the United States Supreme Court, who decided that the Indians' claim should have been made many decades earlier in order to have gained permanent rights to their ancestral home. Despite this unfortunate result, the lives of most Indian residents did not change much during the ensuing decades, and their community continued to be known as the "Tejon Reservation" to most Kern County residents.

A schoolhouse was built by 1921 to provide for the education of Tejon Indian children. Many older children attended the Sherman Institute in Riverside. The Indian community consisted of forty-six people in six residences by 1948, nearly all of whom were of Kitanemuk ancestry. A major earthquake in 1952 destroyed the last remaining adobe homes, but some Kitanemuk families continued living on the ranch, and one of these still resides there. The Tejon Canyon rancheria itself has been abandoned for several decades with only the schoolhouse and cemetery remaining as testimony to the Indian community that once existed there.

Many people of Kitanemuk descent still reside in Kern County, not far from their ancestral homeland. No recent population figures are available because unfortunately the Kitanemuk tribal name has been absent in government documents. The Kitanemuk have been variously classified as "Tejon Indians," "Piutes," and in the 1972 California Indian Judgment Roll as "Yokuts." These designations are not entirely inaccurate because of intermarriage among Indians with various tribal backgrounds within the Tejon community. It is noteworthy that the California Indian vaquero tradition remains strong among the present Kitanemuk, five generations after its emergence as a principal means of livelihood on Rancho El Tejon in the mid-nineteenth century.

John R. Johnson

See also California Tribes

Further Reading

Anderton, Alice Jeanne. "The Language of the Kitanemuks of California." Ph.D. diss., University of California, Los Angeles, 1988.

Blackburn, Thomas C., and Lowell John Bean. "Kitanemuk." *Handbook of North American Indians.* Vol. 8. *California.* Ed. Robert F. Heizer. Washington, DC: Smithsonian Institution (1978): 564–69.

Giffen, Helen S., and Arthur Woodward. *The Story of El Tejon.* Los Angeles, CA: Dawson's Book Shop, 1942.

Harrington, John P. *The Papers of John Peabody Harrington in the Smithsonian Institution.* Vol. 3. *Southern California/Basin.* Eds. Elaine L. Mills and Ann J. Brickfield. Millwood, NY: Kraus International Publications, 1981.

Latta, Frank F. *Saga of Ranch El Tejon.* Santa Cruz, CA: Bear State Books, 1976.

KLALLAM

The Klallam Indians traditionally inhabited the southern shores of the Strait of Juan de Fuca from Hoko River to Discovery Bay in Washington State. Although the spelling "Clallam" is most frequently encountered in the literature, we will follow the spelling the contemporary Klallam use. The Klallam were considered one of the most aggressive tribes in the western Washington State area, expanding their territory in the 1800s to Beecher Bay on Vancouver Island, and to the areas of Port Townsend and Hood Canal. The word "Klallam" is said to derive from *Nuxsklai'yem* meaning "Strong People." At the time of the treaties in the 1850s the Klallam were inhabiting over a dozen villages. From these winter village sites the Klallam frequented fishing and other resource gathering locations throughout their traditional territory.

History

Contact with Europeans began with the Spanish and British explorations in the early 1790s and became fairly regular after the establishment of Hudson's Bay Company trading posts in the area. Frequent mention is made of Klallam trading at Fort Langley, established in 1827; Fort Nisqually, established in 1833; and Fort Victoria, established in 1843. The Klallam signed the Treaty of Point No Point with the United States on January 26, 1855. Over the objections of the Klallam, the treaty stipulated that they were to remove to the Skokomish Reservation on southern Hood Canal, but very few ever did. Throughout the late 1800s and early 1900s, the Klallam remained in most of their traditional village locations, successfully resisting repeated attempts to remove them to the Skokomish Reservation. In 1874 the Klallam from the village at Dungeness purchased 210 acres east of Port Angeles, where they established a thriving community, known as Jamestown. The Jamestown community held the land privately and participated in local industry, the men fished and logged and the women worked in canneries. Other Klallam settlements eventually consolidated by the 1930s, and in 1936 and 1937, under the Indian Reorganization Act, the federal government purchased land at the mouth of the Elwha River, west of Port Angeles, and at Port Gamble, on Hood Canal, establishing the Lower Elwha and Port Gamble Klallam reservations. The Port Gamble and Lower Elwha Klallam tribal governments were organized under the Indian Reorganization Act in 1939 and 1968 respectively. The Port Gamble Klallam have had a Constitution since 1939, the Lower Elwha since 1968. The Klallam were party to land claims cases against the United States in the 1950s (Indian Claims Commission, Docket 134), in which the three groups combined for this purpose. After various considerations, the Klallam were awarded $385,820 in 1970. The Jamestown Klallam had long resisted intervention by the Bureau of Indian Affairs, but in 1975 they adopted a Constitution and in 1980 the Jamestown Klallam received federal recognition, the major impetus for seeking recognition coming from the desire to participate in commercial fishing under the 1974 western Washington fishing rights case.

The Klallam

Division	Reservation (acres)	Land Area	Population
Klallam	Jamestown	12	240
	Lower Elwha	443	530
	Port Gamble	1,301	860

Recent History

The three Klallam tribes each have their own elected council which governs the affairs of their respective reservations. In addition, the tribes participate in the inter-tribal Point No Point Treaty Council, which deals with problems that face the tribes as a whole, particularly fisheries management and enhancement. The Klallam tribes possess treaty-assured fishing rights guaranteed by the 1974 Boldt Decision

(*United States v. State of Washington*, 384 F. Supp. 312 [1974]), which allocated 50 percent of the commercial harvest of salmon to western Washington treaty tribes. Under Phase II of the Boldt Decision the treaty tribes have some say over development activities which might jeopardize the quality of the environment which supports the salmon runs. The Klallam tribes have taken an active role in resource protection and enhancement. They operate several salmon hatcheries and many of their tribal members are active in commercial fishing. The basis of their economic life is the commercial fishery, including salmon, crab, and other species of commercially valuable fish and shellfish. Unemployment rates vary from 21 percent at Jamestown, to 64 percent at Lower Elwha, and 74 percent at Port Gamble. Health care and other social services are provided by state and federal agencies on each of the reservations. Tribal development is limited to small-scale enterprises, such as smoke-shops, typical of reservation communities in the Northwest, and traditional crafts, such as wood carving.

Culture

The Klallam are of the Coast Salish language family, originally speaking a dialect of "Straits Salish," although there are few speakers of Klallam today. The religious life of the Klallam is dominated by Christianity. There are a number of members of the Indian Shaker Church, which has been active among the Klallam since the late 1800s. Children are educated in nearby public schools although the Port Gamble Klallam have a tribal preschool.

Daniel L. Boxberger

See also **Fishing and Hunting Rights; Washington State Tribes**

Further Reading

Eells, Myron. "The Twana, Chemakum, and Clallam Indians of Washington Territory." *Annual Report of the Smithsonian Institution for the Year 1887*. Washington, DC: (1889): 605–81.

Gunther, Erna. *Klallam Ethnography. University of Washington Publications in Anthropology* 1: 5. Seattle: University of Washington (1927): 127–314.

Suttles, Wayne. "The Central Coast Salish." *Handbook of North American Indians*. Vol. 7. *Northwest Coast*. Ed. Wayne Suttles. Washington, DC: Smithsonian Institution (1989): 453–75.

KLAMATH

Historically the Klamaths have lived in the Cascade Range in present-day south central Oregon and northern California. Following a treaty in 1864, the federal government created the Klamath Reservation in what is now southern Oregon. Members of Klamath, Modoc, Pit River, Shasta, and Northern Paiute, the Yahooskin Band of Snake Indians and other groups settled on the reservation. By the end of the nineteenth century, these groups collectively became known as the Klamath tribe. Several anthropologists note that the tribe refers to themselves as Maklaks, or the "people." The name Klamath is of uncertain origin.

History

On October 14, 1864, the Klamaths through treaty (16 Stat. 718) ceded to the United States over 13 million acres of high, semiarid lands east of the Cascade Mountains. In exchange the Klamath retained about 1.9 million acres for the creation of their reservation on February 17, 1870 (16 Stat. 383). Several disputes arose over reservation treaty boundaries which remained unsettled until the twentieth century. Erroneous government surveys in 1871 and 1888 excluded some Klamath lands from the reservation. The federal government agreed on June 17, 1901, to compensate the Klamaths nearly half a million dollars for these omitted lands. Further disagreements ensued over land within the reservation itself. Prior to the 1864 treaty, the State of Oregon conveyed land patents to a land company to construct a never used Oregon Central Military Road. Of the land, 111,358 acres lay within the newly created Klamath Reservation. The Klamath initiated several suits to void the land patents. In February, 1904, the Supreme Court ruled in the Indians' favor. The land company on August 22, 1906, agreed to exchange the land patents in the heart of the reservation for 86,418 acres of prime forest land in the reservation's northeast corner. The Klamaths sought fairer compensation in the courts. After a lengthy battle, on April 25, 1938, the Supreme Court upheld an additional Court of Claims award of $5,313,347. In recent decades the Klamaths have received several other claims related to the creation of the Klamath Reservation. In 1964 the Indian Claims Commission agreed to award the Klamaths $2.5 million for land ceded in 1864 (Docket 100). The Claims Commission in 1969 also granted close to $4.2 million additional compensation for nineteen boundary survey errors (Docket 100–A).

Allotments on the Klamath Reservation, like on most other Indian reservations, occurred in the period from 1895 to 1910. Nearly 180,000 acres were allotted to 1,174 Klamaths. Unallotted, or tribal surplus lands, however, were not opened to outside settlement. The Klamath peoples as a result retained large stands of valuable ponderosa (yellow) pine. Commercial harvests from the stands later became an important source of tribal income. The Klamath Reservation remained federally recognized until 1954. Congress in that year passed Public Law 587, otherwise known as the Klamath Termination Act, which ended the federal government's administrative responsibilities to the Klamath and transferred these to state and local governments. The Termination Act also provided for relinquishment of federal trust over Klamath land and the distribution of tribal income on a per capita basis.

The idea of some form of termination for the Klamath Reservation was not new. Rich timber holdings had long made them a target for withdrawal. The termination movement, however, gained momentum after 1945, largely as a result of the leadership of tribal politician Wade Crawford. His insistence that the Klamaths were ready for termination ensured immediate action. Crawford and his followers were vehemently opposed by veteran tribal leaders Boyd J. Jackson, Dibbon Cook, Jesse L. Kirk, Sr., and Seldon E. Kirk.

Congressional supporters of the Klamath Termination Act hoped the law would appease both tribal factions. The law allowed tribal members the option either to withdraw from the tribe and receive their pro rata share of tribal assets, or to remain with the tribe and have their claim to the unsold portion of the reservation placed under trust. The law provided a four-year transition period lasting until August 13, 1958. Carrying out Public Law 587 proved difficult. Efforts by various lobbyists produced two amendments to the original termination law. The greater revision came in 1958, as Congress agreed to several key changes. New provisions authorized the sale of timber tracts to private buyers through competitive bids equal to or above the market value. Purchasers were required to adhere to sustained yield and other conservation measures. Unsold tracts would be sold to the Forest Service to create a national forest (Winema National Forest). The federal government would purchase the Klamath marsh and manage it as a wildlife refuge. Final termination was postponed until April 1, 1961.

Elections in 1958 effectively ended the Klamath Reservation. In that year, 1,659 Klamaths (77 percent) voted to withdraw from the tribe and receive a per capita payment of $43,000. The government, in order to pay these individuals their share of the tribal estate, sold 717,000 acres of their 862,000 reservation. The remaining 474 members (23 percent) continued their tribal status, hoping to survive economically on the 145,000 acres still held by them. In 1974, however, these last holdouts voted to sell the remainder of the reservation for per capita shares of $173,000.

While federal recognition was terminated in 1954, Klamath identity remained resilient. In 1975, the Klamath readopted its 1953 Constitution and functioned as a tribal government. Federal courts in the middle to late 1970s acknowledged Klamath treaty rights to hunt and fish and water claims. Eventually on August 27, 1986, Public Law 99–398 restored the Klamath tribe to federally recognized status.

Current Situation

Termination proved costly to the Klamaths. Prior to termination, the Klamath were among the most self-sufficient tribes in the United States. In 1993, having lost their land base, the 2,700 enrolled Klamath, 1,600 of them living in Klamath County, Oregon, face severe economic problems. Recent droughts and complicated conservation issues have further hurt the Klamaths' ability to compete. Current statistics reveal that 70 percent of the Klamaths live below the poverty level. Submission by the Tribal Council to Congress in late 1992 of a thirty-year economic self-sufficiency plan attempts to revive a sluggish post-termination Klamath economy. Presently an eight-member business committee chosen by popular vote of the general council directs Klamath affairs. The general council includes all enrolled adult members of the tribe. The Klamaths have had a Tribal Council since 1908, and a Constitution since 1929. Since restoration of tribal status, Tribal Chairman Charles E. Kimbol, Sr., and other present leaders, worked to meet daily needs and provide for their constituents. Home improvement programs, construction of a new dental facility, and plans for new tribal offices and a cultural center seek to improve present living conditions. Forty years after termination, the Klamaths face an uncertain future. Yet the resourceful and adaptive nature of the Klamath people in the face of adversity ensures the continuance and persistence of the tribe as the twentieth century draws to a close.

Culture

Participation in the annual August sucker ceremony, a traditional event to assure favorable sucker (fish) runs, basketweaving classes and translation of textbooks into the Penutian language helps secure cultural continuity. Beadwork, arrowhead-making, and ornamental usage of bone among the Klamaths are among the crafts taught to new generations. An annual all-Indian basketball tournament in February and March, the Klamath Propriety Powwow on December 31, to usher in the new year, and Treaty Days in August, to celebrate restoration of tribal status, help promote community life. Religion among the Klamaths contains elements of Christianity, Catholicism, Shakerism, and traditional Native practices.

Thomas W. Cowger

See also Government Policy: Termination and Restoration

Further Reading

Hood, Susan. "Termination of the Klamath Tribe in Oregon." *Ethnohistory* 19 (Fall 1972): 379–92.

Spier, Leslie. *Klamath Ethnography. University of California Publications in American Archeology and Ethnology* 30. Berkeley: University of California, 1930.

Stern, Theodore. *The Klamath Tribe: A People and Their Reservation*. Seattle: University of Washington Press, 1965.

KOASATI

See Alabama-Coushatta

KONKOW

See Maidu

KONZA

See Kaw

KOOTENAI

See Confederated Salish and Kootenai Tribes; Kutenai at Bonners Ferry

KOYUKON

See Alaskan Athabaskans

KUMEYAAY

In 1769, Kumeyaay (also, Diegueño, Kumiai, Kamia, and Ipai/Tipai) land extended approximately fifty to seventy-five miles both north and south of the Mexican border and from the California coast almost to the Colorado River. The tribe's language belongs to the Yuman branch of Hokan. While they were divided into as many as fifty bands, two tribal chiefs, *Kuchut kwataay*, were responsible for intertribal diplomacy, military operations, ceremonies, marriages, trade relations, and judging interband disputes. All tribal members shared specific national territory which included beach strands, the Sierra Juarez, desert areas, trails, and sacred places. In addition, each band of the tribe had from ten to thirty miles of a river basin. Some band land was jointly used, but most was divided into family holdings. The *Kwaaypaay* (band leader) and council of environmental specialists directed plant husbandry, desert and mountain corn farming, erosion and water management, controlled burning techniques, and economic and religious activities. They also judged intraband disputes. Patrilineal sibs crosscut bands; each band had lineages from several sibs.

History of the Kumeyaay Bands

Southern inland Kumeyaay avoided the Mission San Diego and led revolts to free their relatives who were forced to labor there. Only after 1870 did settlers begin to take their land. In contrast, Northern and Coastal Kumeyaay had early contact with the mission where they learned Spanish. After their first contact with Americans in 1846, they also learned English. These groups were the recipients of several 1875 executive order reserves. Indian agency schools were operating on these reservations by 1883.

Under the 1891 Act for the Relief of Mission Indians, eleven inadequate reservations were trust patented. The commission charged with reserving land stated "many scattered groups exist and should move to Capitan Grande [reservation]," located in the territory of the Capitan Grande and Los Conejos bands. However, the reserved land was too small to support the bands already there. Many small bands remained landless.

The 1891 commission also met the people of San Pascual Indian Pueblo who had been evicted from their adobe homes in 1871. Their reservation was mislocated in Luiseño territory on four hilltops, inadequate for one farm. As a result, members were scattered. In 1954 their descendants united to reclaim the hilltops as their heritage. The Bureau of Indian Affairs (BIA), which accepted their claim only after band members demonstrated proof of descent, then added nonmembers to the band "administratively."

Four bands on former Mexican rancho grants participated in *Barker v. Harvey*, also known as the Cupeño case, which was to determine if land rights held by certain Indian groups under Mexican law would be sustained by the United States Supreme Court now that the territory was within the United States. In May 1901, in what has been termed a "political decision," the Supreme Court denied Indian rights to this territory and evicted them. In 1903 land at Pala was purchased and the army moved the San Felipe Band and the Cupeño there; other bands fled to Santa Ysabel or Mesa Grande.

Until 1910 many Kumeyaay starved on inadequate reservations. The able-bodied worked on ranches for food. Bad publicity finally forced the Indian Office (later the Bureau of Indian Affairs) to buy land to enlarge some reservations. For the agent's convenience, families with children were taken from Cuyapaipe and La Posta reservations to land purchased at the Campo Reservation. Most reservations sustained a few domestic animals, subsistence farms, and some cash crops; many were far from markets, and water was either scarce or stolen. By 1965 the BIA had tried to sell both Cuyapaipe and La Posta, claiming no descendants existed; descendants of those who had been moved to Campo reclaimed them.

Of those bands without a reservation, Jamul members worked for John Spreckels, who owned the Jamul Rancho and was the proprietor of Spreckels Sugar. They camped near their cemetery which was close to a corner of the rancho. Spreckels assured them they would not be evicted, and in 1912 deeded 2.5 acres of "cemetery and approaches" to the Catholic Bishop. In 1970 the Jamul band joined the San Diego Intertribal Council and asked the California Indian Legal Services to help them obtain federal recognition, which they achieved in 1975.

Still others without reservations lived around the edge of Mission Bay, San Diego, or Coronado working as laborers or maids. By 1910 most had fled as refugees to Kumeyaay (Kumiai in Spanish) villages in Baja California which had enough land. The Baja Kumeyaay did not feel pressure from the growing Mexican population until 1950. With the help of Rosalie P. Robertson, a descendant of southern California Kumeyaay leaders, the Kumeyaay in Baja California acquired Mexican government recognition of their villages and land rights around 1975. The Instituto Nacional Indigenista (INI) continues to validate boundaries and provides agricultural and irrigation aid, along with school and health services. Cross-border marriages and ceremonies, regular occurrences in the first half of the twentieth century, became more difficult after 1950 when officials tightened the border. By 1970 the Immigration Service made border-crossing by close relatives impossible.

Tribal Government

By 1891, southern California tribal and band leaders of the Cahuilla, Cupeño, Luiseño, and Kumeyaay no longer functioned openly because the agent required each band to annually elect a "captain who must obey the agent or be removed." Real leaders sought knowledge about the new laws which enclaved them. Over the years, they created several organizations opposing the BIA. One, the Mission Indian Federation (MIF), became well known. However, many saw that the MIF non-Indian councilor was defrauding Indians. Most reservations had two or more opposing groups: those who felt they must obey the BIA and those who opposed it; between them, they slowed or stopped BIA policies they saw as detrimental. After the 1953 passage of Public Law 280, civil and criminal jurisdiction was turned over to the state. This removed Bureau interference except for maintenance of the land's trust status. As organized opposition was no longer needed, it soon withered.

New leaders sought solutions to problems created by Public Law 280. They also faced continuing problems in the areas of sovereignty, economics, education, and health. While developing new, competent band leadership, some sought specialized education to provide specific knowledge to reservation governments. Jointly, the bands are reviving the tribal level organization as it originally functioned to manage tribal sacred places, religious and cultural needs, and protect ancestral places.

Most of these sovereign reservations elect a chairman and council, have articles of association or constitutions, and enrollment regulations listing membership requirements. Each examines development proposals based upon acreage, population, and access to highways; each tries to implement what it considers the best for the group. For example, Sycuan Reservation has restaurants, a casino, bingo, and off-track betting establishments to support its members. It also has a fire department, security force, health clinic, library, preschool, college scholarships, membership housing, cultural programs, and hires 800 people besides its own members. Viejas, Barona, Campo, and Santa Ysabel reservations have started various projects to achieve similar economic development, which will support members and maintain cultural preservation. Viejas and Campo reinstituted traditional Kumeyaay erosion and wet meadow protection measures for their land.

Most bands have tribal halls, senior programs, libraries, preschools, and cultural and tutoring pro-

Figure 1
KUMEYAAY RESERVATIONS, San Diego County, California

	Executive Order	Trust Patent	Acres	Allotted Acres	Members[1]
Campo	— purchase	1893, 1907 1911	15,400.00	0	213
Manzanita	—	1893	3,579.38	0	52
La Posta	—	1893	4,500.00	0	13
Cuyapaipe	—	1893	4,100.13	0	16
Sycuan	1875	1893	640.00	259.43	120
Jamul	(church 1912)	1975	6.03	0	52 ?
Capitan Grande	1875 1883	1894	15,753.40	0	no residents now dam site
Viejas	purchase	1932	1,609.00	0	180
Barona	purchase	1932	5,902.66	0	450
Inyaha-Cosmit	1875	1893	800.00 80.00	0	16
Santa Ysabel	1875	1893, 1926	15,526.00	0	950
		total of 3 separate parts: Santa Ysabel 1, 2, 3			
Mesa Grande	1875 1883	1894 1925 1989	120.00 80.00 800.00[2]	0	300 ?
San Pascual	—	1910 1911	1,379.58	0	200 +
Laguna	—	1892		(voluntarily terminated in 1938)	

Source: Tribal Office Data
[1]*Membership often does not include children*
[2]*Land provided by the Bureau of Land Management*

grams; all encourage their youth to attend college. Charged with providing safe domestic water since 1969, the Indian Health Service has drilled wells, established water systems, built septic tanks, and more recently, staffed clinics on Santa Ysabel and Sycuan. The seven southern bands joined to purchase centrally located land and build the Southern Indian Health Council to serve members, also maintaining a branch clinic at Campo.

Figure 2
Kumiai Farming Reservations (Ejidos) in Baja California

Name	Size	Population
Juntas de Nehi	11,590 hectares	not available
San José La Zorra	3,595 hectares	90
San Antonio Necua	63,043 hectares	144
La Huerta	6,268 hectares	148
San José Tecate[1]	not available	not available

Source: Instituto Nacional Indigenista and Instituto Nacional Antropología e Historia.

[1] Not recognized by Instituto Nacional Indigenista.

Continuing Concerns in the Twentieth Century

Prime concerns are maintenance of sovereignty, trust status of land, water rights, and economic independence. Additional concerns include improved health, medical care, education, cultural maintenance, housing, and the environment. Diabetes is a major health problem which is related to the change of diet to food of European origin.

Over the years, reservations have had water or land stolen by neighbors: fences were "walked in," springs were expropriated, streams were dammed above reservations, or ground water was destroyed by nearby wells. The BIA has not corrected original survey errors. Major pollution and erosion from freeway drainage are damaging several reservations. Two sections of Mesa Grande land were mis-patented to Santa Ysabel as Santa Ysabel 1 and 2; the error has not been corrected. A number of reservations, Cuyapaipe, La Posta, Injaja-Cosmit, and Mesa Grande, for example, lack legal access roads either to the whole reservation or to separate parts.

The Kumeyaay are patriotic and volunteer for military service. They want their sovereign rights as American Indian nations in the larger nation. Most integrate Catholicism with Kumeyaay religion. They use sage smoke and Kumeyaay sacred songs to bless new developments, cultural events, and install officials. Most ceremonies are private. They are proud of their basket artistry.

In 1900 tribal leaders were Pione Largo (Hilmeiup) of Cuyapaipe, and Cenon Duro (Mutawheer) of Mesa Grande. Cenon was followed by Thomas Couro (Curcur) and Pione by his son, Jose Largo. Although Jose Largo's granddaughter, Rosalie P. Robertson, said that Ku-meyaay women were not chiefs, she was recognized as a leader by all needing help.

Florence Connolly Shipek

See also **California Tribes; Luiseño**

Further Reading

Carrico, Richard K. *Strangers in a Stolen Land: American Indians in San Diego 1850–1880*. Sacramento, CA: Sierra Oaks Publishing, 1987.

Couro, Ted, and Christine Hutcheson. *Dictionary of Mesa Grande Diegueño*. Banning, CA: Malki Museum Press, 1973.

———. *Let's Talk Iipay Aa*. Banning, CA: Malki Museum Press, 1975.

Shipek, Florence Connolly. *Pushed into the Rocks: Southern California Indian Land Tenure, 1769–1986*. Lincoln: University of Nebraska Press, 1988.

———. *Delfina Cuero: Her Autobiography, An Account of Her Last Years and Her Ethnobotanic Contributions*. Menlo Park, CA: Ballena Press, 1991.

Williams, Anita Alvarez de. *Primeras Pobladores de La Baja California: Introducción a la Antropología de la Península*. Mexicali: Tall Graf del Gobierno del Estado, 1975.

KUTCHIN

See Alaskan Athabaskans

KUTENAI AT BONNERS FERRY

The Bonners Ferry Kutenai are one of seven bands of Kutenai located in Montana, Idaho, and British Columbia. Their language is regarded as an isolate but may be related to either Algonquian or Salishan languages. The Kutenai resemble the other Salishan cultures of the northeastern Plateau and are very conservative and private in their religious practices and in other aspects of their culture. The impact of Christianity has been very minimal.

The Kutenai community in Boundary County, Idaho, is located about 30 miles from the Canadian border and contains about 4,000 acres. The tribe has a total of about 200 tribal members, half of whom reside on the reservation. After the Kutenai had refused to move to the Flathead Reservation, those near Bonners Ferry were provided with individual allotments in 1895. Each family received an eighty-acre tract. The community lies along the Kutenai River, which historically has flooded but is now contained by diking. The general area is known as the Little Panhandle of Idaho. Of an original fifty-eight allotments, twenty have been sold to whites, leaving the following pattern of land ownership:

	Acres
Indian Allotments	3,973
Government-Owned Land	13
Total	3,986

The Bonners Ferry community is closely related to the Canadian Kutenai at Creston, British Columbia, who have supported them as have the Elmo Kutenai, located on the Flathead Reservation in Montana. Residents must possess at least one-fourth degree of Kutenai legal heredity to be eligible for enrollment. The tribe elects four council members to handle its business under a Constitution approved on June 6, 1947.

Tribal members filed a successful claim with the Indian Claims Commission (Docket 154) claiming title to 1,160,000 acres in northeastern Idaho and northwestern Montana. A judgment of $425,000 was awarded on April 25, 1960. On September 20, 1974, the tribe gained national attention by its "Declaration of War between the Kutenai Nation and the United States of America." In October 1974 President Gerald Ford signed a bill creating a 12.5-acre reservation for the tribe. As a result, the Kutenai received new houses, paved roads, and a community center. The tribe has begun a program of economic development under the direction of its Council, and is currently engaged in managing its successful motel in Bonners Ferry, Idaho, as well as in developing a fish hatchery program as part of the Upper Columbia United Tribes Organization. Increasingly, the Bonners Ferry Kutenai are taking active roles in northwest regional Indian organizations such as the Affiliated Tribes of Northwest Indians. They currently retain much of their traditional culture and many speak their native language. They engage in an active ceremonial life visiting other Kutenai bands with whom they are intermarried, especially with the Crestan and Elmo bands.

Deward E. Walker, Jr.

***See also* Confederated Salish and Kootenai Tribes**

Further Reading

Boas, Franz. *Kutenai Tales.* Bureau of American Ethnology Bulletin 59. Washington, DC: U.S. Government Printing Office, 1918.

Malouf, Carling. "Early Kutenai History." *Montana Magazine of History* 2:2 (Spring 1953).

Turney-High, Harry Holbert. *Ethnography of the Kutenai.* Memoirs of the American Anthropological Association, no. 56. Menasha, WI: AAA, 1941.

Walker, Deward E., Jr. *Indians of Idaho.* Moscow: University of Idaho Press, 1978.

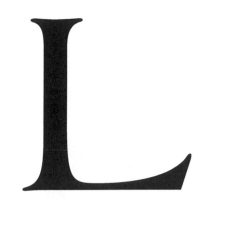

LAGUNA

See Pueblo of Laguna

LAKOTA

Lakota is the Native term for both the language and the people commonly called western "Sioux," and the largest division of the *Oceti Sakowin* or "Seven Fireplaces." Lakota is also synonymous with *Titunwan* meaning "Prairie Dwellers," anglicized as Teton.

Sometime around A.D. 1000, the Seven Fireplaces migrated from their native home in the southeast to the current state of Minnesota, where they resided in the general vicinity of Mille Lacs. The original confederation was composed of seven nations that spoke three mutually intelligible dialects of the same language classified generically as Siouan. The *Isanti* (Santee) comprised the *Mdewakantunwan, Sisitunwan, Wahpetunwan,* and *Wahpekute,* and spoke the Dakota dialect; the *Ihanktunwan* and *Ihanktunwanna* formed the middle division called *Wiciyela* and spoke Nakota. The Teton were the seventh division and spoke Lakota. The term "Sioux," which is now considered a derogatory name despite its popularity, is a French corruption of the Algonquian term *nadowesiuh*, meaning "snakes" or "adders," a reference to the Seven Fireplaces used by their enemies, the Ojibwa.

Around the middle of the eighteenth century, the Lakota migrated westward to the Great Plains in pursuit of buffalo in what are now South Dakota, Montana, Wyoming, and Nebraska. By 1778, they had discovered the Black Hills which were soon to become their spiritual center, and whose ownership continues to be contested between the Lakota and the United States government even to this day. During this period of time, the Teton subdivided again into seven tribes called *Oglala* "They Scatter Their Own"; *Sicangu* "Burned Thighs" also known by the French term, Brule; *Hunkpapa* "End Village"; *Mnikowoju* "Plant Beside the Stream"; *Itazipco* "No Bows," also called Sans

Arcs in French; *Oohenunpa* "Two Kettles"; and *Sihasapa* "Black Feet."

The Lakota are the classic Plains Indians, fully mobilized on horseback, tipi-dwellers and buffalo hunters extraordinaire. They allied with the Cheyenne and Arapaho, but were generally hostile to other tribes of the region. They are best known for the Red Cloud Wars of the 1860s, named after the great chief of the Oglalas, which culminated in the Treaty of Fort Laramie in 1868, marking the only time that American Indians won a war against the United States government. As a result of that treaty, they were placed on the Great Sioux Reservation, which occupied approximately half the state of South Dakota and parts of Wyoming and Nebraska. In the early 1870s, gold was discovered in the Black Hills, bringing white miners to the region in violation of treaty rights. When Indians attacked the miners, the government provided army protection under the command of George Armstrong Custer. Later in 1876, Custer and the Seventh Cavalry were sent to find Teton and other Indian "hostiles" who were hunting buffalo off the reservation. Their encounter resulted in the annihilation of Custer and most of his regiment by Crazy Horse, Sitting Bull, Rain in the Face, and Gall, and eventually led to the dispersal of the Indians, some to Canada. That same year the United States purchased the Black Hills from the Lakota, but because the required number of signatures were not received, the Lakota have been litigating the transaction ever since.

Following was a quick succession of incidents, including the assassination of Crazy Horse in 1877, and the surrender of Sitting Bull in 1881. Between 1888 and 1890, the Lakota under the guidance of the medicine men Short Bull and Kicking Bear became involved in the religious movement of the Ghost Dance, ending in the Wounded Knee massacre of Big Foot and 260 men, women, and children on December 29, 1890, an event that was partly precipitated by the assassination of Sitting Bull a few days earlier.

Toward the end of the nineteenth century, a number of events took place to alter the traditional lifestyle of the Lakota. In 1887, the Dawes Act was passed and so-called excess land was removed from parts of the Great Sioux Reservation, dividing it into a number of smaller ones. The Oglalas consequently were assigned to the Pine Ridge Reservation, the largest of the Lakota reservations occupying Shannon, Jackson, and Bennet counties and second in size only to the Navajo Reservation. The Sicangu were placed on the adjacent Rosebud Reservation located in Todd County, and the Hunkpapa on the Standing Rock Reservation partly located in Corson County in South Dakota, and Sioux County in North Dakota. Adjacent to Standing Rock, the Mnikowoju, Sihasapa, Oonenunpa, and Itazpico were assigned to the Cheyenne River Reservation, occupying Ziebach and Dewey counties, while two smaller reservations, Crow Creek and Lower Brule, located in parts of Lyman and Buffalo counties, serve as home to a miscellany of the above tribes. Some Lakotas, mainly Hunkapapas, also resided on the Standing Buffalo Reserve in Saskatchewan, where they fled after the Custer battle. The reservation land today represents approximately 18 percent of the state of South Dakota, not counting lands reserved in the eastern part of the state, as well as other states where members of the Seven Fireplaces continue to reside.

Since the late 1880s, Lakota children were educated mainly at St. Francis Mission on Rosebud, Holy Rosary Mission on Pine Ridge, and St. Joseph's Mission near the Crow Creek and Lower Brule reservations, as well as at schools operated by the Bureau of Indian Affairs (BIA) on all the reservations. Schools were run military style under the direction of an army officer. Boys were taught vocational skills while girls learned domestic chores.

1900 to 1950

During the first quarter of the twentieth century, most lived on allotted land and tipis soon gave way to government-issue wall tents and then to log cabins. Horse and wagon became the main mode of transportation, until they were replaced by automobiles. But Lakota social organization remained intact despite the prevalence of missionization and public school education. Most Lakotas were evenly divided between membership in the Roman Catholic Church and the Episcopal Church, although other denominations actively proselytized. However, Native religion under the auspices of medicine men continued to be the predominant form of worship. Although the Sun Dance and other religious ceremonies officially were banned by the federal government, most continued underground. Similarly, the major form of political organization, the *tiyospaye*, or band, under the leadership of a chief or head man, flourished. The BIA maintained offices on all the reservations, and "boss" farmers were employed in all of the districts to supervise the training of men and women in agriculture and animal husbandry.

Since the Lakota were renowned horsemen, they took easily to a cowboy way of life, and much of what originally was recognized as cowboy culture was slowly integrated into their tribal way of life. However, the transition from hunting buffalo to eating domestic beef and other government rations was much more difficult. To help further the transition, beef was allotted to individual heads of households who rode down the cattle let out of pens as if they were hunting buffalo. The women quickly moved in after the kill and butchered the beef just like in early days. The general diet was poor, owing to inferior foodstuffs distributed by the federal government; proper refrigeration did not exist until much later in the century.

Despite hostilities with the United States government during the latter part of the nineteenth century, thousands of Lakotas volunteered to fight in World War I. This participation was partly responsible for the continuation of many of the earlier warrior traditions, since returning soldiers were treated as warriors complete with honor songs, giveaways, and special ceremonies. In 1924, partly as a recognition of their participation in World War I, Lakotas, along with members of other tribes who were not already American citizens, were granted citizenship.

During the interim between World Wars I and II, many Lakotas became successful ranchers and farmers, and agriculture and ranching became the major form of economics. However, the depression of the late 1920s and 1930s dealt a severe blow to the Lakota reservations, and many were never able to recover. Without proper capital to start their herds again, most land-rich Lakotas began to lease their lands to more prosperous white ranchers and farmers, a practice that has continued through to the present day.

In 1934 the Indian Reorganization Act was adopted by the Lakotas and all the reservations soon fell under the jurisdiction of a Tribal Council composed of an elected board and district representatives. A tribal court system was also established to handle domestic cases such as child custody, and other minor crimes such as drunken and disorderly conduct, while major crimes fell under the jurisdiction of the federal government.

Although the Indian Reorganization Act was an attempt to give Lakotas more control of their lives, there continues to be a conflict between the Tribal Councils and traditional Lakota political organization. Originally, each of the major *tiyospayes* that settled on the reservations were governed by a *wicasitancan*, or "chief" who had made his reputation as a hunter or warrior before the establishment of the Great Sioux Reservation. When hunting was replaced by government commodities, and warfare abolished as a result of the Treaty of 1868, the system of leadership based on ability was replaced by hereditary leadership, sons and nephews often assuming the role of their deceased fathers and uncles. Today there is frequent disagreement between the Tribal Council and the traditional leadership, as to who controls the grassroots people living in the reservation districts, and, in many cases, impasses are formed when Lakota custom dictates that the traditionalists should be respected and their ideas given priority over those of the Tribal Council.

As subsequent wars ensued, Lakotas again joined the armed forces and fought in World War II, Korea, and Vietnam. Partially through this involvement they maintained their sense of identity as warriors, and many of the religious and secular ceremonies associated with warfare continued to be important despite the attempt of the federal government to assimilate them into mainstream American society.

Social Organization

Partly owing to the relative isolation of the reservations from mainstream American life, many Lakotas managed to hold onto their traditional language and culture throughout most of the first half of the century. Some however were fearful that their culture would give way to the white man's influence, particularly with respect to language and the pervasive kinship system which was perceived to be one of the major differences between white and Indian culture. Young people were reminded about who their relatives are and to show respect for them.

Many traditionalists today continue to hold first allegiance to the *tiyospaye*, the band, which continues to operate under the administration of traditional leaders and medicine men. Christian churches that had been established in the districts where each of the *tiyospayes* lived have become the center of organization for traditional culture, as well as newly introduced Euroamerican culture. For example, churches provide facilities for meetings of the local *tiyospayes*. Respecting the power of the white man's god, many traditional Lakota attend church services in order to try to understand it. The churches also have become the centers for many ceremonies, not all of which are entirely Christian. For example, wakes, funerals, and memorial feasts, traditionally sacred rituals of the Lakota, are now conducted on church premises, and the dead are buried in church cemeteries. Although marriages are frequently conducted by church officials, nominal Catholics married nominal Episcopalians in order to continue following traditional rules which prohibit marriage between members of the same *tiyospaye*.

The 1950s

By the middle of the twentieth century, many of the survivors of the Wounded Knee massacre, and several from the Custer battle, were still alive and greatly contributed to the continuity of Lakota culture through reciting and reenacting their personal experiences of early reservation days. Relatives of the Big Foot band of Mnikowoju from Cheyenne River, and now their descendants, continue to make annual pilgrimages to the Wounded Knee massacre site at Pine Ridge, recounting the narrow escapes and tragic deaths of their relatives at the hands of the military. Today, younger generations of Lakotas continue to ride the 200 miles from Cheyenne River to Pine Ridge on horseback through freezing weather to honor the spirits of their relatives massacred there.

The 1950s also found Lakotas recovering from World War II. Men and women in the military returned to the reservations often to find that the skills that they had learned in the service were not useful or required back home. During this period of time, many took advantage of the federal government's relocation program, which encouraged young married couples to migrate to the cities where they were assisted in finding work and housing. Although the program was superficially successful, 75 percent of the Lakotas returned to their reservations after spending approximately three months in urban areas where they were frequently regarded as outsiders and treated as inferiors.

The 1960s and 1970s

Although many experts predicted that Lakota culture was in the process of vanishing, the 1960s had a dramatic effect on ensuring that the traditional culture was to be consciously kept alive. Although many American Indians vowed not to intervene in the Black Power and Brown Power movements, toward the end of the 1960s and beginning of the 1970s, many Lakotas became involved in what was to be known as the Red Power movement. In 1972, they participated in the pilgrimage to Washington, D.C. called "The Trail of Broken Treaties," which resulted in the siege and takeover of the BIA. In January of 1973, under the auspices of the American Indian Movement (AIM) whose leader was Russell Means, an Oglala, several hundred Lakotas from the Pine Ridge Reservation set up a camp at the Wounded Knee massacre site. They took white hostages from the local trading post and remained at Wounded Knee for seventy-one days surrounded by federal marshals and state militia. In what was to have been a symbolic statement of continued federal injustices to all American Indians, two persons were killed and one wounded during the standoff.

Wounded Knee II, as it was called, has had a profound effect on Lakota people, particularly on the Pine Ridge Reservation where frequently members of the same family were on opposing sides. As a result of the divisive effect the Wounded Knee occupation had on the people, the Sun Dance, which had been one of the major public ceremonies performed annually for all Lakota on the Pine Ridge Reservation, was difficult to reinstate as a single event. Beginning in 1974, smaller Sun Dances began to be held on all the major Teton reservations, some by invitation only. The largest of these Sun Dances, held at Three Mile Creek under the direction of the late medicine man Frank Fools Crow, became associated with the original AIM movement, but continues to be the most popular. However, in 1976 the Sun Dance performed at Green Grass on the Cheyenne River Reservation, the community in which the original sacred pipe of the Lakota Nation is kept, drew as many as three hundred dancers.

The second half of the century also saw the abolishment of the boarding school system, which was replaced by bus service to day schools. At the same time, two-year colleges were established at Pine Ridge, Rosebud, Cheyenne River, and Standing Rock. Oglala Lakota College at Pine Ridge has become a four-year college, and Sinte Gleska College at Rosebud has received university status, mainly owing to the dedication of their presidents, Elgin Bad Wound and Lionel Bordeaux, respectively.

Economic Conditions

The economic situation on all South Dakota reservations has continued to suffer severely. Unemployment figures have reached 80 percent, and those Lakotas who do not work for their respective tribes are on federal entitlement programs. The people still continue to receive commodities from the federal government, and children are fed at school during the year. During the summer time, there are numerous traditional feasts associated with sacred ceremonies and frequently entire buffalo or cattle are cooked and distributed to the visitors. The Lakota custom of *wateca* or taking home surplus food is still an integral feature of traditional feasts, thus ensuring that people will have something to eat for a few days following the feasts.

Although some small businesses have been established on the reservations, most are short-lived. With the few exceptions of gas stations, convenience stores, and arts and crafts stores, almost all businesses such as restaurants, supermarkets, and other retail stores are owned by whites, most of whom live off the reservation. Leasing land is still the most prevalent way of earning a meager living.

The Lakotas in the 1990s

Health conditions fall far below the national average and there are high incidents of diseases and illnesses related to poor diet and acute alcohol consumption including high rates of fetal alcohol syndrome. In 1952 the Public Health Service set up hospitals and clinics on most of the Lakota reservations, and the federal government maintains contracts with other hospitals and physicians when special medical services are required.

The Lakotas continue to be aware of their special history and culture and have integrated them into local education. Classes in Lakota arts, music, dance, language, treaties, and history are taught in all the major school systems and local traditionalists are employed as cultural teachers. Although almost all the major denominations of Christianity have been established on reservations, Lakota people still follow their traditional religion under the leadership of medicine men. Included in the more important religious ceremonies still conducted among the Lakota are the annual Sun Dance, vision quests, sweat lodges, puberty ceremonies for females, memorial feasts and wakes, and *Yuwipis*, a Lakota form of traditional healing.

It is estimated that perhaps as much as half of the Lakota population resides off the reservation for at least part of the year. Many go away to college, or to cities such as Minneapolis, Chicago, Denver, Rapid City, and San Francisco to obtain employment. Most, however, come back to the reservations for summer visits, and usually return permanently once they have retired from their jobs off the reservation.

Lakotas continue to be highly regarded by other American Indian people mainly because of their reputation as great warriors and orators in the past, and many Lakotas hold important positions in American Indian programs on and off their reservations. Among those best known are Ben Reiffel, the first Lakota to become a member of the United States Congress, and Thomas Shortbull, the first Lakota to be elected to the South Dakota State Senate. The Delorias, a prominent family originally from Standing Rock, have made contributions to religion, science, and law. Vine Deloria, Sr., was a well-known Episcopalian minister, and Ella C. Deloria was a linguist who made many contributions to Lakota language and culture. Vine Deloria, Jr., is a well-known political activist who has fought for the rights of Indian people throughout the nation.

Lakotas are particularly known for their contributions to traditional and contemporary arts. Of the better known star quilters is Bessie Cornelius, who founded Lakota Studios, and the popularity of Lakota silverwork has been greatly inspired by the work of Mitchell Zephier. A number of Lakota painters and sculptors have formed an artist's guild called The Dream Catchers, which includes Arthur Amiotte, Vic Runnels, Robert Penn, Donald Montileaux, Don Ruleaux, Richard Red Owl, Joanne Bird, Don Brewer, Gladys Ecker, Robert Freeman, Ed Two Bulls, Martin Red Bear, and S. Zephier.

The Lakotas are also leaders in the powwow circuit, a special Indian form of public celebration in which people gather to dress up in costumes and sing and dance on weekends in both summer and winter. Reminiscent of prereservation days, many of the Lakota powwows emphasize old warrior traditions focusing on the achievements of Lakotas in World Wars I and II, Korea, and Vietnam. A Lakota Vietnam Powwow is held every year on the Pine Ridge Reservation. Powwows are also held on patriotic and Christian holidays, as they have been ever since the turn of the century when Lakotas were permitted to celebrate Indian style as long as it was on an American holiday. Today, the largest outdoor event is the Oglala Nation Powwow, held on the first weekend in August, in which thousands of people from all over the world attend.

William K. Powers

The Lakota

Division	Reservation	Population	Economics
Oglala	Pine Ridge	23,000	Land lease
Sicangu	Rosebud	18,000	Land lease
Hunkpapa Mnikowoju Oohenunpa Sihasapa	Standing Rock	6,700	Land lease
Itapzico	Cheyenne River	6,000	Land lease
Misc.	Crow Creek	3,300	Land lease
Misc.	Lower Brule	1,500	Land lease

Population figures are rough estimates based on information provided by the Bureau of Indian Affairs.

See Sioux Federation map for reservation locations

See also **Black Hills; Dakota; Yankton and Yanktonai**

Further Reading

Densmore, Frances. *Teton Sioux Music.* Bureau of American Ethnology Bulletin 61. Washington, DC: U.S. Government Printing Office, 1918.

Hyde, George E. *Red Cloud's Folk.* Norman: University of Oklahoma Press, 1937.

Nurge, Ethel ed. *The Modern Sioux: Social Systems and Reservation Culture.* Lincoln: University of Nebraska Press, 1970.

Powers, Marla N. *Oglala Women in Myth, Ritual and Reality.* IL: University of Chicago Press, 1986.

Powers, William K. *Oglala Religion.* Lincoln: University of Nebraska Press, 1977.

LAND CLAIMS

Rarely has a conqueror granted the conquered the right to seek restitution or redress for the loss of territory. Under American law, the United States acquired tribal territories—nearly two billion acres—mostly through treaties of land cession. Such acquisitions were not altogether free of duress or force, and some territory was taken by military intervention. Only a small number of tribes east of the Mississippi River secured reservations, but most tribes in the West negotiated reservations, many containing several thousand acres. Generally, it has been assumed that the bulk of Indian lands became irredeemable America, that is, acreage not restorable to the tribes. The official view, as well as that of most scholars, has held that the Indians lost far too much land wrongly—e.g., taken by confiscation or unconscionable payments—and ultimately some restitution seemed appropriate.

When Congress established the Indian Claims Commission in 1946 (ICC), it fully recognized that some land claims had already been filed through the United States Court of Claims (now called the United States Claims Court), but that less than successful, piecemeal approach did not resolve the demands made by numerous tribes. Prior to the ICC, Indian monetary or land claims against the federal government were barred, unless Congress passed special jurisdictional acts; various claims had come before the Court of Claims regularly by the 1880s. However, Congress opened the door to all classes of claims by granting the ICC a broad mandate that encompassed far more than land claims. Early on, the commissioners determined that they would award money, but concluded that the return of title to land was beyond their charge, despite the fact that the courts had already acknowledged not only title based on government negotiations (*recognized* title), but also title based on aboriginal occupancy not confirmed by treaty (*Indian* title). The significance of only making monetary awards instead of reinstating title to land should not be minimized, since it foreshadowed other disappointments expressed by the tribes. Of course, tribes were encouraged to seek congressional restitution. As Vine Deloria, the noted legal scholar of the Standing Rock Sioux, observed, the idea was that once claims were adjudicated and monies accepted, the tribes had to forego forever any further claims to territory. In some

ways, this explains today why those Sioux tribes who have won a claims suit over the taking of the Black Hills in South Dakota have refused to accept the monetary award, which exceeds $100 million. Acceptance virtually forecloses on their ever gaining back a land restoration within those hills.

The national map of adjudicated land claims reveals the extent of the ICC's activities for more than three decades; the commission retired in 1978, but unresolved cases went forward to the United States Claims Court. Cases adjudicated since that date are not reflected on the map, such as the Zuni award in 1991 for the loss of some 5 million acres.

Motivation for Claims and Adjudication

If the tribes hoped for land restorations for their "day in court," the government perhaps had other motives. Some critics view the government as benevolent by granting permission to pursue litigation against the nation. Certainly, the distribution of monetary awards—more than a billion dollars in total—must be regarded as justiciable. A portion of this monetary award went to tribes for so-called "taking" cases; tribes and bands in California and Nevada represent good examples of taking, in the absence of treaties or other negotiated settlements. Another sum was paid to tribes whose title was proven.

Observers have long questioned government motives for the ICC, pointing to parallel efforts to "terminate" the trusteeship of various tribes in the hope someday of ending the guardian/ward relationship. To clear the air of conflict over land claims would surely be a first step toward separating the tribes from trusteeship. It makes sense that the government could not sever the tribes from their trustee without having "cleaned up" historic business. Moreover, a somewhat less emphasized concern focused on the confused "title cloud" that allegedly had hung over vast acreage in the nation, and land claims adjudication would go a long way to lifting this onus in terms of how property institutions would flourish in the various states. Critics of land claims adjudication well argue that little more than monetary gain was made by the tribes at the expense of Indian pride and loss of place, and that perhaps only when tribes retained sizeable amounts of money, rather than dissipating it among tribal members, have constructive improvements on reservations resulted from land claims.

The Land Claims Process

The presentation of a land claim by a tribe has always taken into consideration fundamental economic, ethnographic, geographic, historic, and legal facts, necessitating that research dip back well into the past, specifically to the time of taking. Most tribes retrieved information from the official records—that is, the treaties of land cession and the stream of laws that methodically diminished tribal holdings. The treaties had been rendered into mappable form (by C.C. Royce in 1899) and each cession (several per

Indian Land Claims: Adjudicated Areas

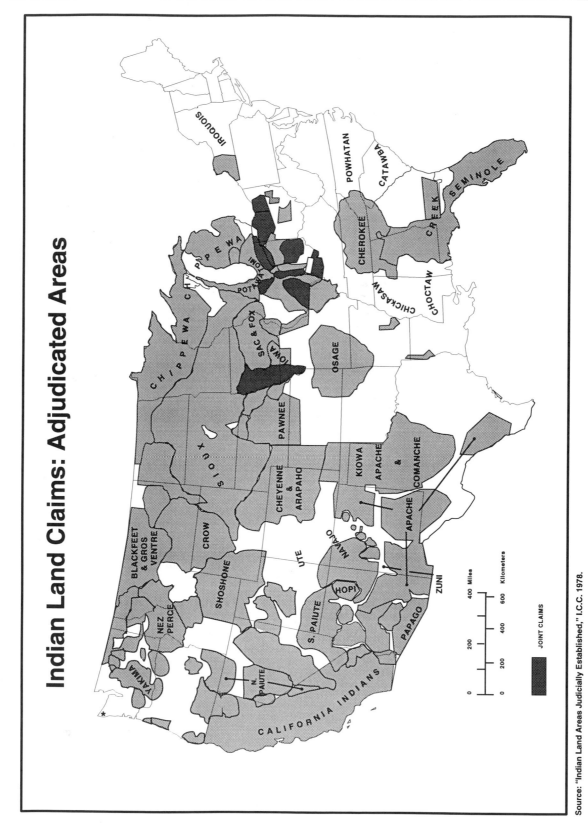

Source: "Indian Land Areas Judicially Established," I.C.C. 1978.

At this scale, we could not show the many claims adjudications for the area northwest of Washington.

tribe in most instances) bear "Royce" numbers. These maps and their corresponding numbers identify *recognized title*, which normally included ceded lands and residual tribal territory as a reservation; sometimes, reservations were established out of the public domain. Ethnographers, ethnohistorians, and other scholars soon identified the role of *Indian or original title* to land not identified at the time of treaties. Researchers had to provide more than just sufficient proof that a given area did indeed belong to a given tribe. Ethnographic and geographic reconstruction carefully identified, expanded, and delimited the bounds of Indian title lands. The ICC subtracted lands proven to have been occupied or utilized by, or sufficiently in conflict between, two or more tribes. Thus, former tribal areas came under careful review, were verified through a combination of cartographic, documentary, ethnographic, and other means, and adjudicated as part of tribal territory. But claims litigation involved much more than just this research.

The ICC did not decide in favor of all land claims, nor did it sustain all demands in any one claim. Of more than 600 dockets filed (several per tribe), at least 200 were dismissed, and 342 received favorable discussions. However, the ICC established premises for the reduction of funding as based on net acreage. Some cases—for example, those of eastern tribes—did not meet the stipulations of the law; other tribes did not demonstrate sufficient proof of "exclusive" occupancy, a condition the ICC made mandatory. Some acreage was, in a sense, chipped off a claim, reducing the total territory on which monetary awards would be based. Moreover, the acreage of existing reservations was subtracted from the total, and offsets to awards were deducted on the basis of total government spending over the decades for a given tribe. As based on historic and economic data provided by expert witnesses, a dollar value per acre *at the time of taking* was reached; as a rule, since the bulk of Native territory was ceded in the nineteenth century, valuation was necessarily low, ranging from under one dollar to about five or six dollars. Nevertheless, total awards reached into the millions, even after offsets and legal and research costs. In many cases, the claims process went on for several years, and this would diminish the net income to a tribe. Normally, the bulk of the funds were paid per capita to tribal members, based upon a roll call approved by the secretary of the interior. Individual Indians often received a pittance; in California, for example, as low as $150 and as high as $650.

Case Studies

Despite common elements, every land claim has exhibited a certain uniqueness; these sample cases reflect various factors including the distinctive aspects of "taking" by unconscionable means and tribal claims to title of land.

Pueblo Indians. Along with the Sioux claims to the Black Hills and other tribal claims, those claims initiated by the Pueblo Indians were precursors of the litigation brought before the ICC. Subsequent to the Treaty of Guadalupe Hidalgo, Congress confirmed Hispanic land grants to the Pueblo Indians. However, under early United States administration, tribal lands were deemed disposable and hence subject to non-Indian acquisition. Thus, these Indians were not protected by the United States as a trustee. It was not until 1913, in *United States v. Sandoval*, that the Supreme Court ruled that Pueblos were entitled to the same protections as other tribes. Consequently, the Bureau of Indian Affairs (BIA) sought to reclaim lands lost to squatters and even many parcels legally deeded. Since some 12,000 non-Indian persons would be affected by changes in title, non-Indian claimants urged Congress to confirm all claims (this was the so-called Bursum Bill). However, in 1924, passage of the Pueblo Lands Act sought to quiet title by accepting only a minority of non-Indian claims and otherwise providing for monetary compensation. It took until 1938 to adjudicate all titles and evict non-Indians without patents. The Pueblo Indians purchased some lands, and by 1944, the total land restoration program aggregated 667,479 acres.

Navajo Indians. Navajo land claims fairly typify tribal claims to title in lands that today may be held in the private sector or in the public domain, or as part of other Indian reservations. Typical problems included the overlap of territorial claims with adjacent tribes, and conflicts in the wording of laws or treaties that generated land disputes later on. Historians consider the Navajos latecomers to the Southwest, for they arrived within the claims area in the fifteenth century. Thus, in their territorial relations with the Hopi, to pick one neighbor, they are newcomers whose claims seem overextended. As of 1992, the Hopi had filed an appeal to the decision to grant Navajos another 16,000 acres of lands held by law in joint usage with the Hopi. The Navajo were known to have spread essentially west/southwest of Dinetah.

By the Treaty of 1868, they ceded considerable acreage, and a reservation was established. Despite their claims—to some areas long abandoned and otherwise also claimed by earlier inhabitants—the ICC rejected much acreage as heavily overlapping those of their neighbors. Apache claims on the south were stronger as were those of adjacent Pueblos on the east. The ICC also excluded lands well within the migration area, for in 1882 an executive order establishing the Hopi Indian Reservation sustained recognized title to that tribe. The commissioners did acknowledge the historic area north of the San Juan River in Utah, where archeology had revealed some two hundred aboriginal sites. The government succeeded in reducing the claim area to half of an original 40 million acres. Much buffer area remained unadjudicated because of nonexclusive occupancy by various plaintiff tribes. A portion of the area remained unlitigated because the Zuni had yet to bring

NAVAJO LAND CLAIMS

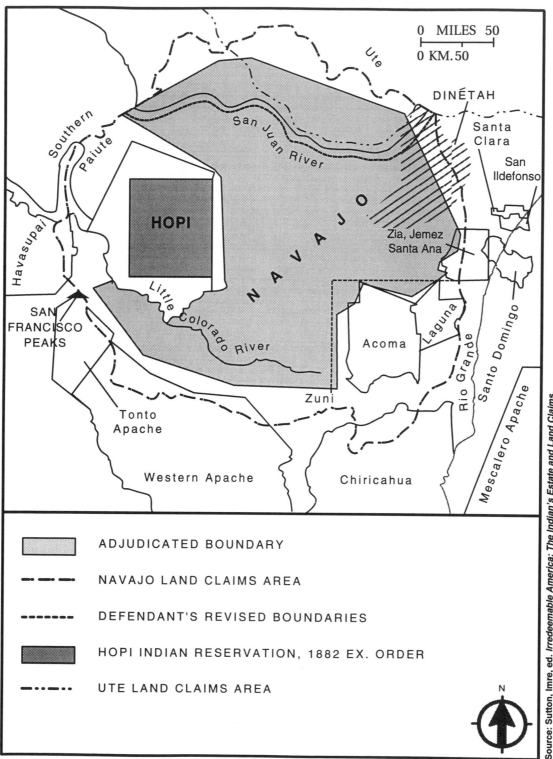

ADJUDICATED BOUNDARY

— · — · — · NAVAJO LAND CLAIMS AREA

· · · · · · · · DEFENDANT'S REVISED BOUNDARIES

HOPI INDIAN RESERVATION, 1882 EX. ORDER

— · · — · · — UTE LAND CLAIMS AREA

Source: Sutton, Imre, ed. *Irredeemable America: The Indian's Estate and Land Claims.*
Albuquerque: University of New Mexico Press, 1985. © 1985 Native American Studies, University of New Mexico.

*Claims of adjacent tribes are not shown on this map. It also excludes reference to the Hopi-Navajo land dispute at
the western end of the Navajo claims area.*

suit (post 1980). Navajo land claims only reflected lands not restored under the Treaty of 1868.

The California Claims. Most land claims were based upon treaties of land cession that had been *confirmed* by Congress. However, several land claims cases resulted from the failure of Congress to confirm treaties, or when the government seized tribal land by conquest or otherwise permitted entry onto the land as if it were already public domain. In 1851 the United States Senate did not ratify eighteen treaties with various California Indian bands, who, however, complied with treaty provisions (see "Indian Land Cessions in California" map). Two consolidated claims cases evolved as a consequence of this unconscionable act of Congress, which chose to support citizen reaction to the possible creation of reservations of vast acreage. The first claims case, litigated before the United States Court of Claims subsequent to congressional passage of a jurisdictional act (1928) which granted the "Indians of California" the right to sue the government, awarded the Indian plaintiffs in 1944, but final payments extended to 1970. This case only dealt with some 8,619,000 acres, or lands within the *nonceded* or reserved portions of the treaty areas, minus 611,226 acres of former rancherias and contemporary reservations. In a subsequent case, the plaintiff bands claimed the remaining 91,765,000 acres of *ceded* lands in a suit before the ICC (1964), which also was decided in their favor. Although the government had established many small reservations, these cases reflect the unconscionable taking of land without compensation of money or sufficient acreage. Today, a few Indian communities continue to reject monetary awards, still hoping for a modicum land restoration (e.g., the Pit River Indians in northern California).

Land Restoration

A few tribes have received land restorations, but not by virtue of successful litigation before the ICC, but rather via the federal district courts and/or the United States Supreme Court, or via Congress. For example, Congress restored 185,000 acres to the Havasupai even though the ICC had already awarded the tribe money. Other land restorations reflect separate lobbying and congressional action, as in the case of Blue Lake, 48,000 acres, Taos; and Mt. Adams, 21,000 acres, Yakima.

Most recently, the Zuni regained Kolhu/wala:wa, involving some 10,000 acres. Such restorations too often return only minimal acreage and restrict tribal use to traditional religious activities. Yet separate litigation did not lead to any restoration of land sought by Navajos and Hopi within the San Francisco Peaks in Arizona, which are perceived as sacred ground to these and other nearby tribes. On the other hand, the Passamaquoddy and Penobscot of Maine received funds from Congress in order to purchase some 300,000 acres, and the Narragansett regained 1,800 acres. By 1975, the restoration of some so-called "surplus" lands accounted for around 300,000 acres, and various purchases or transfers added additional acreage (e.g.,

61,000 acres to the Warm Springs; 2,700 to Northern Paiute/Western Shoshone; and more than 20,000 to other Pueblos). The Alaska Native Claims Settlement Act (1971) ultimately will transfer some 40 million acres to Native corporations. Despite these and other purchases, transfers, and restoration, indigenous America still only represents about 4 percent of the continental United States. Moreover, since the ICC did not address the adjudication of the loss of millions of acres of allotted lands, such claims continue in the courts (e.g., the White Earth Indian Reservation in Minnesota).

Western Shoshone Claim. Legal scholars point to *United States v. Dann* (1985) because this claims case raises other issues over the meaning of aboriginal or Indian title. This case intertwines the question of monetary award and land restoration. The Dann Band of Western Shoshone brought suit in the federal courts to partially set aside a decision by the ICC (1962), which, in awarding the Western Shoshone tribe (as represented by another band, the Te-Moak), extinguished Indian title to some 24,396,403 acres, including land the Danns continue to occupy. By virtue of the decision, the Bureau of Land Management ordered the Danns off of lands forming part of a grazing district in Nevada. The Danns had argued unsuccessfully that their tract of land should be excluded from the ICC decision, for the ICC lacked the authority to extinguish Indian title. However, the courts held that claims cases are decided in terms of an entire tribe, not individuals. The uniqueness of this claim rests with the fact that the whole tribe allegedly accepted the monetary award and the loss of title to land, but the Dann Band continues to contend that it has a right to occupy lands they perceive as unextinguished Indian territory. As with other Indian groups, the Dann Band must seek congressional resolution of their claim.

Comments

Critics do not agree whether the claims process has constituted a success story. While most Indians have accepted their monetary awards, a small number did not, but of those who did, many probably never fully comprehended the implications of the award, nor the total judicial process. Claims adjudication did manage to "quiet" title to millions of acres of irredeemable America, but it did not provide for a nice neat finale to the Indian land question. Not only have cases continued in the Claims Court, but "statute of limitation" cases, so-called 2415 cases, plague the courts. These cases include important conflicts over land tenure, including allotments, matters of trespass, and the like. Meantime, conflicts over water rights between tribes, local citizens, and state and local governments have begun to preempt the litigious process.

Imre Sutton

See also **Alaska Native Claims Settlement Act; Black Hills; Indian Claims Commission; Navajo-Hopi Land Controversy**

INDIAN LAND CESSIONS IN CALIFORNIA

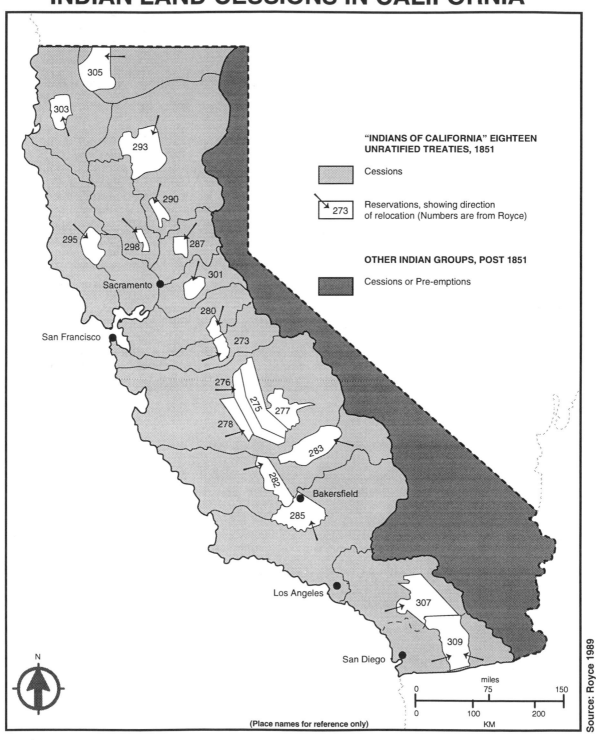

"INDIANS OF CALIFORNIA" EIGHTEEN
UNRATIFIED TREATIES, 1851

Cessions

273   Reservations, showing direction
of relocation (Numbers are from Royce)

OTHER INDIAN GROUPS, POST 1851

Cessions or Pre-emptions

Sacramento

San Francisco

Bakersfield

Los Angeles

San Diego

miles
0   75   150

0   100   200
KM

(Place names for reference only)

Source: Royce 1989

INDIAN LAND RESTORATIONS

Yakima ●

0 MILES 20

0 KM. 20

GIFFORD PINCHOT N.F

Yakima River

Toppenish ●

MT. ADAMS
WILDERNESS

YAKIMA INDIAN RESERVATION

MT. ADAMS

MOUNT ADAMS & YAKIMA INDIAN RESERVATION

FORMERLY WILDERNESS   EXISTING WILDERNESS   — — — — YAKIMA NEW BOUNDARY

WHEELER PK. ▲

CARSON

BLUE LAKE

NATIONAL

Rio Pueblo

Taos Pueblo

FOREST

Taos (City)

N

BLUE LAKE & TAOS PUEBLO

ORIGINAL TAOS LAND   LANDS RESTORED   — — — — N.F. BOUNDARY CHANGES

Source: Sutton, Imre, ed. *Irredeemable America: The Indian's Estate and Land Claims.* Albuquerque: University of New Mexico Press, 1985. © 1985 Native American Studies, University of New Mexico.

The Yakima restoration was made by executive order, May 1972, placing about half of Mt. Adams within reservation boundaries. The Blue Lake restoration transferred 48,000 acres of Carson National Forest by order of Congress in 1970. In turn, the tribe waived any further claims to the townsite of Taos.

Further Reading

Royce, Charles C., comp. "Indian Land Cessions in the United States." *Bureau of American Ethnology 18th Annual Report 1896–1897, Part 2*. Washington, DC: U.S. Government Printing Office, 1899.

Shattuck, George C. *Oneida Land Claims: A Legal History*. NY: Syracuse University Press, 1991.

Sutton, Imre, ed. *Irredeemable America: The Indians' Estate and Land Claims*. Albuquerque: University of New Mexico Press, 1985.

U.S. Indian Claims Commission. *Final Report*. Washington, DC: U.S. Government Printing Office, 1979.

Vecsey, Christopher, and William A. Starna, eds. *Iroquois Land Claims*. NY: Syracuse University Press, 1988.

LANDLESS CHIPPEWA

See Ojibwa: Chippewa in Montana; Ojibwa: Chippewa in North Dakota

LANGUAGES

At the beginning of the twentieth century, most Indian people in the United States spoke the traditional language of their tribe, although many spoke English as a second language. It is important to realize, however, that none of these languages was widely spoken; over three hundred distinct languages were represented at the turn of the century in a total Indian population of no more than one million. A few languages, such as Navajo and Chippewa, could claim fifty thousand or more speakers, but most were spoken by a thousand people or fewer. In some places along the Pacific Coast, relatively dense Indian populations resulted in half a dozen or more mutually unintelligible languages being spoken in areas as small as a county (e.g., Humboldt County, California).

The number of Indian languages is matched by their structural variety. In the Americas as a whole, Indian languages exhibit a range of differences in both phonology and grammar equaling that of the major linguistic areas of Eurasia or Africa. Just within the United States the differences are enormous. There are languages like Wintu and Takelma, with phonetic systems and grammars resembling classical European languages of the Greek or Latin type; languages like Lakota and Choctaw, with relatively simple phonetics and an "agglutinative" type of word formation; languages like Haida and Navajo, whose underlying monosyllabic structure and tonal distinctions are reminiscent of the languages of East Asia; languages like Makah and Shuswap, with intimidating arrays of consonants and highly complex patterns of word formation, rivalled in these respects only by the languages of the Caucasus; and many other languages, like Karuk, Yana, and Seneca, whose peculiarly American structures are unparalleled elsewhere in the world.

The reasons for these enormous structural differences remain unclear. One possibility is that the Western Hemisphere was entered by a number of distinct waves of migration from Eurasia over the Bering Strait (or the Bering Strait land bridge), beginning as early as forty thousand years ago and continuing into relatively recent times. These waves, originating in different parts of the Eastern Hemisphere, could have brought a varied selection of language types into the Americas, which then diversified further after arrival. Another view, more in accord with recent studies of the genetics of American Indian populations, argues that nearly all Native American language families descend historically from the language of a single immigrant population, or closely related groups of such populations. If so, this initial settlement must have been quite early—at least thirty to thirty-five thousand years ago—if the observed linguistic diversity is to be accounted for.

The Study of Indian Languages

Although American Indian languages had been the object of casual scholarly attention for centuries (Thomas Jefferson was an avid collector of Indian vocabularies), it was not until the last quarter of the nineteenth century that this activity became focused and professionalized. The Smithsonian Institution took the lead in this effort, particularly its Bureau of American Ethnology, which was created in 1879. Under the direction of John Wesley Powell (1834 to 1902), the Bureau accumulated extensive data on most of the Indian languages of the United States and, largely on the basis of vocabulary lists, Powell made his still-useful classification of North American Indian languages into fifty-eight families (or "stocks").

Despite these advances in classification, accurate information on the grammatical structures of individual Indian languages was quite rare before the twentieth century. While a number of lengthy and detailed studies had been compiled by missionaries and others, most of these writers were hampered by an ethnocentric view of linguistic structure. They often forced English, French, or Latin categories on languages whose actual organizing principles were quite different. Franz Boas (1856 to 1942) is generally acknowledged to have been the first scholar to seriously investigate American Indian languages on their own terms, and the "Introduction" to his *Handbook of American Indian Languages* (1911) remains an important statement of the principle of linguistic relativism. Boas trained his students at Columbia University (where he began teaching anthropology in 1897) to carry out intensive work on Indian languages, whatever their anthropological specialty. They routinely collected long narrative texts from phonetic dictation, compiled grammatical sketches and dictionaries, and often acquired a speaking knowledge of the Indian languages with which they worked. The most linguistically talented of Boas' students, Edward Sapir (1884 to 1939), carried Boas' plan to brilliant fulfillment with several languages, including Wishram Chinook, Takelma, Yana, Southern Paiute, Nootka, Sarcee, Kutchin, Hupa, and Navajo. In his own teaching, at Chicago and later at Yale, Sapir exercised considerable influence on the development of scientific linguistics, and together with the Germanic philologist-turned-American Indianist, Leonard Bloomfield (1887 to 1949), he made the study of American Indian languages the central focus of the field for several decades. Numerous grammars, dictionaries, and comparative studies were written during this period.

During the second half of the twentieth century, the study of American Indian languages has become more peripheral to the main concerns of linguistics. However, a steady growth in the number of students entering the field has led to great strides being made in the formal description of many Indian languages. In 1921, A.L. Kroeber counted six men in North America seriously interested in, and adequately trained for, American Indian linguistics. At the end of 1993, the Society for the Study of the Indigenous Languages of the Americas—the international scholarly society for American Indian language research—had over 700 active members, two-thirds of them residing in the United States, where most of them worked on North American languages.

The most important recent development in the study of American Indian languages has been the entrance into the field of a number of Native Americans. Although still accounting for only a small percentage of the research being done, Native American linguists usually bring to their work a deep commitment to the preservation of traditional languages and a personal desire to gain fluency in them. These concerns have had an impact on the whole of American Indian linguistics, which is gradually shifting its primary emphasis away from mere utilization of the "exotic" data of American Indian languages to construct theoretical models of language, and toward more thorough documentation (i.e., exhaustive dictionaries), the collection and analysis of oral literature, and developing strategies for preservation.

Decline and Extinction of Indian Languages

The small scale of Indian communities, and the intimate linkage between traditional languages and specific territories and modes of life, has made American Indian languages particularly vulnerable to replacement by English. Most of this loss has taken place during the present century, largely as a result of political and economic changes beyond the control of these small groups.

Until well after the Civil War, the fundamental relationship between whites and Indians in the United States was one of considerable hostility, often marked by the forced removal of Indian people from desirable territory and their resettlement beyond the frontier. Except for missionaries, few whites were aware of the nature and complexity of Indian cultures. With the establishment of the reservation system in the 1870s, progressive sentiment in the United States became inclined to see the "civilization" of Indian peoples as a feasible goal, and the persistence of traditional

lifeways as a major hindrance to this development. Indian cultures and languages became the target of outright suppression through a series of high-minded but arbitrary governmental actions, culminating in the Dawes Act of 1887. A system of boarding schools was created, at first under the control of missionaries but later directly managed by the Bureau of Indian Affairs, where the exclusive use of English was rigorously enforced. These institutions had only begun to have their effect at the turn of the century, but by the 1920s they had made serious inroads on the use of Indian languages, even in remote reservations.

By 1950, most American Indian languages were no longer being learned by children. Today (1993), although approximately one hundred fifty Indian languages are still spoken in the United States, many of these are nearly extinct, and fewer than fifty are spoken widely in their communities. Even fewer—perhaps no more than twenty—continue to be learned by children and are thus assured of survival into future generations. The languages most likely to persist are Yup'ik Eskimo in Alaska; Cherokee in Oklahoma; Choctaw in Mississippi; Mikasuki (Seminole) in Florida; and several languages in the Southwest, including Cocopah, Keres, Havasupai-Hualapai-Yavapai, Hopi, Jemez, Mescalero Apache, Tiwa, Navajo, Tohono O'odham (Papago), Western Apache, Yaqui, and Zuni. These represent only nine of the fifty-eight language families of the Powell classification: Eskimo (Yup'ik), Iroquoian (Cherokee), Muskogean (Choctaw, Mikasuki), Yuman (Cocopah, Havasupai-Walapai-Yavapai), Keresan (Keres, Jemez), Uto-Aztecan (Hopi, O'odham, Yaqui), Athabaskan (Mescalero, Navajo, Western Apache), Tanoan (Tiwa), and Zunian (Zuni). Although no Algonquian language in the United States is likely to survive very far into the twenty-first century, a few Cree and Ojibwa-speaking communities in Canada will probably maintain their language. The other forty-eight North American language families all seem likely to become extinct, including such formerly widespread groups as Siouan (where even Crow and Lakota are no longer being learned by children), Salishan, and Caddoan. The vast diversity of languages in Oregon and California is threatened with total extinction. Already gone are Yukian (Wappo and Yuki), Chimariko, Shasta, Takelma, Kalapuya, Coos, Alsea, Siuslaw, Yana, Costanoan, Salinan, Esselen, and Chumash. The rest are spoken only occasionally by a few older people, except for Warm Springs Sahaptin in Oregon, which is still used by many adults but apparently by no children.

Efforts to Preserve Indian Languages

The efflorescence of political and social activism on the part of minority ethnic groups within the United States, beginning in the 1960s, was reflected in many Native American communities in a heightened concern for the preservation of traditional culture. This concern, coupled with the ready availability of federal and state funding for educational initiatives, most importantly the 1968 Bilingual Education Act (Title VII of the 1965 Elementary and Secondary Education Act), prompted many tribes—and groups working with and on behalf of tribes—to set up Indian language programs in the public schools. In many cases, these programs were part of larger efforts at preserving and transmitting various elements of traditional culture (music, ceremonies, handicrafts, etc.). The linguistic sophistication of both teaching materials and teaching methods in these programs was uneven. In some instances, particularly where professional linguists were centrally involved in the planning and implementation of programs, the quality of the efforts was quite high. Notable examples were the Peach Springs Bilingual/Bicultural Program (a Title VII Bilingual Education Act project for the Hualapai Tribe, Arizona); the Alaska Native Language Center (supported by the State of Alaska on behalf of all Indian, Eskimo, and Aleut groups in the state); and the Makah Language Program (begun under a grant from the National Endowment for the Humanities to the Makah Tribe of Neah Bay, Washington).

A major focus of nearly all these programs was literacy in the traditional language. This required, in many instances, the development of adequate practical orthographies, and much attention was paid to their design. By 1992 nearly every Indian language still in use was equipped with at least one orthography, and not infrequently several. In those situations (mainly in the Southwest) where Indian children still acquire their traditional language before entering school, classroom training in Indian-language literacy has been at least partially effective, although its effect on the overall fluency of the children is uncertain. On the other hand, despite the best efforts of teachers and curriculum developers, most Indian children who have not already acquired their language before entering school do not acquire it later in the classroom. The linguistic accuracy and pedagogical sophistication of a given teaching program seems largely unconnected with its success or failure in this regard.

During the last decade, some Indian language educators and others—particularly young adults deeply committed to the preservation of an Indian identity—have questioned the efficacy of any language (or language and culture) program that is tied to the context of Euroamerican schooling and focused mainly on developing literacy. Instead, they have suggested strategies of language and culture retention that rely primarily on oral transmission in culturally relevant situations, such as "culture camps" and "immersion" programs where children are brought together for extended periods with fluent, traditional elders who interact with them only in an Indian language.

There are signs that such community-based efforts, supported by an increasing number of Indians trained in linguistics, may actually stem the tide of language extinction in a number of cases, even where only a handful of fluent speakers have survived. Thus, Tolowa, an Athabaskan language of northwest California for which only three or four native speakers survived into the 1980s, has now been acquired as a second language by a talented and dedicated young man, who is now successfully teaching it to the children of the community. Such efforts will probably be much more frequent in future decades, and their ultimate effect remains to be determined.

Victor Golla

Further Reading

Bauman, James J. *A Guide to Issues in Indian Language Retention*. Washington, DC: Center for Applied Linguistics, 1980.

Boas, Franz, ed. *Handbook of American Indian Languages*. Bureau of American Ethnology Bulletin 40, pts. 1,2. Washington, DC: U.S. Government Printing Office, 1911–1922.

Campbell, Lyle, and Marianne Mithun, eds. *The Languages of Native America: Historical and Comparative Assessment*. Austin: University of Texas Press, 1979.

Leap, William. "American Indian Languages." *Language in the USA*. Eds. C.A. Ferguson and S.B. Heath. New York, NY: Cambridge University Press (1981): 116–44.

Leap, William, and Robert St. Clair, eds. *Language Renewal among American Indian Tribes: Issues, Problems, and Prospects*. Rosslyn, VA: National Clearinghouse for Bilingual Education, 1982.

Zepeda, Ofelia, and Jane H. Hill. "The Condition of Native American Languages in the United States." *Endangered Languages*. Eds. R.H. Robins and E.M. Uhlenbeck. Oxford, England and New York, NY: Berg (1991): 135–55.

LAW

The History and Origins. The primary legal doctrines defining the modern-day relationship between Indian tribes and the federal government were developed in a series of early nineteenth-century Supreme Court cases authored by Chief Justice John Marshall. The first and most important of these doctrines, the congressional Plenary Power doctrine, holds that Congress exercises a plenary authority in Indian affairs. The second of these core doctrines, the Diminished Tribal Sovereignty doctrine, holds that Indian tribes still retain those aspects of their inherent sovereignty not expressly divested by treaty or congressional statute, or implicitly divested by virtue of their status as diminished sovereigns under United States law. The third and final of these foundational doctrines, the Trust doctrine, holds that in exercising its broad discretionary authority in Indian affairs, Congress and the executive branch are charged with the responsibilities of a guardian acting on behalf of its dependent Indian wards.

Most lawyers who practice in the field of modern-day federal Indian law are largely unaware of the long and complex history behind these foundational doctrines. The legal tradition informing these doctrines emerged during the Christian European Crusades to the Holy Lands of the eleventh through thirteenth centuries. These holy wars of conquest and colonization declared by the Roman Catholic Church were fought under a legal theory which held that the pope in Rome, as Christ's vicar on earth, could authorize Christian princes to raise armies and reclaim lands and property held unlawfully by "heathen and infidel" non-Christian peoples who violated Church-declared principles of "natural law."

Throughout the medieval era, European Christian assertions of power and jurisdiction in non-Christian territories were justified according to principles derived from this crusading era legal tradition. This same medievally derived legal tradition of crusading conquest, and colonization was utilized by Spain in the late fifteenth century to acquire papal recognition of its title to the territories "discovered" by Christopher Columbus in the New World. In 1493 at the Spanish Crown's request, Pope Alexander VI donated the entire New World to Spain and placed the indigenous tribal peoples of all the territories discovered or to be discovered in the region under Spain's jurisdiction and guardianship.

The origins of the legal principles defining the modern-day relationship between Indian tribes and the federal government can be traced directly from this legal tradition of crusading conquest, and colonization against normatively divergent non-Christian peoples carried from the Old World by the European colonizing nations. Following Spain's "discoveries," other Christian European monarchs soon sought to secure rights and privileges in infidel-held territories around the world under the theory of a European Christian nation's superior rights of self-rule and jurisdiction over the territory and resources held by non-Christian "savages." From the initial settlement of its first permanent colony at Jamestown in the early seventeenth century, England, for example, justified its colonization of North America on the legal basis of the English Crown's superior rights of sovereignty in lands discovered by its subjects, which were occupied by "infidels and savages."

Johnson v. M'Intosh and the Doctrine of Discovery

In the 1823 case of *Johnson v. M'Intosh*, 21 United States (8 Wheat.) 543 (1823), the United States Supreme Court formally incorporated the medievally derived European legal tradition justifying conquest and colonization of non-Christian peoples into United States federal Indian law. *Johnson* involved the question of whether Indian tribes possessed the rights to complete sovereignty over the lands they occupied since time immemorial, or whether Christian European "discoverers" of those lands held superior rights.

Chief Justice John Marshall, writing for a unanimous court, held in *Johnson* that under Europe's Law of Nations, discovery of territory in the New World gave the discovering European nation superior rights to the lands occupied by "savage" Indian tribes, "a people over whom the superior genius of Europe might claim an ascendancy."

As Marshall explained, under the European Doctrine of Discovery, the rights of the Indians "to complete sovereignty, as independent nations, were necessarily diminished, and their power to dispose of the soil at their own will, to whomsoever they pleased, was denied by the original fundamental principle, that discovery gave exclusive title to those who made it." Future relations between the discovering European nation and the tribes were matters of purely domestic concern to the colonizing European sovereign. The rights thus acquired being exclusive, no other power could interpose between them. Under *Johnson*'s holding, therefore, the United States, as successor in interest to Great Britain's rights of discovery over North America, possessed the superior title to lands occupied by Indian tribes within its recognized borders.

The Cherokee Cases

Marshall's two subsequent opinions for the Court in the Cherokee cases, *Cherokee Nation v. Georgia*, 30 U.S. (5 Pet.) 1 (1831), and *Worcester v. Georgia*, 31 U.S. (6 Pet.) 515 (1832), refined the basic premises of superior United States rights and diminished Indian sovereignty over Indian lands under the Discovery Doctrine announced in *Johnson*. The two related cases arose out of the State of Georgia's attempts to abolish the tribal government of the Cherokee Nation and distribute its lands under state jurisdiction, in violation of several treaties between the United States federal government and the tribe.

In 1830 the tribe filed an original action in the United States Supreme Court, *Cherokee Nation v. Georgia*, challenging Georgia's assertion of lawful authority within the Cherokees' territorial borders. Chief Justice Marshall's opinion in this landmark decision in federal Indian law ruled that the court lacked jurisdiction to hear the case because the Cherokee Nation was not a "foreign nation" within the meaning of Article III of the Constitution's grant of judicial power. Rather, Marshall ruled, the tribes within the boundaries of the United States were regarded as domestic, dependent nations. "They occupy a territory to which we assert a title independent of their will, which must take effect in point of possession when this right of possession ceases. Meanwhile they are in the state of pupilage. Their relation to the United States resembles that of a ward to his guardian." (30 U.S. [5 Pet.] 1, 17–18 [1831].)

A year later in 1832, in the second of the Cherokee cases, *Worcester v. Georgia*, Marshall announced one of the most important and frequently analyzed Supreme Court decisions in modern federal Indian law. In holding that Georgia had no right to arrest Samuel Worcester, a white missionary, for failure to obtain a license from the state in order to reside on the Cherokee territory, Marshall declared the following principles:

> The Cherokee Nation, then, is a district community, occupying its own territory, with bound-

aries accurately described, in which the laws of Georgia can have no force, and which the citizens of Georgia have no right to enter, but with the assent of the Cherokees themselves, or in conformity with treaties, and with the acts of Congress. The whole intercourse between the United States and this nation is, by our Constitution and laws, vested in the government of the United States. (Id. At 31 U.S. [6 Pet.] 515, 560 [1832]).

Application of the Marshall Principles

The decision in *Worcester* affirming Cherokee rights of sovereignty over the tribe's reservation was never enforced by the Court. The Cherokees, and the other southern tribes, despite the Supreme Court's decision, were forced under duress to leave their homelands, and march on the Trail of Tears to the Indian Territory across the Mississippi River. The Marshall trilogy of cases, however, did provide federal Indian law jurisprudence with an important conceptual framework. Marshall's concepts of exclusive federal authority in Indian affairs, domestic dependent nation status for tribes, and the guardian-ward analogy have continued to be cited by courts and policy makers over the course of more than one hundred fifty years as the unquestioned basis for defining the federal-tribal relationship.

This framework, however, has proven itself to be more readily adaptable to justifying shifting congressional policies towards Indian tribes over the course of history, than of generating any set of consistently applied principles protective of Indian tribal rights and status. During the late nineteenth and early twentieth centuries, for example, reformers in Congress and elsewhere in the nation concluded that the hundreds of Indian reservations established by treaties with Indian tribes had failed in the reformers' ultimate goal of "civilizing" the Indians. Congress responded to this perceived failure by increasing its power and control over the reservation and reservation land base. In 1885, for example, Congress passed the Major Crimes Act, extending United States criminal jurisdiction over a list of enumerated major crimes committed by one Indian against another in Indian country. This first major law asserting federal jurisdiction over purely Indian matters within the reservation was followed by the General Allotment Act of 1887. The act, in effect, sought to encourage the destruction of tribalism and the assimilation of Indians into white "civilization" by parceling out treaty-guaranteed reservation lands to individual tribal members in severalty. To further accelerate the process of disintegration of tribalism and the treaty-guaranteed tribal land base, the act provided for the sale of "surplus" tribal treaty lands to desirous white homesteaders. During the half-century in which the Allotment Act was in effect as the federal government's official Indian policy (1887 to 1934), the total of Indian tribal land holdings was reduced from 138 million acres to 48 million acres.

The late nineteenth and early twentieth century era of assimilationist legislation and allotments produced several significant Supreme Court decisions that have continued to exercise a profound influence on modern federal Indian law doctrine. In *United States v. Kagama*, 188 U.S. 375 (1886) the Supreme Court upheld Congress' power to enact the Major Crimes Act in light of its guardianship responsibilities for its "weak and diminished" Indian wards. In *Lone Wolf v. Hitchcock*, 187 U.S. 553 (1903), the Supreme Court upheld Congress' plenary power to breach a treaty with an Indian tribe if necessary to facilitate the allotment of the tribe's reservation. The *Lone Wolf* court's holding that Congress' exercising of its guardianship responsibilities over Indians raised political questions, essentially insulated congressional actions affecting tribal rights and property during the late nineteenth and early twentieth centuries from judicial scrutiny, and invested Congress with wide latitude in managing Indian affairs.

Congressional and Executive Branch Policy

The legal rights and status of American Indians in the twentieth century have been no less subject to the shifting moods and prejudices of the dominant society as reflected in congressional Indian legislation. In 1934, Congress enacted the Indian Reorganization Act (IRA), which represented a dramatic reversal of the Allotment Act policy of assimilation of tribal Indians. The IRA sought to revive tribal self-determination by encouraging tribes to enact tribal constitutions and create elected tribal governments in order to exercise greater control over the reservation. Yet, within two decades of the IRA's passage, Congress after World War II embarked on a much different policy—tribal termination. House Concurrent Resolution 108, adopted in 1953, declared the "sense of Congress" in support of ending the federal government's trust responsibilities and supervision of Indian tribes "as rapidly as possible." Under this new policy, approximately one hundred nine tribes and bands were terminated, and state jurisdiction and taxing authority imposed over their disestablished reservations.

The federal government, responding to intense opposition from Indian tribes, abandoned the termination policy, and in the 1960s moved to strengthen tribal governments. Tribes were incorporated into the Great Society programs of the Johnson presidential administration, and congressional legislation and policy began to recognize the permanency of Indian tribes in the federal system. In 1970, President Nixon delivered recommendations to Congress outlining the current federal Indian policy of self-determination for Indian tribes. Many of these recommendations were incorporated into the Indian Self-Determination and Education Assistance Act of 1975, a landmark piece of legislation aimed at expanding tribal governmental control over federally funded programs on the reservation. Subsequent congressional legislation has continued to promote the policy of tribal self-determination. The Indian Child Welfare Act, for example, strengthened tribal jurisdiction over child custody proceedings and adoptions involving Indian children. The Indian Tribal Governmental Tax Status Act of 1982 extended to tribes many of the same federal tax advantages and benefits historically enjoyed by states and local governments.

The Role of the Courts

Courts, particularly the United States Supreme Court, have continued to play a central role in defining and shaping American Indian legal rights and status during the twentieth century. In the area of congressional plenary power, for example, the Supreme Court has somewhat retreated from the principle laid down in *Lone Wolf v. Hitchcock*, granting a judicial presumption of congressional good faith to acts affecting treaty-protected property. In *United States v. Sioux Nation*, 448 U.S. 371 (1980), the Sioux tribe was awarded damages totaling more than $100 million for Congress' taking of the Black Hills in violation of the 1868 Fort Laramie Treaty. (See also *Delaware Tribal Business Comm. v. Weeks*, 430 U.S. 73 [1977], which holds that the plenary power of Congress "does not mean that all federal legislation concerning Indians is . . . immune from judicial scrutiny.")

The Court in the twentieth century has perhaps been most active in the field of Indian law in defining the scope of tribal authority and jurisdiction over the reservation. *Williams v. Lee*, 358 U.S. 217 (1959), relied on the Marshall cases in holding that the State of Arizona could not exercise civil jurisdiction over a contract occurring on the Navajo Reservation between a tribal member and a non-Indian merchant. Citing the federal government's support of the development of Navajo tribal courts, the Supreme Court held that absent governing acts of Congress, the test for determining when states could exercise jurisdiction on the reservation, was whether the state action would interfere with the right of reservation Indians to make their own laws and be ruled by them. Subsequent Supreme Court decisions have further refined the scope of tribal versus state control over the reservation by focusing on the extent of federal acts and treaties preempting state jurisdiction in Indian country, informed by the backdrop of tribal sovereignty. See also *McClanahan v. Arizona State Tax Commission*, 411 United States 164 (1973).

Significant doctrinal developments have also occurred in the area of the scope of tribal jurisdiction over non-Indian conduct on the reservation. A series of cases, beginning with *Oliphant v. Suquamish Indian Tribe*, 435 U.S. 191 (1978); and continuing with *United States v. Wheeler*, 435 U.S. 313 (1978); *Montana v. United States*, 450 U.S. 544 (1981); *Brendale v. Confederated Tribes and Bands of Yakima Indian Nation*, 109 S.Ct. 2994 (1989); and *Duro v. Reina*, 110

S.Ct. 2053 (1990), have interpreted the scope of tribal jurisdiction over non-members narrrowly, significantly weakening tribal control over the reservation environment. Under these decisions, Indian tribes, because of their diminished sovereign status under the Doctrine of Discovery, are not permitted to exercise criminal jurisdiction over non-Indians on the reservation. Tribes under these decisions also are severely restricted in exercising civil regulatory jurisdiction over nonmembers, who own land in fee simple on the reservation by virtue of prior allotment policies.

The Court has also been active in defining the contours of the Trust doctrine in Indian law during the twentieth century. *Morton v. Mancari*, 417 U.S. 535 (1974), established that congressional legislation befitting Indian tribes as a group is not violative of the Constitution's prohibitions on invidious racial discrimination, but rather, is justified under Congress' unique trust responsibilities for supporting tribal self-determination.

The Trust doctrine has also played an important role in the series of highly controversial decisions by federal courts during the past several decades recognizing treaty-based Indian hunting and fishing rights; see, for example, *Washington v. Washington State Commercial Passenger Fishing Vessel Association*, 443 U.S. 658 (1979); and with regard to rights to critical natural resources, particularly water, see, for example, *Arizona v. California*, 373 U.S. 546 (1963). These treaty-rights cases relied on several Supreme Court precedents issued earlier in the century, such as *United States v. Winans*, 198 U.S. 371 (1905), and *Winters v. United States*, 207 U.S. 564 (1908), requiring a liberal construction of treaty language in favor of Indian rights by virtue of the Indians' unequal bargaining position in most treaties, and the United States' trust responsibilities to the tribes. Similarly the United States trust responsibility to Indian tribes was relied on by the courts in a major land claim involving the Passamaquoddy Tribe of Maine (see *Joint Tribal Council of Passamaquoddy v. Morton*, 528 F.2d 370 [1975]).

Two important cases decided by the Court involving Indian religious freedom and rights—*Employment Division Department of Human Resources of Oregon v. Smith*, 110 S.Ct. 1595 (1990), and *Lyng v. Northwest Indian Cemetery Protective Association*, 485 U.S. 439 (1988)—have removed the protection of the United States Constitution's First Amendment guarantees of freedom of religion from Indian traditional religious practices. In *Smith*, a case involving the sacramental use of peyote by members of the Native American Church, the Supreme Court held that the First Amendment does not bar application of a state's criminal law prohibiting use of peyote to religiously motivated action. In *Lyng*, the Court held that the federal government did not burden Indian religious practices by construction of a road on federal land through an area regarded as a sacred site by a California Indian tribe.

Robert A. Williams

See also Civil Rights; International Law; Sovereignty and Jurisdiction; Treaties

Further Reading

Burke, Joseph C. "The Cherokee Cases: A Study in Law, Politics, and Morality." *Stanford Law Review* 21(1969): 500–31.

Cohen, Felix S. *Felix S. Cohen's Handbook of Federal Indian Law*. Ed. Rennard Strickland. Charlottesville, VA: Mitchie/Bobbs, Merrill, 1982.

Getches, David, Charles F. Wilkinson, and Robert A. Williams, Jr. *Cases and Materials on Federal Indian Law:* 3d ed. St. Paul, MN: West Publishing Co., 1993.

Hoxie, Frederick. *A Final Promise: The Campaign to Assimilate the Indians, 1880–1934*. Lincoln: University of Nebraska Press, 1984.

Williams, Robert A. *The American Indian in Western Legal Thought: The Discourses of Conquest*. Oxford, England and New York, NY: Oxford University Press, 1990.

LENAPE

See Delaware; Powhatan/Rénape Nation

LIPAN APACHE

See Apache; Plains Apache; Tonkawa

LITERATURE

In the twentieth century Native Americans continue to perform their traditional oral literatures while increasing numbers of them have become highly polished and sophisticated writers. Especially during the last thirty years, tribes and individuals have initiated strong efforts to maintain and restore their oral traditions. Because they reflect the basic beliefs of tribal life, ceremonies, stories, songs, and oratory remain an important part of Native American life, both on and off the reservation.

Oral Literature

During the first half of the twentieth century, many Indians trained in anthropology or linguistics collected and translated oral literatures. Among these are Ella C. Deloria (Sioux), William Jones (Fox), Archie Phinney (Nez Perce), John N.B. Hewitt (Tuscarora), Francis LaFlesche (Omaha), William Morgan (Navajo), and Arthur C. Parker (Seneca). Contemporary scholars like Ofelia Zepeda (Tohono O'odham) carry on this tradition.

Among the Native Americans who have published valuable but less scholarly collections are Percy Bullchild (Blackfeet), George Clutesi (Tlingit), Jesse Cornplanter (Seneca), Charles A. Eastman (Sioux), E. Pauline Johnson (Mohawk), James LaPoint (Sioux), Mourning Dove (Colville), and Vi Hilbert (Lushootseed). Narratives published under the aegis of individual tribes include *The Way It Was, Inaku Iwacha: Yakima Indian Legends* (1974), project director Virginia Beavert; and *Nu Mee Poom Tit Wah Tit (Nez Perce Legends)* (1972), compiled by Alan P. Slickpoo, Sr., et al. Schol-

ars have increasingly recognized the need to discuss the cultural and performance dimensions of oral literatures. *Yaqui Deer Songs/Maso Bwikam* (1987), by Larry Evers and Felipe Molina (Yaqui), is an especially fine example of a bilingual text that pays appropriate attention to these aspects.

Autobiography

Because it is both oral and written, autobiography constitutes a bridge between these two forms of literature. The narrated or "as-told-to" autobiography has retained the popularity it gained in the nineteenth century. In the first half of this century, anthropologists edited increasing numbers of life histories, primarily those written by males, as they recorded tribal traditions. Among the narrators who collaborated with scholars to create excellent ethnographic autobiographies are Sam Blowsnake [Big Winnebago and Crashing Thunder] (Winnebago); Mountain Wolf Woman (Winnebago); Maria Chona (Papago); John Stands in Timber (Cheyenne); James Sewid (Kwakiutl); Left Handed (Navajo); Albert Yava (Tewa/Hopi); and Severt Young Bear (Sioux). *Me and Mine* (1969) by Helen Sekaquaptewa and Louise Udall typifies the form of autobiography in which the narrator tells his or her life history to a friend. The most literary as well as the most widely read of these autobiographies is *Black Elk Speaks* (1932), narrated by Black Elk to John C. Neihardt. Less polished but delightful is *Lame Deer: Seeker of Visions* (1972) by John Fire [Lame Deer] (Sioux) and Richard Erdoes. The latter has also recorded the story of activist Mary Crow Dog in *Lakota Woman* (1990). Several tribal oral life histories, particularly those of the Southwest, have also been recorded: *Navajo Stories of the Long Walk Period* (1973), edited by Ruth Roessel; *Stories of Traditional Navajo Life and Culture* (1978), edited by Broderick H. Johnson; *The Zunis* (1972), edited by Alvina Quam; and *Yaqui Women* (1978), edited by Jane Holden Kelley.

Some Native Americans recorded their own accounts, which were later edited by scholars. Among these are *The Warrior Who Killed Custer* (1968) by Chief Joseph White Bull, which contains his drawings of the events; *Sun Chief* (1974) by Don Talayesva (Hopi), extensively revised and restructured by Leo W. Simmons; *The Autobiography of a Yaqui Poet* (1980) by Refugio Savala, edited with far less intrusion by Kathleen Mullen Sands. Important for the study of Indian women is *Mourning Dove: A Salishan Autobiography* (1990) by Mourning Dove (Christine Quintasket, Colville, 1888 to 1936), which Jay Miller edited from her drafts and fragments.

Increasing numbers of American Indians have published their own written autobiographies. One of the first and most popular of these twentieth-century autobiographers is Charles A. Eastman (Sioux, 1858 to 1939), whose *Indian Boyhood* (1902) describes his life as a traditional Santee Sioux from childhood to age fifteen and whose *From the Deep Woods to Civi-*

lization (1916) chronicles his experiences in the white world. Other Sioux autobiographers who published their life histories during the first half of this century are Luther Standing Bear (ca. 1868 to 1939) and Zitkala-Sa (1876 to 1938). Francis LaFlesche (Omaha, 1857 to 1932) describes in *The Middle Five* (1900) his experiences at a Presbyterian mission school in Nebraska. Others who have written autobiographies include James Paytiamo (Acoma; b.ca. 1890); Anna Moore Shaw (Pima, b. 1898); Ted Williams (Tuscarora, b. 1930); and James McCarthy (Papago, b. 1895). As was true in the nineteenth century, most of the narrated and written autobiographies of this century have focused on the individual's place within the tribal culture. Consequently, they usually include considerable ethnohistorical information and many stories and songs.

One of the best literary and philosophical autobiographies is *Talking to the Moon* (1945) by John Joseph Mathews (Osage, ca. 1894 to 1979), which is strongly influenced by Osage culture as well as by the writers Thoreau and John Muir. An equally sophisticated autobiographer is N. Scott Momaday (Kiowa, b. 1934). His *The Way to Rainy Mountain* (1969) chronicles the Kiowa's origin and migration to Oklahoma, their life both before and after the reservation period, and his own quest for his tribal roots. Momaday's *The Names* (1976) is a fascinating account of both sides of his family as well as a poignant description of his boyhood. *Interior Landscapes* by Gerald Vizenor (Ojibwa, b. 1934) is a moving, witty, and satiric account of the author's youth and his experiences as a soldier, a social worker, journalist, and writer. In *Bloodlines* (1993), Janet Campbell Hale (Coeur d'Alene-Kootenai, b. 1947) creates a beautifully written memoir of her family and of her own life, chronicling how she triumphed over growing up in a dysfunctional family to become a successful writer. Many Native American authors have published poignant and revealing autobiographies in *I Tell You Now* (1987), edited by Brian Swann and Arnold Krupat.

Fiction

Twentieth-century Native American authors increasingly wrote fiction, particularly novels. Many of these deal with the quests of mixed-blood protagonists to find their places in society and with the importance of oral tradition to the survival of tribalism. In the first half of the century, E. Pauline Johnson (Mohawk, 1861 to 1913), Mourning Dove, John Joseph Mathews, and D'Arcy McNickle (Cree-Salish, 1904 to 1977) incorporate these themes into their fiction. Johnson's *Moccasin Maker* (1913), one of the first collections of short stories and essays by a Native American woman, focuses on the experiences of Canadian Indian and non-Indian women. Several of her heroines are mixed-bloods betrayed by their white lovers or husbands. Much of this volume was originally published in *Mother's Magazine* in the United States. One of the earliest novels by an American Indian woman is *Wynema, a Child of the Forest* (1891) by Sophia Alice Callahan (Creek, 1868 to 1893), which describes the acculturation of a white teacher to Creek life and of Wynema to that of the southern gentry. Another is Mourning Dove's *Cogewea, the Half-Blood* (1927), written in collaboration with Lucullus V. McWhorter. Here, Mourning Dove combines the portrayal of a strong-willed, well-educated heroine, who temporarily rejects her tribal heritage with plot elements from Westerns.

Mathews' *Sundown* (1934) focuses on the problems of a mixed-blood Osage whose abandonment of his ancestral past and inability to adjust to the white-dominated present result in alcoholism. Mathews' earlier *Wah'Kon-Tah* (1932), the first book by an Indian to be a Book-of-the-Month selection, is a fictional account of the Osages' struggles to retain their traditions after they were forced onto reservations. Even more sophisticated is McNickle's *The Surrounded* (1936), which chronicles the dilemma of a mixed-blood hero inadvertently caught up in unpremeditated murders that his mother and girl friend commit. His strongly traditional mother and a tribal elder lead the protagonist back to the Salish culture he rejected. Equally powerful is McNickle's posthumously published *Wind from an Enemy Sky* (1978), which depicts the difficulties of representatives from Indian and non-Indian cultures to communicate with each other. McNickle also wrote *Runner in the Sun* (1954), a novel for young people that evokes the life, customs, and beliefs of the ancient cliff dwellers in what is now northwestern New Mexico.

Closer in theme to mainstream American fiction of the 1930s is *Brothers Tree* (1935) by John Oskison (Cherokee, 1874 to 1947), a fine example of the regional novel and a vivid portrait of a part-Cherokee family trying to regain its Oklahoma land and its values. During the 1920s, Oskison wrote a series of what he called "southwestern" potboilers. An example of the ethnographic novel is *Waterlily* by Ella Deloria (Sioux, 1888 to 1971), completed by 1944 but not published until 1988. This fascinating portrayal of nineteenth-century Sioux life chronicles Waterlily's life from birth through adulthood. The most prolific novelist during the 1930s was [George] Todd Downing (Choctaw, 1902 to 1974), who wrote nine mystery novels, including *Murder on Tour* (1931), *The Cat Screams* (1934), and *The Lazy Lawrence Murders* (1941). Most were set in Mexico. *The Mexican Earth* (1940), a travel book, contains his most poetic prose.

Satire

During the first half of the century, American Indian authors wrote in other genres as well. Alexander Posey (Creek, 1873 to 1908) and Will Rogers (Cherokee, 1879 to 1935) were accomplished satirists. Both were undoubtedly influenced by columnists writing political dialect humor in Oklahoma Indian newspapers at the end of the nineteenth century. Using real Creek elders as characters and writing in Creek-style

English, Posey, a great admirer of Robert Burns, satirized the politics of Indian Territory in his *Fus Fixico Letters* (1902 to 1908; rpt. 1993), edited by Carol Hunter (Osage) and Daniel F. Littlefield, Jr. (Cherokee). National and international politics was the main theme of Rogers' satire. His books and miscellaneous writings are now being published as *Complete Works*, edited by Joseph A. Stout.

Poetry

Little poetry was published by Native American writers during this period. Johnson's *Flint and Feather* (1912) included *White Wampum* (1895) and *Canadian Born* (1903). Posey's poetry was published posthumously in *The Poems of Alexander Posey* (1910), which primarily consisted of romantic descriptions of nature written in his youth. An example of Indian dialect poetry is *Yon-doo-shah-we-ah* (1924) by Bertrand N.O. Walker [Hen-toh] (Wyandot, 1870 to 1927), which contains some interesting character sketches and narratives.

The most sophisticated poet of this period is [Rolla] Lynn Riggs (Cherokee, 1899 to 1954), whose *Iron Dish* (1930) contains delicate lyrics and imaginative descriptions of nature. During the first half of the twentieth century, Riggs was the only major Native American dramatist. He is best known for *Green Grow the Lilacs* (1931), the powerful folk drama that became the hit musical *Oklahoma!* Also widely praised were his *Borned in Texas*, produced as *Roadside* (1930). His only play on an Indian theme is *Cherokee Night* (1936), about the Oklahoma mixed-bloods sense of cultural loss.

Post 1960 Literature

In the late 1960s, new Native American writers emerged. The first of these to achieve national recognition was N. Scott Momaday, whose *The House Made of Dawn* (1968) won the Pulitzer Prize. Both in this novel and in *The Ancient Child* (1989), Momaday describes the ritual quests of mixed-blood protagonists, one a World War II veteran and the other a middle-aged artist, to achieve healing through immersion into tribal myths and rites. Another powerful fiction writer is Leslie Marmon Silko (Laguna, b. 1948). Her *Ceremony* (1977) demonstrates the healing power of tribal storytelling by reuniting a mixed-blood World War II veteran with his tribe at the end of the novel. Her *Almanac of the Dead* (1991) continues the ritual quest theme in an epic novel that traces the conflicts between and confluences of Native and non-Native cultures of the Americas and the Southwest. Her short stories and her poetry are collected in *Storyteller* (1981). Paula Gunn Allen (Laguna-Sioux, b. 1939) brings a feminist perspective to her treatment of the ritual quest in *The Woman Who Owned the Shadows* (1983).

In *Winter in the Blood* (1975), James Welch (Blackfeet-Gros Ventre, b. 1940) focuses on a nameless hero's search for the truth about his family background and about his fierce Blackfeet grandmother's early life. In Welch's *The Death of Jim Loney* (1979), a mixed-blood protagonist also seeks information about his Indian family and the white father who psychologically abandons him. The search for identity is also the theme of Welch's *Indian Lawyer* (1990), in which a successful Blackfeet lawyer becomes ensnared in a blackmail scheme that forces him to decide who he is and what he wants.

Native Americans have incorporated themes other than the ritual quest in their novels. Louise Erdrich (Ojibwa, b. 1954) focuses on family and community interrelationships in *Love Medicine* (1984), *Beet Queen* (1986), and *Tracks* (1988). Set in Erdrich's native North Dakota and part of a projected series of four novels, they have gained Erdrich national recognition. *Tracks* and *Love Medicine* chronicle the interrelationships between members of a North Dakota Chippewa tribe from 1912 to 1983. *Beet Queen* deals primarily with the relationships between non-Indian characters in the off-reservation town of Argus. Set on a Montana reservation, *A Yellow Raft on Blue Water* (1987) by Michael Dorris (Modoc, b. 1945) portrays three generations of women torn apart by secrets but bound by kinship. Erdrich and Dorris, who are married and collaborate on each another's works, have co-authored *The Crown of Columbus* (1991), which humorously describes the adventures of a mixed-blood anthropologist as she copes with both her children and her WASP, academic lover while tracking down Christopher Columbus's lost diary.

Among the few historical novels by an Indian is Welch's *Fools Crow* (1986), which vividly describes the impact of white settlement on a Montana band of Blackfeet in 1870. Robert J. Conley (Cherokee, b. 1940) uses the historical novel form in his *Mountain Windsong* (1992), the love story of a couple separated by the Trail of Tears.

Vizenor's novels are sharp and perceptive satires of Indian-white relations and of modern society. His *Griever: An American Monkey King in China* (1987), describes the adventures of a mixed-blood Indian who teaches English in a Chinese university and triumphs over Chinese bureaucracy as he becomes transformed into a Monkey King, the Chinese trickster. His *Trickster of Liberty: Tribal Heirs to a Wild Baronage at Petronia* (1988) depicts a whole family of Indian tricksters who rebel against conventional systems and establish ingenious enterprises. Vizenor takes on the Columbus mythology in *The Heirs of Columbus* (1991), in which a "cross-blood" trickster descendent of the explorer establishes a tribal nation where "humor rules and tricksters heal." He asserts that the Maya created Columbus, and solves the mystery of some missing artifacts.

Thomas King (Cherokee, b. 1943) also uses the trickster as a motif in *Green Grass, Running Water* (1993), an hilarious tale in which King interweaves Indian stories with satires of how whites portray them in books and film. The cast of memorable Indian characters include a stubborn man who leaves his professorship to halt the operation of a huge hydro-electric dam flooding Blackfoot land, a determined woman Indian studies professor who wants to bear a baby but not be burdened with a husband, and a resourceful mother who supports her family by running the Dead Dog restaurant, where she convinces gullible tourists that they are eating authentic Indian dog meat dishes. Identity is the focus of King's *Medicine River* (1990), which combines humor and realism. Set near the Blackfoot reserve in Alberta, it describes his mixed-blood protagonist's attempts to understand his family background and to cope with the schemes of a bumbling friend. The Canadian Broadcasting Company has filmed King's television screenplay of the book.

Identity is also the major focus of two powerful, realistic novels by Louis Owens (Choctaw-Cherokee, b. 1948), *Sharpest Sight* (1991) and *Wolf Song* (1991). *The Sharpest Sight* portrays the quests of two protagonists, a mixed-blood Choctaw and a Chicano, to find their roots and to solve the murder of the Indian protagonist's brother. *Wolf Song* chronicles the growing commitment of a returned college student to his tribal community in Washington and to his dead uncle's battle to save the wilderness from destruction. In *From the River's Edge*, Elizabeth Cook-Lynn (Sioux, b. 1930) movingly portrays the attempts by a Dakota cattleman to regain his culture and his honor after his tribal way of life and his cattle have been stolen.

In the *Jailing of Cecelia Capture* (1985), Janet Campbell Hale portrays the attempts of an urban Indian woman to restructure her life. This novel and her earlier *Owl Song* (1974) about a young boy are among the few works dealing with urban Indians. Anna Walters (Otoe-Pawnee, b. 1946) blends mystery and Navajo-white relations in her *Ghost Singer* (1988), which attacks whites' inhumane practice of storing Indian skeletons and possessions in museums. Other American Indian novelists include Hyemeyohsts Storm (Cheyenne, b. 1935), whose *Seven Arrows* (1972) aroused controversy because of its treatment of Cheyenne religion. His *The Song of the Heyoehkah* (1981) deals with a heroine's quest for ritual knowledge to become a shaman. The only novel by an Eskimo writer is Markoosie's *Harpoon of the Hunter* (1970).

One of the few American Indian mystery writers is Martin Cruz Smith (Senecu del Sur-Yaqui, b. 1942) who has achieved national acclaim for four mystery novels, two of which have Indian themes. Both his *Nightwing* (1977) and *Stallion Gate* (1986) have Indian protagonists who struggle to become reunited with their tribes and traditions. *The Indians Won* (1970) deals more directly with Indian issues. Far different are Smith's *Gorky Park* (1981) and *Polar Star* (1989), which deal with characters from both the Soviet Union and the United States.

Short Fiction. Indian authors have also written much short fiction. Silko's short stories, which strongly reflect Laguna traditions, are collected with her poetry in *Storyteller* (1981). Simon Ortiz (Acoma, b. 1941)

has also published two books containing his short fiction: *The Howbah Indians* (1978) and *Fightin'* (1983). Cook-Lynn has gathered her stories about contemporary Sioux life in *The Power of Horses* (1991). Walters's short fiction is contained in her *The Sun Is Not Merciful* (1985). Conley has published his short stories, which include reinterpretations of traditional stories, in *The Witch of Goingsnake and Other Stories* (1988). Allen adapts traditional stories from various tribes in her *Grandmothers of the Light* (1991).

Nonfiction. Gerald Vizenor's *Wordarrows* (1978), *Earthdivers* (1981), and *The People Named the Chippewa* (1984) combine satiric short fiction and nonfiction. The most widely published Indian writer of non-fiction prose is Vine Deloria, Jr. (Sioux, b. 1933). His works that combine political insight, wit, and satire are *Custer Died for Your Sins* (1969), which contains an interesting essay on Indian humor, and *We Talk, You Listen* (1970). He has also written numerous books on American Indian religion, philosophy, Indian-white relations, and politics. Michael Dorris's *The Broken Cord: A Family's On-going Struggle with Fetal Alcohol Syndrome* (1989) portrays the author's efforts to raise his adopted son, Adam, a victim of the syndrome.

Poetry. Since 1968, Native Americans have become prolific writers of poetry that reflects considerable variety in theme and form. Among the most widely published are Paula Gunn Allen (Laguna-Sioux), Jim Barnes (Choctaw), Barney Bush (Shawnee), Diane Glancy (Cherokee), Joy Harjo (Creek), Linda Hogan (Chickasaw), Maurice Kenny (Mohawk), Duane Niatum (Klallam), Simon Ortiz (Acoma), Wendy Rose (Hopi-Miwok), Carter Revard (Osage), Ralph Salisbury (Cherokee), Luci Tapahonso (Navajo), and Ray Young Bear (Mesquaki). Though primarily fiction writers, Louise Erdrich, N. Scott Momaday, Leslie Silko, James Welch, and Gerald Vizenor have also published poetry. Other talented poets include Sherman Alexie (Spokane-Coeur d'Alene), Peter Blue Cloud (Mohawk), Joe Bruchac (Abenaki), Elizabeth Cook-Lynn (Sioux), Diane Burns (Ojibwa-Chemehuevi), Gladys Cardiff (Cherokee), Anita Endrezze-Danielson (Yaqui), Nia Francisco (Navajo), Lance Henson (Cheyenne), Adrian Louis (Paiute), William Oandasan (Yuki), and Mary Tall Mountain (Athabaskan).

The forms of contemporary Indian poetry vary from traditional chants and songs to highly individualistic verse. Many Indian poets incorporate into their poems tribal myths such as creation and emergence, earthdiver, and the trickster. Common themes include a sense of loss of tribal roots, often associated with a specific space that is part of the history of the author's tribe, and closeness to nature and animals. Native American poets also deal with the problems of identity that mixed-bloods face, the sense of displacement that urban Indians experience, and the injustice inflicted on their people by the dominant society. They describe how the family, as well as tribal values, provides Native Americans with the sources of strength to withstand attempts to alter their culture. Native

American women poets frequently focus on the role of women. Many pay tribute to the grandmothers who traditionally helped raise the children and educated them in tribal culture. Although much of Indian authors' poetry deals with Indian themes, increasingly writers are turning to other subjects as well. Several Indian women writers have focused some of their recent poems on their reactions to maturation and aging.

Increasing numbers of Native Americans are beginning to write dramas. Gerald Vizenor, Linda Hogan, and Thomas King have written plays and screenplays. Among the best-known contemporary dramatists is Hanay Geiogamah (Kiowa-Delaware, b. 1945). His *New Native American Drama* includes his satiric dramas *Foghorn*, *49*, and *Body Indian*. Other published dramatists include Bruce King (Oneida, b. 1950), *Dust Off* (1982), and William S. Yellow Robe, Jr. (Assiniboine, b. 1960), *Snaky/Slant Six: An Anthology* (1990). The Native Writers' Circle of the Americas has published a *Directory of Native Writers*, available from Greenfield Review Literary Center in Greenfield Center, New York.

A knowledge of the rich oral and written literary heritage created by Native Americans is essential to understanding twentieth-century American Indian life. Fortunately, this heritage is gaining an appreciative general audience and increasingly is being introduced into literature courses and texts.

A. LaVonne Brown Ruoff

Further Reading

Allen, Paula Gunn. *The Sacred Hoop: Recovering the Feminine in American Indian Traditions.* Boston, MA: Beacon, 1986.

Bataille, Gretchen M., and Kathleen Mullen Sands. *American Indian Women: Telling Their Lives.* Lincoln: University of Nebraska Press, 1984.

Brumble, H. David, III. *American Indian Autobiography.* Berkeley: University of California Press, 1988.

Owens, Louis. *Other Destinies: Understanding the American Indian Novel.* Norman: University of Oklahoma Press, 1992.

Ruoff, A. LaVonne Brown. *American Indian Literatures: An Introduction, Bibliographic Review, and Selected Bibliography.* New York, NY: Modern Language Association, 1990.

Vizenor, Gerald, ed. *Narrative Chance: Postmodern Discourse on Native American Literatures.* Albuquerque: University of New Mexico Press, 1989.

Wiget, Andrew O. *Native American Literature.* Twayne's United States Authors 467. Boston, MA: Twayne, 1985.

LITTLE SHELL BAND OF CHIPPEWA

See Ojibwa: Chippewa in Montana; Ojibwa: Chippewa in North Dakota

LOWER UMPQUA

See Confederated Tribes of the Coos, Lower Umpqua, and Suislaw

LOYAL SHAWNEE

See Shawnee in Oklahoma

LUISEÑO

The Luiseño (San Luiseño, Juaneño) occupied about 1,500 square miles of coastal southern California, north of the Kumeyaay, holding most of the San Luis Rey River and Santa Margarita River drainages. Their language belongs to the Cupan group of the Takic subfamily. Formerly a tribal leader managed military, diplomatic, trade, and religious relations with other tribes. Each patrilineal band was governed by a *noot* with a council of environmental specialists, and held ten to thirty miles of a river basin, with coastal and mountain sites for other resources. They used plant husbandry, inland corn agriculture, water and erosion management, and controlled burning agricultural techniques.

It was not until 1875, however, when tribal Chief Oligario Calac went to Washington, D.C. to see the president that land was reserved for them by executive order. Due to publicity from Helen Hunt Jackson, additional lands were reserved in 1882 and 1883; but all the Indians knew that executive orders were not secure titles. Finally in 1891 the Act for the Relief of Mission Indians created five Luiseño reservations. All except the Pechanga Reservation (the Temecula Band) retained part of their original farmland. By provisions in this Act, the Pala and Pechanga reservations were allotted immediately. The rest were delayed. In 1927 the Bureau of Indian Affairs started to allot Rincon and La Jolla reservations, ignoring existing improvements. Mission Indian Federation members sued to stop allotment and lost.

Another band, the Puerta La Cruz, participated in the Cupeño case to retain their land on Warner's rancho. After losing the case in the Supreme Court, the army took them all to Pala in 1903 where the original Luiseño Reservation of Pala was joined to purchased land, which was then allotted to the Cupeño, Luiseño, and Kumeyaay relocatees.

After receiving trust patents, those on reservations along the San Luis Rey River planted fruit trees and market and subsistence crops. By 1910, their average annual income matched or exceeded that of small, local non-Indian farmers. They raised cattle, horses, chickens, and kept bees; some leased farm land outside the reservations; most worked part-time for nearby ranchers and farmers. Pechanga residents, lacking adequate water and land, were starving until the Kelsey Tract was purchased, enabling some to farm. Most worked off-reservation.

Water continues to be a constant concern. In 1894 the agent required La Jolla "leaders" to sign a contract allowing Escondido to take "winter storm water" from the river; but only storm water was allowed downriver. In 1924, a dam built above La Jolla took all the water to Escondido. Six miner's inches was to go to Rincon, but none to La Jolla or Pala.

LUISEÑO RESERVATIONS, San Diego/Riverside Counties					
	Executive Order	Trust Patent	Acres	Allotted Acres	Members[1]
La Jolla	1875 (as Potrero)	1892	8,891	634	532
Rincon	1875 (as Potrero) 1881	1892	4,280	351.81	600+
Pauma-Yuima	purchase 1903 Mission Reserve	1892 1973	250 3.5 5,627.25 (from Mission Reserve)	0	237?
Riverside County Pechanga Kelsey	1882 1907 purchase	1893 1988	4,093.80 235 305[2]	1,233.02	694
MIXED: Cupeño (majority), Luiseño, Kumeyaay Pala	1875 purchase 1903	1893} 1903} 1973	3,438.77 3,761.4 (Mission Reserve)	1,174.29	475?
Source: Tribal Office Data [1]Membership often does not include children. [2]Acreage provided to the band by the Bureau of Land Management.					

Because Rincon seldom received the six inches, the ground water dropped and farming ceased. In 1916, the owner subdivided the rancho surrounding Pauma-Yuima to sell for orchards. Non-Indian orchardists took all the Pauma-Yuima water. Pauma's prosperous orchards died, and by 1955 all were working off-reservation. Many lost domestic water and could not live on their land. In 1951, a claim for the stolen reservation water (Docket 80A) was added to the Mission Indian Land Claim. After a 1973 hearing, the Federal Power Commission required Escondido to regularly release six miner's inches from the dam. After many testimonies, the San Luis Rey Case (80A1) was settled out of court in 1985. The bands received several million dollars for past damages and the federal government promised 16,000 acre-feet of other water. As of 1993 the water has not yet been provided. Due to geologic faults, Escondido may no longer keep the dam "full" but must release some water to the river. While insufficient, with this water economic development began; homes were built and members live again on the reservations. The San Luis Rey Band and Pechanga are in Docket 80A2, the water case ongoing since 1985. On Pechanga, water remains a problem since suburban development covered the valley, using local and imported water and changing the land's shape and drainage, depleting ground water and increased erosion. Even with the Indian Health Service (IHS) responsible for domestic water, some lack running water.

Each sovereign reservation elects a tribal chairman and council. Most have articles of association or constitutions, and enrollment regulations prescribing membership requirements. Most have developments such as campgrounds, orchards, stores, and forest plantations that produce some income. All plan for economic independence and employment for members. All have senior programs, preschools, libraries, cultural and tutoring programs, and encourage youth to attend college. All except Pechanga (with its own clinic) belong to the North County Luiseño Clinic on Rincon. The reservations in Docket 80A1 (Pala, Pauma, Rincon, La Jolla, and San Pascual [Kumeyaay]) organized the San Luis Rey Indian Water Authority to manage water, approve developments, and distribute benefits from the settlement for past damages.

The Luiseño are patriotic and volunteer for the armed forces. They want to protect their sovereign rights within the nation. Most combine Catholicism with their traditional religion. Special events and projects are blessed with burning sage, Catholic and Luiseño sacred songs are sung, and Catholic rituals are performed. Many sacred events are private. All work to protect off-reservation sacred sites, cultural remains, crematoriums, and cemeteries, and the reburial of ancestral remains is required.

Florence Connolly Shipek

See also **California Tribes; Cupeño; Kumeyaay**

Further Reading
Bean, Lowell J., and Florence C. Shipek. "The Luiseño." *Handbook of North American Indians.* Vol. 8. *Califor-*

nia. Ed. Robert F. Heizer. Washington, DC: Smithsonian Institution (1978): 550–63.

Boscana, Father Geronimo. *Chinigchinich: A Revised and Annotated Version of Alfred Robinson's Translation of Father Geronimo Boscana's Historical Account of the Belief, Usages, Customs, and Extravagancies of the Indians of This Mission of San Juan Capistrano Called the Acagchemem Tribe.* Ed. P.T. Hanna. Santa Ana, CA: Fine Arts Press, 1933.

Hyde, Villiana Calac, and R.W. Langacker. *An Introduction to the Luiseño Language.* Banning, CA: Malki Museum Press, 1971.

Shipek, Florence Connolly. *Pushed Into the Rocks: Southern California Indian Land Tenure 1769–1986.* Lincoln: University of Nebraska Press, 1988.

LUMBEE

The majority of the 40,000 members of the Lumbee Tribe of Cheraw Indians reside in Robeson County, North Carolina, where they have lived since at least the mid-eighteenth century. Residing in the marshlands that once constituted much of the county's territory, the Lumbees developed a tightly organized community, one that was affected adversely by the racist attitudes and laws of antebellum North Carolina. Unlike the Cherokees, the tribe was never subjected to removal, but like the Cherokees who failed to remove, they survived the era because of their isolation.

During the Civil War Lumbees were pressed into military service by the Confederacy. By the end of the Civil War, Lumbee opposition to this led to an outbreak of violence, led by a tribal leader, Henry Berry Lowerie. Over the course of ten years, from 1864 to 1874, Lowerie led a band of followers against, first the Confederacy, then the local authorities, and finally the Reconstruction civil authorities. As is fitting a culture-hero, Lowerie's rebellion ended with the capture or death of most of his followers and his mysterious disappearance.

With the end of Reconstruction the Lumbees began pressing their claim for state recognition and the establishment of their own school system. In 1885, the state legislature granted both requests, and for the next eighty years the Lumbees operated their own school system, which included a teacher training institution.

During the same period, the tribe sought federal recognition. In 1953, the state recognized the tribe under the name Lumbee; in 1956, the United States Congress granted recognition under the same name, but the victory proved to be hollow because the act prohibited the Lumbees from receiving federal services.

A resurgence of racism in the 1950s brought the Lumbees national recognition. In January, 1958, the Ku Klux Klan announced that it was going to hold a cross-burning rally in the town of Maxim within the Lumbee territory. Although warned against holding the rally, the Klan persisted, and on the designated evening members began gathering for the rally. So did the Lumbees, who quickly overran the Klansmen and drove them from the field, ending Klan activity in Robeson County.

In 1968 leaders of the tribe decided that the informal organization under which they were operating was no longer adequate. They formed a nonprofit corporation to manage the tribe's affairs—the Lumbee River Regional Development Association (LRDA). This organization consists of fourteen elected directors representing nine districts in Robeson County. They, in turn, elect a chairperson, vice chairperson, and an executive director. Directors are elected for staggered three-year terms.

Over the past one hundred years the Lumbees have produced a large number of important political leaders. These included W.L. Moore, James Oxendine, James Dial, and Preston Locklear, who fought to establish the tribal school system, and D.F. Lowry, James Chavis, and Joe Brooks, who fought for federal recognition in the 1930s (although not together). D.F. Lowry was also instrumental in the passage of the Lumbee Acts in 1953 and 1956.

In the 1960s the Lumbees struggled unsuccessfully to maintain their school system and to preserve the identity of Pembroke State University as a tribal symbol. This latter successful fight was led by Janie Maynor Locklear, Danforth Dial, Helen Scheirbeck, Luther M. Moore, and W.J. Strickland. In 1974 a group of Lumbees sought to have Congress clarify the meaning of the 1956 act. The effort was initiated by Brantley Blue, Linda Oxendine, Jo Jo Hunt, Purnell Swett, and Rod Locklear. Over the years, this struggle has been taken up by a number of other individuals including Arlinda Locklear, Ruth Locklear, Emma Lee Locklear, Cynthia Hunt, Reverend Samual Wynn, William J. Revels, Ruth Dial Woods, Rod Locklear, Adolph Blue, and Judge Dexter Brooks.

As part of the effort to clarify its status, the tribe sought federal recognition through the Bureau of Indian Affairs; however, after the necessary documentation was prepared, it was stopped by a solicitor's opinion which stated that the tribe was not eligible for administrative recognition. Throughout the twenty years of the effort to clarify its status, two individuals have stood out: Adolph Dial and Julian Pierce. Dr. Dial, professor emeritus of Native American studies at Pembroke State University and member of the North Carolina State Legislature, has been a leader in the fight for recognition and educational opportunities. Julian Pierce led Lumbee River Legal Services, Inc., until his death in 1988, at the hands of an assassin. He led the struggle for recognition, organized a community health program, and provided legal assistance to a broad spectrum of the community. Above all, he was a focus for tribal identity.

That identity is manifested most clearly in Robeson County, North Carolina, and particularly in the southern reaches of the county, in settlements that are almost exclusively Lumbee, named Saddletree, Pembroke, Prospect, Union Chapel, Moss Neck, and

Harper's Ferry, to mention but a few. It shows itself in a variety of ways. First and foremost are the kinship networks, which incorporate thousands of people within a close social milieu. Hundreds of family members live near each other and maintain daily contacts. They join together for weddings, funerals, anniversaries, homecomings. Those living out of the community return regularly to participate, traveling from Baltimore, Philadelphia, Detroit, and other locations to visit with family. Marrying-in is the rule, rather than the exception.

A second factor is religion. Most Lumbees belong to one of more than 120 all-Indian churches located in Robeson County. All Protestant, they run the gamut of religious doctrine, but all share and are limited to a common pool of membership—the Lumbee Tribe of Cheraw Indians. Many celebrate an annual homecoming that brings together thousands of tribal members, who attend from all over the United States and from all parts of the community. One does not have to belong to a particular church to attend its homecoming. The churches serve as religious and social centers; many of the most prominent Lumbee leaders receive their training and organize their efforts through the churches. Finally, there are specific activities that express tribal identity. These include an annual homecoming and parade in July; the schools, which are predominantly Lumbee, both students and teachers; and a local Indian newspaper. Together these elements maintain the insularity of the Lumbee tribe and the strong sense of its members as Indian people.

Jack Campisi

Further Reading

Blu, Karen. *The Lumbee Problem: The Making of an American Indian People.* New York, NY: Cambridge University Press, 1980.

Dial, Adolph L., and Davis K. Eliades. *The Only Land I Knew: A History of the Lumbee Indians.* San Francisco, CA: Indian Historian Press, 1975.

Evans, William McKee. *To Die Game: The Story of the Lowry Band, Indian Guerrillas of Reconstruction.* Baton Rouge: Louisiana State University Press, 1971.

Stanley, Samuel, and William C. Sturtevant. "Indian Communities in the Eastern States." *Indian Historian* (1968): 15–21.

Swanton, John R. *The Indians of the Southeastern United States.* Bureau of American Ethnology Bulletin 137 (1946). Washington, DC: Smithsonian Institution Press, 1979.

LUMMI

Prior to the signing of the Treaty of Point Elliott and the creation of the Lummi Reservation at the mouth of the Nooksack River, the Lummi Indians inhabited the area of the northern San Juan Islands and adjacent mainland from Bellingham Bay to Point Roberts in northwest Washington State. The name "Lummi" is derived from the name of one of the dominant Lummi villages, xʷlalƏmƏs, which means "facing one another," and refers to the singular pattern of the placement of longhouses in the village. From their winter villages, the Lummi traveled seasonally to fishing, shellfishing, and plant gathering sites. According to oral tradition the Lummi moved into the area around the mouth of the Nooksack River in the early 1700s, displacing the people living there. Testimony given in the 1920s indicates the Lummi were inhabiting nineteen villages at treaty time.

History

Prior to the establishment of non-Indian settlements in Bellingham Bay in the 1850s, the Lummi were frequent visitors to Hudson's Bay Company posts. After ratification of the Treaty of Point Elliott in 1859, the Lummi Reservation became the home of most members of the tribe. The assimilationist policies of the federal government were such that the Lummi were expected to adopt agriculture as their main means of livelihood. Nevertheless, the Lummi continued to travel to off-reservation fishing and gathering sites, especially their reef net locations. Reef netting was an extremely productive form of fishing that not only met their needs for subsistence but enabled the Lummi to participate in the development of the early commercial salmon fishery of western Washington. Gradually, however, commercial interests squeezed the Lummi out of the industry by usurping the Lummi reef net locations. This was the object of a court case in the 1890s, when the Lummi sought to protect their treaty assured fishing rights to reef net locations at Point Roberts (*United States v. Alaska Packers Association*, C.C. Wash. 79F 152 [1897]). The Lummi were party to land claims cases in the 1930s (*Dwamish et al. v. United States*, 79 Ct. Cl., No. F-275 [1934]) and in the 1950s (Indian Claims Commission, Docket 110). The latter resulted in a $57,000 award in 1970, which the Lummi have refused to accept because they considered it to be far too low. The Lummi have had a Tribal Council since 1925 and a Constitution since 1948. In 1969, the Lummi tribe constructed a state of the art aquaculture project on reservation tidelands which today spawns oysters for planting in reservation waters and salmon for release into the Nooksack River. Throughout the 1900s the Lummi have persistently fought for protection of their treaty fishing rights, and continue to play an important role in the fishing industry of the Northwest, participating in the crab, herring, halibut, and other fisheries in addition to the salmon fishery.

Recent History

The Lummi Nation is governed by an eleven-member Business Council selected by popular vote of the General Council. The General Council is composed of all enrolled adult members of the tribe. In 1992 the total enrolled population was 3,200, of whom approximately one-half were living on the reservation. In 1974, the Lummi participated in a lawsuit against the State of Washington (*United States v. State of Washington*, 384 Supp. 312 [1974]) over treaty fishing rights which culminated in a court mandated allocation of the commercial salmon harvest of Washington State. The recent history of the Lummi is characterized by their involvement in fisheries and other resource-related issues including a landmark decision in 1988 determining that income generated from a treaty right is not subject to federal taxation. The Lummi have been a dominant force in the salmon fisheries through their strong commercial fishing fleet and their participation in management activities through the Northwest Indian Fisheries Commission. The Lummi Nation has attempted to promote further development on the reservation by investing in diverse economic enterprises such as a gaming casino and "spin-off" development from the commercial fisheries including processing operations and plans to construct a marina. Nevertheless, figures issued by the Bureau of Indian Affairs indicate that the Lummi Reservation has a 70 percent unemployment rate. In recent years the Lummi have developed educational programs which include facilities for Lummi students to attend school on the reservation, from preschool through community college. The Northwest Indian College, a two-year community college which started on the Lummi Reservation, is branching out to other Indian communities in the Northwest. Northwest Indian College is one of twenty-four, tribally controlled community colleges in the United States. The tribe publishes a weekly newspaper, the *Squol-Quol.*

Culture

The Lummi are of the Coast Salish language family, originally speaking a dialect of "Straits Salish," although there are few speakers of Lummi today. The Lummi have for years had an active program in the tribal school system to keep the language and other traditions alive. Traditionally Lummi women were skilled weavers making baskets of cedar bark and other plant materials, and producing blankets woven of mountain goat or dog wool. These skills are kept alive by a small group of weavers on the reservation. The traditional religion of spirit dancing is an integral part of the Lummi community, and there are several practitioners of traditional healing. In addition to the Spirit Dance Religion, there are a number of Indian Shakers active at Lummi as well as several denominations of Christianity, most prevalant among them is Catholicism. Several dozen Lummi take part in "war canoe racing" with other Salish tribes. Using fifty-foot cedar dugout canoes, these races take part in different Native communities most every summer weekend.

Daniel L. Boxberger

See also **Fishing and Hunting Rights; Washington State Tribes**

Further Reading

Boxberger, Daniel L. *To Fish in Common: The Ethnohistory of Lummi Indian Salmon Fishing.* Lincoln: University of Nebraska Press, 1989.

Stern, Bernhard J. *The Lummi Indians of Northwest Washington.* New York, NY: Columbia University Press, 1934. Reprint. AMS.

Suttles, Wayne. "Economic Life of the Coast Salish of Haro and Rosario Straits." Ph.D. diss., University of Washington, Seattle, 1951. New York, NY: Garland Publishing, 1974.

———. "Post-Contact Culture Change among the Lummi Indians." *British Columbia Historical Quarterly* 18:1, 2 (1954): 29–102.

MAHICAN

See Mohegan; Stockbridge-Munsee

MAIDU

The term Maidu is derived from the Native word commonly translated as "person" or "human," although it appears to be inclusive of all living beings. Maidu has become a somewhat generic term used to describe three distinct Maiduan speaking peoples, who have historically been identified by the following terms: Maidu (Northeastern Maidu, or Mountain Maidu) of Plumas and Lassen counties; Konkow (Northwestern Maidu, Concow, or Koyongkauwi) of Butte and Yuba counties; and Nisenan (Southern Maidu) of Yuba, Nevada, Placer, Sacramento, and El Dorado counties.

In reality each of these language divisions, which are all of the Penutian family, were further divided into an estimated twenty dialects. In times past, there may not have been any common identity such as a "nation" of people. Instead, it appears that there were numerous autonomous communities who had some linguistic and social ties with their neighbors. Each community had specific terms for self-identification, and some of these terms continue to be used today by tribal members.

Several Maiduan groups entered into a treaty relationship with the United States government in 1851, when eighteen treaties were made throughout California. The fact that none of these treaties were ever ratified by Congress led to litigation and redress through the United States Court of Claims. Hearings began in 1927; in 1971, a per capita settlement was made of $37,630,781.74, or approximately $660 per person. However, during the early portion of the twentieth century, most Maiduan people found themselves living on the outskirts of American towns without any recognized legal ownership of their lands. The only segment of the Maiduan population living on a federal reservation at the beginning of the twentieth century were some of the Konkow, who had been forcibly removed to Round Valley in Mendocino County during 1863.

Beginning in 1906 and extending through 1937, a series of acts were passed by Congress to purchase tracts of land for "homeless Indians" in California. All of the current as well as terminated rancherias within the Maiduan area were established through this process. Three former rancherias are seeking to reverse their terminated status, and four additional groups have filed for federal acknowledgment. A large majority of today's approximately 2,500 Maiduan people continue to live within the areas occupied by their ancestors.

Because of the small land base and limited resources available, there is little or no economic development taking place within Maiduan communities. Unemployment is relatively high and many of the jobs that Native peoples had during the first quarter of the century are being done by migrant laborers. Several of the lumber mills and timber operations in northern California have either shut down or reduced their operations, resulting in a scarcity of work for men who had been previously employed in the field.

The experiences of Maiduan peoples in the American education system have been varied. At the turn of the century many children attended the boarding schools at Greenville, Stewart (Nevada), and Chemawa (Oregon). There are numerous stories of children running away from these schools. Treatment of students was known to be harsh, and racism confronted children on many fronts. Native language, worship, hairstyles, and articles of dress were forbidden, and infractions were often met with corporal punishment. Despite these conditions, elders who attended boarding schools often attest to the good education they received. Among today's Maiduan population, a high dropout rate and poor economic conditions have contributed to major underrepresentation in institutions of higher education. Some Maiduan people find the educational system biased and much of the curriculum insensitive to Native perspectives of history, values, and worldview. Loyalty to one's people might sometimes be expressed by dropping out of school, especially if the school is perceived as something which educates according to the values and perspectives of a system largely developed and controlled by Euroamericans. Recently, however, Maiduan communities have been making strides at retention in the schools, and Native recruiters from local universities have been succeeding at enrolling more high school graduates into college. Local community-based programs such as the Roundhouse Council have developed a preschool and after school tutoring services for students; over the past ten years, the graduation rate of Maidu children from high schools in their service area has risen.

The availability of quality health care remains a concern. Where tuberculosis was a scourge during the first half of the twentieth century, diabetes has become a major health problem among Maiduan people today. The most active of the health care agencies is Northern Valley Indian Health, which has clinics in Oroville and Greenville with service open to the entire Indian community, regardless of tribal affiliation.

Despite conditions adverse to maintaining a traditional culture, there continue to live within Maiduan people some distinct cultural values and expressions. While most people under the age of sixty have very little knowledge of the language, there is still a value in the fragmentary knowledge that does exist; children are often given Maiduan names and certain phrases or words continue to be used by many. The survival of what was once a very rich ceremonial life has suffered various fates throughout Maidu country. At Chico, a major center for ceremonial dances in the upper Sacramento Valley, the tradition ended rather abruptly with the death of hereditary headman Holi Lafonso in 1906; the following year, much of their ceremonial regalia was sold to Stewart Culin of the Brooklyn Museum. In Auburn, a similar scenario unfolded when much of the ceremonial dance tradition there came to a close around 1940, shortly after the death of Jim Dick, the local hereditary headman. Among the Mountain Maidu, the Bear Dance has been an important, vital aspect of both ceremonial and social life through most of this century. In 1988, the site for one of the more widely attended Bear Dances changed ownership and the gathering was prohibited; alternate sites on United States Forest Service lands have been sought. In Placer County several ceremonial dances were reinstituted beginning in 1973, primarily through the instruction and guidance of Konkow elder Frank Day. A ceremonial roundhouse was built near Clipper Gap in 1976, but torn down a year later at the insistence of Placer County, due to the structure's failure to meet county building codes. Today, people from several Maidu, Konkow, Nisenan, and Miwok communities participate in a renewed ceremonial tradition. Acorn, Flower, Toto, Deer, Bear, Coyote, and other ceremonial dances are often held from September through May.

Religious traditions and beliefs are no longer quite as open and obvious as in earlier times. For numerous reasons, much of the Maiduan community has found it necessary to practice their traditional beliefs internally, or take them underground. Where once the religious philosophy was manifested in observable everyday events and grand ceremonial performances within the context of village life, today much of this tradition is played out privately within each person as they have come to understand it. Ceremonial dinners honoring the fall acorn harvest, and the earth's renewal in the spring, are observed in several communities. Grass game, a form of gambling, with its genre of luck songs remains a popular activity at gatherings. A few individuals practice the art of basketry, and most of them have benefited from the instruction of elder Maidu weaver Lilly Baker.

Several Maiduan individuals are making an impact in the contemporary art world. The works of artists Harry Fonseca, Dal Castro, Frank Tuttle Jr., and the late Frank Day have been exhibited and published widely throughout the United States and Europe over the past twenty years.

Brian Bibby

See also **California Tribes**

Further Reading

Dixon, Roland B. "The Northern Maidu." *Bulletin of the American Museum of Natural History* 17:3 (1905): 119–346.

Hill, Dorothy J. *The Indians of Chico Rancheria.* Sacramento: State of California Resources Agency, Department of Parks and Recreation, 1978.

Roberts, Helen H. *Concow-Maidu Indians of Round Valley—1926.* Ed. Dorothy J. Hill. Chico: Association for Northern California Records and Research, 1980.

Shipley, William, ed. and trans. *The Maidu Indian Myths and Stories of Hanc'ibyjim.* Berkeley, CA: Heyday Books, 1991.

Simpson, Richard. *Ooti: A Maidu Legacy.* Millbrae, CA: Celestial Arts, 1977.

Wilson, Norman L., and Arlean Towne. *Selected Bibliography of Maidu Ethnography and Archeology.* Sacramento: State of California Resources Agency, Department of Parks and Recreation, 1979.

MAKAH

The Makah, or qʷidičča?a·tx̌, meaning "People of the Cape," were also known in the early historic period as Klasset or Classet; both are derivatives of the name ʔa·?asa·tḥ, a Nootkan name which means "people to the south." The Makah Tribe of Indians is the sole representative of both the Nootkan cultural complex and the Wakashan language family in the United States. Prior to contact with non-Indians, Makah people lived in five coastal villages which were occupied throughout the year: Ozette, Tsoo-yess, and Whyatch were on the Pacific Coast, while Neah Bay and Biheda bordered the Strait of Juan de Fuca. These five semi-autonomous villages were linked by a common language, Makah, and by kinship and marriage.

By 1853 the traditional village system showed signs of stress. Biheda had been abandoned as a result of a devastating smallpox epidemic, and Neah Bay began its rise as the most central of Makah villages. The Treaty of Neah Bay, signed in 1855, established the boundaries of the Makah Reservation, but did not recognize the multiple village system. Subsequent expansion of the reservation boundaries to include villages other than Neah Bay occurred in 1872 and 1873, via three executive orders. The fifth village of Ozette, which is furthest from Neah Bay, was not added to the Makah Reservation. Rather, a separate Ozette Reservation was created by executive order in 1893, to accommodate sixty-four Makahs who declined to move to Neah Bay. By 1917, the remaining Makahs moved to Neah Bay to comply with strict school attendance policies and to avail themselves of the conveniences Neah Bay could offer, like Washburn's Store (est. 1902).

Over the next two decades, many striking changes affected life on the Makah Reservation. Commercial logging began in 1926, and provided the tribe with a source of income for tribal members in addition to traditional fishing occupations. Logging ventures also provided motivation for the construction of the first paved road to the reservation in 1931. In the following year, Washington State built a public elementary and high school on the reservation after receiving a gift of land from Luke Markistum, a Makah. This arrangement guaranteed Makah children a public school education without the trauma of boarding school, traveling long distances, or family displacement.

Changes were also affecting the tribe's governing structure. The Makahs voted to accept the Indian Reorganization Act in 1934, developed their Constitution in 1936, and ratified the corporate Charter in 1937. These documents provided for a five-person Tribal Council; members serve staggered three-year terms and are elected by eligible tribal voters. The Charter provides that the chairman is elected by vote of the five Tribal Council members at the beginning of each calendar year.

Makah Tribal Council representatives began to address issues surrounding the treaty rights of members, and applied experiences garnered during the turbulent 1940s to this quest. The Makah land claim filed with the Indian Claims Commission (Docket 60) was eventually separated into Docket 60 and Docket 60-A. The former requested redress for loss of sealing and halibut rights and was dismissed in 1959. After years of negotiating, the federal government and the tribe reached a compromise regarding Docket 60-A, and the tribe received title to two offshore islands, Tatoosh and Waadah via PL 98-282 in 1984.

While Docket 60-A moved slowly through the federal system, the tribe concentrated on securing its treaty fisheries and was a participant in *United States v. Washington* in 1974. Because the Makahs had an active and healthy interceptive fishery prior to the Boldt Decision, the case did not benefit the Makahs as much as the Puget Sound tribes. Some tribal members believe that the Boldt Decision adversely affected the tribe because the decision favored terminal fisheries and gave no credit to tribes which had flourishing marine economies prior to the decision.

In addition to the defense of treaty fishing rights, Makah priorities extended to the preservation and management of the tribe's ancestral language and culture, the education of Makah people, and the development of economic opportunities for tribal members. In 1970, a severe storm exposed archaeological artifacts from the Ozette village; Makahs collaborated with Washington State University to excavate and conserve over 55,000 artifacts preserved when a catastrophic mudslide buried a section of Ozette long before contact with non-Indians. The extraordinary Ozette excavation and the resulting collection prompted the tribe to build the Makah Cultural and Research Center, which stores, exhibits, and interprets the tribe's artifacts on the reservation. Over 250,000 people have visited the museum since it opened in 1979, generating tourist revenue as well as jobs for tribal members.

The tribal members' interest in cultural resources extends to the language as well. Only a dozen Native speakers of Makah still exist. To preserve this vanishing resource, the Makah Cultural and Research Center staff have operated a language preservation program since 1978. The Makah Language Program operates education and research programs which teach Makah to children, while working with elders to produce a grammar and a dictionary.

January 1992 tribal census data indicate that there are 1,869 members of the Makah tribe; approximately 1,079 enrolled members live on the 27,000-acre reservation, along with 300 other Indians and 325 non-Indians. The largest proportion of the 442 households on the reservation are concentrated in Neah Bay, although families still live at other winter village sites. The average unemployment rate is approximately 51 percent, and fluctuates seasonally; approximately 49 percent of reservation households have incomes classified below the poverty level. The highest employment rates occur in the summer, when ocean fishing, tourism, and logging are at their respective peaks. Stable employment opportunities exist primarily with tribal government and its related operations, the Indian Health Service clinic, the Neah Bay public school system, and the year-round retail businesses on the reservation. The tribe is involved in aggressive economic development efforts to increase employment, and is exploring plans to develop a destination resort and a marina with a safe harbor.

Ann M. Renker

See also **Washington State Tribes**

Further Reading

Kirk, Ruth. *Hunters of the Whale.* New York, NY: Harcourt, Brace and Jovanovich, 1974.

Marr, Carolyn. *Portrait in Time: Photographs of the Makah by Samuel G. Morse, 1896–1903.* Seattle, WA: Allied Printers, 1987.

Pascua, Maria. "Ozette: A Makah Village in 1491." *National Geographic Magazine.* Vol. 180, no. 4. (October 1991): 38–53.

Renker, Ann, and Erna Gunther. "Makah." *Handbook of North American Indians.* Vol. 8. *Northwest Coast.* Ed. Wayne Suttles. Washington, DC: Smithsonian Institution (1990): 422–30.

Renker, Ann, and Greig W. Arnold. "Exploring the Role of Education in Cultural Resource Management: The Makah Cultural and Research Center Example." *Human Organization* 47:4 (1988): 302–7.

Ruby, Robert, and John A. Brown. "The Makah." *A Guide to the Indian Tribes of the Pacific Northwest.* Norman: University of Oklahoma Press (1986): 125–28.

MALISEET

The Houlton Band of Maliseet (pop. 554) is a federally recognized tribe, governed by an elected Tribal Council (chair plus six members), serving staggered four-year terms. With seven bands in Canada, it forms the Maliseet Nation (pop. 3,000). Aboriginal Maliseet lands are divided by the Northeast United States–Canada boundary, but the 1794 Jay Treaty gives them free border-crossing rights. In the 1870s, when logging and potato farming transformed the region, several Maliseet-hunting families settled along the Meduxnekeag River at the edge of Houlton. Without a reservation, the small community was frequently forced to relocate, until settling at "Hungry Hill" above the town dump. Women worked as housecleaners while men did mill-work, odd jobs, and some hunting and fishing. Both also made baskets and picked "fiddle-heads" (an edible fern) to survive.

In 1970, Maliseets and other off-reservation Natives formed the Association of Aroostook Indians to improve their social situation and to gain recognition for their Native rights. In 1973, they won access to services through Maine's Department of Indian Affairs, as well as Indian scholarships and free hunting and fishing licenses. In 1979, during the Maine Indian land claims negotiations, Maliseets protested that Penobscot claims overlapped with their lands. One component group, newly incorporated as the Houlton Band of Maliseets, gained inclusion in the 1980 Maine Indian Land Claims Settlement Act as the sole successor to the Maliseet Nation in the United States. While various unaffiliated Maliseet families in the region were not included and remain without the benefits of formal Indian status, this "tribe" received $900,000 to buy up to 5,000 acres of trust land, plus entitlement to federal services (health, education, and child welfare), funding for housing, and loan guarantees for economic development.

Despite federal recognition, they remain fully subject to state jurisdiction and must make payments in lieu of state property taxes. Since 1988, they own a new tribal center built on their own land (currently about 800 acres) near Houlton. Although high unemployment (56 percent) and alcoholism persist, the band has thirty-six people on its payroll with an annual budget of $1.75 million, engages in economic development projects, and is building fifty new homes on its land.

Harald E.L. Prins

See also **Passamaquoddy; Penobscot**

Further Reading

Erickson, Vincent. "Maliseet-Passamaquoddy." Ed. Bruce G. Trigger. *Handbook of North American Indians.* Vol. 15. *Northeast.* Washington, DC: Smithsonian Institution (1978): 123–36.

McBride, Bunny. "Promises to Keep, Part 3." *The Maine Times* 19:15 (January 16, 1987): p. 14

Maine Indian Program. *The Wabanakis of Maine and the Maritimes: A Resource Book about Passamaquoddy, Maliseet, Micmac, and Abenaki Indians.* Bath, ME: New England Regional Office of the American Friends Service Committee, 1989.

Nicholas, Andrea B., and Harald E.L. Prins. "The Spirit in the Land: The Native People of Aroostook." *The County, Land of Promise: A Pictorial History of Aroostook County.* Ed. Anna F. McGrath. Norfolk, VA: The Donning Company Publishers (1989): 18–37.

Wherry, James D. "The History of Maliseets and Micmacs in Aroostook County, Maine." U.S. Senate. *Proposed Settlement of Maine Indian Land Claims: Hearings before the Select Committee on Indian Affairs.* 96th Cong., 2d sess., S.2829. Vol. 2. Washington, DC: U.S. Government Printing Office (1980): 506–609.

MANDAN

See Three Affiliated Tribes

MANSO

See Tortugas; Ysleta del Sur Pueblo

MARICOPA

See Pee-Posh

MASHPEE

See Wampanoag

MATTAPONI

This Mattaponi group lives on a state reservation of about 125 acres in King William County, Virginia. It is inhabited by about sixty people, with many more living off the reservation. Residents live under the Treaty of 1677, which makes their government autonomous from that of the county surrounding them. Tribal officers include a chief, assistant chief, and three or more councilors, who meet as needed in gatherings closed to all but qualified voters. Voters are Mattaponi-descended males, eighteen or older, who live on the reservation at least six months per year. Serious judicial cases go to the county superior court; legal questions that the council and four white trustees cannot solve go to Virginia's attorney general; urgent problems go directly to the governor. The tribe maintains personal contact with the governor by "paying tribute" in game each November, as required by the treaty.

A late nineteenth century spinoff from the Pamunkey Reservation nearby, the Mattaponis got their own state school around 1920, and their own Baptist congregation in 1932. High school courses were added in 1958, but the school was closed in 1966; children now attend county public schools.

Homes on the reservation were wired for electricity around 1950 and paved roads were built in 1956. In the mid-1970s, after joining the Coalition of Eastern Native Americans and learning grant-writing techniques, the tribe received several grants for education and community improvement. Then-Chief Curtis L. Custalow, Sr., also became active in the Native American Rights Fund, serving for several years on its board.

Traditional culture remains only in a few crafts (pottery, beadwork). Language and lifeways today are those of their Anglo neighbors. Most adults work at salaried jobs off-reservation.

Helen C. Rountree

See also **Upper Mattaponi**

Further Reading

Mooney, James. "The Powhatan Confederacy, Past and Present." *American Anthropologist*, n.s. 9 (1907): 129–52.

Rountree, Helen C. "The Indians of Virginia: A Third Race in a Biracial State." *Southeastern Indians Since the Removal Era.* Ed. Walter L. Williams. Athens: University of Georgia Press (1979): 27–48.

———. *Pocahontas's People: The Powhatan Indians of Virginia Through Four Centuries.* Norman: University of Oklahoma Press, 1990.

———. "Indian Virginians on the Move. "*Indians of the Southeastern United States in the Late 20th Century.* Ed. J. Anthony Paredes. Tuscaloosa, AL and London, England: University of Alabama Press (1992): 9–28.

Speck, Frank G. *Chapters on the Ethnology of the Powhatan Tribes of Virginia.* Indian Notes and Monographs 1:5. New York, NY: Museum of the American Indian, Heye Foundation, 1928.

MENOMINEE

Before first contact with European explorers in the seventeenth century, the Menominee (Menomini) people lived in a nearly 10 million acre area of lakes, rivers, and forests extending along Lake Michigan, roughly from Milwaukee into upper Michigan, and west as far as central Wisconsin. By the mid-nineteenth century, a succession of treaties signed with the United States reduced the tribe's aboriginal homeland to a 233,900-acre reservation located in northern Wisconsin, about forty-five miles west of Green Bay.

Fortunately, the tribe still possessed nearly 350 square miles of prime timber. Aided by the United States Forest Service, the tribe initiated sustained-yield management of their forest in 1908. The Bureau of Indian Affairs (BIA) helped construct a sawmill that became the major source of income and employment. The BIA, however, failed to train Menominees for higher-level positions in the management of sawmill operations or in forest management. Alleging mismanagement of their timber resources, the Menominees filed a suit against the federal government in 1934 in the United States Court of Claims. After seventeen years the court ruled in favor of the tribe and awarded the Menominees $7.65 million.

By 1951 the Menominee Indians were among the most self-sufficient tribes in the United States. They owned a 220,000-acre forest and a sawmill representing a capital investment of $1.5 million. Moreover, they had accumulated $10 million on deposit in the United States Treasury. Unfortunately, the Menominees' image as one of the most "advanced" Indian tribes in the nation marked them as prime targets for "termination," a 1953 government initiative that was one of the most ill-considered congressional experiments in the history of national Indian policy.

When the Menominee Termination Act was signed by President Dwight D. Eisenhower on June 17, 1954, the Menominee became one of the first tribes slated for termination. Although the act was not fully implemented until 1961, many of the negative effects of the policy surfaced years before the final termination began. Expenses involved in the preparation for termination nearly exhausted the tribe's cash assets in the United States Treasury. When a lack of funds forced the closing of the tribal hospital, tuberculosis became a major health problem. Menominee children were no longer legally recognized as members of the tribe if their birthdays fell after the date of closure of the tribal rolls in 1954. Badly needed sources of leadership were depleted when economic decline and rising anxieties about their future led many younger and better-educated Menominees to leave their reservation for the cities. When the Menominee Reservation was finally terminated on May 1, 1961, it became a new Wisconsin county. Quickly tagged by state officials as "an instant pocket of poverty," Menominee County and its residents faced an extremely uncertain and unpromising future.

The new county's tax base was totally inadequate to support needed government services, and the standard of living in the county remained the lowest in the state. After ten years of continuous direct and indirect federal and state aid, the county could not raise the revenues necessary to receive matching federal grants-in-aid.

Faced with the near certainty of fiscal collapse by the late 1960s, Menominee leaders made a momentous decision. They began developing and selling waterfront lots on the county's lakes and rivers to non-Indians. Tribal reaction to the sale of tribal land to whites, coupled with the possible loss of political control over their own affairs as large numbers of non-Menominees established year-round residences and became a voting majority within the county, triggered the rise of a new tribal organization in 1970 called the Determination of Rights and Unity for Menominee Shareholders (DRUMS). DRUMS demanded that Congress establish a new trust relationship characterized by Menominee self-determination over tribal affairs.

For a century and a half, the federal government had assumed a paternalistic responsibility for the welfare of Indians. Ironically, this same sense of federal responsibility helped make Menominee restoration possible. Because of it, Congress and the BIA were vulnerable to the claim by DRUMS that the federal government had a special obligation to rectify the damaging effects of its termination policy on the Menominees. Even policy makers who considered Indian assimilation inevitable were persuaded that the Menominees should be returned to their reservation and allowed the same privilege granted to other tribes—the freedom to play a determining role in the pace and methods for achieving their own assimilation.

Beginning in 1970, DRUMS organized a broad constituency both within and around Menominee County. It utilized public demonstrations, favorable media coverage, and court actions to delay the development and sale of Menominee land. DRUMS leaders such as Ada Deer, a former chairperson of the Menominee tribe, and in 1993, the assistant secretary for Indian Affairs in the United States Department of the Interior, lobbied in Wisconsin and Washington to gain gradual state and federal backing for the organization's goals. Success came on December 22, 1973, when President Richard M. Nixon signed the Menominee Restoration Act into law, which restored federal recognition and protection to the Menominee and reestablished nearly all of their former reservation. The act also provided concrete evidence to all Native Americans that the era of Indian termination was over.

Today the Menominee people are building a new foundation of economic and political strength to support the growth of greater tribal self-determination in the years ahead. As of 1992, enrolled Menominees number more than 7,100 (up from 3,270 in 1957) with 3,400 tribal members living on the 233,900-acre reservation. While the Menominee forest remains central to the uniqueness of the tribe as a people, the reservation is also a major center for new economic development supported in large part by the establishment of extensive tribal gaming operations in 1987. In addition to being the largest single employer on the reservation, proceeds from gaming provide major funding for an array of health and welfare services, economic development programs, and other forms of community investment. Elected leaders are using the resources provided by their gaming operations to invest in the future.

Above all else, the experience of termination in the 1970s produced a foundation for lasting self-determination in the form of the new Constitution and Bylaws of the Menominee Indian Tribe. Adopted in 1977, the Bylaws provide for an elected nine-member Tribal Legislature, a tribal chairperson elected by the Legislature (Glen Miller in 1993), a tribal judiciary, and a general council.

With the restoration of tribal status, Menominee culture is holding its own. Although most members belong to either the Catholic, Presbyterian, or Assemblies of God churches, the traditional Big Drum Religion is also practiced. The tribe has preserved or restored the Menominee clan structure, clan figures, and the Menominee creation and origin story. The Menominee language is in use and taught in tribal schools and at the College of the Menominee Nation near Keshena. The Menominee Nation Powwow has been held annually since 1977.

The Menominee face a diversity of challenges. They must find ways to promote continued economic growth, combat chronic drug and alcohol abuse, and work to preserve their Native language, heritage, and culture. They must resolve conflicting interests within the tribe and, at the same time, rebuff repeated external challenges to sovereign rights guaranteed by existing treaties with the United States. The model of governance in place today sustains the tribe as a competitive equal with other units of local and state government. The Menominee Nation is prepared to meet the challenges of survival in the twenty-first century.

Nicholas C. Peroff

See also **Government Policy: Termination and Restoration; Natural Resource Management**

Further Reading

Keesing, Felix M. *The Menomini Indians of Wisconsin: A Study of Three Centuries of Cultural Contact and Change.* Memoirs of the American Philosophical Society 10. Philadelphia: The Society, 1939.

Menominee Tribal News. Keshena, WI, 1976–ongoing.

Ourada, Patricia K. *The Menominee Indians: A History.* Civilization of the American Indian 146. Norman: University of Oklahoma Press, 1979.

Peroff, Nicholas C. *Menominee DRUMS: Tribal Termination and Restoration, 1954–1974.* Norman: University of Oklahoma Press, 1982.

Spindler, George, and Louise Spindler. *Dreamers without Power: The Menomini Indians.* New York, NY: Holt, Rinehart, and Winston, 1971.

MENTAL HEALTH

Native Americans are among the most impoverished ethnic groups in the United States. Many live in isolated and rugged areas where the climate is often harsh, economic opportunities limited, and transportation to obtain services and basic necessities is lacking. A large number of Native American families live without adequate nutrition, shelter, safe water supply, or modern sanitation facilities.

Historically, Native Americans have been confronted with being repeatedly driven from their homelands, exposed to new diseases, discriminated against, lost support and security from severely weakened nuclear families, tossed in the throes of economic impoverishment, and experienced the psychological consequences of an imposed dependent status. The negative impact of these difficult life circumstances has contributed to putting Native Americans at high risk for mental disorders. However, they are presently the fastest growing ethnic minority, with about one-half of their number aged eighteen years or younger. This suggests a resiliency and core of strength that can be relied on to favorably resolve their present difficulties.

Types of Mental Disorders in Native Americans

Many people believe that mental disorders are more prevalent among Native Americans, but documentary information is lacking. Native Americans suffer from the same disorders as the dominant population, and rates for schizopheniform, somatization, and personality disorders are comparable. Rates for cognitive impairment disorders seem to be slightly higher, possibly a consequence of alcoholism. Experience suggests substance abuse may be three times more common in some Native American communities, and anxiety and affective disorders (depression) may be two times more prevalent. Demoralization, an impairing condition that does not always receive psychiatric attention, is widespread.

Suicide, alcoholism, and violence appear to occur more frequently among Native Americans, becoming almost epidemic in some areas and a major concern in all areas. Rates for these disorders are presented in figures 1, 2, and 3.

Clearly, the major health problem confronting Native Americans is the destructive impact of alcoholism. Although deaths from alcoholism are probably more accurately reported for Native Americans than others, the amount of alcoholism is unacceptable and is a first priority for the Indian Health Service (IHS).

Suicide, alcoholism, and violence are especially prevalent in youth and are related to the degree of tribal integrity. Tribes with more traditional cultural organizations have lower rates for these disorders. Encouragingly, there has been a decrease in the amount of these disorders over the past ten years.

Native Americans most frequently request assistance for depression, anxiety, violence, substance abuse, and family conflicts. Mental disorders in Native Americans are identifiable by the same signs and symptoms and respond to the same treatment modalities as do those seen in other ethnic groups.

Mental Health Problems in Native Americans

Although Native Americans suffer from a higher rate of mental illness than most other ethnic groups, there has been no evidence to support a genetic or constitutional predisposition. The greater amount of mental illness seems to be a consequence of the difficult life circumstances and associated pressures which impinge on many Native Americans.

Individuals and communities vary in their ability to cope with these pressures. Some show only mild and brief consequences with few impairments. For others, the degree of stress is so severe that they become significantly impaired. The types of stress become organized about several major themes and play an etiological role in the development of specific disorders.

Hopelessness is a state in which individuals experience a feeling of futility, lose hope, see themselves swept along by the tide, and feel powerless to intercede. Hopelessness can grow from repeated experiences of failure, such as having to make continual major readjustments with no time for a stabilizing period of success, having promises repeatedly broken, and when there is a lack of education. Isolation, lack of economic resources, disenfranchisement, and limited opportunities also contribute to a feeling of futility and despair. From a clinical perspective, hopelessness is significantly associated with such disorders as depression, melancholy, and demoralization. Efforts to counter feelings of despair and despondency can lead to self-medicating behaviors of substance abuse. Acceptance of powerlessness to change a situation of endless gloom may be taken as justification for self-destructive behavior, including suicide.

Desperation is a condition in which there is a perceived threat, a fear of possible loss of control which brings an urgency to act before it is too late. Because it is more discouragement than abandonment, desperation can be episodic. Desperation can evolve from long-term experiences of harassment, discrimination, exploitation, enforced dependency, encroachment, and isolation. Feelings of desperation are frequently identifiable in such disorders as anxiety and obsessive/compulsive reactions. It also has a component of violence, including suicide, other self-destructive behavior, assault, phobias, and sleep disturbances. To a lesser extent, desperation is implicated in rage outbursts, mild depressive disorders, and substance abuse.

Family dissolution has been the most damaging to the mental health of Native Americans. The family is normally a protective haven, a refuge in which individuals are given nurturance, support, and understanding. For many Native Americans, the impact of the Anglo culture has created a profound identity crisis which carries over into the family and the community. Prior to the coming of the Europeans, Native Americans were a resourceful and competent people, living in close harmony with their surroundings. Men and women had tasks essential to the survival of the family and the community. With spreading Euroamerican control, these energetic, self-sustaining Native American communities were changed into dependent, restricted enclaves lacking opportunities. The security of tribal organization was lost. Tribes were forced to look to the agency, the representative of the federal government, for food, clothing, and shelter. What might appear on first glance as benign treatment soon proved to be devastating for Native Americans.

Unable to perform their traditional roles, many Native Americans lost their sense of purpose. There was often little for adults to do. The boring and sedentary lifestyle in a bleak setting often led to feelings of despair and resentment. Attempts to find relief in constructive activities were not always successful. Men and women lacked special skills and training for new jobs. Even when they sacrificed to acquire an education, the most favorable of these underdeveloped communities could provide jobs for only 10 to 30 percent of the residents. Efforts to relocate to off-reservation sites met with discrimination and loss of community supports. These failures added to the despair and resentment.

Adults caught up in cultural transition could not be strong role models. The more severely affected families became dysfunctional, no longer able to serve as a safe refuge. Many adults and children turned to substance abuse to relieve intolerable pressure and pain, self-medicating with alcohol, the most destructive legacy of the contacts with the European settlers. The debilitating consequences of this addiction added fresh fuel to an already rapid downward cycle. Family dissolution is an ingredient in all psychopathology, but it is of even greater importance in the treatment and prevention of mental illness.

Community Efforts to Address Mental Illness

Conditions of desperation, hopelessness, and family dissolution have been cited as consequences of contacts between Native Americans and settlers. They have contributed to psychopathology in tribal communities by fostering feelings of low self-esteem, anger, powerlessness, and despondency. Once started, de-structive patterns take on a self-perpetuating quality, making it difficult to intervene.

To break the cycle, all potential resources should be mobilized. There must be a strong desire to change. Individuals and communities need to gain a sense of control over their lives, directing their own destinies. Once empowered, they develop the self-confidence to evaluate their situation, identifying problems and noting available assisting resources. Then begins the lengthy and difficult process of implementing the changes needed to improve the quality of life in the community.

Several tribal communities have started programs to reduce mental illness. The Flathead Indian community in Montana, for example, troubled by increases in alcoholism and violence, scheduled an open community meeting to discuss how they might improve the quality of life in the community. Participants decided to look to their traditions and culture for resources to deal with current problems. Blending the input from elders with that of younger professionals, they devised a plan for regaining control of their lives by taking strength from ancient spiritual customs and beliefs. The mental health services delivery system was reorganized with elders assuming greater responsibility for assisting the youth. Traditional methods for maintaining a strong healthy mind/body were added to the available treatment methods.

The Jicarilla Apache Reservation in northern New Mexico experienced an epidemic of suicides among high school students. Alarmed tribal leaders called a

Figure 1
Suicide Deaths and Mortality Rates[1]
American Indians and Alaska Natives, and U.S. All Races, 1955–1988

Calendar Year	Indian and Alaska Native Number	Indian and Alaska Native Rate	U.S. All Races Number	U.S. All Races Rate	U.S. Other Than White Rate	Ratio Indian to: U.S. All Races	Ratio Indian to: U.S. Other Than White
1988....	221	14.5	30,407	11.4	6.9	1.3	2.1
1987....	221	15.0	30,796	11.7	6.9	1.3	2.2
1986....	211	15.0	30,904	11.9	6.8	1.3	2.2
1985....	204	14.1	29,453	11.5	6.7	1.2	2.1
1984....	181	12.9	29,286	11.6	6.6	1.1	2.0
1983....	196	14.7	28,295	11.4	6.4	1.3	2.3
1982....	178	13.6	28,242	11.6	6.4	1.2	2.1
1981....	191	15.5	27,596	11.5	6.8	1.3	2.3
1980....	173	14.1	26,869	11.4	6.7	1.2	2.1
1979....	188	16.1	27,204	11.7	7.9	1.4	2.0
1978....	150	14.0	27,294	12.0	7.4	1.2	1.9
1977....	199	20.5	28,681	12.9	7.8	1.6	2.6
1976....	168	17.9	26,832	12.3	7.6	1.5	2.4

[1]Age-Adjusted Rate per 100,000 Population
The age-adjusted suicide death rate for American Indians and Alaska Natives has decreased 32 percent since its peak in 1975 of 21.2 deaths per 100,000 population. The Indian rate for 1988 was 14.5 compared to the U.S. All Races rate of 11.4.
Source: Indian Health Service, U.S. Department of Health and Human Services. Trends in Indian Health Service— 1991. Rockville, MD.

community-wide meeting. At the meeting, the IHS was asked to provide technical assistance to the committee formed to address the problem. The resulting comprehensive plan included a community-wide traditional reaffirmation and forgiveness session, setting up telephone hot lines, instructing parents and youth in methods for recognizing behavior indicative of suicide intent, and preparing parents to assume greater responsibility for youth activities.

The Winnebago Indian community in Nebraska, distressed with the magnitude of substance abuse and related problems, organized local resources to deal with this pervasive health problem. Seeking new approaches that might prove more effective, social and psychologically oriented agencies in the community were linked with the local general medical hospital. Hospital staff were trained in counseling alcoholic individuals. The complex physiological changes associated with alcoholism were aggressively attended in the hospital, and patients' families were actively involved in the treatment regimen. Although dealing with the most difficult cases, the program soon documented an amazing rate of success with a condition often regarded as intractable. In 1992, the program was chosen from more than 300 federally funded programs to receive the award for excellence in the treatment of alcoholism.

These programs have common origins resulting from community action. Although they often turned to elders for direction, the initial impetus came from youth in the community.

Governmental Programs and Perspectives

Indian Health Service. It is encouraging to see communities taking responsibility for addressing their mental health needs. Tribes, however, are not currently in a position to do it all for themselves. They must have help from multiple sources. The IHS Mental Health Program is the primary source to which Native Americans look for assistance. Mental health services are available in each of the 147 health care centers operated either by the IHS or tribes. A health care center, with a trained professional staff, provides comprehensive services to a population in a defined geographic area. A large number, 57 percent, of the mental health staff are Native Americans. The typical program offers crisis oriented outpatient services on request, and on-call emergency services outside usual clinic or hospital hours.

State Agencies. Where there are no federal reservations, Native Americans, like other citizens, are eligible for mental health services from the state in which they reside. Where there are federal reservations, the lines of service delivery by the state are more complex. Native American communities often take a position that they are sovereign nations whose boundaries cannot be violated by the states. Such a position can preclude state agencies from bringing services to reservation residents, unless the tribe is willing to relinquish some of its sovereignty in negotiations. This situation has been a particular problem in involuntary commitment of mentally ill persons

---

Figure 2
Homicide Deaths and Mortality Rates[1]
American Indians and Alaska Natives, and U.S. All Races, 1955–1988

| Calendar Year | Indian and Alaska Native | | U.S. All Races | | U.S. Other Than White | Ratio Indian to: | |
	Number	Rate	Number	Rate	Rate	U.S. All Races	U.S. Other Than White
1988....	214	14.1	22,032	9.0	28.2	1.6	0.5
1987....	199	14.1	21,103	8.6	26.4	1.6	0.5
1986....	240	16.3	21,731	9.0	27.2	1.8	0.6
1985....	191	14.3	19,893	8.3	24.4	1.7	0.6
1984....	189	14.5	19,796	8.5	24.9	1.7	0.6
1983....	217	16.4	20,191	8.6	26.4	1.9	0.6
1982....	188	14.9	22,358	9.7	30.0	1.5	0.5
1981....	207	17.9	23,646	10.4	33.0	1.7	0.5
1980....	212	18.1	24,278	10.8	35.0	1.7	0.5
1979....	209	18.9	22,550	10.4	36.0	1.8	0.5
1978....	218	21.2	20,432	9.6	33.4	2.2	0.6
1977....	197	20.9	19,968	9.6	34.5	2.2	0.6
1976....	185	21.6	19,554	9.5	36.4	2.3	0.6

[1]*Age-Adjusted Rate per 100,000 Population*
The age-adjusted homicide death rate for American Indians and Alaska Natives falls between the rates for the U.S. Other than White and U.S. All Races population. In 1988, the Indian rate was 14.1 deaths per 100,000 population compared to 28.2 for the U.S. Other than White, and 9.0 for the U.S. All Races populations
Source: Indian Health Service, U.S. Department of Health and Human Services. *Trends in Indian Health Service—1991.* **Rockville, MD.**

to a hospital for treatment. Some states have refused to credit the action of tribal courts in ordering such persons into state hospitals for treatment.

Urban Indians

Approximately one-half of Native Americans now reside off reservations, primarily in larger cities. Many relocated seeking greater opportunities than are available on most reservations. It is unfortunate that federal policies which did little to address the economic deprivation existing on reservations also failed to support relocation. Persons moving from the reservation faced the loss of benefits in the form of education, health care, shelter, and subsistence. The loss of health care placed particular hardships in view of the high cost of medical care and the intensity of stress associated with relocation.

Beginning in 1980, the IHS added the Urban Health Care Branch with responsibility for providing health services to Native Americans residing in urban centers. In l992, thirty-four such centers were in operation, funded from a budget of $17.1 million, about 1 percent of the total IHS budget. The meager funding limits the Urban Health Care Centers to acting as referral centers which locate free or low cost sources of health care and direct Native American clients to these agencies. Mental health services have not regularly been a part of the programs, but in 1992 each Urban Center was given approximately $30,000 to make a survey of needs for mental health care.

Figure 3
Alcoholism Deaths and Mortality Rates[1]
American Indians and Alaska Natives,
and U.S. All Races, 1969–1988

	Indian and Alaska Native		U.S. All Races		Ratio American Indian and Alaska Native, to U.S. All Races
Calendar Year	Number	Rate	Number	Rate	
1988....	389	33.9	16,882	6.3	5.4
1987....	288	25.9	15,513	6.0	4.3
1986....	272	24.6	15,525	6.4	3.8
1985....	281	26.1	15,844	6.2	4.2
1984....	316	30.0	15,706	6.2	4.8
1983....	293	28.9	15,424	6.1	4.7
1982....	298	30.7	15,596	6.4	4.8
1981....	338	35.8	16,745	7.0	5.2
1980....	382	41.3	17,742	7.5	5.5
1979....	398	45.1	17,064	7.4	6.1
1978....	437	54.5	18,490	8.1	6.7
1977....	429	55.5	18,437	8.3	6.7
1976....	425	58.2	18,484	8.6	6.8

[1]*Age-Adjusted Rate per 100,000 Population*
In 1988, the age-adjusted alcoholism death rate for American Indians and Alaska Natives was at its highest level since 1981. It was 33.9 deaths per 100,000 population or 5.4 times the U.S. All Races rate of 6.3.
Source: Indian Health Service, U.S. Department of Health and Human Services. *Trends in Indian Health Service—1991.* **Rockville, MD.**

Outlook for Mental Health Services

A branch of the IHS, the fledgling Mental Health Programs Branch, which first appeared in 1965, has grown considerably. The expansion has not been sufficient to keep pace with the rapidly growing Native American population. A number of crucial issues must be resolved if the mental health needs of Native Americans are to be met.

First, the federal policy of keeping Native Americans in restricted, hopeless, and dependent circumstances has contributed heavily to a rate of mental disorders that is two times the national average. Reservations cannot support today's rapidly increasing populations. The reservations must be rendered hospitable, accommodating, and favorable for achievement, or a program of planned relocation with appropriate supports must be implemented.

Second, increased resources for mental health programs are crucial. The IHS Mental Health Program has demonstrated progress in reducing mental health problems even though it is only funded at about one-half the ascertained level of need. Additional staff and facilities are needed to continue improving the quality of mental health care. Persons with specialized training for serving children, dysfunctional families, and mobilizing community resources must be added to the present professional staff. It is encouraging to note the growing number of Native Americans entering programs offering training in the health professions. Important components essential to a full range of services are not available in most Native American communities. Shelter care, transitional living, self-help groups, residential care for children, vocational training, day care, and foster home placement are conspicuously absent. Funds are also needed for planning, training, and community education about mental health.

A final issue is the prevention of mental illness at the grass-roots level. Although tribal and IHS programs must continue to provide services to Native Americans in crisis, prevention efforts will be the most successful means to reduce mental illness. Native Americans themselves are in the best position to take action for dealing with the pathology stemming from cultural identity confusion. Several communities have demonstrated the ability to organize resources for coping with such major problems as violence and substance abuse. Increased funding and expanded support systems will contribute to improved mental health care, but only Native American communities can recreate a climate for positive self-esteem and confident know-how. By examining traditional and contemporary cultures, Native Americans can build a strong new status, integrating the best features from each culture. In taking these initiatives, they can restore their well-being and security, significantly reducing the amount of depression, violence, substance abuse, and other psychological problems presently curtailing the happiness and progress of individuals and communities.

George McCoy

See also Alcohol Abuse; Families; Health; Indian Health Service

Further Reading

Berlin, Irving N. "Effects of Changing Native American Cultures on Child Development." *Journal of Community Psychology* 15:3 (1987): 299–306.

May, Philip A. "Suicide and Self-Destruction." *American Indian and Alaska Native Mental Health Research* 1 (1987): 52–69.

Meinhardt, Kenneth and William Vega. "A Method for Estimating the Underutilization of Mental Health Services by Ethnic Groups." *Hospital and Community Psychiatry* 38 (1987): 1186–90.

Reiger, Darrel A., et al. "One-Month Prevalence of Mental Disorders in the United States. *Archives of General Psychiatry* 45 (1988): 977–86.

Trimble, Joseph E. "Self-Perception and Perceived Alienation among Indian Groups." *Journal of Community Psychology* 15 (1987): 316–32.

MERIAM COMMISSION

Formally designated as the Survey of Indian Affairs, the Meriam Commission's investigation of Indian conditions and administration in 1926 to 1927 exposed severe problems and helped effect subsequent reforms.

The investigation was in response to a barrage of earlier criticism against federal Indian policies by reformer John Collier. Starting with his 1922 agitation against legislation on disputed Pueblo land titles, Collier's unrelenting attacks essentially centered on the incompetence of federal Indian administration, its many failures to protect Indians, and its assimilationist goals. Collier, instead, espoused cultural pluralism or greater toleration for Indian heritage. Conversations in early 1926 among Thomas Jesse Jones of the Phelps-Strokes Fund, W.F. Willoughby, director of the Institute for Government Research (IGR), and Lewis Meriam, an IGR subordinate, led the three men to suggest a general investigation to Secretary of Interior Hubert Work. After several planning sessions, on June 12, 1926, Work formally requested the IGR to conduct the survey with Meriam as the director.

The IGR arrangement with Work included Meriam's selection of staff members, completion of the work within a year, access to Bureau of Indian Affairs (BIA) records, and full cooperation of BIA field personnel. The investigation's general approach ignored how much BIA administration had improved over time, in favor of evaluating how its services compared to those provided to non-Indians by private or public agencies. John D. Rockefeller, Jr., provided $125,000 to fund the project. Meriam was well qualified to head the survey. He held degrees in English and government from Harvard and had graduated from two law schools. An experienced statistician and expert in government job classification, Meriam, like many progressives, strongly believed in scientific administration, expertise, and efficiency. He assembled the following staff: Ray A. Brown, law professor at the

University of Wisconsin, *legal aspects*; Edward Everett Dale, historian at the University of Oklahoma, *economic conditions*; Emma Duke, American Health Association, *Indian migrants to cities*; Herbert Edwards, National Tuberculosis Association, *health*; Fayette Avery McKenzie, sociologist at Juniata College, *existing records*; Mary Louise Marks, social statistician at Ohio State University, *family life and women*; W. Carson Ryan, Jr., education professor at Swarthmore College, *education*; and William J. Spillman, Bureau of Agricultural Economics, *agriculture*. Henry Roe Cloud, noted Winnebago educator, proved "invaluable" as the group's advisor and intermediary in meetings with Indians.

The Commission began field work in November 1926 and during the next seven months it traveled 25,000 miles and visited 95 jurisdictions in the Far West and Great Lakes regions. The Commission seldom worked as a group or held formal staff meetings. When it arrived at a location, the specialists usually broke off as individuals or small groups to visit BIA facilities pertinent to their interests and to question agency workers, Indian leaders, and local whites. Commission members then met at night or while traveling to compare notes and make plans. After completing field work in June, 1927, they returned to Washington and drafted their report which Meriam and two staffers edited. The 872-page report, *The Problem of Indian Administration*, appeared the following February.

Although generally moderate in tone, the report boldly announced that "an overwhelming majority of the Indians are poor, even extremely poor, and they are not adjusted to the economic and social system of the dominant white civilization." The later chapters severely criticized BIA education, health care, and economic failures. The report characterized Indian schooling as grossly inadequate in preparing students for life on or off reservations and scored boarding schools for overcrowding, deplorable health conditions, and inadequate diets. BIA health care was censured for shockingly high disease rates, services woefully below minimum standards, and failure to undertake preventive medicine. Indian poverty was attributed to mistaken past policies, especially land allotment, forced patenting, and leasing. On the issue of cultural pluralism, the report equivocated by recognizing Indians' pride in their heritage, but it warned that Indians had lost their past means of subsistence and must adjust to the "predominating civilization of whites."

The major recommendations of the report focused on improving BIA administration and services by increased funding and greater efficiency. This moderate approach ignored any radical restructuring of the BIA or its policy philosophy. The single most important recommendation was the creation of a division of planning and development within the BIA to provide badly needed expertise and greater continuity of planning for reservations. The report also requested an emergency appropriation of $1 million to improve the diet of boarding school students. Some of the most interesting (but usually overlooked) findings in the report deal with Indian out-migration because of reservation destitution. One topic which baffled the commission was the technically complex subject of Indian irrigation. Two experts, Porter J. Preston and Charles A. Engle, conducted a separate investigation and released a critical report in mid-1928.

Assessing the results of the Meriam Commission will always be problematic. The report received a generally positive response by government officials and most Indian reformers. Collier's reaction, however, was mixed, and he began lobbying for a Senate investigation even before the report was released. He apparently sensed that the recommendations would fail to support his contention that radical changes were needed. In any case, Congress in early 1928 approved an investigation by a subcommittee of the Senate Indian Affairs Committee which ran intermittently until 1943. The Meriam Report, however, offered a handbook of reforms for the Hoover administration, from 1929 to 1933. Indeed, the appointments of Charles J. Rhoads as Indian commissioner and J. Henry Scattergood as assistant commissioner were largely based on their support for the survey findings. Meriam took a leave of absence, and with a Rockefeller grant, spent the next four years working within the Interior Department to implement the recommendations. Although he was unsuccessful in achieving the division of planning and development, he convinced Secretary of Interior Lyman Wilbur to reorganize the BIA in 1931, and to appoint several younger and more capable administrators to top posts. BIA funding rose from $15 million in 1928 to $28 million in 1931, but hiring additional personnel and raising salaries absorbed most of the increase. Little went to Indians. After 1933, when Collier became Indian commissioner, the impact of the Meriam Report became even more tenuous, although it had laid a groundwork for the Indian New Deal.

Donald L. Parman

See also **Bureau of Indian Affairs; Educational Policy; Government Policy**

Further Reading

Critchlow, Donald T. "Lewis Meriam, Expertise, and Indian Reform." *The Historian* 47 (1981): 325–44.

Parman, Donald L., ed. "Lewis Meriam's Letters during the Survey of Indian Affairs 1926–1927." *Arizona and the West* 24:1, 2 (1982): 253–80, 341–70.

Philp, Kenneth R. *John Collier's Crusade for Indian Reform 1920–1945.* Tucson: University of Arizona Press, 1977.

The Problem of Indian Administration. Baltimore, MD: Johns Hopkins Press, 1928. New York, NY: Johnson Reprint Corporation, 1971.

Prucha, Francis Paul. *The Great Father.* Vol. 2. Lincoln: University of Nebraska Press, 1984.

MESCALERO

See Apache

MESQUAKI

(Also known as Fox, and Sac and Fox of the Mississippi in Iowa). Federally recognized as the "Sac and Fox of the Mississippi in Iowa," the Mesquaki Nation (the "Red Earth People") live primarily on or near their tribally owned settlement located near Tama, on the Iowa River, in central Iowa. Although closely associated with the Sacs (the Sac and Fox Indians), the Mesquaki remained behind when the Sacs were removed from Iowa in the mid-nineteenth century. In 1857, the Mesquaki purchased the first eighty acres of land which forms the nucleus for their present settlement. Additional purchases have increased the size of the land base to 4,535 acres, and since this land was purchased with Mesquaki funds, it is known as the "Mesquaki Indian Settlement," and not a reservation. All of the acreage is owned by the tribe and none has been allotted.

The trust title for the Mesquaki Settlement originally was held by the State of Iowa, but in 1896 it was transferred to the United States Department of the Interior. Championing a program of assimilation, the Bureau of Indian Affairs (BIA) immediately opened a boarding school for Mesquaki children in the neighboring town of Toledo, but many Mesquaki refused to enroll their children. After a series of legal confrontations, federal officials opened a day school on the settlement in 1912. The day school temporarily closed in 1937, but Mesquaki parents complained and one year later the BIA opened a larger day school, enrolling Mesquaki children through the eighth grade. Disputes regarding education reemerged in the 1950s and 1960s, but today the Sac and Fox Settlement School, a bilingual and bicultural institution, continues to enroll children from the pre-kindergarten years through the eighth grade. Older students continue their education at boarding schools or in secondary schools in neighboring communities.

During the early twentieth century the Mesquaki Settlement was governed by a traditional Tribal Council led by Pushetonequa, whom the government recognized as chief, and who was a leader of the "progressive" or Youngbear faction. They were opposed by the Oldbears, a group of more traditional Mesquaki led by Mosquibushito. In 1937, the Mesquaki established a new tribal government under the Indian Reorganization Act. The new Constitution provided for statutory regulations and the establishment of a seven member Tribal Council containing a chairman, vice chairman, treasurer, and secretary. Tribal Council members are required to be enrolled members of the tribe and must reside on the settlement. Since the late 1940s, the rivalry between the Youngbears and the Oldbears has continued in contests over Council seats and in other arenas of tribal politics.

During much of the twentieth century some Mesquaki have cultivated and harvested crops of corn and soybeans on part of their settlement. Others have worked as agricultural laborers or sought employment in the communities that surround them. Part of the tillable lands on the settlement have been leased to non-Indian farmers. During the 1980s, the Mesquaki established an Economic Development Zone along Highway 30 on the northern border of the settlement, and opened a bingo facility there in 1987. Following this facility's success, the tribe erected a new, enlarged building in 1989, and in 1993 the tribe plans to develop a casino and reorganize the whole enterprise as the Mesquaki Bingo and Casino, under the Indian Gaming Regulatory Act. The Mesquakis anticipate that additional businesses such as a hotel and restaurant will be constructed in the Economic Development Zone.

Although the Mesquaki have recently embraced a broad spectrum of economic opportunities, they remain a rather conservative people who are proud of their continued cultural survival. The Mesquaki have retained their kinship ties and a sense of family pervades the settlement. Religious ceremonies from Christian, Native American Church, and Drum Society traditions still form the focus of much social activity. The annual Mesquaki Powwow is held in August each year and attracts many Mesquaki, other tribespeople, and non-Indians. The Mesquaki boasted a total enrollment of 1,027 members in 1991, 812 of which lived on the settlement or in neighboring communities. The remainder are scattered throughout the United States.

R. David Edmunds

See also Ribbonwork; Sac and Fox

Further Reading

A Brief History of the Sac and Fox of the Mississippi in Iowa. Tama, IA: Sac and Fox of the Mississippi in Iowa, ca. 1980.

Gearing, Fred O. *The Face of the Fox.* Chicago, IL: Aldine Publishing Company, 1970.

Gearing, Fred O., Robert McC. Netting, and Lisa R. Peattie, eds. *Documentary History of the Fox Project, 1948–1959: A Program in Action Anthropology.* IL: University of Chicago, 1960.

McTaggart, Fred. *Wolf That I Am: In Search of the Red Earth People.* Boston, MA: Houghton Mifflin, 1976. Norman: University of Oklahoma Press, 1984.

MÉTIS

See Cree; Ojibwa: Chippewa in Montana; Ojibwa: Chippewa in North Dakota

MEWUK

See Miwok

MEXICAN KICKAPOO

See Kickapoo in Oklahoma and Texas

MIAMI

Historically there was one Miami tribe whose homeland was principally in what is today known as Indiana, western Ohio, and eastern Illinois. By treaty and force, the Miami were divided into two groups in 1846. More than 600 were removed by canal boat to a reservation in Kansas and later moved again to Ottawa County, Oklahoma, where they and their close "cousins," the Peoria, Wea, and Kaskaskia, purchased 6,000 acres of land from the Shawnee. Left behind, primarily in Allen, Huntington, and Miami counties of north central Indiana, were more than 1,500 tribal members whose chiefs were granted private reserves. The lands of both groups were eventually allotted to various families and were mostly lost to land speculators and tax sales, leaving both the Oklahoma and Indiana Miami largely without land by 1930.

Twentieth-Century History

Both groups were federally recognized tribes until 1897, when a United States assistant attorney general signed an administrative order ending tribal status for the Indiana Miami. Officials of the Bureau of Indian Affairs claimed that those Miami who had been removed to Kansas and Oklahoma were the "official" Miami Nation, and the only group entitled to federal recognition and benefits.

After allotment land losses the Miami drifted away from their former reservation lands. The Indiana Miami were forced to leave their traditional homeland by 1900 in order to survive. The Oklahoma Miami, despite dispersing from their former Oklahoma reservation, have retained their federal status as a recognized tribe. This has provided them with health care, education, and legal protection not available to their Indiana kinfolk.

In 1937, tribal members in Indiana organized the Miami Nation of Indians of the State of Indiana, Inc., a not-for-profit corporation, as a vehicle for fundraising and cohesiveness. Frances M. Shoemaker was chosen principal chief in 1949 and remained in that position until his retirement in 1993, at which time he became chief of the Elders Council. To provide a focal point for his people, Chief Shoemaker and the tribe organized a pageant with more than thirty participants portraying Miami history and culture. Revenues were used to fund legal expenses in the fight to restore federal recognition. The pageant continued for nearly two decades during the mid-twentieth century. An even older tradition is the nearly one-hundred-year-old Miami picnic and reunion held on the third Sunday of each August, in Wabash City Park. The picnic and twice annual general meetings have been the threads of continuity that have held Miami tradition and culture together in Indiana.

The Miami Tribe of Oklahoma occupies a fairly new tribal headquarters in Miami, Oklahoma. In addition to office spaces for tribal officials, there is a library, a gathering room, and gift shop where tribal crafts are sold, and a modern kitchen and dining area where over 200 elders are fed each day. The Oklahoma Miami have also constructed a 40- by 120-foot brick longhouse about five miles north of the city. Meals are served to elders there on a daily basis, too, and the elders teach traditional crafts to those interested. Most official tribal meetings are held at the longhouse, which also houses many significant remembrances of the tribe's past.

Government

Raymond O. White, Jr., a descendant of Miami chiefs Richardville and LaFontaine, became tribal chairman of the Miami Nation of Indiana in 1980, and was appointed principal chief upon Frances Shoemaker's retirement in February 1993. As tribal chairman, he provided leadership for three primary efforts: restoring federal recognition, initiating economic development, and regaining tribal land. The principal chief is very powerful and to overturn his veto of Council action requires a 100 percent majority vote of the Council. The principal chief serves for life as do all Council members, who are chosen by their clans. The governance structure was revised in April, 1993, eliminating the position of tribal chairman and providing for a vice-chief, principal chiefress, and spiritual leader. Between 500 and 800 people attend twice yearly general tribal meetings. The Miami Tribal Council determines the tribal roll as permitted in the Treaty of 1854, and members are officially enrolled by the tribal secretary and historian. Total enrollment in 1992 was 6,000; about 2,500 people were living in Indiana, while the remainder were residing in other states.

The Miami Tribe of Oklahoma has a constitutional government, which is headed by Principal Chief Floyd E. Leonard, a descendant of Tau-Cum-Wah, the sister of the great Miami War Chief Little Turtle. Second chief is David L. Olds, Shelva Mitchell is secretary, and Jane Otho Downing and Judy Davis serve as Council members. All business of the tribe is transacted by the above-named Council, which meets monthly or as needed. The enrolled membership meets annually to elect new representatives and to make changes in the tribe's Constitution. In the early 1990s, the Miami Tribe of Oklahoma was in the process of adopting a new tribal constitution to update the previous document and to allow for such elements as a tribal court system.

Current Situation

The Miami Nation of Indiana has spent most of the twentieth century in a struggle to regain federal recognition. In June of 1992, the Branch of Acknowledgment and Research of the Bureau of Indian Affairs notified the Indiana Miami that their petition for federal recognition had been finally rejected, ending a ninety-five-year administrative battle. In August of 1992, the Miami, joined by the Native American Rights Fund, decided to sue the federal government asking for a summary judgment overturning the 1897 administrative dissolution order and reinstating federal recognition. Decisions are expected in 1993.

In 1990, the Miami Nation acquired three brick structures in Peru, Indiana. The largest of these buildings now houses the Miami tribal offices, job training programs, a day-care center, a tribal museum, social welfare programs, and a large gymnasium/auditorium where meetings and tribal gaming operations are located. Miami bingo has provided funds for tribal operations, legal expenses, economic development, and land acquisition. In August of 1992, the Miami acquired a thirty-eight-acre tract of land along the Mississinewa River near Peru, directly across from Seven Pillars of the Mississinewa, a Miami sacred and historical site. Their intent is to construct a modern longhouse on the property where they can meet and maintain their culture, arts, and crafts.

The Miami Tribe of Oklahoma has been successful in several economic ventures. They own a profitable trucking line, transporting their primary commodity of gasoline and fuel nationally. In addition, they have purchased and renovated a thirty-unit motel and supper club seating one hundred twenty people on Grand Lake of the Cherokees in Oklahoma. These facilities are located in a high-traffic tourism area, and also in close proximity to several Native American bingo operations. Miami businesses are prospering and more are planned for the future.

The Miami Nation of Indiana has survived one hundred years of deliberate governmental attempts to eliminate its existence, and present generations have redoubled their efforts to preserve Miami heritage and birthrights. The Miami Tribe of Oklahoma has survived its exile from its homeland and obtained an important place among the thirty-nine sister tribes of Oklahoma. The two Miami tribes were founding sponsors of the Minnetrista Council for Great Lakes Native American Studies in Muncie, Indiana, which is "dedicated to preserving and promoting Woodland Native American Culture." They have since been joined by twenty-four other tribal groups with roots in the southern Great Lakes region.

Nicholas L. Clark, Sr.

See also **Oklahoma Tribes; Peoria**

Further Reading

Baxter, Nancy Niblack. *The Miamis!* Indianapolis: Guild Press of Indiana, 1987.

Carter, Harvey Lewis. *The Life and Times of Little Turtle: First Sagamore of the Wabash.* Urbana: University of Illinois Press, 1987.

Godfroy, Clarence. *Miami Indian Stories.* Comp. and ed. Martha Una McClung. 1961. Winona Lake, IN: Light and Life Press, 1987.

Rafert, Stewart J. "The Hidden Community: The Miami Indians of Indiana, 1846–1940." Ph.D. diss., University of Delaware, 1982.

———, ed. *Miami Testimony Pursuant to Congressional Legislation of June 1, 1872 Concerning Partition of the Me-Shin-Go-Me-Sia Reserve, Miami and Grant Counties, Indiana.* Indianapolis: privately printed by the Minnetrista Cultural Center, Muncie and Indiana Humanities Council, 1991.

MICCOSUKEE

The Miccosukee Tribe of Indians of Florida was founded in 1962. Until that time, its members had been considered a part of the Seminole tribe, to whom they are closely related through language, culture, and kinship. By the 1950s a great majority of the Seminoles resided on federal reservations and had begun to acculturate rapidly. However, a group of Mikasuki-speaking Indians who still lived in the Everglades wanted to preserve their traditional lifestyle and religious values, and follow the political leadership of their medicine men and council. They appealed to the federal government for separate recognition, and after much struggle were allowed to draft a Constitution and form their own government. The new tribe adopted the spelling Miccosukee for their political entity; this also differentiated them from the Mikasuki language, which is spoken by most Seminoles as well.

Most of the 400 enrolled members live in modern housing near the tribal headquarters complex, which is located forty miles west of Miami. The tribe operates its own educational, health, and recreational programs, as well as police protection and a court system. Although the tribal government leaders are elected, politics within the tribe are dominated by close-knit family and clan affiliations. For over twenty years the Miccosukees were headed by Chairman Buffalo Tiger, who was instrumental in founding the tribe.

Today the Miccosukees exercise control over about 200 thousand acres of wetlands, most of which are suitable primarily for hunting or fishing. One third of this is a federal reservation. The tribal enterprises, which include a restaurant and service station complex, as well as a tribal culture center, are primarily oriented towards tourism. Individual members still operate airboat rides and gift shops, and Miccosukee arts and crafts such as patchwork clothing and basketry are highly prized by tourists and collectors alike. The tribe has recently opened a bingo hall on land nearer to metropolitan Miami, where they expect to emulate the economic success from bingo enjoyed by the Seminoles.

Harry A. Kersey, Jr.

See also **Seminole**

Further Reading

Covington, James W. "Trail Indians of Florida." *Florida Historical Quarterly* 58 (1979): 37–57.

Kersey, Harry A., Jr. *The Seminole and Miccosukee Tribes: A Critical Bibliography.* Bloomington: Indiana University Press, 1987.

———. "Seminoles and Miccosukees: A Century in Retrospective." *Indians of the Southeastern United States in the Late 20th Century.* Ed. J. Anthony Paredes. Tuscaloosa, AL and London, England: University of Alabama Press (1992): 102–19.

Lefley, Harriet P. "Effects of a Cultural Heritage Program on the Self-Concept of Miccosukee Indian Children." *Journal of Educational Research* 67 (1974): 462–66.

Sturtevant, William C. "Creek into Seminole." *North American Indians in Historical Perspective.* Eds.

Eleanor B. Leacock and Nancy O. Lurie. New York, NY: Random House (1971): 92–128.

West, Patsy. "The Miami Indian Tourist Attractions: A History and Analysis of a Transitional Mikasuki Seminole Environment." *Florida Anthropologist* 34 (1981): 200-24.

MICMAC

Located in northern Maine, the Aroostook Band of Micmacs (pop. 482) gained federal recognition of its tribal status in 1991. Together with 28 other bands, all of which are based in Canada, it forms part of the Micmac Nation (pop. 25,000). They have free border-crossing rights guaranteed under the 1794 Jay Treaty. Traditionally a migratory people subsisting on hunting and fishing, the Micmacs have been allied with the Penobscot, Passamaquoddy, and Maliseet in the Wabanaki Confederacy since the seventeenth century. Until recently, they formed a landless and scattered community.

Their subsistence was primarily based on crafts (especially splint basketry) and seasonal labor (logging, river-driving, blueberry-raking, and potato-picking). More than half are at least "half-blood" and still speak the native language. In 1970, with other off-reservation Natives, they formed the Association of Aroostook Indians (AAI) to combat poverty and discrimination. Lobbying for their Native rights, they gained state recognition of their tribal status in 1973, becoming eligible for Maine's Department of Indian Affairs (DIA) services (emergency health care, food, transportation, and fuel), Indian scholarships, and free hunting and fishing licenses. Due to inadequate resources, documentation of Micmac history in Maine was not available when the state's other tribes participated in the 1980 settlement of the Maine Indian land claims (which also resulted in the DIA's closing).

Dissolving the AAI, the band incorporated the Aroostook Micmac Council in 1982, headquartered in Presque Isle. It is governed by a biannually-elected president, and an eight-member board of directors. It formed a successful mail-order basketry business and sponsored a documentary film about their community. In 1991, with scholarly and legal support (through Pine Tree Legal Assistance, the state's federally funded legal aid agency), it persuaded the federal government to pass The Aroostook Band of Micmacs Settlement Act. Signed into law by the president, it provides not only acknowledgment of its tribal status, entitling members to certain federal services and benefits, but also a $900,000 land acquisition fund to purchase 5,000 acres (trust lands), as well as a $50,000 property tax fund. As a result, the band and its lands now have the same status as other Maine tribes, and their lands accorded federal recognition under the terms of the Maine Indian Claims Settlement Act of 1980.

Harald E.L. Prins

See also **Passamaquoddy; Penobscot**

Further Reading

McBride, Bunny. "The Micmac of Maine: A Continuing Struggle." *Rooted Like the Ash Trees: New England Indians and the Land.* Ed. Richard G. Carlson. Naugatuck, CT: Eaglewing Press (1987): 35–39.

——. *Our Lives in Our Hands: Micmac Indian Basketmakers.* Gardiner, ME: Tilbury House, 1991.

Maine Indian Program. *The Wabanakis of Maine and the Maritimes: A Resource Book about Passamaquoddy, Maliseet, Micmac and Abenaki Indians.* Bath, ME: New England Regional Office of the American Friends Service Committee, 1989.

Prins, Harald E.L. "Tribulations of a Border Tribe: A Discourse on the Political Ecology of the Aroostook Band of Micmacs, 16th–20th Centuries." Ann Arbor, MI: University Microfilms International, 1988.

Prins, Harald E.L., and Karen L. Carter. *Our Lives in Our Hands.* Watertown, MA: Documentary Educational Resources, 1985. Film. 50 min.

MIGRANTS AND REFUGEES

Since its early establishment in the Americas, European colonialism has intentionally practiced a policy of dismemberment of indigenous territories and dislocation of their people. The nation-states that followed the formal political independence from the European metropolis continued and refined this conception of colonial administration, disregarding the principles of ethno-linguistic unity and coherence, consolidating instead a fragmented and deeply divided mosaic of Native local communities. Regional divisions and national borders split entire indigenous nationalities into various uncommunicated segments: Quechua and Aymara Indians are found in the territories of Bolivia, Peru, Chile, Argentina, and Ecuador; Mapuches share the Chilean and Argentinian sides of the Andes; Guajiros occupy the peninsula by the same name that is divided by the border of Colombia and Venezuela; Campa-Asháninka, Matsés-Mayoruna, and Cashinahua are in Peru and Brazil; Miskito are in Nicaragua and Honduras; and Nahuas and Mayas of different linguistic subdivisions live all throughout Central America and Mexico. The United States-Mexico border is no exception—a longstanding history of frontier conflicts and tense relations between the two countries has produced a complex map of ethnic distribution where Yaquis, Opatas, Apaches, Kickapoos, Pimas, Papagos (Tohono O'odham), and other Indian societies share the territory of both nation-states in similar conditions of subordinate minority. The list is far from being complete, for almost everywhere in the Americas the original indigenous ethnic and bioregional territories have been subjected to processes of institutionalized disjunction.

Since the post-World War II years, the old structural tendency of Euroamerican nation-states of establishing and expanding an integrated and interdependent (albeit antagonistic and competitive) global division of labor has increased rapidly, producing two concomitant phenomena. On the one hand, states and transnational corporate interests have developed a new modality of international division of use and appropriation of the environment. Indigenous territories and resources are increasingly becoming the target of recolonization efforts. The Amazon region is perhaps the most eloquent example of this renewed assault on Indian space and resources. On the other hand, the liberal idea of a "free" work market developing as an inherently circumscribed, homogeneous human mass exclusively subject to a particular state administration is also being contested by recent developments.

During the last decades we have witnessed processes of massive transfer of cheap and controllable foreign labor from economically depressed regions and countries to more developed ones. This is the latest manifestation of a trend toward the internationalization of the division of labor, which has been steadily built during five centuries of colonialism. The Indian people of Latin America are a substantial part of this rearrangement of the national and international labor market. Today, between 40,000 and 60,000 Mixtec, Zapotec, Chinantec, and Trique Indians from the southern Mexican State of Oaxaca are working in the agricultural fields of California, Oregon, and Washington, and in the service sector of Los Angeles and other urban areas of California. Recently, Maya speakers from the Tzeltal and Tzotzil communities of the State of Chiapas, Mexico, have begun the migration cycle to the United States. Mixtecs and Zapotecs from Oaxaca are also migrating to the fields of the southeastern states and the urban areas in Illinois. This massive Mexican Indian presence in the United States labor market is essentially due to economic reasons: indigenous people from impoverished and ecologically devastated regions of Mexico migrate cyclically to the United States to earn some dollars that are almost entirely sent as remittances to their families and communities. A recent estimation established that the Mixtec Indians' remittances of one year to their communities in Oaxaca are equal to the entire annual budget of the State of Oaxaca.

Economic deportation is not limited to Mexican Indians. Recently, a group of one thousand Quechua sheepherders from the central Andes of Peru were brought to Nevada by Basque ranchers as highly specialized rural workers, well adapted to the rough conditions of life at high altitude.

The new assaults on Indian territories and resources perpetrated by the expanding national and transnational enterprises throughout Latin America have been particularly violent in Guatemala and Central America, where brutal repression has accompanied the occupation and expropriation of Indian lands. An estimated 100,000 Maya Indians have been massacred in Guatemala during the last forty years. In the early 1980s more than 70,000 Guatemalan Maya Indians sought refuge across the border of Mexico. An estimated 40,000 were relocated in refugee camps by the Mexican government; others remained hidden in the jungle of southern Mexico or interspersed with

Mexican indigenous people and mestizo peasants; finally a constant flow of Maya Indian political refugees began to reach the United States border, making its way deep into the country. Kanjobal Indians from the Guatemalan highlands are living in Indian Town (Florida), and communities of exiled Quiché, Keqchis, Ixils, and Mams are dispersed throughout the peripheral states of the country. As in the case of the other indigenous people from Latin American countries, the United States Census Bureau does not identify these groups as ethnically different and of Indian ancestry; they are, in a sense, invisible indigenous people that are deeply impacting, with their Indian culture, the multicultural character of the popular and Native American sectors of the country.

Stefano Varese

***See also* Chicanos as Indians; Indian Identity**

Further Reading

Douglas, Massey, et al. *Return to Aztlan: The Social Process of International Migration from Western Mexico.* Berkeley: University of California Press, 1987.

Kearney, Michael, and Carole Nagengast. "Anthropological Perspectives on Transnational Communities in Rural California." *CIRS Working Paper* (1988).

Spicer, Edward. *Cycles of Conquest.* Tucson: University of Arizona Press, 1962.

Stuart, James, and Michael Kearney. "Causes and Effects of Agricultural Labor Migration from the Mixteca of Oaxaca to California." *Working Papers in U.S.-Mexican Studies*, No. 28. San Diego: University of California, 1981.

MILITANCY

See Red Power

MILITARY SERVICE

During the twentieth century, the military and military service has had a profound and lasting impact on American Indians and American Indian life. As the nation's largest single employer, the military is also the largest trainer of personnel, and a major provider of higher educational benefits. These functions and extramilitary activities have also dramatically shaped Indian affairs. Recent estimates from the Veterans Administration and United States Census data suggest that there are 160,000 living veterans who are American Indians. This represents approximately 10 percent of all living Indians. Moreover, when this figure is compared to the percentage of non-Indian veterans in the general population, Indians were three times as likely to have served in the military as non-Indians in the twentieth century. Indians have participated in all the major declared and undeclared wars in which American military personnel have fought. The conditions, however, governing their participation changed as federal legislation affecting their legal status changed. In 1917,

a sizable number of American Indians, perhaps as many as one-half of the Indian population, were not citizens and thus not eligible for the draft. Nevertheless, approximately 10,000 Indians served in World War I. The contributions of these Indians led Congress in 1924 to grant all Indians blanket citizenship. In the period between World Wars I and II, little thought was given to how the Indians' new legal status would alter their relationship to the federal government in the event of another war. When America's first peacetime draft was enacted in the fall of 1940, there were 4,000 Indians in the military; by war's end, approximately 25,000 Indians had served.

Although no firm figures exist, it has been estimated that between 10,000 and 15,000 American Indians saw action in Korea, and that over 42,000 Indian military personnel were stationed in southeast Asia during the Vietnam War. Estimates of Indian participation in the military after it became an all-volunteer force in 1972 have ranged between 20,000 to 30,000. This figure still represents a significant percentage of the total Indian population, as contrasted with non-Indian military personnel as a percentage of the total population.

Indians have served in the military throughout our nation's history, but their participation in the armed forces during World War II marked a turning point in Indian/white relations. This war marked the single largest exodus of Indian males from the reservations. The impact of World War II on Indian affairs, however, cannot be understood solely in terms of numbers. Military service provided an unparalleled opportunity for Indians to compete in an arena where their skills as fighters inspired respect. Because Indians did not usually serve in segregated units like their Black counterparts, there was considerable contact between whites and Indians, and this contact apparently reinforced white images of Indians as fierce warriors. It was not surprising that Indians in the military, regardless of rank, were indiscriminately called "chiefs" by their white buddies. And, commanding officers frequently observed that Indians made "perfect soldiers." Since no scientific studies exist of the capacities of Indian soldiers, compared to whites, it is difficult to know whether these observations reflected the pervasiveness of white stereotypes rather than Indians' actual performance. Indians from tribes with a bona fide warrior tradition, such as the Sioux, volunteered in disproportionate numbers and excelled in the front lines. Nonetheless, members of those tribes without this fighting reputation, including the Five Civilized Tribes of Oklahoma and the Navajo, exhibited similar stereotypical behavior.

While Indians saw action in all branches of the armed forces during World War II, and while the total number of Indians who enlisted in the Marines never reached more than 800, the experiences of Indian Marines came to represent the contributions of all Indians in the military. The Marines were an "elite" corps, supposedly composed of the best soldiers. Given the Indians' warrior-like reputation, the Marines naturally welcomed Indians into their ranks. The Navajo Code Talkers, a special communication unit which worked behind enemy lines and used the Navajo language to report on Japanese troop maneuvers, won high praise from their commanders and were credited with providing critical information which helped the Allies in the South Pacific. From the ranks of this group came several tribal leaders, including former Navajo tribal chairman and national Indian leader, Peter MacDonald.

It is also not surprising that one Indian Marine, Ira Hayes, a full-blood member of the small Pima tribe in Arizona, emerged the most famous Indian soldier of World War II, if not in American military history. A paratrooper, Hayes landed in February of 1945 on Iwo Jima. There he took part in an attack on Mount Suribachi during which six Marines raised the United States flag on the summit of the volcano in the midst of heavy fire. An *Associated Press* photographer snapped a picture at the moment the flag was raised, and it quickly became one of the most inspiring war photographs ever taken, catapulting the event and its participants into national prominence. Because he was an Indian, Hayes received special attention. His struggle to raise the stars and stripes appealed to the sentiments of white America—Hollywood could not have created a better advertisement of a people united against a common foe. Before Iwo Jima, Ira Hayes was just another Marine who happened to be an Indian. Afterwards he personified the hoped for assimilation of Indians into the mainstream of American life. During the remainder of his brief life, Hayes struggled with the unwelcome notoriety that accompanied this memorable picture. Destitute and suffering from alcoholism, he died in 1955 at the age of thirty-three.

In contrast to Indian Marines, Indian sailors did not make headlines, although nearly three times as many served in the Navy. Although there are no statistics regarding the number of Indians who served as commissioned officers, an Oklahoma Cherokee, Joseph ("Jocko") Clark, reached the rank of admiral. All told, Indians from more than thirty tribes served in the Navy, the majority hailing from smaller bands in California and the Pacific Northwest, although members of New York State tribes served in both the Navy and the Merchant Marines. Indians also served in the Army Air Corps, the precursor to the Air Force, during World War II. The most highly decorated Indian aviators came from the more assimilated tribes in Oklahoma, Texas, and Wisconsin, and had graduated from Bureau of Indian Affairs schools in California and Kansas.

Military service during World War II did more than provide an arena in which Indians and whites could perform as equals on the battlefield. One of the most significant side benefits of Indian participation in the military was the fact that thousands of young Indian men and women made a decent living for the first time in their lives. While it was not much by white standards, the average Indian soldier's monthly income allowed him or her (several hundred Indian women saw duty as nurses, and in the auxiliary "Wacs" and "Waves") to buy all kinds of consumer goods and still send something home for the family. Suddenly radios, heaters, phonograph records, and refrigerators started turning up on the reservation. Indians could acquire the goods and services of white society, thus bringing the outside world still closer to home. By 1944, the average Indian's income was $2,500—two and one-half times that of 1940. Military life provided a steady job, money, status, and a taste of the white world to previously isolated and unassimilated Indians.

The more Indians dealt with other soldiers, the more they began to understand the differences between living on and off the reservation. They wrote home telling friends to "cooperate with the white man on the reservation to bring education and prosperity to our uncivilized people." Indian soldiers urged their siblings to use education and learn English to prepare themselves for the problems which faced reservations after the war. Increased contact with whites in the military also stimulated changes in the habits and outlook of Indian soldiers. Thousands married non-Indians, converted to Christianity, and permanently relocated off the reservation once the war ended. When whites perceived these changes, they assumed that Indians were ready and indeed wanted to assimilate into the larger society. In other words, trade one way of life for another.

Few Indian soldiers, however, made the same assumption. In the immediate postwar years, Indian veterans fought for basic civil rights and in 1947 mounted a vigorous campaign in the Southwest to win suffrage in Arizona and New Mexico. Indian veterans, accustomed to drinking freely in the military, also successfully challenged an 1802 law which prohibited Indians from having access to liquor either on or off the reservation. These efforts, however, were not perceived by Indians as signifying a rejection of tribal life. Instead, former soldiers were now transformed, in many instances, into tribal leaders, and wanted the full benefits of United States citizenship in addition to their legally recognized tribal status. Representative of this new group of young leaders was Joseph Garry, an ex-Marine who was chairman of the Coeur d'Alene Tribal Council in Idaho and head of the National Congress of American Indians, and who led the fight in the early 1950s against assimilationist federal efforts to liquidate reservations and divide tribal assets among individual Indians.

Interestingly, recent United States Census data confirms that the most significant public policies promoting higher education among American Indians were not the recent initiatives of the 1960s and 1970s, but instead were the opportunities made available through the post-World War II GI Bill. The impact of the GI Bill was significant, but limited, in that Indian women in the same age cohort did not have the same opportunities. Although Indian women served in the uniformed services during the war, the majority of them who contributed to the war effort did so in the war industries, working in defense plants as riveters, inspectors, and machinists to replace men who had enlisted. Nevertheless, these gender-specific benefits testify to the continuing impact of military service on American Indian life.

Indian soldiers participated in all of the subsequent conflicts that have been fought since World War II. In 1950, when Congress began to push for the termination of federal supervision over the tribes, Indians inadvertently lent credence to assimilationist hopes by supporting the war effort in Korea and volunteering by the thousands to serve. As in World War II, Indian soldiers soon became known for their patriotism, and their commanders, who held similar stereotypes to their World War II counterparts, assigned Indians to the most dangerous combat missions. Typically, the non-Indian press called attention to individual acts of Indian bravery as a way to demonstrate that Indians were ready to lay down their lives for their country. Thus, indirectly, Indians in the military were used to support legislation designed to weaken tribal life. Also, like their World War II counterparts, Indian soldiers in Korea subscribed to a philosophy that exemplary service in the military would lead to greater equality and opportunity once the war ended. By and large, this proved to be the case for Indian veterans in the 1950s.

The same pattern, however, did not hold true for Indians who served in the military during the Vietnam War. Despite the fact that Indians continued to distinguish themselves in combat, there appears to have been deep disappointment among Indian Vietnam veterans that military service did not lead to increased economic opportunity. In fact, unlike veterans of other wars in this century, the men who fought in Vietnam were generally not treated as heroes by the larger society when they returned home from Southeast Asia. Because they had fought an unpopular war, the Vietnam veterans' experiences would just as soon be forgotten by the larger society. This led many Indian Vietnam veterans to reexamine their status in American society, and from this reexamination, many emerged as leaders of militant Indian rights organizations, and especially, the American Indian Movement (AIM). On the reservations, Indian Vietnam veterans often joined with the most traditional tribal elders to attempt to recreate indigenous warrior societies. As the historian Tom Holm points out, "Many of these veterans also consciously sought to link their efforts to assert tribal sovereignty to the decolonization struggles of other peoples." So, by the mid 1970s, many of these younger Indian veterans embraced the Vietnamese war of liberation which they had earlier fought against.

Alison R. Bernstein

See also Government Policy: Termination and Restoration; Navajo Code Talkers

Further Reading

Bernstein, Alison R. *American Indians and World War II.* Norman: University of Oklahoma, 1991.

Holm, Tom. "Fighting a White Man's War: The Extent and Legacy of American Indian Participation in World War II." *Journal of Ethnic Studies* 9 (1981): 69–81.

———. "Patriots and Pawns: State Use of American Indians in the Military and the Process of Nativization in the United States." *The State of Native America: Genocide, Colonization, and Resistance.* Ed. M. Annette Jaimes. Boston, MA: South End Press, 1992. 345–70.

Tate, Michael. "From Scout to Doughboy. The National Debate over Integrity—American Indians into the Military, 1891–1918." *Western Historical Quarterly* 17 (October 1986): 417–37.

MIMBREÑO

See Apache

MINERAL RIGHTS

See Mining

MINING

The mining of natural resources on Indian lands in this century has created a paradox of tragedy and a debated blessing. Left with barren lands undesirable to white settlers, a strange irony emerged with the turn of the century: one-third of the nation's coal in the West, 3 percent of America's oil and gas, and 37 percent of potential uranium rest underground, property of America's poorest minority—the American Indians—whose tribal nations are forced to make major decisions about the natural resources on their homelands.

The resources needing protection are vast. The Four Corners area of the Southwest is the largest strip-mining operation for coal in the world, where sixteen-story draglines like huge monsters scoop 325 tons of Mother Earth in a single pass. Tribal lands in Oklahoma, Wyoming, Montana, and the Dakotas are also intensive mining and oil drilling sites, where energy companies compete with each other for Indian leases. Today, in the Black Hills of the Sioux in South Dakota, more than twenty-five energy companies compete for legal rights to mine the beautiful sacred area, and Chippewa groups in northern Wisconsin presently face energy companies eagerly looking at their lands.

Since 1900 the issue of mining has produced numerous problems for the Indian nations, especially causing factionalism about whether or not to mine tribal natural resources. Views have polarized, with some more traditional people who believe that mining desecrates Mother Earth on one side, while the opposite side, often composed of more progressive Indians, is convinced that mining revenue can pay for needed programs such as education, the elderly, health care, and business ventures. Presently almost 50 of the more than 300 federally recognized tribes possess substantial natural resources on their lands, primarily located west of the Mississippi River, where many were forcibly removed from the 1830s until the 1880s.

Further war against Indians and more harmful federal Indian policies reduced tribal land ownership shamelessly so that American Indians now own only an estimated 2.3 percent of the land in the continental United States. Remarkable changes in industrialization at the turn of the century, followed by World War I, propelled the United States to become one of the world's most prosperous nations. The ensuing materialism during the Roaring Twenties was heightened by the increasing popularity of automobiles and a fledgling airplane industry. The need for fossil fuels paralleled a growing demand for oil and coal, much of it found on Indian lands.

Mineral Rights in the Early Twentieth Century

In these early decades, oil companies invaded Indian country, particularly in Oklahoma, where the Osages had more than 3,000 oil wells drilled on their lands, making them the "richest people in the world," and leading to debauchery. Nearby, the Muskogee Creeks and the Seminoles experienced a similar onslaught of oil companies during the optimistic era of wildcat drilling that made Texas famous. While the Elk Hills (California) and Teapot Dome (Wyoming) scandals captured national headlines and led to the indictment of Secretary of Interior Albert Fall, officials benignly neglected the unconscionable exploitations in Indian country.

Due to the trust relationship between the tribes and the United States, the secretary of the interior had immense power as the final authority for allowing mining companies to extract natural resources from the tribes. The Indian Oil Leasing Act passed by Congress in 1927 empowered the secretary of the interior to negotiate on behalf of the tribes, resulting in long-term oil leases on treaty reservations, which netted small royalties. Eleven years later, the Indian Lands Mining Act of 1938 allowed unallotted lands within reservations, or lands owned by a tribe, group, and Indian trust lands, to be leased for up to ten years, with the approval of the secretary of the interior. Unfortunately for the tribes, the lengthy leases remained in effect when the nation began demanding uranium in 1955. The tribes lost undetermined amounts of their natural resources, including timberlands, wildlife, and water, before the 1960s when various American Indians protested against violation of their rights and treaties.

Intertribal Organizations

Energy companies continued extracting tribal natural resources at huge profits until tribes of the northern plains began to discuss their common problems involving mining on their lands. Tribal fears compelled leaders to form the Native American Natural Resources Development Federation (NANRDF) in 1974, to protect reservations from the mining companies. Other tribes, especially in the Southwest, seeing the northern plains effort, advocated an organization for all tribes who wanted protection from the mining companies and the poor leasing practices of the secretary of the interior.

In 1975, twenty-five tribes formed the Council of Energy Resource Tribes (CERT), which replaced NANRDF. CERT, its headquarters in a suburb of Denver, Colorado, installed Peter MacDonald as the chairman of its advisory committee. The member tribes agreed to act as a united front to protect their natural resources, to renegotiate their leases, and to demonstrate that their level of expertise was such that they no longer required the Department of Interior to represent them.

CERT demonstrated its value during the energy crisis of 1973, and again in 1978 when the Organization of Petroleum Exporting Countries (OPEC) called for an oil embargo against the United States. In response to America's growing need for energy and the energy crisis, President Jimmy Carter instituted the Department of Energy to oversee the development of synthetic fuels as frustrated anti-OPEC Americans became energy conscious.

Striving to become more effective in protecting Indian natural resources, CERT opened an office in Washington, DC, to lobby on behalf of the tribes and discuss tribal control over natural resources with key federal officials. At the apex of its activities, CERT operated a $2.5 million budget with a staff of sixty-five workers, called "the best that money could buy," including business experts, engineers, geologists, and attorneys, most of whom were non-Indians. With CERT's assistance, the membership grew to more than thirty tribes, and presently has forty-three tribes in its organization.

Tribes Increase Control of Mineral Resources

The tribes have advanced considerably in expertise, carefully negotiating their natural resources in spite of continued internal factionalism. Under effective leadership, some tribes have renegotiated leases and assumed more control over their natural resources, especially under the current policy of self-determination, implemented via 1975 congressional legislation as the Indian Self-Determination and Education Assistance Act. The Assiniboine, Sioux, and United States Energy Corporation formed the first joint company. The Blackfeet tribe formed joint companies with Blocker Drilling Ltd. and Damson Oil Corporation. Mining royalties have enabled the tribes to invest in needed programs for their people. Health clinics, elderly care, educational scholarships, and vocational training are some of the general programs that tribes have been able to offer their communities since the 1970s.

Further negotiations between the Indian nations and energy companies followed in the 1980s. And the tribes demanded more. Some tribes, like the Blackfeet, worked out joint ownership agreements with energy companies. Other tribes reached agreements whereby the companies train Indians in the mining business at management and administrative levels. Some tribes, like the Navajo, considered assuming total control over the mining of their natural resources and all aspects of the mining procedure, especially at the end of the decade when oil prices reached over forty dollars per barrel. In 1993, half a dozen tribes exercise complete control over mining operations on their reservations, including the Navajo, Crow, Northern Cheyenne, and the Three Affiliated Tribes at Fort Berthold.

Relevant Court Cases and Legislation

On January 25, 1982, the Jicarilla Apache won an important case in the Supreme Court (*J. Gregory Merrion and Robert L. Bayless, et al. and Amoco Production Company and Marathon Oil Company v. Jicarilla Apache Indian Tribe*) allowing it to impose a severance tax on energy companies mining on their reservation. This ruling upheld the sovereign status of the Jicarillas. Indian self-determination over the management of their natural resources was enhanced when Congress passed the Indian Mineral Development Act of 1982, Title II under the Federal Oil and Gas Royalty Management Act of 1982, and the Indian Tribal Governmental Tax Status Act of 1983. In 1983, the Jicarilla Apache drilled oil and gas wells using tribal funds, and Fort Peck Reservation tribes formed a joint venture with United States Energy Corporation. In 1985, the United States Supreme Court ruled in *Kerr-McGee Corp. v. Navajo Tribe* that the Navajo Tribe had the right to impose a value-added or business activity tax and a property tax without the approval of the secretary of the interior—a victory for Indian sovereignty and the tribes.

Managing Mineral Resources in the Late Twentieth Century

The last decade of the twentieth century represents a battleground for tribes to protect their natural resources. A 1981 Linowes Commission report on the management of oil fields and auditing practices in the Department of Interior disclosed that Indian country was losing hundreds of barrels of oil through theft and fixed bookkeeping. At best, the Commission slowed down the energy companies, which still mine coal as quickly as possible on reservations and divert needed water from tribal lands for mining—all for capitalistic greed to extract tribal natural resources as fast as possible for huge profits.

Under the advice of CERT, the tribes strive to work out agreements for reclamation, stressing the environmental program of the federal government, and demand increasing control over mining operations. Such a pressurized dilemma has forced the tribes to learn quickly with millions of dollars at stake for irreversible amounts of natural resources. Sophisticated tribal leadership experienced with memories of victimization in the name of capitalism, now operate with the vigorous shrewd attitudes of modern corporations, representing an inspired Indian leadership.

Donald L. Fixico

See also Council of Energy Resource Tribes; Natural Resource Management; Water Rights

Further Reading

Ambler, Marjane. *Breaking the Iron Bonds: Indian Control of Energy Development.* Lawrence: University of Kansas Press, 1990.

Debo, Angie. *And Still the Waters Run: The Betrayal of the Five Civilized Tribes.* NJ: Princeton University Press, 1940.

Fixico, Donald L. "Tribal Leaders and the Demand for Natural Energy Resources on Reservation Lands." *The Plains Indians of the Twentieth Century.* Norman: University of Oklahoma Press (1985): 219–35.

Reno, Philip. *Mother Earth, Father Sky, and Economic Development: Navajo Resources and Their Use.* Albuquerque: University of New Mexico Press, 1981.

Wilson, Terry. *The Underground Reservation: Osage Oil.* Lincoln: University of Nebraska Press, 1985.

MISSION EDUCATION

See Churches and Education

MISSION INDIAN FEDERATION

The Mission Indian Federation was a reform organization born out of the heavy-handed abuses of the Bureau of Indian Affairs (BIA) suffered by reservation populations throughout southern California. The evolution of this powerful organization came about during one of the most politically and culturally repressive eras of United States-Indian relations. The Federation was significantly different from other pro-Indian reform groups. While it possessed a non-Indian figurehead, its all Indian membership insured it would address a considerably wider scope of social and political issues touching the day to day lives of southern California Indians.

The Federation grew out of a collaboration between a non-Indian named Jonathan Tibbet of Riverside, and a number of local Indians. Bitter veterans and non-citizen Indian draft resisters joined together for a three-day organizing conference at Tibbet's home in November of 1919. Denouncing the incompetent administration of the BIA that had routinely allowed non-Indians to usurp Indian lands and water, the organization was formally established with a president, two vice-presidents, a secretary-treasurer, and chief of police. The position of chief counselor to the organization was given to Tibbet. When Tibbet died in 1930, leadership in the organization was assumed by the tireless organizer Adan Castillo, a Cahuilla and Luiseño of the Soboba Indian Reservation, who served as president from 1920 until his death in 1953.

Three types of meetings were regularly held: the executive council met monthly for routine business; semiannual conventions were open to all members; and special conferences might be called in emergency situations. The Federation published a regular newsletter, *The Indian*, from April 1921 until 1924; it resumed again somewhat irregularly from that date up to 1967.

The Federation's goals included securing tribal lands and water rights, resurveying reservation boundaries, full citizenship rights, the elimination of the BIA, and legislation guaranteeing Indian self-determination. Throughout the 1920s it gained widespread support on the numerous southern California Indian reservations. Even the Walpi and Supai of Arizona joined. Urban Indians from Los Angeles formed a branch and were officially recognized as Federation delegates.

One of the earliest issues tackled by the group was an effort to seek compensation for lands promised to the California Indians by the eighteen treaties in which they surrendered claims to large sections of their territories in exchange for 7.5 million acres of reservation lands. While Congress never ratified the treaties or provided the promised reservations, the Native groups were forced to abandon their old habitats. When the state agreed to represent these California Indian land claims, the Federation vigorously pushed for legislation to allow Indians to hire their own attorneys. Instead, the case was prosecuted by the Attorney General of the State of California. It came to a controversial settlement in 1944.

When the BIA failed to provide police protection for reservation religious, social, and cultural events, the Federation organized an armed police force to maintain order and protect lives. These and other acts of self-reliance were seen as threatening to the authority of the BIA. In 1921, the federal Justice Department had fifty-seven Federation leaders arrested for "conspiracy against the government." Non-Indian reformers joined in an ultimately successful effort to have the charges dropped.

The Federation also fought an ultimately successful campaign to slow down and finally stop the allotment of reservation lands under the Dawes Act of 1887. When Roosevelt's New Deal reform created the Indian Reorganization Act, which proved to be yet another government subterfuge to extend BIA control over Indian lands and lives, the Federation launched a vigorous legislative campaign to overturn its paternalistic overtones.

Following World War II, the Federation joined with other California Indians in a new land claims case under the newly formed Indian Claims Commission Act of 1946. That case also came to a controversial settlement in 1970, and a small per capita distribution was made. The Federation took credit for the establishment of Public Law 280 in California, which took control of civil and criminal jurisdiction away from the federal government and placed it in the hands of local officials.

Unfortunately, the Mission Indian Federation did not survive the termination programs and bitter land claims battles that dominated Indian policy from 1955 to 1970. Leadership split in 1963 and the organization ceased to function after 1967. The optimistic self-determination of the Federation's vision for a bright Indian future was best summarized by president Adan Castillo who wrote in 1945:

> To say that the record of Indian wardship is disgraceful is an understatement. With rare interludes, it has been disgraceful through all administrations. The past is irrevocable. The present and future lie in our hands. The bonds of Indian wardship must be broken forever. (*The Indian* 7 [November 1945])

Edward D. Castillo

Further Reading

Castillo, Edward D. "Twentieth-Century Secular Movements." *Handbook of North American Indians.* Vol. 8. *California.* Ed. Robert F. Heizer. Washington, DC: Smithsonian Institution (1978): 713–17.

The Indian. Riverside, CA: Mission Indian Federation,1921–1945.

Monguia, Anna Rose. "The Mission Indian Federation: A Study of Indian Political Resistance." Master's thesis, University of California, Riverside, 1975.

MISSION INDIANS

See California Tribes

MISSIONS AND MISSIONARIES

The history of relations between Native persons and missionaries in the twentieth century must be seen as a protracted struggle between those who would encourage a Native identity and those who would repress it and foster assimilation. Concomitantly, during the same period, Native Americans have asserted their right to full participation and leadership within the Christian Church, over and against missionaries and ecclesiastical hierarchies, which have failed to recognize that right. In order to understand this tug-of-war, however, it is necessary to look back to the latter half of the previous century.

In the late 1870s, D.P. Kidder of Drew Theological Seminary wrote of missions to America's indigenous peoples:

> In no part of the world have there been greater personal sacrifices or more diligent toil to Christianize savages with results less proportioned to the efforts made. Without enumerating ... causes, the fact must be recognized that throughout the whole continent the aboriginal races are dying out to an extent that leaves little present prospect of any considerable remnants being perpetuated in the form of permanent Christian communities. Still missions are maintained in the Indian territories and on the reservations, and the government of the United States is effectively cooperating with them to accomplish all that may be done for the Christian civilization of the Indians and Indian tribes that remain.

The cooperation spoken of by Professor Kidder was the new Indian policy inaugurated by Ulysses S.

Grant upon his assumption of the presidency. Pursuant to this "peace policy," members of Christian denominations replaced military personnel in the recommendation and review of policies on reservations. Churches were also asked to nominate Indian agents in the hope of weeding out corrupt personnel. As a result, thirteen denominations were given exclusive control over seventy-three agencies. Other churches were prohibited from interfering in matters on another's reservation, and could only enter with the permission of the church within whose jurisdiction the reservation lay. Among the various denominations participating were the Quakers (who first urged the program), the Catholics, the Episcopalians, the Methodists, and the Lutherans. President Grant also created the Board of Indian Commissioners, composed of wealthy Christian laymen, to exercise joint control with the secretary of the interior over procurement and disbursement of funds for reservations.

Under this system of "ecclesiastical serfdom," which allowed no choice of Christian association, assimilationism was the rule. Traditional spiritual practice was forbidden. Reservation schools became little more than adjuncts of the church, where attendance at religious services was compulsory.

The eighteen years from the implementation of the peace policy in 1869 until 1887 represented the high point of Christian missions to Native Americans. In the latter year, however, the passage of the Dawes Act provided for allotment of parcels of land on reservations to individual Indians. The Curtis Act in 1898 applied the same principle to Indian Territory. Unexpectedly, the legislation led to a decided decline in Christian religious fervor among Natives.

The Acts provided that any "surplus" lands not individually allotted could be made available for white settlement. As a result, a steady influx of settlers began. These homesteaders broke many of the strict rules of conduct the missionaries had taught. Natives, who had never controlled their own churches, now saw themselves outnumbered in many congregations. By 1934, approximately two-thirds of the land held by Natives prior to severalty was in white hands. As Natives increasingly became outsiders in mission churches, a general disillusionment with Christianity settled in among them.

In 1906 the Indian Mission Conference of the Methodist Episcopal Church (South) changed its name to the Oklahoma Conference. The effect was abandonment of the denomination's work among Native Americans in the West (although between 1906 and 1912 several Methodist churches were built among the Lumbees in North Carolina, and the northern Methodist Episcopal Church continued work among some tribes). At the time, the Indian Mission Conference had about 5,000 members and 17 Native clergy. The abandonment led to a loss of about half of these Indian members. Other denominations, all of whom largely perpetuated the assimilationist ideal, experienced similar declines. A period of consolidation, which would continue into the 1940s, began.

In 1908 most Protestant agencies joined the Home Missions Council of the newly founded Federal Council of Churches (FCC). The Committee on Indian Affairs of the new body coordinated evangelistic activities among Natives. In 1950, the FCC became the National Council of Churches (NCC) and shortly thereafter a special office for Native matters passed out of existence.

In 1918 an important first step was taken toward greater autonomy for Native people within denominational Christianity. The Brewer Indian Mission (forerunner of the current Oklahoma Indian Missionary Conference) separated from the East Oklahoma Conference of the Methodist Episcopal Church (South). It reported 82 churches, 124 clergy, and 2,702 members. The Mission gave greater freedom to Native pastors, who were no longer merely assistants to white missionaries and who could now preach sermons in the language of the people. Despite such gains, it should be pointed out that at the same time, the denomination was funding the Willis Fulsom Training School, an assimilationist institution in Smithville, Oklahoma, serving Choctaw, Creek, Cherokee, and Siouan children as well as whites. The guiding belief of the school was that educating Natives and whites together was the best way to ensure that the former became good citizens and did not "go back to the blanket."

Throughout the first third of the century, the Bureau of Indian Affairs (BIA) supported the churches' assimilationist push. Indicative of its attitude was a 1921 memorandum from Commissioner Charles H. Burke which told reservation superintendents to prepare Natives for United States citizenship by cooperating with missionaries to teach their charges the "higher" concepts of family values. Burke believed "the Indian must be assimilated if he is to survive." That same year, 26 Protestant denominations reported 32,164 members and 80,000 constituents on 161 reservations; and Catholics reached 61,456 Native Catholics at 149 missions. (There were 40 reservations with no resident Christian missionary presence.) Three years later, Congress passed the Indian Citizenship Act. It was the high-water mark of assimilationism. Despite such policies, however, traditional practices survived and became the basis of later Native renewals.

After taking office in 1933, President Franklin D. Roosevelt appointed John Collier to head the BIA. Believing in "cultural freedom and opportunity" for Natives, Collier was determined to "recognize and respect the Indian as he is." Under his leadership, the Indian New Deal abolished the Board of Indian Commissioners, because of its consistent support for assimilation. It attacked the reservation monopolies of various denominations and ended compulsory attendance at church services in the BIA schools. Collier opened reservation facilities to all religious leaders, traditional and Christian, and left Natives free to support any they wished.

The relaxation of reservation monopolies led other denominations, particularly Pentecostal and evangelical, to develop Indian ministries. The Church of God, the Church of Christ, and the Assemblies of God are among those who have obtained Native adherents. In 1940, for instance, Assemblies of God missionaries arrived on the Nez Perce Reservation in Idaho and established a church. Fundamentalist, and strongly assimilationist, they made limited inroads among Roman Catholic Church members (traditionally, the most tolerant of syncretic belief and practice), but did well among Native Presbyterians and Methodists. Congregants tended, however, to maintain membership in their natal churches and merely attended the Pentecostal services. In 1944, the Church of God of Anderson, Indiana, a Wesleyan Holiness sect, followed suit. While its patterns of acceptance paralleled those of the Assemblies of God, it proved more successful due to its greater tendency to accept Native customs. Both denominations, however, maintained white leadership.

The advent of these Pentecostal and evangelical denominations among the Natives initially led mainline Native congregations to move to a less expressive, more "white" mode of worship. This trend was influenced by the closure of some schools specifically set up for the training of Native pastors. According to Deward Walker, Jr., among the Nez Perce, for example, "The new seminary-trained, Native ministers de-emphasized the older, emotional, and fundamentalist preaching which had characterized the earlier, locally trained preachers." Throughout the 1940s, there remained a widespread belief among non-Natives that there was a dearth of capable Indian leadership.

The increase in the number of denominations engaged in Native missions did little, however, to mask an overall trend of decline in Christian practice among Native persons. In 1950, although there were ten additional Protestant denominations reporting Indian missionary activities (compared to 1921 above), total communicants numbered only 39,200 with an additional 140,000 constituents. While staff remained predominantly white, a 1958 study by the NCC disclosed a less antagonistic attitude toward Native culture and belief. Among Protestants and Catholics, only 35 percent and 44 percent, respectively, supported a strict assimilationist stance. Majorities in several denominations found elements of Native teaching compatible with Christianity: the Episcopalians, 81 percent; Congregationalists, 75 percent; Roman Catholics, 74 percent; and Methodists, 53 percent. In some, however, a majority considered Native religion and ritual "almost entirely unreconcilable" with Christian faith: the Southern Baptists, 100 percent; Reformed, 89 percent; Presbyterians, 70 percent; and American Baptists, 55 percent. During the same period, a few independent Native Christian churches sprang up. The congregations, usually split-offs from organized denominations, had Native leadership and were generally more tolerant of traditional and syncretic practice and belief. Although they often grew and spread along kinship lines, at least some engaged in evangelical activities, even among different tribes.

Termination and relocation programs created new challenges for missionaries, many of whom began to view their role as pastoral more than evangelical. The Oklahoma Indian Mission, for example, sent a pastor to organize work in a Dallas relocation center. Relocation left many smaller, rural churches with few potential leaders and decreasing financial resources.

One of the odder aspects of the opening up of reservations was the reemergence of the Church of Jesus Christ of Latter-Day Saints among Natives. The Mormons consider Indians to be the Lamanites of *The Book of Mormon*, Hebrews who traveled to North America over a 1,500-year period, but who had become "loathsome" and "full of mischief" and "idle" through their "abominations and loss of belief." They thus perpetuated the old slur that Native Americans were descendants of the Ten Lost Tribes of Israel, a belief perpetuated by those who could not accept that indigenous peoples could develop any degree of "civilization" without fertilization from the Old World.

Mormons had ceased Native missions in the 1890s after controversy over their supposed involvement in the Ghost Dance. In 1942, however, a Navajo woman in Shiprock, New Mexico, pleaded with them to send missionaries. As a result, they organized the Southwest Indian Mission, the first Mormon Native American activity in five decades. The program, greatly expanded in the 1950s, consisted of four parts: first, the missions to Natives assisted in farming, cooperative and business enterprises, and educational and recreational programs; second, the Indian Seminary Program was instituted, in which more than 25,000 youths received religious instruction and participated in organized activities; third, special programs were offered at Brigham Young University for the research of Indian history and culture and for support of the approximately 500 Natives who enrolled there annually; and fourth, the Indian Placement Program was implemented, which over a period of 25 years, placed over 60,000 youths with Mormon families during the school year. This last program began phasing out in the 1970s amid criticism of the removal of children from their families and tribal cultures.

Another innovative program began in the late 1970s when the Mennonite Central Committee in Akron, Ohio, sent volunteers to work with a number of tribes in Louisiana. These volunteers worked on recognition petition research, genealogy, and development of crafts cooperatives. They were, however, strictly prohibited from proselytizing. While programs they began are still in operation, they are now administered and run by Natives, and there are currently no such volunteers in the Indian communities.

Among Natives, self-determination has remained a high priority. Capable leaders, both traditional and Christian, have always asserted the peoples' right to religious sovereignty. But the civil rights movement of the 1950s and 1960s provided a new impetus to their assertion of leadership within the Christian community. Since the 1950s, Native churches increasingly have been served by Native clergy, and a number of prominent Native voices have emerged in several denominations. Among these many persons are Homer Noley (head of the National United Methodist Native American Center and the first Native person to serve in an executive staff capacity on one of that denomination's general boards), George Tinker (a Lutheran theologian and professor at Iliff School of Theology), Steve Charleston (Episcopalian bishop of Alaska), William Baldridge (American Baptist theologian and professor at Central Baptist Theological Seminary), and George Patrick Lee (the first Native American to become a member of the Mormon's First Quorum of the Seventy).

Through powerful voices such as these, Natives continue to claim their right to a Christianity of their own over and against missions which are often managed in a way virtually unchanged from the nineteenth century. For instance, at the 1991 Biennial Meeting of the American Baptist Church, Baldridge and Kim Mammedaty issued a statement calling upon the denomination to bring its missionaries home and to halt the "spiritual oppression" of Natives. Similarly, in 1992, its Native American International Caucus saw to it that the United Methodist General Conference adopted a comprehensive plan for Native American ministries, including an acknowledgment that non-Natives in the denomination had "failed to recognize that Native Americans are full participants in the church."

As the twentieth century draws to a close, a number of denominations estimate significant numbers of Natives on their membership rolls: Roman Catholics (285,354); Mormons (75,000); Episcopalians (35,000, and 100 clergy); United Methodists (17,500, and 100 clergy); Presbyterians (9,864); American Baptists (2,000, and 22 clergy); United Church of Christ (1,684); Evangelical Lutherans (1,295). Increasing numbers of Natives, however, particularly young people, are questioning the validity of Christianity as the imported religion of their colonizers. As of this writing, its continued vitality remains in doubt.

Jace Weaver

See also Churches and Education; Religion

Further Reading

Arrington, Leonard J., and Davis Bitton. *The Mormon Experience: A History of the Latter-Day Saints.* 2d ed. Urbana: University of Illinois Press, 1992.

Bode, Marilyn, et al. *Christians and Native American Concerns in the Late 20th Century.* WA: Church Council of Greater Seattle, 1981.

Bowden, Henry Warner. *American Indians and Christian Missions.* Chicago History of American Religion. Ed. Martin E. Marty. IL: University of Chicago Press, 1981.

Noley, Homer. *First White Frost: Native Americans and United Methodism.* Nashville, TN: Abingdon Press, 1991.

Walker, Deward E., Jr. *Conflict and Schism in Nez Perce Acculturation: A Study in Religion and Politics.* Reprint. Moscow: University of Idaho Press, 1985.

MITCHIF

See Cree; Ojibwa: Chippewa in Montana; Ojibwa: Chippewa in North Dakota

MIWOK

The term Miwok refers to an extensive language family covering a wide geographic area in central California, from the coast to the Sierra Nevada mountains. The following articles cover the people living in different ecological niches.

COAST MIWOK

The people known as the Coast Miwok lived along the Pacific Coast of California from what is now Sausalito, to Duncan's Point, including Bodega Bay, Tomales Bay, and along the San Pablo Bay, inland to the area around Sonoma, including Petaluma and Novato. This area was heavily impacted by Europeans, starting in the late 1500s, with the voyages of Sir Francis Drake and Sebastián Rodríguez Cermeño. Further contact came with the missionization efforts from San Francisco, San Rafael, and Sonoma Missions, and the Russian use of land at Fort Ross and Bodega. The Coast Miwok were forced from their village communities and through intermarriage, disease, and murder, severely reduced in numbers. Much of what is known about Coast Miwok life was recorded by Isabel Kelly, an ethnographer and archaeologist, in a series of interviews conducted in 1931 to 1932 with Coast Miwok descendants, Tom Smith from Bodega Bay, and María Copa Frías, from San Rafael and Nicasio.

The Coast Miwok, sometimes calling themselves Pomo or Mexican, continued to live in their traditional homelands working in local sawmills, fishing, or as agricultural laborers. The 1923 Kelsey census included lists of "homeless" Tomales and Bodega Indians. In the 1950s, they were terminated by the federal government and were no longer recognized as California Indians.

In June 1992, in response to activities from a Pomo group in northern Sonoma County who proposed to develop reservation land in Coast Miwok traditional territory, Coast Miwok descendants organized a nonprofit organization called the Federated Coast Miwok. They hold regular meetings and have created Bylaws for their organization; they are pursuing federal acknowledgment. Many Coast Miwok descendants, including Greg Sarris, David Peri, and Kathleen Smith, among others, have been recognized as outstanding scholars.

Victoria Patterson

See also California Tribes

Further Reading

Collier, Mary E.T., and Sylvia Barker Thalman, eds. *Interviews with Tom Smith and Maria Copa: Isabel Kelly's Ethnographic Notes on the Coast Miwok Indians of Marin and Southern Sonoma Counties, California.* San Rafael, CA: Miwok Archaeological Preserve of Marin, 1991.

Kelly, Isabel. "Coast Miwok." *Handbook of North American Indians.* Vol. 8. *California.* Ed. Robert F. Heizer. Washington, DC: Smithsonian Institution (1978): 414–25.

LAKE MIWOK

Lake Miwok is one of seven Miwokan languages whose use forms a belt across Central California from Marin County in the west to the Sierra Nevada mountains in the east. The Lake Miwok, located south and east of Clear Lake, were isolated from other Miwok speakers because they were surrounded by the Wappo, Southeastern Pomo, and the Patwin. However, their language is closely related to the Coast Miwok spoken from Marin to Bodega Bay. They traveled often to Bodega Bay to collect clam shells, seaweed, and shell fish, and were in contact with these other Miwok speakers.

The Lake Miwok encountered the earliest foray of Europeans into the area when the Luis Arguello expedition came upon the villages of Cawiyomi and Oleyomi near Middletown in 1821. In the 1820s, Mission San Francisco de Solano began to baptize many Lake Miwok from Pope Valley and Middletown. In 1848 Mariano Vallejo signed a peace treaty with eleven chiefs, most of whom were Lake Miwok, but during the American period, Lake Miwok people suffered the same hardships and tragedies of other northern California Indians.

After the turn of the century, surviving Lake Miwok and Pomo people received 189 acres as Middletown Rancheria, under the federal act which appropriated funds for homeless California Indians. The Lake Miwok worked as seasonal agricultural laborers, but continued to use traditional medicinal springs, native plants, and foods. They traveled to the coast, to Clear Lake, and to Stonyford to trade, and their geographical position made them excellent middlemen for an extensive trade network. Lake Miwok territory included many mineral and hot springs which were developed by Americans as resorts. The Indians' original rights were at least acknowledged by Harbin Hot Springs, for example, which gave the Lake Miwok "a privilege—for only 25 cents we could stay there and close the place if we wanted."

The current Middletown Rancheria is recognized by the federal government, has a tribal government, and has worked to develop innovative educational programs in local schools.

Victoria Patterson

See also **California Tribes**

Further Reading

Barrett, Samuel A. "The Ethnogeography of the Pomo and Neighboring Indians." *University of California Publications in American Archaeology and Ethnology* 6:1 (1908): 1–332.

Callaghan, Catherine A. "Lake Miwok." *Handbook of North American Indians.* Vol. 8. *California.* Ed. Robert F. Heizer. Washington, DC: Smithsonian Institution (1978): 264–73.

Peri, David W., Scott M. Patterson, and Susan L. McMurray. *An Ethnographic and Historical Cultural Resources Study of the Aminoil, Little Geysers, Ford Flat, Cobb Mountain (Units 16, 18, 19, 20, 21) Geothermal Leaseholds Sonoma and Lake Counties, California.* Rohnert Park, CA: Sonoma State University, Department of Anthropology, The Ethnographic Laboratory, 1978.

SIERRA MEWUK

Mewuk means "People" in the Native language of the Mewuk (Miwok). The Sierra Mewuk homeland is in the Sierra Nevada foothills of central California. The Northern, Central and Southern Mewuk are divided linguistically as well as geographically: Northern Mewuk are located in Amador County and parts of El Dorado and Calaveras counties; Central Mewuk are found in parts of Calavaras County and Tuolumne County; and the Southern Mewuk reside in Mariposa County.

The land of the Sierra Mewuk became the setting for the Gold Rush with the discovery of the "Motherlode" in 1848 by the gold miners. Some 8,000 Mewuk lived on the lands before contact, but by the 1910 census the population had dwindled to less than 700. Devastation from killing, introduced diseases, and the scattering of the Mewuk into hiding helped destroy a once thriving homeland. Today the Sierra Mewuk still inhabit their ancestral grounds despite the many obstacles. The 1990 census identified a total Mewuk (including Coast and Lake Miwok) population of 3,381.

Although there were many negotiated treaties recognizing tribes of California in the nineteenth century, they were refused ratification by the federal government. Obligations that the federal government felt to the Native people of California led to the 1928 Congress permitting the California Indians to sue the United States for compensation promised but denied. The resulting cases were not resolved until 1972, when many of the California people, including the Mewuk, were given $.47 an acre for California land. Also to pacify the Native people, the government set aside land for various reservations and/or rancherias during the early years of the twentieth century. However, not all California Native people were recognized in these ways. Today, we still have many tribes seeking recognition or "untermination"; Mewuk are among those tribes. The American Indian Council of Mariposa County, Calavaras Band of Mewuk, and the Ione Band of Mewuk still fight today in courts and the government systems trying to become federally recognized. Many people from these bands have gone to Washington, D.C., to represent their people in this plight and to date have not been successful. The process has been long and costly.

The only federally recognized Mewuk groups are the Tuolumne Band of Mewuk and the Jackson Rancheria. There are four land bases and/or rancherias to whom recognition has not been given. These four include: Sheep Ranch Rancheria, which houses only a cemetery; Shingle Springs Rancheria, which has a

Tribal Council and a mixture of Mewuk and Maidu people residing there; Buena Vista Rancheria, which has only one individual identified as a living descendent of the original Indian distributees; and Chicken Ranch Rancheria, which is located on 2.85 acres of land with a resident population of seven. This tribe was restored to recognition after a class action suit was won in 1983 (*Tillie Hardwick v. United States*). Today, a bingo parlor stands on this land.

Of the federally recognized rancheria tribes there are two Mewuk bases: Jackson Rancheria and the Tuolumne Band of Mewuk on the Tuolumne Rancheria. Jackson Rancheria was established in 1895 and has 330 acres on which 35 to 40 families live. They have a Tribal Council with a Constitution and Bylaws. Approximately 150 Mewuk live on the 335.77 acre Tuolomne Rancheria with over 200 more living within the surrounding areas. They have an organized Tribal Council and a Constitution and Bylaws that were approved in 1936.

The Tuolumne Rancheria is home to the Tuolumne Indian Health Center, established in 1969. It has grown to have two satellite clinics in Jackson and Mariposa. These clinics serve Native American people from all four counties: Mariposa, Amador, Calaveras, and Tuolumne. Medical and dental services are provided. Community outreach services help to provide services to patients in the clinics and in their homes, and help with other programs by offering assistance with health and social services. Also provided are substance abuse services; services are provided to individuals and their families. There is on-site counseling as well as support groups and area resources are available. These facilities have increased the awareness of good health and dental care and have conducted their programs in support and respect of the traditions and beliefs of Native California people. Both the medical and dental health care offices help to provide training and jobs for the local Mewuk. When the facilities were first established, medical assistance training was provided and many jobs were created for the local Mewuk.

The densely forested land in and near Mewuk territory has provided many jobs through logging and lumber-related industries, which are a major employer for the people residing in the three northern counties. In the Southern Mewuk area, Yosemite National Park employs many descendants of the First People. The Mewuk have been fighting unsuccessfully for land claims in Yosemite for many years.

There have been many obstacles that the Mewuk have had to surmount. Government Indian schools insisted that Native people not speak their language in the schools, thus making the young people attending school lose the use of their Native tongue. Today, few of the elders under the age of sixty have retained the Mewuk language. As the elders pass on, so does the language. Language restoration projects are being implemented using tapes, video, and the assistance of the few remaining fluent speakers. Young people are retaining some of the language through these projects. The Northern Sierra Mewuk Language Program was one such project.

There are few elders left who remember the correct forms of traditional ceremonial dance. Traditionally, when a "headman" or "captain" of a dance house died, the roundhouse was also destroyed and rebuilt. The leaders today are chairmen and tribal council members; there is no headman or captain, only descendants who do not practice the "old ways." Today, however, there are a few dance groups composed of young people who have learned traditional dance steps and more importantly the songs for these dances. With help and guidance from a few elders, dance shall continue to be present. Tuolumne Mewuk Rancheria has a *Hungi* (dance house, roundhouse) and, although its use has been limited, it still stands as a reminder of the old ways. Only in recent times has the house been once again danced in.

One important celebration that takes place each year on the Tuolumne Rancheria is the Acorn Festival, given on the second weekend in September. The weekend of dance honors the acorn crop, and acorn soup (*nupa*) is made every year and offered to all who partake in the festivities (the black acorn was once the main food staple for the Mewuk). On the fourth weekend of September a Big Time celebration is given at Grinding Rock State Historical Park (Chaw'se), hosted by the Amador Tribal Council. Many central California dance groups are invited to participate; Mewuk, Maidu, and Pomo people join in celebration. With the help of Native people, the state park has built a roundhouse. Although it is more structured than traditional houses because of the implementation of state codes, nonetheless the dance house still holds traditional value to the Native people. At Chaw'se, they also help to keep the social importance of a gathering alive by having a field for playing Indian football, a game played in a manner similar to soccer. The traditional handgame is played there. It involves the singing of songs and guessing of bones; there are two marked and two unmarked bones, and two teams play against each other for the money in the "pot." Social games, as well as the dancing and gathering of many Californians, make Chaw'se a very successful event.

To coincide with this Big Time at Chaw'se, for the last five years there has been a Native American Invitational Art Show, featuring artists of Native descent focusing on the Native people in the surrounding areas. Many local artists come to show their traditional and contemporary paintings, carvings, basketry, and other mediums. Basketry that once was a necessity has now become an art form. Though there are few weavers of Mewuk descent, interest has grown in the last three years and baskets are once again being made with traditional materials by women from Amador, Calavaras, and Tuolumne counties in traditional ways.

Mewuk means "People." Today's Mewuk see the importance of the survival of their culture and continue striving to keep the Mewuk culture alive and well in the Sierra Nevada foothills of central California.

Jennifer D. Bates

See also **California Tribes**

Further Reading

Barrett, Samuel A., and Edward W. Gifford. "Miwok Material Culture." *Public Museum of the City of Milwaukee Bulletin* 2:4 (1933): 117–376. Yosemite National Park, CA: Yosemite Natural History Association, 1959.

Hart, Merriam C. *The Dawn of the World; Myths and Weird Tales Told by the Mewan Indians of California.* Cleveland, OH: Arthur H. Clark Company, 1910.

Levy, Richard. "Eastern Miwok." *Handbook of North American Indians.* Vol. 8. *California.* Ed. Robert F. Heizer. Washington, DC: Smithsonian Institution (1978): 398–413.

MODOC

The Modoc homeland included the present border between California and Oregon, lands marked by the majestic mountains of the Cascade Range, including the sacred site of Mt. Shasta. The Modocs lost all of their land under the terms of the Council Grove Treaty of 1864. The government removed the Modoc to the Klamath Reservation in Oregon, which they shared with the Klamath and Paiute. The Modoc call themselves "Ma Klaks," but their Klamath neighbors called them "Mo Adok."

Today, the Modocs are divided into two distinct groups due to historical events. Discontent on the Klamath Reservation led Keintpoos, or Captain Jack, to flee; from 1872 to 1873 these Modoc fought an unsuccessful war with the United States, following which the government hanged Captain Jack and three others, sent two Modoc to prison on Alcatraz Island, and exiled 153 others to the Quapaw Agency in Indian Territory. About 100 Modoc remained on the Klamath Reservation.

At the Quapaw Agency, the Modoc became farmers and ranchers. Their children attended schools there, where they were taught farming, ranching, and business techniques along with the usual reading and writing. Some of the people became Christians. Over the years, the government permitted some Modoc to return to the Klamath Reservation, but others chose to remain in Oklahoma. At the turn of the twentieth century, about fifty Modoc lived on the Quapaw Agency. They were assigned allotments of varying sizes, and tried to eke out a living by farming and ranching.

The division of Modoc lands under the General Allotment Act began in 1891, and the United States Congress recognized the educational and economic efforts of the Oklahoma Modoc by ordering their enrollment in 1909. Some were enrolled in Oklahoma, while others were added to the rolls of the Klamath Reservation in Oregon, permanently dividing the people into two distinct groups. The Modoc in Oregon received a portion of the claims payments awarded to Indians residing on the Klamath Reservation, amounting to $15 per person per year. Every Modoc in Oregon also received between $240 and $500 each year for timber leases. By 1940, each Modoc in the Northwest received an annual income of $800 for timber leases.

Modoc men and women served in the armed forces during World War II and took jobs in defense plants. On August 13, 1954, the federal government terminated the Klamath and Modoc Indians with Public Law 587. Losing their tribal status were fifty-five Modoc in Oklahoma and seventy-five to one hundred Modoc who were living on the Klamath Reservation. Individual Modocs received $45,000, but their federal status and rights to Indian health, education, and legal benefits were lost. Their lands were now taxable.

In 1967, the Modoc joined forces with the Wyandottes, Peorias, and Ottawas in northeast Oklahoma to form an intertribal council. The Modoc organized a new tribal government with Vernon Walker and Bill Follis serving as important early chairs. In 1978 Follis became the first federally recognized chief since 1880, when Bogus Charlie died. The current leader of the Oklahoma Modoc, Follis, is a rancher and businessman in Miami, Oklahoma, and was instrumental in the fight to reinstate his people as a tribe. In 1978 the government recognized the Modoc Tribe of Oklahoma, and approved their Constitution in 1991.

There are about 200 enrolled Oklahoma Modoc in the early 1990s, including some living with their relatives in Oregon. The tribe owns its headquarters in Miami, as well as a church, cemetery, and eight acres of land. Individual tribal members own private lands and businesses, and work in a variety of occupations as farmers, ranchers, clerks, secretaries, health officials, college professors, and government workers.

Under the leadership of tribal historian Patricia Trolinger, the Modoc are currently busy creating a library and archive of family photographs and letters. The tribe has applied for an educational grant to work with elderly Modoc to recover and retain portions of their Northwest language, family histories, and oral traditions. The Modoc share many beliefs with their kinsmen in Oregon, and some return to the Northwest to attend Modoc ceremonies. They also borrow from the Indians around them in northeast Oklahoma, taking part in area powwows, dancing, singing, drumming, and participating in the rich spiritual traditions of the eastern Oklahoma Stomp Dance.

Clifford E. Trafzer

See also **Allotment; Federal and State Recognition; Government Policy: Termination and Restoration; Klamath; Oklahoma Tribes**

Further Reading

Faulk, Odie B., and Laura E. Faulk. *The Modoc.* New York: Chelsea House, 1988.

Murray, Keith A. *The Modocs and Their War.* Civilization of the American Indian 52. 1959. Norman: University of Oklahoma Press, 1989.

Ray, Verne. *Primitive Pragmatists: The Modoc Indians of Northern California.* American Ethnological Society Monographs 38. 1963. Seattle: University of Washington Press, 1973.

Stern, Theodore. *The Klamath Tribe: A People and their Reservation.* American Ethnological Society Monographs 41. Seattle: University of Washington Press, 1965.

Wright, Muriel Hazel. *A Guide to the Indian Tribes of Oklahoma.* Civilization of the American Indian 33. 1951. Norman: University of Oklahoma Press, 1986.

MOHAVE

See Colorado River Indian Tribes; Mojave

MOHAWK

The history of the Mohawks of Akwesasne (meaning "Where the Partridge Drums") dates from around 1755, when a group of Christian Mohawks from the French Mission at Caughnawaga migrated to St. Regis, a point on the St. Lawrence River just southwest of Cornwall, Ontario, and ten miles east of Massena, New York. The French Jesuits had encouraged the migration of this small party because of population pressure at the Caughnawaga Mission, and the need to follow activities of the British along the St. Lawrence frontier. The St. Regis Mission is the oldest permanent settlement in northern New York, predating non-Indian settlement by almost fifty years.

As the Akwesasne Mohawk community straddles the Canadian-United States border along the 45th parallel, much of the political economic and social economic life of the Mohawks has revolved around trying to minimize the artificial barriers constructed by the international border. On the American side of the border, 5,638 enrolled Mohawks live on approximately 14,648 acres south of the St. Lawrence River; on the Canadian side, 7,671 Canadian Mohawks live on 7,400 acres along the southern bank of the St. Lawrence River and on Cornwall Island. The international border is only part of the jurisdictional problem for Akwesasne Mohawks. The Mohawks have three governmental bodies and reside in two provinces of Canada and two counties of New York State. Their children attend three different school districts and the community receives its services from different Indian bureaucracies in Ottawa and Washington. Until recently, if a female Mohawk from Canada married an American Mohawk man, the woman would lose her Indian status by virtue of marrying a non-Indian as defined by the Indian Act of Canada.

Prior to the twentieth century Akwesasne was primarily a farming, fishing, and trapping community. Mohawk men supplemented their incomes by working in the lumber camps of the Adirondacks in the late fall and winter, while Mohawk women wove splint and sweet grass baskets, which have become internationally recognized for their quality and artistic design. Three trustees, appointed by the State of New York in 1802, governed the American Mohawk tribe and twelve life chiefs led the Canadian band until 1878, when the Indian Act of Canada imposed elected band counselors on all Indian bands. All the Mohawks were predominantly Catholic, and both sides of the reserve worshipped at the St. Regis Mission Church, which dates from 1792.

During this century, Mohawks in Canada and the United States have undergone major changes in their community and lifestyle. Farming, fishing, and logging no longer dominate as the primary occupations. There is only one working farm at Akwesasne and the lucrative dairy cattle and sport fishing industries have been decimated by the construction of the St. Lawrence Seaway in 1954 and the pollution generated by major industries along the St. Lawrence River between Cornwall, Ontario, and Massena, New York. The introduction of the chainsaw revolutionized logging and ended the life of Adirondack logging camps and Mohawk employment there.

The era of steel bridges and skyscrapers opened up new careers for Mohawk men. For seventy-five years Mohawks from Akwesasne and Caughnauwaga (Canadian Mohawks from the Kahawakee Reserve near Montreal) have been prominent ironworkers in Canada and the United States. Until recently, before the construction business flattened out, as many as 50 percent of the adult men at Akwesasne worked in high steel. They constitute a large part of the membership of Local 440 (Utica) of the Ironworkers of America. Ironwork is a source of immense cultural pride and self-esteem among Mohawk people. Akwesasne Mohawk ironworkers have participated in almost every large steel construction project in North America. This constant contact with the non-Indian world by large elements of the Mohawk population has had a significant influence on Mohawk cultural values and lifestyle.

The Longhouse Religion of the Iroquois did not arrive at Akwesasne until 1934. For many years, the Longhouse followers were a distinct religious and political minority on the reservation. Traditional Mohawk values and culture were given a boost by the founding of the Akwesasne Counselors Organization in the 1930s by Ray Fadden (Aren Akweks), who did much to reintroduce the teaching of Mohawk language, history, and culture into the school curriculum. Since the civil rights movement of the 1960s, participation in Longhouse ceremonies and activities has increased considerably. The North American Indian Traveling College, founded by Ernest Benedict; the publications *Akwesasne Notes* and *Indian Times*; and the Akwesasne Freedom School are all prime examples of the growth of traditional values and practices at Akwesasne.

Two events in 1968 propelled the Akwesasne Mohawks into national prominence and Indian leadership. In May, 1968, the Mohawk Parents Committee, led by Minerva White and Chief John Cook, boycotted the Salmon River School and called state and national attention to the failure of Indian education. On November 18, Canadian and American Mohawks at Akwesasne blockaded the Cornwall International Bridge, which abuts on Mohawk territory, over the alleged failure of Canada to abide by treaty rights given to Mohawks in the 1794 Jay Treaty. Prominent in the treaty rights blockade were Ernest Benedict and Mike Mitchell, the grand chief of the Akwesasne Band of Mohawks in Canada in 1992.

If there has been a success story at Akwesasne in this century, it has been in the field of Native American education. In less than twenty years, the Mohawks reduced an 80 percent Indian student dropout rate in 1968 to less than 10 percent. In addition to the Freedom School mentioned earlier, Mohawks embarked upon a broad program of educational reform at all levels: preschool, elementary, secondary, college, and adult education. Today, over two hundred Mohawk youths attend college regularly. The Mohawk language, history, and culture are taught in the schools and in the Upward Bound Program, which Mohawk youth attend at St. Lawrence University. Mohawks raised the money and constructed the first Indian library on a reservation in the country. In addition, the tribe has an active educational program in health care and substance abuse at the new health and rehabilitation center.

Political differences continue to plague the community. In 1980, a traditional party takeover of the tribal headquarters was prompted by tribal police attempting to retrieve chainsaws confiscated by traditionalists from a tribal clearing party. A violent confrontation was averted when the New York State police stopped a tribal march on the barricaded traditional stronghold at Racquette Point. One legacy of that confrontation has been the absence of tribal police at Akwesasne since 1980. Currently, the New York State Police patrol the reservation.

A more serious conflict arose in July 1989, when the FBI and the New York State Police raided several privately owned Mohawk casinos in a predawn raid and seized several illegal gambling devices. At the height of their operation, the casinos employed almost 700 Mohawks. For the next nine months pro- and anti-gambling factions mobilized their forces, and the reservation became an armed camp with random shootings, illegal barricades on state highways, Molotov cocktails, power outages, and vehicle rammings. The two main factions were the warriors, who defended the gambling, and the antigambling traditional forces. The violence culminated with the murder of two young men during a night of violence on May first. Canadian military and New York State Police were summoned, and a reservation-wide curfew was instituted. The barriers were dismantled, but no effort was made to disarm the heavily armed reservation forces. The casinos remain closed, but two tribal bingo halls are operating again.

Other outstanding political issues at Akwesasne besides gambling are state taxation of sales on the reservtion, pollution, contraband cigarettes, land claims against the state of New York, and police protection.

Political differences and factionalism have been a way of life at Akwesasne for over fifty years. The introduction of the gambling issue highly inflamed existing differences and brought the reserve, both Canadian and American sides, to the brink of civil war. Today only a healthy outside police presence and the closure of the casinos maintain an uneasy calm. Recent elections confirm that opposing factions are nearly evenly divided. Without a political

consensus, outstanding tribal issues cannot be resolved. The large land claim suit against New York State (13,000 acres) languishes, and the future of legalized gambling remains clouded. The longstanding issue of Mohawk sovereignty and New York State civil and criminal jurisdiction on the reservation remains unresolved. Illegal cigarette trafficking on the reservation is at an all-time high, and local non-Indian merchants are up in arms at cut-rate prices for gasoline and cigarettes on the reservation.

Prominent traditional leaders at Akwesasne today are Jake Swamp, Tom Porter, and Brad Bonaparte. Leading tribalists are Chief David Jacobs, Eli Tarbell, former Chief Leonard Garrow, and Gil White. Rosemary Bonaparte was the first Mohawk woman elected as a tribal chief and Margaret Lazore served as tribal clerk for many years and is the unofficial tribal historian. Leaders in Mohawk education are Minerva White, Lincoln White, Salina Smoke, Solomon Cook, the late Chief Larry Lazore, Ernest Benedict, and William Mitchell.

Robert N. Wells, Jr.

See also **Ironworkers; Iroquois Confederacy**

Further Reading

Fenton, William N., and Elisabeth Tooker. "Mohawk." *Handbook of North American Indians.* Vol. 15. *Northeast.* Ed. Bruce G. Trigger. Washington, DC: Smithsonian Institution (1978): 466–80.

Frisch, Jack. "Revitalization, Nativism and Tribalism among the St. Regis Mohawks." Ph.D. diss., Indiana University, 1960.

Hauptman, Laurence M. *The Iroquois Struggle for Survival: World War II to Red Power.* NY: Syracuse University Press, 1986.

Matthiessen, Peter. *Indian Country.* New York, NY: Viking Press, 1984.

Wilson, Edmund. *Apologies to the Iroquois.* New York, NY: Farrar, Straus and Cudahy, 1960.

MOHEGAN

The Mohegan tribe originated in upstate New York along the shores of Lake Champlain in the prehistoric period. They migrated to their current land base in southeastern Connecticut around the time of contact with the Europeans. As an Algonquian-speaking group, they share many cultural similarities with all southern New England Indians. Despite conflict, land loss, and periods of extreme poverty, the Mohegan have endured the centuries and today they count 976 members on their tribal roll. About 550 of these members live in the traditional homeland of New London County, Connecticut. The Mohegan are currently in the final stages of a battle for federal recognition and land.

Mohegan land claims began in the seventeenth century, when the Sachem Uncas and his sons alienated thousands of acres of land to the colonists. Six hundred acres of these lands, which are owned by the State of Connecticut, are still contested today. Beginning with the late nineteenth century the Mohegan began to file suits and petitions for the return of their Native lands.

One of the tribal members who attempted to regain tribal lands during the twentieth century was John Hamilton. Hamilton was a colorful and contentious figure, who was often at odds with his own people because of his self-proclaimed sachemhood. Nevertheless, Hamilton's legal initiative in the late 1960s led to the filing of two suits against the State of Connecticut (for violation of the Non-Intercourse Acts) for recovery of 600 acres.

To counter Hamilton's claims that he spoke for all Mohegans as their sachem, tribal members created a constitutional government with majority-elected Tribal Council officers from 1970 to 1980. In 1984, under the leadership of Courtland Fowler, this duly elected group submitted its petition for federal recognition. In 1989, the Mohegans received a proposed finding against their federal acknowledgment. The Branch of Acknowledgment and Research (BAR) alleged that from the 1940s through the 1970s the Mohegans did not maintain a cohesive community and political influence. The Mohegan immediately challenged the proposed finding by submitting additional documentation. In March 1994 the BAR granted the Mohegan federal recognition. The land suits remain unresolved as of this writing.

The Mohegan have been both politically and socially active throughout this century thanks in part to the pan-Indianism that began around 1910. The Mohegan were motivated to initiate tribal and intertribal political councils and to revive traditional arts, languages, and organizations. In 1920 the Mohegan formed the Mohegan Indian Association to "preserve the integrity of the tribe and to effect certain aims along social and legal lines," according to anthropologist Frank G. Speck. In 1923, the Mohegans became involved with the Algonquin Indian Council of New England. Three Mohegan were chosen as officers of this council.

Frank Speck worked with the Mohegan during the first half of this century and became a close friend of the Tantaquidgeon family. Current Mohegan medicine woman, Dr. Gladys Tantaquidgeon, worked with Speck as his research assistant at the University of Pennsylvania. Afterwards, she was employed by the Bureau of Indian Affairs as a social worker and then as a Native arts specialist in the West. In 1931, Gladys and her brother Harold opened the Tantaquidgeon Indian Museum. That institution is still a focal point for the tribe.

During the twentieth century the Mohegan celebrated the annual Wigwam festival. This celebration has roots in the Green Corn festivals of pre-Columbian times. This event was held until 1956 and then revived in 1992 as The Wigwam Pow Wow. It involves construction of a brush arbor and the preparation of Native foods like *yokeag* (parched ground corn) and succotash. This annual event has become an important opportunity for Mohegan from all over the country to come home and review kinship ties. It is also a tribal moneyraiser, because Native foods and arts are sold to the public.

Today's Mohegan Tribal Council, governed by a Constitution, represents the tribe at the state and federal levels in issues related to land, recognition, burials, education and socio-economic development. The Mohegan Council of Elders serves as a constitutional review board.

Some of the most important symbols of Mohegan identity in the twentieth century include the Mohegan Church, the Tantaquidgeon Museum, and Fort Shantok Tribal Burial Ground, all of which lie in the heart of the Mohegan homeland. The church has been a focal point of tribal activity since its inception in 1831. An eagle feather hangs above the pulpit symbolizing traditional tribal values. The church is the only property which the Mohegan hold in common today.

The Mohegan message for the twentieth century is as follows: We visualize that the tribe will be self-sufficient and able to provide education and employment opportunities to all . . . and that we will be as we have been in the past, now and in the future—a friend to all.

Laurie Weinstein

Melissa Fawcett

Gladys I. Tantaquidgeon

Further Reading

Fawcett-Sayet, Melissa. *The Lasting of the Mohegans.* Knoxville, TN: Snowbird Publications, forthcoming.

Griner, Jerome. "Petition for Federal Recognition" [and other documents]. Submitted by the Mohegan Tribe to the United States Department of the Interior. Vol 1. Concerning Criteria Set Forth in 25 CFR 83.7. Washington, DC: Bureau of Acknowledgment and Research, Bureau of Indian Affairs, Dec. 17, 1984.

Simmons, William. *Spirit of the New England Tribes: Indian History and Folklore, 1620–1984.* Hanover, NH and London, England: University Press of New England, 1986.

Speck, Frank. "Native Tribes and Dialects of Connecticut: A Mohegan-Pequot Diary." *Bureau of American Ethnology 43rd Annual Report 1925–26.* Washington, DC: The Bureau (1928): 199–287.

Weinstein, Laurie. "Land, Politics, and Power: The Mohegan Indians in the 17th and 18th Centuries." *Man in the Northeast* (Fall 1991): 9–16.

MOHICAN

See Mohegan; Stockbridge-Munsee

MOJAVE

The Fort Mojave Reservation, along the Colorado River in the three states of California, Arizona, and Nevada, was established by War Department General Order No. 19 of August 4, 1870, and by Executive Order of February 2, 1911. The United States government resolved the status of the Fort Mojave tribe to be that of a sovereign nation. The tribe is federally recognized with authority to establish, regulate, and administer statutes and other legislation appropriate to its unique tribal tenets and culture, while also adhering to the Articles of the Constitution of the United States.

The Mojave (*Ahamakav*, "People Who Live Along the River"), are one of the few tribes on aboriginal lands today. Historically Mojave homelands encompassed territory along the Colorado River from present-day Hoover Dam downriver beyond Blythe, California, a distance of approximately 200 miles. Vast territory inland to the west was also occupied by Mojave settlements and camps. Although throughout the centuries following the coming of the Europeans the federal government methodically displaced tribes from their ancestral homes by force and at their discretion, the Mojave were able to remain on their aboriginal land, although this is presently but a fraction of the original territory.

A number of tribes in Arizona comprise the Yuman linguistic family to which the Mojave belong: Yavapai in Prescott; Pee-Posh (Maricopa) in Gila River; Quechan in Yuma; Hualapai in Peach Springs; and Havasupai in Supai. The Mojave are the largest of the group. The language department of the AhaMakav Cultural Society provides classes in Mojave throughout the year, more so during the months when school is not in session.

At the beginning of European immigration to the West (i.e., settlers, trappers, missionaries), passage through Mojave territory did occur. In spite of uncivil behavior attributed to the tribe, the people were of a peaceful and generous demeanor. Confrontation was the result of provocation, attacks, or unjustified imposition upon the tribe. Guides from the tribe led travelers safely through harsh mountain and desert terrain via springs along the Mojave Trail to the Pacific Coast. They also guided Father Francisco Garcés on his expedition from the Pacific Coast to the Sante Fe missions. Don Juan de Oñate, governor of New Mexico in 1604, was the first white man to make an appearance among the Mojave people at the site of the Bill Williams and Colorado River confluence.

The fine physique of the Mojave men seemed to surprise the foreigners, and their physical prowess amazed them. Their physical stature was an average six feet in height; they were recognized, even among the Southwest tribes, as great runners. The people traveled widely, and their songs relate this. Subsistence was dependent upon fishing, hunting, trapping, and seasonal farming, using overflow waters of the Colorado River. Surplus harvest was stored for sparse winter months.

Dreams are an integral part of the Mojave culture. It is through dreams that special powers of healing and foresight into the future are received. Events even of our present-day experience were foretold long, long ago.

From the lofty and majestic *Avi kwa 'ame* overlooking the valley of the Mojave came the teachings and instructions of the Creator Mutiviyl through his son Mustamho. This is the sacred land of the Yuman people. As are all Natives of this country, the Mojave are aware of the stewardship responsibility to the environment, to all living things upon the earth, below the earth, and above the earth. The Yavapai, the Pee-Posh (Maricopa), the Quechan, the Hualapai, the Havasupai, and the Mojave, all of one beginning, share similar religious beliefs.

Mojave population in early history is estimated at 7,000 members, but cannot be confirmed; there was no appropriate census. Although the majority of this very large tribe lived on the Colorado River, many other members were widely dispersed throughout and occupied the vast low desert and high desert. Current tribal enrollment is 967 citizens, the greater number being local residents. Others live in proximity to the reservation. Still others, in pursuit of employment opportunities or higher education, reside elsewhere.

Around 1860 the United States government persuaded Chief Arateba and some tribal members to relocate sixty miles downriver in Parker, Arizona. In 1865 the Colorado River Indian Reservation was established. The majority of the tribe, however, chose to remain with Chief Homose Kohote (hereditary chief) who refused to make the transition and vowed to forever remain in the Mohave Valley.

The Fort Mojave Constitution mandates seven Council members elected at large to staggered four-year terms. Planning and administering under tribal regulations, in addition to considering the regulations of federal, state, and county governments of California, Arizona, and Nevada, has made tribal governance a comprehensive and complex responsibility.

Pete Lambert (*Sukulyi Hi-ar*) was the last chief of the Fort Mojave Tribe. Upon his death in 1947, the centuries-old traditional rule was no more. The advent of the foreigner, his adverse tenets, lifestyle, and subjugation had increasingly hindered and eventually ended Mojave autonomy and self-rule. Leadership involvement in intergovernmental relationships encompassing federal, state, county, and tribal entities is now imperative.

Frances Wilbur Stillman (Malyika Chupek), born and reared among her people, became the first Fort Mojave tribal chairman in 1957. Ever aware and understanding of her people's needs and hopes, she brought about opportunities for education, employment, and self-determination. Nora McDowell Garcia, current chairperson, completed her third term in June, 1993. A number of ambitious and challenging projects have been initiated during her administration.

The tribe maintains its own police force and trial and appellate court, with jurisdiction over civil and (limited) criminal cases. Public education through high school is available in Needles, California; Mohave Valley, Arizona; and Bullhead City, Arizona. Federal Indian boarding schools may also be attended.

Housing for eligible tribal members is provided through the Fort Mojave Tribal Housing Authority (Department of Housing and Urban Development). There are presently 184 homes on the reservation.

Agriculture remains a major tribal business and source of income. Total agricultural land base is 15,000 acres or 41 percent of the reservation land. Most of the farms are in Arizona, with some acreage in California. Cotton is the main crop.

Economic development of new projects on the reservation has concentrated on telecommunications, water, sewer, gas, and electricity. Tribal enterprises may form and operate under the corporate Charter of the Fort Mojave tribe. Other tribal enterprises include housing developments, a car wash, smoke-shop, gas station, and an auto racetrack.

A most ambitious development enterprise has been embarked upon, utilizing the tribe's entire 3,998 acres of Nevada land: It is the creation of a new community, Aha Macav. Recreation, commercial, residential, and casino facilities are provided for in the master plan. This concept is unique in its foundation and implementation. In connection with the enterprise, the tribe has issued revenue bonds for a water and sewer project, which is the first ever issued by an Indian tribe.

Elda J. Butler

See also Arizona Tribes; Colorado River Indian Tribes; Yavapai

Further Reading

Smith, Gerald A. *The Mojave Indians.* Bloomington, CA: San Bernardino County Museum Assoc., 1977.

Stewart, Kenneth M. "Mohave." *Handbook of North American Indians.* Vol. 10. *California.* Ed. Alfonso Ortiz. Washington, DC: Smithsonian Institution (1983): 55–70.

MONACAN

The Monacan Indian Tribal Association, a state-recognized enclave since 1989, is based in Amherst County, Virginia, with many members living in nearby Lynchburg. The total enrollment is about 300.

Today's Monacans are probably descended from a variety of piedmont and mountain Indian groups, including the historical Monacans. The group first reached the public eye in a horridly derogatory book, by eugenicists Estabrook and McDougle (1926). An M.A. thesis two years later tried to set the record straight using cultural explanations for a "backward" way of life, but that work remains unpublished. The tribe has been trying to live down its early twentieth-century reputation ever since.

An Episcopal mission to the tribe was founded in 1908 and staffed first with deaconesses and then with priests from the church army. The current priest spearheaded the move toward incorporation and state recognition in the 1980s; the mission's parish house is now the tribal center. There had been a county-supported school, later staffed by mission personnel, near the mission site since the 1860s; it remained a tribal school until the advent of integration.

The people are governed in tribal matters by an elected chief, assistant chief, secretary, and treasurer; there are also several informally appointed elders. These functionaries meet on the average of once a month in closed sessions. Elections are held when an office becomes vacant. Tribal meetings are called, usually monthly, and are closed to outsiders.

The people's traditional culture has long been superceded by Anglo ways. There has been some move since state recognition to revive some crafts and reconstruct the group's history.

Helen C. Rountree

Further Reading

Hantman, Jeffrey L. *When a People Came from under the World: Archaeology and Ethnohistory of the Virginia Monacan.* Charlottesville: University of Virginia Press, forthcoming.

Houck, Peter W. *Indian Island in Amherst County.* Lynchburg, VA: Lynchburg Historical Research Co., ca. 1986.

Rountree, Helen C. "Indian Virginians on the Move." *Indians of the Southeastern United States in the Late 20th Century.* Ed. J. Anthony Paredes. Tuscaloosa, AL and London, England: University of Alabama Press (1992): 9–28.

MONACHE

See Mono: Western

MONO, EASTERN

See Paiute: Owens Valley

MONO, WESTERN

The twentieth century has brought enormous changes to the Western Mono (Monache) community. The opening of the century found a large proportion of the population living in their traditional homes in the south central Sierra Nevada of California, in Madera and Fresno counties. Economic pressures and government policies, particularly regarding the education of Indian children, coalesced to bring the people out of their mountain fastness into closer proximity with and under the control of the dominant society in the early 1900s. Four major Western Mono communities, based on the traditional band/settlement structure, formed and persist today, including from north to south: the Num (Mona), focused around the town of North Fork; the Posgisa on the Big Sandy Rancheria near Auberry; the Holkoma on the Cold Springs (Sycamore) Rancheria near Tollhouse; and the Wobonuch focused in the town of Dunlap.

Like many California peoples at the turn of the century, the Western Mono bands were essentially landless, with no "legal" claims to their territory. Under increasing political pressure in part brought by the Northern California Indian Association, a Protestant activist organization, the federal government created three small rancherias for the Mono early in the second decade of the century. Additionally, a number of individuals in each of the communities were able to acquire land through the allotment process. A Presbyterian mission and boarding school for girls was established in North Fork, and the American Home Baptist Mission Society established churches and schools at Big Sandy, Sycamore, and Dunlap. Many families moved close to these schools so their children could attend, although a number of children were sent to federal boarding schools, such as Sherman Institute in Riverside, or Carson in Nevada.

The rancherias have never offered an economic base for the people, thus contributing significantly to the persistent problem of unemployment. Men have typically earned wages particularly as loggers, but also as general ranch hands, ropers, sheep shearers, miners, and wood choppers. Logger's families moved back to their mountain homes during the summer logging season, and were thus able to follow traditional gathering patterns. Women took on domestic jobs or worked in local hotels, hospitals, and convalescent facilities, and whole families also moved seasonally to the Central Valley to pick crops. World War II marked many changes in the communities, including loss of population to urban areas which promised jobs, an increase in higher education for many, and the entrance of more women into a larger job market as well as increasingly into tribal administration.

While the early 1950s witnessed termination of two of the rancherias, North Fork and Big Sandy, there has been a strong resurgence of both political activity and expression of cultural values. Under the leadership of Ron Goode, the North Fork community (membership approximately 600) is actively seeking federal recognition. The health needs of the community are served by a well-established regional health clinic offered by Central Valley Indian Health Services. A senior citizen's lunch program is available for the elders, who very much enjoy the regular visiting it provides, and the children have a Head Start program which has operated for twenty years. Big Sandy (membership approximately 200) was officially unterminated in the mid-1980s, and with the guidance of tribal administrator Linda Alec has undertaken a successful housing program. The Cold Springs Rancheria (membership 275), led by Frank Lee, had maintained its federal status and was able to take immediate advantage of Housing and Urban Development opportunities for new housing early in the 1980s. The Wobonuch, led by Dock Dick and his family in Dunlap (membership of approximately 80), are pursuing federal recognition in order to be eligible for federal housing and educational programs.

Cultural life, in addition to being practiced daily with the family, is expressed through activities of the Sierra Mono Museum, established twenty years ago, solely owned and operated by the Mono people and located in North Fork. It maintains a number of collections and displays, supports demonstrations of traditional arts and skills, and gives classes in traditional culture such as basketmaking, beadwork and language. The Museum holds a popular event, the Annual Indian Fair Days, every August with traditional food, arts and crafts, dances and songs, and baseball games. Big Sandy and the Wobonuch are currently cooperating in a National Park Service grant to preserve culture including language, traditional foods, basketry, and ethnohistory. Each of these four Mono communities is committed to cultural preservation and has taken an active role in the protection of their cultural resources and sacred lands.

Helen McCarthy

See also **California Tribes**

Further Reading

Gayton, Anna. "Yokuts and Western Mono Ethnography." *University of California Anthropological Records* 10:1–2 (1948): 1–302.

Gifford, Edward W. "The Northfork Mono." *University of California Publications in American Archaeology and Ethnology* 31:2 (1932): 15–65.

McCarthy, Helen. *A Political Economy of Western Mono Acorn Production.* Ph.D. diss., University of California, Davis, 1993.

Spier, Robert F.G. "Monache." *Handbook of North American Indians.* Vol. 8. *California.* Ed. Robert F. Heizer. Washington, DC: Smithsonian Institution (1978): 426–36.

MOTION PICTURES

See Public Image; Films and Video

MUCKLESHOOT

The Muckleshoot Indian Reservation is located on Muckleshoot Prairie on a hill between the Green and White rivers near Puget Sound in King County, Washington. One version of the meaning of Muckleshoot, originally pronounced *Buklshuhls*, is "from a high point from which you can see." The Muckleshoot spoke a dialect of Lushootseed, a Salish language.

The Muckleshoot tribe has confirmed that it was a participant in the Point Elliott Treaty of 1855. An executive order in 1874 established definite boundaries for the reservation. The original 3,332 acres were mostly allotted and were quickly alienated from the tribe. As of 1975, there were 1,201 acres of trust lands on the reservation interspersed with non-Indian farmlands. The lands have always been fractionated.

The Muckleshoot tribe, which has 1,000 enrolled members in 1993, has been affected by the assimilationist policies of Euroamericans. Muckleshoots suffered under the Bureau of Indian Affairs school system, were not allowed to speak their own language, could not gamble or practice their own religion, and watched the decimation of the forests, the rivers, the fisheries, and entire families.

Land Claims

The Muckleshoots were denied their land claims in the United States Court of Claims, but in 1959 the Indian Claims Commission ruled that the tribe occupied 101,620 acres of aboriginal land valued at $86,377. That amount was awarded to the tribe and provided the initial funds for tribal efforts to buy back some of the lost lands. Acquiring a larger land base continues to be a priority.

Tribal Government

The Muckleshoot tribe is governed by the Tribal Council, whose members serve three-year terms. The chairman, vice-chairman, and secretary-treasurer are elected by the Council. Its Constitution, since amended, was approved in 1936 under the terms of the Indian Reorganization Act.

Education

Education has been a priority with the Muckleshoots, who first used funds available through the 1934 Johnson-O'Malley Act (J-OM) in 1963 to begin a Muckleshoot Head Start program, enrolling thirty-five to forty-five children, aged three to five years. In 1993, this program is still in place. The J-OM program operates in the local school district and is successful in graduating a few Indian students each year. The Muckleshoot Tribal School began in 1985, and in 1994 expects to enroll sixty-five students from kindergarten through fifth grade. The short-term goal is to acclimate the students to public schools and give them the desire to pursue higher education. The long-term goal is to have in one building a comprehensive educational program including GED classes, reading assistance, Muckleshoot language and culture programs, and other daily activities for people from ages five to sixty-five.

Economic Development

Fishing has always been central to Muckleshoot culture. The Judge Boldt Decision made in the United States District Court in 1974 reaffirms the treaty rights of Native Puget Sound people to fish. At the time of the decision, the Muckleshoot tribe owned fifty-one acres in common ownership. From 1976 to 1977, the Keta Creek Rearing Station on the Green River began a program of salmon hatching. In 1981, the holding tanks were expanded and enabled the rearing of about 50,000 chinook, coho, and chum salmon, half of production, as well as steelhead trout for release into the Keta Creek system. Additional rearing tanks contain golden and eastern brook trout, which are donated to Trout Unlimited for release into lakes, primarily in King County.

In September 1989 the White River Hatchery was completed following a legal settlement with the Puget Power utility company. In 1990, 350,000 springer salmon were released. This number had increased to 650,000 by 1993. The goal is to renew the springer run before more of the elders die. In the summer of 1993, an employee was placed in the mountains at Huckleberry Pond to acclimate 150,000 springers to be released below the dam on White River.

Muckleshoot Enterprises began with the construction of the first smoke-shop in the early 1970s. Now located near the highway, it is a combination smoke-shop, liquor, and convenience store. In 1985, the company added the Muckleshoot Indian Bingo Hall to its activities. With a 1,450 seating capacity, it remains a thriving business. The first Muckleshoot business manager was named in 1993, and a casino is in the planning stages.

While the tribe has taken aggressive steps to provide its members with job opportunities, unemployment remains a problem. Much of the work is seasonal, and the unemployment rate often reaches 75 percent.

Child Welfare

The Muckleshoot Group Home was developed by the tribe in about 1979, in response to the Indian Child Welfare Act of 1978, to prevent the continued removal of Indian children from their natural parents for placement in non-Indian foster homes, and to return foster care jurisdiction to the tribe. The home licenses Indian foster homes, gives family counseling and other related services, and houses a varying number of children at any time.

Religion

The Indian Shaker Church has a substantial membership among the Muckleshoot. Its church is open to everyone for occasions such as baptisms. While many Muckleshoot were practicing Catholics earlier in the century, there is no longer a Catholic church nearby. The Pentecostal church is active on the reservation in the late twentieth century.

After resisting decimation and destruction for more than one hundred years, the Muckleshoot tribe is regaining its lands, renewing the fisheries, and educating and rearing its own children. Members are also attempting to relearn the language, maintain traditional skills, and retain Muckleshoot values and beliefs to enter the twenty-first century.

Lorraine J. Cross

See also **Washington State Tribes**

Further Reading

Cohen, Fay G. *Treaties on Trial: The Continuing Controversy Over Northwest Indian Fishing Rights.* Seattle: University of Washington Press, 1986.
Cross, Virginia, and Pat Noel. *Muckleshoot Today.* WA: Auburn School District No. 408, 1985.
Noel, Patricia Slettvet. *Muckleshoot Indian History.* WA: Auburn School District No. 408, 1980.
Ruby, Robert H., and John A. Brown. *A Guide to the Indian Tribes of the Pacific Northwest.* Rev. ed. Norman: University of Oklahoma Press, 1992.

MUSEUMS

Throughout the twentieth century, thousands of museums of every type and size found in the smallest towns and the largest urban areas have collected and exhibited Native American objects. During most of this century, the collection, research, and exhibition of Native American materials by museums was done unilaterally without any significant contribution from or consultation with Native American communities. Significant new relationships between museums and Native Americans have begun to emerge only within the past few decades, largely as a result of a few innovative museum programs, the emergence of tribally operated museums and growing tribal community political strength, and changing museum attitudes hastened by federal legislation on key cultural issues such as religious freedom and repatriation.

By the beginning of the twentieth century, extensive Native American anthropological collections had been assembled and were located in such large museums as the Smithsonian Institution, whose one million specimens included a significant Native American element, and the Field Museum, with its enormous anthropological collection legacy from the 1893 World's Columbian Exposition. Large-scale collecting associated with museums continued to be a major research professional activity across the nation, from new collections for the American Museum of Natural History, the Heye Foundation's Museum of the American Indian, and for university museums at schools, such as Harvard and the University of California. At the same time, smaller-scale collecting was being actively pursued by most other museums on an important regional basis. Major expositions were also to be organized regularly, for example: the St. Louis World's Fair in 1904, Seattle's Alaska-Yukon Exposition of 1909, and San Francisco's Panama Pacific of 1915. These national and regional expositions continued to amass anthropological materials which often went at fairs' end to museums. In all these instances, the collecting activity was driven by a sense of urgency related to the commonly held belief that Indians would soon be extinct (either literally as distinct peoples or as distinct cultures). Few laws restricted collecting for research, and it was not really expected that Native peoples would or could have any important objections to research work, which was an inherently noble, ethical, and social positive activity. Although it is impossible now to estimate accurately, it is probable that by the close of the first few decades of the twentieth century, the vast majority of all existing Indian ethnographic artifacts made prior to 1900 were in non-Indian possession. This collecting and exhibition activity by museums did certainly help to define Indian arts as collectibles and spur the local community production of goods to meet this public commercial interest. In other words, museums helped create an ethnic art market in Native American arts in many parts of the country, especially for the new tourism that came with the expansion of railroads.

It is also true that by the beginning of the century, most museums with Native American materials were using nearly all of the distinctive types of museum exhibits that would eventually be created in this century. The most common exhibit format was perhaps most often found in the small community museum, which simply displayed, in a "potpourri" style, all of what was usually a small and random selection of objects with relatively little interpretive information.

Beyond this, most turn of the century "professional" museum exhibits organized objects in either geographical and/or typological order, with the latter sometimes arrayed to illustrate changes in technology or style through time. But in short order, museums began to present Native American materials in other ways, including, for example, the life-group display and the culture area array. The typological display had often showed massed quantities of artifacts of a particular type (e.g., axes) without regard to provenience, whereas these new display forms either presented material depicting cultural assemblages from societies falling within a geographically defined cultural area, or simply by representative single cultural units, such as a tribe. In either mode, a life-group display was a very popular innovation, usually presenting a representative family or other mannequin grouping in a dwelling or other typical setting, engaged in relevant activities and surrounded by appropriate tools, animals, plants, and so on. One of the first of these diorama or "slice of life" displays was an Arctic Inuit scene created by the famous early museum anthropologist Franz Boas, with a cutaway igloo and icy scene complete with an invisibly suspended bird, all of which enthralled viewers.

These displays, repeated during the Depression through scores of miniature diorama scenes made by Works Progress Administration artists for museums, and since the Depression in both miniature and full scale, have remained one of the most popular forms of museum exhibit. In some cases new versions of the diorama have been created with appropriate sound effects, such as the buffalo hunting scene at the Milwaukee Public Museum, or the very recent Tahitian street scene in the Field Museum's Pacific Islands exhibit. Other early displays focused attention on technology, such as how pottery was made, or how tools were produced and used. In all of these varied efforts at presenting the nature of Indian life and arts to the public, museums did not seek Indian assistance or perspectives. Sacred materials as well as human remains from ancient and not so ancient burials were placed on display as commonly as everyday utensils or other mundane artifacts. Native American materials with considerable aesthetic quality remained within the crafts realm, and well beyond that of fine art. Similarly, museum records and exhibit labels rarely identified individual Indian artists or artisans.

In most of these exhibits, Indians were presented in ways that made it clear they were a part of the past (and often a very ancient past), or were perhaps at best archaic reminders of a bygone era trying to adapt to today's modern, civilized world. Their arts and technologies were viewed as being as much primitive and aesthetically lacking as they were romantic, while information on their religious beliefs, philosophies, political or social organizations were usually absent altogether. The profoundly exotic, curio quality of Indian life presented by museums reflected, as museums often do, attitudes held by members of the general public. It was not expected that Indians would visit museums, take part in museum educational programs, collaborate in significant ways in museum research, or otherwise be concerned or involved with museum affairs except as subjects of museum-directed research (although in one case Lumbee came to the Smithsonian for tests to support their claims for federal recognition as a tribe).

It was in the post-World War II era that a number of new developments began which would change in important and fundamental ways the relationships between museums and Native Americans. These developments included new consultative approaches to exhibits, research, and community projects, Native American representation in museum affairs, new cultural property legislation, and the creation of significant numbers of new tribally operated museums and other new organizations and institutions focused on Native American interests.

Increasing international concern during the 1960s about the looting of archaeological sites, and debate about what steps could be taken to curb the illicit trade in these and other artifacts, led to the 1970 UNESCO Convention in Paris on the means to halt this trade, including the massive and highly destructive illegal trade in pre-Columbian materials from both North and South America. Although the United States did not pass its own legislation in this area until 1982 (and many other major world powers not at all), many museums immediately instituted new collecting policies and procedures designed to deter the acquisition of illicitly obtained specimens. These actions were matched by supporting statements and new ethical policies by major anthropological, archaeological, and museum associations.

The growing professional and legal sensitivity over issues of aboriginal title, wrongful acquisition, and cultural patrimony were highlighted by increasing Native American attempts to seek the repatriation of objects of great community value, most often continuing religious value. Perhaps the most significant example of these efforts was the repatriation of sacred war gods to the Zuni from the Denver Art Museum and other institutions beginning in 1978. On the national level, the North American Indian Museums Association, with about 100 members, was established in 1978, and in 1981 published not only a directory but also guidelines for non-Indian museums to use when asked to repatriate materials. The significance of this movement to recover access to and use of sacred materials and even to religious sites was recognized in 1978 with passage of the American Indian Religious Freedom Act. While this did not lead to large-scale transfers of objects from museum collections to tribes, it did focus clear attention on a set of issues of great concern to Native American communities, especially concerns about human remains and sacred objects. By 1980, there was well-established resistance within the museum community to the possible repatriation of collections and, since this perspective was hardly unanimous, associated sharp debate on the merits of repatriation. In 1990, mu-

seum attempts to deter legislation authorizing repatriation failed with the passage of the Native American Graves Protection and Repatriation Act (P.L. 101-106).

The escalation of Native American attempts to seek a definitive resolution to repatriation in the twenty-odd years preceding passage of P.L. 101-106 did meet with an increase in efforts by a number of museums to be more responsive to Native American concerns. These efforts were in part reactions to Native American interests regarding control over research activities and museum portrayals of Indians. By the 1970s, for example, Native American communities in the United States and Canada had begun to create research agreements for scholars seeking permission to carry out investigations in the community, including museum-based research. On the other side, a number of museums had developed consultative and collaborative relationships with Indian communities in the creation of new exhibits. Institutions as diverse as the Heard Museum, Harvard's Peabody Museum, and the Museum of Anthropology at the University of British Columbia are all examples of this kind of exhibit development. In other cases, the 1970s saw important collaborative research programs underway, such as that at the Royal British Columbia Museum, as well as major outreach programs such as the Burke Museum's work with the Makah Tribe in creating a new Cultural and Research Center and training its staff.

The results of these varied efforts were important for both museums and the Native American communities in showing what could be accomplished. The resulting new exhibits, for example, presented Indians not simply as the dead remnants of a historical past, but as dynamic and contemporary people strong in their cultural traditions and innovative in adapting to new artistic, social, and material conditions and opportunities. Harvard's 1974 Tlingit Aanee show, heralded as the first major exhibit that actively involved tribal members in the planning and execution of the display, presented scenes of traditional and contemporary life side by side, as did the 1980 California Academy of Sciences' Hopi Kachina exhibit, which also took pains to explore a religious tradition in ways approved by community leaders. From these, it is a short step to exhibits such as the 1989 Burke Museum's Washington State Centennial exhibit, "Time of Gathering," where Native Americans selected the artifacts, prepared special interpretive panels, received commissions for contemporary art works for the exhibit, and took part in the associated educational program. And, on an even larger-scale collaboration, the creation of the California State Indian Museum and its proposed larger California Indian Museum system is an example of extensively shared responsibilities, in this case between a widespread Native American community and a state government agency.

Other new exhibits have also focused on singularly important traditional artists and their works, such as the basketry of Datsolalee, or the carvings of

Youngdoctor or Willie Seaweed. Indian protests in the 1960s about museum exhibits of Indians were usually focused on a lack of Indian input and/or perspective, but the 1980s saw a protest against a museum exhibit for quite different political reasons. This was the 1988 Lubicon Lake Indian band protest against the Glenbow Museum's exhibit, "The Spirit Sings," created in association with the Calgary Winter Olympics. This protest, intended to bring attention to a land claim conflict, gained international attention and led to some museums withdrawing earlier offers of loaned material for the exhibit, even though an Indian advisory panel had been involved in the planning. A final intriguing element to this protest was the involvement of a museum corporate sponsor, who was also involved in commercial activity on Lake Lubicon lands.

In many parts of North America, new approaches to exhibits were contemporaneous with increased Indian usage of museum collections in creating new community language programs, art programs, history projects, and general education programs, contributing to the further movement of the Indian art "renaissance" that had begun in the 1960s in areas such as the Northwest Coast and the Southwest, and to the further development or expansion of Indian arts and cultural organizations. The Institute of American Indian Arts, for example, was established in 1962 as a major national center for training young Indian, Eskimo, and Aleut artists in all of the expressive arts. This highly innovative Native American project included training for those who wished to work on the museum side of the arts, a kind of training that would only later become available through university and university museum programs, through museum organizations, such as the workshops sponsored in the 1970s and 1980s by the British Columbia Museums Association, or through internships and assistance provided by the innovative Indian programs of the Smithsonian Institution's Office of Museum Programs. The latter also offered and continues to offer assistance in the development of community research projects, including museum development projects. In some cases, community research projects led directly to the establishment of museums, e.g., the oral history project of the Suquamish tribe and their museum. Community perspectives on their own past, often reasserted by the creation of a tribal museum, led to tribal museum exhibit interpretations that were sometimes quite different than what had been seen in non-Indian museums. Most significant in this respect was often the presentation in new tribal museums, ranging from the Native American Center for the Living Arts in New York to the Yakima Nation Museum in Washington, of Indian worldviews about man-land relationships, and related religious ideologies, including origin accounts of the people.

Within the museum profession in the post-World War II period, Native American materials were slowly transformed from their earlier anthropological artifact and crafts status to one of art objects with recognized aesthetic merits. The increasing interest of art museums after the 1950s in creating their own Native American collections and in producing exhibits of Indian materials continues today, along with the increase in the number of contemporary Indian artists working in modern, as well as traditional, media, and creating very modern as well as traditional forms of expression sought after by collectors and museums. This, combined with more sophisticated museum exhibits and the marketing of those exhibits and associated wares in museum gift shops, has helped to fuel the expansion of new public awareness about Indian arts and support the growing number of new Indian artists and artisans, whose creative work has become increasingly featured in popular publications and magazines aimed at the general public, and as features of local, state, and regional tourism campaigns, including some tribal tourism projects. In museums with anthropological collections, the extensive kind of ethnographic collecting that had been carried out prior to World War II essentially ceased, and museums became far more reliant on donated or purchased collections of widely varying quality and significance, thereby sparking new questions and explorations about the nature and future directions of museum-based anthropological research.

The incorporation of Native American perspectives into the museum establishment represents another development in recent decades. The significance of this trend goes well beyond consultation on exhibits or other museum-specific projects. Notable among the many examples of this larger arena of involvement are the 1990 Native American policy discussions and recommendations with the National Park Service ("Keepers of the Treasures"), Native American participation in the American Association of Museums' 1984 Commission on Museums for a New Century, the 1989 First Nations-Canadian Museums Association Task Force, and the extensive Native American input into the creation of the Smithsonian Institution's new National Museum of the American Indian. The importance of this new level of Native American inclusion in museum affairs is well characterized by the American Association of Museum's call, subsequent to the passage of repatriation legislation, for a new partnership between Native Americans and museums, and by the determination of many Native American individuals and organizations that such partnerships will be meaningful.

As we come to the last few years of the twentieth century, a new museum is being created that may further advance the concept of Native American community and museum partnership, and lead to additional dramatic changes in museum-Native American relationships. With 1989 congressional approval, the Smithsonian Institution has embarked upon the establishment of the National Museum of the American Indian. Based on several years of intensive consultation with Indian communities, it is proposed that the museum be different in several important respects, including: (1) the presence of a significant number of Native Americans on the staff; (2) ongoing community consultation in the development of the museum and its programs; (3) public programs which will include not simply artifacts per se, but also the presentation of living arts, including literature and drama; (4) significantly more attention paid to varied community wishes in the handling and use of tribal materials; (5) far greater community access to museum collections for ceremonial, research, and other purposes; and, for example, (6) access to dynamic outreach programs designed to link community and museum resources for educational and social purposes, including the support of local language programs.

With the creation of the National Museum of the American Indian, the relationships between museums and Native Americans in the twentieth century comes full circle, from the museum as an alien and distant institution uninterested in community concerns and perspectives, to a point where museums have begun to restore many of the most important objects of ongoing importance to their original owners, have become responsible to community concerns and perspectives on museum interpretations and research, and have begun to develop meaningful partnerships of interests and shared responsibilities for precious cultural resources of value to both museum and community.

James D. Nason

See also **Anthropologists and Native Americans; Archaeology; Repatriation of Human Remains and Artifacts; Tribal Museums**

Further Reading

Ames, Michael M. *Cannibal Tours and Glass Boxes: The Anthropology of Museums.* Vancouver: University of British Columbia Press, 1992.

Cole, Douglas. *Captured Heritage: The Scramble for Northwest Coast Artifacts.* Seattle: University of Washington Press, 1985.

Horse Capture, George P. *The Concept of Sacred Materials and Their Place in the World.* Cody, WY: The Buffalo Bill Historical Center, 1989.

Messenger, Phyllis Mauch, ed. *The Ethics of Collecting Cultural Property: Whose Culture? Whose Property?* Albuquerque: University of New Mexico Press, 1989.

"Museums and the First Nations." *Muse* 6:3 (October 1988).

Parker, Patricia L., ed. *Keepers of the Treasures: Protecting Historic Properties and Cultural Traditions on Indian Lands.* Washington, DC: National Parks Service, 1990.

MUSIC

In Indian music, the voice is the most important instrument. The music includes solo pieces, responsorial songs in which the leader and chorus take turns, unison chorus songs, and multipart songs usually accompanied by either rattle or drum, or both rattle and drum. The singers typically perform in Native languages, but include "vocables" (nontranslatable syllables, such as *he, ya, ho, we,* etc.) to carry the melody.

Musical instruments include a variety of rattles, drums, scrapers, flutes and whistles, and the Apache fiddle. Individuals use vessel rattles (a vessel enclosing pebbles, fruit seeds, or other noisemakers with a handle) made of carved wood, baskets, gourds, bark, rawhide, moose feet, clay, metal salt shakers, turtles, cow horns, copper, coconut shells, or buffalo tails. Other rattles are strung and attached to the bodies or clothing of dancers, made from cocoons, deer hoofs, tin cans, turtles, petrified wood, sea shells, or metal cones. A few of the latter also contain pebbles or seeds; i.e., cocoons, turtles, or tin cans. In addition, one can string shells, bird beaks, deer hoofs, or cocoons on sticks or hoops and play each by hand to accompany singing. Other instruments such as rasps, bullroarers, flutes, whistles, musical bows, fiddles, and clapping sticks are less common.

Indian music is composed of many forms ranging from simple short songs with many repetitions, to lengthy song cycles that take several days to perform with almost no repetitions. Scales, rhythms, and meters vary according to area, tribe, ceremony, and sometimes from individual to individual.

In the style of the Plains Indian powwow, one of the most widespread forms, the leader usually starts the song as high as he can, his chorus then answers him, and all sing the melody together, descending throughout the middle and last sections, coming to rest on the lowest or next to lowest note, often more than an octave lower than the start. All singers then repeat the middle and last sections before repeating the whole. The most common form can be shown as AA´BCB´C´AA´BCB´C´, etc. Besides the sounds of the accompanying drum and the ankle bells on the dancers (and sometimes the whistles), the "pulsation," or intentional quivering of the voices, enhances the sound.

Many of these musical characteristics—the words, the number of repetitions, the instruments, and the way the singers work together—come from worldview and, except for church music, depend largely on the dance, thus growing out of long-lasting religious and social customs. While some songs have divine or ancient origins, Indian composers and singers have always been important in creating and passing on the music through oral tradition. Music that is best known to the public comes from non-private ceremonies and social occasions, but equally important are songs for medicine, prayer, initiation, hunting, trying to control nature, putting children to sleep, telling stories, performing magic, playing games, and flirting. In performing these songs and dances, the Indians of today pledge their ties to a living history.

While people revere the older songs and forms, certain changes occur. Modern instrument-makers incorporate bells, tin cans, salt shakers, rubber, and plastic materials into musical instruments and dance costumes. Composers add English words to Rabbit Dance, Forty-nine, and peyote songs. American popular melodies such as "Dixie," "Jambalaya" and "Sugar in the Mornin'" have found their place in contemporary

Indian songs. Singers regularly make new songs that become popular and spread across the country through the powwow circuit. Often these changes meet conflicting audience responses.

Although Indian ways of life have changed considerably in the twentieth century, Indian music is still integral to almost every Indian activity. The Indian of today may sing the same ceremonial songs his ancestors sang before contact with whites as in the Cahuilla Bird Dances; he may sing new songs composed in the old style as in the San Juan Pueblo Turtle Dance; or he may sing songs that combine Indian themes and motifs with non-Indian instruments and harmonies as in the music of XIT, a 1970s Indian rock group.

Native Music

Retention. Many Indians living on reservations or in rural areas practice the ancient religions and music that are necessary to Indian life. These traditional activities are regionally or tribally specific, and the leaders perform them in Native languages following age-old calendars and belief systems. A few examples of retention would include but would not be limited to the following: Southern California, Cahuilla Bird Dance; Great Basin, Ute Bear Dance; Northwest Alaskan Eskimo, Northern Lights Dance; Northwest Coast, Kwakiutl Potlatch; Eastern Woodlands, Iroquois Midwinter; Southeast, Creek Green Corn ceremony; Plains, Blackfeet Medicine Lodge; Pueblo, San Juan Deer Dance; Southern Athabaskan, Navajo Enemyway ceremony.

Although lullabies and courting songs are rare, handgame songs are widespread. The handgame or stickgame as a social and sometimes religious activity is a guessing game found in the Northwest Coast, California, the Plateau, the Great Basin, the Southwest, the Plains, and the Northeast. Customarily, the players employ songs to coincide with the hiding of an object or the mark on a stick, and the game cannot exist without the music. The melodies tend to be narrow in range with short repeated phrases sung by a chorus to insure good luck. On the Northwest Coast and in northern California areas, stickgame songs employ more complicated rhythms than in other areas and often contain multi-part singing. In the Great Basin and central California, men and women have different songs and play separate games. Instrumental accompaniment can be supplied by drums, sticks, rattles, or clapping sticks.

While Eskimos do not have the same guessing game, they have other musical games such as the women's throat games of Baffin Island, the hopping, chasing, string figure, and pebble-juggling games of northwest Alaska, and the insult-singing contests of the Netsilik. In the southeastern United States, ballgame songs and dances precede and follow the highly ceremonial stickball game of the Cherokee, Creek, Choctaw, and Seminole. Some of these songs are similar in style to other southeastern Indian dance music, yet other songs resemble curing or hunting songs. Unique to the ballgame songs in the Southeast is the participation of women vocalists—not as an adjunct to the men, yet as an integral part of the ceremony. Although one can find these ballgames in the twentieth century, some practitioners perform only for "show," and thus do not use the full complement of songs and dances.

Preservation and Revival. Starting in the 1970s, many Indian groups have tried to preserve the unique knowledge of their elders. Some younger musicians have fervently begun recording traditional music and instructions for performance. These efforts represent a new trend by Indian people themselves to gather recordings from archives, make recordings of elders, and combine the two to recreate or preserve some partially remembered dance or ceremony. The Federal Cylinder Project at the Library of Congress and the California Indian Project at the Lowie Museum have returned many old recordings to these tribal groups.

The renewed interest in Indian flute playing represents another revival. Doc Tate Nevaquaya, a Comanche and first-year recipient of a National Heritage Fellowship from the National Endowment for the Arts, through his recordings and personal efforts has taught several Indian young men to play old songs, compose new songs, and adapt Indian vocal melodies and non-Indian songs such as hymns for the flute. Among the other Indian flutists who have enjoyed success as concert artists are Kevin Locke (also a National Heritage Fellowship recipient); R. Carlos Nakai; Edward Wapp, Jr.; John Rainer, Jr.; Gordon Bird; Fernando Cellicion; Robert Tree Cody; Herman Edwards; Daniel C. Hill; Frank Montano; Cornel Pewewardy; D.M. Rico; Stan Snake; Douglas Spotted Eagle; Robert Two Hawks; Woodrow Haney; and Tom Ware. Nakai also composes and performs in ensembles with synthesizers and other electronic or amplified instruments, carrying the music forward into contemporary life. A few of the other flutists also cross over to "contemporary" or "new age" styles.

Performance in Nontraditional Settings. Indian singers and dancers often perform out of context for non-traditional reasons. In the 1990s, Indian traditional singers and dancers perform at Indian, county, and crafts fairs, receptions, national Indian conferences, political rallies, museum and college programs, political demonstrations, graduation ceremonies, tourist attractions, and in various Indian education programs. Traditional Indian music is now widely taught in schools ranging from preschool to university levels. These unusual circumstances have spawned a class of almost "professional musicians." Usually these entertainers augment their modest incomes by public performances. Most of these performers are careful to present the songs properly, to perform only the more secular selections from their repertoire, and to explain the original contexts of the music.

The widespread use and diffusion of Indian styles have created an interest among the Indian record-buying public. It is common to find Indian people listening informally to recordings of Indian music. They may be learning the songs or merely enjoying themselves. Many Indian people also take their tape recorders to powwows, stomp dances, and other Indian gatherings to record music for pleasure. Six commercial record companies cater to this Indian market.

Pan-Tribal Music. Although Indian tribes perform music unique to their own traditions, some tribes have adopted music and accompanying religious ceremonies from others. The most important ceremonies that diffused pan-tribally were the Sun Dance, the Ghost Dance, and the Native American Church or Peyote Religion. In each ceremony, there is some borrowing along with incorporation of local styles.

Of these three only the Ghost Dance has almost disappeared. The Sun Dance, after spreading from its origins in the central plains north into Canada with the Plains Cree and Plains Ojibwa, south into Indian Territory with the Kiowa, west into Idaho with the Kutenai and Shoshone, and east into South Dakota and Minnesota with the Santee Dakota, finally began to vanish from the Great Plains by the end of the nineteenth century. Beginning in the 1970s, the Sun Dance has seen a revival in the Plains, in the mountains with the Utes and Shoshones, and, newly transplanted, in California.

Some modern Sun Dance performances retain the old ways, some revive ceremonies that were temporarily forsaken, and some borrow the ceremony from the Plains to benefit Indians of all tribes. The Sun Dance Religion requires that candidates for redemption do not withdraw from the world but live here and struggle for the good of all. Proper life requires a good heart, sacrifice for others, and selfless behavior toward family, kin, and friends, and the entire Sun Dance community.

These values draw Indians, young and old, from the cities and rural areas to the Sun Dance. Regardless of its sponsorship, by an ancient tribal group, or by a modern organization like the American Indian Movement, the music is so sacred that only the social songs have been released on commercial recordings. The style echoes that of other Plains social dance songs.

Peyote Religion and music are also widespread. Urban Indians participate in ceremonies near their cities, while reservation and rural Indians set up tipis in their yards. Peyote music is so popular that dozens of albums have been released by the two major Indian record companies, Indian House and Canyon. Among these are singers from tribes whose indigenous ways contrasted greatly. The general musical style, as defined by David McAllester, applies to all areas where one finds peyote music. Generally, peyote music is fast, uses a ceremonial water drum and rattle to accompany the singers, and the melody descends. The speed and driving pulse of the drum characterize the music.

Powwows (urban, reservation, and rural) are the locus for most other pan-tribal music. The singers and dancers at powwows, whether urban or rural, represent many tribes. Sponsored by an organization or club, each powwow group raises money and plans months ahead for this major event. The planners take great care in choosing a good "head singer," "head man dancer," and "head woman dancer." The emphasis is on singing and dancing, but the powwow is a gathering that includes activities like feasting, giveaways, arts and crafts sales, raffles, and the crowning of a princess. The singers perform Plains Indian music, northern, southern, or both, with some regionally specific music and dance performed before, after, or as an interlude during the powwow.

To open many powwows in the southern Plains, and sometimes in the cities, members of a Gourd Clan may dance. Gourd dancers represent southern Plains warrior societies, and the members of this honor brotherhood have prescribed clothing and use special rattles and fans. In contrast to the general powwow fare of War Dances, Fancy Dances, or Grass Dances, the Gourd Dance seems slow and the songs extremely long. The music resembles other southern Plains music, but uses a narrower vocal range. The dance is also less vigorous as are most honoring dances.

Frequently, the dancers warm up with Round Dances before the formal opening of a powwow (after the Gourd Dance, if it is performed), and Round Dances may be interspersed among War Dances, Grass Dances, Trick Songs for contests, etc. These social dances, together with the Oklahoma Two-Step, Rabbit Dance, and Owl Dance, offer a chance for audience members to participate freely. At these times, visitors can dance without observing all the formal costuming and etiquette requirements for the more serious dances.

Extra dances might include the Navajo Ribbon Dance, the Swan Dance, the Hoop Dance, the Shield Dance, or one of the Pueblo Buffalo Dances. These dances in a powwow setting are strictly for show, and often the dancers receive payment for demonstrating them. In recent years, most powwow clubs have added contests to attract the best dancers and singers. The men's War Dance or Fancy Dance contests offer the top prize money, sometimes one thousand dollars or more.

In the complex social and religious setting of the powwow, the leaders choose the head singer and head dancers not only for their superior knowledge of song and dance repertoire, but also for their community status and network of family and friends. If these powwow leaders have prestige and command respect, other good singers and dancers will join to show their support. Becoming a head singer requires a strong voice, musical talent, a superior memory, and an ability to guide the group of singers constituting the "Drum."

The Forty-nine Dances, performed mostly by young people after powwows, are social in nature and may last all night. The dress is casual, and the drum, central to most Plains music, may be replaced by any sonorous surface. Done mostly for fun, the dances and songs may contain words about love, sweethearts, and problems. Changing the words to fit the locale or tribe involved is common; e.g., Oklahoma may become New Mexico, or Kiowa may become Pueblo, etc.

These pan-tribal (or pan-Indian) songs contain many vocables (or nonlexical syllables). Because the styles spread across geographical and tribal boundaries, using vocables allows a group of singers from different tribes and language families to sing together with ease. When songs at any of the above gatherings are specific to one language, many singers drop out.

Because of Indian migration to cities and towns, and because of generations of intermarriage with Indians of other tribes and with non-Indians, many young people have never experienced traditional Indian life and have come to rely on powwows, Indian community organizations, and Indian studies programs as sources for reinforcing their "Indianness." Music and dance have contributed greatly to the search for identity by these young Indians. "Drums," or groups of Indian men singers, have sprung up in community centers across the nation. Although the purpose of these Drums is to perform at powwows and other gatherings, the result is a weekly or monthly intertribal gathering of men who practice songs from various tribes in northern or southern Plains style. In the past, young women participated only in dancing, doing beadwork, or practicing other Indian crafts, but recently women have taken a visible role in singing and composing, often joining male Drums or creating their own.

Innovations

Protestant Hymns and Gospel Music. When Christian missionaries began trying to convert and "civilize" Indians, many recognized that the Indians' love of music could be employed to aid in the effort. Although missionaries first translated hymns into Indian languages in the first part of the nineteenth century, Indians soon began translating and composing their own texts to recognized Christian hymn melodies. Later, Indian Christians composed tunes and texts of their own.

In the 1990s, the Indian churches provide a place for worship, a meeting place for Christians, and a locus for Indian singing. In rural and reservation areas, worshipers attend services held in Native languages with songs in those languages, and ministers who are local men with some theological training. In the cities, intertribal groups of Indians come together within specific denominations. Usually conducted in English, these urban services feature songs both in English and in Native languages, and the ministers are usually well-educated Indians.

The "sings" or "singings" held at these churches draw Indians from far and wide. Indian choirs, quartets, trios, duets, and soloists travel far to participate in them. Although some groups sing unaccompanied, many use piano, guitar, bass fiddle, organ, or other available Western instruments for accompaniment. In the 1990s, some singers use tape-recorded sound tracks or even synthesizers and electronic keyboards. Many groups harmonize, but in much of the Christian music, early Indian vocal techniques remain. We still hear leader-chorus responsorial patterns, upward-gliding attacks and downward-gliding releases to musical phrases, and generally nasal voice production. The themes of the songs represent basic human needs and communication with God and are not always direct translations of their English counterparts. Just as traditional ceremonies and urban powwows draw Indians together, so do Indian churches, especially through their music. Several choirs and quartets have published commercial recordings.

Intertribal Choirs and Bands. At Indian schools throughout the country, intertribal choirs and bands enjoy popularity. Depending on local tastes, the choir may perform Western popular music, Christian music, or indigenous Indian music in new choral arrangements. The bands range from marching bands to jazz swing bands with corresponding repertoires. Louis Ballard, a Quapaw-Cherokee composer, did much to promote Indian choral singing. By traveling throughout the country, presenting Indian music workshops, conducting Indian choirs, and producing records and films, Ballard spread his idea of using Indian motifs in traditional Western forms.

Among the school choirs gaining recognition and producing record albums are Brigham Young University, the Institute of American Indian Arts, Santa Fe Indian School, Fort Lewis College, and Bacone College.

Professional Musicians. Professional Indian musicians perform in many styles, e.g., classical, jazz, country, folk/protest, contemporary, rock, rap, and new age. Some blend Indian tunes with mainstream rhythms, instruments, and styles. Most use some instruments or melodies from traditional Indian music. Among these are Tom Bee, Robby Bee, Joe Manuel, Sand Creek, Winterhawk, Cody Bearpaw, Borderline, El Cochise, Eddie and Brian Johnson, Joe Montana and the Roadrunners, Jimi Poyer, Rockin' Rebels, Wingate Valley Boys, Jim Boyd, Arliene Nofchissey Williams, Vincent Craig, Chief Dan George, Burt Lambert and the Northern Express, Frank Montano, Tomas Obomsawin, A. Paul Ortega, Sharon Burch, Jim Pepper, Buddy Red Bow, Joanne Shenandoah, Gene T, Buffy Sainte-Marie, Bruce Hamana, Floyd Westerman, the Fenders, Undecided Takers, the Navajo Sundowners, the Zuni Midnighters, Apache Spirit, Louis Ballard, Brent Michael Davids, XIT, Redbone, Billy Thunderkloud, and John Trudell.

Chicken Scratch (*waila*), the popular dance music of the Indians of southern Arizona, relies heavily on European dance forms such as polkas and schottisches. Similar to Mexican-American Norteño music, employing guitars, concertina, and saxophone, Chicken Scratch finds popularity among the Tohono O'odham (Papago), Pima, Quechan (Yuma), and Yaqui.

The Alaskan Kutchin Indians also dance to European fiddle-guitar music imported by Scottish settlers from the Orkney Islands. In addition, Indian fiddlers and guitar players can be found almost everywhere. During the Cherokee National Holiday in Tahlequah, Oklahoma, a national Indian fiddler's contest is held annually.

Like other Americans, Indians and Eskimos will sing or dance to almost any variety of music that catches their fancy, while reserving their own music for special occasions. Indian musicians have composed music to fit the times, while keeping many of their old styles, forms, and contexts that reinforce traditional values. Music pervades Indian life starting from creation stories and ending with death and memorial. American Indian music is important not only because it influences modern American society, but also because it emphasizes the traditions and values of Indian people. This oral tradition has survived solely because the music and dance were too important to be allowed to die.

Charlotte Heth

See also Dance; Powwow

Further Reading

McAllester, David P. *Peyote Music.* Viking Fund Publications in Anthropology, 13. 1949. New York, NY: Johnson Reprint, 1971.

Nettl, Bruno, Charlotte Heth, and Gertrude P. Kurath. "American Indians." *The New Grove Dictionary of American Music.* Vol. 2. London, England: Macmillan Press (1986): 460–79.

Smyth, Willie, ed. *Songs of Indian Territory: Native American Music Traditions of Oklahoma.* Oklahoma City, OK: Center of the American Indian, 1989.

Vander, Judith. *Songprints: The Musical Experience of Five Shoshone Women.* Urbana: University of Illinois Press, 1988.

Vennum, Thomas. *The Ojibwa Dance Drum: Its History and Construction.* Smithsonian Folklife Studies 2. Washington, DC: Smithsonian Institution Press, 1982.

Selected Discography

American Indians Play Chicken Scratch. Canyon C6120, 1974.

Comanche Peyote Songs. Indian House IH 2401–2402, 1969. K.D. Edwards.

Heth, Charlotte. *Songs of Earth, Water, Fire, and Sky: Music of the American Indian.* New World Records NW 246, 1976. Reissued on CD as 80246–2, 1991.

———. *Powwow Songs: Music of the Plains Indians.* New World Records NW 343, 1986. Reissued on CD as 80343–2, 1991.

Isaacs, Tony. *Handgame of the Kiowa, Kiowa Apache and Comanche,* Vols. 1–2. Indian House IH 2501–2502, 1969, 1974.

Nevaquaya, Doc Tate. *Comanche Flute Music.* Folkways Records FE 4328, 1979.

Smyth, Willie, ed. *Songs of Indian Territory: Native American Music Traditions of Oklahoma.* Oklahoma City, OK: Center of the American Indian, 1989. Cassette.

Helen C. Rountree

Further Reading

Rountree, Helen C. "The Indians of Virginia: A Third Race in a Biracial State." *Southeastern Indians Since the Removal Era.* Ed. Walter L. Williams. Athens: University of Georgia Press (1979): 27–48.

———. "Ethnicity Among the 'Citizen' Indians of Virginia, 1800–1930." *Strategies For Survival: American Indians in the Eastern United States.* Ed. Frank W. Porter. New York, NY: Greenwood Press (1986): 173–209.

———. *Pocahontas's People: The Powhatan Indians of Virginia Through Four Centuries.* Norman: University of Oklahoma Press, 1990.

———. "Indian Virginians on the Move." *Indians of the Southeastern United States in the Late 20th Century.* Ed. J. Anthony Paredes. Tuscaloosa , AL and London, England: University of Alabama Press (1992): 9–28.

Speck, Frank G. *Chapters on the Ethnology of the Powhatan Tribes of Virginia.* Indian Notes and Monographs 1: 5. New York, NY: Museum of the American Indian, Heye Foundation, 1928.

NACHITOCHES

See Caddo

NAMBE

See Pueblo of Nambe

NANSEMOND

The Nansemond Indian Tribal Association has been a state-recognized enclave since 1985. Incorporated as a tribe in 1984, it is centered in the Bowers Hill-Deep Creek area of the City of Chesapeake, Virginia; many members today live in the Norfolk-Portsmouth-Virginia Beach metropolitan areas. The tribe's total enrollment is about 100.

Today's Nansemonds are descended from an English-Nansemond marriage of 1638; the group has been Christianized since about that time. It received a Methodist mission in 1850, and though the church is now an independent United Methodist congregation, the church building serves as a place for tribal meetings. The tribe had its own county-supported grade school from the 1890s until about 1900, and again after a fight from 1922. Those living in the cities sent their children to white schools.

There are monthly tribal meetings, closed to outsiders; the Tribal Council meets in private in a member's house. The chief, assistant chief, secretary, treasurer, and five councilmen are elected every four years by all enrolled, Nansemond-descended adults aged eighteen and over. The tribe has associate memberships for spouses and honorary memberships for outsiders rendering significant services. Chief Emeritus Oliver L. Perry has represented both the tribe and the Indian people of Virginia at several successive Governors' Interstate Conferences on Indians.

Traditional culture remains only in a few crafts (beadwork, wooden-and-ceramic pipemaking, and pottery). The tribe puts on a festival in early September, but has no dance group of its own as of 1991.

NANTICOKE

The Nanticoke, an Algonquian tribe, were living along the shores of Chesapeake Bay when Europeans settled in the tidewater area of what is now Maryland and Delaware. Today's Nanticoke, with a population of about 1,000, live in a spatially defined community near Millsboro, Delaware.

Like many other tribes in the eastern United States, the Nanticoke have never been officially recognized as a trust status tribe by the federal government. Without this relationship, the Nanticoke have not been eligible to receive any benefits or services provided through the Bureau of Indian Affairs. Deprived of their right to such benefits in the areas of health, education, and economic development, the Nanticoke have successfully relied on their self-sufficient character to meet the needs of their people.

From 1855 to 1965 the identity of the Nanticoke was continually questioned. On several occasions, they had to use legal means to define their identity officially or lose their distinctive status permanently. In February, 1922, with the help of anthropologist Frank G. Speck, the Nanticoke Indian Association received a charter of incorporation from Delaware. Russel Clark was elected chief, and E. Lincoln Harman became assistant chief. The Nanticoke Indian Association quickly sought to renew interest in the old Indian traditions. The members of the association decided to hold a festival, which resembled the traditional campfire powwows of most Algonquian tribes, and which became an annual get-together.

After Chief Russel Clark died, he was succeeded by his sons, Ferdinand and Robert. In 1932 another son, Charles C. Clark, became chief, and served until his accidental death in 1971. During this period, interest in the Association and tribal activities waned. In the late 1970s, however, the Nanticoke began anew to explore their own past. The establishment of the Nanticoke Indian Heritage Project in 1977 has resulted in an inventory of the cultural resources of the community, the establishment of the annual Nanticoke powwow, and the creation of the Nanticoke Indian Museum. Kenneth Clark, who became chief of the Nanticoke in 1975, and the new Tribal Council continue to encourage the exploration of the tribe's history and cultural heritage.

Frank W. Porter III

Further Reading

Porter, Frank W. *The Nanticoke.* New York, NY: Chelsea House Publishers, 1987.

Weslager, Clinton A. *The Nanticoke: Past and Present.* Newark: University of Delaware Press, 1983.

NARRAGANSETT

The Narragansett Indian Tribe numbers over 2,400 individuals, most of whom live in the state of Rhode Island. The tribe owns two land parcels: 1,800 acres held in federal trust within the town of Charlestown, and, in Westerly, several hundred acres donated to the tribe by Irving and Arlene Crandall in 1991. The Narragansetts have lived continuously in this area for many centuries, long before the colony of Rhode Island was established in 1636. They were detribalized by the Rhode Island General Assembly in 1880, and all tribal land, except a two-acre parcel containing the meeting house/church and cemetery, were sold at public auction. The Narragansetts, however, maintained a tribal identity and in 1978 regained some of the land lost during detribalization. In 1983, they obtained tribal recognition from the United States government.

Between 1892 and 1937, several unsuccessful land claim attempts were made. These "Shore Claims," made by Gideon and George Ammons, Abraham Champlin, Daniel Sekater, and Joshua Noka, included a strip of coastal land from Westerly to Pawtucket. After the Rhode Island Supreme Court denied the claim in 1898, the Narragansetts asked the Bureau of Indian Affairs (BIA) for help in the matter. The BIA, however, argued that the federal government could not intervene because the Narragansetts had been deposed in colonial times and did not have a legal relationship with the United States government. In the 1970s, led by Eric Thomas and Ella Thomas Sekatau, the tribe claimed successfully that the state had violated the Non-Intercourse Act of 1790, and that lands were illegally auctioned during detribalization. The 1978 settlement agreement returned 1,800 acres of public and private land in Charlestown.

Although the Indian Reorganization Act of 1934 did not pertain to the Narragansetts, the tribe incorporated in that year and set down Bylaws. The Bylaws affirmed the existence of an elected Tribal Council and chief sachem, and formally recognized the positions of tribal medicine man and a nonsectarian Christian leader called a prophet. Philip Peckham was elected chief sachem and William Wilcox was named chief medicine man, a position now held by his grandson, Lloyd "Running Wolf" Wilcox. Joseph Hazard and Valencia Thomas preside over Christian services.

Tribal elections are held every two years. Decision making is vested in the Tribal Council and chief sachem with committees and staff assigned various program areas. Major decisions require the approval of the tribal body. Committees deal with topics such as natural resources, health, education, economic development, and cultural resources. Currently, the tribe is exploring the feasibility of developing a fishery and high-stakes gambling as ways to achieve economic self-sufficiency.

In 1985, the anthropological-archaeological committee, chaired by the understudy to the chief medicine man, John B. "Mudjekewis" Brown III, was created to report to the Tribal Council on issues such as repatriation and efforts to work with non-Indian archaeologists. The Narragansetts participated in one of the first reburials of skeletal remains in the United States in 1971, when anthropologist William S. Simmons returned the remains from a Narragansett cemetery he excavated in the 1960s.

Each summer the annual August meeting and powwow is held on the meeting grounds, a place used for the gathering since at least 1740 when the original church was constructed. Traditional Narragansett and non-sectarian Christian ceremonies take place, and other Indian tribes and non-Indians are invited to attend. Other annual ceremonies recall traditional gatherings, e.g., the fall harvest held at the longhouse in October, or they commemorate past events, e.g., the 1675 surprise attack and massacre of Narragansetts in the Great Swamp by English soldiers.

Tribal representatives are active in the non-Indian community, giving lectures and cultural demonstrations to school groups, university classes, and at other public events. Other tribal programs provide food for elderly tribal members, tutoring for children, and health care.

Paul A. Robinson

Further Reading

Simmons, William S. *Spirit of the New England Tribes: Indian History and Folklore, 1620–1984.* Hanover, NH: University Press of New England, 1986.

———. *The Narragansett.* New York, NY: Chelsea House Publishers, 1989.

NATCHEZ

When first observed by the French in the late seventeenth century, the Natchez Indians lived on the east side of the Mississippi, about 150 miles northwest of New Orleans. They were the last of the mound-building Indians who kept alive an elaborate system of religion and monarchy into the European period.

After the French attacked them viciously between 1716 and 1729, the survivors took refuge among the Chickasaws and the Mvskoke Creeks. They constituted three to five towns among the Creeks through the removal period, and in Indian Territory formed communities in the eastern part of the Creek Reservation, near the Cherokees.

By the time of allotment in 1906, the Natchez of Indian Territory were so intermarried with the Creeks and the Cherokees that they never sought a separate legal identity of their own. According to Archie Sam, their last great leader who died in 1986, by the time separate federal recognition was offered in 1937, there was only one ceremonial ground left, the Medicine Spring site near Gore, Oklahoma, and only a handful of Native speakers. The last ceremony at Medicine Spring was in 1976. The last fluent speaker was Watt Sam, Archie Sam's uncle, who died in 1965.

Although few remnants of Natchez culture still persist in the communities, where the Native languages are now Muskogee and Cherokee, fragments of Natchez ceremonies and traditions are preserved among their former neighbors. Mvskoke Creeks of the Arbeka Stomp Grounds, where there are many people of Natchez descent, still sing Natchez songs and preserve their stories, although no longer told in the Natchez language. The Red Bird Smith ceremonial grounds of the Cherokees preserve some rituals and artifacts left to them by Natchez ceremonial leaders.

John H. Moore

See also **Oklahoma Tribes**

Further Reading

Campbell, Janet, and Archie Sam. "The Primal Fire Lingers." *Chronicles of Oklahoma* 53:4 (1976): 463–75.

Van Tuyl, Charles D. *The Natchez: Annotated Translations from Antoine Simon le Page du Pratz's Histoire de la Louisiane.* Oklahoma Historical Society Series in Anthropology, No. 4. Oklahoma City, OK: The Society, 1979.

NATIONAL CONGRESS OF AMERICAN INDIANS

The National Congress of American Indians (NCAI) is the oldest national pan-Indian political organization. It was founded in 1944 when eighty Indians belonging to more than fifty tribes met in Denver, Colorado, to establish a broadly based, nonpartisan organization that would work within the white political system to improve the status of Indians.

The founding of the NCAI represented a turning point in Indian affairs as Indians emerged as skilled political organizers and lobbyists for their own interest at the federal level. Participation in World War II as soldiers and in defense industries as wage earners, coupled with recent experience gained as a result of the Indian Reorganization Act (IRA), convinced a new generation of Indians that they could determine their own destiny. The NCAI borrowed much of the phi-

losophy, early personnel, and tactics from the Indian New Deal. The constitution and bylaws were modeled on those of the tribes that had voted to accept John Collier's version of Indian self-government, namely IRA-sponsored tribal councils.

Not surprisingly, the commissioner's Special Assistant D'Arcy McNickle, a member of the Flathead tribe, played a critical role in the early planning stages of the NCAI. McNickle convened a small group of Indian bureaucrats within the Bureau of Indian Affairs (BIA) in the spring of 1944, and the group took on the task of launching a new national Indian organization. While these planners supported the Indian New Deal, they believed that a successful Indian advocacy effort had to represent both New Dealers and those who opposed the previous ten years of Indian reform. In preparation for the Denver meeting, the BIA's Minnesota field representative drafted the NCAI's provisional constitution, including a preamble which stated the NCAI's broad goals. Prominent among these goals were a commitment to preserve Indian cultural values and, at the same time, secure the individual rights and benefits to which Indians were entitled as citizens of the United States. This emphasis on both tribal and civil rights reflected the fact that the NCAI's founders did not oppose the voluntary integration of Indians into the mainstream of American society, as long as it did not threaten the survival of tribal societies. Over time, the leadership of the NCAI found that convincing the white political establishment that these two goals were not contradictory proved difficult.

The NCAI's first president, Napoleon Johnson, a Cherokee from Oklahoma, a district court judge, and a New Deal Democrat, discovered that while white society applauded the creation of the NCAI, it saw the Congress solely as a vehicle for "freeing Indians" from federal supervision. The NCAI's early strong support for an Indian Claims Commission was simplistically interpreted by leading white congressional leaders as integrationist. These leaders assumed that after Indians had their "day in court," they would willingly leave their reservations. In fact, the NCAI's advocacy of an Indian Claims Commission stemmed more from its concern to preserve Indian treaty rights and tribal sovereignty. Protecting the tribes required the adjudication of longstanding claims against the United States government. Importantly, when the Indian Claims Commission Act was passed by Congress in 1946, both the NCAI and the act's more integration-minded backers claimed a victory.

In the immediate postwar years, both the NCAI and white politicians had no difficulty focusing on a mutually acceptable political agenda. White politicians joined the NCAI to bring pressure on Arizona and New Mexico to extend the franchise to Indians in 1948. In 1949, as further evidence of the NCAI's growing reputation, when the secretary of the interior appointed a National Advisory Committee on Indian Affairs, the only two Indians he chose to serve on the seven-member board were influential figures in the

NCAI. They were Ruth Bronson, the NCAI's executive secretary, and Louis Bruce, a member of the NCAI's council who, twenty years later, became commissioner of Indian affairs under President Richard Nixon.

By 1950 the NCAI had established itself as the Indian voice in Indian affairs, although few would argue that its power to influence the direction of federal policy had been tested. In general, the NCAI lent Indian support for legislation already desired by a growing integrationist movement among whites. The ease with which the NCAI worked with Congress and the executive branch during its early years helped the fledgling lobby group win credibility in Washington. These early victories, however, masked real differences between NCAI's underlying philosophy of tribal self-determination and that of congressional leadership, differences which later emerged during the Eisenhower administration in the battle over termination.

In July 1953, over the NCAI's strong objections, Congress approved a resolution calling for the removal of federal supervision and the dissolution of BIA control over several tribes, including the Klamaths of Oregon and the Menominees of Wisconsin. This bipartisan legislation became the centerpiece of federal Indian policy for the next two decades, and as such, the focus of the NCAI's attention. During the height of the termination drive, the NCAI was headed by Joseph Garry, an ex-Marine and chairman of the Coeur d'Alene Tribal Council in Idaho. Garry proved the right man for the job, since opposition to termination was particularly strong among tribes in the Northwest. In early 1954, the NCAI mapped out a strategy for opposing termination which argued that Congress was acting in a unilateral fashion and only Indians had the right to terminate federal supervision. By using this familiar democratic principle, namely, securing the consent of the governed, the NCAI managed to delay and eventually derail the momentum for termination. By 1958 the NCAI's argument that no tribe should be terminated against its will became official governmental policy.

The 1960s were a period of transition for the NCAI. There were no major legislative battles like termination around which to rally. Also, the organization could not retain its position as the sole voice of Indian opinion in Washington. A variety of newer, and in most cases, more militant national Indian organizations began to emerge and challenge the NCAI's politics. The American Indian Movement (AIM) and the National Indian Youth Council (NIYC) represented a younger, more radical Indian constituency, which accused the NCAI of being too tied to Washington politics and out of touch with grassroots Indian needs and constituencies.

Differences in both philosophy and political tactics between the NCAI and AIM came to a head in 1973, when AIM members took over the hamlet of Wounded Knee to protest the actions and authority of Richard Wilson, the chairman of the Pine Ridge Sioux Tribal Council. AIM claimed that Wilson had bought his election as tribal chairman and was guilty of mismanagement, fraud, and denying certain Oglalas the rights to free assembly, due process, and protection from unreasonable searches and seizures. During the occupation of Wounded Knee, the NCAI defended Wilson and the elected Tribal Council, stating that AIM had violated tribal sovereignty by interfering with the established elected tribal government. NCAI's defense of Wilson had the effect of distancing the organization from both liberal white and Indian groups who saw Wilson as an antidemocratic Indian strongman.

Following the Wounded Knee occupation, the NCAI experienced difficulty trying to lead a broad political coalition on behalf of Indians. In the late 1970s, the NCAI's support for plans to extend federal recognition to nonrecognized tribes was actively opposed by the National Tribal Chairmen's Association (NTCA), a federation of tribal leaders established in the early 1970s with support from the BIA. NTCA was formerly allied with the NCAI, but it feared that the NCAI's support of smaller, eastern, nonfederally recognized tribes would dissipate resources away from the larger tribal communities west of the Mississippi. NCAI's approach to extend federal recognition was adopted by the executive branch following protracted and often contentious negotiations among and between the Indian leaders themselves.

Also, NCAI's influence waned in the 1980s as the pattern of Indian advocacy shifted away from the legislative arena into the judicial. NCAI was not as well positioned as was the Native American Rights Fund (NARF), a nonprofit legal services organization founded in 1970, to carry forward successfully the legal battles for Indian rights and claims to resources. Even when legislative action was needed, congressional staff who formerly always consulted NCAI leadership first, now turned equally to NARF for its legal expertise. Importantly, NARF, NCAI, and the NTCA represented different Indian constituencies and power bases so that no one organization could supplant the other. And when NARF's legal victories set off a number of attempts to deny Indians the right to control their resources, NCAI stepped in quickly to mount an antibacklash movement.

In its nearly one-half century of existence, NCAI went from being the unquestioned voice of the Indian people, to serving a more circumscribed, but no less valuable role. NCAI's membership in the 1990s includes approximately 200 tribes and 1,500 individual Indian members. The organization receives its support from federal government contracts, membership dues, and private philanthropy. In 1992 its budget was approximately $800,000. As the largest membership-based Indian advocacy organization, it has proven to be the most durable and consistently reliable source of Indian input into the policy-making process at the federal level.

Alison R. Bernstein

NATIONAL INDIAN YOUTH COUNCIL 373

See also **American Indian Movement; Government Policy; National Indian Youth Council;
Native American Rights Fund; Organizations
and Tribal Cooperation**

Further Reading

Bee, Robert L. *The Politics of American Indian Policy.*
Cambridge, MA: Schenkman Publishing, 1982.

Bernstein, Alison R. *American Indians and World War II:
Towards a New Era in Indian Affairs.* Norman:
University of Oklahoma Press, 1991.

Hertzberg, Hazel. *The Search for an American Indian
Identity: Modern Pan-Indian Movements.* NY: Syracuse
University Press, 1971.

Parker, Dorothy R. *Singing an Indian Song: A Biography
of D'Arcy McNickle.* Lincoln: University of Nebraska
Press, 1992.

NATIONAL INDIAN EDUCATION ASSOCIATION

During the latter 1960s Indian education was not a part of any agenda relating to American Indians. This sparked an effort by several American Indian educators to explore ways of attracting national attention to the educational needs of Indian communities throughout the United States. The 1969 report of the United States Senate Special Subcommittee on Indian Education, *Indian Education: A National Tragedy—a National Challenge* (the Kennedy report), and the emergence of Indian educators in various states, led to the first national Indian education conference in Minneapolis in 1969. Against this backdrop, the National Indian Education Association (NIEA) was founded in Minnesota in 1970.

Initial founders and incorporators were Will Antell, who was also president from 1970 to 1972, Rosemary Christianson, and Elgie Raymond, along with a seventeen-member board of directors. The purposes, according to the original articles of incorporation, were: (a) to plan, sponsor, and conduct an annual national conference on American Indian education; (b) to provide a source and opportunity to promote the exchange of ideas, techniques, methods, and principles of research, planning, coordination, education, and participation in the establishment, operation, and improvement of services needed to enhance the social and economic well-being of American Indians; (c) to foster innovation, planning, and research in the fields of elementary, secondary, and higher education; and (d) to further understanding, assistance, and support of the educational, social, economic, and other needs of American Indians.

NIEA has consistently been involved in influencing federal Indian education policy. For example, William Demmert and Will Antell were asked by Senators Kennedy and Mondale to assist the United States Senate in writing the Indian Education Act of 1972, known then as Title IV and amended later as Title V. Between 1970 and 1978 more Indian education legislation was passed by the United States Congress than

any period in American history. NIEA continues to testify in Congress regarding Indian education and related legislation.

In 1991 the mission statement was revised to reflect the need for excellence through the promotion of quality education for all American/Alaska Native people, protecting and maintaining traditional cultures and values, while providing skills for living in a changing world on a national and international level.

NIEA has played an active role in shaping current trends in Indian education. Indian self-determination is reflected in educational policies in public schools, such as tribally administered elementary and secondary schools, as well as in over twenty tribal colleges. The White House Conference on Indian Education held in 1992 was promoted and funded as a result of NIEA's efforts.

Presently, NIEA has 2,500 members. It convenes a national annual conference and publishes a newsletter several times a year. Public service materials, announcements, and brochures are distributed along with legislative updates and calls to action. Future plans call for an Indian educational resource base to be in place by 1994.

From its humble beginnings in the basement of the home of Will Antell in Stillwater, Minnesota, to its national recognition and prominence in its present location in Washington, D.C., NIEA continues to serve as a voice of commitment to the education of American Indian/Alaska Natives into the 1990s and the twenty-first century.

Will D. Antell

See also **Educational Policy; Indian Education Act**

NATIONAL INDIAN YOUTH COUNCIL

The National Indian Youth Council (NIYC) is an Indian advocacy and service organization based in Albuquerque, New Mexico. An incorporated charitable institution, NIYC is directed by a nine-person board of Native Americans from throughout the United States. Its periodical publication, *Americans Before Columbus*, covers a broad range of issues concerning Native Americans and has a circulation of about 20,000.

The second oldest national Indian organization in the United States, NIYC was founded in the aftermath of the 1961 Conference on American Indians in Chicago. The Chicago Conference, coordinated through the University of Chicago's anthropology department, brought together government bureaucrats, scholars, and representatives of Indian tribes to develop an overall strategy statement on Indian policy for presentation to the newly installed administration of John F. Kennedy.

A group of young Indians attended the Conference uninvited and transformed it into a vehicle for a new form of Indian activism. The young Indian activists—many of them college educated—promoted a statement that was substantially incorporated into a declaration adopted by the Conference and that would become the philosophical impetus for the creation of NIYC. The statement declared "the inherent right of self-government" of Indian people and that they "mean to hold the scraps and parcels [of their lands] as earnestly as any small nation was ever determined to hold to identity and survival." The statement additionally rejected "paternalism, even when benevolent" and affirmed a reliance on traditional Indian values, "a universe of things they knew, valued, and loved."

The group of young activists were encouraged by tribal elders who attended the Chicago Conference and organized a subsequent meeting in Gallup, New Mexico. The Gallup meeting of August, 1961, resulted in a constitution and bylaws for the founding of NIYC. The new organization acknowledged the role of younger Indians in setting the course for the future of Native peoples and committed itself to providing leadership to meet ensuing challenges. Clyde Warrior, Shirley Hill Witt, Mel Thom, and other individuals who became well known in Indian country, were among the founding members of NIYC.

Through the 1960s NIYC helped forge an Indian movement that included acts of protest and civil disobedience. NIYC became particularly involved in efforts to secure the treaty hunting and fishing rights of northwestern tribes. NIYC helped organize Indian "fish-ins" in defiance of Washington State authorities seeking to deny treaty fishing rights, and in 1964 NIYC organized a march and demonstration at the state capital in Olympia. Although NIYC was concerned primarily with distinctly Indian issues, the organization aligned itself and participated in the civil rights movement led by African Americans. NIYC members participated in "freedom rides" in the American South and in Martin Luther King's walk to Montgomery, Alabama in 1965. In 1968, NIYC was the Indian coordinator for the Poor People's Campaign.

During the 1970s, NIYC expanded its activities into the realm of environmental issues. It helped organize Indian constituencies, staged demonstrations, and produced literature in opposition to resource development projects perceived as threatening to Indian environments. Environmental issues were the springboard for the development of the legal advocacy wing of the organization. NIYC attorneys filed several lawsuits on behalf of Indian communities against coal strip mining, uranium mining, and milling on Indian lands.

NIYC's evolution continued through the 1980s to the present. The organization developed a comprehensive program to promote Native American participation in the political process. NIYC has organized voter registration drives on reservations, conducted polls to assess Indian political behavior, and has successfully prosecuted several lawsuits to eliminate state and local practices that disadvantage Native American voters. NIYC also has led or participated in litigation concerning Native American religious freedom and treaty hunting rights. In 1984 NIYC achieved consultative status with the United Nations Economic and Social Council. Since then NIYC regularly has utilized United Nations human rights machinery to advocate Indian causes. The organization also has counseled the Miskito Indians of Nicaragua in their efforts to secure self-government and resource rights. NIYC continues to operate a job placement and training program for off-reservation Indians in New Mexico under the federal Job Training Partnership Act.

S. James Anaya

See also **American Indian Chicago Conference; Fishing and Hunting Rights; International Law; Organizations and Tribal Cooperation; Red Power**

Further Reading

Jacobson, Marcus E. "'Rise Up, Make Haste. Our People Need Us!' The National Indian Youth Council and the Origins of the Red Power Movement." Manuscript available from the National Indian Youth Council.

Steiner, Stan. *The New Indians.* New York, NY: Dell Publishing Co., 1968.

Wilkinson, Gerald T. "Activities of the National Indian Youth Council." Available from the National Indian Youth Council, 318 Elm Street S.E., Albuquerque, NM.

NATIVE AMERICAN CHURCH

See Peyote Religion

NATIVE AMERICAN PRESS ASSOCIATION

See Periodicals

NATIVE AMERICAN RIGHTS FUND

The Native American Rights Fund (NARF) was established in 1970 by a Ford Foundation grant as a national Indian rights organization dedicated to addressing major Indian legal problems and providing competent and ethical legal representation for Native Americans who would otherwise be unable to afford such representation. Located in Boulder, Colorado, with branch offices in Washington, D.C. and Anchorage, Alaska, it originated as a project of the California Indian Legal Services (CILS)—one of many legal service programs launched in the 1960s as part of the federal government's War on Poverty. CILS's success in representing Indian tribes and people with limited financial resources caused other Native Americans and tribes throughout the country who were facing legal issues similar to those faced by California Indians to voice their support for a national organization that would address their legal concerns. NARF thus began as a program dedicated to assuring that Native Americans, nationwide, would receive justice within the American legal system.

Goals

NARF's goals are to secure the sovereignty, natural resources, human dignity, status, and traditional ways of life for Native Americans. In so doing, NARF tries to maintain an apolitical posture and concentrate on issues which will be of lasting benefit to all tribes.

Organization

NARF is a nonprofit corporation funded by private foundations and corporations, government grants, and individual contributions. It is governed by a thirteen-member board of directors, formerly called the steering committee. The all-Indian board sets NARF's priorities and policies. Members are chosen on the basis of their involvement in Indian affairs, knowledge of the issues, and tribal affiliation for wide geographical representation. Their leadership, credibility, and vision are essential to NARF's effectiveness in representing its Native American clients.

To achieve NARF's goals and determine the types of cases NARF will handle, the board of directors has defined five priority areas: 1) Preservation of Tribal Existence; 2) Protection of Tribal Natural Resources; 3) Promotion of Human Rights; 4) Accountability of Governments; and 5) Development of Indian Law.

NARF's day-to-day operations are led by an executive director, and with the assistance of a support staff of legal secretaries and administrative assistants, a staff of approximately fifteen lawyers handle the legal cases and legal matters.

NARF also maintains the National Indian Law Library (NILL), founded in 1972 as the first national collection of legal materials devoted exclusively to Indian law. Besides NILL, NARF also maintains another important Indian resource facility—the Indian Law Support Center (ILSC). Funded by the federal Legal Services Corporation, it provides legal research, advice, materials, and often serves as cocounsel in cases handled by Indian legal services programs.

NARF Legal Cases

Cases in which NARF has participated concern all issues of Indian law which focus on the five major priority areas. The issues, for the most part, are part of the legacy of two centuries of treaty formulation between the United States and Indian leaders, which recognizes Indian tribes as sovereign governments within the boundaries of the United States. Some of the cases in which NARF has played an active role include the following:

1) Preservation of Tribal Existence. NARF has handled many cases that focus on tribal sovereignty issues, economic development, federal recognition and restoration of tribes, preservation of Native traditions, enforcement of treaty rights, and protection of tribal lands. Many of these cases have established strong precedents on which others have been built.

NARF's tribal sovereignty cases often involve federal and state governments in litigation to resolve conflicts concerning a tribe's authority to regulate its internal affairs and activities on the reservation. For example, in one important case of this kind—the Supreme Court case of *Solem v. Bartlett*—NARF challenged South Dakota's criminal jurisdiction over 1.6 million acres of Indian land that had been opened in 1908 to non-Indian settlement, and won a unanimous decision from the Court rejecting state jurisdiction in favor of federal and tribal control.

NARF's tribal sovereignty cases also involve jurisdictional issues and regulatory conflicts in areas such as taxation, and hunting and fishing. In the 1985 tax case of *Montana v. Blackfeet Tribe*, NARF attorneys and the Blackfeet tribe successfully challenged the state's authority to tax the tribe's oil and gas royalties. The Supreme Court ruled that the State of Montana did not have the authority to tax the tribe.

In the 1973 case of *United States v. Michigan*, NARF attorneys helped the Bay Mills Chippewa Indian community secure their treaty fishing rights in the Great Lakes and limited the state's power to regulate treaty fishing.

Many of NARF's recognition and restoration cases involve either persuading the federal government to formally acknowledge a tribe's sovereign status or persuading the federal government to restore a previously terminated trust relationship between the tribe and the federal government. NARF represented the Menominee and Siletz tribes in gaining restoration, and represented the Kickapoo of Texas, the Gayhead Wampanoag, the Pascua Yaqui, and other tribes in gaining recognition.

NARF has also been instrumental in providing legal representation to Alaska Native villages on crucial sovereignty rights issues in Alaska. In a 1989 case in which NARF represented a Native village—*State of Alaska v. Native Village of Venetie*—a federal appeals court held that the tribal status of Alaska Native villages must be determined according to the rules applicable to tribes in the lower forty-eight states.

2) The Protection of Tribal Natural Resources. Besides helping tribes protect their sovereignty, NARF attorneys also assist tribes in maintaining their self-sufficiency through the preservation of their land, water, and other natural resources.

In one important land case in 1970, the Army Corps of Engineers attempted to condemn Winnebago Reservation land which bordered a proposed recreation and flood control project on the Missouri River. The Winnebago Tribe of Nebraska faced the possible loss of a sizeable portion of their tribal lands. Six years later, with the help of NARF attorneys, an appellate court ruled that the Corps had no authority to violate the tribe's treaty—one which guaranteed the Winnebago ownership of the land forever—and the project was stopped.

In another significant land case—*Passamaquoddy Tribe v. Morton*—NARF attorneys and Maine's Passamaquoddy tribe helped to establish the legal precedents for the Passamaquoddy and other eastern tribes to obtain—through future court cases—thousands of acres of their lost lands.

NARF has also been instrumental in helping tribes establish and protect their water rights, and has worked to ensure that the federal government fulfills its treaty responsibilities as established by a 1908 Supreme Court decision—later known as the Winters Doctrine—which ruled that when reservations are established, sufficient water to make the reservations liveable must be reserved. NARF has represented and continues to represent many tribes in significant water cases in nearly every state throughout the West, including the *Arizona v. California* case, the Pyramid Lake Paiute cases in Nevada, the Northern Cheyenne and Rocky Boy efforts in Montana to establish their water rights, the Nez Perce litigation in Idaho, and many others. In several cases, successful congressional water rights settlements have been achieved for tribes including the Fort McDowell Mohave-Apache in Arizona, San Luis Rey tribes in California, Pyramid Lake Paiute Tribe, Northern Cheyenne, and the Colorado Ute tribes.

3) The Promotion of Human Rights. NARF cases often focus on securing and maintaining basic human rights for Native Americans in areas concerning religious freedom, education, health, housing, welfare, and the rights of Indian inmates.

In many cases NARF attorneys have successfully defended Native Americans' religious sites and freedom to practice their traditional religions and ceremonies. In one case, after a long, nine-year legal battle, NARF attorneys successfully assisted the Kootenai tribes in blocking construction of a proposed hydroelectric plant which would have directed Montana's Kootenai River around Kootenai Falls—an important religious site for the tribes.

In the area of education, NARF attorneys in the early 1970s participated in revising the Johnson-O'Malley funding regulations that serve as guidelines for distributing certain Indian education funds to public schools. Previously, the funds had been misused and Indian children had not received the full benefits to which they were entitled.

4) The Accountability of Governments to Native Americans. A significant number of NARF's cases focus on ensuring that both the federal and state government carry out their trust responsibilities, in recognizing and honoring the unique federal rights and immunities of the tribes and Indians within their respective borders. In one such case of this type—*Covelo Indian Community et al. v. Watt*—NARF attorneys showed that the federal government was not fulfilling its responsibility to resolve more than 17,000 Indian damage claims. As a result, the United States District Court in Washington, D.C., ordered the federal government to either litigate the claims or submit legislative proposals to resolve them. Congress subsequently extended the statute of limitations and directed that the claims be handled in a timely manner.

NARF also works closely with other national Indian organizations and tribes to ensure that federal Indian policies are consistent with the federal government's legal responsibilities to tribes.

5) The Development of Indian Law. Over the years, NARF attorneys have been instrumental not only in helping to establish favorable court precedents in critical areas of Indian law, but also in distributing much useful information and materials to others who also endeavor to further Indian rights. Prior to the founding of NARF, Indian law was a relatively new or uncommon field of study in the law schools. NARF helped to change that situation by making Indian law a routine part of the curriculum in law schools, and by undertaking crucial projects for the growth of Indian law such as:

- The establishment in 1972 of the Indian Law Support Center (ILSC), which provides support and technical assistance to local legal services and attorneys serving Indians nationwide;

- The establishment of the National Indian Law Library (NILL), which was the first national collection devoted exclusively to Indian law and is used by attorneys, judges, students, researchers, historians, and Indian organizations and tribal courts;

- The establishment of an Indian Lawyer Intern Program for Indian law school graduates;

- The participation in the formation of the American Indian Bar Association.

Important Individuals Who Have Helped NARF

There have been many individuals who have played a role both in the establishment and direction of NARF and in its successes in the courtroom. David Getches, currently a professor at the University of Colorado School of Law, was the founding director. With the help of the first attorneys hired for the project—Robert Pelcyger, John Echohawk (Pawnee), Bruce Greene, Joe Brecher, and Charles Wilkinson—the project quickly began handling some of the major Indian law cases in the country. The staff was soon joined by many of the newest Indian law school graduates—Yvonne Knight (Ponca-Creek), Walter Echo-Hawk (Pawnee), Browning Pipestem (Otoe-Osage), Doug Nash (Nez Perce), and Leland Pond (Assiniboine). John Echohawk, one of the original staff attorneys, became the first Indian director in 1973. Echohawk continues to lead the organization and has become a nationally known advocate for Indian tribes. In all, over forty attorneys have worked for NARF, and of these, more than half have been Native Americans and have since become the leading scholars and practitioners in the field of Indian law.

The board of directors has also played a critical role in the development and guidance of the organization. David Risling, Jr. (Hupa) was the first steering committee chairman. Risling and the many Native Americans who have served on the steering committee and the board of directors, throughout NARF's twenty-two years of operation, have provided and continue to provide the leadership, guidance, and wisdom that has made NARF the successful and effective national Indian legal organization that it is today.

Jeanne S. Whiteing

See also **Civil Rights; Law; Sovereignty and Jurisdiction; Treaties**

Further Reading

"NARF Celebrates Its 20th Anniversary." *NARF Legal Review* 15 (Summer 1990): 1–4.

NARF 20th Anniversary Report. Boulder, CO: Native American Rights Fund, 1990.

NILL Catalogue: An Index to Indian Legal Materials and Resources, Vol. 1. 1973–74. Boulder, CO: NARF.

NATURAL RESOURCE MANAGEMENT

Tribal governments have developed reservation natural resource management programs in an attempt to encourage self-sufficiency and to provide employment for tribesmen. As large land holders, tribes direct resource development on 2.7 million acres of farmland, 44 million acres of grazing land, and 5.3 million acres of commercial forests. A variety of resource programs simultaneously occurs on these lands and nearly all require water. Excluding water improvements and farming and ranching operations, tribal resource management programs emphasize hunting and fishing regulation, forests and woodlands projects, and energy development.

Some tribes possess substantial natural resource development potential and consider tribal control over those assets essential. Control enables tribal leaders to make decisions that reflect local economic and culture concerns. In addition, both resource allocation and control are necessary for tribal self-sufficiency because of the monetary and the subsistence benefits tribesmen gain from regulating reservation wildlife and fisheries, forests and woodlands, and energy resources.

Hunting and Fishing Resource Management

Tribal allocation of hunting and fishing resources is an immemorial tradition. After the creation of reservations and the growing emphasis on making tribesmen farmers, they continued to hunt and to fish throughout the nineteenth century for subsistence and trade. As hunting and fishing resources diminished, tribal governments began to manage these assets by controlling tribal consumption and use of wildlife resources. Today, tribal game departments distribute these assets to members and non-members by issuing hunting and fishing licenses.

Adjustment of tribal fishing and allocating practices occurred in the nineteenth century. As early as 1881, the Quileute of Washington refused to sell coho and chinook salmon to outsiders because of dwindling runs. Another frequent tribal regulatory practice was to remove fish weirs from rivers and permit Pacific salmon, not needed for consumption, to spawn. The continual pressure on the fisheries forced the Quinault to end Sunday fishing, and the tribe required tribal fishermen to maintain 75-foot channels between their fishing nets in 1907.

Because of treaty rights, tribal hunting and fishing activities, which are property rights, extend beyond reservation boundaries. Since tribes retained hunting and fishing activities on territory exclusive of the land title, they clashed with state game officials because tribesmen neither purchased state licenses nor complied with state seasons and limits. State arrests and equipment seizures forced tribesmen from off-reservation fishing and hunting locations in the twentieth century. This temporarily ended tribal management of off-reservation resources and restricted their management decisions.

Tribes in Oregon and Washington resisted state encroachment on their fishery. Eventually the conflict reached federal court in the case *United States v. Washington*. In 1974, Judge George H. Boldt reallocated the Northwest fisheries. Based on tribal hunting and fishing property rights, Boldt ordered the State of Washington to insure that the tribes received 50 percent of the catch. As a result, the Northwest Coast tribes became active managers of the region's on- and off-reservation fisheries. Western Washington tribes created the Northwest Indian Fisheries Commission in 1975 and the Columbia River Inter-Tribal Fish Commission to address collective tribal management responsibilities. By 1987, Washington tribes operated twenty-eight fish hatcheries that produced 63 million salmon and steelhead annually.

Unlike off-reservation management, where tribes regulate tribal members, tribal governments retain authority over both tribal members and nontribal members hunting or fishing on the reservation. Early in the twentieth century, few tribal restrictions applied to either tribal or nontribal members who hunted or fished on reservations. Tribal regulatory control, through licensing, increased after World War II as tribes enacted comprehensive reservation hunting and fishing ordinances. Greater tribal restrictions limited both tribal members and nontribal members use of the resources, and different regulations governed each.

Reservation leaders now began to consider hunting, fishing, and associated outdoor recreation as potential revenue sources for tribal treasuries. Tribes required both tribal and nontribal users to obtain permits. Funds received paid administrative costs associated with game and fish management. Once a tribe began issuing licenses, it created enforcement departments, often consisting of a single tribal warden, to insure compliance. The Confederated Salish and Kootenai Tribes in Montana initially employed a single tribal game warden to enforce game and fish laws and to establish game seasons and bag limits. This warden shared an office with the tribal police and handled all wildlife issues.

The importance of tribal wildlife resources increased and tribal management changed to reflect that trend. The Indian Self-Determination and Education Act of 1975 provided assistance by authorizing tribes to contract with the United States for funds to support tribal operations. Many tribes took that opportunity to improve reservation wildlife programs. The Confederated Salish and Kootenai Tribes created the Enforcement and Wildlife Division to force compliance and to collect wildlife research data essential to managing these resources. To compliment this growing interest in wild lands, the Tribal Council also created a member-only wilderness area. This illustrates tribal management of wildlife resources according to cultural values.

The White Mountain Apache have developed a comprehensive wildlife resource management program on their 1.6 million acre Arizona reservation. The tribe's Game and Fish Department manage bear, elk, javelin, and mountain lion for trophy hunting. These are controlled hunts, and a tribal warden guides a hunter. To insure success, recent regulations limited bull elk permits to thirty-two annually and provided that no bull with less than six points was killed. This control demonstrates the extent to which the White Mountain Apache shape reservation game management programs.

Sharing wildlife management information is important to tribes. Tribal game managers chartered the Native American Fish and Wildlife Society to share knowledge and to discuss issues crucial to tribes.

Timber Management

A tribe's decision to enhance wildlife habitat limits its options to pursue different natural resource development on the same land. This is especially true for reservation forest and woodland properties. When tribal managers decide to either increase or preserve wildlife and fisheries habitats, options decrease.

Unlike wildlife resources, which were considered tribal property, reservation timber resources remained with the land and under United States control. The Supreme Court in *United States v. Cook*, 1873, declared that timber was part of the land and could not be severed without United States authorization. The decision limited tribal logging to clearing land for agricultural purposes. Gradually, tribal management of reservation timber evolved from the tribes as recipients of decisions to decision makers.

Congress ordered reservation land allotted in the nineteenth century forcing the Indian Service to establish a timber program based on obtaining wood products for farming operations. As a result, logging was not pursued as a reservation industry. In this push to allot and reduce reservation land bases, valuable timbered lands were lost.

Only a few reservations established ongoing logging operations. At the turn of the century, the Menominee developed a tribal sawmill and employed tribal members to work the forests and the mill. This was an exception because the government often sold tribal timber to outsiders who also cut the logs.

The Department of the Interior initiated a forestry program in 1910, by hiring a professional forester to monitor logging contracts, to improve fire protection, and to reduce timber trespass. Congress also expanded tribal logging and authorized the sale of green-standing timber from both unallotted lands and allotted tribal lands. Regulations governing res-

ervation logging were approved in 1911, and required the Indian Service to deduct administrative expenses from the timber sale for expenses accrued from supervising reservation logging. Subsequent legislation in 1920 established a maximum deduction of 10 percent.

These deductions were deposited in an Indian Service account and reappropriated back to reservations, based on budgets that foresters prepared. The few timber rich tribes, such as the Menominee and Klamath, resented this intrusion into tribal sovereignty and claimed the deductions reduced their ability to control tribal timber programs. As an alternative, the Klamath supported legislation in a 1929 bill to incorporate the tribe and to give the corporation control over the timber.

The Indian Reorganization Act of 1934 emphasized greater tribal timber conservation. The law authorized the management of tribal forests on the principle of sustained yield. The legislation also encouraged tribesmen to assume greater control over reservation resources, including timber; however, the administration of the Indian Reorganization Act failed to increase tribal control over reservation timber. As a result, timber tribes continued to clamor for greater control of their forests.

Substantial changes in timber control were made in the 1970s. Congress modified the administrative fee deduction in 1972, reducing the charge assessed against timber sales proportionally to tribal contributions to the reservation forestry program. The Indian Self-Determination and Education Assistance Act of 1975 granted tribes greater authority to manage their timber resources. Under the legislation, tribes contracted with the Bureau of Indian Affairs (BIA) for forestry funds. Two decades later in 1990, Congress passed the National Indian Forest Resources Management Act, which increased tribal management and provided monetary support for reservation forestry activities.

Today tribes determine the best use of reservation wood lands, draft forestry budgets, and establish cutting rates. As a result, each tribe's management reservation plan varies from moderate to intensive. Often, tribal logging decisions are socially driven and designed either to maintain tribal employment or to preserve cultural landmarks and wildlife habitat.

Timber tribes created the Intertribal Timber Council in 1979 to assist in forestry management decisions. This organization promotes the development of tribal forest industries and reservation wood products and encourages tribes to conduct studies of reservation forests and woodlands.

Energy Resources

Tribal involvement in reservation energy resource management began in 1891. In that year, Congress passed a general leasing act authorizing tribes to lease tribal lands. Congress intended the legislation to open large tracts of reservation grasslands to outside lease. Also, Congress recognized that tribes held power to control outside access, by either denying or granting leases for coal, natural gas, and oil. Initially, very little energy leasing occurred, because so many other land holders possessed both the resources and the willingness to lease lands cheaply for energy purposes.

Tribal lease approval powers remained limited for decades. Congress strengthened tribal leasing powers in Section 16 of the Indian Reorganization Act of 1934 prohibiting the leasing of tribal lands "without the consent of the tribe." Four years later, Congress passed the Omnibus Tribal Leasing Act of 1938 that stipulated that tribal leases would require competitive bidding and that successful bidders would post bonds. Under this act, which governed tribal energy leases for the next forty-five years, tribal management of reservation energy resources still remained marginal.

Tribal energy resources, which are private property, were managed by the Department of the Interior. The Department's limited goal was to gain the maximum economic benefits from the resources for the tribal landowner. Through the first half of the twentieth century, the BIA negotiated the leases and the United States Geological Survey provided limited technical expertise and lease supervision.

This conservative system was not prepared for the erratic, but profitable, energy markets that emerged in the late 1960s and early 1970s. Historically, the United States placed little emphasis on energy resources because the tribesmen were presumably going to be farmers. On the other hand, the tribes possessed important quantities of energy resources. The Department of the Interior estimated in 1975 that the tribes possessed 3 percent of the nation's oil and natural gas reserves, and 13 percent of the coal reserves.

The comptroller general reported in 1976 that tribal oil and mineral resources were underdeveloped, thus depriving tribes of potential revenue. Unfortunately, the BIA did not possess accurate information on the extent of reservation energy resources, and this lack of information made resource development planning difficult. The comptroller general added that the United States Geological Survey failed to monitor reservation lessor contract compliance, production, and collect royalty payments. The Geological Survey also ignored land reclamation compliance, a crucial concern for tribes when the effects of development can be dangerous to the community's health and cultural survival.

These mismanagement problems convinced tribal leaders of the need to gain greater control of reservation energy development. The BIA made the first step and drafted regulations in 1977 requiring reservation development to comply with the Surface Mining Control and Reclamation Act of 1977. This was not enough. Tribal leaders wanted the 1938 law changed because the act preserved long lease terms and low royalty rates. These provisions hurt the tribes during the boom and bust years of the 1970s. In 1982, Congress passed the Indian Mineral Development Act,

permitting tribes to become developers of their own resources and negotiators of their own contracts. Now, management of tribal mineral resources resided in tribal hands. Tribes now assumed greater risk with the potential for greater profits and, it was hoped, less environmental damages.

Tribes needed energy resource information to make sound decisions. As a result, in 1975, twenty chartered tribes created the Council of Energy Resource Tribes, enabling member tribes to share information and expertise.

Conclusion

Tribes have gained greater control over natural resources during the twentieth century. As tribes assumed management of natural resources, they have established their own priorities for the utilization of natural resources that reflect contemporary tribal goals.

Richmond L. Clow

See also **Environmental Issues; Fishing and Hunting Rights; Mining**

Further Reading

Ambler, Marjane. *Breaking the Iron Bonds: Indian Control of Energy Development.* Lawrence: University Press of Kansas, 1990.

Boxberger, Daniel. *To Fish in Common: The Ethnohistory of Lummi Indian Salmon Fishing.* Lincoln: University of Nebraska Press, 1989.

Hess, Bill. "Apache Elk." *Field and Stream* 86 (May 1981): 52–53, 96, 98.

Kinney, J.B. *Indian Forest and Range: A History of the Administration and Conservation of the Redman's Heritage.* Washington, DC: Forestry Enterprise, 1950.

Newell, Alan S., Richmond L. Clow, and Richard N. Ellis. *A Forest in Trust: Three-Quarters of a Century of Indian Forestry, 1910-1986.* U.S. Department of the Interior, Bureau of Indian Affairs, Division of Forestry, Washington, DC, 1986.

NAVAJO

The Navajos (Navahos, Navajoes, Dineh or Diné, i.e., "the People") occupy the largest reservation in the United States: 28,803 square miles. Situated on the Colorado Plateau, the Navajo Reservation takes up the northeastern portion of Arizona, the northwest corner of New Mexico and a strip of Utah south of the Colorado River. The current reservation encompasses a substantial part of the Navajos' traditional lands, an area defined by the four sacred mountains: *Sisnaajiní* ("Horizontal Black Belt") or Sierra Blanca Peak in Colorado to the east; *Tsoodził* ("Tongue Mountain") or Mount Taylor in New Mexico to the south; *Dook'o'słííd* ("Light Shines From It") or San Francisco Peaks in Arizona to the west; and *Dibéntsaa* ("Big Mountain Sheep") or Mount Hesperus in the La Plata Mountains of Colorado to the north.

Elevation across the reservation ranges from just under 5,000 to 11,300 feet, with desert grassland, Colorado Plateau desert scrub and piñon-juniper-sagebrush vegetation zones below 7,500 feet, ponderosa pine and Douglas fir in a transitional zone to about 9,500 feet, and spruce, fir, and aspen in the higher elevations. Annual precipitation ranges from 6 to 16 inches below 7,500 feet, and from 15 to 40 inches in the higher elevations. Mean monthly temperatures range from 32 to 77 degrees fahrenheit in the lower elevations, and from 25 to 65 degrees fahrenheit above 7,500 feet.

Three smaller segments of the reservation are located in New Mexico: Ramah, Alamo, and Canoncito. The reservation is divided into five agencies, Tuba City, Chinle, Fort Defiance, Shiprock, and Eastern Navajo, and twenty-three land management districts. The number of council delegates is proportional to the population in each district. The smallest political unit is the local community or chapter. Two or more chapters form a tribal election district. There are 109 chapters and 37 districts.

Twentieth-Century History

The formation of the tribal government, the discovery and development of energy resources on the reservation, the extension of reservation lands, overgrazing by livestock and forced stock reduction, the Navajo-Hopi land dispute, and the Navajos' contribution to World War II are the important events and issues of Navajo history in this century. The most important theme throughout is the reestablishment of tribal sovereignty.

Traditionally, the Navajos were governed by an informal system of headmen and clan leaders, the *naat'áanii*, "the ones who orate." The *naat'áanii* met at irregular intervals, usually two to four years, at the *naachid*. Decision making was based on persuasion and consensus, rather than coercion and majority rule.

Modern Navajo tribal government has its roots in the 1922 Business Council, selected by the secretary of the interior to approve oil leases. In 1923, a three-man Council consisting of Chee Dodge, Charlie Mitchell, and Dugal Chee Bekiss was appointed. On July 7, 1923, Dodge, a Catholic and leader of a more traditional faction, was elected chair of the Council, which was composed of twelve delegates and twelve alternates. As a youth, Dodge became proficient in both English and Navajo and served as the interpreter for the army post at Fort Defiance. Jacob C. Morgan, council member from the San Juan Agency, opposed the council's plan for distributing oil royalties to the rest of the tribe. Morgan, a Christian Reformed missionary and leader of a more progressive faction, advocated greater localism. Dodge, Morgan, and their respective followers later divided the tribe over the adoption of a reorganized Council in the 1930s.

As early as 1894 there was evidence that the reservation was badly overgrazed. In 1926, the Council passed a resolution to limit horses and seek a voluntary reduction of sheep. That same year, Deshna Clah Cheschillige was elected chairman. In 1927 the first local chapters were started by John Hunter, agent of the Leupp jurisdiction. Although Navajos have traditionally been matriarchal, women did not receive the right to vote in tribal elections until 1928. In 1932 the first Navajo lawyer, Thomas Dodge, was elected chairman. Three years later, the Navajo people rejected the Indian Reorganization Act (IRA), the pet project of Commissioner of Indian Affairs, John Collier.

Collier intended the IRA to enable tribes to establish constitutional governments. Unfortunately, the act became identified with a very unpopular policy: forced stock reduction. The Navajos saw their herds of sheep, goats, and horses as a form of wealth, and needed the sheep for feeding guests at ceremonies and for paying singers' fees. The government could not afford to ship the mutton to market and many sheep were slaughtered and left to rot. Embittered by the sight of their sheep, shot and bloating in the sun, the Navajos rejected the IRA in 1935. The following year the Tribal Council appointed a constitutional assembly consisting of seventy delegates from across the reservation. Chee Dodge, Albert "Chic" Sandoval, and Father Berard Haile helped select the delegates. With Henry Taliman and Roy Kinsel as chairman and vice-chairman, a Constitution was drafted that was almost identical to the one proposed under the IRA. On Collier's recommendation, Secretary of the Interior Harold Ickes rejected the draft on the grounds that the Navajos were not yet able to govern themselves, and issued a set of Bylaws creating a new Tribal Council in 1938.

Morgan was elected chairman and Howard Gorman vice-chairman, in 1938. They served until 1942, when Chee Dodge was reelected with Sam Ahkeah as vice-chairman. Four years later Ahkeah was elevated to the chairmanship with Dodge as vice-chairman, a position he held until his death in 1947.

World War II and the following years brought rapid changes to the Navajo people. For the first time, substantial numbers of Navajos were being employed as wage earners in defense depots and munitions plants, and meeting an increased demand for workers in agriculture, in construction, and on the railroads. The most famous contribution of the Navajos to the war effort was a special group of Marines known as the Navajo Code Talkers. The Navajo Code Talkers developed a coded form of the Navajo language to transmit messages that the Japanese could not decipher. By the end of the war, 450 men were recruited into the 382nd Platoon. Despite the part the Navajos played in the war, the states of New Mexico and Arizona discouraged Navajo participation in state elections.

The termination policy of the 1950s aimed at ending the trust relationship between the federal government and Indians. Realizing that they could not turn to the states for essential services, the Navajos decided to take on as much of the responsibility as they could. From the mid 1950s on, Navajo tribal government increased its control over natural resources. Using royalties from oil, coal, and uranium mining and establishing forestry as a tribal enterprise, subsequent administrations embarked on a program of increased self-determination.

Paul Jones, elected as chairman in 1954, extended the Council business sessions and advocated the use of oil revenues to set up a tribal scholarship fund. He hired Norman Littell as chief counsel for the tribe. Littell, a critic of John Collier's philosophy, worked with the tribe in enacting regulations that would ensure tribal autonomy.

The plentiful jobs of the war years evaporated like flood waters in the desert. Congress enacted the Navajo-Hopi Long Range Rehabilitation Act in 1950. Under this act, $88 million was appropriated to be spent over the next ten years for road and school construction, irrigation projects, and the development of wells and springs.

In the 1950s tribal activity increased. The tribe's budget increased sharply from $1,022,674 in 1954 to $3,254,325 in 1957. In 1958 the Tribal Council approved a $12 million budget, in which $5 million was earmarked for college scholarships alone. Such growth was made possible by an increase in royalties from energy resources. In 1956 the Aneth, Utah oil fields alone generated over $34 million in revenues for the tribe. Similarly, revenues from uranium mining increased ten fold from 1950 to 1954. Instead of a per capita distribution of this income, the Tribal Council developed reservation infrastructure and established a generous scholarship program, which today is nearly depleted.

As part of this aggressive program, the tribe began to revive local government through the chapter system. To this end the Tribal Council passed a series of resolutions in the mid-1950s providing salaries for local chapter officials and requiring monthly chapter meetings. The Council also appropriated funds for the construction of new chapter houses. By the 1960s almost every chapter had a new building which also served as a community center.

In 1959 the tribal court system was established and the tribe adopted the law and order regulations of the Department of the Interior as the basis for the Navajo Tribal Code. This set the responsibility for law enforcement—with the exception of major crimes—squarely on the shoulders of the tribe.

Paul Jones served as chairman for eight years and was succeeded by Raymond Nakai in 1962. Nakai served two terms and was defeated by Peter MacDonald in 1970. Nakai's administration was characterized by an increase in tribal service programs such as the Office of Navajo Economic Opportunity (ONEO, established in 1965), *Dinébeiina Nahiilna be Agitahe*, the tribally sponsored legal aid program (DNA, established in 1966), as well as heated debates over strip mining on Black Mesa.

Peter MacDonald, a proponent of greater tribal control of Navajo resources and a strong supporter of the DNA, brought about a greater stabilization of the judiciary and of the tribal police, as well as more tribal control over education and health care. He was re-elected in 1974 and again in 1978 for a precedent-

breaking third term. MacDonald served as the first head of ONEO in 1965, and since has dominated Navajo political life for more than a generation.

In 1982 Navajo voters elected Peterson Zah, who slashed his own salary and those of his top aides and tried to halt a 25 percent pay raise for the Tribal Council. In 1986 MacDonald soundly defeated Zah in the primary and won in the tribal elections.

Population

Low population density, poor roads, and a suspicion of outsiders have bedeviled attempts to obtain an accurate count of the Navajo population. When the reservation was established in 1868, there were about 9,000 Navajos. Over the past 130 years, the population has seen a phenomenal increase to 146,001 according to the United States 1990 Census report, showing an average annual growth rate of 2.31 percent. The census report, however, does not include Navajos living away from the reservation; it also does not distinguish between Navajo and non-Navajo Indians living on the reservation. A more accurate estimate of the population is made by using the number of registered voters, 104,963. Since the median age is 18.7 years, this number accounts for slightly less than half of the total population. This indicates that a more accurate estimate should be well above 200,000, and certainly not less than 195,938, the sum of registered voters and reservation school enrollment. Figures 1 and 2 present the distribution of the Navajo population throughout the United States.

Figure 1
Navajo Population

Geographic Region	Population
Northeast	493
Midwest	1,606
South	2,508
West	154,024
Total U.S. Population	158,631

Figure 2
Western States with Largest Navajo Populations

California	6,030
Colorado	2,086
Arizona	76,642
New Mexico	57,919
Utah	9,178

Source: U.S. Census Bureau: *Characteristics of American Indians by Tribe and Selected Areas, 1980.* Washington, D.C.: U.S. Government Printing Office, 1989, p. 28.

Current Situation

Tribal Government. On December 15, 1989, the Tribal Council reorganized the government of the

Navajo Nation. Effective April 1, 1990, this resolution established three branches of government, the executive, the legislative and judicial branches, mirroring the organization of the United States federal government. The offices of president and vice-president replaced those of chairman and vice-chairman. This reorganization also established a separation of powers and a system of checks and balances, created the Office of the Speaker of the Council, and reduced the number of standing committees from eighteen to twelve.

Contemporary Leaders and Issues. In the spring of 1989, the Navajo people were thrown into a crisis as Tribal Chairman Peter MacDonald became the subject of United States Senate hearings concerning the purchase of the Big Boquillas Ranch, land intended for relocatees from the former Joint Use Area. MacDonald relinquished leadership in 1989. Leonard Haskie filled in as chair until tribal elections could be held. Peterson Zah was elected and took office in 1990.

In a separate case, MacDonald was convicted in tribal court of accepting bribes and kickbacks from business associates. On May 27, 1992, the United States District Court in Prescott, Arizona, found MacDonald guilty of sixteen out of thirty-one counts of extortion, fraud, conspiracy, and racketeering. Still serving a sentence in tribal jail, MacDonald faces a maximum sentence of 110 years in federal prison. On November 13, 1992, the same court convicted MacDonald and six others on charges of conspiracy in connection with a July 20, 1989, riot at Window Rock. The clash at tribal headquarters left two MacDonald supporters dead and six wounded, including three tribal police officers. Sentencing in this last case has not yet been handed down.

The Navajo-Hopi land dispute continues to plague these two tribes. In July 1992 the Hopis accused the Navajos in United States District Court in Phoenix of causing $56.9 million worth of damages to land the Hopis received in the 1979 partition of the former Joint Use Area (JUA). The Hopis attributed the cause of the damages to overgrazing. One proposed settlement would allow Navajos now living on Hopi lands to remain for the next seventy-five years. In exchange, the Navajos would be required to purchase approximately 408,000 acres of federal, state, and private land north of Flagstaff, at a price far below its actual worth. Formulated in strict secrecy, revelation of this plan in November 1992 created an uproar among private land owners and business leaders in the Flagstaff area. This controversial plan was awaiting congressional approval in early 1993. This lawsuit is but one part of a much larger land case pending before the District Court.

Economic Development. Dependence on agriculture and livestock, which characterized the early part of this century, has declined. Job opportunities are scarce on the reservation. In 1991, 36.52 percent of the work force was unemployed. The per capita income of the Navajo Nation—including non-Navajos—was just under $6,000 for the same year as reported in a Department of Economic Development survey. The tribe has invested heavily in attracting "clean" industries such as General Dynamics and Fairchild Semi-Conductor Corporation. Fairchild closed its Shiprock plant after a takeover by the American Indian Movement (AIM) in 1975. Recent cuts in defense spending cast doubt on General Dynamics' situation on the reservation.

Education. There are four school systems operating side-by-side on the reservation: Bureau of Indian Affairs schools, public schools, community controlled contract schools, and private and mission schools. Recent statistics appear in figures 3 and 4. The Navajo Nation was the first to open a tribally controlled college, Navajo Community College, which opened in 1969 and was accredited in 1976. The main campus is in Tsaile, Arizona, with a branch in Shiprock, New Mexico, along with four regional centers. The Mission Board of the United Presbyterian Church, U.S.A., opened the College of Ganado in 1972. This Indian controlled college was accredited in 1979.

Health Care. Navajo Area Indian Health Service (NAIHS), the second largest of twelve Indian Health Service (IHS) administrative units, is composed of eight service units. Six of these service units have hospitals, and two have ambulatory care clinics. The service units are linked by paved roads, by air transport, and by telephone communication. Public Health Service nurses are assisted by Navajo drivers/interpreters who help the nurses arrive at remote homesites, navigate unpaved roads, and assist in communicating with the relatively large number of older Navajos who speak little or no English (figure 5).

NAIHS has been successful in reducing the incidents of infant morbidity and mortality through its Navajo Area Perinatal Program. Infant mortality has declined steadily from 46.2 percent in 1965, to 11.8 percent in 1984. As with the Navajo population as a whole, the majority of infant deaths are linked to social and environmental factors, which account for about 40 percent of all Navajo deaths. Alcoholism accounts for the majority of these deaths, at a rate that is about twenty times the national average. Because the traditional ceremonial complex is mainly concerned with healing, there is a continuing dialogue between traditional practitioners and Western health care providers.

Culture

Language. The Navajo language belongs to the Apachean complex of dialects, the southern-most extension of the Athabaskan linguistic family. The Franciscan friars of St. Michael's Mission were the first to develop an orthography and to compile a dictionary of the language, *The Ethnologic Dictionary of the Navajo Language*, published in 1910. The Navajo language is very much alive and, according to the 1980 census, is spoken by 114,626 people, 26,949 of whom speak little or no English (figure 5).

Religion. Navajos participate in one or more religious systems: traditional ceremonies, the Native

Figure 3
School Enrollment

Grade Level	Public	Private	Total
Nursery	1,324	853	2,177
K – 8	32,004	4,340	36,344
9 – 12	12,195	1,109	13,304
College	——	——	4,756
Total	45,523	6,302	56,581

Source: U.S. Census Bureau: *Characteristics of American Indians by Tribes and Selected Areas, 1980*. Washington, DC: U.S. Government Printing Office, 1989.

Note: Navajo Nation Department of Economic Development reports a total enrollment for the 1991–92 school year of 71,490, but did not have the breakdown by grade level.

Figure 4
Schools on the Navajo Reservation

Type of School	Pre	Elementary	Middle	High	Total
Child Develop. Division	148	—	—	—	148
Contracted Schools	—	11	8	13	32
B.I.A.	—	46	24	8	78
Private/ Christian	—	16	10	9	35
Public	7	88	38	25	165
Total	155	161	80	55	461

Source: Navajo Nation Department of Economic Development, 1992.

Note: Of 109 communities (chapters) on the reservation, many have no schools. In reporting these figures, some schools combined grade levels so that some schools were counted three or four times, accounting for the larger number of total schools.

Figure 5
Language Usage on Navajo Reservations

	Ages 5–17	Ages 18+
English only	11,446	9,358
Other than English*	41,231	75,210
Native Language*	41,018	73,618
English not well or not at all	8,407	18,542
Total population by age group	52,677	84,568

Source: U.S. Census Bureau: *Characteristics of American Indians by Tribes and Selected Areas, 1980*. Washington, DC: U.S. Government Printing Office, 1989, p. 283.

*Other languages not specified.

American Church, and Christianity. Most traditional ceremonials are primarily concerned with the restoration and maintenance of health. This main group forms a complex of some twenty-four chantways which are further divided into about sixty-two branches, depending on the gender of the patient and the gender of the protagonist in the myth sung during the ceremony. Some others, the Blessingway group, are also concerned with securing blessings such as wealth and security and are the ceremonials used for the blessing of a new home and the girls' puberty ceremony. Still others belong to a group of mostly obsolete war ceremonials, the Enemyway. The whole intention in this ceremonial complex is to maintain and restore *hózhǫ́*, which may be translated as balance, beauty, or harmony. Traditional ceremonies are performed by *hataałii* or "singers" who may specialize in one or more ceremonials or "chants." Many Navajos see their traditional ceremonies more in terms of health care than religion, and see it as essential that they be cured at a sing, even when being treated by Western practitioners. The perception of traditional ceremonies as health care also justifies participation in other religious systems.

The Native American Church (NAC), or Peyote Religion, was introduced to the Navajos from the Utes in Colorado in the mid-1930s. Peyote ceremonies are held in either a traditional home (hogan) or a Plains-style tipi, with tipis becoming more common in recent years. On the Navajo Reservation, there are a variety of altar shapes being used including full moons, stars, and books. The Peyote Religion shares some of the concerns of the complex of traditional ceremonies. The emphasis, however, is not so much on individual welfare as on the people as a whole.

The intoxicating effects of peyote drew suspicion from traditionalists when it was first introduced on the reservation. Although there were as yet no tribal regulations prohibiting peyote on the reservation, two roadmen were arrested in 1938. Two years later, the Tribal Council placed a ban on peyote. Possession, sale and use of the cactus was illegal on the reservation until October 9, 1967, when the Tribal Council exempted members of the Native American Church from prosecution.

Although Spanish friars first contacted the Navajos in the eighteenth century, and Presbyterians established a mission at Fort Defiance in 1868, it was not until the late 1800s that Christianity established much of a foothold among the Navajos. By 1912 very few Navajos had joined any of the several denominations represented on the reservation. Despite this, in the early years of the century, missions were contributing to the well-being of the Navajos by constructing hospitals (the Episcopalians at Fort Defiance and at Shiprock, and the Presbyterians at Ganado) and schools. The missions also provided Navajos with opportunities for wage work.

A comprehensive survey of Navajo participation in Christian churches has not been carried out since 1977. According to this survey, roughly 10 percent of Navajos attend church regularly (figure 6).

Social Organization. Traditional residence patterns are flexible and have changed over time. There is a strong preference for matrilocal, postnuptial residence in groups of two or more households, which have sometimes been called "outfits." Descent among the Navajos is matrilineal. The primary social unit is the extended family with closest kinship ties to one's mother's clan (mothers).

Arts and Crafts. Rugweaving and silversmithing are the crafts of primary economic importance to the Navajos, and are so well known that they hardly need introduction here. In recent years, there has been a revival of pottery making. Traditional pottery is a rather coarse redware, usually in the form of a cooking pot, with a pointed base or a water jar, sometimes with an incised or bias relief decoration that is waterproofed with piñon pitch after firing. Contemporary potters are presently producing dazzling designs based on sandpaintings. Some basketweaving is still being done, but many of the baskets used in ceremonies are obtained from the Utes. Sandpaintings, once restricted to ceremonial use, are also significant items on the commercial market. Navajos have become involved in the fine arts as well. Carl Gorman, his son, R.C. Gorman, David Chethale Paladin, and Andy Tsihnahjinnie stand out among them.

Music has always played an important part in Navajo ritual and social life. Traditional instruments include drums made from deer hide stretched over a pot, and rattles made from rawhide, deer hoofs, or gourds. Traditional social songs, peyote songs from the Native American Church, Navajo versions of Christian hymns, and modern Navajo music are available as commercial recordings.

Kristie Lee Butler

Figure 6
Christian Churches on
the Navajo Reservation

Roman Catholic[1]	
Parishes	16
Chapels	14
Resident priests, sisters, lay brothers	48
Regular attendance at Mass	1,323
Navajos attending Mass in bordertowns	283
Navajos attending Mass twice yearly	2,498
Total active community	4,023
"Camp" churches (nondenominational)	
Total units	104
Average total attendance	3,068
Navajo pastors	103
Anglo pastors	4
Church of Jesus Christ of Latter-day Saints (Mormons)	
Total units	47
Attendance	2,573
Protestant (all denominations)	
Total units on reservation	235
Units in border towns	750
Average regular attendance	9,276
Native pastors	106
Anglo pastors	119

Source: David R. Scates: *Why Navajo Churches are Growing: The Cultural Dynamics of Navajo Religious Change.* Grand Junction, CO: Navajo Christian Churches, 1981.
[1]*Scates estimates that there are over 30,000 unchurched Navajos (out of his estimated population of 180,000) of Catholic heritage.*

The author would like to acknowledge Mr. Tribhuban Choudhary, statistical technician for the Navajo Nation Department of Economic Development, for providing figures 1-6 and for suggesting alternatives for estimating the population. United States Census figures released after this article was written show that 219,198 people throughout the United States claimed to be Navajo in the 1990 Census.

See also **Arizona Tribes; Drypainting; Mines; Peyote Religion; Navajo Code Talkers; Navajo-Hopi Land Controversy; Textiles**

Further Reading

Bailey, Garrick, and Roberta Glenn Bailey. *A History of the Navajos: The Reservation Years.* Sante Fe, NM: School of American Research, 1986.

Benedek, Emily. *The Wind Won't Know Me: A History of the Navajo-Hopi Land Dispute.* New York, NY: Alfred A. Knopf, 1992.

Goodman, James M. *The Navajo Atlas: Environments, Resources, People and History of the Diné Bikeyah.* Norman: University of Oklahoma Press, 1982.

Haroldson, Sixten S.R. "Health and Human Services Among the Navajo Indians." *Journal of Community Health* 13:3 (1988): 129–42.

Iverson, Peter. *The Navajos: A Critical Bibliography.* Bloomington: Indiana University Press, 1976.

———. *The Navajo Nation.* Albuquerque: University of New Mexico Press, 1981.

Ortiz, Alfonso, ed. *Handbook of North American Indians.* Vol. 10. *Southwest.* Washington, DC: Smithsonian Institution (1983): 489–683.

NAVAJO AND HOPI RELOCATION COMMISSION

See Navajo-Hopi Land Controversy

NAVAJO CODE TALKERS

The Navajo code, one of the few unbreakable codes in the history of warfare, played a vital role in America's victory in the Pacific during World War II. The idea for the code originated with Navajo-speaking Philip Johnston, an engineer in Los Angeles who was raised on the Navajo Reservation where his father had been a missionary. Johnston was concerned about United States military setbacks owing to communication leaks. The Japanese knew in advance the time and direction of American attacks and the force that would be committed to them. Codes were broken almost as fast as they were worked out. Johnston suggested that Marines use the Navajo language as the basis of a code. At that time, it was virtually an unwritten language. Johnston knew few people in the world understood the complex syntax and tonal qualities of the Navajo language. The same word spoken in four different alterations in pitch or tone of voice had four different meanings. Skillful as the Japanese cryptographers were, it was unlikely they would understand Navajo.

In February 1942 Johnston convinced Marine communication officers to witness several Navajo friends transmit English messages into Navajo and back into English. After the successful demonstration for Major General Clayton B. Vogel, Marine Corps Commander at Camp Elliott, north of San Diego, the Marine Corps authorized an official program to develop and implement the Navajo code. By April of 1942, Marine Corps recruiters had traveled to New Mexico and Arizona communities on the Navajo Reservation and selected twenty-nine Navajos, some as young as fifteen years old. This first group of Navajo Code Talkers, fluent in Navajo and English, were put through rigorous physical training and instruction in methods of communication. They then set about constructing and mastering the code in Navajo, which they then transmitted in simulated battles. After training, twenty-seven of the Code Talkers were shipped to Guadalcanal to begin implementing the code in a combat area. Two remained in the United States to work as recruiters and instructors. Later, in the fall of 1942, the Marine Corps enlisted Philip Johnston to train Navajos in using the code established by the initial twenty-nine recruits.

The Code Talkers came up with a foolproof system, which they memorized, that described complex military operations. They designed an alphabet to spell out words for which no code terms could be devised.

A	Wol-la-chee	Ant
B	Shush	Bear
C	Moasi	Cat
D	Be	Deer
E	Dzeh	Elk
F	Ma-e	Fox
G	Klizzie	Goat
H	Lin	Horse
I	Tkin	Ice
J	Tkele-cho-gi	Jackass
K	Klizzie-yazzie	Kid
L	Dibeh-yazzie	Lamb
M	Na-as-tso-si	Mouse
N	Nesh-chee	Nut
O	Ne-ahs-jah	Owl
P	Bi-so-dih	Pig
Q	Ca-yeilth	Quiver
R	Gah	Rabbit
S	Dibeh	Sheep
T	Than-zie	Turkey
U	No-da-ih	Ute
V	A-keh-di-glini	Victor
W	Gloe-ih	Weasel
X	Al-an-as-dzoh	Cross
Y	Tash-as-zih	Yucca
Z	Besh-do-gliz	Zinc

Thus the word "Saipan" was spelled: *dibeh* (sheep), *wol-la-chee* (ant), *tkin* (ice), *bi-so-dih* (pig), *wol-la-chee* (ant), *nesh-chee* (nut). Code Talkers chose alternative words for E-T-A-O-I-N, the six most frequently used letters in the English language. Instead of using ANT for A to spell out a code word, they also used APPLE or AXE for A.

The Code Talkers searched for Navajo words, many taken from nature, that had logical associations with military terms and names of places. Thus, the code word for observation plane became *ne-as-jah* or owl in Navajo; *besh-lo* or iron fish became the code word for submarine. An aircraft carrier became *tsidi-ney-ye-hi*, which means bird carrier. The Navajo word for potato meant grenade, the Navajo word for egg meant bomb, turtle became tank, and whale was a battleship. The Navajo word for India (*Ah-le-gai*) meant white clothes. The Navajo for America (*Ne-he-mah*) meant our mother. The Code Talkers substituted clan names for military units. By the end of the war, 411 terms carried information past Japanese intelligence. The code was so successful that the Japanese failed to decipher a single syllable from thousands of transmitted messages. In fact, Navajos who understood Navajo words never could make sense of the code.

Eventually, some 400 Navajos served in the Code Talker program. Assigned to the Third, Fourth, and Fifth Divisions of the United States Marines, they served in many campaigns in the Pacific theater, usually in two-men teams conversing by field telephone and walkie-talkie to call in air strikes and artillery bombardments, direct troop movements, and transmit other sensitive military information. Between 1942 and 1943, they transmitted hundreds of radio messages to American troops. The code was effective in reporting the location of enemy artillery and in directing fire from American positions.

It was at Iwo Jima, however, where the Code Talkers immortalized themselves. "Were it not for the Navajos," said Major Howard M. Conner, communication officer of the Fifth Marine Division at Iwo Jima, "the Marines would never have taken Iwo Jima." The entire military operation was directed by orders communicated by the Navajo Code Talkers. During the first forty-eight hours, while the Marines were landing and consolidating their shore positions, six Navajo radio nets operated around the clock. They sent and received more than 800 messages without error. When the Marines raised the American flag on Mount Suribachi, the Code Talkers relayed the message in the Navajo code: sheep-uncle-ram-ice-bear-ant-cat-horse-itch.

After the war ended, the Marine Corps kept the code classified "top secret" until the 1969 annual reunion of the Fourth Marine Division Association in Chicago. There, the Marine Corps honored Philip Johnston and some of the Code Talkers with bronze medallions. The Navajo Code Talkers Association, which numbers around 230 members, grew out of this reunion. Their "permanent home" at the Gallup-McKinley County Chamber of Commerce houses historic photos, posters, trophies, radios, and other valuable items. A congressional act and a 1982 presidential proclamation finally informed the world about the invaluable contributions of the Code Talkers.

The Navajo Code Talkers are a source of pride for the Navajos. They are called on to participate in public ceremonies and parades all over the country. Books, curricular materials, and a record by Vincent Craig, a son of one of the Code Talkers, have been produced to honor them. In March of 1989, the Navajo Code Talkers were honored with the dedication of a sculpture in Phoenix, Arizona, the nation's first permanent tribute to them. Developers of the Phoenix Plaza— BetaWest Properties, Inc. and the Koll Company— commissioned sculptor Doug Hyde, who created a fourteen-foot-high sculpture of a young Indian boy holding a flute in his hand. The flute, among many Native Americans a communication tool, is used to signal the end of confrontation and the coming of peace. Surely, the Code Talkers contributed to these goals during World War II.

Arlene B. Hirschfelder

See also **Military Service; Navajo**

Further Reading

Bixler, Margaret T. *Winds of Freedom: The Story of the Navajo Code Talkers of World War II.* Darien, CT: Two Bytes Publishing, 1992.

Hafford, William E. "The Navajo Code Talkers." *Arizona Republic* (February 1989): 36–44.

Kawano, Kenji. *Warriors: Navajo Code Talkers.* Flagstaff, AZ: Northland Publishing Co., 1990.

Lagerquist, Syble. *Philip Johnston and the Navajo Code Talkers.* Billings, MT: Council for Indian Education, 1983.

Paul, Doris A. *The Navajo Code Talkers.* Bryn Mawr, PA: Dorrance and Co., 1973.

Watson, Bruce. "Navajo Code Talkers: A Few Good Men." *Smithsonian* (August 1993): 34–43.

NAVAJO-HOPI LAND CONTROVERSY

The struggle for land and resources between the Hopi and Navajo is rooted in cultural differences and expanding tribal populations. This conflict intensified with the American imposition of reservation systems on both tribes in the last century.

The traditional Hopi land base, called *tutsqua* by the Pueblo villagers, extended roughly from the Grand Canyon, south to the Mogollon Rim, west to what is now called Williams Mountain, and east towards modern-day Ganado, near the contemporary boundaries of northwestern New Mexico and northeastern Arizona. Hopi believe that their ancestors emerged from a hole in the ground near the confluence of the Colorado and Little Colorado Rivers. They explain that a divinity named Masau'u, "Lord of This World," instructed them in the proper way to live, and delineated their land boundaries.

Hopi speak a Shoshonean language from the Uto-Aztecan superfamily. The San Francisco Peaks, Arizona's highest mountains, are sacred to the Hopi, for they believe that they are the perpetual home of the kachinas, mystical nature spirits integral to Hopi religion.

The Hopi evolved theocratic city-states as governing systems. Each Hopi village is independent, ruled by priests, called *monqwis* in Hopi. In the mid-twentieth century, the United States government imposed a tribal council system, establishing a rough Hopi confederation. Tribal Council representatives are elected by their respective villages, and the theocratic system remains intact.

For centuries and even today Hopi considered any non-Hopis entering their territories as intruders. But they established trading relations with the Rio Grande Pueblos, the Paiutes, Havasupai, and Hualapais. Hopi traders, *puchteca*, traveled from their mesa homelands along established routes south into Mexico, west to the Pacific, east to the Great Plains, and north into the Rockies. Three of America's oldest communities, dating back to A.D. 1200, are the Hopi villages of Oraibi on Third Mesa; Shungopovi on Second Mesa; and Walpi on First Mesa.

The Navajo, linguistic relatives of the Pacific Northwest's Athabaskan whalers and totem-carvers, are cousins to the Southwest's only other Athabaskan speakers, the Apache. The Navajo call themselves *Dineh*, "The People." Their ancestors established their homeland, *Dineh bi keyah*, between the Four Sacred Mountains of Sierra Blanca Peak and Mount Hespherus in southwestern Colorado, Mount Taylor in western New Mexico, and the San Francisco Peaks in the west, near modern-day Flagstaff.

The *Dineh* believe that they emerged as a people in the heart of the Four Corners region and were instructed by their divinities, the Holy People, in the proper way to live. They say the Holy People gave them the land between the four mountains, and the Dineh inner sanctum lies in the San Juan Basin, in *Dinetah*.

The ancestral Athabaskans (Navajos) came to the "House Made of Dawn" later than the Hopi and other Puebloan folk. Many Pueblos, including the Hopi, Zuni, and Acoma, viewed the *Dineh* as enemies. However, some Navajo clans developed trading alliances with some Hopi villages. But since there was no one unified Navajo or Hopi nation, and no binding agreements made for all, not all Navajo lived in peaceful coexistence with the Hopi.

The Hopi and Navajo evolved different concepts of land acquisition and land ownership. Hopi developed the concept of a closed universe. Following the guidelines of the Keeper of this World, the Great God *Masau'u*, religious societies and clans maintained shrines and made pilgrimages to shrines delineating boundaries of the Hopi *tutsqua*. Clan lands radiated out from autonomous villages. Hopis did not need to be physically residing on these clan lands in order to claim rightful possession.

THE NAVAJO AND HOPI RESERVATIONS JOINT USE AREA

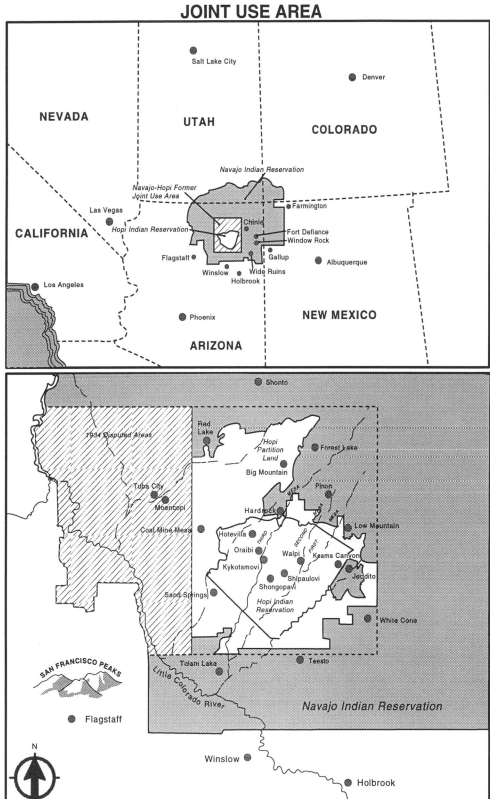

Source: Benedek, Emily. *The Wind Won't Know Me.* New York: Alfred A. Knopf, 1992. Copyright © 1992 by Emily Benedek. Reprinted by permission of Alfred A. Knopf.

In the Navajo way, certain clans were entitled to certain lands within the Four Sacred Mountains, but not all the lands had been claimed by all the clans, particularly in sparsely populated western areas of *Dineh bi keyah*. Prior to European contact, the majority of Navajo people resided within the old *Dinetah*, the inner sanctum of Navajo land that is drained by the San Juan River. Navajo and Hopi reached basic territorial understandings that were enforced by armed strength on occasion. But unlike the Hopi, who believed in a closed, limited universe, the Navajo believed in an expanding universe within their sacred homeland. They pushed out against the boundaries of their world. In the Navajo way, land not within established Navajo clan boundaries could be settled: a Navajo house, or hogan, could be built upon the land, a ceremony would be held afterward, and the land could be held and used by the Navajo occupants. This concept is not dissimilar to the Euroamerican idea of "homesteading."

Elements Contributing to Territorial Stress

From the time of Hopi-Navajo contact, intertribal relations were strained. But four elements led to greater territorial stress between the two tribes after European invasion. These elements were the introduction of sheep and European livestock to the region by the Spanish; the stress of Spanish-New Mexican land usurpation in eastern *Dinetah*; the long-term growth of Navajo and Hopi populations, escalating in the twentieth century; and the imposition of the reservation system onto the Navajo and Hopi peoples by the United States government in the late nineteenth century.

Spanish livestock enabled the Navajo to become the foremost pastoral people of the New World, and the neighboring Hopi adopted pastoralism as well. Sheep and goats need large tracts of grazing lands; thus, Spanish pressure and the taking of large amounts of Navajo land by Spanish adventurers put pressure on both Navajo and Hopi populations. Displaced Navajos began settling on Hopi and Zuni land. Pressure from the Utes in the northern area of *Dinetah* forced some Navajo resettlement on Hopi land. The single largest contribution to Navajo-Hopi stress came after the wars between the Navajo and the "New Men," the Americans of the United States, and after the signing of the Treaty of 1868, which freed the Navajo from captivity on eastern New Mexico.

During the years from 1863 to 1868, Anglo, Spanish, and Pueblo volunteers under the command of Kit Carson had systematically rounded up over 75 percent of the Navajo population and marched them into concentration camps at Fort Sumner in eastern New Mexico. The Navajo leaders signed the Treaty of 1868 to free their people from captivity and return home; they did not understand that they were signing away their old way of life.

When the Navajo returned from captivity, they started a new period in history that marked the beginnings of a unified Navajo Nation. The Treaty of 1868 limited Navajo land to a small rectangle of land, the bulk of the old *Dinetah*, straddling the Arizona-New Mexico border. But contact with whites had taught the Navajo leaders (*naat'áanii*) how to deal with Americans, and the Navajos had a treaty which guaranteed them certain rights and recognition from the United States Congress.

During the period from 1868 to 1991 the Navajo land base has been extended over fifteen times, with presidential and/or congressional approval. In an attempt to regain their old land boundaries Navajo land expansion has come largely at the cost of what Hopi consider as their traditional land base.

The Hopi Reservation Is Established

The Hopi did not war with the United States and they received no treaty or formal recognition. When the Navajo returned from captivity Navajo families settled onto what Hopi viewed as their land. The Hopi sent numerous delegations to Washington, D.C., complaining about Navajo and Mormon incursions into their *tutsqua*. On December 16, 1882, President Chester Arthur delineated by executive order a small rectangle in the center of the Hopi homeland as a reservation, "set apart for the use of the Moqui, and other such Indians as the Secretary of the Interior may see fit to settle thereon." At the time of the decree, there were several hundred Navajo living on what the United States has declared to be the Hopi Reservation. Despite Hopi complaints, the Navajo did not move. Some of their descendants still reside on Hopi reservation land.

As Navajo and Hopi populations recovered and expanded, as farming and herding continued to be integrated in the lives of both peoples, tensions increased between the two. At the turn of the century there were approximately 2,000 Hopi and 7,500 Navajo; today there are 10,000 Hopi and 275,000 Navajo. Both tribal land bases are strained to the breaking point and both tribes stress that they need more land. The Navajo have consistently added to their land base since 1868, but Hopi have not.

Healing v. Jones, 1962

Tribal tension reached a breaking point in 1958, when the Navajo and Hopi councils requested congressional permission to sue each other in federal court. In 1958, Congress authorized a three-judge district court to hear tribal complaints. This was the first time in United states history that one Indian tribe sued another.

In 1962 the judges ruled that both tribes had rights to land on the 1882 Hopi Reservation. The decision, called *Healing v. Jones,* after the names of the two tribal chairmen, stated, "Navajos had squatted on Hopi lands, and because the Secretary of the Interior had never taken . . . action to remove them they had acquired 'squatters rights,' to a one-half interest in the Hopi reservation, surface and subsurface on a share and share alike basis."

The Americans applied Euroamerican rules of jurisprudence at the request of the Hopi and Navajo tribes in an attempt to settle the dispute. The judges established exclusive Hopi rights to Grazing District 6, and established a Joint Use Area for the two tribes. This decision satisfied neither tribe, and the two tribes took each other to court and mounted expensive lobbying and public relations campaigns.

The 1974 Partition of the Hopi Reservation

In 1974 Congress enacted Public Law 93-531 and partitioned the 1882 Hopi Reservation. The Navajo tribe gained title to half of the Hopi Reservation, some 911,000 acres. This law established the precedent of Indian tribes receiving land instead of money as a result of court action. It is an important precedent, and other tribes have since benefited from this action.

In amendments to the 1974 Navajo-Hopi Land Settlement Act, the Navajo tribe also received 400,000 acres of replacement land for Navajo relocatees—some 75,000 acres of this land is a coal mine in New Mexico. No Navajo relocatees reside there. Congress established the federal Navajo and Hopi Indian Relocation Commission to assist Indians in the move, in finding replacement homes, and in gaining the $5,000 relocation bonus for signing up to move prior to July 6, 1986.

Upon partition of the land, complaints from both tribes were raised in the media. Navajos and Hopis both claim religious ties to the land. A center of Navajo resistance to relocation is the Big Mountain area, some thirty miles north of Third Mesa, on a road that leads to the coal mines of Black Mesa. Reporters from all over the world have visited with the Big Mountain Navajos, most of whom have now signed up for relocation. But a group of some fifty resisters maintain that they will never relocate. Some 5,000 Navajos and 100 Hopis were affected by relocation; all Hopis have moved, but approximately 225 Navajos remain on Hopi land.

Court-Ordered Mediations

In October 1992, as a result of federal court-ordered mediations, the Hopi and Navajo tribes reached an agreement in principle, which would bring relocation to an end and allow the Navajo to remain on Hopi land for at least seventy-five years. This agreement said that Hopis would receive about 400,000 acres of land around the San Francisco Peaks area in return for allowing Navajo to lease Hopi partition lands. This was the first time the two tribes had agreed to anything land-related in a century of fighting. But the non-Indian majority of Arizona, led by Senator Dennis DeConcini and Governor Fife Symington, denounced the plan and led efforts to undermine the agreement. To date, the Hopi still have received no replacement land for the loss of half of their reservation.

Land is life and identity to the Hopi and the Navajo. After a century of conflict, and decades of legal battles, the struggle for land and resources between the two tribes continues, despite tribal efforts to find common ground.

Catherine Feher-Elston

See also **Hopi; Land Claims; Navajo**

Further Reading

Benedek, Emily. *The Wind Won't Know Me: A History of the Navajo-Hopi Land Dispute.* New York, NY: Alfred A. Knopf, 1992.

Bureau of Indian Affairs. *Chronology of Events in the 1882 Executive Order Area.* Washington, DC: U.S. Government Printing Office, 1989.

Correll, J. Lee, and Alfred Dehiya. *Anatomy of the Navajo Reservation: How It Grew.* Navajo Times Publishing, 1972. Rev. ed., 1978.

Feher-Elston, Catherine. *Children of Sacred Ground: America's Last Indian War.* Flagstaff, AZ: Northland, 1988.

Kammer, Jerry. *The Second Long Walk: The Navajo-Hopi Land Dispute.* Albuquerque: University of New Mexico Press, 1980.

Parlow, Anita. *Cry, Sacred Ground: Big Mountain, U.S.A.* Washington, DC: Christic Institute, 1988.

NEWSPAPERS

See Periodicals

NEZ PERCE

The Nez Perce are closely linked by culture and language to other Sahaptian speakers of the Plateau. They traditionally ranged throughout the Northwest and western Great Plains and relied on an economy of fishing, hunting, gathering, and animal husbandry based on their large horse herds. They were the most numerous and militarily powerful of the Plateau tribes. The Nez Perce Reservation is situated in north central Idaho in the counties of Nez Perce, Lewis, Clearwater, and Idaho. The western section of the reservation is a short distance from the Snake River and the state of Washington, where Lewiston, Idaho, and Clarkston, Washington, meet. The topography is varied, cut by the Snake and Clearwater rivers and other small streams with numerous valleys and high prairie areas, rising to rugged mountain country with excellent stands of timber. Kamiah, Lapwai, Nez Perce, Cottonwood, Orofino, Culdesac, and Winchester are principal village settlements on the reservation.

In a treaty signed on June 11, 1855, the Nez Perce ceded to the United States several million acres in Oregon, Washington, and Idaho, but reserved over 8 million acres as an original reservation. On June 9, 1863, a second treaty reduced the reservation drastically and eventuated in the War of 1877, which is often associated with Chief Joseph, missionary-induced factionalism, and the Seven Drum Religion (and its antecedents). Current land ownership is as follows:

	Acres
Tribal Land	31,872
Allotted	59,102
Government-Owned Land	1,711
Total	92,685

The Nez Perce were initially sympathetic to Christianity and supported white settlement in the region until the Treaty of 1863. Missionary conversion to Christianity resulted in factionalism as well as in the partial loss and readaptation of various cultural traits during the later nineteenth and early twentieth centuries. The Nez Perce language is not spoken by most tribal members under thirty years of age. For most, English has become their primary language. Despite this, the revitalization of Indian culture witnessed throughout western North America after World War II, and especially after 1960, has also been apparent among the Nez Perce. An accelerating revitalization of traditional arts and crafts, dance, and certain traditional religious practices has been underway for several decades and supported by the Seven Drum Religion and its leaders. This parallels a growing political awareness and activism apparent in such areas as assertion of the tribe's reserved treaty rights, assertion of legal jurisdiction on the reservation, and various efforts to reform and strengthen their schools, health programs, and economy.

Some three thousand Nez Perce are now enrolled in Idaho. (A small number are enrolled on the Colville Reservation and are descended from a part of the Chief Joseph band that returned from Oklahoma in 1885.) Approximately one thousand five hundred maintain permanent residence on the Idaho reservation. One-fourth degree Nez Perce heredity is required for enrollment. The tribe rejected the Indian Reorganization Act and John Collier's Indian New Deal. The present Constitution and Bylaws were adopted on April 2, 1948, and ratified by the tribe in general assembly on April 30, 1948. The principal governing body is the Nez Perce Tribal Executive Committee, whose members are elected at large. The General Council has only limited powers under the present Constitution of 1948. The Executive Committee administers and guides tribal economic development, human and natural resources programs, and the investment of income and assets of the tribe. The tribe also possesses a court system, an Indian Health Service program, and various enterprise programs.

The Nez Perce have received financial settlements from several Indian Claims Commission awards, as well as from the Celilo settlement stemming from the inundation of fishing sites by construction of the Dalles Dam. They continue to play a major role in the political life of the Columbia River Basin, having protected their treaty and demonstrated their influence in major fishing cases such as *United States v. Washington* (1974) and *United States v. Oregon* (ongoing since 1968). They have been active participants in the Basalt Waste Isolation Project, under provisions of the Nuclear Waste Policy Act, and other projects focused on the Department of Energy Hanford Reservation.

They are currently engaged in numerous projects to rehabilitate their salmon and steelhead runs, through membership in the Columbia River Inter-Tribal Fish Commission, and are supported in these activities by such agencies as the Bonneville Power Administration, under provisions of the Northwest Power Act. They are active members of the Affiliated Tribes of Northwest Indians and of various other Idaho and Northwest Indian organizations. They exert influence at the national level through groups such as the National Congress of American Indians. A land reacquisition program is underway, as are an ambitious forestry management program and a cultural resource preservation and management program. There are ambitious plans for future economic development including a gambling enterprise and tourist enterprises. The recent federal approval of the Nee-Mee-Poo Trail and expansion of the Nez Perce National Historical Park are part of an overall strategy for development. The tribe has also begun to write its own history and revive its language through special programs. Most important for the tribe's future are the current negotiations of its water rights, as part of the Snake River water rights negotiations affecting several Idaho tribes.

The Nez Perce maintain an active schedule of social events. On Lincoln's birthday, dance contests and celebrations are held. During the first week of March, the tribe holds the E-Peh-Tas dances and celebration. In May, a spring toot festival is held, while in early summer the Talmaks celebration is held, an annual camp meeting for Presbyterian church members. Pi-Nee-wau Days, held in August, feature parades, dances, and a general celebration. The Mud Springs celebration at Craigmont stresses traditional gambling, dancing, and similar activities. Thanksgiving Day is celebrated, as are Christmas and New Years as part of Presbyterian and Catholic church life.

Deward E. Walker, Jr.

Further Reading

Josephy, Alvin M., Jr. *The Nez Perce Indians and the Opening of the Northwest.* New Haven, CT: Yale University Press, 1965.

Slickpoo, Allen P., Sr., and Deward E. Walker, Jr. *Noon Nee-Me-Poo. We, the Nez Perces.* Lapwai, ID: Nez Perce Tribe of Idaho, 1973.

Spinden, Herbert Joseph. *The Nez Perce Indians.* Memoirs of the American Anthropolgoical Association, Vol. 2, pt. 3. Menasha, WI: AAA, 1908.

Walker, Deward E., Jr. *Conflict and Schism in Nez Perce Acculturation.* Moscow: University of Idaho Press, 1985.

Walker, Deward E., Jr., and Haruo Aoki. *Nez Perce Oral Narratives.* Berkeley: University of California Press, 1989.

NIPMUC

At first contact with Euroamericans, the Nipmuc (Nipmuck, Nipnet), lived in eastern Massachusetts, northeastern Connecticut, and northern Rhode Island. By 1800 they were practically landless and became Massachusetts citizens in 1869. Following the Act of Enfranchisement (1869), individuals received state aid as citizens.

In the 1970s creation of the Massachusetts Commission on Indian Affairs reaffirmed state stewardship. During the twentieth century social activities and public education were led by individuals among the Nipmuc, especially Zara Ciscoe Brough. Some helped found the Council of New England Indians in the 1920s, later forming a Nipmuc chapter. Under Brough's direction, the Nipmuc petitioned for federal acknowledgment in the 1980s. The petition will be resubmitted in 1993. Today, the tribe has no land but two parcels are held privately for its use: the Hassanamesit (two acres), in Webster, Massachusetts, and the Chaubunagungamaug Reservation (about ten acres), in Thompson, Connecticut.

The Nipmuc Tribal Acknowledgment Project, in Worcester, Massachusetts—headed by Thomas L. Doughton, tribal historian and genealogist—is funded by grants and private support. Project work has confirmed about 1,400 members, 80 percent living locally, and plans economic and social development. The tribe hopes to acquire land; no land claims are current. The project will publish information on Nipmuc history and culture, including the forthcoming *Days of Hassanamesit*, by Zara Ciscoe Brough.

In 1991 the tribe recreated their government, electing an Acting Council. Following ratification of their Constitution, tribal government will probably consist of a sachem, chairman, vice-chair, and Council of thirteen.

The Nipmuc maintain distinct social groups: the Hassanimisco band of Grafton, Massachusetts (Chief Natachamin); and the Chaubunagungamaug band of Webster, Massachusetts (Chief Wise Owl). The bands sponsor powwows, festivals, and ceremonial events. Tribal elders carry on ceremonies and sweat lodge activities. Through the Algonquian School in Providence, Rhode Island, Spotted Eagle Brown and Little Crow Hendries keep language, crafts, and traditional philosophy alive.

Ann McMullen

Note: While many sources document the early history of the Nipmuc, written sources for the twentieth century are few. The information above was supplied by Thomas Doughton, who, in 1993, is currently preparing a history of the Nipmuc for publication, and was gleaned from flyers and pamphlets printed by the Nipmuc Tribal Acknowledgment Project.

NISENAN

See Maidu

NISQUALLY

The Nisqually Indian Reservation is located in Thurston County in western Washington State. Ap-proximately four-and-one-half river miles of the Nisqually River flow through the reservation. The occupied portion of the reservation, which is west of the Nisqually River, lies in an elongated corridor, one mile across, wedged in between two segments of land occupied by Fort Lewis, the second largest military base in the United States.

The traditional lands of the Nisqually people had once included the entire Nisqually River Basin. The Treaty of Medicine Creek, signed on December 26, 1854, the Indian War of 1855 to 1856, and the Executive Order of January 20, 1857, reduced the tribal holdings to a 4,700-acre reservation, of which 3,300 acres lay on the Pierce County side of the Nisqually River and 1,400 acres on the Thurston County side. In 1918, when the Fort Lewis military base was established, that portion of the reservation on the Pierce County side was condemned and the people forced to vacate their homes.

Traditional History

The Nisqually are speakers of Nisqually, a Coast Salish language, who take their name from *squalli*, the Indian name for the prairie grass that grows profusely on the vast prairies that border both sides of the lower river. The prefix "*nis*" was later added to bring about the name "Nisqually."

With Mount Rainier in the background and the marine waters of Puget Sound in the forefront, the traditional Nisqually people utilized their vast land area to gather and preserve a bountiful food supply, which included deer and elk, roots and bulbs, nuts and berries, and an assortment of seafood. The western red cedar provided planks for winter homes, logs for dugout canoes, and bark for clothing and baskets. Tools and utensils were made of wood, bone, or stone. Cattail mats and items made of buckskin were also utilized. Salmon, the predominant Nisqually food item, filled the streams and bay to form a basic part of a triad, which today continues to permeate the foundation of tribal life—the land, the river, and the salmon.

Twentieth Century

Reservation life brought many changes. The tribal lands, allotted in 1881, provided homes for fifty-three heads of families. Although the prairie land proved to be poor farmland, the salmon remained plentiful. The beginning of the twentieth century found the Nisquallies with a 4,700-acre reservation with a population of 107. They found themselves caught between two worlds—staying on the reservation with little means of support or leaving home to seek employment as timber workers or as harvest hands. The children, required to attend government boarding schools, brought a new dimension to the tribal structure. Henry Martin, a product of the boarding school system, emerged to direct the tribe through these dark years as a leader and interpreter. When he died in 1918, Peter Kalama, another graduate, became the tribal leader until his death in 1946.

The 1930s found tribal children able to attend public schools with the government supplying Johnson-O'Malley funds to local school districts to offset the tribal tax-free land base. On June 18, 1934, Congress adopted the Indian Reorganization Act, whereby tribes could reorganize and write a constitution, enroll their members, and legally carry on business with outside agencies. The Nisqually Constitution, adopted on July 27, 1946, established a system of government that provided for the election of a tribal chairman, a Business Committtee, and requirements for tribal enrollment. The first enrollment numbered sixty-one individuals. The first hurdle of the new organization was to define their traditional land area for the Indian Claims Commission. Their claim for the entire Nisqually River Basin was reduced to 167,350 acres. Eventually an award was accepted by the tribe.

After the conclusion of World War II the population of western Washington increased as did the number of non-Indian commercial fishermen. The Nisqually Indian fishermen were informed by state authorities that they must limit their fishing to on-reservation fishing; their fishing rights did not extend to off-reservation fishing. This led to several years of confrontation in the 1960s between tribal fishermen and state fishery regulatory officers on the banks of the Nisqually and Puyallup Rivers, which culminated in the famous fishing rights case *United States v. Washington*, climaxing in the Boldt Decision on February 12, 1974. The decision interpreted the Treaty of 1854 to read that the western Washington treaty tribes did indeed retain the right to fish in their "usual and accustomed" off-reservation fishing areas. Nisqually member Billy Frank, Jr., today presides as chairperson of the Northwest Indian Fisheries Commission, which was set up to manage the off-reservation fishery for tribes affected by the Boldt Decision in the Puget Sound waters.

More Recent Events

In 1974 the Nisqually people created a comprehensive development plan, which included an on-reservation tribal headquarters. With the 1918 condemnation of two-thirds of the reservation, only a small nucleus of tribal members remained in the area. In 1976, under the guidance of Zelma McCloud, tribal chairperson, and George Kalama, treasurer, monies were applied for and granted to cover the expenses of buying fifty-three acres of land adjacent to the reservation, and to build a tribal headquarters there. It was completed in 1978. Today the tribal campus offers services in education, medical and dental health care, commodities, senior lunches, and Head Start programs, as well as a tribal police force, a library, trading post, a bingo hall, and a natural resources center to oversee the operation of two tribal fish hatcheries. The tribe employs approximately ninety people. Tribal members also work in the fields of education, social work, and medical services. Several operate small businesses. Traditional tribal ceremonies and crafts are being revived. Many Nisqually tribal members participate in the Indian Shaker Church, the Nisqually Indian Church (Assemblies of God), the Catholic Church, and others.

Throughout the past eighteen years tribal enrollment has increased to 390, with a quarter blood quantum requirement. One hundred and twenty on-reservation homes have been built, and improved roads and water systems have been installed. Tribally owned lands within the reduced portion of the reservation have grown from a two-and-a-half-acre cemetery in 1974, to 459 acres in 1992. Tribal allotted and trust lands total 900 acres. Chairman Dorian Sanchez has recently been reelected to a new two-year term. The tribal chairman and an elected Business Committee carry on the business of the tribe under the original Constitution, which places most of the decision making under the general membership.

Cecelia Svinth Carpenter

See also **Fishing and Hunting Rights; Washington State Tribes**

Further Reading

Barnett, H.G. *Indian Shakers*. Chicago: Southern Illinois Press, 1972.

Carpenter, Cecelia Svinth. *They Walked Before: Indians of Washington State*. Tacoma: Washington State Historical Society, 1977. Tahoma Research Press, 1988.

Haeberlin, Hermann, and Erna Gunther. *The Indians of Puget Sound*. Seattle: University of Washington, 1930. Reprint 1952.

Smith, Marian W. *The Puyallup-Nisqually*. New York, NY: Columbia University Press, 1940. Reprint. AMS Press, 1969.

United States v. State of Washington. United States District Court, Western District of Washington. St. Paul, MN: West Publishing Co., 1975.

NOMLAKI

See Wintun

NOOKSACK

The Nooksack are a Coast Salish tribe located in northwestern Washington State near the modern city of Bellingham. After years as an unrecognized tribe, federal recognition and a small reservation were gained in 1973. Since then, the Nooksack tribe has become an important partner in managing fisheries and other resources in the area, and a provider of services to its members.

The Nooksack traditionally occupied the watershed of the Nooksack River from the high mountain area surrounding Mt. Baker, to the salt water at Bellingham Bay, and extending north into Canada in the Sumas area. They spoke a distinct separate Salishan language, *Lhéchalosem*, referred to in English as Nooksack. The precontact population before 1800 is estimated to have been about 1,100; early epidemics reduced this to the first historic estimate of 450 made in 1857. The population continued to decline with only 207 persons counted in 1923.

The Nooksack were one of many Indian groups which were party to the Point Elliott Treaty of 1855, in which title to the land of much of western Washington was exchanged for recognition of fishing, hunting, gathering rights, and a guarantee of certain government services. The Nooksack were not granted a reservation. They were expected to move onto the Lummi Reservation, but chose instead to remain near their traditional village locations. In the 1870s and 1880s adult male Nooksacks were able to claim homesteads, with 37 claims filed and trust title granted to 3,847 acres. Some 2,400 acres remained in trust in 1990, although much of this is of little economic use due to complex multiple heirship.

Twentieth-Century History

Since the Nooksack were not granted a separate reservation, they were no longer considered a tribe by the Bureau of Indian Affairs, yet they continued to function as a tribe. In 1926 they met under the leadership of George Swanaset to join in the *Dwamish, et al. v. the United States* case before the Court of Claims; in 1935 the Nooksack tribe voted to accept the Indian Reorganization Act, but was not permitted to organize under the act since it was not a recognized tribe. In the 1950s the tribe under the leadership of Joe Louie pursued a land claim case with the Indian Claims Commission (ICC). The ICC decided in 1955 that the Nooksack were indeed a tribe of Indians whose lands had been taken without compensation, but that they only "exclusively occupied and used" a small portion of their traditional territory. It was further decided that the value of the lands at the time of the treaty was $.65 per acre and only this amount would be paid. A payment of $43,383 for 80,000 acres of the 400,000 acres claimed was provided by Congress in 1965. This money was distributed in equal portions on a per capita basis to each recognized descendant of the Nooksack tribe of 1855.

Late in the 1960s the tribe gained new leadership from two persons who returned after working for many years in the Seattle area. Roy George became tribal chairman and later the director of the Small Tribes Organization of Western Washington. Mickey Roberts became director of the Nooksack Community Action Program and worked closely with the elders group in the effort to gain federal recognition. In 1970 the tribe gained title to four buildings on an acre of land, which became the Nooksack Reservation. In 1973 full federal recognition was granted. In 1974 the Nooksack tribe joined the *United States v. Washington* case as a treaty tribe with fishing rights for enrolled members.

The Nooksack tribe is governed in 1993 by an eight-member elected Tribal Council headed by tribal chairman Hubert Williams. As of August 1991, there were 1,168 enrolled members of the tribe, about half of whom live on or near Nooksack trust lands. The reservation in 1993 included only the twelve-acre tribal center location, although reservation status is expected soon for sixty acres of tribally owned trust land. Tribal programs and enterprises employed seventy persons, including non-Nooksacks, prior to the opening of a large gaming hall in 1993. A major focus in tribal programs is land and resources with a special emphasis on fishing. Fishing in the Nooksack River and salt water areas is an important source of income and food for many families. The tribal fisheries program regulates fishing and works to enhance fish runs and protect the environment which the fish depend upon. The tribe works closely with local, state, and federal agencies to review proposed timber harvests and developments and evaluate their impact on water quality, fisheries, and cultural sites.

A second major area of concern is cultural survival and education. There are no remaining speakers of the original Nooksack language. To promote cultural survival, the tribe has begun an inventory of cultural sites of historical and continuing importance. Protection of these sites will preserve links to the traditional past and enable the continued practice of the traditional religion.

Health and housing are also serious concerns to the tribe. The Nooksack Tribal Clinic supplements the Indian Health Service unit, located thirty miles away on the Lummi Reservation. Even so, access to health care continues to be a serious problem due to a serious shortage of funds. The tribe also has programs in mental health and substance abuse. Housing is in short supply and often crowded. Because of problems in dividing multiple heirship lands, the tribe has taken an active role in building houses for individual purchase at cluster sites. It is difficult to keep up with demand, as many people want to move back to the tribal area and many new young families are starting.

Culture

To a casual observer the lives of Nooksack Indians in the 1990s might appear little different from their neighbors. Hidden behind the similarities is a distinct Indian culture.

Nooksack people have strong family ties through large extended families at Nooksack, and links with families in other tribes. The extended families are essential units of economic and emotional support, although affected by problems of crowded housing and high levels of unemployment. The Nooksack tribe forms a distinct community focused on the tribal center and its programs, and on the tribally owned and maintained cemeteries. Funerals are major gatherings to show respect toward another family, build a sense of community, and remember links to the past.

Religion is a strong force in the lives of Nooksack Indians today, both unifying and dividing people. Four forms of religion have strong followings with considerable overlap of participants in the first three: Indian tradition associated with the smokehouse, the Indian Shaker Church, the Methodist Mission, and the Pentecostal Church. Indian traditional religion continues in specially constructed ceremonial houses similar to traditional longhouses (also called smokehouses), where large gatherings are held through the winter months for *syo'wen*, spirit dancing. Related but sometimes separate activities are ritual burnings for the dead, and namings and memorials similar to earlier potlatches.

Nooksack people are also active participants in the secular summer gatherings of northwest Indians, which are focused on canoe races and also include gambling games, Indian dancing, and traditional foods. Several Nooksacks are artists producing ceremonial drums, woodcarvings, and canoes. These activities and products further reinforce a separate Indian identity in the 1990s.

Allan Richardson

See also **Washington State Tribes**

Further Reading

Amoss, Pamela. *Coast Salish Spirit Dancing.* Seattle: University of Washington Press, 1978.

Jeffcott, Percival R. *Nooksack Tales and Trails.* P.R. Jeffcott, 1949.

Richardson, Allan. "Longhouses to Homesteads: Nooksack Indian Settlement, 1820 to 1895." *American Indian Journal,* 5:8 (August 1979): 8–12.

ODAWA

See Ottawa

OFFICE OF INDIAN AFFAIRS

See Bureau of Indian Affairs

OGLALA

See Lakota

OHLONE

See Costanoan/Ohlone

OJIBWA

Known variously as the Anishinabe, Chippewa, Chippeway, Mississauga, Ojibway, Ojibwe, Otchipwe, and Saulteaux, this large tribe resides on lands across the upper plains and midwestern states, from Montana to Michigan. One of the Three Fires, the Ojibwa avoided removal and remain in their traditional homeland. Treated here by state, there are actually twenty-five separate tribal entities or reservations across the region.

CHIPPEWA IN MICHIGAN

Seven distinct tribes comprise the twentieth-century Michigan Chippewas. Each modern tribe is the descendant of and political successor to historic nineteenth-century bands, who have continued to reside in or near their historic village sites from the beginning of United States jurisdiction in Michigan to the present. There have been several spellings of this tribal name throughout its modern history, with most groups favoring either Chippewa or Ojibwa. The most consistent translation of the name over time connects the word with an Ojibwa root word meaning "puckered up" and refers to the gathered stitching of the Chippewa-style moccasin.

The Upper Peninsula of Michigan has the largest number of Chippewas. The four bands there are

Keweenaw Bay Indian Community, the Lac Vieux Desert Band of Lake Superior Chippewa, Bay Mills Indian Community, and the Sault Ste. Marie Tribe of Chippewa. The Saginaw Chippewa Tribe are the only Chippewa tribe in the Lower Peninsula with an identity completely distinct from the neighboring Ottawa. As the name the Grand Traverse Band of Ottawa and Chippewa Indians implies, this band is composed of historically distinct bands from two tribes whose identities have combined in a new political unit. The Grand Traverse community is most closely affiliated with the neighboring Ottawa communities. The Burt Lake Ottawa and Chippewa are also a composite band (see figure 1).

Figure 1

Tribe (Reservation Name)	Location (Town)	Trust Land	Enrolled Members
Lac Vieux Desert	Watersmeet	368 acres	241
Keweenaw Bay Indian Community	Baraga/ L'Anse	5,000 tribal 8,000 allotted	3,102
Bay Mills Indian Community	Brimley	278,000 acres	950
Sault Ste. Marie Band of Chippewa	Sault Ste. Marie	1,265 acres	20,632
Saginaw Chippewa (Isabella)	Mt. Pleasant	806 acres	2,199
Grand Traverse Band of Ottawa and Chippewa	Suttons Bay	600.6 acres	2,311
Burt Lake Band of Ottawa and Chippewa	Brutus	(no trust land) 20.5 acres owned	over 500

Between 1795 and 1864, the Michigan Chippewa bands signed treaties that ceded title to their land and reserved to the bands distinct rights and properties. Allotment schemes implemented in the 1850s and 1860s led to massive fraud that ended with Indians owning little of the lands reserved for them by treaty. Indian claims to land within their reservations have been widely discussed within the Chippewa communities. In the 1991 case *Keweenaw Bay Indian Community v. State of Michigan*, file no. M87–278–CA2 (784 F. Supp. 418), the United States courts upheld the integrity of this Chippewa reservation by finding that the parcel had a strong external boundary containing three townships of land constituting "Indian country." A similar case is now being brought by the United States on behalf of the Saginaw Chippewas. Other Michigan Chippewa tribes hold only small amounts of trust land.

By the beginning of the twentieth century, the individual bands owned little trust property. As the

Michigan Chippewa lost their land base during the late nineteenth century, the United States slowly abandoned responsibility for fulfilling their trust relationship with the tribes. Throughout the twentieth century, the tribes have invested a great deal of political and economic resources to reestablishing their right to self-government. The poverty that had characterized Chippewa communities at the end of the nineteenth century deepened throughout the Great Depression. The Wheeler-Howard Act of 1934 promised the Indian communities access to government programs that could alleviate their suffering. All of the Upper Peninsula Chippewa and the Saginaw Chippewa wrote constitutions and established formal tribal governments under this act. While local constituents in the 1930s often pursued "recognition" for economic relief, they achieved a more important result—reestablishing the federal trust and restoring a government-to-government relationship with the United States. The United States purchased and took land into trust, providing bands who had lost their entire land base with a center for their cultural, political, and economic activities. In 1991, the United States Congress recognized the Lac Vieux Desert Chippewa as a tribe separate from the Keewenaw Bay Indian Community and allowed them to establish their own independent government.

Among the treaty rights preserved by the Michigan Chippewa are the right to fish in Great Lakes waters ceded by various treaties, and the right to hunt and collect on ceded lands. Living in rural settings, the Chippewa bands have historically continued to mix their traditional hunting, trapping, and gathering with seasonal wage labor. Along the shores of Lake Superior they supplemented their income with commercial fishing and work in shipping. All of the bands relied on income from lumbering. During the first two decades of the twentieth century, conservation officers employed by Michigan enacted and enforced legal codes that restricted Chippewa access to their lake and inland resources. From the 1920s until the 1970s, Indians insisted that their treaty-based rights had been infringed on by Michigan. In the 1979 case *United States, et al. v. Michigan, et al.*, file no. M-26–73CA (W.D. Mich., May 7, 1979), federal courts upheld this right. Since this ruling, the Michigan tribes have operated according to their own conservation codes and regulations, which allow them to exercise their rights without depleting the resources.

The Ottawa and Chippewa bands of the Lower Peninsula also petitioned for reorganization, but adverse administrative decisions in Washington during the 1930s and 1940s limited the number of "nonreservation" tribes eligible to reestablish self-government, preventing their recognition. The Chippewa joined with the Ottawa in the 1970s to pursue claims before the Indian Claims Commission, which were ultimately successful. The focused efforts of the unacknowledged tribes helped to preserve their autonomy and sense of polity through the 1970s. The Grand Traverse Ottawa and Chippewa were not allowed to reestablish their governmental rights until 1980. They were the first tribe "acknowledged" through the controversial Federal Acknowledgment Process. The Burt Lake Ottawa and Chippewa are currently seeking restoration of their governmental powers through the same process.

During World War II many Michigan Chippewa men served in the United States Army. Other members found employment in wage labor jobs that had previously been reserved for non-Indians. After the war, increased mobility drew people from the Indian communities to downstate cities—Flint, Detroit, Lansing, Grand Rapids, Green Bay, and Milwaukee. Families regularly traveled between their tribal communities and their urban homes for church-organized camp meetings and retreats, family occasions like weddings and funerals, powwows and events that emphasized their Indian identity, and political meetings. Tribe members had access to better education, broader economic options, and greater political skills. Every community has used these new skills to its advantage.

Throughout the 1950s and 1960s, tribal governments organized and funded incentives to raise the standards of living on their reservations. In less than twenty years the Michigan Chippewa tribes built modern tribal centers with administrative responsibility for tribally owned housing, health care, and educational systems. For the first time in nearly a century, it was possible for tribal members on most reserves to find more than subsistence wage jobs in their home communities. Substantial numbers of tribespeople have reestablished homes within the Indian communities. All of the federally acknowledged tribes are currently operating casinos and are enjoying unprecedented financial independence. Ottawa and Chippewa casinos are a $41.8 million a year industry employing about 2,000 people. Thirty-seven percent of the people working in gaming operations were on welfare or other forms of government assistance and another 31 percent had been unemployed before getting their gaming-related jobs. The Upper Peninsula and Lower Peninsula tribes have become the largest employers of Indians and non-Indians within their regions.

Each Chippewa community maintains strong links to the culture and worldview of its ancestors. The role of these traditions in social events, political structures, and the arts is still evolving. The traditional Midewiwin Society continues its work throughout the state. In addition tribes host intertribal powwows, sweat lodges, and talking circles. Chippewa people from Michigan also travel to Big Drum ceremonies across the United States. The Bay Mills Indian Community sponsors and operates its own junior college that gives their young people the opportunity to sharpen their skills in a culturally relevant curriculum. The Sault Ste. Marie Chippewa cohost a biannual conference that encourages scholars to research

OJIBWA RESERVATIONS AND GROUPS

Sault Ste. Marie

Saginaw (Isabella)

Burt Lake

Grand Traverse

Bay Mills

MICHIGAN

Keweenaw Bay

Lac Vieux Desert

Ontonagon

Sokaogan

Red Cliff

Bad River

Lac Du Flambeau

Lac Courte Oreilles

St. Croix

WISCONSIN

Grand Portage

Fond Du Lac

Mille Lacs

Bois Forte

Leech Lake

MINNESOTA

Red Lake

White Earth

Turtle Mountain

NORTH DAKOTA

Rocky Boy

MONTANA

N

Federal Indian Reservations

Source: Based on maps from U.S. DEPARTMENT OF THE INTERIOR BUREAU OF INDIAN AFFAIRS

and present information on subjects related to the tribes.

James M. McClurken

See also **Ottawa/Odawa: Odawa in Michigan**

Further Reading

Cleland, Charles E. *Rites of Conquest: The History and Culture of Michigan's Native Americans.* Ann Arbor: University of Michigan Press, 1992.

Tanner, Helen Hornbeck, ed.*The Ojibwas: A Critical Bibliography.* The Newberry Center for the History of the American Indian Bibliography Series. Bloomington: Indiana University Press, 1976.

———. *Atlas of Great Lakes Indian History.* Civilization of the American Indian 174. Norman: University of Oklahoma Press, 1987.

Vecsey, Christopher. *Traditional Ojibwa Religion and Its Historical Changes.* Memoirs Series. 152. Philadelphia, PA: American Philosophical Society, 1983.

Wheeler-Voegelin, Erminie, et al. *Chippewa Indians* 5. New York, NY: Garland Publishing, 1974

OJIBWAY IN MINNESOTA

Ojibway is generally interpreted as "To Roast Till Puckered Up," referring to the puckered seams of moccasins, or as a mispronunciation of *O-jib-i-weg*, "Those Who Make Pictographs." Chippewa, widely used in treaties and other official documents, is a corruption of the early spellings Ojibway or Otchipwe. Anishinabe (Anishinabeg, plural) is the name by which the people call themselves and indicates "Original or Spontaneous Man" or "The People."

There are seven Ojibway reservations in Minnesota—Bois Forte, Fond du Lac, Grand Portage, Leech Lake, Mille Lacs, and White Earth (comprising the Minnesota Chippewa Tribe), and Red Lake, all located in the northern half of the state. Land losses by the turn of the twentieth century as a result of allotment were so massive that today the reservations are a fraction of their original size. Enrolled members in the Minnesota Chippewa Tribe totaled 40,000 in 1993, while the separately governed Red Lake numbers 7,940. The total population of Minnesota Indians of all tribes in 1900 was estimated at about 9,000.

The present political organization was greatly influenced by the Indian Reorganization Act of 1934. The original Constitution and Bylaws of the Minnesota Chippewa Tribe (MCT) were ratified in 1936. The six-member reservations of the MCT sought a single consolidated tribal government without relinquishing governance at the local level. Each member reservation elects its own tribal council, generally called the Reservation Business Committee, which governs locally as well as provides representation to the consolidated organization, which is governed by a Tribal Executive Committee.

The MCT governing body has the power to administer funds, manage tribal resources, enter into contracts with individuals or organizations, pass laws regulating the use of lands under its jurisdiction, and conduct other business to promote the interests of tribal members. The headquarters of the MCT is in the community of Cass Lake on the Leech Lake Reservation. The elected Tribal Council or Reservation Business Committee is headquartered in communities of each member reservation. Local councils also exist at the community levels on the reservations. The president of the Minnesota Chippewa Tribe in 1993 was Darrell Wadena, the White Earth tribal chairman.

The remaining reservation, Red Lake, maintains its own separate tribal government. Originally based on a traditional system with hereditary chiefs and their appointees, the governmental system was changed in 1959 to a format similar to those adopted under the Indian Reorganization Act. Gerald Brun was the tribal chairman in 1993. Red Lake is also unique in that it is considered "closed," having never been subject to state jurisdiction. The reservation successfully opposed the allotment policy that so drastically reduced the land bases of other tribal groups. Although the band ceded land to the federal government in the nineteenth century, aboriginal lands surrounding Lower Red Lake and a portion of Upper Red Lake were kept intact and are today tribally owned. The total area under the jurisdiction of the Red Lake Band of Chippewa is over 500,000 acres (comparable in size to the state of Rhode Island), while combined acreage still under tribal jurisdiction of the six reservations of the Minnesota Chippewa Tribe is considerably less.

Land Holdings

Member Reservations of the Minnesota Chippewa Tribe

Reservation	Date Est	Original Acreage	Remaining Acreage Tribal Trust Lands		
			Tribal	Allotted	Total
Bois Forte	1866	103,863	30,354	11,504	41,863
Fond du Lac	1854	97,800	4,784	17,034	21,818
Grand Portage	1854	56,512	37,679	7,086	44,844
Leech Lake	1864	677,099	15,448	12,075	27,527
Mille Lacs	1855	Disputed	3,781	68	3,849
White Earth	1867	709,467	54,125	1,953	56,078
TOTAL MCT		1,644,741	146,171	49,720	195,979

Red Lake Band of Chippewa Indians

Reservation	Acreage of Tribal Trust Lands		
	Tribal	Allotted	Total
Red Lake	564,426	102	564,528

Source: *Indians in Minnesota* by Elizabeth Ebbott. Copyright © 1971, 1974, 1985 by the League of Women Voters. Published by the University of Minnesota Press.

The twentieth-century Ojibway are a diverse group active in contemporary society. The determination of the people to maintain their culture and improve conditions facing tribal members and the land is manifested in many ways. Fond du Lac recently opened a new $7 million community college building. Mille Lacs tribal leaders are negotiating a proposal with the federal government to settle an 1837 treaty involving hunting and fishing rights. The White Earth Land Restoration Project, founded by tribal member Winona LaDuke, is seeking to regain land lost during the allotment period.

As in other areas of the United States, Indian gaming operations have proliferated across Minnesota. Casinos such as Fortune Bay at Bois Forte, Grand Portage Casino and High Stakes Bingo at Grand Portage, and Shooting Star at White Earth are generating substantial amounts of revenue in the state. Other enterprises center around traditional activities. The Red Lakes Fisheries Association, established in 1929, serves as a cooperative for Red Lake's tribal members to market fish. Manitok, Inc., is a White Earth company that processes and distributes wild rice as well as produces and markets other local products.

Tribal cultural activities such as powwows, exhibitions, and storytelling are held throughout the state. The Ojibway language, once targeted for extinction, is currently taught both on and off the reservations at a number of schools and colleges. Tribal elders such as Ignatia Broker (White Earth) and Maude Kegg (Mille Lacs) have written award-winning books based on cultural traditions. (*Night Flying Woman: An Ojibway Narrative*, St. Paul: Minnesota Historical Society Press, 1983; *Portage Lake: Memories of an Ojibwe Childhood*, Edmonton: University of Alberta Press, 1991, respectively). Other twentieth-century Ojibway authors include Kim Blaeser, Gordon Henry, Winona LaDuke, Jim Northrup, John Rogers, Denise Sweet, and Gerald Vizenor. Their work continues that of earlier figures such as the nineteenth century Ojibway legislator and historian William W. Warren (*History of the Ojibway People*, 1855. St. Paul: Minnesota Historical Society Press, 1984). The legacy of early tribal newspapers such as *The Tomahawk* at White Earth is represented today by the numerous contemporary news publications produced both on and off the reservations.

Other noted twentieth-century Ojibway include painters and sculptors such as Frank Big Bear, David Bradley, Patrick DesJarlait, Sam English, Florian Fairbanks, Carl Gawboy, Bambi Goodwin, Robert Rose Bear, and Kent Smith. Terri Brightnose, Duane Goodwin, Frances Keahna, and Ruth Waukazo are renowned for their baskets, moccasins, shawls, beadwork, and other traditional arts.

The Minnesota Ojibway have also produced leaders who are active locally, regionally, and/or nationally on behalf of Indian people. They include Dr. Kathleen Annette (White Earth), the first Minnesota Ojibway woman to become a medical doctor and currently administers a regional Indian Health Service office; Will Antell (White Earth), whose work has included serving as director of the National Indian Education Association as well as in top-level state education positions; Leon Cook (Red Lake), who has served as president of the National Congress of American Indians; and Roger Jourdain (former tribal chairman at Red Lake), who was instrumental in establishing the National Tribal Chairmen's Association.

Paulette Fairbanks Molin

***See also* Fishing and Hunting Rights**

Further Reading

Buffalohead, W. Roger, and Priscilla Buffalohead. *Against the Tide of American History: The Story of the Mille Lacs Anishinabe.* Cass Lake: Minnesota Chippewa Tribe, 1985.

Ebbott, Elizabeth. *Indians in Minnesota.* Ed. Judith Rosenblatt. 4th ed. Minneapolis: University of Minnesota Press, 1985.

Tanner, Helen Hornbeck. *The Ojibwas: A Critical Bibliography.* Bloomington: Indiana University Press, 1976.

To Walk the Red Road: Memories of the Red Lake Ojibwe People. Project Preserve, Red Lake High School. MN: Red Lake Board of Education, 1989.

Vizenor, Gerald. *The People Named the Chippewa: Narrative Histories.* Minneapolis: University of Minnesota Press, 1984.

CHIPPEWA IN MONTANA

The Chippewa arrived in present-day Montana in four separate migrations, but most of these people originated with the Pembina Band of Chippewa from the Red River Valley of the north, extending from Lake Winnipeg in Manitoba, Canada, to the confluence of the Red and Red Lake rivers on the North Dakota-Minnesota border, before a boundary between Canada and the United States existed. As a result of interrelationships fostered by the fur trade, French trappers frequently intermarried with the Chippewa and Cree Indians. These part-French, part-Chippewa or Cree people and their descendants refer to themselves as the Métis or Mitchif.

During the early nineteenth century, the woodland Chippewa, Cree, and Métis moved west from the Red River Valley area when furs and food diminished due to overtrapping of game. These people fully adapted to the Plains Indians' buffalo culture, hunting as far west as the Milk and Judith rivers in Montana, and became known as the Plains Ojibwa.

Rocky Boy Chippewa-Cree

Following Métis leader Louis Riel's failed attempt to create a Native state in 1868 in what is now Canada, about 4,000 Chippewa-Cree from the Pembina Band moved west into land that eventually became Montana. By the early 1880s, the United States began rounding up what it considered to be "Canadian" Indians living in Montana, particularly the Cree. Because of the close relationship of the Chippewa and Métis with the Cree, they were also forced into Canada and many of their homes were burned. Over time, many of these Chippewa and Métis later returned to Montana and settled in communities throughout the state.

In 1885, after the Métis, Cree, and Chippew under Louis Riel's leadership in Saskatchewan again took part in a failed rebellion against the Canadian government, Chippewa Chief Stone Child, or Rocky Boy, led his people south into Montana. Some Métis who had been burned out in the earlier Cree roundup joined with Chief Rocky Boy and his community, while others went south into present-day Lewistown, Montana. Cree Chief Little Bear joined Rocky Boy's group of Chippewa and Métis in 1910. After many years of diplomatic struggle, the Rocky Boy and Little Bear groups received land south of the Bear Paw Mountains near Havre. This is the only Chippewa-Cree reservation in Montana.

Today, the 3,100-member Rocky Boy Chippewa-Cree Reservation is governed by a written Constitution executed by a Business Council with one chairperson, John Stonechild, and eight Council members. The Chippewa-Cree have also established a tribal court with one chief judge presiding.

Intermarriage between the reservation's Chippewa, Cree, and Métis residents has blurred distinctions among the three groups. The reserve uses three languages: English, Cree, and Mitchif. Today's members practice a variety of religions, including Christianity, the Native American Church, the Sun Dance, and other traditional ceremonies. Kenneth Gopher, John G. Meyer, and Russel Standing are traditional religious leaders.

The Rocky Boy Chippewa-Cree Development Company (CCDC) manages tribal resources. This group is striving to meet the need for Chippewa-Cree beadwork, noted nationally for its colorful beauty and floral designs. The CCDC organized the Bear Paw Propane Company, and owns a casino with electronic poker and keno games. The tribe also has skiing, camping, and fishing facilities.

Stone Child Community College is a tribally controlled institution of higher education that was established in 1982. The Rocky Boy government has guaranteed 75 percent employment for the graduates of the college. The tribal government, college, and industry are the main employers of the reservation population.

Little Shell Band of Chippewa

The second distinct migration of Chippewa into Montana occurred when the Little Shell Band of Chippewa arrived due to a number of treaty negotiations between the Turtle Mountain Band of Chippewa in North Dakota and the federal government. In 1882 the federal government issued an executive order recognizing the Turtle Mountain Band's claim to twenty townships in north central North Dakota. In 1884, the United States government decided that the Turtle Mountain Reservation was too large. Many of the

Little Shell people were in Montana on one of their frequent buffalo hunting trips and so were not present for the census, and the United States refused to count many of the Mitchif and Little Shell followers as part of the Turtle Mountain Chippewa. As a result, despite there being approximately 5,000 Turtle Mountain Chippewa living in Montana at this time, the North Dakota reservation was reduced from twenty to two townships, with the "surplus" land transferred to the public domain.

Little Shell took his people to the Milk River near Fort Belknap in Montana to seek a reservation where their other Chippewa and Cree relatives lived. Although Little Shell later returned to his home in North Dakota, many of his followers remained near the Fort Belknap Reservation on the Milk River. Some settled in other areas of Montana, such as at Havre, Great Falls, and Helena. Until his death in 1900, Little Shell travelled between the Montana communities and the Turtle Mountain Reservation trying to negotiate enrollment criterion and an acceptable site for his people's reservation. Today, descendants of the Little Shell Band reside within non-Indian towns and communities in Montana.

The Little Shell Chippewa are governed by a Constitution and Tribal Council. The Council is comprised of a chairperson (Debbie Swanson in 1993) and eight Council members. Their central office is located in Havre, with an economic development office in Helena.

Landless Chippewa

The Landless Chippewa came to Montana following the buffalo. These Chippewa-Cree settled in regions where the buffalo were plentiful. Unlike the other Plains Indians, they built cabins and stayed in their communities for short durations, returning to Turtle Mountain in North Dakota or moving to other Chippewa-Cree and Métis communities where they had relatives. One notable group led by Pierre Berger took twenty-five Métis families from the Milk River area to present-day Lewistown, Montana. In 1879, shortly after their arrival, a trader established a trading post there and the community grew. Today, these Landless Chippewa reside in many towns in north central Montana with no reserve or trust lands.

Some of Little Shell's descendants and some of the Landless Chippewa are seeking recognition from the United States as a distinct tribe. Because this group is currently involved in the federal recognition process, no population or land holdings statistics are available.

Turtle Mountain Allotment Community

The last group of Chippewa to enter Montana is the Turtle Mountain Allotment Community. After the 1892 negotiations at Turtle Mountain, many of the band's members were required to take allotment lands on the public domain in western North Dakota and eastern Montana. Nearly 2,000 allotments of 160 acres each were distributed in Montana. Although many of these people returned to North Dakota following the loss of their allotments, some did not. This group's central government is in Trenton, North Dakota. There are about 1,000 Turtle Mountain Chippewa living in the Montana Allotment Community. These people are employed by local businesses, hospitals, and the community government. Many are farmers and ranchers. In 1993 their chairperson was Everett R. Enno.

Because all of the Montana Chippewa have a common origin, they have familial relations among all four groups. They have common cultures and languages: Chippewa, Cree, and Mitchif. Many have moved freely between their respective communities; Little Shell's followers have moved to the Rocky Boy Reservation, and Rocky Boy tribal members have moved to Little Shell communities.

In the 1990s, there has been a renaissance in Montana Chippewa communities due to the revitalization of the tribes and their cultures, languages, religions, and values. Traditional and mainstream education and economic self-sufficiency are the foci of these four communities. The elders and young are working together to learn about each other and contribute to the rebirth and survival of the entire community. Modern technology coupled with traditional products provides the economic structure for the Montana Chippewa.

Alysia E. LaCounte

See also **Allotment; Cree; Federal and State Recognition; Indian Identity; Tribal Colleges**

Further Reading

Burt, Larry. "Nowhere Left to Go: Montana's Crees, Metis, and Chippewas and the Creation of the Rocky Boy Reservation." *Great Plains Quarterly* 7:3 (1987): 195–209.

Camp, Gregory S. "Working Out Their Own Salvation: The Allotment of Land in Severalty and the Turtle Mountain Chippewa Band, 1870–1902." *American Indian Culture and Research Journal* 14:2 (1990): 19–38.

Dusenberry, Verne. "Waiting for a Day That Never Comes: The Dispossessed Métis of Montana." *The New Peoples: Being and Becoming Métis in North America.* Eds. Jacqueline Peterson and Jennifer S.H. Brown. Lincoln: University of Nebraska Press, 1985. 119–36.

Howard, James Henri. *The Plains-Ojibwa or Bungi: Hunters and Warriors of the Northern Prairies, with Special Reference to the Turtle Mountain Band.* Anthropological Papers 1. Vermillion: South Dakota Museum, University of South Dakota, 1965. Reprints in Anthropology 7. Lincoln, NB: J & L Reprint, 1977.

Murray, Stanley N. "The Turtle Mountain Chippewa, 1882–1905." *North Dakota History.* 51:1 (1984): 14–37.

Thackeray, Bill, ed. *The Métis Centennial Celebration Publication.* N.p. 1979.

Wheeler-Voegelin, Erminie, and Harold Hickerson. *The Red Lake and Pembina Chippewa.* New York, NY: Garland Publishing, 1974.

CHIPPEWA IN NORTH DAKOTA

The Chippewa peoples of North Dakota have a long and rich history on the northern plains. However, these Algonquian-speaking peoples did not originate in this part of North America, but eventually came to the northern Great Plains from the eastern Great Lakes region in the late 1600s. By the time the United States government came to terms with the Plains Chippewa, it found itself dealing with the Pembina and Turtle Mountain Chippewa.

By the last quarter of the nineteenth century the Turtle Mountain Band sought to obtain official recognition from the United States government as a distinct entity; it was not until 1882 that they finally received federal recognition and a reservation. Located in the north central portion of the future state of North Dakota, the reserve was twenty townships in size, and included a fair portion of the Turtle Mountain region in Rolette County. The reservation was reduced to only two townships in 1884, when the government decided that most of the Métis (mixed-blood) population were Canadian in origin.

During the remainder of the 1880s and 1890s, Chief Little Shell led the Turtle Mountain band in its efforts to reinstate the original reservation size, reenroll their Métis relatives, and obtain fair compensation for their 10-million-acre land claim. Federal Indian agents hand-picked tribal members known to back the government's position, and the Agreement of 1892 was duly signed and sent on to Congress where it was fought over for the next twelve years, finally being ratified with minor changes as the Act of 1904. The Turtle Mountain Band received $1 million for their 10-million-acre land cession, giving rise to the nickname "Ten Cent Treaty" for its ten cents per acre price. The reservation remained at the size of two townships, however, and the Métis remained unenrolled. Enrolled members of the Turtle Mountain tribe in 1900, living both on and off the reservation, numbered 2,429.

The Burke Act of 1906 was part of the overall reformist legislation of the time and sought to shorten the twenty-five-year trust period for Native Americans considered to be ready to take on the responsibilities of living in the white world. Many members of the band were considered "competent" by these standards, and thus were given a patent-in-fee simple allotment of reservation land. One of the chief problems, however, lay in the small size of the reservation. The government solution was to allot as many tribal members as possible from reservation land, and then provide the remainder of the allotments out on the public domain. This policy would scatter the band across North Dakota, Montana, and even South Dakota.

The 1917 Bureau of Indian Affairs Declaration of Policy further served to break up the reservation by allotting fee patents based on blood quantum rather than competency. If a tribal member had at least one-half white blood, he or she would automatically be given a patent-in-fee simple. Members of the Turtle Mountain and Pembina bands were overwhelmingly mixed-blood, allowing them to be among the first fee patents issued and speeding up the already precipitous loss of their lands. Between 1917 and 1920, many of these Turtle Mountain and Pembina Chippewa allottees made the long trek back to what was left of their North Dakota reservation after having lost their allotments because of their inability to pay the taxes suddenly due. Most of them stayed with relatives on or near the reservation, or with families who had managed to keep their land in places like Trenton, North Dakota, and Graham Island, near Devils Lake, North Dakota.

The years between 1935 and 1953 saw attempts made to purchase land on and near the reservation in an effort to improve the lot of the numerous landless tribal members. Many Turtle Mountain Chippewa left the reservation in the 1930s and 1940s in search of work elsewhere. Those who stayed behind continued to suffer the ravages of poverty and economic depression, even when the rest of the country went back to work during the war years. In 1940, Governor John Moses authorized a special study of the overall situation on the remote reservation, and the findings were anything but positive. The Moses Report restated that the greatest need was for more land. At this time, there were 7,000 Turtle Mountain Chippewa in Rolette County.

As the 1950s dawned the Turtle Mountain Chippewa were early targets of the next new Indian policy, that of termination. Their rejection of the 1934 Indian Reorganization Act and their survival since caused many in the Bureau of Indian Affairs and Congress to consider them ideal candidates for this new approach to Indian affairs. However, when the Menominee suffered the ravages of termination, it gave the government pause in its haste to implement the policy on other groups, and the Turtle Mountain Band was saved from its disastrous reach.

In the 1970s, President Richard Nixon's new Indian policy of self-determination sought to allow for tribal sovereignty within the boundaries of the reservations while providing federal help in attracting businesses and constructing decent housing. The Turtle Mountain Band began making strides toward a greater degree of self-sufficiency with the construction of a tribally owned manufacturing company with military contracts, a Bulova watch factory built in the 1950s (since bought by other interests) and a shopping mall in Belcourt.

In the 1990s the Turtle Mountain Band is engaged in efforts to bolster and encourage economic development to provide jobs for people which will outlast government programs. The reservation headquarters of Belcourt, North Dakota is home to Turtle Mountain Community College, and help is offered to students wishing to transfer to other colleges and universities in the region. The tribe has also gone into the casino business, which has been a growing source of income. However, questions concerning sovereignty and "gambling compact" agreements with the state remain to be resolved. Another positive development in the late 1980s was the federal government's recognition of the unfairness of the Ten Cent Treaty. Members of the tribe who could prove they were at least one quarter Pembina or Turtle Mountain Chippewa received a pro-rated monetary disbursement.

Reservation land holdings total over 45,000 acres, of which just over 33,000 is Indian controlled. The tribal headquarters of Belcourt is the largest town on the reservation, with a population of 2,000. The band is administered by a nine-member Tribal Council led by a chairperson and is organized according to a 1959 Constitution and Bylaws. Except in unusual circumstances, elections are held in May during even-numbered years. The tribe administers a wide range of programs and actively participates in federal programs.

In the early 1990s the Turtle Mountain Reservation had a population of approximately 10,000, with total tribal enrollment over 25,000. The Chippewa and Mitchif languages are still spoken in the Turtle Mountain vicinity. Mitchif is a creole language with its roots in English, French, Chippewa, and Cree. Most people are Roman Catholic, with a few practicing more traditional religious customs. Turtle Mountain author Louise Erdrich has based many of her fictional works in North Dakota Chippewa communities.

Gregory Camp

See also **Ojibwa: Chippewa in Montana; Tribal Colleges**

Further Reading

Camp, Gregory S. "Working Out Their Own Salvation: The Allotment of Land in Severalty and the Turtle Mountain Chippewa Band, 1870–1920." *American Indian Culture and Research Journal.* 14:2 (1990): 19–38.

Howard, James Henri. *The Plains-Ojibwa or Bungi: Hunters and Warriors of the Northern Prairies, with Special Reference to the Turtle Mountain Band.* Anthropological Papers 1. Vermillion: South Dakota Museum, University of South Dakota, 1965. Reprints in Anthropology 7. Lincoln, NB: J & L Reprint, 1977.

Schneider, Mary Jane. *North Dakota Indians: An Introduction.* Dubuque, IA: Kendall/Hunt Publishing, 1986.

ANISHINABE IN WISCONSIN

Although they were never organized as a single political entity, the Anishinabe (also known as Ojibwa and Chippewa) are one of the most numerous cultural and linguistic groups indigenous to the North American continent. Today, bands of Anishinabe live on reservations and reserves in the Great Lakes region of the United States and Canada. In Wisconsin, there are six Anishinabe reservations located in the northern part of the state. These reservations are part of the southwestern Chippewa, and form the Lake Superior Tribe of Chippewa Indians: Bad River, Lac

Courte Oreilles, Lac du Flambeau, Red Cliff, St. Croix, and Sokaogon.

In protest to an order for removal issued in 1850, the Anishinabe entered into the Treaty of 1854, which established the Bad River, Lac Courte Oreilles, Lac du Flambeau, and Red Cliff reservations. The Sokaogon and St. Croix reservations were established by the secretary of the interior in 1938. While the original acreage of all six of the reservations totalled 285,734 acres, the current total held in trust is about 161,737 acres. Of this, 86,492 acres are tribally owned lands, while 75,242 acres were allotted to individual tribal members. Individual reservations vary greatly in size and tribal ownership (figure 1).

Total membership in the Wisconsin Anishinabe tribes is 16,507, but only about 8,355 of those actually reside on one of the reservations. Many have moved away to seek employment, education, and other opportunities. Towns and cities in Wisconsin with large Indian populations include Ashland, Bayfield, Hayward, and Milwaukee. However, travel between the towns and the reservations is frequent, both to visit family and in conjunction with Anishinabe social events such as powwows, softball tournaments, hunting, wild ricing, and fishing.

Each Anishinabe reservation is governed by a Tribal Council organized under the provisions of the Indian Reorganization Act of 1934. Tribal Council memberships range in size from five to twelve members, each headed by a chairman or president. These tribal governments administer federal programs (health, social services, housing), and also develop plans for tribal business ventures such as bingo. Tribal courts are expanding their civil jurisdiction to include Indian child welfare, small claims, and the development of air and water standards. In addition to these individual tribal governments, recent years have seen the proliferation of larger intertribal organizations to deal with issues of concern to the Indian population in the region as a whole. For example, the Great Lakes Inter-Tribal Council, headquartered at Lac du Flambeau, links the Anishinabe to other tribes in Wisconsin.

Treaty rights became a controversial issue in the 1980s and 1990s as a result of the United States Court of Appeals reaffirming off-reservation hunting and fishing rights. The Voigt Decision of 1983 (*Lac Courte Oreilles Band, etc. v. Voigt*, 700 F.2d 341 [1983]) affirmed that when the Anishinabe ceded their lands in treaties made with the United States, they reserved the right to hunt, fish, and gather on lands that they sold. This ruling, in conjunction with others decided in additional states, paved the way for a series of court cases and Anishinabe grass-roots mobilization, as well as anti-treaty activism among non-Natives in the state. Thomas Maulsen, from Lac du Flambeau, has been instrumental in organizing the Anishinabe to defend their treaty rights. The Great Lakes Indian Fish and Wildlife Commission (GLIFWC) was formed in 1984 to "provide coordination and services for the imple-

mentation of treaty rights to fish, hunt, and gather in the treaty-ceded territory, and to represent tribal interests in natural resource management in the ceded territory." The GLIFWC is based on the Bad River Reservation, and its natural resource management program includes biological services, conservation enforcement, public information, policy analysis, and natural resource development. In addition, each Anishinabe band has its own natural resource programs and conservation codes to manage hunting, fishing, and gathering on and off the reservations. In Wisconsin alone, Anishinabe hatcheries released 48,903,676 fish into reservation waters in 1991.

Another major development among the Anishinabe is the establishment of Lac Courte Oreilles Community College (LCOCC), a tribal college that provides educational and vocational training for Wisconsin Indians. The curriculum includes coursework in Native cultures, arts, and languages. LCOCC is also the home of WOJB, a public radio station that caters to the interests of Indians throughout the state, and of Gaiashkibos, current president of the National Congress of American Indians and Lac Courte Oreilles tribal chairman.

Unemployment, which has always been high, has been greatly impacted with the advent of bingo and other gaming operations that provide employment and income for the reservations. All six reservations have at least one casino, and the tribal members are concerned about accountability and reinvestment of casino profits. In April, 1993, the State of Wisconsin passed a referendum for a constitutional amendment banning gambling. This is a potential source of conflict for the tribes and the state. Other sources of individual income are commercial fishing industries owned and operated by tribal members, and arts and crafts shops throughout the reservations, but many people are fairly well assimilated into the economic life of northern Wisconsin, which is mostly seasonal.

With the forced assimilation policies of the late nineteenth and early twentieth centuries, the Anishinabe people have experienced a significant loss of their traditional culture. However, with improvements in opportunities for American Indians in general, the Anishinabe are now reclaiming their language, art, religion, and other traditions. Both Lac du Flambeau and Red Cliff have tribal museums. The "Three Fires Society" claims to be a modern Midewiwin, but this is disputed by many traditional families. Nevertheless, unadvertised Midewiwin lodges do exist on various reservations, and the Big Drum Society is also restricted to those invited to participate. The number of participants of these two traditional religions is unknown. However, a large portion of the Anishinabe population are not involved in organized religion as it is perceived by non-Indians. Depending on the beliefs of an individual, singing, hunting, fishing, and other daily activities may or may not have religious connotations. Christian sects have a long history of competition for government funding on the reservations. The response to the Catholic Church today is not much different than in non-Indian communities; church attendance is on the decline.

The Chippewa language is pretty much gone as a first language, but many people know enough words to more or less understand it. Efforts are being made to reverse this trend, as the language is taught in Head Start classes on the reservations, and adults can take language classes at Northland College and Lac Courte Oreilles Community College.

In recent years, community members have organized an annual powwow circuit sponsored by individual Anishinabe reservations. The size of the powwows has grown, and can be as large as 250 dancers and ten drums. One of the oldest and most popular powwows that takes place over the summer months is the Honor the Earth Powwow, at the Lac Court Oreilles Reservation.

The Anishinabe have been successful in adapting their traditional culture to the contemporary world. It would seem fair to say that although modified by technology, traditional forms of hunting, fishing, and wild rice gathering have remained intact as important expressions of culture for the Anishinabe of Wisconsin.

Brian Baker

Rick Eckert

Percent of Tribal Members Living on Reservations

Reservation	Reservation Population	Tribal Membership	Percent on Reservation
Bad River	1,538	4,475	32%
Lac Courte Oreilles	2,279	4,068	56%
Lac du Flambeau	1,420	2,706	52%
Red Cliff	1,471	2,830	51%
Sokaogon	413	1,399	59%
St. Croix	1,288	759	??

Calculated from community profiles.

Local Estimates of Reservation Indian Population and Labor Force Statistics for Indians Living On or Adjacent to the Reservations

	Unemployed Percent			Percent Earning $7,000+		
Reservation	1981	1991	Percent Change	1981	1991	Percent Change
Bad River	46	81	+35%	27	9	-18%
Lac Courte Oreilles	61	59	-2%	19	14	-5%
Lac du Flambeau	42	44	+2%	33	30	-3%
Red Cliff	57	54	-3%	25	21	-4%
Sokaogon	64	48	-16%	14	17	+3%
St. Croix	63	53	-10%	26	27	+1%

Calculated from BIA data.

Department of the Interior Lands Under Tribal Jurisdiction

Reservation	Original Acreage	Current Acreage	Percent Decrease
Bad River	124,234	56,897	55%
Lac Courte Oreilles	69,000	48,295	31%
Lac du Flambeau	73,000	44,919	39%
Red Cliff	14,500	7,881	46%
Sokaogon	2,000	1,694	16%
St. Croix	2,400	2,051	15%

Reservation	Tribally Owned Acreage	Percent	Individually Owned Acreage	Percent
Bad River	28,813	42%	33,083	58%
Lac Courte Oreilles	22,429	46%	25,865	54%
Lac du Flambeau	30,542	68%	14,377	32%
Red Cliff	5,963	76%	1,917	24%
Sokaogon	1,694	100%	0	0%
St. Croix	2,051	100%	0	0%

Great Lakes Agency, BIA, Ashland, WI, December 31, 1991.

See also **Environmental Issues**

Further Reading

Barnouw, Victor. *Wisconsin Chippewa Myths & Tales and Their Relation to Chippewa Life: Based on Folktales Collected by Victor Barnouw, Joseph B. Casagrande, Ernestine Friedl, and Robert E. Ritzenthaler.* Madison: University of Wisconsin Press, 1977.

Danziger, Edmund Jefferson. *The Chippewa of Lake Superior.* Civilization of the American Indian 148. 1979. Norman: University of Oklahoma Press, 1990.

Ritzenthaler, Robert E. "Southwestern Chippewa." *Handbook of North American Indians.* Vol. 15. *Northeast.* Ed. Bruce G. Trigger. Washington, DC: Smithsonian Institution (1978): 734–59.

Vennum, Thomas. *Wild Rice and the Ojibway People.* St. Paul: Minnesota Historical Society Press, 1988.

OKLAHOMA TRIBES

See Alabama-Coushatta; Apache; Arapaho; Caddo; Cherokee; Cheyenne; Chickasaw; Choctaw; Comanche; Creek/Mvskoke; Delaware; Iowa; Kaw; Kickapoo in Oklahoma and Texas; Kiowa; Miami; Modoc; Natchez; Osage; Otoe-Missouria; Ottawa in Oklahoma; Pawnee; Peoria; Plains Apache; Ponca: Southern; Potawatomi in Oklahoma; Quapaw; Sac and Fox; Seminole in Oklahoma; Seneca-Cayuga; Shawnee in Oklahoma; Tonkawa; Wichita; Wyandotte; Yuchi

FEDERAL INDIAN GROUPS OF OKLAHOMA

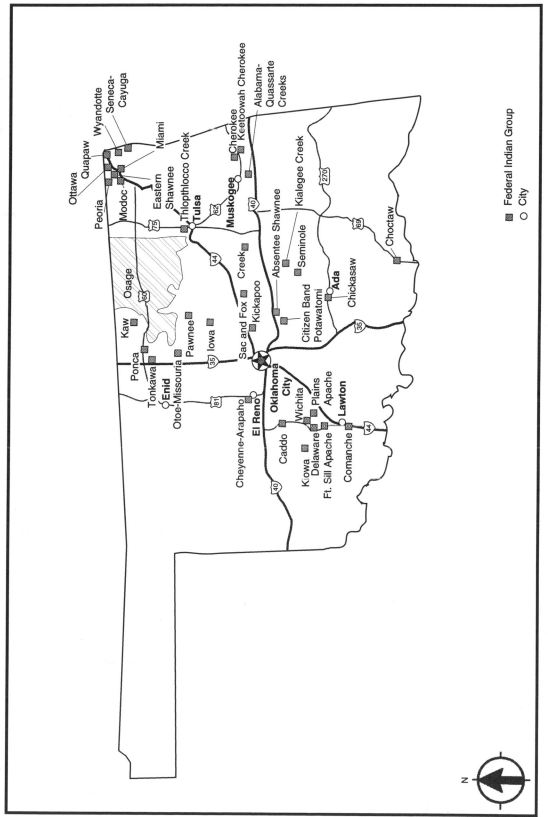

■ Federal Indian Group
○ City

Source: *Discover Indian Reservations USA: A Visitor's Welcome Guide*; edited by Veronica E. Tiller. Denver: Council Publications; 1992.

OMAHA

The Omaha Tribe of Nebraska is one of five tribes (the others are the Ponca, Osage, Kansa, and Quapaw) that speak languages of the Dhegiha Siouan group. Prior to the seventeenth century, the ancestors of these tribes lived east of the lower Ohio River valley in Indiana and Kentucky. The name Omaha comes from *Umon'hon*, a word in their language that means "against the current" or "upstream." Omaha tradition describes how they and the Quapaw ("with the current" or "downstream") separated when crossing the Ohio River in southern Indiana, some time after they had left their homeland to the east. After parting from the Quapaw, the Omaha and Ponca followed the Des Moines River to its headwaters in what is now northwestern Iowa. By the 1770s, the entire tribe of 3,000 people had settled on the Missouri River at a place they called *Ton'wontonga*, "Big Village," near the present town of Homer, Nebraska.

Since signing a treaty in 1854, the tribe has resided on the Omaha Reservation in northeastern Nebraska. In 1882, Congress passed the Omaha Allotment Act, a predecessor to the General Allotment Law (The Dawes Act) of 1887. Despite opposition by some traditionalists, Omaha lands were divided into individual allotments by Alice Cunningham Fletcher, an ethnographer hired to administer the program. Fletcher went on to collaborate with tribal member Francis La Flesche (1857 to 1932) in documenting traditional Omaha ceremonies and government. Their joint publication, *The Omaha Tribe* (1911), is a classic example of detailed ethnographic reporting.

Francis La Flesche was one of the first Native American ethnographers; he went on to document traditions of the Osage tribe as well as his own. In addition to his ethnographic work, he held a law degree and wrote a book describing his school days, *The Middle Five* (1900). His sister, Susan La Flesche Picotte (1865 to 1915) was the first Native American woman to obtain a degree in medicine. In 1889, Dr. Picotte began a medical practice on the Omaha Reservation. In 1913 she was responsible for building a tribal hospital in Walthill, Nebraska.

Thomas L. Sloan, another pioneering Omaha, was an 1889 graduate of Hampton Institute in Virginia. He held a law degree and was mayor of Pender, Nebraska. In the 1920s, he was president of the Society of American Indians. Hiram Chase also held a law degree, defended members of the Native American Church, and served as county attorney of Thurston County, Nebraska.

Throughout the twentieth century, Omahas have resisted efforts to reduce the size of their reservation or limit their sovereignty. The reservation is now about fifteen by twenty square miles and consists of 52,000 acres. In 1970, the tribe gained civil and criminal jurisdiction from the State of Nebraska, and now administers its own law enforcement and judicial system. During the 1970s, it pursued claims to Blackbird Bend, an area once theirs which is now in Iowa because of a shift in the Missouri River's course. The tribe was successful in bringing its case to the Supreme Court.

Omahas now govern themselves through an elected council of seven members and a tribal chairman. Approximately 6,000 people are enrolled as tribal members, up from a population of 3,500 at the turn of the century. About half of enrolled Omahas live on the reservation, where employment includes tribal service occupations, agriculture, and small businesses. Educational and health care facilities include elementary and high schools and a health care center, which provides extended care and diabetes treatment. Approximately 50 percent of Omahas spoke their language in the 1980s and language training is provided in the schools.

In 1989, through the efforts of tribal chairman Doran Morris and tribal historian Dennis Hastings, the tribe obtained the return of its Sacred Pole (*Umon'hon'ti*, the "Real Omaha," an emblem of tribal unity), from Harvard University's Peabody Museum, where Francis La Flesche had placed it for safe keeping a century earlier. Plans are under way to build an interpretive center on tribal land to house the Sacred Pole and other historic items, such as the Sacred White Buffalo Hide, which the tribe recovered from the Museum of the American Indian in 1991. Omahas were instrumental in drafting legislation requiring the return of human remains held by academic institutions. Since obtaining control of these remains, members have collaborated with researchers at the University of Nebraska at Lincoln in studying human remains from the former village site of Ton'wontonga. The remains were reburied on the reservation with appropriate ceremony in 1991.

When Omahas gave up nineteenth-century tribal ceremonies, many of them turned to the Native American Church, handgames, and the Gourd Dance for spiritual meaning. They also continued the annual *He'dewachi* gathering, which now takes the form of the Omaha tribal powwow held in late summer each year. Omaha music, particularly the *Hethu'shka* or warrior songs, has been influential among participants in the Plains powwow tradition throughout the twentieth century. Powwow dancing and the presentation of gifts by families remain an important part of Omaha identity.

Robin Ridington

See also **Powwow; Repatriation of Human Remains and Artifacts**

Further Reading

Barnes, R.H. *Two Crows Denies It: A History of Controversy in Omaha Sociology.* Lincoln: University of Nebraska Press, 1984.

Fletcher, Alice C., and Francis La Flesche. "The Omaha Tribe." *Bureau of American Ethnology 27th Annual Report 1911.* Lincoln: University of Nebraska Press, 1992.

Lee, Dorothy Sara, and Maria La Vigna. *Historical Recordings from the Fletcher/La Flesche Collection.* Booklet. *Omaha Indian Music.* Washington, DC: American Folklife Center in cooperation with the Omaha Tribal Council. Library of Congress, 1985.

Mark, Joan T. *A Stranger in Her Native Land: Alice Fletcher and the American Indians.* Lincoln: University of Nebraska Press, 1988.

Myers, Thomas P. *Birth and Rebirth of the Omaha.* Lincoln: University of Nebraska State Museum, 1992.

Welsch, Roger L. *Omaha Tribal Myths and Trickster Tales.* Chicago, IL: Sage Books, 1981.

ONEIDA

The Oneida tribe at the time of contact (early seventeenth century) occupied an area of land around Oneida Lake extending north to Lake Ontario and the St. Lawrence River, and south to the Delaware River. The tribe's name is an anglicized version of the Oneida's name for themselves—*Onvyo?teaka?*—meaning "People of the Standing Stone." The tribe has had regular contacts with Europeans since at least 1634, and possibly as early as 1616, when Champlain attacked a village thought to be Oneida located near Nichols Pond, in Madison County.

During the eighteenth century the Oneidas were at first loyal to the English in the struggles with the French and later loyal to the colonists during the Revolutionary War. In return for their loyalty the national government extended to the Oneidas protection of their territories, but this did not prevent the State of New York from "buying" much of their land in contravention of federal treaties and laws.

By the middle of the nineteenth century the Oneidas had lost most of their land in New York. In the 1820s, half (600) of the Oneida tribe moved to Wisconsin, settling in the area of Green Bay. In 1993, their reservation comprises 2,200 acres. In the 1840s, another 400 members of the tribe moved to Canada, occupying land they purchased near London, Ontario. The remaining 200 or so tribal members either stayed around the city of Oneida or moved to the Onondaga Reservation outside of Syracuse.

Thus, from these movements, three separate Oneida communities emerged, each with a political system modified by the events specific to its history. Wisconsin evolved a bilateral descent system with an elective council, and in 1937 adopted an Indian Reorganization Act (IRA) Charter. The 11,000-member tribe governs itself under the IRA Constitution under which they established a Business Committee. At least twice a year, the tribe holds a general meeting that has the authority to make laws and rules, and to override the actions of the Business Committee. The entire Business Committee is subject to election every three years. It consists of a chairman, vice-chairman, secretary, and treasurer, and five members elected-at-large.

Many members of the Wisconsin community belong to Episcopal and Methodist churches. There are also adherents of the Longhouse Religion of Handsome Lake. While there are few native Oneida speakers today, the tribal school has classes in the Oneida language. An active arts and crafts program encourages beadwork, silverwork, and carving skills. The tribe sponsors a large annual powwow.

The Ontario Oneidas, who number 3,000 in 1993, maintained a traditional political system based upon hereditary chiefs until 1934, when the Canadian government intervened in a growing factional dispute and installed an elective system consisting of twelve councilors and one chief. But the government's solution did not resolve the conflicts on the reserve. Many individuals continued to adhere to a traditional system centered in the Longhouse Religion of Handsome Lake, and this organization continues to exert a strong influence on the government of the reserve, although it is not recognized by the Canadian government.

The third Oneida community is located on thirty-two acres of land near Oneida, New York. It has had a tumultuous history since World War II. In the 1940s and 1950s, it was led by two sisters, Mary Winders and Delia Waterman. Mrs. Winders died in the 1950s, and the tribe's leadership was taken over by Mrs. Waterman's daughter and son-in-law, Geralda and Jake Thompson. They organized an elective system, which was challenged by descendants of Mrs. Winders, led by her daughter Gloria Halbritter. After a long and at times violent battle, Halbritter prevailed and instituted what she considers a traditional system consisting of sachems and clan mothers. This system is presently functioning, although there is still a split within the tribe. Tribal members, who number 700 in 1993, belong to various Christian denominations. In addition, many individuals adhere to the Longhouse Religion.

In this century each of the three Oneida tribes has had a number of important leaders. For the Wisconsin Oneidas, there has been Oscar Archiquette, Irene Moore, Norbert Hill, Purcell Powless, Gordon McLester, and Rick Hill. In Ontario, Demas Elm led the Longhouse followers until his death in the 1970s; Evan John, although a devout Christian, was a leader in the medicine society. In New York, besides the individuals previously mentioned, the most important leader until his death in 1991 was Richard Chrisjohn. Born on the Oneida reserve in Canada, he moved to New York in the 1930s and married one of Mrs. Winders' daughters. He was a fluent speaker of Oneida and a skilled carver.

At present the two Oneida tribes in the United States have established gaming facilities and are using the revenues from these enterprises to purchase land and acquire assets. Most tribal activities are financed from these revenue sources. The Ontario Oneidas are dependent upon Canadian government funding. All three tribes are involved in a lawsuit against two counties in New York for lands taken in the eighteenth and nineteenth centuries. Although they have won twice in the United States Supreme Court, the case has dragged along for more than twenty years without resolution.

Jack Campisi

Further Reading

Campisi, Jack. "Oneida." *Handbook of North American Indians.* Vol. 15. *Northeast.* Ed. Bruce G. Trigger. Washington, DC: Smithsonian Institution (1978): 481–90.

Campisi, Jack, and Laurence M. Hauptman, eds. *The Oneida Experience: Two Perspectives.* NY: Syracuse University Press, 1988.

Foster, Michael K., Jack Campisi, and Marianne Mithun, eds. *Extending the Rafters: Interdisciplinary Approaches to Iroquoian Studies.* Albany: State University of New York Press, 1984.

Shattuck, George. *The Oneida Land Claims: A Legal History.* NY: Syracuse University Press, 1991.

ONONDAGA

The Onondagas, the "firekeepers" of the Iroquois Confederacy, today occupy a reservation of 6,100 acres just south of Syracuse, New York. This reservation is what remains of a 100-square-mile tract set aside for the tribe in the 1788 state Treaty of Fort Schuyler, most of which was ceded to the state in a series of transactions from 1795 to 1822. Tribal enrollment is estimated to be 1,600. In addition, the Six Nations Reserve in Ontario is home to more than 500 Onondagas, descendants of refugees who had fled into Canada following the American Revolution.

Considered by some to be the most conservative of the several Iroquois tribes, the Onondagas have consistently asserted their sovereignty, regarding themselves as an independent nation, in the face of counterassertions by the federal government and New York State. The contentious relationship that prevails among these competing sovereigns has its roots in the post-Revolutionary period, when New York usurped federal authority in its taking of, and ultimately claiming jurisdiction over, Onondaga lands.

Efforts to allot Onondaga lands, part of a national policy of assimilation that arose in the 1800s, continued into the twentieth century, but were resisted at every turn. The unilaterally imposed 1924 Indian Citizenship Act was repudiated by a majority of Onondagas. They opposed federal legislation that in 1948 and 1950 extended state jurisdiction over Iroquois lands. Similar attempts to control Indian affairs in the state had been made in 1888, 1906, and 1915.

The Onondagas voted overwhelmingly against the Indian Reorganization Act of 1934, and worked in vain with other Iroquois for its repeal. As part of the Confederacy, they also challenged the Selective Service Act, arguing unsuccessfully that they were a foreign nation and that the Indian Citizenship Act was unconstitutional. Resistance to the draft was to continue. Nonetheless, the Iroquois people, as is the case with American Indians in general, have voluntarily served in the Armed Forces in numbers proportionally higher than any other ethnic group in the United States.

Onondagas such as George Thomas, Joshua Jones, Andrew Gibson, and George A. Thomas represent a succession of prominent leaders from before the Depression and through the war years. Both Thomases and Jones held the title of *Tadodaho*, the spiritual leader of the Confederacy. Others, such as Irving Powless, Sr., and Leon Shenandoah, emerged in the post-war period with the growth of a unity movement, sparked by the League of Nations Pan-American Indian organization. Today Shenandoah holds the *Tadodaho* title.

In the 1960s and 1970s the Onondagas took the lead in the unity movement, assuming political pre-eminence among all the other Iroquois tribes, especially those allied in the Confederacy. Activists such as Oren Lyons, Irving Powless, Jr., and others, became the tribe's most influential voices. Onondaga concerns have become increasingly indistinguishable from those of the Confederacy Council, which continues to promote its hegemony over all the Iroquois tribes.

Over the last two decades, Onondaga political activism has resulted in the return of wampum belts, which had been held for many years by the New York State Museum. A school boycott in the early 1970s, organized by Lloyd Elm, called attention to the educational concerns of the tribe, and forced negotiations with the State Education Department. A kindergarten through eighth grade school continues to operate on the reservation. During this same period, the tribe fought state attempts to acquire reservation land for the widening of Interstate 81. Governor Nelson Rockefeller met with the Onondaga chiefs to settle this dispute. Today, the Onondagas are contemplating a land claim against the State of New York, following the lead of the Cayugas, Oneidas, Mohawks, and the Stockbridge-Munsees.

The Onondagas are governed by a Council of hereditary chiefs selected by clan mothers, which conducts both the secular and religious affairs of the tribe. All of the Onondaga chiefs must be followers of the teachings of Handsome Lake, thus linking them to the Longhouses on the other Iroquois reservations. At the same time, the chiefs represent the tribe at Confederacy councils, and have been dominant in their affirmations of traditional Iroquois ideology and culture.

Descent is reckoned matrilineally, which also determines tribal membership. A portion of the population speaks Onondaga, although tribal business is conducted primarily in English. The community has produced a number of renowned artists and athletes, and is noted as a training ground for world-class lacrosse players.

There is significant unemployment at Onondaga. Those who hold jobs work in nearby Syracuse as tradespeople, in construction (especially high steel) for the railroad, or in the service industry. Others have entered the professions including school administration and teaching.

William A. Starna

See also **Iroquois Confederacy**

Further Reading

Blau, Harold, Jack Campisi, and Elisabeth Tooker. "Onondaga." *Handbook of North American Indians.* Vol . 15. *Northeast.* Ed. Bruce G. Trigger. Washington, DC: Smithsonian Institution (1978): 491–99.

Hauptman, Laurence M. *The Iroquois and the New Deal.* NY: Syracuse University Press, 1981.

———. *The Iroquois Struggle for Survival.* NY: Syracuse University Press, 1986.

———. *Formulating American Indian Policy in New York State, 1970–1986.* Albany: State University of New York Press, 1988.

Vecsey, Christopher, and William A. Starna, eds. *Iroquois Land Claims.* NY: Syracuse University Press, 1988.

ORGANIZATIONS AND TRIBAL COOPERATION

Indian society is communally and socially based. The values of cooperation and sharing and the processes of coalition building and decision making by consensus provide Indian people with a primary orientation towards an appreciation of group formation. Indians have organized into groups for their mutual welfare for hundreds of years. The All Indian Pueblo Council, established prior to 1500, and the Haudenosaunee (Iroquois League), in existence for more than 500 years, are the oldest continuous organizations in North America, and they are organizations formed by smaller tribal nations and groups to protect their interests. These and scores of other organizations exist today, each devoted to the fulfillment of a variety of differing tribal objectives, including political, regional, economic, social, educational, cultural, and spiritual.

At the national level are such important political organizations as the National Congress of American Indians (NCAI), which today represents the interest of approximately 150 tribes, and the National Indian Youth Council. The National Tribal Chairmen's Association (NTCA), established in 1971, was another important national organization, serving as a lobbying organization for tribal government officials for more than two decades. NCTA, instrumental in obtaining the first contractual programs from the Bureau of Indian Affairs (BIA) in the 1970s, sponsored conferences on topics essential to the improvement of life in Indian country, and acted as an intermediary between the BIA and the tribes.

The National Indian Youth Council (NIYC), another national organization, was established in 1961 to provide a national vehicle for a younger and more militant Indian voice. The NIYC involved itself in a number of political endeavors from fish-ins, to law-

suits, to voter registration drives, to lobbying efforts before the United Nations. Americans for Indian Opportunity (1970), a national advocacy and consulting group created by LaDonna Harris, has worked over the last two decades in the areas of tribal resource development, environmental protection, and tribal governance.

In addition to forming national organizations, tribes often have entered into regional alliances to better serve their people's needs. The Wabanaki Confederacy and the Muskogee Confederacy are historical examples of such arrangements. The All Indian Pueblo Council (AIPC), mentioned above, today represents the interests of nineteen Pueblos. The AIPC is currently engaged in a number of areas, including the expansion of its museum facility, the protection of Pueblo water rights, and the improvement of educational, economic, and health care for Pueblo Indians.

USET, or United South and Eastern Tribes, Inc., headquartered in Nashville, Tennessee, serves as a liaison and sponsorship body for twenty tribes in the south and eastern part of the United States. The Great Lakes Inter-Tribal Council (1961) represents ten federally recognized tribes located in Wisconsin. For the last thirty years, this state-chartered organization has worked to preserve the inherent sovereignty of its members, to improve the economic and social conditions of all members, and to educate the general public about Indian status, rights, and needs. Other regional organizations assisting tribes in the 1970s and 1980s include the Intertribal Council of California, the Nevada Inter-Tribal Association, Oklahomans for Indian Opportunity, Inc., and the Five Civilized Tribes Foundation, Inc.

The Alaska Federation of Natives (AFN) was the first state-wide body representing the Inuits, Indians, and Aleuts of Alaska. Formed in 1966 as a response to the threatened loss of Native lands under the Alaskan Statehood Act, the AFN was instrumental in obtaining passage of the 1971 Alaska Native Claims Settlement Act and the bill's 1990 revisions. Named as the administering agency for claims settlement under the 1971 act, the federation has worked to educate Alaska Natives and to assist Alaska's established villages and the regional corporations, such as the Aleut Corporation and Sealaska, to develop and productively manage the resources of its stockholders. In addition, most states support agencies designed to work with the Indian nations found within their respective states, including the Maryland Indian Commission, the Michigan Commission on Indian Affairs, the Connecticut Indian Commission, and the Massachusetts Commission on Indian Affairs, to name a few.

Tribal individuals have also established a number of important agencies whose objective is to pursue the legal protection and expansion of Indian legal rights. The Institute for the Development of Indian Law and the Indian Law Resource Center, both originally located in Washington, D.C., as well as the International Indian Treaty Council, have worked with tribes, other Indian groups, and international organizations to protect and to further the legal status of American Indians. The Institute for the Development of Indian Law is responsible for furthering the understanding of Indian legal rights among the dominant and tribal populations. The Indian Law Resource Center played a central role in the late 1970s in bringing the issue of indigenous rights to the international community, lending assistance in lobbying for the creation of the United Nations Working Group on Indigenous Populations. The National American Indian Court Judges Association (NAICJA, 1970), an outgrowth of Arrow, Inc. (1949), has worked on tribal and national levels to improve the quality of legal services on reservations. Since its inception, NAICJA has educated hundreds of tribal judges in various aspects of constitutionalism and jurisprudence. The American Indian Law Center, in association with the University of New Mexico Law School, has educated scores of young Indian lawyers over the last two decades, many of whom are now the tribal attorneys and judges on their respective reservations. Other Indian organizations devoted to the legal field are the Indian Legal Curriculum and Training Program, and the National American Indian Court Clerks Association.

Another very important group of Indian organizations are those devoted to the protection, and in some cases, development of the tribal natural resource base. Tribes possess both renewable resources, such as fisheries, forests, water, and game; and nonrenewable resources, such as oil, gas, coal, and uranium. The Council of Energy Resource Tribes (CERT), the most well known of the tribal organizations, is devoted to the management of tribal energy resources. Two important resource groups, active in the late 1980s, include the Intertribal Agriculture Council and the Tribal Timber Consortium, the former designed to improve the agricultural potential of tribal lands, and the latter to promote the latest timbering techniques and forest management. Today the National American Indian Cattlemen's Association promotes ranching on reservations.

The Columbia River Inter-Tribal Fish Commission, the Northwest Indian Fisheries Commission, the National Coalition to Protect Indian Treaties, and the Great Lakes Indian Fish and Wildlife Commission are some of the several intertribal organizations which Indian leaders have established to manage and protect vital tribal fishing treaty rights. Acknowledged as treaty protected rights by the Supreme Court in a series of decisions beginning in the late 1960s, tribes have worked prodigiously to protect their access to fish and to ensure the continued existence of fish habitat. The Columbia River Inter-Tribal Fish Commission (1977), for example, was instrumental in the passage of the Northwest Electric Power Planning and Conservation Act, and the United States-Canada Salmon Interception Treaty, both laws of extreme

importance in the maintenance of the fragile salmon ecosystem.

Tribal organizations formed to assist tribes in improving their social, educational, and health status include the National Indian Education Association (1970), the Association of American Indian Physicians, the National Indian Council on Aging, the American Indian Science and Engineering Society (AISES), and the Association of American Indian and Alaska Native Social Workers, among others. The National Indian Council on Aging, located in Albuquerque, New Mexico, has worked on behalf of elderly American Indians since its inception in 1976. The Council is composed of forty individuals and serves as a liaison between tribes and advocacy organizations, distributes information and technical services to local tribal agencies working with the elderly, and lobbies for the passage of relevant legislation. The Association of American Indian Physicians (1971) devotes its energies to the improvement of Indian health care and the education of Indian health care workers. The American Indian Science and Engineering Society has worked for more than fifteen years to increase the number of Indians in the science and engineering fields. Through its sponsorship of conferences, science fairs, college chapters, and scholarships, the AISES has assisted more than 500 Indians to careers in the fields of architecture, engineering, and science.

Other tribal organizations work to protect the artistic heritage of tribal cultures and to promote the work of Indian artists. The Indian Arts and Crafts Board, a federally funded agency established by John Collier in 1935, is among the oldest of these groups. The Southwestern Association on Indian Affairs (SWAIA), founded even earlier in 1922, today sponsors a number of activities and groups whose work serves to preserve the artistic heritage of southwestern Indian people. In recent years, SWAIA has sponsored a national conference of Indian storytellers; a youth/elder conference, the large Santa Fe Powwow attended by more than 10,000 individuals, the first National American Indian Student Art Exhibition and Sale, and the ongoing activities of the Indian Market Community Circle, which preserves and advances Indian art through the publication of their magazine *Indian Market*. The Institute of American Indian Arts and the Institute for the Study of Traditional American Indian Arts have assisted Native artists to train others and to exhibit their craft. The Inter-Tribal Indian Ceremonial Association and the American Indian Dance Theatre are other well-respected organizations promoting traditional Indian dances and ceremonies.

Spirituality remains at the core of Indian culture and existence. Towards this end, tribal religious leaders have joined together in any number of religiously based organizations devoted to the spiritual well-being of Indian people. Examples include the Bureau of Catholic Indian Missions, the National Indian

Lutheran Board, Nations Ministry, and the Council for American Indian Ministry.

Sharon O'Brien

See also Alaska Federation of Natives; Alaska Native Regional Corporations; American Indian Law Center; American Indian Science and Engineering Society; American Indian Treaty Council; Americans for Indian Opportunity; Council on Energy Resource Tribes; Indian Arts and Crafts Board; Institute for the Development of Indian Law; Institute of American Indian and Alaska Native Culture and Arts; Iroquois Confederacy; National Congress of American Indians; National Indian Education Association; National Indian Youth Council; Native American Rights Fund; Pan-Indianism

Further Reading

Cole, Katherine W., comp. *Minority Organizations: A National Directory.* Garrett Park, MD: Garrett Park Press, 1978.

Danky, James, ed. *Native American Periodicals and Newspapers, 1828–1982: Bibliography, Publishing Record, and Holdings.* Comp. Maureen Hady. Westport, CT: Greenwood Press, 1984.

Encyclopedia of Associations. Detroit: Gale Research, issued annually.

La Potin, Armand S., ed. *Native American Voluntary Organizations.* Westport, CT: Greenwood Press, 1987.

Littlefield, Daniel F., Jr., and James Parins, eds. *American Indian and Alaska Native Newspapers and Periodicals, 1826–1985.* 3 vols. Westport, CT: Greenwood Press, 1984–1986.

For additional information, readers should also consult the newsletters, periodicals, and annual reports published by many Indian organizations.

OSAGE

A Siouan-speaking people, the Osage believe they migrated from the banks of the Ohio River to what is now Missouri hundreds of years ago, and were first encountered by Europeans in 1673 in their villages along the Osage River. In 1825, the tribe was resettled on a large reservation located in the extreme southern portion of what became the Kansas Territory in 1854. The Osage made a final move in 1871, selling their Kansas reserve and purchasing from the Cherokee a new reservation in northeastern Indian Territory, later Oklahoma.

On their last reservation, the Osage settled in five villages which contained twenty-four clan organizations within a general framework of two basic divisions, the *Tzi-sho* ("Sky People") and *Hunkah* ("Earth People"). The Office of Indian Affairs counted 3,679 full-bloods and 280 mixed-bloods and intermarried citizens (white men married to tribal women and accepted into the tribal community) in 1871. Smallpox epidemics and continued intermarriage with non-Indians resulted in a population count of 2,229 in 1906, with the tribe approximately half mixed-bloods and half full-bloods.

Two interrelated events occurring ten years apart were to irrevocably shape the course of twentieth-century Osage life and culture. The first was the discovery of oil beneath the reservation in 1896, and the second was the 1906 Osage Allotment Act. The secretary of the interior granted a single drilling company oil and natural gas leasing rights to all of the eastern half of the approximately 1-million-acre reservation for ten years beginning in 1895. As a result of this monopoly operation's slow development progress, the Osage received little in the way of royalties until the 1920s. Nonetheless, many saw the potential for future wealth by 1900, which greatly affected the issue of Osage land allotment.

The Osage were the last tribe to agree to allotment and were able to use to their political advantage the eagerness of Congress to complete the elimination of tribally held lands, a condition of statehood for Oklahoma. All of the surface area of the reservation was divided among the 2,229 individuals listed on the 1906 annuity roll. By the 1960s, almost half of the allotted parcels had been alienated in one manner or another, and by 1993 only about one-third were still owned by Osage individuals. Besides the individual allotments, there are three 160-acre communally held village sites at Pawhuska, Hominy, and Grayhorse, Oklahoma, plus a larger site for tribal government at Pawhuska. Any Osage can still live without charge at the so-called "Indian towns," even if they own allotted lands elsewhere in Osage County. The Pawhuska site consists of about 700 acres in 1993 and includes a golf course, cemetery, tribal offices, and a reservoir.

Most significant, however, was the provision in the Allotment Act that the mineral estate of the former reserve would remain tribally owned. Only the 2,229 original allottees or their designated heirs, also known as "headright holders," would share in the division of income derived from mineral exploitation. The increased demand for oil and natural gas, coupled with the elimination of the earlier monopoly and the opening of the western half of the mineral estate, led to tremendous tribal wealth in the 1920s. Surrounding tribes boasted individual wealthy members whose mineral rights adhered to personal surface allotments, but the Osage benefited as a group. Open air auctions for lease rights were held at the Pawhuska Indian Agency, and drillers paid as much as a million dollars for the privilege of trying to find oil. If they were successful, the Osage received one-sixth the value of subsequent petroleum production as a royalty. The Great Depression of the 1930s witnessed a precipitous fall in the price of petroleum and a consequent drastic drop in tribal royalties. Osage oil revenues remained small in the postwar period, until a resurgence in the early

1980s due to the Arab nations' price-fixing. Royalty payments have fallen off again in the 1990s, and the future of the Osage oil fields is uncertain.

Billed nationwide during the 1920s as "the richest people in the world," the Osage discovered their bonanza to be a mixed blessing. Guardians appointed to handle the accounts of the tribespeople judged to be "legally incompetent" often proved corrupt and cheated their wards out of fortunes. In one notable case, over twenty murders resulted from a plot to transfer headrights into the hands of schemers. Marriages of financial convenience made by unscrupulous non-Indians often ended in expensive divorces or planned violence. Fears that their white husbands might unduly influence tribal politics, whose main function was the council's granting of oil leases, caused a considerable delay in the eventually successful campaign for the enfranchisement of Osage women.

Tribal government and society were drastically altered by the oil wealth. Alcoholism and drug abuse were rife. Osage politics is still almost completely shaped by the overriding concerns of oil leasing and headright payments. The primary business of the tribal government is the perpetuation of this system and management of the mineral estate, which is still tribally controlled. Since original allottees or those inheriting from them are the only Osage who can vote in tribal elections or hold office on the Business Council, there has inevitably come into being a "have-not" younger generation. There has been much continuing internal dissension over the issue of governance as many of the 11,000 tribally enrolled Osage in 1993 are excluded from participation, since most are not headright holders. Consequently, the majority of Osages are shut out of their own governance. On the bright side, personal wealth has enabled many Osage to insulate themselves from the majority culture's demands for change from traditional ways. This has not been as prevalent since the 1960s.

Full-blood Chief Fred Lookout and mixed-blood Councilman John Joseph Mathews led the tribe's attempts to deal with the harsh economic changes of the Great Depression. Many Osage took part in New Deal-era work programs and the tribe received a federal grant to build a museum, the nation's first tribally owned institution. However, the tribe's preoccupation with oil matters caused it to be largely kept out of the Indian New Deal in the 1930s. With the coming of war in 1941, Osage men and women joined the armed services and worked in war industries. Clarence L. Tinker rose to the rank of major general in the Army Air Corps, the first Indian to reach that rank since the Civil War.

Today, Osages hold the same kinds of jobs as the rest of rural Oklahoma, except that some work for the tribal agency and, more recently, run the legal tribal bingo games in Pawhuska. There are a number of people engaged in farming and ranching, and those eligible still receive headright incomes from oil and gas which vary in size enormously, although royalty income has dropped in the last few years as oil prices have stabilized.

The bulk of the Osage live in Oklahoma, especially Osage County, but many are scattered throughout the Indian nations and beyond. Osages are predominantly Catholic with a Protestant minority, but many follow the Peyote Religion—sometimes simultaneously with Catholicism. It is estimated that there are fewer than 300 fluent Osage speakers in 1993. There was a resurgence of traditional culture in the 1970s and 1980s with language classes, crafts classes, and increased attendance at peyote meetings, but oil matters continue to preoccupy many. Every year, however, large numbers can be found during the month of June in attendance at the *I'N-Lon-Scha* dances held on successive weekends at the three Indian towns, visible proof of an enduring tribal culture. Although these are the only regularly scheduled dances, individual Osage may dance at pan-Indian powwows across the country.

Terry P. Wilson

See also Mining; Natural Resource Management; Oklahoma Tribes

Further Reading

Baird, W. David. *The Osage People*. Phoenix, AZ: Indian Tribal Series, 1972.

Mathews, John Joseph. *Osages: Children of the Middle Waters*. Civilization of the American Indian 60. 1961. Norman: University of Oklahoma Press, 1982.

Wilson, Terry P. *Bibliography of the Osage*. Native American Bibliography Series 6. Metuchen, NJ: Scarecrow Press, 1985.

———. *The Underground Reservation: Osage Oil*. Lincoln: University of Nebraska Press, 1985.

OTOE-MISSOURIA

Originally two separate tribes, the Otoe lived along the Nemaha and Platte rivers in eastern Nebraska, while the Missouria occupied the lower Missouri River Valley, from the mouth of the Grand River to the modern Kansas City region. Hard pressed by the Sacs and Foxes, the Missourias joined forces with the Otoes in 1796, and during the 1850s the two tribes ceded their lands in eastern Nebraska for a reservation of 162,000 acres along the Big Blue River in southern Nebraska and northern Kansas. Disputes over acculturation split the Otoe-Missouria people into two factions: the Coyote Band, who attempted to retain a more traditional way of life; and the Quaker Band, who were more willing to walk the white man's road. After two additional land cessions in 1876 and 1881, the tribe sold their lands in the Big Blue Valley and purchased 129,000 acres in north central Oklahoma. By 1882, almost all Otoe-Missouria had moved to Indian Territory.

At first the Coyote Band established a separate village on the Iowa Reservation along the Cimarron River, but by 1900 most had joined with their kinsmen at the Otoe-Missouria agency at Red Rock in modern Noble County, Oklahoma. There the Otoe-Missouria followed a bumpy road toward acculturation. About twenty-five students annually attended the Otoe-Missouria Boarding School, a Quaker school whose curriculum was modeled after similar institutions in neighboring white communities. By 1900 the tribe had established a court system where respected leaders such as White Horse, Wayhonaryea, and Joe John served as judges for both civil and criminal cases. The courts were assisted by a formal reservation police force, which enlisted about one dozen Otoe-Missouria officers. Meanwhile, many Otoe-Missouria farmers tended individual farms, cultivating crops of wheat, corn, oats, and potatoes.

During the 1890s the Otoe-Missouria repeatedly rebuffed federal attempts to allot their reservation, but by 1899 the reservation was divided among 514 individuals. However, the Otoe-Missourias were able to retain their surplus unallotted land, and in 1907 this acreage was divided and added to the tribespeople's individual allotments. Oil was discovered in the Red Rock region in 1912, and between 1917 and 1921 unscrupulous federal officials terminated the trust status for many mineral-rich Otoe-Missouria allotments. Over 90 percent of these lands passed from Indian control, but the tribe protested and in 1922 federal officials renewed the trust status of the remaining tribal allotments until 1932.

Many Otoe-Missouria left the Red Rock region during the Great Depression of the 1930s and moved to cities such as Oklahoma City or Tulsa. A traditional people, the Otoe-Missourias initially refused to establish a formal constitutional government under the Oklahoma Indian Welfare Act of 1936, and it wasn't until 1984 that they finally did so. Many members of the tribe served in the armed forces during World War II, and following the war, a number of the returning veterans formed the Otoe Indian Credit Association. In the 1950s, the tribe was actively pursuing nine land claims before the Indian Claims Commission, and in 1953 they were the first tribe to receive a favorable decision on the basis of aboriginal use and occupancy, commonly known as "Indian Title." Congress appropriated $1,556,000 in payment, which, after lengthy discussion, the tribe elected to receive in per capita payments. Another payment in 1964 was also divided on a per capita basis.

During the 1970s, the Tribal Council began to purchase former Otoe-Missouria lands and added them to the tribe's land base. Federal grants were secured to provide for a series of economic training programs, as well as for the remodeling of tribal office facilities and the construction of a cultural center, senior citizen's center, and a tribal enterprises building. Other funds provided for the employment of community health representatives, and tribal members were hired to provide nursing, counseling, and ambulance services. The Otoe-Missourias were one of the first Oklahoma tribes to establish income-generating bingo.

The modern Otoe-Missouria Tribe consists of about 1,550 enrolled members, half of whom live in the Red Rock region. Tribal members meet regularly at the cultural center for ceremonies and social gatherings, and kinship and family ties remain strong. The Otoe-Missouria Chapter of the American War Mothers provides the tribe with benevolence and leadership, and the people assemble in mid-July each year for the Otoe-Missouria Powwow. Some tribespeople attend Protestant or Catholic religious services, while others are members of the Native American Church. The Otoe-Missouria people have successfully integrated themselves into the larger social and economic patterns prevalent in Oklahoma, but they remain Otoe-Missouria, a people proud of their tribal traditions.

R. David Edmunds

***See also* Oklahoma Tribes**

Further Reading

Chapman, Berlin Basil. *The Otoes and Missourias: A Study of Indian Removal and the Legal Aftermath.* Oklahoma City, OK: Times Journal Publishing Co., 1965.

———. *History of the Otoe and Missouria Lands.* New York, NY: Garland Publishing, 1974.

Edmunds, R. David. *The Otoe-Missouria People.* Phoenix, AZ: Indian Tribal Series, 1976.

Hopkins, Kenneth Noel. "Temporary Refuge: Otoe-Missouria Indians on the Big Blue Reservation, 1854–1881." Master's thesis, Texas Christian University, 1980.

Whitman, William. *The Oto.* Columbia University Contributions to Anthropology 28. New York, NY: Columbia University Press, 1937.

OTTAWA/ODAWA

ODAWA IN MICHIGAN

The Odawa or Odawu (meaning "Trader" or "At-Home-Anywhere People") or Ottawa (the anglicized version) Nation traces its origins to Manitoulin Island (where many still live), the east and north coasts of Georgian Bay, and the Bruce Peninsula in Ontario. After contact, they moved from Ontario into the Upper and Lower Peninsula of Michigan, Wisconsin, Illinois, Indiana, Ohio, Pennsylvania, Kansas, and Oklahoma. For the past 300 years, many Odawa have lived in the northern lower peninsula of Michigan, which has become the adopted "Odawa homeland."

Historically, the Odawa included the Little Traverse Bay, Burt Lake, Little River, Grand Traverse, Grand River, Roche DeBoeuf, and Blanchard's Fork bands. From 1837 to 1854 the threat of removal was greatest for all the Odawa, and relations between the Roche DeBoeuf and Blanchard's Fork and the other bands became very strained because of opposite viewpoints on removal and assimilation. On October 30, 1831, the approximately 500 members of the Roche De Boeuf and Blanchard's Fork bands of Odawa signed a treaty with the United States government that gave them a reservation in Kansas where they remained from 1836 to 1867, until their relocation to Oklahoma from 1867 to 1869. The other Odawa were successful in staying in Michigan despite not being granted a permanent reservation because of a last minute rider on their legislation.

In the 1990s, the Michigan Odawa bands were living in various counties in the lower peninsula of Michigan.

Burt Lake:	Charlevoix, Cheboygan, and Emmet counties
Grand River:	Kent, Ottawa, and Muskegon counties
Grand Traverse:	Benzie, Grand Traverse, Kalkaska, Leelanau, and Manistee counties
Little River:	Manistee and Mason counties
Little Traverse Bay:	Charlevoix, Delta, Emmet, Mackinac, and Schoolcraft counties

Government Relations

The Michigan Odawa bands have had a long history with the United States government, having been party to thirty-two different treaties. The federal government wanted to bypass having to contact all of the Ottawa and Chippewa groups whenever it entered into treaties with these peoples. To that end, Washington created a fictional entity called "the Ottawa and Chippewa Bands." Article 5 of the 1855 Treaty of Detroit with the Odawa and Chippewa dissolved this nonexistent "tribe." Over the years, federal officials who never read the treaty field notes claimed that the Ottawa had been terminated. The Michigan Odawa have never been terminated by Congress, yet they are treated as such by the Bureau of Indian Affairs (BIA). This error has cost the Odawa access to federal funding for many education, housing, economic development, and medical service programs.

Since the nineteenth century, the Odawa nations have been seeking legal redress for allotments illegally taken, annuity payments that were never received, traditional lands sold at way below market value, inadequate schooling of their youth, and the abandonment by the United States government of their trust relationship. In 1905, Simon Keshigobenese, John Kewaygeshik, and John Miscogon were instrumental in helping successfully sue the federal government in the United States Court of Claims. The Durant Roll, which documented and made payments to all of the Michigan Odawa who were the descendants of the Odawa and Ojibwa parties to the 1855 Treaty of Detroit, was created in 1910. Odawa population in Michigan at this time was about 6,000.

Since 1935, and as recently as the 1980s, the Michigan Odawa have requested that the United States government recognize them under the Indian Reorganization Act (IRA). John Collier, architect of the IRA, was unable to get Congress to appropriate the funds needed to establish social aid and economic programs for all of the tribes that applied. As a consequence, despite meeting the government's requirements for reorganization under the IRA, the Odawa application was rejected. Collier rationalized that since the Odawa were Michigan citizens, they would at least have access to Michigan economic and social assistance. However, racism and discrimination would deny many Odawa from much needed health and human services. Consequently, because the Odawa could not receive governmental services and the local economy was impoverished, many Odawa people were forced to move to urban areas in the 1940s.

Twentieth-Century Issues

Throughout the twentieth century, the Michigan Odawa have asserted their treaty protected rights to hunt, fish, and gather on public land in their ceded territories. They have risked arrest and seizure of their equipment. The Northern Michigan Ottawa Association (NMOA) was created in 1948 to represent all the Michigan Odawa bands in federal, state, and local litigations. Besides winning two Indian Claims Commission cases in 1971, NMOA leaders Robert and Waunetta Dominic worked with state and local officials regarding Indian hunting and fishing rights. The arrests temporarily stopped with the 1979 decision in *United States, et al. v. Michigan, et al.*, file no. M26–73 C.A. (W.D. Mich., May 7, 1979), but have recently resumed. The late Chief Judge Noel Fox reinterpreted the tribes' relationship with the United States government, correcting a century of misunderstanding. He stated:

> . . . The U.S. wanted to handle disputes arising as a result of the 1855 treaty on a localized basis and sought to avoid the need for calling a general convention of the Indians to resolve future problems, and the Indians of the treaty area wished to be treated with locally and not as an artificial "Ottawa and Chippewa nation."
>
> This—and only this—is what Article 5 accomplishes.

Judge Fox further stated:

> . . . Even if the Treaty of 1855 were the only source of the tribe's federal relationship, the treaty provision would not end aboriginal federal rights or prevent recognition of a modern tribal group as a political successor in interest.

The Michigan Odawa should have been added to the BIA list of federally recognized tribes in 1979 following Judge Fox's decision. However, the only Odawa band that is federally recognized is the Grand Traverse Band of Ottawa and Chippewa Indians (GTB). After the Dominics died (Robert in 1976 and Waunetta in 1981), the GTB broke away from the NMOA and sought federal recognition. Leelanau County GTB members Dodie Harris, Lou Scott, and Greg Bailey, with the assistance of Michigan Indian Legal Services (MILS) attorney Eleesha Pastor, delivered their federal recognition petition to the Department of Interior, and on May 27, 1980, their tribe was granted federal recognition. In 1982, they purchased 12.5 acres in Peshawbestown and gained trust and reservation status for their land. The Little Traverse Bay Bands of Odawa has received funding since 1990 from the Administration for Native Americans to form a locally based tribal government. Other Odawa bands are also organizing themselves to preserve Odawa culture, political, and economic rights.

Culture

Many elders are still fluent in the Odawa language, but two generations of boarding school restrictions on speaking the language has resulted in fragmentary knowledge among middle-aged Odawa. All of the Michigan bands are currently conducting classes aimed at restoring the language among present and future generations.

The majority of Odawa communities in Michigan are Christian, but interest in traditional religions is growing, and many people blend both Christian and traditional Odawa beliefs and values. Gatherings such as feasts, powwows, ghost suppers, and naming ceremonies still flourish.

Traditional expressions of art continue to be produced, such as black-ash baskets, birch-bark containers, frames, and other objects, maple-sugar products, porcupine quillwork, sweetgrass baskets, pottery, woodcarving, and buckskin clothing. Odawa youth are blending these traditional art forms with contemporary designs, such as quilled jewelry, beaded tennis shoes, hair combs, jean jackets, baseball caps, ribbon shirts, paintings, carvings, and sculpture.

In the 1990s the Odawa continued to fight for federal acknowledgment to reinstate their trust relationship as the political successors to the Odawa signatories of the 1836 and 1855 treaties. The Odawa will continue to pursue federal acknowledgment through the Branch of Acknowledgment and Research, but there are many financial and emotional hardships and lengthy time intervals involved that plague the process.

By 1993 there were approximately 10,000 Odawa. In the late twentieth century, many Odawa returned to their traditional homes for weddings, funerals, vacations, and retirement. Despite low wages and lack of economic opportunities, many Odawa are willing to sacrifice material things to move back to their communities and live closer to their extended families. With a land base and adequate resources for economic development and education projects, Michigan Odawa can finally gain the self-sufficiency their ancestors had always wanted for their descendants.

Patricia A. Dyer

See also **Ojibwa: Chippewa in Michigan;
Potawatomi in Southern Michigan**

Further Reading

Doherty, Robert. *Disputed Waters: Native Americans and the Great Lakes Fishery.* Lexington: University of Kentucky Press, 1990.

Dyer, Patricia. "The Northern Michigan Ottawa Association." Master's thesis, Michigan State University, forthcoming.

Feest, Johanna E., and Christian F. Feest. "Ottawa." *Handbook of North American Indians.* Vol. 15. *Northeast.* Ed. Bruce G. Trigger. Washington, DC: Smithsonian Institution (1978): 772–86.

McClurken, James M. "We Wish To Be Civilized: Ottawa-American Political Contests on the Michigan Frontier." Ph.D. diss., Michigan State University, 1988.

———. *Gah-Baeh-Jhagwah-Buk – The Way It Happened: A Visual Culture History of the Little Traverse Bay Bands of Odawa.* East Lansing: Michigan State University Museum, 1991.

Weeks, George. *Mem-ka-weh: Dawning of The Grand Traverse Band of Ottawa and Chippewa Indians.* Traverse City, MI: Village Press, 1992.

OTTAWA IN OKLAHOMA

The history of the Ottawa tribe of Oklahoma may be traced to tribal homelands on Manitoulin Island and the Bruce Peninsula on northern Lake Huron. The name Ottawa is from the Algonquian term *adawe*, which means "to trade" or "to buy and sell." The Ottawa were well noted among their neighbors for their trading skills and intertribal relations.

Although the great body of the Ottawa tribe remained on the lower peninsula of Michigan, the Roche DeBoeuf and Blanchard's Fork bands of Ottawa living south and west of Lake Michigan were removed by treaty with the United States to Iowa after 1833, and again shortly thereafter to Kansas. The approximately 500 tribal members who were removed from Michigan resided on their reservation in Kansas until 1867, when those who did not wish to accept individual allotments of land relocated to Indian Territory. The purchase of land for the tribe from the Shawnee in Indian Territory was arranged by Ottawa Chief John Wilson. This land consisted of approximately 14,860 acres in the extreme northeastern corner of Indian Territory, between Spring River on the east and the Neosho River on the west. By 1891, under the General Allotment Act of 1887, 157 Ottawa were allotted land in severalty, with the bulk of their land placed on the open market. At the turn of the century, there were 170 Ottawa in Indian Territory.

After their removal from Kansas, the Ottawa filed a claim against Ottawa Baptist University at Ottawa, Kansas. Through the claim, the Ottawa sought to receive the educational rights guaranteed them by an 1862 treaty in which 20,000 acres of tribal land in Kansas were set aside as a foundation for a school to benefit the Ottawa. The Ottawa also sought to recover the land occupied by the university, as well as other tribal lands sold illegally by Indian agents. In 1965, the claim was settled; the final award paid to the tribe for the land and withheld treaty funds totaled $406,166.19.

In 1905 the Ottawa joined the other tribes of Indian Territory in supporting the establishment of a separate Indian state to be named "Sequoyah." Many leaders of the Indian tribes feared the Anglo-American settlers of Oklahoma Territory would dominate them if the Oklahoma and Indian territories were combined to form a single state. However, this proposal failed in Congress. Upon Oklahoma's declaration of statehood in 1907, the Ottawa became citizens of the new state.

At this time, the Ottawa were prospering in the areas of business and agriculture. Due to prolonged association with Anglo society, the Oklahoma Ottawa had attained a high level of acculturation. Most of the tribe spoke English as their primary language, and by the 1960s there were few Ottawa speakers in the tribe. During World War II, the tribe contributed to the war effort by providing defense plant workers and servicemen. One Oklahoma Ottawa, Joseph J. King, was killed in combat while serving with the armed forces.

In 1936 the tribe was organized under the Oklahoma Welfare Act. Two years later the Ottawa were issued a charter of incorporation, which was ratified by the tribe in 1939. However, during the Eisenhower administration, the Oklahoma Ottawa were targeted for termination and lost their federal status in 1956.

In 1967, the Oklahoma Ottawa joined several of their neighbor tribes to form the Inter-Tribal Council. The council provides a framework to secure federal and state assistance for the tribes. In 1978, following several years of lobbying by officials of the Inter-Tribal Council, President Jimmy Carter signed a bill restoring federal recognition to the Ottawa, Modoc, Wyandotte, and Peoria.

With the encouragement of Chief Clarence E. King and second Chief Charles Dawes, the Ottawa experienced a cultural renewal during the 1960s. Customs such as the baby-naming ceremony were resumed by tribal members. The tribe began a new tradition by holding the first of their annual powwows in 1964. The Oklahoma Ottawa powwow has continued, and usually takes place over the Labor Day weekend.

According to the 1990 census there are currently 367 Ottawa in Oklahoma, concentrated primarily in the region of Miami. The tribal offices are located in Miami and the Ottawa tribal cemetery is maintained on ten acres of land in Ottawa County. Charles Dawes is chief of the Oklahoma Ottawas in 1993.

John R. Lovett

See also **Oklahoma Tribes**

Further Reading

Nieberding, Velma. *The History of Ottawa County*. Miami, OK: Walsworth Publishing Company, 1983.

Unrau, William, and Craig H. Miner. *Tribal Dispossession and the Ottawa Indian University Fraud*. Norman: University of Oklahoma Press, 1985.

Wright, Muriel. *A Guide to the Indian Tribes of Oklahoma*. Civilization of the American Indian 33. 1951. Norman: University of Oklahoma Press, 1986.

Owens Valley Paiute

See Paiute: Owens Valley

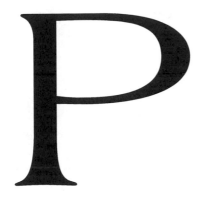

PAINTING

Ceremonial painting and the chronicling of tribal and personal martial accomplishments originated in a time beyond the recall of written or oral history. Native American secular depictions of customs and ceremonies, genre renditions, and deliberately composed, purely aesthetic compositions are relatively recent developments.

Around 1882 Choh, a Navajo in Arizona, was drawing mounted warriors, trains, birds, and frogs. In the Plains, towards the end of the nineteenth century, in the so-called "ledger drawings," war accounts were often accompanied by nostalgic works depicting subjects such as courting and hunting scenes rendered in an increasingly realistic manner with few if any of the ancient pictographic conventions. Particularly noteworthy is the work by Plains prisoners in Fort Marion, St. Augustine, Florida (1875 to 1878), because some of this art evidences an obvious concern with balance, symmetry, and rhythm, all characteristics of later developments.

Jesse Walter Fewkes commissioned Hopi artists in Arizona for the first ambitious publication of Southwest Native American art, "Hopi Kachinas, Drawn by Native Artists," published in the *21st Annual Report of the Bureau of American Ethnology, 1899–1900* (Washington, 1903). From 1901 to 1902 Kenneth Chapman of the Museum of New Mexico collected drawings from Apie Begay, a Navajo living in western New Mexico, who was drawing on paper secular interpretations of personages from Navajo sandpaintings used in healing ceremonies. Around that time, with the encouragement of sympathetic teachers, drawing and painting was also taking place in a number of Indian schools. There is work from Zuni Pueblo in the Denver Art Museum, bearing the date 1905. The Smithsonian Institution has work by Hopi students at Sherman Institute, California, done in 1908. Work, apparently not extant, was purchased in Nambe and Cochiti Pueblos in New Mexico circa 1909 to 1912. By the fall of 1910, Alfredo Montoya (d. 1913) of San Ildefonso had sold drawings of ceremonial dancers, which are now in the collections of the Museum of New Mexico. By 1917, Awa Tsireh (Alfonso Roybal) of San Ildefonso (ca. 1895 to 1955) is reported to have sold paintings. Shortly before his death, Crescencio Martinez of San Ildefonso (d. 1918) painted an extensive series of paintings illustrating the winter and summer ceremonies for Edgar B. Hewett, Director of the School of American Research and the Museum of New Mexico.

Early Painters

In the Fall of 1918 Elizabeth DeHuff, the wife of the superintendent of the Santa Fe Indian School, sought out talented students to provide her with souvenirs of the dances she had not been allowed to photograph. She emphasized that she wanted the students to capture the feel and movement of the Pueblo dances. She assembled several students, including Velino Herrera, Zia (1902 to 1973); Fred Kabotie, Shungopovi, Arizona (1900 to 1986); and Otis Polelonema, Shungopovi, Arizona (1902 to 1981) for daily informal painting sessions for which she provided supplies but no instruction. When she discovered that the work of these students was being sought after and eagerly purchased in Santa Fe, she arranged for an exhibit in the Museum of New Mexico held in April 1919. It attracted critical and public attention. John Sloan, president of the Society of Independent Artists, arranged for the collection, augmented by works of Awa Tsireh and Crescencio Martinez supplied by Hewett, to be displayed at the Society's Fourth Annual Exhibition held in March, 1920, in New York City. The collection received favorable reviews in, among other publications, *The New York Times* and *Dial* magazine. Because the works were well-received, similar collections were also exhibited in the 1921 and 1922 annuals of the Society.

Following the success of the first generation of Pueblo painters developed at the Santa Fe Indian school, other artists living in New Mexico Pueblos began to paint. These included: Tonita Peña, San Ildefonso (1895 to 1949); Encarnacíon Peña, San Ildefonso (1902 to 1979); Julian Martinez, San Ildefonso (1897 to 1943); Oqwa Pi (Abel Sanchgez), San Ildefonso (1899 to 1971); Wo-Peen, San Ildefonso (1907 to 1990); Richard Martinez, San Ildefonso (1904 to 1987); Romando Vigil, San Ildefonso (1902 to 1978); and Pan Yo Pin (Thomas Vigil), Tesuque (1889 to 1960).

In the 1880s on the Plains, Indian scouts and old warriors drew in ledger style. In Oklahoma, Silverhorn, younger brother of Kiowa artist Ohettoint, a returned Fort Marion prisoner, filled sketchbooks with bold decorative compositions for sale. Other drawings continued to be made within a traditional tribal context, such as the sketchbook by Red Hawk and other artists recovered from the scene of the massacre of Wounded Knee. In 1897, James Mooney of the Smithsonian Institution commissioned the returned Fort Marion prisoners Paul Zotom (1853 to 1913),

Tonita Pena (San Ildefonso Pueblo). "Eagle Dance," 1934. Private collection. Photo courtesy of the Native American Painting Reference Library.

Jerome Tiger (Creek-Seminole). "My People Awaits," 1966. Private collection. Photo courtesy of the Native American Painting Reference Library.

Ohettoint (1852 to 1934), and Silverhorn (1861 to 1940) to paint miniature tipis and shields. Later, Silverhorn produced works for Mooney and Colonel Hugh L. Scott, illustrating aspects of Kiowa culture including the Sun Dance, Ghost Dance, peyote rituals, and Kiowa myths and folklore.

The ledger drawing style was carried into the second decade of the century by artists such as Amos Bad Heart Bull, Oglala Sioux (1869 to 1913), who filled a ledger book with over 400 drawings covering the history, customs, and religion of the Teton Sioux. The work was done over a twenty-year period starting in 1891 and continuing until shortly before his death. Two Oklahoma artists who started painting around the turn of the century are Earnest Spybuck, Absentee Shawnee (1883 to 1949) and Carl Sweezy, Arapaho (1881 to 1953). Spybuck, who was not influenced by the Plains tradition, painted in a Euroamerican naive style, emphasizing detail and naturalistic renderings. Sweezy, who worked mostly in oils, used a modified ledger drawing style.

Oscar Jacobson and the Kiowa Six

Around 1918, Susie Peters, a government field matron to the Kiowas, began encouraging a number of Kiowa youngsters with gifts of crayons and paints. In the late 1920s, she brought a group of six of her proteges to the attention of Professor Oscar B. Jacobson, head of the art department at the University of Oklahoma, who invited them to paint in a special workshop where he and his assistant, Dr. Edith Mahier, helped them define and refine their style. While their paintings are indebted to Plains antecedents, their affinity to contemporary popular art, particularly costume and stage design, is evident. These Kiowa paintings, usually of single figures or small groups, reflect a twentieth century Plains emphasis on elaborate and decorative costumes. Many depict the dance, particularly powwow or contest dancing, as an individualistic virtuoso performance. These artists, who set in motion what is now recognized as the "Renaissance of Southern Plains Painting," are Spencer Asah (1905 to 1954), James Auchiah (1906 to 1974), Jack Hokeah (1902 to 1969), Stephen Mopope (1900 to 1974), Lois Smoky (1907 to 1981), and Monroe Tsatoke (1904 to 1937).

Jacobson arranged for a series of exhibits in museums and universities and a showing of their art at an international art exhibit held in 1928 in Prague, Czechoslovakia. In 1929, *Kiowa Indian Art*, a limited

Harry Fonseca (Nisenan-Maidu). "Coyote Koshares No. 9," 1983. Private collection. Photo courtesy of the Native American Painting Reference Library.

edition folio of their work, was published in France. In 1931, the widely traveled landmark exhibit "The Exposition of Indian Tribal Arts" included selections of both Pueblo and Oklahoma Indian paintings.

The Studio at Santa Fe Indian School

By 1930, following a reversal of a long-standing governmental policy designed to encourage assimilation into white society by discouraging the expression of Native American cultures, programs were started to develop Indian art and handicrafts. In the spring of 1932, a group of established southwestern Native American artists and one Plains artist, Jack Hokeah from Oklahoma, painted murals in the dining room of the Santa Fe Indian School. September 1932 saw the establishment of the "Studio" at the Santa Fe Indian School dedicated, according to Dorothy Dunn, its founder, to "recover, maintain, and develop" Indian art. The movements encouraged by Mrs. DeHuff and Professor Jacobson had involved only a handful of painters in informal, short-lived programs which were not officially part of a curriculum. Conversely, Dorothy Dunn's program provided an official institutional setting that catered to as many as 300 students over an extended period of time. Her students, most of whom were in grade school, were considerably younger than Mrs. DeHuff's or Jacobson's students. Under Dunn's leadership (1932 to 1937), many promi-

Stephen Mopope (Kiowa). "Eagle Dancer," ca. 1930. Private collection. Photo courtesy of the Native American Painting Reference Library.

nent southwestern artists developed, including: Narciso Abeyta, Navajo (b. 1918); Harrison Begay, Navajo (b. 1917); Allen Houser, Apache (b. 1914); Gerald Nailor, Navajo (1917 to 1952); Oscar Howe, Sioux (1915 to 1983); Quincy Tahoma, Navajo (1921 to 1956); Andy Tsinajinnie, Navajo (b. 1918); and Pablita Velarde, Santa Clara (b. 1918). Although Dorothy Dunn left the Studio in 1937, it continued functioning with her methods of instruction until 1962. Under the later direction of Geronima Montoya, San Juan (b. 1915), one of Dunn's students, several notable artists emerged, particularly in the early years, including Gilbert Atencio, San Ildefonso (b. 1930); Joe Herrera, San Ildefonso (b. 1923); and Ben Quintana, Cochiti (ca. 1923 to 1944).

Art in Oklahoma

In the 1930s, the Kiowa style was widely emulated, particularly in Oklahoma where many new artists initially started painting in that manner. Gradually, they developed distinctive new styles. A major influence on developments were noted artists Acee Blue Eagle, Creek (1907 to 1959); Woody Crumbo, Creek-Potawatomi (1912 to 1989); and Richard West, Cheyenne (b. 1912). In 1935, Blue Eagle became the first head of a newly organized Indian art department at Bacone College (then an elementary and secondary school), in Muskogee, Oklahoma. Woody Crumbo held the position from 1938 to 1941. Dick West served as chairman of the Bacone art department from 1947 to 1970. West, who has considerable art training, is a versatile artist who has mastered a variety of styles ranging from the earlier realistic to the abstract and contemporary. Ruth Blalock Jones, Delaware-Shawnee (b. 1939), studied at Bacone and in 1993 is chair of its art department. Artists who studied at Bacone include: Terry Saul, Choctaw-Chickasaw (1921 to 1976); Solomon McCombs, Creek (1913 to 1980); Joan Hill, Creek-Cherokee (b. 1930); Virginia Stroud, Cherokee-Creek (b. 1951); and David Williams, Kiowa/Kiowa Apache/Tonkawa (1933 to 1985). Archie Blackowl, Cheyenne (1911 to 1992) and Fred Beaver, Creek (1911 to 1980) also started painting in the 1930s and 1940s. Noted artists who began painting in the 1950s and 1960s include Doc Tate Nevaquaya, Comanche (b. 1932) and Bert Seabourn, Cherokee (b. 1931).

Styles of Painting

For several decades after the 1930s, Native American painting continued to develop along the lines established by its early founders. Paintings tended to emphasize details in costumes and decorations, but foreground, background, and perspective were absent. Paintings were basically flat with color applied in discrete areas without shading. Subject matter was restricted to realistic, if stylized, treatments of genre scenes, and depictions of Indian lifestyles, including nineteenth-century and contemporary customs and ceremonies.

A major trend began in the direction exemplified by the works of Blackbear Bosin, Kiowa-Comanche

(1921 to 1980), Oscar Howe, Rafael Medina, Zia (b. 1929), and Jerome Tiger, Creek-Seminole (1941 to 1967). These artists had increasing technical proficiency and individuality, imbuing many of their works with emotion and drama. The subject matter, rather than portraying specifics, is often more generalized as they attempt to convey spiritual and mystical impressions. Bosin and Howe, for example, refer to customs and ceremonies, but usually do not actually portray them. Medina does not paint the sacred clowns (*koshare*) officiating at a Pueblo dance, but paints them close-up, out of context, amidst conventional Pueblo decorative pictorial elements, in order to emphasize the mystery and awe surrounding this most sacred of Pueblo characters. Tiger's many "Trails of Tears" (the exodus from the Southeast to exile in Oklahoma) are free of documentary particulars so that they become generalized universal statements about oppression, suffering, alienation, and despair. Bosin, Howe, and Medina originally painted in styles similar to those of the 1930s and 1940s. As they matured, they incorporated elements of symbolism, cubism, and surrealism in their work.

Innovation and the Institute of American Indian Arts

Oscar Howe's eloquent protest in 1958 against the rejection of his entry to the Philbrook Museum's annual Indian competition on the grounds that it was not "traditional Indian art," resulted in the lifting of restrictions against new and innovative styles and a broadening of subject matter. In 1962, this new direction in Indian art was championed by a Bureau of Indian Affairs governmental school, the Institute of American Indian Arts (IAIA), which replaced the Santa Fe Indian School. It emphasized a contemporary approach using American and European styles. In content, the school also introduced social commentary, protest, and activist issues.

The most successful and influential artist ever associated with the IAIA is Fritz Scholder, Luiseno (b. 1937). As an IAIA instructor, he set out to inspire his students to paint the Indian "real" not "red," deliberately avoiding stylistic and psychological cliches. His startling, sometimes starkly repelling images, reflecting stylistic influences from Thiebaud, Diebenkorn, and especially Bacon, illuminate the paradoxes and agonies of contemporary life. They were in marked contrast to some of the idealized, romantic, and sentimental conceptions being done at the time. Unlike Scholder, who admittedly had limited exposure and experience with Native American culture, T.C. Cannon, Kiowa-Caddo (1946 to 1978), identified strongly with traditional values. He also used contemporary mainstream styles and made personal statements with wit, anger, and affection about the dilemmas and paradoxes of maintaining a sense of Native American identity. Other artists who developed at the IAIA include Earl Biss, Crow (b. 1947); Delmar Boni, Apache (b. 1948); David P. Bradley, Ojibwa (b. 1954); Ben-

jamin Buffalo, Cheyenne (b. 1948); Earl Eder, Sioux (b. 1944); Henry Gobin, Tulalip (b. 1941); Benjamin Harjo, Jr., Seminole-Shawnee (b. 1945); King Kuka, Blackfeet (b. 1946); Linda Lomahaftewa, Hopi (b. 1947); Parker Boyiddle, Kiowa-Wichita (b.1948); Kevin Redstar, Crow (b. 1943); and Richard Ray Whitman, Yuchi-Pawnee (b. 1949). The IAIA's successful promotion of new subject matter executed in contemporary styles helped gain acceptance for many other artists not connected with the school. Among them, Richard Danay, Mohawk (b. 1942); R.C. Gorman, Navajo (b. 1932); Harry Fonseca, Maidu (b. 1946); Helen Hardin, Santa Clara (1943–1984); Michael Kabotie, Hopi (b. 1942); George C. Longfish, Seneca/Tuscarora (b. 1942); Dan Namingha, Hopi (b. 1950); Jaune Quick-to-See Smith, Cree-Shoshone, (b. 1940); and Frank LaPena, Wintu-Nomtipom (b. 1937).

Painting in the 1990s

Today many Native American artists are no longer limited to the modest remuneration from the curio stores, trading posts, expositions, and contests, which historically were their major outlets. Buoyed by in-

T.C. Cannon (Caddo-Kiowa). "Waiting for the Bus: Anadarko Princess, 1933," 1977. Private collection. Photo courtesy of the Native American Painting Reference Library.

creasing national and international interest in contemporary Indian painting, an increasing number of art galleries display and promote their work. While earlier artists tended to be self-taught, many artists today have earned undergraduate and graduate art degrees. There is no readily identifiable subject matter or style characterizing the work of current Native American painters. Native American sensibilities are presently being expressed in a very wide range of styles and subject matter, from new interpretations of the old nostalgic standards, to the latest postmodernist allusions and parodies.

Arthur Silberman

See also Art; Institute of American Indian and Alaska Native Culture and Arts

Further Reading

Dunn, Dorothy. *American Indian Painting of the Southwest and Plains Areas.* Albuquerque: University of New Mexico Press, 1968.

Silberman, Arthur. *One Hundred Years of Native American Painting.* Oklahoma City: Oklahoma Museum of Art, 1978.

———. "A Selection of Native American Art." *Tamaqua* 2 (Winter/Spring 1991): 47–87.

Tanner, Clara. *Southwest Indian Painting.* Tucson: University of Arizona Press, 1968.

Taylor, Joshua, et al. *Fritz Scholder.* New York, NY: Rizzoli, 1982.

Wallo, William, and John Pickard. *T.C. Cannon.* Oklahoma City, OK: Persimmon Hill, 1990.

PAIUTE

People known as the Paiute occupied a vast area of the American West in precontact times, ranging from what is now central Oregon in the north to southern California in the south, and extending east across the Great Basin as far as southeastern Wyoming. In the twentieth century there are Paiute groups in Oregon, California, Nevada, Arizona, Idaho, and Utah. Anthropologists employ three cultural designations for the numerous Paiute groups: Northern Paiute, Owens Valley Paiute, and Southern Paiute. The articles in this section follow this pattern.

NORTHERN PAIUTE

The term Northern Paiute is applied to both a linguistic and a cultural group in the western Great Basin. Also sometimes referred to as Paviotso (a term that is less favored today), the cultural entity and the language should be distinguished from Owens Valley Paiute to the south, and Southern Paiute to the southeast. Special care should also be taken in associating the names Mono, Snake, Bannock, and the variant spellings of "Paiute," especially as seen in the older literature, with this group. The name Mono is sometimes mistakenly applied to the Northern Paiute people, who live near Mono Lake, California, in addition to its more proper application to people in the southern Sierra Nevada. The term Snake, and especially Oregon Snake, was also used in the nineteenth-century literature, but was more generally applied to Northern Shoshone people to the east. The Bannock are Northern Paiute speakers who moved from the Oregon area to Idaho by the mid-1700s, and now reside on the Fort Hall Reservation. And the variant spellings of "Paiute" have been indiscriminately applied to Northern Paiute, Owens Valley Paiute, and Southern Paiute people from the time of the first European encounter in the 1700s. Geography is often the only referent of value in determining if a "Paiute" group is Northern Paiute. Today, the people themselves use the term Paiute without a modifier other than for reservation community (e.g., Pyramid Lake Paiute Tribe), although they are generally aware of the linguistic and cultural differences that set them apart from the other two groups who also use the name.

In the early nineteenth century the Northern Paiute people occupied a very large area that paralleled the eastern slopes of the Sierra Nevada and Cascade ranges from roughly Mono Lake in California to the John Day River in Oregon. In the north, the territory was roughly 400 miles wide, but it tapered to an area roughly 75 miles wide below Mono Lake where it adjoined that of the Owens Valley Paiute. Eastern neighbors of the Northern Paiute were the Shoshone people of central Nevada and Idaho, also close linguistic kin. Western neighbors included the Washoe people centered at Lake Tahoe, as well as Pit River groups, none of whom were linguistic relatives. In the early nineteenth century, all Northern Paiute groups were hunters, gatherers, and fishermen, with the balance of each pursuit to the total subsistence system being related to local geography. All continued to pursue aspects of traditional economies well into the twentieth century, although most were greatly modified after about 1870.

Beginning in the mid-nineteenth century, the large land area that was Northern Paiute territory was systematically eroded by Euroamerican encroachment and by the establishment of federal reservations. By the start of the twentieth century, less than 5 percent of the original area remained in Indian control. Two large reservations were established in Nevada (Pyramid Lake and Walker River) in 1859, a third in Oregon (Malheur) in 1871, and a fourth in Nevada (Stillwater) in 1891. The original plan was to settle all Northern Paiute people on these large reserves, but as each was already the home of a recognized Northern Paiute subgroup, others generally refused to move to them for fear of encroachment, but also because they would be abandoning their own traditional territories. Thus, many people remained in place, often establishing small settlements on the outskirts of Euroamerican towns. From these, they worked a variety of wage labor jobs for town residents, who thus were not particularly eager that the Indian people be removed. The abandonment of two old military posts in the 1890s allowed for two small reservations to be established for landless groups in northeastern California

Northern Paiute Reservations, Populations, and Economic Resources

Tribe	Res. Land in Acres	Population Enrolled	Population Res.[1]	Government	Economic Resources
Nevada					
Pyramid Lake	475,162	1,798	829	Council of 10	I-80 Smoke-shop, Campground; PLITE; Hay, Cattle
Walker River	320,512	1,555	822	Council of 7	Cattle, Hay; Smoke-shop, Mini-mart; Truck-stop; Cafe; Feedlot
Yerington Reservation and Colony	1,156 9.5	659	354	Council of 7	Market; Dairy Queen; Smoke-shop
Fort McDermitt	35,183	689	645	Council of 8	Cattle, Hay
Fallon Reservation and Colony	5,480 60	900	885	Council of 7	Smoke-shop
Lovelock Colony	20	110	93	Council of 5	None at present
Reno-Sparks[2] Colony	1,956[3] 28	724	598	Council of 7	3 smoke-shops; Mall; Printing
Summit Lake	10,208	112	9	Council of 5	None at present
Winnemucca Colony	340	17	(144)	Council of 5	None at present
California					
Bridgeport Colony	40	96	60	Council of 5	None at present
Cedarville Rancheria	17	22	12	?	None at present
Fort Bidwell	3,335	162	89	Council of 5	None at present
Oregon					
Burns Colony	751 11,031[4]	356	170	Council of 5	Food processing business
Warm Springs Confederated Tribes[5]	641,035	123	55	Council of 3 Chiefs, Representatives	Resort; Sawmill

[1]Resident figures may or may not include nonmembers, but usually do not.
[2]Has more than one tribe (Washoe).
[3]New lands acquired and separated by several miles from the Colony.
[4]Allotted lands still held privately but without residents.
[5]Includes three tribes (Wasco, Warm Springs, Northern Paiute), with population figures given for Northern Paiute only; one chief is Northern Paiute.
Sources: Nevada Indian Commission, 1992; USBIA "Indian Service Population and Labor Force Estimates," 1991; individual tribes, 1992.

and northern Nevada (Fort Bidwell and Fort McDermitt). The period from roughly 1910 to the early 1930s saw a resolution to the problem of other landless groups with the establishment of most of the federal "colonies" adjacent to Nevada, California and Oregon towns (see figure). Colonies have land bases of from ten to forty acres, and have federally recognized tribal governments; but until recent years, they have been too small to attract much attention for federal support services.

Twentieth-Century Issues

The twentieth century history of the Northern Paiute people is largely coincident with reservation and/or colony history, and no two entities have proceeded exactly alike. Major issues in which each has been involved to greater or lesser degrees are those of water, land, and services, and more recently, economic development.

Water Rights. Given that much of Northern Paiute aboriginal territory was desert steppe, it nonetheless attracted a variety of Euroamericans interested in farming, ranching, and urban settlement, and there has been an almost continuous struggle somewhere in Northern Paiute country over water. Pyramid Lake, Walker River, and Fallon (formerly Stillwater) reservations each sit at the end of large rivers that afford upstream users many chances to divert that precious commodity. In good years as well as drought years, the reservations get what remains to sustain fisheries (Pyramid Lake, Walker River), waterfowl habitat (Fallon), and farms (all three). Litigation over water rights began early in the twentieth century for Pyramid Lake and Walker River, as each attempted to establish rights to water for farmlands and domestic supplies, then the only recognized legitimate uses. Walker River filed and lost several suits against upstream users starting in 1902, and only succeeded in getting a reservoir to control seasonal water distribution to its farmlands in 1937. In 1905, Derby Dam was built on the Truckee River, diverting much of the river's flow away from Pyramid Lake into the Carson River basin. In 1913, the Orr Ditch suit was filed against upstream Truckee River users, and in 1926 temporary operating orders gave the majority share of the water to those users. Pyramid Lake received water rights sufficient to irrigate only a small portion of the existing reservation fields, and nothing to sustain the lake and preserve its outstanding trout fishery. (It was not until 1955 that some recognition was given to water rights for the fishery—agricultural and domestic uses still remaining the primary criteria for distribution of water until then.)

The Stillwater Reservation faced similar difficulties over water, although with a different solution. The original reservation (1891) was composed of allotments of 160 acres each, given to 50 individuals, but without any water guarantee. A few years later, another 146 allotments were made. This proved totally unworkable, so in 1906, these allotments were exchanged for allotments of 10 acres each with water rights. Although this vastly reduced the land area of the original reservation, it gave the people the chance to make agricultural improvements impossible before. However, a water right does not guarantee delivery, especially in drought times. Thus, the Fallon Reservation has also been involved in litigation through the years to obtain its rightful property. All three reservations remained concerned in the 1960s and 1970s about the various versions of a bistate water compact that would have divided the waters of the Truckee, Carson, and Walker rivers between Nevada and California. Pyramid Lake and Fallon have been active participants to protect their rights in the negotiated settlement for the Truckee River Compact in the 1980s and early 1990s. In 1991, the compact confirmed their water rights and authorized compensation for rights not properly delivered in the past.

Land Issues. Land issues have also been important to all Northern Paiute tribes since the founding of the reservations and colonies. The entire Malheur Reservation in Oregon was returned to the public domain in the early 1880s as a result of the Bannock War of 1878, in which some reservation residents participated. After internment on the Yakima Reservation for five years, former reservation residents dispersed to Pyramid Lake and Fort McDermitt in Nevada, the Miller Creek extension of the Duck Valley Reservation in Idaho, Warm Springs Reservation in Oregon, Fort Bidwell Reservation in California, and to the Burns area in the former Malheur district. Other land cessions have been less drastic, but nonetheless important. The General Allotment Act of 1887 resulted in the loss of some 286,000 acres of the Walker River Reservation in 1906. Some of these lands, as well as others, were later restored or added to the reservation. Pyramid Lake lost a 20,000-acre timber reserve in the late 1800s, and another 22,000 acres from the 1880s to 1906 to homesteaders and the railroad on the southern end of the reservation. The reductions at Fallon left it with roughly 10 percent of its former land base. All of the large reservations also dealt continually with cattle trespass, attempts at non-Indian homesteading, and poaching on fish resources (especially Pyramid Lake). In the 1930s and 1940s, reservation residents began to run their own cattle, and tribal councils under the Indian Reorganization Act began to take firmer control over land issues, thus alleviating the situation.

Entitled Services. The definition and delivery of entitled services has been a major issue for colony residents in the twentieth century. Although the larger reservations also have had trouble with schools, health care, police jurisdiction, housing, and sanitation and utility services, it has been the colonies that have felt the impact most. Because of small land bases, and their proximity to towns, they have often been at the center of jurisdictional problems between state and local governments and the federal system. In 1964, this situation was remedied at least in part with the formation of the Inter-Tribal Council (ITC) of Nevada, an overarching body that gave the small groups a much larger voice. Through the years, the ITC has managed various larger Housing and Urban Development, Public Health Service, and other projects so that smaller communities could more fully participate. Although still active, ITC now plays less of a role as the smaller tribes have gained their own strength and experience.

Education. Educational services also have been intermittent on most reservations and colonies. In the late 1870s and early 1880s, day schools were established at Pyramid Lake and Walker River. They were not established until much later on the other reservations and colonies: e.g., Lovelock in 1907, Fallon Reservation in 1908, Reno-Sparks in 1928, and Burns in 1931. Stewart Institute, a boarding school for Nevada Indians, was established in 1890 at Carson City, Nevada, and many Northern Paiute people attended through the years. In the 1950s, it was opened to a wider United States Indian population, and ultimately closed in the 1970s. Additional Northern Paiute students attended other federal boarding schools well into the 1950s, when local schools began to educate Indian students.

Economies. With reservation confinement and non-traditional forms of education came many changes in the cultural past. A number of traditional subsistence pursuits had to be abandoned or modified, as the people no longer had access to the resources, or the resources were destroyed by non-Indian users. Pyramid Lake and Walker River remained active fisheries, making good profits for individual fishermen selling fish in local towns, until upstream diversion of water and non-Indian poaching caused rapid declines in the 1920s. Most reservations lacked sufficient large and small game animals, birds, waterfowl, or seed and root crops to do more than provide partial support for residents. Some continue to take these resources elsewhere on public lands, with or without required permits, as much as a mark of ethnic identity as for subsistence. New modes of subsistence are from raising cattle and hay (larger reservations), wage work in a variety of professions, and in some cases, from tribal businesses.

Religion

Reservation confinement also brought attempts at missionization to most Northern Paiute communities. Although the denominations differ across the region, most people today participate in some form of Christianity. Some also retain aspects of their Native religions, kept alive in prayer, story, and song. Native doctors, or persons of supernatural power, were active throughout the 1930s, but declined in numbers after that time. Today, only a few such persons are present in the region.

Other Northern Paiute people participate in nonlocal Indian religious movements, such as the Native American Church, the Sweat Lodge movement,

and the Sun Dance. The Native American Church was promoted in the 1930s and 1940s in much of the area, but did not gain a large following. Today, there are a few members on most reservations. The Sweat Lodge movement, originally brought to the Wind River Reservation in Wyoming and disseminated to the Northern Paiute from there, is active principally in Nevada. The Sun Dance was introduced at Fort McDermitt in 1981, and has been active there since that time. Sun Dances have also been held at Walker River and at a few non-reservation locations in Nevada.

Social and Political Organization

Social organization probably has been least altered from older patterns. Independent and extended families remain the most cohesive units in Northern Paiute society. People gain much of their strength from kin associations. Although young people have married outside their tribe with more frequency in recent years, a number of marriages are still to local non-relatives. Knowledge of kinship terms is declining, however, as Native language use declines. A number of middle-aged and most elderly persons still remember proper reckonings.

Political organization has changed considerably, from a precontact system of headmanship, to the emergence of chiefs over mounted raiding bands in the 1860s and 1870s, back to a system of headmanship in early reservation years, and then to elected tribal councils in the 1930s. Most Northern Paiute communities are organized under the Indian Reorganization Act of 1934 at present, and hold elections for council positions every two to three years (figure 1). Councils function as business corporations, handling tribal funds and enterprises, overseeing tribal resources, and working for the improvement of living and working conditions. Since the 1960s, women have been as active as men on councils, and have held most important leadership positions. Although the opinions of elders are still highly respected, most council members today are younger people.

The Late Twentieth Century

Reservations and colonies changed in appearance, particularly in the late 1960s, 1970s, and 1980s, as most completed successful projects to improve housing and other basic services (electricity, phone, plumbing). Houses built in the early part of the twentieth century were replaced with modern three- to four-bedroom houses, many arranged on smaller lots along paved streets. Allotted reservations, such as Walker River, Fallon, and Fort McDermitt, constructed some houses in dispersed patterns, but a more urban character was imparted to all colonies and some reservation areas after this time. Reservation and colony lands also began to fill up, and new patterns were thus required. Reno-Sparks Colony, a large population base on a small land holding (twenty-eight acres) in the middle of an urbanized area, successfully negotiated for a large addition to its land base in a rural area

(Hungry Valley) in the 1980s. This addition has greatly alleviated the overcrowding this community was feeling through the 1980s. Most groups have also constructed multi-purpose facilities, tribal offices, and occasionally clinics on their lands, so that services are closer at hand.

Multipurpose facilities often house cultural and language programs. Each group has had some experience with these since the 1970s, but lack of funds or consistent funds has plagued them all. The Yerington Paiute tribe produced a dictionary and grammar for its language program in the 1980s, as well as a series of workbooks and story books. Fort McDermitt produced a bilingual reader. Language loss is accelerating, however, and only at Fort McDermitt are young children learning to speak their Native language.

Economic development has been the biggest tribal priority during the 1980s, and it continues to gain much attention in the 1990s (figure 1). Smoke-shops have had good success at Pyramid Lake, Reno-Sparks, and Fallon Colony, as have minimarts at these locations. Pyramid Lake also operates two fish hatcheries as a tribal business (PLITE) that employ tribal members to raise fry to repopulate the lake. Business parks have fared less well, often due to isolation of the reservations or lack of land. Economic depression in the early 1990s was causing Fort McDermitt to consider hosting a monitored retrievable storage facility for high-level nuclear waste on its reservation. Others were doing what they could to attract businesses, and with them, jobs, to their localities. Native artisans who manufacture traditional willow and beaded baskets, buckskin gloves, moccasins, and other items are few in the 1990s, but produce excellent work. Some, but by no means all, are able to support themselves through sales.

Health concerns parallel those for jobs and economic development in the 1990s. Substance abuse is coupled with high unemployment on several reservations, and tribes have put what resources they have, along with federal dollars, into programs to attempt to remedy the situation. Although more young people are graduating from high school than in years past, the rate is still low in some areas, and ability to get employment thus hampered. Tribes themselves have become the major employers of their high school and college graduates, but they cannot provide for all. More and more young people are thus leaving the reservation communities to try to find employment in urban areas, and this contributes to a decline at home. It also stresses family relationships, although many return for important events such as births, marriages, and funerals. All of these communities have weathered change before, and with the increased abilities and power now vested in their leadership, they will do it again. Old values coupled with new skills will see them through.

Catherine S. Fowler

Further Reading

Fowler, Catherine S., and Sven Liljeblad. "Northern Paiute." *Handbook of North American Indians*. Vol. 11. *Great Basin.* Ed. Warren L. d'Azevedo. Washington, DC: Smithsonian Institution (1986): 435–65.

Hittman, Michael. *A Numa History: The Yerington Paiute Tribe.* Yerington, NV: Yerington Paiute Tribe, 1984.

Johnson, Edward C. *Walker River Paiutes: A Tribal History.* Schurz, NV: Walker River Paiute Tribe, 1975.

Knack, Martha C., and Omer C. Stewart. *As Long as the River Shall Run: An Ethnohistory of Pyramid Lake Indian Reservation.* Berkeley: University of California Press, 1984.

Numa: A Northern Paiute History. Reno: Inter-Tribal Council of Nevada, 1976.

OWENS VALLEY PAIUTE

The people called Owens Valley Paiute in the mid-nineteenth century controlled a tract of land some one hundred twenty miles long by twenty to forty miles wide, encompassing the headwaters and terminus of the Owens River and paralleling the eastern slope of the Sierra Nevada in southern California. In addition to being called Owens Valley Paiute, they also occasionally have been referred to as Eastern Monos, Northern Paiutes, or merely Paiutes. Part of the confusion in names results from the recognition of certain linguistic and cultural similarities and differences with their neighbors: their language is essentially the same as that spoken by the Mono or Monache people west of the Sierra Nevada, while their culture is similar to that of the Northern Paiutes of Nevada and beyond. The people refer to themselves as Paiutes, although they recognize their language affiliation with the Mono or Monache. They also share environmental features and a northern border with the Northern Paiutes, and there remain many ties in that direction. However, they set themselves apart both linguistically and culturally from the Southern Paiute to the south and east.

Today the Owens Valley Paiute control a small fraction of their former lands. They live on four small tracts of reserved land within the Owens Valley: at Bishop, Big Pine, Lone Pine, and Fort Independence. A fifth small reservation is located outside the valley to the northeast of Bishop at Benton. All of these reservations were set aside after 1900, the population receiving little attention from the federal government before that time. In 1897, Indian day schools were in operation at Bishop and Big Pine, and one was opened at Independence a few years later. In 1902, a portion of what had been Camp or Fort Independence, a military post, was officially set aside for use by local Indians. In 1912, an executive order withdrew several tracts of lands near Bishop, Big Pine, and Lone Pine for consideration for reservation status and, ultimately, allotment. A small reserve was also set up at Benton in 1915, the same year the Fort Independence Reservation, including the lands reserved earlier, was officially established. Circumstances in later years would cause a few additions to these reserved lands, but mainly deletions.

The Owens Valley Paiute in precontact times had been hunters and gatherers, and occasionally fishermen. They also had irrigated, by means of an extensive system of ditches, tracts of land in various places in the valley that contained wild seed and root crops. For the most part, the twentieth-century reservations did not include these former tracts of irrigated lands, and they were also too small for people to continue any but an occasional pursuit of hunting, gathering, or fishing. Nor were they conducive to ranching, a common mode of subsistence for non-Indians who settled in the valley in the middle and late 1800s. Thus, the residents of the newly reserved lands became small-scale farmers and gardeners, and continued wage work in the towns and on the ranches, a pattern they had begun after the 1870s. Some families continued to live off-reservation in various parts of the valley on homesteads. Western Shoshone families from the southern part of Owens Valley, as well as areas to the east, also moved to the reservations, so that the communities now reflected mixed tribal origins.

The history of Owens Valley and all of its residents in the twentieth century has been intimately linked to that of the City of Los Angeles and its quest for water. From 1905 nearly to the present, the city has attempted, with considerable success, to acquire land and water throughout the Owens Valley and north into the Mono Lake Basin. These acquisitions have included Indian lands almost from the beginning—nineteen parcels held by individual Indian people before 1913. However, in 1937, the biggest exchanges and reductions in Indian lands occurred, by an act of Congress. In that year, all of the lands reserved by previous executive orders were exchanged for 1,391 acres already owned by the City of Los Angeles, along with the promise of new housing, fencing and some outbuildings, limited farm equipment, and consoli-

dated water rights. The lands exchanged in Bishop included several scattered tracts, thus bringing together Indian holdings into one reservation. Those at Big Pine and Lone Pine also consolidated some former holdings. Fort Independence voted against the exchange with the city, and retained its former reservation (see figure). The City of Los Angeles in return acquired several thousand acres of valuable watershed property in the northern part of the valley, as well as Indian water rights in several valley locations.

By the end of the 1930s, the City of Los Angeles owned 95 percent of the farmland and 85 percent of all town property in the valley. Although they leased some lands and water to local farmers and ranchers, this ownership effectively ended the local farming and ranching economy in which Indian people had participated as wage laborers. A few Indian people went to work for the Los Angeles Department of Water and Power, but these jobs hardly offset the losses. Promised improvements were made on the reservations, however, and the people adjusted as best they could. In the 1970s and 1980s, the valley's economy began to rebound as tourism developed.

The five reservations are presently governed by elected tribal councils (Fort Independence has a Business Council). However, the valley as a whole is also governed by the Owens Valley Paiute-Shoshone Board of Trustees, a body made up of certain numbers of council members from the reservations at Bishop, Big Pine, and Lone Pine (Fort Independence if a quorum is needed). The Board is responsible for administering programs that affect all Indian people in the valley, and in some cases, Inyo County in general. It operates a cultural center, gymnasium, and educational center on the Bishop Reservation, and oversees the Toiyabe Indian Health Project, which serves the entire area. The Board, as well as the separate reservations, sponsors cultural programs such as

Owens Valley Paiute Reservations, Populations, and Economic Resources

Tribe	Reservation Land in Acres	Population Total	Population Reservation	Government	Economic Resources
Bishop[1]	875	1,350	430 est.	Council of 5	Mini-storage; Teleworks center
Big Pine[1]	279	413	220 est.	Council of 5	Industrial park
Lone Pine[1]	237	296	190 est.	Council of 5	None at present
Fort Independence[1]	352.24	123	75 est.	Business Council of 3[2]	None at present
Benton	160	84	40 est.	Council of 5	None at present

[1]*Also under the Owens Valley Paiute-Shoshone Board of Trustees.*
[2]*General Council, made up of all members 21 years of age and older.*
Sources: USBIA "Indian Service Population and Labor Force Estimates," 1991; individual tribes.

yearly powwows (Bishop and Big Pine), handgame tournaments, arts shows, and exhibits at the museum and cultural center, etc.

All reservation communities report a high rate of Native language loss, and each has sponsored public or private programs in an attempt to revive language skills. Other cultural activities that are being revived or retained by families or communities include traditional funeral observances (Cry ceremony), pine nut and other Native food harvesting, basketry (to a limited extent only), hide working, beadwork, handgames, and singing. Employment in arts or crafts is limited, however, and most people continue to work in the local tourist-related businesses, in mining, or as service providers either through the tribes, the county, or the state.

Catherine S. Fowler

See also **California Tribes; Shoshone: Western**

Further Reading

Busby, Colin I., John M. Findlay, and James C. Bard. *A Cultural Overview of the Bureau of Land Management: Coleville, Bodie, Benton, and Owens Valley Planning Units, California.* Bakersfield, CA: Bureau of Land Management Cultural Resources Publications, Anthropology-History, 1980.

Kahrl, William L. *Water and Power: The Conflict Over Los Angeles' Water Supply in the Owens Valley.* Berkeley: University of California Press, 1982.

Liljeblad, Sven, and Catherine S. Fowler. "Owens Valley Paiute." *Handbook of North American Indians.* Vol. 11. *Great Basin.* Ed. Warren L. d'Azevedo. Washington, DC: Smithsonian Institution (1986): 412–34.

Steward, Julian H. "Ethnography of the Owens Valley Paiute." *University of California Publications in American Archaeology and Ethnology* 33:3: 233–350.

Walter, Nancy Peterson. "The Land Exchange Act of 1937: Creation of the Indian Reservations at Bishop, Big Pine, and Lone Pine, California through a Land Trade Between the United States of America and the City of Los Angeles." Ph.D. diss., Union Graduate School, Columbus, 1986.

SOUTHERN PAIUTE

Southern Paiute is a linguistic and cultural group in the northern Southwest and the southeastern Great Basin area. Both the language and the ethnic group are frequently referred to simply as "Paiute," not to be confused with the Northern Paiutes, a related but separate group who speak a mutually unintelligible language. In the mid-nineteenth century, when sustained contact with Euroamericans was just beginning, Southern Paiute territory covered a large contiguous area in Arizona, Utah, Nevada, and California. However, the ten modern Southern Paiute groups retain only a tiny portion of this land and tribal members now live in widely separated communities both on and off the reservations. Five Utah based Paiute bands or groups, Shivwits, Indian Peaks, Cedar City, Koosharem, and Kanosh, recently united to form a larger tribal entity, the Paiute Tribe of Utah. The San Juan Paiute Tribe's communities are located in both Arizona and Utah, within the presently constituted borders of the Navajo Reservation. The Kaibab Paiute Tribe has a reservation on the "Arizona Strip" north of the Grand Canyon. The three Southern Nevada tribes are Moapa, Las Vegas, and Pahrump. Pahrump is the only modern Southern Paiute political group that is not recognized by the federal government. It has, however, initiated a process to become federally recognized. One additional group, the Chemehuevi, are historically Southern Paiute and speak Paiute. However, because of their long-term association with the Colorado River Mohaves and their lack of association with other Southern Paiute groups, they will be mentioned only peripherally in this article.

Situation at the Onset of the Twentieth Century

By the beginning of the twentieth century, Paiute life had changed irrevocably. They had lost control over most of their traditional land to incoming groups. Diseases introduced by these groups had led to sharp declines in population. Paiutes lost land to miners and ranchers in California and Nevada, Mormon farmers in Utah and Arizona, and Navajos in what was to become the Western Navajo Reservation. In 1900, only Moapa had been allocated a reservation. This reservation was originally intended to accommodate all the Paiute groups, but by the turn of the century the efforts of local settlers had "successfully" reduced its size until it was insufficient to support even the Moapa band. Although the San Juan also lost land to Navajos and Mormons, they were the only Southern Paiute group that still retained access to much of their traditional land.

Many Paiutes continued to hunt, gather, and farm when they could, but the traditional resources remaining under Paiute control were no longer plentiful enough to supply all their subsistence needs. To support their families Paiutes were also selling crafts, working as farm and ranch hands and as domestics, and in the case of the San Juan, raising sheep and goats. Although eventually most Paiute groups were allocated small reservations, these were never large enough to allow them to return to a self-sufficient lifestyle.

Twentieth-Century History

Paiutes received very little government attention during the beginning and middle parts of the twentieth century. The educational, health, and economic needs of the Paiute people were ignored by the federal government and to a large extent by the state and local governments as well. Especially during the early part of the century, schooling was sporadic. Between 1900 and 1940 government-run day schools were established at Las Vegas, Shivwits, Moapa, and Kaibab, lasting from one year (Las Vegas) to about thirty years (Kaibab). When a day school was not available, some

Figure 1 Modern Organization of Southern Paiute Tribes				
Tribe or Band	Type of Government	Number of Council Members	Title and Name of 1992 Tribal Head	Funding for Tribal Head
Paiute Tribe of Utah	Council	6	Chairperson Geneal Anderson	Serves as Enrollment Officer
Shivwits Band (Utah)	Council	4	Chairman Mart Snow	Not paid
Indian Peaks Band (Utah)	Council	4	Chairperson Jeanine Borchardt	Not paid
Cedar Band (Utah)	Council	5	Chairman Marcus Bow	Not paid
Koosharem Band (Utah)	Council	4	Chairperson Vera Charles	Not paid
Kanosh Band (Utah)	Council	4	Chairman Mckay Pikyavit	Not paid
Kaibab (Arizona)	Council	7	Chairperson G. Bullett Benson	Paid with tribal funds
Moapa (Nevada)	Council	6	Chairperson Rosalyn Mike	Paid with tribal funds
Las Vegas (Nevada)	Council	7	Chairperson Alfreda Mitre	Paid with tribal funds
San Juan (Arizona & Utah)	Council	8	President Evelyn James	Serves as Enrollment Officer
Pahrump (Nevada)	Council	5	Chairperson Richard Arnold	Not paid

Source: Data supplied by the Southern Paiute BIA Field Station at Cedar City, Utah, September, 1992.

Figure 2 Southern Paiute Reservations, Populations, and Economic Resources				
Tribe	Reservation Land Area in Acres	Population Total	Population Reservation	Economic Resources
Paiute Indian Tribe of Utah[1]	32,458.00 (owned separately by the five bands)	609	438	Farming; Mining lease; Cattle lease; 2 Cut and Sew operations
Kaibab (Arizona)	120,840.00	212	84	Farming; Fruit trees; Campground
Moapa (Nevada)	71,950.65	273	186	Farming; Gift-shop; Mini-mart; Sand and gravel; Fireworks
Las Vegas (Nevada)	3,852.68	71	52	Smoke-shop; Mini-mart
San Juan (Arizona & Utah)	Does not have a separate reservation yet	221	115 living on traditional land	Basket-weaving co-op
Pahrump (Nevada)	Does not have a separate reservation yet	70	50 living on traditional land	None at the present

Source: Data supplied by the Southern Paiute BIA Field Station at Cedar City, Utah, September, 1992.
[1]Includes the five bands.

Paiute children were sent away to government boarding schools. Many Paiute children sent to boarding schools never returned to their home communities; some died from diseases caught at school, while others simply never returned after graduation. Throughout the first half of the twentieth century, Paiutes continued to die from disease in relatively high numbers. Poor nutrition and housing, and the lack of modern sanitation, led to endemic tuberculosis, frequent pneumonia, whooping cough, and high death rates from epidemics of influenza and measles. It was not until the 1930s (and in some communities until the 1950s) that the Paiute birth rate began to exceed the death rate.

Well into the middle of the century, most Paiutes were still serving as an underemployed pool of unskilled rural labor due to discrimination, inadequate educational opportunities, and the lack of an adequate resource base. Some groups even lost what little government support was available. The San Juan Paiute Reservation was returned to the public domain in 1922, only a year after an oil company expressed interest in drilling on their land. Despite a continuing San Juan presence, in 1933 the land was made part of the Navajo Reservation based on the Navajos' arguments that "Indians" had used the land from time immemorial and that therefore it should be returned to the Navajo Reservation. Indeed, after the consolidation of the various Navajo reservations in the mid-1930s, the needs and even the existence of the San Juan Paiutes were rarely noted.

In 1954, the Utah Paiutes were "terminated." The goal of termination was to remove Indian tribes from federal supervision and their land from trust status. Although the Utah groups did not meet the government's own economic or educational criteria, four Paiute bands were terminated: the Shivwits, Indian Peaks, Koosharem, and Kanosh. The Cedar City band was not terminated because it had no official status nor any trust land.

Not until the 1960s did Southern Paiute fortunes begin to take a turn for the better. Southern Paiutes had filed a claim with the Indian Claims Commission for compensation for lands that were illegally taken, and in 1965 were awarded a $7,253,165.19 court judgment. Paiutes who were members of groups without trust lands (reservations) received $7,522 each. Bands with trust lands voted on the distribution of the award. Moapa and Kaibab, for example, both decided to allocate a large portion of the money to economic and social development, creating projects which have provided income to the tribes and employment to their members.

During the 1970s, the Utah Paiute bands established a legal corporation which in addition to developing economic projects succeeded in reversing termination and in restoring their trust status. On April 3, 1980, the Paiute Indian Tribe of Utah Restoration Act was passed. This act restored the four terminated bands to federally recognized status and confirmed

the status of the Cedar City band. In addition, although each band kept its own government, the act united the five bands into one recognized tribe with a Tribal Council. During the same period the San Juan tribe began working on formal federal recognition through the Bureau of Indian Affairs' (BIA) Federal Acknowledgment Project. The San Juan tribe received final approval from the BIA for federal recognition, effective on March 28, 1990. While working on their federal recognition case in the 1980s, the San Juan also were involved in the Navajo-Hopi-Paiute land claims case. They testified in federal district court to their use of the reservation created by the 1934 Act in January 1990 and received the judge's opinion concerning their 1934 land use in July 1992.

Government

Most Southern Paiute tribes organized formally under the Indian Reorganization Act (IRA) of 1934. However, neither Pahrump nor San Juan were able to take advantage of the IRA option, and the original Utah bands had to reorganize after termination under the Paiute Restoration Act of April 3, 1980 (figure 1).

Although present-day Paiute communities have a form of government based more or less on the federally imposed model with a council and a chairperson, traditional beliefs about leadership and authority still inform their political practice. Traditionally, Paiute leaders were better viewed as spokespersons representing the group, rather than as independent decision makers. Leaders lasted only so long as they expressed the wishes of their followers. Most decision making was actually done by the consensus group composed of all adults. Modern Paiute governments with their written constitutions and elected officials still work in many ways like the more traditional governments. Leaders who veer significantly from what the group wishes do not remain in official position long, elected term or not. Also a number of informal political processes, such as "committees" of elders, greatly influence the course of political events. In fact, the Kaibab recently rewrote their Constitution to incorporate a number of these informal political processes.

Contemporary Issues

All the tribal governments are working on economic development projects to produce both revenue for the tribe and jobs for its members, but the type of development depends in part on the tribal land area, its situation, and the tribal population (figure 2). Although tribal members generally desire development, it has sometimes proved to be a divisive issue. In 1991, Kaibab, for example, turned down a hazardous waste incinerator project, but only after over a year of intratribal dispute. The project would have built the largest hazardous waste incinerator in the West on the Kaibab Paiute Reservation. Since the tribe was at the time having financial difficulties, accepting a project that would have made every Kaibab Paiute rich was especially tempting.

In addition to development issues, tribal governments are concerned with projects in health and education. Paiutes have much higher rates of certain diseases (e.g., adult onset diabetes) than non-Paiute communities. School children from Paiute communities are also very likely to be "at risk" educationally. Most communities have Community Health Representatives (CHRs) who monitor individuals with health problems (frequently diabetes related), provide in-home care, and set up needed health screenings and programs. These communities also have programs for their elderly, including craft programs, hot lunches, cut firewood, special housing, etc. Paiute communities have attempted to develop various educational programs for adults and ones for their children. Although various educational programs for adults and college scholarships are sometimes available, the relatively small size of most Paiute resident communities makes the development of bilingual and bicultural programs in the schools difficult.

Culture

A casual visitor to most Southern Paiute communities would find that the visible characteristics of the communities differ little from those of the non-Paiute communities which surround them. Although housing and clothing styles may resemble those of nearby communities, Paiute community organization and interaction clearly are founded on Paiute traditional culture. Traditional kinship principles and ideas about leadership and governing affect the character of community life. Paiutes from all groups also agree on the importance of traditional Southern Paiute language, rituals, and storytelling, although not all the groups have retained the same level of traditional knowledge.

The Paiute kinship system extends close ties to a wider network of people than does the Anglo one. Since the Paiute incest taboo forbids young people to marry a kinperson and since many Paiutes in their own community will be related to them, Paiute young people often have to look to other communities to find a non-kinperson to marry. The cumulative effect of Paiute kinship beliefs is to enlarge the number of people to whom one is related (consanguineally and affinally) and upon whom one can depend. A San Juan Paiute proverb states that "your friend is your enemy." This is interpreted by the San Juan to mean that your relatives are the only people upon whom you can truly count. Kinship networks also contribute to a certain community character. Children often move in with other relatives for varying amounts of time, sometimes at the child's wish and sometimes at the other relative's wish. Individuals and families move to other communities to be with different kin. Material possessions are frequently shared within large extended families, so that a present given to a Paiute in Kaibab may soon show up in Moapa, or two related families might even agree to swap houses. Close ties among kin, however, sometimes lead to distrust between unrelated families and political factions in the communities.

The Paiute language is spoken in varying degrees by members of the different tribes. Only in the San Juan tribe are children still learning the language as a first language. Southern Paiute is spoken by many older people in other Paiute communities, but the active or passive knowledge of the language among younger Paiutes varies by family. Many of the tribes are trying to record the language and hope to develop programs to encourage younger speakers.

Paiute Rituals

Various traditional Paiute rituals are still practiced today by some Southern Paiutes. Briefly described here are three of these rituals: the menarche and first childbirth rites of passage; and the Cry.

Clearly, one of the oldest of Southern Paiute rituals is the menarche ritual, conducted for a girl at the time of her first menstruation, and its symbolic twin, the rite of passage conducted for a couple after the birth of their first child. After the early decades of this century, these two rituals fell into disuse in nearly all of the Southern Paiute communities, although certain practices such as the abstention from cold water after childbirth may still be followed in a number of communities. For the San Juan, however, these two rituals have continued in an unbroken tradition from the nineteenth century to the present day. Among the San Juan, the menarcheal girl is isolated for four days in a separate room or separate area of a one-room house. Her male and female elders instruct her about the responsibilities and duties of a young woman, and about the taboos she must observe during these four days, such as not touching her face or hair with her hands, not eating animal foods, and not drinking cold liquids. In addition, she must run to the east at sunrise, and to the west at sunset. On the morning of the fifth day, several rituals are conducted to bring the overall ritual to closure. These include bathing the girl in cold water; dressing her in clean clothes; putting red ocher or white clay pigment on her cheeks; feeding her rabbit or sheep liver wrapped in cedar and other bitter herbs and having her spit some into the fire; singeing or cutting the ends of her hair; and "massaging" her body to shape it into its proper adult shape.

Although hospital births are now the norm among the San Juan Paiute and the parts of the birth customs dealing with the actual birth can no longer be followed, the first childbirth continues to be an important rite of passage for young men and women in the San Juan community. The parturient woman observes dietary taboos on meat, salt, and cold water for thirty days and the taboo on touching her head or face except with a scratching stick. If there is a husband living with her, then he, too, observes these same taboos, for four days or up to the full thirty-day period. In addition, his wife's kin instruct him on his new role as father and give him various daily tasks. He must also run each morning toward sunrise and each evening toward the sunset. At the close of the thirty days, the couple bathe in cold water, have their faces painted with red ocher and the tips of their hair clipped, and are given the ritual meal of liver with cedar leaves to spit in the fire.

Some time prior to 1870, the Cry ceremony and the Cry songs that form its ritual backbone were introduced to the Southern Paiutes of Las Vegas, Pahrump, and Moapa as a memorial ceremony by the Chemehuevi, who had themselves adopted it earlier from the Mohave. By the 1890s, the Cry had become an integral element of community life in all the Paiute groups with the exception of the San Juan, who still do not consider the Cry to be a part of their traditional way. A memorial Cry consists of groups of singers singing song cycles and a "giveaway" of valuables to the guests. Although in the past Cry ceremonies lasted several nights, today they last one or sometimes two nights and are performed the night before a church funeral, as well as a year or so later as a memorial. On the last night from sunset to sunrise, two song cycles, the Salt Songs, and the Bird Songs, are sung by two groups of singers. Friends and family paying their respects give emotional speeches about the deceased person during pauses between songs.

Southern Paiute belief and ritual is grounded in a mythological cycle of stories often called Coyote Tales or Winter Stories. These stories describe a myth-time peopled with mythological characters who have the names of animals but act like people. These stories set forth standards of proper and improper behavior, and provide cosmological explanations for the origins of life crisis rituals and prescriptions. In addition to this important genre of stories, Southern Paiutes tell legends which take place in real time but often include supernatural elements, as well as a number of other types of stories such as ghost stories, funny stories, historical stories, etc.

Traditional Paiute storytelling is still a part of most of the Southern Paiute communities. A few of the groups are attempting to videotape their stories to save for future generations or to use in Paiute cultural programs for their youngsters. Only San Juan storytellers still tell the traditional stories in traditional settings to an audience of family members of all ages. Coyote and the other myth-time characters are still familiar to many Paiute children, however, as stories continue to be told in English.

Pamela A. Bunte

Robert J. Franklin

See also **Arizona Tribes; Chemehuevi; Colorado River Indian Tribes**

Further Reading

Bunte, Pamela A., and Robert J. Franklin. *From the Sands to the Mountain: Change and Persistence in a Southern Paiute Community*. Lincoln and London: University of Nebraska Press, 1987.

Euler, Robert C. *Southern Paiute Ethnohistory*. University of Utah Anthropological Papers 78. Salt Lake City: University of Utah Press, 1973.

Kelly, Isabel T. *Southern Paiute Ethnography*. Glen Canyon Series 21. University of Utah Anthropological Papers 69. Salt Lake City: University of Utah Press, 1964.

Kelly, Isabel T., and Catherine S. Fowler. "Southern Paiute." *Handbook of North American Indians*. Vol. 11. *Great Basin*. Ed. Warren L. d'Azevedo. Washington, DC: Smithsonian Institution (1986): 368–97.

Knack, Martha C. *Life Is with People*. Socorro, NM: Ballena Press Anthropological Papers 19, 1980.

PAMUNKEY

The Pamunkey Indian tribe's land base consists of a reservation on the Pamunkey River in King William County, Virginia. It contains approximately 1,200 acres and dates from a 1677 treaty with the British Crown. Thirty families reside on the reservation, and many tribal members live in nearby Richmond and Newport News. Other tribesmen are scattered in New Jersey, New York, and Pennsylvania. The tribal roll has not been updated in several years; however, the estimate in 1991 was 450.

The Pamunkey have a long history of contact with the State of Virginia. Every autumn the Tribal Council pays tribute to the governor of Virginia, in the form of freshly killed game, upholding the requirements of the 1677 treaty.

In 1855 the Richmond and York River Rail Road (now the Southern Railway) encroached on Pamunkey lands by laying tracks across the reservation. This issue was litigated in 1979, and a monetary settlement and leasing agreement was quickly reached between the tribe and Southern Railway. The agreement was ratified by the United States Congress in 1980. A second small land claim languishes in court.

The twentieth-century chiefs include: Theodore T. Dennis (1898 to 1902); George M. Cook (1902 to 1942); Tecumseh D. Cook (1942 to 1984); William H. Miles (1984 to 1990); and William P. Miles (1990 to the present). Tribal affairs are handled by an all-male Pamunkey tribal government consisting of seven councilmen, a Pamunkey Indian Baptist Church Governing Board, six tribal non-Indian trustees appointed by the Tribal Council, and numerous committees which are created to fill special needs.

Today the Pamunkey Indians are deeply involved in preserving their surviving traditions. The Pamunkey Indian Museum, built in 1979 under the direction of Warren Cook, leads this effort. Two videos have been produced recently: "The Old Ways: The Pamunkey Indian Women's Pottery Guild" (Pamunkey Museum/Cinebar, 1988); and "The Ways of Our Fathers" (Pamunkey Museum/Cinebar, 1990). The latter video documents Pamunkey deadfall traps, turtling, and shad fishing. In 1985, the Museum also published a major pamphlet on Pamunkey pottery entitled *The Pamunkey Tradition: Documenting the Past*. The museum is visited by large numbers of school children who are given tours and instruction concerning Pamunkey culture.

While the Pamunkey Indians have been able to find regular employment in the public sector since World War II, this has not always been the case. Much of surviving Pamunkey culture is indebted to a subsistence lifestyle centered around pottery making, fishing, hunting, and trapping. As long as anyone can recall, the Pamunkey Indians have made a living from the Pamunkey River and its environs. While the men turned to their boats, the women made pottery. By 1900, pottery making was in a serious decline, and in 1932 the state employed a teacher to revive the tradition. Since then, the Pamunkey Pottery Guild has made and marketed Pamunkey wares. Today two types of pottery are constructed and sold at the Museum: traditional wares burned in an open fire, and schoolhouse pottery which is painted, glazed, and kiln fired.

Thomas J. Blumer

Further Reading

Pollard, John Garland. *The Pamunkey Indians of Virginia.* Bureau of American Ethnology Bulletin 17. Washington, DC: U.S. Government Printing Office, 1894.

Rountree, Helen C. *Pocahontas's People: The Powhatan Indians of Virginia through Four Centuries.* Norman: University of Oklahoma Press, 1990.

———. "Indian Virginians on the Move." *Indians of the Southeastern United States in the Late 20th Century.* Ed. J. Anthony Paredes. Tuscaloosa, AL and London, England: University of Alabama Press (1992): 9–28.

Speck, Frank G. "Chapters on the Ethnology of the Powhatan Tribes of Virginia." *Indian Notes and Monographs* 1:5. New York, NY: Museum of the American Indian, Heye Foundation, 1928.

Stern, Theodore. "Pamunkey Pottery Making." *Southern Indian Studies* 3 (1951): 1–78.

PAN-INDIANISM

Pan-Indianism refers to a process by which Native North Americans have elected, sometimes voluntarily, sometimes under coercion, to transcend the particularities of their cultural-national heritage, creating instead a single overarching sense of "Indianness," shared by all indigenous peoples on the continent. It is, as a number of analysts have observed, an extremely complex social phenomenon, containing as it does not only the potential for a strengthening of Native America vis-à-vis the dominant Euroamerican culture, but the elements of a system with which Euroamerica can more efficiently subordinate Indians, and even the seeds of destruction for many individual Native nations. Correspondingly, it is seen differently by different people in different parts of the country.

In seeking to pick up the threads of Pan-Indianism, its historical development and its present breadth and direction, many observers have located the roots of the idea in a pre-Columbian trend among Native peoples of the Northeast to broaden their concep-

tions of themselves, overcoming specific intergroup divisions to establish new forms of unity. "There was," to quote Cherokee anthropologist Robert K. Thomas, "wholesale institutional adoption of captives from other tribes and, at the very least, incipient confederacies were forming which included tribes which spoke different languages." Early evidence of this tendency may be found in the forging of the Haudenosaunee or "Five Nations Iroquois Confederacy" in the Northeast at least as early as A.D. 1350. Another example is in the alliance made by the various Pueblos of present-day New Mexico and Arizona, a matter which resulted in their unified and temporarily successful revolt against Spanish rule in 1680.

The trend toward Pan-Indianism was accelerated during the seventeenth century as Indians increasingly banded together to resist the early phases of European invasion along the eastern seaboard. One outcome of this process was a political/military alliance of midwestern peoples in 1763 under the Ottawa leader, Pontiac, and an accompanying intertribal religious movement. Later, during the early part of the nineteenth century, a similar movement headed by Tecumseh, a Shawnee leader, involved a still larger number of eastern peoples and marked the beginning of the great intertribal councils of the period. Still later, on the Great Plains, the Pan-Indianist dynamic was given even greater impetus, probably because wholesale adoption of the horse by the peoples of that region allowed for accentuated mobility, regularized intergroup communications, and a heightened capacity for mutual military defense. Examples include the relationship between the Comanches, Kiowas, and Kiowa Apaches on the southern Plains from roughly 1830 to 1875, and that of the Lakotas, Cheyennes, and Arapahos to the north, from about 1840 to 1877.

Up to this point, it is evident that the Pan-Indian impulse assumed the form of a pattern of alliances serving to preserve and enhance, rather than to diminish, the autonomy and integrity of each participating indigenous people. With the end of the Indian Wars, however, the federal government began to pursue its own notion of Pan-Indianism, one which featured the sort of "supratribalist" amalgamation of Native peoples advocated by a group of influential whites known as the "Friends of the Indian." At a series of conferences conducted at Lake Mohonk, New York, the Friends developed what they felt were "humane and enlightened alternatives" to the posture of outright physical extermination advocated by the army (e.g., General Philip H. Sheridan) and those aligned with it (e.g., future President Theodore Roosevelt), and which at the time constituted the core of the United States policy towards Indians.

In essence, the Friends' main lobbying organization—the so-called Indian Rights Association, founded in 1882—recommended that Washington take steps to undermine whatever internal cohesion remained in individual indigenous nations. Simultaneously, they argued, Indians should be carefully conditioned to view themselves as a more-or-less homogeneous ethnic group "naturally" subsumed within the "broader" and "inherently superior" Euroamerican society. Interested mainly in absorbing the residue of conquered lands and peoples, United States policy makers quickly advanced these ideas as an agenda of wholesale "assimilation" of Native peoples.

The first half of the Friends' assimilationist equation was addressed through legislation, such as the 1885 Major Crimes Act (which made Native peoples subject to Euroamerican law, even within their own territories); the 1887 General Allotment Act (which replaced traditional Native systems of collective occupancy of land with Euroamerican notions of individuated ownership); and, eventually, the 1924 Indian Citizenship Act (which incorporated indigenous people directly into the United States polity, whether they desired such inclusion or not). At the same time, an across-the-board program requiring compulsory attendance at boarding schools—where Indian children from various peoples were deliberately intermixed, isolated from their homes and communities for years on end, systematically "deculturated," and then steeped in the values and mores of Euroamerican tradition—was aimed at accomplishing the second half.

All of this greatly increased the rate at which Pan-Indian sensibilities were embraced, a matter witnessed by the proliferation during the late nineteenth and early twentieth centuries of a number of explicitly supratribal social and spiritual expressions. Perhaps most notable in the social connection was the steadily rising popularity of intertribal powwows. The spread of the Native American Church, often called the "Peyote Religion," exemplifies the spiritual dimension. In a somewhat more political vein, a group which included many highly acculturated individuals including Arthur C. Parker (Seneca), Charles Eastman (Santee Dakota), Charles E. Daganett (Peoria), and Carlos Montezuma (Apache) collaborated in 1911 to found the first genuine Pan-Indianist organization on a national basis, the Society of American Indians. Subsequently, a number of comparable groups were created, including the All Indian Pueblo Council (1919), Grand Council Fire of American Indians (1923), Indian Association of America (1932), and the Indian Confederation of America (1933).

Eventually, this trend fostered the creation of a whole cluster of federally supported supratribal entities, most of them finding their birth in the Indian Reorganization Act of 1934, and Indian Commissioner John Collier's Indian New Deal programs of the late 1930s. These include the National Congress of American Indians (NCAI, founded in 1944), National Indian Education Association (NIEA, founded in 1970), National Tribal Chairmen's Association (NCTA, founded in 1971), Native American Rights Fund (NARF, founded in 1970), and the Council of Energy Resource Tribes (CERT, founded in 1976).

Meanwhile, the logic of socio-cultural, political, and economic integration had reached the point where Congress in 1953 adopted House Resolution 108, a measure through which the United States assigned itself the prerogative to dissolve selected Native nations altogether. Over the next decade, 109 indigenous peoples was summarily "terminated," often declared "extinct" by legislative fiat, their members usually scattered to the winds. This was coupled with a wider program dubbed "relocation," through which large numbers of Indians were encouraged to leave their reservations for urban locales where they typically ended up jumbled together in impoverished inner city Indian ghettos. The scale upon which this process was pursued is evidenced in the fact that, by 1980, the United States Census Bureau reported more than half of the country's 1.6 million identified Indians had been dispersed into cities where they were not only "intertribalized," but subsumed within the far greater mass of Euroamerican, African-American, Asian American, and Latino populations.

Faced with this sort of frontal assault on the very existence of their constituency, such groups as NCAI were compelled to mount a relatively fierce resistance. Nonetheless, NCAI's method—aligning itself with liberal Democrats as an expedient to countering the terminationist sentiments associated with conservative Republicans in Congress—served in the end more to perfect than to dismantle the structure of federal power over Indians. In effect, the *quid pro quo* involved in bringing termination to a halt was NCAI's endorsement of the Democratic Indian Civil Rights Act of 1968, a bill which mired Native North America even more deeply in the bog of United States jurisdiction and control. This was followed, in 1975, by acceptance of the Indian Self-Determination and Education Assistance Act, a measure designed to make Native people themselves responsible for administering a whole range of federal programs.

The supratribalist version of Pan-Indianism's participation in the ongoing erosion of indigenous rights, always under the mantle of protecting them, led to an explosive frustration within important sectors of many Native communities during the 1960s. In rejecting supratribalism as the domain of "sell-outs" and "Uncle Tomahawks," a number of those sharing this perspective began themselves to hammer out a concept of Pan-Indianism which had far more in common with that of Pontiac and Tecumseh than with the more recent and federally sanctioned manifestations of the NCAI, NTCA, NARF, and CERT. By 1961, the first organizational expression of this new "Red Power" tendency, the National Indian Youth Council (NIYC), had appeared. It was followed, over the course of the decade, by other groups like the American Indian Movement (AIM, founded in 1968) and Indians of All Tribes (founded in 1969), the International Indian Treaty Council (IITC, founded in 1974), and Women of All Red Nations (WARN, founded in 1975).

By-and-large, the Red Power alternative, although it is composed of people representing diverse Native peoples, has been marked by an uncompromising reassertion of the prerogatives of each indigenous nation in its own right and a concomitant willingness to offer direct physical challenges to any United States denial of these prerogatives. The advent of groups like NIYC, AIM, and WARN, despite insistent denunciation of them by federal authorities and supratribalist organizations alike, has had an undeniably positive effect in instilling the kind of pride and dignity among Indians which comes with a sense that at least some among them retain the capacity to "stand on their own two hind legs and fight back in the manner of our ancestors." It was this, perhaps more than anything else, which Thomas concludes, that, whatever else may be said of it, Pan-Indianism remains "a vital social movement which is forever changing and growing."

M.A. Jaimes

See also **American Indian Movement; Council of Energy Resource Tribes; Government Policy; Indian Rights Association; International Indian Treaty Council; National Congress of American Indians; National Indian Education Association; National Indian Youth Council; Native American Rights Fund; Organizations and Tribal Cooperation; Peyote Religion; Powwow; Red Power; Society of American Indians**

Further Reading

Cornell, Steven. *The Return of the Native: American Indian Political Resurgence.* London, England and New York, NY: Oxford University Press, 1988.

Hertzberg, Hazel W. *The Search for American Indian Identity: Modern Pan-Indian Movements.* NY: Syracuse University Press, 1971.

Stewart, James H. "Urbanization, Peoplehood and Modes of Identity: Native Americans in Cities." *Identity and Awareness in Minority Experience.* Eds. George E. Carter and James R. Parker. LaCross: Institute for Minority Studies, University of Wisconsin (1975): 108–36.

Svenson, Frances. "Ethnicity versus Communalism: The American Indian Movement and the Politics of Survival." *The Mobilization of Collective Identity: Comparative Perspectives.* Eds. Jeffrey A. Ross and Ann Baker Cottrell. Langham, MD: University Press of America (1980): 65–88.

Thomas, Robert K. "Pan-Indianism." *The Emergent Native Americans: A Reader in Culture Contact.* Ed. Deward E. Walker, Jr. Boston, MA: Little, Brown & Co. (1972): 741–46.

Papago

See Tohono O'odham

PASSAMAQUODDY

The Passamaquoddy (meaning "Pollock-Spearing Place") have two reservations located in Maine's poorest and easternmost county. Sipayik (pop. 560), the main village since 1770, is established at Pleasant Point Reservation (225 acres), a promontory in Passamaquoddy Bay. Fifty miles inland is Motahkokmikuk (pop. 550), situated in Indian Township, a 23,000-acre reservation of thick forest on the Schoodic Lakes chain. Founded in 1852 by a conservative faction following a political quarrel (the "War of the Flags") with their more progressive opponents at Sipayik, it consists of two neighborhoods, separated by a seven-mile paved road: Peter Dana Point at Big Lake; and the Strip, near the town of Princeton, overlooking Lewey Lake. Since 1900 the tribe has grown from 460 to about 2,500 members, about half of whom live off the reservations. Membership is based on birth, but adoption is possible for those of at least one-quarter Indian blood. Each reservation has a biennially elected government, consisting of a governor, lieutenant governor, and a six-member council. The supreme governing body is the sixteen-member Joint Tribal Council, cochaired by the governors from both reservations. It makes decisions on matters that concern the tribe as a whole. A tribal representative at the Maine State Legislature is chosen alternately between the two reservations. Although the current elective government was introduced in the 1870s, following the death of the last Passamaquoddy life-chief, its political structure has frequently been modified.

The tribe made a treaty with Massachusetts in 1794 (which failed to be ratified by the United States Congress), relinquishing aboriginal title to its lands in return for several islands, a 23,000-acre township, and some small tracts, including 10 acres on Pleasant Point, which increased to 99 acres in 1801. In 1820, when it gained statehood, Maine became the tribe's guardian and enforced all its laws on the reservations, approved any changes in the operation of tribal government, dispatched an Indian agent to oversee the elections, etc. Three years later, the tribe gained non-voting representation to the Maine legislature. In 1856, using proceeds from the sale of timber, grass, etc., from tribal lands, the state established a Passamaquoddy Trust Fund to finance emergency aid for the needy. In 1929 the tribe fell under the Forestry Department, followed by Health and Welfare in 1932. From 1936 onwards the state issued them free hunting and fishing licenses. During World War II, the United States government took part of Indian Township to serve as a German POW camp, later selling it off to non-Indians. In 1953, as the last state to ratify the 1924 United States Indian Citizenship Act, Maine permitted the tribe to vote in state elections. A special Department of Indian Affairs was founded in 1965, but was abolished in 1981 when the state was replaced by the federal government as trustee.

Despite railway connections established in the nineteenth century, both reservations turned into deprived enclaves. Sipayik traditionally depended on the sea (weir-fishing, lobstering, clamming, and seal and porpoise hunting) and later specialized in commercial scale basketry for the nearby sardine fisheries. Motahkokmikuk relied more on hunting and trapping, succeeded by some farming, logging, and sportsguiding. Both also engaged in migrant labor (raking blueberries and picking potatoes), and making items such as sweetgrass and splint baskets, rustic furniture, canoe paddles, axe handles, snowshoes, moccasins, and Christmas wreaths. By the 1960s many people began to abandon the reservations to escape growing economic and cultural poverty, leaving only some 300 at Sipayik and 200 at Motahkokmikuk.

Then came a radical reversal when the people of Motahkokmikuk discovered that the state had sold or leased off some 6,000 acres at Indian Township. In 1964 fifty Native Americans under Governor John Stevens staged a protest against further encroachment, starting what became a major Native rights struggle. Eight years later Native American Rights Fund (NARF) attorney Thomas N. Tureen filed suit for the tribe against the United States Department of the Interior (*Passamaquoddy v. Morton*). He argued that the 1790 Trade and Intercourse Act also applied to the Passamaquoddy and Penobscot, entitling them to a federal trust relationship. The federal district court ruled in their favor, which affirmed that they might have a valid claim to about two-thirds of Maine. While the Justice Department was forced to sue the state for $300 million and 350,000 acres, complex out-of-court negotiations led to the 1980 Maine Indian Claims Settlement Act, in which each tribe dropped its claims in exchange for $13.5 million in funds and $26.5 million to purchase 150,000 acres as trust land. Both gained a unique status as both a federally recognized tribe and a municipality—that is, with the exception of jurisdiction over its domestic relations and small claims between members, and the right to try misdemeanors and minor infractions in their tribal courts, they are subject to the civil and criminal jurisdiction of the state. Members do pay state taxes on income earned on the reservations. Although the tribes set their own rules of fishing, hunting, and trapping, Maine's basic regulatory laws still apply on tribal lands, as monitored by the Maine Indian Tribal State Commission. Until the Passamaquoddy ratify their new tribal constitution, relevant state laws already on the books will continue to be observed.

Today, in addition to their reservation lands, the Passamaquoddy have purchased about 134,000 acres of trust land, including 1,000 acres adjacent to Pleasant Point, 6,000 acres of blueberry barrens and forest located northwest of Indian Township, and in western Maine along the Quebec border. They have had considerable success with capital investments (e.g., the Dragon Cement Plant—sold after only five years, earning them $60 million in 1988—and Northeastern Blueberry Farms). They run a high-stakes bingo operation, own two radio stations, operate a cable television program, and have some small businesses. They also own a lucrative patent on a scrubber designed to control coal emissions that cause acid rain. Based on trust fund interest and investment dividends, tribal members receive quarterly per capita payments (about $250) and an occasional bonus.

Once eligible for federal funding and services (housing, education, health care, social services, etc.), the Passamaquoddy's annual budget mushroomed from a few thousand dollars to about $4 million. With new offices, a health center, primary school, and modern homes to replace old shanties, tribal government has become by far the largest and best-paying employer. New housing and free health care have drawn many members back to the reservation, and new work opportunities have lowered unemployment from about 80 to 30 percent. Although formal education began in 1824, few ever completed school until Maine Indian scholarships became available in 1934. Now, many are enrolled in the university. While few of the young speak Passamaquoddy, half of all adults still know the language. To preserve its heritage, the tribe had its language codified in the 1970s and employed bilingual educators to teach the Native tongue, as well as its history, arts, and crafts. Other important cultural resources include the Wapohnaki Museum at Sipayik, and the annual Indian Days celebrations, which have taken place since 1965 and include ceremonial dances, crafts sales, and traditional food. Finally, while anti-Indian prejudice has eased, major social problems still haunt the tribe, including high alcoholism. But, after four centuries of European contact, there is hope for the tribe's cultural survival.

Harald E.L. Prins

See also Penobscot

Further Reading

Brodeur, Paul. *Restitution: The Land Claims of the Mashpee, Passamaquoddy, and Penobscot Indians of New England.* Boston, MA: Northeastern University Press, 1985.

Luckhardt, Joan C. "Passamaquoddy Indians and Local Whites: Interconnections and Conflicts within a Changing Political Economy, 1600–1983," Ph.D. diss., Rutgers University, 1985.

Maine Indian Program. *The Wabanakis of Maine and the Maritimes: A Resource Book about Passamaquoddy, Maliseet, Micmac, and Abenaki Indians.* Bath, ME: New England Regional Office of the American Friends Service Committee, 1989.

Stevens, Susan M. "Passamaquoddy Economic Development in Cultural and Historical Perspective." *American Indian Economic Development.* Ed. Sam Stanley. The Hague, Netherlands and Paris, France: Mouton, 1978.

U.S. Congress. Senate Select Committee on Indian Affairs. *Hearings on Proposed Settlement of Maine Indian Land Claims.* 96th Cong., 2d sess. S. 2829. 2 vols. Washington, DC: U.S. Government Printing Office, 1980.

PATWIN

See Wintun

PAUGUSSETT

The seventeenth-century Paugussett (Paugasuck) were a loose confederation of five Algonquian-speaking tribes—the Pequannock, Wepawaug, Naugatuck, Pootatuck, and Paugussett—with lands in what is now

Fairfield County, Connecticut. Following the Pequot War, white settlement began, with Native lands sold and confiscated. Seventeenth-century reservations dwindled until the Golden Hill Paugussetts, descendents of the Pequannock tribe, held only one quarter of an acre in 1875, the oldest reservation in the United States. The tribe was brought under state trusteeship in 1886, and the quarter acre in Trumbull, Connecticut, was administered by the State Parks and Forests Agency.

Stewardship was transferred to the Department of Welfare in 1941, which discouraged tribal members from inhabiting tribal lands. Members of the Sherman family continuously occupied the quarter-acre reservation. In 1973 the commissioner of the Department of Environmental Protection shared jurisdiction over the reservation with the Connecticut Indian Affairs Council (CIAC). The Golden Hill Paugussetts became members of the CIAC in 1974, represented by Aurelius Piper (Big Eagle) who succeeded Edward Sherman (Black Hawk) as chief. In 1976 a neighbor claimed ownership of the reservation. The tribe came together and, with support from other groups and American Indian Movement (AIM) members, won the suit. A building was finished in 1975 to serve as a home for the chief, a tribal school, museum, and office. Renewed action of the same suit failed again in the 1980s. In an effort to gain a larger land base, the tribe received a 1979 grant from the Department of Housing and Urban Development, purchasing 69 acres in Colchester, which was later expanded to 108 acres. The land has been developed with wildlife areas and trails, and a tribal business is under construction.

The tribe's more than one hundred and twenty members (with approximately eighty-five living locally) have been trying to gain federal acknowledgment since 1982 and are currently preparing a petition. In 1992 the tribe brought suit to claim ninety-one acres in Bridgeport, part of one of their original reservations. The tribe hopes to gain federal acknowledgment, use settlement monies to purchase more land, and plans construction of a casino, as well as tribal social programs. Tribal members are engaged in a variety of activities, including crafts, drumming, and sweat lodge ceremonies, as well as public education and counseling. Many are actively involved in AIM, and others work for Native American rights and sovereignty.

Ann McMullen

Further Reading

Guillette, Mary E. "Golden Hill Paugussett Tribe." *American Indians in Connecticut: Past to Present*, GH1-17. Hartford: Connecticut Indian Affairs Council, 1979.

Smith, Claude Clayton. *Quarter-Acre of Heartache*. Blacksburg, VA: Pocahontas Press, 1985.

Wojciechowski, Franz L. *The Paugusseett Tribes: An Ethnohistorical Study of the Tribal Interrelationships of the Indians in the Lower Housatonic River Area.*

Nijmegen, The Netherlands: Catholic University of Nijmegen, Department of Cultural and Social Anthropology, 1985.

PAWNEE

The Pawnee tribe is divided into four bands: Pitahawirata, Kitkahahki, Chaui, and Skidi. In 1893 their 203,020-acre reservation in north central Oklahoma was allotted to 820 individuals with the surplus 171,088 acres open to non-Indian sale and settlement. Today a tribally owned reserve of a few hundred acres on the site of the old Pawnee Indian School contains the tribal offices, the ceremonial roundhouse, the community building, the Roam Chief Recreation Building, and campgrounds where tribal meetings and dances are held. Although Pawnees continue to live in the area, the majority reside in other parts of the state or in cities throughout the United States.

The Pawnee Agency of the Bureau of Indian Affairs supervises sales of Pawnee trust land or its leasing for agricultural use, or oil and gas exploration. Indian funds obtained from these sources and the annual annuity of $30,000 (Treaty of 1857) are dispersed per capita by this agency. Various claims against the United States government for tribal funds owed the Pawnee have been made since the 1920s. In 1966, the Indian Claims Commission awarded $7,316,098 ($6,400,000 after various costs were subtracted) to be paid to the tribe for aboriginal lands in Kansas and Nebraska ceded to the United States in the last century. In the 1970s, the Pawnees also successfully pressed for return of certain tribal reserve lands given by the United States government to the city of Pawnee, Oklahoma. In 1992, the state government and Indian tribes of Oklahoma discussed the issues of tribal sovereignty versus state's rights pertaining to taxation on Indian-run reservation business sales (smokeshops), and the building of gambling casinos.

In the 1980s and 1990s tribally sponsored public bingo games provided some funds for tribal government expenses and other projects. Grants from the United States government and other sources have enabled the Pawnee to institute programs for assisting tribal members, such as transportation and noon meals for the elderly. Drug and alcohol abuse programs, food commodity programs, Indian Health Service clinics, child welfare, mental health, and job skill training programs have existed at various times.

The present tribal government, established by the Oklahoma Indian Welfare Act of 1934, contains two eight-member governing bodies: the chiefs or Nasharo Council and the Business Council. The chiefs are chosen by their bands and the Business Council is elected at large. The tribal government endeavors to protect tribal members' rights, promotes economic development, and serves as an intermediary with the United States government. Both men and women are qualified to serve. Conflict with the Bureau of Indian Affairs and power struggles between the two councils have occurred. The Tribal Constitution and Bylaws have been amended from time to time to meet changing conditions.

In less than a century, the tribal population dropped from 10,000 to 600 in 1906. Poor living conditions, untreated diseases, hunger, and starvation resulted from inept government policies and practices. Tribal health and economic conditions have improved since the beginning of the twentieth century, and the population rebounded to about 2,500 Pawnees by the early 1990s.

Despite a high unemployment rate around Pawnee itself, individual Pawnees have been employed in the past and present as farmers, housepainters, surveyors, artists, silversmiths, beadworkers, professional traditional dancers, and members of the armed services. Men worked on the Civilian Conservation Corps during the Great Depression and several left Oklahoma during World War II to work in the defense industry. Many of these people did not return to Oklahoma after the war. The tribe had its first medical school graduate in the 1980s, Dr. Charles Knife Chief. John Echohawk, director of the Native American Rights Fund, is only one of several Pawnee attorneys promoting Indian rights.

Pawnees have attended Pawnee Indian School, Carlisle Indian School, Haskell Institute, and Chilocco Indian School, learning labor and other skills. Later in the century, many men and women who had served in the armed forces took advantage of the GI Bill and attended college. Continued participation in higher education is funded by government grants.

The tribe maintains some aspects of its cultural heritage. However, the use of the language is gradually disappearing. Attendance at the government schools listed above usually resulted in punishment of students using their Native languages. Until the 1990s, Pawnee singers understood the language of their songs, but memorization without comprehension now often occurs among many younger singers.

Pawnee social clubs and groups sponsor various events. The Pocohontas Club, the Service Club, and the War Mothers Club help with tribal functions. The Pawnee Veterans Organization is probably the most important group, sponsoring the annual four-day Pawnee Homecoming in July. Money for this and other events is raised throughout the year from donations, suppers, and handgames. Various Pawnee cultural activities survive, including war dances, round dances, a modified Ghost Dance, handgames, the Young Dog Dance, and the Kitkahahki War Dance. Other dances such as the Pipe, Buffalo, Bear, and Doctor Dances were performed until the owners of these dances and ceremonies died early in the twentieth century. Men, women, and children attend dances dressed in either everyday clothes or dance outfits and are accompanied by men singers seated around a large drum. Food is provided by tribal members and a meal is prepared and served for all participants.

The Native American Church and Christian churches (including fundamentalist sects) have members among the Pawnee. Formerly, traditional Pawnee religion was noted for its ceremonial complexity, its Sacred Bundles, and the importance of anthropomorphic figures in nature and the heavens, of which *Tirawahut*, an abstraction similar to the Judeo-Christian "God," was preeminent.

Martha Royce Blaine

See also **Oklahoma Tribes; Powwow**

Further Reading

Blaine, Martha Royce. *The Pawnees: A Critical Bibliography.* Bloomington: Indiana University Press, 1980.
———. *Pawnee Passage, 1870–1875.* Civilization of the American Indian 202. Norman: University of Oklahoma Press, 1990.
Champe, John Leland, and Franklin Fenenga. "Notes on the Pawnee." *Pawnee and Kansa (Kaw) Indians.* New York, NY: Garland Publishing, 1974.
Hyde, George E. *The Pawnee Indians.* New ed. Civilization of the American Indian 128. Norman: University of Oklahoma Press, 1974.
Weltfish, Gene. *The Lost Universe, with a Closing Chapter on the Universe Regained.* 1965. Reprinted as *The Lost Universe: Pawnee Life and Culture.* Lincoln: University of Nebraska Press, 1977.

PECOS

See Pueblo of Jemez

PEEDEE

The PeeDee (which is also spelled Pee Dee or Peedee) of South Carolina are not to be confused with the PeeDee of the colonial period, for the contemporary group is related to the Lumbee Tribe of North Carolina. Members of this largest Indian tribe in South Carolina live in four counties: Chesterfield, Dillon, Marlboro, and Marion. The principal PeeDee communities include Pleasant Hill, Sand Hill, Latta, and the Locklear Indian Community. Other population concentrations are located in Bennettsville, Clio, McColl, and Little Rock.

The tribal roll contains about 2,500 names. As of 1993 the elected chief is Rodney Roller and the blood or hereditary chief is David Locklear. The Council consists of both chiefs, a secretary/treasurer, and three council members who are elected at large. The tribe attempts to have representatives from the major communities serve on the Council.

The PeeDee are currently seeking state recognition. A major goal is to establish a center where the Council will have meeting rooms and office space. In recent years, the tribe has participated in the Job Training Partnership Act and the VISTA/ACTION program.

The PeeDee Wind Walkers dance troop is well known throughout the region. Other cultural activities include bead, leather, and feather work. The dancers make all their own regalia. The tribe also publishes the *PeeDee Indian Association Pathfinder Newsletter.*

Thomas J. Blumer

Further Reading

Taukchiray, Wesley DuRant. *Peedee*. Wesley D. White Papers, Series 2. Charleston: South Carolina Historical Society.

Taukchiray, Wesley DuRant, and Alice Bee Kasakoff. "Contemporary Native Americans in South Carolina: An Overview." *Indians of the Southeastern United States in the Late Twentieth Century*. Ed. J. Anthony Parades. Tuscaloosa, AL and London, England: University of Alabama Press (1992): 72–101.

PEE-POSH

Near Phoenix, Arizona, lives one of the smallest yet most persistent Native American groups in the United States—the Pee-Posh, otherwise known as the Maricopa. Of the 797 Pee-Posh nationwide (1990 census), most live in the Maricopa Colony three miles west of Laveen on the Gila River Indian Reservation (GRIR). These Pee-Posh are descendents of the Yuman subgroups Kavelchadom, Kahwan, and Halyikwama. The second largest concentration of Maricopa live at Lehi, on the nearby Salt River Reservation. They trace their ancestry to another Yuman subgroup, the Halchidhoma. Although both groups share their reservations and have close relations with their neighbors, the Akimel O'odham (Pima), the Pee-Posh have their own unique heritage.

First identified as the Cocomaricopa by the Spanish, this Yuman-speaking group originally lived in the lower Colorado River valley region. By the late seventeenth century pressure from other Yuman groups forced the Cocomaricopa to migrate up the Gila River. The first bands reached the present area of the GRIR by the mid-eighteenth century, where they formed a confederation with another farming group, the Akimal O'odham (Pima). United States citizens moving west developed an alliance with the confederation, which provided the United States Army, forty-niners, ranchers, and pioneers with protection and foodstuffs. On February 28, 1863, to cement the powerful confederation's cooperation, the United States government shielded Pee-Posh and Akimal O'odham (Pima) lands from white encroachment by establishing the GRIR.

Although their land was now protected, the Pee-Posh still faced a series of traumatic challenges in the late nineteenth century. These sedentary farmers had to deal with an aggressive American culture, an unequal market system, and deadly diseases which cut the Pee-Posh population in half by 1900. The most significant issue the Pee-Posh had to cope with was the increased competition for water. Because white farmers upstream near the new settlement of Florence diverted the Gila River, many of the Pee-Posh under their leader Juan Cheveria, along with some Akimal O'odham (Pima), moved to the confluence of the Gila and Salt rivers. This settlement which became present-day Laveen was known as the Maricopa Colony. Meanwhile, the Halchidhoma relocated to the Salt River around the present site of Lehi. These two moves enabled the Pee-Posh to continue farming while the fields of their Piman neighbors died of thirst. In June of 1879, President Rutherford Hayes extended federal protection to the Pee-Posh bands by enlarging the GRIR and establishing the Salt River Reservation.

Though influenced by external pressure, the members of the confederation had maintained a nominal independence. Around the turn of the century, however, the situation began to change as the Bureau of Indian Affairs (BIA) increased its efforts to assimilate the Pee-Posh. With this goal in mind, the BIA allowed American cultural institutions to make inroads on the reservation. Around 1899 Presbyterian missionaries established the first Christian church at the Maricopa Colony. Acceptance or rejection of the new faith created a rift (or exacerbated an existing rift) within the community. A year later a day school was established at Laveen. Eventually children were also sent to the Phoenix Indian Boarding School.

In 1915 the BIA stepped up its assimilation efforts by introducing the allotment policy to the GRIR. Previously the Pee-Posh lived in family-style clusters. Individual families claimed particular fields, yet the whole community cooperated in planting and harvesting the crops. In hopes of breaking up the tribal community and thus accelerating assimilation, the BIA allotted each Pee-Posh two ten-acre plots—one irrigated and one undeveloped. Several Pee-Posh were fearful that the policy would threaten the existing social structure; thus they opposed the land distribution idea. Others, who had become members of the Presbyterian Church, worked for the government, or were intertwining in the outside market favored allotment. When the time for allotment came, many of the strongest opponents were jailed long enough for allotment supporters to be assigned the best lands in the Colony. Besides inflaming a preexisting division in the community, many older Pee-Posh directly blamed allotment for breaking up family clusters, which weakened the kinship structure, thus intensifying social problems.

In addition to their culture, Euroamericans also threatened Pee-Posh water rights. In the late nineteenth century, non-Indian development of an irrigation system in the Salt River Valley reduced the amount of water flowing downstream to the Pee-Posh. If it were not for a 1902 Arizona court decision that upheld Pee-Posh water rights, it would have been cut off completely. Nevertheless Pee-Posh water was again endangered in 1917, when the government turned the Salt River Project (SRP) over to private interests. The SRP launched an aggressive water development program by constructing three dams on the Salt River below the existing Roosevelt Dam. By 1930, this stopped the Salt River surface water from flowing down to the Maricopa canals. In response, the BIA forced the SRP to supply well water to the Pee-Posh. Unfortunately, the subsurface water proved too brackish for growing edible foods, forcing the people to switch to the cash crops of cotton and small grains.

By the 1930s the emphasis switched from forced assimilation to reservation development. The completion of the Coolidge Dam on the Gila River in 1930 allowed GRIR Superintendent A.H. Kneale to irrigate over 50,000 acres. This only nominally impacted the Pee-Posh, since they did not get any of the water from this project. The Pee-Posh continued to rely on the Salt River and wells. Likewise, a series of New Deal government programs promoted several public works projects, but few of them were executed in the Laveen area. On the other hand, numerous Pee-Posh did secure much needed employment through such government programs as the Civilian Conservation Corps-Indian Division. The biggest New Deal event to affect the reservation was John Collier's Indian Reorganization Act (IRA). Through this Act, the Akimal O'odham and Pee-Posh formed the Gila River Indian Community (GRIC) in 1934, based on a Constitution which established seven districts linked together by a reservation-wide Council. Unfortunately, because the Pee-Posh dominated only one of the seven districts, many feel they have not always been fairly represented. For several years, the Yuman speaking Pee-Posh did not even participate in the tribal government, especially since the council meetings were held in the Pima dialect until 1949.

When World War II started, around ninety Pee-Posh volunteered for the armed services while others found jobs in the growing war industry. The trend to secure employment off the reservation continued after the war, partly due to conditions on the GRIR. As the small allotments became fragmented due to inheritance, the Pee-Posh found it increasingly difficult to make a living through farming. To deal with the agricultural situation, several Pee-Posh decided to consolidate their allotments and form an informal cooperation known as the "Farm Chapter." This association slowly expanded until the 1980s, when it became the Maricopa Indian Cooperative Association. The successful endeavor today manages around 1,200 acres, paying each allottee a percentage of the profit. Meanwhile the Pee-Posh turned to off-reservation jobs to supplement their allotment income. The overall majority went to work in Phoenix, but in the early 1950s, the BIA launched the relocation program, which helped Native Americans get established in other urban areas such as Los Angeles. Although the program failed due to poor planning and lack of funding, it helped several Pee-Posh enter the wage economy. Most eventually returned to Arizona, yet this program did reflect a growing trend of Pee-Posh pursuing work outside of the Salt River area. Today, Pee-Posh are found from Michigan, to Florida, to Hawaii, with the largest concentration outside of Arizona in California.

In the 1950s the Pima-Maricopa tribe took advantage of the Indian Claims Commission Act of 1946, and brought suit against the government for land lost to encroaching whites. In 1970 the Commission finally ruled in favor of the Indians, but the amount of compensation money, once divided up to each tribal member, was exceedingly small.

To help bring jobs to the reservation itself, GRIC tribal government in the mid-1960s launched "It Must Happen," a program designed to take advantage of the Great Society. With federal aid, three industrial parks were opened in the reservation. In hopes of attracting a tourist industry, the Gila River Arts and Craft Center was also opened. Since then, it has helped preserve aspects of both Pee-Posh and Akimal O'odham culture. Since many Pee-Posh already worked in Phoenix, the employment efforts did not affect them as much as the social programs, such as the introduction of Head Start. In addition, through the Community Action Project, District Seven developed a community center which today provides a central hub for the Maricopa Colony. In the 1970s the Department of Housing and Urban Development launched a housing effort on the reservation, which replaced the Maricopa's "sandwich" style adobe homes. Unfortunately many of the new homes are substandard and not suited to the Arizona climate.

Today, despite becoming full participants in the Phoenix job market, the Pee-Posh still cling to their cultural heritage. This includes cultural arts by such artists as Ida Redbird. Though the amount of acreage possessed by Pee-Posh is unclear, they do dominate District Seven of the 372,000 acre GRIR. Educationally, the children either attend off-reservation public schools, BIA schools, or the Catholic school at St. Johns. Although not chartered separately from their Akimal O'odham neighbors, the Pee-Posh do function as a cultural unit within District Seven of the GRIC. The Pee-Posh have not lost their language or heritage, even though a cultural retention program has not been initiated. In an effort to mix old ways in with today's world, the youth have organized a youth council and formed the Estrella Mountain Dancers. The people's decision-making forum is an open community meeting advised by the Maricopa Resident Board and an informal council of elders. This group now faces a myriad of difficulties. Some are continuous problems, such as their fight for water. In an ongoing suit, the GRIC is trying to secure a portion of the water from the Central Arizona Project. Other problems are new, brought on by their increased interaction with the urban world—crime, drug abuse, alcohol, and diabetes. Despite these challenges, the Pee-Posh are facing their problems much as they always have—as a proud and independent people with a unique culture and history.

Peter MacMillan Booth
Ralph Cameron

See also **Arizona Tribes; Pima; Water Rights**

Further Reading

Dobyns, Henry F. *The Pima-Maricopa.* New York, NY: Chelsea House Publishers, 1989.

Ezell, Paul H. *The Maricopas: An Identification from Documentation.* University of Arizona Anthropological Papers No. 6. Tucson: University of Arizona Press, 1961.

Hackenburg, Robert. *Aboriginal Land Use and Occupancy of the Pima-Maricopa Indians.* New York, NY: Garland Publishing, 1974.

Harwell, Henry. "Maricopa Origins: An Ethnohistorical Approach to a Riverine Yuman Community." Ph.D. diss., Indiana University, 1979.

Harwell, Henry O., and Marsha C.S. Kelly. "Maricopa." *Handbook of North American Indians* Vol.10. *Southwest.* Ed. Alfonso Ortiz. Washington, DC: Smithsonian Institution (1983): 71–85.

Spier, Leslie. *Yuman Tribes of the Gila River.* New York, NY: Cooper Square, 1970.

PEIGAN

See Blackfeet

PEMBINA BAND OF CHIPPEWA

See Ojibwa: Chippewa in Montana; Ojibwa: Chippewa in North Dakota; Cree

PEND D'OREILLE

See Confederated Salish and Kootenai Tribes; Kalispel

PENOBSCOT

The Penobscot Indian Nation is headquartered on the Indian Island Reservation (315 acres), near Old Town, Maine. Penobscot (from *Panawahpskek*) translates as "Where the Rocks Spread Out." This tribe owns about 200 islands in the Penobscot River, between Old Town and Medway and up both the east and west branches of the river to Chesunkook Lake and Mattagamon Lake. It also holds large tracts of trust land (55,000 acres) in Penobscot County, and at Alder Stream in western Maine, plus fee-simple lands (38,000 acres), including part of Carrabassett Valley near Sugarloaf ski resort.

Its democratic government, which calls for biennial elections of governor, lieutenant governor, and a (nonvoting) tribal representative to the Maine legislature, was established following the death of their last life-chief in 1870. It also includes an elected Tribal Council of twelve members, serving (staggered) four-year terms, plus a police force, tribal court, and a primary school.

Penobscot numbers have grown dramatically this century, from 389 in 1910 to 1,984 in 1991. Although 60 percent live in Maine, only 25 percent live on the reservation. Tribal membership is based primarily on birth, but can also come through adoption, provided one possesses at least one-quarter Indian blood. While there are still some "full-blood" Penobscots alive today, over half the tribe is between one-quarter and one-half blood quantum.

In the late 1700s growing outside pressure on Penobscot territories undermined their traditional subsistence based on trapping, hunting, fishing, and gathering. In 1796 they signed a treaty with Massachusetts, relinquishing aboriginal title to much of their land in exchange for annuities (corn, cloth, blankets, ammunition, silver dollars, tobacco, etc.), reserving for their own use only the Penobscot River islands, including the one on which their main village was located, and some large tracts upriver for hunting. This treaty was never ratified by the United States Congress, as mandated by the Trade and Intercourse Act of 1790.

In 1820 Penobscots came under control of the new State of Maine, which gained custody of all the tribe's holdings. An Indian agent, appointed by the governor, was charged with running its affairs. In 1833 Maine sold about 100,000 acres of the tribe's remaining hunting lands, leaving them with less than 5,000 acres (about 200 small islands in the river above Old Town, some of which were assigned to individual tribesmen). Trust fund interest went toward paying the agent and to the chief, who divided it among his people.

Since land loss thwarted traditional subsistence patterns, nineteenth-century Penobscots turned to farming or seasonal wage labor as loggers, river-drivers, and hunting guides. Many became artisans, making baskets, canoes, moccasins, snowshoes, knick-nacks, etc. Basketry emerged as a key income source, and tribespeople often traveled long distances by train to sell their work in New England's tourist haunts. In part to enhance craft sales on the homefront, the tribe began promoting the reservation as a tourist attraction in the 1920s, holding elaborate Indian pageants with special costumes and dances. Increasingly, Penobscots also found employment in a local canoe factory, or in the region's lumber, shoe, and textile industries. In the 1930s, the reservation was hard hit by the Depression and a culture of poverty developed.

In 1950, heralding a new era in Penobscot community life, the small ferry was replaced by a new, one-lane bridge between Indian Island and the mainland. In 1954, thirty years after they had gained United States citizenship, the Penobscots finally obtained voting rights in state elections. Fearing what they saw as a threat to their tribal sovereignty, they asserted themselves as the Penobscot Nation and began researching their historical claims. With renewed pride in their heritage, they made common cause with other Maine Indians in a push for improved state services, which resulted in the founding of a new Department of Indian Affairs in 1965.

In 1972 they joined their Passamaquoddy neighbors in a massive land claim against the state (*Passamaquoddy v. Morton*). Seven years later they gained federal recognition. In addition to a federally funded tribal health care system, recognition provided the tribe with access to large-scale funding for community projects such as new tribal offices, low income housing, and a sewer system. As their annual budget ballooned ($3 million in federal grants and $2 million in state funds) and the number of tribal government employees rapidly climbed from 10 to 110, Penobscot leadership became more powerful than ever before.

In 1980 a two-thirds majority of the tribe voted to settle their land claims against the state in the Maine

Indian Claims Settlement Act, which gave the Penobscot Reservation all the powers of a municipality. While allowing a considerable measure of jurisdiction to the State of Maine, it retained many powers over internal tribal matters. The Penobscots received $40.3 million, of which $12.5 million was placed in a permanent federal trust fund from which members receive modest quarterly dividends, while another $1 million was invested in a special fund for the elderly. The remainder was earmarked for the acquisition of 150,000 acres of trust land, on which the tribe sets its own hunting and fishing regulations.

So far, the Penobscots have purchased 55,278 acres of trust land and 69,485 acres of fee-simple lands, of which some is mortgaged to provide cash or as collateral for tribal investments, while other parts are used for development projects. Considerable income comes from lands leased to logging operations. The tribe operates its own audio-cassette manufacturing plant on Indian Island. Offering work to more than 150 people, many of whom are Penobscots, it has contributed to lowering unemployment from 35 to 15 percent. Other ventures have been less successful and the tribe must still overcome major problems, including poverty and alcoholism.

As acculturation began in the 1600s much of the traditional culture was lost by the mid-1800s. However, remnants of Penobscot culture do survive. While only few Penobscot elders still know their ancestral Abenaki tongue, the tribe makes serious efforts to preserve the language and teach the few remaining traditions, including crafts, songs, and dances. Also, though most Penobscots have been Roman Catholics for centuries, there is renewed interest in Native spiritualism.

Harald E.L. Prins

See also **Passamaquoddy**

Further Reading

Brodeur, Paul. *Restitution: The Land Claims of the Mashpee, Passamaquoddy, and Penobscot Indians of New England.* Boston, MA: Northeastern University Press, 1985.

Ibelle, William. "In Search of the 20th Century Penobscot." *Salt* 5 (Winter 1983): 30–72.

Maine Indian Program. *The Wabanakis of Maine and the Maritimes: A Resource Book about Passamaquoddy, Maliseet, Micmac, and Abenaki Indians.* Bath, ME: New England Regional Office of the American Friends Service Committee, 1989.

Speck, Frank G. *Penobscot Man: The Life History of a Forest Tribe in Maine.* Philadelphia: University of Pennsylvania Press, 1940.

U.S. Congress. Senate. Select Committee on Indian Affairs. *Hearings on Proposed Settlement of Maine Indian Land Claims.* 96th Cong. 2d sess., S.2829. Washington, DC: U.S. Government Printing Office, 1980.

PEORIA

The Peoria (*Piwarea*, meaning "He Comes Carrying a Pack on His Back") originally lived in the Prairie du Chien area of Wisconsin and were part of the Algonquian-speaking Illinois Confederacy. After moving to southern Illinois and then ceding that land in the early nineteenth century, the Peorias amalgamated with the Kaskaskias (another tribe of the Illinois Confederacy) and settled on land by the Marias des Cygnes River in Kansas.

Following the Civil War, they were forced to surrender their lands in Kansas in 1867, and were moved to the northeastern corner of Indian Territory (Oklahoma), where they joined the Miami, Wea, and Piankashaw tribes as the "United Peoria and Miami Tribe." In 1893 their Oklahoma lands were allotted, and in 1907 the tribe's remaining lands were placed within the jurisdiction of Ottawa County, Oklahoma.

As part of the termination program of the Eisenhower administration, the Peoria's tribal status was terminated in 1950. Living in a rural area, the Peorias were unable to maintain themselves without federal assistance, and tribal leaders fought termination as a violation of their treaty rights with the United States. As a result, the Peoria tribe was restored as a federally recognized tribe in 1978. Outstanding claims by the Peorias and other tribes of the Miami and Illinois confederacies were resolved by the Indian Claims Commission in 1974.

Today the Peoria maintain a tribal office in Miami, Oklahoma, where they own 38.79 acres of land. Under the Oklahoma Indian Welfare Act (Thomas-Rogers Act) of 1936, the tribe produced a Constitution in 1939 and incorporated as the Peoria Indian Tribe of Oklahoma. A second Constitution, ratified in 1981, provides for a tribal Business Council composed of a chief, a second chief, a secretary-treasurer, and two Council members. All are elected to staggered four-year terms. Rodney Arnette is the current tribal chairman, elected in 1982. Regular meetings of the Business Council are held monthly.

From a turn of the century population of 448, total tribal enrollment in 1993 is 2,000 people, with 400 residing in the trust area. The Peorias' tribal population includes members of the Kaskaskias and other Illinois tribes, as well as Weas and Piankashaws. Tribal members own several businesses in Ottawa County, and the employment rate for the tribe is 88 percent. Many work in Tulsa. The Peoria are affiliated with the other tribes of Ottawa County (Miamis, Ottawas, Senecas, and Quapaws) in efforts to promote business interests and cultural concerns.

The Peoria are largely assimilated into mainstream American life and most are Christians. The tribe helps sponsor the annual "Indian Heritage Days" in June at Miami, Oklahoma, in conjunction with other tribes of Ottawa County, and individual Peorias are participants in the Quapaw tribal ceremonials held on the Fourth of July weekend near the town of Quapaw, Oklahoma. Although little of the Illinois culture and language remains, the Peoria have maintained the traditional songs and dances of the Illinois people which are presented at the Quapaw ceremonials, and some efforts have been made in recent years to revive the traditional Calumet Dance, first mentioned by Father Marquette in the seventeenth century. During the 1970s and 1980s the Peoria Indian Tribe of Oklahoma has sought to revive traditional arts and crafts and produce a tribal history, as well as to promote awareness of their place in American history to the general non-Indian public.

Thomas F. Schilz

See also Miami; Oklahoma Tribes

Further Reading

Confederation of American Indians. *Indian Reservations: A State and Federal Handbook.* Jefferson, NC: McFarland & Co., 1986.

Leitch, Barbara. *A Concise Handbook of Indian Tribes of North America.* Algonac, MI: Reference Publications, 1979.

Libby, Dorothy, and David Stout. *Piankashaw and Kaskaskia Indians.* New York, NY: Garland Publishing, 1974.

Peoria Tribe. *The Peorias: A History of the Peoria Tribe of Oklahoma.* Eds. Dorris Valley and Mary M. Lembcke. Miami: Peoria Tribe of Oklahoma, 1991.

Strickland, Rennard. *The Indians in Oklahoma.* Norman: University of Oklahoma Press, 1980.

PEQUOT

The Pequots, also known as the Mohegan-Pequots, occupied the Thames River drainage basin for some time prior to European contact. The language of the Mohegan-Pequots, along with all southern New England Indian groups, is part of the Eastern Algonquian language family.

Today, there are two separate Pequot Indian tribes in Connecticut: the federally recognized Mashantucket (Mushantuxet) or Western Pequots of Ledyard, Connecticut; and the state-recognized Paucatuck or Eastern Pequots, who occupy a nearby land base, the Lantern Hill Reservation in North Stonington. These two communities had the same history until the mid-1660s. The Mashantucket Pequots were granted land at Mashantucket in 1666. In 1683, the Paucatuck or Eastern Pequots were provided with a reservation on the east side of Long Pond in North Stonington, Connecticut.

Until recent decades, the twentieth century was a period of continuing decline for the Pequots. Early in the century their major cottage industry, basketmaking, declined because of the deaths of the principal practitioners. The anthropologist, Frank Speck, estimated that there were twenty-five members at Mashantucket in 1907.

By the mid-1920s, Atwood I. Williams (Chief Silver Star) began acting as spokesman for some of the Pequots. Williams seems to have been recognized by some as sachem over the Paucatuck and Mashantucket Pequots until the mid-1930s, when John George became the recognized spokesman for the Mashantucket Pequots. Williams continued as one of the leaders of the Paucatuck (Eastern) Pequots.

Meanwhile, externally imposed conditions, including the manipulation of tribal membership of both groups by the state's agent and the deterioration of existing housing, as well as the state's refusal to allow the construction of new housing, had the combined effect of producing artificially limited on-reservation populations throughout the twentieth century.

The Paucatuck or Eastern Pequots at Lantern Hill

The twentieth century for the Eastern Pequots is a story of survival. Led in the early twentieth century by individuals such as Ephraim Williams, their spiritual leaders included members of the Sebastian family, who have been instrumental in forging new directions in the second half of the century. Efforts began in the 1970s to gain federal recognition. Neese Mattucks drafted the original recognition petition, filed in 1989, which is under revision by tribal researchers. In 1993 Roy Sebastian, Chief Hockeo, is chief and tribal chairman. There are about 18 homes on the 226-acre reservation, whose exact acreage is in dispute. For the 564 members, a principal issue is the ongoing conflict with the State of Connecticut over Native rights on the reservation and issues relating to land claims. Factionalism within the tribe has not made the resolution of these issues any easier. Tribal elders, however, continue to provide leadership. Some have knowledge of aspects of the Pequot language, which is well-documented in written form, which they pass on when appropriate.

The Mashantucket Pequots

Although John George was the acknowledged Mashantucket leader after the mid-1930s, actual community leadership rested in the hands of the half-sisters Elizabeth Plouffe (nee George) and Martha Langevin Ellal until their deaths in the early 1970s. Amos George became the Mashantucket Pequot tribal leader after the deaths of Plouffe and Ellal. In 1974, the Mashantuckets reorganized their tribal government and established a written Tribal Constitution. Their preliminary tribal membership rolls listed fifty-five members in 1974. Richard Hayward was elected as chairman of the Mashantucket Pequot Tribal Council at the annual tribal meeting in 1975 and continues in that office in 1993.

Remembering the stories told by the older generation of leaders (Plouffe and Ellal), Hayward and others conducted more research into the history of land transfers to non-Indians. They became convinced that the land had been stolen, and they were able to enlist the aid of Thomas N. Tureen, working for the Native American Rights Fund, to institute in 1976 a suit over the lands taken from the tribe. Years of negotiation and politicking followed until 1983 when the United States Congress enacted the *Mashantucket Pequot Indian Land Claims Settlement Act* (Public Law 98–134, Title 25 U.S.C.A. § 1751–1760), which settled the tribe's land claim and provided federal recognition to the Mashantucket Pequot Tribe, establishing an important precursor for the tribe's economic resurgence.

While the changes that the Mashantucket Pequot Tribe has experienced since federal recognition have been experienced elsewhere, few other reservations can attest to changes as dramatic as at Mashantucket. The tribe's land base has gone from 214 acres in 1983 to its 1991 total of 1,795 acres. In 1993 there are about 282 enrolled members. A number of economic development initiatives have been implemented and on-reservation employment has undergone a dramatic increase. Following the lead established by other federally recognized tribes, the Mashantuckets began a high stakes bingo operation on their reservation which has become enormously successful. After complex negotiations with the State of Connecticut, a gambling casino opened on the reservation in 1992. In the late twentieth century, they are an economic force in the broader non-Indian community of southeastern Connecticut.

James D. Wherry

Further Reading

DeForest, John W. *History of the Indians of Connecticut from the Earliest Known Period to 1850.* Hartford, CT: W.J. Hamersley, 1851. Hamden, CT: Shoestring Press, 1964.

Hauptman, Laurence M., and James D. Wherry, eds. *The Pequots in Southern New England: The Fall and Rise of an American Indian Nation.* Norman: University of Oklahoma Press, 1990.

Jennings, Francis. *The Invasion of America: Indians, Colonialism, and the Cant of Conquest.* New York, NY: W.W. Norton, 1975.

PERIODICALS

Native American newspaper and other periodical publishing began in 1828 with the establishment of the *Cherokee Phoenix,* a newspaper, at New Echota, Cherokee Nation. Publishing by Native groups or individuals was an oddity until the late nineteenth century, when a flurry of publishing activity occurred, especially in Indian Territory (now Oklahoma). What appeared to be the beginning of a strong Native press was undermined by federal policies aimed at assimilating Native Americans into American society. As a result of such policies, Native societies, and therefore Native publishing, entered a period of decline, from which they did not begin to recover until after World War II. Since then, the Native press has grown rapidly and today appears to be entering a period of stability and increased professional growth.

During the nineteenth century, little Native publishing occurred outside of Indian Territory. The *Cherokee Phoenix* had suspended publication before Cherokee removal to the West, but in 1844 the Cherokees established its successor, the *Cherokee Advocate,* to inform the Cherokee people of their government's actions and of the American policies affecting them. Except *Copway's American Indian* (1850) in New York, other early Native newspaper publishing

occurred only in the Choctaw and Chickasaw nations. In the late nineteenth century, however, the Native press proliferated in Indian Territory as a result of federal policy aimed at allotment of land and statehood for the Territory. Cherokees established a number of newspapers, such as the *Indian Chieftain* (1882) and the *Arrow* (1888). Creeks established the *Indian Journal* (1876), Choctaws began the *Atoka Independent* (1899), and Osages published the *Wah-sha-she News* (1893). Breakup of the tribal land titles and Oklahoma statehood undermined these beginnings of a strong Native press. Similar economic, social, and cultural changes prevented its development elsewhere.

The Native press of the first four decades of the twentieth century was a product of late nineteenth-century Indian policy. Native communities were demoralized by an eroded land base, poverty, poor health, and cultural loss that were byproducts of allotment, off-reservation boarding schools, and other assimilationist policies of the late nineteenth century. For the most part, Native newspaper and other periodical publication was dominated by publishers and editors who were assimilationists, many of them graduates of the off-reservation boarding schools, where they had learned printing. Their publications were not tribal, serving not only the Native community, but the local non-Native community as well. Most newspaper publishing occurred in eastern Oklahoma, formerly Indian Territory, and included titles such as the *Adair Weekly Ledger* (1904) and the *Claremore State Herald* (1905). Elsewhere, Roy Stabler edited the *Winnebago Chieftain* (1907) in Nebraska; Webster Hudson, the *Quileute Independent* (1908) and the *Quileute Chieftain* (1910) in Washington; H.C. Ashmun, the *Odanah Star* (1912) in Wisconsin; Peter Navarre, the *Rossville Reporter* (1913) in Kansas; and William Pugh, the *Martin Messenger* (1914) and the *Shannon County News* (1930) in South Dakota. Magazines such as the *American Indian Magazine* (1913) of the Society of American Indians, and Lee Harkins' *The American Indian* (1927) urged full citizenship rights and the economic mainstreaming of Native Americans. Others went further and were more strident, insisting on the abolition of the Bureau of Indian Affairs, opposing attempts by reformers in the 1920s and 1930s to reverse assimilationist policies and to revitalize Native communities, and attacking the administration of Indian affairs by John Collier. Such publications include Carlos Montezuma's *Wassaja* (1916), William L. Paul's *The Alaska Fisherman* (1923), the California Indian Rights Association's *California Indian News* (1935), and the American Indian Federation's *The First American* (1937).

Just as federal Indian policy had influenced the Native press in the past, during the twenty years following World War II it did much to shape the press as it exists today. Relocation policy began a process of urbanization of the Native population that continues today, and termination policy put reservation residents on notice that the federal government intended to sever its responsibility for Indian affairs. Urban as well as reservation leaders felt the need to keep communities informed, especially concerning termination efforts. One result was increased pan-Indian activity, exemplified in publications such as the *Bulletin* (1947) of the National Congress of American Indians, and urban newsletters such as the *Chicago Warrior* (1955) and the Seattle *Indian Center News* (1960). A second result was the revitalization of the tribal or Indian nation press. Some newspapers established in that era remain in print today, e.g., *Ute Bulletin* (1950), *Char-Koosta News* (1956), *Navajo Times* (1959), *Tribal Tribune* (1961), *Fort Apache Scout* (1962), and *Jicarilla Chieftain* (1962).

The decade following 1965 was perhaps the most intense period for Native periodical publishing. In addition to continued urbanization, Great Society legislation, especially the Economic Opportunity Act and the Elementary and Secondary Education Act of 1965, transformed the publishing scene by channeling federal funds to Native communities and organizations, resulting in proliferation of newsletters and newspapers aimed at specialized audiences. In addition, a rising sense of Indian nationalism, cultural awareness, and growing demands for self-determination resulted in an activist press such as *Akwesasne Notes* (1969) and the establishment of a national Native monthly, *Wassaja* (1973). The early 1970s witnessed the development of specialized publications in fields such as law, health, and literature, and the establishment of the American Indian Press Association (1971). The Alaska Native Claims Settlement Act of 1971, which established the thirteen regional Native corporations, resulted in a flurry of publishing activity among Alaska Natives. Most publications begun in this period were related to specific programs or policies and funded wholly or in part by funds from outside the Native communities. Thus most were short-lived, failing to survive the slow withdrawal of federal funds from social and economic programs in the late 1970s and the slashing of federal budgets in the early 1980s. However, Native communities had become accustomed to receiving news publications, and their demand for news remains strong today.

In recent years Native publishing has begun to overcome many of the problems that had beset it throughout its history. Funding was often uncertain, whether the source was local or outside the Native community. Those publications that survived budget cuts in the 1980s have become more securely based through advertising or commitment of local funds. Limited funding and a lack of trained journalists often resulted in inexpensive, unprofessional-looking publications. Today, the increased number of professionally trained Native journalists, improved computer technology, and the Native American Journalists Association (established in 1984) ensure a broader, more in-depth coverage of local, regional, and national Native news. In addition to tribal and Native nation newspapers, many independent publications have firmly established themselves, such as the excel-lent national weekly *Indian Country Today* (formerly *The Lakota Times*), published by Tim Giago; the twice monthly *News from Indian Country*, published by Paul DeMain; the urban monthly, *The Circle*; and quarterly magazines such as *Turtle Quarterly* and *News from Native California*. There are also first-rate academic journals such as *Akwe: kon Journal* (formerly *Northeast Indian Quarterly*), *Wicazo Sa Review*, *American Indian Culture and Research Journal*, and *American Indian Quarterly*, and professional publications such as the American Indian Science and Engineering Society's *Winds of Change*.

Yet problems remain. Funding for tribal or Native nation publications depends on economic rise and fall. Independent publishers who depend on advertising are also vulnerable to economic trends. Editors of publications funded by local Native American governments or agencies usually have little editorial license, and tribal governments remain capable of shutting down presses or removing editors, as has been demonstrated in recent years at the *Navajo Times* and the *Mandan, Hidatsa and Arikara Times*. Thus the question of freedom of the press on Native controlled land remains a debated issue. However, it is constantly on the agenda at meetings of the Native American Journalists Association, which, under the leadership of Tim Giago, Mark Trahant, and Paul DeMain, has taken a firm stand in its favor.

Despite obstacles, Native newspaper and other periodical publishing has achieved a high degree of sophistication and professionalism. Publishers have the technical capability and the know-how to focus on the major issues that confront their constituencies on local, regional, and national levels. They have established information networks not only among themselves, but with organizations involved in the worldwide Indigenous Peoples' Movement. Thus, the Native press appears to be coming into its own as a source of empowerment for Native communities. Extensive collections of the products of Native presses are housed in the American Native Press Archives at the University of Arkansas at Little Rock, and in the newspapers and periodicals section of the Wisconsin State Historical Society. Much of what future generations know about Native communities of the late twentieth century will be found in such collections.

Daniel F. Littlefield, Jr.

See also Radio and Television

Further Reading

Danky, James P., ed. *Native American Periodicals and Newspapers, 1828–1982.* Comp. Maureen E. Hady. Westport, CT: Greenwood Press, 1984.

Littlefield, Daniel F., Jr., and James W. Parins, eds. *American Indian and Alaska Native Newspapers and Periodicals, 1826–1924.* Westport, CT: Greenwood Press, 1984.

———. *American Indian and Alaska Native Newspapers and Periodicals, 1925–1970.* Westport, CT: Greenwood Press, 1986.

———. *American Indian and Alaska Native Newspapers and Periodicals, 1971–1985.* Westport, CT: Greenwood Press, 1986.

Murphy, James E., and Sharon M. Murphy. *Let My People Know: American Indian Journalism, 1828–1978.* Norman: University of Oklahoma Press, 1981.

PEYOTE RELIGION

Peyotism is an American Indian religion based upon the sacramental use in ritual of the peyote plant. Peyote is a small, spineless cactus having psychedelic properties, which grows in a limited area principally in northern Mexico and southern Texas. It is light green in color, segmented, about one to two inches across, growing singly or in clusters close to the ground from a long tap root. It is harvested by cutting off the tops of the clusters, leaving the root to produce more "buttons," as the tops are usually called. The buttons are generally dried before being eaten, are extremely bitter, and frequently produce vomiting. They also produce a pleasant euphoria, an agreeable point of view, relaxation, colorful visual distortions, and a sense of timelessness that are conducive to the all-night ceremony of the Native American Church. To the church's members, peyote is the essential ingredient, the sacrament. Peyote is not habit-forming.

Archaeology indicates that peyote was used by the inhabitants of Mexico 10,000 years ago. It was used as a medicine to be taken internally or as a poultice on sores, to foretell the future, to find lost objects, as a stimulant during strenuous activity, such as travel or war, and in group religious ceremonies when supernatural aid was sought. Peyote and peyote ceremonies became known to the Indians of the western United States in the nineteenth century when the horse enabled the Plains Indians to travel widely into the southern United States and Mexico, peyote's natural habitat.

In the last quarter of the nineteenth century, when the Plains Indians and remnants of many other great tribes were forced onto reservations in Oklahoma, a peyote ceremony was observed among them that continues today in the Native American Church. This ceremony is of Native origin, rooted in aboriginal Mexican ceremonies with possible additions from newly acquired Christianity. Its immediate predecessor was probably the ceremony of the Carrizo Indians, who lived along the Rio Grande, and the ceremony found its way into Oklahoma principally by way of the Lipan and Mescalero Apache, the Caddo, the Karankawa, and Tonkawa tribes of southern Texas and New Mexico. It was first described by anthropologist James Mooney in 1890 after attending meetings with Kiowa Indians in Oklahoma.

The ceremony generally begins around nine o'clock on a Saturday night. A tipi or brush enclosure is the preferred setting, the opening toward the east. In the center is constructed a shallow fire-hole, and beside it a low crescent-shaped mound of sand, the altar. At the beginning of the meeting, the fireman, who sits at the door with a pile of kindling, lights the fire. The peyotists enter and sit in a circle, the roadman (chief of the meeting) sits west of the center, facing east, the chief drummer to his right, and the cedarman to his left. A large peyote button is placed on the altar. The ceremony consists of praying, singing to the drum and rattle, eating peyote, which is passed around, each person taking four buttons at a time, and in some meetings, smoking ritual cigarettes passed through the cedar smoke from the fire. The roadman leads the meeting in praying, singing, eating more peyote, etc., but all adult members take turns in all activities. At midnight, there is a pause when people are free to move about. The meeting commences again after the roadman has blown his eagle bone whistle to the four directions, and continues until dawn when another break occurs in order for a ritual taking of water and food: parched corn, sweetened meat, and fruit. Again the meeting continues until the sun is fully up, about nine or ten in the morning. The meeting breaks up after the final traditional song, and the peyotists leave the tipi and partake of a full breakfast and informal conversation.

Each peyotist brings to the meeting certain sacred paraphernalia consisting of feather fans, which they use to fan smoke from the sacred fire toward themselves, and gourd rattles to aid in singing. Sometimes an ill person is brought to meetings to receive special prayers and peyote, but, whether to cure a particular person who is ill or just to assuage the worries or heal the ailments of those present, a peyote meeting is always considered a curing ceremony. The music is traditional and a song is always sung four times, four being the sacred number throughout the ritual. The ambience of the meeting is serious and devout.

Although the present ritual is similar to the early ritual in most respects, time has brought some changes. Two variations developed early: the Half Moon or Tipi Way, and the Big Moon or Cross Fire Way, the main distinction between them being the use of tobacco in the Half Moon ceremony, whereas the use of tobacco is minimal, if at all, in the Big Moon ceremony. Although the traditional setting is still preferred, today it is sometimes necessary to hold the ceremony in a house. Then, either the fire and sand altar must be contained in a metal vessel, or they are dispensed with entirely and the Chief Peyote rests on an embroidered altar cloth on the floor. But even if the ceremony is held in a house, the participants sit in a circle on the floor, the roadman facing east with the chief drummer to his right, and the cedarman to his left.

Within a few years after peyotism was observed in Oklahoma, it spread to nearly all the tribes in western Oklahoma: it spread to the Comanche, the Kiowa, the Kiowa-Apache, the Wichita, the Delaware, the Southern Cheyenne, the Southern Arapaho, the Osage, the Tonkawa, the Quapaw, the Seneca, the Ponca, the Kaw, the Otoe, the Pawnee, the Sac and Fox, the Iowa, the Kickapoo and Shawnee in Oklahoma, and beyond

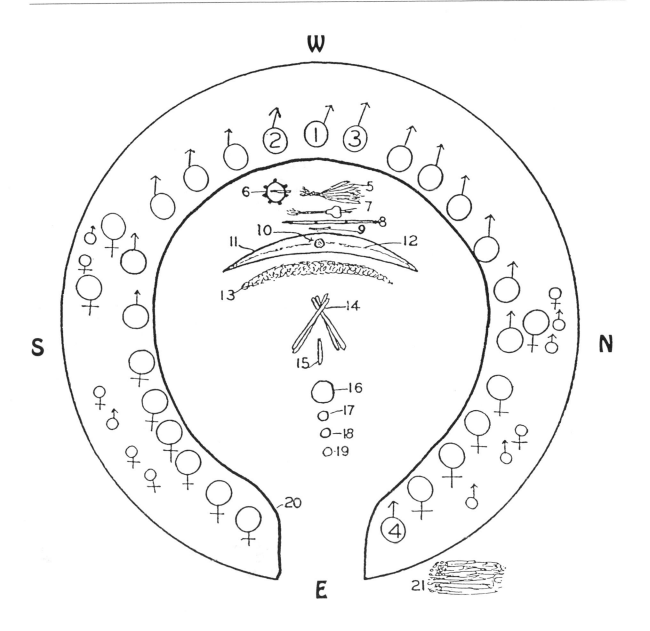

Figure 1
ARRANGEMENT OF TIPI

1. Chief	8. Staff	15. Fire-stick
2. Chief-drummer	9. Whistle	16. Water
3. Cedarman	10. Chief peyote	17. Maize
4. Fire-chief	11. Sand moon	18. Fruit
5. Fan	12. Peyote road	19. Meat
6. Drum	13. Ash moon	20. Rope
7. Rattle	14. Fire	21. Wood pile

Oklahoma to the Winnebago, the Omaha, the Prairie Potawatomi, the Kaw, the Fox, the Menominee, the Chippewa, the Ponca, the Sioux, the Northern Cheyenne, the Crow, the Northern Arapaho, the Wind River Shoshone, and the Ute. It was spread by dedicated missionaries and by personal contact through chance visits to peyote meetings. Its appeal was not 100 percent; it never gained more than 90 percent participation on a single reservation, and the percentage was more likely to be 35 to 50 percent. Nevertheless, it soon became a significant force, much opposed by Christian churches and the Bureau of Indian Affairs (BIA). Every effort was made to suppress it. Suppression began early in Oklahoma in the Court of Indian Offenses, which not only forbade the use of peyote but confused peyote with mescal beans. Later, governmental authorities equated peyote with alcohol and sought suppression under the Prohibition Law of 1897. Unsuccessful in halting the spread of peyotism, in 1912 an effort began in earnest to get a strong federal law against peyote. This action was led by the BIA, the Board of Indian Commissioners, the Bureau of Catholic Indian Missions, the Society of American Indians, the Lake Mohonk Conference, and many other such groups, as well as individual missionaries, psychologists, chemists, educators, and Indian non-peyotists, who all maintained that peyote was addictive and that it harmed peyotists mentally and physically.

In 1918 specific legislation to outlaw peyote was considered by the United States House of Representatives. Indian peyotists and certain whites, particularly anthropologists who had studied peyotism, attended meetings, and knew that peyote was not habit-forming, that it did not make the Indians lazy or crazy, that, in fact, it was a moral support to many troubled Indians, testified on peyote's behalf. They strongly argued that peyote helped Indians to overcome their worst enemy—alcohol; they said that peyotists did not drink. The bill was defeated. It was then that the peyotists of Oklahoma, in order to make their religion more acceptable to the white population, organized and incorporated the Native American Church (NAC), the purpose of which was "to foster . . . the religious belief of several tribes of Indians . . . in the Christian religion with the practice of the Peyote Sacrament as commonly used among the adherents of this religion in the several tribes of these Indians . . . and to teach . . . morality, sobriety, industry, kindly charity and right living and to cultivate a spirit of self respect and brotherly union among the members. . . ."

Anti-peyote legislation continued to be sought. Although always defeated at the national level, over the next few years Utah, Colorado, Nevada, Kansas, Arizona, Montana, North and South Dakota, New Mexico, and Wyoming passed laws prohibiting possession of peyote. However, since state laws had little jurisdiction on Indian reservations, peyotism continued to flourish, and many new churches were incorporated with similar aims as the NAC of Oklahoma. By the middle of the century it had spread to the Bannock and Shoshone of Idaho, the Cree, the Blackfeet, the Assiniboine, the Goshute, the Western Shoshone, the Washoe and Northern Paiute, the Southern Paiute, the Taos, and the Navajo.

Peyotism met a new obstacle when it spread to the Pueblo tribe of Taos in New Mexico, and the Navajo in Arizona. Among the Indians of the Plains, tribal organization was loose, the chief of the tribe being more or less a distinguished citizen. He led, but only as long as he was followed. Among the Plains Indians there were many non-peyotists, and peyotism was often denigrated but meetings were never interfered with and peyotists were never persecuted by fellow tribesmen. The Pueblos, on the other hand, were tight theocracies and the Tribal Council ruled with an iron hand. The small band of peyotists at Taos were forbidden to meet by the Tribal Council and were punished by fines, confiscation of property, break-up of meetings, and jail terms until, this time, the United States government stepped in to defend the peyotists. John Collier had become head of the BIA in 1932, bringing a new appreciation of Indian culture to that office. Much of the persecution of the Taos peyotists had been due to interfering whites, and Collier was able to promote a more conciliatory attitude on the part of the Taos non-peyotists.

On the Navajo Reservation peyote was also forbidden by the Tribal Council, which passed a resolution stating "Any person who shall introduce into the Navajo country, sell or use or have in possession . . . the bean known as peyote shall be deemed guilty of an offense against the Navajo tribe and upon conviction . . . shall be sentenced to labor for a period not to exceed nine months, or a fine of $100.00 or both." This action resulted in many arrests, fines, jail terms, and court cases over the next twenty-seven years, until, in 1968, the Navajo Nation accepted for the first time the United States Bill of Rights which guarantees religious freedom.

Today peyotism is practiced throughout the western United States with little interference. In 1944 the NAC of Oklahoma became the NAC of the United States. In 1955, the NAC of the United States became the NAC of North America, several Canadian churches having joined the parent organization. At that time, sixty-six groups returned a questionnaire sent out by anthropologist and peyotist J. Sidney Slotkin, inquiring as to the number of people using peyote as a sacrament, and 7,218 were listed as members. The questionnaire covered groups in Saskatchewan and Alberta, Canada, and included the states of California, Idaho, Arizona, New Mexico, Colorado, Wyoming, Montana, North Dakota, South Dakota, Nebraska, Kansas, Oklahoma, Texas, Minnesota, and Wisconsin. Today, peyote meeting are also held in Nevada, Utah, Oregon, and Washington. It has been estimated that the Native American Church has 200,000 members with innumerable branches, the NAC of North America and the NAC of Navajoland being the largest.

It was never an exclusive religion; members are free to belong to other churches, and they do. It is always a curing ceremony as well as a social and spiritual experience. Use of alcohol is forbidden. There is no written theology; it is always spread by missionaries. Today the Chief Peyote often shares the space of honor on the altar with the Bible.

Since 1978 with the passage of the American Indian Religious Freedom Act, the practice of peyotism by American Indians is generally protected by law. Occasionally, Indians are still arrested for possession of peyote, since peyote is classified as a dangerous substance and forbidden under the Drug Abuse Control Act of 1965. However, when Indians show that possession of peyote is for use as a sacrament in a peyote ritual, there is usually no trouble. Most states have rescinded their earlier anti-peyote laws. One state that has not is Oregon, and recently, the United States Supreme Court upheld the State of Oregon in a case that concerned the firing and denial of unemployment compensation to two peyotists. The decision stated that in spite of free exercise of religion guaranteed by the Bill of Rights, still a state may fire individuals without compensation who break a state law, even though they do so in the practice of their religion. This decision is being strongly criticized by the white community, as well as the Indian, as a step backward in America's commitment to the right of freedom of religion.

Omer C. Stewart

Further Reading

Aberle, David F. *The Peyote Religion Among the Navajo.* 2d ed. Viking Fund Publications in Anthropology, Vol. 42. IL: University of Chicago Press, 1966.

Anderson, Edward F. *Peyote: The Divine Cactus.* Tucson: University of Arizona Press, 1980.

LaBarre, Weston. *The Peyote Culture.* 4th ed., enl. New York, NY: Schocken Books, 1975.

Slotkin, J. Sydney. *The Peyote Religion: A Study in Indian-White Relations.* Glencoe, IL: Free Press, 1956.

Stewart, Omer C. *Peyote Religion: A History.* Norman, OK and London, England: University of Oklahoma Press, 1987.

PHOTOGRAPHY

The earliest known photograph of a Native American was taken in Great Britain sometime between October 1844 and April 1845, when photographers David Octavius Hill and Robert Adamson made a portrait of the Reverend Peter Jones, the son of a Welshman and a Mississauga Indian woman. Since then, professional photographers, missionaries, anthropologists, government agents, and tourists have visually recorded almost every aspect of Native American life. Today, more than 145 years later, Native Americans continue to be highly popular subjects for photography. Now, however, there are a growing number of Native photographers who use the camera for their own creative and documentary purposes.

Earliest Photographs of Native Americans

In the United States many of the earliest portraits of Native Americans were made as records of diplomatic delegations to Washington, D.C. In the 1850s scores of Indian leaders traveled to the capital to negotiate treaties with the federal government. Typically, their visits to Washington were not complete without a sitting at a photographic studio. Many of the delegation photographers became well known for their portraits of Indians, including Alexander Gardner, Charles M. Bell, A. Zeno Schindler, and Mathew B. Brady.

After the Civil War the federal government sent several expeditions to survey and document the resources in the West. Three of the best-known, nineteenth-century photographers of Indians in the West accompanied these expeditions—Timothy O'Sullivan, William Henry Jackson, and John K. Hillers. These documentary photographers combined professional technical skills and artistic vision to create memorable portraits and images of Indian life. Critics observe, however, that these photographers often chose not to record such grim realities as hunger and dislocation, as Native Americans were pushed off their lands by white settlement and the Indian Wars.

Other nineteenth-century photographers of Native Americans included commercial photographers who traveled through the countryside and set up studios in frontier towns. These photographers, like many of the delegation and survey photographers, often sought to market the images of Indians they took. Typically, their photographs expressed, both visually and through their captions, attitudes of racial superiority common to many whites in that era. These images often recreated conventional stereotypes of Native Americans that followed established conventions in painting and drawing, dating back to the earliest contacts between Euroamericans and Native peoples.

Jesse Cooday (Tlingit). "Clear Cut Columbus," 1993. Detail. Mixed media. Courtesy of the artist.

Glenda J. Guilmet (Taino heritage). "Shadow Dance #1," Copyright © Glenda J. Guilmet 1988. Courtesy of the Sacred Circle Gallery of American Indian Art, Seattle, Washington.

Photography Enters the Twentieth Century

At the turn of the century many anthropologists, missionaries, and Indian agents took up photography as the equipment became more portable. Their images often reflect their particular political or social outlook, whether it was to document "primitive" Native lifestyles and the decline of traditional culture, or to promote the benefits of assimilation.

Pictorialist photographers like Edward S. Curtis and Joseph K. Dixon pursued a different agenda in their romantic photographs made in the early twentieth century. These photographers felt a social obligation to preserve and record a world that was undergoing profound technological and social change. Curtis, probably the best-known photographer of Indians in this century, undertook a monumental effort to document the traditional culture of North American Indians through the creation of nearly 40,000 photographs depicting some 80 tribes. In his zeal to preserve his image of the past in the face of rapid change, Curtis sometimes used costumes and props. Some critics have objected to this creation of "documentary fiction." Joseph K. Dixon and others were convinced that the solution to the desperate conditions of reservation life lay in citizenship for Native Americans. Dixon hoped to directly influence social policy by evoking nostalgic images of the past in his photographs of Native peoples during the Wanamaker Expeditions from 1908 to 1917.

Several contemporary photographers continue to make a career out of photographing Native Americans. Some, like Richard Erdoes and Ulli Steltzer, have sought to work closely with Native peoples to create a more authentic record of their lives. Others, such as John Running, specialize in lush color images of Indians that appeal to the notion of Indians as the exotic "other."

Native American Responses to Photographers

Over the years, and depending on the tribe, the individual, the photographer, and the circumstances, Native Americans have had different reactions to photography and the presence of photographers within their midst. In the earliest periods, some Native peoples feared the camera, concerned that the creation of the images might in some way rob the subject of his or her soul or self. Others, however, found photographs fascinating and sought to have their pictures taken. In more recent years, Native Americans have expressed a dislike for photography because of the stereotypic qualities of many photographs, whether of the "Io, the poor Indian," or "noble savage" varieties. Others resent the commercial exploitation of photographs that have been taken of Native Americans and their communities. Often, Euroamerican photographers achieved fame and fortune as a result of their photographs, while their Native subjects were rarely compensated or even asked for their permission for publication of the images.

Often Native Americans have resented the intrusions by photographers into their communities, as much as the creation of the photographs themselves. In the Southwest, for example, at the turn of the century scores of professional and amateur photographers descended upon the Hopi and the New Mexico Pueblos to photograph ceremonial dances. According to contemporary accounts, the crush of photographers and other spectators was often so great that the dances were impeded and interrupted. In addition, commercial photographers often marketed many of these photographs of sacred ceremonies as evidence of the primitive and "wild" nature of the tribes. As a result of these experiences, the Hopi and many of the New Mexico Pueblos banned photography of ceremonies in the 1910s and 1920s. Nonetheless, curious and insensitive individuals continue to try to photograph ceremonial events. In 1984, the Santa Fe *New Mexican*, a daily newspaper, photographed dances at Santo Domingo Pueblo from a low-flying plane and published them a few days later. The *New Mexican* issued a partial apology only after Santo Domingo filed a $3.5 million lawsuit against the paper for invasion of privacy and trespassing.

Despite these negative experiences, Native peoples, like many others, appreciate the power of photography to record events and traditions, to make statements, and to preserve memories. They also appreciate its possibilities as a medium for artistic expression and communication.

Native American Photographers

Although it is not certain when Native peoples began taking photographs (Sitting Bull may have taken a photograph of a photographer in 1882), a few were active by the early twentieth century. Some, like George Hunt, a Kwakiutl assistant trained by anthropologist Franz Boas, made many photographs of community life for outside uses. Others like George Johnston, a Tlingit in the Yukon Territories in Canada, apparently taught themselves the medium, probably after encounters with itinerant professional photographers. For more than forty years, Johnston recorded life in his community and sold photographs in his trading post. The work of these individuals, and possibly many others, is only now coming to be more widely known through research and exhibitions.

Today Native photographers such as Victor Masayesva, Jr. (Hopi), Jolene Rickard (Tuscarora), Jesse Cooday (Tlingit), Pena Bonita (Mescalero Apache), and Zig Jackson (Mandan) seek to integrate their personal vision as artists with the inspiration they draw from their tribal heritage. When they photograph fellow tribal members and community activities, the images reflect a level of intimacy and trust rarely evident in images by outside photographers. Unlike Native painters and sculptors who draw from established traditions, Native photographers, working in a variety of genres, face the challenge of developing a culturally responsive aesthetic for the medium. Yet they seek foremost to be known as photographers, rather than as "Indian" photographers.

In 1982 Flathead artist Jaune Quick-to-See Smith curated a traveling exhibition of Native American photography. This exhibition drew public attention to the work of both aspiring professional and amateur Native American photographers. In 1985 Native photographers formed the Native Indian Inuit Photographers Association (NIIPA) to advocate for their interests and needs. Based in Canada, NIIPA organizes and tours exhibitions, holds seminars and workshops, maintains a directory, and provides networking through its annual meeting. It is developing a Quincentennial project tentatively called "See Through Our Eyes," which will feature works of approximately thirty-five Native, United States, and Canadian photographers in a book and traveling exhibition. This project, which will result in thousands of negatives, will offer a definitive statement on Native photography, and how Native photographers view themselves and their communities at the close of the twentieth century.

Natasha Bonilla Martinez

See also Art; Public Image

Further Reading

Banta, Melissa, and Curtis M. Hinsley. *From Site to Sight: Anthropology, Photography and the Power of Imagery.* Cambridge, MA: Peabody Museum Press, 1986.

Fleming, Paula R., and Judith Luskey. *The North American Indians in Early Photographs.* New York, NY: Dorset Press, 1986.

Hill, Rick. "In Our Own Image: Stereotyped Images of Indians Lead to New Native Art Form." *Muse* (Winter 1988): 32–37.

Lippard, Lucy R., ed. *Partial Recall; With Essays on Photographs of Native North Americans, by Suzanne Benally, et al.* New York, NY: The New Press, 1992.

Lyman, Christopher M. *The Vanishing Race and Other Illusions: Photographs of Indians by Edward S. Curtis.* Washington, DC: Smithsonian Institution Press, 1982.

Masayesva, Victor, Jr., and Erin Younger. *Hopi Photographers, Hopi Images.* Tucson: Sun Tracks/University of Arizona Press, 1983.

Silver Drum: Five Native Photographers. Hamilton, Ontario: Native Indian Inuit Photographers' Association, 1986.

PIANKASHAW

See Miami; Peoria

PICURIS

See Pueblo of Picuris

PIEGAN

See Blackfeet

PIMA

Twentieth-century archaeologists have postulated that the Tohono O'odham ("Desert People") and the Akimel O'odham or Akimel Au-Authm ("River People") are the probable descendants of the prehistoric people called Hohokam. The Hohokam practiced irrigation agriculture utilizing an extensive system of canals stemming from rivers crossing the arid environment throughout the Gila and Salt River valleys in Arizona.

By the time of European contact in the late 1600s, the once thriving culture of the Hohokam was reduced to small villages occupied by O'odham-speaking groups (Uto-Aztecan linguistic family), who were given the names Pima and Papago by the Spaniards. O'odham-speaking people first experienced the influence of old world cultures with the introduction of Christianity, livestock, grain crops, metal implements, and cannon shot. With the intimidating support of musket balls and Spanish swords the Pima and Papago tribes accepted change and Christianity.

The emergence of the American political system in the eigthteenth and nineteenth centuries brought about the United States federal government reservation system as a way of dealing with the aboriginal people. The reservation system brought about starvation, disease, and the infamous hostilities with various Native tribes and the United States Cavalry. In general, the practice of acculturation by religious and governmental leaders on the remnant tribes in North America had near devastating effects and far-reaching impact into the next hundred years.

The present-day Pimas reside along the dry Gila and Salt rivers in central Arizona. Gila River Indian Community was formally established by Congress on Febrary 28, 1895, on 374,361 acres of land. The Salt River Pima-Maricopa Indian Community was established on June 14, 1879. The communities of Salt River and the Gila River are also the present-day home to the Pee-Posh ("the People"), more commonly known as Maricopas.

The Gila River Indian Community

The administration of tribal government is headquartered in Sacaton, Arizona, 40 miles south of the greater Phoenix metropolitan area. Approximately 9,540 tribal members reside on the reservation with an estimated 2,000 residing off the reservation. Tribal government consists of three branches: legislative, judicial, and executive. The legislative branch is composed of seventeen elected Tribal Council members from the seven districts within the reservation boundaries. The judicial branch includes the Community courts, which are delegated the authority to administer justice in cases involving violations of federal law and the Community's law and order code. The jurisdiction of tribal courts in certain cases extends beyond the physical boundaries of the reservation. For example, tribal courts become involved in the placement of their children in order to comply with the federally mandated Indian Child Welfare Act (ICWA). In this instance, the decision of the tribal courts take precedent over placement by state social service agencies and courts. The executive branch includes the duties and responsibilities of the governor's office. The governor's office is responsible for carrying out the policies and direction of the Tribal Council or legislative branch. The governor is also the head of the Community's administrative and programmatic units.

As it was 2,000 years prior, agriculture continues to play an important role in the economic life of Gila River Indian Community. Tribal and independent agricultural or irrigated lands total 34,000 acres and are concentrated between 1,000 and 1,500 feet above sea level. Future goals for land and water use include charting additional acreage for agricultural purposes, establishing cropping patterns, and developing a more efficient water delivery system for the development of 10,000 acres of the Community's irrigable lands. Today's Community members understand the intrinsic value of their land and water. In 1968 the Community established the Gila River Farms and a Farm Board to oversee its operation. As a Community enterprise the purpose of the Farms is to promote economic development, to provide business training to the Council and other members, to provide a means of tribal income, and to provide employment opportunities for tribal members. The Farms include six ranches and two profit centers. Crop production on the 16,000 acres includes cotton, alfalfa, wheat, barley, melons, grapes, citrus, onions, and lettuce. The Gila River Farms is maintained by 145 full-time and 285 seasonal workers. The total operating budget is approximately $8 million.

Other areas of tribal economic development include the development of three industrial parks. Aluminum extrusion and fabrication, warehousing, a brass foundry, concrete batching, feedmilling, resource recovery, telecommunications, and manufacturing are a few of the industrial activities occurring at the Community's industrial parks.

The Gila River Arts and Crafts Center located on a major interstate attracts tourism. The Center features a gift shop, restaurant, museum, and Heritage Park. The park is of special interest to tourists and local Community members because of its representation of 2,000 years of Pima/Maricopa life since the days of the Hohokam. Attracting large-scale commercial recreation is the Community's Firebird International Raceway Park. Firebird offers a motor-sport facility that features Pro-National Hot Rod Association drag-racing, a 120-acre boat racing lake, and an outdoor amphitheater, Compton Terrace, which has been the stage for top performing artists.

The Gila River Indian Community has authorized the formation of Gila River Telecommunications, Inc. (GRTI). This is a tribal corporation, charted under federal Indian laws, which has developed and operates a complete telecommunications system to serve subscribers residing on the reservation. GRTI has made it possible for individual members of the Community to speak long-distance to the rest of the world with state-of-the-art telecommunications equipment and technology.

Located on the northern portion of the reservation is a private commercial airfield (Memorial Airfield) with an 8,500-foot runway. The airfield was first constructed as a training facility during World War II. The Community, in conjunction with the Federal Aeronautics Administration, is planning to develop an airport master plan in order to take advantage of the opportunity to relieve air traffic congestion at the airports in the greater metropolitan Phoenix area.

Gila River Indian Community provides educational programs and ancilliary services directly and indirectly to approximately 8,000 preschool and school-aged children. Early childhood programs such as Head Start and school-initiated preschool programs are available to young Community members. The reservation has three Bureau of Indian Affairs funded schools within its boundaries. There are ten elementary and secondary school districts that border the Community's land and serve students from Gila River. In the 1991 to 1993 academic year Gila River had forty-nine students enrolled in colleges and universities and twenty-six students enrolled in vocational training programs. The Community also provides several supplemental programs to its students. These programs include Library Media Services, services to disabled children, alcohol/substance abuse prevention programs, and counseling/home liaison services.

Youth development on the reservation is of vital importance. The Tribal Council established and sanctioned the Akimel O'odham/Pee-Posh Youth Council in 1987 to provide leadership training and a means for youth to formally voice concerns and opinions to the Tribal Council. The Youth Council remains committed to utilizing the collective talents and energies of its members for building stronger families and communities.

The Indian Health Services, United States Department of the Interior, provides health care to the Community from the local Sacaton service unit and the Phoenix service unit. The tribe also receives health related services from the United States Department of Health Services. In 1980 a twenty-bed HuHuKam Memorial Hospital was completed after nearly a decade of planning and development. Gila River Indian Community members have had a history of unusually high rates of diabetes in comparison to the Anglo population. To address the alarming rate of diabetes among Community members, the Native American Dialysis Center was opened in July 1989. This facility, privately owned and operated, provides dialysis services to Native American patients from the Community and off-reservation localities.

Salt River Pima-Maricopa Indian Community

The Salt River Pima-Maricopa Indian Community was established on June 14, 1879. The reservation encompasses 52,600 acres of land and is situated on the eastern edge of the greater Phoenix metropolitan area. The on-reservation population is approximately 5,000 members. For generations the Pimas and Maricopas farmed along the banks of the Salt River providing grain crops to the newly arrived settlers in the settlements of Phoenix and the river crossing town of Tempe.

The Community is governed by a president, vice-president, seven council members, a Community manager, and complete governmental service. They voted on and adopted a Constitution and Bylaws as part of the Indian Reorganization Act on June 15, 1940. The Police Department has twenty-four officers, and the Fire Department has twenty firefighters. The Community offers many facilities including six parks, two swimming pools, a library, a museum, two golf courses, four baseball diamonds, four recreation centers, and two theater complexes.

Economic development has taken on many forms. The Salt River Indian Community is unique for the intensive urbanization surrounding its borders. About 12,000 acres are now under agricultural cultivation. The Pavilions, a 140-acre retail center, is the nation's largest commercial development ever built on Indian lands. The Community also mines sand and gravel on and off Indian land and operates a comprehensive solid waste disposal operation serving the Community and nearby cities. There is a tribally owned cement plant and a golf course. The construction of the Pima Freeway along nine miles of the western boundary is attracting new businesses to the Community.

Education is very important. There are numerous elementary schools, junior high schools, high schools, and boarding schools, along with special education schools and a Head Start program available to Community students. The latest figures available show 965 students enrolled. The Community has a public library and the Hoo-hoogam Ki Museum displays the rich tradition of the Pima-Maricopa people. The museum highlights the superb Pima basketmaking tradition, which continues today and also features a restaurant serving authentic Indian foods. The Community has a monthly newpaper called *The Au-Authm Action News*.

There are many recreational opportunities available. The Verde and Salt rivers provide popular fishing, boating, and tubing activities. Well-known pow-wows take place in April, September, and November of each year.

The United States Public Health Service provides out-patient care in a clinic environment and operates a hospital in Phoenix. The Community Health Center and Dialysis Treatment Center, operated by the Kidney Disease and Hypertension Center, provide in-patient medical care to Community members.

The "Man in the Maze" is the tribal symbol of the Community. This legend has been retold for generations as a guidepost through life's journey. The legend demonstrates the choices in determining the paths leading to dreams, goals, and ultimate destination. As a Community, the Salt River Pima-Maricopa people are influenced by the rich heritage of their ancestors. With this, they continue in balance and harmony as they prosper as one nation.

Gilbert C. Innis

Office of Community Relations,
Salt River Pima-Maricopa Indian Community

See also **Arizona Tribes; Indian Child Welfare Act; Pee-Posh**

Further Reading

Ortiz, Alfonso, ed. *Handbook of North American Indians.* Vol.10. *Southwest.* Washington, DC: Smithsonian Institution (1983): 125–36; 149–216; 212–16.
Russell, Frank. *The Pima Indians.* Tucson: Univer Arizona Press, 1975.
Shaw, Anna Moore. *A Pima Past.* Tucson: University of Arizona Press, 1974.
Webb, George. *A Pima Remembers.* Tucson: University of Arizona Press, 1959.

PINAL

See Apache

PIRO

See Tortugas; Ysleta de Sur Pueblo

PISCATAWAY

In southern Maryland there are presently several hundred individuals living in different communities who embrace a Piscataway Indian identity. There are numerous theories as to the origin of these people, which suggest a racial mixture of Indian, Black, and white. A thorough examination of ethnohistorical sources has shed considerable light on the development of these Piscataway Indian communities. The present-day Piscataway population originated in Charles County, Maryland, prior to 1778, evolved from multiple origins, and developed from socially disapproved interracial unions.

During the contact period, several tribal groups lived along the small streams and swampy tracts of land along the Potomac River. By the end of the seventeenth century, the population of these tribes had been severely reduced. They were forced to band together and were assigned to reservations. Following Bacon's Rebellion, many of these groups (including the Piscataway) emigrated to Pennsylvania and Virginia. The remnants of several of these individual tribes, however, remained in southern Maryland. By the middle of the nineteenth century, many of these Indian families had become tenant farmers, and gradually accumulated enough capital to purchase their own property.

In time several Indian communities developed. The nineteenth-century settlement pattern reflected the precontact location of tribal villages in southern Maryland. William H. Gilbert, who did a detailed study of the Indian population of southern Maryland in the 1940s, concluded that "little remains today of the Indian heritage among these people. In fact, there seem to be no unifying cultural traits to bind them into a common unity distinct from Whites and Negroes." Many simply referred to themselves as "Indians" with no tribal designation. There was, however, a small group led by Phillip Proctor (who later assumed the name Turkey Tayac), who strongly identified themselves as direct descendants of the Piscataway Indians.

In the 1970s considerable factionalism and hostility developed among the Piscataway regarding the tribal identity of the Indian population, and who had a legitimate right to be chief of the Piscataway people. the death of Turkey Tayac, his son, Billy Red-claimed to be the hereditary chief of the ibe. A dispute about the legitimacy of this claim resulted in a division among the Piscataway into two factions who eventually took their claims to court. In an out-of-court settlement, the litigants created the Maryland Indian Heritage Society, which would be led by Hugh Proctor, and the Piscataway Indian Nation, Inc., which would be led by Billy Tayac. In 1981, a third Piscataway political organization, the Piscataway-Conoy Confederacy and subtribes, were formed. Mervin Savoy of Indian Head is tribal chairwoman of the Confederacy. Each of the groups is currently preparing petitions for federal recognition.

The estimated population of the Piscataway Indians of southern Maryland, according to the state's Commission on Indian Affairs, is between 5,000 and 7,000. However, membership in each of the three Piscataway organizations is 100 to 200. While they do not have any land base or live in recognizable communities, they are bound by family ties and group membership in their respective tribal organizations.

Frank W. Porter III

Further Reading

Ferguson, Alice L.L. *The Piscataway Indians of Southern Maryland.* Accokeek, MD: Alice Ferguson Foundation, 1960.

Gilbert, William H. "The Wesorts of Maryland: An Outcasted Group." *Journal of the Washington Academy of Sciences* 35 (August 1945): 237–46.

Harte, Thomas J.C. "Social Origins of the Brandywine Population." *Phylon* 24 (1963): 369–78.

Porter, Frank W. *Maryland Indians: Yesterday and Today.* Baltimore: Maryland Historical Society, 1983.

PIT RIVER

The Pit River Tribe (also known as Achumawi and Atsugewi) is composed of eleven bands, each band constituting a small territorial division along the Pit River and its tributaries in northeastern California. The eleven bands are often distinguished by their languages, Achumawi and Atsugewi, two closely related members of the Palaihnihan branch of the Hokan linguistic family. Nine bands (Ajumawi, Astarawi, Atwamsini, Ilmawi, Hammawi, Hewisedawi, Itsatawi, Madesi, and Kosalektawi) spoke related dialects of Achumawi, and the Atsugewi and Aporige bands spoke Atsugewi, and often the Achumawi language as well. The terms Achumawi (Achomawi) and Atsugewi are also used to designate the two groups of Pit River Indians.

From an estimated precontact population of 3,000 Pit River Indians, their number had been reduced to approximately 1,000 according to the 1910 United States Census. During the nineteenth century, they endured disease, military conflict, displacement by white settlers, and the forced removal of many Pit River Indians to the Round Valley Reservation. But the landless Pit River people clung to the fringes of their territory, and finally after 1897, the Dawes Act allowed them to acquire land as individual allotments.

The vast majority of California allotments were located in northeastern California. Although most of the available land was agriculturally marginal, many Pit River people applied for parcels with the help of educated leaders such as Charlie Green. They tended to select parcels that clustered in their traditional band territories, often near their former settlements. In this way the Pit River people reinforced their band ties and continued to supplement their diet by collecting in familiar areas. For various reasons many Pit River Indians could not maintain ownership and allotments were sold. Between 1917 and 1930 many allotments along the Pit River were acquired by representatives of Pacific Gas and Electric Company prior to hydroelectric development in ways which, to the Pit River people, were questionable. By 1950 few of the former allotments were still retained.

Another type of land base resulted from the C.E. Kelsey Census of 1905–1906, which revealed a large number of landless Pit River people. Seven small rancherias were established in Pit River territory between 1915 and 1938. None of these rancherias were suitable for intensive agriculture and all were very small except for XL Rancheria. Neither of the Atsugewi bands received rancheria land.

In the California Indian land claims cases, the tribe presented its own cases beginning in 1919, since Pit River territory had not been included in the eigh-teen unratified treaties from 1851 to 1852. Charlie Green went to Washington under the auspices of F.G. Collett's Indian Board of Cooperation and for years dedicated his efforts to the land claims issues. The tribe finally appointed him an honorary chief and tribal delegate but he died in 1950, long before the case was settled. After the Indian Claims Commission Act of 1946, the Pit River Tribe was allowed to file claims as a separate tribe (1951), present their case (1957), and receive a favorable ruling (1959). But they were urged to support and join a joint compromise settlement for all the Indians of California in 1963 and did so despite a bare majority vote and serious internal conflict. This decision, and dissatisfaction with the settlement, created years of disharmony between the disparate groups who were divided primarily by upriver and downriver bands.

By 1966 members of the Pit River, primarily the younger downriver members and the Atsugewi, began civil rights demonstrations and political activism concerning the usurpation of their tribal lands. The Pacific Gas and Electric Company was a traditional opponent and demonstrations against the National Park Service, the Forest Service, and others followed. The civil disorder focused on issues of tribal sovereignty, the free practice of Indian religion and self-determination. The Pit River people began to unite and organize around the concepts of traditional Pit River territory and political consolidation.

The Pit River Tribe first received formal recognition in 1976 and its Constitution was accepted in 1987. Current tribal rolls include 1,350 members, of which 706 are voting members. The Tribal Council meets at least eighteen times a year and each of the eleven bands is represented by one vote. Tribal leadership is striving to create a unified government and community that continues to recognize and respect band differences. With the rancherias and tribal membership stretched across Modoc, Lassen, and Shasta counties, the difficulties of tribal participation in community projects and tribal operations is a serious handicap today.

Unemployment has always been a serious problem in the northeastern region of California and it has worsened as the logging industry declined. The most recent Pit River labor force report (1983) states that 59 percent of the potential work force is unemployed and most regional employment opportunities are seasonal. The tribe harvests one crop of hay per year from the XL Rancheria, but has the potential for two annual crops.

Health conditions have vastly improved since the 1920s when influenza, smallpox, and tuberculosis outbreaks plagued the area. Indian doctors were a real alternative to the inadequate medical system well into the mid-twentieth century and continue to be in occasional use. The Pit River Tribe has its own health clinic in Burney near tribal headquarters. The clinic is a member of the California Rural Indian Health Board, as is the clinic in Alturas used by the upriver bands. Health conditions have recently been improved by the construction of two wells and additional sanitation services for Atsugewi homes in the Hat Creek area, but many homes are still substandard. The health clinic has a drug and alcoholism program but needs more financial assistance with this problem.

In Alturas, Fall River Mills, and Hat Creek, there are Indian Mission churches. The Indian Mission or Pentecostal Church blended Christianity and some aspects of the traditional belief system by the 1920s. Before 1930, Indian children were schooled at these missions or in distant boarding schools, such as Fort Bidwell or Sherman Institute. The churches still have an active membership, but have never completely replaced an adaptive traditional system which draws continued energy from attachment to the land. The Pit River Tribe sponsors a tribal powwow annually which is a popular regional event. The Pit River people are strongly united in their attachment to their ancestral lands and the preservation of sacred places, an example of which is their recent and ongoing opposition to economic development on Mt. Shasta.

Nancy H. Evans

See also **California Tribes**

Further Reading

Garth, T.R. "Atsugewi." *Handbook of North American Indians.* Vol. 8. *California.* Ed. Robert F. Heizer. Washington, DC: Smithsonian Institution (1978): 236–43.

Kniffen, Fred B. "Achomawi Geography." *University of California Publications in American Archaeology and Ethnology* 23:5 (1928): 297–332.

Olmsted, D.L., and Omer C. Stewart. "Achumawi." *Handbook of North American Indians.* Vol. 8. *California.* Ed. Robert F. Heizer. Washington, DC: Smithsonian Institution (1978): 225–35.

Voegelin, Erminie. "Culture Element Distributions XX: Northeast California." *University of California Anthropological Records* 7:2 (1942): 47–252.

PLAINS APACHE

The Indians officially known as the "Plains Apache Tribe of Oklahoma" have been known to outsiders by a confusing variety of names during their history. Their name for themselves is *Na-i-shan Dene,* meaning "Our People." In the past they often appear to have been known to other tribes and Europeans by names that also meant "Apaches" generally, making it difficult to identify the *Na-i-shan Dene* in early documents. They are believed to be the "Apaches del Norte," whose arrival in New Mexico with a group of Kiowas was recorded early in the nineteenth century, and as the "Plains Lipans," who arrived on the northern frontier of Texas with their Kiowa and Arapaho allies during the same time period. During the nineteenth century, they came to be known to Americans as the "Prairie Apaches" or "Plains Apaches," and finally, on into the twentieth century, as the "Kiowa Apaches." This last, misleading, name is unacceptable to them; they generally nowadays call themselves Plains Apaches or simply Apaches.

Tribal traditions specify a northern Plains, rather than southwestern origin, and ethnographic and linguistic studies portray them as a Plains tipi-dwelling, buffalo-hunting people, who spoke an Apache language distinct from that spoken in the Southwest. They gradually moved southward from the Missouri River region until they were settled on the Kiowa-Comanche-Apache Reservation (KCA) in present southwestern Oklahoma in the late nineteenth century. That reservation was allotted in 160-acre parcels to individual members of the three tribes in 1901, with the remainder of the land open to citizen settlement. Two Plains Apache population centers developed a few miles west of the towns of Apache and Fort Cobb, Oklahoma, and these people are sometimes referred to respectively as the Cache Creek and Washita Apaches.

The Plains Apaches entered the twentieth century depleted in numbers by epidemics and inundated by a flood of settlers drawn to the former KCA reservation. Their history in this century has been characterized by a dramatic growth in population and gradual adjustment to living in the larger society. The tribe's population has grown from about 150 members at the turn of the century, to their nearly 1,400 descendants in 1993, a result in part of high rates of intermarriage with Indians of other tribes. The Plains Apaches' economy has shifted from dependence on per capita payments and the leasing of allotted land toward greater involvement in the broader economy.

The best-known tribal leader of the twentieth century has been Gonkon, or Apache John, who was selected to represent the tribe in protesting the Jerome Agreement, which allotted the Kiowa-Comanche-Apache Reservation in severalty. The Plains Apaches have benefited from the same land claims settlements as the Kiowas and Comanches and own some property in common with them. A tribal government was organized in the 1970s to administer federal programs and manage other tribal business. The tribe now has an administrative complex in Anadarko, Oklahoma, which is used for Apache language classes and other educational and social purposes. They also own a convenience store in Anadarko and a dance ground west of Fort Cobb, where major ceremonials are held in June and August. Their most pressing economic problem is lack of employment opportunities.

The Plains Apaches have a rich repertory of traditional music and often excel in arts and crafts. Many of them are noted as traditional Indian singers, drummers, and dancers. The two chapters of the *Manatidie,* or Blackfeet Society, are much in demand to dance at the powwows of other tribes in addition to their own people's celebrations. Members of the tribe have been particularly noted for the excellence of their beadwork, silverwork, featherwork, painting, and woodcarving. While they participate fully in the southern Plains Indian social and religious milieu of western Oklahoma, traditionalist Plains Apaches still recognize their kinship with both the southwestern Apaches and the Sarcee of Alberta, Canada.

Michael G. Davis

See also **Apache; Comanche; Kiowa; Oklahoma Tribes**

Further Reading

Beatty, John. *Kiowa-Apache Music and Dance*. Occasional Publications in Anthropology. Ethnology Ser. 31. Greeley: Museum of Anthropology, University of Northern Colorado, 1974.

Davis, Michael G. "The Cultural Preadaptation Hypothesis: A Test Case on the Southern Plains." Ph.D. diss., University of Oklahoma, 1988.

McAllister, J. Gilbert. "Kiowa-Apache Social Organization." *Social Anthropology of North American Tribes*. Ed. Fred Eggan. Enl. ed. IL: University of Chicago (1955): 97–169.

Mooney, James. *Calendar History of the Kiowa Indians*. Bureau of American Ethnology, 2nd Annual Report 1898. Washington, DC: Smithsonian Institution, 1979.

———. "Kiowa Apache." *Handbook of American Indians North of Mexico*. Ed. Frederick W. Hodge. Bureau of American Ethnology Bulletin 30. Vol. 1. 1907–1910. 6th ed. Totowa, NJ: Rowman and Littlefield, 1979.

PLAINS OJIBWA

See Ojibwa: Chippewa in Montana

POETRY

See Literature

POJOAQUE

See Pueblo of Pojoaque

POKAGON POTAWATOMI

See Potawatomi in Southern Michigan

POMO

Pomo is the name given by linguists to speakers of seven related but mutually unintelligible languages, further designated by geographical prefixes indicating their locations relative to each other: Northern Pomo, Central Pomo, Southern Pomo, Southwestern (Kashaya) Pomo, Eastern Pomo, Southeastern Pomo and Northeastern Pomo. Pomo-speaking people have traditionally lived in what is now called Lake, Mendocino, and Sonoma counties in northern California and still reside there today. The people generally referred to themselves with the name of the village community they came from, and today use the name of their rancheria in much the same way. For example, the Yokaya (after whom the Ukiah Valley was named) now call themselves the Yokayo Band of Pomo Indians; the Shanel (from Hopland) now call themselves the Hopland Band of Pomo Indians. According to the 1990 census, 4,766 people identified

themselves as Pomo. Following are the current federally recognized reservations and rancherias which are either Pomo or include significant Pomo membership: Hopland, Guidiville, Pinoleville, Coyote Valley, Redwood Valley, Sherwood Valley, Manchester/Point Arena, Potter Valley, and Round Valley (Little Lake Pomo) in Mendocino County; Cloverdale, Dry Creek, Stewarts Point, and Lytton in Sonoma County; Robinson, Upper Lake, Big Valley, Elem Indian Colony, Scotts Valley, and Middletown in Lake County; and Grindstone in Glenn County.

The struggle for a permanent land base and tribal identity has characterized Pomo life in the twentieth century. After the great disruption of Pomo culture caused by disease, enforced incarceration on federal reservations, the regrouping of people prompted by the Bole Maru, or 1870 Ghost Dance, and the inevitable takeover of Indian land by homesteaders, the Pomo of Mendocino County began to form new coalitions and contrived to buy back their land in the late 1870s through the 1890s. Groups of people pledged their labor to non-Indian landowners in exchange for land or pooled their money to purchase property outright. In 1878 a group of Northern Pomo people bought seven acres in Coyote Valley. In 1880 another Northern Pomo group bought 100 acres along Ackerman Creek, now known as Pinoleville. In 1881 Yokayo Rancheria was financed primarily by Central Pomo-speaking people and is still retained as private property today; the Yokayo Band of Pomo Indians is currently seeking federal acknowledgment. It is an example of one of the longest held, communally owned pieces of property in California. In 1892 Potter Valley Rancheria was bought. Sherwood Rancheria and Yorkville Rancheria were also privately purchased.

By the turn of the century, however, most of the Pomo private property had been lost through foreclosure or mortgage debt. Although the California Indian population was reduced to an estimated 16,500 at that time, 11,800 of the survivors were considered "landless." Public attention was drawn to the desperate plight of the so-called "landless Indians," and Congress in 1905 authorized an investigation of their living conditions. C.E. Kelsey, an attorney from San Jose and officer of the Northern California Indian Association, was appointed special agent to investigate and develop a plan to improve their lives.

Kelsey, after traveling the state, recommended that Congress buy small parcels of land for these "homeless" Indians meeting the following four criteria: that there be sites for houses, that the land be irrigable, and that a proper supply of water and wood be available. A series of appropriation acts for land purchases was passed starting in 1906 and followed by almost yearly appropriations through 1934, when the Indian Reorganization Act was passed, which contained separate authority for the acquisition of land for Indians. Between 1906 and 1913 Kelsey himself purchased land in northern and central California pursuant to the acts. In Mendocino County, Kelsey helped to acquire land for the Potter Valley Band of Pomo Indians, Redwood Valley Rancheria, Pinoleville Rancheria, Guidiville Band of Indians, Hopland Band of Pomo Indians, Coyote Valley, and others. The Yokayo Band maintained their own property, Yokayo Rancheria, despite the hardships of interband conflicts, mortgage payments, and a constant need for tax money. Land for Pomo Indians was also purchased in Lake and Sonoma counties.

Most Pomo people at the turn of the century depended on native plants, fish, and game for subsistence. The variety and the amount eaten corresponded to age, i.e., the older people relied more heavily on Native foods than the younger people, with each subsequent generation relying less on traditional food resources and more on store bought foods like dried beans, rice, coffee, sugar, and flour. Acorns, however, continued to be the most extensively utilized traditional food. The Pomo people have maintained traditions that have become part of contemporary life. These include living on shared land in close communities; the importance of family relationships; seasonal trips to the coast; the eating of Native foods; continued use of Pomo languages; and participation in Pomo dances, songs, and games.

There were only a few opportunities for earning money open to Pomo people. They lived on isolated rancherias on the outskirts of communities that were strongly segregated. Local businesses displayed signs that said, "No dogs or Indians allowed." Restaurants would not serve Indians nor would schools and churches in town allow them to attend. Their transportation was limited to horse and wagon and later to substandard automobiles. Many Pomo men and women worked in the hop fields. Others earned money by cutting firewood for large buyers, such as the state hospital in Talmage. Women wove baskets for collectors and were employed as laundresses until they were displaced by Chinese laundries.

The early twentieth century was characterized by some important legal challenges initiated by Pomo Indians. In 1907 an Eastern Pomo, Ethan Anderson, won a court case giving nonreservation Indians the right to vote. In 1923 Stephen Knight in Mendocino County challenged the state school segregation laws and in an out-of-court settlement forced a local public school to admit his daughter. His case had been preceded by one in Lake County where Pomo parents sued a local school district that refused entrance to their children. In that case, however, the school board exercised a legal option to establish a separate school for Indian students. Knight later took on the City of Ukiah, when he challenged the segregation policy of the local movie theater on behalf of his granddaughter. Many self-help groups such as the Pomo Mothers' Club, Society of Northern California Indians, and the Indian Board of Cooperation were started by and/or heavily supported by Pomo people.

The Depression and local prejudice pushed many young Pomo women to seek employment in the Bay Area in the 1930s, where they were hired, with the help of the Bureau of Indian Affairs (BIA) and the Oakland YWCA, as domestics. Pomo men were able to find local employment as migrant field workers and ranch laborers. World War II led to greater employment opportunities and many Pomo people left Lake, Mendocino and Sonoma counties to serve in the armed forces and to work in war-related industries.

In the 1950s a new federal Indian policy which emphasized assimilation and the end of government supervision began to make itself felt among the Pomo. It was vigorously opposed by California's Indians at first, but in 1958 the California termination bill (H.R. 2824) was passed affecting forty-one California rancherias including many Pomo rancherias. These rancherias held lengthy discussions and most voted to terminate their federal relationship in exchange for deeds and promises of BIA-funded capital improvements. The termination process continued throughout the 1960s. In the 1970s it became apparent that the BIA had not fulfilled its obligations for such improvements as roads, domestic water, and irrigation systems. Several Pomo rancherias successfully sued the government to amend their terminated status as a result of these omissions. In the 1980s a suit was filed by Tillie Hardwick from Pinoleville Rancheria in Mendocino County on behalf of herself and others to "unterminate" themselves. Evidence was presented by California Indian Legal Services citing the failure of the BIA to live up to their termination agreements. The settlement of *Tillie Hardwick v. United States* resulted in a judgment restoring federal recognition to seventeen rancherias, which included many Pomo properties. This quest for the restoration of federal recognition continues to the present day.

In addition to the ongoing Pomo struggle for recognition and land on the part of individual bands was the creation of an Indian land base in Sonoma County through the establishment of an Indian center called Ya-Ka-Ama. It has grown to be a model center with its native plant nursery, economic development projects, and educational and cultural programs. Another pan-Pomo project is the Intertribal Sinkyone Wilderness Council, a group of tribal people in Mendocino County who are attempting to restore a heavily logged area of public land as a model of traditional Indian land use and modern native plant restoration techniques.

Throughout the twentieth century Pomo people have maintained their culture and sense of identity through music, dance, and traditional crafts such as basketry. Pomo basketweavers are internationally known. Elsie Allen, Laura Somersal, Mabel McKay, and others have been immortalized by museums and private collectors alike. Pomo dancers perform at all ceremonial gatherings and several rancherias have reconstructed their sacred dance houses. Several linguistic projects have resulted in Pomo orthographies, Pomo language education programs, and a continuing number of books published about Pomo languages.

Victoria Patterson

See also California Tribes

Further Reading

Barrett, Samuel A. "The Ethnogeography of the Pomo and Neighboring Indians." *University of California Publications in American Archaeology and Ethnology* 6:1 (1908): 1–332.

Bean, Lowell John, and Dorothea Theodoratus. "Western Pomo and Northeastern Pomo." *Handbook of North American Indians.* Vol. 8. *California.* Ed. Robert F. Heizer. Washington, DC: Smithsonian Institution (1978): 289–305.

Kaplan, Victoria Dickler, et al. *Sheemi Ke Ianu: Talk From the Past, A History of the Russian River Pomo of Mendocino County.* CA: Title VII Project of Ukiah Unified School District, 1984.

McLendon, Sally, and Michael J. Lowy. "Eastern Pomo and Southeastern Pomo." *Handbook of North American Indians.* Vol. 8. *California.* Ed. Robert F. Heizer. Washington, DC: Smithsonian Institution (1978): 306–23.

Patterson, Victoria. "Virgilia Knight, et al. v. Carroll School District." *News From Native California* 1:6 (January/February 1988): 7–10.

———. "Indian Life in the City. A Glimpse of the Urban Experience of Pomo Women in the 1930s." *California History* 71:3 (Fall 1992): 402–11.

PONCA

The split of the Ponca people into the northern tribe in Nebraska and the southern tribe in Oklahoma was the result of the United States government assigning the Ponca Reservation in Nebraska to the Sioux. Forced to relocate to Oklahoma in 1876, thirty Ponca returned to Nebraska three years later and eventually were permitted to remain in their homeland. From this separation grew the two separate political entities of today, with the Southern Ponca remaining the larger tribe.

NORTHERN PONCA

The Northern Ponca Tribe of Nebraska is a Plains tribe of the Dhegiha group within the Siouan language family. Most likely emanating from the middle Mississippian cultures of the Eastern Woodlands, the Ponca and their close relatives the Omaha probably appeared on the Plains around A.D. 1200 to 1300, after which time these two groups parted ways, the Ponca settling near what is now Niobrara, Nebraska.

Four treaties were negotiated between the federal government and the Ponca, the second two resulting in the loss of much of their 2.3 million acres of tribal land. Having a reservation of only 96,000 acres, the Ponca suffered a final blow in the inadvertent assignment of their land to the Sioux in the Fort Laramie Treaty of 1868. Devastated by the reduction of their land base, the Ponca were in a politically weakened position and were ordered to move to Indian Territory in Oklahoma in 1876 to 1877. The Ponca chiefs went south to explore the territory, but, finding it unacceptable, they petitioned to return and remain in the north. Their request was denied, and the Ponca were forced south. However, a group of Ponca led by Chief Standing Bear, finding their new homeland to be inhospitable and wishing to return to their original homeland to bury their dead, defied government orders and headed north. They were arrested, taken into custody, and detained on the Omaha Reservation in Nebraska, where the resulting famous Trial of Standing Bear of 1879 established the Ponca's legal entitlement to their homeland on the Nebraska reservation. The Ponca who stayed in Oklahoma became known as the Southern Ponca Tribe.

The Ponca remaining in the north became the Northern Ponca, settling on their 26,236–acre reservation in Knox County, Nebraska. As with other tribes, the allotment of land to individuals as a result of the Dawes Act of 1887 seriously undermined tribal traditions and structure, further weakening the group. The Northern Ponca remained on what was left of their reservation, until the termination policy of the 1950s targeted them, among others. Four hundred forty-two Ponca were removed from the tribal rolls and dispossessed of their last 834 acres of land by 1966. The termination bill contained a provision, however, for the Ponca to retain their traditional burial ground. Despite their termination, a group of Ponca remained in the Nebraska and South Dakota areas, determined to reverse this devastating act. They organized and incorporated, forming the Northern Ponca Restoration Committee (NPRC) in 1986. Under the strong leadership of NPRC members Deb Wright, Fred LeRoy, and Marshall Prichard, the approximately 890 members of the Northern Ponca sought and obtained recognition from the State of Nebraska in 1988 and pursued congressional restoration. In October of 1990, President George W. Bush signed the Northern Ponca Restoration Act, returning the Ponca to eligibility for services in health, education, and employment. Since restoration, they have been able to reacquire 413 acres of their former reservation land, and in 1993 are in the process of acquiring two additional tracts—the 160-acre former Standing Bear Ponca Agency and the Black Ghost allotment of 253 acres. If acquired, such land would be taken into trust by the secretary of the interior after review by the solicitor general.

Spiritual ties to the aboriginal homeland and tribal cemetery persist, serving as a focal point for the regional development of a tribal center and museum. The Ponca have a strong cultural identity and continue to practice their traditions. The *Hedushka* (War Dance) Society continues, with annual powwows featuring Ponca regalia, ritual paraphernalia, and traditional singing and drumming. The Northern Ponca Sun Dance is no longer practiced, but tribal members participate in sun dances held by other tribes. The Peyote Religion was introduced to the Ponca in the early 1900s and has remained an important element in religious activity throughout the twentieth century. The recent return of the Omaha Sacred Pole is of great interest to the Ponca as well, since it is likely that the pole was cut before the Ponca/Omaha split, and so also belongs to the Ponca. The Ponca language is still spoken by a few elderly people, and is closely related to the Omaha language, which is thriving.

Today the Northern Ponca reside in twenty-four different states, but over half of the tribal members continue to reside in the states of Nebraska, South Dakota, and Iowa. Most have achieved a high school education, but continue to be burdened by poor health and high unemployment rates. Like other American Indian groups, the Ponca population has disproportionately high rates of diabetes and hypertension. Eligibility for health care services now promises a higher standard of health for the Northern Ponca and their descendants.

Most Poncas today believe that termination had a damaging effect on their ability to maintain their culture and resulted in the loss of some of their heritage—knowledge of their cultural practices, language, and the loss of a political identity. While the majority of Ponca believe that a reservation near the town of Niobrara, Nebraska, should again be established, the conditions imposed on them by their restoration makes that unlikely. However, the Northern Ponca have renewed their trust relationship with the federal government and are undertaking tribal cultural and economic development.

The Ponca are in the process of establishing a new tribal government in the early 1990s and currently have an Interim Tribal Council based in Niobrara, Nebraska. Former Northern Ponca restoration activist Deb Wright serves as the chairperson. The Interim Council is working on a Tribal Constitution, which will be submitted to the Bureau of Indian Affairs for approval and to tribal members for ratification. An economic development plan, whose goal will be to provide employment opportunities for tribal members, was submitted to Congress in October 1993.

Elizabeth S. Grobsmith

Beth R. Ritter

See also **Omaha**

Further Reading

Cash, Joseph H., and Gerald W. Wolff. *The Ponca People.* Phoenix, AZ: Indian Tribal Series, 1975.

Grobsmith, Elizabeth S., and Beth R. Ritter. "The Ponca Tribe of Nebraska: The Process of Restoration of a Federally Terminated Tribe." *Human Organization* 51 (1992): 1–16.

Howard, James H. *The Ponca Tribe.* Bureau of American Ethnology Bulletin 195. Washington, DC: U.S. Government Printing Office, 1965.

Olson, James S., and Raymond Wilson. *Native Americans in the 20th Century.* 1984. Urbana: University of Illinois Press, 1986.

Tibbles, Thomas Henry. *The Ponca Chiefs: An Account of the Trial of Standing Bear.* Ed. Kay Graber. Lincoln: University of Nebraska Press, 1972.

SOUTHERN PONCA

The Ponca Tribe of Oklahoma, or the Southern Ponca, is located in north central Oklahoma, a few miles south of Ponca City. The Ponca have four treaties with the United States; the last two defined their reservation in their traditional homeland of northeast Nebraska. The Sioux Treaty of 1868, however, confused the land issue. An administrative blunder included all the Ponca lands within the treaty lands of the Sioux. Rather than correct the error, the United States government forced the removal of the majority of Ponca to Indian Territory in 1877, where a new reservation was established adjacent to the Arkansas and the Salt Fork Rivers. In 1878, Chief Standing Bear and sixty-five of his followers returned to Nebraska to bury his eldest son. This event resulted in the separation of the Ponca into separate northern and southern tribes.

By 1905 the Southern Ponca reservation had been allotted to individuals, but a strong anti-allotment faction emerged among the more traditional members which fractured the tribe. Many of the allotted lands were leased to a non-Indian family that owned the 101 Ranch, who then developed oil wells and operated a wild west show.

During this period of internal strife and external pressure, Robert Buffalohead brought the Peyote Religion to the Ponca in 1902, having learned the ritual among the Cheyenne. By 1916 more than half of the Ponca population of 630 were participants of the new religion. Two Poncas were involved in establishing the Native American Church in 1918; Frank Eagle was elected the church's first president, Louis McDonald was elected treasurer. Today, Poncas are also members of various Christian denominations, including Methodist, Nazarene, Baptist, Full Gospel, and Catholic.

In 1950 the Ponca developed a Tribal Constitution and Bylaws under the Oklahoma Indian Welfare Act of 1936. The government consists of a seven-member Tribal Business Committee and defines criteria for membership in the tribe. During the 1960s and 1970s, the Ponca Tribal Housing Authority was formed, and a new community developed at White Eagle with subsidized houses and rental duplexes for the elderly. A health clinic was built and leased by the tribe to the Indian Health Service. The former school at White Eagle was renovated and became the Tribal Affairs Building. A new cultural center with cooking facilities and a gymnasium was constructed. And, in association with other tribes in north central Oklahoma, the Ponca have established a Court of Indian Offenses.

But in the 1970s and 1980s, factionalism and disharmony characterized tribal government. As the Ponca Tribal Business Committee assumed the responsibilities for managing up to sixteen federal programs—health, nutrition, food distribution, alcohol and drug abuse, child welfare, legal services, higher and adult education, training and employment, rehabilitation of housing, and law and order—accusations of mismanagement and dishonesty led to several recall elections. By 1990 the tribal government had become more complex, with departments for accounting, planning, grants and contracts, and a tax commission.

With the reduction of federal funding that began in the early 1980s, the Business Committee began a search for other sources of revenue to fund tribal initiatives. Ponca bingo generated a few jobs and over one million dollars for tribal operations in 1983. Smoke-shops have also brought in revenue for the tribe. However, these activities, on which no state taxes are collected, have brought the Ponca tribe into conflict with the Oklahoma Tax Commission.

The Ponca have served in all United States military conflicts of the twentieth century, and in 1919 Ponca veterans founded American Legion Post 38 (the Buffalo Post), and the wives and mothers formed an auxiliary unit and a chapter of the Gold Star Mothers. The annual Ponca powwow has been held in late August since 1877, when it began as a harvest celebration. In the 1930s, it honored Ponca children leaving home to attend boarding schools. It is now an inter-tribal event that features Ponca War Dance songs.

The Ponca Indian War Dance Society, formed in the 1950s as a revival of the *Hethuska* Society, sponsors a spring and fall dance each year. As part of a Mother's Day dance in 1983, the Ponca Indian Women's Society revived the Scalp Dance, which had not been performed since the end of World War II. It is now performed on a regular basis. Other tribal organizations and families sponsor special dances throughout the year to honor achievements by members of the tribe. The traditional shinny game has also been revived, and is played on four consecutive Sundays each spring in White Eagle. As a result of contacts made at meals served for the elderly at a federally funded nutrition program on the reservation, a Ponca elders organization has formed. Members participate in tribal events and sponsor handgames.

The Ponca have never been a large tribe, and the enrolled population in 1993 is 2,360. In 1978 there were only twenty-four full-blood Poncas. As the full-blood population has declined, there has also been a loss of speakers of Ponca, a Dhegiha Siouan language related to Omaha, Osage, Kansa, and Quapaw. By the early 1990s, only a few older tribal members remained fluent in the Ponca language.

Donald N. Brown

See also Oklahoma Tribes

Further Reading

Brown, Donald N., and Lee Irwin. "Ponca." *Handbook of North American Indians.* Vol. 13. *Plains.* Ed. Raymond J. DeMallie. Washington, DC: Smithsonian Institution, Forthcoming.

Howard, James H. *The Ponca Tribe.* Bureau of American Ethnology Bulletin 195. Washington, DC: U.S. Government Printing Office, 1965.

Howard, James H., and Gertrude P. Kurath. "Ponca Dances, Ceremonies, and Music." *Ethnomusicology* 3 (1959) : 1–14.

Jablow, Joseph. *Ethnohistory of the Ponca.* New York, NY: Garland Publishing, 1974.

POOSEPATUCK

See Unkechaug

POPULATION

There is considerable scholarly debate as to the size of the Native population of aboriginal America north of Mexico. Estimates have ranged from scarcely one million inhabitants to many millions. Early in the twentieth century, James Mooney of the Smithsonian Institution estimated individual tribal populations, summed them by regions, and arrived at a total of only about 1.15 million Native Americans (American Indians, Eskimos, and Aleutian Islanders) north of the Rio Grande at the time of, as he expressed it, "first extensive European contact." According to Mooney, the dates of extensive European contact with the regions varied from 1600 to 1845. Thus his estimate did not necessarily refer to aboriginal populations, although Mooney did assert that Native Americans experienced little, if any, population reduction prior to their first extensive contact with Europeans.

Scholars in subsequent decades generally reaffirmed Mooney's low population estimate. In 1966, however, Henry Dobyns used ratios of depopulation for this area of between 9.8 million and 12.15 million, and in 1983 Dobyns used depopulation rates (from epidemics) and environmental carrying-capacities to assert there were some 18 million Native inhabitants north of Mesoamerica (an area which included northern Mexico as well as present-day United States, Canada, and Greenland). Other scholars have arrived at estimates falling between those of Mooney and Dobyns. In the mid-1970s, for example, Douglas Ubelaker of the Smithsonian Institution summed tribal estimates from the *Handbook of American Indians North of Mexico* to arrive at an aboriginal population north of Mexico of 1,850,011; in the early 1980s, I assessed the population at 1,845,183 using a linear depopulation trend. Ubelaker has more recently revised his population estimate slightly upward to 1,894,350. In my most recent work in 1987, *American Indian Holocaust and Survival*, I analyzed these and other population estimates and concluded the aboriginal population north of present-day Mexico numbered over 7 million people in 1492, somewhat over 5 million for the coterminous United States, and somewhat over 2 million for present-day Alaska, Canada, and Greenland combined. Subsequent scholarly work will likely produce more consensus in the aboriginal population estimates for America north of Mexico.

There is consensus that Native populations experienced drastic declines following contact with European and African populations. Explorers and colonists from the "Old World" brought their diseases to the so-called "New World," diseases which caused massive population reductions of the Native peoples of this hemisphere. Smallpox, measles, the bubonic plague, cholera, typhoid, scarlet fever, diphtheria, pleurisy, mumps, whooping cough, pneumonia, malaria, yellow fever, and various venereal diseases, possibly including syphilis, infected Native Americans though their contacts with Europeans and Africans. (Tuberculosis was likely present among Native Americans as well as peoples of the "Old World" prior to 1492.) Native Americans had few really serious diseases of their own—probably in part because of fewer domesticated animals and areas of population concentration and possibly because of less overall population density—and were newly exposed to European and African diseases. Exposure to the new diseases often produced "virgin soil epidemics," in which a large percentage of the population was infected at the same time. The diseases also often infected the same Native American groups over and over again. Smallpox, for example, was epidemic among American Indians of present-day United States from its introduction in the early 1500s until after the mid-1800s.

It was not only disease that reduced Native populations here, however. To disease as a cause of population reduction must be added the effects of warfare, including genocide, the massive removals and relocations Native Americans ultimately experienced, and the general destruction of Native ways of life. Through increased mortality and decreased fertility these factors reduced the size of Native populations from the early 1500s to around the turn of the present century.

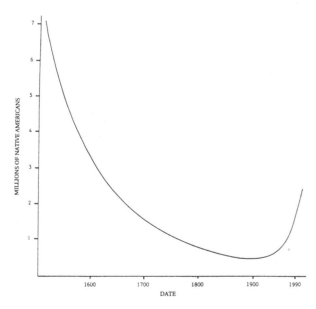

It was then, around 1900, that the Native American population reached its low point or "nadir" of perhaps only around 250,000 in the United States, and not much more than 100,000 in Canada (and around 10,000 in Greenland).

Native Americans have experienced a remarkable population recovery during the twentieth century (figure 1). In part, this population recovery was a result of decreased mortality rates and associated increases in life expectancy, as the effects of "Old World" diseases and the other reasons for population reduction were lessened. It also resulted from intermarriage with non-Native peoples and changing fertility patterns during the twentieth century, whereby Native American birth rates have remained higher than birth rates for the total North American population. Regular decennial census enumerations indicate a population growth to 1.96 million by 1990 for the United States. (The 1990 census count included over 1.8 million American Indians; the rest were Eskimos and Aleutian Islanders.) To this may be added some 740,000 Native Americans in Canada in 1986, 575,000 American Indians, 35,000 Eskimos (Inuit) and 130,000 Métis. Also added to this would be perhaps 30,000 Native Americans in Greenland. The total then becomes around 2.75 million.

Today, Native Americans are distributed unevenly throughout North America. In general this is a reflection more of events subsequent to the arrival of Europeans and others, than of distribution patterns existent at the time non-Native populations arrived in the Western Hemisphere. In the United States, for example, the 1990 census enumerated the largest number of American Indians in the states of Oklahoma, California, Arizona, and New Mexico. Similarly, around one-fourth of all American Indians enumerated in the 1990 census lived on the 278 American Indian reservations (or "Pueblos" or "rancherias") in the United States, or on closely associated "tribal trust lands." The largest of these was the Navajo Reservation: 143,405 Native Americans resided there, along with 5,046 non-Indians. These reservations are concentrated in the western United States. Around 60 percent of the Native American population of Alaska in 1980 (21,869 American Indians, 34,144 Eskimos, and 8,090 Aleutian Islanders) lived in what are called "Alaska Native Villages." Directly comparable data for Canada is not available, given differences in how Canadian Native American populations are defined, as explained below. Canadian provinces with the largest number of "registered" Indians are Ontario, British Columbia, Saskatchewan, and Manitoba. Similarly, many Canadian Native Americans live on "reserves": about 70 percent of the registered Indian population live on the 2,272 Canadian reserves.

The twentieth-century increase in the Native American population reflected in United States censuses was also a result of changes in the identification of individuals as Native American. For example, since 1960, the United States Census has relied on self-identification to ascertain an individual's race. Much of the increase in the American Indian population from 523,591 in 1960 to 792,730 in 1970, to 1,366,676 in 1980, to 1.8 million in 1990, has resulted from individuals identifying as non-Indian in an earlier census but as American Indian in a later census. It has been estimated, for example, that as much as 60 percent of the population "growth" of American Indians from 1970 to 1980 may be accounted for by these changing identifications! (Important to note in this regard is that the 1980 United States census obtained information that some 7 million Americans had some degree of Native American ancestry. [Native American ancestry ranked tenth in the total United States population in 1980. In descending order, the nine leading ancestries were: English, German, Irish, African American, French, Italian, Scottish, Polish, and Mexican.])

There are in existence today more than 300 American Indian tribes in the United States "recognized" by the federal government and receiving services from the United States Bureau of Indian Affairs. (There are also some 125 tribes seeking federal recognition and dozens of other groups who might do so in future years.) The Bureau of Indian Affairs generally requires a one-fourth degree of American Indian "blood" ("blood quantum") and/or tribal membership to recognize an individual as American Indian. However, each tribe has a particular set of requirements, typically including a "blood quantum" for membership (enrollment) of individuals in the tribe. Requirements vary widely from tribe to tribe. For example, some tribes require at least a one-half Indian (or tribal) blood quantum, many tribes require a one-eighth blood quantum, some tribes require a one-eighth or one-sixteenth or one-thirty-second blood quantum; many tribes have no minimum blood quantum requirement, but only require some degree of American Indian lineage.

Around 1980 the total membership of these approximately 300 tribes was about 900,000. Therefore, many of the 1.37 million individuals identifying as American Indian in the 1980 census were not actually enrolled members of federally recognized tribes. In fact, only about two-thirds were. Such discrepancies have varied considerably from tribe to tribe. Most of the 158,633 Navajos enumerated in the 1980 census and the 219,198 enumerated in the 1990 census were enrolled in the Navajo Nation; however, only about one-third of the 232,344 Cherokees enumerated in the 1980 census and the 308,132 enumerated in the 1990 census were actually enrolled in one of the three Cherokee tribes (The Cherokee Nation of Oklahoma, the Eastern Band of Cherokee Indians [of North Carolina], or the United Keetoowah Band of Cherokee Indians of Oklahoma). Thus the Navajo Nation is the American Indian tribe with the largest number of enrolled members, but more individuals identified as "Cherokee" in the 1980 and 1990 censuses than as any other American Indian tribal affiliation.

Officially, to be an Indian in Canada one must be registered under the Indian Act of Canada. A person with Indian ancestry may or may not be registered, and categories of Canadian Indians include: "status" (registered) Indians, individuals registered under the act, and "nonstatus" (nonregistered) Indians, individuals never registered or who gave up their registration (became "enfranchised"). Status Indians may be further divided into "treaty" or "nontreaty" Indians, depending on whether their group ever entered into a treaty relationship with the Canadian government. Of the 575,000 American Indians in Canada in the mid-1980s, some 75,000 were nonregistered and some 500,000 were registered. The "Métis" are a group of individuals of Indian and white ancestry who are not legally recognized. Today, there are 596 bands of Canadian Indians. In the early 1980s, most bands contained fewer than 500 members; only eight bands contained more than 3,000 members: Six Nations of the Grand River (11,172), Blood (6,083), Kahnawake (5,226), Iroquois of St. Regis (4,098), Saddle Lake (4,020), Wikwemikong (3,493), Blackfoot (3,216), and Lac La Ronge (3,086). (The largest "group" of Canadian Indians in terms of language and culture are the Chippewa-Ojibwa. Adding the Ojibwa in the United States to them would make a total population [registered and nonregistered] which might rival the over 300,000 self-declared Cherokee in 1990.)

Coinciding with the twentieth-century population recovery of Native Americans have been increases in the proportion of the Native American population living in urban areas of the United States and Canada. According to United States Census data, less than one-half of one percent of American Indians in the United States lived in urban areas in 1900; by 1950 this had increased to only 13.4 percent; by 1990, however, slightly over 50 percent of all American Indians lived in urban areas. (This compared with around 75 percent of the total United States population living in urban areas in 1990.) Cities in the United States with the largest Native American populations in 1990 were New York City, Oklahoma City, Phoenix, Tulsa, Los Angeles, Minneapolis-St. Paul, Anchorage, and Albuquerque. Somewhat less than one-half of Canadian Native Americans live in cities. Canadian cities with the largest Indian populations are Vancouver, Edmonton, Regina, Winnipeg, Toronto, and Montreal. Ensuing decades will evidence a continued involvement of Native Americans in the cities and towns of the United States and Canada. This will have a profound effect upon the Native American population as urban involvement will influence fertility and mortality rates, patterns of intermarriage with non-Native peoples and tribal identity.

Russell Thornton

See also **Urbanization**

Further Reading

Dobyns, Henry F. *Native American Historical Demography: A Critical Bibliography.* Bloomington: Indiana University Press, 1976.

———. "Native American Population Collapse and Recovery." *Scholars and the Indian Experience*. Ed. William R. Swagerty, Bloomington: Indiana University Press, 1984. 17–35.

Johansson, S. Ryan. "The Demographic History of the Native Peoples of North America: A Selective Bibliography." *Yearbook of Physical Anthropology* 25 (1982): 133–52.

Snipp, C. Matthew. *American Indians: The First of This Land*. New York, NY: Russell Sage Foundation, 1989.

Thornton, Russell. *American Indian Holocaust and Survival: A Population History Since 1492*. Norman: University of Oklahoma Press, 1987.

———. *The Cherokees: A Population History*. Lincoln: University of Nebraska Press, 1990.

Verano, John W., and Douglas H. Ubelaker, eds. *Disease and Demography in the Americas: Changing Patterns before and after 1492*. Washington, DC: Smithsonian Institution Press, 1992.

POTAWATOMI

Like their close allies the Odawa, these Great Lakes people saw their numbers divided as a result of forced relocations between their traditional woodlands homeland and locations in the southern plains. Signatories to fifty-three treaties with the United States, the majority of the Potawatomi today belong to the Oklahoma and Kansas tribes, although there are recognized and unrecognized groups scattered through northern Indiana, Michigan, and northern Wisconsin. More closely allied today with neighboring tribes in their regions than with their relations across the country, the five articles here separately address the tribes in Oklahoma, Kansas, Wisconsin, Northern Michigan, and Southern Michigan.

POTAWATOMI IN KANSAS

The Prairie Band of Potawatomi is one of a score of Potawatomi groups in the United States and Canada. With roots in the southern Great Lakes, ancestors of the modern Prairie Band came to northeast Kansas in 1847. Their eleven- by eleven-mile reservation is located in Jackson County, about twenty miles north of Topeka, Kansas.

Led by Wakwaboshkok, the Prairie Band fiercely resisted the Dawes Act of 1887, but by 1895 all tribal members had been forced to accept individual allotments. By 1900, the Tribal Council had ceased functioning. The United States government disbanded the Potawatomi Agency in 1903 and stopped treaty annuities in 1909. Only 43 percent of their former lands remained in Potawatomi hands by 1925, and by 1962 this number had fallen to 22 percent. Much of this was owned by absentee Potawatomi who leased their allotments to non-Indians. The tribe held a mere ninety acres in common. By 1977, however, about one-fourth of the reservation was again Indian-owned, although most was still in highly reduced, "checkerboarded" allotments. Tribal holdings totaled 890 acres, or slightly more than 1 percent of the reservation. The tribe borrowed federal funds in 1982 to buy another 1,500 acres of their former land in order to start a tribal farm.

For the first third of the twentieth century, the reservation population hovered around 650; another 150 tribal members lived elsewhere. The people subsisted by farming, hunting and trapping, leasing their lands, and working at wage labor. The Prairie Band suffered greatly during the drought and Great Depression of the 1930s, and conflict and disorganization marked this period. Tribal leadership took the form of an advisory council to the Bureau of Indian Affairs (BIA) superintendent, but it did little other than pursue land claims against the United States government. The Prairie Band Potawatomi rejected the Indian Reorganization Act of 1934.

In August of 1953, the "Potowatamie Tribe of Kansas and Nebraska" was singled out for termination. Tribal chair Minnie Evans, along with James Wahbnosah and John Wahwassuck, testified before a joint hearing of the House and Senate Subcommittees on Indian Affairs in Washington, D.C., in February 1954. Their determined opposition, in conjunction with the neighboring Kansas Kickapoo, enabled the Kansas tribes to escape termination.

Supported by the BIA, progressive band members passed a modernized tribal Constitution in 1961, and the official tribal rolls that year listed 2,101 members. Only a fraction lived on the reservation, however. The 1990 United States Census counted 1,079 people on the Prairie Band Reservation; 503 (47 percent) were Native Americans. The remainder of Jackson County contained an additional 219 Indian people. The reservation population, both Indian and non-Indian, is young: 36 percent are under the age of 18; only 12 percent are age 60 or older. The per capita income of Indians living on the reservation is $4,846, and 43 percent of the Indians have incomes below the federal poverty level. Educational levels are also low: of Indians 25 years of age and older, 37 percent do not have a high school diploma and only 2 percent have a college degree.

The 1970s saw many of the Prairie Band become active in local and national Indian affairs, such as obtaining state approval for hunting and fishing rights. But in 1972, spurred by increased tribal activism and factionalism, the BIA suspended their Constitution and placed the tribe under its direct control. Not until 1976 was a new Constitution adopted and a Tribal Council seated.

Economic opportunities on the reservation are limited and unemployment is high. Bingo has been a major tribal enterprise for several years since the late 1980s, and in 1992 the Potawatomi signed a compact with the governor of Kansas to build a casino on the reservation. The state legislature and attorney general opposed the agreement, however, and the state Supreme Court voided the compact. The Prairie Band Potawatomi filed a federal suit which was still pending in 1993.

Throughout the twentieth century, reservation-based Prairie Band Potawatomi have remained culturally conservative. A survey in the mid-1970s found that Potawatomi was still spoken in 44 percent of

POTAWATOMI RESERVATIONS, COMMUNITIES, SETTLEMENTS, ENCLAVES IN THE UNITED STATES

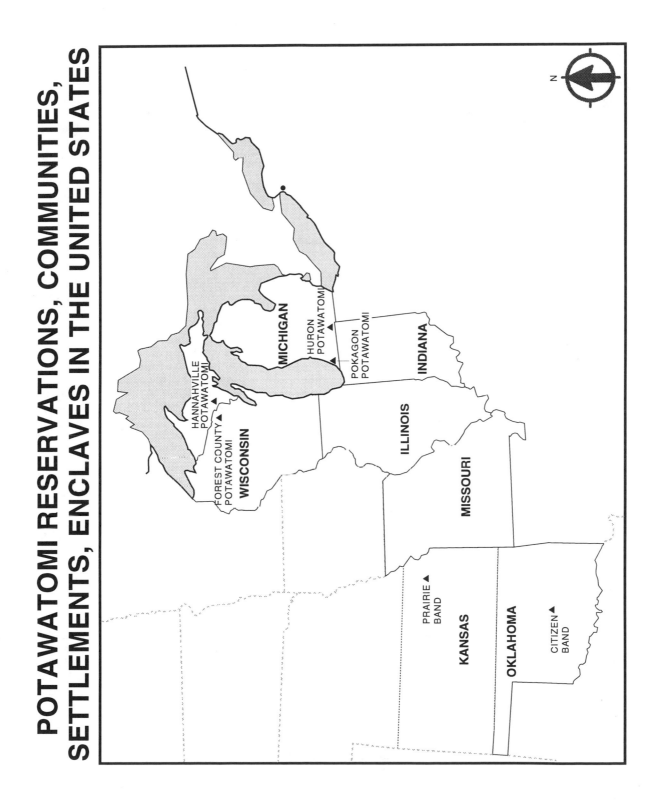

reservation households, and 22 percent of the reservation population considered themselves fluent or competent speakers of the language. Fluency declines with age, however, and the tribe has initiated steps to provide Potawatomi language instruction for the young.

Most tribal members belong to one of two Native religions. The Drum Religion, or Dream Dance, originating among the Santee Sioux in 1872, came to the Prairie Band in the 1880s and their reservation remains the locus of this religion. In 1910, a tribal member named Skishkee brought the Native American Church to his people from Oklahoma, and in 1925 the "Native North American Church of God" was incorporated in Kansas. Under threat of prosecution in 1981, the Prairie Band Potawatomi of Kansas and Kickapoo tribal and religious leaders succeeded in getting a Kansas law amended to allow the use of peyote in Native American Church services.

Donald D. Stull

See also **Kickapoo in Kansas**

Further Reading

Clifton, James A. *The Prairie People: Continuity and Change in Potawatomi Indian Culture, 1665–1965.* Lawrence: Regents Press of Kansas, 1977.

Herring, Joseph B. *The Enduring Indians of Kansas: A Century and a Half of Acculturation.* Lawrence: University Press of Kansas, 1990.

Neshnabek, the People. Prod. Donald D. Stull. University of California Extension Media Center, 1987. Videocassette. 30 min.

POTAWATOMI IN NORTHERN MICHIGAN

Ancestors of the Hannahville Potawatomis originally lived in Illinois and Wisconsin. The 1833 Treaty of Chicago required the Wisconsin Potawatomis to move west of the Mississippi River, but ancestors of the modern Hannahville Potawatomis refused to move. These people gradually migrated north and east from their original Wisconsin homes. Some stopped for periods of time at points along the Menominee River, and at Manistique and Nahmah in northern Michigan. A number continued eastward into Canada.

By 1853 the main body of Potawatomi refugees remained around the Cedar River. Ottawa and Chippewa families as well as Potawatomi families who returned from Canada joined the refugee community. In 1883 Peter Marksman, a Chippewa preacher and political leader at Keweenaw Bay, became interested in the plight of the refugee community. He found them unoccupied land near the town of Harris and lent the Indians money to begin building a permanent settlement. Community members named their settlement Hannahville after Marksman's wife.

In 1913 the United States Congress formally acknowledged the existence of the community by purchasing land for them. The land was not in a single block, but consisted of small parcels scattered among non-Indian holdings around the towns of Harris and Wilson, Michigan. The Hannahville Potawatomi reorganized under the Indian Reorganization Act, adopting a Constitution and Bylaws on July 23, 1936. A Council of twelve was primarily responsible for assigning land to their members on a lifetime basis. They also held the authority to approve timber permits, loans, and the building of homes, and assumed all additional powers vested in the tribe by Congress throughout the twentieth century.

During the late nineteenth century, Hannahville community members made their living by raising fields of corn, squash, beans, pumpkins, potatoes, and other vegetables. They supplemented their income with seasonal wage labor, primarily in lumbering. During the first two decades of the twentieth century, this economic base slowly eroded as the Indians tried to farm land with declining fertility. The State of Michigan further limited the tribe's well-being by restricting hunting and fishing to prescribed seasons and by license. By 1910 lumber mills had sawed the best quality timber and closed, leaving the Indians with little cash income. State and local governments refused tribal members even the most basic services of road maintenance throughout the 1930s. Inadequate transportation prevented the Indians from traveling to urban areas for employment.

Throughout the 1940s the Indians had access to only local seasonal wage labor cutting pulp wood working for non-Indian farmers. Of the 142 people who lived at the Hannahville Potawatomi Indian Community in 1949, forty people had cash income. Twelve of these people lived by welfare, four mixed welfare and part-time jobs, three worked part-time at a local sanitorium, three worked off the reservation, and four depended entirely on odd jobs. Tuberculosis was a continual health problem in the community. Because of their poverty, non-Indian neighbors assigned the Hannahville Potawatomis a second-class status. Indian children were unable to participate equally in public school activities. Local news coverage characterized the Hannahville people as a problem confronting nearby non-Indian communities.

The Bureau of Indian Affairs Michigan Agency all but abdicated their trust responsibilities to the band after 1929. One investigator who conducted extensive studies at Hannahville in 1949 reported that the "community's prospects for the future are certainly not bright. . . . Short of finding oil on the reservation, or a new and attractive means of employment in the area which would serve to pull them out into the larger society, they will continue much as they are— a minority and an underprivileged group." The relatively static population figures for the reservation support this statement. In 1975, the population of the Hannahville Reservation remained virtually unchanged from that of 1949. Although the reservation contained 3,411 acres, the land supported a population of only 185 Indian residents. Today, the tribe has 836 members, 397 of whom live on the reservation. The reservation contains 3,200 acres of trust land.

Throughout the 1960s and 1970s, the Hannahville Potawatomi Tribal Council took bold initiatives to meet their needs. Working with a reinvigorated Michigan Agency, the council created alcohol treatment, day care, educational, and legal aid programs for tribal members. They devised economic development plans that allowed the tribe to manage its forest, farm, wildlife, and human resources to benefit the entire community. They attracted federal funds for tribal housing. Still, working with the limited resources of their reservation, the community faced high unemployment and emigration of its members. In 1990 the tribe devised a new way to create jobs on the reservation. They opened the Chip-in Casino at Escanaba. For the first time in the twentieth century, Hannahville Potawatomi Indian Community members have regular employment on the reservation. The tribe has adequate capital to invest in their future.

Twentieth-century reports on the Hannahville Potawatomi Indian Community have all emphasized the high value placed on Native American concepts. The Hannahville Potawatomis have traditionally viewed themselves as a community of family members. Although the community includes several families who sometimes compete for the right to make political decisions, they have usually avoided factional rivalries and power struggles. Community members have consistently emphasized the value of the Potawatomi language, cosmology, and practical use of natural resources. A core of elders continues to speak their Native language, and a new generation of young people are being instructed. Christian and traditional religious leaders both practice in the community. For seventeen years the Hannahville Potawatomi Community has hosted the Great Lakes Powwow, continuing traditions in song, dance, and art.

James M. McClurken

Further Reading

Tiedke, Kenneth E. *A Study of the Hannahville Indian Community, Menominee County, Michigan.* Special Bulletin of the Michigan State College Agricultural Experiment Station 369. East Lansing: Michigan State College, 1951.

U.S. Department of the Interior. Bureau of Indian Affairs. Planning Support Group. *Statistical Data for Planning: Hannahville Reservation.* Report no. 229–3. Billings, MT: The Group, 1975.

POTAWATOMI IN SOUTHERN MICHIGAN

The name Potawatomi has no literal translation. From the early 1600s to the present, the tribal name has commonly been translated "People of the Place of the Fire," "Keepers of the Sacred Fire," or "The Fire Nation," referring to an historical relationship with the neighboring Ottawas and Chippewas and the Potawatomis' responsibility for maintaining a council fire that united these peoples. During the mid-nineteenth century, two bands of the larger Potawatomi tribe refused to leave their Michigan villages and hunting territories for a Kansas reservation. The descendants of the Potawatomis who stayed in southwest Michigan and northern Indiana call their tribal political organizations the Potawatomi Indian Nation, Inc. (The Pokagons) and the Nottawaseppi-Huron Potawatomi Band (The Huron Potawatomi). Members of both of these bands refer to themselves by the traditional name *Nishnabek*, "The People."

The core population of each Michigan Potawatomi band resides near the locations of their nineteenth-century villages. The Pokagons live in Berrien, Cass, and Van Buren counties, near the towns of Berrien Springs and Dowagiac, in the extreme southwest quarter of Michigan's lower peninsula and St. Joseph County of northern Indiana. The Huron Potawatomi band live in Barry and Allegan counties, near the towns of Athens, Hopkins, Bradley, Shelbyville, and the city of Hastings, all in south central Michigan. Throughout the twentieth century, especially after World War II, the rural Potawatomis have lived seasonally or permanently in nearby cities. South Bend, Indiana, as well as Grand Rapids, Lansing, Battle Creek, and Kalamazoo, Michigan, have significant Potawatomi populations.

Huron Potawatomi

The center of Huron Potawatomi polity and culture is the 120-acre Pine Creek Reservation near Athens, Michigan. Eighty acres of this parcel were purchased in 1845 by Moguago and Pamptopee, band leaders whose people had been forcibly rounded up by the United States Army in 1839 and had escaped from their federal conducting agents in Illinois and returned to Michigan. The State of Michigan donated another 40 acres and took the 120-acre parcel into trust in 1848.

In 1849 a Methodist Episcopal Mission was established on the reserve. A long series of Potawatomi lay preachers assured that messages delivered from the pulpit were meaningful to the Indian members, and that political leaders continued their traditional role as religious leaders as well. The church served as a cultural center on the reserve throughout the nineteenth and twentieth centuries. Church-sponsored camp meetings continue to facilitate annual gatherings of the Huron Potawatomi with their dispersed kin from Pokagon and Walpole Island, Canada. At these meetings, marriages are arranged, history is conveyed between generations, and traditions of pre-Christian cosmology and beliefs are passed between generations. The tradition of annual gatherings continues at the band's annual powwow, held near the site of the former Nottawaseppi Reservation at Burlington.

The Huron Potawatomis are currently unrecognized as a tribe by the United States. Congress appropriated money in 1902 for what federal officials believed was a final cash payment to settle nineteenth-century claims. After that time, the federal government withdrew their trust relationship with the band.

Still, the kin-based political structure that characterizes bands has continued throughout the nineteenth and twentieth centuries. Leadership rested in the heads of prominent families—the Pamptopee (Pamp), Wesaw, Mandoka, Medawi, Mackety, and Chivi families, among others. In 1970 the band formalized their tribal government, electing a chairman and representatives, and incorporating under the name Huron Potawatomi, Inc.

Pokagon Potawatomi

The Pokagon Potawatomis are the descendants of and political successors to two communities built on land purchased by band members near Catholic churches at Silver Creek, near Dowagiac, and at Rush Lake, north of Waterviliet. The Pokagons have no land in federal or state trust and are not federally recognized. From their base communities, the nineteenth- and early twentieth-century Pokagons carried on an economy mixing traditional gathering of cranberries, blueberries, maple sugar, and other natural resources, with small game hunting and subsistence agriculture. These people added to their cash income by working their own farms or hiring out as wage laborers on farms owned by their non-Indian neighbors. The Pokagons continue to recognize the historic importance of these joint economic pursuits today, as reflected by the name of their community powwow—*Kee-Boon-Mein-Ka*, or "We Are Finished Picking Blueberries." Following World War I, some Pokagon families obtained jobs in local industry, though the numbers of Potawatomis employed outside of the rural economy was small before World War II.

Like the Methodist Church among the Huron Potawatomi, the Catholic Church has served the Pokagons as a center for social and political gatherings throughout the nineteenth century and into the twentieth, providing the opportunities for socialization that have kept the Potawatomi identity and cultural knowledge alive. As early as 1866, the Pokagon Potawatomis created a formal government with an elected seven-member Business Council headed by a chairman and a chief, who pursued a number of claims against the United States in the nineteenth century. The leadership of the Pokagons, also like that of the Huron Potawatomi, rests in the heads of the families who comprise the band. The names of Pokagon, Alexi, Williams, Topash, Winchester, Rapp, Wesaw, Quigno, Chushaway, Motay, Hamilton, Mixe, Bozil, Person, Sawalk, Ance, Seton, Wagin, Knap, Shagonaby, and White Pigeon appear and reappear in the historic record throughout the nineteenth and twentieth centuries.

Reestablishing a government-to-government relationship with the United States has been the most difficult political struggle faced by these Potawatomi bands during the twentieth century. In 1934 the Nottawaseppi-Hurons and Pokagons informed the United States of their desire to organize a tribal government under the Wheeler-Howard Act. The Pokagons actively argued their case with federal officials regularly between 1935 and 1942. An administrative decision was made in Washington to limit the number of nonreservation tribes "recognized" under Wheeler-Howard, and the Southern Michigan Potawatomi were denied federal status. World War II drew many Potawatomi men and women away from their rural communities for military service or for work in industry. The result was a brief hiatus in Potawatomi political activity. After 1946 both Potawatomi bands filed successful suits before the Indian Claims Commission, but payment remains incomplete. Political actions and events around these suits provided an organizing issue that helped perpetuate the need for band government despite a more geographically dispersed membership.

The creation of the Federal Acknowledgment Project and the Branch of Acknowledgment and Research within the Bureau of Indian Affairs has allowed both bands to directly pursue a restored government-to-government relation with the United States. Through the 1980s, each band has dedicated substantial political and economic resources toward achieving recognition. The Nottawaseppi-Hurons petition is now being actively considered by the Bureau of Indian Affairs, and the Pokagons are awaiting consideration. In the meantime, each band Council is an active governmental unit working within the community to meet the needs of its members. The Councils emphasize human services—education for their members, family counseling, programs to fight substance abuse, and economic development.

Modern Potawatomi people in both communities are concerned with maintaining their distinct cultural identity; their language, arts, and ceremonies that symbolize the forces of a Potawatomi worldview. To quote a Michigan Potawatomi resident, "The most meaningful aspect of life as a Potawatomi today is the culture. We are learning the language and dancing the powwows. Underlying it all is the practice of spiritual ways. The sacred sweat lodge and longhouse ceremonies have returned."

Thomas W. Topash

James M. McClurken

See also Ojibwa: Chippewa in Michigan; Ottawa/Odawa in Michigan

Further Reading

Clifton, James A. *The Pokagons, 1683–1983: Catholic Potawatomi Indians of the St. Joseph River Valley.* Lanham, MD: University Press of America, 1984.

Clifton, James A., George L. Cornell, and James M. McClurken. *People of the Three Fires: The Ottawa, Potawatomi, and Ojibway of Michigan.* Grand Rapids: Michigan Indian Press, Grand Rapids Intertribal Council, 1986.

Edmunds, R. David. *The Potawatomis: Keepers of the Fire.* Civilization of the American Indian 145. Norman: University of Oklahoma Press, 1978.

POTAWATOMI IN OKLAHOMA

Originally inhabiting southern Michigan, northern Indiana, northern Illinois, and southeastern Wisconsin, the forefathers of the Citizen Band Potawatomi Indian Tribe of Oklahoma were related to the Ottawas and Chippewas. During the colonial period they developed close political, economic, and consanguine ties to the French, and by the early nineteenth century many individuals of mixed Potawatomi-French ancestry had emerged to positions of leadership. Active participants in the fur trade, the Potawatomi were removed to Kansas during the 1830s, where they eventually settled near St. Mary's Mission, on the Kansas River west of present-day Topeka. Prospering as merchants and farmers, the Citizen Band split from the Prairie Band of Potawatomis in 1861 and accepted both individual land allotments and United States citizenship. During the 1870s the tribe was moved to a new reservation in Indian Territory, which they temporarily shared with the Absentee Shawnee. Between 1875 and 1889 this reservation was also allotted, and by 1900 most members of the Citizen Band were living on individual allotments in modern Pottawatomie County, Oklahoma. However, many of the Potawatomi allotments contained only marginal agricultural land, and during the first quarter of the twentieth century many of the 1,768 tribal members sold their allotments and turned to careers in business or industry.

Since many of the Citizen Band were Catholic, much of their religious and social life centered around Sacred Heart Abbey (formerly Sacred Heart Mission), a Benedictine institution near Asher, Oklahoma. The abbey sponsored separate boarding schools for Potawatomi boys and girls, and in 1910 the Benedictines opened St. Gregory's College at Shawnee, Oklahoma, which also educated Potawatomi students.

Because the Citizen Band Potawatomi were acculturated and relatively well educated, many found employment in Oklahoma's emerging urban centers and the tribespeople began to disperse. During the Dust Bowl, many Potawatomi, like other "Okies," fled the state for a new life in Texas or California. Consequently, the sense of community among them declined and their political cohesion fragmented. Although the tribe adopted a Constitution in 1938 under the Oklahoma Indian Welfare Act of 1936, many members did not participate in tribal government until the 1970s, when the five-person Tribal Council and the elected Business Committee were rejuvenated.

Embarking upon a vigorous new program of political and economic reform during the 1980s, the Citizen Band emerged as one of the foremost proponents of Native American entrepreneurship. Located on a tract of tribally owned land just south of Shawnee, Oklahoma, their tribal center currently includes tribal offices, a convenience store, a restaurant, a golf course, a gaming hall, a bank, and a museum and gift shop. The Potawatomi recently purchased forty acres of private land to add to their tract of land where the tribal center is located, and a modern gaming casino is under construction. The tribe administers its own senior citizen center, day-care facilities, and health services. A major employer in Pottawatomie County, the tribe currently provides work for over one hundred fifty people and administers a summer youth program that provides training or employment for sixty young people.

Led by John Barrett, the tribal Business Committee has aggressively campaigned to broaden the base of tribal government, and during the 1980s and 1990s the Business Committee has repeatedly traveled to meet with tribal members residing in California, Texas, Kansas, and other locations. In response, tribal enrollment has expanded to almost 18,000 members, and although many do not live in Oklahoma, participation in tribal elections, council meetings, and government has steadily increased.

Most Potawatomi are Christian, with Catholic ties that extend back into the French period, but a small minority are members of the Native American Church. Some tribal traditions have been lost, but the tribe has established a tribal archive and has sponsored research and programs exploring their past history. The tribal powwow, held each June, remains the focus of much tribal activity and has emerged as one of the largest such celebrations in the state.

At the close of the twentieth century, the Citizen Band Potawatomi present a case study in acculturation. Almost all are of mixed lineage and many are well-educated individuals who pursue careers as successful professionals and business men and women. Combining the tribe's traditions of successful entrepreneurship with modern business acumen, they have utilized expanding definitions of tribal sovereignty to establish themselves as an economic force in east central Oklahoma. Indeed, the Citizen Band Potawatomi of Oklahoma combine much of the new and the old, and in the process may be expanding the parameters of Native American identity.

R. David Edmunds

***See also* Oklahoma Tribes**

Further Reading

Cash, Joseph H. *The Potawatomi People (Citizen Band).* Phoenix, AZ: Indian Tribal Series, 1976.

Edmunds, R. David. *The Potawatomis, Keepers of the Fire.* Civilization of the American Indian 145. Norman: University of Oklahoma Press, 1978.

———. "Two Case Studies." *The Wilson Quarterly* 10 (1986): 132–42.

———. *Kinsmen Through Time: An Annotated Bibliography of Potawatomi History.* Native American Bibliography Ser. 12. Metuchen, NJ: Scarecrow Press, 1987.

Murphy, Joseph. *Potawatomi of the West: Origins of the Citizen Band.* Shawnee, OK: Citizen Band of Potawatomi, 1988.

Sherard, Priscilla Mullin. *People of the Place of the Fire.* Oklahoma: privately printed by the author, 1976.

POTAWATOMI IN WISCONSIN

The Forest County Potawatomi live in three communities within a twenty-mile radius in southern Forest County in northern Wisconsin. Most of these people, originally from southern Wisconsin near Lake Geneva, are descendants of those who did not make the move to Kansas in 1836 as a result of the 1833 Treaty of Chicago and of the few Potawatomi who returned from Kansas. The largest community is located at Stone Lake (Lake Lucerne) near Crandon, the county seat. The smaller communities are near the towns of Blackwell and Wabeno/Carter.

The Potawatomi are an Algonquian-speaking group with close ties with the Chippewa and Ottawa tribes, with whom they formed a powerful confederacy. The name Potawatomi means "Keeper of the Fire," referring to the tribe's role as caretaker of the confederacy's sacred fire.

Historically it is estimated that the Potawatomi numbered about 15,000 people at their zenith and controlled nearly 30 million acres of land in the Great Lakes region. Potawatomi lands in Wisconsin were acquired by acts of Congress on June 23, 1913. The intent was to purchase 11,786 scattered acres and allot them to individuals to encourage the rapid assimilation of the Potawatomi among non-Indian settlers by not concentrating the people in Indian communities. However, the Indian Reorganization Act of 1934 brought the policy of allotment to a halt, and today most of the land is under tribal ownership. Today the majority of the 461 Potawatomi who reside on or near the reservation live close to the main roads and towns in their own communities. Total tribal enrollment is 741, up from a 1908 population of 457.

Traditionally, leadership was carried out by hereditary chiefs, but self-appointed chiefs became the rule in the early twentieth century. Simon Kahquados was one of the most well known of these, acting in a leadership role for fifteen years until his death in 1930. He made several trips to Washington to argue for recognition of Potawatomi treaty rights.

The Forest County Potawatomi Community is a federally recognized Indian tribe, governed by a General Council made up of all tribal members of voting age under the Indian Reorganization Act of 1934. Day-to-day operations are carried out by an Executive Council, which is composed of six elected individuals serving staggered two-year terms. Elections are held annually. The tribal chairman in 1994 is Al Milham.

Because of their small numbers and isolated location, the Forest County Potawatomi have retained much of their traditional culture. The language remains in common use. Both the Peyote Religion and the Medicine Drum or Lodge Society had many adherents well into the late twentieth century, and other Potawatomi religious traditions still being carried out in the 1950s included the Dream Dance, War Dance, Wabeno adoption ceremony, and the Naming Feast.

The lumber industry was the major economic force in the first half of the twentieth century and still provides some work for individuals. However, the tourist industry has become more prominent.

The Forest County Potawatomi own two casinos, one in Milwaukee and one in Carter, Wisconsin, which provide the tribe's major source of income. They also own a gas station, lease a smoke-shop to an individual, and have their own logging crew and small excavating company. The tribe is in the process of building a motel adjacent to the casino in Carter.

Steve A. Woods

See also **Natural Resource Management**

Further Reading

Ritzenthaler, Robert E. *The Potawatomi Indians of Wisconsin.* Bulletin of the Public Museum of the City of Milwaukee 19:3 (1953): 99–174. Milwaukee, WI: North American Press, 1962.

Salzer, Robert J. "Bear-walking: A Shamanistic Phenomenon Among the Potawatomi Indians in Wisconsin." *Wisconsin Archeologist* 53:3 (1972): 110–46.

POTTERY

Pottery emerges at different times in the archaeological record of the area that is now the United States. Pottery dating to 2400 B.C. has been excavated in the southeastern United States at Stallings Island, Georgia. In the Northeast, the earliest confirmed evidence occurs about 1,000 years later, while in the Southwest the earliest sites with pottery date to about 200 A.D.

Pottery making flourished as groups made the transition from hunter-gatherers to farmers. The agriculturally based cultures of North America used pottery for domestic, trade, ceremonial, and funerary purposes. The pottery of the Anasazi, Mogollon, and Hohokam cultures in the West reached its highest level of development in technology, design, and decoration before the arrival of the Spanish in 1540. Sophisticated stamped pottery from the Southeast also reached its zenith in pre-Columbian times. European contact significantly changed the social and material aspects of these cultures. Copper, cast iron, and enamel containers replaced Native use of pottery for domestic purposes, while cultural disruptions severely impacted on other uses. The Historic Period (1540 to 1880) was characterized by immense upheaval, dislocation, and population reduction. Eastern potters were impacted more than those in the West, and only the Catawba of South Carolina maintained a technologically pure Native American pottery tradition up to the present.

The Early Tourist Trade

When the railroad connecting the East and West Coasts opened in 1880, American and European tourists began to descend upon the Southwest. While they were fascinated by Indian pottery, they were primarily interested in purchasing small painted items as souvenirs. Responding to the tourist market and encouraged by traders at the trading posts, the impoverished Pueblo potters began to make curio pottery such as cups, plates, ashtrays, cowboy hats, incense burners, candle holders, canoes, and pitchers decorated with Indian motifs. The interest of archaeologists, collectors, and museums in the more traditional styles of earlier periods was not enough to support a market for the older styles or to encourage new forms and other experimentation. Quantity replaced quality. Materials and production methods, however, had not changed, insuring an uninterrupted pottery tradition in the West.

Long before the southwestern tribes turned to tourist wares that facilitated the survival of their traditions, eastern tribes faced the problem of competition from non-Indian potteries and factory-produced iron kettles and pans. Only the Catawba and Pamunkey found a solution. The Pamunkey peddled utilitarian vessels to farmers in the Virginia Peninsula. This trade was destroyed by the arrival of the railroad in the 1850s, and the tradition languished until the 1930s. For the past sixty years, the Pamunkey have used a commercial kiln, glazes, and paints. The Catawba also benefited from peddling their traditionally made utilitarian pottery to farmers throughout both Carolinas. When roads enabled tourists to reach the Great Smoky Mountains in the late 1920s, the Catawba also began to produce inexpensive tourist wares. They continue to peddle their wares in a limited way.

Pottery Making in the East

The Catawba are the only eastern potters with a fully intact aboriginal tradition. They continue to dig clay, process it by an ancient recipe, follow Mississippian culture construction techniques, burnish their wares with heirloom quartz pebbles, incise their vessels with design motifs of great antiquity, and burn their pottery in an open fire outdoors. The resulting wares are mottled red, grey, and black. Some fifty Catawba potters produce about one hundred shapes including traditional cooking pots, water jugs and jars, eastern-style peace pipes, snake effigy pots, and a wide assortment of traditional smoking pipes. Catawba incising represents a direct link with the pre-Columbian past. The Catawba tradition was carried into the twentieth century by a stellar group of master potters including Martha Jane Harris, Sarah Harris, Rachel and John Brown, Sallie Gordon, Margaret Brown, Epp Harris, Susannah Owl, and Nettie Owl. Today's potters, which include Georgia Harris, Nola Campbell, Earl Robbins, Mildred Blue, and Catherine Canty, take their skills from the earlier generation.

Traditional pottery of the eastern Cherokee in North Carolina, represented by the Katalsta family's high quality stamped-design ware, died out around 1900. It was replaced by pottery of the Catawba tradition, due to the efforts of two highly respected

Nampeyo (Hano Pueblo, Hopi, Arizona), ca. 1910. Courtesy of the Museum of New Mexico, 88771.

Julian and Maria Martinez (San Ildefonso Pueblo), ca. 1941. Courtesy of the Museum of New Mexico, 68362. Photo by Wyatt Davis.

Robert Tenorio (Santo Domingo Pueblo). "Pot #350," 1987. Courtesy of the School of American Research, SAR 1987-8-1.

Helen Cordero (Cochiti Pueblo). "Story Teller," 1969. Earthenware, 10 3/4 inches high. Courtesy of the U.S. Department of the Interior, Indian Arts and Crafts Board, W-D 70.44.1.

Marie Z. Chino (Acoma Pueblo). Earthenware bottle, slipped and painted, 1963. 9 inches high. Courtesy of the U.S. Department of the Interior, Indian Arts and Crafts Board, W-65.7.13.

Catawba potters, Susannah Harris Owl and Nettie Harris. Residing on the Cherokee Reservation, they shared their pottery making skills, instructing Cherokees in their tradition. Kamie Owl Wahnetah, Ella Arch, Rebecca Youngblood, and others followed. They excelled in this "new" tradition, and established modern pottery making on the Cherokee Reservation.

Resurgence of Pottery Making in the Southwest

Decline in the quality and amount of Indian pottery reached a low point by 1920, among most of the pottery making tribes. Concern about the decline resulted in action by archaeologists, collectors, and traders, among others, to encourage the revival and improvement of pottery making. Excavations in 1895 at Sikyatki, a fifteenth-century ruin near Hopi First Mesa in Arizona, by ethnologist Jesse Walker Fewkes indirectly resulted in a revival of Pueblo pottery that extended throughout the eastern and western Pueblos. From Sikyatki burials, Fewkes excavated a unique, beautiful, and well-executed style of pottery with motifs of stylized birds, butterflies, and animals painted in hues of red and brown on a yellow background. An accomplished and respected Hopi/Tewa potter, Nampeyo, and her husband Lesou, were already using designs from prehistoric pottery shards from the Hopi mesas. Lesou worked at the Sikyatki site, which gave them an opportunity to study the unique designs on intact pottery. From this experience, and observations from other sites in the Hopi area, Nampeyo and Lesou developed their own interpretative expressions of the Sikyatki designs. They adapted the classic Sikyatki low, wide-shouldered jars and bowls, applying designs artfully and precisely. Executing these new designs as an aggregate of the old, combined with their own creativity and excellence in execution, they transformed a craft into art, initiating a revival of Sikyatki pottery.

Another accomplished pottery family, Maria and Julian Martinez from the Pueblo of San Ildefonso in New Mexico, introduced a new style of black pottery. In 1918 or 1919 Maria and Julian, through experimental firing, developed the matte-black-on polished-black style of pottery that would bring focus and excitement to the Pueblo pottery industry. Their unique pottery, with Maria making the pot and Julian executing the designs, was an instant success. They joined the other innovative potters of the early twentieth century in setting the stage for a pottery revival among several of the southwestern tribes.

For the first half of the twentieth century, pottery making was kept alive by a few dedicated potters, like Nampeyo and Maria, who were appreciated and supported by a small, constant market of tourists and collectors. These included Margaret Tafoya, Jessie Garcia, Lucy Lewis, and Marie Z. Chino. By the 1960s there was a second resurgence of Native pottery making in the Southwest. Led primarily by potters at the Pueblos of Santa Clara and San Ildefonso, both the quality and quantity of the pottery produced increased. Public interest in all forms of Pueblo pottery expanded dramatically, and by 1980 most of the Puebloan groups in New Mexico, and the Maricopa, Navajo, and Hopi in Arizona, were producing pottery of quality. Record sales of pottery by Native Americans in recent years reflect this interest.

Pottery Forms

Today's potters continue to make most pottery forms used by their ancestors. These include bowls, jars, seed jars, dippers, canteens, ladles, pipes, figurines, and miniature versions of these forms. The more popular Pueblo pieces are forms of jars, bowls, and figurines, especially storytellers. In the 1960s Helen Cordero (Cochiti Pueblo) created the popular "storyteller" figurine—a hand-molded figure with one or more children attached—an image drawn from the memory of listening to her grandfather tell stories. Marie Romero (Jemez Pueblo) has made several sets of clay figures depicting Pueblo activities such as rabbit hunting and corn grinding. Nativity scenes or *nacimientos* are another popular form made in recent years by potters at the Pueblos of Jemez, Santa Clara, Cochiti, Tesuque, Acoma, San Ildefonso, San Juan, and Taos, and occasionally by Navajo potters. Jars, bowls, containers, pans, animal effigies and pipes are the most common forms produced by the Cherokee, Catawba, and Pamunkey in the Southeast.

Pottery Making Techniques

Modern potters who follow the technology of their ancestors use one of three common methods to make pottery: the coil method, where the pot is built with coils of clay and smoothed with a scraper; the coil method with paddle and anvil, where coils are flattened by pounding the outside of the pot while holding a solid object against its inside wall; and the modeling or molding method, where the clay is shaped and pinched by hand. Pueblo potters use the coil method; most other groups employ the paddle and anvil; and all groups mold pottery, especially when making small pots and figures. The potter's wheel was never used in prehistoric America and is not used by traditional southwestern Native American potters today. Glazing was also unknown to these potters; however, some prehistoric groups in the Southwest used glazed paints to apply designs.

Traditional pottery, that is pottery made following the basic steps used by ancestral potters, is still being made by some groups. Steps include collecting and preparing indigenous clays, tempers, and paints; constructing and decorating the pot; and outdoor firing. Today some potters take shortcuts, using commercial clay and paints, and electric or gas fired kilns.

Pots are fired using a variety of Native fuels. Potters at the New Mexico Pueblos of Santa Clara, San Ildefonso, and occasionally Santo Domingo and San Juan use the non-oxidizing method of smothering the fire with manure to produce black pottery. All other pottery is oxidized, not smothered. The same red clays that fire black during the non-oxidizing method fire red in the presence of oxygen. Other colors are achieved with clay, vegetal materials, and minerals that are collected locally.

Eastern potters use high carbon fuels such as pine needles, deciduous leaves, coniferous wood, and coal to produce dark shades of pottery. The Catawba retain all the steps in their ancient tradition. The Pamunkey continue to dig native clay, but use a combination of modern and old construction techniques. Most Pamunkey pottery is decorated with commercial paints, glazed, and baked in an electric kiln. Most Cherokee potters today use commercial clays, the potters' wheel, and some lingering Catawba construction techniques.

Pottery Designs

Designs on pottery are based more on tradition than symbolism. Most pottery made today can still be identified with a particular tribe or tradition. This is especially true of Pueblo pottery. Potters are strongly influenced by old and new traditions associated with their Pueblo. Potters marrying into another Pueblo often adopt that Pueblo's traditions. Elizabeth Medina, originally of Jemez, became an accomplished potter learning the Zia tradition from her mother-in-law, Sofia Medina, a master traditional potter.

Catawba potters such as Sara Lee Ayers, Evelyn George and Georgia Harris continue to incise their pottery with traditional line drawings of a limited corpus of motifs. Members of the Cherokee Bigmeat family often embellish their wares with ancient stamped designs either by impression or incising. The Pamunkey generally paint their wares with pan-Indian designs, or sometimes decorate with Woodland incising.

There are symbols that are used by certain family groups: the tadpole by the Nahohai family at Zuni; the water serpent (*avanyu*) by Albert and Josephine

Anna B. Mitchell (Oklahoma Cherokee). Left: red on buff jar with Cherokee scroll and "step to the mounds" designs; right: Cherokee stamped blackware with strap handles, ca. 1993. Courtesy of the potter.

Vigil at San Ildefonso; the bear paw by Margaret Tafoya's family at Santa Clara; and the serpent on Woodland revival pottery made by Catawba potter Georgia Harris.

Pueblo potters decorate their pottery by painting, carving, and incising designs before firing. For a polished surface, a stone is rubbed over the surface of the pot before firing. Traditional Navajo potters such as Rose Williams, Faye Tso, and Lorena Barlett often applique a design below the vessel rim. Navajo potters like Bertha and Silas Claw have begun to deviate from tradition by painting designs after firing, while others like Chris McHorse are stone polishing to a high finish.

Learning Pottery Techniques

Generally, potters learn the craft from their mother or another relative; however, a few are self-taught or learn in school. Nontraditional technology has influenced Native American pottery making, providing opportunities for creativity by nontraditional ceramic artists. Craft groups provide instruction, networking, and sharing of skills, materials, and marketing opportunities. They are especially prevalent in the East, where the Catawbas in South Carolina, the Mattaponi and Pamunkey in Virginia, the Cherokee in North Carolina, and the Coushattas in Louisiana have established groups.

Some reservation schools in the Southwest include pottery in their curricula. Jennie Laate, an Acoma potter who married into the Zuni Pueblo, was given permission to make pottery in the Zuni style and invited to teach traditional pottery technology at Zuni High School in 1973. At her retirement in 1989 she estimated that she instructed 2,000 students in traditional pottery techniques, collecting indigenous clay, temper, and paints on the reservation and forming and firing the pots.

Economic Importance of Pottery

Pottery sales over the past decade account for a high percentage of income in several households at the Pueblos at Hopi (First Mesa, Hano and Pollaca), Santa Clara, Jemez, San Ildefonso, and Acoma. There are professional full-time potters at these and other Pueblos who have realized prices of more than $1,000 for a single piece. Most potters, however, sell their pottery for far less. Pamunkey prices, for example, range from $2 to $75, and Catawba prices range from $10 to $500.

More pottery is being made today than at any time since the arrival of Europeans in the New World. Today, potters have easy access to markets and cooperatives, and collectors continue to visit them at the reservation throughout the year. They also sell their work at special events like the annual Santa Fe Indian Market, cultural fairs, commercial galleries, and museums. Currently, there is a strong market domestically and internationally for good Native American pottery.

Modern-Era Pottery

Interest in contemporary Native American pottery sparked a dramatic transformation that has attracted collectors willing to pay prices commensurate with high quality. By the 1980s, most of the Puebloan groups in New Mexico and the Hopi in Arizona were producing collector grade pottery. The Cherokee and Catawba also maintained their high standard of excellence.

There are scores of modern-era potters who are recognized for their abilities to produce fine pottery, in addition to those already mentioned. Marie Z. Chino of Acoma, for example, was a prize winner at the first Southwest Indian Fair in 1922. She was one of the first to work with the prehistoric traditions, using fine-line designs executed in black on a white kaolin clay slip. Marie, along with Lucy Lewis and Jessie Garcia, had established this style of pottery at Acoma by the 1950s, each passing their knowledge on to their children and grandchildren, most of whom are recognized potters. On the Maricopa Reservation Ida Redbird was the master potter who, along with her students, sustained the Maricopa pottery tradition.

Anna Belle Sixkiller Mitchell of Vinita, Oklahoma, is an extraordinary Cherokee potter. She takes a scholarly approach to researching prehistoric Woodland pottery. Her bowls and vases, executed by traditional methods and in hues of tans, browns, and black, are designed by incising, stamping, and applique. Anna Belle's pottery, along with other recognized potters, is sought by collectors and museums. She travels extensively, speaking about her Cherokee heritage and encouraging others.

Robert Tenorio, a master potter from Santo Domingo Pueblo, learned pottery making from his great maternal aunt, Lupe Tenorio, who died in 1990. One of the skills she taught was the preparation of black paint from the Rocky Mountain bee plant (*Peritoma serrulatum*), with a cream slip prepared from greenish bentonite clay obtained from nearby Cochiti Pueblo. Robert uses only traditional designs, complying with traditional expectations, applying them on bowls, flared-rim *ollas*, and canteens. Designs are geometric and half circles with motifs of birds and floral patterns painted in red and black on the cream slip. Robert's achievements have initiated a pottery revival at his Pueblo that includes his grandmother, Andrea Ortiz (who died in 1993), and sisters Paulita, Hilda, and Mary.

The art of pottery continues to flourish in the late twentieth century. The achievements of the Native American potters discussed above, and their numerous contemporaries, are a tribute to the perseverance of their cultures, and to their individual creativity.

John W. Barry

See also Art; Catawba

Further Reading

Barry, John W. *American Indian Pottery*. Florence, AL: Books Americana, 1981.

Batkin, Jonathan. *Pottery of the Pueblos of New Mexico, 1700–1940*. CO: Taylor Museum, Colorado Springs Fine Arts Center, 1987.

Blumer, Thomas J. "Catawba Influence on Cherokee Pottery." *Appalachian Journal* 14:2 (1987): 153–73.

Fewkes, Vladimir. "Catawba Pottery-Making, with Notes on Pamunkey Pottery-Making, Cherokee Pottery-Making, and Coiling." *Proceedings of the American Philosophical Society* 88 (1944): 69–124.

Peckham, Stewart. *From This Earth: The Ancient Art of Pueblo Pottery*. Santa Fe: Museum of New Mexico Press, 1990.

Richmond, Stephen, and Mollie Blankenship. *Contemporary Artists and Craftsmen of the Eastern Band of Cherokee Indians*. Cherokee, NC: Qualla Arts and Crafts Mutual, 1987.

Trimble, Stephen. *Talking with the Clay: The Art of Pueblo Pottery*. Santa Fe, NM: School of American Research, 1987.

POVERTY

See Economic Conditions

POWHATAN-RENÁPE

The Powhatan-Renápe Nation consists of approximately 600 people of Virginia Native American ancestry, who mainly live in the Delaware Valley of Pennsylvania and New Jersey, intermarried often with related Nanticokes from the state of Delaware and Indians from other tribes. The ancient name Renápe (pronounced rain-ah-pay), meaning "human beings," was used by most of the Algonquian-speaking groups from North Carolina to New Jersey, except where an "L" dialect led them to say Lenápe.

The Renápe of Virginia, usually referred to as Powhatans after the home village of a famous leader (Powhatan or Wahunsonakok), consists today of the Chickahominy, Eastern Chickahominy, Mattaponi, Pamunkey, Nansemond, Upper Mattaponi, and Rappahannock subgroups. Beginning as early as the 1770s many Powhatans began to leave Virginia to move to New Jersey, probably because of a steady loss of land. This movement was accelerated during and after the Civil War, when Renápe fled north to escape the warfare and subsequent discrimination against most Native Americans as free persons of color, whether part-African or not.

The Philadelphia-Camden region and especially the Pennsauken neighborhood of Delair became the focus for a steady migration of Powhatan people. In the Delaware Valley they preserved their sense of being Native people, developing a very tight network of families. Charles Juancito, a son of one of the early migrants, began formally organizing in the 1930s, and by the 1960s the "Powhatan Indians of the Delaware Valley" operated in Philadelphia as well as New Jersey. The name was changed to the Powhatan-Renápe Nation in the 1970s, and in 1981 the 350-acre Rancocas Indian Reservation was obtained from the State of New Jersey.

The reservation includes natural habitat and wildlife areas, along with an education center, a newly completed museum, a ceremonial mound, and a traditional-style village. The Powhatan-Renápe Nation is led by Chief Roy Crazy Horse and a council of nine.

Jack D. Forbes

Further Reading

Attan-Akamik Newspaper. Rancocas, NJ: Powhatan Press, ca. 1970 to date.

Forbes, Jack D. "The Renápe People: A Brief Survey of Relationships and Migrations." *Wicazo Sa Review* 2 (Spring 1986): 14–20.

POWWOW

Derived from the Algonquian, *pauau*, meaning any gathering of people, the word since has been applied to any number of generalized activities of both Indian and non-Indian focus. Today, Euroamericans use the term to signify any kind of meeting, caucus, or social event. However, from an American Indian perspective powwow as a relatively modern term refers to any tribal or intertribal secular event that features singing, dancing, honoring ceremonies, and giveaways, occasionally interposed with prayers and speeches in the Native language or English.

Although a number of powwows are open to the public, most are held for the benefit of tribal members. Men, women, and children take part anywhere from a few days to a week dancing all day and night in outdoor arbors during the summer, gymnasiums and schools during the winter. An entrance fee is normally charged for tourists, but small tribal powwows are gratis. The organizers of powwows are usually a committee of men and women chosen for their interests and abilities.

Of particular importance to the contemporary powwow are the spectacularly-constructed dance costumes for men, women, and children. These costumes have changed over the past century, some reflecting older, traditional styles, others associated with ongoing dance fads of the mid-twentieth century. All costumes are worn in conjunction with specific styles of singing and dancing, and are required when participating in dance contests. The only other persons to wear costumes are important chiefs and other tribal or community leaders. Singers and spectators normally are attired in mufti.

Powwows are perhaps the most public and dramatic expressions of American Indian identity in the twentieth century and are held on a calendrical and sometimes ad hoc basis. They are equally at home in large cities such as Denver, Bismarck, Rapid City, Tulsa, and Oklahoma City, reaching as far as Los Angeles and New York. Originally a dance associated with the Great Plains, today powwows are held in nearly every major city in the United States and Canada, and in many European cities where American Indians are invited to participate.

Origins

Most experts agree that the modern-day powwow had its origin in a religious ceremony of the Pawnee sometime before the mid-nineteenth century. The oldest form of the dance is the Pawnee *Irushka*, meaning "they are inside the fire," and commonly translated "warrior." The name pertains to a vision in which the founder discovered humans dipping their hands into boiling water and playing with fire. They told the man that they had a new dance to teach him and proceeded to hold him over hot coals causing him to scream. After this he was taught the songs and dance and told that he should take it to the people. The humans in the vision then turned into birds and animals and left.

The man did not sleep well that night because he dreamed of the fire ordeal. The next day he went out to a hill to fast and met a man who asked him to follow him. They came to a place where the same humans who had appeared in the vision were sitting around a fire singing and laughing. Again he was given the fire ordeal, and again the humans turned into animals and birds and disappeared. But this time one man stayed. He said that in a fight he had lost his scalp lock and could never go back to his people because of the disgrace. Some birds and animals however had taught him to make a headdress from deer hair, turkey, and eagle feathers that resembled a scalp lock. The deer hair was woven together to resemble the roached mane of a horse. In the middle of the headdress was a bone spreader made from the shoulder blade of a deer. A two-inch shank bone was placed in the center and an eagle feather inserted. The animals and birds also taught the man to make other things to be worn in the dances. All these things he gave to the initiate, who in turn taught them to his people. The headdress, called a roach, represented the fire ordeal of the *Iruska*. The red deer hair represented the fire and the black hair was symbolic of the smoke. The bone shank represented the special medicine given to the originator, and the eagle feather represented the man standing in the center of the fire. In addition, the man was given a "crow belt," which today emerges as the modern-day "bustle" worn by powwow dancers.

The dance soon diffused to the nearby Omaha, who transformed the sacred ceremony to one celebrating warfare. The Omaha and other Siouan-speakers called the dance *Hedushka* or *Helushka*, a dialectal variant of the original.

Some formal positions in the newly organized ceremony under the Omaha included the owner of the drum, leaders of the society, male and female singers, tail dancers, whip dancers, and a number of lay members. Each officer occupied a special place at the *Hedushka* dance, which was later held in a multisided dance house. When the singers began, the whip bearers encouraged the dancers by nudging them with the special emblem of their office, a whip whose wooden handle resembled the hind leg of a rabbit.

As the dance diffused westward among the Plains tribes, the Pawnee fire ordeal was reenacted. Dancers lined up to dance around a kettle of boiling meat allegedly thrusting their bare hands and arms into the water. It is said that they rubbed their hands with a special medicine to prevent them from scalding. A man singled out for bravery was elected to dance the tail, or encore of the dance, alone. During the *Hedushka* ceremonies there was much speech making and giving away of blankets, horses, and other gifts, and the festivity was concluded with a feast. Among some tribes dogs were cooked and eaten.

Diffusion of the Dance

After the middle of the nineteenth century, most Plains tribes were confined to reservations. During this time, the *Hedushka* began to spread across the Plains reaching approximately thirty tribes residing between the Canadian border, Rocky Mountains, Mississippi River, and Oklahoma. The dance soon became a medium by which one-time enemies established peace.

As the dance moved westward, each tribe that learned it from its neighbor named it after some peculiar characteristic. For example, the Canadian Dakota and Lakota called it *Helushka*, a dialectal variation of the original. The Lakota of the Pine Ridge and Rosebud reservations called it by two names, the Omaha Dance (after the tribe that taught it to them), and the "Grass-tucked-in-the-belt" Dance (after the Omaha custom of wearing braided prairie grass to symbolize scalps once taken on the warpath). Among the Shoshone and Arapaho, it was called the Wolf Dance, the wolf symbolizing the scout or warrior on the warpath. The Lakota of Standing Rock as well as the Blackfeet, Cree, Assiniboine, and Three Affiliated Tribes called it the Grass Dance.

On the southern Plains, the dance took on a new distinction probably as a result of non-Indian promoters who employed Indians in Wild West and other arena shows for the enjoyment of Easterners and Europeans. They called it the "War Dance," a term which stuck through most of the twentieth century. In Oklahoma, sometimes called "the cradle of powwowing," the dance took on two main types of characteristics, the "fancy dance" of the Kiowa, Comanche, Kiowa-Apache, and southern Cheyenne and Arapaho, as opposed to the more conservative "straight dance" of the Osage, Otoe, Quapaw, Ioway, Missouri, and Ponca (and once again the Pawnee and Omaha).

It is difficult to know precisely when the term powwow came into use, but it was sometime around the turn of the century in Oklahoma. In fact, it was not until the mid-1950s that the terms powwow and War Dance became popular outside Oklahoma. At this time individual tribal members began traveling between reservations and other Indian communities to participate in powwow contests, and gradually the term powwow caught on. While there was once a general tendency for song styles created in Canada and North Dakota to diffuse southward, even as far as Oklahoma, and dance styles popular in Oklahoma to gravitate northwards, there has been an increasing amount of uniformity in dance and costume style since the 1970s. The southern Lakota reservations, such as Pine Ridge and Rosebud, as well as urban centers, such as Tulsa, Oklahoma City, Denver, and Rapid City, since have served as conduits through which styles of singing, dancing, and costumes pass.

Powwow Styles

As the *Hedushka* society diffused, songs and dances took on regional and individual characteristics. However, the major symbol of the male dancer, the roach and crow belt, remained fairly constant throughout the Great Plains area. To these basic articles were added other accessories that developed over time, changing sometimes each season with some new design element. Through the mid-twentieth century, the dance costumes for men and women remained rather constant with the major distinction on the southern Plains being the fancy and straight forms of the dance, and on the northern Plains a retention of characteristic tribal forms.

Since 1955 there has been a tendency toward the development of six basic styles of dance costuming, three for males and three for females. These styles of costumes have regional origins and are particularly significant during dance competitions when there is a strong coordination between the types of songs, dances, and costumes. Although at one time before 1955 it was possible to distinguish tribal affiliation mainly on the basis of women's attire, since then the stylistic differences have become more absolute, focusing on traditional costumes for males and females, that is, those types of costumes reminiscent of the latter part of the nineteenth century, even though some of these traditional costumes have become modernized. Fancy dance, originally a feature of Oklahoma fast dancing, includes neck and back bustles as well as the traditional roach. The straight dance outfit featuring a single-feather roach, or otter turban, with no feathers other than fans and stylized feathers worn at the base of the roach, usually the tail feathers of a flicker, plus accessories made from trade cloth and an otter fur drag worn down the back of the dancer, is considered a traditional costume.

Since the 1960s there has been an ongoing development that reached its peak in the 1980s and still continues, namely, the Grass Dance costume for males, consisting of the traditional roached headdress but no feathers other than fans. The major feature of this costume are ribbon and yarn fringes that generously adorn the dancer. Two more styles have developed for females, the Shawl Dance consisting of elaborately beaded, sequined, or otherwise decorated shawls worn over an ankle- or knee-length dress, which identifies the female fancy dancer. The last style is that of the Jingle Dress, a plain ankle-length dress made from taffeta or buckskin to which are attached, in various patterns, rolled lids from snuff cans. A single eagle plume adorns the dancer's head, and she carries an eagle wing fan. The dance style is rather stiff, but the movements are quick.

Each style requires different types of dance movements. Traditional dancers dance proudly with an air of distinction; fancy dancers whirl about furiously

Grass Dance, Oglala Nation Powwow, Pine Ridge, SD, August 1992. Photo courtesy of William K. Powers.

Men's Fancy Dance, Oglala Nation Powwow, Pine Ridge, SD, August 1992. Photo courtesy of William K. Powers.

Traditional (Straight) Women's Dance, Oglala Nation Powwow, Pine Ridge, SD, August 1992. Photo courtesy of William K. Powers.

Jingle Dance, Oglala Nation Powwow, Pine Ridge, SD, August 1992. Photo courtesy of William K. Powers.

keeping in time to a quick tempo; Grass dancers bend, lean, and shake to slower songs using the long fringes of their outfits to disguise tricky foot movements; Jingle-dress dancing combines sedateness with speed. All powwow dances are free-style, men and women dancing either in a clockwise or counterclockwise direction depending on local custom. Each style also has an occasional binary form called "Crow Hop" in the north and "Squat" or "Hummingbird Dance" in the south, where the first half of the dance, the dancers shake their bells while in a squatted position in time to a drum tremolo, and in the second part arise and dance in powwow style.

Powwows traditionally begin with a grand entrance followed by a flag raising ceremony and a short invocation. War dances then follow, interspersed with Round Dances, Rabbit Dances, Two Steps, and other specialties. The singers and dancers break for the noon and evening meal, and then resume dancing, sometimes until the early morning.

Generally in the north songs are sung in a higher register and in a clearer falsetto by a group of men seated around a bass drum, each singer keeping time with a drumstick. Female singers frequently join them in the chorus. In the south, the register is lower, tempo faster, but the composition of the song groups the same. Songs are similar in structure despite the differences in performance style. Thus, dancers from

any part of the country can participate wherever powwows are held and keep time with the songs.

Giveaways

One of the highlights of the powwow, whether tribal or intertribal, is the custom of giveaway in which an individual or family presents to another individual or group of individuals such things as quilts, kitchen ware, blankets, footlockers, plastic wash tubs, and other miscellany. The giveaway is a means of recognizing others, particularly those who have been helpful through a period of mourning, or who have somehow distinguished themselves in the military, graduating from school, or somehow providing leadership to a community or to the tribe.

The giveaway is an old custom on the Plains, one which has persisted as a traditional Indian means of honoring someone. In the old days, horses and beaded articles were the major items given away, and in some cases they still are. However, economic conditions have somewhat restricted the nature of the items to be given away, and many are bought at local dry-goods stores.

Although there are some regional and tribal differences, the giveaways normally take place in the afternoon. The announcer makes known to the audience the reason for the giveaway, who the donors and recipients are, and then calls for an honor song. The singers, usually chosen by the donors, sing an appropriate song after which they too become recipients of a donation, usually cash. At the conclusion all participants in the giveaway shake hands with each other, and the ceremony ends and dancing resumes.

Dance Contests

Although dance contests have been popular in Oklahoma since the turn of the century, it was not until the mid-1950s that they became popular on virtually all reservation and Indian communities. Today, many old timers feel that competitions have taken something away from earlier traditions. Nonetheless, most powwows feature contests in the belief that without them the best dancers will not come, nor will the sponsoring tribe or committee draw large crowds.

Again as with other features of the powwow there are some local variations. Generally all contests are organized around age, sex, and dance (hence costume) style. There are usually four categories: tiny tots, in which little boys and girls may participate together if there are only a few; boys and girls; young men and women; and elder men and women. Each age group participates in contests for win, place, and show, in traditional, fancy, Grass, Jingle, and Shawl dancing.

At large powwows there may be hundreds of dancers participating, so that contests are run in heats during the afternoons and evenings of the last several days. On the last night, finals are held.

Powwow contests are judged by older men and women, most of whom have been powwow champions. Each of the dancers must register before the

Traditional (Straight) Men's Dance, Oglala Nation Powwow, Pine Ridge, SD, August 1992. Photo courtesy of William K. Powers.

Shawl Dance, Oglala Nation Powwow, Pine Ridge, SD, August 1992. Photo courtesy of William K. Powers.

powwow begins, and each is given a number which is affixed permanently to their costume. Dancers are judged on their individual ability to master the particular style in which they compete, to keep good time with the song, and to end precisely on the last beat of the drum. Dancers are automatically disqualified if they lose an article of costuming during the contest, or if they overstep the last beat. They also are expected to participate fully in the entire powwow, and not only in the competitions.

During the actual competition, the judges surround the dancers and watch each of them through their respective heats carefully. Clipboards in hand, they rank each of the dancers accordingly and note their numbers on a pad. At the end of the final competitions, the numbers are tallied and dancers notified. Frequently the winners of the competitions provide a short solo dance in front of a cheering audience.

Significance

In summary, the powwow is the key symbol of twentieth century American Indian identity. Although frequently seen as a "Pan-Indian" movement, the powwow actually enables members of tribes to relate to others of different tribes in order to perpetuate contemporary American Indian culture on a grand and public scale. At the same time, American Indians participate in rich and tribally distinct cultures which continue to flourish.

William K. Powers

***See also* Dance; Music**

Further Reading

Black Bear, Ben, and R.D. Theis. *Songs and Dances of the Lakota.* Rosebud, SD: Sinte Gleska College, 1976.

Koch, Ronald P. *Dress Clothing of the Plains Indians.* Norman: University of Oklahoma Press, 1977.

Powers, William K. *War Dance: Plains Indian Musical Performance.* Tucson: University of Arizona Press, 1990.

Wissler, Clark. "General Discussion of Shamanistic and Dancing Societies." *American Museum of Natural History Anthropological Papers* 11:12 (1916): 853–76.

PRAIRIE APACHE

See Plains Apache

PRISONS AND PRISONERS

American Indian prison populations are on the rise, a direct reflection of the increase in alcohol and drug abuse so prevalent in Indian communities, both on the reservation and in urban areas. Although many reservations in the United States are technically "dry," alcohol is easily obtained through bootlegging or in nearby off-reservation towns. American Indians who are convicted of felonies committed on reservation (trust) land generally go to federal prisons—unless the state is one in which jurisdiction over tribes has been transferred to the state. If a Native American is from a reservation but is convicted of a crime off the reservation, the prisoner is incarcerated in a state correctional institution. Tribal courts have jurisdiction over tribal members who commit misdemeanors on the reservation, and may impose penal sentences upon them of up to six months and/or up to a $500 fine. Indians comprise approximately 2.5 percent of federal prison populations, despite the fact that they only make up about 1 percent of the United States population.

States having high numbers of incarcerated Indian inmates are mostly in the Plains area, including Montana, Nebraska, North Dakota, Oklahoma, South Dakota, Minnesota and Wyoming. In the Southwest, Arizona and New Mexico have relatively large numbers of Indian prisoners, as in the Northwest, in states such as Idaho and Washington. Alaska is the state with the largest population of Indian (Alaska Native) prisoners—over 30 percent.

Indian prison populations may be routinely underestimated, since some Indians identify themselves as being a member of a particular tribe—e.g., Navajo or Lakota—rather than the more generic term Native American. Also, some individuals prefer not to specify their ethnic heritage when coming into prison, thinking such identification may have disadvantages. Correctional authorities may assume some Indian prisoners are Hispanic or African-American based on their appearance, when culturally they identify more with their Native American heritage.

Indian prison populations tend to be very young, an outcome directly influenced by the large amount of alcohol and drugs used at very early ages on America's reservations. The teenage pregnancy rate among American Indians is the highest of any in the country; this situation, coupled with extremely high rates of fetal alcohol syndrome, yields devastating results to the overall health of reservation populations. It is estimated that the average age for the beginning of substance abuse among Indians is twelve, with a large proportion of those children using inhalants such as Lysol spray, correction fluid, spray paint, or gas, which can cause severe neurological damage, aggressive behavior and brain damage. Experimentation with drugs such as marijuana often begins at age eight or nine among Indian children, younger than in non-Indian communities. Early substance abuse not only has profound effects on children's growth physiologically and developmentally, but also is compounded by undeveloped decision-making abilities and inexperience, deepening the victimization of children. The impact of drug and alcohol use on the stability of the Indian family is also severe, contributing to the ultimate delinquency and incarceration of many Indian youth. Termination of parental rights due to alcohol use in the family often results in children being raised in foster care or institutions, placing them further at risk for anti-social behavior. Physical and emotional abuse play strong roles in the alienation of children from their families and result in a deepening of their involvement in substance abuse and crime. Because of the frequency with which legal infractions occur, families seldom stigmatize delinquent acts. Children who observe the regularity of close relatives' incarceration grow up thinking such conviction is a normal part of growing up.

American Indians may have large representation in America's prisons in part because they have the highest crime rates of any ethnic group in the United States. Rape, suicide, and homicide are almost always alcohol-related and appear to involve relatively youthful perpetrators; suicide among Indian youth definitely appears to be on the rise, particularly in reservation communities. Alcohol plays a major role in accidents, drunk driving, assault, and minor legal violations as well. While national statistics on reasons for incarceration are not available, the Nebraska Indian prison population may be a reasonable model of the kinds of crimes committed by this population. In this population, burglary, robbery, and first degree sexual assault are the crimes Indians most frequently serve time for, followed by first-degree assault, first-degree murder, and third-degree assault. While this may vary from prison to prison, the extremely violent nature of crimes committed is positively correlated with alcohol and drug use. Most prisoners freely admit their chemical dependence and the role alcohol and/or drug abuse played in the commission of offenses.

Indian prisoners, as with most ethnic groups, profit from identification with their ethnic group during incarceration, and often undertake responsibility for their education and rehabilitation through cultural and spiritual activities in prison. Native American offenders exhibit considerable variability with regard to their familiarity with their own traditions and culture. Those who have knowledge of their language and customs often become the teachers. Those who know little of their ethnic heritage frequently begin a long process of learning about their culture, which instills pride, improves feelings of self-esteem, and increases the likelihood of a successful rehabilitation. Most prisons in the United States with any sizeable Indian population have Native American social or religious groups or clubs, e.g., Native American Spiritual and Cultural Awareness Group (Nebraska), Native American Council of Tribes (South Dakota), Many Feathers Club (Utah), Lakota Oyate-ki Culture Club (Oregon), etc. These groups serve important roles in the political, social, and ideological adjustment to incarceration. Litigation against correctional authorities has resulted in most of these prisons allowing some form of American Indian religious observances, the most common of which is the Sweat Lodge ceremony, prayer with the Sacred Pipe, and visits from spiritual members of the community, perhaps medicine men. In Nebraska, minimum-custody Indian prisoners have been permitted to travel out-of-state to participate in the annual Sun Dance on the Rosebud Sioux Reservation in South Dakota.

Lawsuits by Indian inmates against correctional authorities have been filed in Connecticut, Idaho, Indiana, Iowa, Kansas, Nebraska, North Dakota, Ohio, Oklahoma, Oregon, South Dakota, Utah, and Washington, among others. The first state prison to permit the use of the sweat lodge was Nebraska. This established a precedent for other prisons in the United States, and now sweat lodge structures in different prison facilities exist in approximately twenty-one states. Religious freedom lawsuits are filed throughout the United States by prisoners who believe that their constitutionally guaranteed rights to religious freedom have been infringed upon. The difficulties in conducting Indian religious activities in prison are many, and often result in conflict due to cultural misunderstandings. Care in the handling of religious articles, such as the Sacred Pipe or in the use of (burning) plants such as sage, sweetgrass, or cedar, are the sources of continual grievances of discrimination and harassment. Proper protocol in and around the sweat lodge is also problematic, as prison security routines (e.g., conducting "count") are not always compatible with proper ritual observance at the sweat lodge.

Prisons with sizeable Indian populations attempt to avoid some of these problems through training or orientation programs for their correctional employees and administrators. This may range from special classes to inviting Native American spiritual leaders, guests or inmates delegated to provide sensitization. Prisons sometimes claim that their staff does not understand Indian affairs and so depend on outside training to help better serve the Indian population. Seminars, films, videotapes, and lectures on Indian culture help to offset some of these problems.

Most prisons with relatively large numbers of Indian inmates permit Indian clubs or groups which meet weekly and sponsor occasional celebrations such as the powwow, handgame, or special feasts of traditional foods. A special Indian advisor or religious coordinator is often employed to facilitate their needs, although these may be handled by the prison chaplain as well. Native American Church ceremonies are performed at several prisons; however, no prison permits the use of peyote in its services. Some prisons allow lower custody inmates to travel away from the prison to attend special religious events in the community, but only where security accommodations can be made.

Indian inmates generally regard parole with reserve, and often opt to serve their entire sentence rather than having to comply with all the stipulations imposed by them in the parole process. This preference can be explained, in part, by the high recidivism rates for Native Americans. In Nebraska, although Indian recidivism rates appear to equal those of other ethnic groups (24 percent), activities of ex-offenders appear to result in reincarceration in approximately two-thirds of the cases. Nearly always this is due to a return to alcohol use—that is, recidivism in drinking appears to result in recidivism to incarceration. Indian prisoners who watch "brothers" (fellow Indian inmates) return to prison following their release on parole are discouraged, and decide that they are likely to spend less time in prison overall if they complete their entire sentence ("jam" out) and be completely free, rather than be released conditionally and risk parole violation and extension of the sentence beyond the original one. Serious parole violations may also result in additional new charges being filed (e.g., escape) which, if the inmate is convicted again, may add consecutive "time" to the original sentence.

Although it is more difficult to obtain drugs or alcohol in prison than on the street, it is by no means impossible. Indian inmates claim to be able to obtain these substances through correctional officers or those delivering services to the institution. Even without such availability, Indian prisoners make "hooch," a homemade alcoholic beverage made from fruit, yeast, and sugars. In Nebraska 40 percent of Indian inmates freely admitted continuing to use such substances in prison. Although the goal of most Indian prisoners is to remain sober upon release from prison, in fact, few had real opportunities in prison to consciously develop strategies and skills to reinforce their sobriety upon release from the institution. Many inmates believe they leave prison with fewer social skills than those with which they came in, have more anger as a result of prison living, and have learned to master techniques of being "cons."

The problems of continuing alcohol and drug use and parole failures are good indications of the absence of real rehabilitation in prison. Although most state prisons have programs aimed at rehabilitation, such as Alcoholics Anonymous or Narcotics Anonymous, prison overcrowding results in most programs being overenrolled or unavailable. There are waiting lists to be admitted to special programs (e.g., sex offender programs), and what programs are available are "generic"—that is, geared for the masses rather than individuals with shared problems. Indian prisoners tend to shy away from these programs. They find it difficult to be full participants when correctional officers are present, when those in attendance represent a cross-section of the entire prison population, and when they perceive that the model is one based largely on Judeo-Christian, rather than Indian, ideology. Although Indian Alcoholics Anonymous programs do exist in some states, seldom are such programs available inside the prisons. Indian prisoners generally prefer to address the causes of their incarceration—largely crimes attributed to alcohol abuse—either in an exclusively Native American context, which is difficult to achieve in prison, or with Indian counselors or para-professionals, who may be able to relate more easily to the unique experiences of American Indians. With increasing pressure on state budgets, counseling, therapy and other rehabilitative activities in prison are necessarily limited to groups, not individuals, and cannot be targeted at one particular cultural group. As a result, many Native Americans do not participate in them and leave prison without having really addressed the nature of their crime or the factors leading up to its commission.

Elizabeth S. Grobsmith

See also **Alcohol Abuse; Families; Mental Health**

Further Reading

Grobsmith, Elizabeth S. "The Impact of Litigation on the Religious Revitalization of Native American Inmates in the Nebraska Department of Corrections." *Plains Anthropologist* 34 (1989): 135–47.

———. "The Relationship between Substance Abuse and Crime among Native American Inmates in the Nebraska Department of Corrections." *Human Organization* 48 (1989): 285–98.

———. *Indians in Prison.* Lincoln: University of Nebraska Press, forthcoming.

Grobsmith, Elizabeth S., and Jennifer Dam. "The Revolving Door: Substance Abuse Treatment and Criminal Sanctions for Native American Offenders." *Journal of Substance Abuse* 2 (1990): 405–25.

Hall, Roberta. "Alcohol Treatment in American Indian Populations: An Indigenous Treatment Modality Compared with Traditional Approaches." *Annals of the New York Academy of Sciences* 472 (1986): 168–78.

Weibel-Orlando, Joan. "Treatment and Prevention of Native American Alcoholism." *Alcoholism in Minority Populations.* Eds. Thomas D. Watts and Roosevelt Wright, Jr. Springfield, IL: Charles Thomas, Publishers (1989): 121–39.

PUBLIC IMAGE

Undoubtedly the "discovery" of the Americas is one of the most epochal episodes of recent human history. As Columbus himself would muse, "the world is small." But as the events of the 1992 Columbus Quincentennial would show, there was no consensus about his public image as a symbol of discovery. Rather, the events of the Quincentennial became a national forum for reanalyzing the process of Western civilization and the reciprocal role of indigenous people in this process.

Columbus' medieval mindset refused to acknowledge the obvious—that the Americas were already populated by intelligent people whose communities were rooted in a long history of settlement. Rather, in Columbus' revisionist mindscape, this Eden was populated by exotic creatures of every sort, some of whom were beings "closer to men than animals." American Indians were typecast as being "gentle and fearful," "wild and heathen," and, as seen by their nakedness and "lack of distinctiveness," nothing more than nymphs of nature.

The theme was thus set for the just conquest of the New World. The rationale would be repeated in some variant thereafter by every subsequent adventurer and colonist. It became the strategic and sustaining stereotype, which persists even within our contemporary public image of American Indians.

> Columbus did not discover a new world; he established contact between two worlds, both already old.
> (From the *Spanish Seaborne Empire,* 1966, J.H. Parry)

Romantic images of the settlement of the West abound throughout popular literature. Quite simply, the colonialists created the frontier from an image that was consistent with their actions. They glorified the conquerors and their ruthless campaigns against the American Indian. The devastation which was wrought upon the indigenous people was justified as necessary for settlement. They extolled the virtues of the settler for having brought civilization to the wilderness.

The notion of civilization was sustained by a powerful myth. Christians were holy, white, and civilized. Indians were idolatrous, dark, and savage. The Greeks had invented the term "barbarian" to apply to outsiders. By the time it had been used to describe the indigenous people of the Americas, it also meant morally inferior. Thus, the Americas were made to become a virgin wilderness, inhabited by a barbaric nonpeople called savages.

> Book Order: Klamath Indians: A Century of Tradition.
> Remarks: HAS NEVER BEEN PUBLISHED DUE TO A LACK OF COOPERATION BY INDIANS who do not like whites writing about them but seem unable to do it themselves. ORDER IS [sic] CANCELLED
> (Excerpted from bookseller's purchase order, 11/01/91)

Ultimately, the Indian persona was divided into two distinct genre. One persona was that of the "good" Indian. An example was the Delaware Indian Chief ("Saint") Tammany, who had welcomed William Penn and his followers in the 1680s. As a supporter of the settlers, he and Christopher Columbus became the guiding heroes of the Tammany Society. Good

Indians, therefore, were collaborators, subservient, and disposed toward accepting Anglo ways.

The other persona was the "bad" Indian. They were portrayed as warlike, obstinate, ignorant, and untrustworthy. Upon them was waged a "just war." "The only good Indian is a dead Indian." Based on this popular sentiment, Natives in real life were hunted down mercilessly. Those who were captured were often imprisoned, tortured, and enslaved. Those who escaped were subject to a bounty. During 1756, the Pennsylvania Council established the price of a scalp of an Indian male over twelve years old as $130, a woman $50. As late as the 1870s, a bounty of $250 was offered for an Apache scalp in the territory of Arizona.

> "Nophaie, you come with the white man's vision of the future," he asserted. "Yes. You were taught to see with your heart. The white education taught Nophaie to see with his mind."
>
> "The sun of the Indian's day is setting," replied Doetin, mournfully. "We are a vanishing race."
>
> (From *The Vanishing American*, Zane Grey, 1925)

In the eighteenth century, the embodiment of American virtues and values became the farmer. Farmers were held in high esteem because of the campaign they waged against the wilderness. As tillers of the soil, they were perceived as worker ants—tirelessly transforming fallow lands into productive real estate. Through raw strength, their efforts ushered America into modernity. Indians, on the other hand, were the lazy hunters and slovenly keepers of the wilderness. They became the antithesis of progress.

With the advent of industrialism, the demographics of the nation shifted away from the rural communities to the urban centers. The wage economy gave rise to the emergence of the leisure class, and Indians and their isolated communities became a popular subject of picturesque tourism and exotic exhibitionism. Frequently, they were promoted as a "vanishing race," and a significant industry was created among artisans to reconstruct and depict a pristine tribal culture. The painter Frederic Remington and the photographer Edward Curtis were among the most prolific artists in depicting idyllic reconstructions. Other entrepreneurs, such as George Catlin, a noted nineteenth-century artist, and William "Buffalo Bill" Cody, exploited America's curiosity by staging frontier reenactments for the curious public.

Eventually, the popular media met the growing demand for adventurism by fabricating a totally new myth, the "cowboy." Battles between the hero cowboy and the enemy Indian became a metaphor for the domination of good over evil. The Indian, who in the end always died, was a downtrodden trophy for a superior race annihilating an inferior one. Christian values and Darwinian principles were thus projected upon the "taming" of the West. The cowboy became a national symbol and even homicidal outlaws like Billy the Kid and Jesse James were unduly romanticized. Such revisionism, in fact, became the de facto ethos of American society.

With the advent of the moving picture, Hollywood capitalized on the fictional cowboy. In 1903, Edwin S. Porter originated the western movie in his film *The Great Train Robbery*. A sensational hit, a whole new genre of films called the B-Western was to follow. As typified in the screenplays directed by John Ford, the 1950s "shoot-em-up" images droned in the Indian psyche like a festering toothache. The formula was simple—the posse and/or cavalry comes to the rescue, saving innocent denizens from the throes of marauding Indians.

Eventually, the depiction of the Indian became a sustaining industry. In Hollywood, movies about Indians were accomplished largely through the casting of non-Indian actors. "Playing Indian" became a national obsession and organizations such as the Boy and Girl Scouts of America appropriated Indian folklore for their activities. Even adults participated in their own fantasy pageants. Annually, for example, the Smoki People—"white men and women from all walks of life of Prescott, Arizona"—reenacted a Hopi Snake Dance as well as other "ancient, mystic rites and ceremonies" of the Southwest Indians.

Beginning with the civil rights movement, some advances were made in reversing the stereotypical images of American Indians. Incidents such as the 1969 occupation of Alcatraz Island, the takeover of the Bureau of Indian Affairs headquarters in 1972, and the FBI confrontation with Indian activists at Wounded Knee, South Dakota, in 1973 served to bring attention to the plight of contemporary Indians. In time, many elements of these important struggles were forgotten. Laden with liberal guilt, public sympathy gradually moved toward revisionist history. Such was the case in the Oscar winner for Best Picture of 1990, *Dances With Wolves*. A thinly veiled plot reveals a romantic portrait of Lakota Sioux life. Its theme continues to be the heroics of a maverick army officer who rescues a captive Anglo maiden from her adopted tribe's impending annihilation.

> Pity the Indians and buffalo of outer space....
>
> (From *Indian Voices: The First Convocation of American Indian Scholars,* 1970)

The television cult series "Star Trek" has coined outer space as "the final frontier." According to authoritative scientists, outer space is nature's vacuum—a void comprised of nothingness. Given such logic, mankind is poised to repeat the same grievous history of conquest. One of the greatest challenges which lays ahead for Euroamerican society, however, is not the exploration of outer space. It is the reeducation of its children about the value of cultural diversity. Judging from widespread attitudes held within mainstream America, that task will be monumental.

The most recent wave of sports hysteria attests to this problem. Mascots of teams such as the Redmen, the Redskins, the Seminoles, the Braves, the Scalpers, the Utes, and the Chiefs continue to dominate the media. Far from benign, the mascots are/were personified through idiotic caricatures such as Willie Wampum (Marquette University), Chief Noc-A-Homa (Atlanta Braves) and Chief Iliniwek (University of Illinois). These, in turn, inspire fans to display their team loyalty with demeaning gestures such as the infamous "tomahawk chop." Together, they perpetuate outmoded stereotypes, rather than the purported positive and heroic stature of American Indians that they claim to be honoring.

Similarly, images such as the Mazola and Land o' Lakes Indian maidens, the Mazda Navajo jeepster, Mohawk tires, and the Santa Fe railway chief continue to ply the commercial trade of the public mystique. The so-called Santa Fe artistic style as well as new-age environmentalism, mysticism, and spirituality have dominated the mass market to an even greater extent. "Tribalism" as a vogue lifestyle portends the onset of social elitism. Fakes, opportunists, and the medicine-show people continue to indoctrinate the unwary.

The fact of the matter is that as long as indigenous imagery and thought continues to be preempted by nonindigenous people, the interpretation will be fundamentally equivocal. The stereotype of the Indian long ago diverged from the reality of contemporary tribal people. The themes have been exhausted and there is little chance for any more innovation and meaning among such static images. The task, therefore, is to stop Indian stereotypes from being perpetuated.

> George Lucas [Star Wars] is an amateur anthropologist and he owes his inspiration for the Force to the American Indian concept of life force. "Originally," Lucas said, "the phrase was going to be, May the life force be with you . . ."
> (From an interview by Gene Siskel, *Chicago Tribune*, 1983)

In the face of the exotic and primitive, the outsider draws on their own preconceptions and experiences to selectively appropriate elements of the "Indian." The consequent image may be a subjective interpretation, the purpose of which is to corroborate the outsider's viewpoint. I refer to this process as "revisionism" and it, more often than not, entails remaking Native people apart and separate from their own social and community realities.

Native societies have a complex pluralistic human settlement history, and are characterized by subtle cultural transformations and the constant adaptation of new cultural traditions among distinct communities. Many of these transformations have emerged from the interaction of diverse indigenous and Euroamerican communities. The ability of people and their communities to adapt outside traditions has been ignored as a result of image-making intended to portray "authenticity." By deconstructing the Native mystique, it can be seen that both the social scientist and the entrepreneur contribute equally to such revisionism.

There are two distinctive and often parallel aspects of this authentic image-making. One was promulgated by social scientists in the fields of anthropology, ethnography, and history. The other was developed by entrepreneurs of the tourism and film industries. Among social scientists, Native peoples became a "living laboratory." Among entrepreneurs, Native peoples became a "living backdrop." In both instances, however, the investigations were dominated by outsiders who were looking for their own affirmation of a primitive and exotic humanscape.

Native people have, by and large, resented being cast into such a static mold. They reject being placed within the living laboratories and the living backdrops of non-Indians. As a result of the attempts by Native governments to counteract this image and diversify their economies, many Native peoples have now chosen to regulate their own tourist enterprises and museums. This is a relatively new phenomenon and comes in the epoch of the Columbus Quincentennial. The critical question that remains is whether Native peoples will defer to the outside revisionist image or whether they will revise their own images in a manner which is acceptable to them.

Whether the dominant image is the war-bonnet, face-painted, and buckskin clad "chief" or the erotic, grass-skirt garlanded Hawaiian "hula-girl," the irony is that many Native people continue to cater to such images. There is no consensus among Indians about this type of activity. Many reservation communities are divided and factionalized over the exploitation of their own cultural images. Although attempts have been made by some tribal governments to regulate the use of sacred images and symbols, other tribes such as the Cherokee tribe of North Carolina have made a profitable enterprise from manufacturing stereotyped "Indian toys."

By and large, however, many Native people choose to play an invisible or non-existing role in controlling aspects of such exploitation. Whereas non-Indian communities like Sedona, Arizona, and Santa Fe, New Mexico, procure the bulk of their commerce with the merchandising of "authentic" Indian arts, very little of this marketing-hype is present in the reservation communities. In a larger sense, Native people prefer to protect their communities from crass commercialism. The reservation becomes "spiritual," and such spiritualism is an integral part of the amenity of its sense of place.

Although the regulation of outside commercialism of Indian culture has been largely informal, the most challenging aspect among American Indians today is how they will deal with revising their own images. As "insiders," how much cultural information will they be willing to divulge and under what pretext? How will they "revise" their own image while at the same time coping with the same issues that confront conservators today? Will they allow themselves to continue to be "living museums" or will they choose to stage pageants and reenactments designed to shroud their real community presence and deflect tourism away from their private lives? By addressing these and other important questions, they will undoubtedly be able to both demystify the Indian mystique and contribute to their own revision of the prevailing stereotypes.

> While American Indians have a grand past, the impact on their culture on the world has been slight. There are no great American Indian novels, no poetry. There's no memorable music. Their totem poles do not rank with the statuary of Greece and there's no American Indian art, except for some good craft work in wool, pottery and silver. Their genius was for living free in a wild state—without damaging the ozone layer.
> (Andy Rooney, Columnist, 3/25/92)

The other challenge to Native people is mainstream society itself. The unfortunate reality of the youth of a monocultural, mainstream America is that the great majority are ignorant and unappreciative of cultural diversity. The ideal of humanity has been lost in the colonial and neocolonial morass of individual competition and consumer avarice. And from a pragmatic standpoint, monocultural youth in the diversified context of a world whose pluralistic communities are the majority, will doubtless not be tolerated. Rather ironically, America's cultureless youth are thus faced with the prospect of becoming the next generation of stereotyped savages in the post-Quincentenary epoch.

Theodore S. Jojola

See also Film and Video; Literature; Newspapers and Journals; Photography; Radio and Television

Further Reading

Hirschfelder, Arlene B. *American Indian Stereotypes in the World of Children: A Reader and Bibliography.* Metuchen, NJ: Scarecrow Press, 1982.

Sale, Kirkpatrick. *The Conquest of Paradise: Christopher Columbus and the Columbian Legacy.* New York, NY: NAL/Dutton, 1991.

Scholder, Fritz. *Indian Kitsch: The Use and Misuse of Indian Images.* Flagstaff, AZ: Northland Press, 1979.

Slapin, Beverly, and Doris Seale. *Through Indian Eyes: The Native Experience in Books for Children.* Philadelphia: New Society Publishers, 1991.

Viola, Herman J., and Carolyn Margolis, eds. *Seeds of Change: A Quincentennial Commemoration.* Washington, DC: Smithsonian Institution Press, 1991.

Weatherford, Jack. *Indian Givers: How the Indians of the Americas Transformed the World.* New York, NY: Crown, 1988.

Yewell, John, Chris Dodge, and Jan DeSirey. *Confronting Columbus: An Anthology.* Jefferson, NC: McFarland & Co., 1992.

PUBLIC LAW 280

See Government Policy: Termination and Restoration

PUBLIC SCHOOLS

Developing an educational system that will support the contemporary needs of the American Indian and Alaska Native is a difficult task. There is need for a system that will promote development of the intellectual, social, cultural, and economic well-being of each individual, and serve as a symbol for the tribes of their ability to survive the invasion of millions of people from other countries.

In a quick review of the history behind the presence of American Indians and Alaska Natives in public schools, this article uses two states as illustration: New York, one of the original thirteen colonies; and Alaska, the last state to enter the Union with an Indian population. To review the history of public education for American Indians in the fifty states would be a mammoth undertaking. This sample shows that it is difficult to generalize.

New York

In the state of New York there were no specific provisions for Indians to attend public schools until 1846. Before then Indian children were permitted to attend public schools in communities that were near Indian reservations. The schools submitted counts of Indian children and received state funding whether the students attended school or not. In 1846 New York enacted legislation that limited the count of Indian children for public school funding to students that actually attended school at least three months of the previous year. This marked the beginning of direct state public resources for the education of Indian children on reservations in New York. In 1856 Indian schools were placed under the direct charge of the first superintendent of public instruction.

In 1904 New York enacted legislation that provided for compulsory education of Indian children on Indian reservations. This legislation extended the school year for Indian children (September through July) and made school compulsory for children of six to fourteen years of age. This lengthened the school year two more months annually and gave Indian children two more years of schooling than was provided for other children in the state. The legislature intended to limit the influence of the home on the students, and place students more directly under the influence of the school and teachers. Ironically there was no appropriation for enforcing the legislative requirements. The segregation of Indian students on reservations in reservation schools led to a decline in the quality of schools Indian children attended, in part because less monies were spent for maintenance, repairs, and school operations, including teacher's salaries. As early as 1913 state annual reports on the status of the education of Indians recommended that Indian children attend white schools (an annual report ending July 31, 1915, stated that "It is good educational policy to have Indian children in school with white children whenever it is possible to do so. . . . This mingling of Indian and white children . . . is of great benefit to Indian pupils in learning the language and customs of the people with whom they must live in business and social relations." The policy of integrating Indian children into public schools really began with the closing of the Tonawanda Reservation schools in 1930 and 1931, and the busing of the children to public schools in Akron. Tuition and transportation costs were paid by the state to the school district.

Alaska

In Alaska three types of schools were established during the Russian trade period. Public schools, created under the Russian-American Company, religious schools created under the Russian-Greek Orthodox Church, and government schools. Company schools were designed for training future personnel. Government schools were available for the sons of company officials, and religious schools were designed to christianize the Natives by teaching them to read the scriptures.

During the time between the Treaty of Cession signed by the United States and Russia on March 30, 1867, and the appointment of Dr. Sheldon Jackson as a general agent of education for the State of Alaska on April 11, 1885, by the United States commissioner of education, missionary schools replaced the Russian schools. With the appointment of Dr. Jackson as general agent of education, the establishment of public schools in Alaska was ensured. The first public schools were mission schools subsidized by the federal government, but by 1899, local communities were authorized to set up school boards and establish schools. The first problem reported concerning the education of Native children in the public schools occurred in 1902, when the city of Nome neglected to make provision for Eskimo children to attend the local school.

With the passage of the 1905 Nelson Act, schools for white children outside of incorporated towns fell under the authority and responsibility of the governor of Alaska as an ex-officio superintendent of public instruction. The education of Native Alaskans remained the responsibility of the United States secretary of interior. This was the beginning of Alaska's two separate school systems. The United States Congress in 1917 authorized Alaska's territorial legislature to establish schools under the authority of local governments. White children, as well as Native children and children of mixed blood whose parents had adopted customs of the white population, were eligible to attend.

Conclusions

In reviewing the events of Indian students attending public schools in New York and in Alaska, several findings emerge. First, Indians began attending public schools in different ways in different states. Second, racial conflicts often surfaced and the climate in the school was not always pleasant for Indian students. Third, segregated schools emerged, not only in federal schools, but in mission and public systems as well.

There was a clear underlying philosophy of separating the Indian child from the influences of the Native community whenever possible. This separation was seen as a way of accelerating the civilization or acculturation of the Indian child, moving children away from their Native cultures, and christianizing them.

It is an established policy that today states are responsible for the education of all of its citizens. Theoretically this included all Indians after the Indian Citizenship Act of 1924. Even though many Indians had become citizens prior to that legislation, states were reluctant to provide a public education for Indian students without the presence of federal monies. As early as 1890 the Indian Service began a policy of federal reimbursement for the cost of public schools educating Indian students.

In 1891 the federal government formally began moving Indian children to public schools through a system of contracts, and by the time the Meriam Report was published in 1928, there were more Indian students in public schools than in Bureau of Indian Affairs (BIA) schools. Approximately 90 percent of Indian students are now in public schools according to the *Indian Nations At Risk* report of 1991.

The Johnson-O'Malley Act of 1934 (JOM), as amended, authorized the secretary of interior to enter into contracts with tribes, schools, states, and private institutions to provide Indians with education and social services, formalizing the practice of paying for the public cost of educating Indians.

Congress passed the Federally Impacted Areas Act (P.L. 81-874) in 1950, and the School Facilities Construction Act (P.O. 81-815) in 1953. Both acts as amended provide public school districts federal support because of nontaxable federal land (including reservations) in or near the school districts serving students whose parents live and/or work on those lands. P.L. 874 is used for the operations of schools, and P.L. 815 for the construction of schools.

Title I of the Elementary and Secondary Education Act of 1965, as amended, was proposed by President Lyndon Johnson to overcome poverty. It was designed to provide compensatory educational programs and improve academic performance for educationally disadvantaged students using poverty as a means for identifying students. Except for a change from Title I to Chapter I, a decrease in rules and regulations (resulting in less paper work), and a requirement to show that students are improving academically in order to continue, ESEA has remained intact. This and the Bilingual Education Act provide both BIA and public schools monies for Indian students in rural and urban areas.

The Indian Education Act of 1972 (P.L. 92-318 as amended) was the result of a national study carried out by the United States Senate through a special subcommittee on Indian education. The report, called

Indian Education: A National Tragedy—A National Challenge (the Kennedy report), called for support to public schools, Indian contract schools, Indian tribes and organizations (as a priority), and other groups to plan and implement programs that meet the unique educational, language, and cultural needs of Indian students. It also called for adult education and training that would lead to employment. It originally missed the importance of professional programs that offered terminal degrees.

Congress enacted the Indian Self-Determination and Education Assistance Act of 1975 to provide Indian tribes an opportunity to practice self-determination. It requires federal agencies to contract with tribes the responsibility for administering federal services to the tribe. The law authorizes appropriations for public school construction on or near Indian reservations, and supplements funds available under P.L. 815 (Impact Aid).

There are between 400,000 and 500,000 Native students in elementary and secondary schools. Approximately 50,000 of these are in BIA, private, and Indian contract schools. Until the implementation of the Indian Education Act of 1972, the only accurate counts for the numbers of Indian students in public schools came from the JOM and P.L. 874 counts.

Combined, the statutes and laws enacted for public education services to Native students are comprehensive and provide for all the necessary programs and authority needed to meet the educational program and construction needs of Indians. The Snyder Act (1921) actually provides all of the authority required to meet both the unique and basic educational needs of Indian students. P.L. 874, the Johnson-O'Malley Act, and the Indian Education Act of 1972 provide a wide range of educational program options. P.L. 815 and the Indian Self-Determination Act are adequate for meeting the needs of school construction (with the possible exception of Indian community colleges). These programs, along with the Elementary Education Act of 1965, cover BIA school students, as well as all urban and rural Indian students attending public schools. Unfortunately, these laws are not usually fully funded.

What then is the problem encountered by Native communities and students with schooling? The problem appears to be the inability of public schools to build educational systems serving Native children that the students are comfortable in and that build upon their tribal identities. There is, of course, another problem: one of creating schools that build a sense of ownership in the school. All of the reports on Indian education that have been reviewed for this article, starting with the Meriam Report of 1928, and ending with the *Indian Nations At Risk* report, point out consistent themes and recommendations. These include the following:

1. A lack of teachers that are trained to work with Native students, including insufficient numbers of Native teachers.

2. A lack of attention being paid to the development of Native language and culture for academic, as well as tribal reasons.

3. Overt and covert racism and a school atmosphere that is not a safe and/or a comfortable place to be in for many Native students.

4. The lack of a well-developed language base among many children that allows for the development of the conceptual and analytic skills important to a formal education (a more recent position).

5. Family or community-related health and social barriers that many students must overcome.

6. School facilities that are aesthetically unpleasing and buildings that are unsafe.

7. School curriculum that is not consistent with the historical perspectives of Native students, as well as other minorities.

In the twenty years since the publication of *Indian Education: A National Tragedy—A National Challenge*, and the subsequent legislation, the Indian Education Act of 1972, a significant number of models and projects with evidence of effectiveness have been developed. Examples include the Santa Fe Indian School in New Mexico; the St. Regis Mohawk project with their local public school; and the RAPS program in Alaska, which is a partnership between government agencies, Native corporations, and schools. In addition, several exciting things have developed. There are more parents involved in the education of their children, larger numbers of Indian students are going to college and graduating, greater numbers of Indian teachers are in the classroom, and public school administrations are beginning to recognize that they must change if they are to succeed in educating the multi-cultural mix of students that they are responsible for. Finally, there has been a significant move towards Indian control of BIA and public schools in rural Indian communities.

When one considers that 85 to 90 percent of the Indian student population is in public schools—with the significant growth of the Indian sovereignty movement; with the lack of an Indian professional community of teachers, doctors, scientists, engineers, etc.; and with few tribal resources remaining after the treaty-making period because of major concessions made to the federal government—one must ask whether public schools as we know them are capable of meeting their responsibilities to the American Native community.

The answer is probably not—at least not until some significant change takes place.

William G. Demmert, Jr.

See also **Bureau of Indian Affairs Schools; Educational Policy; Indian Education Act, 1972; Johnson-O'Malley Act**

Further Reading

Birdseye, Ruth A. *Indian Education in New York State 1846–1953–54.* Albany: The University of the State of

New York, The State Education Department, Division of Elementary Education, Bureau of Elementary School Supervision, 1955.

Cohen, Felix S. *Felix S. Cohen's Handbook of Federal Indian Law.* Ed. Rennard Strickland. Charlottesville, VA: Mitchie/Bobbs-Merrill, 1982.

Deloria, Vine, Jr. *Legislative Analysis of the Federal Role in Indian Education,* Department of Health, Education, and Welfare, Office of Education, Office of Indian Education, Washington, DC, 1975. 2mf ERIC ED 113 114.

Demmert, William G., Jr. "Native Education: The Alaskan Perspective." *Indigenous Peoples and Education In The Circumpolar North.* William G. Demmert, Jr. Godthab, Greenland: Gronlands Seminarium, 1986.

Indian Nations At Risk: An Imperative for Educational Reform. Final Report of the Indians At Risk Task Force, U.S. Department of Education. Final Draft. June 13, 1991.

Szasz, Margaret C. *Education and the American Indian.* 2d ed. Albuquerque: University of New Mexico Press, 1979.

PUEBLO OF TIGUA

See Tortugas; Ysleta Del Sur Pueblo

PUEBLOS

The entries that follow concern the Pueblo communities which are located along the Rio Grande and its tributaries in New Mexico. Pueblo cultures may appear to be homogeneous but they are quite distinctive with regional, linguistic, and social variations. These Pueblos have existed for centuries and were thriving communities at the time of Francisco Vásquez de Coronado's expedition in 1540 to 1542 to the region. They continue to be evolving vital communities today. There are eighteen Pueblo communities discussed in this section.

The Pueblo communities of Ysleta del Sur and Tortugas, which have histories quite separate from the others located along the Rio Grande, are discussed elsewhere in the encyclopedia. Hopi and Zuni are also discussed elsewhere as they do not naturally fall into this group.

ACOMA

Acoma (Akoma, Acu, Acuco, and other variations of these spellings appear historically and in modern-day conversations) denotes in the Keresan language the "Place That Always Was," or "Home for Many Ages." The name refers to the village and people who occupy the Acoma Mesa, or *peñol*, which is 357 feet high and about 60 miles west of Albuquerque, New Mexico, and 12 miles south of Interstate 40. The reservation includes the villages of Acomita and McCartys, where most of the people live throughout the year. A small number continue to reside at Acoma (Sky City) voluntarily and by appointment, where since 1982 they have been visited annually by more than one million vacationers, most of them during the summer months.

The *peñol* and Sky City are thought to be the oldest inhabited sites in the United States, first reported by Fray Marcos de Niza in 1539 and then visited by Francisco de Coronado's army in 1540. These and subsequent relations with Spaniards in the sixteenth century was where the Spanish title "Kingdom of Acu" originated. The Spaniards believed that 5,000 to 10,000 warlike people occupied a very large area in this kingdom. These early descriptions of Acoma supported modern Indian claims to traditional lands comprising some 5 million acres and numerous villages, which are no longer part of the aboriginal domain. Acoma has since recovered half a million acres of the original 5 million.

The Acoma people are peace-loving and seek by nonaggressive means to restore their aboriginal lands. Finding no resolutions before the Court of Claims in 1890s, nor before a Pueblo Lands Board in 1924, the Acoma began a complicated, time-consuming land claims petition before the Indian Claims Commission in 1948, presenting the petition before the Commission on August 9, 1951. After hearings in 1952, 1953, 1954, 1957, and 1961, the Indian Claims Commission declared the Acoma had aboriginal title to the lands, waters, and minerals claimed, and the United States agreed to a settlement of $6,107,157, made to Acoma in 1970. No lands were exchanged as a result of the claim.

Now the Acoma are determined to restore their aboriginal lands by purchasing ranches and properties bordering the reservation. In 1977 the tribe purchased the Berryhill, or Bibo, ranch that included 13,860 acres to the west of the reservation. This was followed with the acquisition of the Kowina Foundation Purchase in 1979, including extensive ancestral ruins of that name, a museum complex located there, and 83.80 acres, again to the west.

In 1978 the Acoma purchased the large Wilson ranch, also known locally as the B-15, to the east and south of the reservation. Then in 1982 the tribe added 291.84 acres to the west through purchase of a farm from Pete Baca, Jr. In 1982 the Acoma bought the land north of the reservation incorporating a business complex, just north of Acomita, at the Acomita turnoff at Interstate 40. In all, there were 236.4 acres on which were situated a trading post, warehouse, restaurant, twenty-five unit mobile home and RV park site, and a Chevron service station. Former Governor Merle L. Garcia championed the purchase of this area, because the Pueblo considered the Los Cerritos property, as it was called, the cornerstone of Acoma economic development efforts.

The last and largest purchase occurred in 1988, when tribal Governor Ray A. Histia consummated the Red Lake ranch purchase of 114,342 acres to the south of the reservation. The tribe was able to retrieve valuable religious sites through these purchases. The Tribal Council created a position of ranch manager to oversee the ranches and tribal herds gathered there.

The greatest disappointment came during Governor Stanley Paytiamo's time in office, when the

490

RIO GRANDE PUEBLOS

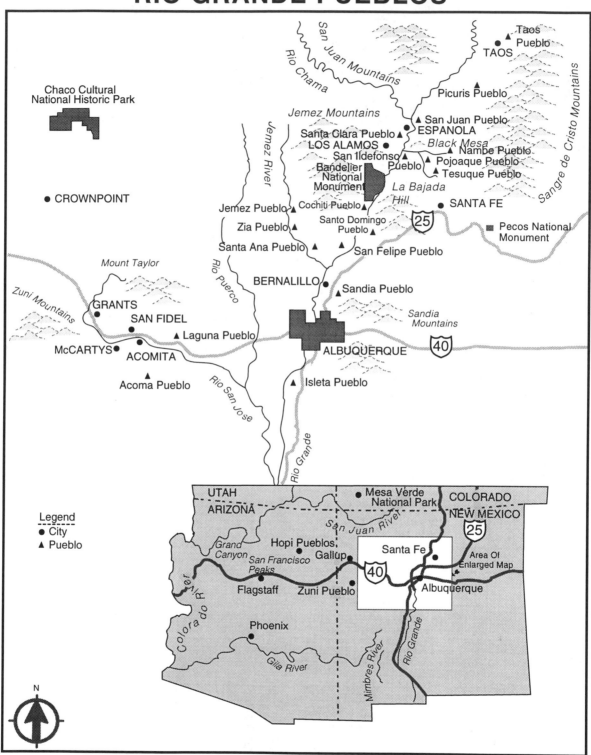

Source: TRIMBLE, STEPHEN. TALKING WITH THE CLAY: THE ART OF PUEBLO POTTERY SANTA FE: SCHOOL OF AMERICAN RESEARCH, 1987. Courtesy of the School of American Research. Map by Carol Cooperrider.

United States government ignored Acoma's interests to the west of the reservation and State Road 117, and established a 253,000-acre natural conservation area and 115,000-acre El Malpais National Park by act of Congress, signed by President Ronald Reagan, January 1, 1988. The law blocked any future Indian ownership of these lands. The Acoma would have finally settled for 12,000 acres, more or less along the same state road, but this petition was disregarded.

In recent years the tribe added significantly to its enterprises and human services. There is a new governmental complex not far from Acomita, to the west on the same road. There is a large, attractive visitors center, museum, and lunchroom at the base of Acoma *peñol*, with bus service for the many visitors to Sky City. Pottery making and vending are major cottage industries. Local farming dwindled over the past fifty years because of increased pollution to the San Jose River waters caused by the growing town of Grants, but ranching has increased significantly. During the early part of this century, sheep husbandry gradually gave way to cattle, particularly after 1930 and loss of the eastern wool markets.

The Tribal Council created Acoma's first school board on April 19, 1978, to oversee programs at the Sky City Community School, Acomita Day School, and Laguna-Acoma High School. Bilingual and minority language efforts resulted in the first Acoma-Keresan dictionary among other learning programs for the young. Adult education and higher education endeavors are leading to the elimination of illiteracy and channeling monies to students who qualify for college and university education and who wish to attend. Social services now include a senior center, individual and family counseling, child welfare and protective services, health care (including reaching out to remote areas), and drug and alcohol programs.

On April 13, 1971, the tribe adopted its first code of law and order. Passage by the Council established the first permanent court system with an attending judge, trial by jury, and a published list of reservation offenses. Juvenile alcoholism has caused the greatest concern, but most offenders receive help from the entire court staff, as well as the police department, who attempt to work with victims toward finishing their education or finding employment.

Acoma opened its first hospital on June 26, 1976, located on the reservation and operated jointly as the Acoma-Canoncito-Laguna Hospital. The three tribes furnished members to a joint hospital board: Acoma, Canoncito Navajo, and Pueblo of Laguna—all primary beneficiaries. The hospital offers total health care including dental care, a complete pharmacy, laboratory services, community health nursing, mental health care, environmental health concerns, and nutritional and social services in general. The main hospital also contains a ritual curing room at the request of user tribes, a special alcohol and drug treatment center known as "Sunrise," and a special ward for kidney dialysis equipment furnished and operated by the Rehobeth Christian Hospital, Gallup, New Mexico.

The ancient theocratic governmental system is still in force with clan members holding authority over governmental appointments and land allocations. These appointments include a governor, first and second lieutenant governors, a sheriff and two deputies, an interpreter, and a secretary. These officials along with the Acoma Tribal Council direct all civil affairs for the tribe. *Caciques* (religious leaders) also appoint councilmen of which there are twelve, who serve indefinite terms and they in turn appoint a bonded treasurer who serves an indefinite period. Each tribal member is affiliated with one of the eighteen or nineteen clans, of which several are reduced to only a few members and appear to be disappearing.

The population is estimated at around 4,000 from just below 500 in 1900. The Pueblo's census continues to be considered, while a constitutional committee is attempting to define tribal membership. Unemployment continues to be a worrisome problem; the governors have reported over 60 percent of adults are without jobs, especially following some nearby mine closings. Much effort is made to employ tribal members on the reservation since many are being forced to seek work elsewhere and to leave their homes.

Ward Alan Minge

Further Reading

Dillingham, Rick. *Acoma and Laguna Pottery*. Santa Fe, NM: School of American Research Press, 1992.

Garcia-Mason, Velma. "Acoma Pueblo." *Handbook of North American Indians*. Vol. 9. *Southwest*. Ed. Alfonso Ortiz. Washington, DC: Smithsonian Institution (1979): 450–66.

Minge, Ward Alan. Acoma: *Pueblo in the Sky*. Rev. ed. Albuquerque: University of New Mexico Press, 1991.

Sedgwick, Mary K. *Acoma, The Sky City: A Study in Pueblo-Indian History and Civilization*. Cambridge, MA: Harvard University Press, 1926.

White, Leslie A. *The Acoma Indians: People of the Sky City*. Glorieta, NM: Rio Grande Press, 1973.

COCHITI

Cochiti Pueblo lies on the west bank of the Rio Grande in north central New Mexico, about twenty-five miles southwest of Santa Fe. This site has been occupied by these Indians since before the coming of the Spaniards in A.D. 1540. The village is near the center of the reservation, a tract of over 50,000 acres, roughly divided by the Rio Grande, flowing from north to south and traditionally providing irrigation water for the Cochiti fields.

The 1990 census tallied 1,199 for Cochiti, an increase from the 1980 figure of 918. Linguistically, these Indians belong to the Eastern Keresan language group, a cluster of five Pueblos. While these tribes share an appreciable number of culture traits and patterns, each tribal culture is distinct, characterized by a unique assemblage of traits.

Suggestions have been made that the eastern Keresan-speaking Pueblos, together with the two western Keresan-speaking tribes, Acoma and Laguna, are affiliated with other North American Indian language groups; most authorities, however, are content to have the Keresan linguistic group stand alone. In the past, most Cochiti commonly used three languages—Keresan, Spanish, and English. Today, only some of the older generation are able to use Spanish.

As of this time the smaller tribes such as the Cochiti are concerned with the imminent loss of their Native language. Increasing numbers of marriages with non-Keresan spouses, the adverse effects of television including almost total programming in English, and more frequent employment away from the reservation have all contributed to this growing concern. As the Indians recognize, the loss of their language means the loss of their ceremonies, and the loss of ceremonies means the loss of their culture—their way of life.

The Cochiti are served by the mission and attending priests of San Buenaventura, the patron saint. The Cochiti consider themselves to be "good Catholics" and follow Catholic practices for baptisms, confirmations, marriages, and burials. Among the older people, these rites are at times augmented by calling on the services of one of the Native medicine, or curing, societies. While these medicine men are ever fewer in number, their services are still valued. In some cases, the people utilize modern medical personnel and facilities as well as calling on the traditional practitioners. For some time now, babies have been born in hospitals, most commonly in Santa Fe, and visiting nurses and doctors care for many ailments and diseases. Tribal health has improved greatly in recent decades.

Similarly, there has been a steadily growing interest in formal education. Most young people complete their high school training, for the most part busing daily to the Bernalillo Public High School, twenty miles away. Some families, however, prefer sending their young to St. Catherine's Indian School, a boarding school in Santa Fe. An increasing number of these graduates, both young men and young women, continue to college—either at the smaller institutions in New Mexico or out-of-state colleges. The armed services continue to be attractive to many of the Cochiti.

Upon completion of these college or service years, the young Cochiti Indians may remain away from the Pueblo where they can find more advantageous employment. On the other hand, a fair percentage return home where they engage in some form of craft, often in collaboration with a spouse, involving pottery making, silversmithing, drummaking, painting, etc. Others succeed in finding gainful employment in nearby communities.

As far as Native ceremonialism is concerned, leadership shifts in specific circumstances from the headmen of the medicine or other secret societies to the headmen of the kivas. The kiva groups take the lead in celebrating various Catholic feast days, including the major July 14th observance of the Feast of San Buenaventura. In addition to these church-oriented celebrations, there are also Native dances, such as hunting, or animal dances.

Although some individuals no longer participate in tribal ceremonies, many belong to either the Turquoise or the Pumpkin Kiva. These moiety affiliations are acquired by children from their fathers. If there should be trouble between a member and the leadership, it is possible to change from one kiva to the other, with the consent of the two sets of leaders. Such a request, while not common, is virtually never refused, as the principal objective of these leaders is to keep the tribal member, and often his family as well, active in the ceremonial life of the tribe.

This is in contrast to the clan system, which includes about a dozen clans, where membership is acquired from the mother at the time of birth. These matrilineal units are not as significant as they were in former years; they tend to be exogamous insofar as marriage is concerned. However, with a somewhat elaborate ritual, it is possible for a person to change from his natal clan to another. This is more often done in the case of a woman, as one might expect from the matrilineal clan structure; after the adoption ceremonies, subsequent children inherit the new clan from her.

While some tribes have followed a written Constitution in their political organization for a number of years, the Cochiti still follow an unwritten set of regulations or policies, which might well be termed "common law." Problems are solved on the basis of precedent; as time goes along and new situations confront the Cochiti, the Tribal Council discusses the matter until a consensus is reached—and this then takes on the status of precedent. This is the traditional way of reaching decisions, but under the pressures of today's demands, decisions are sometimes made by a majority opinion at the present time.

In terms of arts and crafts, Cochiti has long been recognized as the home of drummakers, whose products are of great interest to other tribes as well as to tourists. In addition, there are the potters whose pieces are eagerly sought after; perhaps most popular among these items are the "storytellers," first created some years ago by Helen Cordero, but now fashioned by many others, both at Cochiti and in other Pueblos. Widely recognized silversmiths and painters, including Tonita Peña, Joe H. Hererra, Manuel "Bob" Chavez, and others, have achieved prominence.

Charles H. Lange

See also **Pottery**

Further Reading

Goldfrank, Esther S. *The Social and Ceremonial Organization of Cochiti.* Memoirs of the American Anthropological Association 33. Menasha, WI: AAA, 1927.

Lange, Charles H. *Cochiti: A New Mexico Pueblo, Past and Present.* Austin: University of Texas Press, 1959. Albuquerque: University of New Mexico Press, 1990.

———. "Cochiti Pueblo." *Handbook of North American Indians.* Vol. 9. *Southwest.* Ed. Alfonso Ortiz. Washington, DC: Smithsonian Institution (1979): 366–78.

ISLETA

The large Isleta Reservation stretches across the fertile bottomland of the Rio Grande about twelve miles south of Albuquerque, New Mexico. The Pueblo is named after the seventeenth-century Spanish Mission, San Antonio de la Isleta, later referred to as San Augustine de la Isleta after it was refounded in 1710 following the Pueblo Revolt of 1680. The main village is located on the west bank of the Rio Grande, with two farm villages on the east side of the river.

Based on 1988 statistics the Bureau of Indian Affairs (BIA) estimated that Isleta's Reservation included 211,037.01 acres under tribal trust with 7.99 acres owned by the government for a total of 211,045 acres. Of this total, 33,088 acres are forested areas, which are included in the 202,073 acres used for range land.

During most of the nineteenth century, Isleta's population grew slowly until the 1890s, when there was a rapid increase probably reflecting an influx of people from Laguna. Population statistics vary depending on the source. In 1966, 2,231 were enrolled at Isleta with approximately 1,974 actually in residence. According to the 1990 United States Census of Housing and Population, Isleta has a total population of 2,915, of which over 92 percent are American Indian. In 1993, according to the census office of Isleta Pueblo, 3,971 members were officially enrolled; however, the exact number of members actually living in the Pueblo was unknown.

Land Claims, Water Rights, and Economic Development

Land claims and water rights are among the two most important human rights issues for Native Americans in the twentieth century. Isleta brought a claim for fair and just compensation for the loss of land to Spanish land grants before the Indian Claims Commission in 1959. The first claim was for the Peralta Tract of 14,710.85 acres, which was part of the Lo de Padillo Grant containing 51,940.82 acres, made on May 14, 1718. A second claim was for the Bosque de los Piños involving 2,582.78 acres, which was part of the original Antonio Gutierrez and Joaquin Sedillo grants aggregating 22,636.92 acres, made on November 5, 1716. Each claim had a different set of facts surrounding the situation, thus requiring a separate decision by the Commission. In the end, both claims were dismissed because it was determined that Isleta had been given almost all of the Peralta Tract and the appropriate compensation when they sold it. The Commission felt that the second claim could not be sustained by the evidence presented.

Not gaining much success in land claims, Isleta has fared better in their right to water for irrigation. A political subdivision of the state of New Mexico, the Middle Rio Grande Conservancy District (MRGCD), was formed in 1925 to provide flood protection and improve irrigation along the Rio Grande in the central part of the state. In 1928, authorization was given to the secretary of the interior to enter into a contract with the MRGCD for conservation, irrigation, and drainage improvements, as well as flood control on Pueblo land. Six Pueblos were located within the district including approximately 21,000 acres of irrigable Pueblo land. The statute provides that at least 8,346 of those acres are "prior and paramount to all other rights of the district," and are "not subject to loss from nonuse and abandonment as long as title to the land is in the hands of the Indians." Although this statute demonstrates the state's concern to protect the irrigation rights of the Indians, nothing in the 1928 Act defines the rights of the Pueblos to water other than that delivered by the district.

Isleta has been more successful in consolidating land allotments into commercial farms than any other Pueblo. By the 1960s about 75 percent of the farm lands had been rehabilitated and organized into sizeable units that could be farmed efficiently with modern machinery. Because of its proximity to Albuquerque, Isleta is in a favorable position to supplement farming and grazing income with wage work.

The majority of men and women commute to Albuquerque to work at Kirtland Air Force Base, for the BIA, or in other urban businesses. Isleta has flourished economically with a successful cattle range operating on the reservation, and about 5,000 acres of farmland under irrigation.

The availability of local jobs has kept the unemployment rate down. In 1988 the Department of the Interior estimated the unemployment rate for the Pueblo at 22 percent. Government funds permitted the preparation of twenty acres for public recreation and fish ponds. An electronic company and welding supply company established themselves in the Pueblo in 1974. The industrial complex where Interstate 25 crosses the reservation assures further tribal income and employment possibilities. Isleta has also gained income by leasing out 7,259 acres to 54 businesses, including signboard permits, according to 1989 records of the Department of the Interior.

Tribal Government and Community Life

After long years of strife, dissension, and factionalism, Isleta Pueblo adopted a Constitution in 1947. Under this Constitution, each man twenty-one years or older can vote for his choice for governor the first ten days of December. The incumbent governor plus the three men receiving the highest number of votes become the four candidates for governor. On January first, another vote takes place, and the candidate with the highest number of votes becomes governor, the second highest, president of the Council; and the third, vice-president of the Council. The governor chooses four members of the Council and the president and vice-president each chooses three Council members. The governor also appoints the first and second lieutenant governors, the sheriff, the secretary, and the treasurer.

The Isleta child is born into a bilaterally extended family in which there is no differentiation in kinship terminology between relatives on the mother's or father's side. Farmlands are usually inherited by the males in the Pueblo. Besides the family, a child receives membership in a Corn group, which are ritual units that function in personal rites such as baptisms, marriage, death, etc., as well as solstice rituals which are of importance to the entire Pueblo.

Each infant is made a member of a moiety, a dual system found among other Rio Grande Pueblos. The first child goes into the father's moiety, the second into the mother's, and the third into the father's, with a ceremonial father from that moiety as the child's sponsor. The child receives his moiety name during the spring ceremony when the irrigation ditches are opened or during one of the semiannual retreats and purification rituals.

According to United States Department of the Interior statistics, in 1988, 253 students were enrolled in BIA elementary schools, which includes grades one through six. Isleta families usually send their children to Los Lunas or Albuquerque to go to junior high and high school.

Religion and Ceremonial Life

Each moiety is in charge of ritual requirements for the Pueblo as a whole, during the particular season it represents, winter or summer. In addition, each moiety is responsible for one major dance a year. Ceremonies marking the transfer of this responsibility from one moiety to the other are held in late March and late October.

A unique feature at Isleta is that the Corn groups, which are similar to clans, select their own captains, who are responsible for the ceremonies and dances for the year. These captains are then confirmed by the governor and Council. In the 1960s religious leaders were still very influential; nevertheless, since the adoption of the Constitution, they do not have as much overt political power as they did formerly.

Isleta Today

Isleta has had a long history of factionalism, which culminated in the adoption of the 1947 Constitution. Dissension developed again in the 1960s between the progressives and the conservatives concerning the development of Pueblo resources, the development of recreation opportunities, the importance of education, and the necessity of making decisions about industrialization, and pressures from Albuquerque's expansion.

Isleta has been able to take advantage of the economic and commercial opportunities provided by its proximity to Albuquerque and its location along Interstate 25. Artists such as Estella and Robin Teller and Herman and Betty Lente make pottery; Joseph and Veronica Moquino make jewelry; Andy and Roberta Abeita are sculptors; and Jessie Overstreet, Margaret Ojola, and Margaret Zuni make traditional clothing for sale in village curio shops as well as for larger shops in Albuquerque. Several Isleta women bake Pueblo bread, pies, and cookies for local retailers in the village and along the Interstate. Although the arts and crafts production and bread baking provide income, it is not enough to provide for a family and is primarily a supplement to the total household income. Those members not involved in farming or local enterprises continue to work primarily in Albuquerque.

A revival of ceremonialism in the past few years has raised concerns from the young educated members as to how to retain the values of the old way, which they value and respect, while acquiring an education and an understanding of the non-Pueblo world in which they must work. This is a concern voiced by many young Native Americans throughout North America, who are struggling to find a balance between two very different worlds, with beliefs and values that often oppose each other.

Shelby J. Tisdale

Further Reading

DuMars, Charles T., Marilyn O'Leary, and Albert E. Utton. *Pueblo Indian Water Rights: Struggle for a Precious Resource.* Tucson: University of Arizona Press, 1984.

Ellis, Florence Hawley. "Isleta Pueblo." *Handbook of North American Indians.* Vol. 9. *Southwest.* Ed. Alfonso Ortiz. Washington, DC: Smithsonian Institution (1979): 351–65.

Smith, Anne M. *New Mexico Indians.* Museum of New Mexico Research Records No. 1. Santa Fe: Museum of New Mexico, 1966.

U.S. Indian Claims Commission. *Commission Findings on the Pueblo Indians.* New York, NY: Garland Publishing, 1974.

JEMEZ

The Pueblo of Jemez (pronounced He-mish) is one of nineteen Pueblos located in New Mexico. It is a federally recognized American Indian tribe with just over 3,000 tribal members. Most members reside in the village known as Walatowa (a Towa word meaning "This Is the Place.") Walatowa is located in Sandoval County, New Mexico, within the southern end of the majestic Cañon de San Diego. It is located approximately fifty-five miles northwest of Albuquerque and approximately seventy miles southwest of Santa Fe.

The Pueblo of Jemez is a dependent sovereign nation with an independent government and tribal court system. Our secular tribal government includes the Tribal Council, the Jemez governor, two lieutenant governors, two *fiscales*, and a sheriff. Our second lieutenant governor is also the governor of the Pueblo of Pecos. Traditional matters are still handled through a separate governing body that is rooted in prehistory. This traditional government (the Supreme Council) includes the *cacique* and other spiritual and society leaders, a war captain, and a lieutenant war captain. Through perseverance, our people have managed to preserve our traditional culture, religion, and knowledge regardless of outside pressures. We have also preserved our complex language, a language that anthropologists and linguists refer to as Towa. Jemez people are the only individuals that speak this language and, in fact, to prevent exploitation by outside cultures, traditional law forbids our language from being translated into writing.

Having originated from a place in the underworld called *Hua-vu-na-tota*, our ancestors, the Jemez Nation, migrated to the Cañon de San Diego region from the Four Corners area in the late fourteenth century. By the time of European contact in the year 1541, the Jemez Nation was one of the largest and most powerful of the Puebloan cultures occupying numerous villages that were strategically located on the high mountain mesas and in the canyons that surround the present village of Walatowa. These stone-built fortresses, often located miles apart from one another, were as high as four stories and often contained over 2,000 rooms. These are now some of the largest archaeological ruins in the United States. Situated between these "giant Pueblos" were literally hundreds of smaller one- and two-room houses that were used by the Jemez people during spring and summer months as base-camps for hunting, gathering, and agricultural activities. Our spiritual leaders, medicine people, war chiefs, craftsmen, pregnant women, elderly, and disabled lived in the giant Pueblos throughout the year. Warriors and visitors could easily reach at least one of the giant Pueblos within an hour's walk from any of the smaller seasonal homes. Cliff dwellings were also built along the sides of the adjacent cliffs to guard access to springs and religious sites, to monitor strategic trail systems, and to watch for invading enemies. In general the Jemez Nation resembled a military society that was often called upon by other tribal groups to assist in settling hostile disputes.

Our people first experienced contact with Europeans when Spanish conquistadors and the Coronado Expedition arrived in the year 1541. The Expedition soon left the area and exactly forty peaceful years went by before contact between our two groups was experienced again. This occurred when the Rodriguez-Chamuscado Expedition entered the area in 1581, followed by the Espejo Expedition in 1583. In the year 1598 a detachment of the first colonizing expedition under the direction of Don Juan de Oñate visited the Jemez, and the Franciscan priest Fray Alonzo de Lugo was assigned to our people. He built the area's first church at the Jemez village of Giusewa (now Jemez State Monument). According to our intricate oral history and early written Spanish records, such as the reports from the Espejo Expedition in 1583, the Jemez Nation was an estimated 30,000 strong at the time of Spanish contact. This information indicates that the population of the Cañon de San Diego was probably three times larger than what it is today. Unfortunately, the peace between our differing cultures did not last long, and the Jemez population was soon decimated as a result of warfare and diseases introduced by the Europeans.

During the next eighty year, numerous revolts and uprisings occurred between the Jemez people and the Spanish, primarily due to Spanish attempts to Christianize our people by force and congregate them into one or two villages where the Franciscan missions were located. As a result, numerous people were killed on both sides, including many of the Franciscan priests. By the year 1680 the hostilities resulted in the Great Pueblo Revolt, during which the Spanish were expelled from the New Mexico province through the strategic and collaborative efforts of all Pueblo Nations. By 1688 the Spanish had begun their reconquest by force under General Pedro Reneros de Posada, acting governor of New Mexico. By 1692 Santa Fe was again in Spanish hands under Governor Diego de Vargas. Four more years would pass before the Jemez Nation was completely subdued and placed under Spanish rule. Soon afterwards the vast majority of the extensive Jemez domain was taken from our people by the Spanish clergy and military, and our ancestors were concentrated into the single village of Walatowa where we reside today. As a result the most significant of our ancestral Jemez sites are now located just out of view of the Pueblo of Jemez, on federal lands that are no longer controlled by our people. Regardless, our ancestral lands are still held in the highest esteem by the Jemez people and not a week goes by that they are not paid tribute to through our prayers and religious offerings.

In the year 1838 Jemez culture became diversified when the Towa-speaking people from the Pueblo of Pecos (located east of Santa Fe) resettled at the Pueblo of Jemez in order to escape the increasing depredations of the Spanish and Comanche cultures. Readily welcomed by our ancestors, the Pecos culture was rapidly integrated into Jemez society, and in 1936, both cultural groups were legally merged into one by an act of Congress. Today the Pecos culture still survives at Jemez, its traditions have been preserved, and as previously noted, the Pueblo of Jemez still honorably recognizes a governor of the Pueblo of Pecos.

The majority of Pueblo members are engaged in agricultural and livestock industries and arts and crafts production. Those members who are employed outside the Pueblo hold many positions in high-technology fields at Los Alamos Laboratories and at computer companies in Albuquerque and Santa Fe, and still others hold government positions with the Bureau of Indian Affairs (BIA) and the United States Forest Service.

Presently, our people are internationally known for their arts and crafts. Pottery bowls, seed pots, sgraffito vessels (elaborately polished and engraved), wedding vases, figurines, holiday ornaments, and our famous storytellers are now in collections throughout the world. In addition Jemez artisans create beautiful basketry, embroidered woven cloth, exquisite stone sculptures, moccasins, and jewelry. Our people are also known as runners, many of whom still hold unbroken records at major national events. We continue to set records as each new generation enters track and field competition.

A variety of educational opportunities are available for Jemez children. The Head Start program at the Pueblo has teachers and teachers' aides from the community. There is a BIA day school and a public school for elementary and secondary grades.

Traditional dances are held throughout the year at Jemez, many of which are not open to the public. However, the public is welcome to share in many of our events, including the Nuestra Señora de Los Angeles Feast Day held on August 2 (the "Pecos Feast"), the San Diego Feast Day held on November 12 ("Jemez Feast"), and the Nuestra Señora de Guadalupe Feast Day," which occurs on December 12. Additional events open to the public take place at various times throughout the Christmas Holidays. The Jemez Pueblo Visitors Center is currently in development.

William J. Whatley

Further Reading

Sando, Joe S. *The Pueblo Indians*. San Francisco, CA: Indian Historian Press, 1976.

———. "Jemez Pueblo." *Handbook of North American Indians*. Vol. 9. *Southwest*. Ed. Alfonso Ortiz. Washington, DC: Smithsonian Institution (1979): 418-29.

———. *Nee Hemish: A History of Jemez Pueblo*. Albuquerque: University of New Mexico Press, 1982.

LAGUNA

The Pueblo of Laguna, whose residents are Keresan-speaking, is located forty-five miles west of the city of Albuquerque, in the northwest region of New Mexico.

The area consists of massive hematite and quartz sandstone mesas and basalt lava beds, which are a source for building many Pueblo homes. Laguna consists of six separate villages, closely related geographically, in a total land area of 528,079.60 acres. Laguna is a thriving people with an active government, economic opportunity, and a long-lasting regard for their traditional culture.

The whole of Laguna has grown significantly over the past century as a result of land purchases made by the Laguna government. Net area of a United States government survey in 1898 was 17,328.91 acres. The most recent land purchase was that of 2,245.28 acres on July 28, 1983. All lands on the reservation are available for use by all tribal members. Laguna has also grown in population. Over the past fifty years, the Pueblo has more than doubled in size from 3,297 members in 1954 to 7,023 according to the 1992 Laguna Pueblo census.

Old Laguna is the village that was originally recognized by the Spanish on July 4, 1699. The Pueblo is said to have been formed by refugees from the Pueblo Revolt of 1680. No written records of Laguna prior to 1699 exist; however, studies done by Florence Hawley Ellis suggest definite habitation before Spanish recognition. From residents of Old Laguna, the villages of Mesita, Paguate, Paraje, Encinal, and Seama were formed.

Although part of a larger whole, the six villages of Laguna are autonomous to a degree. The people of each village elect two officers, with the exception of Laguna and Paguate, due to a larger population, who elect four. The officers, known as *mayordomos*, are responsible for allocating plots of land to those who wish to farm or build homes. The village officers also oversee the upkeep of the intricate irrigation system, which runs along the fields of each village. Weekly meetings are held in the six villages with the *mayordomos* presiding. There, a report of the recent Tribal Council meeting is presented. Village residents attend not only to be informed, but to voice opinions, ideas, or complaints.

On a higher level, the tribal government of Laguna consists of a twenty-one member Council; two representatives from each village and nine staff members who are elected at large. The staff members include a governor, first lieutenant governor, second lieutenant governor, treasurer, secretary, and others. The government is bound to protect and govern its people through the Pueblo of Laguna Constitution, which was adopted in revised form from the Indian Reorganization Act in 1958. Another revision of the fifteen-article Constitution was made in 1984. Land leasing, water and mineral rights, membership, per capita distribution, elections, and jurisdiction are all included in the Constitution with other critical specifications. The Tribal Council and other employees affiliated with the government are exclusively housed in one building in Old Laguna.

In addition to government occupations, other sources for employment in Laguna Pueblo are through the Laguna Police Department, Laguna-Acoma High School, Laguna Elementary School, Casa Blanca Commercial Center (a tribally owned shopping center), Laguna Rainbow Elderly Center, a newly built junior high school, Laguna Industries, and the Laguna Construction Firm.

Laguna Industries is, as yet, the largest source of employment on the reservation. Holding contracts with the United States Army, Laguna Industries constructs communication shelters at a minimal cost to both parties. The business is located near Mesita and employs over 300 workers.

Between the years of 1953 and 1983 mining operations were conducted continuously in the largest open-pit uranium mine in the world. Leasing lands near Paguate, the Anaconda Mineral Company, a division of Atlantic Richfield Company, extracted 25 million tons of jackpile uranium from three open-pit and nine underground mines during its twenty-nine years of operations. The ore was transported daily to Anaconda's Bluewater Mill near Grants, New Mexico, where it was refined.

During that time Anaconda employed as many as 800 workers in and around the Laguna area. When mining ceased on March 31, 1982, as a result of a depressed uranium market, the Pueblo's income was reduced by an estimated $8 million annually. Five years later plans for the Laguna Reclamation Project went into effect. Anaconda, responsible as lease holder, is funding $45 million with additional funding through Laguna and the federal government to complete the project. Reclaiming the mine area is said to last twelve years from its starting date of October 1987. Employment through the Laguna Construction Firm for sixty-five Laguna members will last for the duration of the project.

As important as the economic and governmental aspects of Laguna, the people's ability to carry on ceremonial traditions is extraordinary. Ancient dances and village feast days are still held as part of an ongoing celebration of life. Due to missionary activity starting in the sixteenth century, each village has a Catholic mission named exclusively for its patron saint. In honor of each saint, an annual feast is held within each village.

The largest feast celebrated is that of Old Laguna. Held on September 19, the feast day commemorates the death of Saint Joseph; the mission is named San José. Yearly on this day, the saint's statue is taken out of the church and placed in the village plaza, in a shrine which is erected specifically for the feast day. Ceremonial dances are held throughout the day in front of the shrine. Outside the plaza, the two main roads of Old Laguna are lined with stands of vendors selling their wares. Local artists, silversmiths, potters, and makers of traditional clothing display and sell their work—a way of livelihood for many who live on the Pueblo. Every house is bustling with visitors as traditional foods are served. Every village celebrates its feast day in a similar way.

Along with the feast days, the six villages hold several sacred ceremonial dances throughout the year. These particular dances require an intense cooperation within the entire village, and are closed to the public. Signs located at the entrance to the village announce this activity.

Debra Toya

Further Reading

American Indian Policy in the Twentieth Century. Ed. Vine Deloria, Jr. Norman: University of Oklahoma Press, 1985.

Churchill, Ward, and Winona LaDuke. "Native America: The Political Economy of Radioactive Colonialism." *Critical Issues in Native North America* 2. IWGIA Document 68 (1991): 25–67.

Dale Edward Everett. *The Indians Of The Southwest: A Century of Development under the United States.* Norman: University of Oklahoma Press, 1949.

Ellis, Florence Hawley. "Laguna Pueblo." *Handbook of North American Indians.* Vol. 9. *Southwest.* Ed. Alfonso Ortiz. Washington, DC: Smithsonian Institution (1979): 438–49.

NAMBE

One of the Tewa Pueblos of the northern Rio Grande region, Nambe is located approximately fifteen miles north of Santa Fe, New Mexico. The Spanish name for Nambe is a rendition of the Tewa name nanbe, which translates as *nan*, "earth," and *be*, "roundness." The people of Nambe probably mixed with their Spanish-American neighbors to a greater degree than other Pueblos. Apart from the amount of the Native Tewa language used in Council meetings, Spanish and English are used more often than Tewa. The current trend is toward more English being spoken in the Pueblo. This trend has probably been associated with the lack of a strong ceremonial life at Nambe.

Land Claims, Water Rights and Economic Development

Land claims and water rights are two of the most important human rights issues among Native Americans of the twentieth century. Proof of continuous occupancy on Pueblo lands and the associated water rights play an important role in the success of these claims. Results of several test excavations at Nambe revealed that the present-day Pueblo site has been occupied continuously for over five-and-one-half centuries. Recently the Bureau of Indian Affairs (BIA) estimated that Nambe land totaled 19,124.01 acres, of which, 9,333 acres are forest areas and 93 acres are being leased out to 21 businesses.

The Pueblo of Nambe petitioned the Indian Claims Commission for the return of 45,000 acres near the Santa Fe Ski Basin that they claimed was taken from them in 1905 by Santa Fe County without payment or compensation. The Nambe Reservation (6,500 acres), established by Executive Order of President Theodore Roosevelt on September 4, 1902, and the so-called Nambe Pueblo Grant (13,000 acres), patented by the United States in 1864, lie within the claimed area.

The boundaries of the claimed area were defined by how the land was used by the members of Nambe Pueblo. Information concerning the boundaries of the area of occupancy and aboriginal use was transmitted from generation to generation by the Pueblo's grandfathers. As stated in the Indian Claims Commission documents, old Pueblo officials took the new war captains and governors around Nambe lands and identified each boundary marker delineating the area of Nambe land use.

The Commission was of the opinion that the Nambe Pueblo land had been taken without compensation on October 12, 1905, when it was proclaimed a part of the national forests. They authorized proceedings to determine the exact acreage of the tract and its fair market value at the time of taking.

In further efforts to obtain the land, Nambe Pueblo rejected the government's offer of a cash payment in December 1976. Today Nambe primarily consists of open grazing land and forests that produce noncommercial timber, with about 300 acres suitable for farming. The Pueblo also leases approximately 2,000 acres from various government agencies, such as the Forest Service, for grazing purposes.

With the exception of Nambe Falls, a tourist attraction, the economic assets of Nambe are limited.

Nambe offers camping, fishing, and sightseeing at the Nambe Falls Recreation Area, and there is some farming and grazing, but the main source of income is wage work. Presently many tribal members work at Los Alamos National Laboratory, in Santa Fe, in Espanola, and for the Eight Northern Indian Pueblos Council. In the meantime, plans are being drafted and submitted to various agencies for economic development, such as expansion of tourist facilities and augmenting irrigable land acreage.

Tribal Government and Community Life

Nambe is considered a rather modest community that includes a well-maintained village with a traditional core. A combination of old and new ways are used to conduct village business. Since 1960, a governor and four officials have been elected although there is no written constitution. Even though the officials meet with these governors on business, voting is restricted to the groups of governors. Meetings are opened in the Tewa language, but actual business may be carried out in Tewa and/or English. Although they may not have the ritual knowledge that traditional Pueblos consider requisite for responsible tribal officers, young men play a large part in tribal government at Nambe.

In general children of female members married outside the Pueblo are not enrolled unless voted in by the Pueblo Council; on the other hand, children of male members are automatically enrolled. There was a population growth in the 1970s, which was probably a result of a combination of several factors including more job opportunities both in and outside the Pueblo, increased health facilities, and improved housing.

Nambe was the first Pueblo to accept federal government housing from the Department of Housing and Urban Development in 1967. They built the type of low-cost housing found on other reservations in the Southwest. In March 1993, according to Nambe Pueblo Government Office, there were 630 enrolled members of Nambe with approximately 487 living in the Pueblo. The 1990 United States Census of Populations and Housing indicates that there are 1,402 people living at the Pueblo and on Nambe trust lands. Of this total 63 percent are Hispanic and 5 percent are white or Black, who either live on Pueblo lands or have married into the Pueblo.

Since there are no schools in Nambe Pueblo, children are bused out to public schools in Espanola where they usually complete high school as well as taking some post high school training. Like Native peoples throughout the country, members of Nambe are finding that they can recapture their past and identity by maintaining group cohesiveness. For this reason, several members are returning to the Pueblo and more young people are staying.

Religion and Ceremonial Life

Most of the inhabitants of Nambe are predominantly Roman Catholics, although several are Protes-

tants. The only ceremony held by Nambe other than a tourist-oriented dance held each July fourth, at Nambe Falls, is their feast day held in honor of Saint Francis on October 4, which includes a Catholic mass and traditional Indian dances.

Nambe Today

The dual moiety system found in other Tewa Pueblos is virtually nonfunctional at Nambe. Much more emphasis is placed on the nuclear family as the basic social and economic unit, and some kinship terms have practically disappeared.

Like many of the other northern Pueblos, Nambe has demonstrated a continued interest in carrying on an artistic heritage. In 1993 Nambe had sixteen artists working in a variety of media. Some of the artists include Virginia Gutierrez, Ernest and Connie Mirabal, Lawrence and Kathleen Perez, Pearl Talachy, Gloria Yellow Leaf Trujillo, Lonnie Vigil, and Robert Vigil, who make pottery using both traditional and contemporary methods and designs; Margie and Dave Garcia, and Roderick and Lela Kaskella, who produce fine silver and gold jewelry; Lucia Jimenez, Angie Peña, LaVern Porter, and Elaine Rodriquez are weavers; Ernest Mirabal, Jr. is a sculptor; and Naomi Romero works with beads and leather. Although most of these artists have not been able to make a living from the sales of their arts and crafts, it has provided an outlet for carrying on the heritage of Pueblo artistic traditions while encouraging innovation.

Nambe's existence as a Pueblo is precarious; nonetheless, the recent revival of ceremonialism, the arts, the Pueblo ownership of over 19,000 acres of unallotted land, and the recent land claim are factors that help to preserve its identity.

Shelby J. Tisdale

See also Water Rights

Further Reading

Ellis, Florence Hawley. "Nambe: Their Past Agricultural Use of Territory." *Water Rights Studies of Nambe, Pojoaque, Tesuque, and San Ildefonso Pueblos.* Manuscript. Bureau of Indian Affairs, United States Department of the Interior. 1967.

Kelly, Henry W. "Franciscan Missions of New Mexico, 1740–1760." *New Mexico Historical Review* 15:4 (1940): 345–68.

Smith, Anne M. *New Mexico Indians.* Museum of New Mexico Research Records, No. 1. Santa Fe, 1966.

Spiers, Randall H. "Nambe Pueblo." *Handbook of North American Indians.* Vol. 9. *Southwest.* Ed. Alfonso Ortiz. Washington, DC: Smithsonian Institution (1979): 317–23.

U.S. Indian Claims Commission. *Commission Findings on the Pueblo Indians.* New York, NY: Garland Publishing, 1974.

PICURIS

Also known as San Lorenzo de Picuris, it is the second smallest of the Rio Grande Pueblos (elevation,

7,300 feet) and is located in a secluded mountain valley fifty miles northeast of Santa Fe and twenty-four miles southeast of Taos, New Mexico. The Bureau of Indian Affairs (BIA) reported a population of 226 in 1991. About half are not permanent residents of the Pueblo. This community of scattered one-story adobe houses has barely survived as a viable entity since settlement (A.D. 1275 to 1350), in spite of two crucial facts characteristic from the early 1700s—namely, geographic isolation and a small population. In the year of the 1680 Pueblo Revolt, the population was estimated at 3,000. Subsequent revolts against the Spanish led to the abandonment of the Pueblo in 1696 and a flight to the Plains from which a Spanish expedition returned 300 to Picuris in 1706. The population has since fluctuated from a high of 400 in 1744, to a low of 91 in 1890. Small size has been a catalyst for significant change in spite of strong ethnic persistence in the twentieth century, including their northern Tiwa language, Picuris.

Geographic isolation has also been important to Picuris history. The Coronado expedition of 1540 and other Spanish forays missed Picuris completely until Gaspar Castaño de Sosa's 1591 expedition found its mountain location. It was then, and remains, well off the main artery of travel from Santa Fe to Taos. In fact, the Picuris often refer to themselves as the "People of the Hidden Valley."

Their small reservation (14,960 acres) is surrounded by rural Spanish American settlements and homesteads. Only 260 reservation acres are arable. Traditional farming, stockraising, and hunting have been almost completely abandoned. Wage work is usually obtained only by leaving the Pueblo on a permanent or semipermanent basis, which has contributed to the steady exodus of the on-reservation population. For those remaining, federal aid and assistance programs, plus some income from the sale of crafts, particularly their fine micaceous pottery, are the primary sources of support. In 1953 the BIA day school was closed, forcing Picuris children to attend school in the nearby Spanish American community of Peñasco. Given the somewhat strained relations between the two peoples, this was not an ideal situation.

Compared to a large conservative Pueblo like Taos, other changes at Picuris constitute drastic departures from Pueblo norms. The traditional Council of ceremonial leaders headed by the *cacique* was replaced in the 1960s by the governor as the head of the Pueblo. This was partially due to abandonment or lapses in ceremonial activities reducing the importance of religious leaders. The Council is now composed of all males, eighteen years or older, who annually vote in the governor, war chief, and their staffs. With only a small number of experienced males, the same individuals are elected repeatedly to serve in secular government. The office of secretary-treasurer, created in the 1970s, is staffed by a woman. Pueblo norms rarely allowed women to serve in any governmental capacity.

A bilateral kinship system with families in neolocal residence remains the basis of social organization, but without the emergence of strong extended family units, given there are so few families in the first place. In the 1940s and 1950s Picuris was a rather desolate place culturally. The annual feast day of San Lorenzo was poorly attended and executed, in spite of encouragement that all tribal members return to the Pueblo and participate. Economically, the situation was so bad that the BIA and the Red Cross came on occasion to distribute emergency rations of food and clothing. Locally, health care continues to be practically nonexistent. The seriously ill must be transported to Taos or Santa Fe.

In the 1960s, due to an avid pursuit of federal aid programs and other assistance, the situation began to turn around. The Picuris assisted a professional archeologist in excavating their old village site at the northern edge of the Pueblo. One kiva, replete with ancient wall murals, was fully restored and the ruins are now used for paid guided tours. The Pueblo was able to build a small museum and cultural center in which to display the artifacts uncovered by the excavations. They created a lake close to the village, stocked it, and collect fees for fishing. They also opened a restaurant serving Pueblo Indian foods, and in 1988, allowed a film company to videograph the public portions of their ceremonial dances, something usually prohibited in most Pueblos. With these commercial ventures, the Picuris are maximizing in every way the resources they have or can obtain.

These activities have energized the Pueblo. Ceremonies long lapsed have been restored. Only one kiva was used in 1959. Now, four are in seasonal use and the annual celebration of San Lorenzo Day is again intact. Their isolation still restricts many tourists from going to Picuris, but compared with the past, the increased numbers are significant. In the summer of 1992, the Indians contracted with a small Eastern college to hold an anthropological field school in the Pueblo. The students were housed by Picuris families and engaged in cultural investigations, something unheard of in the other Pueblos.

A tragedy occurred in 1985 when the west wall of the 1776 mission church collapsed. The Pueblo had hard-plastered the mission in the 1970s. Internal deterioration of the original adobe walls resulted in irreparable damage. By 1988 nothing was left; however, the Picuris immediately began a rebuilding campaign. This ambitious project helped to solidify the community, strengthened their identity as Picuris Indians, and brought them a great deal of favorable publicity and support. More importantly, this small tribe has survived the onslaughts of the past against incredible odds, fueled in part by isolation and underpopulation. Shrewdly exploring all available sources of support, they are trying mightily to insure their survival into the twenty-first century. In a spring, 1992, advertisement in the local *Taos News*, the Pueblo listed all their tourist attractions. One item in the ad indicates they are tuned in to the wider world around them. It states: "Major Credit Cards Honored."

John J. Bodine

Further Reading

Brown, Donald N. "Picuris Pueblo." *Handbook of North American Indians.* Vol. 9. *Southwest.* Ed. Alfonso Ortiz. Washington, DC: Smithsonian Institution (1979): 268–77.

Schroeder, Albert H. *A Brief History of Picuris Pueblo: A Tiwa Indian Group in North Central New Mexico.* Series in Anthropology, No. 2. Alamosa, CO: Adams State College, 1974.

Siegel, Bernard J. "Social Disorganization in Picuris Pueblo." *International Journal of Comparative Sociology* 6:2 (1965): 199–206.

POJOAQUE

Pojoaque or *Po suwae geh,* meaning "Water Drinking Place," is one of the eight northern Tewa Pueblos of New Mexico. Located approximately sixteen miles north of Santa Fe near the junction of US Route 285 and State Route 84 on 11,601.44 acres, Pojoaque is the smallest of the New Mexico Pueblos. Abandoned during the early part of the nineteenth century, Pojoaque is developing its culture and economy.

Twentieth-Century History

The history of Pojoaque Pueblo before European contact is similar to that of the other New Mexican Pueblos. Pojoaque was once the center for all the surrounding Tewa Pueblos and enjoyed political, cultural, and religious independence with ample resources to sustain its agriculturally based economy. Arrival of the Spanish to northern New Mexico in the sixteenth century initiated change. Spanish colonization and suppression resulted in the Pueblo Revolt of 1680, which was successful in removing the Spanish from the Rio Grande Valley. Spanish rule, however, was reestablished under the campaign of 1692 to 1694. During this period Spanish retribution further reduced and scattered the Pojoaque people. Spanish Governor Francisco Cuerbo y Valdez resettled Pojoaque with five families in 1706, and by 1782 it had a resident priest. Pojoaque's population was seventy-nine in 1712, declining to forty by 1890, a fraction of its population before European contact.

Petra Montoya Gutierrez, a Pojoaque who was living at Santa Clara Pueblo in 1993, was born at Pojoaque in 1907. Her father Antonio Jose Montoya was a leader at Pojoaque until his death in 1911. When her mother died in 1913, Petra was adopted by a Santa Clara Pueblo family. Petra confirmed that there were no kiva ceremonies performed at Pojoaque in the twentieth century. The Pueblo was likely abandoned sometime around 1922 after its leaders had died.

Pojoaque's land was officially granted by a land grant from Spain and Mexico; however, the records were lost. In 1856 Pojoaque petitioned the United States suveyor general and the land grant was confirmed by act of Congress in 1858. Pojoaque's governor, along with other Pueblo governors, received their land patents from President Lincoln during ceremonies at Washington, D.C. in 1864. At the same ceremony each governor received a silver-headed cane that to this day symbolizes the political recognition of the Pueblos.

Antonio Jose Tapia, a Pojoaque who had left the Pueblo in 1912 to work in Colorado, and one of the three remaining Pojoaques who lived at the Pueblo, returned to Pojoaque in 1932. Disturbed by reports that Nambe Pueblo was enchroaching on Pojoaque land, and that a Spanish and American settlement had been established thereon, Antonio led a relentless struggle to regain control of the Pojoaque lands for Pojoaques. His efforts were successful. Landgrabbers and livestock were evicted and the Pueblo was fenced by 1934.

Current Situation

Pojoaque is administered by a governor, secretary, and treasurer. The Council consists of the officers and any Pojoaque, male or female, of eighteen years of age or more, who are in attendance at the Council meetings. Elections are held annually. In 1974, Pojoaque became the first Pueblo to elect a woman governor, and since then other women have served as governor and held other offices. A major responsibility of the governor and the other two officers is managing its commercial developments along US Route 285. Their commercial enterprises in 1993 include a mobile home and recreational vehicle park, restaurant, auto store, plaza supermarket, and other service stores. Pojoaque also operates an official state tourist center, the Poeh Cultural Center and Museum, and an arts and crafts shop. The enterprises have been successful in providing jobs and revenue, with the latter distributed equally among tribal members.

The Pojoaque Valley School Community Complex is located on land leased from the Pueblo. Arts and trade schooling is available in Santa Fe, with tribal scholarships available for those who wish to pursue trade and professional training beyond high school.

Pojoaque's tribal roles have been steadily increasing from the fourteen who were living at the Pueblo in 1914, to one hundred four in 1970, and to approximately two hundred in 1993. The majority of its members live in the Pueblo, the others in Santa Fe and Santa Clara Pueblo. Pojoaques today are a proud mixture of Tewa, Tiwa, and Spanish.

Health care is available in the nearby towns of Espanola and Santa Fe. United States Public Health Service professionals and facilities, and public clinics and hospitals, provide high-quality care. There are no special health problems unique to the Pojoaque.

Culture

Community life includes social and business activities and interactions with families at other Pueblos, especially Santa Clara. Most traditional community activities of the past have not as yet been revived at Pojoaque. A senior center adjacent to the governor's office provides for social interactions, and most Pojoaques are members of the Pojoaque Roman Catholic Church. Their language is no longer spoken; however, some speak Santa Clara Pueblo Tewa, which is similar. Pojoaques take pride in their Tewa heritage and maintain their cultural identity through participation in religious and social events at other Tewa Pueblos.

On October 27, 1973, the Pojoaque people danced publically for the first time in the twentieth century. This event, made possible by the assistance of other Pueblos, was one of great pride that introduced the beginning of a cultural revival. A kiva-type building has been constructed, and although Pojoaque lacks a kiva society and therefore lacks the capability to conduct religious kiva society ceremonies, the building will support other Pojoaque activities. The Pueblo celebrates the Feast of Our Lady Guadalupe on December 12, with the Butterfly Dance supplemented by the Eagle and Buffalo Dances. Pojoaque also celebrated All Kings Day in 1993 with Buffalo and Eagle Dances.

Joe and Thelma Talachy are two Pojoaque traditional potters who are well known for their polychrome coiled pottery. Two of their eighteenth-century revival Pojoaque polychrome *olla* jars are part of the Museum of New Mexico's collection. Thelma's mother Petra Montoya Gutierrez taught her daughters pottery skills and each produces fine pottery. Other recognized Pojoaque potters and artists reside at the Pueblo, and at Santa Clara Pueblo and Santa Fe.

Visitors to Pojoaque will find a proud, friendly people who welcome the opportunity to share their friendship. Pojoaque's successes in recent years are apparent, and they are regaining economic prominence in the northern Pueblo region.

John W. Barry

Further Reading

Lambert, Marjorie F. "Pojoaque Pueblo." *Handbook of the North American Indians.* Vol. 9. *Southwest.* Ed. Alfonso Ortiz. Washington, DC: Smithsonian Institution (1979): 324–29.

Sando, Joe S. *Pueblo Nations: Eight Centuries of Pueblo Indian History.* Santa Fe, NM: Clear Light Publishers, 1992.

SAN FELIPE

The Keres-speaking Pueblo de San Felipe, also known as San Felipe Pueblo, is located on the west bank of the Rio Grande in a narrow area between the river and the cliffs of Black Mesa to the west. A cottonwood bosque, or grove, and the Pueblo's farmlands border the river valley. Beyond are semiarid to arid grasslands, hills, and mesas. The average annual rainfall is less than fifteen inches. San Felipe is in Sandoval County in New Mexico, which has over 20 percent Native American population, among the highest in the state, with seven Pueblos, three Navajo chapters, and a portion of the Jicarilla Apache Reservation as stated in the 1990 United States Census.

Many San Felipe people consider descriptions of their traditional way of life to be attempts to destroy their identity as a people. For that reason, the focus here is on major issues in the Pueblo's interaction with the outside world, as identified by several tribal leaders. It is based on interviews, congressional testimony, and government documents. The structure of tribal government has been described elsewhere by the San Felipe Tribal Council (see Deloria).

Twentieth-Century History

San Felipe's land base has a net area of 48,929.90 acres, comprised of the original Spanish grant made in 1689 and patented in 1864, private claims acquired for the Pueblo, acreage added through an executive order in 1902, and other acquisitions made during this century, according to the Bureau of Indian Affairs (BIA).

Although population data is inconsistent, it is clear that since 1900 San Felipe has steadily grown from about 500 to over 2,500. The highest growth rate occurred between 1950 and 1980, and there was a slight slowdown between 1980 and 1990 (figure 1).

Figure 1
San Felipe Population, 1900–1991

Year	Population
1900	514
1900–05	475 (annual avg.)
1910	490
1920	542
1930–32	555 (annual avg.)
1940–42	697 (annual avg.)
1948–50	784 (annual avg.)
1950	815
1963	1,273
1964	1,327
1968	1,542
1970	1,632
1975	1,924
1976	2,088
1980	2,145
1981	2,151
1989	2,398
1991	2,619

Source: Adapted from Farah and McDonald: Table 3, n.p.

Farming has been an important occupation at San Felipe throughout this century, although Pueblo members increasingly have been employed in nearby urban areas since the late 1950s. In 1900 the Pueblo cultivated 1,200 acres of wheat, corn, melons, hay, and alfalfa and tended 1,000 head of cattle and sheep. By 1979, although many San Felipes continued to farm, the amount of land cultivated had declined to 425 acres and less than one quarter of the irrigable farmland was in use (figure 2).

According to BIA Labor Force estimates for 1991 based on tribal data, 25 percent of the Pueblo's potential work force of 1,551 earn over $7,000 annually. The unemployment rate, which excludes those who have become discouraged and are no longer seeking work, is 34 percent (figure 3). An active informal economy based on subsistence farming, hunting, pinon-picking, crafts work, and trading continues to be important.

Figure 2
San Felipe Land Being Farmed as a Percent of Available Farmland

Year	Available Farmland (Estimated Acres)	Land Being Farmed (Acres)	Estimated Percent of Available Farmland Actually in Use
1900	@ 3,000	1,200	60 (est.)
1920	1,097	817	75
1927	4,116	1,111	27
1936	3,333	1,284	39
1943	3,836	1,425	37
1970	1,670	362	22
1979	1,872	425	23

Source: Adapted from Farah and McDonald: 218, 222, appendices B and C.

Figure 3
San Felipe Resident Population and Labor Force Status, January, 1991

Labor Force Status (For 16 Year Olds and Over)

a. 16 Years Old and Over	1,698
b. Unable to Work (Student, Caring for Children, Disabled, Retired)	147
c. Total Employed	937
d. Percent Aged 16 to 64 Earning $7,000 Plus	25 %
e. Number Not Employed but Able to Work	614
f. Number Seeking Work	479
g. Number Left Work Force Due to Discouragement	135
h. Unemployment Rate (Percent Seeking Work)*	34 %

Source: Adapted from Indian Service Population and Labor Force Estimates, 1991.

Note: Data sources include tribal statistics; surveys conducted by the tribe; school records; employment records; tribal membership rolls; and BIA program services records. In the majority of cases, data is estimated.

*Those not seeking work include those who have been discouraged from seeking work, have no available work opportunities, or no means of transportation. They are omitted from the Burea of Labor Statistics' definitions of "Labor Force" and "unemployed."

Current Issues

Water. The growth of metropolitan areas in the Southwest since mid-century has increased demand for scarce water resources. The San Felipe people believe that water is not a commodity, but the basis of their spiritual salvation. Not until 1979 was the first Indian, Frank Tenorio of San Felipe, elected as a board member of the Middle Rio Grande Conservancy Dis-

trict, an organization founded in the 1920s to construct flood control and irrigation systems in a region that includes six Pueblos. Tenorio has stated: "This is an age of specialization and categorizing, but Pueblos do not look at water as an isolated or unconnected thing. Water is an essential part of our body. The land is our flesh, the culture is our soul, and water is the blood that sustains our life. For the body of our peoplehood to survive we must have all these . . . ."

Sovereignty. There have been constant threats to San Felipe's sovereignty during the twentieth century. For example, in 1943 New Mexico Senator Clinton Anderson introduced House Resolution 323 to authorize exploration of dam sites on Pueblo land. The Bureau of Reclamation identified San Felipe as an ideal dam site and attempted to survey the plaza. In a letter that year to the commissioner of Indian affairs, Governor Don Sanchez wrote:

> Only the Indians of this Pueblo can express [the] tragic feelings of the loss of our beloved lands and homes and all that is thereon. We feel that it is unjust to deny our children's rightful heritage. Our lands, homes, and our religion are so bounded together that we have on our lands the sacred places, a shrine for prayer, and meditation. These Holy places are in immediate danger if the dam is constructed here. New homes and villages will require to be built. Gone are the Priests who knew the ceremonies for building new Pueblos and removing these sacred shrines. Much suffering will occur among us if we are moved to other locations.

A massive lobbying effort at the national level by Pueblo leaders and interpreters from San Felipe, Cochiti, and Santo Domingo as well as non-Indian advocates led Anderson to withdraw the bill. Some of the most effective letters were written by San Felipe servicemen fighting overseas, which included at least thirty men out of the Pueblo's total population of fewer than 700.

There have also been ongoing conflicts over jurisdiction. For example, as recently as 1978, the New Mexico legislature seriously discussed a state Senate Joint Resolution that proposed an amendment to the New Mexico Constitution to limit federal jurisdiction over Indian lands in New Mexico and give the state civil and criminal jurisdiction over tribes. The resolution was tabled indefinitely.

Education. San Felipe has pursued several educational goals since World War II: improved educational skills for young people; increased involvement in and control of schooling at both public and tribal contract schools; and upholding the federal government's historic responsibility for Indian education. "I feel that education is the basis of all life, all living," said Frank Tenorio, chairman of the school board at the tribally operated Albuquerque and Santa Fe Indian Schools (1976 to 1981). "These are our children, and if we don't fight for them, who will?"

In the early 1900s San Felipe children could attend the BIA elementary school at the Pueblo and the federal boarding school in Albuquerque. Both were federally controlled and denied parents and communities a voice in the educational process. When the BIA attempted to shift responsibility for education to the states in the 1950s, it encouraged San Felipe students to attend newly built public schools at Santo Domingo Pueblo and Bernalillo. These schools were largely financed with federal funds tied to Indian enrollment, such as the Johnson-O'Malley Act (1934), but had no Indian representation on school boards.

San Felipe successfully protested the BIA's closing of the elementary school at the Pueblo in the late 1950s and requested a new school building, which was finally constructed in 1978. In 1989 San Felipe, along with four other Pueblos in Sandoval County, successfully challenged under the Voting Rights Act the at-large method of electing members to the Bernalillo Municipal School District (*Bowannie v. The Bernalillo Municipal School District*). Since 1991 Lawrence Troncosa of San Felipe has been a board member of the Bernalillo Public Schools. Today most students in grades kindergarten through sixth attend the BIA-run San Felipe school or nearby public Algodones Elementary School, while grades seven through twelve go to the tribally run Santa Fe Indian School or the public Bernalillo High School.

Voting. Indians were granted the right to vote in New Mexico state elections in 1948, and San Felipe became a precinct in the late 1950s. However, court cases in the 1980s are proof of persistent discrimination at the state and local level against the potentially powerful Indian vote in Sandoval County. In 1984 the State of New Mexico was found to be in violation of the Voting Rights Act, because the state's legislative redistricting plan diluted the voting strength of Indians in Sandoval County (*Sanchez v. King*). In 1988 the United States Justice Department sued the state of New Mexico and Sandoval County for violating the constitutional voting rights of Indians—particularly the Keresan Pueblos such as San Felipe—alleging that "American Indians in Sandoval County have suffered a long history of official discrimination affecting the right to vote" (*United States of America v. State of New Mexico*). This case was resolved in 1990 by a settlement agreement between the state and the Keres-speaking residents of Sandoval County.

Federal Programs. Beginning in the 1960s San Felipe participated in many "Great Society" programs including Head Start, Youth Development, and Home Enrichment. According to a former governor, "The Office of Economic Opportunity provided the stage for the development of skills that enabled Indians to run their own affairs. These programs brought tribes into federal circles to benefit their peoples. It was the beginning of doing for yourselves what the BIA had always done before." This collaboration continues to be effective: in 1987 the entire Pueblo worked together to make 20,000 adobe bricks and construct a new Head Start building.

Culture. Throughout this century outsiders have attempted to delve into the religious and ceremonial life at San Felipe. The tribal leadership sees this as an infringement that threatens the well-being and continued survival of the community. As Governor Joseph V. Sanchez testified before the Senate Committee on Indian Affairs on April 14, 1980, "We consider any attempt to teach or convert by any means that which we consider our salvation an intrusion into our private religious rights. . . . The reason we have prevailed in continuing our religious pursuits is that we have guarded them closely and will continue to do so with all intensity."

Turquoise, shell, and silver jewelry have been made throughout this century for domestic and commercial use. Jewelers include Richard I. Chavez, Rama Chavez, Nellie Ramone, Charlene Reano, Charlotte Reano, and Louis Padilla. Most other traditional arts at San Felipe are made for use within the Pueblo. Potters active before 1950 include Pietra Sandoval, Josefita Lucero, and Mary Lucero. Some potters working after 1950 are Marcelina Calabaza, Candelaria Montana, Lupe Lucero, R. Candelaria, Simon and Mary Small, and Cynthia Chavez. Nat Valencia is a skilled moccasin maker; other individuals weave woolen belts, embroider kilts and mantas, and do beadwork.

Sally Hyer

Further Reading

Aberle, S.D. *The Pueblo Indians of New Mexico: Their Land, Economy and Civil Organization*. Memoirs of the American Anthropological Association 70. Menasha, WI: AAA, 1948.

Deloria, Vine, Jr. *Of Utmost Good Faith*. San Francisco: Straight Arrow Books, 1971.

Farah, Phillip, and Brian McDonald. *Economic Impact of Alternative Resolutions of New Mexico Pueblo Indian Water Rights*. Vol. 2, *Final Report*. WRRI Project No. B-064–NMEX. Albuquerque: Bureau of Business and Economic Research, Institute for Applied Research Services, University of New Mexico, 1983.

Strong, Pauline Turner. "San Felipe Pueblo." *Handbook of North American Indians*. Vol. 9. *Southwest*. Ed. Alfonso Ortiz. Washington, DC: Smithsonian Institution (1979): 390–97.

U.S. Department of the Interior, Bureau of Indian Affairs. *Indian Service Population and Labor Force Estimates*. Washington, DC, January 1989; January 1991.

White, Leslie A. *The Pueblo of San Felipe*. Memoirs of the American Anthropological Association 38. Menasha, WI: AAA, 1932.

SAN ILDEFONSO

On the eastern apron of the Jemez Mountains lies the Parijito Plateau and situated nearby is the Pueblo of San Ildefonso, whose Native name is Powhoge, translated as "where the water cuts down through." One of six Tewa Pueblos along the northern Rio Grande in New Mexico, this village, 25 miles northwest of Santa Fe, has 26,197 acres of surrounding land and a population of 1,457 according to the 1990 census, an increase of almost three times the 1980 count. The small Spanish villages of Jacona, Jaconita, and El Rancho are in the vicinity, and the Tewa Pueblo of Santa Clara, about ten miles to the north, is adjacent to San Ildefonso lands.

Homes are generally low adjoining adobe structures situated around two large plazas, with additional housing edging towards State Road 502. Today, houses have modern conveniences such as indoor plumbing, electricity, television, and other appliances. Presently, there are several shops within homes, selling arts and crafts to the public.

Education has become an important component of daily life with a Head Start program located near the governor's office. The Pueblo Day School, north of the San Ildefonso church, teaches grades one through six after which children are sent to the Pojoaque School District. High school students may also attend St. Catherine's School in Santa Fe, Santa Fe Indian School, and later enroll in colleges or the Institute of American Indian and Alaska Native Culture and Arts.

History

It is believed that certain clans migrated from areas north of Mesa Verde around A.D. 1300, and settled close to their present location occupying villages known today as the ruins of Sankewi, Otowi, and Potsuwi. Prior to Spanish occupation, once again, the people relocated. A 1694 attack by De Vargas caused inhabitants to defend themselves by fleeing atop Black Mesa. After two years they surrendered, returning below just north of their previous home; the act of moving north rather than south has been considered a break in tradition.

Since that time, due to diseases introduced by outsiders, a high mortality rate reduced the people to 161 according to an 1864 census. By the beginning of the twentieth century as their population grew ever smaller, factionalism and superstition divided San Ildefonso. At this time, the *cacique* and governor decided to return the people to their pre-Spanish site in the South Plaza. Some families followed, but the majority preferred to remain behind. The Summer Moiety incorporated the few remaining Winter families as they divided themselves into the North and South Plaza People, each maintaining their own secular and religious officers—another indication of what Alfonso Ortiz would consider "dynamic and flexible Tewa dual organization."

Political Organization

San Ildefonso maintains a dual organization now not described through moieties, but through household placement (North and South Plaza People). There is only one *cacique*, a life-time position, for the Summer People, who annually appoints a governor. The governor is confirmed by the Council of *Principales*, composed of former governors, and it is his job to mediate relationships with the outside world as well as internal disputes. He is assisted by two lieutenants; a war captain, who is appointed annually with both religious and civil duties; warriors, who assist the war captain; *fiscales*, whose primary duty is to bury the dead; and a police officer who occupies a largely honorary position.

Social Organization

San Ildefonso's kinship system is based upon simple bilateral arrangement, which distinguishes age and uses separate terms for mother and father, but makes no distinction between paternal and maternal descent. Kinship terms also reflect affectionate attitudes. For example:

> If a boy has a cousin or friend of whom he is fond, he will call him older or younger brother, depending on their relative ages. If he merely likes the other, he will call him uncle, or nephew, indicating whether the other is the father's older or younger brother and older or younger than the speaker. (Whitman 1947:75)

Marriage can occur with a member of the Pueblo or with an outsider. After a mutual agreement by both families, an Indian ceremony takes place—followed shortly by Catholic rites.

Ceremonial Organization

Christianity has played an important role in the lives of the people of San Ildefonso since conquest. It initially created severe problems but ultimately coexists with Native religion. For example, in attempting to defy the Spanish, the people in 1696 burned their Catholic church but it was later rebuilt in 1717. Eventually, a syncretization between Pueblo (underground) and Roman Catholic (above ground) religion resulted.

There are two medicine societies that deal with illness, unusual events, and exorcise witchcraft. Increasingly, however, people are using the federally maintained Indian Hospital in Santa Fe for health matters.

The *cacique* acts as religious head based upon a paternalistic hierarchy with his two life-time assistants—the right- and left-hand man. There are three kivas: the north kiva; the round, highly photographed kiva in the South Plaza; and a square kiva to the southwest. Many public and closed ceremonies take place during the calendar year, with January 23rd as the major feast day honoring their patron saint. The night before, *luminarios* or small bonfires illuminate the plaza and village. Later, *Kossa* (clowns) and animal dancers perform. The following morning, a Buffalo-Deer Dance occurs at dawn lasting approximately one and one-half hours, after which a Comanche Dance takes place in the plaza that afternoon.

The *Kossa* Society is not moiety based, and is the only Clown Society at the Pueblo. San Ildefonso no longer has a *Kwirana* Society. The *Kossa* have weather and fertility functions associated with the Water Serpent and bringing rain for crops. They also act as War Dance assistants, serve as managers, and police various ceremonies.

Economy

In 1846 the United States won the Southwest from Mexico, and subsequently a large influx of traders and merchants settled there and introduced a cash economy instead of the barter system, which had been the dominant way of life. Until the later part of the nineteenth century, Pueblo men had been involved with subsistence agriculture and hunting, while women concentrated on related household activities. During World War II, some Pueblo members began to earn a living at the laboratories at Los Alamos or in nearby Santa Fe, with farming becoming almost nonexistent except for ceremonial purposes.

Pottery both for utilitarian or sacred purposes has occupied a significant role in Pueblo life, documented as early as A.D. 100 to 400. With the opening of the Santa Fe Trail in 1821 and the introduction of commercial tinware, hand-coiled pottery production severely declined. Although potters at this Pueblo had been well known in the late 1800s for creating polychrome pottery, archaeologists in the early 1900s, excavating nearby ruins found sherds, which became a catalyst for Maria and Julian Martinez to revive pottery making, eventually bringing about the innovation of a highly polished blackware. Making polished black- or redware involves a process that creates a smooth surface with a matte painted or incised design, an extremely popular and highly regarded commodity. Fired at low temperatures, many innovative as well as traditional pieces are made for the tourist trade as art objects, rather than for use as utilitarian wares. The revival of the arts and crafts market in the early 1900s creatively stimulated some Pueblo men to assist their wives in designing and painting pottery. This production became and remains even today a lucrative source of income. In addition, beginning in the early 1900s when the new tradition of painting on paper was born, San Ildefonso has produced such renowned painters as Crescencio Martinez (Ta'e) and Alfonso Roybal (Awa Tsireh).

Patricia Fogelman Lange

See also Pottery

Further Reading

Edelman, Sandra A. "San Ildefonso Pueblo." *Handbook of North American Indians*, Vol. 9. *Southwest.* Ed. Alfonso Ortiz. Washington, DC: Smithsonian Institution (1979): 308–16.

Harrington, John. *The Ethnogeography of the Tewa Indians.* Bureau of American Ethnology, 29th Annual Report 1907–1908. Washington, DC: U.S. Government Printing Office (1916): 37–636.

Hewett, Edgar Lee. *Antiquities of the Jemez Plateau, New Mexico.* Bureau of American Ethnology Bulletin 32. Washington, DC: U.S. Government Printing Office, 1906.

Ortiz, Alfonso. *The Tewa World: Space, Time, Being, and Becoming in A Pueblo Society.* IL: University of Chicago Press, 1969.

Sando, Joe. *Pueblo Nations: Eight Centuries of Pueblo Indian History.* Santa Fe, NM: Clear Light Publishers, 1992.

Ward, John. "Census of the Indian Pueblos within the Territory of New Mexico from 1790 to 1864." Cambridge, Mass. Harvard University. Peabody Museum of Archaeology and Anthropology. Spinden, Box 1, 1864.

Whitman, William III. *The Pueblo Indians of San Ildefonso: A Changing Culture.* Contributions to Anthropology no. 34. New York, NY: Columbia University, 1947.

SAN JUAN

San Juan Pueblo is the northernmost of six Tewa-speaking communities in north central New Mexico. It is located on the east side of the Rio Grande, about one-half mile north of its confluence with the Rio Chama. Known in the Tewa language as Okeh Owinge (translated as "Okey Pueblo"), San Juan is called the Mother Village of the Tewas in creation stories. The resident population has slowly been increasing from a total of 422 in 1920, to 2,301 people in 1991. The Pueblo land grant presently includes 12,234 acres, of which approximately 2,000 are irrigable. Largely an agricultural community in the past, most of the modern-day income is derived from wage work in nearby cities, government and tribal jobs in the Pueblo, and arts and crafts. Native religion as well as the Catholic Church remain strong elements in the lives of the people.

In 1598, under the leadership of Don Juan de Onate, the Spanish bestowed the name San Juan Bautista (St. John the Baptist) on the Pueblo. This Indian community also became known as San Juan de los Caballeros because its people were highly regarded as "gentlemen" by the Spanish. At that time (1598), the first Spanish capitol, San Gabriel, was established at the site of the old Tewa Pueblo of Yunge Owinge, west of the Rio Grande on San Juan Pueblo land.

Twentieth-Century History

Until the 1940s farming, cattle raising, and trade had been the economic mainstays of the tribe, supplemented by wage work. World War II began to change this balance and by the mid-1960s, wage work, most of which was found in Santa Fe, Espanola, or Los Alamos, had become dominant. After the passage of the Economic Opportunity Act of 1964, a great number of federally funded programs were initiated at San Juan. In 1965 San Juan and the other Tewa Pueblos formed Neighborhood Youth Corps in their villages and, in the same year, the Eight Northern Pueblos Community Action Program was created. In the late 1960s and into the 1970s grants were given to San Juan for various Pueblo construction jobs including a youth center, a senior center, tribal offices, a tribal court, a law and order department, a warehouse, and a post office. In the 1970s San Juan, as well as the other Pueblos, received fully funded grants from the federal government, channeled through the Eight Northern Indian Pueblos Council, for job training and educational development. One such program, the Eight Northern Pueblos Artisans Guild, existed in San Juan from approximately 1972 to 1982. Here, government-funded art classes were taught and students were paid to attend. Later, the Guild became a retail outlet for the art produced by its students. Since the Guild always relied on government funding, it was forced to close when that funding ended in the early 1980s.

From the mid-1960s to the mid-1970s a number of other federally funded jobs were created in or near the Pueblo by the Departments of Commerce; Health, Education, and Welfare; Housing and Urban Development (HUD); and Labor. The Tribal Council also expanded into many new areas and employed numerous tribal members in a variety of committee or program duties.

In the early 1980s federal funding for many of these programs was reduced and in some cases eliminated. Federal grants during the Reagan-Bush administrations became matching grants. San Juan, as well as other tribes in the area, has had great difficulty finding matching money, thus projects often have not materialized. Due to federal budget cuts the tribal economic situation has become much more difficult during the 1980s and early 1990s.

In the 1950s and 1960s vocational training and employment programs relocated some San Juan people to large western cities. By the 1970s and 1980s, many of them had become disillusioned and returned to the Pueblo. In the early 1990s, due to recession and rising unemployment, a new trend is appearing: some San Juan residents are beginning to farm again. This includes retirees who lived elsewhere but have returned to the Pueblo to farm.

Housing

With both the young people and retirees returning to San Juan and many young couples starting families, there has been great pressure to provide adequate housing. In the 1960s as a result of federal Housing and Urban Development (HUD) programs, many new single-family homes were built in housing developments, which sprang up away from the center of the village. The old adobe houses around the plazas gradually were abandoned and fell into disrepair because of the lack of resources to maintain or refurbish them.

In the 1990s HUD houses built in the 1960s and 1970s are falling apart because of substandard construction materials. Some need to be condemned. Since HUD will not take responsibility for those that are fully paid off and there are no available funds to rectify these problems, there is presently no recourse for their owners. Due to federal budget cuts no new HUD homes have been built at San Juan since 1984 or 1985. Rather, families have been buying mobile homes and placing them on their land. An occasional family will build a more traditional adobe home, but costs and construction time greatly limit the number who can afford to do so. Presently, the tribe has a federal grant to rehabilitate about twelve houses a year. Houses around the central plazas are slowly being refurbished, as are a few located elsewhere in the village.

Water Rights

Aboriginal water rights, established legally through the Treaty of Guadalupe Hidalgo in 1848 and later recognized by the United States Supreme Court, allow Indian peoples to have first claim to the water available to them. In the 1990s, the Aamodt Water Suit (which has been ongoing for over twenty-five years and involves the Tesuque Valley, twenty miles south of San Juan) is challenging this ruling. In this case, the State of New Mexico wants to gain control of Pueblo water rights, limiting them to historical or present use, and wants to place control of both surface and ground water with the State Engineer. Indian water rights have always been and still are determined solely by federal law. The allocation of Rio Grande water rights to San Juan Pueblo is pending, awaiting a final decision in this case.

In a second water rights issue, the tribe is currently negotiating with the federal government on water from the San Juan-Chama Rivers Diversion Project. Although already awarded a water allocation, the tribe is negotiating to use a limited number of acre-feet of water for which it can afford maintenance costs. San Juan wants to maintain the option, however, of increasing the acre-feet of water it may use, if the need arises in the future and if it can pay the increased maintenance costs. This water rights issue is presently unresolved.

Four irrigation ditches on San Juan Pueblo land are still in operation and provide water for agriculture: the Acequia Madre (the mother ditch), the San Rafael Ditch, the Chamita Ditch, and the Upper Alcalde Ditch. The Pueblo has first rights to this water; neighboring Hispanic communities have second rights. Several wells on San Juan land provide water for domestic use.

Land Issues

In 1689 during the Spanish occupation, 17,544 acres were designated as the San Juan Pueblo Land Grant by Governor Domingo Jironza de Cruzate. Title to this land was later guaranteed by the Treaty of Guadalupe Hidalgo in 1848. In the late 1800s and early 1900s, however, due to trespassing and gradual encroachment by outsiders, the San Juan land base decreased. As a result of the Pueblo Lands Act of 1924, decisions by the land board reduced the San Juan Pueblo Land Grant to 12,234 acres. Recently trespass surveys have been done and in the last eight years a small amount of land along the Rio Grande has been returned to the tribe. In general, Hispanic and Pueblo neighbors live peacefully together and tribal land problems are arbitrated and settled through negotiation by the Tribal Realty Officer, the Tribal Council, and the Bureau of Indian Affairs.

San Juan Pueblo is considered tribal trust land that is still controlled by the Bureau of Indian Affairs (BIA). Each family living in the Pueblo has the right to live on and use a piece of land, which was assigned to the family by the BIA in the 1930s. This land can be left to family descendants or can be sold or traded to other Pueblo persons living in the village. Non-Indians cannot acquire it. Some pieces of land were not assigned but were left as common grazing lands which could be used by anyone in the village. Both situations still apply in the 1990s.

There are no current land claim issues in negotiation. In the 1950s and 1960s the tribe was unable to regain control of land north and west of the Pueblo, which is still being used for religious and ceremonial purposes. Some of this land is currently owned by the Forest Service, which has issued permits to the tribe so members can continue to use it for sacred purposes.

Current Situation

Tribal Government. San Juan tribal government basically includes three categories of officials: 1) civil officers; 2) tribal religious leaders; and 3) Catholic Church officers. The civil government, formally established by the Spanish in the early 1600s, includes a governor, two lieutenant governors, and a sheriff. These officials, who handle all contemporary, nonreligious affairs, are appointed for a one-year term by the tribal religious leaders and may be reappointed an unlimited number of times. The Tribal Council, also part of the civil government, is composed of the current governor, lieutenant governors, sheriff, all former governors, and the male heads of the religious societies of the village. Women have not been appointed as tribal officers nor do they serve on the Tribal Council. Other tribal program administrators' positions have been more recently created to meet tribal needs. They are selected by a personnel selection committee and hold office until they resign, retire, or are asked to step down.

Native religious leaders are rooted in the traditional San Juan socio-religious organization. The most important of these leaders hold office for life and are responsible for selecting other Native officers as well as the civil and Catholic officers. War chiefs, considered a part of the group of Native officers, are selected by the Native religious leaders and hold these positions for one year. War chiefs have a variety of religious and ceremonial duties and also maintain order in the village. Catholic church officers (*fiscales*) are appointed by the Native religious leaders, but have duties relating primarily to Catholic religious activities in the village. These individuals are not involved in the workings of the civil government.

In 1976 a more recent governmental addition, a tribal court, modeled on other tribal law courts, was approved by the Tribal Council. Previously, the tribal governor had served as judge. The change was from a Native traditional court to a court of common law, which handles small misdemeanors and civil cases— hearing mostly criminal, traffic, DWI, domestic, child abuse, and divorce cases. Since October 1984, the San Juan court has become a full-time operation. The tribe contracts with the BIA, which provides limited funding for the court and also for law and order through the tribal police. Since the BIA does not pay for incarceration and the tribe has no money to do so, the judge must be creative in sentencing offenders. Traditional cases are still sent to the governor and former governors, who continue to make decisions in these instances. This respected group of men serves as an appeals court for the tribal court. Their decisions are final, and there is no higher court of appeal.

Economic Development and Conditions. Currently a number of tribal business enterprises bring steady, yearly income to the tribe. These include the tribally owned Shell Service Station; the San Juan bingo operation; the Blue Rock Office Complex, which houses the Northern Pueblos Agency of the BIA; and the San Juan Tribal Lakes Recreation Area, which includes year-round trout fishing and a picnic area. The tribe is currently expanding and improving this latter resource.

The Pueblo also receives income from leases to the Eight Northern Indian Pueblos Council for office space, to the United States government for the post office, and to Duke City Lumber Company for a lumber mill. Income derived from these sources has been used to help start up other small businesses and to support the tribal government and administration. The most recent project is a newly completed gymnasium for general tribal use. Contracts the tribe holds with the federal and state governments bring funds necessary to run programs such as social services, law and order, tribal courts, senior services, education, and tribal administration.

Owning and managing its own businesses and employing its own people is the essence of the tribe's business philosophy and goals. Business operations are not under the control of the Tribal Council; rather a Business Development Board, a business manager, and staff bear this responsibility.

Employment. The total number of San Juan tribal members employed in 1991 was 567 out of a resident population of 2,132. Those earning $7,000 or more per year numbered 453 (Department of Interior, BIA estimated Labor Force Statistics, 1991). In 1992 San Juan had thirty-four people employed at the Eight Northern Pueblos Indian Council Offices, forty in tribal businesses, and thirty-three who worked as tribal employees. Incomplete figures from the 1990 census basically support these figures and add comparable numbers of people working in education and health services in the area.

Many tribal members work independently as artists and craftsmen. Well over one hundred are members of the Oke Oweenge Cooperative, where they volunteer one day a week and sell their art work as well. This organization, begun in 1968 by Geronima Cruz Montoya, is totally self-sustaining, raises operating funds mostly through grants and sales of art work, offers members opportunities to learn new art forms or improve those they already know, and provides an outlet for the sale of their work. San Juan pottery is probably the best known of its art forms. The Pueblo presently has approximately sixty potters who derive part of their income from pottery sales. Of these, about thirty are members of the Co-op; the others work independently.

Health care. No professional medical health care is presently available at San Juan Pueblo. The nearest clinic is at Santa Clara Pueblo, approximately ten miles away, and the nearest hospital is the Public Health Service Hospital in Santa Fe, approximately thirty miles away.

Since about 1970 San Juan has had a Community Health Representative Program, which is funded annually by the Indian Health Service. The representative, not medically trained but from the Pueblo, arranges health education programs and performs many kinds of community health outreach activities, including making doctor's appointments and transporting patients to them.

Several serious diseases are a major concern at San Juan. These include hypertension, diabetes, and kidney disease. Teen pregnancy and drug and alcohol abuse are other problem areas. The New Moon Lodge, an alcohol treatment center under the auspices of the Eight Northern Indian Pueblos Council, Inc., has been located in San Juan Pueblo for approximately ten years. Overall the health picture at San Juan is gradually improving as people learn to utilize available services.

Education. San Juan has two grade schools: a public day school and a BIA day school. Funding ended in 1990 for the formerly thriving bicultural, bilingual education program at the BIA school, much to the chagrin of many parents and teachers. The public San Juan Elementary School presently has an enrollment of approximately one hundred twenty students from kindergarten to sixth grade; the BIA school has fewer. A Head Start program is still funded and continues as a strong, necessary educational tool. Upon completion of grade school, parents may send their children to the Espanola Junior and Senior High Schools, or to boarding school at the Santa Fe Indian School or at St. Catherine's School, also in Santa Fe.

According to a sampling of the Pueblo population done as part of the 1990 census, 38 percent of the population living at the Pueblo over the age of 25 graduated from high school. Of these high school graduates, approximately 96 percent attended college, with 9 percent obtaining associate degrees, 4 percent receiving bachelor's degrees, and 14 percent attaining graduate or professional degrees. The accuracy of these percentages is difficult to verify, since there are three different figures for the total Pueblo population: 2,301 (the tribe's figure for 1991); 1,276 (the 1990 census total); and 2,132 (the Department of the Interior, BIA Estimated Labor Force Statistics, 1991).

Individual families still continue to teach their children the language and the culture. This has always been and still remains the duty of the family. In many cases, however (as a result of single-family HUD housing units), grandparents no longer live in the same house with their grandchildren, so the young do not necessarily grow up hearing and speaking the Tewa language. Families now exert more effort in teaching the customs, traditions, and ceremonies to their young, because modern conditions and the presence of television, compact discs, transistor radios, etc., provide strong competition. Overall, however,

education by the families has been successful, and the culture has remained strong.

Culture. San Juan Pueblo has not been immune to the investigations of various social scientists over the past one hundred years or so. Much cultural material has been gathered by a number of these people, who have published their findings without the approval of the tribe. Thus there exist cultural and ceremonial descriptions, photographs, recordings, translations of songs, folktales, and myths, which were provided by knowledgeable San Juan individuals, but not with the understanding that the information would be published and become available to the world at large. Recently, there has been a reevaluation of these materials by the tribe, which now holds ultimate authority over what it will allow to be published. San Juan is checking each new manuscript closely and must approve every one. At present, publication of material concerning the culture is not allowed.

Many of San Juan's old traditions have survived, yet like any other community in the United States, the culture is continually undergoing change and is being modified. The old exists side by side with the new. The central area of the old village is being refurbished and is still in use, yet tribal government offices, located nearby, were built within the last fifteen to twenty years. The traditional ceremonies are still performed every year, with some portions reserved for Pueblo members only, while others are open to the public (see figure). Pueblo members maintain their ties to Native life and traditions while holding jobs as scientists or engineers at the Los Alamos National Laboratories, while working for the government, or while carrying jobs in health, education, or business in Santa Fe, Espanola, and in San Juan. The people of San Juan Pueblo are maintaining the best and most meaningful parts of their traditional culture while adapting parts of the Anglo culture that they find necessary for their survival. Presently, they are doing well in both worlds.

Linda J. Goodman

Annual San Juan Calendar of Public Ceremonies*

January 1, New Years Day	Installation of new officers
January 6, Three Kings' Day	Various Dances
Late January	Cloud Dance or Basket Dance
Mid-February	Deer Dance
Early March	Yellow Corn Dance or Butterfly Dance
June 13, San Antonio Day	Green Corn Dance
June 23	Buffalo Dance, Foot Races
June 24, San Juan Day	Comanche Dance and Buffalo Dance (alternate throughout the day)
September	Harvest Dance (performed once every 2 or 3 years)
December 24, 25, Christmas	Matachines Dance
December 26	Turtle Dance

*The San Juan Ceremonial Calendar usually includes, but is not limited to, the above dances.

See also **Land Claims; Water Rights**

Further Reading

Dozier, Edward P. "The Rio Grande Pueblos." *Perspectives in American Indian Culture Change.* Ed. Edward H. Spicer. IL: University of Chicago Press (1961): 94–186.

———. *The Pueblo Indians of North America.* New York, NY: Holt, Rinehart, and Winston, 1970.

Dutton, Bertha. *Pocket Handbook of Indians of the Southwest.* Santa Fe, NM: Southwest Association on Indian Affairs, 1965.

Ortiz, Alfonso. "San Juan Pueblo." *Handbook of North American Indians.* Vol. 9. *Southwest.* Ed. Alfonso Ortiz. Washington, DC: Smithsonian Institution (1979): 278–95.

Sando, Joe. *Pueblo Nations: Eight Centuries of Pueblo Indian History.* Santa Fe, NM: Clear Light Publishers, 1992.

Many thanks are due to the 1992 tribal officers and program administrators of San Juan Pueblo who gave freely of their time and knowledge and provided facts, figures, and information concerning the recent history and current situation at San Juan. This article could not have been written without their generous help.

SANDIA

Spanish for "watermelon" (Zandia, Çandia), Sandia's name in its Tiwa dialect is *Nafiat*, meaning "sandy place." It is located about thirteen miles north of Albuquerque, New Mexico, between State Road 313 and Interstate 25 in the shadow of the Sandia Mountains to the east. The extremely rugged west face of the mountains is the most prominent feature. The mountains rise to an elevation of 10,538 feet and then fall to a sandy plain, which is bounded by the Rio Grande on the west. Sandia, located on the plain, maintains numerous sites of traditional cultural and religious importance in the mountains. Its people utilize the mountain foothills for grazing land, herbs and plants, and springs. Over one hundred distinct plant species which grow in the foothills and the mountains are still utilized. The natural resources of the community include woodlands, rangelands, farmlands, water, wildlife, and sand and gravel deposits.

The total reservation acreage is 22,884. Approximately 2,000 acres are suitable for farming and 6,000 for rangeland. All such land is fully utilized. The residential area is currently 170 acres and will increase as homes under construction are completed.

The old village has a central plaza and is located on a plain near the Santa Fe Railroad tracks. The Sandia mission church, Nuestra Señora de los Dolores de Sandia ("Our Lady of the Sorrows of Sandia") and St. Anthony, is located to the north of the old Pueblo. The mission church is the second one built at Sandia with the original serving as the Pueblo cemetery. Newer housing units have been built on the sand hills to the east of the old village. Many families maintain a home in the village, which they use during feast days, and another home in the newer residential areas. Sandia has a community center, a swimming pool, and offices for tribal administration. A wellness center for the community is in the planning stages at this time.

Early History

Archaeological evidence indicates that the site of Sandia has been occupied since at least A.D. 1300 and perhaps earlier. It is likely that Sandia was one of the villages visited by Coronado during his *entrada* of 1540 to 1542. It was one of approximately twenty Southern Tiwa villages stretching south along the Rio Grande in the province which Coronado called Tiguex. Sandia was not identified by its current name until the seventeenth century. The Pueblo became the site of a mission and a major Spanish administrative center during the 1600s. The many villages of Tiguex became depopulated and reduced by the Spanish. At the time of the Pueblo Revolt in 1680, only four Southern Tiwa villages survived: Sandia, Alameda, Puaray, and Isleta. Sandia was the largest with a population of 3,000. The people of Sandia participated in the Pueblo Indian Revolt of 1680, which threw off the yoke of Spanish oppression. Their Pueblo was burned by the Spanish retreating from Santa Fe. The Pueblo was also burned by Otermín during early attempts at reconquest by the Spanish in 1681 and 1682. The people of Sandia fled to the Sandia Mountains, according to their oral tradition and Spanish documents. Later, they became refugees as their village had been destroyed. They made their way to the Hopi mesas and there were assigned land and founded the village of Payupki on Second Mesa. According to oral traditions of the Hopi, this area has always been multiethnic with villages of Zuni, Keres, Tiwa, and Tewa origin, and the Hopi have accommodated not only the Southern Tiwa survivors, but also some of the Tewa refugees from the Rio Grande basin. The Sandias visited Hopi and their village site in 1987 and were shown their old lands.

After New Mexico was reconquered by the Spanish beginning in 1696, the lands which had belonged to Sandia and to the other nearby villages gradually were reoccupied by Spanish settlers. Beginning in 1740 a Spanish missionary petitioned the Crown to allow the refugees at Hopi to resettle their ancestral site of Sandia. In 1742, 441 Tiwas and Hopis came to the Rio Grande but were not permitted to settle at Sandia. The petition was finally granted in 1748, and a written land grant was made to Sandia which specifically located the Rio Grande as their boundary on the west, and the Sierra Madre of Sandia ("y por el Oriente la Sierra Madre llamada de Sandia") the Sandia Mountains on the east. The original settlers were 350 people comprising 70 families. Because some of the lands of the Pueblo had already been occupied by the Spanish settlers, they were given permission to water and graze their stock on the west side of the river and on additional land to the north and south.

When New Mexico became a part of the United States as a result of the Treaty of Guadalupe Hidalgo in 1848, the United States legally agreed to recognize all valid Spanish land grants. Sandia's 1748 land grant papers were conveyed to Washington, where a fraudulent copy was translated, which altered the southern boundary of the Pueblo lands, but which retained the wording making the eastern boundary the Sandia Mountains. Congress confirmed the grant by statute in 1858. The errors were compounded when the official government surveyor, Ruben E. Clements, surveyed the land only to the base of the Sandia Mountains, rather than to the crest of the mountains, which was standard Spanish practice that had been followed in other grants where mountains were named as boundaries. The grant was patented to Sandia Pueblo in 1864, which confirmed a reduced land area cutting off some of Sandia's rightful land to the south and to the east. Sandia's land base became significantly contracted once again as a result of these errors, setting the stage for twentieth-century problems and attempts to recover their rightful granted lands. As a result of these frauds, Sandia lost access to thousands of acres of land and the resources of water, grazing land, timber, mineral deposits, game, and plant resources.

Twentieth-Century History

At the turn of the century, Sandia's population had been significantly reduced through war, illness, and loss of resources. There were doubts on the part of some outsiders whether Sandia would survive. The Pueblo was a farming and ranching community, but the continued encroachment on its lands and waters by squatters made life very difficult. Sandia pursued a policy of trying to regain its land. The Pueblo Lands Board was established by the federal government to settle Pueblo land claims once and for all and to clear title to lands for white and Hispanic settlers. Sandia attempted through this board to regain lands which had become incorporated into the town of Bernalillo to the north and inhabited by various settlers to the south, but despite their claims they lost significant amounts of land to non-Pueblo people.

The Pueblo has been fighting through legal and administrative remedies to regain title to the land from the foothills to the crest of the Sandia Mountains. This land is currently under the administration of the United States Forest Service, which has also released some of the land to private developers. Important religious and cultural sites in this area are very heavily impacted by development, increased recreational "improvements," and other activities which radically change their character, making the practice of Sandia religion and culture very difficult. The Pueblo has pursued an aggressive policy of legal action in their attempts to preserve the impacted areas in a pristine form through establishing alliances with environmental and cultural preservation groups in the region.

As upstream settlers became more and more numerous, the amount and quality of water for the Pueblo declined and farmland became increasingly salty. Much of the Pueblo's bottom land and *bosque* near the Rio Grande is so encrusted with salt today that it is unusable. While Sandia has an adequate water supply today, there may be problems for the future. Sandia's underground water is being depleted by industrial and commercial development and expansion to the south; the Pueblo is attempting to protect and claim this resource.

Sandia's religious practices require a pure water supply in the Rio Grande suitable for primary contact. The Pueblo has brought legal action against developers polluting river water and has attempted to have the Environmental Protection Agency (EPA) enforce Clean Water Act standards. It has also created its own water quality standards which have been approved by the EPA. It is one of the first tribes in the United States to have Treatment As State (TAS) status, which provides the same authority for tribes as for states. The water quality standard for Sandia is a stricter standard than that of the State of New Mexico. Isleta Pueblo, the other Southern Tiwa community, was the first tribe in the United States to enact a water code which is also quite strict. The Rio Grande Pueblos are all net receivers of polluted water from other users, but do not discharge in the Rio Grande. The tribes' efforts in water quality are providing for a cleaner, less polluted river for all users of the Rio Grande, a major environmental accomplishment.

Current Situation

The Pueblo has a governing system that has adapted to different outside systems of government with which it must interact. The major positions are the governor, lieutenant governor, war chief, and lieutenant war chief and their staffs. These officials normally serve for one year. The outgoing officials choose possible candidates and the *cacique* (the major religious leader) also chooses, with the *cacique* making the final selection of officers, who are then notified that they have been selected. The position of *cacique* is part of the traditional religious system and is a lifelong position. The governor represents the community to the outside world and is the person to whom all official business is directed. The war chief and his staff guard and protect the Pueblo and members of religious societies while they are doing their work for the community, such as dances and ceremonies, and also have responsibility for the area outside the village proper. Former governors and war chiefs make up the Council, which is an advisory and decision-making body. The sacristan is responsible for care of the church, preparation for Catholic masses and ceremonies, and aspects of care for the dead who are buried in the Pueblo cemetery.

As the issues facing the community have become more bureaucratic and complex, additional positions have been added in tribal administration. These include the tribal administrator, treasurer, business and economic developer, tribal planner, comptroller and staff, and positions involving realty, tribal courts, and grants and contracts. These positions are filled with highly educated, qualified persons normally from the community who serve for multiple years at the pleasure of the Council.

At the present time the economy of the Pueblo depends upon sand and gravel leases on lands in the southern portion of the reservation, reservation bingo which draws from the Albuquerque metropolitan area, tax ordinances, a trading post specializing in Indian arts and crafts, recreational fishing ponds, and a few small businesses. The Pueblo is near closing on the purchase of Coronado Airport, which adjoins Pueblo land to the south and has freeway access. The tribe is engaged in planning for continued economic development.

An exit from Interstate 25 allows access to the southern part of the reservation and its bingo parlor and the Albuquerque metropolitan area provides a ready market for bingo. The bingo parlor has been a tremendous success for Sandia. It has provided 135 jobs to the community at all levels of ability and education. While it has not always made money, the tribe has supported the operation because it employs so many tribal members. Currently, the tribe is suing the governor of New Mexico for his failure to sign a gaming compact with the tribe as the federal law governing gaming has mandated.

Many Sandias are employed by the federal government, in the private sector in the Albuquerque metropolitan area, and in tribal enterprises. Unemployment is a low 2 percent of the work force. Sandia has a very highly educated population with a number of tribal members with college educations and advanced degrees. One of the objectives of the Pueblo is to increase its economic base by developing commercial and industrial facilities on the southern boundary of the reservation, where it meets the expanding metropolitan area.

The Pueblo has a growing population. Total tribal enrollment in 1993 is 481 persons; 233 males and 248 females. The on-reservation population is 266. There are 127 family groups according to the 1993 Bureau of Indian Affairs census. The great majority of the population is young, although there is a very active group of elders in the community.

The health status of the community has become a focus of concern. The Pueblo has noticed a significant increase in cases of hypertension, and also diabetes and its consequences, such as blindness, amputations, and the need for dialysis. This has been especially evident in recent years as the population has moved more toward white collar jobs and away from active occupations such as farming. Sandia Pueblo is planning a new health clinic, which will replace the old one located in the tribal administration building. The community has also completed plans for a wellness center, which will provide space for a weight room, a game room, offices for counselors, and classroom space.

The Pueblo of Sandia has produced leaders known at both state and national levels. Domingo Montoya served as governor of the Pueblo several times, was then appointed to the Indian Affairs Commission of New Mexico, and also served as chairman of the All Indian Pueblo Council, an organization of the nineteen Pueblo tribes in New Mexico. Esquipula Chaves was very active in dealing with Pueblo affairs at the local, state, and national levels. Patrick Baca served as a county commissioner for Sandoval County, and is currently the secretary of labor for the State of New Mexico. Andres Lauriano served the Pueblo as governor and war chief for many years and was also instrumental in the Sandia language preservation program. Frank Chaves is emerging as a leader in the area of Indian gaming.

Culture

Sandia is a small, closely knit community with strong ties to neighboring Pueblos, such as Isleta and San Felipe, and the nearby small town of Bernalillo. Its members are very religious, practicing both Catholicism and the traditional religion. Sandias not living in the village return for the Pueblo's annual feast day of San Antonio on June 13, celebrated with a Corn Dance and offering a feast to all friends and relatives on that day. Dances such as the Eagle, Buffalo, and others are held on January 6, when the new Pueblo government is installed in office. Traditional dances and ceremonies are held throughout the year and also may be given when a marriage occurs. Matachines may be danced at marriages or on other special occasions. The community is dedicated to the preservation of its traditional religion and has devoted immense resources in an attempt to protect its off-reservation traditional sites needed for religious practice.

Sandias speak a dialect of the Southern Tiwa language. Another dialect is also spoken at Isleta, a village to the south of Albuquerque. This language belongs to the Tiwa subfamily of the Tanoan language family, which also includes the subfamilies of Tewa and Towa, also spoken in the Pueblos. The Tiwa subfamily includes two other languages spoken at Taos and Picuris in the northern part of New Mexico. These languages are not mutually intelligible with Southern Tiwa. Since the 1960s the Pueblo has engaged in a variety of efforts to preserve their language and currently runs language programs for children and adults. Elders in the community normally speak Sandia, Spanish, and English. Middle-aged tribal members speak Sandia and English with a few speaking Spanish as well. Many younger people do not speak Sandia, although they may understand it and there is a strong desire to learn to speak it. The community is exploring different means to preserve their language.

Sandia kinship is bilateral. Two moiety groups, Turquoise and Pumpkin, are found in the community and children are assigned to these groups alternately. Five Corn groups also exist in the community, which have important religious, curing, and personal functions. Most families today are nuclear and live in single-family homes. In many families both parents work and care for the elderly is becoming a problem, particularly for elders who are disabled. The community is considering a nursing home to provide local care for those elderly whose families are unable to care for them.

Sandia has been noted in the past for its basketry, although this craft is no longer practiced. Pottery making was revived in the 1960s, but has again declined. Some Sandias make jewelry and there are several artists and sculptors in the community.

The Future

Sandia is a community committed to planning for its future and defending its culture and heritage as it becomes surrounded by development. It is very deeply traditional and uses every means available to ensure its survival and continued quality of life now and into the future. The Pueblo has articulated the following goals:

1. To improve the quality of life for individuals and collectively.

2. To remain sensitive to tribal customs, traditions, values, and other human and environmental considerations.

3. To improve the capacities and longevity of the tribe's human and natural resources through positive proactive measures.

Elizabeth A. Brandt

See also Hopi

Further Reading

Brandt, Elizabeth A. "Sandia Pueblo." *Handbook of North American Indians.* Vol. 9. *Southwest.* Ed. Alfonso Ortiz. Washington, DC: Smithsonian Institution (1979): 343–50.
Simons, Suzanne Lee. "The Cultural and Social Survival of a Pueblo Indian Community." *Minorities and Politics.* Ed. Henry J. Tobias and Charles E. Woodhouse. Albuquerque: University of New Mexico Press (1969): 85–112.

SANTA ANA

This Pueblo is one of the most religiously conservative tribes of the Keresan-speaking people. They live in several "farm villages" on the Rio Grande near Bernalillo, New Mexico, but return to their traditional home on an approximately 63,000-acre reservation, some 10 miles northwest on the Rio Jemez, for religious celebrations. Sand dunes have covered their ancestrally irrigated fields, and dry farming ceased to be very productive as the climate dried, forcing them to find irrigable farm land elsewhere. The reservation land does not even support cattle grazing well.

When the Santa Anas migrated from the Galisteo basin between A.D. 1200 and 1300, they stopped at the confluence of the Rio Grande and Rio Jemez before moving to the present location of Old Santa Ana, Tamaya. In the late seventeenth century, they began returning to those Rio Grande farm lands, but returning late, they had to buy back their land from Spanish settlers.

Both Native sacred buildings and the Pueblo's Catholic church are located in Tamaya, where the Spaniards found these people in 1598. Since practicality demands they live near their fields, each Santa Ana family today maintains two houses, one in the old village and another in one of the farm villages of Chicali, Rebajani, or Ranchitos, collectively known as Los Ranchitos.

Tamaya has changed over the years from several-story high apartment blocks clustered about the plaza (the predominant architecture in 1776 and before), to several parallel rows of mostly connected one-story adobe homes around the plaza. Though all the houses in Ranchitos have utilities, Tamaya has only several water hydrants which in 1992 were put on a solar powered subsidiary pumping system. Installed in the 1950s, the dike guarding Tamaya from encroachment from the Jemez River Dam, and a later community building now used only for storage, are the two most modern changes in this village. Two circular large kivas stand toward the west and south of the village, and several square religious society houses nestle unobtrusively among the residences. The thick-walled adobe Catholic church, built in 1706 and rebuilt in 1734, stands north of the Pueblo, but the convent is now gone. Some corrals are still maintained around the outer edges of the village, but are rarely used.

In Ranchitos, the tribal administration offices are clustered with the clinic, elderly meal center, traditional officers' building, intergenerational center and Head Start building. The tribal court, maintenance building, swimming pool, Blue-Corn Mill, and the green house complex (established between 1985 and 1986) are located at a slight distance. Across the Rio Grande, where Santa Ana established a golf course and an upscale restaurant between 1986 and 1990, there are also commercial offices, a pro golf shop, a snack building, and a discount smoke-shop.

Here, like in many other Rio Grande Pueblos, the government is divided between internal and external jurisdiction. Present government combines the traditional tribal theocracy, the secular government decreed by Spain in 1620, and a modern administrative structure for maintenance of day-to-day operations. The governor, Secular Council, and aides handle external affairs; the administrative staff handle day-to-day operations; and the traditional Religious Council, *cacique (gowiye),* war captains, aides, *fiscales,* plus a drum roller and sacristan handle internal affairs. Except for annual appointment by the theocracy of officers (other than the *cacique,* drum roller, and sacristan), there is very little interaction between the two segments of government. Members of the Secular Council, though formerly past governors, are now all male heads of families. In 1979, Santa Ana established an administrative staff to provide a stable governmental continuum and conduct federal programs. By 1992 this staff had increased from nine to thirty.

Pueblo life, which is nominally Catholic, still revolves around traditional religious functions which made agriculture supplemented by hunting successful for large Pueblo populations in a marginal desert. They feel the maintenance of a harmonious equilibrium between man and the universe is necessary to avoid illness, famine, or other disaster. Because the people move to Tamaya for religious activities, these activities have been concentrated around Catholic and national holidays, which are supplemented by Native observances. Such ceremonies are under the control of the *cacique*, Religious Council, religious officers, and the religious societies.

The heads of the medicine societies (Fire, Flint, Snake, *Kwinic Cikame*, and *Kwinic Hakawa Cikame*) compose the Religious Council. Each society has its particular responsibility toward the welfare of the tribe, *Koshire* and *Quirana* (the two Clown societies), Medicine, Warrior, Hunter, and Kachina societies still exist. There is a brief description of these, their responsibilities, and the calendar in the *Handbook of North American Indians*.

The last installed *cacique* (*Tcraikatse* at Santa Ana, or "head priest") died before 1910, and was succeeded by his senior assistant (called *gowiye* at Santa Ana). There is some indication that only the head of the Scalp society (which died out) who in Santa Ana was also a member of the *Kwinic Hakawa Cikame* society, could officially install a *cacique* into office. Lacking installation, the subsequent *caciques* have actually been *gowiye* (the senior assistant to the *cacique*).

Prehistorically the Santa Ana people used dry farming on the hills behind the village and along the trail between Tamaya and Ranchitos. Ditch irrigation was used on fields in the floodplain south of Tamaya as early as 1300 and later at Los Ranchitos. By 1890 only guards occupied Tamaya during the growing season. The Santa Anas also herded sheep and cattle, but by the 1960s most farming and herding had died out. People worked in Bernalillo next to Ranchitos, and in Albuquerque eighteen miles south. Many people still hold positions in teaching, nursing, computer programming and in the clerical, construction, or similar fields in Albuquerque.

In 1985 dormant farmlands were revived into large commercial fields using organic and Xeriscopic technology as an economic endeavor to maintain the Pueblo's river water rights. Their greenhouse specializes in retail and wholesale of Xeriscape, drought tolerant plants of the Southwest, though they also grow seedlings for Pueblo plantings of chili, plus herbs and vegetables for the restaurant. With the establishment of the Blue-Corn Mill and commercial blue corn fields, the tribe's farming has expanded from a small local market to an international one. The ultimate intention of this agricultural effort is to create a stable economic base within the community, which will provide tribal employment while accommodating the Native calendar rather than merely federal holidays.

There is not much income from Native crafts. Porfirio Montoya perpetuated Spanish straw inlay on crosses and boxes until his death, and his nephew Elmer Leon continues the art. Eudora Montoya, his wife, was the sole remaining traditional potter until she encouraged a revival in the 1970s.

In 1707 the population of the Santa Ana was listed at 340; it gradually rose to 550 in 1890, but then disease ravaged the people, dropping the population to 298 in 1864, and 236 by 1930. With improved health care, the population increased by 52 percent between 1950 and 1968 up to 456 and according to the Santa Ana governor's office, it went up another 28 percent by 1992 to 629. Most of these people live in Ranchitos, and if they work off-reservation, they commute.

There is a Head Start program at Ranchitos, but older children generally attend Bernalillo or Albuquerque public schools. Higher education is heavily encouraged by the elders and many attend the University of New Mexico or the Technical Vocational School in Albuquerque.

Andrea Hawley Ellis

Further Reading

Ellis, Florence Hawley, and Andrea Ellis Dodge. *The Early Water Works of Three Jemez Valley Pueblos: Jemez, Zia, Santa Ana*. Pt. 1. Report for the U.S. Attorney's Office District of New Mexico, in Albuquerque for use in *Abouselman v. United States Government* (1987). Albuquerque, NM: Florence Hawley Ellis Archives.

Strong, Pauline Turner. "Santa Ana Pueblo." *Handbook of North American Indians*. Vol. 9. *Southwest*. Ed. Alfonso Ortiz. Washington, DC: Smithsonian Institution (1979): 398–406.

White, Leslie A. *The Pueblo of Santa Ana, New Mexico*. Memoirs of the American Anthropological Association 60. Menasha, WI: AAA, 1942.

SANTA CLARA

In the Tewa basin, north and west of Santa Fe in the Rio Grande valley, New Mexico, there are six Tewa-speaking Pueblos of which Santa Clara Pueblo is the second largest. Its population of over 2,000 is second to that of the San Juan Pueblo, numbering well over 2,000. The other Tewa-speakers are from the Pueblos of San Ildefonso, Tesuque, Nambe, and Pojoaque.

Santa Clara Pueblo is situated on the west bank of the Rio Grande, a few miles south of the junction of the Rio Chama, from the northwest, and the Rio Grande, from the north. The northern edge of the Pueblo borders on the southern boundary of Espanola. The village is essentially at the location where the Spanish under Coronado first found it in 1540 to 1541. The reservation contains almost 46,000 acres, of which about 700 are irrigated fields, and the remainder range land and forest. A small hospital is located in the Pueblo. To an increasing degree, the economy has been shifting in the post-World War II period from agricultural pursuits to crafts, principally pottery, and wage earning at nearby Los Alamos, Espanola, and Santa Fe. A number of Santa Clara potters have been and continue to be widely recognized for the unusually high quality of their wares, especially the polished black pieces.

While retaining much of the traditional culture, a number of Santa Clara Indians have degrees in higher education, including a number of doctorates. Several of these individuals continue to participate regularly as dancers or chorus members when Native ceremonies are held. The basic ceremonial organization has rested on a patrilineal moiety, or dual-kiva, system, the tribe being divided into Summer and Winter groups. Upon marrying, the bride shifted over to the husband's kiva.

These Summer and Winter kiva groups at Santa Clara Pueblo served as governing bodies responsible for the management and conduct of civil matters and also ceremonial activities. The political organization represented a blend of the Native structure and that imposed by the Spanish authorities. Accordingly, the kiva, or moiety, headmen functioned as tribal chiefs, alternating in sharing the responsibilities of governing in the course of a year. The Summer headman ruled from spring to fall, and the Winter headman, the remainder of the year. As Arnon and Hill pointed out, "The moiety priests [headmen] held themselves aloof from affairs of ordinary men but selected the secular officials and had final authority in all matters, sacred and profane." Through the years, the Winter kiva group has been the more progressive, and the Summer, more conservative.

While the Spanish authorities had intended to replace the Native governmental and ceremonial system with their own officials and policies, this did not happen. Instead, the Indians assumed the new roles with their own officials and carried on their activities essentially as before.

This traditional pattern of Santa Clara political organization became nonfunctional and obsolete during the period between 1894 and 1935, when the tribe experienced a major schism. In addition, in the early 1930s, new controversies arose and both factions, Summer and Winter, divided again. These four divisions finally agreed to request arbitration by the Indian Service in Santa Fe. This development resulted in 1935 in the adoption of a written Constitution under the Indian Reorganization Act of 1934.

This form of government is still comparatively rare among the Pueblo Indian tribes; actually, Santa Clara was the first tribe to adopt a written Constitution. Dr. Edward Dozier, a Native of Santa Clara Pueblo, explained the reasons behind such schisms:

> It is opposition to the compulsory dictates of the Pueblo authorities which has brought about dissatisfaction and discord in the past as well as at present. Forced participation in all communal activities and the prohibition of all deviant behavior, though designed to discour-

age the rise of dissident groups, have often had the opposite effect and have resulted in frequent factional disputes.

While the 1935 Constitution certainly did not do away with all conflicts, a major result was the separation between religious and secular matters and participation in ceremonies became voluntary. The document set forth guidelines for an initial nomination of officers—each of the four parties could submit nominations for governor, lieutenant governor, secretary, treasurer, interpreter, and sheriff. Each group was also to elect two representatives to the Tribal Council. Actually, there has never been a ballot of four full slates. Instead, there have been two full slates of candidates, to which the factions not submitting nominations lend their support.

The "election" procedure adopted by the Council, at the behest of the Bureau of Indian Affairs, was actually a compromise—the "election" considered candidates nominated by the kiva groups, and these were carefully selected with confidence that they would maintain a conservative position regarding any problem that might arise.

The Tribal Council is authorized to designate election procedures; actually, the Constitution gives complete governing power to the Council, which is composed of all the officers mentioned, including the eight representatives. The Council holds both legislative and judicial powers, as noted above.

The schisms occurring at Santa Clara Pueblo are a classic illustration of the types of disputes that have resulted in the formation of factions. The whole history of intra-Pueblo conflicts demonstrates the resiliency of these cultures. In former times, similar controversies undoubtedly led to physical separation of the factions—with new villages frequently resulting when agreement or conformity could not be attained. In recent years, however, it has been customary for a tribe to forcibly evict individual dissidents, or these malcontents have voluntarily left the community for a more peaceful life elsewhere.

Traditionally, the perpetuation of Pueblo Indian tribes such as Santa Clara has illustrated the cohesive nature of these communities, and the complex system of checks and balances necessary for a harmonious and functioning social and cultural entity.

Charles H. Lange

Further Reading

Arnon, Nancy S., and W.W. Hill. "Santa Clara Pueblo." *Handbook of North American Indians.* Vol. 9. *Southwest.* Ed. Alfonso Ortiz. Washington, DC: Smithsonian Institution (1979): 296–307.

Dozier, Edward P. "Factionalism at Santa Clara Pueblo." *Ethnology* 5:2 (1966): 172–85.

———. *The Pueblo Indians of North America.* New York, NY: Holt, Rinehart and Winston, 1970.

Hill, W.W. *An Ethnography of Santa Clara Pueblo, New Mexico.* Ed. Charles H. Lange. Albuquerque: University of New Mexico Press, 1982.

Parsons, Elsie Clews. *The Social Organization of the Tewa of New Mexico*. Memoirs of the American Anthropological Association 36. Menasha, WI: AAA, 1929.

Sando, Joe S. *Pueblo Nations: Eight Centuries of Pueblo Indian History*. Santa Fe, NM: Clear Light Publishers, 1992.

SANTO DOMINGO

The Pueblo of Santo Domingo lies on the east bank of the Rio Grande in north central New Mexico, about thirty-five miles southwest of Santa Fe. The village, with a 1990 population figure of 2,851 (a slight decrease from the 1980 figure of 2,857), is the largest of the five Eastern Keresan-speaking Pueblos today. These Indians have long been recognized for their ultraconservative stance on almost all issues. Neighboring tribes at times have ridiculed the Santo Domingo Indians for their conservative attitudes; for the most part, however, they have envied the ability of the Santo Domingos to hold to their traditional ways.

The Santo Domingo Reservation contains over 71,000 acres, straddling both the Rio Grande and Interstate 25. At least two earlier Santo Domingo villages, called Gipuy, were located successively along the banks of the Arroyo de Galisteo, a few miles northeast of the present-day village. These sites were destroyed by flooding of the Galisteo. Prior to the abandonment of these Pueblos, however, it was there that the sixteenth-century Spanish expeditions first found the Santo Domingos.

Again the tribe moved west—to the east bank of the Rio Grande, about a mile west of the present Pueblo. This village was called Kiwa, the name of their present-day village as well. Kiwa was again periodically subjected to additional flooding. An especially severe flood in 1886 washed away much of the village as well as the mission church; this resulted in another move, farther back from the river, to the site occupied at the present time.

Situated on the east side of the Rio Grande, Santo Domingo has figured prominently throughout historic times. Initially this location proved to be more advantageous than the positions of neighboring San Felipe and Cochiti Pueblos on the west side of the river. Before the coming of the Americans, Santo Domingo was a stopping place on the Camino Real, running from Mexico and El Paso through Albuquerque and on up to Santa Fe and Taos. This important line of travel was long ago replaced by subsequent highways, including the present-day Interstate 25, which bypasses Santo Domingo Pueblo just a few miles away.

At present, Santo Domingo Pueblo is arranged along nine east-west streets with a north-south street at each end. As the population has grown, additional houses have appeared around the edges of this nucleus as well as along the roads leading in and out of the village. The lines of contiguous houses between most of the east-west streets have been named (Cochiti Row, Santo Domingo Row, Zia Row, Jemez Row, Santa Ana Row, and San Felipe Row—all Keresan-speaking Pueblo tribes except for Jemez).

The mission church of Santo Domingo (Saint Dominic) and the municipal building (tribal offices) are located to the east of the main Pueblo and across the irrigation canal—a physical separation as well as a symbolic division vis-a-vis the heart of the village. The day school was recently removed from just east of the church, to its present location several miles away and only a few hundred yards from Interstate 25. An automobile service station and a small museum and visitors' center are between the school and the highway, and an extensive series of booths has been built in recent years as a base for an annual arts and crafts fair. A community building serves as a clinic for visiting nurse services, doctors, and dentists.

In addition to these manifestations of modern American culture, there are conveniences in the homes such as refrigerators, washing machines, television sets, and other appliances as well as telephones. The great majority of these items have been added in the years since World War II.

Despite these changes, Santo Domingo has retained much of the old ways. They govern themselves by the annually appointed major officers—war captains, governors, and *fiscales*—backed by the Tribal Council composed of all men who have served in any of these six offices and who serve for life. There is no written constitution for the tribe, and decisions are made according to precedent, or common law, insofar as this is possible. When confronted with new situations and problems, the council and officers debate the issues until a solution is found. In the interest of conserving time (a new concept in itself!), majority rule is sometimes resorted to rather than depending on the time-consuming traditional rule of unanimity.

Economically the people of Santo Domingo have been relatively well off; there are over 3,500 acres of irrigated farmland and about 65,000 acres of open grazing lands. The men and women are widely recognized for their craft products: pottery, jewelry, woven belts, and leather moccasins and leggings. The men regularly range far—to Arizona, California, Colorado, and Oklahoma—trading Santo Domingo products as well as serving as middlemen for Navajo blankets and other items not produced locally. A considerable amount of this commercial activity takes place in Santa Fe and Albuquerque as well.

Such travels and contacts have provided many insights into "the other way of life." Being selective from among both the new things and ideas as well as the old, the Santo Domingos have maintained their own core values to an almost unparalleled degree. With the confidence emanating from tribal pride and the prestige accorded to Santo Domingo leaders, it is quite common to find these men assuming leadership roles in such inter-Puebloan affairs as the All-Pueblo Council, or as members of delegations sent to Washington from time to time to plead the Puebloan case before federal agencies, including congressional committees.

At home the Santo Domingo tribe may be characterized as a theocracy with the *cacique* as the head. He is sometimes referred to as *yaya*, or "mother," as he is considered to represent the Corn Mother, or *Iyatiko*. The *cacique* is the ceremonial leader of the tribe, the chief, or *hochanyi*. As head of the Flint Medicine Society, he is also the principal medicine man. While commonly referred to as an annual election of tribal officers, there is a designation, or selection, announced by the heads of the two medicine societies each December. The Flint headman names the two war captains and ten young men, *gowachanyi*, as their helpers. These officials are indigenous, with primary roles in the preservation and protection of the tribal theocracy and general tribal culture.

The *Shikame* Society headman names the two governors and their six assistants, *capitanes*; he also names the two *fiscales*, and their four helpers, *bishgari*—these six having charge of matters pertaining to the mission church.

Santo Domingo is organized in a dual, two-kiva system, the Turquoise and the Pumpkin, with membership reckoned patrilineally, through the father. In addition, there are some twenty exogamous matrilineal clans. Marriages are becoming more frequent with outsiders; however, at Santo Domingo there is considerable pressure against these unions.

Charles H. Lange

Further Reading

Lange, Charles H. "Santo Domingo Pueblo." *Handbook of North American Indians*. Vol. 9. *Southwest*. Ed. Alfonso Ortiz. Washington, DC: Smithsonian Institution (1979): 379–89.

White, Leslie A. "A Comparative Study of Keresan Medicine Societies." *Proceedings, 23rd International Congress of Americanists*, 1928. New York, NY: ICA (1930): 604–19.

———. *The Pueblo of Santo Domingo, New Mexico*. Memoirs of the American Anthropological Association 43. Menasha, WI: AAA, 1935.

TAOS

(Also known as San Geronimo de Taos.) This large, multistoried Pueblo with its spectacular backdrop of the Sangre de Cristo Mountains is 70 miles up the Rio Grande from Santa Fe in north central New Mexico. Inhabited since A.D 1350, the Pueblo is only three miles from the Hispanic/Anglo town of Taos, bringing the three peoples into daily contact, but the degree of ethnic separation remains profound. On a reservation of 95,000 acres and at the base of the Indians' sacred Taos Mountain, the Pueblo itself (elevation, 7,098 feet) is divided into two four- and five-storied adobe house blocks built on either side of the small Rio Pueblo de Taos. Outside ladders are still used to reach the upper floors. Electricity and running water are not permitted inside the old village. A mecca for tourists since early in the twentieth century, over one million visitors come through Taos today. In a very real sense, Taos Pueblo has become a living monument to the persistence of the American Indian for Indians and non-Indians alike. The Pueblo has been nominated as a World Heritage site.

The Taos Indians were always in the forefront of revolts against Spanish domination, and in 1847 joined Mexican settlers in their last armed rebellion—this time against the fledgling American government. However, this was by no means their last battle. The twentieth century has witnessed a continuous parade of legal skirmishes over land encroachment, political sovereignty, water rights, and a host of other issues. None is more dramatic than the battle for Blue Lake, their most important religious shrine twenty miles above the Pueblo behind Taos Mountain. In 1906 Blue Lake and 48,000 acres of surrounding aboriginal use area were incorporated into the Carson National Forest. For sixty-four years the Indians waged a legal war against the government, until finally winning restoration to their reservation in 1970. Significantly, this marked the first time in the United States–Indian relations that land instead of monetary compensation was returned to an American Indian tribe. The issue that finally won the battle was the plea for religious freedom.

Through it all, the sophistication of the Indians in dealing with local, state, and the national government grew immeasurably. No more than a few Taos could use English proficiently in 1900. In 1993 the majority do so. While expert legal counsel is still sought, the Taos have learned to communicate and resolve many of their external problems themselves. But they have never relinquished the core values of their culture, nor abandoned the use of Taos, their Tiwa-based language. Their noted conservatism is partly attributable to maintaining their traditional governing system with its overlay of Spanish-imposed officials. Taos is governed by an all male Council of Elders (which numbers around sixty): this includes the *cacique*, the top religious leaders of the six kivas, plus kiva initiated men who have served as governor, lieutenant governor, war chief, or lieutenant war chief. The latter four are charged with the daily public affairs of government, both on and off the reservation. However, these officers serve only one-year terms and then join or rejoin the Council. They may serve again in subsequent posts, but never for the same position in consecutive years, making it impossible for an individual to consolidate any lasting power and therefore difficult to identify "the leaders" in the usual sense. With its structure of checks and balances and, given that all important matters must be referred to the Council, Taos government has been a powerful conservative force in directing and controlling change.

Loyalty to a closed system and a rule of secrecy adhered to by all Taos Indians never to reveal anything intrinsic to Taos culture have been incredibly potent weapons against outside interference, as well as strong tools to quell internal dissent. At least since effective Spanish presence (around 1600), factionalism has been nearly ubiquitous at Taos, but factions are usually politically and religiously powerless. Many obvious material changes have occurred since 1900, but cultural identity, a worldview stressing a strong sense of community, and loyalty to one's extended kin, are largely intact.

Traditionally an agricultural and hunting people with stockraising in a supplementary role, the Taos have largely abandoned those pursuits for wage work, active participation in government self-help projects, and various forms of welfare. Many young and middle-aged adults must leave Taos for employment elsewhere, but achieving ever higher levels of education is equipping a number for economic survival. One important source of revenue in recent decades has been tourism. Charges to enter the Pueblo, more to take photographs, and the sale of arts and crafts out of home curio shops have been important to the tribe, individual artists, and other entrepreneurs. However, the Taos people are economically far from well off by national standards. Their special advantages have helped, but they remain a poor people.

In 1910 Taos had a population of 515, which has steadily risen to a Bureau of Indian Affairs reservation resident population toll of 1,601 in 1991. Another 500 tribal roll members are not resident on or near the reservation, due primarily to longstanding depressed economic conditions in north central New Mexico. Nevertheless, the number of people identifiable as Taos has increased fourfold in the twentieth century. Health care has been much improved, although many people suffer from the same medical problems familiar on other reservations, e.g., diabetes. A very pernicious disease has been alcoholism, annually taking its toll if not directly, then indirectly, due to exposure or vehicular accidents. It is also at the root of many marital problems, and a determining factor in the breakdown of a number of families. The Pueblo has an active Head Start program and a day school for the primary grades. Most students go to high school in the town of Taos, and a smaller number go to various Indian boarding schools.

Positively, the bilateral kinship system creates strong extended family ties at this clanless Pueblo. The kiva-based religion maintains a rich ceremonial life including the August tribal pilgrimage to Blue Lake. Since the 1970s a renewed commitment on the part of many younger people to their identity as Taos Indians may mean that the knitting of this community is stronger now than in past decades.

The Taos Indians are an active tribe with a vibrant culture that has withstood incredible pressures to assimilate over the past four centuries of European contact. At the twenty-year commemoration of the return of Blue Lake held in September 1991, the tribe coined a slogan befitting the occasion, "Blue Lake—a Symbol of Perseverance." It could just as well be applied to the Pueblo of Taos itself.

John J. Bodine

See also **Sacred Sites**

Further Reading

Bodine, John J. "Taos Pueblo." *Handbook of North American Indians*. Vol. 9. *Southwest*. Ed. Alfonso Ortiz, Washington, DC: Smithsonian Institution (1979): 255–67.

Fenton, William N. *Factionalism at Taos Pueblo, New Mexico*. Anthropological Papers 56. Bureau of American Ethnology Bulletin 164. Washington, DC: U.S. Government Printing Office (1957): 297–344.

Gordon-McCutchan, R.C. *The Taos Indians and the Battle for Blue Lake*. Santa Fe, NM: Red Crane Books, 1991.

Parsons, Elsie Clews. *Taos Pueblo*. General Series in Anthropology 2. Menasha, WI: G. Banta Publishing Co., 1936. New York, NY: Johnson Reprint, 1971.

TESUQUE

Southernmost of the Tewa-speaking Pueblos, Tesuque is approximately nine miles north of Santa Fe, New Mexico. The name Tesuque is a Spanish rendition of the Tewa word *tecuge* meaning "structure at a narrow place." Established in 1694, the present-day village of Tesuque is located along the Tesuque River. Land holdings consist of 17,024.41 acres, 16,706.36 of which are from the original Spanish grant, and additional acreage includes the 318.05-acre Aspen Ranch, a compensation purchase made in 1937 after the Pueblo Lands Act of 1924. In 1988 the Bureau of Indian Affairs (BIA) reported that 600 acres of land was being used for farming, 392 for open grazing, 350 for commercial timber, and 15,547 for noncommercial timber.

The 1990 United States Census of Population and Housing counted a total population of 697 for Tesuque Pueblo and trust lands. Of this total 33 percent were American Indian and 40 percent were of Hispanic origin. Because of Tesuque's proximity to Santa Fe, there are a large number of non-Indians both living on Pueblo lands as well as intermarried into the Pueblo. According to Tribal Council records, as of March 1993 there were 488 enrolled members at Tesuque with applications for enrollment still pending. Most of the enrolled members live in the Pueblo.

Land Claims, Water Rights, and Economic Development

Claims to land and water have become major human rights issues among Native Americans in the twentieth century. Like other Native peoples, the Tesuque community has had to struggle to keep enough land and water to support their way of life. In this century, Tesuque has come under tremendous pressure to give up or lease water and land to outsiders. There was plenty of water in the Tesuque River for tribal members to irrigate their land until 1906, when Anglo settlers moved into the Tesuque Valley, buying and tracking land. By 1917 Tesuque had fallen on hard times because many of the new settlers had redirected the river water to their farms and orchards.

A concrete diversion dam was constructed in 1923 to provide as much water as possible for Tesuque's main irrigation ditch. By 1928 small ranches owned by Spanish-Americans were being bought by Anglo-

Americans to use as summer homes, and new land was being brought under cultivation. To supply more water to the Pueblo, the Indian Irrigation Service constructed an infiltration basin near the river in 1929 to 1930 and a second basin in 1934 to 1935, thus alleviating former shortages.

Tesuque is a member of the Eight Northern Indian Pueblos Council, which was formed in 1965 as part of the Office of Economic Opportunity Program. In 1968 Tesuque received permission from the secretary of the interior "to enter into 99-year leases with external non-Indian interests, for the development of tribal lands and other resources," in the hope of generating tribal revenues and providing employment opportunities.

In the spring of 1970 an agreement was signed by Tesuque officials which would permit the Sangre de Cristo Development Company of Santa Fe to "lease 1,345 acres of Tesuque land, with an option of an additional 3,700 acres, for recreational, commercial, and economic development." The plan included an eighteen-hole golf course, restaurants, hotels, tennis courts, and stables, as well as residential lots. After evidence of deception and bad faith on the part of the non-Indian signatories surfaced, tribal members had the lease canceled in 1976.

In 1988 Tesuque had leased out ninety-six acres to thirty-two businesses, which ranged from horse stables and camping areas, to small commercial businesses such as service stations, convenience stores, and specialty stores. As Santa Fe continues to grow, the demand for Tesuque's water and land will undoubtedly increase.

The economy of the Pueblo has improved somewhat with the increase in tribal businesses and land leases. Like several other tribes throughout the country, Tesuque owns and operates a bingo casino on the highway between Santa Fe and Espanola. In January 1989 the unemployment rate as reported by the United States Department of the Interior for Tesuque Pueblo was 43 percent. Although the unemployment rate is high by national standards, it is lower than most of the other Tewa Pueblos.

Tribal Government and Community Life

Despite being surrounded by Spanish and Anglo influence, Tesuque is the least known and most conservative of the Tewa Pueblos. Although it is involved in developing its resources, it remains relatively conservative today. Pueblo government is based on Spanish institutions which are now thoroughly integrated into their own political-religious system. Pueblo officials are elected by the two moiety heads, and consist of a governor, which rotates among four men; two lieutenant governors, one of which acts as sheriff; two *fiscales*, who act as church caretakers, administrative assistants, and help with irrigation ditches; and a treasurer. Elections are held in December and the installation of officers occurs in January for a term of one year. The Tribal Council, which acts as liaison between the Pueblo and outside contacts, is comprised of tribal officers, former governors, and the war chief.

Around 1923 a day school was established with a capacity for thirty students. In 1966 children attended the BIA-operated day school for the first six grades then went on to St. Catherine's, a Catholic boarding school, or to public junior and senior high schools in Santa Fe. As of 1988 Tesuque had forty-three students enrolled in its elementary school.

Religion and Ceremonial Life

An annual outdoor kachina dance is held in October, at which time the Pueblo is closed to outsiders. Compared to other Pueblos, the presence of a kachina cult at Tesuque is defined as weak. Although they have resisted conversion for centuries, by the twentieth century Catholic religious practices had become incorporated into Tewa ceremonialism. Primarily Roman Catholic, Tesuque holds a feast day on November 12 in honor of its patron saint, San Diego, which combines a Native dance with a church service.

Arts

Tesuque is popularly known for the "Rain God" figurines made in the late 1800s to sell to tourists as they passed through the Lamy train station; however, they never achieved the quality or significance of some of the other Pueblo pottery. A recent revival of traditional wares produced by Tesuque potters can be observed at both the Eight Northern Pueblos Indian Market and the Santa Fe Indian Market. Today, there are approximately ten members of Tesuque involved in pottery making, including Ignacia Duran, Shirley Duran, Reyes Herrera, Helen Herrera, Thelma Tapia, Theresa Tapia, Beatrice Touix, Priscilla Vigil, Ignacia and Alice Vigil. There are artists working in other media as well, for example, Joseph Herrera is a woodcarver, Paul Vigil a painter, Connie Vigil does beadwork, and Beatrice Tioux weaves belts. Art production has not yet developed commercially in terms of becoming an important source of income, but as the artists improve the quality of their craft they may see some economic benefits in the future.

Shelby J. Tisdale

Further Reading

Aberle, Sophie. *The Pueblo Indians of New Mexico: Their Land, Economy, and Civil Organization.* Memoirs of the American Anthropological Association 70. Menasha, WI: AAA, 1948.

Edelman, Sandra A., and Alfonso Ortiz. "Tesuque Pueblo." *Handbook of North American Indians.* Vol. 9. *Southwest.* Ed. Alfonso Ortiz. Washington, DC: Smithsonian Institution (1979): 330–35.

Ellis, Florence Hawley. "Tesuque: Past Use of Farm Lands and Water." Water *Rights Studies of Nambe, Pojoaque, Tesuque, and San Ildefonso Pueblos.* Bureau of Indian Affairs, U.S. Department of the Interior, Washington, DC, 1967.

Parsons, Elsie Clews. *The Social Organization of the Tewa of New Mexico*. Memoirs of the American Anthropological Association 36. Menasha, WI: AAA, 1929.

Smith, Anne M. *New Mexico Indians*. Museum of New Mexico Research Records, 1. Santa Fe, NM: The Museum, 1966.

ZIA

Zia Pueblo, located in the Upper Sonoran Desert life zone, seventeen miles from Bernalillo, New Mexico, is one of five extant Keresan-speaking villages. Besides English most adults speak Keresan and some Spanish.

The old village is on a knoll above the Rio Jemez, in the center of the oldest portion of the tribe's very dry, 121,577-acre trust lands, and spreads newer arms both north and westward. In the subdivision south of the river toward Highway 44, a small cooperative grocery shares the tribal office and community buildings, but other commerce is discouraged.

Since 1978 a community building containing a museum, library, and cultural center; clinic; maintenance building; warehouse; gymnasium; firehouse; and tribal offices have been built. The thick-walled adobe Catholic church was built before 1613, rebuilt in 1680, and stucco plastered in 1973. During the 1980s existing traditional religious buildings expanded by 25 percent to accommodate recent and expected population increases. Both the circular "big kivas" were extensively renovated in the 1940s. The Turquoise kiva was entirely rebuilt in 1974, and the Pumpkin kiva (called the Wren kiva in the 1940s) was rebuilt completely in 1988. Each of the seven square society "little kivas," the two practice houses, and *Hochanyitsa* (tribal officer's chambers), have also been renovated and expanded.

Further anticipated population increases will be accommodated through the establishment of a new village beginning in 1993 near the site of Kawasiya Zia II (LA 377) on the mesa to the east. The prehistoric site, previously occupied between about A.D. 1515 and 1800, will be preserved, not built over. The Bureau of Indian Affairs (BIA) is building a bridge and paving the road between the two villages, a Housing and Urban Development (HUD) grant exists for the first twenty-three houses, and a Community Development Block Grant (CDBG) is being used for the establishment of all the infrastructure utilities. This new village is on the BIA list for construction of a kindergarten through eighth grade day school sometime during the 1990s.

In 1692 a Spanish mass baptism made the Zia Roman Catholic, but this did not erase the old ways. Zia sustains an elaborate, centuries-old cultural and religious design that has made successful gardening by large populations possible in a marginal desert. Their view sees things not merely as good or bad, but as disturbing or maintaining a harmonious equilibrium between man and the universe. Native social controls encourage standards and practices thought to maintain that balance, and thus avoid illness, famine, or other disaster.

Though designed for a larger population and thus allowing for present and future population expansion, the existing group feels that the well-being of their people, animals, crops, and culture rests on perpetuation of the old system. This requires cooperation among the eleven religious societies (Flint, *Koshairi*, *Kwiraina*, Giant, *Kapina*, Fire, *Shima*, Snake, *Katsina/Gomaiyawic*, *Hoaina*, and Hunt), the *cacique* group (three members), the two war chiefs, their four assistants, and the residents. These societies have either remained stable or increased in size over the last fifty years.

A brief description of the religious organization exists in the *Handbook of North American Indians* and need not be repeated, except to point out changes or corrections. The Warrior (Scalp) Society has died out or been altered in Zia (1916) and other Pueblos, leaving no one qualified to initiate the head *cacique* (called at Zia the *tiamunyi*). His duties are now performed by the senior *cacique's* assistant (called the *tcraikatsi* at Zia). The Snake Society now shares a "little kiva" within the village, as do several other societies. The *Hochanyitsa* has never been privately owned, but was lived in for some years by one *cacique* who owned no other house.

In 1620 the Spanish king decreed yearly elections of a governor and other secular officers within each Indian Pueblo. This imposed secular government over the older theocratic Pueblo system. Government is conducted through three groups: a Secular Council, governor, including his lieutenant and assistants to handle external affairs; plus the traditional Religious Council, war captains, and their aides to handle internal affairs; and a secular hiered staff. Officers are appointed by the Religious Council annually. Membership in the Zia Secular Council is composed of male tribal members over eighteen years of age.

In most Pueblos taxes are paid by holding a tribal office, and doing assigned, usually unpaid, community services, such as irrigation ditch maintenance, plastering of community buildings, participation in community religious duties, and ceremonial dances held regularly in the plaza. Political office is not a sought-after lucrative position, but simply a public duty performed by most responsible tribal males sometime during their lifetime. During World War II, monetary compensation rather than labor as taxes was permitted, when the tribal member was employed by the armed services. This practice persists as fines for nonparticipation.

In 1973 Zia established an administrative staff to provide a stable governmental continuum. By 1992, this staff had increased from a part-time treasurer to fourteen full-time staff members with occasional part-time help. Pueblo membership ordinances established in 1979 restrict tribal membership to hereditary Zias and their Indian spouses. In 1990, Zia added each person's Native name and clan to the census documents. Until this project, the Zia dialect of Keresan was unwritten. Past leaders had to remember each person's Native name and clan, for community work cannot otherwise be legally assigned. As the tribe grew, and Native names were only used ceremonially, memory slips led to inequalities in certain types of community contributions.

Prehistorically and into the twentieth century, the Zia used dry farming on the hills behind the village and ditch irrigation in the floodplain. After the Spanish introduced sheep and cattle in 1598, emphasis shifted toward the pastoral. By the mid-twentieth century herding dominated the economy. The 1950s brought a marked decline of income from sheep, and by the 1960s there were no sheep raised at Zia. But herding of cattle persisted and in 1989, since more families wanted cattle than the land permitted, a grazing ordinance and permit procedure was established. In the 1980s Albuquerque, approximately thirty-five miles to the southeast, and Rio Rancho, fifteen miles southeast, became Zia's major trade and employment centers.

Though the main income is from wage jobs, farming, ranching, and crafts provide both a secondary income and a small domestic opportunity to tie the people to their earlier lifestyle. There are some fifty women making traditional pottery, plus painters (watercolor, acrylic, oil), sculptors, and others tanning buckskin, making moccasins and kilts, weaving, and sewing. These Native crafts are dying out in many other Pueblos.

The Zias hope to bequeath to their children this unique lifestyle along with the education necessary to cope in the outside mainstream society. In 1992 they opened a new small museum. As part of the celebration, they held an all-day crafts and dance festival exhibiting their unique Crow Dance, which had not been publicly performed for twenty-eight years, and the colorful Buffalo Dance. This festival raised the seed money of a perpetual college scholarship fund for their young people.

Diary accounts written on Espejo's 1582 expedition to New Mexico indicated Zia's population was "more than four thousand men over fifteen years of age, and women and children in addition," reflecting a conservative estimate of slightly over 7,000. In 1890 the demise of Zia, then numbering only 96 people, of which only 20 were able-bodied men, was freely predicted. Between 1910 and 1920, the population increased 30 percent and had quadrupled to 400 by 1960, doubling again by 1992, thus producing a large percentage of young people in the present village.

In 1992 the Pueblo had 720 residents with an 820 total population. Families in the 1940s often bore fifteen children, usually raising only about six. Before 1900 the Pueblo child mortality rates required such a birth rate. With improved health care, more children have survived, rescuing this tribe from extinction. Now, those children are creating their own families, but generally they bear only two or three children.

Andrea Hawley Ellis

Further Reading

Dodge, Andrea Ellis. "Changes in Some Social Functions and the Associated Buildings in Zia since the Predicted Demise of Zia in 1894." Ms. in the Florence Hawley Ellis Archives, Albuquerque, NM and the Zia Library, 1988.

Ellis, Florence Hawley. *Anthropological Evidence Supporting the Land Claim of the Pueblos of Zia, Santa Ana, and Jemez.* Report to the Indian Land Claims Commission, Washington, DC, 1956.

Hoebel, Adamson E. "Zia Pueblo." *Handbook of North American Indians.* Vol. 9. *Southwest.* Ed. Alfonso Ortiz. Washington, DC: Smithsonian Institution (1979): 407–17.

Stevenson, Matilda Coxe. *The Sia.* Bureau of American Ethnology, 11th Annual Report 1889–1890. Washington, DC: U.S. Government Printing Office (1894): 3–157.

White, Leslie A. *The Pueblo of Sia, New Mexico.* Bureau of American Ethnology Bulletin 184. Washington, DC: U.S. Government Printing Office, 1962.

PUYALLUP

The Puyallup are part of the Southern Coast Salish culture complex in the Puget Sound basin in what is now Washington State. Their first recorded contact with Western culture occurred in 1792, by members of the George Vancouver expedition, representing Britain. They first formalized relations with the government of the United States in 1854 through the Medicine Creek Treaty.

In 1886, prior to the General Allotment Act, the federal government declared tribal members citizens, allotted 17,463 acres of reservation land to 167 individuals, and reserved the remaining 585 acres in trust. By the end of the first decade of the 1900s, questionable tactics had virtually extinguished all tribal ownership of allotted and trust property. The remaining tribal members were left without a land base and were trapped between subsistence living and the introduced cash economy. The tribe's federal court protests fell upon deaf ears.

Twentieth-Century History

In 1929 the remaining Puyallup trust land was the site of the first Indian hospital in the Northwest. From 1939 to 1980, virtually the only lands under tribal control were cemetery sites, one adjacent to the Indian hospital. In 1939 the Interior Department purchased thirty-eight acres (the bulk of trust property) and built the largest Indian health facility in the Indian Service. This facility served Natives from Alaska and at least four other states, but was closed in 1959 by the federal government despite serious Indian health needs and protests by several regional tribes. The Northwest is without an Indian hospital to this day.

In 1973 the Puyallup tribe organized a campaign to recover the hospital site from the State of Washington, which had purchased it from the federal government for one dollar in 1961. A group of Puyallup, including Ramona Bennett, chairwoman of the tribe at that time, staged an armed but peaceful occupation of the facility in 1976. After a second occupation of the facility by the tribe in 1980, the site was transferred back to trust status (consistent with a federal-tribal agreement) based upon an unreported decision by Judge Tanner in *United States v. Washington* (1980) in which he ruled that the transfer of the land from the federal government to the state was invalid. In 1976, the Puyallup began to operate the first Indian medical clinic in the nation under the provisions of the federal Indian Self-Determination and Educational Assistance Act. This medical clinic was established within reservation boundaries on their remaining trust land adjacent to the former Indian hospital. The Takopid Health Center, completed in 1993 and funded by the Indian Health Service, offers a wide range of health care to individuals representing over 250 tribes and bands throughout the United States.

The number of enrolled members of the tribe totaled 1,544 in 1990. The number of Indians and Alaska Natives, representing a wide variety of tribal backgrounds, living on or near the Puyallup Reservation, was over 10,000 in the same year. Most of the reservation is non-Indian owned (99 percent in the late 1980s). Thus, the Puyallup are embedded in an unusual social situation. They are a reservation community, partially assimilating a major Northwest city (Tacoma) and three other smaller cities. Parts of these incorporated areas are within the boundaries of the federally designated reservation. The Puyallup provide social, health, and educational services to a large urban Indian community, in addition to providing support to surrounding tribal entities.

The Puyallup are primarily urban dwellers who have been allowed almost no land base during most of the twentieth century. Despite this fact they have maintained their distinct cultural identity and an unbroken relationship with the federal government. Though their relationship with local and state governments has often been adversarial, they have managed to become leaders in the struggle to reaffirm fishing rights, to educate their children in their own schools, and to revive their cultural ceremonies. At the same time, they have maintained and expanded a health care system for the Indians in the community.

Culture

Puyallups hold a wide range of standard Western religious beliefs, and some are members of the Indian Shaker religion. Precontact beliefs persist in the form of winter spirit dancing and traditional healing ceremonials. Their continuing kinship interactions with neighboring tribes, who endured less acculturation pressure, has assured their ability to reintroduce traditional ceremonials such as the first salmon ceremony and healings within their own land base. Of particular significance is the institution of an annual powwow celebrating the return of the Indian hospital lands and facilities to tribal control. The original language (Lushootseed), though taught in schools and surviving as place names, is not spoken generally.

Their spiritual revival is intricately linked to the protracted struggle to regain aboriginal fishing rights, which began in the mid-1950s with the first arrests of Puyallup tribal members for "illegal" fishing. By 1964 this struggle led to a fish-in, which culminated in the arrest of Robert Satiacum (Puyallup) and Marlon Brando (the actor), among others. These acts proved to be the rallying point for the ongoing revival of ceremonial and cultural activities, and the ultimate return to trust status of some of their reservation property.

The Puyallup have shown a persistent ability to endure, adapt, and change despite concerted efforts toward assimilation and the decimation of their land, economic, and subsistence base. The revitalization of their culture gained momentum in the 1960s. This movement eventually led to the reestablishment of their fishing rights in 1974, through the decision of Judge George Boldt of the United States District Court of Western Washington. The reaffirmation of their land base, the emergence of their contemporary health care and social service system, the establishment of a tribal school system (kindergarten through community college), and the completion in 1990 of the largest Indian land claims settlement in history with local non-Indian governments and residents within reservation boundaries, all are related to their desire to preserve their subsistence and spiritual relationship to the salmon.

Economic Development

In order to enhance the depleted salmon population, they have created a fisheries division that released 1,356,706 salmon and steelhead in the spring of 1991. They continue to fight the destruction of wetlands and the degradation of water quality in their salt water and riverine ecosystem. They have justly demanded the creation of a new wetland area as a component of the recent land claims settlement.

The negotiated land claims settlement in 1990 also enabled the further expansion of their land base, the creation of an endowment fund for social and health services, the awarding of small business loans to tribal members, and the creation of a series of development projects including a marina and a bingo palace. The current trust land base of the tribe does not exceed 1,000 acres.

Recent benchmarks in their modern history include the development of Puyallup International (a business investment and development arm), recognition in 1989 of their Chief Leschi Tribal Schools through a presidential citation for its model antidrug program (PRIDE), establishing the first tribally controlled Indian Health Service unit in the Puget Sound region in 1989, and various other awards including national recognition for a model mental health day treatment program in 1992.

George M. Guilmet
David L. Whited

See also **Fishing and Hunting Rights; Indian Health Service; Washington State Tribes**

Further Reading

American Friends Service Committee. *Uncommon Controversy: Fishing Rights of the Muckleshoot, Puyallup, and Nisqually Indians.* Seattle: University of Washington Press, 1970.

Cohen, Fay G. *Treaties on Trial: The Continuing Controversy over Northwest Indian Fishing Rights.* Seattle: University of Washington Press, 1986.

Guilmet, George M., and David L. Whited. *The People Who Give More: Health and Mental Health among the Contemporary Puyallup Indian Tribal Community.* American Indian and Alaska Native Mental Health Research, The Journal of the National Center Monograph Series 2:2 (Winter 1989). Denver: University Press of Colorado, 1989.

Smith, Marian W. "The Puyallup of Washington." *Acculturation in Seven American Indian Tribes.* Ed. Ralph Linton. New York, NY: D. Appleton-Century (1940): 3–36.

———. *The Puyallup-Nisqually.* Columbia University Contributions to Anthropology 32. New York, NY: Columbia University Press, 1940. New York, NY: AMS Press, 1969.

QUAPAW

When first encountered by Europeans in the 1670s, some 15,000 to 20,000 Quapaws resided in villages in what is now Arkansas, near the confluence of the Mississippi and Arkansas rivers. Treaties signed in 1819, 1824, and 1833 first reduced the extent of ancestral lands and then provided for the removal of the entire tribe to the northeastern corner of Oklahoma, near present-day Miami.

When the twentieth century dawned, most of the Quapaws were still in northeastern Oklahoma, but not on a reservation. In 1893, the tribal leadership had taken the unprecedented action of allotting its own reserve in 240-acre parcels, to the 230 enrolled members of the tribe.

The discovery of rich lead and zinc deposits on some of these allotments shaped the course of Quapaw history through the 1930s. Defrauding the Quapaws was the usual order of business in the mining district. The federal government ignored the problem until 1908, when it began to take its guardianship responsibilities seriously. For the Quapaws, this belated action meant higher royalties, bonus payments, revocation of fraudulent leases, and protection from local, state, and federal taxes. So obvious were the benefits that, in 1921, the tribespeople petitioned to extend restrictions on certain allotments for an additional twenty-five years. Congress consented, taking similar action again in 1939 and 1970.

If federal intervention benefited the Quapaws, it also curtailed their personal freedom. For Chief Peter Clabber (1893 to 1926) and others, it meant the loss of control of both their leases and the revenue derived from them. Operators paid royalties directly to the agency, which were then distributed to beneficiaries only upon personal application. These procedures notwithstanding, the Quapaws still managed to engage in an orgy of spending in the 1920s that depleted most of their individual accounts.

The property holdings of some Quapaws made the Tribal Council wary of any proposal designed to alter the status quo of tribal life or government. Consequently, the tribe rejected the Indian Reorganization Act of 1934 and then refused to organize under the terms of the Oklahoma Indian Welfare Act passed two years later. The leadership filed a land claim under the provisions of the Indian Claims Commission in 1946, an action that in 1954 resulted in a favorable judgment against the federal government of nearly $1 million. Seven years later, that money was paid out to 1,199 individual Quapaws, but not before the traditional leadership was replaced in 1956 by a new Business Committee composed of elected members.

The Indian Claims Commission award revitalized the Quapaws both as a people and as a community. Led by Robert Whitebird from 1956 until 1968, the Business Committee responded to this surge of interest and rising expectations with confidence and effectiveness, even avoiding termination in the 1950s. In the late twentieth century, the tribe of 1,927 manages varying enterprises, ranging from a bingo parlor to a quick-stop gasoline station, a nationally acclaimed powwow (a major social event in northeastern Oklahoma), and a gleaming new headquarters southeast of Quapaw, Oklahoma.

There is very little traditional culture left. A handful still speak the language, and some of the older women give out Quapaw names. The "Big Moon" variant of the Peyote Religion was introduced to the Quapaws by John "Moonhead" Wilson in the late 1890s. Victor Griffin, later chief of the tribe from 1929 to 1958, became Wilson's most earnest disciple. The widespread acceptance of peyote caused the Tribal Council to withdraw its support of St. Mary's of the Quapaw in 1927, a Catholic mission school that had operated among the tribe for thirty-five years. By the 1990s, however, peyote was no longer a significant spiritual force. All of the roundhouses were gone and Christianity was pervasive.

W. David Baird

See also **Oklahoma Tribes**

Further Reading

Baird, W. David. *The Quapaw Indians: A History of the Downstream People.* Civilization of the American Indian 152. Norman: University of Oklahoma Press, 1980.

Nieberding, Velma. *A History of Ottawa County.* Miami, OK: Walsworth Publishing Company, 1983.

Westbrook, Kent C., and J.A. McEntire, III. *Legacy in Clay: Prehistoric Ceramic Art of Arkansas: Exhibit and Catalogue.* Little Rock, AR: Rose Publishing Company, 1982.

Wright, Muriel H. *A Guide to the Indian Tribes of Oklahoma.* Civilization of the American Indian 33. 1951. Norman: University of Oklahoma Press, 1986.

QUASSARTES

See Alabama-Coushatta

QUECHAN

The Quechan (Yuma) Nation consists of about 3,000 people and a 33,000-acre reservation in southeastern California, just across the Colorado River from Yuma, Arizona. A small portion of the land also lies in Arizona. Approximately 8,000 acres are allotted to individuals, but held in trust by the federal government.

The Colorado River has been a key factor in the Quechans' history. In precontact times it irrigated their fields with rich silt during its springtime floods. The Quechans also controlled one of the few Colorado crossings in the east-west routes of commerce, giving them a strategic importance in precontact trade, and later traffic with Spanish, Mexican, and Anglo interlopers.

By the early 1900s, the Quechans' reservation had lost much of its most fertile land along the river due to a fraudulent "agreement" with the federal government in 1893. This agreement featured coerced and forged signatures of tribal members, and promised the Indians irrigation water in return for cession of their "excess" land that remained after individual allotments were issued. The irrigation system was not constructed as stipulated, but some of the "excess" land—the most fertile acreage in what is now known as the Bard District—was sold to whites at bargain prices. In 1978, 25,000 acres of the former reservation were finally restored to the tribe after years of frustrating effort by its leaders. Unfortunately, water rights to the restored portion have not been granted. Without adequate water the land is economically marginal. The tribe has taken the water issue to court, but finds itself continually pitted against powerful agricultural and urban interests (including greater Los Angeles and Phoenix) also demanding a greater share of the already oversubscribed Colorado's water.

During this century tribal relations with the federal government and efforts to build a strong economic base for the Quechans have pivoted on what rich agricultural land still remains in the tribe's domain. Bureau of Indian Affairs superintendents controlled the land's development until the late 1930s; the best land was not farmed by the Indians themselves, but was leased out to Anglo farmers while the Indians languished in poverty. Most of the prime land is still leased, despite the tribe's efforts to create a tribally managed agricultural cooperative in the late 1960s and early 1970s. That effort failed, along with a large hydroponic tomato-growing enterprise that succumbed to the competition of cheaper produce imported from Mexico and the effects of a destructive blight. The tribe's agricultural enterprises are slowly rebuilding.

Meanwhile, the tribe has cashed in on the gambling operations that have attracted non-Indians to reservations across the country. It has also built modern trailer parks to lure the large numbers of winter residents who come to the Yuma region from colder climates. It continues to search for economic ventures that will generate much-needed permanent jobs for its members. Its reservation is ideally situated along a major rail route through the Southwest and an interstate highway between Phoenix and San Diego. Federal, state, and tribally funded jobs have been the economic foundation of the Quechans since the mid-1960s.

About two-thirds of the tribe's members live on or near the reservation. A seven-member Tribal Council includes a full-time president and vice-president, who serve four-year terms; the other five Council members are elected biennially. A strong egalitarian ideal dominates council behavior and tribal politics in general. Both men and women have served as council presidents and members. The tribal government has become diversified and complex since the mid-1960s; tribal presidents now must interact skillfully with officials at state and federal levels, as well as oversee the operation of a variety of tribal administrative, economic, educational, and health programs.

Adult-onset diabetes continues to be one of the most alarming health problems for the people. There is a small hospital facility on the reservation, but seriously ill diabetics must be treated either in nearby Yuma or at the large Indian Health Service facility in Phoenix. New homes and an improved water and sanitation system have improved the living conditions of the people; again, their most pressing material need is for jobs offering a secure future.

Most of the adults on the reservation still speak their Native language in addition to English, and younger people are actively interested in keeping the language alive. Everyone still enjoys congregating at the dancing grounds to dance a hop-and-shuffle step to lively songs such as "Bird" or "People" (this last accompanied by tin-can rattles). Their traditional ritual is most apparent today in funeral and mourning ceremonies, which include sacred song cycles by male singers and dancing by women in brightly colored long dresses and beaded shawls. Most often the dead are still cremated, and much of their personal property is destroyed in the funeral pyre. In the past all remains of the pyre were brushed smooth so as to eliminate all physical reminders of the deceased's existence. Today family members often provide small grave markers near the special building reserved for funeral services. The people are frustrated by the continuing loss of intimate knowledge of traditional rituals as the elderly ritualists themselves pass away.

Many Quechans were baptized into Christian faiths as children; Catholic, Methodist, Mormon, and Nazarene congregations meet on the reservation. But for many of the middle-aged and elderly, the Christian faith supplemented rather than supplanted traditional beliefs that include the concept of special personal power received in particular types of dreams. The Quechans still retain some knowledge of their traditional system of patrilineal clans, named for totems such as snake, coyote, frog, or corn. Until the early 1900s, some clans tended to be localized in one of the five or six Quechan settlements along the Colorado and lower Gila rivers. Two members of the same clan could not marry. Couples today often ignore the marriage-regulating functions of clans. There is still great formal respect paid to elderly members of the tribe, who comprise a special organization known simply as "the old people." As in the past, eloquent speakers of the Native language are closely heeded; this is one of the manifestations of their personal dream power.

Robert L. Bee

See also **Arizona Tribes**

Further Reading

Bee, Robert L. *Crosscurrents Along the Colorado: The Impact of Government Policy on the Quechan Indians.*Tucson: University of Arizona Press, 1981.
———. "Quechan." *Handbook of North American Indians.* Vol. 10. *Southwest.* Ed. Alfonso Ortiz. Washington, DC: Smithsonian Institution (1983): 86–98.
———. *The Yuma.* New York, NY: Chelsea House Publishers, 1989.
Forbes, Jack D. *Warriors of the Colorado: The Yumas of the Quechan Nation and Their Neighbors.* Norman: University of Oklahoma Press, 1965.
Forde, C. Daryll. *Ethnography of the Yuma Indians.* University of California Publications in American Archaeology and Ethnology 28, no. 4. Berkeley: University of California Press, 1931. 83–278.

QUILEUTE

The Quileute Nation (also kʷoʔlí·yotʼ, Quilléayute, Quillehute, Quilahute, Kwille´hiūt, and Kwe-dée-tut) historically inhabited the drainages of the Quillayute River system and adjacent Pacific Ocean coastline of the western Olympic Peninsula of Washington State. The rich natural environment allowed development of a broad base of maritime, littoral, riverine, and terrestrial subsistence activities that utilized the entire expanse of the Quillayute River watershed. Permanent settlements were maintained along coastal and inland rivers. Additional sites were used seasonally for fishing, hunting, and gathering. The Quileute language, also spoken by the Hoh and the Chemakum (now politically extinct) make up the linguistically isolated Chimakuan family.

History

The numbers and effects of late eighteenth-century European contact were limited by the lack of safe anchorages. In 1855, M.T. Simmons negotiated the Treaty with the Quileute, Etc., 1855, which called for removal to the Quinault Reservation (established in 1873). However, the Quileutes were given assurances of continued residence, and no movement occurred except for consolidation in the village of La Push at the mouth of the Quillayute River. The economically important camas prairies were homesteaded by whites, and the town of Forks now sits on the largest prairie.

In 1889, a small one-square-mile reservation was created at La Push by executive order. Because the treaty assumed relocation, Quileutes are eligible for membership at either La Push or Quinault. Near the turn of the century, some Quileutes took allotments in the public domain (now mostly lost), and after 1910 some received eighty-acre timber allotments on the Quinault Reservation. The tribe incorporated in 1937 and the Tribal Council has five members elected to two- and three-year terms. Members in 1993 were Douglas Woodruff, Sr. (chair), Chris Penn, Sr., William Penn, Bonita Warner, and Leo Williams. Heritable chieftainships are noted but not effective. The opinions of elders have a subtle, but important, effect on decisions, especially those affecting traditional cultural life.

Current Situation

Population has risen considerably from the estimates of 252 in 1889 and 285 in 1945. Current tribal enrollment, requiring 50 percent blood quanta, or 25 percent conditioned by place of birth and/or residence, is 874 in 1992. Less than half, about 350, live in La Push, which has a total population of 400. Protestant (Assemblies of God), Indian Shaker Church, and traditional religious practices coexist in the community. While clear distinctions may be made, individual practice often laps over the boundaries.

Important land issues include location of the reservation boundary and ownership of former allotments and residences that were subject to adverse taking. Resource protection and off reservation utilization present continuing issues since treaty rights provide protection for usual and accustomed practices.

The reservation economy has depended largely on fishing, but continued decreases in salmon runs dominate the future scenario and outweigh the benefits received from the 1974 Boldt Decision which allocated 50 percent of harvestable fish to treaty fishermen. Indian participation in the logging industry has been limited. Sales on timber allotments have provided unpredictable windfalls to some tribal families. A number of jobs are provided by the tribal government and tribal school financed by the Bureau of Indian Affairs. The tribe also oversees a fish hatchery, fish processing facility, harbor, restaurant, and tourist resort.

Culture

A reservation school was run from 1882 until about 1946. In 1979, the Quileute tribal school began operation under a Native school board and provides education through the eighth grade. The associated enrichment program focuses on cultural education and has been a major benefit to the tribe. A nationally recognized language program has produced a number of textbooks and computerized instruction at a time when only a few Native speakers remain. Instruction in dance, song, carving, weaving, gathering, and other activities, including their relationship with traditional philosophy and metaphysics, has been important in building cultural self-esteem.

The Quileute Tribe took the lead in encouraging canoe building and ocean voyaging among Washington tribes in the 1989 "Paddle to Seattle." Some twenty tribes participated in this event, which generated plans for an international gathering of canoe tribes. In 1993, nineteen canoes made the long voyage, once common, to the 'Qátumas festival hosted by the Heiltsuk Band in British Columbia. This "Paddle to Bella Bella" was a major event for strengthening indigenous unity and renewing the cedar canoe culture on the Northwest Coast.

The 1980s have seen increased practice of the potlatch. This traditional feast and gift-giving ceremony marks significant events such as name-givings, funeral memorials, and marriages. The strong power at these potlatches was still experienced into the 1940s, but by the 1960s the ceremony was nearly abandoned. Recent use of the potlatch both reflects and encourages a rekindled interest in the tribe's traditional social and spiritual life, and in the family-owned songs, dances, and society memberships. In the face of economic and self-esteem challenges, the Quileutes are fortunate that adaptation to the industrial world has been relatively recent, and the memories of the elders still bridge the gap to the old ways and provide a beacon for the future.

Joseph Lubischer

See also Hoh; Washington State Tribes

Further Reading

Pettit, George A. *The Quileute of La Push, 1775–1945.* University of California Anthropological Records 14:1. Berkeley: University of California Press, 1950. Millwood, NY: Kraus Reprint, 1976.

Powell, James V. "Quileute." *Handbook of North American Indians.* Vol. 7. *Northwest Coast.* Ed. Wayne Suttles. Washington, DC: Smithsonian Institution (1990): 431–37.

QUILLWORK

The art of using porcupine quills as a decorative medium is an ancient one in North America. Quillwork predates European contact; it had great artistic and technical influence on the subsequent development of beadwork. Quillwork was a mature art form as evidenced by its geographical distribution, technical development, and aesthetic value. Unfortunately, it is also a fragile art form, and few early examples have survived.

When manufactured glass beads were introduced by non-Indians, beadwork became the preferred medium and gradually replaced quillwork as the principal decorative technique. By the early twentieth century quillwork production was limited to a few tribes located in the northern Plains, northern California and eastern Canada.

Starting in the 1960s when the Indian Arts and Crafts Board began to systematically encourage local quillworkers, the quantity of quillwork for sale increased on a few reservations. At this time a few families among the Lakota/Dakota of North and South Dakota were the principal makers of quilled items, and the majority of their output was marketed to the non-Indian curio market. The Lakota of the Pine Ridge and Rosebud reservations were the most prolific quillers. Beadwork remained the preferred decorative medium for most Indians, although there was an increase in the use of quilled items made by a small number of specialists. In northern California basketmakers continued to use porcupine quills as a decorative element, but otherwise porcupine quills were no longer used in the traditional arts. Quilled boxes were made by some Micmac specialists in eastern Canada, where a few businessmen and museums encouraged sales by carrying items in their shops. And there were a few quillworkers in north central Canada who occasionally made objects for a weakly developed market. Other than the few Indian quillworkers, there were a number of non-Indian hobbyists who learned quillwork as part of their interest in Indian material culture.

The number of quillworkers nationally was increasing dramatically by the 1970s. Most of their production was made for sale to tourists, although growing numbers of Indians were using quilled items in combination with or exclusive of beadwork. In 1972 the Sioux Museum and Craft Center in Rapid City, South Dakota, staged a major exhibit of quillwork based on its permanent collection and has exhibited quillwork frequently since. A major boost to the recognition of quillwork as an important art form occurred when Alice New Holy from the Pine Ridge Reservation was given a National Heritage Fellowship by the National Endowment for the Arts in 1985. The New Holy family was widely known as important quillworkers in their community. New regional and national markets for quillwork were established, which encouraged its production and increased the number of active quillworkers.

Presently, the number of active quillworkers continues to increase nationally, particularly in the northern Plains where quillwork has been reestablished on the majority of the reservations. Formal classes in quillwork are part of the curriculum in several tribally controlled community colleges on reservations. They have been offered as special classes in numerous urban Indian centers, and in some Indian studies programs on college campuses. This development has facilitated the acquisition of basic quilling skills as potential students are no longer restricted to informal instruction. In communities where there are no active quillworkers willing or able to instruct students, formalized classes offer another opportunity for perpetuating the art form. There are now many quillworkers in urban areas. A number of traditional art forms utilizing quills are revitalized, as in northern California where quill ornamentation on objects can again be found. Although the total number of quillers has increased, the major producers of quillwork are still centered on reservations in the northern Plains and eastern Canada. Many American Indians use or own quilled objects, as well as many non-Indians, although beadwork continues to be the preferred decorative medium for the great majority of Native people.

Formerly the quills were dyed with mineral or vegetal colors and used in combination with undyed quills to create patterns of dazzling variety. Modern quillworkers use commercial dyes to achieve the same effects. There are over fifty separate techniques used in creating quilled objects. These fall into five major technical categories: wrapped, sewn, woven, pierced, and strung. Currently, the most commonly used techniques are wrapped and sewn work, although there is growing interest in the production of strung work because of its efficiency. Today's quillworkers are extremely inventive and create new ways of decorating contemporary items that were never part of traditional material culture. Quilled baseball caps, cigarette lighters, picture frames, and combs are a few

examples of the continuing vitality of quill artists. While most of the contemporary quill production is in small objects like bracelets, combs, earrings, and small pouches, there is a limited production of major quilled items like men's shirts, leggings, pipebags, and saddle bags. These items are very costly because of the labor needed to produce them and are generally sold to museums or collectors.

The manufacture and sale of quilled objects is the principal income for a number of families in the northern Plains and eastern Canada. Whereas quillwork used to be an art form that was primarily or exclusively practiced by women, modern quill artists include a number of males. Quillwork has been incorporated into multi-media works by a few artists working in the medium of painting. Contemporary quillwork continues to evolve as an art form, making unique contributions to modern Indian cultures.

JoAllyn Archambault

See also Art, Beadwork

Further Reading

Lyford, Carrie. *Quill and Beadwork of the Western Sioux.* Lawrence, KS: Haskell Institute, 1940.

Orchard, William C. *The Technique of Porcupine-Quill Decoration among the North American Indians.* New York, NY: Museum of the American Indian, Heye Foundation, 1916.

Quillwork by Native Peoples in Canada. Toronto: Royal Ontario Museum, 1977.

Taylor, Colin. "Early Plains Indian Quill Techniques in European Museum Collections." *Plains Anthropologist* 7 (February 1962): 58–69.

Whitehead, Ruth Holmes. *Micmac Quillwork: Micmac Indian Techniques of Porcupine Quill Decoration, 1600–1950.* Halifax: The Nova Scotia Museum, 1982.

QUINAULT

The Quinault are a nation of more than 2,400 members, 1,400 of whom live on the Quinault Reservation, a triangular area between the Pacific Ocean and the high, snow-capped Olympic Mountains in Washington State. The reservation includes 340 square miles of evergreen forests, five rivers, and 24 miles of ruggedly beautiful coastline on the Pacific Ocean. As a result of the United States government allotment policy and federal court interpretation of the Quinault River Treaty, persons of Quinault, Queets, Quileute, Hoh, Chinook, Chehalis, and Cowlitz ancestry are enrolled members of the Quinault Indian Nation. The Quinault Nation's population center, Taholah, is at the mouth of the Quinault River as it flows into the Pacific Ocean. Queets Village, which is smaller, lies on the other side of the reservation near the mountains.

The first recorded contact between Quinaults and Europeans was in 1780 when a Spanish ship laid anchor on the coast just south of the Quinault River mouth. The Spanish received a hostile response to their visit. Over the next seventy-five years the Quinault kept

Quillwork medallion by Alice New Holy (Lakota) executed on rawhide in red and white porcupine quills. White beads are used in fringe and necklace. Private collection. Photo by Donald Tenoso.

their distance from the growing non-Indian settlements. Under pressure from the United States government, the Quinault River Treaty was signed by the Quinault, Quileute, and the Hoh on July 1, 1855. In wthis treaty the Quinaults gave up a vast territory, but reserved the most ceremonially and economically important lands for their own use. Quinaults living outside this area were encouraged by the United States government to settle on the reservation through incentives of money, goods and services. On November 4, 1873, the President of the United States signed an executive order signaling recognition of Quinault sovereignty over the Quinault Reservation.

The government moved in 1907 to divide the Quinault Reservation into individual allotments in accordance with the 1887 General Allotment Act. One of the major intents of the Allotment Act was to break up reservation land into individual allotments that could be farmed. Since the Quinault beaches and timberland were not suited for farming, the chief of the Indian Forestry Service intervened and in 1914 was successful in halting allotment.

Dividing Quinault lands into small parcels began again in 1924 when Tommy Payne, a member of the Quileute tribe located on a reservation north of the Quinault, filed a lawsuit to resume allotments. The federal court agreed that Quinault lands could be allotted to allow timber cutting. This case opened the Quinault to new lawsuits by individuals without reservation lands seeking to get valuable timber allotments on the Quinault Reservation. The United States Supreme Court decided *Halbert v. United States* in 1931, allowing members of the Chehalis, Chinook, and Cowlitz tribes the right to claim parcels of land. Although representatives of these tribes had refused to relocate their people on the Quinault Reservation during the Chehalis Treaty negotiations of 1855 and immediately after the 1873 presidential order, three generations later individuals from these tribes led the movement to divide the remainder of the Quinault reservation lands. Since there was no requirement that individual allottees live on the lands they acquired, few moved to the reservation. By 1933 the United States government had approved 2,340 individual allotments, using all the tribes' reserved lands. Allottees were allowed to apply for status as Quinaults and many have become enrolled Quinaults.

The allotment process, combined with irresponsible Bureau of Indian Affairs (BIA) management of lands leased to timber companies, resulted not in Indian farmers or Indian businesses, but in large areas of clearcut hills and valleys. The environmental destruction from clearcut logging and the leaching of cedar slash which was not removed almost destroyed the fish spawning habitat, sharply reducing salmon runs on the Quinault Reservation. The most direct consequence of allotments was the movement of Indians off the reservation to nearby towns. Almost half the Quinault Nation's population now lives off the reservation.

On August 24, 1922, the Quinault people documented for the first time the shape and character of the modern Quinault Nation when the Bylaws governing the Tribal Council of the Quinault Indian Reservation were signed into law. These established an elective government ruled by a Tribal Council made up of voting members of the nation, and a Business Committee composed of a president, vice-president, secretary, treasurer, and five council members. The Quinault government continued to evolve for the next forty-three years during which the Tribal Council made adjustments and amendments to the Bylaws. The Quinault Tribal Council formally ratified all adjustments and amendments for the Bylaws on May 22, 1965, and ratified the Constitution of the Quinault Indian Nation on March 22, 1975.

Salmon fishing, seafood processing, forest products and lumber are the main economic activities on the Quinault Reservation. While several large commercial timber companies cut hundreds of thousands of board feet of timber from lands inside Quinault territory, these companies have little direct impact on the tribal economy. Tribal members find employment largely off the reservation. The single largest employer on the reservation is the Quinault government—employing many tribal members in social and health delivery programs, fisheries management, and forest management. The Quinault government sponsors a seafood processing plant, two restaurants, two food markets, and assorted small enterprises which produce wood products. Quinault's private sector economy is very small, with fewer than twenty tribal members owning businesses. Recognizing the importance of retaining the integrity of their community, Quinault government policies have discouraged non-Indian business enterprises and, as a result, only a few residents of the village of Taholah are non-Indian.

The Quinaults have a long history of interest in education and control their own schools. They have had a public grade school since 1920 and their own school board since 1957. Quinault culture, including language instruction in their Salishan language, is integrated into the curriculum. Since 1991 they have also had their own high school and increasing numbers of graduates are entering colleges for professional training.

The Quinaults are among the first tribes in the Northwest to fully exercise sovereignty over their territory. In 1969 they gained national attention through the closure of their beaches to all but tribal members to preserve the habitat. During the same year they also stopped the construction of a state road through their reservation, when the state would not agree to tribal control of access and rights of way. After twenty years of logging (from 1950 to 1971) under the BIA leasing policies, less than 1 percent of the clearcut land had been replanted. In 1971 the Chow Chow Bridge spanning the Quinault River was blockaded to stop the transport of logs as a protest to the decimation of the reservation's forests and fisheries. Beginning in 1970 with an Economic Development Administration project, the Quinaults began a study and rehabilitation program for reservation streams and forests, which evolved into the Quinault Department of Natural Resources. Since 1974 the Quinaults have been involved in reforesting their land and have three major facilities for fish propagation. The major thrust of Quinault economic policy is to regenerate abundant fishruns and forests which can provide employment for future generations.

Chief Taholah (Taxola, circa 1850), after whom the main Quinault village is named, continues to have a powerful influence on the Quinault Nation. Harry Shale, Horton Capoeman, James (Jug) Jackson, Pearl Baller and Joe DeLaCruz are Quinault's modern leaders who closely identify with their nineteenth-century Quinault forerunner. On May 5, 1984, a traditional potlatch ceremony was conducted to name Oliver Mason, the great-great-grandson of Chief Taholah, the hereditary chief of the Quinault tribe. The potlatch passing the title of chief from Jackson to the Mason family was the first ceremony like it on the Quinault Reservation since 1926. Joe DeLaCruz has been Quinault tribal chairman for over twenty years and has achieved distinction in his role as an office holder in national Indian organizations and an outspoken leader on behalf of Indian rights.

The Quinaults are participating in a federal self-governance project in which the government provides funding directly to tribes to develop and manage their own programs. Joe DeLaCruz was one of the principal architects of this new approach, and the Quinaults were instrumental in getting the program approved. This compact is intended as a first step in working toward a relationship with the federal government, in which tribal sovereignty is reinforced and the BIA is restructured to be more responsive to Indian communities. The Quinault Indian Nation has opened a new chapter in its political relations with the United States.

Rudolph C. Rÿser
Marilyn G. Bentz

See also **Chinook; Washington State Tribes**

Further Reading

Adamson, Thelma. *Folk-Tales of the Coast Salish.* Memoirs of the American Folk-Lore Society 27. 1934. New York, NY: Kraus Reprint, 1969.

Bentz, Marilyn. "The World View of Young Quinault Indians." PhD. diss., University of Washington, 1984.

Capoeman, Pauline K., ed. *Lands of the Quinault.* Seattle, WA: Quinault Indian Nation, 1990.

Hajda, Yvonne. "Southwestern Coast Salish." *Handbook of North American Indians.* Vol. 7. *Northwest Coast.* Ed. Wayne Suttles. Washington, DC: Smithsonian Institution (1992): 503–17.

Jones, Joan Megan. *Basketry of the Quinault.* Taholah, WA: Quinault Indian Nation, 1977.

Olson, Ronald LeRoy. *The Quinault Indians.* Seattle, WA: University of Washington Publications in Anthropology 6:1 (1936): 1–190.

Quinault Natural Resources. Taholah, WA: Quinault Forestry Department, 1978–ongoing.

RACE RELATIONS

Race relations today for Native Americans involve contacts not only with people of European, African, Asian, and Polynesian-Pacific ancestry, but also relations with people of part-Native ancestry such as the so-called Latinos and Hispanics, as well as Mexican-Americans, Chicanos, mestizos, and Métis (half-breeds or, as I prefer, double-breeds) and people of part-African ancestry. Race probably played no part in traditional indigenous thinking except in the old meaning of race, i.e., to speak of the Irish race, the Cherokee race, or the Mexican race, meaning by that term simply a stem or branch of something larger.

The new concept of race as referring to separate, distinct divisions of humankind is a product of European rationalism and classificationism of the late eighteenth and nineteenth centuries. Closely correlated with the capture or purchase of non-whites for use as slaves and with the rise of the British, French, Spanish, and German empires came the popularization of this idea of "race," and the development of racism as a system of ideas and actions. Both have had a significant impact upon indigenous Americans.

In the early part of the twentieth century most Native Americans were subject to numerous racist laws and practices which had been adopted at various dates beginning in the seventeenth century in the English colonies, and as early as the sixteenth century in Spanish-held areas. In general, the early 1900s saw restrictive laws continuing in the United States, laws which, for example, blocked in many states intermarriage between Native Americans and people of European ancestry (or, in Louisiana and Oklahoma, between Native Americans and Africans). Those scholars who have argued that the United States' policy towards Native people was one of "assimilation" in this period must recognize that in many states Indians (especially if of "full-blood") could not go to school with white children or marry white persons.

Many aspects of federal Indian policy also smacked of racism. For example, the fact that full-bloods were less able to secure full title to allotted lands and were more restricted as "wards" than were lighter mixed-bloods illustrates a policy which can be called racist. Moreover, the discrimination practiced against "Freedmen" and "colored" citizens of the Five Civilized Tribes in the early 1900s, denying them future trust status and the right to document Native ancestry in the enrollment process, serves to reinforce the above interpretation.

United States federal Indian policy has essentially been built upon the principle that Native people did not constitute "persons" within the meaning of the Fifth and Fourteenth Amendments to the United States Constitution, thereby effectively depriving them of the protection of their traditional property rights, the equal protection of the laws, and the right to vote as citizens (until after 1924). It is hard to imagine not being "a person" when alien immigrants and nonhuman corporations were so defined by the Supreme Court, but such are the lengths to which racism can go when the confiscation of someone else's property is the object in view.

Most Native Americans in the early twentieth century were still persons of very definite nonwhite features and, usually, dark reddish-brown skin color. On the East Coast and in Louisiana and Oklahoma, some also had part-African features. These racial differences are vital if one is to understand the manner in which Indian individuals have often been treated, as, for example, in being prohibited from staying in white motels or eating in white restaurants or going to school with white children. Very often Mexicans of Indian extraction or appearance have experienced the same kind of discrimination and segregation.

In spite of the development of a racial caste system, a great deal of intermixture between Europeans and Native Americans has commonly occurred in the United States region. Many of the mixed-bloods formerly passed into white society so as to be able to escape from discriminatory statutes and prejudice. Since the 1960s, on the other hand, there has been a tendency for some of the descendants of the above to publicly reassert their Native identity. Other mixed-bloods always remained as members of tribes, sometimes intermarrying with full-bloods, but sometimes marrying each other and non-Indians, and coming to constitute almost a separate caste (as is true in Latin America).

As Native nations lost their independence and came under United States political control, the white superstructure stimulated and encouraged a system wherein mixed-bloods have often been favored over darker people, especially since the mixed-bloods often have an influential white father or other relative, became Christian, and/or spoke English, French, or some other European language. Thus by possessing a combination of biological and cultural features favored by whites, people of mixed European-American ancestry have often acquired dominance on Indian reservations and have usually excelled in education and as spokespersons, writers, businesspersons, and government employees. It is to be suspected that mixed-bloods (except for those who are part-African) continue today to receive better treatment at the hands of non-Indians than do darker, more "full-blood" looking persons. (This is, incidentally, not necessarily because mixed-bloods seek better treatment. White people simply react better, as a group, to people who resemble them racially and culturally.)

The Spanish Empire established an elaborate caste system based upon race in its territories. Many people of Native American origin in the United States originate from Mexico, Guatemala, El Salvador, and other regions where they have been strongly programmed by five centuries of racism. Thus "Indian" features and even the very term "indio" are regarded in largely negative terms. "Indian" has come to mean "backward" (or worse) and "rural" to many middle- and upper-class Latin Americans. For this reason, many Mexican-Americans, and other persons derived from former Spanish colonies, are ashamed to be seen as being "Indian," and are also prejudiced against original American facial features, hair color, and skin color.

Persons from proud, traditional, indigenous communities in Meso-America seem to wish to retain their Native identity in the United States, but many other persons from Spanish-speaking areas or marginalized communities seem to wish to deny a Native affiliation. Thus the popularity of terms such as "Latino" and "Hispanic" (Spanish, Spanish-American, Spanish origin), which seek to "sanitize" the mixed-blood with a European name. Latin, Hispanic, and Spanish all refer strictly to Europe and to European peoples. Mexican and Chicano, on the other hand, are American terms referring to the ancient Nahua-Aztec people (Mexica, pronounced Meshika).

Relations between Native Americans from the United States and persons of Mexican or Latin American origin are often close, a great deal of intermarriage having taken place from California to Nebraska and Texas to Virginia. Nonetheless, tension also exists because Native people resent the fact that many Indian-looking Latin Americans deny that they are Indian. On the reverse side, some United States federally recognized Indians discriminate against Mexican Indians, and do not want more Native people to be recognized in the United States. Tensions also exist wherever Spanish-speaking persons have come to occupy a middleman role as shopkeepers, traders, tavern operators, etc. (These roles are almost always occupied in Mexico as well by persons who are identified as white or mestizos, rather than Indian, with similar tension and antagonism.)

Indigenous Americans in the western United States have also intermarried with Chinese and Hawaiians (mostly pre-1900) and with Filipinos. Intermarriage with Black Africans has also been extensive, but is mostly pre-1907 (Oklahoma) or pre-1900 (East Coast).

The United States federal government has, since 1978, used its official system of "racial" classification to undercount Native Americans by arbitrarily denying all South American Indians the right to be classified as American Indians. Moreover, virtually all Mexican and Central American Indians, along with the above, are being classified as Hispanic because of their country of origin.

At the same time that Native people are being "disappeared" as Hispanics, there is considerable evidence that the United States Immigration and Naturalization Service is using Native American racial features as perhaps the main criteria for rounding up so-called illegal aliens from Mexico and Guatemala. Moreover, it is significant that during the 1980s and early 1990s the overwhelming majority of Indian-derived Guatemalans were denied asylum as refugees by United States officials, while the overwhelming majority of Eastern European (Soviet) applicants were being accepted. This occurred in spite of the fact that the genocide and racism directed against indigenous people in Guatemala has been well publicized, with at least a million Mayan persons forced to become refugees. European white immigrants were almost always primarily "economic" refugees in contrast, especially after "Perestroika" commenced.

Thus it would appear that anti-Indian racism is alive and well in spite of the popularity of *Dances With Wolves*.

Jack D. Forbes

See also **Chicanos as Indians; Indian Identity; Migrants and Refugees; Red-Black People**

Further Reading

Debo, Angie. *And the Waters Still Run*. NJ: Princeton University Press, 1940.

Forbes, Jack D. *Aztecas del Norte: The Chicanos of Aztlan*. Greenwich, CT: Fawcett Publications, Premier Books, 1973.

———. "Undercounting Native Americans: The 1980 Census and the Manipulation of Racial Identity in the United States." *Wicazo Sa Review* 6 (Spring 1990): 2–26.

Morner, Magnus, ed. *Race and Class in Latin America*. New York, NY: Columbia University Press, 1970.

RADIO AND TELEVISION

For most of the twentieth century, Native American communities were not involved in radio or television communications. Existing radio and TV coverage was performed by Anglo radio and television personnel.

In the 1970s the federal government saw the need for Native people to document their own history, customs, and language. The Bureau of Indian Affairs (BIA) purchased video cameras and recorders and gave this equipment to Native American tribes. It was a fine gesture, but the BIA did not provide any training funds. Without funds to train their people, most tribes just stored the equipment away in backrooms and never used it. Some tribes did take advantage of the equipment given to them and started small, limited video production departments. They used education and job training aid programs to acquaint their people with this new technology. Some of the original projects are still going today, notably within the Muskogee Creek and the Northern Ute nations.

During the last half of the 1970s, tribal councils recognized the need for self-control of media matters. Tribal radio stations began to appear with help from the United States government through the Commerce Department's National Telecommunications and Information Administration (NTIA), Public Telecommunications Facilities Program (PTFP). This program helps groups purchase equipment for radio stations, providing a more cost efficient way for tribes to take control of their own community information system.

In Alaska in the early 1970s there were two Native and one non-Native public radio stations operating. The purpose of the stations was to inform Alaska Native communities about political issues that affected their communities' land and how the legislature was handling it. The three stations hired a reporter to cover the legislature, the beginnings of the Alaska Public Radio Network.

One of the first tribal radio stations to go on the air in the lower forty-eight states was KTDB, 89.7 in Pine Hill, New Mexico, which signed on in 1972. Its stated mission is "to provide information, local, state and national and educational programming in the Navajo language." There are twenty-six tribal public radio stations and one tribally controlled commercial radio station operating in Indian country today.

Over the years, different organizations have been formed to address the need for tribal communications. The earliest was the Alaska Public Radio Network (APRN), formed in the early 1970s. In 1986, APRN started National Native News, the only nationally broadcast daily news program specifically covering Native issues. APRN has started educational training programs that address the needs of Native radio across the country. Its Alaska Native Fellowship Program (ANFP), a recruitment and one-year, full-time, on-the-job training program for radio staff, started in 1983. APRN's Indigenous Broadcast Center (IBC) started in 1991. Through its facilities and programs, IBC is helping to strengthen Native-controlled radio stations, recruit young people for media careers, and aid tribal people working in the field.

The Native American Public Broadcasting Consortium (NAPBC) started in 1978, founded on the need for balanced programming in public television. NAPBC addresses its mission by providing Native American video programs to public television stations around the country. They also fund program productions for the Public Broadcasting System (PBS).

Native American independent video and audio producers saw the NAPBC in a larger context, as an advocate not only for television, but also for radio. To address this new role, NAPBC started its radio training project in 1984. The mission of the project was to train young staff and management personnel in on-site production, supervisory techniques, and management skills. By 1986, this project changed direction. Training was still the main focus, but production took on more importance. In 1992 the American Indian Higher Education Consortium (AIHEC) and the NAPBC started the Telecommunications Project. The American Indian Radio on Satellite (AIROS) project will begin as a major cooperative undertaking by NAPBC, APRN, and the Indigenous Communications Association, in 1993.

Tribal radio stations had been operating independently of each other and had no major organization with which to network. In the late 1980s they tried unsuccessfully to organize. Station representatives met at Wingspread Conference Center in Racine, Wisconsin, in 1990. The Indigenous Communications Association (ICA), a Native communications network, was the result of that meeting. This new organization struggled for two years. In 1992, with the help of NAPBC, the tribal radio stations met a second time to strengthen ICA. Its mission is to address the issues that impact tribal radio stations and network with one another, APRN, and NAPBC.

Tribally controlled television stations in the United States are almost nonexistent. Alaska again is leading the way with its efforts to bring this new technology to Native communities. Many tribes are looking into different types of technology to use on their reservations. Low power television, satellite transmission, and the Rural Television Network options are open, but funds and personnel are not available. Some tribes have partnered with other groups to establish cooperative tribal use of time and materials at an existing television station. Most notable here is KRSC TV-35 in Claremore, Oklahoma, an educational licensed station of Rogers State College, serving northeastern Oklahoma. It also serves the needs of the six indigenous nations in that area. The Navajo Nation also produces its own style of television on its tribally owned station NNTV-5, Window Rock, Arizona.

Native American communications still have a long way to go. In the United States, there are only a few Native American professional broadcasters in television and radio compared to other ethnic groups. Training is the real need, but not the only issue that faces tribal television and radio. Organizations like APRN, NAPBC, and ICA that serve Native communications needs daily are making headway for others to follow. Native Americans are just now taking control of their own electronic destiny, and with time, new forms of communication will be theirs.

Matthew L. Jones

See also Film and Video; Periodicals

Further Reading

Kaplin, Diane. "Electronic Smoke Signals." *Main.* (July/August 1992): 1, 8.

RAMAPOUGH

The Ramapough Mountain Indians, descendants of coastal Algonquians, have over 2,500 enrolled members. For over 200 years, the Ramapough homeland has been located on the New York and New Jersey State borders from Split Rock, New York, near Suffern, to Green Mountain Valley and Fyke Creek near Darling, New Jersey. Today most of the Ramapough people are located in the village of Hillburn, New York. During the past century many families have relocated to Mahwah, New Jersey, where the tribal offices are located.

The Ramapough Nation was incorporated in 1978 and recognized by the state legislature of New Jersey in 1980. It is governed by an elected chief, subchiefs, and Council. Enrolled members sixteen years and older may vote. Beginning in 1981 the Ramapough began administering Title V Indian Education programs in the Ramapo and Ringwood area school systems.

The Ramapough sponsor an annual fall powwow held in late September or early October. The powwow, which is viewed by the Ramapough as a homecoming event, features American Indian dancers from various nations and arts and crafts made by Native people.

News related to tribal meetings, social gatherings, tribal and individual achievements, and American Indian concerns and issues are printed in *The Drum Beat*, a bimonthly newsletter.

The Ramapough Mountain Indians petitioned the United States federal government for recognition in May of 1990. Their proposed finding received a preliminary denial in late 1993. As of this writing it is too soon to know the final outcome of their petition.

Naomi Caldwell-Wood

Further Reading

The Drum Beat. Mahwah, NJ: Ramapough Mountain Indian, 1990–ongoing.

Leese, Marianne, ed. "The Ramapough Mountain Indian." *Woodsmen, Mountaineers and Bockies: The People of the Ramapos*. New City, NY: The Historical Society of Rockland County (1985): 45–51.

Salomon, Julian Harris. *Indians of the Lower Hudson Region: The Munsee*. New City, NY: Historical Society of Rockland County, 1982.

RAPPAHANNOCK

The United Rappahannock Tribe, a state-recognized enclave since 1983, was incorporated as a tribe in 1921 and again in 1976. It is located in Essex, Caroline, and King and Queen counties in Virginia. The tribe's total enrollment is about 150.

The Rappahannocks had no school at all, except for a tiny informal one run by a tribal member until the 1950s. This was due to the fact that not one of the three counties they lived in was willing to establish a school for the fragment of the group living within its boundaries. The small grade school they finally obtained was closed in 1964. They had no tribal Baptist church until 1964, and then not all tribal members enrolled in it.

The tribe is governed by a chief, assistant chief, and eight to ten councilmen who are elected for three-year terms by all enrolled, Rappahannock-descended adults aged eigthteen or over. There are closed Tribal Council meetings quarterly; general tribal meetings are held irregularly, as necessary. The tribe has worked toward establishing a tribal center for some years.

Traditional culture remains only in a few crafts (some beadwork and pottery). There are two dance groups, one with accompanying drum, which perform in pan-Indian style at many Indian and non-Indian festivals throughout the region. Otherwise, the people's language and way of life is that of their Anglo neighbors.

Helen C. Rountree

Further Reading

Rountree, Helen C. "The Indians of Virginia: A Third Race in a Biracial State." *Southeastern Indians Since the Removal Era*. Ed. Walter L. Williams. Athens: University of Georgia Press (1979): 27–48.

———. "Ethnicity Among the 'Citizen' Indians of Virginia, 1800–1930." *Strategies for Survival: American Indians in the Eastern United States*. Ed. Frank W. Porter. New York, NY: Greenwood Press (1986): 173–209.

———. *Pocahontas's People: The Powhatan Indians of Virginia Through Four Centuries*. Norman: University of Oklahoma Press, 1990.

Speck, Frank G. *Chapters on the Ethnology of the Powhatan Tribes of Virginia*. Indian Notes and Monographs 1:5. New York, NY: Museum of the American Indian, Heye Foundation, 1928.

———. *The Rappahannock Indians of Virginia*. Indian Notes and Monographs 5:3. New York, NY: Museum of the American Indian, Heye Foundation, 1928.

RED-BLACK PEOPLE

Tens of millions of persons living in the Americas (as well as others found in parts of Africa and Europe) are biologically of both Native American and African ancestry, often mixed with European as well. Such persons are especially common in the United States of America, Brazil, Venezuela, Panama, Colombia, Surinam, Puerto Rico, other Caribbean islands, Belize, the Caribbean coasts of Honduras and Nicaragua, and parts of Peru and Mexico. Considerable Native American ancestry from Brazil also exists in Ghana, Angola, and other parts of West Africa.

Many persons of African-Native American mixture do *not* identify as Native American, while others *strongly* identify with their indigenous American nation or community. Thus Red-Black people do not comprise a single ethnic group, but instead are simply a heterogeneous biological population with numerous cultural dissimilarities.

"Red-Black" or "Black-Red" is the direct translation of a Yuchi term (*Goshpi-tcha'la*) used formerly to refer to persons of mixed Native American and Black African ancestry in Oklahoma. Contrary to popular stereotypes, such persons (also known as *mulatos*, *zambos*, *lobos*, and *chinos* in Spanish-speaking Latin

America; *cafusos, caborés,* and sometimes *cabras* in Brazil; and *kaboegroes* and *muratos* in Surinam) are extremely numerous from the United States southward to Argentina. When mixed also with European ancestry, such persons are commonly known as *pardos, grifos,* or *mulatos* (or mestizos in Brazil), and people of color in the Caribbean.

Contacts between Africans and Americans may have commenced in the period from 1000 to 500 B.C., as evidenced by the huge Olmec stone heads of southern Mexico, which have African or perhaps Polynesian-like features. Since 1493 the two peoples have been in continuous contact, not only in the Americas but also in Spain, Portugal, the Canary Islands, West Africa, and other places where American slaves were shipped by the Spaniards and Portuguese or where Native Brazilian troops were used by the Dutch.

Red-Black people do not fall into any single category insofar as social identification and culture are concerned. In the United States, for example, scholarly studies since the 1920s have found that from 30 to 70 percent of African-Americans knew of Native American ancestry and that, at least in the Deep South, having American ancestry was more common than having European ancestry. Large numbers of African-Americans have continued to identify themselves as being part-Native, such as singers Pearl Bailey, Marian Anderson, Lena Horne, and Tina Turner. In fact, when one considers the massive intermixture of indigenous Americans and Africans in the Caribbean during the sixteenth and seventeenth centuries, coupled with a similar phenomenon in South Carolina, New England, and elsewhere at a later date, one must conclude that most African-Americans are part-Native American (although the actual percentage of indigenous ancestry may be slight in many cases).

But the vast majority of African-Americans do *not* belong to "Indian" communities, nor do they attempt to identify themselves as "Red-Black." Thus, they stand in contrast to several other categories of Native American-African mixed people, including individual persons today who attempt to define themselves as being *both* African and Native American, and who try to maintain connections with both Black and indigenous communities or kinfolk.

Another category of part-African persons are those individuals who reside in or stem from a Native American community and who identify as Indian or Native. These people, who are often first-generation mixed-bloods, are sometimes discriminated against for part-African features, but often are well accepted whenever they have sufficient kinfolk in the Native community. Groups as diverse as the Papago, Navajo, Ojibway, Sioux, and Caddo, among many other tribes, have at least a few members today who are part-African.

The next category consists of nations or communities where virtually the entire population is mixed American-African and where some ambiguity exists about whether the people are Indians or not. Such groups might include the so-called "Seminole Ne-

groes" of Brackettville, Texas, and Coahuila, some mixed communities of Delaware, North Carolina, and Virginia (ones which have not organized modern tribal associations), the so-called "Creole" population of the east coast of Nicaragua, and the Garifuna ("Black Carib") people of Belize, Honduras, and Guatemala. The latter are a special case, since their language is Native American, while their ancestry is perhaps more African than American. Many Garifuna are now living in Los Angeles, Memphis, and elsewhere in the United States. (Ironically, the historically related Carifuna of Dominica Island in the Antilles have lost their language, while apparently retaining a greater degree of indigenous American ancestry.)

Next it is appropriate to mention the many recognized Native Americans of the eastern United States who live on or near state-recognized reservations, or whose organized existence has long been acknowledged by scholars and by state and federal authorities. Most of these groups, found in Massachusetts, Rhode Island, Connecticut, New York, New Jersey, Delaware, Maryland, Virginia, eastern Tennessee, North Carolina, South Carolina, and Louisiana, have long provided asylum for "foreign" Indians, other people of color, and for whites seeking a respite from the racism found outside of Indian towns and homelands. As a result many of these freedom-loving tribes have absorbed varying amounts of African ancestry. This fact has not, however, made them "biracial" or "triracial" communities, since they have stubbornly adhered to a solid identity as Native Americans in spite of great obstacles. (Nonetheless, some individuals may have been forced to identify as African-American or as Caucasian when living away from home, in order to survive economically and/or socially.)

It should be stressed that most *surviving* Native communities in the above states have been ones which have attempted at various times (especially since 1865) to discourage intermarriage with African-Americans so as to avoid being reclassified as Black by white officials and legislators, or being simply overwhelmed by African ancestry due to the sheer size of the nearby Black populations. The threat of reclassification has been real (as in Virginia in the 1920s to 1950s), and some tribes were officially deprived of Indian status because of the allegation of having become Negro (such as the Gingaskin tribe of Virginia in the nineteenth century).

Finally, we must take note of central and eastern Oklahoma, where state law after 1907 prohibited the marriage of Native Americans who were *not* part-African with Native Americans who *were* part-African, or with any other persons of African ancestry. The State of Oklahoma attempted to break up the Muskogee, Cherokee, Seminole, Choctaw, and Chickasaw nations by driving a solid wall of segregation in education and social relations between former tribal citizens of non-African and part-African ancestry. This process was made easier because the federal government, when forcibly dividing up Indian lands in the early 1900s, did not give "Freedmen" who were citizens of the Five Civilized Tribes the right to document any Native American ancestry, in the cases which I have seen. Thus these "colored citizens" could be excluded from the programs of the Bureau of Indian Affairs, even though many doubtless were part-Native American by blood. Many Red-Black persons who formerly spoke Native languages have seen their children and grandchildren become simply African-Americans. Nonetheless, a degree of African ancestry is still to be found among many tribes in Oklahoma (although some groups are very reluctant to discuss the subject because of white prejudice and the recency of legal discrimination).

It should be noted that the Miskitu Nation of eastern Nicaragua, along with a number of other Indian groups in Central and South America, has absorbed African ancestry, while still retaining a strong identity as a nation of Native people. As knowledge increases, it is to be expected that more and more persons will come to accept African-Native American mixed-bloods as readily as they now accept European-Native mixed-bloods.

Jack D. Forbes

See also **Chicanos as Indians; Indian Identity; Race Relations**

Further Reading

Forbes, Jack D. *Afro-Americans in the Far West.* Washington, DC: U.S. Government Printing Office, 1969.
———. *Black Africans and Native Americans.* Oxford, England: Basil Blackwell, 1988.
———, ed. *The Indian in America's Past.* Englewood Cliffs, NJ: Prentice Hall, 1964.
———. "The Manipulation of Race, Caste, and Identity: Classifying Afroamericans, Native Americans, and Red-Black People." *Journal of Ethnic Studies* 17 (Winter 1990): 1–51.
———. *Africans and Native Americans.* Champaign: University of Illinois Press, 1993.
Katz, William L. *Black Indians: A Hidden Heritage.* New York, NY: Atheneum, 1986.
Wright, J. Leitch. *The Only Land They Knew: The Tragic Story of the American Indians in the Old South.* New York, NY: Free Press, 1981.

RED EARTH PEOPLE

See Mesquaki

RED POWER

The Red Power movement of the 1960s emerged as a direct response to implementation of federal termination and relocation policies during the 1950s. It was also a reaction to the broader socio-economic context, which found Native America by far the poorest, most disempowered, least educated, most malnourished and disease-ridden, and consequently shortest-lived sector of United States society. The slogan "Red Power"—plainly borrowed from the most militant wing of the African-American civil rights movement—reflected an increasingly pronounced sensibility among younger Indians, particularly college students, that what was needed in the face of their people's desperate circumstances was someone to take a strong stand in defense of Indian rights.

The American Indian Chicago Conference

If there was a founding moment for the movement, it came in the American Indian Chicago Conference during the summer of 1961, when a group of Native students including Clyde Warrior (Ponca), Herbert Blatchford (Navajo), Shirley Hill Witt (Mohawk), Vivian One Feather (Navajo), and Mel Thom (Paiute) openly revolted against the authority of older Indian leaders, whom they described as being "Uncle Tomahawks" and "sell-outs to the white establishment." The group formed itself into an autonomous youth caucus during the conference, hammering out and subsequently publishing a seminal manifesto entitled *A Statement of Indian Purpose.* They then repaired to the University of New Mexico where, in August, they founded the National Indian Youth Council (NIYC), an organization which was to serve as the cutting edge of Red Power politics throughout the remainder of the decade. Blatchford was named as director, Thom—nicknamed "Mao Tse Thom"—as chair, Clyde Warrior as president, and Shirley Hill Witt and Joan Noble (Ute) as vice-presidents.

National Indian Youth Council

During its first three years of existence, NIYC devoted itself mainly to recruitment and consolidation of a membership base, publishing a regular organizational newspaper entitled *ABC: Americans Before Columbus*, and forging theoretical positions. Speeches and articles by organizers had considerable influence among Indian youth, bringing NIYC membership to an estimated 5,000 at the end of 1963. Certain of the radicals' themes also had a noticeable impact in academia, finding their way into essays by established scholars, such as Cherokee anthropologist Robert K. Thomas. In early 1964 the NIYC leadership decided it was time to launch its first direct action program.

Fish-Ins in Washington State

The setting was western Washington State, a locale in which a number of small, almost landless, Native nations possessed unequivocal treaty rights to pursue traditional subsistence fishing for salmon and steelhead in their "usual and accustomed places." State officials, however, had increasingly suppressed these rights throughout the twentieth century, largely as a boon to the ever-growing, non-Indian commercial fishing industry. Despite almost continuous appeals from the Indians, the federal government—which had committed itself to enforcing the relevant treaty provisions in exchange for land cessions—had done nothing to correct the situation. As a result, the fishing nations had been left virtually destitute, and apparently without recourse.

In March 1964 NIYC organized what it called a "fish-in," sending volunteers out onto the Quillayute River to fish in defiance of Washington State regulations. When state police and game wardens arrived to arrest the NIYC volunteers, local Indians, who had gathered in large numbers along the shoreline to observe the event, began to taunt them. Shortly, local fishers began to replace the NIYC members as they were arrested, and by the end of the day literally hundreds of Native people were asserting treaty rights by fishing, whether the state liked it or not. The wardens and police retreated in disarray. The event sparked a rash of comparable actions involving several thousand Indians on several other rivers over the next several months. NIYC then called a national meeting on Puget Sound, attended by representatives of fifty-six indigenous nations across the United States, to organize a support network which would allow the peoples of the Pacific Northwest to undertake an extended fish-in campaign.

Not only did the other Indian nations rally to the cause, but it garnered the support of a number of non-Indian religious organizations, such as the American Friends Service Committee, and celebrities like Dick Gregory, Marlon Brando, and Jane Fonda. Over the next several years, despite escalating levels of official repression, much of it violent, the fishing rights struggle not only continued, but spread eastward to the larger Yakima and Colville reservations. Young grassroots leaders like Janet McCloud (Tulalip), Ramona Bennett (Puyallup), and Sid Mills (Yakima) emerged to carry the campaign to new levels of intensity.

The Boldt Decision

In 1974, confronted by the specter of an apparently endless conflict on the rivers, Federal District Judge George H. Boldt rendered a decision, upheld by the Supreme Court in 1978, that the indigenous nations of Washington held not only the right to fish, but to a full half of the annual fish harvest in the state. The state government was thus legally compelled to finally negotiate an arrangement acceptable to the Indians, a matter showing clearly that NIYC's strategy of direct action was well-founded and effective.

Indians of All Tribes

The NIYC brand of Red Power politics also set an example for groups outside the organization. In 1964, for example, a small group of Lakotas living in San Francisco occupied the former federal prison on Alcatraz Island, arguing that the abandoned facility was theirs under provision of Article 6 of the 1868 Fort Laramie Treaty. Although the courts declined to uphold their position, and the group was quickly removed by United States marshals, 1969 saw a much larger force calling itself Indians of All Tribes (IAT) retake the island under much the same premise. This time the occupiers, led by a Mohawk named Richard Oakes, announced they were prepared to defend themselves against eviction. Ultimately, the occupation lasted a year and a half, ending in June 1971. Having successfully negotiated an arrangement with the Nixon administration (later reneged on by the government), wherein Alcatraz would be converted into an Indian school and culture center, IAT then shifted its attention to support the Pit River Nation of northern California in a series of confrontations with police attempting to enforce the Pacific Gas and Electric Corporation's "ownership" of Indian land. Such tactics were also employed in occupations of abandoned federal facilities in Chicago during 1969, and a portion of the Fort Lawton Military Reservation near Seattle in 1971.

Mohawk Blockade of the Cornwall Bridge

The Mohawks of upstate New York, divided from their Canadian cousins by the international border running along the St. Lawrence River, blockaded the Cornwall Bridge in 1968. At issue was the Indians' right under the 1794 Jay Treaty to freely travel back and forth, a traffic systematically curtailed by Canadian authorities. Although a number of Indians were arrested as a result of this action, the Canadian government found it impossible to prosecute. An arrangement more-or-less complying with the treaty terms was subsequently negotiated. During this time, the Mohawks established *Akwesasne Notes*, which became the quasi-official organ of Indian militancy everywhere in North America.

The tone, tenor, and tempo of Red Power activism also had the effect of pulling some of the more conventional Native organizations into stiffer posture. For instance, the historically rather staid National Congress of American Indians (NCAI) had by the late 1960s named as its executive director Vine Deloria, Jr., a young Lakota firebrand who was shortly to author *Custer Died for Your Sins* and *We Talk, You Listen*, bestselling books, which laid the details of the movement's agenda before a truly mass audience for the first time. All told, the dynamic of Red Power thus wielded a considerable impact in terms of convincing Congress to enact progressive legislation, such as the 1968 Indian Civil Rights Act (which ended termination as a federal policy, specifically repealing Public Law 280), and the Indian Education Act of 1972. By the latter year, the early elements of Red Power had been largely supplanted by the more coherent and unified American Indian Movement (AIM), a formation which came to be known as "the shock troops of Indian sovereignty." Undeniably, however, it was the pioneering efforts of groups like NIYC and IAT which set the stage for what was to come.

Ward Churchill

See also **Alcatraz Occupation; American Indian Chicago Conference; American Indian Movement; Fishing and Hunting Rights; Government Policy; Indian Education Act, 1972; International Indian Treaty Council; National Indian Youth Council; Russell Tribunal; Trail of Broken Treaties; Wounded Knee II**

Further Reading

American Friends Service Committee. *Uncommon Controversy: Fishing Rights of the Muckleshoot, Puyallup and Nisqually Indians.* Seattle: University of Washington Press, 1970.

Blue Cloud, Peter, ed. *Alcatraz is Not an Island.* Berkeley, CA: Wingbow Press, 1972.

Deloria, Vine, Jr. *Custer Died for Your Sins: An Indian Manifesto.* New York, NY: Macmillan Publishers, 1969.

Josephy, Alvin M., Jr. *Red Power: The American Indians' Fight for Freedom.* New York, NY: McGraw-Hill Publishers, 1971.

Steiner, Stan. *The New Indians.* New York, NY: Harper & Row, 1968.

RELIGION

American Indian religions have undergone considerable change in the twentieth century, under duress from mainstream American culture. Many American Indians have become Christians, although a substantial number of these continue to engage in aboriginal religious expressions. Prohibitions against the free exercise of Indian religions in the early part of the century have given way to popular appreciation of Indian spirituality in recent years, and Indians have revived some aspects of their traditional religions as a dimension of cultural and political revitalization since the 1960s. Today there is a range of religious orientation in various Indian communities.

Aboriginal Indian religions north of Mexico were locally produced modes of relationship between communities of associated individuals and their ultimate sources of life. Each tribal group conceived of these sources as spiritual entities—persons and powers—which the community attempted to engage as relatives, and which revealed themselves through the forms of the natural world: winds, sun, thunderers, animals, corn, etc. The proper relationships of these entities to human and nonhuman beings constituted to each community a way of life. North American tribal religions were performative, oral, and variable within each community, as each generation drew upon tradition in order to create its own religious forms derived from experience. Although each community practiced its own religion, its own way of life, intertribal contacts were constant, producing diffusion of many religious traits. Emergence myths, bear ceremonialism, shaking tent divination, green corn fasts and feasts, sun dances, vision quests, guardian spirit complexes, and totemism are only several of the most salient features common to many Indian tribes.

At the turn of the twentieth century, North American Indian religious traditions were under duress. The aboriginal patterns of subsistence—the gathering, hunting, fishing, and farming economies that had developed over thousands of years—were either deteriorating or were already devastated by the American juggernaut. Indian religious beliefs and practices had been based upon these activities of sustenance, and the demise of the material bases left many religious expressions without a frame of reference or an immediate purpose. In addition, the kinship communities that were bound together through spiritual and ritual commonality were losing their cohesion and autonomy under United States (and Canadian) pressure. Around 1900 anthropologists were attempting to "salvage" the remains of the "disappearing" Indian ways of life. These scholars often found it difficult to reconstruct aboriginal religious beliefs and activities, or to find informants who could speak knowledgeably about the religious life of former times.

The United States (and Canadian) Indian bureaucracies were intent upon eradicating Indian paganism" in its most apparent forms. From 1881, the United States Bureau of Indian Affairs (BIA) had been issuing directives to its agents to prohibit Indian "dancing," "giveaways," and other religious behaviors. Indian police arrested sundancers, potlatchers, ceremonial clowns, etc., and courts of Indian offenses sentenced them to prison terms and awarded fines. The continual target for these attacks was the Plains Sun Dance, which was forced into disuse or seclusion. The persecution functioned as part of the general United States aggression against Indian ways of life.

As aboriginal religions were being undermined, new religious movements were evolving. The various prophet cults, eschatalogical rituals, ghost dances, etc., of the late nineteenth century continued to exert an influence on Indian rituals and values in the twentieth century. The famous Ghost Dance initiated by the Paiute Wovoka led to the most infamous assault on Indian religious practitioners in 1890 at Wounded Knee (Pine Ridge, South Dakota), where the United States Cavalry gunned down several hundred Sioux ghost dancers. The Peyote Religion—with its cultus of sacramental ingestion of the mildly hallucinogenic cactus, *Lophophora williamsii*—was already well developed in Indian Territory, the Southern Plains, and the Southwest. Its emissaries traveled to Indian communities throughout the western half of the United States (and into Canada), bringing with them a semichristianized ethos of peace and Native solidarity, as well as a myth-ritual complex that postulated a divine universe concerned about the Indians' welfare, and which communicated with them through the mediation of peyote.

Some new religions, e.g., the Indian Shakers of Washington State (begun by Squaxin Indians, John and Mary Slocum in 1882) were explicit in their use of Christian theology and liturgy, perhaps in order to protect themselves from governmental persecution. Others, like the Bole-Maru cult in California, were grounded primarily in Native form and function. All addressed the crises of the Indian ways of life, for example, the degenerative state of Indian health. Some of these movements fell into immediate disuse; others persist to the present day. Some were reintegrated into tribal traditions; others criticized traditions. Some remained local phenomena; others spread from tribe to tribe, becoming pan-Indian in ideology and performance.

American institutions helped foster this pan-Indianism. Boarding schools brought Indians together from a variety of tribes. Railroads, mail service, the English language, reservations (not to mention Indian Territory), all served as the infrastructure through which intertribal marriage occurred. Pan-Indianism did not nullify local aspects, but sometimes enhanced them, sometimes submerged them. Regional patterns substituted for village distinctiveness, and certain characteristics of an Indian religiousness began to take shape. A self-conscious idealization of the "old ways" took place, as religious visionaries, prophets, and functionaries took aim at American culture. In this regard, Mother Earth became the transcendent icon for an environmentalist, kinship-based, pan-Indian religiousness.

Under these forces, local tribal religions withered in the first half of the century. In some communities—particularly those with less cogent means of local authority—the various aspects that had characterized the religious matrix atrophied and even ceased to function. Some tribal peoples ceased telling their ancient myths, or began to regard them as fictional fables (or indecent tales), rather than revelations of sacred knowledge. Many rituals disappeared from use, as specialists died without passing down authorization to the next generation. Some rituals became incomprehensible to those who continued to carry them on in truncated form. Vision quests for guardian spirits ceased to occur, as youths spent their formative years in boarding schools, and as non-Indians intruded into the wild areas inhabited by the spirits. Faith in the medicinal prowess of local healers underwent severe damage, as newly introduced diseases (such as tuberculosis, or the influenza epidemic of 1918) defied traditional curing techniques. Ecstatic soul-flight and sorcery came to be regarded by some as superstitious notions, under the skeptical influence of outsiders. The balanced interplay between individual beliefs and community worship came unglued as Indian social systems collapsed under pressure from missionary, educational, medical, and bureaucratic intrusions.

Yet, there was religious persistence in many Indian communities, especially those with organized social structures, priesthoods, and institutionalized means of apprenticeship. The Pueblo liturgical year continued to address the needs of tightly knit, agricultural communities. Navajo singers continued to treat numerous diseases with rituals based on mythological models. Potawatomi elders continued to lecture their congregations at naming ceremonies, funerals, and other rites of passage of the individual life-cycle. Lakota holy men continued to smoke their prayer-filled pipes. Ojibwas continued to dread the appearances of preternatural *windigos* (cannibal spirits). Sweat lodges, midwinter thanksgivings, midsummer busks, animal-bone ritualism, kiva organizations,

etc., persisted, as did Indian spirituality, yearning for expression.

In some cases the twentieth century brought about increased institutionalization of Native forms, such as the bishops of the Indian Shaker Church, or the state-by-state incorporation of the Native American Church (Peyote Religion), beginning in 1918, or the more recent Medicinemen's Association among the Sioux. These legal structures seem to have been designed not for the needs of the believers, but rather as protective devices against attacks from non-Indian authorities, although sometimes the attackers have been tribal governments, e.g., the Zuni and Navajo Tribal Councils that attempted to prohibit peyotism.

At the same time, Christianity became by the twentieth century the traditional religious expression of tens of thousands of Indians. In some communities, Christians (at least in name) constituted two-thirds of the Indian population. The Penobscots and Passamaquoddies of Maine, and the Pueblos of New Mexico, had embraced Catholic religiousness (willingly, or under coercion) in the seventeenth century, and although non-Christian religiousness persists among these peoples, so does Catholicism. The Houma Indians of Louisiana intermarried with Frenchmen in the eighteenth century, adopting not only their names and language, but also their Catholicism. The Cherokees converted to various Protestant modes in the early 1800s and have regarded those denominations as their own to this day. Even for those tribes who encountered Christianity for the first time only in the mid-nineteenth century, like the Skagits of Washington or the Sioux of the Dakotas, the twentieth century has witnessed Christian fervor and several generations of continuous Christian culture. The search for the unreconstructed aboriginal in the twentieth century—e.g., the Lakota Sioux holyman of *Black Elk Speaks* (1932)—often turns up a Christian, in Black Elk's case, a committed Catholic catechist.

In 1934 Commissioner John Collier ordered an end to BIA prohibitions against Indian religions. Despite opposition from Christian missionaries and BIA personnel, Collier's directive regarding Indian religious freedom resulted in the resurfacing of religious phenomena that were thought by outsiders to have disappeared. Plains Indians once again celebrated Sun Dances in public. The World War II years and the postwar policies of relocation and termination set back the resurgence of the 1930s. The ideology of the melting pot in the 1950s made distinctive Indian expressions unfashionable, and the increasing urbanization of Indian populations led to an unsettling of kinship-based, nature-directed religious forms.

Nevertheless, two related movements of the 1960s—the pan-Indian political activism (grounded to some degree in the Black civil rights movement and mainstream "counterculture"), and the pan-religious ecumenism of American Christian churches following the Second Vatican Council (1962 to 1965)—opened the way for Indians to reassert their "traditional" values and spirituality (suffused as they were with Christian elements) in an atmosphere of toleration and even support from non-Indians. One can find, for example, that an Iroquois community (St. Regis), founded by zealous Catholic Mohawks in the mid-eighteenth century, began to feel the impact of "traditional" Longhouse practitioners who drew upon the semi-aboriginal, semi-Christian pronouncements of the early nineteenth century Seneca visionary Handsome Lake. These Longhouse activists were asserting treaty rights against the obstructions of the United States and Canada, and their political goals fitted their religious ideology. Over the 1960s and 1970s, "St. Regis" became "*Akwesasne*" (a Mohawk term) in common parlance, and a struggle ensued between the longhouse and the church for the hearts and souls of the local Iroquois. In similar fashion, traditionalists asserted their powers of prophecy and authority in diverse tribal groups, such as the Hopis of Arizona, the Miccosukees of Florida, the Ojibwas of Minnesota, and the Creeks of Oklahoma. These traditionalists have had an undisguised political agenda of increasing Indian sovereignty, and their religious expressions have sometimes taken a "fundamentalist" tone, i.e., they have claimed to possess a set of explicit truths that are not to be subject to criticism or deviation, and which serve as radical critiques of modern American culture, from which they feel besieged. The American Indian Movement (AIM) employed a superb exponent of this radicalized neo-orthodoxy in the spiritual politics of the late Creek medicine man, Phillip Deere. By the early 1980s, Deere was hosting an annual youths and elders conference on his land in Oklahoma, at which he exhorted "born-again pagans" from across North America to live an environmentally conscious, kinship-based, ritually purified life. These conferences dovetailed with gatherings of the International Indian Treaty Council (the foreign policy wing of AIM), at which Deere and others represented themselves as the protectors of Mother Earth against the encroachments of the United States and other imperialist nations. Such religious activists expedited the revival of sweat lodges, vision quests, pipe ceremonialism, etc.

The Second Vatican Council of the early 1960s helped produce in American Christianity a revolutionary open-mindedness toward all religious cultures. Not only Catholics, but also mainline Protestants, came in the 1970s to reconsider their missionizing tactics among American Indians. Many Christian organizations apologized for their past intolerance, and encouraged the expression of Native cultural (and religious) forms in Christian worship. While Indian scholars such as Sioux Vine Deloria, Jr. (the son of two prominent Christians) were excoriating the Christian crushing of Indian religions, the Christian ministers in the field were setting about to "inculturate" the local liturgies: calling for sacred pipes to be smoked on the altars, for example. Dialogues took place between medicine men and clergymen. Christian

Indians who had hidden from whites their use of traditional religious forms were now inviting priests and nuns to come in to sweat, smoke, and pray with them.

Given the freedom to express their Indian religiousness within a Christian context, some Indian ritualists have chosen to "compartmentalize" their religious lives, keeping separate their Native and Christian faiths, employing them alternatively as the need arises. Others have practiced "syncretism" openly, combining their Indian and Christian beliefs and practices into a single religious way of life. On some reservations, there are Christian sweat lodges, Christian vision quests, and Christian healing masses.

John Hascall, an Ojibwa medicine man and Catholic priest, has travelled to Indian communities throughout the United States and Canada for the past decade, combining his Native Midewiwin and his charismatic Catholicism into an appeal for Indians to heal their alcoholism and feelings of inferiority through self-esteem and divine aid. Hascall's program is similar to those employed by various twelve-step sobriety programs, but with a spiritual orientation, e.g., the Pilgrimage of the Blackfeet in Montana, and the Sacred Circle therapy of the Great Lakes and Plains Indians.

The effects of vocal traditionalism and post-Vatican II pan-religious ecumenism are now felt in "new age" spirituality across America, where some non-Indians are turning to supposed Indian traditions (the "Hopi Way," the "Navajo Way," etc.) and purported Indian spokespersons (Sun Bear, Lynn Andrews, etc.) for inspiration to heal the malaise of post-modern America. It is an irony not lost on contemporary Indians that the century that began with the suppression of Indian religions is coming to a close with the romanticizing of those same forms of spirituality. Indian religious practitioners began the century as outlaws; today they are exemplars.

Despite the liberalization of American attitudes toward Indian religions in recent decades—as expressed in the 1978 American Indian Religious Freedom Act, for example—there are still situations in which Indian religious practice is obstructed by United States policies and by the American way of life. Indians find themselves infringed in their sacramental use of peyote; they are prevented from performing sweats and other rituals in prisons and other authoritarian institutions; their ancestral remains are unearthed by pothunters and stored in museums, alongside sacred artifacts that have been taken from the Indian communities that produced (and continue to revere) them; their sacred sites (burial grounds, vision questing areas, etc.) are desecrated by dams, roads, ski resorts, etc. Although greater sensitivity has been evident in recent years regarding the repatriation of religious artifacts and bones, the two most recent Supreme Court cases involving Indian religious rights—*Lyng v. Northwest Indian Cemetery Protective Association* (1988) and *Employment Division v. Smith* (1990)—demonstrate little understanding or concern for Indian religion on the part of the American judicial elite.

The religious patterns of contemporary Indian peoples vary from place to place, and often from person to person. The Hopis in Arizona continue to communicate with their deities through community-wide ceremonials. Clans are still responsible for particular rituals throughout the round of the liturgical year. The rituals (and the clans themselves) have the ultimate aim of assuring fertility in the world and in the tribe. Each February kachinas (masked impersonators of the deities) enter the kivas (underground chambers that recall the underworld from which the Hopis emerged in primordial time) to perform Bean Dances, in order to expedite the germination of bean seedlings. In August, during the non-kachina season, Hopis dance the Snake ritual in the plazas, in order to show reverence for chthonic powers that provide crops with strength. Hopi men still make pilgrimages to the *sipapu* ("the place of emergence") in the Grand Canyon, where they collect salt for their villages. Some Hopis are Christians (e.g., Mormons); however, aboriginal religiousness still flourishes in public and in secret.

The Houma Indians of Louisiana achieve their spiritual goals of binding themselves to God and to each other through the American Christian calendar; Easter, Christmas, All Saints Day, and the Feast of Christ the King are some of their holiest days. They worship in Christian churches with their non-Indian neighbors, engage in ecumenical dialogue, make pilgrimages to Medjugorje in Yugoslavia in the hope of encountering the Virgin Mary face-to-face. Their foremost religious leader is their Native Catholic priest, Roch Naquin, who is director of the Cursillo Movement in the Diocese of Houma-Thibodaux, and who blesses the fishing boats of his parishioners every spring.

At San Ildefonso Pueblo in New Mexico, Catholicism also runs strong; however, the ancient masked dancers of the kiva societies make regular displays of their spiritual prowess: on the Feast of San Ildefonso, January 23, animal dancers come down from the hills at dawn and perform homage to the natural world throughout the day, stopping for a time in the morning to allow the community to attend Mass in the village church. The Catholic realm and the realm of the deer and buffalo impersonators come together for one juncture after Mass, when the Catholic priest greets the dancers at the church gate. For the most part, the San Ildefonso Indians live two parallel, compartmentalized religious lives, in a pattern that goes back to the late seventeenth century.

At Pine Ridge, South Dakota, the Lakota Sioux both compartmentalize and syncretize their Native and Christian traditions. In addition, there exists a substantial Peyote Religion which overlaps the other two. In the course of a year, a Lakota may participate in many sweats (non-Christian and Christian), numerous pipe ceremonies (including some in church), a number of sun dances, weekly Christian worship, and an occasional *Yuwipi* rite, at which spirits are summoned to aid the community, as well as a number of all-night peyote rituals. Some Lakotas emphasize the continuity between these various modes of religiousness; others keep them separate in concept and practice.

At Lummi, in the northeast corner of Washington State, Nooksack and other Coast Salish people gather for a lengthy memorial service for a recently deceased man. The ceremonial time is divided among Christian pentecostals, Indian Shakers, traditional *seeyowin* (spirit) dancers, and representatives of a new religious sect from the Yakima Reservation—a combination of Shaker and spirit dancer traits, called the Seven Drum Religion. Each group takes its turn in helping send the soul of the dead safely to the other world, and in comforting the living. In the Coast Salish communities of Lummi, Tulalip, Swinomish, and others, spirit dancers still train novices in the art of receiving songs from the ancestors and the spirits of nature. "Babysitters" initiate these Red and Black Paint "Babies" through fasting and sometimes rough sensory bombardment, until the initiates holler their spirit songs in smokehouses during the winter ceremonial season. Masters of *Squeedeelich* (power boards) are able to use their spirit powers to perform divination: recovering lost bodies and souls.

In New York City, Chicago, Denver, Los Angeles, and in numerous other urban environments, some American Indians assimilate to mainstream religious culture, attending a variety of Christian churches, or abandoning the trappings of organized religion. Others make regular visits to their reservation homelands to participate in rituals, and participate in urban sweat lodges, powwows, peyote services, and healing ceremonies. For the majority of contemporary Indians, the city is the setting for various religious ways of life.

Christopher Vecsey

See also American Indian Religious Freedom Act; Indian Shaker Church; Missions and Missionaries; Peyote Religion; Sacred Sites

Further Reading

Beck, Peggy V., and Anna L. Walters. *The Sacred: Ways of Knowledge, Sources of Life*. Tsaile, AZ: Navajo Community College, 1977.

DeMallie, Raymond J. *The Sixth Grandfather. Black Elk's Teachings Given to John G. Neihardt*. Lincoln: University of Nebraska Press, 1984.

Hultkrantz, Åke. *The Study of American Indian Religions*. New York, NY: Crossroad, 1983.

Vecsey, Christopher. *Handbook of American Indian Religious Freedom*. New York, NY: Crossroad, 1991.

RELOCATION

See Government Policy; Urbanization

REPATRIATION OF HUMAN REMAINS AND ARTIFACTS

An important issue facing Native Americans in the twentieth century is the repatriation of Native American human remains, associated grave goods, and cultural artifacts. Although no even reasonably accurate figures exist, it has been estimated that the remains of as many as 600,000 Native Americans are held in university, museum, historical society, and private collections in the United States, and as many as 2 million are held worldwide. How many associated grave goods and cultural artifacts are held is pure speculation. Moreover, it is estimated that the remains of hundreds of Native Americans and associated artifacts are uncovered every year. Most American Indian and other Native American peoples (that is, Native Hawaiian Islanders as well as Eskimos and Aleuts) attach an important spiritual quality to the human remains of their ancestors and consider many of their cultural artifacts as sacred. That ancestral remains and sacred objects are held by museums, scholarly and other institutions, and even private individuals, is a source of considerable discomfort to Native peoples. That many of these were obtained illegally adds to this discomfort, as well as legitimizes claims for repatriation of any Native American human remain or artifact. Perhaps of even more importance, many Native Americans think that treating their human remains as objects of curiosity or even scientific study is not respectful to them or their ancestors.

Native Americans feel that repatriation must occur despite any scholarly or public good that may be derived from the remains or objects and the study of them. In contrast, many scholars and other people argue that the scientific and public values of the remains and artifacts outweigh any claim Native Americans may have on them. They argue that the scientific value is important not only to the public at large, but also to Native peoples themselves as scholars attempt to reconstruct histories of Native Americans. Human skeletal remains have become even more important as objects of study, they assert, given recent advances and probable advances in scientific technology. These advances include the detection of immunoglobulins and DNA sequencing from bone, which could enable scholars to establish past disease experiences, in the former instance, and establish generic relationships among populations, in the latter instance. Moreover, science progresses and unforeseen as well as foreseen advances will enable scholars to learn increasingly more from the remains. Similarly, there are those who argue that cultural objects of Native Americans now existing in museums and educational institutions belong not only to Native Americans but to all Americans, even all peoples of the world. They are part of the heritage of all people, not only Native American people.

Native American remains and Native American artifacts have been objects of study and intrigue to non-Native Americans for centuries. The excavation of Native American burial sites and mounds dates from the eighteenth century. Thomas Jefferson excavated burial mounds on his property in Virginia, and in so doing Jefferson became the "father of American archaeology." He wrote of his excavation, "I conjectured that in this barrow might have been a thousand skeletons." The Smithsonian Institution opened in 1846 and provided further impetus for the development of American archaeology. Important, of course, were Native American remains and cultural objects. In 1868 the surgeon general of the United States ordered that a collection of Native American crania be developed for study, supposedly to determine if Native Americans were "inferior" to other Americans. As a result over 4,000 Native American skulls were collected—from burial scaffolds, graves, and battlefields—and sent to the Army Medical Museum. Other museums participated in the endeavor of collecting Native American skeletal remains, including the American Museum of Natural History and the Field Museum of Chicago.

Virtually all of the 4,000 crania at the Army Medical Museum were eventually transferred to the Smithsonian's National Museum of Natural History to add to the remains of approximately 14,500 other Native Americans there. This supposedly represents the largest single collection of Native American remains in the United States, followed by some 13,500 held by the Tennessee Valley Authority, and approximately 11,000 held by the University of California (mostly at its Berkeley campus).

During the past few decades, Native American groups and individuals have increasingly demanded that ancestral remains and sacred objects be returned to them for proper disposal or care. Recently, Native Americans in the United States have been successful in obtaining the passage of federal and state laws not only preventing the further disenfranchisement of remains and objects, but also repatriating remains and objects to appropriate tribes and individuals. Native peoples in Canada have also raised similar issues, but such changes in Canadian law have not yet occurred. Landmark state legislation in the United States was Nebraska's 1989 Unmarked Human Burial Sites and Skeletal Remains Protection Act. In so passing the Act, Nebraska became the first state with a general repatriation statute. It provides for the protection of unmarked burial sites throughout the state and the repatriation (within one year of a request) to relatives or American Indian tribes of human remains and associated "burial goods" held in state-sponsored or state-recognized public bodies.

During the twentieth century, the federal government has increasingly enacted legislation aimed at protecting the rights of Native American groups vis-à-vis ancestral remains and sacred objects. Recently, such legislation has often been the result of an increased vocalness and political sophistication on the part of the Native American groups themselves.

Native groups have successfully lobbied lawmakers and obtained public support for their repatriation efforts in recent decades. Twentieth-century legislation may be dated from the Antiquities Act of 1906, which granted the federal government jurisdiction over all aboriginal remains and artifacts on federal property. Other important legislation in this regard includes the Historic Sites Act of 1935 (supplemented by the Reservoir Salvage Act of 1960), the National Historical Preservation Act of 1966, the Department of Transportation Act of 1966, and the National Environmental Policy Act of 1969. In 1978, the American Indian Religious Freedom Act was passed; it specifically addressed Native American cultures. This was followed shortly after by the Archaeological Resources Protection Act of 1979, which specifically mandates that the American Indian Religious Freedom Act be considered in the disposition of archaeological resources. Recently even more important federal legislation was enacted. The first was Public Law 101-185 in 1989, which established the National Museum of the American Indian as part of the Smithsonian Institution. A component of this law mandated the return of Native American human remains and funerary objects held by the Smithsonian to appropriate individuals and groups. In 1990, Public Law 101-601, the Native American Graves Protection and Repatriation Act, was established. It specifically considers the disposition of Native American human remains and artifacts in federal agencies (other than the Smithsonian), *as well as* in institutions receiving federal support. It increases the protection of Native American graves on federal and tribal land, makes the commercial traffic of Native American remains illegal, requires the inventory and repatriation to culturally affiliated tribes or descendants of all collections of Native American remains and associated funeral objects held by federal agencies and federally funded museums (and universities), and requires the repatriation of Native American sacred objects and cultural patrimony under certain conditions. ("Cultural affiliation" is defined to mean: "that there is a relationship of shared group identity which can be reasonably traced historically or prehistorically between a present-day Indian tribe or Native Hawaiian organization and an identifiable earlier group.") Recently, the Smithsonian Institution made the decision to adhere to Public Law 101-601 as well as Public Law 101-185, thereby extending the mandate of repatriation to include not only human remains and funerary objects, but also sacred objects and objects of cultural patrimony to Native American groups. The National Museum of the American Indian Act of 1989 (Public Law 101-185) contains a provision whereby a Repatriation Review Committee be appointed "to monitor and review the inventory, identification, and return of Indian human remains and Indian funerary objects." This committee is to be composed of five individuals, at least three of which are to be selected from individuals nominated by Native American groups themselves.

The Committee was impaneled in March 1990: four of the five members were selected from those nominated by Native American groups, and two of these are American Indians. Specifically, the committee's duties, as stated in Public Law 101-185, are: "(1) with respect to the inventory and identification, ensure fair and objective consideration and assessment of all relevant evidence; (2) upon the request of any affected party or otherwise, review any finding relating to the origin or the return of such remains or objects; (3) facilitate the resolution of any dispute that may arise between Indian tribes with respect to the return of such remains or objects." The collections of the Smithsonian's newly created National Museum of the American Indian, however, are not under the purview of this committee; rather, the Museum's repatriation activities are the responsibility of its own board of trustees. The Museum's repatriation policy was established early in 1991, and it has its own policy and procedure for "(1) the repatriation of Native American human remains and funerary objects; (2) the repatriation of objects of religious, ceremonial and historical importance to Native American peoples, communally owned tribal property, and other property acquired by or transferred to the Museum illegally."

In accordance with its own established procedures, some of the approximately 18,500 skeletal remains in the collections of the National Museum of Natural History have been repatriated by the Smithsonian to Native American groups, including some to Hawaiian Islanders. To date, the largest number of repatriated remains have been returned to Larsen Bay, Alaska—756 skeletal specimens (not necessarily whole skeletons). These were part of a site on Kodiak Island excavated by the Smithsonian physical anthropologist Ales Hrdlicka between 1932 and 1936, which yielded in excess of 5,000 artifacts and several hundred human remains. (Decisions regarding the return of artifacts and other skeletal remains from this site are currently pending.) The Smithsonian has also returned sets of human remains to the Sisseton-Wahpeton Sioux (of South Dakota), and the return of remains to Pawnee, Cheyenne-Arapaho, and Nevada Indian groups are currently being considered. Other museums, institutions, agencies, and collectors have also returned Native American skeletal remains. For example, California Indian remains have been repatriated to appropriate groups by the Catholic church, and the State of Nebraska has returned Pawnee and Omaha remains.

Various cultural and sacred objects have also been returned, by the Smithsonian and other museums, institutions, and private individuals. For example, wampum belts have been returned to the Iroquois, medicine bundles and prayer boards have been returned to the Navajo, Hopi, and Mohawk, a Sacred Pole has been returned to the Omaha, as have the skeletal remains and burial offerings of almost one hundred Omaha held by the University of Nebraska, and several dozen Zuni War Gods have been repatriated to them (these represent virtually all such War Gods known to exist).

As it has developed, the repatriation of human remains became polarized between advocates of reburial and advocates of study and preservation in repositories. Little compromise has occurred. Recently, however, many would argue that compromise to one degree or another is not only necessary but desirable. New, creative ways of Native Americans and scholars, particularly physical anthropologists, relating to one another are necessary. Science and scholarship have much to offer to Native Americans, as Native Americans attempt to recapture their lost histories. Native Americans are no longer powerless in American society; they are important actors in shaping their own destinies, and their wishes must be respected.

Russell Thornton

See also **Archaeology; Museums**

Further Reading

American Indian Sacred Objects, Skeletal Remains, Repatriation and Reburial: A Resource Guide, 1992 Update to 1990 Guide. Comps. Rayna Green and Lisa Thompson. Washington, DC: The American Indian Program, National Museum of American History, Smithsonian Institution, 1992.

Layton, Robert, ed. *Conflict in the Archaeology of Living Traditions.* London, England: Unwin Hyman, 1989.

Price, H. Marcus, III. *Disputing the Dead: U.S. Law on Aboriginal Remains and Grave Goods.* Columbia: University of Missouri Press, 1991.

"Repatriation of American Indian Remains." Spec. ed. *American Indian Cultural and Research Journal* 16 (1992).

Ubelaker, Douglas H., and Lauryn Guttenplan Grant. "Human Skeletal Remains: Preservation or Reburial?" *Yearbook of Physical Anthropology* 32 (1989): 248–82.

RESERVATIONS

Reservations constitute a fundamental aspect of the past and present history of Indian-White relations. Broadly defined, Indian reservations are land areas that as a result of Euroamerican colonization and partial extinguishment of Indian aboriginal title were expressly set aside or acquired for the occupancy and use of Indian tribes (and their remnants).

Early reservations were created by the colonies and some were subsequently recognized by state legislatures as state Indian reservations. The 1990 United States Census listed twelve state reservations. In 1990 their combined total Indian population was reported at less than 1,000 residents.

By far greater and more significant is the number of existing federal Indian reservations; except for the Annette Island Indian Reserve of some 1,200 Tsimshians, Haidas, and Tlingits in southeastern Alaska, all federal reservations are located in the lower forty-eight states, mostly west of the Mississippi River, and in the Great Lakes region (see maps). In 1990 the Bureau of Indian Affairs (BIA) recognized 287 land areas as federal Indian reservations (reservations proper, Pueblos, rancherias, etc.), with a total resident Indian population of about one million, nearly half the total American Indian population.

Federal Indian reservations were established or confirmed after 1778 by federal treaty or statute conferring to the occupying tribe(s) recognized title over lands and resources within their respective boundaries. Recognized title is a full property right protected by the Fifth Amendment.

Before the turn of the century, 56 of the 162 federal reservations then existing were established by executive order, giving rise to the question of whether Indian title was held to be permanent. The permanency of the federal reservation tenure, whether based on treaty, congressional act, executive order, or a combination thereof, was recognized under the General Allotment Act introduced in 1887. After 1919, reservations could only be established by act of Congress.

Over 56 million acres of mostly reservation land are today held in trust by the United States for tribes and individual Indians. About 82 percent of this Indian estate is owned by tribes, a little over 17 percent by individual Indians, and less than one percent by the government. In the case of communally owned tribal lands, individual tribal members are generally granted so-called "assignments" for the purpose of erecting a residence or conducting subsistence and other economic activities. Tribal assignees have surface use rights over their respective assignments, according to the terms of the license issued by the tribe. Indian tribes exercise powers of self-government over their respective reservations, within the jurisdictional limitations set by Congress.

The largest federal reservation is the 16-million-acre Navajo Reservation in Arizona, New Mexico, and Utah, home to some 200,000 Navajos. The Navajo Reservation is unique in that after its establishment in 1868, it was progressively expanded by executive orders and acts of Congress until it completely engulfed a small enclave of Southern Paiutes (who were granted federal recognition in 1990) and, more significantly, it surrounded traditional Hopi land. The ambiguous wording of the 1882 executive order establishing a reservation for the Hopi "and such other Indians as the Secretary of the Interior may see fit to settle thereon" eventually led to the modern Navajo-Hopi land dispute. The passage in 1974 of the Navajo-Hopi Settlement Act (P.L. 93-531), and subsequent partition of the two tribes' Joint Use Area, was followed by the disruptive relocation of several hundred Navajo families from Hopi Partition Land, and by the resistance to removal of a core of Navajo traditionalists. The issue remains unsettled in 1993.

Also in Arizona are some of the largest reservations, including Tohono O'odham (2.7 million acres, about 17,000 Papago), San Carlos (1.8 million acres, 7,800 San Carlos proper, Pinal, and Arivaipa Apaches), and the adjoining Fort Apache (1.6 million acres, 12,000 White Mountain Apache). Other large reservations are Uintah and Ouray (1 million acres, over 3,000 Northern Ute residents) in Utah; Wind River (1.8 million acres, 7,000 Eastern Shoshone and Northern Arapahoe) in Wyoming; Crow (over 6,600 residents) and Fort Peck (6,700 Assiniboine and Sioux) both in Montana, each comprising about 2 million acres; Colville (1.4 million acres, 4,400 descendants of a dozen confederated Salish and Sahaptian-speaking tribes) and Yakima (one million acres, 13,000 descendants of fourteen confederated Yakima tribes) in Washington State; and three Teton Sioux reservations in South Dakota, namely, the famous Pine Ridge Reservation (1.5 million acres, home to some 20,000 Oglalas), Cheyenne River (1.4 million acres, 12,000 Minneconju, Sans Arc, and Two Kettle Sioux), and Standing Rock (one million acres, over 5,800 Hunkpapa and Sihasapa [Blackfeet] Sioux), which extends into North Dakota. By contrast, California rancherias and many of the smaller reservations in California, Nevada, Oregon, and Washington are less than 1,000 acres with only a few hundred Indian residents or less.

As a consequence of allotment, most reservations have a large number of non-Indian residents, many of whom own or lease land within their boundaries. The BIA estimated that by 1980 non-Indians comprised nearly half the residents on federal Indian reservations. Although in theory the presence of non-Indian land owners and lessees on Indian reservations does not alter the status of reservations as defined by law, it has contributed to jurisdictional ambiguity and continuing disputes between tribal, federal, and state authority. Combined with the checkerboard and fractionate ownership pattern present on practically all the midwestern, Plains, and Pacific Northwest reservations, this situation has considerably hampered tribal economic development.

Under attack from allotment at the turn of the century, revived in the 1930s and 1940s by tribal reorganization, again threatened by termination in the 1950s, Indian reservations have, during the second half of the twentieth century, strengthened their role as a focal point for the retention of American Indians' separate tribal identities, and for the consolidation of tribal self-determination. The persistence of unique tribal traditions and dozens of distinct tribal languages still spoken on reservations perpetuate the reservation-tribe axiom.

At the same time, since the 1970s, reservation tribalism has also been paralleled by, and to some extent has merged with, the modern pan-Indianism of the Plains-styled "powwow culture." Mixed blessings have come to the reservations from massive federal subsidies, which are partially responsible for lack of economic self-sufficiency, and growing bureaucratization of tribal governments; together with the ever-present paternalism of the BIA this situation has fostered what has been labeled the "hostile dependency" of reservation Indians towards the dominant society. As history shows, white colonization and inconsistent federal policies are indeed largely responsible for the anomalous socio-cultural, economic, and political status of today's Indian reservations.

Origins and Background

In its purpose the reservation concept has today completed a full cycle, undergoing a series of periodic changes that have reflected the Indian policies of the colonial powers and of the United States. Still, in its theoretical basis, the principle of reserving specific areas for the ownership, occupancy, and use of Indians has remained essentially unaltered, stemming from the fundamental recognition by Euroamericans that American Indians, though originally regarded as culturally inferior, constitute distinct socio-political entities possessing natural "right of soil." White newcomers eagerly pursued the acquisition of the Indian right of the soil, not only by legal purchase and exchange through treaties and agreements, but often illegally by force. As a result, only a fraction (less than 5 percent) of the aboriginal American Indian land base remains today under Indian control; reservations are one tangible expression of this control, which, due to historical circumstances, is subject to the plenary powers of Congress and limited by past and present legislation.

The recognition and protection of Indian property and rights, although inconsistently applied, was initially the primary reason for establishing areas exclusively reserved for Indians. Spain issued land grants to the Indian Pueblos of the Southwest that were later honored by Mexico and the United States. The colonies reserved lands for Indians to regulate trade and to protect them from encroachment by other tribes and settlers.

As pressure on Indian lands grew, in 1763 the British Crown assumed central control of Indian affairs and established a boundary line along the Appalachians separating the colonies from "Indian country," reserved exclusively for the Indians. After independence, the United States, too, adopted a national Indian administration through the Constitution, which gave Congress plenary powers over Indian affairs. Federal Indian policy initially aimed at preserving a permanent, separate "Indian country." But the failure of four Congressional Trade and Intercourse Acts to safeguard Indian territorial integrity led in 1823 to the recognition by the Supreme Court that the United States, as successor and inheritor of England's title of discovery, was entitled to extinguish by purchase, exchange, or conquest the recognized Indian right of occupancy.

Between 1820 and 1840 numerous eastern and midwestern tribes were forcibly removed west of the Mississippi (regarded as a "permanent" Indian frontier), to Indian Territory, an area originally comprising most of present-day Nebraska, Kansas, and Oklahoma, and reduced to part of the latter after 1865.

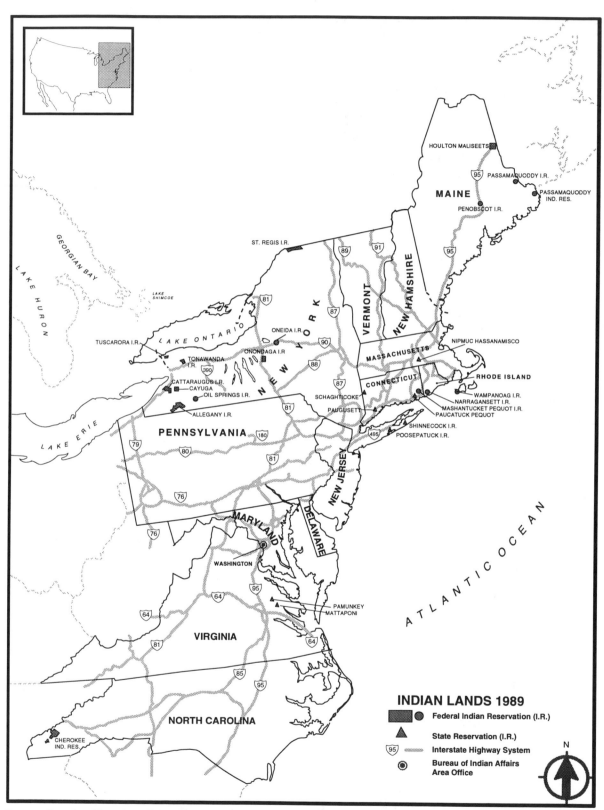

GEORGIAN BAY

LAKE SIMCOE

LAKE HURON

LAKE ONTARIO

LAKE ERIE

HOULTON MALISEETS

PASSAMAQUODDY I.R.

PASSAMAQUODDY IND. RES.

MAINE

PENOBSCOT I.R.

ST. REGIS I.R.

NEW HAMPSHIRE

VERMONT

N E W   Y O R K

TUSCARORA I.R.

TONAWANDA I.R.

ONEIDA I.R

ONONDAGA I.R

NIPMUC HASSANAMISCO

MASSACHUSETTS

CATTARAUGUS I.R.

CAYUGA

OIL SPRINGS I.R.

CONNECTICUT

RHODE ISLAND

ALLEGANY I.R.

SCHAGHTICOKE

PAUGUSETT

WAMPANOAG I.R.

NARRAGANSETT I.R.

MASHANTUCKET PEQUOT I.R.

PAUCATUCK PEQUOT

PENNSYLVANIA

SHINNECOCK I.R.

POOSEPATUCK I.R.

NEW JERSEY

DELAWARE

MARYLAND

WASHINGTON

ATLANTIC OCEAN

PAMUNKEY

MATTAPONI

VIRGINIA

INDIAN LANDS 1989

Federal Indian Reservation (I.R.)

State Reservation (I.R.)

Interstate Highway System

Bureau of Indian Affairs Area Office

NORTH CAROLINA

CHEROKEE IND. RES.

N

Source: Based on Maps from U.S. DEPARTMENT OF THE INTERIOR BUREAU OF INDIAN AFFAIRS

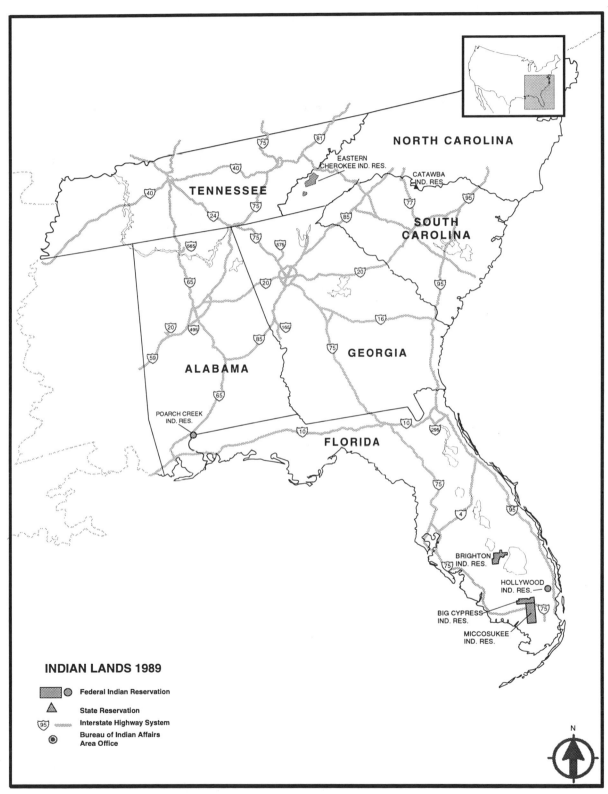

INDIAN LANDS 1989

- Federal Indian Reservation
- State Reservation
- Interstate Highway System
- Bureau of Indian Affairs Area Office

Source: Based on Maps from U.S. DEPARTMENT OF THE INTERIOR BUREAU OF INDIAN AFFAIRS

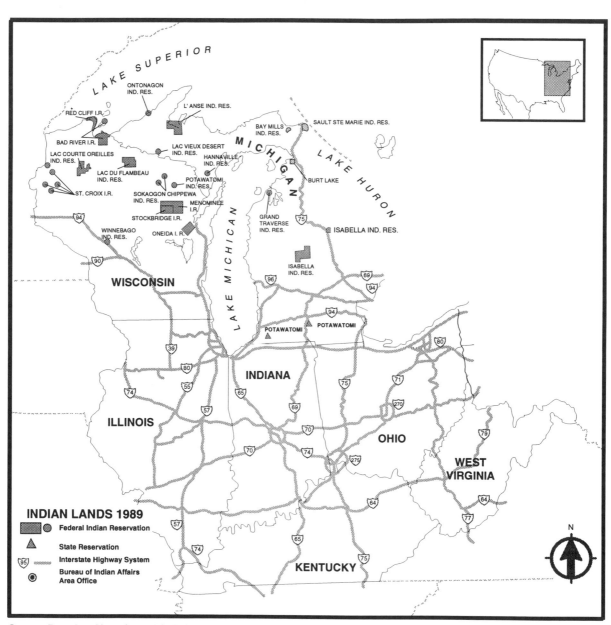

Source: Based on Maps from U.S. DEPARTMENT OF THE INTERIOR BUREAU OF INDIAN AFFAIRS

ARKANSAS

LOUISIANA

MISSISSIPPI

MISSISSIPPI
CHOCTAW IND. RES

TUNICA-BILOXI IND. RES.

COUSHATTA IND. RES.

CHITIMACHA IND. RES.

INDIAN LANDS 1989

Federal Indian Reservation

State Reservation

Interstate Highway System

Bureau of Indian Affairs
Area Office

N

Source: Based on Maps from U.S. DEPARTMENT OF THE INTERIOR BUREAU OF INDIAN AFFAIRS

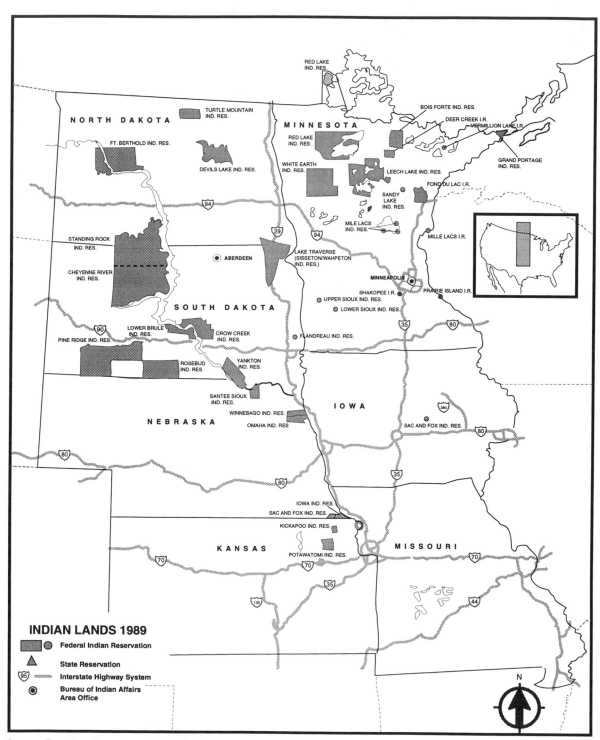

INDIAN LANDS 1989

Federal Indian Reservation

State Reservation

Interstate Highway System

Bureau of Indian Affairs Area Office

Source: Based on Maps from U.S. DEPARTMENT OF THE INTERIOR BUREAU OF INDIAN AFFAIRS

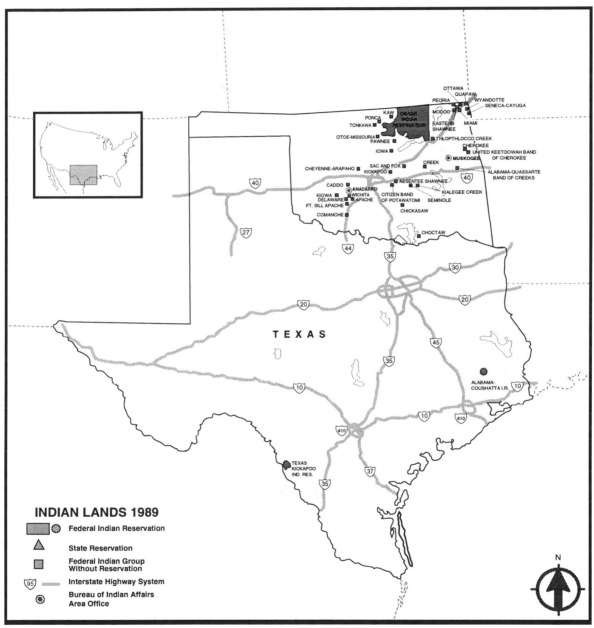

INDIAN LANDS 1989

Federal Indian Reservation

State Reservation

Federal Indian Group
Without Reservation

Interstate Highway System

Bureau of Indian Affairs
Area Office

Source: Based on Maps from U.S. DEPARTMENT OF THE INTERIOR BUREAU OF INDIAN AFFAIRS

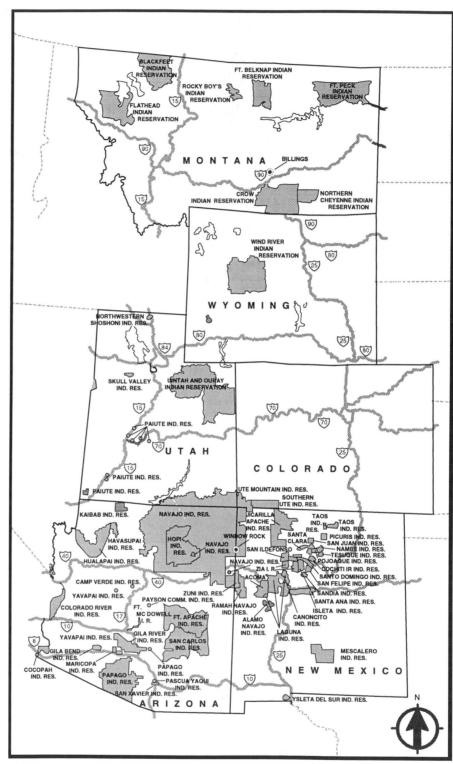

INDIAN LANDS 1989

▨ ⬤	Federal Indian Reservation
▲	State Reservation
⑨⑤ ~~~	Interstate Highway System
◉	Bureau of Indian Affairs Area Office

Source: Based on Maps from U.S. DEPARTMENT OF THE INTERIOR BUREAU OF INDIAN AFFAIRS

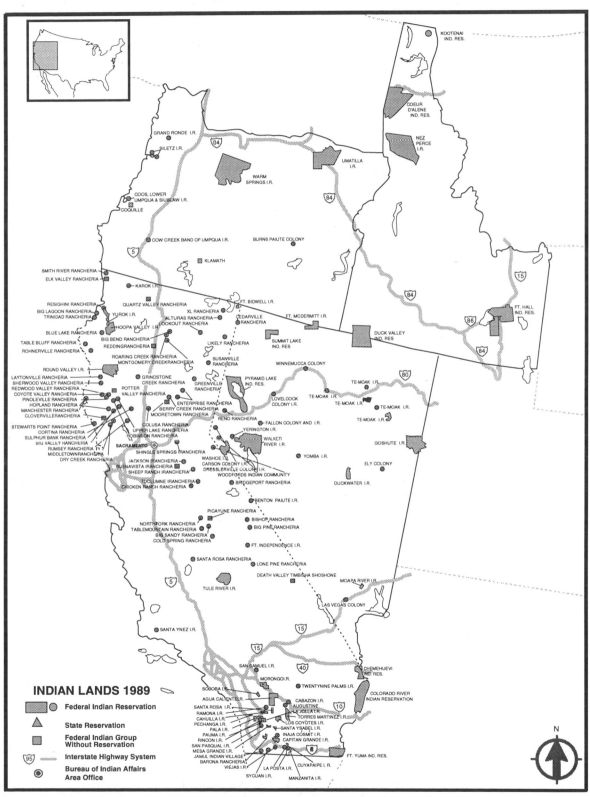

INDIAN LANDS 1989

Federal Indian Reservation

State Reservation

Federal Indian Group
Without Reservation

Interstate Highway System

Bureau of Indian Affairs
Area Office

Source: Based on Maps from U.S. DEPARTMENT OF THE INTERIOR BUREAU OF INDIAN AFFAIRS
For Alaska and Washington State lands see maps on pages 8 and 686

By the mid-nineteenth century, under pressure from a growing and westward moving American population, the government replaced the idea of a vast western Indian country "protected" by a single Indian frontier, with the policy of forcing tribes onto selected reservations; these "islands" of land were to be reserved for Indians and administered for them by white superintendents and agents of the Indian Office.

The confinement of Indians to reservations was pursued through an intense treaty-making policy, backed by military force. Between 1778, date of the first United States treaty with the Delaware, and 1871, when Congress unilaterally ended nearly a century of treaty-making, some 370 treaties brought Indian tribes under the trusteeship of the United States, requiring massive, repeated Indian land cessions, and defining the nature and extent of the lands and rights tribes were to reserve onto themselves. The reservation system opened millions of acres of ceded Indian lands to white settlement, facilitated government control over tribes, increased Indian dependency, and laid the basis for the policy of forced assimilation. With reservation life, American Indians entered a period of profound socio-psychological and economic disintegration, increased tribal factionalism, and erosion of traditional tribal authority. Only to a limited extent during reorganization, and eventually more consistently with self-determination, was this trend partially reversed.

Jurisdiction

Reflecting the inconsistency of federal Indian policy, the jurisdictional question on Indian reservations became ambiguous and contradictory, as it remains today. Original exclusive tribal jurisdiction within reservation boundaries was expressly limited in 1885 by Congress with the passage of the Major Crimes Act (23 Stat. 385). The following year, in *United States v. Kagama* (118 U.S. 375), the Supreme Court reversed its earlier 1883 decision in *Ex parte Crow Dog* (109 U.S. 556), and upheld the exercise of congressional power over Indians and their reservations while restricting that of the state (to crimes between non-Indians and selected civil matters).

In theory, as summarized in 1977 by the American Indian Policy Review Commission, "in the absence of express Federal statutes altering the jurisdictional pattern, Indian reservations are geographic areas, governed by tribal law, where State and Federal jurisdiction do not reach." However, both the Congress and the Supreme Court have repeatedly limited tribal sovereignty and jurisdiction. In the 1978 *Oliphant v. Suquamish Tribe* (435 U.S. 191) the High Court found that a tribe has no criminal jurisdiction over non-Indians within the reservation boundaries. And recently, in 1992, the Supreme Court upheld a tax imposed by Yakima County, in Washington State, on land privately owned by Indians on the Yakima Reservation. The Court based its opinion on the century-old General Allotment Act, which in the Court's view allows Yakima County to impose a property (ad valorem) tax on reservation land patented in fee to individual Yakimas pursuant to the act. Thus, a century after allotment, the property of Indian families and the sovereignty of tribes are again threatened by the dominant society, in violation of Indian rights that reservation boundaries were supposed to delimit and protect.

Allotment

By the end of the nineteenth century, rather than safe-havens, reservations had turned into confined areas of neglect and despair for some 250,000 "vanishing" American Indians. Reservations were now perceived as an obstacle to Indian "civilization" and progress. Dissatisfaction with the reservation system and pressures from the states to open Indian lands to white settlement led to the passage in 1887 of the General Allotment Act, or Dawes Act (24 Stat. 388). More than 100 reservations saw much of their communally owned lands broken up in individual tracts of 160 acres or less.

Particularly significant was the reduction of the Great Sioux Reservation into six separate allotted reservations in 1889 (25 Stat. 888). With the sole exception of the Osage, a few years prior to Oklahoma statehood in 1907, the reservations of the several tribes concentrated in Indian Territory, including those of the Cherokee, Chickasaw, Choctaw, Creek, and Seminole (the so-called Five Civilized Tribes), were dissolved and redefined as "historic areas." During less than 50 years of allotment, tribal holdings went from over 136 million acres in 1887, to about 48 million in 1934, when the policy was abandoned.

An indirect, positive sideline of allotment (with its emphasis on making self-sufficient farmers out of all Indians) was the 1908 *Winters* decision (207 U.S. 564), in which the Supreme Court recognized by necessary implication the water rights of reservation Indians.

Tribal Reorganization

The failures of allotment and forced assimilation, deplorable living conditions on Indian reservations marked by widespread disease, malnutrition and even starvation, plus the urgent need for a reform of the Indian office were denounced in 1928 by the Meriam Report. The Indian New Deal inaugurated in 1934 under Commissioner John Collier brought a major change with the Indian Reorganization Act (IRA) (48 Stat. 984) in the perception and administration of Indian reservations. Reservations were now seen as a potential basis for tribal reorganization, revitalization of tribal, social and cultural traditions, identity and values, and for the strengthening of tribal governments.

The IRA stopped allotments and introduced land reclamation, conservation, and economic development projects. Between 1935 and 1937 alone, over 2 million acres were added to the total Indian land holdings. Tribes also regained control of 7 million acres of grazing land that had been leased to white cattlemen. The ban on traditional ceremonies was lifted, and improvements were made in Indian education and health. Better qualified BIA personnel were hired in Washington or assigned to the reservations. In 1936, the Oklahoma Indian Welfare Act (49 Stat. 1967) restored tribal governments, but not their reservations, to the Oklahoma tribes.

Termination and Restoration

The political and cultural strengthening of tribes, the persistence of their unique identity, and the consolidation of their separate land base were antithetic to the assimilationist philosophy of the American melting pot. The special "quasi-dual citizenship" status of Indians, as both members of tribes and as United States citizens (fully since 1924), was regarded as contradictory and anachronistic in a modern and prosperous America. Following World War II, the government pursued the withdrawal of its federal trusteeship over tribes; reservations were once again perceived as an obstacle to the "emancipation" of Indians. In 1953, House Concurrent Resolution 108 declared the congressional intent to make American Indians "subject to the same laws and entitled to the same privileges and responsibilities as are applicable to other citizens of the United States." Soon thereafter, Congress passed Public Law 83-280 (67 Stat. 588), terminating federal supervision and control over selected tribes, and granting most criminal and civil jurisdiction to certain named states.

The Menominee, Klamath (including Modoc and Yahooskin), the Alabama-Coushatta, Southern Paiute, Mixed-Blood Ute, Confederated Tribes of Siletz Indians, Confederated Tribes of the Grand Ronde Community, Catawba and Ponca tribes, plus some forty California Indian rancherias were terminated and their reservations dissolved. Nonreservation Oklahoma tribes like the Wyandotte, Peoria, and Ottawa were also terminated.

By the mid-1960s the policy was abandoned; a decade later, starting with the Menominee in 1973, many of the terminated tribes and rancherias began to be restored to federal trust, including the Siletz in 1977, Ottawa, Peoria and Wyandotte in 1978, the Paiute Tribe of Utah in 1980, Confederated Tribes of Grand Ronde in 1983, Klamath in 1986, and the Ponca Tribe of Nebraska in 1990. Where applicable, congressional restoration also called for the subsequent establishment of a reservation.

In strictly numerical terms, the effects of termination were limited; between 1953 and 1964, only some 13,000 of a total Indian population of 450,000, and less than one-and-one-half million acres of reservation land (about 3 percent of total Indian trust land) were affected. As a policy, however, termination had a strong psychological and political impact on American Indians who unified against it and contributed to its defeat. Similarly negative in its socio-psychological effects, though limited in its quantitative impact, was a parallel program administered by the BIA during the termination years. A policy of actively assisting reservation Indians to relocate to urban areas was pursued to alleviate the chronic reservation problems of unemployment, lack of educational opportunities, poor living conditions, and inadequate medical care, now compounded by a rapidly growing reservation Indian population (see figure). In less than ten years, a little over 33,000 reservation Indians participated in the program. Confronted with the hard reality of urban life, with a culture so different from their own, and often facing racial discrimination, many relocatees eventually left the cities and made it "back to the rez."

Estimates of Indian Population Residing on or Adjacent to Federal Reservations

Year	Rounded Estimate	Source
1900	250,000	Commissioner of Indian Affairs
1920	334,000	Commissioner of Indian Affairs
1940	382,000	Commissioner of Indian Affairs
1960	473,000	Bureau of Indian Affairs
1980	750,000	Bureau of Indian Affairs
1990	950,000	Bureau of Indian Affairs

Includes historic areas of Oklahoma.

Problems and Prospects

The partial reflux to the reservations helped educate urban and reservation Indians, at a crucial time of growing Indian political consciousness, about their rights and the unfulfilled responsibilities of the federal government. The resulting climate of Indian militancy of the 1960s and 1970s contributed to the passage in 1975 of the Indian Self-Determination and Education Assistance Act (P.L. 93-638), setting the stage of the new policy of government-to-government relations with the tribes adopted by the Reagan and Bush administrations and subsequently upheld by President Clinton. But Indian militancy also highlighted the tensions and contradictions present on reservations. The bureaucratic control still exercised by the BIA, interference of state and federal authority in tribal affairs, and pressures by private corporate interests often compound historically rooted tribal factionalism (usually between, but not limited to, sociological full-bloods and sociological mixed-bloods) and exacerbated the power struggle for political and economic control of many reservations' rich mineral, timber, and water resources.

The pervasive split and antagonism between the elected Tribal Council and the traditional leadership at the Hopi Reservation, the now "historic" 1973 occupation of Wounded Knee on Pine Ridge Reservation by members and supporters of the American

Indian Movement, the recent ousting on corruption charges of Navajo Chairman Peter MacDonald, and confrontations between opposite Mohawk factions at St. Regis Reservation are examples of the internal strife affecting numerous reservations.

Internal problems are compounded by increased tension between reservation Indians and surrounding white communities over treaty-based Indian fishing, hunting, and trapping rights that extend outside of the reservation boundaries, particularly in western Washington and the Great Lakes area. The animosity has fostered the stereotypical perception that reservation Indians are "privileged" with respect to the wider American citizenry. A growing movement among rural white Americans, backed by political opportunists, is again calling for abrogation of treaty rights and termination of Indian reservations. This call for termination is also supported by those who perceive the reservation status as a main cause of pervasive dependency and apathy among today's reservation Indians.

Regardless of undeniable overall progress since the days of abuse and neglect of a century ago, in the closing decade of the twentieth century, Indian reservations continue to offer a contradictory scenario. The poverty rate is more than double the national figure. Unemployment remains over 50 percent on most reservations; chronic unemployment is accompanied by chronic alcoholism, in a vicious cycle of cause and effect that brings deaths, disintegration, and violence to many Indian families. Nearly one-fourth of reservation Indian housing units are still substandard. The increasing institutionalization of child care and elderly care reflects the reduced traditional role of the extended family and kinship network in caring for the young and old in modern reservation life.

Despite these and similar problems, nearly half the total American Indian population in the United States continues to reside on reservations. The Indians' strong sense of "place" is tied to tribal identity and culture; the reservation is synonymous with home, family, community, and tribe. A number of tribes require birth on the reservation as one of their criteria for tribal membership. Pervasive among American Indians is the intrinsic religious nature of the land; its sacredness is reflected in tribal ceremonies and traditional initiation, puberty, and curing rituals performed periodically on reservations. The new pride in tribal identity and "Indianness" of the last three decades has promoted intergenerational ties, with a positive image projected on elderly tribal members, regarded as a living link with the tribal past, and keepers of the tribal language and traditions. Annual ceremonies and social gatherings on reservations bring families together and strengthen kinship networks and reciprocal obligations, balancing somewhat the negative impact on Indian families of alcoholism, unemployment, and partial acculturation to white individualism.

Economic considerations reinforce socio-cultural motivations in keeping or bringing Indians back to the reservation: tribal and federal programs, from education to medical care, from housing to a variety of food and other assistance programs for the poor, provide reservation Indians with a safety-net not available off the reservation. The reservation status exempts resident Indians from federal income taxes on income from trust lands; from state income taxes on income earned on the reservation; from state sales taxes on transactions made on federal reservations; and from local property taxes, although the recent Supreme Court decision could jeopardize this aspect of reservation immunity from taxation. Thus, to the uncertainty of limited opportunity in the white man's world, many American Indians prefer the relative "security" of poverty on their reservations.

During the 1980s reservation status prompted tribes to open their own gaming activities, particularly bingo, which are now operant on some one hundred and fifty reservations in 24 states. Despite the contingent and unpredictable nature of the gaming-generated revenues, the opposition to gambling of a certain segment of the tribal population, and the danger of organized crime moving onto reservations, such activities have had an immediate beneficial impact on reservation economies.

While historically rooted problems continue to affect reservation life, some younger resident Indians find themselves increasingly unable to cope with life off the reservation; the "rez" seemingly offers partial "protection" from the modern white world and its contradictions. In doing this, the reservation system may contribute to creating new generations of Indians who are socially dysfunctional with regard to the dominant society. A viable policy of tribal economic development and self-sufficiency that emphasizes exchange with, rather than dependency on, the dominant society may be an alternative to the negative effects of chronic dependency and reservation isolationism. Fortunately, also, growing numbers of educated American Indian professionals are committing themselves to work on the reservation for the benefit of the tribal community.

An American Indian historian, Donald L. Fixico (Sac and Fox), recently introduced the concept of "parallel coexistence" in describing the aspirations of today's Indian tribes; for better or worse, since their establishment, reservations have been the basis for the parallel status of American Indians. The extent to which new generations of American Indians working for the improvement of Indian life on reservations will be able to safeguard these same reservations from the threat of neo-termination advocated by modern critics of Indian treaty rights and self-determination, will depend both on the will of Indian people, and the future direction of federal Indian policy.

Cesare Marino

See also **Allotment; Economic Conditions; Economic Development; Federal and State Recognition; Fishing and Hunting Rights; Gaming; Government Policy; Indian Country;**

Meriam Commission; Navajo-Hopi Land
Controversy; Sovereignty and Jurisdiction;
Treaties; Urbanization

Further Reading

Castile, George Pierre, and Robert L. Bee, eds. *State and Reservation: New Perspectives on Federal Indian Policy.* Tucson: University of Arizona Press, 1992.

Lopach, James J., Margery H. Brown, and Richmond L. Clow. *Tribal Government Today: Politics on Montana Indian Reservations.* Boulder, CO: Westview Press, 1990.

Matthiessen, Peter. *Indian Country.* New York, NY: Viking, 1984.

Presidential Commission on Indian Reservation Economies. *Report and Recommendations to the President of the United States.* Washington, DC: The Commission, 1984.

Sturtevant, William C., ed. *Handbook of North American Indians.* Washington, DC: Smithsonian Institution, 1978–ongoing.

Sutton, Imre. *Indian Land Tenure: Bibliographical Essays and a Guide to the Literature.* New York, NY: Clearwater, 1975.

U.S. Dept. of Commerce. *Federal and State Indian Reservations and Indian Trust Areas.* Washington, DC: U.S. Government Printing Office, 1974.

RESTORATION

See Government Policy: Termination and Restoration

RIBBONWORK

Ribbonwork is a hybrid craft combining European materials and techniques with Native American designs. Its origin is found in the applique and other needlecrafts of colonial North Americans, as well as in the Native American crafts of paint, quills, beads, weaving, and birch-bark cutouts. The development of the craft among Native Americans followed European settlers as they moved ever westward.

Ribbonwork has a 3,000-mile distribution, from the St. Lawrence Seaway, throughout the Great Lakes area, and into Oklahoma; specimens in museum collections represent more than forty different nations. Ribbonwork also has a two-hundred-year history—from its earliest practice, to its highest development in the nineteenth century, to its decline in the early twentieth century, and finally to its reemergence during the rise of the Native American civil rights movements of the 1970s. To understand who makes and uses ribbonwork today, it is necessary to understand the history and distribution of the craft as it developed.

The earliest use of ribbons can be found as simple uncut fabric decorations and is found among many groups that never developed formal ribbonwork. True ribbonwork is made of brightly colored silk ribbons, cut and sewn into strips which are then attached to items of clothing and other paraphernalia. There are four styles of ribbonwork.

Winnebago shawl, early twentieth century. Ribbonwork in Developmental style, combined with Positive style in traditional manner. Courtesy of the Denver Art Museum, 1950.54. Photo by Otto Nelson.

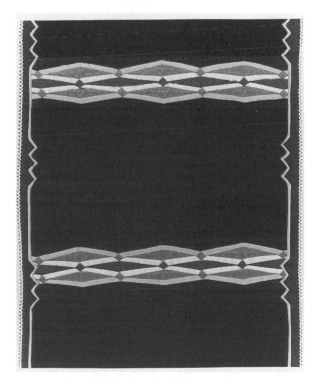

Detail from Osage breechcloth in Shingled style of ribbonwork made by Georgeanne Robinson. Howard Collection. Courtesy of the Milwaukee Public Museum, 64586.

The simplest and earliest style is made of ribbons cut in simple saw-tooth designs, applied to a base cloth or another ribbon. Native Americans in Maine and neighboring areas of Canada made the most elaborate panels of "Developmental" style.

Another early style of ribbonwork is made in successive layers of Developmental strips, like the shingles of a roof. This "Shingled" style appears early among the Iroquois and Miami, where it reached a high level of elaboration, with many layers of ribbons (sometimes more than thirty-five), a variety of colors, and numerous detailed designs. Oklahoma Osage and Delaware ribbonworkers today specialize in this Shingled style, and some modern artisans produce ribbonwork that rivals earlier masterpieces.

The other two styles of ribbonwork are each made of two pairs of ribbons, joined along a center seam. If the top layer of ribbons creates the figure of the design, then the style is called "Positive"; if the bottom layer of ribbons creates the figure of the design, then the style is called "Negative."

Positive style apparently developed in the early to mid-nineteenth century from quilting patterns (the quilting, not the piecing) in the western Great Lakes area. Positive figures tend to be floral and curvilinear and are reminiscent of many other Victorian designs, including architectural embellishments and furniture. Positive style ribbonwork was highly developed among the Menominee and Winnebago, who still make it today in Wisconsin. It is the most commonly made style of ribbonwork among modern craftsmen. Negative style figures tend to be geometric. This style appears to be the last to develop, and its origin may be found among the Osage and Delaware of Oklahoma in the late nineteenth century.

Following the dislocations of the nineteenth century, ribbonwork appears to have declined among many of the original producing groups. By the twentieth century, the ribbonwork tradition was carried on by only a few practitioners, and the craft had died out among many nations.

During the 1930s interested government agents worked with individuals in Oklahoma to collect information about ribbonwork and at the same time to reintroduce the traditional craft to people who had forgotten it. The ultimate influence of non-Indians on this process has yet to be determined, but by the middle of this century Native Americans were visiting museums, inspecting traditional items, and re-creating them on their own initiative.

By the mid-1970s there were a number of well-known fine ribbonwork craftsmen in Oklahoma and

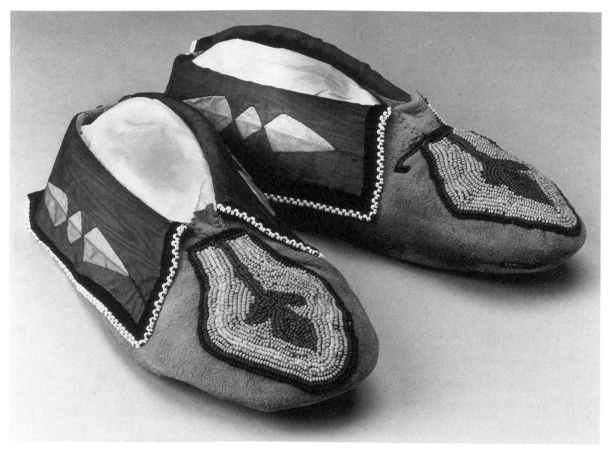

Delaware mocassins, 1970. Ribbonwork done in Negative style by Nora Thompson Dean. Howard Collection. Courtesy of the Milwaukee Public Museum, 64792.

Kansas, representing Delaware, Kickapoo, Osage, Pawnee, Sac and Fox, and other tribes. They made fine pieces for personal use as well as for sale. Museums and Indian agencies were teaching the traditional craft, while non-Indians produced a similar product for profit. In addition, hobbyists tried their hands at ribbonwork for their "authentic" costumes.

The mid-twentieth century production of ribbonwork saw a number of differences from its traditional form. Originally, all ribbonwork was hand sewn, frequently with ornamental embroidery on Positive-style pieces. Ribbonworkers were female, learned the craft from women relatives, and specialized in their own tribe's styles and designs. Designs belonged to the person who created them, and they were sometimes named.

Pieces produced primarily for traditional, ceremonial, and domestic purposes demanded high quality execution, which took great time and labor for production. Many modern craftsmen continue to create fine pieces in their tribal styles for a specialized market that discriminates on the basis of authenticity.

However, as public interest in Native American crafts generated a wider market for ribbonwork, pressure to produce the craft for economic profit meant that its quality frequently declined. Many who had no interest in making the craft before (including men) became producers; some entrepreneurs were not even Indians, and some set up small shops and hired non-Indian seamstresses.

The introduction of the sewing machine allowed mass production with fewer ribbons, simpler figures, and less embellishment. Simple Positive strips are the most commonly made style of ribbonwork among all craftspeople, especially those who use a sewing machine to do the applique. Sometimes craftspeople used cotton and synthetic yard goods instead of silk ribbons to make nontraditional items such as pillow shams, quilts, curtains, and European-style clothing. Although some of this work was quite good, those entrepreneurs who made no effort to follow the rigours of traditional production flooded the market with inferior products. Certainly, they did not follow traditional tribal identification with certain styles, and the craft had not been passed down from one generation to another.

As the fad for ethnic goods wanes, these inferior products have passed from the market. Meanwhile, Native Americans, connoisseurs, and the general public still appreciate well-made, traditional ribbonwork. The many examples of elaborate and technically accomplished museum and modern specimens demand our respect and admiration.

D.K. Abbass

See also Art

Further Reading

Abbass, D.K. "Contemporary Oklahoma Ribbonwork: Styles and Economics." Ph.D. diss., Southern Illinois University, Carbondale, 1979.

———. "American Indian Ribbonwork: The Visual Characteristics." In *Native American Ribbonwork: A Rainbow Tradition.* Ed. George Horse Capture. Cody, WY: Buffalo Bill Historical Center, 1980: 31–43.

———. "American Indian Ribbonwork." *Lore: Quarterly of the Milwaukee Public Museum* 36 (Summer 1986): 8–15.

Horse Capture, George C., ed. *Native American Ribbonwork: A Rainbow Tradition.* Cody, WY: Buffalo Bill Historical Center, 1980.

Marriott, Alice. "Ribbon Applique Work of North American Indians, Part I." *Oklahoma Anthropological Society Bulletin* 6 (1958): 49–59.

Pannabecker, Rachel K. "Ribbonwork of the Great Lakes Indians: The Material of Acculturation." Ph.D. diss., Ohio State University, 1986.

Sac/Fox ribbonwork dress, pre-1960. Ribbonwork done in Positive style by Mabel Harris. Attached to modern dress by Alice Marriott. Courtesy of the Oklahoma Museum of Natural History, University of Oklahoma, NAM 10-7-8.

ROCKY BOY CHIPPEWA-CREE

See Cree; Ojibwa: Chippewa in Montana

RODEOS

"The immense popularity of rodeo and the marked preoccupation with it throughout the American Great Plains is a phenomenon . . . for here is an event which obviously holds deep meaning for a large segment of the regional population," writes Elizabeth Lawrence. "The contests and performances of rodeo are remarkably patterned and repetitive, comprising a kind of ritual event which serves to express much that is significant not only in the lives of its participants and audiences, but also within the society that endorses it."

Indian people have long held the belief that there is a sacredness and unique relationship with animals. This belief is evident in their philosophy, religion, and spirituality; it continues to exist today. Animals were also vital to Indian lives for food, transportation, economic livelihood, and social position. On the Plains, the concern with the human-animal relationship expanded into acknowledging those who displayed horsemanship skills. Plains Indian equestrian skills equalled those of the best horsemen anywhere.

Rodeos, events that are intensely competitive and interactive, are closely linked to the cowboy and ranch life introduced by Euroamericans in the nineteenth century. Initially, Indian rodeo was an unorganized activity generally conducted at the local community level by ranchers and livestock owners. It was often held in conjunction with horse racing activity. Its origin dates back at least to the 1940s, when contests were held in the Southwest, the Northwest, and Great Plains states. Since then, Indian rodeo has continued to grow and gain popularity in both Indian and non-Indian communities.

Small rodeos are held in conjunction with Indian fairs and powwows. The number of contestants and the size of the purses have increased, necessitating the development of rules and regulations. Most rules are patterned after those of the Professional Rodeo Cowboys Association. As a result, regional organizations with rules to regulate rodeo events have emerged throughout the United States and western Canada.

Rodeo events include saddle bronc, bareback bronc and bull riding, calf roping, team roping, steer wrestling, and ladies' barrel racing. Youth events include boys' steer riding and girls' break-away calf roping and barrel racing. Notable Indian rodeo contestants and performers include Jackson Sundown, Will Rogers, Tom Three Persons, Kenny McLean, Larry Condon, Joe Chase, Pete Fredericks, Howard Hunter, Leo Camarillo, Tee Woolman, and Bobby Harris.

By the late 1960s, there were several regional all Indian rodeo organizations at various stages of development. In an effort to elevate the growth and development of Indian rodeos to a higher level of competitive expertise and progress, the Indian National Finals Rodeo was established in 1976. Initially partially federally funded, the event brought about an annual contest of the leading contestants of regional Indian rodeo organizations to compete for world championships in the seven major events. Its popularity has also drawn interest from corporate sponsorships and broad community support in Albuquerque, New Mexico, where it is held annually in November. Approximately 2,000 Indian rodeo contestants are members of regional Indian rodeo organizations. There are one hundred and fifty all-Indian rodeos held annually, that generate one million dollars in purses and awards.

Jay Harwood

See also Sports and Games

Further Reading

Lawrence, Elizabeth Atwood. *Rodeo: An Anthropologist Looks at the Wild and the Tame.* IL: University of Chicago Press, 1982.

RUSSELL TRIBUNAL

A new kind of activity generated by human rights activists during the 1970s was the tribunal format. The best-known of these that focused on Indians was the Fourth Russell Tribunal on Rights of the Indians of the Americas, held in Rotterdam, The Netherlands, in November 1980. The Russell Peace Foundation of Great Britain supported the tribunal as one of its activities to promote a peaceful world in which human rights are respected. The conference was organized by a coalition of Dutch activists who came together as the Dutch Work-Group Indian Project, and also acted as the tribunal's secretariat. Immediately following the tribunal the group published a seven-volume report.

The tribunal was composed of a distinguished body of international personalities, experts, and jurists. Indian groups from throughout the Western Hemisphere were asked to submit cases in advance, and from the many submitted, fourteen were chosen by the tribunal to be heard in full. Nearly a hundred additional cases were organized by subject matter under eleven topics such as: the seizure of Indian lands, the appropriation of Native resources; extreme oppression as cheap labor; and the pervasive existence of racism.

At the end of the proceedings, the Indian peoples who had brought their cases to the tribunal drew up a collective declaration which summarized the conditions of indigenous peoples in the Americas, denounced government policies of genocide, ethnocide, exploitation by transnational corporations, and the dividing of Indian lands. Specifically, the statement condemned the regimes of Bolivia, Guatemala, El Salvador, and Chile, calling for the overthrow of those military regimes by democratic forces which should include full Indian participation and leadership.

The fourteen specific cases heard by the tribunal covered a broad and complex set of issues, which cross other human concerns such as world peace and disarmament, national liberation, international financing, transnational interventions, and governmental policies. Two of the cases received wide publicity and were generally considered the most serious in terms of the millions of people, not only Indians, affected. One was the case of Guatemala; the other was the case brought by the Western Shoshones from Nevada against the basing of the MX missile in their homeland.

The Guatemalan case, presented by a Quiché Indian from the Committee for Peasant Unity, focused on the Spanish embassy massacre, which had occurred less than a year before the tribunal was held. The massacre occurred when Indians from communities where land had been forcibly seized by the Guatemalan army peacefully occupied the Spanish embassy in the capital. The Spanish ambassador attempted to establish communications with the regime in order to initiate negotiations, but the military authorities rejected his attempt, and without warning, bombed the embassy. Only one demonstrator and the ambassador survived.

The Western Shoshones complained that their land had been forcibly taken from them in violation of their 1868 treaty with the United States, and that territory was being used to construct the MX missile system, the largest construction project in the history of the world. The Shoshones maintained that the development stage alone would deplete the rapidly declining water-table in their territory, and that clearly they would be forced to relocate if sensitive, dangerous weapons were placed all over their land.

The publicity surrounding the Shoshone case, brought to the world community by a small, little-known Indian people, provoked a strong reaction from the international peace movement. Soon after the Russell Tribunal, the United States government ceased to specify where the MX would be placed and construction was postponed.

Overall, the tribunal underscored the effectiveness of testimonial in presenting Indian issues, and numerous other tribunals have been organized since that pioneering one.

Roxanne Dunbar Ortiz

See also **International Indian Treaty Council; International Law**

Further Reading

Dunbar Ortiz, Roxanne. *Indians of the Americas: Human Rights and Self-Determination*. London, England: Zed Press, 1984.

Dutch Work-Group Indian Project. *Report of the Fourth Russell Tribunal on the Rights of Indians of the Americas*. Rotterdam: Dutch Work-Group, 1981.

Stavenhagen, Rodolfo. *Derecho Indigena y Derechos Humanos en America Latina*. Mexico: El Colegio de Mexico, Instituto Interamericano de Derechos Humanos, 1988.

SAC AND FOX

The Sac and Fox Nation is the largest of the three tribes of Sac and Fox. At the time of contact with Europeans (1667), the Sac and Fox were two distinct Algonquian-speaking tribes occupying lands in the Michigan and Wisconsin Great Lakes area. The Sac were called Sauk (*Asa ki waki*, "People of the Yellow Earth"), until the late eighteenth century. The Fox were known as the Mesquaki (*Muskwakiwuk*, "Red Earth People"). After near annihilation, the two tribes joined forces for survival in the early 1700s, though they kept their tribal identities separate.

In 1804 the tribe was removed to Iowa and in 1861 they were forced into Kansas. The tribe was removed yet again in 1869, this time to Indian Territory (Oklahoma). The Sac and Fox land run of September 22, 1891 opened the 759,000-acre reservation area in Payne, Pottawatomie, and Lincoln counties to white settlers. The remaining tribal trust acreage of 986.70 acres and 5.45 tribal fee acreage is located 5.5 miles south of Stroud, Oklahoma, on U.S. Highway 377 (Oklahoma Highway 99) in Lincoln County on the site of the old Sac and Fox agency and town. The water tower base marks what was once the Sac and Fox Mission School. The brick home of Chief Moses Keokuk, built in 1879 and located 2.5 miles west of the nation's offices, is privately owned and listed on the National Register of Historic Places. The tribal headquarters are there, as well as the Black Hawk Health Center, Sac and Fox National Public Library and Archives, the Sac and Fox Police and Court, and the tribal community building. The tribe also maintains offices in Stroud and Shawnee, Oklahoma.

Government

The first tribal Constitution was written and adopted in 1885 and established a court system, a police department, a mission school, and a large farming operation. The current tribal government in Oklahoma was first organized under the Indian Reorganization Act of 1934 and the Oklahoma Indian Welfare Act of 1936, as the Sac and Fox Tribe of Indians of Oklahoma. The latest Constitution was adopted July 24, 1987, and in 1988 the Sac and Fox officially renamed itself the Sac and Fox Nation.

The tribal governing body is the Governing Council, which meets the last Saturday of each August and is composed of the entire tribal membership over the age of eighteen. There is also an elected Business Committee whose five members (principal chief, second chief, secretary, treasurer, and committee member) serve staggered four-year terms and set tribal policies and guidelines. Other committees that assist the Governing Council are the grievance committee, tax commission, housing authority, foster home licensing commission, and industrial development commission. *The Sac and Fox News*, the monthly tribal newspaper, is the newspaper of record for government actions.

There were 467 enrolled tribal members in 1900. Tribal membership in 1992 was over 2,200 persons with 1,554 persons residing in the tribal jurisdiction; less than 100 are full-blood Sac and Fox. As stipulated by the 1987 Constitution, individuals are required to submit documentation to the Business Committee and/or Governing Council verifying that they are at least one quarter Sac and Fox with at least one parent on the current rolls. Although tribal members now live in all parts of the United States and in foreign lands, there are two areas of concentration in Oklahoma itself. The southern group, centered near Shawnee, Oklahoma, is the larger band. The northern group is located around Cushing, Oklahoma.

The Sac and Fox Code of Laws was adopted in 1985. The Sac and Fox Court System was the first complete tribal court system in Oklahoma. The District and Supreme Courts of the Sac and Fox Nation exercise general, civil, criminal, and juvenile jurisdiction in Sac and Fox Indian country.

The Sac and Fox Police Force has five full-time officers and a number of reserve officers. The tribe has entered into a number of cross-deputization agreements with law enforcement agencies in neighboring counties and municipalities. Under the agreements, these counties furnish jail service for tribal offenders.

Twentieth-Century Issues

Tribal members have been employed in a wide range of professions, earning their livings as lawyers, doctors, librarians, agricultural workers, small business entrepreneurs, actors, and workers in local industries. Oil production in Oklahoma provided work in the counties surrounding the traditional tribal area for most of the twentieth century. Oil was struck on the allotments of many tribal members in the early half of the century, affording them a comfortable living, but with the overproduction and price fluctuation in the petroleum industry in the late twentieth century, the job market has been limited in the tribal jurisdiction.

The Sac and Fox Code of Laws was developed to create a favorable climate for the reservation economy and to increase the land base. The tribe regulates businesses on trust land, such as the Sac and Fox Bingo Ordinance, which has allowed a successful bingo operation on tribal grounds for nearly ten years. All tobacco shops within tribal jurisdiction are also regulated by the Code. State-tribal relations in the late twentieth century have been characterized by discussions over taxation and gaming rights. An environmental health problem has recently been discovered. Improper oil production practices over the century have resulted in ground water contamination.

Traditions

The tribal customs of adoptions, naming ceremonies, and seasonal feasts continue to be followed by the eleven clans: Fish, Peace, Fox, Warrior, Bear, Wolf, Thunder, Eagle, Potato, Beaver, and Deer. There are estimated to be only 200 persons who speak the Sauk and Mesquakie languages fluently, but classes are being taught through the tribal library in an effort to preserve the languages.

Although tribal members are generally Christians (mostly Methodist and Baptist), there is a strong Native American Church influence. There are also ceremonial dances that are performed at appropriate seasons and events, such as the Bean Dance and Swan or Crane Dance. Sac and Fox men are known for their traditional and straight dancing, and the women still dance in cloth and ribbon dresses, especially at their large annual outdoor powwow held on the second weekend in July. There is also an annual All-Indian Memorial Stampede Rodeo held each summer.

The Sac and Fox create fine ribbonwork (or applique) on clothing and blankets in floral designs that reflect their woodland heritage. Present-day craftpersons also specialize in beadwork, basketry, and featherwork.

The Sac and Fox National Public Library preserves and encourages tribal traditions through several programs including language classes, archival protection of historical photographs and documents, a video collection of contemporary events, a collection of oral history interviews of elderly members of the tribe, and display cases with changing exhibits of tribal photographs, documents, and artifacts.

The tribal courthouse, the oldest building on the reservation, exhibits several historical photographs and a 1936 wall mural painted by a tribal member as a Works Progress Administration project. The main office building houses several exhibit cases for display of antique beadwork, ribbonwork, old photographs, and artifacts.

Notable people in the twentieth century have included athletes, an ethnologist, and artists. Jim Thorpe, born in 1888 at a Sac and Fox village south of the agency town, attended the Sac and Fox Mission School and later Carlisle Indian School in Pennsylvania. He won gold medals for the pentathlon and de-

cathlon in the 1912 Olympics, and was named the "greatest athlete in the first half of the century" in a 1950 *Associated Press* poll. William Jones was a graduate of both Harvard and Columbia universities. A well-known ethnologist, he died in 1909 while working in the Philippines for Chicago's Field Columbian Museum. Antowine Warrior is a nationally known artist and illustrator of several books. R.G. (Ronald George) Harris, a champion war dancer at national competitions throughout the United States and Canada, has performed at the Red Earth Festival in Oklahoma, Smithsonian Institution events, and the inauguration of President William J. Clinton. Viola Spoon is a master ribbonworker whose blankets and shawls have been featured in state museums. Donald Marland is a craftsman known for his beautiful roach head pieces, which are sought by dancers throughout the United States.

Lana S. Grant

See also **Mesquaki; Oklahoma Tribes; Sports and Games**

Further Reading

Eagle Walking Turtle. *Indian America: A Traveler's Companion.* 2d ed. Santa Fe, NM: John Muir Productions, 1991.

Hagan, William T. *The Sac and Fox Indians.* Civilization of the American Indian 48. Norman: University of Oklahoma Press, 1958.

Numbers #1; Months #2; Seasons #3; Relatives #4; Relatives #5; and *Food #6.* Bookmark: Language Series. Stroud, OK: Sac and Fox Nation. 1992.

The Sac and Fox Nation; The Sac and Fox National Public Library; The Sac and Fox Court: Justice For A Nation. Sac and Fox Brochure Series. Stroud, OK: Sac and Fox Nation. 1989–1991.

The Sac and Fox News. Stroud, OK: Sac and Fox Nation, 1980-ongoing.

Wright, Muriel H. *A Guide to The Indian Tribes of Oklahoma.* Civilization of the American Indian Series 33. 1951. Norman: University of Oklahoma, 1986.

SAC AND FOX OF THE MISSISSIPPI IN IOWA

See Mesquaki

SACRED SITES

Land and natural formations are inextricably intertwined with the practice of traditional Native American religions. The relationship between physical areas and traditional religions is a basic and essential component of those religions.

Unlike Western religions, tribal religions are not theological in the sense of incorporating a set of established truths about God and God's relationship with humanity. Rather, the continuation of traditional Native religions over time is ensured only through the performance of ceremonies and rituals, which have the ability to generate dreams and visions. These ceremonies and rituals are often performed at specific sites. These sites may be places where spirits live, or which serve as bridges between the temporal world and the sacred.

Areas of sacred geography are often related to tribal creation stories and other historical events of religious significance. They may also be sites with special geographical features; burial sites; areas where sacred plants or other natural materials are available; or structures, carvings, or paintings with religious significance that were made by tribal ancestors—for example, medicine wheels and petroglyphs. For some tribal religions, there may be no alternative places of worship. The required ceremonies must be performed at certain places to be effective. In many tribal religions, the location of these sites is a closely guarded secret. It is considered contrary to the beliefs and practices of the religions to discuss such sites with outsiders.

A large number of those sites which are known to be sacred to traditional Indian religions are located on what is currently federal land. Historically, the needs and philosophy of Western society have often conflicted with the use of lands by traditional Indian people. In the case of sacred geography, Western concepts of resource development, e.g., logging, mining, or tourism, may conflict with the preservation of the integrity and sanctity of sacred sites. The goals and needs of those who want to "develop" such lands are generally more readily incorporated into land management policies and decision making than are the religious beliefs of Native Americans affected by that development.

For these reasons, traditional Indian people have been engaged in a decades-old struggle with the federal government (and occasionally state governments) to protect threatened sacred sites. In a few cases, those efforts have been successful. In 1970, President Nixon signed legislation returning part of the sacred Blue Lake in New Mexico to the Taos Pueblo. The lake had been annexed by the United States in 1906. Another example of a successful defense of a sacred site involved Kootenai Falls in Idaho, which was threatened by proposed hydroelectric development in the 1980s. An administrative law judge ruled that the project was against the public interest.

However, most of the disputes between traditional Indian religious practitioners and federal and state governments have been resolved in favor of the government—with a resulting impact upon the ability of practitioners to utilize these sacred sites. For example, cases were decided which permitted the following activities to take place:

- Development of a ski area on the San Francisco peaks in Arizona, sacred to the Hopi and Navajos (*Wilson v. Block*, 1983).

- Construction of viewing platforms, parking lots, trails, and roads at Bear Butte in South Dakota, sacred to many Plains Indians (*Fools Crow v. Gullet*, 1983).

- Flooding of sacred Cherokee sites by the Tennessee Valley Authority (*Sequoyah v. Tennessee Valley Authority*, 1980).

In 1988, the United States Supreme Court directly considered the issue of First Amendment protection of sacred sites (*Lyng v. Northwest Indian Cemetery Prot. Assn.*, 485 U.S. 439). This case involved the construction of a road by the Forest Service in northern California, which the government asserted would improve access to timber and recreational resources. The Forest Service's expert found that the construction of the road was potentially destructive of "ceremonies . . . which constitute the heart of the Northwest [Indian] religious beliefs and practices." Based upon these findings, the federal trial and appellate courts had ruled in favor of the Indian religious practitioners. Those courts had determined that the negative impact upon the religious freedom rights of the practitioners outweighed the government's interest in building the road.

The United States Supreme Court reversed the lower courts, rejecting the application of a balancing test to land management decisions by the government. The Court ruled that unless (1) there was specific governmental intent to infringe upon a religion, or (2) the government's action coerced individuals to act contrary to their religious beliefs, the First Amendment provided no protection against governmental action, which impacted upon, or even destroyed, a Native American sacred site.

The *Lyng* decision also established that the American Indian Religious Freedom Act of 1978 (AIRFA) is not available as an alternative mechanism for protecting sacred sites. AIRFA established a federal policy "to protect and preserve" American Indian religious freedom rights, including "access to sites" and "the freedom to worship through ceremonials and traditional rites." Pursuant to AIRFA, a limited number of administrative regulations and policy statements have been issued which provide some opportunity for Indian input into land management decisions. In *Lyng*, however, the United States Supreme Court held AIRFA to be judicially unenforceable—"it has no teeth" in the words of the Court.

Thus, where governmental actions threaten sacred sites, traditional Indian religious practitioners have no constitutional or statutory legal remedy based directly upon a religious freedom claim. Rather, lawyers representing these practitioners must resort to environmental and historic preservation laws which, at times, may provide an indirect mechanism for challenging land management decisions which impact upon sacred sites.

For these reasons, legislation is currently being considered in Congress which would amend AIRFA to provide aggrieved traditional religious practitioners with a legal cause of action. The legislation would also establish new administrative procedures and modify existing planning processes in order to maximize opportunities for Native American input and ensure full consideration of the impact of governmental activity upon sacred sites.

In 1993, there are a number of sacred sites disputes pending before courts and administrative agencies, such as: (1) Uranium mining is planned at a site in Arizona sacred to the Havasupai tribe; (2) tribes in Montana, Wyoming, Oklahoma, and South Dakota are resisting Forest Service plans to improve access for tourists, develop tourist facilities, and facilitate logging in the vicinity of a sacred Medicine Wheel in Wyoming; (3) oil companies are seeking the right to drill large exploratory wells in the Badger Two-Medicine area in Montana, a pristine site sacred to traditional Blackfeet Indians; and (4) the University of Arizona is building telescopes on Mount Graham, a site sacred to the Apache.

Recent testimony before a House of Representatives subcommittee identified forty-four known sites that are currently the subject of disputes concerning land management or development. As the location of sacred sites is often kept secret by traditional religious practitioners, these sites certainly reflect only a small subset of the total number of sites nationwide. Thus, conflict concerning the use and protection of sacred sites between traditional Indian religious practitioners, developers, and land managers is likely to continue for the foreseeable future.

Jack F. Trope

See also American Indian Religious Freedom Act; Religion

Further Reading

Deloria, Vine, Jr. "Sacred Lands and Religious Freedom." *NARF Law Review* 16 (Spring/Summer 1991): 1–6.

Hirschfelder, Arlene, and Paulette Molin. *Encyclopedia of Native American Religions.* New York, NY: Facts on File, 1992.

Proceedings of the National Sacred Sites Caucus. New York, NY: Association on American Indian Affairs, 1991.

U.S. Federal Agencies Task Force. *American Indian Religious Freedom Act Report.* Washington, DC: The Task Force, 1979.

Vecsey, Christopher. *Handbook of American Indian Religious Freedom.* New York, NY: Crossroad, 1991.

SALINAN

The Salinan, whose precontact population is estimated at 3,000, were profoundly affected by the late eighteenth-century establishment and later secularization of Franciscan missions in their homeland located in south central coastal California. Two major Salinan divisions are recognized. The northern or northwestern group, known as the Antoniaños, was gathered principally into Mission San Antonio de Padua after its 1771 founding in the San Antonio River valley, southwest of present-day King City. The southern Salinan division, referred to as the Migueleños, was associated with Mission San Miguel Arcangel after its 1797 founding in the Salinas River valley near present-day Paso Robles. Under the largely peaceful conquest by the Spanish, acculturation among the "gentle and affable" Salinan was swift and is evidenced, for example, by archaeological remains associated with the neophyte residences at Mission San Antonio.

After the 1834 secularization decree and the cessation of church directed economic pursuits, the disenfranchised Salinan mission Indians largely vacated the mission center communities. One historic community of Migueleño Salinan and other displaced Indian families was established at Raphael Villa's ranch near Cayucos on Estero Bay. Many other Salinan remained in their traditional homeland, holding jobs as *vaqueros* (laborers) or domestics on the large ranchos carved out of the vast mission holdings by the Mexican government. Spanish had become the primary language for many Salinan, and intermarriage with persons of Spanish or Mexican descent was not uncommon. In the more remote areas of this relatively unsettled region, several Salinan families subsisted as small-scale ranchers, supplementing the larder by hunting and collecting of traditional foodstuffs. Many Salinan descendants continued this pattern of livelihood after the Mexican land grants were subdivided and acquired by American interests. By the late 1800s many tracts were consolidated into large cattle operations, and the labor force included many Salinan descendants. Several of the men were highly regarded and sought after as hunting guides by the Americans. These economic opportunities to remain in their traditional homeland were the basis for maintaining close ties with the land and with each other, which has been passed to succeeding generations. The old mission churches and Catholic traditions are also forces which have continued to bring Salinan families together socially to worship and for festivals and ceremonies; the annual fiesta at Mission San Antonio honoring the Feast of Saint Anthony is one such event.

Well remembered by contemporary descendants is the historic Salinan community commonly referred to as "The Indians'" located not far from Mission San Antonio at the foot of Santa Lucia (Serra) Peak, a mountain sacred to the Salinan. The Indians' served as a gathering place for many Salinan families from the 1870s through the 1930s. At the heart of this community were the homesteaded lands of Eusebio Encinales, his wife Perfecta, and their seven children. Many members of this family were important sources of language and cultural data for the seminal ethnology on the Salinan published by J. Alden Mason. The anthropologist and linguist John P. Harrington also interviewed many of the same people between 1922 and 1932; of importance to future studies are the more than 3,500 pages of field notes about the Salinan made by Harrington (now available on microfilm), particularly the ethnogeographic data collected during field trips with the Salinan, which demonstrate a continuity in knowledge of the traditional Salinan landscape and provide information important to archaeology.

The Salinan have never been granted tribal lands, nor have they been organized formally as a group. However, an informal network among Salinan descendants has always been operative, especially among the families who maintained residency in or near the traditional Salinan homeland. Federal tribal recognition is also being actively pursued. In 1993 there are hundreds of individuals who recognize Salinan ancestry, the majority living in the Salinas Valley between Monterey and Paso Robles. Before the late 1960s, when Native American ethnicity became more popularly accepted by mainstream America, persons of Salinan descent often hid or denied their Indian ancestry, identifying themselves as Mexican or Spanish. Among many Salinan descendants today, there is a revitalized interest in learning about Salinan history and culture through archaeology and genealogical, archival, and oral history research; a widespread concern for preservation of the Mission San Antonio and its historic setting, and for protection of ancestral burial grounds; and a growing pride in and desire for recognition of Salinan heritage.

Janet P. Eidsness

See also **California Tribes**

Further Reading

Harrington, John P. *The Papers of John Peabody Harrington in the Smithsonian Institution.* Vol. 2. *Northern and Central California.* Ed. Elaine L. Mills. Millwood, NY: Kraus International Publications, 1981.

Hester, Thomas Roy. "Salinan." *Handbook of North American Indians.* Vol. 8. *California.* Ed. Robert F. Heizer. Washington, DC: Smithsonian Institution (1978): 500–04.

Hoover, Robert L., and Julia G. Costello, eds. *Excavations at Mission San Antonio 1976–1978.* Los Angeles: University of California, Institute of Archaeology, 1985.

Mason, J. Alden. "The Ethnology of the Salinan Indians." *University of California Publications in American Archaeology and Ethnology* 10:4 (1912): 97–240.

Rivers, Betty, and Terry L. Jones. "Walking Along Deer Trails: A Contribution to Salinan Ethnogeography Based on the Field Notes of John Peabody Harrington." *Journal of California and Great Basin Anthropology.* Forthcoming.

SALISH

See **Confederated Salish and Kootenai Tribes**

SAMISH

The Samish Indian Nation is a landless Coast Salish tribe of northwestern Washington State. The majority of tribal members live near the aboriginal homeland in the San Juan Islands and in British Columbia. The tribe's headquarters are in Anacortes, Washington.

A persistent issue for the Samish has been their relations with the federal government. By the 1960s the Bureau of Indian Affairs regarded the Samish as "nonrecognized," and ineligible for services and treaty rights. The Samish were denied the standing of a treaty tribe and therefore rejected as a litigant in *United States v. Washington,* 1974 (the Boldt Decision), which affirmed off-reservation fishing.

Samish have responded to actions of the government and settlers by relocating and reorganizing. Although Samish leaders were party to the Treaty of Point Elliott in 1855, many Samish refused to move to reservations or were excluded when the final borders of the Swinomish Reservation were drawn. Traditional headmen Sam Watchoat and Bob Syithlancoh received trust allotments at the Samish settlement on Guemes Island in 1883, but white settlers forced them out by 1912. The Samish continued to occupy fishing villages on Lopez and Cypress Islands, and some received allotments on the Swinomish Reservation in 1885 and 1905. Efforts to organize politically to protect treaty rights began by 1907, and the Samish joined forces in 1918 with the related Nuwhaha people. The Samish created a Constitution and Bylaws in 1926, and again in 1951, 1965, and 1974. The Samish filed a land claim with the Indian Claims Commission in 1951 (Docket 261), and in 1971 were awarded $5,754 after deductions for governmental services provided since 1855. The tribe refused the award.

Tribal leadership has been persistent and innovative. S.J. Kavanaugh, Samish tribal president, was president of the Northwestern Federation of American Indians (NFAI), an organization which pressed the government to allow tribes to sue for land claims (granted in 1926). Don McDowell also headed the NFAI. Samish supported the Indian Reorganization Act of 1934 and opposed termination of the federal-Indian relationship and the handing over of the trust responsibility to the State of Washington in the 1950s. Laborious efforts to regain recognition characterized the 1970s. The Samish's petition to the federal government in 1975 was turned down without response. A second petition, filed in 1979, was turned down in 1983. The tribe fought this ruling, funded by a grant from the Administration for Native Americans, relying on the Freedom of Information Act to obtain copies of the research conducted by the Branch of Acknowledgment and Research (BAR), which was used as evidence in refusing the Samish petition. Tribal officials regarded the process of reconsideration of Samish status through the BAR to have halted by the mid-1980s and focused on obtaining recognition through court review or congressional action. In 1992 a federal court ordered the Samish case reopened, and materials were made available to the tribe providing an opportunity to reply to the judgment. Among the Samish council members who have led the recognition effort are Mary Hansen, a tribal historian and the secretary for the Intertribal Council of Western Washington Indians in the 1950s; Mary Hansen's son, Kenneth Hansen, former chair of the Small Tribes of Western Washington; and Margaret Green, a longtime chair of the eleven-person Samish Council.

Despite the lack of federal recognition, the 600-member tribe remains active. Potlatch Gifts operates out of the Anacortes headquarters, selling Samish woolen goods and other Indian items. The Northwind Cultural Resource Services offers archaeological expertise, and the tribe envisions a cultural interpretive center. The Samish have long sought cooperative relations with the surrounding community. They operated a community food bank in the 1980s, and erected "The Maiden," a spiritually significant wooden sculpture, in a public location in 1983.

Samish are participants in winter Spirit Dancing. Ceremonial activities place Samish in a network of Coast Salish people of western Washington State and the lower mainland of British Columbia. Samish regularly participate in seasonal Indian activities, including bone gambling, sports, and Indian dancing, and have hosted intertribal war canoe races in Anacortes Harbor. Some Samish belong to the Indian Shaker Church, and many conduct important traditional ceremonies, including the taking of inherited Indian names, "burnings" of possessions of the deceased, memorials, and potlatches. Extended families provide essential economic and emotional support to their members.

Bruce G. Miller

See also **Washington State Tribes**

Further Reading

Bishop, Kathleen L., and Kenneth C. Hansen. "The Landless Tribes of Western Washington." *American Indian Journal* 4:5 (1979): 20–31.
Petition for the Federal Acknowledgment of the Samish Indian Tribe. Anacortes, WA: Samish Tribal Press, 1979.
Ruby, Robert H., and John A. Brown. *A Guide to the Indian Tribes of the Pacific Northwest*. Norman: University of Oklahoma Press, 1986.
Sampson, Chief Martin J. *Indians of Skagit County*. Anacortes, WA: Skagit County Historical Society Series 2 (1972).
Suttles, Wayne P. "The Economic Life of the Coast Salish of Haro and Rosario Straits." Vol. 1. *Coast Salish and Western Washington Indians*. New York, NY: Garland Publishing, 1974.

SAN CARLOS

See Apache

SAN FELIPE

See Pueblo of San Felipe

SAN ILDEFONSO

See Pueblo of San Ildefonso

SAN JUAN

See Pueblo of San Juan

SAN JUAN DE GUADALUPE TIWA TRIBE

See Tortugas

SANDIA

See Pueblo of Sandia

SANDPAINTING

See Drypainting

SANTA ANA

See Pueblo of Santa Ana

SANTA CLARA

See Pueblo of Santa Clara

SANTEE

The Santee Tribe of South Carolina is scattered in Berkeley, Calhoun, and Orangeburg counties with a major population center at Holly Hill, South Carolina. Other individuals are known to reside in the cities of Charleston and Orangeburg, and in the state of Florida. The tribal roll contains approximately 1,000 names. The Santee reorganized in the late 1960s after many years without a tribal government. Chief Hudson Crummie led the group from 1970 to 1985 and was succeeded by Chief Oscar Pratt, who leads the group in 1993.

The Santee Live Oak Indian School was closed in 1966 as a result of integration. Eighty children were enrolled that year. Today the land surrounding the former school and Live Oak Church is held as community property. The two buildings are used for worship services and tribal meetings. The Tribal Council submitted a letter of intent to the Bureau of Indian Affairs (BIA) in June 1979 concerning their desire to seek and obtain federal recognition. The Santees are number fifty-three on the BIA priority list.

No crafts are practiced by the Santee Indians, but they are noted for their distinct English language dialect. No linguistic studies of the Santees have been published to date.

Thomas J. Blumer

Further Reading

Taukchiray, Wesley DuRant. *Santee Tribe*. Series 2, Wesley D. White Papers. Charleston: South Carolina Historical Society.
Taukchiray, Wesley DuRant, and Alice Bee Kasakoff. "Contemporary Native Americans in South Carolina: An Overview." *Indians of the Southeastern United States in the Late Twentieth Century*. Ed. J. Anthony Parades. Tuscaloosa, AL and London, England: University of Alabama Press (1992): 72–101.

SANTO DOMINGO

See Pueblos: Santo Domingo

SAUK-SUIATTLE

The present-day Sauk-Suiattle are the descendants of the Sah-ku-mehu, who were party to the

Treaty of Point Elliott of 1855. Although expected to remove to a reservation away from their upriver homelands, few Sauk-Suiattle ever did so. The name "Sauk-Suiattle" is derived from the two main rivers that run through their traditional territory in Washington State. The Sauk-Suiattle utilized an area encompassing the Sauk and Suiattle rivers' watersheds, from the confluence of the Sauk and Skagit rivers to the crest of the Cascade Mountains. From winter village sites, the Sauk-Suiattle traveled seasonally to fishing, hunting, and plant-gathering locations. The Sauk-Suiattle frequently visited with the Indians east of the Cascade Mountains, traveling over mountain passes for purposes of trade and social interaction.

History

Living in a fairly remote area, the Sauk-Suiattle had little interaction with non-Indians until the 1880s. After ratification of the Treaty of Point Elliott in 1859, the Sauk-Suiattle were to remove to the Swinomish Reservation near the mouth of the Skagit River. Most Sauk-Suiattle stayed in their traditional areas congregating in a winter village on Sauk Prairie, just north of the present town of Darrington. In 1884 non-Indian homesteaders claimed the area of Sauk Prairie and destroyed the Sauk-Suiattle longhouses. The Sauk-Suiattle withdrew to the Suiattle River valley where they filed for individual homestead allotments under the Indian Homestead Act of 1884. Later the Suiattle River area was incorporated into the National Forest system, and from 1915 to 1917 most of the Sauk-Suiattle homesteads were cancelled and the people dispersed to non-Indian communities in the area. The Sauk-Suiattle were party to land claims cases against the United States in the 1950s (Indian Claims Commission, Docket 97). Although the Sauk-Suiattle have always been a separate tribe and have been organized with a tribal government since 1946, the Indian Claims Commission determined that the Sauk-Suiattle were part of the Upper Skagit tribe and included their case with the Upper Skagit's (Indian Claims Commission, Docket 92). This combined claim resulted in an award of $385,471. The Sauk-Suiattle have been federally recognized as a separate tribe since 1973. In 1985 trust land was purchased in the Sauk Prairie area to create the Sauk-Suiattle Reservation.

Recent History

The Sauk-Suiattle have been organized with a Constitution and Tribal Council form of government since 1975. As a western Washington treaty tribe they exercise fishing rights allocated under the 1974 Boldt Decision (*United States v. State of Washington*, Civil No. 9213, 384 F. Supp. [1974]), and participate in comanagement of the Skagit River system with other tribes in the Skagit System Cooperative. There are presently one hundred enrolled members of the Sauk-Suiattle tribe. In addition to salmon fishing, tribal members work in the local logging industry and in other occupations in nearby communities. Unemployment at Sauk-Suiattle is high, at approximately 84 percent.

Culture

The Sauk-Suiattle are of the Coast Salish language family, speaking a dialect of Lushootseed. Unlike many of their Indian neighbors, the Sauk-Suiattle have traditionally been more oriented to the rivers and mountains relying much more on big-game hunting than the coastal tribes. Many Sauk-Suiattle practice the traditional Spirit Dance Religion, although some converted to Indian Shakerism in the early 1900s and some are members of one or another Christian denomination.

Daniel L. Boxberger

See also **Fishing and Hunting Rights; Washington State Tribes**

Further Reading

Bruseth, Nels. *Indian Stories and Legends of the Stillaguamish, Sauks and Allied Tribes.* 1949. Reprint. Fairfield, WA: Ye Galleon Press, 1977.

Collins, June McCormick. *Valley of the Spirits: The Upper Skagit Indians of Western Washington.* American Ethnological Society Monographs 56. Seattle: University of Washington Press, 1974.

Sampson, Martin J. *Indians of Skagit County.* Mount Vernon: Skagit County Historical Society, 1972.

Suttles, Wayne, and Barbara Lane. "Southern Coast Salish." *Handbook of North American Indians.* Vol. 7. *Northwest Coast.* Ed. Wayne Suttles. Washington, DC: Smithsonian Institution (1989): 385–502.

SCHAGHTICOKE

The Schaghticoke (Scaticook, Pisgoch tigoch, meaning "Where the Rivers Meet") Reservation, established in 1752 with approximately 400 acres, is located in the mountainous terrain of northwestern Connecticut. It is bordered on the west by New York State and on the east by the Housatonic River, near the town of Kent.

Once on the reservation, Schaghticoke people were subjected to oppressive control from colonial overseers to state agencies, including the Connecticut State Parks and Forests Agency and the Connecticut Department of Welfare. By 1955 the tribe decided they had had enough. Led by Theodore "Pahia" Coggswell, Howard Harris, and Franklin "Swimming Eel" Bearce, a petition (Dockett #112) was filed with the United States Indian Claims Commission. Both motion and appeal were dismissed. In 1973 Tribal Chairman Irving Harris spearheaded legislation in Connecticut, which created the Indian Affairs Council (PA #73-660), giving seats and a voice to the state's five tribes. Schaghticoke then contacted the Native American Rights Fund to file for still pending recognition and to regain 1,200 acres lost after 1790. In 1980 tribal elections overturned Schaghticoke leadership. Irving Harris lost to Maurice "Butch" Lydem, who promised to work on economic development projects, housing, and employment. There are 350 people on the tribal rolls and in 1991 five families reside on the reservation.

Currently, Schaghticoke is at an important crossroads. Court battles over the state's jurisdiction and tribal factionalism have hampered progress. Recent legislation (PA 85-368) now recognizes the tribe as a self-governing entity.

Schaghticoke maintains its cultural connections to the land through tribal functions and special programs, which bring the children to the reservation to strengthen their ties and identity. Language and ceremonies were suppressed and fragmented for over 250 years until no one remembered. But everyone believes that the land is the culture and the culture is in the land; which is why they are still here today.

Trudie Lamb Richmond

Further Reading

Guilette, Mary E. *American Indians in Connecticut.* A Report for The Indian Affairs Council, Connecticut Department of Environmental Protection, Hartford, 1979.

Richmond, Trudie Lamb. "Spirituality and Survival in Schaghticoke Basketmaking." *A Key into the Language of Woodsplint Basket.* Eds. Ann McMullen and Russel G. Handsman. Washington, CT: American Indian Archaeological Institute, 1987. 123–43.

SCULPTURE

Twentieth-century Native American sculpture is rooted in the earliest artistic impulses of the continent's original peoples, from the monumental earth sculpture of the Mississippian mound builders, to intricately worked stone effigy artifactual tools the Indians sculpted. Much of this great artistic heritage is lost, rotted away by time and the elements. Yet the rare surviving examples of wooden figures from Key Marco and the Spiro Mounds reveal the sophistication of the pre-Columbian sculptor. There is sculptural stonework still in existence, such as the Spiro platform pipes, Eskimo bonecarving, and pottery in human forms, pipes, and amulets. These works are a reminder that the sculpting, carving, and incising traditions are as old as the inhabitants of this continent. Ancient Native sculpture speaks to us of the noblest, as well as the most practical, aspects of life. They tell us how the two—the quest for beauty and the demands of survival—the spiritual and the pragmatic—can come together through the creative impulse of the sculptor.

Native American sculpture survived the European onslaught, adapting as did all of Indian culture. New pressures and new opportunities included the introduction of tools that made sculpting and incising easier. It became a more profitable art with the opening of commercial markets. Indian life and art were changed by the introduction of the gun, the horse, and ardent spirits. This produced revolutions in Plains and other Indian cultures, which are reflected in utilitarian and religious sculptures including horse dance sticks, pipe stems, souvenir hunting sticks, and eating bowls and spoons. Older forms, including clubs, speaker's staffs, masks, and animal effigies, continued to be produced both for spiritual and utilitarian purposes, as well as for Anglo explorers, adventurers, and tourists with their curio and art markets. Slowly, bone and walrus tusk carving, scrimshaw trinkets, argillite characters, pottery effigies, and kachina figures found their way into private collections and public museums. The heroic Northwest totemic carvings of grand scale came to symbolize, for many non-Indians, the highest achievement of Native art. Both the ancient and the transitional sculpture of the Native American influenced the rise of modernism in European sculpture and painting with twentieth-century Western artists such as Moore, Brancusi, Picasso, and Pollock acknowledging the impact of the Native American sculptor upon their own works.

Twentieth-century Native American sculpture was, in turn, influenced by mainstream Western art. The contemporary Indian art world includes sculptors who work exclusively in the traditional Native forms, as

Allan Houser (Chiricahua Apache). "Earth Mother," 1987. Bronze; 41 by 28 by 25 inches. Courtesy of the Montclair Art Museum Permanent Collection, 89.22.

well as many who express their heritage in more modern Western styles. The tension created by these struggles has produced much of what is the very best within twentieth-century Native American sculpture. The twentieth-century Native Fine Arts Movement, including Indian sculpture, is deep and diverse. This sculptural movement has roots in both traditionalism and modernism. It stretches geographically from Alaska to New York, back to the far Southwest, and into the hills of the old southeastern Indian woodlands.

The international art world recognizes Native American sculpture as an important achievement. Two of the dominant figures among twentieth-cen-

tury Native American sculpture are Allan Houser (Apache) and his son Bob Haozous (Apache/Navajo). The Chippewa artist George Morrison is typical of a generation of artists who have taken Native art beyond the world of ethnography. These sculptors have been honored with public commissions for monumental works for major spaces in cities throughout the world.

Allan Houser, who began his art career as a painter at the Santa Fe Studio, is the major figure in the history of contemporary Native sculpture. Equally successful whether working in stone or metal, in abstract or realistic form, Houser's works are always classically elegant, simple, and moving. While the

Roxanne Swentzell (Santa Clara Pueblo). "The Emergence of the Clowns," 1988. Coiled and scraped clay; from left: 58.4 by 33 by 33 centimeters, 43.2 by 55.9 by 45.7 centimeters, 43.2 by 35.6 by 35.6 centimeters, 17.8 by 48.3 by 26 centimeters. Collection of the Heard Museum. Courtesy of the Heard Museum. Photo by Craig Smith.

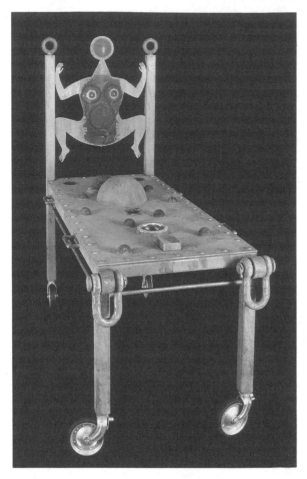

Bob Haozous (Apache-Navajo). "The Abortionist's Bed,"
1990. Cut steel; 2.22 by 2.22 meters. Collection of the artist.
Photo courtesy of the Heard Museum. Photo by Craig
Smith.

George Morrison (Ojibway). "Northwest Area Foundation
Commemorative Totem," 1982. Bronze; 27.9 by 10.2 by
10.2 centimeters. Collection of the artist. Photo courtesy of
the Heard Museum. Photo by Craig Smith.

subject matter is most frequently Native American,
the impact and the issue are always universal. Houser
has dominated Native American sculpture in the last
half of the twentieth century.

The works of Bob Haozous seem destined to
dominate Native sculpture into the twenty-first century. In so many ways, Haozous is the quintessential
Native American sculptor of the modern era. Working
in wood, metal, and stone, he produces shocking
sculpture which questions the value premises of
modern society, both Indian and non-Indian. The
critic Suzanne Deats noted:

> With a background in both worlds—i.e. an
> Indian heritage and European training—
> [Haozous] avoids the obvious solution of work-
> ing in one mode with the superficial trappings of
> the other.
>
> Instead he has chosen a sterner path. He
> puts the two influences on a collision course
> within his artistic concept, then slices through
> them with the same ferocious skill with which

he wields a cutting torch. He reshapes and jux-
taposes the fragments until a third reality
emerges.

The sculpture of George Morrison, the only
Native American artist to have been in New York
at the time of the birth of abstract expressionism,
brings together a unique combination of tribal totemic forms and post-war modernism. His works are
characterized by strength, power, understanding,
warmth, and beauty, whether in natural woods or
cast metal. Morrison has completed more public commissions for Native sculpture than any other Indian
artist.

Bill Reid, a Haida artist in Canada, is the dominant figure in the extension and revival of traditional
Canadian and Northwest Coast Native wood sculpture. Reid produces massive works, drawing upon the
ancient Northwest woodcarving tradition, as well as
tiny jewel-like gold pieces. His work has led to the
founding of a school for modern Canadian totem and
woodwork, which has produced two new generations

of Native artists and kept alive these ancient ways. Alaska and northern Canada have produced a significant body of sculpture as well. Most of these are neotraditional, looking back to the argillite carved and polished work, or the soapstone figures of earlier times. Larry Beck, a Chnagmiut Eskimo, has extended the traditional mask making by constructing his masterful renderings of traditional Eskimo objects using found materials from the modern world—hubcaps, auto mirrors, kitchen utensils, and all the vast flotsam of man-made utilitarian objects.

In recent years, a number of artists have produced sculptured clay works of museum quality. Perhaps the most widely recognized of these is Roxanne Swentzell (Santa Clara), whose Pueblo figures capture the irony, beauty, and vitality of contemporary southwestern Indian culture. Karita Koffey (Comanche) also uses clay to produce fine masks in the sculptural tradition. The Cherokee Bill Glass works in a more monumental form, recreating figures from ancient woodland worlds. Glen LaFontaine's (Cree-Chippewa) are similarly executed but with a greater sense of humor. This school of clay sculpture is reminiscent of the pottery opera singers and circus figures from the Pueblos of the late nineteenth and early twentieth century.

The ironic Indian artist has turned to sculpture to focus upon the tragic and bitter yet humorously reaffirming aspect of contemporary Indian life. Ron Anderson's (Cherokee) "Car Scaffold Burial" is an example of such environmental sculpture, with his Mercury Cougar wrapped in a funerary blanket and hoisted on a traditional Plains burial scaffold. Conrad Houser's (Navajo) and Richard Danay's (Mohawk) works show the double bind of the Indian who must live in both a traditional and a modern world. Danay's "Chief's Chair," for example, places an ancient Aztec leader in a children's wheeled toy with a car phone at his side.

The Northwest Coast mask carving tradition has proven commercially profitable. Perhaps the most

Willard Stone (Cherokee). "Proud Peyote Bird," 1964. Walnut; height 30 1/4 inches. Courtesy of the U.S. Department of the Interior, Indian Arts and Crafts Board, W-64.97.

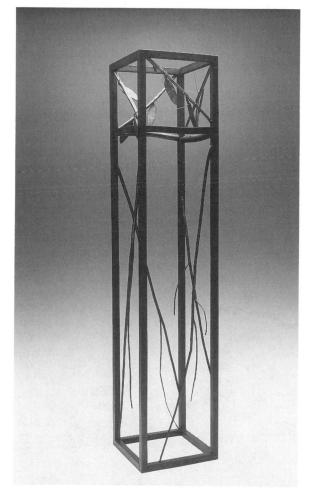

Truman Lowe (Winnebago). "Mnemonic Totem #3," 1989. Bronze; 120 by 25 by 25 centimeters. Collection of the Heard Museum. Courtesy of the Heard Museum. Photo by Craig Smith.

widely known of these commercial carvers is a Cherokee, Donald Smith, who has taken the name Lelooska. His dramatic but innovative work contrasts sharply with adaptations of traditional styles by sculptors such as R.E. Bartow (Yurok) who works with mixed-media in epic creations such as the widely exhibited "Salmon Mask." The Tlingit James Schoppert has recently executed wood sculptures that draw upon his own tribal design heritage, but in dissected and abstracted forms, and others, which are inspired by the southwestern Eskimo of the nineteenth century extending this remarkably surrealistic tradition.

Woodland sculpture of the post-war era draws upon separate traditions, which are united in the works of divergent Iroquoian peoples including the Tuscarora Duffy Wilson and the Cherokee John Wilnoty. Both have created masterly works in stone as well as wood. The woodcarving tradition is best represented by the Eastern Cherokee Amanda Crowe and the late Oklahoma Cherokee Willard Stone. As a young man, Stone began to utilize the grain in the wood to create the pattern and design for works which captured woodland animals and birds. The Cheyenne painter W. Richard West is one of the finest of the Plains wood sculptors, although he was less prolific than one would have hoped. His technical skill was more than equalled by his sense of composition and conception. Unfortunately, his rarely executed works are difficult to locate, but represent twentieth-century Native sculpture at its evocative best. Truman Lowe (Winnebago),

is for his generation what West was to his. Lowe utilizes traditional Native forms and materials to extend utilitarian objects, such as canoes or dwellings, into sculptural works of art such as his architectural construct entitled "Wooden Pole Construction." Susie Bevins-Ericsen (Iñupiat Eskimo) has done much the same with her northern materials and traditions. John Hoover (Aleut), particularly in monumental works such as "Winter Loon Dance," extends traditional forms into theatrical works, which convey the spirit of the old in the strikingly contemporary.

In conclusion, much twentieth-century Native American sculpture has blended the ancient Indian traditions with the modern artistic idiom to produce significant and diverse works of art, with movements ranging from the Northwest Canadian revival, to the contemporary ironic and satirical school. As the Native American moves toward the twenty-first century, Indian sculpture is being commissioned and installed by the non-Indian public in cities throughout the nation and the world. Morrison's totemic poles, Houser's noble madonnas, and Haozous' metallic ecological and environmental monoliths stand where earlier generations might have installed an "End of the Trail" or a "Custer's Last Stand." Today, Native sculpture stands as an artistic and spiritual tribute to the survival of the values of those original and ancient inhabitants of this land.

Rennard J. Strickland

See also **Art**

Further Reading

Archuleta, Margaret, and Rennard Strickland. *Shared Visions: Native American Painters and Sculptors in the Twentieth Century.* Phoenix, AZ: The Heard Museum, 1991.

Duff, Wilson, Bill Holm, and Bill Reid. *Arts of the Raven: Masterworks of the Northwest Coast Indians.* BC: Vancouver Art Gallery, 1967.

Houser and Haozous: A Sculptural Retrospective. Phoenix: The Heard Museum, 1984.

Pearlman, Barbara H. *Allan Houser.* Boston, MA: David R. Godine, 1987.

Standing in the Northern Lights: George Morrison, A Retrospective. Minneapolis: Minnesota Museum of Art, 1990.

Wade, Edwin L., ed. *The Arts of the North American Indian: Native Traditions in Evolution.* New York, NY: Hudson Hills Press, 1986.

Willard Stone: Wood Sculptor. Muskogee, OK: Five Tribes Museum, 1968.

SEMINOLE

The Seminole, descendants of the Creeks who migrated to Florida, occupied reservations in Florida and Oklahoma (where much of the nation had been removed during and following the Second Seminole War, 1835 to 1842) at the start of the twentieth century. The two articles which follow deal individually with the Seminole Tribe of Florida and the Seminole

John Julius Wilnoty (Cherokee). "Up From the Deep," 1971. Catlinite; 14 by 14 inches. Courtesy of the U.S. Department of the Interior, Indian Arts and Crafts Board, W-71.38.1.

Nation of Oklahoma. The Miccosukee Tribe of Indians, whose members were considered part of the Seminole tribe of Florida until 1962, are discussed elsewhere. Other groups who identify as Seminoles but are not currently federally recognized are not included in these discussions.

SEMINOLE IN FLORIDA

The Seminole Tribe of Florida is one of the two federally recognized Indian polities in the southernmost state. Its 2,000 enrolled members still converse in two Native languages, plus English; about a third speak Muskogee or Creek, while the remainder use a Hitchiti language known as Mikasuki. The latter is also spoken by members of the nearby Miccosukee Tribe, to whom they are closely related through culture and kinship. The Seminole land holdings in south Florida encompass five reservations of over 100,000 acres. Two of these, Big Cypress and Brighton, are large rural tracts devoted primarily to commercial agriculture and cattle herding ventures. The small Hollywood and Tampa reservations are located in large urban centers where the tribe engages in high revenue producing business enterprises. A Seminole community near the town of Immokalee was taken into trust status during the 1980s.

Within the last century the Florida Seminoles have undergone several major transformations in their social, economic, and political life. The years between 1870 and 1914 were an era of intensive hunting, trapping, and trading for the Seminoles. They sold alligator hides, bird plumes, and otter pelts at trading posts on the sparsely settled Florida frontier. In return they received guns, ammunition, canned foods, and clothing, as well as bolts of cloth and hand-cranked sewing machines. This trade-based economy collapsed when Florida began to drain the Everglades to promote agriculture, and the international market for Indian goods declined at the beginning of World War I. The 1920s saw the Florida "land boom," which led to further impoverishment and displacement of Indians from their lands. During the Great Depression years and World War II, a majority of the Seminoles relocated to federal reservations in south Florida. There they undertook cattle herding, adopted wage labor, and accepted many of the white man's ways, such as schooling and health care; a large number also converted to Christianity. In the 1950s the Seminoles were one of those Indian tribes scheduled for termination of all services and support from the federal government during the Eisenhower administration. Fortunately, with the support of Florida's congressional delegation and dedicated Indian rights advocates, the tribe evaded termination. To protect their interests, the reservation Seminoles adopted a Constitution and Corporate Charter as authorized by the Indian Reorganization Act of 1934. The Seminole Tribe of Florida received federal recognition in 1957. At that time, the Seminole traditionalists—perhaps a third of the population—were mostly Mikasuki-speakers who retained their camps in the deep Everglades.

This element resisted the social and political acculturational process taking place among their counterparts on the reservations, and in 1962 they formed the Miccosukee Tribe to conserve social and religious values.

The elected Seminole tribal government is composed of two elements. A Tribal Council serves as the general policy-making body for the Seminole people. The Seminole Tribe of Florida, Inc. is a federally chartered corporation, which supervises tribal business enterprises. Economic conditions improved dramatically in the late 1970s with the introduction of two highly profitable ventures. The first was the sale of state tax-free cigarettes in smoke-shops operated on the reservations by Indian owners who pay a fee to the tribe. However, by far the most profitable and controversial Seminole enterprise is unregulated, high-stakes bingo, which reportedly nets the tribe a multi-million dollar annual income. The tribe's right to sell nontaxed cigarettes and operate bingo has been unsuccessfully challenged in federal courts, where Seminole sovereignty was reaffirmed. Today the income from these enterprises supports many tribal social services that are no longer underwritten by the federal government; it also provides a cash dividend for tribal members.

Over the last two decades, the Seminoles have benefited from the progressive leadership of astute and articulate tribal chairmen. These included Betty Mae Jumper, the first woman elected to head the Tribal Council, and a strong advocate of education; Howard Tommie, who pushed the limits of self-determination by introducing both smoke-shops and bingo; and the dynamic James Billie, in his fourth term in 1993, and the architect of extensive Seminole business enterprises.

In recent years new housing, expanded recreational facilities, and community centers have been added on each reservation. Although most Seminole children attend public schools, the tribe operates an elementary day school on the isolated Big Cypress Reservation; youngsters are then bused to the nearest town for secondary school. Many Seminole youngsters now complete high school and a few attend college. Moreover, Seminoles now have viable economic alternatives, which enable younger families to remain among their own people, rather than moving away to seek employment. This has brought greater stability to social life and reinforces the transmission of Native languages and cultural traditions. The historic clan and matrilineal kinship system of the tribe is still observed, although much of the folklore is in danger of being lost to successive generations. The highly regarded Seminole arts and crafts, such as designing colorful patchwork clothing and basketry, are still produced and remain a major source of income for a small group of talented artisans.

Harry A. Kersey, Jr.

See also **Miccosukee**

Further Reading

Garbarino, Merwyn S. *Big Cypress: A Changing Seminole Community*. New York, NY: Holt, Rinehart and Winston, 1972.

Kersey, Harry A., Jr. *Pelts, Plumes, and Hides: White Traders among the Seminole Indians, 1870–1930*. Gainesville: University Presses of Florida, 1975.

——. *The Seminole and Miccosukee Tribes: A Critical Bibliography*. Bloomington: Indiana University Press, 1987.

——. *The Florida Seminoles and the New Deal 1933–1942*. Gainesville: University Presses of Florida, 1989.

——. "Seminoles and Miccosukees: A Century in Retrospective." *Indians of the Southeastern United States in the Late 20th Century*. Ed. J. Anthony Paredes. Tuscaloosa, AL and London, England: University of Alabama Press (1992): 102–19.

Sturtevant, William C. "Creek into Seminole." *North American Indians: Indians in Historical Perspective*. Eds. Eleanor B. Leacock and Nancy O. Lurie. New York, NY: Random House (1971): 92–108.

SEMINOLE IN OKLAHOMA

Originally inhabiting northern Florida, all but a few hundred of the Seminoles were forcibly removed to what is now east central Oklahoma by the United States government, during the course of the Second Seminole War, 1835 to 1842. They settled in their current location, modern Seminole County, Oklahoma, in 1866. An eighteenth century offshoot of the Creeks, the Seminoles also incorporated members of other Eastern Muskogean peoples, such as the Yamasis and Apalachees, and some non-Muskogeans as well. Several Florida Maroon communities, consisting of escaped Black slaves and their descendants, also joined the Seminoles after the American Revolution. Most Seminoles spoke dialects of two related Muskogean languages, Creek (Muskogee) and Hitchiti, and generally followed Creek social and cultural practices.

The primary social, political, and religious groups within the tribe are the *italwas*, called "bands" in English, which are similar to the Creek tribal towns. Band membership is inherited matrilineally. The number of bands shrank from more than twenty-six in the early nineteenth century, to fourteen by the 1890s. Two of these bands consisted of Black Seminoles, called Freedmen. Each band was self-governing, had representatives on the Tribal Council, and possessed a distinct territory.

Allotment

Allotment was the most significant historical event for the Oklahoma Seminoles in the twentieth century. An 1897 agreement with the United States government provided that all tribal lands would be divided and each tribal member would receive an equal share of the lands according to value. Lands for public use and the townsite of Wewoka were reserved from the allotment process. Supplemental agreements signed in 1899 and 1905 provided for the inclusion of children born after the roll was completed and lands were set aside for them. The original allotments, comprising 346,854.39 acres, were completed by 1902, and allotments of 40 acres each were assigned to newborn children in 1905.

The allotment process was scheduled for completion by March 4, 1906, at which time deeds would be issued to the Indians and the tribal government would be extinguished. An act of Congress on March 3, 1901, had made all members of the Five Civilized Tribes United States citizens. In 1907, Indian Territory and Oklahoma Territory entered the Union as the State of Oklahoma, and the Seminoles also became state citizens.

While only 4,223 acres were immediately available for white settlement, the allotment agreement provided that the Seminoles could sell their lands, except for a 40-acre homestead site, following issuance of the deeds. The homestead allotment was inalienable and nontaxable in perpetuity. The Five Tribes Act of April 26, 1906, placed restrictions on the sale of lands by full-blood Indians, though not for mixed-bloods or Freedmen.

The issuance of deeds initiated a period of rapacious land grabbing and fraud by Americans. By 1920 only about one-fifth of all allotted lands remained in Seminole hands. In 1923, the Greater Seminole Oil Field was opened. This event prompted further frauds on the Seminoles and few Indians benefited from the wealth it generated.

Loss of land and lack of economic opportunities in Seminole County contributed to Seminole migration out of the area and to the cities, particularly after World War II. Land loss and migration also contributed to the disappearance of discrete band territories. Today only 35,443 acres of the original allotments remain in Seminole hands.

Tribal Government

Despite the provisions for the extinction of the tribal government, it continued well past that date. John F. Brown, who had been principal chief since 1885, was defeated in the 1901 tribal election by Hulputta Micco, following a scandal concerning the Wewoka townsite. Hulputta Micco died in 1905, however, and the Seminole council elected Brown as his successor; he retained that position until 1915. After 1906, the tribal government had little power or influence. The Indian Reorganization Act of 1934 brought renewed federal recognition of the elected Seminole chief and council, but they primarily served as advisors to the Bureau of Indian Affairs.

The passage of Public Law 91-495 in 1970 led to the adoption of a new Constitution by the Seminoles. Based on traditional precedents, it provides for the election of a principal chief and an assistant chief, who serve four-year terms, and a Tribal Council. The Council consists of three elected representatives from each of the fourteen bands, one of whom is the band chief. The tribe maintains a headquarters office on the outskirts of Wewoka, and another tribal complex at the Mekasuky Mission south of Seminole. The tribe operates various social welfare programs for tribal members. Jerry Haney was serving as principal chief in 1991.

In 1976, the Indian Claims Commission awarded the Oklahoma Seminoles $16 million for lands confiscated in Florida during the early 1800s. Disputes over the allocation of this money severely divided the tribe and led to chronic factional disputes, bringing tribal operations to a standstill in the early 1980s. A final settlement for use of the funds, now grown to $40 million through interest payments, was arrived at in the fall of 1990, as a result of federal legislation.

Economic Conditions

In 1991 there are about 10,000 to 11,000 Oklahoma Seminoles, including 900 to 1,100 Freedmen, up from about 3,000 in 1900. As many as half of the Indians are full-bloods. Per capita income and educational levels are low for all Seminoles and unemployment is high. Oil production and related industries, along with construction, retailing, small manufacturing, and agriculture, provide most jobs. Economic development efforts by the tribe, as well as state and federal efforts, have had little success.

Culture

Despite being interspersed among a much larger white population, the Seminoles remain culturally conservative. While most Seminoles speak English today, many also speak Muskogee and the language is in constant use in the home and elsewhere. Hichiti, however, has essentially died out in Oklahoma. The Oklahoma Seminoles also retain many other traditional beliefs and practices and rarely participate in white institutions, except for school and jobs.

In 1900 most Seminoles followed traditional religious practices, with only a small minority of Christians. Christian churches, particularly the Baptists, won large numbers of converts in the early 1900s, though the distinction between Christian and traditionalist remained vague to the Seminoles prior to the 1930s.

As early as 1900 some of the Seminole bands could no longer support their own stomp grounds. By 1910 only six of twelve grounds still operated. In the early 1950s that number fell to four. Two more closed in the late 1970s, but one was revived in 1976 and continues to exist today, as do two others. Seminole traditionalists from other bands either attend one of these or one of the nearby Creek grounds. These stomp grounds continue to be the sites for traditional religious ceremonies, particularly the Green Corn ceremony (*Apuskita*).

Most Seminoles today are Christians, predominantly Baptists, but also there are some Methodists and Presbyterians. Even Christian Seminoles, however, retain many traditional practices. Services are generally in Muskogee and the layout of Seminole churches resembles that of the stomp grounds. Likewise, each band generally maintains its own church.

Some Seminoles who are church members also attend traditional ceremonies, despite a 1930s church ban on such participation. Many traditional Seminoles attend church services during the winter when there are no traditional ceremonies. Both groups of Seminoles use the services of traditional curers and conjurers.

While most Seminoles know their clan membership, most clan functions have disappeared. Even clan marriage rules are largely ignored. The clans do retain many of their ritual functions, however. Some remnants of matrilineal descent are retained, particularly with regard to band membership. The Oklahoma Seminoles also show a tendency toward matrilocal residence, though economic and residential constraints often make this impossible.

Richard A. Sattler

See also **Allotment; Oklahoma Tribes**

Further Reading

Debo, Angie. *And Still the Waters Run: The Betrayal of the Five Civilized Tribes*. NJ: Princeton University Press, 1940.

Howard, James H. *Oklahoma Seminoles: Medicine, Magic, and Religion*. Norman: University of Oklahoma Press, 1984.

McReynolds, Edwin C. *The Seminoles*. Norman: University of Oklahoma Press, 1957.

Spoehr, Alexander. "Kinship System of the Seminole." *Field Museum of Natural History, Anthropological Series* 33 (1942): 29–113.

Swanton, John R. "Social Organization and the Social Usages of the Indians of the Creek Confederacy." *Bureau of American Ethnology 42nd Annual Report*. Washington, DC: U.S. Government Printing Office (1928): 23-472.

SENATE COMMITTEE ON INDIAN AFFAIRS

The Senate has assigned a standing committee to develop American Indian policy for nearly 150 years, from 1820 through 1945 and since 1977, when the current Committee on Indian Affairs was established as a temporary select panel. It was made permanent in 1984, and the "select" designation was dropped from its title in 1993, following an aborted attempt to abolish it. Its House counterpart existed from 1821 through 1945. The Senate Committee has eighteen members and in 1993 is chaired by Senator Daniel K. Inouye (D-Hawaii).

In 1946 both Houses created Subcommittees on Indian Affairs within the Committees on Public Lands (and Surveys), which became the Committees on Interior and Insular Affairs in 1948 in the Senate and in 1951 in the House. The Senate Subcommittee continued until the Select Committee was organized in 1977, when the Interior Committee was reorganized into the Committee on Energy and Natural Resources. The House Subcommittee existed until 1978 in the

Interior Committee, which changed its name to the Committee on Natural Resources in 1993, and established an eleven-member Subcommittee on Native American Affairs, chaired by Representative Bill Richardson (D-New Mexico).

Early Policy Direction

Much of the Senate's Indian policy direction was settled through its treaty-making authority during the first century, a policy urged by President George Washington to "conciliate the powerful tribes," to maintain "the fixed and stable principles" of treaties and relations with foreign nations and to give "energy to the laws throughout our interior frontier and for restraining the commissions of outrages upon the Indians, without which all pacific plans must prove nugatory." The Senate initiated, over the specific objections of Georgia, the hallmark of federal Indian law, the "Act to regulate trade and intercourse with the Indian tribes," which recognized as valid only those land and other transactions with Indians that were federally approved (Act of July 22, 1790). The "Non-intercourse Act" was made permanent in the Act of June 30, 1834. This law became the basis for federal settlements of legal claims in the 1970s and 1980s by Indian nations to lands in Rhode Island, Maine, New York, Connecticut, and elsewhere in the East. Between 1789 and 1820, the Committee of the Whole Senate deliberated and ratified treaties and considered all Indian legislation and appropriations, only occasionally relying on small ad hoc panels to review specific aspects of treaties and other measures.

The House used its investigatory process as early as 1792 and its authority to initiate appropriations to drive Indian policy, threatening not to fund each ratified treaty as a way of extracting concessions from the Senate and asserting control over Indian affairs. Both Houses have developed as much substantive Indian law of significance through their money bills as through their authorizing panels. The Senate ratified 371 United States-Indian treaties until there were enough appropriate votes in both Houses to end this single-House practice. The 1871 Indian Appropriations Act prohibited further "contract by treaty" with Indian nations, but Congress continued into the 1900s to enact over 100 treaty agreements through the legislative processes of both Houses.

The first chairman of the Senate Committee was Senator David Holmes (R-Mississippi). The committee and subcommittee have been chaired by forty-four senators from four parties (twenty Republicans, nineteen Democrats, three Whigs, two Jeffersonian/ Jacksonians) and from thirty states (five from Missouri; four from South Dakota; three each from Arkansas and Montana; two each from Iowa, North Dakota and Oklahoma; and one each from twenty-three other states). The House panels have been chaired by forty-seven members from three parties (twenty-five Democrats, thirteen Republicans, seven Whigs, and two whose parties are unrecorded) and from twenty-five states (five from Tennessee; three each from Arkansas, Kansas, Minnesota, Montana, New York, and Oklahoma; two each from Indiana, North Carolina, Pennsylvania, South Dakota, Texas, and Washington; and one each from twelve other states). During the same period since 1820, there have been thirty-eight presidents, twenty of whom have been Republicans, twelve Democrats, and six Whigs.

Committees of Senators White and Dawes

Those with the longest tenure as chairman of the Senate panels have been Senators Hugh Lawson White (J/AJ/W-Tennessee) and Henry Lauren Dawes (R-Massachusetts), each of whom served for twelve years. Senator White won the seat vacated by Senator Andrew Jackson (J-Tennessee) in 1825, quickly rising in the Committee ranks to chairman two years later, serving from 1827 to 1832, and from 1834 to 1839. He assumed the chairmanship following a period of intensive warfare and treaty-making in the territories northwest and south of the Ohio River. Between 1800 and 1825, 113 treaties were ratified by the Senate, including nearly 20 negotiated by soldiers who had fought the Indian nations and would later become presidents, such as Generals Jackson and William Henry Harrison.

Senator White was the legislative architect for the Indian removal policy, together with his House counterpart, Representative John Bell (W-Tennessee) (1829 to 1830 and 1835 to 1940) and his predecessor, Representative John Cocke (Tennessee) (1823 to 1826). In his first annual message in December of 1829, President Jackson called for the removal policy, for civilizing the Indians who "retained their savage ways," and for the rights of states to Indian lands. The skids had been so well greased by the president and the Committee chairmen that by February of 1830, removal bills were reported favorably by both committees. (Representative David Crockett was the only member of the delegation to break from the Tennessee block to join the opposition in the two-month floor debates.) The Indian removal bill became law in May of 1830. The president later refused to enforce related Supreme Court decisions to halt removal, despite personal pleas by Chief Justice John Marshall.

Senator Dawes' twelve years as Committee chairman (1881 to 1892) followed an eighteen-year career in the House, where he had chaired the powerful Appropriations, Elections and Ways and Means Committees. Upon his retirement from Congress after thirty-six years of service, Senator Dawes became chairman of the Commission to Administer the Affairs of the Five Civilized Tribes (1893 to 1903). He arrived in Congress in 1857 at a time when the states, homesteaders, and goldminers might as well have been in charge of Indian affairs. In 1850, for example, Congress authorized treaty negotiations with Indians in California, and eighteen treaties were negotiated and sent to the Senate by President Millard Fillmore. However, the

California legislature petitioned the Senate to reject the treaties and remove all the Indians from the state; in 1852 the Senate adopted a resolution refusing to ratify the treaties, with the practical effect of allowing the gold fever to kill or displace 90 percent of California's Indian people. It would take the Colorado Third's slaughter and mutilation along the Sand Creek in 1864 of hundreds of unarmed Cheyenne and Arapaho people, mostly women and children, to capture the attention of Congress about outrages against Indians, which were the subject of a Joint Committee and Special Senate Committees from 1864 to 1867.

After overseeing the House-driven end to Senate treaty-making and the Indian Homestead Act (permitting public lands for Indians who abandoned their tribal ways) in the money bills of 1871 and 1875, Representative Dawes left the House for the Senate. While the House was bent on transferring Indian affairs back to the War Department from the Interior Department, which had acquired its administration in 1849, Senator Dawes focused on "civilizing" the Indians: he helped craft legislation in 1879 for Indian children to be taken from their families for programming in federal boarding schools; in 1883 he worked for courts of Indian offenses that would lead to the outlawing of Indian religions and their "heathen and barbarous customs"; and from 1892 to 1893 he was involved in withholding rations from families who resisted the starve-or-sell/starve-or-school mandates for land cessions and school attendance. The hallmark of Senator Dawes' Committee chairmanship was the General Land Allotment Act of February 8, 1887, in which tribal lands were parceled out to individual Indians.

Indian New Deal Programs

The Indian New Deal programs of the administration of President Franklin Roosevelt—and the Indian Reorganization Act of 1934 steamrolled through Congress by Committee Chairmen Senator Burton K. Wheeler (D-Minnesota) and Representative Edgar Howard (D-Nebraska)—stopped the forced assimilation of Indian people and the erosion of Indian resources. It recognized tribal sovereignty, self-government, and cultural rights, consolidated Indian land holdings and authorized funds for tribal land acquisitions and economic advancement. Within two years of its enactment, however, legislation to undo the new law began to be introduced. As World War II was underway, the tribal structures and federal programs spawned by the New Dealers began to be characterized by many in Congress as "un-American," and inherently communistic and socialistic. Before the war's end, reports from the committee chairman, Senator Elmer Thomas (D-Oklahoma), and the House Select Committee to Investigate Indian Affairs and Conditions, chaired by Representative Karl Mundt (R-South Dakota) of the Indian Affairs and Un-American Activities Committees, set the stage for subsequent legislation to terminate federal-tribal relations.

Senate and House Subcommittees of Public Lands

The Senate and House Committees were relegated in 1946 to Subcommittees of Public Lands, vastly increasing the clout of land and water developers, parks, and wildlife advocates and the mining, utilities, and other special interests over Indian lands that already controlled the Interior Department. The Indian Claims Commission was set up to resolve Indian land claims with cash-only settlements. The Committees on Appropriations, Civil Service expenditures in Executive Departments and Public Lands forced the development of legislation to "terminate" specified tribes, to turn over jurisdiction to states, and to send Indians to "relocation" cities, where the promise of jobs faded and Indians were stranded. In 1957 the Department of the Interior secretary called the termination policy "potentially disastrous," reporting Indian land losses of 2.6 million acres from 1948 to 1957, with 1.7 million lost from 1953 to 1957 alone. These figures did not account for the Indian lands taken or used during the war, mostly in secret by congressional defense and lands committees for the purpose of nuclear and other weapons testing and storage.

Roles of Other Senate Committees

In the 1960s and 1970s other Senate committees began a reversal of termination policies. This primarily included the Judiciary Subcommittee on Constitutional Rights, chaired by Senator Sam J. Ervin (D-North Carolina), in 1961 to 1969 hearings on the constitutional rights of the American Indian; the Labor and Public Welfare Special Subcommittee to Investigate Problems of Education for American Indians, chaired by Senators Robert F. Kennedy (D-New York) and Edward M. Kennedy (D-Massachusetts), in 1967 to 1969 hearings and in the *Report on Indian Education: A National Tragedy—A National Challenge*; and the Judiciary Subcommittee on Administrative Practice and Procedure, chaired by Senator Kennedy, in hearings beginning in 1971 on federal protection of Indian resources. During the late 1960s and early 1970s the Subcommittee on Indian Affairs, chaired by Senator George McGovern (D-South Dakota), crafted legislation ending the termination era and beginning the self-determination policy. In 1975 a two-year study by the American Indian Policy Review Commission, chaired by the subcommittee chairman Senator James Abourezk (D-South Dakota), began an extensive set of hearings that produced a voluminous report in mid-1977. During the same period, the Judiciary Committee held camera hearings with an FBI agent who had infiltrated the American Indian Movement (AIM). AIM leaders had occupied the Bureau of Indian Affairs building in Washington, D.C. in late 1972, and the village of Wounded Knee on the Pine Ridge Reservation in South Dakota in early 1973; both activities called to world attention the emergency needs of Indian people. The Judiciary Subcommittee on Internal Security, chaired by Senator James O. Eastland

(D-Mississippi), issued its *Report on Revolutionary Activities* within the United States in late 1976.

Reestablishment of the Senate Committee

The prominence of Indian affairs in Congress generated by these reports and the recommendation of the American Indian Policy Review Commission, building on that of the earlier Kennedy report that the Senate should reestablish an Indian affairs committee, led to the 1977 creation of the Select Committee on Indian Affairs, whose chairman was Senator Abourezk. The Commission's vice-chairman, Representative Lloyd Meeds (D-Washington), was the lone dissenting voice to its final report; following a year of efforts by Meeds as House Indian Subcommittee chairman to thwart follow-up legislation, Interior Chairman Morris K. Udall (D-Arizona) had the Subcommittee disbanded and all Indian legislation handled through the full Committee. This paved the way for significant legislation to protect Indian religious freedom rights, to promote Indian children and family rights, to provide land and development fund settlements to Indian land claims in the East, and to establish tribally controlled community colleges. In 1979 the United States Commission on Security and Cooperation in Europe recognized Indian international rights under the self-determination and human rights principles of the Helsinki Accords and was able to report that the United States "has recognized that it has not always lived up to its obligations in its protection of the rights of Native Americans to a continuing political existence. The United States Government, however, is improving its performance and attempting to close the gap between policy and practice."

Challenges and Accomplishments in the 1980s

The 1980s signaled an abrupt change in practice, with Congress forestalling President Ronald Reagan's proposed cut of one-third of the federal Indian budget, or $1 billion, in his first budget in 1981, and other administration initiatives to turn over Indian education, resources, and jurisdiction to states. The Senate Select Committee, chaired by Senators William S. Cohen (R-Maine), Mark Andrews (R-North Dakota), and Daniel K. Inouye (D-Hawaii), resisted the full scope of the administration's cuts of the 1980s. However, more than $100 million was cut from an Indian budget that was inadequate to the Indian needs at the outset. With the White House emphasis during this decade of imposing states' rights over Indian matters, several efforts in Congress to wipe out Indian land claims and to negate a Supreme Court decision upholding tribal gambling operations were narrowly averted. By the end of the 1980s Congress had enacted legislation providing some concessions to the states' non-Indian gaming interests, but still recognizing tribal governmental and economic rights, as well as new laws providing for greater tribal autonomy in pro-gram administration; for return of Indian human remains and sacred objects from museums, federal agencies, and educational institutions; for clearly-stated repudiation of the termination policy; for improved health and housing conditions; and for the establishment of a National Museum of the American Indian on the last remaining land on the Capitol Mall. In 1989 and 1990 Congress even apologized for the 1890 Seventh Cavalry Massacre of Lakota People at Wounded Knee and authorized an Indian Memorial along the Little Bighorn River, dropping the name of "Custer" and renaming the national area as the Little Big Horn Battlefield Monument.

The Future

In 1993 a new effort by state governors to gain greater control of tribal gambling revenue and operations also took the form of a planned attempt by Nevada gaming interests to abolish the Senate Committee on Indian Affairs. The planned floor action was not offered by its sponsor, who pursued another strategy, to have the committee abolished by the panel recommending an overall congressional structure reorganization. At the same time efforts are underway to undo the gaming bill that the states hailed as their victory and the legislation they wanted in 1990. The only stated complaint against the Senate Committee on Indian Affairs has been that it has been too much of an advocate for Indians. The matter remained unresolved at the time of this publication.

Suzan Shown Harjo

See also **Allotment; Government Policy; Treaties**

Further Reading

Deloria, Vine. *Custer Died for Your Sins: An Indian Manifesto*. New York, NY: Macmillan, 1968.

Hoxie, Frederick E. *A Final Promise: The Campaign to Assimilate the Indians, 1880–1920*. Lincoln: University of Nebraska Press, 1984.

Prucha, Francis Paul. *The Great Father: The United States Government and the American Indians*. Vol. 2. Lincoln: University of Nebraska Press, 1984.

SENECA

The Seneca Indians presently live in four major political and community groups located in the United States and Canada: the Seneca Nation of Indians, located on three reservations in Cattaraugus and Allegany counties, New York; the Tonawanda Band of Seneca, near Akron, New York; the Six Nations Reserve near Brantford, Ontario; and the Seneca-Cayuga Tribe, located in northeastern Oklahoma. The original homeland for all of these groups was located between Lake Canandaigua on the east, and the Genesee River on the west, in what is now New York State.

Designated as one of the elder brothers in the political organization of the Iroquois Confederacy and occupying the westernmost position in the Confederacy, the Seneca have been a diverse group from the early historic period. Various groups of Seneca were signatories to treaties with the United States beginning with the Treaty of Fort Stanwix in 1784 and ending with the federal treaty with the Tonawanda Seneca in 1857. These negotiations generally resulted in the reduction of Seneca lands in the state of New York and the movement of some Seneca groups out of the state.

The Seneca Nation of Indians

The largest group of contemporary Seneca, the Seneca Nation of Indians, has approximately 6,241 members living on the federally recognized Allegany and Cattaraugus reservations in New York State. The Allegany Reservation is located along the Allegany River in Cattaraugus County, and is the location of the city of Salamanca, New York. The Cattaraugus Reservation, along Cattaraugus Creek and Lake Erie, lies some thrity miles south of Buffalo, New York. This reservation is also occupied by significant groups of Cayuga and Munsee people. The third Seneca Nation reservation, the Oil Spring Reservation in Allegany and Cattaraugus counties, is the site of the first oil discovery in the United States, and has no permanent Seneca residents.

The Seneca Nation of Indians came into being in 1848 with the adoption of a written Constitution which abolished the office of chief, and which created the Seneca republic with a tripartite system of government under a legislative branch comprised of a single Tribal Council, the executive branch consisting of president, treasurer and clerk, and the judiciary branch with two separate court systems. By abolishing the traditional chief system, the Seneca Nation was seen as having withdrawn from the Iroquois Confederacy.

The Cornplanter Grant

A reduced acreage of slightly more than 100 acres remains of the Cornplanter Grant in Pennsylvania, located on the west bank of the Allegany River, a few miles south of the New York/Pennsylvania state line and the Allegany Reservation. Originally presented to the Seneca Chief Cornplanter as a personal possession by the Commonwealth of Pennsylvania, title continues to reside with the 600 or more descendants of Cornplanter. The majority of Cornplanter's heirs are members of the Seneca Nation of Indians or the Tonawanda Band of Senecas.

The Tonawanda Band of Seneca

The second group in New York State is the Tonawanda Band of Seneca, a federally recognized tribe located on the Tonawanda Reservation near Akron, New York. The Tonawanda Seneca number about 1,050. Unlike the Seneca Nation, the Tonawanda Band of Seneca continues with a traditional Tribal Council of eight chiefs, and membership in the Iroquois Confederacy. They retain 7,549 acres of restricted tribal lands.

Other Seneca

The Canadian Seneca, currently numbering some 262 Nigarondasa Senecas, and 331 Konadaha Senecas, originated from the loyalist Iroquois who followed the Mohawk Chief Joseph Brant into Canada following the American Revolution. The fourth group of Seneca are descended from a highly amalgamated group of Iroquois, now called the Seneca-Cayuga Tribe of Oklahoma.

Twentieth-Century History

Throughout the twentieth century, both the Seneca Nation of Indians and the Tonawanda Band of Senecas repeatedly fought against the intrusions of Washington, D.C. and Albany officials into tribal affairs. Both tribal governments successfully and overwhelmingly rejected the Indian Reorganization Act of 1934. They nevertheless lost battles in 1948 and 1950, when Congress unilaterally transferred criminal and civil jurisdiction over American Indian affairs to New York State. Moreover, the Seneca Nation of Indians faced its major crisis of the twentieth century when they could not prevent Washington, D.C. from building the $120 million Kinzua Dam in the 1960s. The dam flooded over 9,000 acres of the Cornplanter tract and Allegany Reservation and disrupted Seneca traditional life and mores. In more recent days, the Seneca Nation of Indians has been preoccupied with settling the thorny problem of 3,000 ninety-nine-year leases on their lands in and around Salamanca, New York. In 1990, the Seneca Nation received a $35 million settlement award from the federal government for its failure to act in the past to protect Indian interests in this matter. In 1992, it received $25 million in direct and indirect monies from New York State in further compensation. The leases have been renewed under new terms with the City of Salamanca.

Both Seneca groups have asserted their economic self-determination in opposing the state's desire to tax reservation sales of petroleum and tobacco to non-Indians. Seneca people today find employment in the nearby cities of Rochester and Buffalo. The Seneca Nation of Indians runs mini-marts in several locations and has bingo operations on the Allegany and Cattaraugus reservations. Its tribal government is also a major employer. Potential casino gambling remains a divisive issue for the Seneca Nation of Indians.

Seneca history of the twentieth century has also been marked by positive achievements. From 1935 to 1941, Arthur C. Parker and the Rochester Museum and Science Center helped initiate a WPA Indian Arts Project which stimulated a renaissance of Seneca arts, especially at the Tonawanda Indian Reservation. Seneca artists such as Sarah Hill, Ernest and Kidd Smith, Jesse Cornplanter, Sanford Plummer, Elon Webster, and Harrison Ground helped revive Seneca arts and became featured artists at the New York State Pavilion at the World's Fair of 1939. As a result of Parker's efforts, those of Namee Hendricks, a local philanthropist, and the intervention of Eleanor Roosevelt, the Tonawanda Indian Community House, another WPA project, was built by Indian labor in the late 1930s. This community house, the first of its kind in New York, still serves the Seneca peoples' health, education, and social service needs.

Recent achievements of the Seneca include the creation of a Seneca Nation health department to deliver services to both the Cattaraugus and Allegany reservations as well as the urban Seneca population in Buffalo, with the establishment of direct clinic services in the city. The Seneca Nation of Indians Health Department has been commended as a model in the Indian health service field.

The Senecas in New York maintain a matrilineal system of kinship determining tribal and clan affiliation. Clan affiliation and traditional religion continue to be important among these Seneca.

George H.J. Abrams

See also **Iroquois Confederacy; Seneca-Cayuga**

Further Reading

Abler, Thomas S., and Elisabeth Tooker. "Seneca." *Handbook of North American Indians.* Vol. 15. *Northeast.* Ed. Bruce G. Trigger. Washington, DC: Smithsonian Institution (1978): 505–17.

Abrams, George H.J. *The Seneca People.* Phoenix, AZ: Indian Tribal Series, 1976.

Wallace, Anthony F.C. *The Death and Rebirth of the Seneca.* New York, NY: Alfred A. Knopf, 1969.

SENECA-CAYUGA

The Seneca-Cayuga Tribe of Oklahoma presently lives on lands in Ottawa County, Oklahoma. The community today is derived from two bands of Iroquois Indians removed from Ohio early in the 1830s. Despite being frequently referred to in the historical record as "Senecas of Sandusky," "Neosho Senecas," "Cowskin Senecas," "Seneca Nation," or simply "Senecas," these Oklahoma Iroquois are linguistically closer to the Cayuga.

The presence of diverse Iroquois peoples emigrating at different times from the east produced political disunity, and Iroquois society in the Indian Territory remained divided. A separate Cayuga tribal structure existed until the mid-1920s, and in a weakened and modified form until 1937. Senecas, on the other hand, were electing a Tribal Council of three councilmen and three chiefs from the 1870s until 1937. The Seneca-Cayuga faced other problems, such as whites who trespassed and stripped timber off their lands, corrupt Indian agents who cheated them of their treaty benefits, illegal grazing, nonpayment of their annuities, federal and local attempts to consolidate them with the Cherokees, and disruptions caused by the creation of Oklahoma Territory. Most importantly, the federal government allotted half of the approximately 65,000-acre Seneca Reservation by 1888. In 1902 and 1903, Washington, D.C. allotted most of the remaining land to the 337 tribal members, desig-

nated 10,000 acres as "surplus," and threw the former reservation open to white settlement. By 1936, when Congress passed the Oklahoma Indian Welfare Act providing for tribal incorporation, educational assistance, and economic development, these Iroquois had only 140 acres of tribal lands left.

In 1937, the Seneca-Cayugas became the first tribe to come under the act, the first of eighteen to adopt a Constitution and Bylaws, and the first of thirteen to ratify a Charter of Incorporation. A Business Committee of five members was soon elected and the newly consolidated tribe, operating as a single entity, started the application process for loans.

Although their tribal land base increased by tenfold in a three-year period as a result of their political unity, the Seneca-Cayuga were nevertheless dispossessed of 281.33 acres in 1940 when the Grand River Dam Authority built its Pensacola Dam. The new government policy of "termination" threatened the Seneca-Cayuga in the 1950s, but unlike their neighbors the Ottawas and Peorias, they successfully resisted by uniting against this policy. More recent developments include the filing of a land claim under the leadership of James Allen, Peter Buck, and Vernon Crow against New York State. Allen and Crow also served in World War II, where Allen was a prisoner of war in Germany and Crow returned home a decorated hero. By 1993 landholdings in Oklahoma consisted of 1,093 acres of trust lands and 2,975 acres of allotted lands.

The 1993 community of 2,460 individuals, with 787 residing in northeastern Oklahoma, has maintained its cultural and religious connections to Iroquois people in the east, especially its kin at the Six Nations Reserve near Brantford, Ontario, and at the Allegany and Cattaraugus Seneca reservations in New York State. There were twelve Oklahoma speakers of Cayuga in 1970. Ruby Charloe Diebold, Bob White, and Reuben Dutch White served as Cayuga language resource people in past attempts to set up a language preservation program. The Seneca-Cayuga maintain Iroquois rituals such as the Green Corn ceremony held in August each year; retain a longhouse; and collect annuity payments from New York State under provisions of the 1788 Treaty of Cayuga Ferry. Many Seneca-Cayuga Indians work in Tulsa and Oklahoma City, and as far away as New York and California. Some in northeastern Oklahoma are involved in the ranching industry.

Laurence M. Hauptman

See also **Cayuga; Oklahoma Tribes; Seneca**

Further Reading

Hauptman, Laurence M. *The Iroquois and the New Deal.* NY: Syracuse University Press, 1981.

———. *The Iroquois Struggle for Survival: World War II to Red Power.* NY: Syracuse University Press, 1986.

———. "The Seneca-Cayuga Reject Termination." *Between Two Worlds: The Survival of Twentieth*

Century Indians. Ed. Arrell Morgan Gibson. Oklahoma City: Oklahoma Historical Society, 1986. 184–201.

Sturtevant, William C. "Oklahoma Seneca-Cayuga." *Handbook of North American Indians.* Vol. 15. *Northeast.* Ed. Bruce G. Trigger. Washington, DC: Smithsonian Institution (1978): 537–43.

SERRANO

The Serrano spoke a Takic language belonging to the Uto-Aztecan language family. Originally occupying much of the Mojave Desert and the San Bernardino Mountains, they had largely disappeared in this area by the beginning of the twentieth century. Some had moved among the Gabrielino, Cahuilla, and other groups. San Manuel Reservation, in San Bernardino, California, near the foot of the San Bernardino Mountains, was established in 1893 and is a Serrano reservation. It has eighty-five members of whom twenty-five live on the reservation. The Serrano also make up a considerable part of the population of Morongo Reservation. Many of them are descendants of John Morongo, who married a Cahuilla woman and became in the 1880s and 1890s an important leader of the reservation that is now named after him. Soboba Reservation also has Serrano members.

The ethnographer and linguist, John Peabody Harrington, interviewed a number of Serrano people in the early years of the twentieth century, preserving in his notes at the Smithsonian Institution a great many Serrano place names and a geographically specific rendering of the Serrano creation story.

The land base at San Manuel (657.93 acres) was never very adequate for agriculture. People there supported themselves largely by wage labor. In recent years San Manuel has established a bingo parlor. At Morongo Reservation, many Serranos belong to the Moravian Church, whereas the Cahuilla are often Roman Catholic. Many Serranos have worked as cattlemen and independent farmers and have played a major role on the Morongo Business Committee. Because there has been extensive intermarriage at Morongo, it is not possible to give an estimate of the percentage of Serranos there.

Morongo Reservation, like San Manuel, has a bingo parlor, which was established under the chairmanship of Robert Martin, a Serrano-Cahuilla. Other well-known Serranos include Ernest Siva, an ethnomusicologist at the University of California, Los Angeles, and the late Sarah Martin, also Serrano-Cahuilla, who was an important ceremonial leader in the first part of the twentieth century. The number of Serrano speakers is now very small and very few traditional rituals survive. Some Serranos continue to sing Bird Songs on social occasions.

Lowell John Bean

Sylvia Brakke Vane

See also California Tribes

Further Reading

Bean, Lowell John, and Charles R. Smith. "Serrano." *Handbook of North American Indians.* Vol. 8. *Califor-*

nia. Ed. Robert F. Heizer. Washington, DC: Smithsonian Institution (1978): 570–75.

Strong, William Duncan. "Aboriginal Society in Southern California." *University of California Publications in American Archaeology and Ethnology* 26:1 (1929): 183–273. Banning, CA: Malki Museum Press, 1987.

SHAKER CHURCH

See Indian Shaker Church

SHAMANISM

See Traditional Medicine

SHASTA

The aboriginal territory of the Shasta Nation is comprised of seven major divisions. Their names and geographic watershed areas in northern California and southern Oregon are: Kahosadi, Rogue River; Kamatwa, Upper Klamath River; Ahotireitsu, Shasta River; Iruaitsu, Scott River; Konomihu, Salmon River; New River Shasta; and Okwanuchu of Squaw Creek, McCloud River, and Upper Sacramento River. In addition, there are two subdivisions: the Achomawi and Atsugewi, Pit River watershed; these two now have their own political identity.

On November 4, 1851, at Fort Jones, California, Commissioner Redick McKee negotiated a treaty with thirteen Shasta chiefs representing the Upper Klamath, Shasta, and Scott River Indians. This signed treaty set aside a reservation for them, but it was never ratified. After the signing of the treaty a barbecue was prepared, the meat and bread poisoned with strychnine. Thousands of Indians feasted and then perished. Vigilantes continued the genocide by attacking the villages, killing and burning as they went. The Shasta had no recourse, since no white man could be convicted of any offense upon testimony of an Indian or Indians. Treaty signer Sun Rise was forced to flee into the mountains for two years before it was safe for him to return to Quartz Valley.

The Rogue River Treaty of 1853 included Shastas; the resulting reservation was abandoned when that group was relocated to the Grand Ronde and Siletz reservations in Oregon. Additional treaties which included Shastas were the Chasta Costa Treaty, 1854, and the Klamath Treaty, 1864, which ceded the California Shasta's aboriginal territory. The Shasta were unaware of this transaction and never received just compensation for loss of their homeland. A reservation was granted to Indian Mary in 1885, now known as Indian Mary Park, in Oregon. Ruffy Reservation was terminated in 1959. The Quartz Valley Reservation was established in 1939, for such Shasta and Upper Klamath Indians speaking the Shasta language who were eligible to participate; it was terminated in 1958 and reinstated in 1983. Two Shasta Indians currently reside there. Some Shastas received allotments under the Dawes Act, but little of this land was able to be retained.

During the 1860s Chief Mungo made a Treaty of Peace and Friendship with the founders of Happy Camp, and with about one hundred residents of Fort Jones. During the latter half of the nineteenth century the head chief was Tyee Jim. After the turn of the century, Wilson Pete and John Courts were representatives. Stanley W. Miller appeared before the Indian Claims Commission and John Carmony served on the Indian Board of Cooperation and journeyed to Washington, D.C. on California land claims business. Clara Wicks, Fred Wicks, and Lawrence Burcell were Shasta representatives for the Quartz Valley Reservation.

Roy V. Hall, Jr., is current chairman of the Shasta Nation. He is assisted by Mary Carpelan, Betty Hall, Sonja Maricle, and Caraway George. Their focus is on federal recognition, archaeology, return of grave goods and ancestral remains. Ninety percent of the Shasta people work in timber related industries, which are currently in decline and thus the economic situation for many Indians has become grim. Health care services for the Shasta have been inadequate, and they have to depend on approval for services from the Karuk Tribal Health Program. Legal proceedings became necessary in one instance to obtain payment for medical services. The Shasta cultural identity has been passed down through individual families. Most have their own collection of artifacts, which include basketry, obsidian blades, woodcarvings, stone implements, and ceremonial dress.

The Shasta Nation is currently petitioning for federal recognition for 1,300 members. It is a member of the Confederated Aboriginal Nations of California, a coalition of Indian nations which is growing spiritually and politically. The California Tribal Status Act in 1992 established a commission comprised of one person each from seven acknowledged tribes, seven unacknowledged tribes, two terminated tribes, and two nonvoting members, representing the Bureau of Indian Affairs and the Indian Health Service. This commission will make recommendations as to which Indian nations meet the criteria for federal acknowledgment. In view of the genocide visited upon them in the last century, the Shasta believe that the very least the United States government can do is acknowledge their past and current existence.

Betty L. Hall

Monica J. Hall

See also **California Tribes**

Further Reading

Hannon, Nan, and Richard K. Olmo, eds. *Living with the Land: The Indians of Southwest Oregon.* Medford: Southern Oregon Historical Society, 1990.

Holt, Permelia Catharine. "Shasta Ethnography." *University of California Anthropological Records* 3:4 (1946): 299–349.

Renfro, Elizabeth. *The Shasta Indians of California and Their Neighbors.* Happy Camp, CA: Naturegraph Publishers, 1992.

Silver, Shirley. "Shastan Peoples." *Handbook of North American Indians.* Vol. 8. *California.* Ed. Robert F. Heizer. Washington, DC: Smithsonian Institution (1978): 211–24.

Zucker, Jeff, Kay Hummel, and Bob Hogfoss. *Oregon Indians: Culture, History, & Current Affairs.* Portland: Western Imprints, The Press of the Oregon Historical Society, 1983.

SHAWNEE

Traditional historic and archeological evidence place the Shawnee on the Ohio River in prehistoric times, where they eventually returned after being pushed south by the Iroquois and then west by the colonists across Pennsylvania with their kinsmen among the Delaware. This location put them in continual conflict with the Europeans and colonists until Tecumseh's death in 1813 broke the solidarity of the Ohio region tribes. Scattered and allied with remnants and refugees of other area tribes, the majority of the Shawnee eventually ended up in Oklahoma in a series of treaties and removals. Today, there are three distinct political entities in Oklahoma—the Absentee Shawnee, the Eastern Shawnee, and the Loyal Shawnee. A Shawnee band consisting of descendants of scattered families who managed to escape the removals of the nineteenth century—the Shawnee Nation United Remnant Band—has achieved state recognition from Ohio.

SHAWNEE IN OHIO

The descendants of Shawnees who survived in the Ohio Valley after Tecumseh's defeat, most of the approximately 600 members of the Shawnee Nation United Remnant Band (URB), are scattered over Ohio and surrounding states. Officially gaining state recognition by Ohio in 1980, the Shawnee Nation URB purchased the first of their tribal lands in 1989. By 1992 the major land holding consisted of 117 acres at Shawandasse just south of Urbana, Ohio, and an additional 63 acres near Chillicothe, Ohio. Efforts to purchase more land continues. Currently no one resides year-round on Shawnee lands; instead, Shawandasse serves as a meeting place for ceremonies, councils, powwows, and youth camps.

The URB can trace its origins to scattered Shawnee settlements in nineteenth-century Indiana under the leadership of Aaron Flowers. Despite attempts to gain security by blending in with white farming communities, these Shawnees also married other Shawnees, preserved ceremonies like the Green Corn, and hid sacred bundles.

One such Shawnee community was Blue River in Hancock County, Indiana. By the 1950s about fifty Shawnees there under the leadership of Reva Pope struggled to preserve traditions like the Green Corn ceremony. With Pope's death in 1959 no efforts were made to continue or revitalize Shawnee traditions until his grandson Hawk Pope (Tukemas) organized the United Remnant Band in 1971, ultimately moving from Indiana to Ohio to return to Tecumseh's homeland.

Hawk Pope continues today as chief. Many of the traditions and ceremonies, such as the Spring Bread Dance, Green Corn ceremony, and Fall Council, are based on Pope's boyhood recollections of such events at Blue River. Most URB members do not have those kinds of personal recollections on which to draw. However, they do have family oral traditions of being Shawnee, despite their integration into the surrounding population.

The URB hopes to transform Shawandasse into a residential Shawnee community. Also taking leadership roles in this effort are Linda Knox (Crow Woman), the "mother of the nation"; Rev. Fred Shaw (Neeake), the principal storyteller; and artist Christy Pope (Meenjip Tatsii), whose pottery has been exhibited in galleries as far away as Oklahoma and Arizona.

Sharlotte Neely

Further Reading

Callender, Charles. "Shawnee." *Handbook of North American Indians*. Vol. 15. *Northeast*. Ed. Bruce G. Trigger. Washington, DC: Smithsonian Institution (1978): 622–35.

Clark, Jerry E. *The Shawnee*. Lexington: University of Kentucky Press, 1977.

Neely, Sharlotte. "The Role of a Leader in Preserving the Tribal Organization of the Ohio Shawnee." Central States Anthropological Society Annual Meeting, Cincinnati, OH 1990.

Pope, Hawk. *Shawnee Nation United Remnant Band: A Brief History of the Present Day Shawnee Tribe of Ohio*. Dayton, OH: Shawnee Nation URB (P.O. Box 162, Dayton, OH 45401), 1989.

———. "Archeological and Pot Hunter Disturbance of Native American Graves." Shawnee Nation United Remnant Band position paper. Dayton, OH: Shawnee Nation URB, 1990.

SHAWNEE IN OKLAHOMA

After years of tribal division and removal, three distinct bands of Shawnee people currently reside in Oklahoma: the Absentee Shawnee, the Eastern Shawnee, and the Loyal Shawnee (often referred to in the past as the Cherokee Shawnee). Although usually traced to the Great Lakes area, the Shawnee spent much of their history in the American South and the word "Shawnee" stems from the Algonquian word *Shawun*, meaning "South," or *Shawunogi* meaning "Southerner." They refer to themselves as *Shawano* and once numbered over 50,000.

Absentee Shawnee

The Absentee Shawnee received title to a portion of a reservation between the north and south forks of the Canadian River near present-day Shawnee, Oklahoma, in 1872. The Citizen Band Potawatomi received title to the rest of the reservation. Most tribal members soon accepted individual land allotments, and by 1900 the majority had succumbed to the processes of assimilation into the American mainstream. Those "progressive" elements of the tribe tended to follow the examples set for them by the thoroughly assimilated Chief White Turkey and Thomas Wildcat Alford. Others belonging to the Big Jim Band opposed acculturation well into the twentieth century. In the 1920s, the Big Jim segment even entertained ideas of moving to Mexico, where they hoped they could maintain their communal way of life. Hard feelings between the two camps kept the tribe's leaders occupied, but hostilities never reached dangerous levels. Educated at Hampton Institute in Virginia, Alford served in various capacities with the Indian Department for most of his life. He believed strongly in the "benefits" of Indian assimilation and achieved considerable success in the pursuit of his goal, described in his 1936 autobiography *Civilization*.

The tribe organized as the Absentee Shawnee Tribe of Indians of Oklahoma under the Oklahoma Indian Welfare Act of 1936. They fall under the federal jurisdiction of the Shawnee Indian Agency, which is part of the Bureau of Indian Affairs (BIA) Anadarko Area Office. Members have adopted a Constitution, Bylaws, and an Executive Committee presided over by a governor. Leroy Ellis served as the governor in 1992. The Absentee Shawnee maintain a tribal court of law and a police force, and provide most of the tribe's health services at their tribal complex just outside of Shawnee. From February 1, 1925, to December 19, 1961, health services were provided in the federal Indian sanitarium that had been erected adjacent to Absentee Shawnee lands. Originally established as a center for the treatment of tuberculosis for Native Americans, it was one of only two such facilities in the country.

The BIA estimated the tribe's population in 1981 to be 1,384. More recent estimates point to a population of over 2,000. Members derive their income from farming, livestock, taxes on oil and gas contracts, small businesses, bingo, and tax-free sales. They also won a claim against the federal government in 1971. Baptist and Friends denominations claim the largest membership among the Absentee Shawnee. The Big Jim Band conducts tribal thanksgiving dances such as the Green Corn Dance in early spring and fall and a ceremonial War Dance in August near Little Axe. Of the three Shawnee bands in Oklahoma, the largest number who speak the Algonquian Shawnee language belongs to the Absentee Shawnee.

Eastern Shawnee

The Eastern Shawnee reside in Ottawa County in northeastern Oklahoma. They belong to the Miami Indian Agency branch of the BIA's Muskogee Area Office. Historically linked with the Seneca tribe, they were known collectively as the United Nation or Mixed Band of Seneca and Shawnee upon arrival in Oklahoma in 1832. Not until an 1867 treaty did the federal government refer to them as the Eastern Shawnee. In 1937, they organized as the Eastern Shawnee Tribe of

Oklahoma under the Oklahoma Indian Welfare Act and officially separated from the Seneca. Members then approved a Constitution and Bylaws and established the Eastern Shawnee Business Committee, then composed of Walter Bluejacket, Thomas A. Captain, Ora S. Hampton, Edward H. Bluejacket, and Edward Dushane. They also approved an Eastern Shawnee Tribal Charter issued by the secretary of the interior in an election held December 12, 1940. George J. Captain served as chief in 1992.

In 1965, 813 members of the tribe shared a claims case award of $110,000 for depredations suffered during the Civil War. The current tribal roll shows 1,550 members. They publish a newsletter, the *Shooting Star*, and employ seventeen office and nutrition staff in addition to twenty-five bingo employees. Their tribal complex, located in West Seneca, Oklahoma, consists of an administration office, a community building, a 750-seat bingo hall, a one-quarter-acre recreational park, and an eye clinic. They provide much of their own health care and operate a nutrition program to feed the elderly. Few of them speak their Native tongue, and most derive their income in the same manner as mainstream Americans.

Loyal Shawnee

The Loyal Shawnee, often referred to as the Cherokee Shawnee, comprised the main body of the Shawnee tribe before the Civil War. Their "loyalty" to the Union cause benefited them little as they were forced from their homes in Kansas after the war and relocated among the Cherokee in Oklahoma by agreement of June 7, 1869. They purchased their land from the Cherokee and were incorporated with the tribe. Their Cherokee enrollment assigns them membership in the Tahlequah Agency branch of the BIA's Muskogee Area Office.

The main body of the tribe is centered in northeast Oklahoma in the town of Whiteoak, although tribal members are scattered throughout the United States. They are not officially organized by the terms of the Oklahoma Indian Welfare Act and have no federally recognized Constitution or Bylaws. For most federal purposes they are enrolled as Cherokee citizens, but they also maintain separate rolls for themselves. These rolls determine those Shawnee who are eligible for federal funds arising from judgments on their claims, which have been awarded in 1929, 1964, 1971, and 1982. Their political structure consists of a General Council that determines those members who should share in tribal funds and financial judgments. A Loyal Shawnee Business Committee, established December 4, 1960, consists of a chairman, a vice-chairman, a secretary-treasurer, a historian, and four elected members serving two-year terms. The present chairman is Don Greenfeather. A grievance committee investigates complaints of misconduct and actions of the Business Committee.

The maintenance of a Loyal Shawnee Cultural Center provides further evidence of their desire to distinguish themselves as separate from the Cherokee, as does their general commitment toward maintaining tribal culture. Each year dances such as the Spring and Fall Bread Dance, the Green Corn Dance, and the Buffalo Dance help to promote cultural and tribal unity, as do the Shawnee ballgames played during these times. Less than a dozen still speak their Native language. The tribe does not vigorously pursue typical reservation income-generating ventures such as bingo and tax-free cigarette sales. Their population is approximately 8,000.

Peter R. Hacker

See also **Oklahoma Tribes**

Further Reading

Alford, Thomas Wildcat. *Civilization, and the Story of the Absentee Shawnees.* As told to Florence Drake. Civilization of the American Indian 13. 1936. Norman: University of Oklahoma Press, 1979.

Chapman, Berlin. "The Potawatomi and Absentee Shawnee Reservation." *The Chronicles of Oklahoma* 24:3 (1946): 293–305.

Hacker, Peter R. "Confusion and Conflict: A Study of Atypical Responses to Nineteenth Century Federal Indian Policies by the Citizen Band Potawatomis." *American Indian Culture and Research Journal* 13:1 (1989): 79–93.

Howard, James Henri. *Shawnee!: The Ceremonialism of a Native Indian Tribe and Its Cultural Background.* Athens: Ohio University Press, 1981.

Parker, Linda. "Indian Colonization in Northeastern and Central Indian Territory." *America's Exiles: Indian Colonization in Oklahoma.* Oklahoma Ser. 3. Oklahoma City: Oklahoma Historical Society, 1976. 104–29.

Wright, Muriel H. *A Guide to the Indian Tribes of Oklahoma.* 1951. Civilization of the American Indian 33. Norman: University of Oklahoma Press, 1986.

SHINNECOCK

Approximately 400 Shinnecocks reside on the Shinnecock Indian Reservation, located on the south fork of eastern Long Island in the Town of Southampton, New York. Hundreds more regularly return to participate in tribal events and family gatherings. The land still owned and occupied by the Shinnecocks is a small portion of their original land base, which reached from Peconic Bay on the north to the Atlantic Ocean to the south, with western and eastern borders defined by relations with neighboring Native people. Settlers of English descent created the Town of Southampton in 1640; by 1703, the lands reserved to the Shinnecock were reduced to fewer than 4,000 acres. Originally set aside as a reservation by the New York Colonial Government, it continues to be recognized by the State of New York. In 1859 the land base was further reduced to fewer than 1,000 acres by town and state actions that were never ratified by the United States Congress. Today, the Shinnecocks maintain their homes, cemetery, powwow grounds, beaches, tribal programs, and offices on the land surrounded on three sides by the Shinnecock Bay. The bay was historically a rich breeding ground for shellfish, but has been increasingly threatened by pollution and the forces of nature. The Shinnecocks continue to guard against encroachment and to protect their natural environment and sites that are sacred to their people.

Shinnecocks are actively involved in their extended families; they celebrate births and support one another in times of death or personal disaster. Their lifestyles, however, have been influenced heavily by the early work of missionaries of the Protestant Reformed tradition, who converted most of them to Christianity, taught them to speak English, and otherwise molded their behavior. The Shinnecock Presbyterian church stands today on the reservation as a descendant of the oldest Protestant mission sites in North America. The church buildings serve as places of worship and a gathering space for educational and social events and tribal business. Two Shinnecocks, a man and a woman, are ordained Presbyterian ministers.

Many Shinnecocks living on the reservation today, or their parents or grandparents, attended elementary school in the schoolhouse on the reservation maintained by the State of New York until the early 1950s. In the 1930s some Shinnecock children were sent to schools on the Cattaraugus Reservation of the Seneca Nation in upstate New York. Today, children attend public schools in the town nearby.

Several annual events draw Shinnecocks together. June Meeting is celebrated on the first Sunday in June, with many people opening their doors for visiting family members and friends; preparing favorite Shinnecock foods such as clam pie, strawberry shortcake, fruit pies, and baked beans; and attending special gatherings at the church for thanksgiving and sharing recollections. The Shinnecocks also have their own Indian Thanksgiving Day, which they now observe on the third Thursday of November, when they honor elders and share fall harvest foods and seasonal favorites such as samp, oyster stew, pumpkin pie, and sassafras tea. A Labor Day Weekend Powwow has been held since the late 1940s. This event is the primary fundraiser for the tribal government and the Shinnecock church. "Powwow" is also an intertribal social event and a major educational and recreational attraction for tourists and other Long Islanders. On December 29 or 30 of each year, some Shinnecocks visit the tribal cemetery to commemorate the Shinnecock men who perished in 1876 while aiding the whaling ship *Circassian*.

Throughout the twentieth century, the Shinnecocks have kept a distinct identity while actively contributing to their communities. Shinnecock men were recognized for their knowledge of the woods and seas. As the economic life of eastern Long Island changed, Shinnecock men worked on the East End's golf courses, and used their woodworking skills to carve decoys, make baskets and scrubs, and cane chairs. Painting,

carpentry, and other building trades continue to be performed skillfully by Shinnecocks. Shinnecock women were hired by the summer resort community for their housekeeping, child care, and needlework skills, and many presently do such work as their primary or supplemental occupation. Today, with increased educational achievement by Shinnecocks and expanded employment opportunities in the county, many find employment in governmental facilities, schools, hospitals, recreational institutions, retail establishments, and in their own small businesses, as well as in the increasing number of tribal programs. All Shinnecocks took pride in the development of the Shinnecock Tribal Oyster Project in the 1970s.

From the 1790s, the Shinnecock government has operated essentially as codified under New York State law. Each year three male Shinnecocks have been elected to serve as trustees by adult Shinnecock men who reside on the reservation. These men have primary responsibility for allotting land to tribal members and other tribal matters. In the 1930s, federal agents administering elections for acceptance of constitutions under the Indian Reorganization Act visited the Shinnecocks, but this community did not vote in those elections or change its style of government. In 1988 a New York State court upheld the status of the Shinnecock as a governmental entity enjoying protection from lawsuits under the doctrine of sovereign immunity. Men who served as trustees during drastically changing times from the end of World War II into the late 1970s include Avery Dennis, the late Charles Kellis Smith, and Harry K. Williams, who has served as ceremonial chief of the Shinnecocks since the death of Henry "Chief Thunderbird" Bess.

The Shinnecocks hold tribal meetings for the discussion of issues such as tribal projects, legal actions and finances, and to give direction to the trustees. Until 1992, only reservation-resident male blood member Shinnecocks were eligible to vote on tribal business. Since then, Shinnecock women can vote in tribe meetings, but not in the election of trustees. Also in 1992, Shinnecock men and women elected a thirteen-member Council, whose stated purposes include assisting tribal trustees and facilitating communications within the community. Council committees and task groups were formed to address Shinnecock concerns. They include health, education, governance, the Oyster Project Committee, and other special committees. The trustee-appointed board of the Shinnecock Nation Museum/Cultural Complex hopes to erect a permanent museum structure within the next few years.

Little has been written about the Shinnecocks, and much that has been written is viewed by Shinnecocks as inaccurate and incomplete, unduly focusing on intermarriage, destructive behavior, and the alleged loss of culture. The Shinnecocks continue to have a strong sense of Native personal identity and community ties. They show vitality in their tribal life and commitment to honoring their heritage and building healthy futures for their children.

Marguerite A. Smith

Further Reading

Deloria, Vine. *Custer Died for Your Sins: An Indian Manifesto*. New York, NY: MacMillan, 1969.

Howell, George Rogers. *The Early History of Southampton, L.I., New York, with Genealogies*. Albany, NY: Weed, Parsons, 1887. Southampton, NY: Yankee Peddler Book Co., ca. 1967.

Hunter, Lois Marie. *The Shinnecock Indians*. Islip, NY: Buys Brothers, 1950.

Spicer, Edward H. *The American Indians*. Cambridge, MA: Belknap Press, Harvard University Press, 1980.

Stone, Gaynell, ed. *The Shinnecock Indians: A Cultural History*. Readings in Long Island Archaeology and Ethnohistory 6 (1983). Suffolk County Archaeological Association.

SHOALWATER

Located thirty-two miles southwest of Aberdeen, Washington, at the Pacific entrance to Willapa Bay, the Shoalwater Bay Indian Tribe lives on a reservation that includes 1,035 acres (335 in uplands and the balance in tidelands). The Georgetown Indian Reservation was established in 1866, the first in the state of Washington set up by presidential order. This group has always been a small enclave, with current tribal roles numbering 150 (1993), approximately 100 of whom live on the reservation, which comprises part of the present-day community of Tokeland.

This amalgamated tribe arose as a result of a devastating "intermittent fever" (malaria) epidemic in the early 1830s, after which Lower Chehalis and Chinookan, and possibly Kwalhioqua, survivors amalgamated into a single community. The main constituent groups were: the Willapa Chinook, Lower Chinookans who spoke Chinook Proper and lived at the time of contact along the southern shores of Willapa Bay in several permanent winter villages (probably all located south of the Newah River); and the Shoalwater band of the Lower Chehalis, a Salishan language group (that also included the Wynoochee, Humptulips, and Grays Harbor Chehalis), who originally lived along the northern reaches of the bay. Whether they included surviving members of the little-known neighboring Kwalhioqua group, Athabaskan speakers whose territory overlapped with that of Lower Chehalis and who may have intermarried with them, is a matter of conjecture.

Cultural Background

Contacts resulting from the maritime fur trade had probably already started to disrupt aboriginal culture patterns by the beginning of the nineteenth century. Earlier descriptions of Lower Chinook culture (by Lewis and Clark, Ross, Cox, Franchere) generally relate to those groups along the lower Columbia, but certainly also apply to the Shoalwater Bay bands as well. Both the Chinookan and Salishan groups share features of the greater Northwest Coast cultural complex and were very close culturally. This included hereditary chiefs (with a noble class, commoners, and slaves), who intermarried and validated their status by the display and disbursement of wealth in the form of food, dentalium shell currency, clothing, canoes, and slaves. For the "men of the bay," hunting land and sea mammals and fishing (by line, seining, dip and scoop nets, and spearing) were important, but the rich beaches provided a predictable annual bounty as well. Women worked the beaches and also gathered berries and dug roots in season. They lived in permanent villages of gable-roofed, upright cedar-plank houses and dressed minimally, with the men often going naked when weather permitted and women wearing short, cedar-bark or silk-grass strip skirts (both sexes wore robes and conical rainhats in colder weather). Their annual cycle included seasonal moves to fishing camps or for gathering, where temporary cat-tail mat huts would be erected. Other traditions have included strapped infants onto board or canoe-cradles (with head-flattening devices in Chinookan families); naming at the end of the first year; puberty ceremonies (often with tattooing) for girls; the possibility (at least for chiefly men) of multiple marriages often with first spouses from another village; and the lifetime acquisition of status and guardian spirit powers (which allowed membership in secret societies). One's father's identities and relatives were the focal kinship relationships, and families lived in multi-generational houses with the most high ranking (oldest fit male with highest status) serving as head of the family.

History

We have a clear picture of a people in transition from the writings of James Swan (*The Northwest Coast; Or, Three Years' Residence in Washington Territory, 1857*), who came to live on Shoalwater Bay (the original name of Willapa Bay) in 1852. Although many aspects of traditional Native life were maintained, and leaders such as the notable Chief Toke continued to appear, white oyster traders had started to exploit the rich beaches of the bay and, using Native laborers, were exporting upwards of 100,000 bushels of oysters per year. The tribe took part in the negotiations with Governor Isaac Stevens in 1855, which were broken off and did not result in a treaty. Thus the Shoalwater Bay group is considered a federally recognized "non-treaty tribe," which deprives them of off-reservation rights to hunting and fishing at traditional sites (although some members have continued to exercise customary subsistence patterns despite the objections of state officials).

The Shoalwater Bay Tribe in the 1990s

Tribal government includes a five-member Tribal Council, elected to staggered two-year terms. The tribal government is the largest employer on the reservation; a number of tribal enterprises are in the planning stages and members currently run three retail businesses on the reservation. In 1981 a land claims settlement reimbursed the tribe for land which had been improperly alienated, and these funds in trust have allowed the tribe to commence buying back original land holdings. Between 1988 and 1992 the tribe experienced a 66 percent mortality rate, resulting in public demands for improved access and delivery of health care. According to the 1990 census, tribal members had the lowest per capita income for adults of any Washington reservation. The Lower Chehalis language, which had replaced general Salishan-Chinook bilingualism by the turn of the century, is incompletely remembered by only a few and is functionally extinct.

Yet, the Shoalwater Bay tribe still represents a distinct community. Shaker officials are called in for healings and funerals, a few families have continued to pass on hereditary names according to tradition, and tribal members maintain an annual cycle of fishing and gathering.

Kenneth C. Hansen

J.V. (Jay) Powell

See also **Washington State Tribes**

Further Reading

Hadja, Yvonne P. "Southwestern Coast Salish." *Handbook of North American Indians.* Vol. 7. *Northwest Coast.* Ed. Wayne Suttles. Washington, DC: Smithsonian Institution (1990): 503–18.

McChesney, Charles E. *Rolls of Certain Indian Tribes in Oregon and Washington.* Fairfield, WA: Ye Galleon Press, 1969.

Silverstein, Michael. "Chinookans of the Lower Columbia." *Handbook of North American Indians.* Vol. 7. *Northwest Coast.* Washington, DC: Smithsonian Institution (1990): 533–46.

Swan, James G. *The Northwest Coast: Or Three Years' Residence in Washington Territory.* New York: Harper, 1857. Seattle: University of Washington Press, 1972.

SHOSHONE

In precontact times, Shoshone speakers inhabited parts of present-day eastern California, eastern Oregon, central Nevada, southern Idaho, northern Utah, and western Wyoming. Though linguistically similar, the Shoshone (also spelled Shoshoni) pursued dramatically different lifestyles based on the varied environments that they inhabited. Today, anthropologists have divided the Shoshone into three groups based on these different environmental adaptations. Those Shoshone living in the Great Basin, who were primarily hunters and gatherers, are known as the Western Shoshone. Those living in the Columbia River Plateau, who relied on gathering plant foods, hunting (including bison), and fishing, are known as the Northern Shoshone. The Shoshone who adapted a Great Plains lifestyle, and relied primarily on bison hunting, are known as the Eastern Shoshone.

The Western Shoshone today live in colonies and reservations in the states of Nevada, Utah, California, and Idaho, some of which they share with the Owens Valley Paiute or the Washoe. Those on the Utah-Nevada border and in Utah are known as Goshute. Most of the Northern Shoshone live on the Fort Hall Reservation in southeastern Idaho, while most of the Eastern Shoshone live on the Wind River Reservation in central Wyoming. The Panamint (or Koso) Shoshone, similar in culture to the Western Shoshone, live in Nevada and eastern California.

Christopher Loether

See also **California Tribes**

EASTERN SHOSHONE

The Eastern or Wind River Shoshone of west central Wyoming are descendants of nineteenth-century bands in the Rocky Mountains and the high Plains, who intermarried with Crow, Nez Perce, and French-speaking Métis. The 1868 Treaty of Fort Bridger established the Wind River Reservation for the Wind River Shoshones and determined its location and borders. Subsequent land cessions diminished the size of the reservation, some of which was restored in 1904. The present size of the reservation is 2,268,008 acres in Fremont and Hot Springs counties, Wyoming. In 1878 the United States government placed a small band of Arapahos on the reservation, which ultimately resulted in their permanent settlement. Today, Shoshones and Arapahos share the reservation: Shoshones live primarily in the west and northwestern area, and Arapahos in the east and southeastern area. Of the individual allotments made in the early twentieth century, few remain at the end of the century.

Twentieth-Century History

1900 to 1938. The period from 1878 to 1902 was characterized by an economic and demographic collapse, bringing the Wind River Shoshone population to an all-time low of 799 in 1902. Huge forced land cessions to whites and the Arapaho, prohibitions of off-reservation hunting, trivial investment, starvation-level rationing, and epidemics of tuberculosis and measles oppressed the Shoshone. They maintained unity and morale, however, through traditional leadership, especially by the Washakie family, and socio-religious innovations, particularly the Peyote Religion. The Episcopal missionary John Roberts aided Shoshone accommodation to reservation life by means of education and religious syncretism. During the period that followed through 1938, Shoshones experienced slow demographic and cultural recovery. Enrolled population reached 1,106 in 1934, 918 of whom lived on the reservation.

1938 to 1976. John Collier's reforms during the New Deal era promoted self-government through a Business Council which managed new resources after 1938. The Shoshone and Arapaho tribes elected their own Tribal Councils, each consisting of six members, one of whom was elected chairperson for a two-year tenure. The two Tribal Councils met separately and also gathered together for meetings of the Joint Business Council. The Business Council managed new resources after 1938, which included a $4.4 million award for lands ceded north of Wind River, activated oil, gas, and uranium mining leases, and expanded livestock ranching. Health conditions improved dramatically in the 1930s, beginning with Dr. Paul Aronson's use of isoniazid to combat tuberculosis. Shoshone women contributed significantly to the eradication of this and other diseases through their efforts in case identification and follow-up. Inspired by an outstanding cadre of female teachers, women became active in a variety of areas of Shoshone life. For example, Maud Clairmont began a long and important tenure on the Shoshone Business Council beginning in the middle 1930s. In 1957, 60 percent of Shoshone income came from leases and tribal funds; 23 percent from wages; and 17 percent from agricultural self-employment. There were 1,699 enrolled Shoshone that year, 1,184 of whom were resident at Wind River. School attendance and performance were improving.

A major aid to cultural vitality during this period was the extensive use, initiated especially by Lynn St. Clair, of the tape recording of songs and other traditional as well as newly introduced materials. The Sun Dance was increasingly intertribal. A new Rocky Mountain Hall provided a tribal social locus. Housing for people at Wind River improved substantially, helped in part by assistance from the Department of Housing and Urban Development programs.

The greatest difficulty of this period was gaining cooperation from white business and political interests, who saw the Indians and their land basically as objects of exploitation. This blocked, for example, the development of tourism on the reservation. Moreover, while young Shoshones felt themselves to be rural Wyoming people, off-reservation jobs remained largely closed, particularly for full-blood Shoshones.

1976 to Date. Since 1976, Wyoming's economy and that of the Shoshone have fared poorly. A major result has been out-migration. Between 1980 and 1990 the population of Fremont County, within which the Wind River Reservation is situated, dropped by 13 percent. Between 1976 and 1988, the total Shoshone resident population fell by 31 percent from 1,725 to 1,185.

In 1988 the Joint (Shoshone and Arapaho) Business Council established the "WINDS" Needs Assessment Task Force, which conducted a comprehensive survey of reservation conditions. For the Shoshone, the needs were great. Poverty and an unemployment rate of 71 percent topped the list of concerns. Housing, transportation, and health care were woefully inadequate.

There has been a concerted effort during this period to keep the Shoshone language alive amongst the younger generation by instituting Shoshone language courses at the Wyoming Indian High School, located on the reservation. The creation of a Shoshone Tribal Cultural Center has also contributed as a source of adult education courses in a variety of Shoshone arts and crafts, such as beadwork, moccasins, and dance bustles, etc.

Culture

Among today's Shoshone, self-identity as a people is maintained by external barriers (hostility to Arapaho, ambivalence toward whites), by family traditions, and by participation in traditional and neo-traditional rituals.

The oldest ritual, the *Naraya* or Shuffling Dance, was performed to ensure abundant food plants, animals, and water, as well as to ward off illness from the community. The ritual disappeared before World War II; however, its rich repertory of songs presenting scenes of the natural world and after life in a highly compressed poetic style of the highest order was preserved by Emily Hill and Dorothy Tappay. Recordings and analysis are now extant.

The principal religious ceremony performed today is the Sun Dance, held each year in late July. Male sun dancers, who seek health for themselves and family members or who seek the power to heal, enter the specially constructed lodge on a Friday evening and remain in it until the conclusion of the ceremony on Monday. They must not eat or drink for the duration, the bulk of which consists of dancing to and from the center pole. It is felt that these sacrifices also contribute to the health and well-being of the entire community.

Changes during and after World War II have impacted on the Sun Dance. Shoshone pride and concern for their servicemen led to the introduction of a special ceremony and song that accompanies the raising of the American flag. There is now more intertribal presence. Indian visitors from surrounding states come to watch, and help sing, and a few even participate as sun dancers. After the ceremony is finished, presents are distributed to visitors from other reservations and people play handgame, a team guessing game. A feast for the community and visitors marks the conclusion of the Sun Dance.

The Peyote Religion, introduced early in this century, is a dominating emotional focus for a minority of both Shoshone and Arapaho. Sacramental use of the drug for tranquility, religious insight, health, and general welfare is its core. Its ritual, led by a roadman and held preferably in a canvas tipi, lasts through a night of prayer and song.

Among secular institutions, the powwow, introduced in 1957 from southern Plains Indians, is the most important. It consists of a weekend of dance contests and games, as well as a concluding feast. For Shoshones, it is a gathering of northern Plains powwow singers and dancers from many tribes, and a time of cultural influence and exchange. Song and dance are at the heart of the powwow. War Dance songs and singing style are as different from Euroamerican music as they could possibly be. This difference is thoroughly enjoyed and asserted. The dance styles and costumes of the War Dance are equally distinct.

A key element of today's culture is the enlarged role of women, evident in many spheres, particularly in music and ceremony. Early in the twentieth century, men and women had distinctly different musical roles, which complemented each other. Men danced the War Dance, and women danced the Women's Dance. Only men played the drum and sang War Dance songs. If women joined in singing, they had their own part an octave higher than the men and entered at a later point in the song.

Soon after the first powwow on the reservation in 1957, women began dancing their own adapted version of the traditional War Dance. Eventually, younger women danced their own version of the fast, fancy War Dance as well. In the early 1970s a Shoshone woman broke the taboo for women when she joined her brothers and father at the drum. Subsequently, a group of sisters formed their own female drum group, performing all the male roles for both song and drum. In 1978 they performed both the Giveaway and Chokecherry Songs at a winter community dance. Because no one else was able to perform on this occasion, their effort made possible the performance of the dances, and therefore the ceremonies. The women broke new ground, but in the service of Indian music—their own Shoshone music—and for their own community. This has been the key for the acceptance of all the changing musical roles for women. Music and dance are essential to the Shoshones' sense of identity and their ongoing bond as a community. To this end, Wind River Shoshone women have lent their support and power and have, in turn, been supported and empowered.

Demitri B. Shimkin

Judith Vander

See also **Arapaho; Gender; Powwow**

Further Reading

Joint Business Council, Wind River Indian Reservation. *Wind River Indian Needs Determination Survey.* Final Report. Fort Washakie, WY, 1988.

Shimkin, Demitri B. *The Wind River Shoshone Sun Dance.* Bureau of American Ethnology Bulletin 151. Washington, DC: U.S. Government Printing Office (1953): 397–484.

———. "Eastern Shoshone." *Handbook of North American Indians.* Vol. 11. *Great Basin.* Ed. Warren L. d'Azevedo. Washington, DC: Smithsonian Institution (1986): 308–35.

U.S. Department of the Interior. Missouri River Basin Investigation Project. *Population and Income Census, Wind River Reservation, Wyoming.* Billings, MT, 1960.

Vander, Judith. *Songprints: The Musical Experience of Five Shoshone Women.* Urbana: University of Illinois Press, 1988.

SHOSHONE-BANNOCK

The Shoshone-Bannock Tribes of the Fort Hall Reservation, also referred to as the Sho-Bans, are located in southeastern Idaho. The reservation's 544,000 acres are home to two Indian tribes, the Shoshone (also known as the Northern Shoshoni) and Bannock.

In precontact times, Shoshone-speaking Indians occupied all of what is now the state of Idaho from the Salmon River south. In the eighteenth century, Northern Paiute speakers, today known as the Bannock Indians, moved into southern Idaho from eastern Oregon, settling primarily in the eastern Snake River plains. The Bannock dialect of Northern Paiute is unique to eastern Idaho. Both the Bannock and Shoshone languages belong to the Numic family within the Uto-Aztecan language phylum. As of 1992, there are approximately 300 speakers of Bannock, most of whom are middle-aged or older. There are approximately 1,500 speakers of Shoshone on the Fort Hall Reservation representing all age groups.

The United States government signed two treaties with the Shoshone and Bannock of Idaho. The first, the Treaty of Soda Springs, Idaho (1863), was never ratified. A second treaty was negotiated in 1868 at Fort Bridger, Wyoming, which established the Wind River Reservation in Wyoming, and the Fort Hall Reservation, originally 1.8 million acres, in eastern Idaho. A smaller reservation, 105 acres, was established in the Lemhi Valley of Idaho in 1875.

The town of Pocatello grew from a railroad station on the Fort Hall Reservation. In 1888, the Indians of Fort Hall agreed to cede 1,600 acres for the establishment of a town. Pressured by the constant growth of the town, the Indians agreed to cede another 418,500 acres of their reservation for $600,000. Congress ratified this agreement in 1900. The so-called "Day of the Run" occurred on June 17, 1902, when approximately six thousand people took part in the land rush.

In 1907 the 474 Shoshone-Bannock living on the Lemhi Reservation were removed to Fort Hall. Some, however, later returned to the Lemhi Valley and settled near the town of Salmon, Idaho, where approximately 160 persons of Lemhi descent were living in the 1960s. By 1993 they were fewer than a dozen.

Religion

The Fort Hall Shoshone-Bannock participated in both the Ghost Dance of 1870 and 1890. The round dance and its accompanying Ghost Dance songs continue to be a part of the eclectic religious life of the reservation. In 1901, the Sun Dance was first introduced to Fort Hall. The Native American Church (NAC) was introduced to Fort Hall in 1915, but was not officially incorporated by the State of Idaho until 1925. However, the transportation of peyote outside reservation boundaries remained illegal. On March 19, 1991, the Idaho legislature approved a bill allowing peyote to be transported across non-reservation land after heavy lobbying by NAC members and Idaho's Indians. The Shoshone-Bannock tribes continue to fight for the protection of their sacred sites throughout the state, such as blocking the development of a housing project at Castle Rock in Boise, which by early 1993 had yet to be resolved.

Today many Shoshone-Bannock participate in a number of religions simultaneously. It is not unusual for people to belong to the Native American Church, participate in the Sun Dance, and attend Christian religious services as well. There are also a number of ceremonials based on the traditional Great Basin round dance, along with traditional healing and sweat lodge ceremonies.

Allotment

The Fort Hall Reservation began to be surveyed in 1892 in compliance with the Dawes Severalty Act of 1887, but allotment was not completed until 1914. In 1907 Congress appropriated $350,000 to begin construction of the Fort Hall Irrigation Project, in order to bring water to the reservation. By 1911, 20,000 acres of Indian land was under irrigation, which allowed the government to go ahead with allotment. Between 1911 and 1913, 1,863 allotments were assigned, totaling 347,300 acres. After allotment, 35,700 acres (nearly 10 percent) of the allotted land was alienated through sales, patents in fee, or certificates of competency before the trend was reversed in 1934 with the passage of the Indian Reorganization Act. As of 1992, 96 percent of the land on the Fort Hall Reservation was Indian controlled, either held in trust by the Shoshone-Bannock tribes or owned by individual tribal members.

Tribal Government

After the passage of the Indian Reorganization Act, the tribes adopted a formal Constitution and Bylaws in 1934. On April 17, 1937, tribal members voted to ratify the Corporate Charter, and the Shoshone-Bannock Tribes of the Fort Hall Reservation became a legal entity.

The main governing body is known as the Fort Hall Business Council. Elections for the Business Council are held every two years. According to the 1990 census, the population of the Fort Hall Reservation was 5,114 persons, of whom 3,035 (59.3 percent) claimed American Indian ancestry. As of 1991 there were 3,528 enrolled members in the Shoshone-Bannock tribes.

Land Claims

In 1946 the Indian Claims Commission was established. A case on behalf of all Shoshone Indians (including the Bannock) was brought before the Commission, which ruled in 1963 in favor of the Indians' claims. A total of $15.7 million was awarded, of which the Fort Hall Shoshone-Bannock received $8,864,000. The Shoshone-Bannock tribes voted to distribute 75 percent of the money on a per capita basis to each of the 2,754 tribal members (including the descendants of the people from the Lemhi Valley), while the remaining 25 percent was used for the benefit of the tribes as a whole. In 1971 an additional $4.5 million was awarded to the Lemhi Valley descendants. Again, 75 percent was distributed on a per capita basis, while the remainder was used to benefit the tribes as a whole.

Economic Development

During the first half of the twentieth century, the main sources of income for the Shoshone-Bannock came from agriculture and livestock (mainly sheep and cattle). Beginning in 1947 the J.R. Simplot Company entered into a contract with the tribes to mine the phosphate located within reservation boundaries. This was followed later by the building of a phosphate beneficiation plant on the reservation by the Food and Machinery Corporation. Both companies have made agreements to hire tribal members as employees, although by the late 1980s the phosphate mine on the reservation was beginning to play out.

In 1978 following an economic development study, the tribes built the Trading Post, a tribally owned and run grocery store. In 1980 they added the Clothes Horse (a souvenir and curio shop), and the Teepee Gas and Diesel Filling Station. The Oregon Trail Restaurant, the Tribal Museum, a steel fabrication business, and the Bannock Peak Truck Stop and Convenience Store subsequently opened on the reservation. The tribal government employed approximately 280 persons in 1991, most of whom were tribal members. The annual operating budget for the tribal government in the same year was close to $13 million, $4 million of which came from the tribes' own resources, and $9 million from federal sources and grants. As of 1993, unemployment on the reservation is around 40 percent.

In 1991 the Shoshone-Bannock began operating high stakes bingo and completed a bingo hall next to the Trading Post complex in early 1992. The State of Idaho attempted twice to stop the bingo operations in court, but lost both times. In the summer of 1992, the Shoshone-Bannock tribes made public their plans to open a casino on the reservation. The State of Idaho opposed the idea, and included in the November 1992 election an amendment to the state Constitution banning casino gambling anywhere in the state. The amendment passed, and as of 1993 the tribes are challenging in federal court the state's right to jurisdiction of such matters on Indian land.

Health care on the reservation is provided by the Indian Health Service in conjunction with the Tribal Health and Human Services Department. A new health clinic was completed in 1990. The leading cause of death on the Fort Hall Reservation is accidents, followed by heart disease, malignant neoplasms, and pneumonia/influenza.

As the twentieth century comes to a close, the Shoshone-Bannock continue to fight county, state, and federal authorities for the rights and privileges guaranteed them by treaty, statutes, and executive orders. The primary concerns of the people are health, education, jobs, and the continued maintenance of their traditions and languages into the twenty-first century.

Christopher Loether

Further Reading

Jorgensen, Joseph G. *The Sun Dance Religion: Power for the Powerless.* IL: University of Chicago Press, 1972.

Madsen, Brigham D. *The Lemhi: Sacajawea's People.* Caldwell, ID: The Caxton Printers, 1979.

———. *The Northern Shoshoni.* Caldwell, ID: The Caxton Printers, 1980.

Murphy, Robert F., and Yolanda Murphy. "Northern Shoshone and Bannock." *Handbook of North American Indians.* Vol. 11. *Great Basin.* Ed. Warren L. d'Azevedo. Washington, DC: Smithsonian Institution (1986): 284–307.

Shoshone-Bannock Tribes. *Shoshone-Bannock Tribes, Fort Hall, Idaho.* Fort Hall Reservation, ID: Tribal Health and Human Services Department, 1991.

WESTERN SHOSHONE

The Western Shoshone people of the intermountain west called themselves the Newe (people). They occupied a large area in the Great Basin, covering the region from southern Idaho (north) to Death Valley, California (south), and from the Smith Creek Mountains and Valley in central Nevada (west) to the area around the present-day Ely, Nevada (east). The Newe called their homeland *Pia Sokopia,* or "Earth Mother."

The Newe created a unique way of life before contact with whites. They divided themselves into small extended family groups who confined themselves to particular places where they hunted and gathered. The family groups had different names, usually based upon a local food resource or a particular occupation or a geographic feature. For example, those in Ruby Valley called themselves the Watatekka ("Eaters of Rye Grass Seeds") and those in Death Valley called themselves the Timbisha, named after Furnace Creek.

The Newe acquired the name Shoshone after early white explorers labeled them as such in the 1820s. Some years later in 1863 the federal government negotiated four separate peace treaties with all the Newe-speaking people in the Far West. It made the Treaty of Ruby Valley with those in northeastern Nevada. Since this treaty site was the furthest west, the government gave the Newe at this place the name Western Shoshone. Over the years the people have accepted this name although they haven't forgotten their traditional names.

Early Twentieth-Century Lands

At the turn of the century only one reservation existed for the Western Shoshone, called the Western Shoshone Reservation. Created by presidential executive order in 1877, it is located in Duck Valley along the Nevada-Idaho border. The Bureau of Indian Affairs (BIA) planned to induce all the Great Basin Shoshones to move there. But the majority refused because of deep attachment to their ancestral locations. By the early years of the century, only one-third had settled Duck Valley, whereas the other two-thirds remained off-reservation, in or near their Native areas. To enlarge the reservation population, the government encouraged Northern Paiutes from Oregon and Nevada to settle Duck Valley in the 1880s and onward. The two tribes organized the Shoshone-Paiute

Business Council in 1936 under the authority of the Indian Reorganization Act (IRA) of 1934. The reservation was renamed the Duck Valley Reservation, also in 1936, and it continues to be the home of Shoshones and Paiutes.

By the early years of this century the federal government accepted the fact that most Western Shoshones did not live on reservation land. At the same time, it was unwilling to create large reservations for them. The government, however, established the Colony Program for Nevada Indians, setting aside small colonies (mini-reservations) on the outskirts of Nevada towns. Three colonies were created for the Western Shoshone in northeastern Nevada: the Battle Mountain Colony in 1917, the Elko Colony in 1918, and the Ely Colony in 1931. These small colonies could accommodate only small numbers of families who worked in the adjacent towns. As the Colony Program was unique to Nevada, the Rancheria Program was unique to California. In 1928 the government established the Indian Ranch rancheria for those Shoshones living in Panamint Valley, California. This rancheria was one of dozens created in California for different tribes in the early twentieth century under the Rancheria Program of 1906. Shoshones shared the Bishop, Big Pine, and Lone Pine rancherias and the Fort Independence Reservation with the Owens Valley Paiutes. By the early 1930s, 4,201 acres of colony, rancheria, and allotment land had been set aside for some Shoshones who chose not to move to Duck Valley. The most recent Shoshone group to achieve federal status are the Timbisha of Death Valley, recognized by the Federal Acknowledgment Project in 1982.

In the mid-1930s the federal government carried out a much greater effort to set aside land for the Western Shoshone. This land reform program, carried out under the IRA, allowed the BIA to purchase land for reservations for those tribal people who had never lived on federal trust land. Three separate Shoshone reservations in Nevada came into existence under the IRA: the Yomba Reservation in 1937, the South Fork Reservation (along with Odger's Ranch) in 1938, and the Duckwater Reservation in 1940. All IRA reservation land totalled 24,000 acres. The Shoshones who settled Duckwater and Yomba created their own separate reservation-based tribal councils with constitutions/bylaws and charters under the IRA. Those who settled South Fork joined the much larger federated council of the Te-Moak Bands of Western Shoshone Indians along with those living on the colonies. These tribal governing bodies still exist today, as do the IRA reservations created in the 1930s and 1940s. There are also Shoshones at Fallon, Walker River, and Fort McDermitt reservations, living with the Paiutes.

Land Claims

One important concern of the Western Shoshone has been the issue of land and treaty claims. In December 1912 the Shoshones held their first of numerous claim meetings. They discussed the provisions of the Treaty of Ruby Valley (1863). This treaty specified that the Shoshones were the owners of a large land base mostly in the eastern half of Nevada. But the United States did not honor the treaty after 1863 and claimed title to the Shoshones' land. The Shoshones requested that the treaty be honored. Finally, in 1946, the federal government created the Indian Claims Commission (ICC) to redress past wrongs committed against the Indian tribes, including the treaty promises the whites had broken. The ICC allowed the tribes to sue the government, for monetary awards only. No land would be returned to any tribe. Nevertheless, the Shoshones filed suit in the 1940s, and in 1979 the government agreed to pay them $26 million for the loss of 24 million acres of aboriginal territory. As of 1993 the Shoshones have not received any money, mainly because a number of them have rejected the money settlement. Instead, they maintain that the government must honor the Treaty of Ruby Valley. They also stress that sacred Mother Earth cannot be sold to the Americans.

Federal Programs

The Western Shoshone continue to be affected by Indian policies coming out of Washington, D.C. Under the Mutual Self-Help Housing Program in the Department of Housing and Urban Development (HUD), which emerged in the early 1960s, many Shoshone families acquired new houses under government supervision. HUD houses, as they are popularly known today, are visible in nearly all Shoshone communities. Under the Office of Economic Opportunity (OEO) of the mid-1960s, the government provided specialized training for tribal adults, preschooling for youngsters, and work opportunities for teenagers. The legacy of OEO is still seen today in the Shoshone communities that operate Head Start programs for preschoolers. In 1975 Congress passed the Indian Self-Determination and Education Assistance Act, which permitted the tribes to take over the functions of the BIA. Under this new order, the tribes, including the Western Shoshone, now receive federal funds ("638 funding") to run their own programs without BIA supervision.

Western Shoshone Leadership

Regardless of the continued presence of the federal government, Shoshone leadership has been highly visible throughout the century. Thomas Premo, Bill Gibson, and Muchuch Temoke were early leaders. The first two were products of the large off-reservation boarding schools: Premo attended the famed Carlisle Indian School in Pennsylvania and Gibson attended the Stewart Indian School in Nevada. When the Indians of Duck Valley organized a Tribal Council in 1911 Premo was one of the prominent leaders. He was also the first chairperson of the Shoshone-Paiute Business Council of Duck Valley in the 1930s. Gibson was prominent in politics in the Elko area. He helped organize the first Shoshone claims meeting of the twentieth century in 1912. In 1929 he recommended that the government establish a reservation in the South Fork Valley, an idea that became reality a decade later. A staunch advocate of treaty rights, Muchuch Temoke of Ruby Valley, in at least three trips to Washington, D.C. (1917, 1919, 1947), argued that the government should carry out the unkept promises of the Treaty of Ruby Valley. His family's hereditary leadership was derived from Old Chief Temoke, the principal signer of the 1863 treaty. In 1916 Muchuch became the traditional chief of Ruby Valley. His son, Frank, became the chief in 1953.

More recently, a number of Shoshone leaders stand out. Mary and Carrie Dann of Beowawe, Nevada, took the federal government to court over the issue of land title. The two sisters, with support from other Shoshones, asserted that the Shoshones had never lost title to their Native territory, and that the United States needed to recognize the Shoshone as the rightful owners of a vast domain in the Great Basin. In a positive victory in 1983 the Ninth Circuit Court of Appeals, in the well-known Dann Decision, ruled in favor of the sisters. Unfortunately, two years later the Supreme Court overturned the lower court's decision. Another Shoshone leader was the late Glenn Holley of Battle Mountain, who helped found the Western Shoshone Sacred Lands Association (WSSLA) in 1974. The WSSLA defended the Danns' position and also rejected the government money settlement for land. In the 1980s Jerry Millett of Duckwater and Raymond Yowell of South Fork were the first and second elected chiefs of the Western Shoshone National Council (WSNC), founded in 1984. The WSNC's major focus has been land claims, and in the early 1990s it continues to reject money for land. Perhaps the best-known leader of recent decades has been Frank Temoke of Ruby Valley. Like the above leaders Temoke has also opposed the government's ICC decisions regarding land claims. Over the years he has sponsored Shoshone fandangos (round dancing, etc.) in Ruby Valley.

Economic Development

Like other tribes across the country, the Western Shoshones have pushed for economic self-sufficiency. Those at the Duckwater, Duck Valley, South Fork, and Yomba reservations have been involved in the cattle business. Cattle ranching has been their main source of income for much of this century. The Battle Mountain, Elko, and Wells colonies have smoke-shops where they sell cigarettes at reasonable prices to both Indian and non-Indian customers. In more recent years some Shoshone communities have established different kinds of economic enterprises: the Battle Mountain Colony now has a convenience store, the Duckwater Reservation owns a catfish farm, and the Duck Valley Reservation operates a tribal farm consisting of 640 acres with a rotating sprinkler system. Regardless of the above economic activities, the

Shoshones, because of their limited land base, still have not achieved self-sufficiency, and the unemployment rate remains high: 47 percent for the Yomba Reservation, 50 percent for the Elko County, and 76 percent for the Ely Colony, all in 1977.

Although Shoshone culture has changed over the years, the people have worked hard to retain some of their Native ways. They still sponsor their traditional Round Dances, Native prayers, and handgames at gatherings called "fandangos." The fandangos are also held at even larger gatherings, including the Ruby Valley Treaty Days and the Great Basin Indian Spiritual conferences, both held throughout the 1980s. These activities give the older people the opportunity to teach Native traditions to the younger generations. Some Shoshone communities are making efforts to preserve the language, part of the Uto-Aztecan language family. The following have offered specialized Shoshone classes at different times in the 1970s and 1980s: the Elko Colony, the Duck Valley Reservation, the Duckwater Reservation, and the South Fork Reservation. The Shoshones also express themselves artistically. Perhaps the best-known artist in recent times is Jack Mallotte of South Fork, who is noted for his graphic art depicting Great Basin themes.

In the closing years of this century all the Western Shoshone communities remain intact. At least two reservations, Duck Valley and Duckwater, have produced tribal histories in the 1980s, which reflect the uniqueness of the Shoshone (Newe) people.

Steven J. Crum

Western Shoshone Colonies and Reservations

Community	Acres	Enrollment
Duck Valley (Idaho, Nevada)	289,819	1,721
Duckwater (Nevada)	3,785	288
Ely (Nevada)	10	274
Timbisha	40	199
Yomba (Nevada)	4,719	192
Te-Moak (Nevada)		*2,078
Battle Mountain	680	*
Elko	193	*
Ruby Valley		*
South Fork	13,050	*
Wells	80	*

Combined population figures for the Te-Moak Bands of Western Shoshone Indians.

See also Paiute: Owens Valley

Further Reading

McKinney, Whitney. *A History of the Shoshone-Paiutes of the Duck Valley Indian Reservation.* Salt Lake City, UT: Howe Brothers, 1983.

Newe: A Western Shoshone History. Salt Lake City: University of Utah Printing Service, 1976.

Newe Sogobia: The Western Shoshone People and Lands. Reno, NV: Western Shoshone Lands Association, 1982.

Steward, Julian H. *Basin-Plateau Aboriginal Sociopolitical Groups.* Bureau of American Ethnology Bulletin 120. Washington, DC: U.S. Government Printing Office, 1938.

Thomas, David Hurst, Lorann S.A. Pendleton, and Stephen C. Cappannari. "Western Shoshone." *Handbook of North American Indian.* Vol. 11. *Great Basin.* Ed. Warren L. d'Azevedo. Washington, DC: Smithsonian Institution (1986): 262–83.

GOSHUTE

The Goshutes are linguistically and culturally a division of the Western Shoshones. The easternmost of the Western Shoshones, they occupied a vast territory in Nevada and Utah extending from the Steptoe Valley in the west to Great Salt Lake. The Goshutes are known by many other names, including Gosiute, Goship, Shoshoni-Goship, and "Desert Ute," a confusion with the Utes which is clearly in error. The Goshute Indians have also been confused with the Paiutes.

The ecology of the Great Basin area permitted only the development of very small local groups or bands, weakly organized, which needed extensive areas to maintain their small populations. The Goshutes were aboriginally divided into small bands or groups often associated with specific gathering places.

History

Protesting encroachment on their lands and the destruction of game and other wild foods, the Goshutes engaged in hostilities, principally attacks on stage lines, mail carriers, and telegraph operators, during the early 1860s. After a particularly disastrous encounter with the United States at Steptoe Valley in 1862, they were ready to sue for peace, but hostilities continued into 1865. It is significant that the Goshute had a separate treaty from that of the other Western Shoshones, both signed in 1863. The Ruby Valley Treaty with the Western Shoshones describes a land distinct from but bordering on the tract described in the Tuilla (now Tooele) Valley Treaty with the "Shoshoni-Goship." The Tuilla Valley Treaty of 1863 did not provide for the cession of any lands. It does, however, provide for the establishment of reservations by the president "as he may deem necessary." Such reservations were not established until early in the twentieth century.

By 1875 the Goshutes were concentrated at Deep Creek (now the Goshute Reservation) and at Skull Valley, both within their aboriginal area. The Confederated Tribes of the Goshute Reservation, which crosses the Nevada-Utah border, was established by executive order in 1914 and expanded in 1920. The documentation for the origin of the Skull Valley Reservation in Utah is somewhat unclear, but by 1918 this reservation was in existence. The two reservations are not politically affiliated. In 1993 there are 413 enrolled members on the Goshute Reservation and 111 enrolled members of the Skull Valley Goshute Tribe.

The Goshute filed a claim with the Indian Claims Commission for compensation for lands and minerals taken without adequate compensation; in 1975 they were awarded $7.3 million.

Political Organization

The Confederated Tribes of the Goshute Reservation, composed entirely of Goshute despite its name, operates under a Constitution and Bylaws adopted in 1940. The Goshute Business Council, its governing body, is composed of five individuals, each with a three-year term: a chairman, vice-chairman, and three members. They are chosen by eligible participants who are age twenty-four or older. The Council, under the direction of the chairman, conducts official business, establishes policy and management procedures, program budgets, and hires and fires tribal employees. The Skull Valley Goshutes elected not to adopt a constitution and bylaws. They wished to remain as traditionalists and follow the 1863 Tuilla Valley Treaty. They have a chairman, vice-chairman, and a secretary-treasurer, each serving a four-year term. All decisions must be voted on by the majority of the enrolled membership.

The Goshute Reservation

The 113,128-acre Goshute Reservation is located in a remote and isolated area in eastern Nevada and western Utah near Ibapah, Utah. The reservation offers no basic economic support system for its members. A major portion of its members have to go out of the area for employment in service areas. A few have a limited number of cattle, which graze on tribal lands, and some farm hay, but these activities are not sufficient and they must also rely on state and tribal assistance. While the tribal government offers some employment, unemployment is a major problem. The area is one of the most scenic in the country, however, and also has great potential for natural resource development.

Most Goshute Reservation residents lived in log cabins until recently when the Shoshone Joint Housing Authority constructed twenty-two homes through a Housing and Urban Development program. Communications are still difficult. Mail delivery is twice a week, and residents need satellite dishes for television reception. There is a paved road to the reservation by way of Wendover, and a dirt road joins the reservation with Schellbourne, Nevada. There is a paved emergency air-strip.

Ibapah has a small elementary school. After sixth grade students are bused sixty miles to Wendover School. Many chose to attend government boarding schools, such as Sherman Indian High School in Riverside, California; Theodore Roosevelt Indian School in Fort Apache, Arizona; or Chemawa Indian School in Salem, Oregon.

Skull Valley Reservation

The 17,000-acre Skull Valley Reservation is located in a remote, isolated area in western Utah near the Dugway Proving Grounds. Twenty-five of the one hundred eleven enrolled members live on the reservation in tribal or mobile homes. Employment is a problem at Skull Valley, which does not receive funding from the Bureau of Indian Affairs other than technical support. The band receives income from leasing land to Hercules (Aerospace Project), which also employs some tribal members. The tribe also operates a convenience store and a seasonal water project. Mail delivery is to nearby towns, and children attend the Dugway School sixteen miles away.

Religion and Culture

Many Goshute people participate in the services of the Native American Church, others attend the Church of Jesus Christ of Latter-Day Saints. They enjoy visiting different reservations to participate in handgames and other activities. Many Goshute do beadwork, make willow and winnowing baskets, and cradleboards. Some artisans scrape and tan deerskin to make buckskin gloves and other buckskin items.

Chrissandra Murphy-Reed

Further Reading

Malouf, Carling. *The Gosiute Indians.* University of Utah, Museum of Anthropology Archaeology and Ethnology Papers 3 (1940): 29–36. Reissue University of Utah Anthropological Papers 3, Salt Lake City, 1950.

———. "The Gosiute Indians." *Shoshone Indians.* New York, NY: Garland Publishing (1974): 25–172.

Reagan, Albert B. *The Gosiute (Goshute) or Shoshoni-Goship Indians of the Deep Creek Region in Western Utah.* Proceedings of the Utah Academy of Sciences, Arts and Letters 11 (1934): 43–54.

Steward, Julian H. *Basin-Plateau Aboriginal Sociopolitical Groups.* Bureau of American Ethnology Bulletin 120. Washington, DC: U.S. Government Printing Office, 1938. Salt Lake City: University of Utah Press, 1970.

Sia

See Pueblo of Zia

Sierra Blanca

See Apache

Siletz

See Confederated Tribes of Siletz

SILVERWORK AND OTHER JEWELRY

Although the use of metal was rare in ancient North America, some copper was common in the Great Lakes and Southeast areas, primarily as a product of cold processing. In addition, a moderate amount of silver and lead was worked in the Southeast. Gold was apparently almost unknown in early days; the small gold ornaments of the Calusa in Florida are thought to have been created from gold obtained from Spanish galleons wrecked enroute back to Spain from Mexico and Peru.

Early peoples did not lack for body and costume adornment; stone, bone, wood, shell, clay and other natural raw materials were readily converted into beads, pendants, rings, bracelets, and armbands by skillful carving, engraving, incising, inlaying, and drilling to transform otherwise bland substances into remarkably attractive ornaments. Feathers, quills, hair and fur likewise were used to embellish the human body and clothing. Many of the products of the early artists were remarkably sophisticated and combined a variety of design motifs and construction techniques, indicating a long period of development.

With the arrival of the Europeans, body decoration changed radically. The introduction of metals in quantity and the technical skills required to exploit them soon developed to a level which allowed Native craftsmen to embark upon a wholly new decorative world. Nor was this restricted to metal; brilliantly colored glass beads, yarns and fibers, porcelain and cloth—almost the entire panoply of European manufacture—was quickly adapted or transformed for Native use. Inevitably, a degree of copying accompanied this adaptation, both as an emulation of the costume of the immigrant colonists, as well as to enhance the appearance of the Native. The result is often bewildering to the ethnologist trying to arrive at an understanding of what is Native and what is derived—and often no less confusing to the Native. And each region made its own selections with varying results, all relatively successful.

Since 1900 contemporary Native American jewelry has grown into a vast productive world; second in economic value only to textiles, it has become the great creative aesthetic force of the Southwest, where silver, and more recently, gold, is the stock in trade of most of the Navajo, Zuni, and Hopi artists; these three peoples produce three-fourths of the Indian jewelry of North America. Rivalling them, but less dominant, are the Santo Domingo, Sioux-Cheyenne-Arapaho beadworkers, and Kiowa-Comanche German silver craftworkers, followed by Northwest Coast and Iroquoian silversmiths. And a more recent addition to the market are several remarkable Eskimo-Aleut silversmiths, who have developed a unique art form of their own. Unfortunately, the southeastern region has not developed a strong contemporary jewelry tradition; the traumatic Trail of Tears removed many of the most talented artists from the region.

Southwestern Silversmiths

Contemporary artists employ a variety of techniques and approaches to their art: Navajo silverworkers use a great amount of cast or handworked silver supporting moderately large turquoise settings, while Zuni taste follows a more intricate pattern of many small turquoise, coral, and jet settings, in which silver is primarily a framing; Hopi silverwork is distinguished by a great use of overlay, with turquoise secondary, if at all. Santo Domingo craftsmen favor minuscule shell beads, known as *heishi*, with equally tiny turquoise, coral, or jet decoration; bone is less commonly used than earlier, as is wood or clay.

The creative vitality of the Southwest is expressed in the great number of innovative artists, each of whom has been responsible for the development of directions as well as designs. The first known Navajo silversmith, Atsidi Sani, gave birth to a whole artistic industry when he learned his skills from a Mexican ironworker around 1853, and taught other Native smiths; in the present century, Ambrose Roanhorse, Fred Kabotie, and Fred Peshlakai have all provided the same influence as teachers of the art; the work of Kenneth Begay raised Navajo silverwork to a height equalled by few; and today, Gibson V. Nez, Cippy N. Crazyhorse, Charly Lee, and Lee Yazzie, to name only a few, are paramount in recognition and reputation. The introduction of a genre form (perhaps influenced by the success of pictorial weaving), which replicates daily life in engraved, cast, or stamped forms on bracelets, pendants, and brooches, is due to Clarence Lee and his son, Richard.

Maurice Maisel was responsible for the installation in the period from 1920 to 1930 of the production

Bill Reid (Haida). Frog brooch. 1959. Gold; 4 cm. Courtesy of the University of British Columbia Museum of Anthropology, A9349.

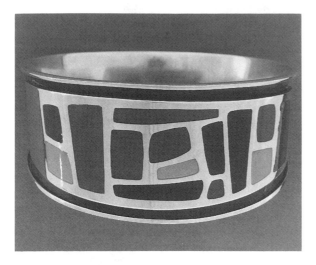

Roger Tsabetsaye (Zuni Pueblo). Bracelet. 1967. Silver, partially sulphurized and vitreous enamel champlevé; width 1 ³/₈ inches. Courtesy of the U.S. Department of the Interior, Indian Arts and Crafts Board, W-69.20.16.

Denise Wallace (Aleut). "Seal Hunt." Sterling silver with sugalite ring with door. Photo courtesy of Gallery 10, Inc., of Scottsdale, AZ, and Santa Fe, NM.

Charles Loloma (Hopi). Inlaid jewelry. Photo courtesy of Gallery 10, Inc., of Scottsdale, AZ, and Santa Fe, NM.

line system in Albuquerque, wherein a number of smiths, mostly Navajo, worked on a piece, passing it from hand to hand for subsequent application of hand stamping, soldering, setting, polishing, with the end result a mélange of individual applications. Many tourists gained their introduction to Indian jewelry from the Fred Harvey Company, who sold it in vast amounts during the heyday of the Harvey Houses, around 1890 to 1940. The Indian Arts and Crafts Board can be credited with establishing standards which raised the quality of silversmithing. Today, there are more Navajo silversmiths than from any other tribe, and the art has become synonymous with them—especially the development of three classic forms: the concha belt; the *ketoh* bowguard; and the squash blossom necklace with crescentic *naja* pendant.

Zuni Inlay. The Zuni people follow closely behind numerically, with a tremendous outpouring of needlepoint, petit-point, and cluster settings in turquoise; and the revival of a prehistoric art form—mosaic work in shell, turquoise, jet, and coral set into a silver framing. Much of this work was heavily influenced in the period from 1920 to 1930 by a white trader, C.G. Wallace, who introduced some design forms, and encouraged the economy. Although many Native smiths now include their families as full- or part-time helper/apprentices, the Zuni have gone beyond most; a large number of the jewelry artists working today are actually a man and wife operating as a unit, with their children becoming apprentices. Some of the major groups most prominent today are the Ondelacy, Calabaza, Tsabetsaye, Quam, Weebothee, Bowannie, and Edaakie families; individuals who are well known for their skills are Carolyn Bobelu, Milford Nahohai, and Robert Kaskalla.

Hopi Overlay. Although the distinct Hopi overlay jewelry existed earlier, it owes most of its development to the influence of the Museum of Northern Arizona. In 1938 a number of motifs designed by Virgil Hubert, the Museum's Anglo curator of art, were given to several smiths, notably Paul Saufkie, Randall Honwisioma, and Wilson Talayumptewa, among others. From this core has grown the style identified with the tribe today, and marked by such outstanding talents as Bernard Dawahoya, Robert Lomadapki, Michael Kabotie, Louis Lomayesva, and Lawrence Saufkie. But the most innovative southwestern jewelry artist was without doubt the late Charles Loloma, a young Hopi who started as a potter, and subsequently transferred his skills to silver and gold jewelry, creating a wholly new and nontraditional technique of setting various stones with great imagination and technical skill. His design forms have become a standard followed by many younger artists throughout the Southwest. Another new technique, the engraving of intricate designs upon the surface of the silver object, is produced by Howard Sice. Other Pueblo artists include Charles Lovato and Gail Bird, both of Santo Domingo.

Silversmiths from Other Geographical Areas

Beyond the Southwest, remarkable work followed the initial influence of Ronald Senungetuk, an Eskimo smith working for the Indian Arts and Crafts Board, whose clean-lined designs became a standard for many Alaska Natives, including Lincoln Wallace, and two Aleut women, Denise Wallace and Gertrude V. Svarny. Separately, Robert Davidson and Bill Reid, both Haida artists, have excelled in cast and engraved jewelry in silver and gold. German silver has been the metal of choice for the late Julius Caesar, Pawnee, and his son Bruce, two artists whose creative peyote designs are widely known.

Jewelry in Other Media

A few artists have developed jewelry designs in other than the more traditional metals. Alfred Zephier, a Sioux, produces work in quills and stone; Patty Fawn Smith, a Cherokee, works in ivory; and Robert Kaniatobe is a Choctaw shellcarver. All are fine examples of the desire to reach beyond the traditional into more innovative exploration. Gender lines are being crossed, as men become involved in the more traditional women's activities, and vice versa—the old rules are falling fast.

Jewelry is one of the major economic bases of support for a large proportion of the Indian peoples of North America; various estimates of cash income exist, none of which are completely reliable, but it is second only to textile production and is followed very closely by pottery. It is not unusual today for silversmiths to receive four to five figure sums for their work—a far cry from the $4 and $5 per item amounts of the 1930s.

The most noticeable direction today is toward continuing experimentation: the creation of intricate pieces of accommodating stones other than turquoise (i.e. diamonds, rubies, emeralds); a greater use of gold; and a steady flow in the production of a less traditional, more European design form.

Frederick J. Dockstader

See also Art; Beadwork; Quillwork

Further Reading

Adair, John. *The Navajo and Pueblo Silversmiths.* Norman: University of Oklahoma Press, 1955.

Bedinger, Margery. *Indian Silver: Navajo and Pueblo Jewelers.* Albuquerque: University of New Mexico, 1973.

Cirillo, Dexter. *Southwest Indian Jewelry.* New York, NY: Abbyville Press, 1992.

Dockstader, Frederick J. "The Centenary of Navajo Silversmithing." *Cranbrook Institute of Science Newsletter* 23:2 (1953): 14–18.

Lund, Marsha. *Indian Jewelry: Fact & Fantasy.* Boulder, CO: Paladin Press, 1976.

Mori, John and Joyce. "Hopi Silversmithing." *Masterkey* 44:4 (1970): 124–42.

Wright, Margaret. *Hopi Silver.* Flagstaff, AZ: Northland Press, 1972.

SIOUX FEDERATION

Written records employ only the term "Sioux" to encompass fourteen tribes whose original territory, comprised of approximately 100 million acres, extended from present-day Wisconsin to the foothills of the Rocky Mountains. "Dakota" identifies the four eastern tribes (Mdewakanton, Wahpekute, Sisseton, and Wahpeton) distinguished by dialect and cultural proclivities, from "Nakotas" who were located near the middle of the territory (Yankton and Yanktonai with Assiniboine), and from "Lakotas" located at the west end (Oglala, Brule, Hunkpapa, Sans Arc, Minneconjou, Two Kettle, and Blackfoot Sioux). "Santee" refers to the Mdewakantons and Wahpekutes. No word exists that includes the Sissetons and Wahpetons together. Twentieth-century reservations are indicated on the following map.

Herbert T. Hoover

See Dakota; Lakota; Yankton and Yanktonai

SIX NATIONS

See Iroquois Confederacy

SKAGIT

See Upper Skagit

SKOKOMISH

The Twana (also spelled Twanoh or, more accurately, Tuanook) were the Salishan people who aboriginally occupied the Hood Canal drainage in western Washington State. Their population was already diminished by a smallpox epidemic when the first direct contact with Europeans occurred in 1792. The Skokomish ("big-river people") were the largest of nine Twana communities, each traveling in warmer weather to hunting, fishing, and gathering sites, then reconstituting in winter at permanent house sites. The Skokomish resided in six settlements along the Skokomish River. The other Twana divisions (the Duhlelap, Dosewallips, Duckabush, Hoodsport, Quilcene, Vance Creek, Tahuya, and Dabob) lived in single-site communities.

The Skokomish Reservation (4,937 acres, or about 7.5 square miles) was established for the Twana at the mouth of the Skokomish River by the Treaty of Point No Point in January 1855. Reservation settlement began in 1859, following ratification by Congress, but several off-reservation settlements persisted. In 1881 there were still ten Twana households near the Seabeck sawmill and three more at Duckabush. All Twana and other reservation residents (including some Chimacum from the Point No Point Treaty, and a number of Steilacoom whose tribe received no reservation from the Medicine Creek Treaty) have been known as "Skokomish" since early reservation times. During the past decade, however, the term "Twana" has gained

Dakota, Lakota, Yankton, and Yanktonai Reservations in the Twentieth Century

Source: Herbert T. Hoover

renewed use in defining the traditional language and culture.

Twentieth-Century History

The loss of Skokomish control over valuable pieces of land within the final reservation boundaries (established by executive order in 1874) has had a negative impact on the community's self-image and restricted economic development. Around the turn of the century, a pickle tycoon from Tacoma purchased the land between the west channel and main channel at the Skokomish River mouth. His alterations to the landscape, including diking and ploughing, led to loss of botanic species such as the sweetgrass (*Scirpus Americanus*) used for basketry. About the same time, traditional activities such as shellfish gathering were restricted because of Washington State claims of jurisdiction over tidelands. During the years from 1926 to 1930, the City of Tacoma put two dams on the North Fork of the Skokomish River. A diversion tunnel was run to a powerhouse on Hood Canal and power lines stretched along the shoreline. Condemnation of land for the Olympic Highway in 1931 resulted in the destruction of important cultural sites and further limitations on saltwater access. Potlatch State Park (113 acres) was opened in 1960 on a choice piece of shoreline property.

Claims and court cases entered into by the Skokomish tribe (such as those before the Court of Claims and Indian Claims Commission) have been attempts to regain control over land and resources or gain compensation for their loss. Their 1965 award of $373,577 was used to purchase land for housing and a fish processing plant. It also provided for per capita payments. An attempt to affirm tidelands ownership (*Skokomish v. France*) ended when the final appeal was lost in 1963. However, the tribe was able to regain embattled fishing rights in 1974 through the decision of *United States v. Washington*.

The best-known leaders in recent times came from a line descending from precontact Hoodsport Twana headmen. George Adams (born 1880) served not only on the Tribal Council but also several terms in the State House of Representatives. His daughter, Georgianna Miller (born 1903), also served on the Tribal Council and was influential in the Mason County Democratic Party. Anna Pavel (born 1930), her daughter, was a tribal judge and later, in the late 1970s, the Tribal Council chairman.

Current Situation

The Skokomish Indian Tribe has over 630 enrolled members and is federally recognized. Its government structure was established in 1938 under the Indian Reorganization Act. The seven members of the Council serve four-year terms. Candidates for open positions are nominated at the annual General Council meeting.

Most tribal members are affected by recent logging and fishing restrictions. To stimulate employment and better living conditions on the reservation, the tribe has purchased property for housing, resource enhancement, and economic development sites. It has a grocery-deli-gas station, fish hatchery, and fish processing plant. The tribe, under the leadership of previous Tribal Council chairman Denny Hurtado (born 1947) and his successor Joseph Pavel (born 1956), is presently working to regain the land at the river delta. Possible uses include an agricultural facility to take advantage of the regained tidelands, a resort, and a museum.

Culture

The Twana Language and Culture Project (1975 to 1980) recorded examples of the language from the final three speakers, created dictionaries and textbooks, and initiated programs in two public school districts and the tribal preschool. A number of traditional ceremonies and practices (such as the naming ceremony, spirit dancing, secret society initiations, and the first salmon ceremony), many not practiced for over seventy years, were reestablished in the late 1970s and early 1980s. Only a Treaty Day Celebration held the final Saturday of January is open to the public. The predominant religions on the Skokomish Reservation are the Indian Shaker Church and the Assemblies of God.

The tribal center houses a display featuring historic photographs, cultural objects, and art, both contemporary and from the late nineteenth century. Basketry and carving projects have stimulated interest in preserving and reinterpreting traditional arts. Today, there are some fourteen individuals who make baskets, the best recorded Twana art, and there is a tribal dance group. The Tribal Council uses a tax on tribal fishing to fund a tutoring program (at a public school on the reservation) that includes arts and crafts education.

Nile Thompson

See also **Washington State Tribes**

Further Reading

Curtis, Edward S. *The North American Indian*. Vol. 9. Norwood, MA: Plimpton Press, 1913. New York, NY: Johnson Reprint, 1970.

Eels, Myron. *The Indians of Puget Sound*. Seattle: University of Washington Press, 1985.

Elmendorf, William W. *The Structure of Twana Culture*. Washington State University Research Studies 28 (3) Monographic Supplement 2. Pullman, 1960. Reprinted in Coast Salish and Western Washington Indians 4. New York, NY: Garland Publishing, 1974. Pullman: Washington State University Press, 1992.

Thompson, Nile, and Carolyn Marr. *Crow's Shells: Artistic Basketry of Puget Sound*. Seattle, WA: Dushuyay Publications, 1983.

SNOHOMISH

The Snohomish (or Sinahomish) Tribe of Indians is a Coast Salish tribe of northwestern Washington State. Tribal members are concentrated on the eastern shore of the Olympic Peninsula, where they displaced the Chimacum in the mid-nineteenth century. Approximately three-quarters of tribal members live within or immediately adjacent to traditional lands.

A reservation in Snohomish territory on the western shore of Hood Canal, provided for in Article II of the Treaty of Point Elliott, 1855, was never appropriated. Instead, a general reservation, intended for several tribes and originally called the Snohomish Reservation, was created at Tulalip on Puget Sound. Allotments of land at Tulalip to Snohomish people between 1883 and 1909 were insufficient, leaving most Snohomish landless. In 1935 the United States government denied off-reservation Snohomish the right to vote on the Indian Reorganization Act. Acceptance of the Act by reservation residents led to the creation of two distinct political groups.

Snohomish living on the Olympic Peninsula established a strong economic base by the late nineteenth century. Members owned farm land, dairy herds, hop fields, logging operations, and other commercial establishments which provided employment for members. Conditions were difficult during the 1930s and 1940s, due to the closing of some Snohomish businesses during the Great Depression; the death of prominent leaders, particularly Bodah Strand in 1928 and state Senator William Bishop in 1934; and the departure of men to fight in World War II.

Snohomish have been leaders in regional political activity throughout the century. Thomas Bishop led landless tribes in asserting treaty rights and in the quest for a land base through organization of the Northwest Federation of American Indians in 1913. Many, including William Bishop, Alfred Van Trojen, William and Jennie Hicks, and Charles Elwell, contributed to creating a formal twentieth-century Snohomish political organization. By 1917 the Snohomish had elected an Executive Board and were incorporated under state law in 1927 and again in 1974. Leaders filed a claim (Docket 125) under the Indian Claims Commission for compensation for lands ceded in 1855, and after offsets, $136,165.79 was awarded to the tribe. A new generation of leaders emerged after World War II, notably Kathleen Bishop, who was influential among landless Indians of the state in the 1960s, and also Clifford Allen, Hank Hawkins, William Matheson, Evelyn Elwell, and Alfred Cooper. Jack Kidder serves as tribal archivist and historian, maintaining records in Anacortes.

The right of Snohomish to fish without a state license was revoked in 1974 following a decision in *United States v. Washington*, which recognized treaty-based Indian fishing rights. Subsequently, other tribes laid claim to Snohomish aboriginal fishing areas. Meanwhile, the Snohomish submitted a claim to federal recognition in 1979, which was denied by the Branch of Acknowledgment and Research of the Bureau of Indian Affairs in 1983. The decision is under appeal.

Monthly Council meetings and annual general meetings of the 902-member tribe are well attended. Cultural traditions and community cohesion are maintained through family ties and attendance at tribal social and political gatherings. Members hold a variety of religious affiliations. There is no one formal tribal center, and meetings are held in several locations within tribal territory.

Bruce G. Miller

See also **Washington State Tribes**

Further Reading

Bishop, Kathleen L., and Kenneth C. Hansen. "The Landless Tribes of Western Washington." *American Indian Journal* 4 (1979): 20–31.

Snohomish Petition to the Office of Federal Recognition. 1979.

Twedell, Colin Ellidge. "An Historical and Ethnological Study of the Snohomish Indian People." *Coast Salish and Western Washington Indians* 2. Ed. David Horr Agee. New York, NY: Garland Publishing (1974): 475–694.

U.S. Department of the Interior, Bureau of Indian Affairs. *Recommendation and Summary of Evidence for Proposed Finding against Federal Acknowledgment of the Snohomish Indian Tribe.* Washington, DC: The Bureau, 1982.

SNOQUALMIE

(Also known as the Snoqualmi, Snoqualmu, Snoqualmoo, Snoqualmook, Snoqualamick, Snoqualamuke, Snoqualimich, Snoqualmish, and Snowqualmiq.) Aboriginally, some 3,000 Snoqualmie Indians inhabited the Snoqualmie and Tolt rivers' drainage systems between Monroe and North Bend, Washington. They reportedly inhabited ninety-six cedar longhouses (100 to 200 by 50 feet) located in sixteen winter villages. They hunted, fished, gardened, and gathered roots, berries, and herbs well into the twentieth century.

By the 1840s the Snoqualmie were united under Chief Pat Kanim, reputed to be "the most powerful" Indian in western Washington. His nephew, Jerry Kanim (1870 to 1956), served as the Snoqualmie chief for the first half of the twentieth century, traveling among his people settling disputes, teaching Snoqualmie law and customs, and assisting his people economically by forming a tribal picking crew harvesting fruit, berries, and vegetables in the Puget Sound region.

Most of the Snoqualmie tribe refused to leave their aboriginal lands in order to move to an overcrowded reservation located on foreign tribal territory, and so ended up as landless Indians when the land allotments were completed on the Tulalip Reservation in 1909. In 1916 the Snoqualmie tribe reorganized their tribal government to form a representative Council fashioned after that of the Euroamerican society, so that they could acquire a checking account, sign legal documents, and conduct their business in accordance with formal legal procedures. They added a written Constitution in 1929.

In 1937, the Bureau of Indian Affairs proposed a 10,240-acre Snoqualmie Reservation along the Tolt River near Carnation, Washington, in the vicinity of their former principal village and home of their chiefly Kanim family. World War II broke out and the proposal was lost in the rush of war mania. After the war the federal government's attention turned to the settlement of claims under the Indian Claims Commission. The Snoqualmie tribe filed a successful claim in 1951 and received a cash settlement in 1968.

Although the Snoqualmie formed a representative Tribal Council in 1916, consisting of chairperson, vice-chair, secretary-treasurer, and four Council positions, Jerry Kanim continued to serve as their chief until his death in 1956. Ed Davis was designated as the honorary chief following the death of Jerry Kanim. Tribal Council membership was eventually expanded to nine. In 1986 the Snoqualmie installed Ernest Barr as chief of the tribe and Kenneth Moses, Ronald Lauzon, James Zachuse, and Patrick Barker as subchiefs, thus restoring their former Council of Chiefs, which served during much of the nineteenth century. Presently, their tribal governance consists of a Tribal Council, a Council of Chiefs, a General Council of all the voting members, and a Council of Elders composed of the "older adults." The tribal office is in Redmond.

Two significant spiritual leaders of the Snoqualmie tribe during this century are Ed Davis (1880 to 1987) and Kenneth Moses (1926 to the present). Ed Davis became a Shaker Indian minister in 1912, and for the next seventy-five years served both the Snoqualmie and Tulalip Shaker Churches. Kenneth Moses is a highly respected "Spirit Doctor" who travels to many Indian homes and reservations throughout the Pacific Northwest. Since the Snoqualmie Indians were one of the landless tribes designated for termination in 1953, they were eventually omitted from the recognized list of tribes. The Bureau of Indian Affairs granted preliminary federal recognition to the tribe on April 26, 1993.

The 1,000-plus members of the Snoqualmie tribe are organized according to historic treaty families. Although the members of these families are becoming increasingly dispersed over the Puget Sound, they continue to meet frequently to discuss family and tribal concerns. Most Snoqualmie are able to trace their descent to one of seven historic treaty families: Davis, Forgue-Louie, Kanim, Harriman, Moses, Tomallum, and Zachuse. Some of these family gatherings are held in specially constructed shelters, with cooking facilities, that are located along scenic streams nestled in the foothills of the Cascade Mountains.

Cultural traditions are maintained in a number of ways. The Tribal Council sponsors traditional arts and crafts classes. The Snoqualmie language, part of the Salishan language family, continues to be spoken by some tribal members. The Washington State Centennial Committee selected the Snoqualmie Tribal Dancers to serve on special occasions as part of the state's centennial celebrations. The 268-foot Snoqualmie Falls, center of the tribe's aboriginal spiritual life, have been designated as the first traditional Native site to be placed on Washington State's register of historic places, and one of the first to be nominated for the National Register of Historic Places. Contemporary religious practices among the Snoqualmie include modified traditional beliefs, the Indian Shaker Church, the Christian faith, and a mixture of all three. Traditional seeking of spirit power is presently limited to its acquisition during smokehouse dancing and power dreams.

The Snoqualmoo band represents a 1988 factional split from the Snoqualmie tribe. Phil Wahl, great-great-great grandson of former Chief Pat Kanim, heads up this new splinter group. Pat Kanim's daughter, Julie Kanim Glasgow, reportedly defied her father in the late 1840s and warned Glasgow of the chiefs' plans to kill him. In turn, Julie was expelled from the tribe but her descendants were readmitted several generations later in the 1980s. However, the reconciliation proved to be relatively temporary. The Snoqualmoo band, with approximately 100 members in 1993, submitted a petition for federal recognition in 1988 as a separate group of Indians from the Snoqualmie tribe.

Kenneth D. Tollefson

See also **Washington State Tribes**

Further Reading
Haberlin, Hermann, and Erna Gunther. *The Indians of Puget Sound.* Seattle, University of Washington Press, 1930.
Tollefson, Kenneth D. "The Snoqualmie: A Puget Sound Chiefdom." *Ethnology* 26:2 (1987): 121–36.
———. "Religious Transformation among the Snoqualmie Shakers." *Northwest Anthropological Research Notes* 23:1 (1989): 97–102.
———. "Cultural Survival of The Snoqualmie Tribe." *American Indian Culture and Research Journal* 16:4 (1992): 29–53.

SOCIETY OF AMERICAN INDIANS

The Society of American Indians (SAI) took shape in the mind of Ohio State University sociologist Fayette Avery McKenzie. His frequent use of Native American issues in his sociology teaching placed him in contact with Carlos Montezuma, Charles A. Eastman, Sherman Coolidge, and Charles E. Daganett. As guest speakers in his Ohio State University classes, these people must have confirmed McKenzie's belief in the viability of a national Native American reform organization. McKenzie hosted a planning meeting in the spring of 1911 to organize a national Indian conference to be held in the early fall of that year. In the Ohio Union at Ohio State University in Columbus on Columbus Day 1911 the American Indian Association took official form. Soon renamed the Society of American Indians, the SAI's place and date of birth underscored its assimilationist thrust.

The Society offered individual—not tribal—membership to Indians and "associate" membership to non-Native persons. It appears that enrollment crested early, with 619 members in 1913. The bulk of the Society's support in that banner year came from its 400 associate members. Indians in the SAI came from many tribes, with Plains and Great Lakes-New York area Indians particularly evident. This concentration seems related to the fact that many Society officers derived from these groups and that SAI annual conferences were almost invariably held in the Midwest. In later years, membership and annual conference attendance from the West increased. Serious efforts were made to draw notable whites into associate membership.

Officers of the Society of American Indians mostly were models of its assimilationist ethos, although in later years personal reverses diminished their devotion to the melting pot. Many had been associated with the Carlisle Indian Industrial School and seemed almost to be under the lifelong tutelage of Richard Henry Pratt. Also, many attended colleges and universities, some completing professional degrees. Important Native American women were among the Society's leadership, including Gertrude Simmons Bonnin, Emma D. Johnson Goulette, Marie L.B. Baldwin, Rosa B. LaFlesche, and the ever-controversial Laura M. Cornelius Kellogg. In all, most of the Society's leaders in their personal and professional lives epitomized Indian assimilation.

Since one of the Society's chief objectives was to educate the American public about the abilities and aspirations of Native American people, its publications circulated widely to public, university, and historical society libraries throughout the United States. Emulating the journals of learned societies, the SAI placed news announcements, conference proceedings, and articles—often glowing, illustrated Indian assimilation "success" stories—in a quarterly magazine, *The American Indian Magazine/Quarterly Journal of the Society of American Indians*, published from 1913 to the early 1920s.

The annual conferences of the Society of American Indians featured a range of special reports, debates, entertainment, and varied diversions, as well as sessions devoted to internal business. Indians and non-Indians alike attended these annual meetings; however, voting was restricted to Native American membership. More than two hundred persons may have attended these annual conferences in the SAI's early years, but attendance dwindled to ninety-five by 1915 and slacked to mere handfuls by the early 1920s. Except for 1917, these conferences were held each "Indian summer" from 1911 to 1923. American intervention in World War I opened deep and jagged chasms of conflict within the Society and forced cancellation of the 1917 conference. The unctuous harmony exuded by many of the Society's annual conference proceedings was hardly omnipresent; in actuality, it was largely immobilized by a triangular stand-off among traditionalists, progressives, and the undecided.

The records of the Society—mainly correspondence—reflect the pervasive dilemma of assimilation versus self-determination. For the most part, the Society's officers and a few key members individually pursued its interests. At times, there were indications of collective decision making; other times, it seemed possible that individuals ran amuck, perhaps driven by personal vendettas as much as by SAI goals. Much of the Society's communication, not surprisingly, was with the Bureau of Indian Affairs (BIA), leading to criticism—especially during the Society's formative years—that it was too heavily influenced by the Bureau and the BIA's Indian employees. It seems evident that the BIA respected the SAI; it invariably launched thorough investigations and issued timely responses to SAI complaints and petitions.

The touting of "self-determination of subject peoples," as one United States World War I intervention objective, gave hope to many Native Americans that whites might call for an easing of the more oppressive BIA policies and practices once the war was over. Although united in these hopes, Indian opinion split concerning roles to be played in the war. Some, believing that Native Americans at the front would advance assimilation and hasten the granting of citizenship, volunteered for military duty. Others, declaring that denial of citizenship relieved them of any wartime obligations, passively—sometimes actively—resisted the war. Arthur Parker and Carlos Montezuma, respectively, took these positions. Parker, using his New York State archeology post as a disguise, set up a spy network to ensure draft registration of New York's Indians. At the same time, Carlos Montezuma urged tribal leaders to ignore the draft. For this, his mail and household were surreptitiously violated by the Federal Bureau of Investigation.

The citizenship question was at the heart of the SAI's difficulties with World War I and, lurking in the citizenship issue, was the assimilation/self-determination dilemma. From the Armistice through the early 1920s the Society paid increasing attention to these matters as it helped mount a movement for universal Native American citizenship. The Indian citizenship bill signed in June 1924 was a victory both for assimilationists and those favoring self-determination. Believing that the Indian franchise was central to assimilation, while recognizing the necessity for preservation of tribal polity and property, the Society—in concert with the American Civil Liberties Union and other groups—helped evolve a position comfortably held by many since 1924.

The ideals of the Society of American Indians were hardly forsaken by the mid-1920s, but its momentum was indeed lost. Wartime ravaged the Society; membership sagged, its founding leadership largely departed its ranks, its magazine became crudely commercialized, and its annual meetings featured tawdry flirtations with fanciful trends. Hardly a history of dashed hopes, however, the story of the Society of American Indians is one of imagination and resilience of persons caught in constricting economic, social, and political conditions where, as Arthur Parker once lamented: "Good marches slowly because its friends drag it by the ankles."

John W. Larner

See also **Government Policy; Pan-Indianism**

Further Reading

Hertzberg, Hazel W. *The Search for an American Indian Identity: Modern Pan-Indian Movements.* NY: Syracuse University Press, 1971.

Iverson, Peter. *Carlos Montezuma and the Changing World of American Indians.* Albuquerque: University of New Mexico Press, 1982.

Larner, John W., ed. *The Papers of the Society of American Indians.* Wilmington, DE: Scholarly Resources, 1987. Microfilm.

Wilson, Raymond. *Ohiyesa: Charles Eastman, Santee Sioux.* Urbana: University of Illinois Press, 1983.

SOVEREIGNTY AND JURISDICTION

When European explorers first encountered the indigenous peoples of the Americas, the aboriginal owners of the New World were organized in a wide variety of political structures. Perhaps the most complex social and political forms of organization were found in Latin America among the Maya, Aztec, and Inca civilizations. Nevertheless, the approximately 10 to 15 million people who then inhabited that portion of North America comprising the United States were organized in a wide variety of political structures. These varied in complexity and expanse from the small fishing villages of the Pacific Northwest, some of which were little more than a few extended families, to the complex confederation of the *Hodenosaunee*, the Iroquois Confederation, perhaps formed after Columbus' first voyage, which allied the five major nations of upstate New York, Southern Ontario, and Quebec into a formidable political and military power, which controlled much of commerce and political interchange among the various tribes of the northeastern section of the continent.

What all of these indigenous political units had in common was that they were independent, self-governing states. At the time of contact, the tribes owed allegiance to no other nation. Tribal polities exclusively occupied or shared with select other tribes a relatively defined geographic area and governed to the exclusion of all other political powers the activities that took place within their territory involving both their members and others. Anthropologists and lawyers have long recognized that from careful analysis of tribal customs and traditions, one can discern a distinct legal regime through which the tribe settled disputes, handled deviant or criminal conduct, arbitrated personal property ownership, allocated rights to use of tribal lands, and structured domestic and communal relations.

Like any process of cross-cultural contact, the importation of white man's law to the red man's land altered both the nature of legal relations of the non-Indian communities and the political structures and law of the indigenous communities affected by such contact. Many important aspects of American democracy, including the confederation form of governance and the paradigm of individual political participation in small meetings, were shaped by the Indian communities with whom the early colonists dealt, particularly by the Iroquois Confederation. Similarly, the colonial laws of England dramatically affected the legal and political status of Indian nations, as developed through non-Indian legal institutions generally with little or no participation of the Indian nations themselves.

Initially European colonial powers had neither the will nor the might to challenge the conception the Indians held of themselves as self-governing, independent polities—nations in every sense of the word. Throughout the colonial period, the English, French, and Dutch in North America dealt directly with the Indian tribes as nations with which they must negotiate for the sale of land and to arbitrate disputes among peoples. Notwithstanding the persistent emergence of military hostilities between Euroamerican settlers and Indian communities during this period, the most common mechanism for redressing disputes and facilitating land cessions from the tribes was the treaty council, at which representatives of the colony and the various tribes would negotiate with one another on terms of political, if not racial, equality.

Doctrine of Discovery

During the colonial period, the European colonial powers were as concerned about encroachment by other European powers as they were by their relations with the Indian nations. They were forced to work out a legal accommodation to facilitate the colonial exploitation of North America through trade, commerce, and ultimately settlement, while attempting to prevent frequent conflicts among themselves. Out of such concerns emerged the doctrine of discovery, under which the first European nation to discover areas of the New World was accorded the exclusive right to colonize that area, and to deal with its aboriginal occupants at all levels, including trade and cession of their lands. The doctrine of discovery was a legal construct worked out among the European colonial powers, particularly among European powers like the English, French, and Dutch, who rejected the right of the Vatican to allocate exploitation of the New World between Spain and Portugal. More importantly, like most legal constructs that have affected Indian tribal sovereignty, the doctrine emerged for the most part without any participation by the aboriginal peoples most affected by its operation.

Long after the doctrine of discovery had its primary effect, Chief Justice John Marshall would explain the doctrine in the famous 1823 decision of the United States Supreme Court in *Johnson v. M'Intosh* 21 U.S. (8 Wheat.) 543 (1823). By denying the right of independent Indian nations to sell or cede their lands to whomsoever they pleased, the doctrine of discovery represented the first legal intrusion on the political independence and sovereignty of the Indian tribes in order to facilitate expanding Euroamerican colonial hegemony over the New World. It would not be the last.

While some have misinterpreted the doctrine of discovery to deny Indian property ownership of the lands they occupied from time immemorial, it did no such thing. Since the doctrine was primarily designed to allocate colonial spheres of authority among European powers, it recognized the legal and political reality that Indians held and owned much of North America. Tribal title originally derived, according to the discovery doctrine, from aboriginal possession, the occupancy of the land by its indigenous inhabitants from time immemorial. This aboriginal title, or Indian title as it was sometimes called, represented an encumbrance on the legal right to the lands acquired by the discovering European nation, and had to be removed before the rights of discovery (also known as a right of preemption or a naked fee simple title) could ripen into a present possessory legal right that would permit European settlers to lawfully displace the aboriginal occupants and owners. According to the doctrine, aboriginal title could be extinguished by voluntary cession from the tribe, voluntary abandonment of the land by its aboriginal occupants, or by conquest, presumably pursuant to a just defensive war. Since the doctrine of discovery recognized the right of Indian tribes to sell their land to the discovering nation, it recognized the tribes as cohesive political and economic units capable of engaging in diplomatic negotiations and economic intercourse with European powers. On the other hand, the requisites of accommodation among competing European states caused the colonial powers to deny Indian nations one essential attribute they recognized in their own conception of sovereignty or nationhood— the right to external affairs powers including the rights to negotiate diplomatically on the basis of equality with other nations of the world, the right to cede land to or acquire land from other nations, and the right to independently make war. While the Indian tribes of the day clearly exercised such powers irrespective of Western legal theory, legal recognition of the existence of full *independent* sovereign existence of the Indian nations would have been incompatible with the mutually exclusive geographic spheres of European dominion that the discovery doctrine sought to create.

Domestic Dependent Nations

While Indian nations have been legally recognized as sovereign political nations since the inception of contact, there has been a reluctance on the part of Euroamerican legal systems to recognize them as *independent* sovereign nations. In the famous case of *Cherokee Nation v. Georgia*, decided by the United States Supreme Court in 1831, Chief Justice John Marshall rejected the argument that the Cherokee Nation was a foreign nation entitled to file an original action in the United States Supreme Court in order to restrain enforcement of laws enacted by the State of Georgia for the purpose of disbanding the Cherokee Nation. Describing the tribe both as a "state" and a "nation," Marshall's opinion for the Court indicated that Indian tribes were *domestic dependent nations*, which had lost those powers of a foreign state that were inconsistent with their dependent status, such as their external affairs powers. He later analogized them to a feudal state of Europe, such as the Principality of Monaco, which maintains sovereign self-governing powers but has lost some of its external affairs powers, relying instead on another sovereign, in this case the United States, for its international protection. Two members of the Court disagreed and thought that Indian tribes legally constituted truly foreign and independent states. The next year, the Supreme Court made clear in *Worcester v. Georgia* that the essential sovereign status of an Indian tribe and the exclusive constitutional commitment of the power to manage Indian affairs to the federal government rendered the Georgia laws invalid and unconstitutional. In recounting the history of Indian tribal sovereignty during the colonial period, Marshall said:

> Certain it is, that our history furnishes no example, from the first settlement of our country, of any attempt on the part of the crown, to interfere with the internal affairs of the Indians, further than to keep out the agents of foreign powers, who, as traders or otherwise, might seduce them into foreign alliances. The king . . . never intruded into the interior of their affairs, nor interfered with their self-government, so far as respected themselves only.

While accurate when written, the Chief Justice's comments indicated the potential for the expansion of United States sovereignty and jurisdiction into two different areas, each of which the Indians resisted: (1) matters involving non-Indians in Indian country; and (2) matters involving Indians, or tribal members, in Indian country. Over the last two hundred years, the federal government has gradually diminished tribal authority in both of these areas, beginning with jurisdiction over non-Indians. During the late eighteenth and early nineteenth century, the United States increasingly sought to curtail and displace the exercise of tribal jurisdiction over white citizens of the United States in Indian country, particularly for criminal offenses occurring in Indian country. During the late nineteenth and twentieth centuries, expanding American political hegemony in Indian country increasingly took the form of assertions of federal, and sometimes state, jurisdiction over some Indian activities in Indian country.

Expanding Nature of Federal Claims and Political Hegemony

Two events during the early nineteenth century illustrate the expanding nature of federal claims to political hegemony in Indian country. Many late eighteenth-century treaties contained provisions like that found in Article VIII of the 1791 Treaty of Holston between the Cherokee Nation and the United States:

> If any citizen of the United States, or other person not being an Indian, shall settle on any of the Cherokees' lands, such person shall forfeit the protection of the United States, and the Cherokees may punish him or not, as they please.

Such provisions, which confirmed the basic territorial conception of sovereignty and jurisdiction claimed by the tribes, began to disappear from treaties negotiated after 1804. At the same time, Congress enacted the Trade and Intercourse Acts, under which the federal government increasingly assumed law enforcement jurisdiction for crimes committed by citizens of the United States in Indian country, even when tribal members were victims. Later, Congress expanded that jurisdiction to include crimes committed by Indians against United States citizens, at least where the offender had not already been punished by the laws of the tribe. The statutory successor of these provisions is still in force and is found at 18 United States Code § 1152.

Second, as a result of the illegal extension by Mississippi of state jurisdiction over the Choctaw Nation and the refusal of the federal government to protect them and enforce their prior treaty rights guaranteeing political autonomy, the Choctaws, like many of the southeastern tribes, later were forced to negotiate a removal treaty with the United States. As part of their forced removal, they ceded their lands in Mississippi in exchange for new homelands in Indian Territory, now eastern Oklahoma. In the treaty negotiated to implement their removal, they sought to protect their understanding of the basic territorial nature of their jurisdiction in the new homelands. Federal treaty commisioners obviously doubted their authority to concede the Choctaw demand. As a result, Article IV of the Treaty of Dancing Rabbit Creek of 1830 rather ambiguously protects exclusive tribal jurisdiction over all matters arising within their new homelands, including obvious Choctaw insistence on the Choctaw right to try white men who came onto their lands and violated their laws:

> The Government and people of the United States are hereby obliged to secure to the said Choctaw Nation of Red People the jurisdiction and government of all the persons and property that may be within their limits west, so that no Territory or State shall ever have a right to pass laws for the government of the Choctaw Nation of Red People and their descendants; and that no part of the land granted them shall ever be embraced in any Territory or State; but the U.S. shall forever secure said Choctaw Nation from, and against, all laws except such as from time to time may be enacted their own National Councils, not inconsistent with the Constitution, Treaties, and Laws of the United States; and except such as may, and which have been enacted by Congress, to the extent that Congress under the Constitution are required to exercise a legislation over Indian Affairs. But

> the Choctaws . . . *express a wish that Congress may grant to the Choctaws the right of punishing by their own laws, any white man who shall come into their nation, and infringe any of their national regulations.*

While the Choctaws could demand complete jurisdiction over "all the persons and property that may be within their limits," the concluding provision of Article IV indicated that by 1830, the federal government regarded the exercise of tribal criminal jurisdiction over white citizens of the United States to be beyond the normal scope of tribal authority, requiring confirmation by an act of Congress for which the Choctaw are still waiting.

Just as the early nineteenth century was a time the federal government expanded its jurisdiction over non-Indians in Indian country at the expense of preexisting tribal sovereignty, the expanding colonial hegemony of the federal government during the late nineteenth and twentieth centuries further curtailed preexisting tribal sovereignty by laying federal claim for the first time to significant powers to govern Indian activities in Indian country. For example, after the United States Supreme Court decided in *Ex parte Crow Dog*, 109 U.S. 556 (1883) that Indian nations had exclusive jurisdiction to punish an Indian for the murder of another Indian in Indian country, Congress overturned that result by enacting the federal Major Crimes Act, now found in amended form at 18 United States Code § 1153, which for the first time extended federal jurisdiction to seven (currently over sixteen) enumerated types of serious offenses when the crime occurred in Indian country and the accused is an Indian. Similarly, in the late nineteenth and early twentieth centuries, the Indian Service sought to displace traditional tribal governments by substituting for them puppet governments in the form of the so-called courts of Indian offenses and Indian Police staffed with personnel subservient to local Bureau of Indian Affairs field superintendents. These institutions enforced a Code of Indian Offenses that proscribed not only crimes like theft and robbery, but also various traditional Indian cultural and religious practices, such as dances, gifts to a family for the marriage of their daughter, potlatches, and the burial or destruction of goods at death. Even as late as the 1940s and 1950s, Congress sought to reassign jurisdiction over Indians for on-reservation crimes and civil causes of action through several tribally specific jurisdiction statutes, various tribally specific termination statutes, and a general jurisdictional statute known as Public Law 280.

As a reward for the distinguished military service displayed by many Indians during World War I, the Citizenship Act of 1924 made all Indians citizens of the United States. This act, however, did not affect the preexisting political and treaty rights Indians held and therefore did not change the sovereignty of Indian tribes or tribal jurisdiction in Indian country.

Jurisdiction in Indian Country

The past two centuries of expanding United States colonial political hegemony over the tribes, and of federal assaults on the principle of tribal territorial sovereignty and jurisdiction over Indian lands, produced the complicated, sometimes irrational, jurisdictional pattern which exists in Indian country today in the United States. Jurisdiction for each question is determined by a complex mixture of factors, including the reservation and land ownership status of the territory where the crime or civil cause of action occurred, the race and tribal affiliation of the parties, the impact of outside governance on tribal self-government, the existence or nonexistence of applicable specific federal jurisdictional or regulatory statutes governing the issue, and the like.

As a general rule, under modern federal Indian law, the only special jurisdictional arrangement that exists for Indians concern crimes or civil causes of action that occurred in whole or in part in Indian country. Indian country constitutes a legal term of art, which is defined in 18 United States Code § 1151 to include all land located within the exterior boundaries of any Indian reservation (including any non-Indian owned parcels or railroad or highway rights of way); any dependent Indian country, irrespective of reservation status; and any individually owned restricted Indian trust allotment, to which Indian title has not been extinguished even if located outside of an Indian reservation. Except where Indians are exercising treaty or statutorily guaranteed off-reservation rights, such as the off-reservation hunting and fishing rights guaranteed to many tribes in the Pacific Northwest region, the Great Lakes, and Wisconsin, Indians, like other United States citizens, generally are subject to federal and state jurisdiction for their off-reservation activities. Thus, while sales of goods to Indians, for example, may be exempt from state sales taxes when occurring on their reservation, Indians pay sales taxes for most off-reservation purchases.

To understand jurisdictional arrangements for on-reservation activities, it is useful to separate criminal jurisdiction, on the one hand, from civil adjudicatory, regulatory, and taxing jurisdiction, on the other. Federal jurisdiction statutes purport to clearly demarcate criminal jurisdiction, while civil adjudicatory, regulatory, and taxing authority in Indian country generally has been subject to case by case adjudication.

Criminal Jurisdiction

Many serious crimes occurring on-reservation are the primary responsibility of the federal government, although discretionary federal refusals to prosecute such offenses occur all too frequently. Under the General Crimes Act, 18 United States Code § 1152, the federal government can prosecute crimes occurring in Indian country committed by non-Indians against the person or property of an Indian, and crimes committed by Indians (who have not already been punished by the laws of their tribe) against the person or property of a non-Indian. In addition, the federal Major Crimes Act now found at 18 United States Code § 1153 permits federal prosecution of Indians for certain enumerated types of serious crime, ranging from murder, kidnapping, and rape, to theft, when the crime is committed in Indian country. Thus, non-Indians who commit crimes in Indian country can be prosecuted by the federal government if the victim of the crime is an Indian, otherwise they can be prosecuted by state authorities. Indians who commit crimes in Indian country can only be prosecuted by the federal government in one of three situations. First, if the crime is one of nationwide application and does not implicate or infringe on any Indian treaty or other right, such as offenses involving murders or assaults on federal officials in the performance of their duties, the federal government can prosecute. Second, if the crime is one committed against the person and property of a non-Indian, and the Indian accused has not already been punished under the laws of the tribe, the federal government has jurisdiction under the General Crimes Act. Third, if the crime is one of the enumerated types of serious offenses specified in the federal Major Crimes Act, federal prosecution is also authorized even if the victim is an Indian.

Indian tribes retain jurisdiction based on their inherent tribal sovereignty to try crimes committed by Indians on their reservation. Such jurisdiction is exclusive over lesser crimes not covered by the federal Major Crimes Act, at least where the victim is Indian. While most tribes are not in fact exercising such authority, the legislative history of the federal Major Crimes Act suggests that Indian tribes retain inherent sovereignty to exercise concurrent jurisdiction over the serious crimes enumerated in that act, although the range of potential punishments they can impose was limited by the Indian Civil Rights Act of 1968 as amended, 25 United States Code § 1302, to a jail term of one year or a fine of $5,000, or both. Furthermore, under the Indian Civil Rights Act of 1968, Indian tribes are subjected to most of the limitations of the Bill of Rights in their exercise of criminal and civil jurisdiction. In *Oliphant v. Suquamish Tribe*, 435 U.S. 191 (1978), the United States Supreme Court ruled, in perhaps its most racist decision of the late twentieth century, that Indian tribes lacked inherent criminal jurisdiction to try non-Indians for crimes committed on the reservation. In *Duro v. Reina*, 495 U.S. 676 (1990), the Court extended that ruling to cover Indians who were not members of the tribe governing the reservation where the crime occurred. Congress has since overturned the *Duro* decision by statute, thereby authorizing tribes to exercise criminal jurisdiction over nonmember Indians, but not non-Indians.

As a general rule, state governments have no criminal jurisdiction in Indian country except for crimes committed by non-Indians against the person or property of other non-Indians. The federal government, however, occasionally has transferred criminal jurisdiction to state governments in tribally specific situations. In the 1940s, Congress enacted such legislation for all reservations in Kansas, the Devil's Lake Reservation in North Dakota, the Mesquaki Settlement (Sac and Fox Reservation in Iowa), and all reservations in New York. Congress also passed legislation terminating a number of designated tribes in the 1950s and all such termination legislation subjecting affected tribal members to state criminal and civil jurisdiction. In addition, during the same period Congress enacted Public Law 280, which originally mandated five states, California, Minnesota (except for the Red Lake Reservation), Wisconsin (except for the Menominee Reservation), Oregon (except for the Warm Springs Reservation), and Nebraska, to assume both criminal and civil adjudicatory jurisdiction and authorized other states not having such authority to voluntarily assume it by affirmative legislative enactment. Certain states, like Washington and Iowa, voluntarily assumed some jurisdiction under Public Law 280. Alaska was added to the list of mandatory states under Public Law 280 when it entered the Union. In 1968 Congress amended Public Law 280 to prospectively require tribal consent through a referendum for any future transfers of jurisdiction to the sates, and to authorize states to retrocede back to the federal government the jurisdiction they already had acquired under Public Law 280. A number of states, including Nebraska and Wisconsin, have retroceded some or all of their Public Law 280 jurisdiction for specific reservations.

Civil Adjudicatory Jurisdiction

In the area of civil adjudicatory authority, federal Indian law generally permits Indian tribes to exercise jurisdiction over any claims arising in Indian country or involving an Indian from the reservation. Many tribes have modern Western-style courts that exercise such adjudicatory authority. These courts generally resemble state or local courts, although the procedure sometimes may be less formal and the substantive law applied may represent a composite of Western legal principles and tribal customary or written law. Like any sovereign government, an Indian tribe need not exercise all sovereign powers which it is capable of invoking, and some tribes through their tribal constitutions or ordinances have decided, as a matter of tribal law, to exercise less jurisdiction than they are afforded under the principles of federal Indian law.

State courts generally have no jurisdiction over claims arising on the reservation, unless the tribe is a terminated tribe or jurisdiction has been transferred through Public Law 280 or some similar federal statute. In general, federal Indian law is said to preempt, that is prevent, the exercising of such state jurisdiction to assure that the Indians can make their own laws and be governed by them. One exception to the general principle of preemption of state court jurisdiction over on-reservation claims permits Indi-

ans, and in particular Indian tribes, to waive their right to seek redress in tribal courts and to sue non-Indians directly in state courts, even when non-Indians could not involuntarily sue tribal Indians in the same forum. The mere fact that a civil dispute either involves Indians or arose in Indian country does not authorize the federal courts to exercise jurisdiction over the dispute. Federal jurisdiction exists over a private dispute arising in Indian country only if the dispute arises under the federal constitution, laws, or treaties or if the parties are citizens from different states and none of the adverse claimants are from the same state.

One productive source of federal civil cases involves cases contesting the authority of state or tribal governments to exercise criminal, civil adjudicatory, regulatory, or taxing jurisdiction. Tribes regularly file suit in federal court contesting the exercise of state power on reservations. In *National Farmers Union Insurance Co. v. Crow Tribe*, 471 U.S. 845 (1985), the Supreme Court also ruled that a non-Indian party could sue in federal court under principles of federal Indian law to contest the authority of the Crow tribal courts to exercise jurisdiction over a civil dispute to which it was a party. The Court nevertheless held that where a non-Indian party seeks to invoke federal court jurisdiction over a claim of lack of tribal jurisdiction, it must first exhaust all available remedies in the tribal courts before the federal court can entertain the dispute.

Regulatory and Taxing Jurisdiction

Regulatory and taxing jurisdiction in Indian country represents an area where the cases and statutes do not provide any bright line tests allocating jurisdiction and sovereignty. Rather, these areas have produced extensive litigation, the results of which often turn on the specific facts of each case. Certain general principles emerge from these cases, however. Indian tribes as sovereign polities generally have authority to tax and regulate activities of both Indians and non-Indians in Indian country, particularly on tribally and individually owned Indian trust land within Indian country. For example, In *Merrion v. Jicarilla Apache Tribe*, 455 U.S. 130 (1982) and *Kerr-McGee Corp. v. Navajo Tribe*, 471 U.S. 195 (1985), the Supreme Court ruled that the inherent sovereignty possessed by Indian tribes permitted the tribes to impose mineral and oil and gas severance taxes and possessory interest taxes on natural resources extracted by non-Indian companies from leased Indian lands. Likewise, in *New Mexico v. Mescalero Apache Tribe*, 462 U.S. 324 (1983), the Court held that the Mescalero Apache tribe could regulate (and the State of New Mexico could not regulate) non-Indian hunting and fishing within the Mescalero Apache Reservation, since the tribe had invested, with federal approval, considerable funds in the development and maintenance of tribal fish and game resources, and had a significant investment in developing a tourist industry that relied in part on these resources.

Generally, states have no jurisdiction to regulate and tax the activities of tribal members in Indian country. Any state exercising jurisdiction in such matters is said to be preempted by federal Indian law. Thus, for example, in *McClanahan v. Arizona State Tax Commission*, 411 U.S. 164 (1973), the Supreme Court ruled that states had no jurisdiction to impose income taxes on tribal members for income earned on their reservation. Recent decisions of the courts, however, have granted state and local governments broader regulatory and taxing power over some non-member activities in Indian country, particularly for matters occurring on non-Indian owned lands within a reservation. The Court held in *Washington v. Confederated Tribes of the Colville Reservation*, 447 U.S. 134 (1980) that the federal preemption of state tax law in Indian country did not prevent states from imposing taxes on non-Indians or Indians who were not members of the governing tribe for purchases of cigarettes on the reservation. States also have been permitted to regulate and tax non-Indians for activities occurring on non-Indian owned land within the reservation. For example, in *Brendale v. Confederated Tribes and Bands of the Yakima Indian Nation*, 492 U.S. 408 (1989), the Court ruled that local county authorities could zone, and Indian tribes could not zone, non-Indian owned parcels of land in open areas of a reservation that had lost their dominant Indian character and included substantial non-Indian ownership and population.

Where, however, the exercise of state authority potentially could interfere with federally supported tribal programs, even state jurisdiction to regulate or tax non-Indian activities in Indian country has been found to be preempted by federal law. In *White Mountain Apache Tribe v. Backer*, 448 U.S. 136 (1980), for example, the Supreme Court ruled that the State of Arizona could not apply its motor vehicle fuel tax and its carrier's gross receipts tax to the activities of a non-Indian trucking firm who hauled tribal timber on a reservation under contract with a tribal timber operation. Significant to the decision in *White Mountain Apache* was the fact that federal statutes and regulations significantly governed the management of and prices charged for tribal timber, and that the ultimate economic burden of the tax would fall on the tribe even though the legal incidence of the tax was technically on the non-Indian carrier. Similarly, in *California v. Cabazon Band of Mission Indians*, 480 U.S. 202 (1987), the Supreme Court ruled that significant financing and other federal support for Indian gaming operations precluded the State of California from enforcing its laws regulating gambling against a tribal gaming operation conducted in Indian country. Thus, state jurisdiction to tax and regulate non-Indians and nonmember Indians in Indian country is determined on a case by case basis, with state claims to jurisdiction being stronger with respect to activities on non-Indian owned lands within reservations, and state power being weakest with respect to activi-

ties occurring on Indian-owned lands, and where significant federal statutory or regulatory authority governs the activity the state seeks to regulate or tax.

Federal regulatory authority in Indian country is often misunderstood. Under the so-called plenary power doctrine, a legally questionable colonialist remnant of expanding federal political hegemony over Indian nations, the federal government claims Congress has complete and relatively unfettered power to regulate or tax any and all activities in Indian country, including legislating to extinguish or abridge the sovereign powers of Indian tribes. In practice, however, the federal government generally has not exercised such broad powers. As a general rule, any federal law of general application applies in Indian country, unless it would interfere with, abridge, or modify a right of Indian tribes on their members derived from treaty, statute, or executive order. Where federal regulatory or taxing laws are inconsistent with traditional Indian rights, the courts will only find that Congress meant to extinguish the Indian right in question where Congress has manifested a clear awareness of and intent to extinguish or modify the Indian right. Such intent may be apparent on the face of the federal statute in question, or it may be derived from the legislative history of the statute in question. Thus, even though Indians held traditional on-reservation hunting and fishing rights, the Supreme Court ruled in *United States v. Dion*, 476 U.S. 754 (1986), that Congress, by enacting amendments to the Eagle Protection Act that explicitly preserved Indian rights to take eagles for ceremonial purposes with a license, had extinguished any preexisting treaty right to take eagles for other purposes. This rule sometimes produces anomalous results. For example, the income derived by Indians from individual trust allotments is deemed exempt from federal income taxes, since federal taxation would be inconsistent with tax free status of such lands promised to Indians in the General Allotment Act of 1887. By contrast, the cases seem to suggest that individual income derived by tribal members from tribally owned lands is subject to federal income taxation since the treaties, statutes, or executive orders establishing the reservation generally contain no promise, akin to that found in the General Allotment Act, of tax-free status. Nevertheless, the prevailing assumption at the time most reservations were created was that Indians were tax exempt in Indian country. This assumption was supported by the so-called "Indians not taxed" clause, or Article I, Section 2 of the United States Constitution, and Section 2 of the Fourteenth Amendment to the Constitution, which excluded so-called "Indians not taxed" from the census for purposes of representation in Congress and imposition of direct taxation.

Conclusion

This survey indicates that Indian tribes began as independent sovereign nations. The process of colonialism initiated by contact between the indigenous inhabitants of the New World, and the Euroamerican colonists from the Old World, gradually changed the legal and political status of Indian tribes from sovereign independent nations to domestic dependent nations. With that externally imposed change in status, the law of the colonizers enforced a gradual diminution in the sovereign powers of tribes and therefore the scope of their jurisdiction. The modern remnant of those colonialist legal doctrines continues to treat Indian tribes as sovereign nations, whose territory is subject to special jurisdictional rules in which the tribe has the primary governance, and the federal government assumes a secondary jurisdictional role. Nevertheless, significant erosion in tribal jurisdiction, often in favor of an enlarged jurisdictional role for state and local government, has occurred throughout the twentieth century, and especially in the last quarter of the twentieth century.

Trial jurisdiction, however, remains the rule for most members of Indian tribes for activities occurring on the reservation. Tribal authority has been partially diminished, however, in favor of the law of the colonizers, federal or state law, for serious crimes, for activities on non-Indian owned lands within the reservation, and for nonmember activities within the reservation. The process of expanding colonial political hegemony over Indian country and its people has continued in United States law through most of the twentieth century, and the remnant of original sovereignty which the laws of the United States accord to Indian tribes is no longer defined in only geographic terms. Jurisdiction in Indian country is determined by an odd, and sometimes irrational, pattern of land ownership and the race or tribal membership of the parties involved in the matter in question. Since Indian tribes, for the most part, were not parties to and rarely agreed with the diminution in their sovereign powers enforced by the laws of the colonizer, not surprisingly they often claim, with significant justification, to retain far greater sovereign powers and jurisdiction than federal Indian law is prepared to concede. This political dynamic inevitably produces tensions and disputes among tribal, federal, and state governments about sovereign powers and jurisdiction denied to the tribes by the colonial justifications accepted by federal Indian law, which the tribes and their members point out they never voluntarily surrendered.

Robert N. Clinton. Copyright © 1992 Robert N. Clinton.

See also **Civil Rights; Law**

Further Reading

Canby, William. "The Status of Indian Tribes in American Law Today." *Washington Law Review* 62 (1987): 1–22.
Cohen, Felix S. *Felix S. Cohen's Handbook of Federal Indian Law.* Ed. Rennard Strickland. Charlottesville, VA: Mitchie/Bobbs-Merrill, 1982.
Clinton, Robert N. "Criminal Jurisdiction over Indian Lands: A Journey through a Jurisdictional Maze." *Arizona Law Review* 18 (1976): 503–83.
———. "State Power over Indian Reservations: A Critical Comment on Burger Court Decision." *South Dakota Law Review* 26 (1981): 434–46.
Clinton, Robert N., Nell Jessup Newton, and Monroe E. Price. *American Indian Law: Cases and Materials.* Charlottesville, VA: Mitchie/Bobbs-Merrill, 1991.
Laurence, Robert. "The Indian Commerce Clause." *Arizona Law Review* 23 (1981): 203–61.

SPOKAN

The Spokan Indians of northeastern Washington spoke a Salishan language shared, in different dialects, with the contiguous Coeur d'Alene, Kalispel, and Flathead, and which was a lingua franca in the northeastern Plateau. The three bands of Spokan occupied the semiarid terraces of the Spokane River. Their dependence upon salmon necessitated a specialized fishing technology, permanent riverine winter village locations, semisubterranean pit houses, extensive use of tules, mutual exploitation of resource areas, leadership through consensus of opinion, a sweat lodge complex, shamanism, and wide utilization of plant and root crops, which were gathered during spring and summer and stored for winter consumption.

Historical Period

The first Euroamerican contact in the area was by Lewis and Clark in 1805 and followed by major smallpox epidemics in 1846 and from 1852 to 1853, which destroyed one-third to one-half of the area's Plateau inhabitants, and gave rise to religious nativistic movements, particularly the Prophet Dance and the Dreamer Cult. First mention of the Spokan was by David Thompson, who surveyed the region from 1808 to 1811 for the Northwest Fur Company. Religious factionalism commenced in 1839 with the Tshimakin Protestant mission, and relations between Euroamericans and the Spokan further deteriorated with the 1847 Whitman Massacre and the abandonment of the Tshimakin mission.

The 1850 Land Donation Act served to increase uncontrolled Euroamerican encroachment by miners and other settlers upon the Spokan, which ultimately led to warfare with the United States Army, and the 1858 military defeat of the Spokan at the battle of Four Lakes by Colonel George Wright. In 1880 the Army established Fort Spokane at the mouth of the Spokane River, and maintained the garrison until 1898 when the War Department turned it over to the Interior Department for the establishment of an Indian boarding school for Colville and Spokan children, until its closure in 1906. With continued encroachment by settlers upon Indian land, and conflict about where the Spokan would be settled, the January 18, 1881, executive order set aside 154,898 acres of public land for the Spokan, establishing the Spokane Indian Reservation. In 1907 the Bureau of Indian Affairs (BIA) gave full agency status to the 600 Spokan with the establishment of the BIA and tribal headquarters in Wellpinit.

Contemporary Period

Further destruction of fish resources was created by the 1908 construction of Little Falls Dam, where a major traditional fishery was located, an area critical not only for salmon but also for trade with other contiguous groups. Even more devastating to the Spokan economy was the August 30, 1935, New Deal authorization for construction of Grand Coulee Dam, a structure that stopped all migration of salmon.

On August 13, 1946, Congress passed an act establishing the Indian Claims Commission, whereby various tribes could present claims for 3 million acres taken and compensation at 1892 prices. The Spokan contended in their claim that their membership was based upon language, settlements, and a sense of social unity, thereby giving them the right to share in tribal property. They further maintained that the 1887 land agreement had been obtained for an "unconscionable consideration" under duress when they ceded 3.14 million acres, being paid $.32 per acre. In December 1966 the Spokan voted 155 to 3 to accept a compromise from the Indian Claims Commission for a settlement of $6.7 million, which was held in trust.

In 1954 rich quantities of uranium oxide and antunite, a secondary uranium-bearing mineral, were discovered on the reservation by two tribal members. The Atomic Energy Commission placed six test holes and guaranteed a private Indian incorporated company a purchase contract after revealing that nine ore bodies found had an estimated wealth of $14 million. Ultimately, two Indian mining companies, Midnight Mine and Dawn Mining, produced ore until the Three Mile Island disaster. Previous claims by enrolled members to the proceeds led to considerable conflict without settlement.

During this period tribal factionalism eventually led to the formation of the Spokane Indian Association, an outspoken group who feared the tribe would not receive all uranium royalties due them, claiming losses through reorganization and sale of stock, particularly since most production shifted from tribal to private land. The conflict with regard to law enforcement and state jurisdiction over uranium, fishing, and hunting rights led the BIA to advance a policy of termination for all the Spokan in December 1955. Ultimately, the Spokan successfully opposed termination of land and Indian status, led mostly by Robert Sherwood, the tribal chairperson.

Although a few older people still make baskets, collect roots, and practice some Spokan customs, for the most part the old ways are lost since only a few speak the language, use the sweat lodge, or practice traditional religion. While many participate in occasional pan-Indian celebrations and are concerned about political and socio-economic sovereignty, only a few younger Spokan are active in revitalizing what are now essentially syncretic ceremonies, such as the Blue Jay Dance and Mid-Winter ceremony. The revitalization of traditional ways, particularly amongst some younger Spokan, is in part due to active involvement by several Plains Indians, who have effectively introduced certain Plains' features and rituals. However, Spokan elders are actively opposed to these non-Spokan influences.

The reservation is organized around an elected Tribal Council with headquarters, community center, museum, and tribal store located in Wellpinit. Both Catholic and Protestant churches exist on the reservation, but not the Indian Shaker or Native American Church. Factions are formed basically along lines of religious affiliation, and between incipient political and geographical groups. Issues of high unemployment, legality of gaming, litigation over loss of fishing sites and resources, and control of cultural resource management are the dominant contemporary concerns. Tribal revenues are generated by land leases, a treated post mill, and a lumber mill capable of processing timber cut on the Spokane Reservation by enrolled members. The Spokan tribe, through revenue settlement from loss of aboriginal and historical fishing sites by Washington Water Power dams, has established a successful fish hatchery, one staffed entirely by enrolled Spokan. Approximately 50 percent of the 2,100 enrolled as Spokan Indians live on the reservation.

John Alan Ross

See also **Washington State Tribes**

Further Reading

Ross, John Alan. "The Spokan." *Handbook of North American Indians*. Vol. 12. *Plateau*. Ed. Deward E. Walker, Jr. Washington, DC: Smithsonian Institution, forthcoming.

Roy, Prodipto, and Della M. Walker. *Assimilation of the Spokan Indians*. Institute of Agricultural Sciences Bulletin 628. Pullman: Washington State University, 1961.

Ruby, Robert H., and John A. Brown. *The Spokane Indians*. Norman: The University of Oklahoma Press, 1970.

Wynecoop, David C. *Children of the Sun: Spokane: A History of the Spokane Indians*. Wellpinit, WA: privately printed, 1969.

SPORTS AND GAMES

A clear understanding of American Indian sports today must start with a review of the role of sports in traditional Indian life. Prevailing attitudes about games and sports in the twentieth century have been strongly influenced by long-standing beliefs about the proper place of these activities in the community.

In the traditional life of most American Indian communities, sports and games have occupied a very prominent role. In fact, accounts provided by oral history, artifacts, ball courts, folklore, and the writings of early travelers, suggest that the importance placed on these activities would be considered excessive, even by today's standards. For Native Americans, however, these activities were steeped in tradition and intimately related to all phases of life, especially to ceremony, ritual, magic, and religion.

Many Native games began as religious rites and evolved into popular sports only over time. Games held a central place in ceremonies and festivals related to war, hunting, harvest, birth, death, and other events important to the community.

Given the great diversity among Indian cultures throughout North America, it would be misleading to sketch a unified picture of Indian sports. Although several games were nearly universally played, many others were limited to one tribe or to a small number of tribes in a given locality. Indian games were generally characterized by extensive spiritual preparation, high standards of sportsmanship, attention to artistic expression through game implements and body decorations, and the placing of wagers on most sports contests.

The most popular of all American Indian sports were ballgames. Among these, the most prevalent was lacrosse, which was invented by the Indians on this continent. Varieties of lacrosse have been played throughout most parts of the United States and Canada. In addition, games of shinny, double ball, and the ancient court ball game were very popular in large areas of the North American continent.

Foot races were among the most universal of all Indian sports. From the time of the earliest contact with outsiders, Indians astonished observers with their extraordinary running feats, particularly in long-distance races. This long-standing tradition of running excellence still serves as a source of motivation and pride for Indian youth.

Gambling among American Indians was nearly universal as a sporting activity. The placing of wagers was evident both in athletic games and in games of chance, which involved dice or stick games. A great deal of leisure time was devoted to these table or blanket games by both men and women. Betting on games of chance or on sporting events was never viewed by Indians as a moral issue, but was customary and a part of the social life of the community. Although gambling did redistribute the wealth somewhat, the goods remained within the community in a kind of circular economics.

American Indian Athletes in the Early Twentieth Century (1900 to 1930)

American Indian sports reached its zenith in prominence and visibility during the early part of the twentieth century. Particularly noteworthy were the athletic teams of the Carlisle Indian School in Pennsylvania, from the 1890s to 1918, and those of the Haskell Institute in Lawrence, Kansas, during the 1920s. John Steckbeck stated in *The Fabulous Redmen* that "for twenty-odd years, the Redmen raced across the stage of big-time football, leaving in their wake many a bewildered team . . . then vanished from the American sporting scene forever." During this period, a number of Indians also excelled in major league baseball and in professional football after it developed in the 1920s. Indian visibility and participation in sports at the national level significantly diminished after 1930.

The prominence of Indians on the national sporting scene was enhanced by the coming together of Indian youth from different tribes to the boarding schools of Carlisle and Haskell. This marked a new phase in Indian relations. The pooling of Indian athletes to compete against non-Indians led to extraordinary success for Carlisle and Haskell sports teams. Strong sports interests, a tradition of participation, and the enthusiasm generated in these new non-Indian games led to unanticipated successes. Though neither Carlisle nor Haskell was ever a true four-year college, they competed against the best college teams of the day.

Unquestionably, the most outstanding Indian athlete was Jim Thorpe of the Sac and Fox Tribe of Oklahoma, who attended and played football and several other sports at the Carlisle School in 1908, 1909, 1911, and 1912. Thorpe won All-American honors at the small Carlisle School and was also the major sports hero of the 1912 Olympics. In addition, Thorpe played major league baseball with the New York Giants, and was a star in the early days of the National Football League. He was president of the league during its first year in 1920. Stories of Thorpe's athletic prowess almost defy belief. For example, he scored 198 points in 1912 against major college football competition, a feat never equalled.

Some measure of Thorpe's status as an athlete can be gathered from the recognition provided by the Associated Press, which in 1950 conducted a poll of 391 sportswriters and sportscasters to determine the greatest football player of the half century (1900 to 1950). Thorpe won with 170 votes, besting second place Red Grange by 32 votes. Remarkably, in 1950, Jim Thorpe was more than thirty years past his peak playing days.

The Associated Press also polled the sportswriters to determine the best *all-around* male athlete of the first half of the twentieth century. Thorpe, with 166 votes more than the runner up, clearly surpassed Babe Ruth, Jack Dempsey, and other prominent athletes in this poll. No doubt, Thorpe's versatility in track, baseball, football, and several other sports contributed to his hands-down victory in the rankings.

Other American Indians achieved national prominence in sports during the early part of the century. Charles A. "Chief" Bender from the Chippewa tribe, Minnesota, was a star pitcher for the Philadelphia Athletics from 1903 to 1917, appearing in five World Series. Bender was elected to the Baseball Hall of Fame in 1953. Joseph N. Guyon of the White Earth Chippewa tribe in Minnesota attended the Carlisle

School and then transferred to the Georgia Institute of Technology. He later played football with several professional teams, including the Canton Bulldogs, the Oorang Indians, and the New York Giants. Guyon was inducted into the National Professional Football Hall of Fame in 1966.

John Levi from the Arapaho tribe of Oklahoma was the most famous of all athletes at the Haskell Institute. Levi won All-American honors in football in 1923, sharing the backfield with Red Grange. Like Thorpe, Levi was a multi-talented athlete playing football, basketball, baseball, and track. Tom Longboat, a member of the Onondaga tribe of New York State and Canada, achieved great fame in middle-distance runs in the eastern part of the United States. He later entered and won the 1907 Boston Marathon in a time nearly five minutes faster than the previous best time in the marathon. Longboat, acclaimed the first "World Professional Marathon Champion," attracted crowds as large as 100,000 people to his races.

John T. "Chief" Meyers, a member of the Cahuilla band of California, attended Dartmouth College, where he excelled in baseball in the early part of the twentieth century. Subsequently, he was a catcher with the major leagues, playing with the New York Giants from 1908 to 1915 and later with the Brooklyn Dodgers.

Louis F. Sockalexis, a Penobscot from Old Town, Maine, entered professional baseball in the late nineteenth century from Holy Cross College, where he served as a pitcher and outfielder. He played outfield with the Cleveland Spiders where he batted .331 in 1897. Part of Sockalexis' legacy was the name "Indians" for the Cleveland team. Known as the Spiders during Sockalexis' years, the team was subsequently called the Bronchos, Blues, and the Naps. In 1915 a Cleveland newspaper held a contest to select a new name and, according to Franklin Lewis's team history, the name "Indians" was selected as a tribute to the popularity of Louis Sockalexis.

Louis Tewanima, a Hopi from the Second Mesa in Arizona, attended the Carlisle School during the same time as Jim Thorpe, from 1907 to 1912. Tewanima achieved distinction as one of the greatest distance runners this country has ever produced. He was a member of the 1908 and 1912 Olympic teams, winning a silver medal for a second-place finish in the 10,000-meter run in 1912, and finishing ninth in the marathon in the 1908 Olympics. He established a world record in the indoor ten-mile run at Madison Square Garden. Tewanima was selected as a Helms Foundation member of the all-time United States Track and Field Team in 1954.

The athletic teams at Indian schools, particularly at Haskell and Carlisle, provided a morale boost and rallying focus for the total Indian population. In addition, a cohesion among Indian tribes was encouraged by these visible successes. The spirit of the total Indian community was lifted by sports success at Indian schools, as well as by those who excelled as members of non-Indian teams or as individual participants.

The Decline of American Indian Sports During the Mid-Twentieth Century (1930 to 1970)

In proportion to the rest of the population, both the number of Indian athletes and the image of the Indian as a superior athlete have declined appreciably since 1930. This decline coincided with restrictions placed on Indian participation in sports events. These restrictions have been both externally and internally imposed.

The closing of the Carlisle School in 1918, and the serious de-emphasis of athletics at the Haskell Institute in 1930, effectively closed off the traditional avenues of sports opportunity for American Indians. Thereafter, Indian athletes had to enroll in non-Indian colleges in order to participate in college sports. As a result of legislative restrictions, informal barriers, and the poor quality of education in Indian schools, entry into major non-Indian colleges was particularly difficult during this period. As a result, athletic participation by Indians at the college level was at its lowest point during the 1930s, 1940s, and 1950s.

In addition, opportunities to develop sports skills through participation in youth training programs and sports clubs have been much more limited for Indians than for non-Indians. Athletic programs such as age-group swimming, gymnastics, tennis, special summer camps for golf, wrestling, ice skating, and organized leagues for youth football, basketball, and little league baseball have simply not been as available for reservation Indians as for aspiring athletes in suburban and urban areas.

As a result of social developments over time, Indians have imposed upon themselves restrictions and a kind of sports isolation. Internal pressures have seriously limited sports participation even at the senior high school level. Further, these constraints have inhibited Indians and discouraged them from leaving the reservation for athletic participation. Those who have the athletic ability to succeed beyond the reservation are often pressured by friends and family to remain as a part of the traditional Indian community.

Still, there were several notable success stories among Indian athletes between 1930 and 1970. Many of these have been in areas in which the sport, or visibility of the sport, was not connected to college participation.

Two of the best-known American Indian athletes during the mid-twentieth century were runners Ellison "Tarzan" Brown and William M. "Billy" Mills. Tarzan Brown, a member of the Narraganset tribe in Rhode Island, excelled in distance running, winning the Boston Marathon in 1936 at the age of twenty-two. In 1939, he again won the Boston Marathon, setting a record for the course.

Billy Mills, a member of the Oglala Sioux tribe in South Dakota, was perhaps the most famous of Indian amateur athletes during the mid-twentieth century. Mills achieved international acclaim by winning a gold medal in the 10,000-meter run at the 1964 Olympics in Tokyo. He set an Olympic record in the process and became the first American to win any Olympic race longer than a mile. In 1965, he set a world record in the six-mile run. Mills attended the Haskell Institute before transferring to the University of Kansas to complete his college career. He has been enshrined into the National Track and Field Hall of Fame and the American Indian Athletic Hall of Fame. A movie of his life entitled *Running Brave* was released in 1983.

Allie P. Reynolds of the Creek tribe in Oklahoma played major league baseball as a pitcher with the Cleveland Indians and the New York Yankees from 1942 to 1954. Reynolds led the American League in strikeouts in 1943 and 1952, and in earned run average in 1952 and 1954. He was voted the nation's professional athlete of the year in 1951. Prior to going into professional baseball, Reynolds attended Oklahoma State University on a track scholarship excelling in the 100- and 200-yard dashes, and in addition was a varsity football player for three years.

Oren Lyons of the Onondaga Nation in New York State attended Syracuse University where he won All-American honors as a lacrosse goal-keeper in 1957 and 1958. His 1957 team was undefeated. Lyons, who comes from a family of superb lacrosse players, also excelled as an amateur boxer in the United States Army and in Golden Gloves tournaments. After spending several years as a commercial artist in New York City, he returned to the reservation where he is a community leader and traditional faithkeeper.

During the 1970s, Gene Locklear, a Lumbee Indian from North Carolina, played major league baseball with the Cincinnati Reds, the San Diego Padres, and the New York Yankees. His best season was in 1975, when he played 100 games and batted .321 with the San Diego Padres. Subsequently, Locklear has achieved significant acclaim as a professional artist living in California. Rod Curl, a Wintu Indian from California, has been a touring professional golfer since the early 1970s. In 1974 he won the Colonial National Open with a four-under-par 276, beating Jack Nicklaus by one stroke. Alex "Sonny" Sixkiller, a member of the Cherokee tribe from Oklahoma, achieved national recognition in the early 1970s as a football player with the University of Washington, where he excelled as quarterback. He played professional football in the National Football League for a short time before his career ended abruptly as a result of injuries.

Sports and Games Today (Since 1970)

During the last two decades, Indians have participated in practically all sports in every region of the country, both as amateurs and as professionals. However, in recent years one major problem in reporting on Indian sports performers has been the lack of a systematic method for identifying people as Indians. Although some have been identified or recognized as Indians, others have not. In former years, it was relatively easy to identify a Native American. Today's increasing interaction among races makes such identification less clear.

Despite the obvious enthusiasm within certain communities for the local teams and heroes, American Indian sports have not been significantly reestablished on a national level. Still, there are cases of noteworthy performances by individuals and teams within particular tribes. These include the exceptional level of play and commitment to baseball among the Choctaws of Mississippi; running excellence among numerous tribes throughout the Southwest, including the Laguna Pueblo distance runners; and basketball play among the Crow tribe in Montana. Not only does the excellent performance of these groups stand out, but the intense level of support on the part of the Indian community is also remarkable.

Athletes in these groups, however, reflect a tendency of Indian athletes in general to restrict their participation to the local scene, hesitating to venture into the regional or national level of competition as is customary for most non-Indian athletes. Those who do venture outside the Indian community have often returned home prematurely. According to sportswriter Gary Smith, there is a cliche among the Crow Indians in Montana to the effect that "every Indian that leaves has a rubber band attached to his back." Very few Indians have exhibited the patience to persist in athletic situations away from the home environment.

In discussions with Indian athletes at the Haskell Indian Junior College in 1984, this author noted that Indians reared on reservations were not confident of moving on to a four-year college competitive level, even though their record of performance would imply their ability to succeed at that level. Athletes growing up in an urban or suburban setting were less prone to restrict their aspirations.

Even though there has not been a major turn-around from the depressed state of Indian sports since the mid-twentieth century, there are several encouraging signs, among which are: (a) The establishment and growing impact of the American Indian Athletic Hall of Fame, located at the Haskell Indian Junior College in Lawrence, Kansas, which has given visibility to American Indian athletic heroes of the twentieth century; (b) The development of national level Indian sports teams and organizations, particularly the Iroquois National Lacrosse Team from New York State, who have been involved in international competition for the past several years; (c) The creation of the National Indian Athletic Association, which has initiated plans to coordinate and promote youth clinics and national championships, and to serve as a resource for Indian sports activities; and (d) The continued high level of interest by Indian youth in activities, including basketball, lacrosse, ice hockey, boxing, rodeo, and running.

Perhaps the most rapidly developing sport among Indian youth in the western part of the United States is rodeo. No fewer than ten regional Indian rodeo organizations are in operation today, culminating in a National Indian Finals Rodeo Championship each year in Albuquerque, New Mexico.

The Native peoples of Alaska and northern Canada continue to gather each year for the "Eskimo Olympics," which feature many competitions indigenous to the area, such as the high kick and the blanket toss. Although they are little known outside Alaska, extraordinary feats of strength, agility, and flexibility are exhibited each year by these superior athletes.

Running is still the most universal of all Indian sports. The New Mexico-based Indian running club, Wings of the West, has won two successive national age group championships recently at the Athletic Congress United States National Cross-Country Championships. Continuing efforts are being made not only to promote excellence among Indian athletes, but also to create a more supportive climate for competitions at the regional and national level. With these initiatives and the returning excellence among these athletes at the local level, there is reason to be optimistic that American Indian sports and games may one day reassume a place of distinction on the national scene.

Joseph B. Oxendine

X.L. Kugie Louis

See also Rodeos

Further Reading

Blanchard, Kendall. *The Mississippi Choctaws at Play: The Serious Side of Leisure.* Urbana: University of Illinois Press, 1981.

Culin, Stewart. *Games of the North American Indians.* Bureau of American Ethnology, 24th Annual Report 1902–1903. Washington, DC: U.S. Government Printing Office, 1907. New York, NY: Dover, 1975

Nabakov, Peter. *Indian Running.* Santa Barbara, CA: Capra Press, 1981.

Oxendine, Joseph B. *American Indian Sports Heritage.* Champaign, IL: Human Kinetics Books, 1988.

Smith, Gary. "Shadow of a Nation." *Sports Illustrated* (February 18, 1991): 60–74.

Steckbeck, John. *The Fabulous Redmen.* Harrisburg, PA: J. Horace McFarland, 1951.

SQUAXIN ISLAND

Squaxins are a people of the water, of the land, and of the sky. We are of the bays, the inlets, and the streams. Our life continues to depend on the stewardship we extend to all the earth.

The Squaxin Island tribal people lived in the temperate forests and along the waters in the southern Puget Sound area in today's Washington State. They carved canoes from cedar logs and traveled throughout the sound to the Pacific Ocean. Their lives were built around the vast resources of the region; they accepted fish, shellfish, animals, and plants as gifts of nature with great respect and appreciation. Their culture, religion, and entire lives were based on the

blessings of the Great Spirit. The island which bears the tribe's name was once used as a prison camp. We know from books and from the stories that have been passed down that atrocities were committed against tribal citizens. But efforts to disperse the tribe were unsuccessful. Today, there are more than 350 surviving descendants.

History and Government

The Squaxin Island Reservation was established on Squaxin Island in 1854 under the Medicine Creek Treaty. Squaxin ancestors, who spoke a southern Coast Salish language, were confined on the island during the Puget Sound Indian War, 1855 to 1856, dispersing thereafter to the surrounding area. In 1882 Squaxin John Slocum reported an extraordinary revelation that led to the founding of the Indian Shaker Church. Soon spreading beyond Puget Sound, it has an active membership throughout the Pacific Northwest in the late twentieth century. Today most tribal members are Protestant.

The tribe is governed by a Tribal Council. Organized under the Indian Reorganization Act of 1934, its Constitution was adopted in 1965. The tribe filed a claim with the Indian Claims Commission (Docket 206), and was awarded $7,662 in 1974, which it initially refused.

Today the tribe retains the use of Squaxin Island for fishing, hunting, shellfish gathering, camping, and other activities. The tribal headquarters are located on tribal trust land at Kamilche, south of Shelton, Washington, which was purchased in the 1970s. The tribe's resource management offices are located here, along with the community center and other facilities.

Priorities

The Squaxin Island people have always distinguished themselves as good stewards of the land and its resources. Virtually every fishery management technique used today has its roots in traditional practices. Management decisions are carefully made in order to consider the impact they will have on seven generations of descendants. Like their ancestors, tribal members celebrate the First Salmon ceremony, an expression of the great respect and brotherhood with which the Indian views the fish and other gifts of nature.

Natural Resource Management

The tribe's natural resource department works cooperatively with the Northwest Indian Fisheries Commission, and local, state, and federal non-Indian governments. It is active in fishery management activities, ranging from hatchery enhancement to environmental protection. Its hatchery produces millions of healthy fish every year. In 1987, for example, the tribe released nearly 2.5 million chum salmon into local area waters.

Clams and oysters are also inseparable parts of the tribe's culture and survival. The Hartstene Oyster Company was acquired in 1976, along with 2,300 feet of tideland frontage, which has been planted with oysters almost every year since. Tribal citizens also harvest shellfish, under tribal permit, on traditional tidelands. They operate the largest tribal salmon and steelhead netpen program in the Northwest, much of it in cooperation with the State Department of Fisheries, to increase commercial and sport fishing.

Environmental Protection

Tribal ancestors left a powerful legacy of respect for the environment, and the Squaxin Island people work hard to continue this tradition. Indian and non-Indian government efforts are combining forces to develop effective environmental protection programs. The "treaty Indian tribes," as historic stewards and present-day comanagers of the fisheries resource, are actively involved in the effort to solve the problems created by pollution. The Squaxin tribe participates in developing programs with the Puget Sound Water Quality Authority and the Timber-Fish-Wildlife Agreement. The objective is not to eliminate jobs or harm Washington State's economy, but to assure that in making today's decisions, there will be resources for jobs and a healthy environment in the future.

We wish to consider the future, we hope for an abundance of clams and salmon for our grandchildren. The homes of the clam people and the salmon people must be respected and protected. They are our relatives, and they provide us food for a healthy and happy life.

Steve Robinson
Dave Whitener
Squaxin Island Natural Resources staff

See also **Washington State Tribes**

Further Reading

Echrom, J.A. *Remembered Drums*. Walla Walla, WA: Pioneer Press, 1989.

Gorsline, Jerry, ed. *Shadows of Our Ancestors*. Townsend, WA: Empty Bowl, 1992.

"People of the Water." A slide, tape, and video production of the Squaxin Island Tribe, 1989.

Smith, Marian W. *The Puyallup-Nisqually*. Columbia University Contributions to Anthropology 32. New York, 1940. New York, NY: AMS Press, 1969.

STEILACOOM

Traditionally, the Steilacoom (also known as Stailakoom or Chillacum) occupied the Tacoma Basin, a territory north from the Nisqually River up to Point Defiance, and inland as far east as the start of the Puyallup River watershed, in western Washington State. The basin contains two major water sources: Chambers Creek (or the Steilacoom River) and the Segwallitchu River. The five divisions of the Indian people included the Steilacoom proper (six sites on Chambers Creek), the Sastuck (three sites on Clover Creek), the Spanaway (at Spanaway Lake), the Tlithlow (at Hillhurst on Murray Creek), and the Segwallitchu (two sites on the Segwallitchu River).

The Steilacoom were the most affected of all western Washington tribes by early white settlement. Within their territory were the first trading post, army post, church, and incorporated town north of the Columbia River. The tribe signed the Medicine Creek Treaty in 1854, but was not given a reservation because of their proximity to planned development surrounding the town of Steilacoom. Following the Territorial War of 1855 to 1856, many Steilacoom families settled on reservations created for other tribes signing the same treaty, including the Puyallup, Nisqually, and Squaxin Island reservations, as well as the Skokomish and Port Madison reservations. Others, those who retained their identity as Steilacoom Indians, remained in their homeland; these are the ancestors of the modern-day Steilacoom tribe.

Twentieth-Century History

With the assistance of the Bureau of Indian Affairs (BIA), the tribe filed a petition in the Court of Claims (No. K-41) in 1929, that was ultimately dropped. In 1937 the BIA suggested that the Steilacoom join with the numerically lesser Nisqually tribe in order to benefit from the Indian Reorganization Act. This bid failed, due to Nisqually concern regarding loss of self-determination. The Steilacoom filed a claim in 1956 under the Indian Claims Commission and won a judgment of $9,246.32, for loss of lands taken under the treaty. The tribe filed for intervenor status in the fishing rights case *United States v. Washington*, but was denied participation. The negative ruling was used by the BIA as justification for withholding acknowledgment status.

At the turn of the century the four main community pockets of the Steilacoom tribe were at Steilacoom, Dupont, Roy, and Yelm. When their main leader John Steilacoom died in 1906, his son was too young to inherit that role. Instead it passed on to his older cousin, Joseph McKay. When McKay transferred to the Puyallup tribe in 1929, his relatives in the Latour family (Rose Andrews and Fred Bertschy and their children) took over the responsibilities until 1951, when they brought in an enrolled Colville Indian, Lewis Layton, to serve as the tribal chairman.

Current Situation

Although the tribe did not receive a permanent reservation, it has maintained political continuity up to the present day. A nine-member Council administers the matters of the tribe. They are elected to three-year terms at an annual general membership meeting. Joan Ortez has served as chairperson since Lewis Layton resigned in 1975.

Presently the greatest issue of the tribe remains the lack of federal acknowledgment status. While continuing to work on an acknowledgment petition, the Steilacoom have joined the Duwamish and Snohomish tribes in a suit to reverse the findings of their attempt to enter the *United States v. Washington* case. The case is based on recent revelations that the presiding judge had Alzheimer's disease when he ruled against the non-reservation tribes. The tribe has never accepted its payment from the Indian Claims Commission. Rather, they have left the money with the BIA until their recognition is confirmed, and they can spend the award plus interest on acquiring a land base.

The tribe has approximately 615 members. About 90 percent of the members descend from members at the time of the treaty, while 10 percent stem from early 1950s adoptions of unenrolled Indians from neighboring tribes. A substantial number live in or near the traditional homeland, with about 47 percent (139 households) residing in twelve community pockets of three to twenty families within Pierce County.

The tribal business office and a museum are located in a cultural center in the town of Steilacoom. The center contains a snack bar and has an available meeting room for rent with catering available. Individual employment has been negatively impacted by cutbacks in logging. Previously 30 percent of the adult population was employed in the timber industry.

Culture

About 20 percent of Steilacoom marriages are to Indians from other tribes. These spouses represent a number of geographic areas: the Southwest (Mescalero Apache, Comanche, and Isleta Pueblo), the Midwest (Sioux and Comanche), dispersed eastern tribes (Cherokee, Seminole, Choctaw, and Delaware) and the Northwest (Tlingit, Makah, Lummi, Nisqually, and Yakima).

The tribe has provided a number of classes including basketry and woodcarving. Knowledge of the Steilacoom dialect of Puget Sound Salish is limited to a few nouns and a small number of ancestral names.

The respect given to elders within the tribe is demonstrated in an annual Elders Feast Day, which generally corresponds with the general membership meeting and the distribution of food baskets at the beginning of winter.

Nile Thompson

See also **Washington State Tribes**

Further Reading

Eells, Myron. *The Indians of Puget Sound.* Seattle: University of Washington Press.

Haeberlin, Hermann, and Erna Gunther. *The Indians of Puget Sound.* University of Washington Publications in Anthropology 4:1. Seattle: University of Washington Press, 1930. Seattle: University of Washington Press, 1952.

Smith, Marian. *The Puyallup-Nisqually.* Columbia University Contributions to Anthropology 32. New York, NY: Columbia University Press, 1940. New York, NY: AMS Press, 1969.

STEREOTYPES

See Public Image

STILLAGUAMISH

The Stillaguamish tribe (also known as Stoluckquamish) of northwestern Washington State takes its name, "River People," from its Southern Coast Salish Lushootseed language. Surrounding tribes traditionally recognized the Stillaguamish as "the Canoe People." The Stillaguamish traditionally occupied the geographic territory from Milltown to McMurray, east to the town of Darrington, south to the Stillaguamish Watershed, northeast to Granite Falls, northwest towards Warm Beach, and including Port Susan. Members of the tribe, 2,000 strong at their peak, lived in twenty-six villages along the north and south forks of the Stillaguamish River.

Before white settlers arrived in the mid-1800s, wealth in the tribal communities was recognized by how much one could give away, not the accumulation of material things. The Stillaguamish, one of the wealthiest tribes in the Northwest, measured their wealth in the plentiful amounts of salmon, deer, elk, roots, berries, and cedar trees that flourished in their river paradise. The Stillaguamish shared their wealth at traditional gatherings by giving away canoes, baskets, and mountain goat hair blankets, and by providing a plentiful feast of fish and game. Salmon was the main source of subsistence for the tribe, especially for those members living down river. Up river inhabitants also hunted for deer, elk, bear, and mountain goats, using the furs for trading with trappers and explorers.

The Stillaguamish tribe and other tribes in Washington signed the Treaty of Point Elliott in 1855. As signatories to the Point Elliott Treaty, the Stillaguamish tribe co-manages the 700-square-mile Stillaguamish Watershed with the State of Washington. The tribe is responsible for providing harvest management, enhancement, habitat protection, and enforcement services for the fisheries resource. For giving up their lands in the signing of the treaty, the tribe received a land claim settlement from the federal government in 1966. Funds received from that settlement were used to purchase the tribe's current land base of sixty acres, twenty acres of which are in trust with the government.

Esther Ross was the tribal leader who took the Stillaguamish into the modern era. Raised in California, she returned to the Arlington area with her mother in the 1920s. She was elected chairwoman in 1926. During the ensuing years, she led the tribe's struggle for federal recognition, and was acknowledged throughout Indian country as a leader in the fight for treaty rights. Ross is well remembered for tossing the bones of a dead ancestor on the desk of Governor Daniel Evans at a 1969 meeting. This dramatic act was an effort to get the tribe's burial grounds restored to them, so their ancestors would be on Stillaguamish soil forever. The Stillaguamish tribe finally was recognized by the federal government in 1976, but the burial grounds were never restored.

Elders of the tribe have indicated that 80 to 90 percent of the tribal population died from "new" diseases brought by trappers and settlers to the area. Currently, there are 184 enrolled tribal members who descend from three main families: the Goodridges, the Smiths, and the Harveys.

In the 1990s, arts and language are taught at the tribal center in Arlington. While very few elders still speak the Lushootseed language, there is currently a program that unites elders with children to teach them the language of the tribe. The Stillaguamish tribe initiated a fisheries management program in 1977, following court rulings by Judge George Boldt in 1974 that were favorable to tribes with treaty fishing rights. The program was set into motion in 1978 with the collection of chum salmon brood stock that were raised at a tribal facility under development on Armstrong (Harvcy) Creek. Presently, the tribe raises approximately 200,000 chinook and coho and 1.5 million chum salmon annually at the hatchery facility.

Tribal leadership in 1993 consists of tribal chairwoman Gail Greger, vice-chairman Gary Tatro, secretary Jody Soholt, treasurer Helen Pierce, and council members Carol Brooks and Donna Soholt.

Brent W. Merrill

See also **Fishing and Hunting Rights; Washington State Tribes**

Further Reading

Bruseth, Nels. *Indian Stories and Legends of the Stillaguamish, Sauks and Allied Tribes.* Fairfield, WA: Ye Galleon Press, 1977.

Meyer, Tony. "Stillaguamish Tribe of Indians." Olympia, WA: Northwest Indian Fisheries Commission, 1987. Brochure.

Suttles, Wayne, and Barbara Lane. "Coast Salish." *Handbook of North American Indians.* Vol. 7. *Northwest Coast.* Ed. Wayne Suttles. Washington, DC: Smithsonian Institution (1990): 485–502.

STOCKBRIDGE-MUNSEE

The Stockbridge-Munsee Band of Mohican Indians trace their roots to the great Mahicans of the East (*Muh-he-con-ne-ok*, "People of the Waters That Are Never Still"). Tradition says a great mass of people moved from the north and west seeking a place where the waters were never still. They found such a place and chose it for their homeland on both sides of the Mahicanituck (later Hudson) River. In 1734 some of the people agreed to let missionaries come among them, and the village of Stockbridge, Massachusetts, became the site of a church and school. The band of Mohicans living there came to be known as the Stockbridge Indians. Landless by 1785, this band moved westward to Stockbridge, New York, at the invitation of the Oneida Indians. Resisting attempts to move them yet again west of the Mississippi River, they finally settled on a reservation in Shawano County, Wisconsin in 1856.

By the 1920s the 500 or so tribespeople were again landless and destitute. Under the terms of the Indian Reorganization Act (IRA) of 1934, the Stockbridge-Munsee reorganized under the leadership of Carl Miller and acquired some 15,000 acres of land, about five-sixths of it submarginal cut-over timber land. By 1937, the people had begun establishing their homes on this land. The approximately 1,500–member Stockbridge-Munsee Band of Mohican Indians is now located in a rural, wooded area in Shawano County, in north central Wisconsin near the village of Bowler. The reservation boundaries encompass two townships, Red Springs and Bartelme, for a total of 46,000 acres. Approximately 16,000 acres of this land is held in trust for the tribe, which has resisted breaking the reservation into allotments.

As a result of the IRA, local government was now in the hands of the Stockbridge-Munsee people. They elected their own tribal government with Harry A. Chicks as tribal president. The second president, Arvid E. Miller, was the leader of his people for twenty-six years. He was a charter member of the National Congress of American Indians (1944), and helped to establish the Great Lakes Inter-Tribal Council in the 1960s.

The Stockbridge-Munsee Tribal Council is composed of seven members. The chairperson and treasurer are elected biannually; the vice-chair and four Council members annually. The Council is responsible for upholding the tribal Constitution and ordinances, and implements a number of programs through various boards and committees. In the late 1970s and 1980s, the tribe joined forces with non-Indian residents in the area to fight the federal government's proposal to locate a low-level radiation dump on the entire Stockbridge-Munsee Reservation and half of the nearby Menominee Reservation. As of 1993, the government was looking elsewhere.

Located on tribal lands are tribal offices, a comprehensive health center, the Ella Besaw Residential Center for the Elderly, a community center for the elderly, a youth center, the Arvid E. Miller Memorial Historical Library Museum, a campground and powwow grounds, and the Mohican Northstar Casino and Bingo Hall. The advent of the casino has dropped Mohican unemployment rates considerably. Other tribespeople are employed in the various tribal programs already mentioned, and there are also several small tribal businesses off the reservation that employ people. Individual Mohicans work in the neighboring communities as teachers and teacher-aides, professors, psychiatrists, attorneys, musician/composers, singers, and actors.

The Stockbridge-Munsee have recently brought back a twelve-day New Year celebration called *W Chin Din.* Some of the people have participated in Sweat Lodge ceremonies. Although there are many faithful Christians who have assimilated into the American mainstream, there is also a great hunger for spirituality among the young people, who are calling on their elders to help them. In recent years, some of the young adults have been studying the Munsee-Mahican language, introducing it to their children, and requesting language classes. The annual All Veterans Powwow is held in early August, attracting drummers, singers, traders, and spectators from all over the country. The Stockbridge-Munsee people have survived centuries of movement and struggle to maintain their identity and pride as a people.

Dorothy W. Davids
Staff, Stockbridge-Munsee Historical Committee

See also **Brothertown; Mohegan**

Further Reading

Brasser, Ted J. "Mahikan." *Handbook of North American Indians.* Vol. 15. *Northeast.* Ed. Bruce G. Trigger. Washington, DC: Smithsonian Institution (1978): 198–212.

Frazier, Patrick. *The Mohicans of Stockbridge.* Lincoln: University of Nebraska Press, 1992.

Savagian, John C. "The Tribal Reorganization of the Stockbridge-Munsee: Essential Conditions in the Re-Creation of a Native American Community, 1930–1942." *Wisconsin Magazine of History* 77:1 (1993): 39–62.

SUISLAW

See Confederated Tribes of the Coos, Lower Umpqua, and Suislaw

SUMAS

See Ysleta del Sur Pueblo

SUQUAMISH

The Suquamish and their ancestors have inhabited the Puget Sound area for thousands of years. They lived in cedar longhouses; Old Man House, the famed spiritual and physical center of the Suquamish people, was said to be 900 feet long and 60 feet wide. Before the coming of the white man, this region was one of the most populated centers north of what is now Mexico City. Approximately 300 years after Columbus' arrival in the Western Hemisphere, Captain George Vancouver and the crew of the *Discovery* sailed into Puget Sound. Shortly after their arrival, diseases such as smallpox, measles, and the flu spread rapidly among the Indian people. Missionaries, most of whom were Catholic, soon began to come into the area. They were among the first to be school teachers and introduced the first boarding schools. Many Suquamish are still Catholic; others are turning to Native religions, such as the Indian Shaker Church. The English language replaced the Puget Sound Salish language, today called Lushootseed, which the Suquamish are now struggling to teach the children and to transliterate into written form.

The Suquamish, Duwamish, and other tribes signed the 1855 Treaty of Point Elliott with territorial Governor Isaac Stevens. Chief Seattle delivered his famous speech at the treaty signing; he has been quoted, both accurately and inaccurately, many times since. The treaty placed the Suquamish on what is now known as the Port Madison Indian Reservation, located on the Kitsap Peninsula in Washington State. The land base within the reservation boundary is 7,811 acres today, but because of the federal government's allotment policy fewer than 3,000 acres remain in trust or in Indian ownership. The Suquamish were involved in a land claim filed before the Indian Claims Commission, and in 1993 there are still land issues under consideration.

Over one hundred years have passed since the Suquamish people began adjusting to white society. While today's culture reflects contemporary society, it retains close ties with the tribal past. The seven-member tribal government, like the earlier chiefs' councils, makes decisions based on the will of all tribal members. It currently operates under a Constitution and Bylaws adopted in 1965.

The Tribal Center and Museum bring together both the present and the past in the form of a working business office and an historical institution. The museum welcomes inquiries into Suquamish history and culture. The tribe celebrates the honored memory of Chief Seattle with the annual Chief Seattle Days, held the third weekend each August. Monthly pow-wows, held at the Tribal Center, are open to the public. The third weekend in April, the tribe hosts the Native American Art Fair, in which Native artists sell their works to the general public. The tribe works continually to expand programs to enhance the environment and natural resources, which are vital to the survival of the Suquamish people's traditional and spiritual lifestyles.

Many of the Suquamish tribe's 780 enrolled members depend on seasonal employment, such as fishing, fireworks, clam digging, and gathering plants for basketry, carving, medicines, and ceremonies. In addition to the Tribal Center and Museum, the tribe has a store, an entertainment center for its bingo operation, a fish hatchery, a human resources center, a law enforcement office, a tribal court facility, and a nature trail.

Suquamish Museum/ Suquamish Tribal Archives

See also **Washington State Tribes**

Further Reading

The Eyes of Chief Seattle. WA: The Suquamish Museum (P.O. Box 498), 1985.

Heuving, J. *Suquamish Today.* Seattle, WA: United Indians of All Tribes Foundation, 1979.

Lane, Barbara. *Identity, Treaty Status and Fisheries of the Suquamish Tribe of the Port Madison Reservation.* Washington, DC: Report for the U.S. Department of Interior, 1974.

Thompson, Nile, and Carolyn Marr. *Crow Shells: Artistic Basketry of Puget Sound.* Seattle, WA: Dushuyay Publications, 1983.

SWINOMISH

The Swinomish (or Squinamish) Indian Tribal Community is a Coast Salish tribe located near LaConner, in northwestern Washington State, composed primarily of aboriginal Swinomish, Kikiallus, Lower Skagit, and some, but not all, of the Samish. Amalgamation of these groups into a single community was a persistent issue earlier in the century. Legislation in 1946 to permit Indian groups to sue the government for treaty-linked compensation led to efforts by Kikiallus, Lower Skagit, and aboriginal Swinomish to file separate suits. These groups unsuccessfully sought independent tribal status during the 1970s, as had the separate Samish tribe. Provisions were made for the 7,448.80-acre Swinomish Reservation under the Treaty of Point Elliott of 1855, which was subsequently modified by an executive order of 1873. The land claim (Docket 293) filed with the Indian Claims Commission was dismissed in 1971.

In the early reservation period, the Swinomish lost most gathering, hunting, and fishing locations, and state efforts to regulate Indian fishing and hunting hindered Indian subsistence efforts after 1905. In 1892, the commissioner of Indian affairs prohibited traditional winter Spirit Dancing, Indian medicine, and plural marriage. By the 1920s conditions for Swinomish were seriously eroded: political autonomy was removed by Indian agents, housing and health conditions were inadequate, and the Bureau of Indian Affairs Tulalip School rejected Indian values and languages. Few Swinomish succeeded in business in the period from 1900 to 1910, although exceptions include Charles Wilbur's farm and Thomas Wilbur's logging business.

Swinomish developed new leadership strategies to improve their conditions in the 1930s, and Tandy Wilbur, Sr., chairman by 1941, was instrumental. A Constitution was established in 1936 under the Indian Reorganization Act (48 Stat. 984), and the Swinomish Indian Senate was created, replacing an earlier Council. Reorganization allowed the tribe to take corporate action for economic benefit. Fish trap and oyster raising businesses made significant profits, partly through sales to the United States Army during World War II. Additionally, the tribe gained control of its legal code, and the selection of police and judges. Thomas Williams served as judge, and Andrew Joe and Al Sampson were police during this period. The Tulalip School was closed and children were sent to the public school in LaConner under the Johnson-O'Malley Act of 1934.

During the Depression, Swinomish men formed Works Progress Administration crews, and built reservation roads and playing fields. National Housing Administration loans allowed construction of a "model village" of eighteen homes, under the leadership of Dewey Mitchell. More homes were built in the 1960s, and again in 1973, under Housing and Urban Development (HUD) funds. An independent housing authority was established, and eventually rental apartment units were built, including one for elders.

The Swinomish used federal War on Poverty funding, during the 1960s to 1980s, to administer Indian Community Action Projects and other programs. An administrative infrastructure was created and four programs established, including Seafoods Enterprise and an alcohol prevention and control program. The pivotal legal decision, *United States v. Washington*, removed illegal state restrictions on treaty-based Indian fishing in 1974 and led to the creation of a sizeable purse-seine fleet. Recently, tribal income has come from the lease of lands developed into marina facilities and housing. Individuals derive income from fishing, farm labor, and lumbering. A modern gambling operation, an Indian arts store, and seasonal firework sales bring in revenue.

Today the Swinomish community provides the approximately 624 tribal members a range of services. The tribe holds memberships in several intertribal organizations, including the Skagit Systems Cooperative, organized in 1976 to regulate and enhance fisheries. The Northwest Intertribal Court System handled 269 criminal and 12 civil cases on the reservation in 1990 under the authority of Swinomish codes and ordinances. The innovative Swinomish Tribal Mental Health Project trains Swinomish people with established community roles as advisers, or "natural helpers," in Western mental health care procedures.

Winter Spirit Dancing activities restrictions were removed in the 1930s and a ceremonial smokehouse was built. Spirit Dancing engages the Swinomish with a network of Coast Salish people from Puget Sound and the lower mainland of British Columbia. Indian Shaker, Catholic, and Pentecostal churches also have congregations. Swinomish people are participants in the summer cycle of war canoe races and powwows. Bone gambling and basketball tournaments are important in these gatherings. The Swinomish Festival is held on Memorial Day and Treaty Days take place in January. English is spoken today, although Northern Lushootseed has not disappeared. Funerals and memorial services continue to be important community events.

Bruce G. Miller

See also **Washington State Tribes**

Further Reading

A Gathering of Wisdoms: A Cultural Perspective. LaConner, WA: Swinomish Tribal Mental Health Project, 1991.

Roberts, Natalie. "A History of the Swinomish Tribal Community." Ph.D. diss., University of Washington, Department of Anthropology, 1975.

Ruby, Robert H., and John A. Brown. *A Guide to the Indian Tribes of the Pacific Northwest.* Norman: University of Oklahoma Press, 1986.

Sampson, Martin J. *Indians of Skagit County.* Mount Vernon, WA: Skagit County Historical Society, 1972.

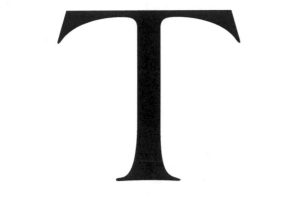

TACHI

See Yokuts

TANACROSS

See Alaskan Athabaskans

TANAINA

See Alaskan Athabaskans

TANANA

See Alaskan Athabaskans

TAOS

See Pueblo of Taos

TAXATION

Taxation of American Indians is a subject that can be summarized in the following general fashion: tribes are not taxable entities; individual tribal members are subject to taxes unless a treaty or statute provides an exemption; states have no taxing authority over Indians in Indian country; and tribes have taxing jurisdiction over both Indians and non-Indians within Indian country.

Article I, Section 2, Clause 3 of the United States Constitution and the Fourteenth Amendment, Section 2, provide for the apportionment of representation in Congress and use the phrase "Indians not taxed." At the time, the phrases recognized that tribes and their members were outside the political jurisdiction of the federal government and the states. This language generated the misleading notion that Indians are not subject to any federal or state taxes.

One early case, *New Jersey v. Wilson*, 7 Cranch 164 (1812), recognized that a tribe and a state could contract to designate tribal lands as tax exempt, and that the exemption would run with the land even to a subsequent non-Indian purchaser.

Indian tribes are not taxable entities under the Internal Revenue Code. The code taxes "individuals" or "persons" which are terms that don't apply to tribes. In passing the Indian Tribal Governmental Tax Status Act of 1982, P.L. 97–473 (codified as amended at 26 U.S.C. 7871 and various sections of 26 U.S.C.), Congress indicated that it was aware of this treatment of tribal governments by the Internal Revenue Service. The committee report on the legislation noted, "The Internal Revenue Code does not specifically exempt Indian tribal governments from Federal taxation; however, the Internal Revenue Service has ruled that Indian tribes are not taxable entities." Congress indicated its intention that this ruling was not to be disturbed by the Indian Tax Status Act by stating, "[t]he bill does not amend the present income tax treatment of Indian tribal governments specified in Rev. Rul. 67–284. . . ." (S. Rep. 97–646).

If a tribal government or a subdivision of that government such as an economic development authority operates a tribal business in Indian country, the income derived from that enterprise would not be subject to federal income taxes. The same tax exempt status applies to a tribally created corporation. In *Mescalero Apache Tribe v. Jones* (411 U.S. 145 [1973]), the United States Supreme Court noted that with respect to a tribal corporation created under the authority of the Indian Reorganization Act "the question of tax immunity cannot be made to turn on the particular form in which the Tribe chooses to conduct its business."

Indians are subject to federal law, including tax law, "in ordinary affairs of life, not governed by treaties or remedial legislation" (*Squire v. Capoeman*, 351 U.S. 1, 6 [1956]). Under the General Allotment Act of 1887 or similar legislation, there are provisions for tax exemption. This legislation provided that the land would be transferred to the allottee at the end of the trust period in fee simple status "free of all charge or incumbrance whatsoever." The United States Supreme Court has concluded that this means Congress intended that no taxes should apply until a patent in fee is issued.

As a consequence of this statutory exemption, individual tribal members are not subject to federal taxes for income that is directly derived from land held in trust for them by the federal government. Tax exempt status applies to trust land whether acquired as an original allotment, or by gift, inheritance, or purchase (*Stevens v. Commissioner*, 425 F.2d. 741 9th Cir. [1971]). The tax exempt status of income does not apply if the trust property is rented from another Indian or the tribe (*United States v. Anderson*, 625 F.2d 910 9th Cir. [1980]). Income directly derived from the land would include rentals, royalties, proceeds from the sale of crops grown on the land including timber, proceeds from the sale of livestock raised on the land, bonus payments for signing a lease, and even proceeds from the sale of the trust land itself. Income directly derived does not include income from commercial businesses such as a restaurant, motel, or craft shop (*Critzer v. United States*, 597 F.2d 708 Ct. Cl. [1979]).

State Taxing Authority

States first attempted to levy ad valorem taxes on these Indian trust allotments without success with the Kansas Indians (72 U.S. [5 How.] 737 [1866]). At the turn of the century, the Supreme Court found the General Allotment Act to have preempted state property taxes on an Indian allotment, improvements, and personal property (*United States v. Rickert*, 188 U.S. 432 [1903]), and continues to recognize such a preemption (*Bryan v. Itasca*, 426 U.S. 373 [1976]).

Today, analysis of state taxing authority is made utilizing two tests. One is called the "infringement" test, and analyzes whether state action infringes on tribal sovereignty and the right of the Indians to make laws and govern themselves (*Williams v. Lee*, 358 U.S. 217 [1959]). The other is the "federal preemption" test, which examines whether state law is preempted by the operation of federal law if it interferes or is incompatible with federal and tribal interests reflected in federal law (*McClanahan v. Arizona Tax Commission*, 411 U.S. 164 [1973]).

Federal preemption has also been found in Indian country with respect to state income taxes (*McClanahan v. Arizona State Tax Commission*, 411 U.S. 163 [1973]), personal property taxes (*Bryan v. Itasca County*, 426 U.S. 373 [1976]), and vendors' license fees (*Moe v. Confederated Salish and Kootenai Tribes*, 425 U.S. 463 [1976]).

Federal preemption has prevented states from imposing gross receipts taxes on non-Indians doing business with Indians in Indian country (*Warren Trading Post v. Arizona Tax Commission*, 380 U.S. 685 [1965], *White Mountain Apache v. Bracker*, 448 U.S. 136 [1980], *Central Machinery Co. v. Arizona State Tax Commission*, 448 U.S. 160 [1980]). Transactions between non-Indians in Indian country are generally subject to state jurisdiction. In some instances transactions between Indians and non-Indians may be subject to state taxation jurisdiction.

The cigarette cases are an area where the states are allowed to exert taxation jurisdiction, even though the sales are by Indians to non-Indians or nontribal member Indians. The United States Supreme Court created this exception because it perceived a lack of reservation generated value in such sales by tribal smoke-shops (*Moe v. Confederated Salish and Kootenai Tribes*, 425 U.S. 463 [1976], *Washington v. Confederated Tribes of the Colville Indian Reservation*, 447 U.S. 134 [1980], and *California State Board of Equalization v. Chemehuevi Indian Tribe*, 474 U.S. 9 [1985]). An Oklahoma tribe tried to distinguish the earlier decisions on the basis that those were states in which P.L. 83–280 was in effect. The United States Supreme Court rejected the argument, found the Oklahoma tribe subject to the cigarette taxes on sales made to non-Indians, and further found the state had a right

without a remedy because the tribe's sovereign immunity from suit prevented the enforcement of any judgment by the state (*Oklahoma Tax Commission v. Citizen Band Potawatomi Indian Tribe*, 111 S.Ct. 905 [1991]).

Tribal Taxing Powers

Tribal powers to tax non-Indians were recognized at the turn of the century (*Buster v. Wright*), and continue to be recognized. The power of tribes to tax cigarette sales to non-Indians has also been recognized (*Washington v. Confederated Tribes of the Colville Reservation*, 447 U.S. 134 [1980]). Tribal severance taxes of a tribe organized under the Indian Reorganization Act have been upheld with the United States Supreme Court recognizing the "power to tax is an essential attribute of Indian sovereignty because it is a necessary instrument of self-government" (*Merrion v. Jicarilla Apache Tribe*, 455 U.S. 130 [1982]). The Court has recognized the taxing powers of tribes who are not organized under the Indian Reorganization Act (*Kerr-McGee v. Navajo Tribe*, 471 U.S. 195 [1985]).

Outside of Indian country, tribes and their members are subject to state and federal taxes on the same basis as any other citizen (*Mescalero Apache Tribe v. Jones, Squire v. Capoeman*). Tribal and tribal member lands owned in fee simple even within the boundaries of Indian country are subject to state property taxes (*County of Yakima v. Confederated Tribes of the Yakima Indian Nation* 502 U.S.___ [1992]).

Indian Tribal Governmental Tax Status Act

In 1982, Congress passed the Indian Tribal Governmental Tax Status Act (Title II, 96 Stat. 2605), and subsequently amended the legislation in 1984 and 1987. This statute and its amendments had the effect of making tribes eligible for the same benefits as states and local governments with respect to tax status. The law gave tribal governments the option to finance commercial and private activities and government functions with tax-exempt bonds. Donations made to tribes would be deductible from federal income, estate, and gift tax liability. Tribal governments would be immune from federal taxes for purchases the Indian governments made on 1) special motor fuels, 2) manufacturers excise tax, 3) communications excise tax, and 4) highway use tax. To qualify for these exemptions, the tribes must be engaged in the exercise of "essential governmental functions."

The Indian Tax Status Act made tribal taxes deductible from federal income taxes. One could also claim credit for contributions made to campaigns for tribal political office. The legislation included provisions for tax-sheltered annuities for personnel such as tribal employees. Income from sickness and disability funds were not to be included in the taxpayer's gross income. There were also provisions for deductions from gross income for expenses incurred in carrying on a trade or business in direct connection with appearing or presenting testimony before tribal governing bodies.

Tax Exempt Status of Fishing Rights

In 1987 the United States Congress also passed legislation to confirm the tax exempt status of Indian fishing rights. P.L. 100–647 provided for Indian fishing rights in subtitle E, 102 Stat. 3640, and stated that there would be no federal or state income tax on the exercise of treaty-related fishing rights. The tribes have contended for years that they had not given any authority to tax to the United States or the states as their treaties were silent on the matter. The United States Internal Revenue Service took the opposite view that the treaties had not granted any exemption, and therefore the income was subject to taxation. Congress took legislative action to side with the treaty tribes.

Kirke Kickingbird

See also Indian Country; Sovereignty and Jurisdiction

Further Reading

Clinton, Robert N., Nell Jessup Newton, and Monroe E. Price. *American Indian Law: Cases and Materials.* Charlottesville, VA: Mitchie Bobbs/Merrill, 1991.

Cohen, Felix S. *Handbook of Federal Indian Law.* Washington, DC: U.S. Government Printing Office, 1942.

Getches, David H., and Charles F. Wilkinson. *Cases and Materials on Federal Indian Law.* St. Paul, MN: West Publishing Co., 1979.

Walker, Hans, Jr. *Federal Indian Tax Rules: A Compilation of Internal Revenue Service Rules Relating to Indians.* Oklahoma City: Institute for the Development of Indian Law, Oklahoma City University, 1989.

TELEVISION

See Radio and Television

TESQUE

See Pueblo of Tesque

TETON

See Lakota

TEXAS BAND OF KICKAPOO

See Kickapoo in Oklahoma and Texas

TEXTILES

Textile arts, while practiced by Native Americans throughout the United States during the twentieth century, are most notably developed in the Northwest coast and the Southwest. Consequently, the articles in this section cover these two areas. The Northwest Coast article also discusses other parts of Indian country where weaving continues to be important.

NORTHWEST COAST AND OTHER AREAS

On the Northwest Pacific Coast, from Alaska to the Columbia River, archaeological evidence indicates that weaving was highly developed centuries before the first European contacts in the 1700s. In historic times weaving was a woman's art, and took the form of ceremonial robes, utilitarian clothing, baskets, hats, tump lines, and woven mats. Weavers employed a variety of locally available materials: spruce root, cedar bark, various kinds of vegetable fibers, strips of fur, and the wool of mountain goat. Early reports refer also to dog-hair blankets in the Vancouver Island area, but no such weavings are known to exist today.

Mountain goat wool, fine and soft, was most readily available on the mainland among the Tlingit/Tsimshian people of the north and the Salishan peoples of British Columbia, and it was in these two regions that distinctive forms of wool weaving for ceremonial use and for utilitarian purposes developed. In the north, a twined robe covered with black geometric patterns similar to those on basketry was observed by eighteenth-century visitors, but production evidently ceased by the 1830s. They were replaced by the well-

Contemporary ravenstail sampler of woven white yarn with black and yellow designs, self fringe and fur, made by Teri Rofkar. Tlingit. Courtesy of the National Museum of the American Indian, Smithsonian Institution, 25/3568. Photo by Karen Furth.

known Chilkat robes, or dancing "blankets." Chilkat blankets, named for the Chilkat Tlingit who produced most of them, incorporated warps, which combined cedar bark with mountain goat hair. Family crest designs, copied from painted pattern boards, demanded a high degree of skill and a considerable investment in time, up to six months to produce a single blanket.

In the Salish area blankets of mountain goat wool and some vegetable fibers were produced for ceremonial clothing, for bedding and for potlatch wealth. Most Salish blankets were plain twill-weave, sometimes adorned with thin stripes of colored wool. A few consisted of elaborately colored and patterned blankets worked in small squares and zig-zag stripes. Always rare, the production of these weavings ceased in the late nineteenth century when Pendleton blankets became widely available.

Other types of weaving produced along the coast included twined robes of yellow cedar bark, some with painted designs; twilled cedar bark mats plaited on the diagonal; hats of spruce root or twined cedar bark; baskets of many varieties; and tump lines twined of commercial yarn or raveled cloth over warps of Indian hemp.

Most weavings were intended for indigenous use, often for ceremonial wear and for potlatch wealth. By the end of the nineteenth century missionization, population loss, changing economies, and denigration (and, in some cases, outlawing) of traditional religious and ceremonial practices had severely affected Native cultures. Most weavers had little incentive to produce woven blankets, nor time to engage in such labor-intensive activity. Button blankets created of trade cloth became a popular substitute in ceremonies which did survive; by the 1920s trade blankets had completely replaced Salish weavings; Western-style clothing was worn by virtually everyone. Many of the spectacular Chilkat weavings were sold to museums and to collectors far from the area. The early years of the twentieth century were a low point for the production of weavings, as well as other arts.

Several factors kept weaving from becoming extinct during these difficult years. The production of baskets for the burgeoning tourist market maintained the knowledge of traditional weaving techniques and provided an important source of cash income for some families. While knowledge of Salish weaving was lost, the creation of a knitting industry in the early 1920s kept alive the skills of spinning and wool preparation. The introduction of domesticated sheep to the area provided a supply of wool for this venture.

During the first half of the twentieth century, in the more remote areas of the Northwest Coast, clan traditions and ceremonial practices did continue, along with the production of weavings for indigenous use. In 1938 a visitor to Klukwan noted that three Chilkat weavers were producing blankets. The Kwakiutl maintained their ceremonial practices also, but the accompanying art forms were carved masks and other

regalia; weaving had been replaced earlier by button blankets.

The founding of the Indian Arts and Crafts Board (IACB) in the late 1930s was an effort to encourage Native artists often by assisting in the formation of craft cooperatives and in the distribution of products to dealers. Its efforts in Alaska centered on baskets, as well as Eskimo carvings and fur clothing. Its support for weaving arts elsewhere included Shoshone, Paiute, and Washoe basketry in Nevada, and groups such as the Choctaw Spinners Association (1937) and the Sequoyah Weavers Association (1939), both in Oklahoma.

Interest in Northwest Coast art, including Chilkat blankets, was stimulated by the 1939 IACB's Indian arts exhibition at the Golden Gate International Exposition in San Francisco. A number of other museum exhibitions, as well as publications, brought an awareness to the general public of indigenous art forms. By the 1960s there was an awakening of pride in Native identity, an increase in potlatching, and a greater participation in other ceremonial activities which required the commissioning of various kinds of regalia, including dancing blankets. Button blankets, which had been produced since the nineteenth century as a substitute for the woven blankets, also enjoyed increased popularity. Made of imported wool broadcloth, button blankets displayed family crest designs rendered in buttons and shells; they are used today as dance regalia alongside woven blankets. In the continental United States the growth of the pan-Indian movement and an interest in powwows also stimulated the production of all kinds of dance gear; for example, on the southern Plains woven scarves became a popular addition to powwow outfits.

In 1976 the Totem Heritage Center in Ketchikan and the Institute of Alaska Native Arts (IANA) in Fairbanks both began operations to preserve indigenous arts by means of workshops and demonstrations; Chilkat weaving is among the workshops which have been offered at the IANA. Wider recognition of indigenous arts by outsiders also stimulated the production of weaving. In the early 1960s two Central Coast Salish women, Adeleine Lorenzetto and Mary Peters, were encouraged by Oliver Wells, a non-Native, to recreate the traditional Salish woven blankets. By careful study and partial unraveling of an old blanket, they were able to discover and replicate the old techniques. Hearing of their experiment, the Hotel Bonaventure in Montreal commissioned six large weavings, establishing a commercial basis for this traditional art. Other Salish weavers began to participate, eventually forming the Salish Weavers Guild in 1971 to market their weavings to museums, gift shops, and galleries.

Museums also became participants in the revival of weavings. In 1986 the Musqueam Indian Band and the University of British Columbia Museum in Vancouver jointly created an exhibit, "Hands of Our Ancestors: The Revival of Salish Weaving at Musqueam." The weavers not only participated in writing the text for the exhibit, but also conducted spinning and weaving demonstrations at the museums. Salish weavings are done today with sheep wool, rather than the now-scarce mountain goat wool, and a number of Salish weavers are experimenting with traditional designs and techniques.

The Tlingit geometric woven robe which disappeared early in the nineteenth century has seen a similar new life. Known today as *yeil koowu* ("the raven's tail") it was replicated by Cheryl Samuel, a non-Native weaver who studied the few remaining examples in museum collections, and who deciphered the intricate twining patterns to recreate new robes and dance leggings. Samuel had done similar work with creating Chilkat blankets, but ravenstail weaving had passed from living memory two hundred years ago, and it required much trial and error before she successfully completed a pair of leggings. By the mid-1980s she was offering weaving classes; to date at least 150 weavers have studied ravenstail weaving. In 1990 the Totem Heritage Center sponsored a gathering of student weavers from Canada and the United States, which resulted in formation of the Ravenstail Weavers Guild, with chapters throughout Alaska and Canada. The guild brings together young weavers and respected elders who provide knowledge of traditional protocols and cultural contexts for ceremonial regalia.

The late twentieth century has seen a revitalization of artistic production on the Northwest Coast, including the weaving arts. With the exception of baskets, which have been made for an outside market for more than a hundred years, the creation of new weavings is primarily for local use and reflects the revitalization of ceremonies and increased interest in maintaining cultural heritage. The production of weavings is embedded in old traditions, but incorporates a number of innovations. Weavers today continue to learn their skills from a single teacher, but the instruction may be in a class, or a workshop, and the teacher may be someone other than a family member, perhaps even a non-Native. Several weavers may work together on a single piece. Weavings are still produced to order, but the client today may be not only an individual from another family, but an outsider—a museum, an art collector, a hotel, perhaps a government agency. The office of the prime minister in Ottawa, for example, displays Salish weavings. The Alaska Native Brotherhood and the Southeastern Alaska Indian Cultural Center participated in the commissioning of a ravenstail weaving. The blanket was presented and danced at the opening ceremonies of the *Crossroads of Continents* exhibition at the Anchorage Museum of History and Art. Another weaving was presented in 1992 in Juneau at "Celebrations," a gathering of Tlingit, Haida, and Tsimshian elders and dancers. The designs on the "Hands Across Time" robe, as it was named, incorporated motifs from the four cultural traditions represented by the weavers: Tlingit, Tsimshian, Haida, and non-Native.

The transition from past to present in Northwest Coast weaving is exemplified in the life and work of Tlingit master-weaver Jenny Thlunault (1890 to 1986). Growing up in the small, traditional village of Klukwan, Alaska, she created throughout her life Chilkat blankets and shirts for ceremonies, for gifts, and as commissions for Native people and non-Native collectors. In 1984 she demonstrated Chilkat weaving at the Festival of American Folk Life in Washington, D.C., an event far removed in place and time from her girlhood home. Weaving arts of the Northwest Coast have similarly traveled far from their place of origin, but have retained their cultural meaning and their beauty.

Weaving in Other Areas

Weaving among other Indian tribes throughout the United States has, in many cases, maintained its integrity while sometimes taking new forms. In 1986 for the American Federation of Arts, Ralph T. Coe produced an exhibition of newly created traditional Native American arts, among them not only a wide variety of woven blankets but numerous textiles. Coe's search for objects for the *Lost and Found Traditions* exhibit made it clear that the weaving arts of the late twentieth century equal, and in some cases surpass, the best of the artistic traditions of the past. A Winnebago beaded sash, Cherokee finger-weaving, an Oklahoma Kickapoo bulrush mat, Yakima twined

Beaded arrowhead sash from woman's wedding outfit. Osage. The sash belonged to Mary Redeagle when she married Paul Beartrack. Courtesy of the National Museum of the American Indian, Smithsonian Institution, 23/7300 D. Photo by Karen Furth.

cornhusk bags, a plain Salish wool blanket, and a Narragansett hemp-twined bag (made of hemp imported from Italy) were on display, testifying to the creative vigor and adaptability of contemporary artists and craftspeople.

Twentieth-century weaving arts have reflected the diverse strands of Indian cultural histories—loss and in some cases extinction, a pride in heritage and maintenance of cultural traditions in the face of opposition, a desire to relearn ancient techniques and express them in contemporary form, and the creation of entirely new artistic forms—for innovation has always been embedded in tradition. The weaving arts have been encouraged, and in a few cases made possible, by outsiders—non-Indian weavers, collectors and other patrons, museums and other educational institutions. But the major contribution has been that of the Native people themselves who, despite adversity, have kept alive artistic creativity and a pride in heritage throughout the twentieth century.

Mary Jane Lenz

***See also* Art; Basketry**

Further Reading

Coe, Ralph T. *Lost and Found Traditions: Native American Art 1965–1985*. New York, NY: The American Federation of Arts, 1986.

Gustafson, Paula. *Salish Weaving*. Vancouver, BC: Douglas & McIntyre, 1980.

Henrikson, Steve. "The Reemergence of Ravenstail Weaving on the Northern Northwest Coast." *American Indian Art* 18 (Winter 1992): 58–67.

Jensen, Doreen, and Polly Sargent. *Robes of Power: Totem Poles on Cloth*. Vancouver: University of British Columbia Museum Note 17, 1986.

Johnson, Elizabeth L., and Kathryn Bernick. *Hands of Our Ancestors: The Revival of Salish Weaving at Musqueam*. Vancouver: University of British Columbia Museum of Anthropology Notes 10, 1986.

Samuel, Cheryl. *The Chilkat Dancing Blanket*. Seattle, WA: Pacific Search Press, 1982.

———. *The Raven's Tail*. Vancouver: University of British Columbia Press, 1987.

Embroidered cotton dance manta. Hopi. ca. 1914. A Hopi bride's white wedding robe may be decorated later with panels embroidered in wool. 44 ¹/₂ by 61 inches. Courtesy of the National Museum of the American Indian, Smithsonian Institution, 23/6428. Photo by Karen Furth.

SOUTHWEST

The textile arts are a centuries-old tradition in the American Southwest, the region that today encompasses the states of New Mexico and Arizona and parts of Colorado and Utah. Pueblo and Navajo peoples have continued to produce handwoven and hand-decorated textiles into the twentieth century, for both local use and the outside market. Contemporary textile artists selectively integrate new materials and designs into their work, contributing to the continued vitality of the craft. Today, handcrafted textiles are visible symbols of ethnic pride, a link to the past and a legacy to be passed on to succeeding generations.

The ancestors of the Pueblos made patterned blankets, shirts, kilts, leggings, carrying straps, sashes, and bags in a variety of finger- and loom-weaving techniques. Textile surfaces were decorated with painted, tie-dyed, or embroidered designs. Cotton from southern Arizona reached the people by A.D. 700, largely replacing wild plant and animal fibers. Two looms were used: the vertical loom for wide articles, the backstrap loom for narrow items.

Beginning in 1598, Spanish settlers provided sheep wool, indigo-blue dye, and commercial cloth, raveled primarily for red yarn. The *sarape*, a blanket of longer-than-wide proportions and the forerunner of the southwestern rug, was a Spanish introduction. In addition, the Spanish introduced knitting with metal needles; knitting and crocheting probably replaced indigenous openwork weaves. Embroidery, a characteristic Pueblo decorative technique, also probably increased in the post-European period.

Unlike Pueblo peoples, the Navajos were relative newcomers to the Southwest, arriving from western Canada by 1500. Navajo women learned how to spin and weave from their Pueblo neighbors, and by 1700 were producing textiles for intertribal trade and trade to the Spanish. The Navajos made the same articles as the Pueblos—shirts, mantas, and breechcloths— with the exception of the *biil*, the two-piece Navajo blanket dress. Navajo textiles also reflect Spanish influence but it was indirect, transmitted to Navajo weavers through their Pueblo teachers. Around 1800 Saltillo blanket styles from northern Mexico provided a new design source, still evident in contemporary serrate-edged patterns.

The flow of factory merchandise that began entering the Southwest in the first half of the nineteenth century dramatically altered both Pueblo and Navajo textile production. Plied wool yarns, synthetic dyes, and factory cloth became widely available. Commercial blankets issued by the government further diminished the need for handwoven garments. At the same time, the arrival of the railroad in New Mexico in the early 1880s opened up a non-Indian market for Indian handicrafts, and led to the development of a new product, the blanket/rug. Reservation traders would act as the primary brokers for the production and sale of Navajo textiles well into the twentieth century.

Twentieth-Century Pueblo Textiles

Pueblo weaving had declined dramatically by the early twentieth century. Only the Hopis and the Zunis, for a short time, continued to produce handspun, handwoven articles, for their own use and to trade to other Pueblos. By 1930, production of the striped rug, made for sale since the late 1800s, had all but ceased. Except for the twill-woven manta, the rectangular blanket worn as a wraparound dress or shawl, traditional clothing was reserved for ceremonies. Women decorated the wool dress with cotton under-dresses, commercial shawls, and aprons.

Production of Pueblo textiles has received new impetus in this century, however. The revival is credited to the intervention of numerous individuals, museums, and government agencies that have provided funding, training, and a market for Indian crafts. Among these efforts were the 1923 establishment of the Indian Arts Fund in Santa Fe, the basis for the collections of the School of American Research, and the work of the Indian Arts and Crafts Board, under the United States Department of the Interior. The Institute of American Indian Arts, formerly the Santa

Woven wool textile with horizontal stripes in olive, gold, gray, and black made by Phyllis Nolwood in 1977. Navajo, Wide Ruins style. 71 1/2 by 46 1/2 inches. Courtesy of the National Museum of the American Indian, Smithsonian Institution, 25/636. Photo by Karen Furth.

Fe Indian School, continues to teach traditional and Euroamerican arts to Indian students. Craft fairs, including the annual Hopi Craftsmen Show, sponsored by the Museum of Northern Arizona since 1930, encourage the use of natural dyes and quality weaving. Native craft guilds such as Oke Oweenge Arts and Crafts in San Juan, and the Northern Pueblo Indian Artisans' Guild, also provide important outlets for the sale of textiles.

Today Pueblo artisans produce traditional-style articles including mantas, kilts, shirts, and warp-patterned sash belts. Most garments are made entirely from commercial cotton or wool fabric, however. Sewing and embroidery are the foremost textile arts among the Rio Grande Pueblos; weaving survives only among the Hopi and in the production of red wool sash belts, also popular sale items. Woven decorated textiles incorporate white cotton string warps, cotton batting for wefts, commercial plied wool yarns, and, increasingly, bright acrylic yarns—sometimes, as is the case with sash belts, in new designs. Traditional garments have been provided by a variety of means throughout the century. Tewa Weavers, in Albuquerque, began producing treadle-woven wool mantas made by Isleta weavers in 1938. Most contemporary embroidery is done on commercial fabric, and cut-out appliqued cloth may be substituted for hand-stitched designs. Embroidered articles made for tourist sale include shirts, vests, and many other clothing and novelty items.

Traditional clothing is highly visible at Pueblo feast days and dances. Women's mantas include the blanket dress with blue edges, the black manta with red embroidered borders, the white cotton manta with panels of wool embroidery, and the white "maiden shawl" with red and blue striped borders. Male dancers wear dark wool or embroidered white cotton kilts and the warp patterned sash belts also used by women to fasten their manta dresses. Hopi men continue to make the plain-weave, white cotton wedding robe, braided cotton sash, and brocaded dance sash; Jemez needleworkers still produce the embroidered white cotton shirt, for which the Pueblo is well known. Crocheted and knitted yarn shirts and leggings may also be seen. Some foreign articles are accepted as traditional today, including the men's white trousers with slit pants and cotton shirts introduced by the Spanish, and the colorful commercial shawl adopted by women.

Some garments retain specific symbolic functions, for example, a Hopi bride may still receive two white cotton mantas, one of which is traditionally buried with her at her death. Cotton, because it is identified with clouds, has religious significance for the Hopi. The long fringe on the Hopi wedding sash symbolizes rain; embroidered cloud and lightning designs, butterflies, and related motifs are also associated with rain and, in a wider sense, the renewal of life. Many contemporary embroidered designs appear on prehistoric textiles.

Pueblo textiles are viewed as conservative, remarkably unchanged over time. Innovation occurs alongside tradition, however. Craftspeople experiment with new forms at the same time that they research long-forgotten techniques. Lucy Yepa Lowden of Jemez and Ramoncita Sandoval of San Juan are master embroiderers. Other San Juan artisans include Gabrielita Nave, Geronima Montoya, Reyes Abeita, Modesta Charley, Piedad Antoine, and Lorencita Bird and her daughter, Evelyn. Many of these individuals have been working since the 1920s, producing traditional-style garments, embroidery, and woven belts; Antoine also makes crocheted socks and leggings. Isabel Gonzalez, of Jemez, one of the youngest of the group, lives in San Ildefonso; her work is distinctive for her color selection and fine technique.

Western Pueblo articles continue to be made primarily for internal use or for trade to Zuni or the Rio Grande Pueblos. In Zuni, Vivian Kaskalla produces fine traditional embroidery on commercial cotton cloth; Zuni high school students, taught by

Pair of crocheted leggings of white cotton string made by Regina Cata in 1959. San Juan Pueblo. These leggings won first prize at the 1959 Gallup Ceremonial. Courtesy of the National Museum of the American Indian, Smithsonian Institution, 23/709. Photo by Karen Furth.

Herrin Othole, weave sash belts. Elmer Sequoptewa, Louis Josytewa, Roger Nasevaema, and Martin Gashweseoma are prominent Hopi weavers whose work reaches an external market.

Ramona Sakiestewa is a professional artist whose tapestries receive wide acclaim in the art world. Drawing on her Hopi heritage as well as professional training, Sakiestewa creates bold images that evoke the hues and forms of the southwestern landscape, prehistoric Pueblo design systems, and Andean textiles researched in Peru. Sakiestewa established her own company, Ramona Sakiestewa, Ltd., in 1981. She produces and markets textiles woven on a treadle loom in natural-dyed and commercial yarns.

In spite of the success of individual artists, concern exists for the future of Pueblo textiles, especially those produced by Rio Grande Pueblo craftspeople. Sales today are insufficient to guarantee the viability of the craft, especially given the skills and time involved. New generations of craftspeople will require training, an expanded market, and sufficient financial return if Pueblo textile arts are to endure.

Twentieth-Century Navajo Textiles

Navajo women produced surplus cloth for trade throughout the historic period. Thus, it was probably not a significant departure when they turned to weaving for an outside Anglo market in the late 1800s. Like their Pueblo counterparts, the Navajos had abandoned the traditional manta and shoulder robe in favor of Anglo-American clothing. Women adopted full skirts and velveteen blouses; men wore cotton trousers and Pendleton blankets. Saddle blankets and sash belts comprised the only loom-woven articles produced for the people, with the exception of the two-piece dress made for special occasions and the articles produced for the Pueblo trade. Weavers concentrated on making rugs.

Woven wool textile in geometric patterns in red, black, and gray, made by Rose Owens in 1981. Navajo. This piece was woven on a wagon wheel as a loom. Diameter, 42 inches. Courtesy of the National Museum of the American Indian, Smithsonian Institution, 25/637. Photo by Karen Furth.

Between 1900 to 1940 reservation traders and weavers worked together to improve yarns and dyes and to develop rug patterns that would sell. Traders discouraged cotton string warps, Germantown yarns, and packaged dyes, urging, instead, a return to handspun wool yarn. The quality of Native wool itself had deteriorated, however, due to crossbreeding of the *churro* with merino sheep. Also, up until 1920, weavers were paid by the pound for rugs they delivered, a practice which did little to foster careful spinning or weaving.

Regional styles based on distinctive combinations of color and design grew up around traders Juan Lorenzo Hubbell in Ganado, Arizona, and J.B. Moore in Crystal, New Mexico. Hubbell revived nineteenth-century blanket styles and, when these proved unpopular, promoted designs with large central patterns on a white, gray, or red ground. Moore introduced bordered geometric patterns and motifs, such as the latch hook and fret drawn from Oriental carpets. Early Crystal rugs were woven in natural wool tones and aniline red; Moore's wife supervised the dyeing of the handspun wool, which was sent East to be cleaned and carded. Both traders placed a high premium on quality; Moore based his prices on size of rug and fineness of weave. Two Grey Hills designs, established in 1925 by Ed Davies at the Two Grey Hills trading post and George Bloomfield from the post at Toadlena, incorporate early Crystal patterns and motifs. Rugs were woven entirely in natural black, brown, beige, and white, as well as lighter shades produced by carding together light and dark wool fibers.

In the early 1920s attention turned to native plant dyes. Mary Cabot Wheelwright, from Boston, worked with trader Cozy McSparron in Chinle to encourage the return to a borderless banded pattern and improved dyes, both synthetic and vegetal. The new interest in vegetal dyes contributed to the development of numerous banded "revival" styles, for example, at Wide Ruins, where Bill and Sallie Lippincott bought a trading post in 1938, and at Nazlini, an area known for its plant motifs. Improved weaving techniques were also integral to Teec Nos Pos rugs, characterized by intricate serrate-outline designs.

Rugs continue to be identified by region, although a large proportion of weavers have never adhered to any particular style. The "storm pattern" is associated with the Western reservation, *ye'ii, ye'ii bicheii*, and sandpainting designs with the Farmington/Shiprock and Lukachukai areas. Striped vegetal and aniline-dyed rugs woven at Crystal since the 1940s are known for their wavy-line effects; raised-outline rugs have been produced regularly in the Coal Mine Mesa area since the 1950s. New styles still emerge, including Burntwater rugs, developed in the early 1970s by weaver Philomena Yazzie and characterized by a combination of Ganado and Two Grey Hills designs woven in pastel plant colors. Pictorials, saddle blankets, twill weaves, and two-faced rugs are specialty weaves not specific to any area.

Rugs are a commercial product; however, the process of weaving is important in Navajo culture, and to individual weavers. Some women will not make *ye'ii, ye'ii bicheii*, or sandpainting designs, traditionally created only in a ritual context. The "weaver's pathway," a short pick of weft in a contrasting color that runs to the textile's edge, represents a way out for the weaver's energy after a rug is completed. Many families respect certain customs surrounding the act of weaving, including not weaving when pregnant and offering special prayers and songs at certain times when a rug is on the loom.

Textile quality and marketing have remained two related, critical issues. In 1935 the Departments of the Interior and Agriculture together established the Southwestern Range and Sheep Breeding Laboratory at Fort Wingate in an effort to restore good wool-producing breeds. A pilot project directed by Lyle McNeal at Utah State University has successfully reintroduced *churro* sheep to reservation weavers; *churro* wool fibers are long and greaseless, ideal for spinning and dyeing purposes. Experiments with dyes made from plant leaves, barks, stems, and roots continue. In 1940, Nonabah G. Bryan, a weaver at the Wingate Vocational High School, published a booklet containing recipes for eighty-six colors. D.Y. Begay, a weaver, has recently conducted dye workshops for the Ramah Weavers Association.

C. N. Cotton, a wholesale dealer in Gallup, advertised Navajo rugs as early as 1896. Both Hubbell and Cotton conducted a mail-order business, publishing illustrated catalogues between 1902 and 1911 that encouraged special orders. Navajo rugs were bought by Fred Harvey hotels, retailers, and, increasingly, by museums, galleries, and collectors across the country. In the 1930s, the Indian Arts and Crafts Board and the Eastern Association on Indian Affairs, the latter a private philanthropic organization, provided support. Today, top weavers take prizes at the Museum of Northern Arizona's Navajo Show and Santa Fe's Indian Market, making a name for themselves and contributing to the value of Navajo textiles in general.

Weaving is still learned at home, but is also taught in some reservation schools and at the community college. It is an important source of income for families, although rarely the only one. In 1973 the Navajo Community College estimated that a woman earned an average of only 30 cents an hour for an above-average rug—this in spite of the growing popularity of Navajo textiles across the country. However, prices are rising. In 1987, a Two Grey Hills tapestry by Barbara Jean Teller Ornelas and her sister, Rosann Teller Lee, sold at Indian Market for $60,000, a record price. The Crownpoint Rug Weavers Auction, a popular outlet, pays weavers 90 percent of the final sales price. Top weavers negotiate their own commission orders and market their own rugs to visiting traders and dealers, sometimes sending their work to Santa Fe or New York for the best price.

Although weavers still call their work "rugs," many pieces are extremely finely woven tapestries designed to be hung on the walls. Tapestry, twill, and two-faced textiles display perfectly straight selvages, a smooth finish, and an ever higher number of wefts per inch. Weavers utilize a wide variety of yarns, in both natural and aniline colors, often in the same piece. Commercially processed yarns resembling single-ply handspun Native wool, developed by Bruce Burnham in Sanders and by the Navajo Wool Grower's Marketing Industry, are especially popular, although other commercial yarns including four-ply knitting worsted are also sometimes used.

Today, Navajo weavers number in the thousands. A recent exhibition of works by thirty-four contemporary Navajo weavers at the Denver Art Museum revealed how difficult it is to single out only a few of the outstanding artists of the 1980s and 1990s. Grace Henderson Nez, Gloria Begay, and Mary Lee Begay represent three generations of weavers from one family who reinterpret nineteenth-century blanket patterns. Several weavers make regional-style rugs, modifying their colors and designs; Bessie Barber has added pictorial motifs and spots of color to Two Grey Hills patterns, creating, with other women in her family, the new Burnham style. Marjorie Spencer and her daughters weave Wide Ruins designs in pastel yarns from Burnham's trading post; Irene Clark produces Crystal "wavy-line" rugs in new shades of gray and tan. Kalley Musial titles her pieces and chooses colors that reflect her moods. In 1984 Mae Jim completed a nine-by-fifteen-foot Ganado rug woven in handspun wool, one of the largest and most important Navajo tapestries on record.

Weavers experiment with colors, forms, techniques, and pictorial images. Rose Owens makes Ganado Red round rugs; Amy Begay produces prize-winning tufted rugs using mohair from her mother's goats. Unique twill-woven, two-faced rugs have been developed by the late Irene Julia Nez and her relatives. Ason Yellowhair and members of her extended family weave stylized patterns containing birds and flowers. The eclectic nature of Navajo weaving is self-evident. New Yorker Gloria F. Ross has commissioned a series of textiles designed by painter Kenneth Noland; works by artists Sadie Curtis, Irene Clark, Mary Lee Begay, and numerous others reveal not only the skill involved but also the ability of Navajo weavers to innovate and adapt.

Women weave because it is a way to make money, because it earns them the respect of their families and communities, and because they enjoy the work. They speak of learning to weave from their mothers or grandmothers, and how important it is that future generations know how to weave. Weaving can make a difference economically, and is related to the role of women in Navajo society. Hope for the future of Navajo weaving is bright.

Eulalie H. Bonar

See also Art

Further Reading

Hedlund, Ann Lane. *Reflections of the Weaver's World: The Gloria F. Ross Collection of Contemporary Navajo Weaving.* CO: Denver Art Museum, 1992.

Kent, Kate Peck. *Pueblo Indian Textiles: A Living Tradition.* Santa Fe, NM: School of American Research Press, 1983.

———. *Navajo Textiles: Three Centuries of Change.* Santa Fe, NM: School of American Research Press, 1985.

Mera, H.P. *Pueblo Indian Embroidery.* Memoirs of the Laboratory of Anthropology 4. 1943. Santa Fe, NM: William Gannon, 1975.

Roessel, Ruth. "Navajo Arts and Crafts." *Handbook of North American Indians.* Vol. 10. *Southwest.* Ed. Alfonso Ortiz. Washington, DC: Smithsonian Institution (1983): 592–604.

Wheat, Joe Ben. "Early Navajo Weaving." *Plateau* 52:4 (1981): 2–9.

THREE AFFILIATED TRIBES

Three tribes, the Arikara (Arickaree, Ree), Hidatsa (Gros Ventres), and Mandan, now officially known as the Three Affiliated Tribes, occupy the Fort Berthold Indian Reservation in western North Dakota. Once geographically separate and linguistically different, these three tribes present a united front to state and federal officials, while internally maintaining separate tribal identities.

At the time of contact with non-Indians, the Arikara, Hidatsa, and Mandan tribes lived in villages along the Missouri River. They hunted buffalo and grew corn, squash, and beans. The Arikara, the northernmost members of the Caddoan language family, were established in central South Dakota. The Mandan and Hidatsa, speakers of related but mutually unintelligible languages, considered themselves allies and occupied five villages near the confluence of the Knife River with the Missouri, in western North Dakota. Relations between the Arikara and the other two tribes were sometimes peaceful and sometimes unfriendly. In 1837 all three tribes were decimated by smallpox and subsequently suffered depredations from enemy tribes. By 1845 a group of Hidatsa determined to find a safer location for their village, moved up the Missouri River and established a village known as Like-A-Fishhook. They were soon joined by other Hidatsa and Mandan. Around this time the Arikara moved north and occupied the area abandoned by the Mandan. Unification of the three tribes began in 1862, when the Arikara moved into Like-A-Fishhook Village.

For forty years Like-a-Fishhook Village was a focus of commerce and government. Traders, army men, and representatives of the Office of Indian Affairs made the village their home while conducting business. The Treaty of Fort Laramie of 1851 recognized the three tribes' claims to more than 12 million acres, but when Fort Berthold Reservation was officially established in 1870 by an executive order from President Ulysses S. Grant, it was only 8 million acres. Another executive order in 1880 and an 1886 agreement to open the land to allotment further reduced the land base to less than 1 million acres, its approximate size today. Even before allotment, Like-a-Fishhook Village was abandoned and the people scattered across the reservation where they established kinship-based communities along the Missouri River. The Arikara lived on the east side of the Missouri in Nishu and Elbowwoods. The Mandan and Hidatsa moved west of the river, where the Mandan settled in Beaver Creek, Red Butte, and Charging Eagle. The Hidatsa lived on both sides of the river in Lucky Mound, Shell Creek, and Independence. In 1910 a large section of land that was wholly allotted to non-Indians was removed from the reservation boundaries.

Unlike the other tribes in North Dakota, the Three Affiliated Tribes accepted the Indian Reorganization Act and formed a representative tribal government. The reservation was divided into districts with representatives elected from each district. A tribal Constitution and Bylaws were drawn up and these, with some amendments, are followed today. As part of the formulation of the government, the tribe officially adopted the name the "Three Affiliated Tribes." In accordance with provisions of the Indian Reorganization Act, the Three Affiliated Tribes incorporated themselves and the tribal government is legally the Three Affiliated Tribes Business Council.

In the 1950s, the Three Affiliated Tribes suffered an economic and social disaster from which they have not yet fully recovered. The Missouri River was dammed and Lake Sakakawea covered the homes and farms of most of the tribal members. Carl Whitman, Jr., led the opposition to the dam and continued to be a respected tribal leader for many years, but the tribespeople were forced to accept the government's offer. Families who supported themselves by ranching and farming along the fertile Missouri bottomlands found themselves moved to the dry, windy uplands. New communities were built, but the exigencies of available land meant that relatives no longer lived near enough to help each other. As a result of the reservoir, an administrative center named New Town, composed of the former tribal headquarters of Elbowwoods and non-Indian towns of Sanish and Van Hook, was established. At the time of its establishment, New Town was not on the reservation and the Three Afilliated Tribes eventually moved their tribal offices to a new building on the west side of the river. A bridge that connected communities on both sides of the river was moved to the northern edge of the reservoir, essentially isolating the southern end of the reservation. New roads and new schools were necessary. The Indian Health Service Hospital was replaced by clinics in the new communities. The tribes received $12 million in compensation for their loss, although an evaluator hired by the Tribal Council placed the loss at more than $20 million. In 1992 the Three Affiliated Tribes received an additional compensation of $143 million to be paid to the tribe in the form of interest.

Today the Fort Berthold Reservation consists of approximately 900,000 acres of land, more than half owned by non-Indians. A small percentage of families make their living by farming or ranching, but tribal and federal governments are the largest employers. Unemployment remains a major problem. In 1993, the tribe opened a high stakes gambling casino, which could provide jobs for many people. Both Indians and non-Indians share a similar western rural lifestyle of small towns and scattered homesteads. The Arikara still live on the east side of the reservoir, near the towns of White Shield, named for a former tribal leader, and Parshall. The Mandan live around Twin Buttes, a small community on the west side of the reservoir and the Hidatsa center on Mandaree. In 1980 the northeastern segment was returned to the reservation, placing New Town on the reservation and more and more Indians now live there, the primary commercial center. The tribal population of the reservation is about 3,000, but tribal enrollment is more than 6,000, suggesting the large percentage of people who live off the reservation.

Each reservation community sponsors a pow-wow every summer and these have become the focus of year-round tribal activities as groups conduct fundraisers. Bingo games, raffles, auctions, and special ceremonies called War Bonnet Dances help to maintain Indian identities. The traditional crafts of pottery making and basketry have disappeared, but beadwork, quillwork, and star-quilt making are common. All the major religious denominations are represented on the reservation. A small number of Three Tribes people are members of the Native American Church. Recently there has been a revival of the sweat lodge and other traditional religious ceremonies. All the tribespeople speak English, but elderly Indian people continue to speak their Native language and from time to time the schools sponsor classes in the languages so many people have some understanding of their traditional language. Intermarriage has eased some of the tribal separateness that once existed, but the three tribes continue to maintain distinct tribal identities through language, customs, and residence.

Mary Jane Schneider

Further Reading

Bowers, Alfred. *Mandan Social and Ceremonial Organization*. IL: University of Chicago Press, 1950.
——— *Hidatsa Social and Ceremonial Organization*. Bureau of American Ethnology Bulletin 194. Washington, DC: U.S. Government Printing Office, 1964.
Meyer, Roy. *Village Indians of the Upper Missouri: The Mandans, Hidatsas, and Arikaras*. Lincoln: University of Nebraska Press, 1977.

Tigua

See Tortugas; Ysleta del Sur Pueblo

TILLAMOOK

Decimated by new diseases and shoved aside by Euroamerican settlers, the Tillamook Indians faced a bleak and difficult existence in the twentieth century. Nominally under the Clatsop Plains Indian Agency in the 1850s, but subsequently affiliated with the Grand Ronde Reservation, to which few if any tribal members removed, the survivors remained as landless people in their old homeland. Families and individuals resided in the watersheds of the Nehalem, Tillamook, Nestucca, Nechesne (Salmon River), and Siletz in northwestern Oregon. Some responded to the ministry of Father Adrian Croquet, Catholic missionary on the Grand Ronde Reservation, who from 1860 to 1898 annually traveled to the coast to seek baptisms and solemnize marriages.

In 1897 the Tillamook joined the Clatsop, Lower Band of Chinook, and the Cathlamet under a jurisdictional act (37 Stat. 578) to litigate for the taking of their lands without ratification of their 1851 or 1855 treaties. Dr. Charles McChesney, supervisor of Indian schools, enrolled fifty-eight tribal members in 1906. Survivors ultimately obtained a token sum of $10,500 in 1913, as a result of this case before the United States Court of Claims.

There is no record of any formal organization of a Tillamook tribe in the twentieth century. Survivors, however, participated in claims litigation pursuant to the Act of August 26, 1938 (40 Stat. 801). In *Tillamook Band of Tillamooks*, Docket 240, before the Indian Claims Commission, they secured a judgment in 1962 of $72,162 for the Nehalem band and $97,025 for the Tillamook band. Tribal informants shared linguistic and cultural information with Franz Boas in 1890; Elizabeth Derr Jacobs in 1933; Homer G. Barnett in 1934; John Peabody Harrington in 1942 to 1943; Leon V. Metcalf in 1951; and Herbert C. Taylor, Jr., and Robert Suphan in the 1950s. The last speakers of the Tillamook Salishan language worked from 1965 to 1970 with Laurence C. Thompson. Congress terminated the federal relationship with the Tillamook in 1956. The descendants have not organized nor sought to secure restoration of status as a tribe.

Stephen Dow Beckham

Further Reading

Boas, Franz. "Notes on the Tillamook." *University of California Publications in American Archaeology and Ethnology* 20:1 (1923): 3–16.

Jacobs, Melville, ed. *Nehalem Tillamook Tales*. Eugene: University of Oregon Books, 1959.

McChesney, Charles E. *Rolls of Certain Indian Tribes in Oregon and Washington*. Fairfield, WA: Ye Galleon Press, 1969.

Seaburg, William R., and Jay Miller. "Tillamook." *Handbook of North American Indians*, Vol. 7. *Northwest Coast*. Ed. Wayne Suttles. Washington, DC: Smithsonian Institution (1992): 560–67.

Suphan, Robert J., and Herbert J. Taylor, Jr. *Oregon Indians I*. New York, NY: Garland Publishing, 1974.

TIPAI

See Kumeyaay

TLINGIT

At the time of first contact with Europeans in the eighteenth century, the Tlingit occupied nearly all of what is today southeastern Alaska, portions of northern British Columbia, and part of the Yukon Territory of Canada. In the mid-eighteenth century, some Haida migrated into southeastern Alaska and their descendants have been neighbors to the Tlingit for several generations. The precontact population was probably between 15,000 and 25,000, but there was no census taken until long after epidemics decimated the Tlingit and other Northwest Coast Indians. Today it is difficult to even begin to estimate the number of Tlingit because, like many other Native Americans, they have intermarried with outsiders and spread around the world. In general, it seems safe to say that today there are approximately 20,000 people who consider themselves to be Tlingit. The Sealaska Corporation, formed under the Alaska Native Claims Settlement Act of 1971 (ANCSA), has about 15,500 registered shareholders, but this number does not include individuals born after 1971. Most Tlingit continue to live in Alaska, but about 25 percent of the shareholders of Sealaska live outside of the state. Most of these Tlingit live in the Pacific Northwest states, principally Washington and Oregon.

The Tlingit language is an isolate showing some grammatical relationship to Athabaskan languages. In the early days of colonization, Tlingits were punished for speaking their language and many began to speak English as their first language. Today there are probably no more than a few hundred Tlingit, nearly all over sixty years of age, who are fluent in the language. It appears that within another generation there may be no more Native speakers of the language.

During the Russian-American period from 1800 to 1867, Tlingits underwent gradual acculturation. The Russian Orthodox religion was widely accepted. With the purchase of Alaska by the United States, other Christian missionaries came into the region. At the present time, nearly all Tlingit people are members of one or another Christian denomination, and the traditional beliefs and practices in shamanism appear to be non-existent.

Traditionally, the Tlingit were a matrilineal society and from the descriptions of the earliest explorers, women were often times in charge of trading expeditions. In modern Tlingit society, most members recognize the principle of matrilineal succession. In the past, the Tlingit society was a moiety system, with one side identified as the Ravens and the other as Eagles, and members of one side had to marry those of the opposite side. Although the more conservative Tlingit still follow the old pattern, a few people have married individuals from their own side. While the extended family and clan system determined much of daily life in the past, today only the more traditional and conservative follow the old social patterns. Many young people are the offspring of intercultural marriages and have little understanding of the old ways.

The Tlingit were always forward-looking pragmatists and very early in their dealings with outsiders learned that they had to adapt or lose out. The Alaska Native Brotherhood (ANB) and Alaska Native Sisterhood (ANS) were originally formed to advocate for equality and human rights. These two organizations were later the driving force behind a land claims settlement. Once a settlement was obtained, the ANB and ANS continued to exist and today provide social activities and some scholarships for the young people.

The initial drive for compensation for the lands taken from them by the creation of the Tongass National Forest in 1907 came from the ANB and ANS. But since non-Tlingit were allowed to be members of these two organizations, a new structure was set up to administer the $7.5 million they received in 1968 for the lands taken. The new organization became the Central Council of the Tlingit and Haida Indian Tribes of Alaska. Today the Central Council functions as a tribal agency and contracts with the Bureau of Indian Affairs and other government agencies to assist with health, education, housing, and related social services. The Southeast Alaska Regional Health Corporation first began as a part of the Central Council, but later became an independent agency and now provides public health services across the region.

As a result of ANCSA, a regional corporation, Sealaska Corporation, and several village corporations were established. Tlingits born prior to December 18, 1971, are shareholders in both the regional and village corporations. But since Sealaska was intended to be a corporation for profit, it has focused its interests on economic development in the areas of fisheries, logging, land development, and investment. Most villages have both a profit and a nonprofit corporation. The regional corporation also supports a nonprofit organization known as the Sealaska Heritage Foundation, which, using its own funds and with grants from various agencies, supports a variety of activities. The Foundation sponsors a project to record and translate Tlingit oratory, a theater group which takes traditional stories and transforms them into stage productions, and post-secondary scholarships to many Tlingit and Haida students. The Foundation has also produced texts and tapes in the Tlingit language, and these materials are being used to teach the language at some high schools and at the University of Alaska Southeast. Every other year the Foundation organizes and supports a celebration, during which time Tlingit, Haida, and other Native Americans gather in Juneau to celebrate their cultural heritage.

From the onset of colonization, the Tlingit people were under pressure to abandon their traditions, customs, and beliefs and to accept Western ways and traditions. Tlingit, like many Native Americans, were treated as socially, intellectually, and culturally inferior people. Some acquiesced to this discrimination and prejudice and completely cast off their old culture. Many others preserved what they could of the old ways, while following a cultural pattern of pragmatism and adaptation, in order to succeed in the world in which they now had to live.

To a certain extent, there is a social-cultural break between urban and rural Tlingit. Many of the urban Tlingit have intermarried with non-Tlingit. They work and live in the towns of southeastern Alaska or in the cities of Washington and Oregon. Some of these urban Indians have managed to preserve parts of their cultural heritage, but to a great extent have been assimilated into the dominant society. Some still suffer the indignities of prejudice and discrimination. On the other hand, in many southeastern Alaskan settlements and a few Canadian villages, Tlingit tend to be the dominant society. Here they continue to depend on subsistence hunting, fishing, and gathering as a major part of their income. They also interact according to traditional social patterns, and may even ascribe to the values and attitudes of their ancestors. In many ways, the village Tlingit have been the ones to preserve the old culture and traditions. Urban Tlingit often return to their home villages, or invite their village relatives to come to the city for social and memorial gatherings.

Alcohol abuse has been a major problem in Alaska for both Natives and non-Natives since the time of first contact. Today, the social problems of modern America, including drug abuse and AIDS, have come to Alaska and afflict both rural and urban, Native and non-Native, residents. Other problems, such as domestic violence, child abuse, and suicide are linked to poverty, discrimination, and economic problems in both the villages and towns of southeastern Alaska.

Fortunately some of the ancient wisdom, knowledge, skills, and values persisted even though the schools and missionaries worked to eradicate the traditional culture. Over the past thirty years, there has been a gradual Tlingit cultural renaissance. The memorial for the dead, which some refer to as the potlatch, is still an important Tlingit social and religious event. The memorial has economic, social, political, and religious implications and has persisted in spite of the efforts of many non-Tlingit to eradicate it. In many ways, it is the one key, sacred event in Tlingit life.

The Tlingit had developed some highly sophisticated art forms, particularly in the areas of woodcarving and the weaving of blankets and robes. In museums around the world, Tlingit art forms a major portion of Northwest Coast collections. With the support of many state and federal agencies, along with local, village, and regional corporation support, Tlingit art is again flourishing. In fact, even non-Tlingit artists have entered the field, and with the help of Tlingit elders and master artists, have mastered many of the traditional art forms.

For many years, the Tlingit people have encouraged the younger generations to pursue a formal education. Today there are Tlingit businessmen, accountants, attorneys, and other professionals. Several Tlingit are school teachers and school administrators. Many Tlingit college students currently seek professional careers in a variety of fields, but a few have revived an interest in their cultural heritage. Hopefully, they will be able to extract and distill the finest parts of Tlingit culture and preserve them for future generations.

Wallace Olson

See also **Alaska Native Brotherhood/Sisterhood; Alaska Native Claims Settlement Act**

Further Reading

Dauenhauer, Nora Marks, and Richard Dauenhauer, eds. *Haa Tuwunáagu Yis, for Healing Our Spirit: Tlingit Oratory.* Seattle: University of Washington Press, 1990.

Emmons, George Thornton. *The Tlingit Indians.* Ed. with additions by Frederica deLaguna and a biography by Jean Low. Seattle: University of Washington Press, 1991.

Olson, Wallace M. *The Tlingit: An Introduction to Their Culture and History.* Auke Bay, AK: Heritage Research, 1991.

TOHONO O'ODHAM

The Tohono O'odham Nation (formerly Papago), located in southern Arizona, is one of the few tribes in the United States that has not had to relocate from their traditional homelands. However, their aboriginal land base has been considerably reduced.

The traditional language of the Tohono O'odham is grouped under the Uto-Aztecan stock, and classified under the Piman language. According to Ruth Underhill, "They had a highly developed Native literature in myth and song recital , in folk stories, and in formalized oratory; they were greatly interested in social gatherings and were especially sensitive to the maintenance of form and custom in social intercourse." Due to outside contact various aspects of the overall social and economic conditions of the tribe have either improved or deteriorated. Contact has been with both Spanish and English-speaking groups of people and has been friendly.

In 1949, the Indian Health Service reported that the Papago Tribe was rated in a "Group III" classification, whereby the tribe would be able to handle its own affairs without federal supervision in approximately twenty-five years. In 1993, the tribe is still under the supervision of the Bureau of Indian Affairs (BIA).

The Tohono O'odham Nation is composed of three reservations established by executive order between 1874 and 1917 to stem encroachment by non-Indians. In 1874 the San Xavier Reservation was created; it is located on the southwestern outskirts of the city of Tucson. The Gila Bend Reservation was established in 1882 with an acreage of 10,235. The Tohono O'odham Reservation, the main reservation located in Sells, Arizona, west of the city of Tucson, was established in 1917 with a total acreage of 2,774,370.

The population of the tribe was approximately 9,700 from 1934 to 1961. The most recent population study was compiled by the Tohono O'odham Enrollment Office in 1991. They cite the population as the following:

San Xavier Reservation	
On-reservation	942
Off-reservation	380
Gila River Reservation	
On-reservation	499
Off-reservation	463
Tohono O'odham Reservation	
Total:	15,295
Total for three reservations:	17,579

Prior to European contact, the tribes already had a sophisticated method of social organization and control. The decision-making process was one that depended on consensus, rather than majority rule. In 1934 the United States Congress approved the Indian Reorganization Act (IRA), which provided tribes the option of organizing themselves under a constitution or rejecting the IRA. In 1937 the Tohono O'odham Nation voted to accept the IRA through a national tribe election, which created the first Tribal Constitution. They elected two representatives from the twelve districts that composed the reservation to serve under one central government. They elected a chairman and vice-chairman to lead the tribe under this new political structure. In addition, each district maintained a local government structure with a distinct relationship with the Tribal Council. In 1986 after fifty-two years, the tribe voted to revise its initial Constitution in a successful national election. The revised Constitution called for the return to the usage of the tribe's traditional name of Tohono O'odham (meaning "Desert People"), instead of Papago. Perhaps the most important element was the creation of a three-branch form of government consisting of the executive, legislative, and judicial. Excerpts from the preamble of this document dictate the mission of the tribal leaders, which is to affirm the sovereign powers of the nation; preserve, protect, and build upon the unique culture and traditions; conserve the common resources; establish a responsive form of government; provide for free expression by the people; promote the rights, education, and welfare of the present and future generations of the people; and show gratitude to *I'itoi*, the traditionally recognized Maker of the Tohono O'odham Nation.

In order to implement the elements of the preamble, one must engage in a process of envisioning what will be taken into consideration in looking at the current economic picture. That includes resources from the copper mine on the main reservation, Indian gaming at the bingo hall, the cattle industry for some districts, a few Indian-owned businesses, a state grocery chain, the Tohono O'odham Utility Authority, the Central Arizona Project for water resources, and the federal dollars that are appropriated to the tribal programs.

Tohono O'odham people, along with the Pima, have historically been well known for their fine coiled basketry. This craft is very much alive today, with Tohono O'odham basketweavers producing more basketry than any other tribe in the United States. Their coiled baskets are made of desert beargrass, yucca, and devil's claw. A wide variety of designs decorate these baskets; lizards, birds, and saguaros are among the most popular motifs.

A hallmark design for Tohono O'odham basketry is the man-in-the-maze pattern, depicting Elder Brother preparing to journey through a life maze. It is unclear where this motif originated; it bears some resemblance to a maze design of uncertain age etched into the wall of Casa Grande, a Hohokam Great House south of Phoenix. It has become the symbol of not only the Tohono O'odham, but the Pima (or Akimel O'odham) as well.

Other Tohono O'odham crafts still produced include horsehair and baling-wire baskets and some polychrome pottery. There are artists on the reservation producing Hopi-style overlay jewelry, paintings and prints, woodcarvings, and other less traditional art forms.

Some of the current health issues include a high incidence of diabetes, obesity, and alcoholism. There is an Indian Hospital in Sells and clinics in San Xavier and Santa Rosa. The majority of children attend elementary and secondary schools on the reservation. There is a BIA boarding school for kindergarten to eighth grade, a high school, and the Santa Rosa Ranch (a day school and boarding school for disabled children).

On January 4, 1993, the University of Arizona's President, Dr. Manuel Pacheco, and his delegation met with the chairman of the Tohono O'odham Nation, the late Josiah Moore, to begin a dialogue about the current and future needs of the tribe in terms of technical assistance available from the university to enhance tribal programs.

There are over thirty programs within the executive branch of the Tohono O'odham Nation. The leadership of these programs identified some areas that needed attention, such as realistic professional development opportunities for their staff members. Some of the strategies include recruitment in and offering of undergraduate and graduate degree programs in a variety of disciplines based on the tribe's specific needs and expectations. Training requests include computer science for all levels of program management. A demand for students with a science and engineering background was voiced by the managers of the water resources programs and the Tohono O'odham Utility Authority. Specialization in accounting and business management skills is needed in such programs as accounting, and grants and contracts. The program leaders expressed a desire for courses to be offered at various sites with an instructor and for the classes to be transmitted to the more remote locations on the reservation.

The development of student internship programs for undergraduate and graduate students attending institutions of higher learning will enhance the research and analysis components in many areas including tribal enrollment, water resources, livestock, health and human resources, development of environmental protection, and civil and criminal codes, to name a few.

Tribal enrollment and the current and future status of the Tohono O'odham membership is one area needing study. In the past, a majority of tribal members were full-bloods. A more recent trend is intermarriage between Tohono O'odham and members of other tribes or non-Indians. According to the tribe's enrollment office, this has a significant impact on both the numbers of individuals enrolled in the tribe and their blood quanta. This trend will impact the future policies of the tribe as an increased membership vies for limited federal and tribal resources. In response to concerns voiced during public hearings, the 1986 Constitution of the Tohono O'odham Nation specified that membership in the tribe shall consist of the following:

> Section 1. (a) All Indians whose names appear on the official census rolls of the Sells and Gila Bend Reservation as of January 1, 1940; (b) All children born to resident members; (c) The Council shall have the power to adopt anyone who is one-half degree or more; and (d) All rights shall be lost or relinquished if a person is enrolled in more than one tribe; however, the person will be provided the opportunity to relinquish his or her rights elsewhere.

The last population study was conducted in 1961 by Robert A. Hackenberg. According to his findings, a total of 9,613 Papagos were surveyed, 8,330 were full-bloods or 86.66 percent; 1,283 or 13.34 percent were mixed-bloods. Hackenberg noted that "Many of the mixed bloods are part Pima Indian, and a smaller number are part Yaqui." In 1934, the estimated population was 5,577; in 1961, 9,614; in 1972, 10,000; and in 1992, it is approximately 15,000 members located both on and off the three reservations. The analysis of tribal membership and future trends is a prime field of study for tribal members pursuing a higher education.

Program leaders have also requested the placement of upper-division undergraduate and graduate interns in appropriate tribal programs to assist with the research and analysis of hydrological, mineral, and economical studies, and reports for litigation purposes. Research skills are being recognized as a valuable tool for tribal members. Native American students with college degrees are being encouraged to rewrite and reassess the resources written about their people by non-Indians.

In order to continue to implement the visions of previous leaders, such as the late Thomas Segundo and the late Josiah Moore, it is felt that the Tohono

O'odham Nation must put education at the forefront of its priorities. Both Segundo and Moore had college degrees and were both employed off the reservation in professional capacities prior to returning to the reservation to serve as chairmen of the tribe. Many tribal members have stated that these two leaders have been the only ones in this day and age who have managed to successfully live and be productive in both the Western and Tohono O'odham worlds. As more and more Tohono O'odham leaders recognize the value of a Western education, we must also be cognizant of the mores of a group of people who have survived five hundred years of encroachment and numerous attempts at assimilation.

Vivian Juan

See also **Arizona Tribes; Higher Education; Indian Reorganization Act**

Further Reading

Blaine, Peter, Sr. *Papagos and Politics.* Tucson: Arizona Historical Society, 1981.

Dobyns, Henry F. *The Papago People.* Phoenix, AZ: Indian Tribal Series, 1972.

Fontana, Bernard Lee. *Of Earth and Little Rain: The Papago Indians.* Flagstaff, AZ: Northland Press, 1981.

Hackenberg, Robert A. *Papago Population Study, Research Methods, and Preliminary Results.* Tucson: Bureau of Ethnic Research, Department of Anthropology, University of Arizona, 1961.

Ortiz, Alfonso, Ed. *Handbook of North American Indians.* Vol 10. *Southwest.* Washington, DC: Smithsonian Institution (1983): 125–48; 161–211.

Underhill, Ruth Murray. *Social Organization of the Papago Indians.* Contributions to Anthropology 30. New York, NY: Columbia University Press, 1939.

———. *Rainhouse and Ocean: Speeches for the Papago Year.* Flagstaff: Museum of Northern Arizona Press, 1979.

TOLOWA

The Tolowa (*Xʉsh*, Tututni, Chetco) live in the coastal redwood forest region of northwestern California and southwestern Oregon. The greater part of their shoreline is immense and rocky, rising steeply nearly 2,000 feet in elevation. The aboriginal homeland of the Tolowa includes the drainages of Chetco, Pistol, Sixes, Winchuk, and Smith rivers and Wilson and Galice creeks. The names given to the Tolowa kin in Oregon who live near the Chetco and Rogue rivers are Chetco and Tututni. The Tolowa language is Athabaskan; however, the term Tolowa was applied to the tribe by the Algonquian-speaking Yurok people of the lower Klamath River. The true Athabaskan term for the Tolowa is *Xʉsh*, or "Person." The larger Athabaskan term *Deni* is used as a tribal name when referring to a person's village affiliation.

The precontact Tolowa (Chetco, Tututni) population is estimated at 4,000. By 1906, only 254 Tolowa were found in the southern aboriginal homeland who had survived the massacres, military destruction, subjugation, and removal to the Siletz and Hoopa Indian reservations during the mid-1800s. The current Tolowa population has reached approximately 1,000.

Under the General Allotment Act of 1887, several individual land allotments were made and the Jane Hostatlas allotment, which is located at the historic fishing weir village of Nelechundun, has continued to be held in Tolowa ownership. The Smith River and Elk Valley rancherias were established after 1906 under appropriation acts for the "homeless" Indians in California. Both rancherias were terminated in 1960. Termination was one of the most destructive policies the federal government forced upon the Tolowa. They survived extermination, relocation, the boarding schools, racism and oppression, but this act removed the home land base and the sense of community. The early 1960s saw a serious erosion of Tolowa identity, tradition, and unity, and isolation between families and the rancherias grew. In response, the Nelechundun landholders in 1973 created the Nele-chun-dun Business Council upon the land base of the Jane Hostatlas allotment, with a constitution, enrollment, and state incorporation, and finally in 1983, with the help of a grant from the Administration for Native Americans, formed the Tolowa Nation and filed for federal acknowledgment. Concurrently, the *Tillie Hardwick v. United States* case was settled, "unterminating" both the Smith River and Elk Valley rancherias, and removing the need for federal acknowledgment. The Constitution of the Howonquet Indian Council of the Smith River Rancheria was approved in 1987, and the enrollment ordinance for accepting and processing membership applications of rancheria and Tolowa members became effective on May 14, 1991.

The Tolowa *Naydosh* (Feather Dance) remains as one of their central traditional spiritual and religious expressions. *Naydosh* embodies the protocol, ceremony, and enactment of renewing Earth Mother and honoring her creation. Earth and the laws to live by were set down for the Tolowa at Yontockett, and the Yontockett town site remains as the spiritual axis for the Tolowa. Prior to the settlers' infernal destruction of Yontockett and 450 Tolowa in 1853 during the climax of *Naydosh*, Yontockett was the largest village and host to the ancient ten-night winter solstice *Naydosh* where tribal members made pilgrimages from the entire region to partake in the ceremony. Similar attacks upon *Naydosh* occurred in 1854 and 1855; *Naydosh* endured under the protection of the treaty negotiated with the settlers by Headmen Guylish and Yu'xasutl of Howonquet in 1855. Federal prohibition of Tolowa dances and religion came in 1923 and federal agents arrested the dance makers and confiscated regalia. *Naydosh* continued to be celebrated, but in private homes and in shortened versions, and it was not again celebrated publicly until the 1950s.

With the suppression of traditional dances and healing, the Tolowa were receptive to the Indian Shaker religion brought from the Pacific Northwest in 1927 by way of friends and relatives on the Siletz Reservation in Oregon. The Tolowa wholeheartedly embraced the healing and culturally inclusive practices of the "Shake" and added new songs, prophecies, and Tolowa protocol. A Shaker Church was built on the Smith River Rancheria in 1932 and the "Shake" has become an integral part of the traditional Tolowa belief system.

Tolowa language preservation and documentation were encouraged in the late 1960s with the support of the Del Norte Indian Welfare Association, and in 1969 the elders began formal class offerings in the public schools. This effort resulted in the creation of two dictionaries, completed in 1983 and 1989. In 1971 two Tolowa gained state teaching credentials for teaching language; a third one received a credential in 1980.

The Smith River Rancheria tribal office was completed in 1986 followed by a medical and dental clinic in 1987. Most recently the tribal center and senior nutrition site have been completed. The Tolowa are entering a new and exciting phase in their history. Perhaps now they can begin to meet and address their social, economic, political, and cultural needs, which had been suppressed during the difficult time of termination.

Loren J. Bommelyn

See also **California Tribes; Indian Shaker Church**

Further Reading

Beckham, Stephen Dow. *The Indians of Western Oregon: This Land Was Theirs*. Coos Bay, OR: Arago Books, 1977.

Bommelyn, Loren, ed. *Tolowa (Tututni) Language Dictionary*. Crescent City, CA: Tolowa Language Committee, 1989.

Drucker, Philip. "The Tolowa and Their Southwest Oregon Kin." *University of California Publications in American Archaeology and Ethnology* 36:4 (1937): 221–300.

Gould, Richard A. "Tolowa." *Handbook of North American Indians*. Vol. 8. *California*. Ed. Robert F. Heizer. Washington, DC: Smithsonian Institution (1978): 128–36.

Norton, Jack. *Genocide in Northwestern California: When Our Worlds Cried*. San Francisco, CA: Indian Historian Press, 1979.

TONGVA

See Gabrielino/Tongva

TONKAWA

Originally settled in Texas, the Tonkawas were part of the southern Plains cultural complex. In the eighteenth century, the tribe was consolidated by the Spanish at the San Gabriel Mission in east Texas, but the mission was abandoned in 1758. With the arrival of the Austin colonists in Texas in 1821, the Tonkawas became allies of the Anglo-Texans against the Wacos and Comanches. Tonkawa warriors fought alongside the Texas Rangers against Comanche war parties in the antebellum period.

The tribe was removed to Ft. Cobb, Indian Territory (Oklahoma), in 1859, but was attacked there in 1862 by Kansas Unionist Indians. The survivors fled to Texas, where they served the Confederacy as frontier scouts. After the Civil War they were scouts for the United States Army, and participated in the last military campaigns against the Comanches and Kiowas. Despite protest by tribal members, Texas politicians, and Army officers, the Tonkawas were removed to the abandoned Nez Perce Reservation in Kay County, Oklahoma, in 1884. Barely fifty-three people remained of an aboriginal population of over five thousand. In 1896 their lands were allotted, and the tribal population fell to thirty-four people by 1921.

The tribe's Constitution, passed in 1938, provides for a president, vice-president, and secretary-treasurer, all elected to two-year terms. Regular meetings of the Tribal Council are held monthly. The 1993 population is 186. The Tonkawas include within their membership the only surviving Karankawas (a coastal tribe from Texas) and a number of people of Lipan ancestry.

Tonkawa landholdings consist of 398.74 acres, of which 238.24 acres are allotted, near the town of Tonkawa in Kay County, Oklahoma. Half an acre is owned by the United States, and the remainder belongs to the tribe as a whole. Tribal members are employed in small businesses in the Tonkawa area and are economically assimilated into the non-Indian community.

The Tonkawas participated in the Pawnee Ghost Dance in the early twentieth century, and some members are active in the Native American Church. The Tonkawa language is extinct. The tribe holds a pow-wow in June of each year near the town of Tonkawa. In recent years tribal members have held ceremonials and educational workshops in Texas cities, including Austin and Port Lavaca.

Thomas F. Schilz

See also **Oklahoma Tribes**

Further Reading

Confederation of American Indians. *Indian Reservations: A State and Federal Handbook*. Jefferson, NC: McFarland & CO., 1986.

Leitch, Barbara. *A Concise Handbook of Indian Tribes of North America*. Algonac, MI: Reference Publications, 1979.

Schilz, Thomas. "People of the Cross Timbers: A History of the Tonkawa Indians." Ph.D. diss., Texas Christian University, 1983.

Strickland, Rennard. *The Indians in Oklahoma*. Norman: University of Oklahoma Press, 1980.

Wright, Muriel H. *A Guide to the Indian Tribes of Oklahoma*. Civilization of the American Indian 33 (1951). Norman: University of Oklahoma Press, 1986.

Tonto

See Apache

TORTUGAS

(Also known as Tigua; Los Indigenes de Guadalupe; Los Inditos de Las Cruces; Piro, Manso, Tiwa Tribe; San Juan de Guadalupe Tiwa Tribe.) The village of Tortugas is located immediately south of Las Cruces, New Mexico. It is composed of two historically distinct areas: San Juan and Guadalupe. Exact landsize for Tortugas is difficult to assess due to the fact that part of the land is deeded to non-Indians. San Juan was founded by Hispanic settlers in 1852. Guadalupe, which is the southern part of Tortugas, was established in 1888 by families descended from Indians of the El Paso area missions. The nucleus of this group was known in the late 1800s as "Los Inditos de Las Cruces." Most members of the original group were Indian families from the Mission of Nuestra Señora de Guadalupe, in what is now Ciudad Juarez, Mexico. The Indians of this mission were of mixed Manso, Piro, and Tiwa ancestry. Families from the Guadalupe Mission included the Abalos, Jemente, Roybal, and Trujillo families. Other Indian families from the Tiwa Pueblo of Ysleta del Sur and the Piro Pueblo of Senecú joined the group. This composite group is popularly known as the Tortugas Indians, despite the fact that most of the Indian families continued to live in Las Cruces instead of Tortugas.

The earliest known leader of "Los Inditos de Las Cruces" was Felipe Roybal, who was the nephew of the last *cacique* (religious chief) at the Guadalupe Mission in Juarez. Felipe Roybal led the effort to establish an Indian community at Tortugas from 1888 to 1896. In 1896 the "Inditos de Las Cruces" became disillusioned with prospects in Tortugas and obtained a lot in Las Cruces to construct a chapel dedicated to Nuestra Señora de Guadalupe. After Felipe Roybal was killed in 1906, plans to build a chapel in Las Cruces were abandoned. The group shifted their efforts back to Tortugas, where they completed a chapel in 1910. In the same year the Guadalupe Day ceremonies, which had been held in front of Saint Genevieve Church in Las Cruces, were moved to Tortugas.

On April 12, 1914, Los Indigenes de Nuestra Señora de Guadalupe, a nonprofit corporation, was formed. The corporation's intent was to construct a Catholic church and cemetery, community buildings, and houses. It also provided for civil officers for the corporation and traditional leaders, such as the *cacique* and war captains. The dual separation of officers continues until today. On September 14, 1914, the commissioners of the Pueblo transferred title of the Pueblo land to the corporation. The corporation in turn deeded the chapel and grounds to the Bishop of Tucson on October 26, 1914.

From the beginning, the corporation and Tortugas were of multiethnic composition. Most of the original corporation members were of Mission Indian descent and lived outside Tortugas in Las Cruces and surrounding areas. No governmental agency has collected any statistics on the Mission Indian descendants in Doña Ana County, nor is there any information currently available concerning how many members of the corporation are of Mission Indian descent. Although census figures exist, there is no way to distinguish Natives from non-Natives within this small village.

During the 1940s and 1950s, rifts occurred between members of the corporation, resulting in a final break by litigation in the 1960s. Many of the Mission Indian descendants are now seeking federal recognition as the Piro, Manso, Tiwa Tribe (or the San Juan de Guadalupe Tiwa Tribe). Those members who remain active in the corporation, which includes both Indians and non-Indians, conduct ceremonies and maintain the public buildings in the village of Tortugas. All land in Tortugas is privately owned, except the public buildings owned by the corporation. Members of the various groups connected with the Tortugas Indians are economically integrated into the greater Las Cruces area. No indigenous languages are spoken at present, although some people may still remember a few words of Tiwa. A few families continue to make traditional pottery for their own use, but not for public sale.

One amazing facet of this multiethnic group is that they have held on to many ceremonies that have since been lost from their parent Indian communities. For years people from Ysleta del Sur have come north to Tortugas to participate in the annual Rabbit Hunt, and its associated ceremony, and the *Baile de Olla*. These ceremonies and dances are kept alive in Tortugas.

The three-day ceremony honoring Our Lady of Guadalupe is held every December 10 through 12. This is the major ceremony of the year and brings former residents from all over the country to renew family and friendship ties. This ceremony is marked by three days of activity. On December 10, an all-night wake (*Velorio*) is held, with the Catholic Rosary interspaced with *matachine* dances by Los Danzantes. December 11 is marked by a pilgrimage to nearby Tortugas Mountain. After a mass is held at the summit, the day is spent making *quiotes* (walking sticks) and *coronas* (head bands) for the pilgrimage back to Tortugas. On the way back down the mountain, participants light bonfires in the shape of a cross. Once they reach the Pueblo, a brief ceremony is held in front of La Casa del Pueblo (community house), where the *quiotes* are deposited by the participants.

December 12 is marked by all-day dancing by the four dance groups. The two corporation groups are Los Danzantes (*matachine)* and Los Indios. The other two groups, Los Aztecas del Carrizo and the Guadalupana Aztecas, were introduced into the village in 1921 by Juan Pacheco, an immigrant from Zacatecas, Mexico. At 4:00 P.M. on December 12, a procession carrying the image of Nuestra Señora de

Guadalupe leaves the church, led by all four dance groups. Halfway through the journey, the procession stops in front of La Casa del Pueblo to change *mayordomos* (sponsors) for the coming year. The procession then proceeds to the church. On January 1 a small procession takes the image from the church back to La Capilla (little chapel), where the image stays until the following December 10. San Juan Day is another time for celebration. The traditional one-day fiesta became a two-day celebration in 1986. This fiesta is held on the closest weekend to June 24.

Patrick H. Beckett

Terry L. Corbett

See also Ysleta del Sur Pueblo

Further Reading

Beckett, Patrick H., and Terry L. Corbett. *Tortugas.* COAS Monograph 8. Las Cruces, NM: COAS Publishing and Research, 1990.

———. *The Manso Indians.* COAS Monograph 9. Las Cruces, NM: COAS Publishing and Research, 1992.

Houser, Nicholas P. "Tigua Pueblo." *Handbook of North American Indians.* Vol. 9. *Southwest.* Ed. Alfonso Ortiz. Washington, DC: Smithsonian Institution (1979): 336–42.

Hurt, Wesley R., Jr. "Tortugas: An Indian Village in Southern New Mexico." *El Palacio* 59 (1952): 104–22.

TRADITIONAL MEDICINE

It is not possible to provide a complete review of traditional medicine for every tribe in North America because there are so many. Some tribes have similar beliefs and languages (Mohawk and Cherokee), while other tribes are very different (Mohawk and Apache). Acknowledging that the word "traditional" means different things to different people, it is still possible to provide several general statements about traditional medicine among American Indians that can be used as guidelines in understanding tribal beliefs about illness and healing.

Common Beliefs About Traditional Medicine

Most tribes have the belief that their medicine people have extra "power" that other tribal members do not have. This power comes from varied sources: a visionary experience that leads one into the study of medicine, such as Black Elk had, for example, or being born into a family that includes generations of medicine people, like Geronimo. Many tribes have both men and women medicine people, but some tribes, such as the Yurok in California, have only medicine women. Many medicine people have a specialty, such as herbalist, bone-setter, midwife, or counselor. A man named Sam, for example, is a traditional Comanche medicine man who was born visionary. Then there is Effie (Hopi), a medicine woman who learned the art of using herbs, and Billy (Sioux), who was born with the ability to

manipulate energy; Ocie (Cherokee) works on bones, and Lola (Apache) is a midwife. Effie, Billy, Ocie, and Lola may or may not be visionary, but they are healers. Each person is effective and useful in what he or she does, and they each have distinct ways of doing their work. They are "medicine" in their cultures; learned, capable individuals who occupy places of respect in their communities.

One must be very careful when using the terms medicine man or woman, healer, or shaman, because these are terms for concepts for which there are no direct translations from tribal languages. Each tribe has a particular title for its healers, a title that is not easily gained, for the knowledge of these professions is closely guarded and many long years of apprenticeship to a seasoned practitioner is needed. Indian people understand that helping someone to heal him/herself is a private, doctor-patient relationship with certain protocol and formality. Ceremonies like "talking circles" or "smudging" (smoking) are intended for helping groups of people to return to harmony, but not for healing.

In many tribes, ethics prohibit healers from charging for their services, although gifts are expected. In other tribes payment is required and there is a standard for gifts that repay the healer for his/her time and skill. When asking a medicine person for assistance, it is appropriate to offer a pouch of tobacco. Today in almost every tribe tobacco is recognized as a gift of respect. Payment or a substantial gift is expected later.

To tribal people, healing cannot be separated from worship or from daily life. Worship is not contained in a building or limited to certain days, but is ongoing every minute of life. Personal health is a continual process of keeping oneself strong spiritually, mentally, and physically, and in doing so, keeping away or overcoming those forces that might make one unwell. To remain well, individuals must stay in harmony with themselves, their environment, and their Creator. Harmony thus becomes a shield against disharmony, which is quite similar to the tenets of behavioral medicine that teach stress control as a means of healthy living. Added to the harmony may be herbs, rebalancing of energy, and rituals of fasting, prayer, and thanksgiving to the Creator.

Staying in harmony is only one part of health; another part is adhering to traditional beliefs and obeying tribal religious tenets. Every tribe has its own unique spiritual tenets or laws that are coupled with the belief that the violation of a tenet has a consequence. For example, the Kiowa believe that a medicine person must not harm (kill) a member of his own tribe with his/her "power," because such an act requires his own life in return. The Yaqui believe that a pregnant woman must not go outside during an eclipse of the moon or her unborn child will be born handicapped (unfinished). Traditional spiritual tenets may require that certain rituals be performed in a prescribed manner (among the Navajo, for example, it is necessary to walk around the fire in the right direction). They may include taboos related to animals (Tohono O'odham will not kill horned toads), family members (many tribes ban marriage between clan relatives), or natural phenomenon such as lightning (Apaches will not go near objects struck by lightning). Consequences of violations include physical or mental illness, disability, continual adverse happenings in one's life, or trauma. The violation must be recompensed before harmony and health can be restored.

The statement above is a source of conflict between traditional people and modern medical establishments. A critically ill, new-born Apache baby was air lifted to a large medical center. The baby's body was covered with designs representing deities and spirit beings, painted with ashes, charcoal, and colored clay. The tiny head was covered with a heavy dusting of corn pollen, used in much the same way as holy water is used in a religious ritual. The painting and dusting had been made in a sacred ceremony in order to "undo" a violation by the baby's father, and needed to remain on the baby's body for four days to complete the "undoing." The symbols were the infant's protection as well as visual representations of the prayers offered in supplication for forgiveness and the return of health. To remove them would be much worse than taking crosses, rosaries, or Bibles from Christian individuals, for it also opened the gates of hell, so to speak, upon this infant. Fortunately, the hospital personnel knew the meaning of the painting and dusting on the baby's body and did not bathe him for the remaining time of the required four days (despite the fact that he was considered unsterile).

Bad Use of Power

Positive healing power has its negative side, which has been identified as "bad use of power" by some Indians because there is no literal translation for tribal concepts on this topic. Most tribes associate using bad power with darkness or night, powers under or down somewhere, and evil. "Bad use of power" illness is considered an unnatural unwellness, where other illnesses are natural consequences of actions, inactions, breaking of taboos, or violating sacred tenets. A medicine person who is strong in working against the "bad use of power" must be sought for assistance to counter the illness that has occurred. However, the only way a "nightwalker" (Hopi term for someone who makes bad use of power) can harm an individual is when that individual's personal and spiritual energy is so low that the "bad power" can affect him. The best defense against "bad power" is the defense against all illnesses: keep one's mind, body, and spirit strong and pure, and keep one's spiritual energy stronger than any force of evil that might threaten it.

Common Spiritual Beliefs

There are a few spiritual and healing beliefs that the majority of tribes hold in common, although each individual tribe expresses the beliefs differently. Probably the most common belief is the concept that there is a Supreme Creator, although many early writers described Indians as "heathen," "idolaters," and "pagan." Most tribal beliefs also incorporate other lesser deities, such as Mary figures (Navajo's Changing Woman, Yaqui's *Maala Mecha*), Jesus figures (Cherokee's Thunder, Pima's *I'itoi*), and mediators between the spirit world and the earth (similar to saints), such as Iroquois False Faces, the visions of which have been given to individuals in dream-visions, and the Hopi Kachinas, who dance to evoke blessings from the Creator.

Many believe that man is a triune being composed of a body, mind, and spirit. Most illnesses are viewed as being directly related to a spiritual cause, creating an imbalance between the body, mind, and spirit. Cause and effect, or action and consequences, have strong implications in healing. Concepts of living are related to beliefs about death. Since there is an absence of certain Biblical concepts in traditional beliefs, such as hell and eternal punishment, the object of life is not to avoid going there. Instead, one should seek to maintain constant, daily harmony and contact with the Creator, to follow all sacred teachings, and to treat all life with respect.

Traditional Medicine in a Twentieth-Century Setting

Before the turn of the century, tribal people had limited access to modern medicine and depended a great deal on traditional healers. In the twentieth century more Indian Health Service hospitals and clinics were built and tribal people began to use non-Indian physicians and modern medicines more frequently. While the concept of being in spiritual harmony was essentially the same as it was in the previous centuries, tribal members were not adverse to seeking medical help at the modern facilities for their physical bodies. Also, there were diseases among tribal people that had not been there before contact with Euroamericans, such as tuberculosis, measles, and whooping cough. The "white-man's" medicine was good for "white-man's diseases," illnesses for which traditional healers often had no medicine and, if epidemic, could wipe out entire villages.

Some traditional aspects of Indian medicine have survived today, such as the use of sweat baths for purification and healing, wearing medicine bags and charms, and the continuation of ancient healing rituals and ceremonies. Traditional healers in some tribes, such as the Quinault and some Eskimo groups, still have the ability to go into a trance and seek information or curing from entities in the "other world." Although there are alarmingly few of them today, medicine men and women are still being born and trained "to medicine" and still work with their tribal people in the 1990s despite many disruptions to their cultures, spiritual beliefs, and traditional ways of life. However, the growing places of many healing herbs, once the apothecary for healers, have been destroyed, reducing the availability of herbs such as wild tobacco, prickly ash, and buffalo gourds. A parallel use of traditional and modern medicine has become quite common in today's world, a system in which traditional medicine is employed to treat the spirit, while modern medicine treats the body or the mind.

All tribal groups experienced major disruption of their culture by the coming of non-Indians to this continent, but some tribes suffered greater losses than others. Many tribes experienced great cultural disruptions when they were removed from their ancestral lands. The Five Civilized Tribes of Oklahoma (Chickasaw, Cherokee, Choctaw, Creek, and Seminole), who originated in the southeastern United States, for example, suffered a great loss of traditional beliefs and ceremonies, perhaps because many sacred ways are rooted in the land itself (certain mountains, lakes, and rivers are sacred; often tribal deity figures live there). Other tribes, such as the Navajo, some of the Sioux, and the Pueblo-dwellers, appear to have retained more of their traditional beliefs and sacred ceremonies, perhaps because they are still living in the land of their ancestors, where their sacred beings reside.

The impact of non-Indian educational systems and outside religions also decimated the ranks of traditional healers. The education systems took children out of the homes, where they were traditionally taught tribal rituals and ceremonies. Missionary activities reinforced the use of modern medicine and the abandonment of traditional ways. These factors contributed to the steady decline in the numbers of traditional healers.

Today, Indian people are caught between two worlds, experiencing the forces of the spirit world, yet bound by the modern technology of communications and transportation that speeds their world far beyond its original bounds. It is often difficult for an American Indian to fit into the modern world as worker, family member, or member of society, without also trying to walk between traditional and modern religion and medicine. Children and young people who are born to medicine, or who are sought out to be healers in their communities, have an even more difficult time trying to bridge the conflicts between their traditional medicine teachings, the television set, and the microwave oven society of the 1990s.

Another reason for the decline in the number of traditional healers is that training healers is a private matter and spans many years, has no classrooms, and frequently must be done by memory alone; therefore transfer of knowledge is difficult. Many young Indians today, when faced with a choice between the television world and the spirit world, choose the modern world. Therefore they are not coming behind the elder healers to learn the ancient arts. The traditional healers we had in the 1970s, like Essie (Pomo), Araphooish (Crow), Edgar Jr. (Comanche), and Yucupicio (Yaqui), have either passed on or are not practicing any more. Many elders fear that by the year 2000 only a handful of the traditional people will exist that hold ancient sacred knowledge of healing.

The Navajo Nation realized this dilemma and established a method within the Navajo Community College by which respected healers from throughout the Navajo Nation were engaged to teach young people the ancient songs and chants of healing. The book *The Sacred Ways of Knowledge: Sources of Life* was published as a text. It is a comprehensive book on belief systems of tribal people. Although formal teaching of "medicine" is not traditional, it has become necessary if tribal religions and healing arts are to be kept alive.

Carol S. Locust

See also **Health; Indian Health Service; Peyote Religion; Religion**

Further Reading

Beck, Peggy V., and Anna Walters. *The Sacred Ways of Knowledge: Sources of Life.* Tsaile, AZ: Navajo Community College, 1977.

Locke, Steve, and Douglas Colligan. *The Healer Within.* New York, NY: E.P. Dutton, 1986.

Locust, Carol. " Wounding the Spirit." *Race, Racism, and American Education. Harvard Educational Review* 58:3 (1988): 315–30.

McNeil, William. *Plagues and People.* New York, NY: Anchor/Doubleday, 1976.

Preston, Robert J., and Carl A. Hammerschlag. "The Native American Church." *Psychodynamic Perspectives on Religion, Sect, and Cult.* Ed. David A. Halperin. Boston, MA: John Wright PSG. (1983): 93–103.

TRAIL OF BROKEN TREATIES

During the decade from 1968 to 1978, four major national events were organized by Native Americans which riveted national and international attention, brought Indians together in a pan-Indian movement, and concretely affected federal Indian policy. These actions were: the seizure and occupation of Alcatraz Island from 1968 to 1970; the Trail of Broken Treaties caravan from San Francisco to Washington, D.C. in the fall of 1972; the Wounded Knee siege from February to May 1973; and the Longest Walk, a seven-month pilgrimage across the continent from February to August, 1978, to protest the 1977 rash of proposed anti-Indian federal legislation. The Trail of Broken Treaties was a turning point in producing concrete proposals and galvanizing the spontaneity of Alcatraz into a program, and led directly to Wounded Knee and the tenth anniversary repetition of the caravan in 1978.

The Trail of Broken Treaties caravan brought hundreds of Indians to Washington, D.C. on November 3, 1972, in a challenge to President Richard Nixon's re-election campaign commitment to "Indian self-determination." The pressure created by several years of volatile Indian demonstrations and demands undoubtedly contributed to Nixon's proclamation of "Indian self-determination." The Indians of the caravan proposed to clarify the meaning of the campaign slogan.

The assembled Indians presented a proposal to the government, the "Twenty Points," which focused on treaties. Seven of the twenty points concerned treaties: demands for resubmission of unratified treaties to the Senate; restoration of the treaty-making process; creation of a treaty commission; creation of a commission to review treaty commitments and violations by the United States; mandatory judicial relief against treaty rights violations; and judicial recognition of the Indian right to interpret their own treaties. The document eschewed the attempts by the states to gain civil and criminal jurisdiction over Indian territories, resources and laws, and insisted on continued federal trust responsibility. Among other points were calls for the abolition of the Bureau of Indian Affairs (BIA), direct Indian representation to the president, and the repeal of past termination legislation.

The classic text on the event is Vine Deloria's *Behind the Trail of Broken Treaties*. Deloria describes the trip across the continent:

> The Caravan began [from San Francisco] in October and wound its way eastward, stopping at every reservation within easy driving distance of the main route. For the first time, people began to realize the extent of discontent existing on the reservations. The Bureau of Indian Affairs had been instructed to refuse to assist any of the different groups that were proceeding east.... The Caravan stopped in St. Paul, Minnesota, to plan the list of grievances and hold workshops on the various phases of the march. In several days of workshops the Caravan members hammered a list of twenty points which they felt fairly and adequately summarized a reform program for the government which would receive strong support from Indians.

Among the organizations involved in the planning of the caravan were the American Indian Movement, the National Indian Youth Council, and the Native American Rights Fund. Numerous other organizations endorsed the concept. Robert Burnette, a Lakota from Rosebud, and Reuben Snake, Winnebago, served as co-chairmen. Anita Collins, Paiute-Shoshone, was secretary and LaVonne Weller, a Caddo and president of the National Indian Youth Council, was treasurer.

On arrival in the capital, around four-hundred members of the caravan peacefully entered the Bureau of Indian Affairs building while their representatives went to negotiate with BIA officials regarding the demonstration. Within a short time, BIA security guards attempt to force the Indians to leave the building. They refused, insisting they would wait for information about the negotiations. When the guards began clubbing the demonstrators, the Indians resisted and forced the guards out of the building. The Indians secured the exits.

Although one aspiration of the caravan project was to garner media attention, they never imagined the scale of coverage that resulted. National attention focused on the event, and public support for the Indians was overwhelming.

After two days, with the Indians still occupying the BIA building, having renamed it "The Native American Embassy," White House representatives agreed to study and respond to the Twenty Points. The Indians vacated the building on November ninth, the White House having promised that no criminal charges would follow. The government provided over $60,000 for the Indians to return to their homes in various parts of the country.

Significantly, the National Tribal Chairmen's Association (NCTA), created under the Nixon administration and federally funded, vehemently opposed the Trail of Broken Treaties, but strongly supported the Longest Walk a decade later. What happened between the two events, both of which were organized and participated in by the very same Indian people? The organization and persistence of the Indian people had come to transform the government entity, and it became a viable reality.

An outcome, ultimately in response to the Twenty Points, was the federal establishment of the American Indian Policy Review Commission, which issued its final report in 1977. The report expressed the essence of the Twenty Points and continues to be accepted as fundamental federal Indian policy. The commission concluded:

> Sovereignty means the authority to govern; to exercise those powers necessary to maintain an orderly society ... the power to enact laws; the power to establish court systems; the power to require people to abide by established laws; the power to tax; the power to grant marriages and divorces; the power to provide for the adoption of children; the power to zone property; the power to regulate hunting and fishing ... When we talk about tribal sovereignty, thus, we are saying a very simple but deeply fundamental thing: Indian Tribes are governments.

Despite setbacks and continued struggle for full Indian treaty and human rights, the Trail of Broken Treaties caravan and the Twenty Points reformulated the terms of the debate, and those terms are no longer in question.

Roxanne Dunbar Ortiz

***See also* American Indian Movement; American Indian Policy Review Commission; Government Policy; Red Power; Treaties**

Further Reading

Akwesasne Notes. *BIA, I'm Not Your Indian Any More: Trail of Broken Treaties*. Mohawk Nation via Rooseveltown, NY: Akwesasne Notes, 1973.

American Indian Policy Review Commission, Final Report. Washington, DC: U.S. Government Printing Office, 1977.

Burnette, Robert, with John Koster. *The Road to Wounded Knee*. New York, NY: Bantam Books, 1974.

Deloria, Vine, Jr. *Behind the Trail of Broken Treaties: An Indian Declaration of Independence.* New York, NY: Delta Books, 1974.

Forbes, Jack. *Native Americans and Nixon: Presidential Politics and Minority Self-Determination, 1969–1972.* Los Angeles: American Indian Studies Center, University of California, 1981.

TREATIES

History

Indian nations engaged in diplomatic relations long before the coming of the Europeans. The Five Nations Confederacy (today the Six Nations), the Council of the Three Fires (Ottawa, Chippewa, and Potawatomi), and the Seven Fires of the Dakota give evidence of sophisticated diplomatic activity in prediscovery times. French and English colonial officials recognized and used the Indian format for reaching agreements and both "covenant chains" and wampum belts were used to record agreements between these nations and the Indian nations with whom they had relationships.

English colonial treaties consisted of military alliances with larger Indian nations, and land purchase agreements with small nations and subdivisions of the larger groups. Treaties would take as long as six weeks to complete since the primary format was discussion of the points of contention and agreement on a course of action. Some treaties made by the southern colonies were put into a formal legal document, but on the whole treaties became the recorded speeches and promises of the Indian and English representatives who did the bargaining. With the outbreak of the Revolutionary War, the continental Congress authorized representatives of the respective states to negotiate treaties of neutrality on their behalf. Every effort was made to secure the American frontier from combined English and Indian attacks. Only in New England was this policy very successful.

In September 1778 at Pittsburgh, the Delawares made a treaty with the United States that was written in formal legal style and language. This treaty has been understood as marking a new phase in the American political relationship with Indian nations, because its terms are precise and capable of specific interpretation by judicial authorities. The formal documentary recording of agreements has since characterized the treaty relationship.

In the post-Revolutionary period, Spain became an active competitor with the United States for Indian loyalties and adopted the American format of formal documents outlining rights and duties in treaties. Mexico, following its successful move for independence, also adopted the American format as did the Russians on the West Coast. Mexican treaties with the American Indian tribes continued until 1875. American states, visiting dignitaries, fur trapping companies, and religious and ethnic colonies also adopted the formal document in their dealings with Indians.

Even before the end of the Revolution, some Indian nations had adopted the written document to record their traditional relationships. Railroad and irrigation companies in the closing decades of the nineteenth century also used the written format, so we have a rather complete record of Indian political relationships with a wide variety of other entities.

The list of Indian treaties, ratified and unratified, provides a guide to the diplomatic activities of the United States with the indigenous peoples. Post-Revolutionary treaties were designed to bring peace to the frontier and transfer the loyalties of the Indians from Great Britain to the United States. Between 1783 and 1809, we see great efforts to restrict Indian nations living east of the Mississippi, and to ensure that the river itself is open to navigation and trade. The Treaty of Ghent, signed December 24, 1814, ended the War of 1812 and required Great Britain and the United States to make peace treaties with the Indian allies of the other country. The United States exploited this requirement and made new treaties with Indian nations living in remote areas on the Missouri and other western rivers.

By 1818 the sentiment in the United States was to remove the eastern Indian tribes west of the Mississippi River, and treaties were made with fragments of the larger nations, particularly the Cherokees, the Miamis, and Ohio Indians, and the Ottawa and Chippewa, to do so. Generally, the treaties made between 1818 and 1835 can be understood as implementing this sentiment and the Treaty of New Echota of 1835, which resulted in the traumatic removal of the major portion of the Cherokee region to Oklahoma, is generally regarded as completing the first effort to remove Indians from the path of American settlement.

The end of the Mexican War and the settlement of the Oregon boundary produced a tidal wave of Indian treaties as the United States aggressively sought to confirm its claim to lands within what is now our continental boundary. Treaty commissions were sent to California and the Pacific Northwest, territorial officials in the Southwest made treaties with the major Indian nations in that region, the Plains Indians met at Fort Laramie for the great Horse Creek Treaty, and in Minnesota two treaties virtually confiscated that area from the Sioux and Chippewa. Many of these 1850s treaties provided for continuing hunting and fishing rights and identified the homelands of tribes. Other treaties such as the 1854 Omaha treaty and the 1855 Michigan treaty attempted to deal with the allotment of lands and the civilization of individual Indians.

The Civil War provided another impetus for treaty-making. In the West, the war was used as an excuse to force Indians from the rich farming and grazing lands, and to open areas for mining and timber exploitation. Many of the massacres of Indians occurred in conjunction with frontier contentions that the Indians were siding with the Confederacy and therefore should be punished. When the Civil War ended, the western frontier was ablaze and a "Peace Commission" consisting of several Civil War generals, most notably William Tecumseh Sherman, and members of Congress, made a series of treaties with the Plains and Mountain Indians from 1867 to 1868. These treaties have since proven to be objects of great controversy because of their sweeping promises of self-government and annuities.

In 1871 the House of Representatives attached a rider to an appropriation act prohibiting the president from recognizing any more Indian nations as having the capability to make treaties with the United States. The rider became the subject of great debate because the Senate saw the condition as unconstitutional and as limiting the power of the president to conduct diplomatic activities. Nevertheless, the Senate receded on the provision and it became law. The executive branch continued to make treaties with Indian nations; Congress continued to authorize treaty commissions to go to specific Indian reservations and seek land cessions and other concessions, and Congress now ratified these treaties by simply incorporating their texts into federal statutes. This practice continued until 1911 and was used, after the General Allotment Act of 1887, to secure Indian agreement to accept allotment of lands and sale of surplus to the government for white homesteaders.

Formal agreements with Indian nations became sporadic and rare between 1911 and 1950 and were generally informal documents or just general council meetings at which the majority of an Indian nation signified its agreement with a proposal from the Congress or the executive branch. Between 1950—when the Cheyenne River Sioux made an agreement to cede lands for the building of dams on the Missouri River—and 1971, when the Alaska Natives agreed to settle all claims to lands in Alaska in return for certain privileges, lands, and compensation, almost all legislation was dependent upon the Indian approval of its contents, although no formal requirement was recognized as being legally necessary.

Since 1971 it has been the practice of the federal government to negotiate settlements with Indian nations in lieu of making a formal treaty or passing unilaterally composed legislation. The settlement act is thus the modern equivalent of the old treaty proceedings. Under a number of recent laws, most particularly the Indian Child Welfare Act of 1978 and the Indian Gaming Regulatory Act of 1988, states and Indian nations have been required to draw up "compacts," which perform the same legal and political function as treaties and agreements. Already there are discussions in a number of the larger Indian nations, particularly those which have been divided into a number of reservations, of renegotiating the treaties and creating a modern legal/political relationship that will be easier to administer and which will spell out rights and responsibilities clearly. Treaties thus remain the most important single device for establishing the unique relationship between American Indians and the United States.

The Status of Indian Treaties

The Constitution declares that treaties are the supreme law of the land and this general description has always been foremost in considering the methods and procedures whereby treaties are understood. Indian nations are not directly mentioned in conjunction with the treaty-making power, but it was standard practice at the beginning of the Republic to deal with Indian nations through treaties and, with the exception of the prohibition on the president's power to recognize political entities for treaty-making purposes, it has never been challenged.

It is important to understand that through treaties, a nation can perform diplomatic functions and promise laws in ways that would be unconstitutional if they were proposed as routine matter of internal law. *Missouri v. Holland* (1919) determined that the Migratory Bird Convention signed with Great Britain enabled the federal government to assume responsibility for migratory birds within the borders of the constituent states even though common law traditions had allocated that subject to the control of the states. A similar doctrine has often been applied with respect to Indian treaties, and the relationship which they have established between Indian nations and the United States, and has been described by courts as "political" and not racial, thus freeing Congress to deal with subjects in a perfunctory manner. Were the Indian relationship not described as "political," Congress would run afoul of constitutional provisions prohibiting discrimination on the basis of race, and perhaps even religion.

This ability of Congress to deal exclusively with Indians has been described as "plenary" in *Lone Wolf v. Hitchcock* (1903) and has resulted in persistent violation of treaty provisions by Congress under the guise of exercising a larger "trust" function with respect to Indians. In general, federal state courts have upheld treaty provisions except in those instances where they have come into direct conflict with later acts of Congress. Thus while courts declare that treaties have "dignity," which is to say, they are to be regarded as valid law at the federal level, treaties are inevitably subject to the political manipulations of Congress and therefore, like all other treaties with foreign countries or groups of countries, Indian treaties have a certain political vulnerability, which ordinary domestic statutes lack.

Over the years the courts have evolved certain kinds of legal doctrines which suggest that the treaty occupies a certain elevated status superior to that of a domestic statute, and consequently most practicing attorneys, elected officials, and Indian leaders go out of their way to deal specifically with treaty provisions. The most basic doctrine is that courts will not go beyond the written evidence to inquire into the validity of treaties. This attitude does much injury to Indian rights when there is clear evidence that the treaty was fraudulent, but it does provide a barrier against unwarranted attack on the treaty itself. Generally, careful historical research can provide the proper context for treaty interpretation, so that in spite of the fraudulent actions of the government a century ago, some measure of justice can be done.

More important in protecting both Indians and their treaties is the doctrine that the movement of rights and benefits in a treaty is from the Indian nation to the United States. Thus, whatever is not specifically surrendered by the Indians at a treaty session is presumed to remain with the Indian nation. This doctrine protects the Indians against the implied erosion of status and rights and helps to dispel the belief that the United States "gave" Indians their land and privileges. This doctrine also proves useful in making the treaties relevant legal documents, since the treaty can be understood, like the United States Constitution, as containing powers that are inherent and not articulated until they are needed.

An additional doctrine, not always followed by the courts or Congress, is the idea that the latest document in time controls the interpretation of the earlier document. Thus a later statute is believed to overrule or amend an earlier treaty and vice-versa. Technically the latest treaty which an Indian nation possesses has the effect of excluding it from previous general legislation. This problem is usually resolved by political means and not by judicial interpretation.

Finally, many treaty texts use deliberately vague language such as "free and undisturbed use of the land," and these phrases are impossible for courts to interpret accurately. They do, however, provide a background in which the United States is charged with upholding the general spirit of the treaty. In some instances, the promise of an education without further elucidation is interpreted today as covering all forms and levels of education, thereby bringing to the Indians a more comprehensive benefit than was perhaps originally intended. These general phrases act to keep the moral diplomatic obligation of the treaty on a high level and enhance its status.

Indian Treaty "Rights"

Federal legal doctrines articulating procedures and describing specific rights, such as hunting and fishing, civil and criminal jurisdiction, and educational and other social services, seem to balance almost precisely with a slight inclination in favor of the Indian tribes. Treaty rights are thus enforceable in federal and state courts, most particularly when they deal with property of the tribal group, and in almost every instance where they deal with hunting, fishing, and gathering rights. Jurisdictional protections and rights to self-government, at least since the adoption of new constitutions which require the supervision and approval of the secretary of the interior, became extremely complicated issues, and tribes do not always prevail in these cases, because the judiciary is rarely knowledgeable enough to comprehend the nature of the legal issue being posed.

The concern of many people is that the "rights" under treaty be recognized and affirmed; this part of treaty law is badly misunderstood by most people. There are three basic kinds of rights contained in every treaty: corporate or national, individual, and property rights. Corporate or national rights consist in preserving the political identity of the community, its right to self-government, and to continued recognition and negotiations. Some rights to hold property, usually real property, are also corporate rights. In *Choate v. Trapp* (1912), the Supreme Court held that the right to hold property in common was itself a property.

Individual rights under treaties usually consist of becoming eligible for allotments, receiving special reservations of land or specific sums in lieu thereof, and floating privileges such as the right, at some point in the future, to choose land or get a per capita share of tribal assets and expatriate the Indian nation. In general, promises of educational, health, and other services are not regarded as individual rights, but as benefits due the Indian nation itself. Since these services are not specifically measured within the text of the treaty and depend upon congressional appropriations for fulfillment, they are not precisely regarded as rights in the sense that they can be enforced through court orders.

Property rights dovetail considerably with corporate rights, and yet in a sense are quite different. The right to hunt, fish, take maple syrup, gather wild rice, or use trees for tipi poles are all included in Indian treaties and are certainly property rights. But in order for individuals to avail themselves of these rights, it is necessary for the Indian government to take action to allocate the resources in a systematic manner.

During the period when Indian reservations were being set aside for Indian nations that had not signed treaties, there was some debate as to whether or not the Indians owned the natural resources on their reservations. After several false starts and bureaucratic bungling, it was ruled that all natural resources existing on the reservations did indeed belong to the Indians who inhabited it. A great deal of research is needed in order to clarify and affirm exactly what kinds of property belong to the Indians on a reservation, or are being described in a treaty. The 1868 treaty with the Sioux gives as the eastern border of the reserved lands the high-water mark of the east bank of the Missouri River. Presumably, that means the Sioux own the whole Missouri River, at least during its sojourn through South Dakota. Courts, Congress, and states attack broad treaty clauses such as this one because they refuse to believe that the Indians should have such a resource.

The increase of technology has placed a burden on the understanding and enforcement of treaty rights. Water rights are now broken down into surface and ground water components, and while it is clear that Indians have rights to water underneath them on the reservation, they are sometimes subjected to state water codes, which radically change the amount of water available and how they can use it. Oil and gas, minerals, and timber are clearly the property of Indians through treaty and through the establishment of reservations. Rights to engage in commercial fishing and rice gathering are generally regarded as originating in treaties, but because these resources are also supervised outside the reservations by state agencies, Indian nations must devote an extraordinary amount of funds to protect this kind of property.

Summary

In recent years the belief in a homogenous federal Indian law, carefully cultivated as a doctrine by Felix S. Cohen in his famous *Handbook of Federal Indian Law*, has been challenged, and the once rigid boundaries placed around the interpretation of Indian treaties has relaxed considerably. Consequently no hard and fast rules of interpretation can be given at the present time. When this shift in emphasis in federal Indian law is coupled with the movement toward renegotiating relationships through settlement acts, only rough approximations of law can be given. Suffice it to say that Indian treaties remain at the very pinnacle of importance in the lives and fortunes of all Indian nations today.

Vine Deloria, Jr.

See also **Fishing and Hunting Rights; Land Claims; Law; Sovereignty and Jurisdiction**

Further Reading

Cohen, Felix S. *Handbook of Federal Indian Law.* Washington, DC: U.S. Government Printing Office, 1942.

Gilbert, Bil. *God Save Us This Country: Tekamthi and the First American Civil War.* New York, NY: Atheneum, 1989.

Jones, Dorothy V. *License for Empire: Colonialism by Treaty in Early America.* IL: University of Chicago Press, 1982.

Jones, Douglas C. *The Treaty of Medicine Lodge: The Story of the Great Treaty Council as Told by Eyewitnesses.* Norman: University of Oklahoma Press, 1985.

TREATY COUNCIL

See International Indian Treaty Council

TRIBAL COLLEGES

Tribally controlled colleges are created and administered by Native Americans. Usually located on reservations, the colleges serve students and communities by emphasizing economic development and cultural awareness. These colleges emerged out of the movement for Native American self-determination. Arguing that past efforts to educate American Indians failed both students and Indian societies, creation of Indian-controlled institutions was proposed by a growing number of tribal leaders and Indian educators during the 1960s.

Guy Gorman, Allen Yazzie, and Dr. Ned Hatathli were among the many people on the Navajo Reservation who promoted the idea of an Indian-controlled college for their community early in that decade. In California, Jack Forbes, along with Navajo artist Carl Gorman, were pursuing the idea of an American Indian university. On the Rosebud Sioux Reservation, Stanley Red Bird and Gerald Mohatt helped generate interest in a tribally controlled college for their reservation.

The first tribal college was eventually founded on the Navajo Reservation in 1968. Frustrated by the high failure rate of Navajo students who went off the reservation to enter college, tribal leaders created their own two-year institution, Navajo Community College. Because it was located within the reservation, students would have fewer of the financial and emotional pressures that many experienced when entering a college or university away from home. Equally important was the college's effort to insert traditional Navajo values in its organization and curriculum.

The Navajo institution was soon followed by other tribal or Indian controlled institutions. In 1990 there were twenty-four tribally controlled colleges in the United States. All colleges offer associate degrees but two colleges, Oglala Lakota College and Sinte Gleska College, now offer bachelor's programs. Recently, Sinte Gleska also began offering an accredited master's program in elementary education. The institutions are located from North Dakota to Arizona, and from California to Michigan. Most are in the northern Plains states (see listing which follows).

The typical tribal college is housed in a collection of donated, rented, or temporary buildings that are, at best, adequate. Little Big Horn College is based in a former gymnasium; the basketball court has become the library and a shower room is now a science lab. Down the road is a former sewer treatment plant, now used by the college as a chemistry lab. Although a new campus is now being built, Fort Berthold Community College's offices and classrooms were for most of its history scattered along a several block section of New Town, North Dakota. There, the basement of the post office was rented for classroom space. Other colleges have buildings that were renovated or constructed by students from their building trades program. Sinte Gleska College has several classrooms and a bookstore that were built in this way.

A few tribal colleges have more spacious facilities. Navajo Community College, for example, has a large campus in the center of the Navajo Reservation that features a six-story administration building designed to be reminiscent of the traditional Navajo structure, the hogan. Surrounding this building are dormitories, classrooms, a gym, and a student center.

But even at the best equipped tribal college, facilities are being strained by climbing student enrollment. In 1981, for example, there was a total full-time equivalent of 1,689 Indian students enrolled in tribally controlled colleges. In 1989, however, the number grew to 5,788, with a total enrollment of approximately 11,000 full- and part-time students. In 1991, total full- and part-time enrollment had climbed to approximately 14,000.

Still, most of the colleges remain small. The largest institution, Navajo Community College, enrolled 3,804 students in 1989. Oglala Lakota College, the second largest, enrolled 1,756 that same year. But most other institutions enroll under 1,000 students; in 1989 Cheyenne River Community College had the fewest students, with 287 enrolling.

Most students are Native American and live in the college's reservation community. As a group, they are older; the average age at many institutions is between thirty and thirty-five. Most, too, are women, many of whom are single parents.

Most presidents and top administrators are Native American, and at all colleges the majority of board members are from the tribe. Most faculty, however, are not Indian, reflecting a shortage of Indians with graduate degrees and the unwillingness of those who are qualified to work at the low pay scales at most colleges.

Tribal colleges differ from other American colleges and universities because they must work to reflect the unique needs of their communities, and making traditional Native American values a part of their curricula and campus environments. Arguing that past efforts to educate Native Americans failed because they did not recognize the economic and cultural needs of their students, tribal colleges work to be responsive to both.

First, each provides a curriculum that celebrates the traditional Indian culture of its students. Not seen as just another area of study, Native American traditions and values are at the heart of each tribal college's structure and identity. All colleges, for example, offer courses in their tribe's language, art, and philosophy. Some, including Blackfeet Community College in Montana, sponsor annual cultural camps where students, tribal members, and visitors can experience what it was like to live in a traditional Indian encampment and earn college credit in the process. Other institutions, stressing the relevance of Native culture in contemporary society, attempt to insert tribal values into every class, including math, science, and business. Turtle Mountain Community College and Navajo Community College have been leaders in the movement to integrate traditional and Western educational models in the classroom.

Colleges also emphasize culture in the services they offer to students. Recognizing that many of their students are unfamiliar with the goals of higher education and are uncomfortable working in a bureaucracy—even one as small as a tribal college—most institutions offer classes in college life, and stress the need for individual counseling.

College administrators know that their students face practical barriers to finishing a degree. Because many reservations are geographically isolated and offer few social services, students may miss class and even drop out because a car needs repair or there is no one to care for their children. Although resources are limited, many colleges offer day care and provide transportation to the college. At least one president visits the homes of students who suddenly stop attending class.

Second, tribal colleges offer training for tribal needs. While courses at these institutions range from certificates in welding to a master's degree in elementary education, each college's curriculum is based on the understanding that most tribal members cannot or do not want to leave their reservation community. Instead, the colleges tailor their course offerings to the needs and opportunities that exist in their communities. The result is that most students who complete a program at a tribal college find employment. A 1989 survey of six colleges found that while reservation unemployment rates can range from 50 to 85 percent, only 12 to 17 percent of tribal college graduates were unemployed.

Third, tribal colleges sponsor research and development programs that directly benefit their reservations. Believing that their responsibility extends into the larger reservation community, all work to generate economic development and combat debilitating social ills. Some work directly with area industries to provide training and research. Little Hoop Community College, for example, works closely with a tribal manufacturing plant that produces a bullet-resistant material for the military, helping it to find a broader market for the product. Others support literacy tutoring and alcohol awareness programs.

A number of colleges also sponsor institutes for the study of community needs. Believing that the history and traditional culture of the northern Plains were not being adequately studied, Sisseton Wahpeton College created an Institute for the Study of Dakota Culture in 1991. Little Big Horn College, meanwhile, supports the Institute for Families and Children which has sponsored meetings on community development and education policy.

In these ways, tribal colleges, unlike most community colleges, also act as research institutions. According to one president, tribal colleges provide for the research and development needs of their tribal nations in the same way the country's large research universities provide the needs of the United States.

Development of tribal colleges and their programs is hampered by a lack of money. Unlike public community colleges, tribal colleges receive little or no state support. Grants from foundations and corporations, while important, do not cover the operating costs of a college. Instead, most tribal colleges rely on federal support through the Tribally Controlled Community College Act of 1978. The money distributed to each college from this act is critical to the survival and growth of the institutions. In addition, the Navajo Community College Act is legislation specifically for that institution and is equally important to its survival.

The Navajo legislation provides money according to need, while the Tribally Controlled Community College Act, under which most tribal colleges are funded, distributes money according to each institution's enrollment. The amount of money dis-

TRIBAL COLLEGES

North Dakota

Fort Berthold Community College, New Town
Little Hoop Community College, Fort Totten
Standing Rock College, Fort Yates
Turtle Mountain Community College, Belcourt
United Tribes Technical College, Bismarck

South Dakota

Cheyenne River Community College, Eagle Butte
Oglala Lakota College, Kyle
Sinte Gleska College, Rosebud
Sisseton-Wahpeton Community College, Sisseton

Montana

Blackfeet Community College, Browning
Dull Knife Memorial College, Lame Deer
Fort Belknap Community College, Harlem

Fort Peck Community College, Poplar
Little Big Horn College, Crow Agency
Salish Kootenai College, Pablo
Stone Child Community College, Box Elder

Other States

Bay Mills Community College, Brimley, Michigan
Crownpoint Institute of Technology,
Crownpoint, New Mexico
D-Q University, Davis, California
Fond Du Lac Community College, Cloquet, Minnesota
Navajo Community College, Tsaile, Arizona
Nebraska Indian Community College,
Winnebago, Nebraska
Northwest Indian College, Bellingham, Washington
Lac Courte Oreilles Ojibwa Community College,
Hayward, Wisconsin

tributed under both acts fluctuates from year to year, but has not kept pace with the rapidly climbing enrollments at most colleges. While the act authorizes payment of $5,820 for each Indian student count, a figure based on an institution's total Indian enrollment, this has never been higher than $3,100 and dropped to $1,964 in 1989.

The colleges work together as the American Indian Higher Education Consortium, to which all tribally controlled colleges belong. They support the cost of a small Washington, D.C. office which monitors legislation relevant to the colleges. The consortium also sponsors *Tribal College: Journal of American Indian Higher Education*, a quarterly magazine that includes scholarship on Indian education, information about the work of the colleges, and articles on the social and economic needs of the Indian society.

In addition, the colleges have also created the American Indian College Fund. Based in New York City, this new project is building an endowment and scholarship fund for the colleges and their students.

Paul Boyer

See also Educational Policy; Higher Education

Further Reading

Carnegie Foundation for the Advancement of Teaching. *Tribal Colleges: Shaping the Future of Native America.* Princeton, NJ: The Foundation, 1989.

Forbes, Jack. *Native American Higher Education: The Struggle for the Creation of D-Q University, 1960–1961.* Davis, CA: D-Q University Press, 1985.

Stein, Wayne. "A History of Tribally Controlled Community Colleges: 1968–1978." Ph.D. diss., Washington State University, 1988.

TRIBAL COURTS

See Tribal Governments

TRIBAL GOVERNMENTS

American Indian tribal governments, in what is now the United States, have existed for thousands of years in some form or another. Like all governments, these early governing structures provided for defense and public safety, allocated resources, and provided for the welfare of their people. The structures and processes of the governments varied depending upon the environment and the needs of the people.

Small bands of the Great Basin states and the California region, for example, were simple, generally composed of the adult or male members meeting in a general council. Decisions concerning where and when to hunt and forage, and when to conduct ceremonies, were decided almost daily. The tribes of the Northeast, Southeast, and Southwest were primarily agriculturalist, living in permanent villages, towns, and pueblos. The feasibility of staying in one place allowed for the development of more complicated and multi-leveled systems of governments. Two Indian governments in particular—the Iroquois Confederacy or Haudenosaunee, comprised of five (later six Indian nations) and the All Indian Pueblo Council, comprised of all the Pueblos—are centuries-old, making them the oldest political organizations in existence in North America.

Despite differing cultures, traditions, and government structures, many (although not all) traditional tribal governments reflected and reinforced similar cultural values of cooperation, responsibility to the community, harmony, and spirituality. Many tribes were democratic, employing systems of checks and balances, so as to prevent abuses of power. Among the Iroquois, for example, the men ruled, but it was the clan mothers who ultimately decided which men were qualified to rule. The Muskogees of the Southeast divided their communities into two moieties, one devoted to war and the other to peace, thereby ensuring a balance between these two proclivities.

Tribal governments, responding to external and internal pressures generated by their interaction with non-Indians, changed most dramatically in the 1800s. The degree of evolution depended on the circumstances and nature of the tribe's contact with non-Indians. Every tribe responded differently. The Indian nations of the Southeast reacted to pressure from white settlers who wanted their lands by adopting many of the political and social institutions of their non-Indian neighbors. The Pueblos of the Southwest erected public governments to deal with outsiders, leaving important tribal matters in the hands of the traditional theocracy. The Lakotas' response was most generally typified by armed resistance.

Opposition, however, for most tribes, proved ineffective. By the turn of the century, the federal government had effectively emasculated the powers of the majority of tribal governments. The Bureau of Indian Affairs (BIA) superintendent or agent on reservations had assumed most of the tribal governing responsibilities. The paternalistic agent distributed rations, handled the tribe's finances, and managed programs aimed at the assimilation of his wards into the white man's culture. Towards this end, the BIA constructed schools to teach "civilization" and English, established courts of Indian offenses, and created Indian police forces to enforce the non-Indians' laws. The practice of one's tribal ceremonies and religion could bring a prison term of ten days. Bureau regulations forbid many traditional practices, including Indian marriages, burial practices, and the wearing of long hair by men.

The government's move to assimilate Indians as individuals into the American mainstream continued unabated until the mid-1930s. In 1933 John Collier was appointed as commissioner of the BIA. A strong advocate of allowing tribes to solve their own problems without government paternalism, he persuaded Congress in 1934 to pass the Wheeler-Howard Act, or as it is commonly referred to, the Indian Reorganization Act (IRA). Although not passed as Collier originally conceived, the legislation provided for the adoption of tribal governmental structures and the provision of economic development loans from a revolving loan fund.

Supporters have hailed the IRA with preventing the total demise of tribal governments by providing a mechanism whereby tribes were able to reinstate governments and regain some control over their futures. Critics have argued that the legislation continued the assimilation process by not resuscitating traditional governments, but by imposing tribal constitutions and governments which reflected non-Indian or Western political values. According to the terms of the legislation, tribes had to vote against acceptance of the act's provision. Tribes who chose not to vote, such as the Hopi, who declined on cultural grounds, were nonetheless considered bound by the legislation.

Hence, modern tribal governments represent a wide range of governing structures. Today, more than half of all tribal governments are constituted under the provisions of the IRA, or according to similar acts, such as the Oklahoma Indian Welfare Act of 1936 or the Alaska Native Claims Settlement Act of 1971. Several Indian nations, such as the Onondaga, the Seneca of New York, many Alaskan villages, and some of the Pueblos have retained their traditional systems. The large Navajo Nation, as well, voted against the provisions of the IRA and today possesses a modified form of its traditional governments.

All federally recognized tribal governments today, despite their form of government, are recognized by the federal and state governments as possessing inherent sovereignty. The United States' recognition of tribal sovereignty is implicitly inferred from the United States' decision to negotiate more than 370 treaties and agreements with Indian nations and tribes, and is explicitly recognized in hundreds of Supreme Court cases, dating from as early as 1830. Tribes are recognized as quasi-sovereign domestic dependent nations. As sovereigns, tribes possess the right to govern their own affairs, including the authority to structure their governments; to regulate membership; to maintain justice; to provide for public safety and welfare; to develop tribal economies and regulate businesses; and to tax. As inherent sovereigns, these governing powers are not powers given to tribes by the federal government, but are powers of government that tribes have possessed from time immemorial.

As of 1990 the federal government recognized 321 tribes in the lower 48 states and 210 Alaska Native governments. In addition, there are several state recognized and over 100 nonfederally recognized tribes. Hence, describing the characteristics and structures of modern tribal governments is virtually impossible, as the variety of tribal governments is equal to the number of tribes. The political description that follows represents and includes only the most common of governmental features.

The most important distinction between most tribal governments and those of the federal and state governments is in the apportionment of the executive, legislative, and judicial functions of government. Whereas the federal and state governments have a clear delineation of authorities, tribal governments more frequently combine the executive and legislative functions into one branch—the tribal council. Some councils, especially those representing small tribes, may also function as the judicial branch. Although many, if not most, tribes operate according to constitutions provided and sanctioned by the BIA, it is this lack of a separation of powers and a system of checks and balances that has generated the most public criticism of tribal governments.

It is the tribal council (or legislature, or business committee) which governs the tribe. Tribal council members are elected at-large or by district, depending on the size of the reservation. Some tribes, such as the Warm Springs of Oregon and Miccosukee of

Florida, include on their councils both elected members and traditional clan representation.

The executive branch usually consists of an elected head (called chief, or governor, or president, depending upon the tribe), an assistant head, a secretary, and a treasurer. These executive officers may be elected by the tribal electorate or elected by the council from among its own membership.

It is in the operation of the judicial branch that one finds the most variety amongst tribal governments. Tribal court systems vary widely depending upon the tribe's size, resources and cultural orientation. As mentioned, the tribal constitutions of small tribes may invest the judicial function in their councils. If a separate court system exists, the council may act as an appellate court. Larger tribes may possess separate courts to hear criminal, civil, juvenile, or appeals. In recent years, some tribal governments, such as those of the Lakota Nation and tribes of western Oklahoma, have formed jointly operating supreme courts. Whether the appellate court is invested with judicial review, i.e., the right to declare council legislation illegal, depends upon the tribal constitution or bylaws.

The laws applied and the jurisdiction of the tribal courts vary according to the tribal constitutions and the tribal laws passed by the council. The Dene Nation, or Navajo tribe, for example, has passed more than twenty codes, ranging from laws dealing with zoning and commercial transactions, to those covering juveniles. Some tribal courts specifically recognize and apply traditional laws and customs in their decision making. The San Juan Pueblo offers its members a choice between having their dispute resolved according to traditional law, or the more non-Indian adversarial judicial forum.

Tribal court systems, of which there are more than one hundred forty in existence, have improved dramatically in recent years. Organizations such as the National American Indian Court Judges Association and the National Indian Justice Center have assisted in the training of tribal court judges.

Tribes protect their lands and maintain justice amongst their members by the exercise of criminal and civil jurisdiction. Over the last hundred years, the federal government has gnawed away at the tribes' once exclusive jurisdiction over its land and people by assuming increased jurisdiction for itself and the states. The implementation of criminal jurisdiction on reservations is today a very complex process of differing and concurrent jurisdictions.

In 1885 Congress passed the Major Crimes Act. Originally covering seven major crimes, the Act now provides the federal government with authority over the prosecution of Indians committing murder; manslaughter; kidnapping; rape; carnal knowledge of any female not the perpetrator's wife and who is under sixteen years of age; assault resulting in serious bodily harm; assault with intent to commit rape; incest; assault with intent to commit murder; assault with a dangerous weapon; arson; burglary; robbery; and larceny.

Congress further complicated tribal jurisdiction over criminal acts with the passage of Public Law 280 in 1953. Although the act did not divest tribes of their authority over lesser crimes, the legislation allowed five states, California, Minnesota, Nebraska, Oregon, and Wisconsin, to assume criminal and civil jurisdiction over Indians and non-Indians on reservations. Another bill, the Indian Civil Rights Act of 1968, has further impacted the administration of justice on reservations. The act's primary function is to ensure that tribal members possess most of the federal bill of rights protection vis-à-vis their governments. The act also prohibited tribes from incarcerating any individual in jail for longer than six months and charging more than $500 in fines—penalties which Congress increased in 1986 to one year in jail and/or $5,000 in fines.

Two court cases have further limited tribal authority in the area of criminal jurisdiction. In 1978, the Supreme Court ruled in *Oliphant v. Suquamish Indian Tribe* that the tribal exercise of criminal jurisdiction over two non-Indians committing crimes within reservation boundaries was inconsistent with their status as domestic dependent nations. In 1990, the Supreme Court in the *Duro v. Reina* case expanded this reasoning to include not only non-Indians, but any nontribal members, whether Indian or not.

Both decisions have impaired tribal sovereignty by limiting important tribal governing authority. Heretofore, the courts had recognized that tribes possessed the authority to exercise all powers of government unless ceded in a treaty, or expressly removed by Congress in legislation. The courts have now added a third criteria for limiting tribal authority: the exercise of any power considered inconsistent with tribal status as domestic dependent nations. Exactly what authorities the courts will determine to be "inconsistent with tribal status as domestic dependent nations," remains unclear.

Tribal authority over civil jurisdiction within reservation boundaries remains more intact, but also no longer exclusive. Tribes continue to possess jurisdiction over Indians and non-Indians in such areas as zoning; family relations, including marriage, divorce, adoption, and the care of juveniles; and the settlement of civil damage suits. The states have gained control over some actions by non-Indians, such as the regulation of hunting and fishing rights on non-Indian lands within reservation boundaries—a ruling which has made the management of wildlife on reservations difficult.

Tribes have fared considerably better in gaining jurisdiction over adoption and foster child care proceedings of tribal children. In the mid-1970s, a study showed that approximately one-fourth of all Indian children were being raised in non-Indian homes. In 1978, strong lobbying efforts by tribes and national Indian organizations such as the National Congress of American Indians and the National Tribal Chairmen's Association, resulted in the passage of the important Indian Child Welfare Act. According to the provisions of the act, tribes have the authority over state courts to determine adoption and child care provisions for their children.

Also in 1978 the Supreme Court affirmed in the *Santa Clara Pueblo v. Martinez* decision that tribes possessed the authority to determine who their children are, i.e, to define their own membership, or tribal citizenry. The case considered the right of the Santa Clara Pueblo to admit as members only those children born to enrolled fathers. The court, in a ruling supporting tribal culture and traditions, ruled that tribal membership laws were not subject to federal equal protection laws.

Enrollment is usually determined by one or a combination of the following requirements: blood quantum; descendancy; or through the paternal or maternal line. The Yakima of Washington, for example, adhere to perhaps the most common requirement, the possession of one-quarter tribal blood. The Cherokee and Muskogee Creek of Oklahoma enroll individuals who can prove descendancy to persons on a set of historic Dawes Land Allotment rolls. The Onondaga Nation, one of the original members of the Iroquois Confederacy, enroll only children born to enrolled mothers.

In 1975 Congress passed a second important piece of Indian legislation in the twentieth century, the Indian Self-Determination and Education Assistance Act. Stating the government's intent "to strengthen the Indian's sense of autonomy without threatening his sense of community," President Richard Nixon proposed the passage of legislation that would allow the tribes to assume control over their own housing, law-enforcement, health, social service, education and community development programs. The congressional drafters intended for the Bureau's role to change from that of a controlling, paternalistic agency charged with running all aspects of reservation life, to a technical advisory agency, responsible for implementing the government's trust responsibility over Indian lands and resources—a goal that has been partially met today.

Since the act's passage, tribes have increasingly assumed responsibility over a multitude of services formerly administered by the Bureau. Although tribal services and programs vary widely, depending upon tribal resources and needs, education is an area of concern to all tribes. In an effort to improve on the statistics that indicate only 52 percent of Indians who enter high school graduate, tribes administer Head Start programs, after school programs, and provide some college and vocational scholarships.

Health care is another very important area of tribal concern. Tribes provide a variety of health programs, such as alcohol, nutrition, prenatal care, dental, and vision care programs. Some tribes are fortunate to have a tribal clinic or Indian hospital near them from where members can obtain medical care.

The future provision of social services, education, and health care programs is partially but intricately tied to the tribes' abilities to improve their economies. Economic development, however, is an all too often elusive objective. Many tribes live in rural areas without a sufficient infrastructure and far from adequate transportation and communication networks. These problems, combined with an unskilled and uneducated labor force, make it difficult to attract businesses.

The Navajo, Apache, and several other tribes are fortunate to possess mineral and energy resources which they are currently developing. Other tribes, such as the Warm Springs and Eastern Cherokees, have entered into the hotel and tourist business. The most profitable business venture of late in Indian country is Indian gaming. In 1987, the Supreme Court held that tribes possess the inherent sovereignty to engage in certain forms of gambling enterprises. Today more than one hundred tribes in twenty-four states have opened bingo halls with varying degrees of financial success.

The authority to tax is another inherent right of governmental sovereigns possessed by the federal and state governments as well as the tribal governments. The right to tax includes the levying of taxes on individuals, businesses, and resources within their reservation boundaries. For the most part, tribes have not utilized this authority. The Oglala Sioux have levied a tax on non-Indians working on the reservation. Other tribes, such as the Navajo and Apache, collect an excise tax on oil and gas taken from reservation lands.

Future tribal governments face many of the same challenges as other governments—the provision of a responsive and able governmental structure and leadership, the improvement of local economies, and the provision of services during difficult economic times. Tribal governments, however, possess an additional responsibility and complicated challenge: the necessity to provide governmental structures and services that reflect and enhance the values and needs of the membership, as well as being responsive to and protective of demands from the outside society. To achieve these objectives, tribes are increasingly coalescing their efforts with state governments and in intertribal and intergovernmental organizations.

In the past, states have presented the greatest threat to tribal existence. As society becomes more complex and interdependent, however, state and tribal governments increasingly cooperate to provide services and programs. For example, in an effort to provide better police protection, tribal police forces and local off-reservation police forces are cross-deputizing their officers, thereby ensuring the more complete protection of all area individuals.

Several tribes have formed regional or tribal coalitions, such as the Intertribal Council of California and the United Southeastern Tribes, which enable them to better service their individual tribes. National Indian organizations have and continue to be of importance in lobbying for Indian rights and goals. CERT, Council of Energy Resource Tribes, is a coalition of nearly forty tribes whose objective is the development of mineral and energy resources. NARF, Native American Rights Fund, is devoted to the protection and representation of Indian legal rights. NCAI, the National Congress of American Indians, functions primarily to lobby for Indian legislation and programs. Tribes are increasingly joining together politically at the international level as well, testifying before the United Nations Working Group on Indigenous Populations, in order to protect the rights of indigenous peoples world-wide.

Sharon O'Brien

See also **Civil Rights; Government Policy; Indian Reorganization Act; Sovereignty and Jurisdiction**

Further Reading

Lopach, James J., Margery Hunter Brown, and Richmond L. Clow. *Tribal Government Today: Politics on Montana Indian Reservations.* San Francisco, CA, Boulder, CO, and London, England: Westview Press, 1990.

O'Brien, Sharon. *American Indian Tribal Governments.* Norman: University of Oklahoma Press, 1989.

Parman, Donald L. *The Navajos and the New Deal.* New Haven, CT: Yale University Press, 1976.

Philp, Kenneth. *John Collier's Crusade for Indian Reform: 1920–1954.* Tucson: University of Arizona Press, 1977.

Philp, Kenneth, ed. *Indian Self-Rule: First Hand Accounts of Indian-White Relations from Roosevelt to Reagan.* Salt Lake City, UT: Howe Brothers, 1986.

TRIBAL MUSEUMS

At mid-century, strong social forces swept across the nation, altering forever the physical environment and the political and economic circumstances under which Native Americans lived. Among the forces were major policy redirections in trust responsibilities toward federally recognized Indian tribes and Alaska Natives, the civil rights movement, demographic shifts, and expanded transportation and communication systems. The changes disrupted centuries-old systems of human relationships through which Native communities had maintained and transmitted traditional cultures, and defined their identity.

The forces also contained new resources, ideas, and attitudes which generated in museums and cultural centers owned and operated by Native Americans. These institutions, commonly called tribal museums, are unique in nature and purpose as a result of the special autonomous status afforded indigenous people in the United States. Their growth and development mirrors rapidly changing needs and aspirations of tribal people and a resurgence in Native American consciousness. The museums' evolution correlates with the restructuring of tribal politics and economics, a process which transformed many

of the cultural roles and responsibilities traditionally held by families and clans, and reshaped them as tribal government functions.

Origins and Purposes

In 1981 approximately forty American Indian and Alaska Native museums and cultural centers in the United States and Canada met the professional definition of a museum. By 1992, the number grew to more than one hundred seventy-five legally organized facilities, most of which are located west of the Mississippi River. Additionally, numerous tribal historical and cultural programs in formative stages of institutional development exist.

Two concepts shape the rationale for establishing Native American operated museums: first is the basic democratic principle that groups have the right to define their own identity, and elements of culture are among the distinguishing factors; second are the social welfare responsibilities of government, which hold that modern nations have an obligation to identify and preserve their culture, and to utilize it in ways that benefit all community members.

The notion of tribal museums took hold in the 1960s because of grassroots efforts by individuals who, often independently of each other, sought methods for making sense out of their changed environment and maintaining their distinct identity. Also contributing were the effects of research into community history, such as that done by the Indian Claims Commission, the United States Office of Education Title III and VII, and Office of Economic Opportunity programs.

However, the idea to actually start a cultural organization in a community only emerges at that moment when heightened sensitivities intersect with critical local events and financial opportunities. Some specific catalysts are:

The impact of commercial development and archaeological excavations. The preservation of material culture is a primary motivation for creating facilities. The Makah Cultural and Research Center in Neah Bay, Washington, began because the tribe decided to store its archaeological collection on the reservation. Tribal museums are also created as a way to balance site conservation and tribal members' rights to privacy with the demands of tourism. The Pueblo of Acoma's Tourist and Visitation Center is a facility that brokers these conflicting needs. Legislation mandating repatriation and storage of archaeological materials continues to drive the need for repositories.

Strong desires to document a presence and to honor the past. The new conditions altered land usage, dispersed families, and led to natural resource disputes and loss of traditional skills. They obliterated community systems for conveying history and beliefs. Museums were selected because mainstream society recognizes them as places which give value and credit achievements. The rationale echoed turn-of-the-century beliefs that since Indians were "vanishing," their physical evidence should be preserved. Several institutions, including the Malki Museum in California and the Yakima Indian Nation Museum in Washington State, were started because collections were offered to the tribes.

Federal funding opportunities. Initiatives such as the Department of Commerce Economic Development Administration (EDA) program in the 1970s spurred development by supporting construction costs. Strategies focused on tourism. EDA encouraged tribes to use museums as assets for generating revenue and stimulating employment. The Gila River Indian Arts and Crafts Center in Arizona selected this approach. It consists of a recreational vehicle parking area, restaurant, performance platform, sales shop, and museum space. The bicentennial of the United States was another funding source. This initiative prompted the Oneida Nation in Wisconsin to build its museum.

Expanded visions for tribal museums as places to serve community, cultural, and educational needs. In the 1980s, the purposes for establishing institutions shifted slowly. Some changes were responses to new funding priorities and federal legislation affirming Native rights and cultural practices. But most reflected enormous increases in overall tribal knowledge about their own internal workings, and the desire to actively control their lives. Two decades of experience had exposed the significance of culture as the core element to give their society structure and meaning. The new perspectives, exemplified by the Colorado River Indian Tribes Museum in Arizona, include management for all aspects of cultural patrimony—objects, archives, language, physical sites, ceremonies—and for their integration into daily life.

Nature and Structure

Each institution's physical format, administrative structure, and programs differ relative to the organizing group's historical and cultural context and resources. Tribal museums vary widely in physical appearance. Some are newly built, while others are renovations of existing structures. They range in size from less than 1,000 to more than 30,000 square feet. Some structures are decorated with Indian motifs or are patterned after traditional building forms. Their locations are either near busy highways or in village areas. Placement reflects political decisions about the museum's purpose and primary audience, and a community's desired public image.

The facilities are financed by tribal government allocations, grants, entrance fees, and sales revenue. Often budgets are inconsistent, causing difficulties in recruiting and retaining staff and in maintaining services. The number of employees fluctuates widely due to seasonal demands and availability of funds. Generally, one or two people are hired full-time. Many facilities rely on job training opportunities to support temporary positions.

Four administrative categories are discernible:

Tribally operated institutions located on reservation land. Tribal councils set overall policies and procedures. A few have created separate boards, with final authority vested in tribal government. Some museums have advisory committees composed of community representatives and, occasionally, noncommunity members with subject expertise.

Pan-Indian operated cultural centers, often situated in urban areas. These are established to meet the cultural, recreational, and social needs of Indians from various tribal backgrounds who live in major cities, and to offer tourists an Indian viewpoint of history and a sales outlet for Native-made arts and crafts. They are legally incorporated not-for-profit, tax-exempt entities, which are guided by boards of directors, a majority of whom are Native Americans. The Daybreak Star Arts Center in Seattle is an example.

Native-controlled cultural organizations that are administratively and/or physically linked to "parent" institutions, which may or may not be Indian owned. Groups who do not have buildings negotiate space and install exhibitions in institutions with related goals. This category includes tribal college museums, such as the Atalona Lodge Museum at Bacone College, Oklahoma, and pan-Indian organizations, such as the Southeast Alaska Indian Cultural Center, which is located in a United States National Park Service building in Sitka.

Family or individually owned museums. These may be located on reservation land or on privately owned sites, and are nonprofit organizations. Exhibitions usually focus on the family who operates it. The Lenni Lenape Historical Society in Pennsylvania illustrates this type.

Tribal museums perform a broad range of functions in pursuit of their goals, including identification, preservation, documentation, research of collections, and presentation of public programs and exhibitions. The degree of involvement in each activity is determined by the purposes for which the museum was created and its resources.

Collections are similar to mainstream museums, but not as extensive in scope or quality. They consist of prehistoric artifacts; historic materials such as tools, weapons, and clothing; household and transportation equipment; musical instruments; recent memorabilia; and ceremonial regalia. If originals are unavailable, replicas and simulations are substituted. Because concepts of culture are integral to the practices of daily life, tribal museums do not make organizational distinctions between disciplines or professions. Activities such as archives, genealogy tracings, and language retention can be museum responsibilities. Increasingly, staff are conducting research. The Suquamish Museum and Cultural Center in Washington State is noted for pioneering methods which use photographs and oral traditions to stimulate and preserve community memories.

Permanent exhibitions, often designed and fabricated by non-Indian firms, occupy major portions of space. Themes focus on creation stories, adaptation and survival strategies, lifestyles before contact, patriotism and loyalty, artistic skills, and relationships with nature and neighbors.

Public programs provide guided tours, opportunities to view performances, and sometimes participatory experiences. Dependence on external funding often dictates that program efforts be geared to non-Indian audiences. However, instances of programming that interact with communities are expanding. In Alaska, the Kodiak Area Native Association links college and high school teachers with tribal elders to reintroduce, as part of the curriculum, training in traditional arts and crafts, such as kayak building. At the Zuni Pueblo, the museum project believes that raising community awareness about environmental issues is one of their important roles.

Impact and Challenges

Viewed narrowly, Native American museums and cultural centers are meeting their objectives as places to store artifacts and honor the past. These first decades have produced a foundation for understanding the broad issues facing tribal museums and for demonstrating possibilities. Moreover, when analyzed within the context of social upheaval, their very survival and proliferation is remarkable.

However, considered from the ultimate purpose—to help understand, practice, and transmit Indian culture and traditions—the reality is that many museums are marginal to the societies they profess to serve and represent. The reasons include the following:

The adoption of policies and organizational models codified by mainstream cultural institutions. Some museological principles are the antithesis of Native American spiritual and cultural mores. Traditionally, for example, knowledge and practices necessary to conduct ceremonies are transmitted in direct person-to-person relationships, and by individual choice. By contrast the process of institutionalizing information expands access and thus conflicts with cultural needs for confidentially. This can alienate segments of the population.

Modes of communication that do not resonate with Native peoples' worldviews. Basic research needs to be undertaken to ensure that the intellectual concepts which form the theoretical basis for museum functions actually express that group's sense of itself. If museums are intellectually organized according to non-Indian schemes, they may convey information that does not reflect Native experiences or values.

Reliance on scholarship lacking in Indian perspectives and collections developed by non-Indians. The predominance of the oral tradition in Native societies as the mode of communication has created gaps in the historical record. Since, for non-Indians, written documentation determines values attributed to objects and events, Indian views are rarely included. A related deficiency is the lack of knowledge about how the act of transmitting recollections and experiences orally influences messages that a listener receives. As understandings about cognitive processes grow and are applied, tribal museums will be better able to communicate meaningfully.

The perception of culture as a function to be funded by nontribal sources. Marketing museum facilities under the guise of financial gain unconsciously diminishes respect for heritage, and obscures their purpose as agents for knowledge and self-esteem. Such attitudes have significant implications for maintaining control of cultural identity.

Tribal museums were never intended, nor is it possible or desirable, to replace the cultural and educational tasks of families and individuals. But, if they are to serve emerging needs, then the museums' practices must be grounded in community traditions and values. Needed are explorations into the interrelationships among culture, institutional structure, intellectual access and autonomy. In turn, such examinations will stimulate the creation of museums recast in ways that are sustainable by their communities and that nurture the daily lives of tribal members.

Nancy J. Fuller
Suzanne Fabricius

Copyright © 1993 Smithsonian Institution

See also **Cultural Revitalization; Museums**

DEFINITION OF A MUSEUM

Museum means a public or private nonprofit institution, which is organized on a permanent basis for essentially educational or aesthetic purposes and which, using a professional staff: (1) owns or uses tangible objects, whether animate or inanimate; (2) cares for the objects; and (3) exhibits them to the general public on a regular basis. An institution which exhibits objects to the general public for at least 120 days a year shall be deemed to meet this requirement. An institution uses a professional staff if it employs at least one full-time paid or volunteer staff person, or the equivalent whether paid or unpaid, primarily engaged in the acquisition, care, or exhibition to the public of objects owned or used by the institution. (Extracted from Museum Services Act, Title II of the Arts, Humanities and Cultural Affairs Act of 1986, Public Law 94–462.)

Further Reading

Fuller, Nancy J. "Native American Museums: Development and Related Issues, A Bibliography." *Council for Museum Anthropology Newsletter* 9 (January 1985): 9–15.

Hill, Tom, ed. *Museums and the First Nations.* Spec. issue of *Muse* 70 (October 1988).

Museums and Native Americans: Renegotiating the Contract. Spec. issue of *Museum News* 70 (January/February 1991).

Parker, Patricia L., ed. *America's Tribal Cultures—A Renaissance in the 1990s.* Spec. issue of *CRM* [Cultural Resources Management] 14:5 (1991).

General Information Resources

Keepers of the Treasures
P.O. Box 151
Hominy, OK 74035

Smithsonian Institution Museum Reference Center
Arts and Industries Building, Room 2235, MRC 427
Washington, D.C. 20560

TRUST RESPONSIBILITIES AND TRUST FUNDS

The federal Indian trust relationship is one of the foundation concepts underlying the political relationship between the United States government and American Indian tribes. The relationship was not created within a single document nor is its scope defined in a single treaty or statute. Specific treaties can be identified as the source for some tribes. For others, executive agreements, legislation, and court decisions create the trust relationship. In *Cherokee Nation v. Georgia*, 30 U.S. 1 (1831), Chief Justice Marshall personified the United States-Indian government relationship when he said of the Cherokee, "Their relationship resembles that of a ward to its guardian." The trust relationship is also known as the guardian-ward relationship, the trusteeship, the trust responsibility, the special relationship, and the unique relationship. In some circumstances, it has not been necessary to use the actual term "trust" to create a legally enforceable duty (*Joint Council of the Passamaquoddy Tribe v. Morton*, 528 F.2d 370 [1st Cir. 1975]).

The American Indian Policy Review Commission, 1975 to 1977, a congressional commission which studied Indian policy, defined the relationship as "an established legal obligation which requires the United States to protect and enhance Indian trust resources and tribal self-government, and to provide economic and social programs necessary to raise the standard of living and social well-being of the Indian people to a level comparable to the non-Indian society."

United States law is clear that the federal government has a strict obligation to protect Indian trust property, using the highest standards of good faith, honesty, skill, and diligence. This means that the Bureau of Indian Affairs (BIA) must exercise the highest standards in such areas as management and accounting for Indian trust funds, and protection and management of Indian lands and natural resources.

Congress is the trustee. The constitutional powers of Congress to ratify treaties and regulate commerce with Indian tribes provide the legal basis for this unique congressional duty (*United States v. Kagama*, 118 U.S. 375 [1886]; *McClanahan v. Arizona State Tax Commission*, 411 U.S. 164, 172, n. 7 [1973]). Congress has delegated the day-to-day functions of implementing the trust responsibilities to the Bureau of Indian Affairs, Department of the Interior. Congress has also delegated certain duties to the Department of Health and Human Services (Administration for Native Americans, Indian Health Service), Department of Education (Office of Indian Education), and the Department of Labor (Indian and Native American Programs).

Generally, both the federal government and Indians agree that the true beneficiary of the trust relationship is the Indian tribe. Individual Indians receive benefits indirectly as members of a federally recognized tribe. These services may extend to Indians whether they live on or off the reservation.

During the last three decades, the executive branch has tried to limit the trust relationship to protect only Indian interests in Indian land or natural resources. The motivation was financial. Various administrations hoped to limit federal budget expenditures. Congress, in a series of legislative acts, has made clear that the trust relationship extends beyond land and natural resources. Examples of this legislation include:

The Indian Self-Determination and Education Assistance Act of 1975 provided a mechanism for tribes to contract with the federal government to perform the services for their people that had been previously provided by the federal bureaucracy. Congress declared its continuing commitment to the trust relationship, which it described as "unique and continuing . . ." (25 U.S.C . 450[b]). In 1988 amendments to the act, Congress renewed its "responsibility to individual Indian tribes and to the Indian people as a whole . . . ."

The *Indian Alcohol and Substance Abuse Prevention and Treatment Act*, 1988, declared that, "the Federal Government has a historical relationship and unique legal and moral responsibility to Indian tribes and their members . . ." (25 U.S.C. 2401[1]). Congress noted that "included in this responsibility is the treaty, statutory, and historical obligation to assist tribes in meeting the health and social needs of their members . . ." (25 U.S.C. 2401[2]).

The *Tribally Controlled Schools Act*, 1988, reemphasized Congress's commitment to the trust relationship "through the establishment of a meaningful Indian self-determination policy for education . . ." (25 U.S.C. 2502[b]).

Trust Funds

Indian trust funds can belong to both tribes and individual members of a tribe. The source of the trust funds belonging to tribes consists of income derived from payments due under treaty obligations; income from the lease of tribal lands for agricultural, ranching, or other purposes; income from lease, bonus payments, delay rental, and royalties for mineral leases; and income from tribal judgment funds won in suits against the government, usually involving claims for the taking of tribal lands. While some statutes have provided for the expenditure of tribal trust funds without tribal consent, the requirement of tribal consent for the use of tribal moneys has been a feature in statutes beginning as early as 1879, and becoming permanent in 1907 (see U.S.C. 140). It has appeared as a requirement in the disposition of tribal assets under the Indian Reorganization Act (25 U.S.C. 476[e]), the advancement by the BIA of tribal funds for purposes to be designated by the tribal governing body (25 U.S.C. 123z[c]), and for the investment of tribal funds at the request of the tribes (25 U.S.C. 162[a]).

Individual Indian trust funds may be derived from tribal income when such income is distributed to individual tribal members (per capita). Income from tribal judgment funds may be distributed on a per capita basis with a certain portion retained by the tribe for programs to serve common needs such as education and economic development. (See the Indian Judgment Fund Distribution Act, 25 U.S.C. 1401.) Some tribes make per capita payments to tribal members from the lease or royalty income derived from tribal lands. More commonly, an individual Indian may derive trust income from the lease of his trust allotment for various purposes. These trust allotments generally derive from implementation of the General Allotment (Dawes) Act or similar legislation. The shares of tribal or trust allotment income due minors and incompetents are held in trust by the government. Payments by the lessee to the government, which in turn forwards payment to the Indian owner, are the source of the myth of the Indians' "monthly check from the government." When these payments are held by the government in Individual Indian Money (IIM) accounts, adult Indians have a right to fill out applications and withdraw funds from their accounts.

Fund Management. In the management of funds of the Indian tribes, the federal government has the responsibility to exercise its fiduciary duties in such a manner that it will maximize Indian trust income by prudent and informed investment (*Cheyenne-Arapaho Tribes v. United States*, 512 F.2d 1390 [Ct. Cl. 1975]).

While the General Allotment Act has been found to create a limited or bare trust relationship, combined with other statutes it has been found to require money compensation when the federal government mismanages Indian land, money, and resources. The Supreme Court found the fiduciary relationship to be undisputed and to arise when the government assumed elaborate control over forests and property belonging to the Indians (*United States v. Mitchell*, 463 U.S. 206 [1983]).

Problems With Fund Management. Problems with the fulfillment of the government's fiduciary duties to tribal governments and tribal members extend to management of mineral resources. In 1989 the Senate Select Committee on Indian Affairs Special Subcommittee on Investigations issued a report which examined the Department of Interior's Mineral Management Service. The special subcommittee found that oil companies were stealing oil from Indian lands by mismeasuring and fraudulently reporting the amount of oil purchased. The report found the Department of Interior was aware of these practices and had failed in its stewardship responsibilities. (Special Committee on Investigations of the Select Committee on Indian Affairs, United States Senate, Final Report and Legislative Recommendations 105, S. Rep. 101–216, 101st Cong., 1st Sess. [1989]).

In April of 1992 the House Committee on Government Operations submitted a report entitled "Misplaced Trust: The Bureau of Indian Affairs Mismanagement of the Indian Trust Fund." The report focused on the continuing management problems of the BIA in handling approximately $2 billion in tribal and individual Indian trust funds. The report emphasized that habitual problems in the BIA's ability to fully and accurately account for trust fund moneys, to properly discharge its fiduciary responsibilities, and to prudently manage the trust funds had not improved since 1985. The report also criticized the BIA's failed attempt to privatize management of Indian trust funds at the cost of $1 million.

Kirke Kickingbird

See also **Bureau of Indian Affairs; Government Agencies; Government Policy; Reservations**

Further Reading

American Indian Policy Review Commission, Final Report. Washington, DC: U.S. Government Printing Office, 1977.

Clinton, Robert N., Nell Jessup Newton, and Monroe E. Price. *American Indian Law: Cases and Materials.* 3d ed. Charlottesville, VA: Mitchie/Bobbs-Merrill, 1991.

Cohen, Felix S. *Felix S. Cohen's Handbook of Federal Indian Law.* Ed. Rennard Strickland. Charlottesville, VA: Mitchie/Bobbs-Merrill, 1982.

Hall, Gilbert L. *Duty of Protection: The Federal Indian Trust Relationship.* 2d ed. Washington, DC: Institute for the Development of Indian Law, 1981.

U.S. Congress. House. Committee on Government Operations. *Misplaced Trust: The Bureau of Indian Affairs Mismanagement of the Indian Trust Fund.* 102d Cong., 2d sess. H. Rep. 102–499. Washington, DC: U.S. Government Printing Office, 1992.

U.S. Congress. Senate. Special Committee on Investigations of the Select Committee on Indian Affairs. *Final Report and Legislative Recommendations.* 101st Cong., 1st sess. S. Rep. 101–216. Washington, DC: U.S. Government Printing Office, 1989.

TSIMSHIAN OF METLAKATLA

The Tsimshian (Tsimpshean) tribe of Metlakatla, Alaska, came from British Columbia, where they lived in villages known as Port Simpson, Metlakatla, and Ckain, which is now Prince Rupert. William Duncan, a missionary, was sent to the Tsimshian area by the Church of England Missionary Society in 1857. Duncan learned the Tsimshian language and developed a Christian colony of Tsimshians to whom he taught the Bible, how to weave and make clothing, how to run gas engines and operate steam boats, and other known trades. He even taught them music and created a small city brass band and a church choir of some sixty voices. Duncan noted that his Christian colony was still exposed to white traders, who sometimes gave liquor for furs, besides utensils, tools, and guns, and so in 1862 he moved his colony to a place near Prince Rupert named Metlakatla. The Tsimshian built an ideal town there and erected a big church that seated 1,200 people and was warmed by many large wood stoves. Duncan had twelve church elders who helped him deliver the Bible messages to about 900 people.

The Metlakatla colony thrived for twenty-five years; all was peaceful in the Christian community until the year 1886 when the Church Missionary Society decided to send a bishop to take over Duncan's missionary work. Duncan went to Washington, D.C., and successfully appealed to President Grover Cleveland to set aside land in Alaska for his community. In 1887 Duncan and approximately 800 people moved from Metlakatla, British Columbia, to Annette Island, about sixteen miles south of Ketchikan, Alaska, and built a new home at Port Chester, later called New Metlakatla. In 1891 Congress established the Annette Island Reserve, which included the entire island. Further, in 1916, President Wilson added 3,000 feet of reserve waters around the island of Annette for exclusive fishing areas of the Metlakatla Natives.

By the time Duncan died in 1918, an anti-Duncan faction under the leadership of Edward Marsden, a Presbyterian minister who was a Tsimshian from New Metlakatla, had emerged. However, Duncan's legacy, in the form of a city government consisting of twelve democratically elected council members, and a commitment to economic self-sufficiency, continues to the present. Perhaps because of this, as well as the early establishment of the Annette Island Reserve including the surrounding waters, the Metlakatla community did not become involved in the land claims issues of the 1960s and was not a participant in the Alaska Native Claims Settlement Act of 1971. According to the 1990 census, the Indian population of the Annette Island Reserve is 1,209; a total of 2,432 people identified themselves as Tsimshian.

Russell Hayward

Further Reading

Beynon, William. "The Tsimshians of Metlakatla, Alaska." *American Anthropologist* 43 (1941): 83–88.
Dunn, John A., and Arnold Booth. "Tsimshian of Metlakatla, Alaska." *Handbook of North American Indians.* Vol. 7. *Northwest Coast.* Ed. Wayne Suttles. Washington, DC: Smithsonian Institution (1990): 294–97.
Garfield, Viola E. "The Tsimshian and Their Neighbors." *The Tsimshian Indians and Their Arts.* Seattle: University of Washington Press (1966): 1–70.

TUBATULABAL

The Tubatulabal inhabit the Kern River Valley, a mountain valley in the southern Sierra Nevada in California. Their ancestral territory included the complete drainage of the North and South Forks of the Kern River, from their sources near Mt. Whitney to about forty miles below the junction of the two rivers. The principal village sites of the Tubatulabal were located throughout the Kern River Valley at an elevation of about 2,500 feet, and temporary camps were made during the seasonal (summer and fall) migrations to the high country. The name Tubatulabal means "pine-nut eaters" and is of Shoshonean derivation. Tubatulabal is one of three Uto-Aztecan linguistic stocks, and differs very greatly from the other two. This implies separateness and antiquity for the Tubatulabal, who are known to have preceded their neighbors to the southeast, the Kawaiisu, to the area.

In 1776 the orderly flow of life was interrupted by the explorations of Padres Francisco Garcés and Pedro Font. Serious disruption had occurred by the 1850s when settlers and miners occupied the Kern River Valley. In 1863, in response to Owens Valley Indians depredations of settlers' cattle, thirty-five to forty unarmed Tubatulabal men were rounded up and shot. Thus began a period of time in which it was clearly not preferable to practice Tubatulabal beliefs, traditions, or even language in public; the missionaries and school teachers of the dominant culture punished and inflicted economic hardship on the people who dared to do so.

The Tubatulabal had a great variety of plant and animal food resources and were fortunate in having both acorns and pine-nuts in their range. The Tubatulabal used many stone tools, principally of granite and obsidian, in hunting and food preparation, and the valley has numerous bed-rock mortars on granite outcroppings. Tubatulabal basketry is similar in fineness to the Panamint Shoshone and Yokuts, and there are numerous rock art sites in the valley, including two solstice sites.

From precontact times to about 1955 the Tubatulabal were loosely governed by hereditary tribal leaders, with leadership generally passing from father to son, with occasional women leaders. The last of the hereditary chiefs was Steban Miranda, who died in 1955. From that time until the late 1960s, leadership of the tribe was carried forward by a Council of Elders of respected families. With the coming of the 1970s, however, it was recognized that the tribe had to become more organized to benefit politically and socially. At this time, due to intermarriage and similarities in culture, the Tubatulabal, the Kawaiisu, and the Canebrake area Koso banded together to form the Kern Valley Indian Community (KVIC) and Council, which gained tax-exempt status in 1987. The KVIC is a member of the Confederated Aboriginal Nations of California, a recently organized coalition of Indian nations. The principal goal of the KVIC is to achieve federal recognition, which would entitle them to reservation status with housing, medical, and educational opportunities for the people. The people believe that they have been previously recognized by the government, as they signed four of the eighteen treaties with California Indians in 1852. These treaties were never ratified and the Tubatulabal received nothing for the land signed away.

Today approximately 400 Tubatulabal still reside in the Kern River Valley, with up to 500 more living elsewhere. Most of the men work on valley ranches as cowboys and ranch hands, or in the logging and construction industries. The women are housewives or are employed in local businesses, restaurants and motels, and the young people often have to leave the valley to seek more lucrative employment or education.

The Tubatulabal have not been idle during the slow, often frustrating task of seeking federal acknowledgment. Under the leadership of their chairman, Ron Wermuth, elected in 1988, they formed a partnership with the United States Forest Service to build a cultural center in the valley to educate the public and their own children as to the rich and unique culture that is theirs. In 1988 Wermuth created the "Monache Gathering," now an annual three-day event involving traditional singers, dancers, and elders. Sweat lodge ceremonies are also part of this gathering. Today the Tubatulabal are active culturally, politically, and spiritually and are a viable Native American community enjoying a renaissance of tradition.

Carol Holmes-Wermuth

See also **California Tribes**

Further Reading

Powers, Bob. *Indian Country of the Tubatulabal.* Spokane, WA: Arthur H. Clark Company, 1981.

Smith, Charles R. "Tubatulabal." *Handbook of North American Indians.* Vol. 8. *California.* Ed. Robert F. Heizer. Washington, DC: Smithsonian Institution (1978): 437–45.

Voegelin, Erminie Wheeler. "Tubatulabal Ethnography." *University of California Anthropological Records* 2:1 (1938): 1–84.

TULALIP

Tulalip is the name of a bay in Washington State. Since ancestors of the tribal members who now live in Tulalip Bay signed the Treaty of Point Elliott in 1855, it is the corporate name of several allied tribes now known as the Tulalip Tribes. The name Tulalip comes from the Snohomish word *Dxləlap*, which means "A Bay Shaped Like a Purse," or a long bay with a narrow opening going far inland. The Tulalip Tribes Reservation is located west of the city of Marysville, which is about forty miles north of the city of Seattle and faces Puget Sound. Residing there are 1,600 of the 2,500 registered tribal members who are predominantly of the Snohomish, Snoqualmie, and Skykomish tribes and their allied nations.

Twentieth-Century History

During the early years of the reservation, Tulalip was the site of a government boarding school for Indian children in western Washington north of Tacoma; it remained their sole source of education until 1938, when children from Tulalip were allowed to attend public schools in the city of Marysville.

Up until 1930, members of the Tulalip Tribes were in the forefront of litigation and other organizational means being utilized to address issues such as land, fishing, educational, and health rights, which had been guaranteed to them by the treaty they had signed. One of these organizations was the Tulalip Improvement Club, later known as the Northwest Federation of American Indians, founded by William and Robert Shelton of the Tulalip Reservation. Robert and others of his generation had served in the army in World War I and had returned with their eyes opened about how the rest of the United States and the world lived. They wanted more land for their reservation and realized they were being denied employment opportunities and health benefits, especially for children and elders. One of the first projects of the Northwest Federation of Indians was to get involved in a court case, which became known as *Dwamish et al v. the United States* 1927, 1934. Arthur L. Griffin presented the case, which contained extensive testimony from members of all western Washington's acknowledged tribes about land areas in aboriginal times, fishing places, and places of occupation and land use. The case was denied by the Washington State Supreme Court in 1927; it was appealed to the United States Supreme Court in 1934 and denied there too. The case contains significant and useful data and preceded in time, substance, and purpose the issues that were brought to the Indian Claims Commission after it was founded in 1946.

Out of the Northwest Federation of Indians grew the first of the Tulalip governing bodies who, having no place to meet and no real sanction until legislation in 1934, met on the beach, sat on logs, and when they could afford it, bought note paper on which to keep minutes of their meetings. This first group included William Shelton, Sebastian Williams, Wilford Steve, Ezra "Art" Hatch, Carl Jones, and Hubert Coy. After the enactment of the Indian Reorganization Act, they changed the name of their governing body to the Tulalip Board of Directors, and it has remained as such to the present day. Today they have six members who are elected every three years and a chairman who is elected yearly. Stan Jones is the chairman in 1993; he has served in that capacity for sixteen years. Other board members are Raymond Fryberg, Herman Williams, Sr., Herman Williams, Jr., Dawn Simpson, Calvin Taylor, and Marie Zachuse.

In recent years the Tulalip Tribes have been less involved in political and Indian rights issues than they have been in developing employment for tribal members on the reservation. They have benefited from the outcome of the fishing rights case known as *United States v. Washington*, in which Judge George Boldt ruled in 1974 that certain Indian tribes in Washington would be restored to their right to harvest half of the salmon runs in the area, as Judge Boldt interpreted the meaning and intent of the 1855 treaty. One of the tribal elders who testified in that lawsuit, even though the Tulalip Tribes chose not to be involved in the original issue, was Harriette Dover, daughter of William Shelton and the only woman to serve on the Tulalip Board of Directors as its chair. Her testimony was instrumental to that decision, which has now become law. In addition she and Marge Williams almost single-handedly made it possible for Tulalip to have an elementary school on the reservation which non-Indian students also attend.

As a result of the 1974 Boldt Decision, Tulalip men and women can now fish at least part-time for a living; with that and other business enterprises they participate in they see an improvement in their 43 percent unemployment rate. Tribal members' employment has centered on labor jobs such as logging and migratory farm labor.

Current Situation

The Tulalip Tribes' Board of Directors have concluded that the best means for tribal members to realize viable employment is for the tribes to establish their own businesses. The fishing rights issue as it was decided in 1974 helped them to turn the corner on this issue. Instrumental in founding these businesses was Clarence Hatch, a recently deceased executive director for the tribes.

The general fund receives monies from land lease agreements with non-Indians who have homes on the reservation, a logging business, a construction company, a smoke-shop, a bingo operation, a marina, and a cafe. The smoke-shop began fourteen years ago and like the bingo operation is located on land just west of Interstate 5, which is a major highway in the area. The bingo operation has been so successful that it provides 40 percent of the operating budget. These monies subsidize tribal programs such as a preschool, elders home, extensive alcohol and drug rehabilitation programs, and educational programs.

The bingo operation has been operating for ten years and is managed by Tulalip tribal member Wayne Williams, grandson of William Shelton. Stan Jones is a member of the United States Gaming Commission; he wanted an operation that would support the general fund and provide additional monies they could use to purchase more land for business ventures, housing sites for tribal members, and social programs.

As a result of the success of the bingo operation the Tulalip Tribes have also opened a casino, the first tribe in Washington to have permission to do so by both state and federal governments. Both the bingo hall and the casino operation are in attractive buildings. The casino, which offers blackjack, craps, roulette, poker, and pulltabs, will have a new wing in early June. Manager Steve Griffiths is non-Indian: his contract stipulates that in three years he will train a tribal member to be the manager. Nine hundred tribal members are employed as a result of these business ventures.

The Tulalip Tribes want to diversify. They plan to build a large golf course on land purchased above the reservation cemetery overlooking the Puget Sound. In addition, they plan to build a business park, envision a second casino, and a high-tech clean industry on a 400-acre site. They may even build a Grand Prix raceway and are considering seeding Tulalip Bay with clam and oyster beds so that tribal members can harvest for both their own or for commercial use. However, most of the developments will center around land areas close to the bingo and casino operations near the Interstate. As Stan Jones commented: "We want to keep the land by the water in its original form. We want to be able to walk through the trees, and we want our children to be able to walk through them and know that we preserved the land for them."

Culture

The Tulalip Tribes are interested in maintaining their heritage. In 1912 William Shelton obtained permission from the superintendent of the reservation, Dr. Charles M. Buchanan, to build a longhouse where they could meet and perform some of their traditional dances and ceremonies. Dr. Buchanan stipulated that they commemorate Treaty Day, January 22, in the longhouse. In 1960 Wayne Williams, Bernie Gobin, and others built an additional community house on the same site. Treaty Day continues to occur on January 22 as do other celebrations, such as Siɔwən (the Winter Dancing Religion), naming ceremonies, the Salmon ceremony, and memorials. This past year, Tulalip hosted a daylong commemoration of Columbus Day, a critical, healing view.

In 1975 Harriette Dover, Morris and Berta Dan, Bernie Gobin, Stan Jones, and several other elders recreated and reinstituted a Salmon ceremony in late June to honor and celebrate the first of the run of the king or chinook salmon: this was a ceremony they had not been allowed to do for at least one hundred years due to suppression by the federal government of traditional Indian religious practices. It is an annual event that attracts several hundred Indians and non-Indians alike.

In recent years the Tulalip Tribes have sponsored courses in beadwork, carving, basketry, and traditional language. Like many other aboriginal people throughout the world they are interested in knowing more about their heritage and they now realize it can be a source of strength for them. Much of their traditional social structure in its kinship and class system is still in place and governs tribal and daily interactions. In the spring of 1993, Grace Goedel began teaching the Snohomish or Lushootseed language in a classroom on the Tulalip Reservation in a program developed by Hank Gobin, the cultural resource specialist for the tribe. There may be as many or as few as fifty fluent speakers of Lushootseed today.

Darleen A. Fitzpatrick

See also Washington State Tribes

Further Reading

Cohen, Fay G. *Treaties on Trial*. Seattle: University of Washington Press, 1986.

Dover, Harriette. *Marching On To Victory*. Seattle: University of Washington Press, 1930.

Haeberlin, Hermann, and Erna Gunther. *Indians of Puget Sound*. Seattle: University of Washington, 1930. Seattle: University of Washington Press, 1952.

Hess, Thom. *Dictionary of Puget Salish*. Seattle: University of Washington Press, 1976.

Radcliff, Rene. "Stan Jones and the Tulalip Tribes: Building a Heritage." *Business Monthly* (May 1993): 22–4.

TUNICA-BILOXI

The Tunica-Biloxi tribe is located in Avoyelles Parish on their 130-acre reservation south of Marksville, Louisiana. The tribe includes 430 individuals of at least one-quarter blood quantum. Once two separate tribes speaking unrelated languages, the Tunica and Biloxi fused in the 1920s, electing Elijah Barbry as their unitary chief.

Throughout the twentieth century efforts to maintain the tribal land base and identity were made by a succession of tribal chiefs: Volsin Chiki, Sesosterie Yuchigant, Elijah Barbry, Ernest Pierite, Horace Pierite, Sr., and Joseph Pierite, Sr. The present reservation is situated on a small portion of an earlier Spanish grant made to the Tunica tribe by Bernardo de Galvez in the 1780s. In 1974 the tribe incorporated, elected a chairman, Joseph Pierite, Jr., and was recognized by the State of Louisiana as a tribe in 1976. In the 1980s the tribe was recognized by the Department of the Interior of the United States.

Under the leadership of Chairman Earl Barbry, Sr., in 1991 the tribe operates a housing authority, maintains its own museum, manages its cattle herd, and also a pecan-processing plant at Mansura, Louisiana.

The traditional New Corn ceremony, the *Fete du Ble'*, is celebrated by the families on the reservation. While that sacred ceremony is not public, a secular festival is held close to the celebration, bringing many local Indians and non-Indians to the reservation for dancing, ballplay, craft sales, and food.

Family traditions maintain tribal crafts, and some individuals retain portions of the tribal musical tradition. A crafts program is being developed to maintain tribal arts and to facilitate marketing.

Tribal leaders have been active in state and national Indian affairs since the 1960s. Elijah Barbry in the 1930s and Joseph Alcide Pierite in the 1960s were early activists struggling for tribal recognition and sovereignty. Chief Pierite carried his activities to national levels, with tribal involvement in the National Congress of American Indians and with the Coalition of Eastern Native Americans. In 1991 the Tribal Council follows these early leads and is active in state and national affairs.

Hiram F. Gregory

Further Reading

Downs, Ernest C. "The Struggle of the Louisiana Tunica Indians for Recognition." *The Southeastern Indians since the Removal Era*. Ed. W.L. Williams. Athens: University of Georgia Press (1979): 72–89.

Faine, Hohn R. *The Tunica-Biloxi Indians: An Assessment of a Louisiana Indian Tribe*. Baton Rouge, LA: The Institute for Indian Development, 1986.

Gregory, Hiram F. "The Louisiana Tribes: Entering Hard Times." *Indians of the Southeastern United States in the Late 20th Century*. Ed. J. Anthony Paredes. Tuscaloosa, AL and London, England: University of Alabama Press, 1992. 162–82.

TURTLE MOUNTAIN BAND OF CHIPPEWA

See Ojibwa: Chippewa in Montana; Ojibwa in North Dakota

TUSCARORA

The Tuscarora are today located on a reservation near Lewiston, New York, and at the Six Nations Reserve near Brantford, Ontario. They are descendants of Native American peoples who lived in eastern North Carolina until the early eighteenth century. As a result of wars of conquest initiated by Carolina colonists, many Tuscaroras fled north and received refuge in Oneida territory. By the 1720s the Tuscarora had been accepted as the sixth nation of the League of the Iroquois, albeit a "nonvoting" member of this confederacy. After the American Revolution, the Tuscarora moved to the area near Niagara Falls and were given a one-mile square tract by the Seneca and a two-mile square tract by the Holland Land Company. They also purchased 4,319.47 acres. Today, there are approximately 1,200 enrolled tribal members in New York living on the remaining 5,689.47 acres of Tuscarora territory, a homeland that is owned in fee simple title with restrictions against alienation to non-Indians.

The Tuscarora are culturally and linguistically Iroquoian. They are a matrilineal society. They are made up of clans and each clan is represented on the Tuscarora Council of Chiefs by a member chosen by the clan mother of that clan. The Tuscarora Council consists of thirteen chieftain titles. The sachems of the Iroquois Confederacy confer titles upon the Tuscarora. Today the Tuscarora are Catholic, Protestant, and Longhouse (Native Iroquoian religion), with the majority of tribal members being of the Protestant faith.

In the twentieth century the Tuscarora have faced many challenges to their cultural and political existence. They overwhelmingly rejected federal efforts to extend the Indian Reorganization Act over them in the mid 1930s. Despite being loyal allies of the United States since 1776, they nevertheless were drafted against their will in World War II. They faced their worst modern crisis in the late 1950s, when Robert Moses and the New York State Power Authority attempted to build a massive reservoir on their lands for the needs of the planned Niagara Power Project. The Tuscarora refused to sell and a court battle and Indian protest ensued; nevertheless, the United States Supreme Court in 1960 allowed the New York State Power Authority to condemn and use Tuscarora land for the reservoir. This bitter loss has helped shape modern Tuscarora existence. In more recent decades, the Tuscarora have faced major internal crises over non-Indians residing on the reservation, as well as individual entrepreneurial efforts to extend cigarette enterprises, gambling, and gas stations onto reservation lands.

Many Tuscarora people work in industrial plants in Niagara Falls and the Buffalo area. Others are employed in construction as roofers, laborers, carpenters, and in structural steel work. There are also Tuscarora people working in education, medicine, and business.

The Tuscarora language is taught in the Tuscarora Indian School. Many people participate in Iroquois festivities with the surrounding Iroquois Nations. A Tuscarora picnic and field day is held each July. It is open to Indians and non-Indians, as is the Tuscarora Community Fair held in October.

Chief Kenneth Patterson

Further Reading

Graymont, Barbara. "The Tuscarora New Year Festival." *New York History* 50 (1969): 143–63.

Hauptman, Laurence M. *The Iroquois and the New Deal.* NY: Syracuse University Press, 1981.

———. *The Iroquois Struggle for Survival: World War II to Red Power.* NY: Syracuse University Press, 1986.

Landy, David. "Tuscarora among the Iroquois." *Handbook of North American Indians.* Vol. 15. *Northeast.* Ed. Bruce G. Trigger. Washington, DC: Smithsonian Institution (1978): 518–24.

Rickard, Clinton. *Fighting Tuscarora: The Autobiography of Chief Clinton Rickard.* Ed. Barbara Graymont. NY: Syracuse University Press, 1973.

TUTUTNI

See Tolowa

TWANA

See Skokomish

UMATILLA

See Confederated Tribes of the Umatilla Indian Reservation

UMPQUA

See Confederated Tribes of the Coos, Lower Umpqua, and Suislaw; Cow Creek Band of Umpqua

UNANGAN

The homelands of the Unangan (Aleut) consist of the volcanic and treeless lands and surrounding waters of the Aleutian, Pribilof, and Shumagin islands, as well as the far western portion of the Alaska Peninsula from Port Moller westward. All Unangan villages are located on either the shores of the Bering Sea or the North Pacific Ocean. It should be noted that the terms "Unangan" and "Aleut" do not have the exact same meaning. The use of Aleut began during the Russian period of Alaskan history; there are conflicting theories about the origin of the word. Now, it is used by many Alaska Natives living in the coastal areas of Prince William Sound west of the Aleutians. Unangan means "People" in our own language. There are three major Unangan dialects which are understandable to anyone speaking any of the dialects fluently. There are approximately 2,000 Unangan living in the homelands, and at least an equal number living in Alaska and the rest of the United States.

The Aleutian climate is windy, wet (including snow), foggy, unpredictable, and in general inhospitable. Severe weather forms over the islands when the cold air from the north violently clashes with the relatively warm air from the south. The Unangan have inhabited the homelands for at least 9,000 years. We have lived off of the extremely rich marine resources (fish, sea mammals, shellfish), birds and, on the eastern islands and mainland, land animals such as caribou, moose, bear, and small game. We were completely dependent on kayaks (*baidarkas, ikiyaks*) to obtain food and other necessities; without the kayak the Unangan culture may not have been able to thrive or survive.

The Russians first made contact with the Unangan in the Shumagin Islands in the 1740s. Shortly thereafter contact was made at Attu on a bay which later came to be known as Massacre Bay, due to a violent clash with the Russians which resulted in the killing of a number of Unangan. The Unangan way of life was forever altered by contact. The Russians' primary mission was the commercial exploitation of sea otters for their pelts. The Unangan were utilized as hunters due to their excellent maritime and hunting skills. The otter was hunted from *baidarkas* from the Aleutians to southeast Alaska, and south to Baja California. Before long most of the people had Russian names and most had been converted to the Russian Orthodox faith; to this day many Unangan have Russian names and most practice Russian Orthodoxy.

As the otter populations declined in the 1820s, the Russians gradually moved east. They continued to have a presence in the Aleutians through the church and educational institutions which remained. The Unangan, whose population likely was between 16,000 and 20,000 prior to contact, now numbered about 4,000. This population decrease resulted from the introduction of European diseases as well as from warfare. Since elders and children are the people most susceptible to disease and since it is the old who carry the knowledge of the culture and the young who are charged with learning from the elders, the Unangan culture was in jeopardy, and many villages simply ceased to exist.

Once the Russians left, the Unangan people were left alone and settled into their traditional lifestyle, which now incorporated some Russian ways. The United States purchased Alaska in 1867, without the consent of Natives, but the purchase had little impact on the Unangan until World War II, when everything changed again. The Japanese attacked the Aleutians and captured Attu, taking the people of Attu to Japan. The United States decided to evacuate all Unangan villages to protect the people from the Japanese, although many non-Unangan were allowed to remain on the islands. The people were interned in southeast Alaska in camps which were mostly located in abandoned canneries. There was no heat, scant food, and little medical care. Disease brought on by the unsanitary conditions of the camps took the lives of many people with those most susceptible again being the elders and young children.

Following the war the Unangan were allowed to go home. However, it took months for the United States government to arrange transportation, and those who made it back found that their homes had been ransacked or destroyed by United States military personnel. The churches had been destroyed and priceless icons stolen. The people of Attu were not permitted to return home because the government said they could not be taken care of as their island was so remote. As a result, the Attu dialect is almost extinct. Villages, some very ancient, were abandoned because there was nothing to go back to and schools and other services were not available in many areas. The impact of World War II was as devastating for the Unangan culture as Russian contact. Few elders remained to pass on the knowledge of the culture. The Unangan population was greatly reduced and many people predicted the demise of Unangan culture.

The economy of the Aleutian Islands was transformed following the war. Customary and traditional hunting and fishing remained a mainstay of the Unangan culture, but a cash economy based on commercial fishing began to develop. Most Unangan, however, were unable to participate in the lucrative portions of the fishery and were relegated, at best, to working long hours for low pay in the canneries. The only economic activity for the Pribilof Aleuts was the taking of fur seal pelts to be sold by the federal government.

In 1971 the United States Congress passed the Alaska Native Claims Settlement Act (ANCSA). The initial drafts of the Act excluded the Unangan people on the grounds that we had too much Russian blood. Following intense lobbying efforts by Unangan and support from other Alaska Natives, we were included in the Act; individuals were required to have at least one-quarter Native blood, rather than one-half, as originally proposed, as a prerequisite to participation in the Act.

ANCSA was significant in that it granted the Aleut Corporation and our village corporations lands which were primarily located in traditional homelands. This provides us with some measure of cultural, economic, and social autonomy. The downside of the Act was that it granted neither land nor resources to village governments. Because village governments are in large part our identity and the only formal entities that are set up to promote our culture and protect our group sovereignty, ANCSA has caused many problems. Tribes in the "lower forty-eight" created corporations as the economic arms of the tribes; however, in Alaska, the regional and village corporations were established separately from the tribes. Since the interests of a corporation are often different than those of a tribe, there have been bitter divisions between some families and within some villages. Added to this is the fact that many villages are state-chartered municipalities, with their own self-interests; thus, it is easy to envision the conflicts which can develop between these entities. In fact, in village Alaska it is not uncommon to see one individual who is a member of the village council, the city council, and the village corporation arguing against himself, depending on which hat he may be wearing at a given time.

Unangan villages are in a state of flux as we try to adapt to the many changes that have been imposed in the last few decades. Our numbers are slowly increasing, which should serve to provide us with a level of population necessary to sustain ourselves. A substantial number of Unangan intermarry, which has the effect of bringing new ideas and different cultures into our communities.

Unangan identity is at an all-time high with more villages reviving and amending tribal constitutions to provide ever greater levels of sovereignty. Tribal courts and other instruments of self-determination are being discussed and considered with great interest. Even in Unalaska, the commercial center of the Aleutians with approximately 225 Aleuts of a total population of over 3,000, the Qawalangan ("Sons of Sea Lions") Tribe is moving to establish cultural and economic self-sufficiency to the Unangan community. Unangan language and culture is being taught to the young in some public schools. The old dances, songs, and other aspects of our heritage are being slowly rediscovered and reintroduced.

Most Unangan recognize that our villages need to develop and sustain a sound economy if they are to remain viable and culturally intact. With few exceptions, the villages are working aggressively, sometimes on their own and sometimes as consortiums, to create economic opportunity. For example, "Community Development Quotas" is a new concept whereby communities bordering the Bering Sea are eligible for a guaranteed share of the allowable bottomfish harvest. Most eligible Unangan villages have banded together with sponsoring seafood companies to guarantee a steady income, training for well-paying jobs in all segments of the industry, and other advantages that will serve to keep our villages functional. The Aleut Corporation, village corporations, and the tribes are in most instances working more closely together than at any time since ANCSA was implemented. It seems that there is a realization that we can only make it as a people if we work together for our common good.

Given the tremendous adversity which the Unangan have faced in the past, and our ability to remain standing when others thought we were down for the count, there is no reason why the Unangan shouldn't be around for, at the very least, another 9,000 years.

Paul R. Swetzof

See also **Alaska Native Claims Settlement Act**

Further Reading

Black, Lydia T. *Aleut Art*. Anchorage, AK: Aleutian/Pribilof Islands Association, 1982.

Jochelson, Waldemar. *Aleut Tales and Narratives*. Eds. Knut Bergsland and Moses L. Dirks. Fairbanks: University of Alaska, Alaska Native Language Center, 1989.

Laughlin, William S. *Aleuts: Survivors of the Bering Land Bridge*. New York, NY: Holt, Rinehart and Winston, 1980.

Oliver, Ethel Ross. *Journal of an Aleutian Year*. Seattle: University of Washington Press, 1988.

Veniaminov, Ivan. *Notes on the Islands of the Unalaska District*. Trans. Lydia T. Black and R.H. Geoghegan. Ed. Richard A. Pierce. Fairbanks: University of Alaska,

Elmer E. Rasmuson Library Translation Program. Kingston, Ontario: Limestone Press, 1984.

UNEMPLOYMENT

See Economic Conditions

UNITED MANSO

See Tortugas

UNITED PEORIA AND MIAMI TRIBE

See Miami; Peoria

UNKECHAUG

The Unkechaug tribe (also Unquachock, Unchechauge, and Unchachage, meaning "Land Beyond the Hill") was also known as Poosepatuck or Patchogue. Located on Long Island on the Poosepatuck Reservation, its land was set aside in 1666. The reservation is still recognized by the State of New York some 325 years later. Today, the 52-acre site at Mastic Neck is bounded on the east by Forge River, on the south by Poosepatuck Creek, and on the west by Mastic Beach. An avenue runs along its northern border.

The tribe's history in the twentieth century has been one of endurance. It successfully resisted a legal move in the 1930s by the State of New York to oust residents from their reservation. During the 1950s, Chief Wild Pigeon (Walter Treadwell, Jr.) rekindled the tribe's interaction with state and local governments. Improved state roads on the reservation resulted, and electricity was brought into the area. The tribal government gave the Suffolk County Police Department permission to enter the reservation (with notification of the Tribal Council of any actions undertaken). The Tribal Council established a working partnership with the Economic Opportunities Commission of Suffolk County during the 1980s, receiving and implementing a major Housing and Urban Development grant for rehabilitating homes on the reservation. The Council also erected a community center. The tribe's seventeenth-century church was destroyed during this time. Today, a new brick church stands near the site of the old one. City water reached the Poosepatuck Reservation in the early 1990s.

The tribe has several programs aimed at assisting its young people, including a high school degree (GED) program, and one for tutoring. Classes in arts and crafts help keep the ties to the past intact. Governance of the tribe is carried out by a chief, three land trustees, a tribal secretary, a keeper of the records, and a keeper of the wampum. The government is elected by certified blood right members, eighteen or older, who have resided on the reservation for a minimum of six months prior to the election. Within the population of approximately 200, there are college graduates, white and blue collar workers, and those who are self-employed. All work in the surrounding community.

Mary Treadwell

See also **Shinnecock**

Further Reading

Douglas, F.H. "Long Island Tribes." *Leaflet* 49. Denver, CO: Denver Art Museum, Department of Indian Art, June 1932. Reprint. January 1973.

Gonzalez, Ellice Becker. "Tri-Racial Isolates in a Bi-Racial Society: Poosepatuck Ambiguity and Conflict." *Strategies for Survival.* Ed. Frank W. Porter. New York, NY: Greenwood Press, 1986. 113–37.

Morice, John H. "Concerning 'An Ethnological Introduction to the Montauk Indians.'" *History and Archaeology of the Montauk Indians.* Readings in Long Island Archaeology and Ethnohistory 3. New York, NY: Suffolk County Archaeological Association (1979): 163–68.

UPPER KUSKOKWIM

See Alaskan Athabaskans

UPPER MATTAPONI

Formerly called the Adamstown Band, this state-recognized enclave (since 1983) was incorporated as a tribe in 1923 and again in 1976 in upper King William County, Virginia, near Central Garage. Many members now live in the Richmond metropolitan area. The total enrollment is about seventy-five.

The tribe had its own grade school sporadically from the 1890s, and continuously from 1917 until integration in 1966. It founded its own Baptist church in 1942. Monthly tribal meetings are held, preceded by closed meetings of the Tribal Council, which is made up of a chief, up to three assistant chiefs, secretary, treasurer, and seven Council members. These officers are elected by all enrolled Upper Mattaponi-descended adults aged eighteen and over. The tribe also has associate memberships for spouses and honorary memberships for outsiders who have been especially useful to the tribe. Since one of its prominent families is also Mattaponi-descended, with potential residence rights on the reservation, the Upper Mattaponis allow dual membership. In 1987 the tribe got their old school building back from the county. They have since refitted it as a tribal center.

Traditional culture remains only in a few crafts (pottery, beadwork, some featherwork). Otherwise the people follow the ways of their Anglo neighbors and have done so since before 1800. The tribe puts on a festival in late May but has no dance group as of 1991.

Helen C. Rountree

See also **Mattaponi**

Further Reading

Berry, Brewton. *Almost White.* New York, NY: Macmillan, 1963.

Rountree, Helen C. "The Indians of Virginia: A Third Race in a Biracial State." *Southeastern Indians Since the Removal Era.* Ed. Walter L. Williams. Athens: University of Georgia Press, 1979. 27–48.

———. "Ethnicity Among the 'Citizen' Indians of Virginia, 1800–1930." *Strategies for Survival: American Indians in the Eastern United States.* Ed. Frank W. Porter. New York, NY: Greenwood Press, 1986. 173–209.

———. *Pocahontas's People: The Powhatan Indians of Virginia through Four Centuries.* Norman: University of Oklahoma Press, 1990.

Speck, Frank G. *Chapters on the Ethnology of the Powhatan Tribes of Virginia.* Indian Notes and Monographs 1:5. New York, NY: Museum of the American Indian, Heye Foundation, 1928.

UPPER SKAGIT

The Upper Skagit Tribe of Indians, located in the Skagit Valley of northwestern Washington State, became "landless" with the cession of lands to the United States after the Treaty of Point Elliott in 1855. Allotments of land made to several Upper Skagits in the 1890s were lost after 1897, with the creation of Washington National Forest. In 1907 and 1909, Upper Skagits received allotments on the Suiattle River. Many of these, too, were cancelled by 1917, and Upper Skagits lost their ability to continue traditional land use patterns. In the meantime, several families made money logging and floating cedar down the river to market. Discussions with the Bureau of Indian Affairs for a reservation on the Suiattle River produced no results.

Early in the century primary sources of income were logging, fishing, and agricultural work. Fishing, however, began to be curtailed by state regulation by 1897. Over time, logging and agriculture declined, and many Upper Skagits left the valley for economic reasons. Upper Skagits challenged fishing regulations in the early 1960s and several were arrested, fined, and jailed for up to ninety days. A landmark judgment, in *United States v. Washington*, 1974, removed state restrictions on Indian fishing and gave half the salmon catch to recognized Indian tribes. Meanwhile, Upper Skagit efforts to claim federal recognition under the Indian Reorganization Act of 1934, headed by Chairman Lawrence (Knuckle) Boome, succeeded in 1974. The tribe thereby became eligible to participate in the treaty-based fisheries, and many members returned to their homeland.

Long-term efforts to force the government to provide compensation for ceded lands began about 1915, with the creation of a council of the hereditary chief and subchiefs. Council Secretary Alice Cuthbert and Charles Boome were long-time leaders. Claims were filed in 1926, as part of *Duwamish et al. v. United States* (79 C. Cls. 530, 1934), and again in 1951 (Docket 92), amended in 1958, under the Indian Claims Commission. In 1968 the tribe was awarded the sum of $385,471, or $271 per capita.

In 1974 a Constitution and Bylaws, created under the provisions of the Indian Reorganization Act, established a new, elected seven-member Council. Women, formerly only nonvoting Council members, were enfranchised and now hold four seats. Council membership remains balanced between the large families. Floyd Williams has served as chairman for much of the period since federal recognition.

In 1981 the tribe purchased seventy-four acres, which were put into trust status and declared reservation land by executive order. Fifty houses, a tribal center, and library were constructed with money from the Department of Housing and Urban Development and other grants. The tribe joined the multitribal Skagit System Cooperative in 1976 to manage treaty fisheries. Also, a tribal court was established within the Northwest Intertribal Court System. Newly developed code protects the rights of individuals, employees, and officials, and guarantees equality of opportunity and religious diversity.

The tribe began the manufacture of replica Northwest Coast bent-wood boxes in 1985 under the direction of Harlan Sam, and a woodshop employing nine tribal members was constructed on the reservation in 1991. By 1992, box sales were projected to exceed $200,000. A fire-fighting crew has gained seasonal employment in national forests, bringing in $118,000 in wages in 1987. In all, the tribe employed fifty people full-time in 1992, thirty-three of whom were Indians; eleven Indians were in professional and administrative positions. The 552-member tribe operated under a $1.2 million budget and has offered its members a range of services, including health care (under arrangement with the Indian Health Service branch), mental health, social, and police services. A day-care center was established on the reservation in 1990. The tribe relies primarily on grants and taxes on treaty fisheries to operate these services.

The tribe, with several adjacent tribes, concluded a long-term multi-million dollar settlement in 1992 with Seattle City Light for the loss of salmon runs due to the construction of dams on the Skagit River in the early twentieth century. Money will go towards protection of fish habitat and cultural resources.

A Shaker Church hall, constructed in the town of Concrete in 1926, was the tribal meeting location until 1984, and services are still held there. In 1986, Lawrence (Okie) Joe opened a *Seowyn* (winter ceremonial) house in Upper Skagit territory, the first since the 1940s, and initiates receive spirit powers there. Pentecostalism gained adherents in the 1980s. Ceremonial giving of inherited Indian names, an infrequent occurrence in the 1970s, is now a frequent occurrence. Funerals remain significant community events, and some families continue the practices of "burnings," giveaways, and memorial services. Elder Vi Hilbert has recorded Skagit stories and taught the Lushootseed language at the University of Washington.

Bruce G. Miller

See also **Washington State Tribes**

Further Reading

Collins, June McC. *Valley of the Spirits: The Upper Skagit Indians of Western Washington.* Seattle: University of Washington Press, 1974.

Fernando, Andres. "Introduction." *Treaties on Trial.* Ed. Fay G. Cohen. Seattle: University of Washington Press, 1986.

Miller, Bruce G. "After the F.A.P. : Tribal Reorganization after Federal Recognition." *Journal of Ethnic Studies* 17:2 (1989): 89–100.

———. "A Sociocultural Explanation of the Election of Women to Tribal Office: The Upper Skagit Case." Ph.D. diss., Arizona State University, 1989.

Robbins, Lynne A. "Upper Skagit (Washington) and Gambell (Alaska) Indian Reorganization Act Governments: Struggles with Constraints, Restraints, and Power." *American Indian Culture and Research Journal* 10:2 (1986): 61–73.

Sampson, Chief Martin J. *Indians of Skagit County.* Skagit County Historical Series 2. Anarcortes, WA, 1972.

UPPER TANANA

See Alaskan Athabaskans

URBAN INDIAN CENTERS

American Indian centers have been established in many urban as well as rural areas throughout the twentieth century. Each state has at least one Indian center with many states having three, four, or as many as ten. They have one thing in common—the desire to provide services and support to Native peoples who find themselves removed from their tribes and reservations. They provide opportunities to share cultural ties and an environment for social events. Many serve as agencies for counseling services in areas such as housing, employment, substance abuse, legal assistance, and education.

The establishment of urban Indian centers, especially in cities like Chicago, Los Angeles, San Francisco, Denver, New York, Boston, Minneapolis-St. Paul, Phoenix, Detroit, and Cleveland, was a direct result of Indian migration to these areas. This migration was due in part to the economic needs of Native peoples and the increasing inability to find viable employment in and around reservations. Another factor was the federal government's relocation and termination policies of the 1950s and 1960s, which sought to move Indians from reservations to the cities. Still another reason was the wider experience gained by American Indians as a result of serving in World War II. These returning veterans often had trouble readjusting into their tribal societies and moved to the cities. Today, nearly one half of all Indians live in cities.

This migration brought with it needs that were not being serviced by existing social service organizations in the cities. Many centers were started by two or three individuals who wanted to share their culture and heritage. They began by organizing social events such as pot-luck dinners or get-togethers to brush up on Indian singing and dancing. Still other centers began by immediately addressing the societal problems evident in the urban areas, like alcoholism, unemployment, and housing needs. Often prominent activists assisted members of an urban Indian community in initiating the establishment of these centers. Russell Means, a leader of the American Indian Movement, worked with the Cleveland Indian Center in the mid-1960s. The Chicago Indian Center, established in 1953, is one of the nation's oldest.

Some urban centers function solely as a referral service to other social service agencies, while others hire staff people to provide those services themselves. Some combine the two. A center may have substance abuse counselors on staff who are sensitive to Native American cultures. Housing discrimination can be a problem in some cities for Indian people, and centers often provide assistance in that area. Employment counseling is also an area in which Indian centers seek to help ease the transition from the rural, family-centered reservations to the larger and impersonal city environment.

The support for Indian centers to provide these services primarily comes from federal government grants. Funding from programs like the Job Training Partnership Act (JTPA) of the Labor Department are eagerly sought by Indian centers. The Department of Health and Human Services is another federal agency with special funding for urban Indians. The size of the local urban Indian community generally determines how aggressively an Indian center will pursue outside funding. The Bureau of Indian Affairs (BIA), however, provides no support to urban Indians. The BIA's relationship is strictly with reservation-based people and federally recognized tribes.

This need for funding by urban Indians has occasionally put unnecessary strains on urban and reservation Indian relations. Because federal funding is limited, urban and reservation Indians are often put in the position of competing for the same monies. Groups often attempt to discredit other Indian organizations in order to lessen the number of qualified applicants for limited funds. Urban Indian centers are constantly emphasizing the increasing need for their services by people who were formerly receiving them on their reservations.

In addition to providing social services, urban Indian centers often get involved in contemporary political issues. In the late twentieth century, many centers have spoken out against the commercialization and misuse of cultural symbols to sell products and the use of Indian stereotypes as mascots for sports teams. They also often take leading roles in demonstrations or calling attention to both local and national issues of importance to American Indians. Many urban centers formed groups in 1992 to offer Indian perspectives to Columbus Quincentennial celebrations.

Besides these community-based urban Indian organizations, the nation's cities are also the homes of Indian organizations whose scope and interests are national, rather than local. These groups are different than Indian centers that serve the local community. Organizations such as the National Congress of American Indians, the United National Indian Tribal Youth, and the American Indian Movement concern themselves with broad political and societal issues, and should not be confused with urban Indian centers.

Urban Indian centers have a unique ability to bring Indians from many different cultures and backgrounds together. Because of their proximity to reservations, some tribal groups are more prevalent than others at particular urban centers, such as the Ojibwa in Minneapolis and the various Iroquois nations in Buffalo. All centers, however, are characterized by their intertribal populations. Indian centers usually have regular access to information about events back on the reservations. Although some cities have neighborhoods where Indians tend to live near each other, others do not. The Indian center may be the only place in the city where an individual can go to see other Indian people and share traditional songs and dances. There are usually activities and gatherings that bring the community's elderly and young people together, ensuring that traditional customs and ways will have a forum for sustenance.

Michele T. Leonard

See also Government Policy; Military Service; Urbanization

Further Reading

Danziger, Edmund Jefferson. *Survival and Regeneration: Detroit's American Indian Community*. Detroit, MI: Wayne State University Press, 1991.

Eagle Walking Turtle. *Indian America: A Traveler's Companion*. Santa Fe, NM: John Muir Publications, 1989.

Fixico, Donald L. *Urban Indians*. New York, NY: Chelsea House, 1991.

Liebow, Edward D. "Urban Indian Institutions in Phoenix: Transformation from Headquarters City to Community." *Journal of Ethnic Studies* 18:4 (1991): 1–27.

Weibel-Orlando, Joan. *Indian Country, L.A.: Maintaining Ethnic Community in Complex Society*. Urbana: University of Illinois Press, 1991.

URBANIZATION

Many American Indian peoples have lived in urban areas for thousands of years. Urban areas and cities developed independently in both hemispheres of the world—in Mesopotamia of the Eastern Hemisphere over 5,000 years ago, and in Mesoamerica of the Western Hemisphere about 3,000 years ago. While American Indian cities were modest by contemporary standards, at the time of Columbus their sizes rivaled cities in the other hemisphere. Indeed, the largest city in the world at that time may have been Tenochtitlan with a population between 150,000 to 300,000.

Various Native American peoples in what is now the United States and Canada also lived in cities in 1492; however, their cities were not nearly as large as those to the south. The largest city that developed in this area was Cahokia, located across the Mississippi River from the present-day city of St. Louis, Missouri.

Cahokia had a population of perhaps as many as 40,000 in about A.D. 1200. Other sizable American Indian cities included Moundville (Alabama) and Pueblo Bonita (New Mexico), though they were not nearly so large as Cahokia.

American Indians became involved very early in cities dominated by Europeans and, later, Americans. American Indians were early residents in colonial cities on the East Coast, in several California cities, in cities in Indian Territory (present-day eastern Oklahoma), and in Arizona and New Mexico, for example. The place of American Indians in such cities is generally overlooked, however.

During the twentieth century American Indians and other Native Americans (Eskimos and Aleuts) have increasingly become residents of the cities of the United States and Canada. As figure 1 illustrates, only 0.4 percent of American Indians in the United States in 1900 lived in urban areas. This percentage increased gradually during the early decades of the century, and at mid-century some 13.4 percent of American Indians in the United States lived in urban areas. Ensuing decades, however, produced more rapid increases in American Indian urbanization: in 1990 over one-half of the over 1.8 million American Indians in the United States lived in urban areas. United States cities with large American Indian populations are Los Angeles-Long Beach, Tulsa, Phoenix, Oklahoma City, Albuquerque, San Francisco-Oakland, Riverside-San Bernadino-Ontario, Minneapolis-St. Paul, Seattle-Everett, Tucson, San Diego, New York, Anaheim-Santa Ana-Garden Grove, Detroit, Dallas-Ft. Worth, Sacramento, Anchorage, and Chicago.

Figure 1
Urban Percentage of American Indian Population in the United States, 1900–1990

Year	Percentage Urban
1900	0.4
1910	4.5
1920	6.1
1930	9.9
1940	7.2
1950	13.4
1960	27.9
1970	44.5
1980	49.0
1990	50.0+

About 40 percent of the .74 million Native Americans in Canada lived in urban areas in 1986, as indicated in the 1986 census. (Some 25 percent of Canadian Native Americans lived in cities with populations greater than 100,000.) This was a significant increase during the preceding decades: only about 30 percent of the Native Americans in Canada lived in urban areas in 1971, and only about 13 percent lived in urban areas in 1961, according to the census of Canada of those years. (In 1971 only a little over 15 percent of Canadian Native Americans lived in cities of 100,000 or more.) Wide variations in urbanization existed among the various groups of Canadian Native Americans, however. Some 70 percent of Canada's nonstatus Indians lived in urban areas in 1981, and some 60 percent of the Métis did; however, only about 30 percent of the status Indians lived in urban areas. (About 20 percent of Canadian Eskimos [Inuit] lived in cities.) Canadian cities with large Native American populations are Winnipeg, Edmonton, Montreal, Vancouver, Toronto, Regina, Calgary, Prince Rupert, Hamilton, London, Saskatoon, and Prince Albert.

The urbanization of Native Americans has been in large part a result of the migration of Native Americans to cities and towns from rural areas, reservations, and reserves (in Canada), rather than a result of differences in natural increases between urban and nonurban populations. In fact, natural increases—differences in births and deaths—are typically higher in nonurban areas. An important factor in this urban migration in the United States has been the Bureau of Indian Affairs' (BIA) relocation program. Begun in 1950, the program assists American Indians in moving from reservations to selected urban areas. The Bureau also provides employment counseling, vocational training, and educational assistance for relocated American Indians. One area selected for relocation was greater Los Angeles, which now has the largest number of urban American Indians. Many American Indians, however, have moved and continue to move to cities in the United States without relocation assistance from the BIA.

Economic factors have generally been considered the primary reason Native Americans move to urban areas, in both the United States and Canada. This is because of a frequent lack of employment opportunities on reservations and reserves and in rural areas, and the perception that urban areas have good employment opportunities. Unemployment rates, for example, are far higher for American Indians on reservations in the United States than for American Indians living in urban areas. Employment opportunities in urban areas are not always realized, however, and many American Indians in the United States have returned to reservations and rural areas after having lived in cities. In fact, many American Indians have followed a circular pattern of movement back and forth between urban and reservation or rural areas. In many instances, such migrants may be merely following job opportunities in cities. As one might imagine, research has indicated that American Indians with vocational skills and training and/or high educational levels are likely to benefit economically from living in urban areas.

Along these lines, three types of American Indian migrants to the United States cities have been identified: (1) those who live in urban areas, but remain oriented to their reservation, and who may move back and forth between the reservation and the city; (2) skilled laborers who move to the city, but live generally on the "fringes" of the city and city life; and (3) "middle class" American Indians who typically live in predominantly white neighborhoods, but may also participate in American Indian cultural and political activities.

Economic reasons have also been found to be important determinants for American Indians in the United States leaving cities, probably because perceived job opportunities often do not materialize. Despite the importance of economic reasons, personal and medical problems (including alcoholism) are generally found to be the most important reasons American Indians say they return to reservations and rural areas. Some studies have indicated that urbanization may result in better health care for American Indians, and consequently a lower incidence of most diseases and decreased mortality rates. Other studies indicate urban American Indians may be deprived of health and mental health services available to reservation residents. For example, free medical care through the United States Indian Health Service is typically not available to urban Indians; often, however, American Indians in urban areas will return to their reservation for health care through the Indian Health Service. Alcoholism, accidents, and suicide continue to plague both urban and nonurban American Indians, nevertheless.

Native Americans in urban areas of the United States and Canada face serious threats to their tribalism and "ways of life." One such threat occurs through intermarriage. In 1970 over one-third of all married American Indians in the United States were married to non-Indians; however, over one-half of those living in urban areas were married to non-Indians, while only between one-fourth and one-fifth of those living in rural areas were married to non-Indians. In 1980, over one-half of *all* married American Indians were married to non-Indians, and the differences between the intermarriage rates of urban and nonurban American Indians continued. Another threat occurs through the loss of tribalism for American Indians in urban areas. For example, American Indians in urban areas are less likely than American Indians in reservation and rural areas to speak an American Indian language as their "mother tongue," or to report a tribal affiliation in United States census enumerations. American Indians in urban areas are also more likely to marry Indians from other tribes than are American Indians living on reservations or in rural areas.

Urban Native Americans in both the United States and Canada do attempt to maintain their tribalism by living in Native American neighborhoods, keeping contacts with their reservations or reserves and extended families, and establishing Native American centers. One important product of Native American urbanization has been the development of a pan-Indian identity and the establishment of pan-Indian organizations for both political and nonpolitical activities. Urban Native Americans have developed dances, powwows, and other social activities which cut across tribal lines. They have also developed pan-Indian "survival schools" and political organizations.

Indeed, the major pan-Indian political movement of recent decades—the American Indian Movement—originated among urban Indians in Minneapolis.

Russell Thornton

See also **Population; Urban Indian Centers**

Further Reading

Snipp, C. Matthew. *American Indians: The First of This Land.* New York, NY: Russell Sage Foundation, 1989.

Sorkin, Alan. *The Urban American Indian.* Lexington, CT: Heath Publishing Company, 1978.

Stanbury, W.T. *Success and Failure: Indians in Urban Society.* Vancouver: University of British Columbia Press, 1975.

Thornton, Russell. "Contemporary American Indians." *Scholars and the Indian Experience: Critical Reviews of Recent Writing in the Social Sciences.* Ed. W.R. Swagerty. Bloomington: Indiana University Press, 1984. 162–78.

———. *American Indian Holocaust and Survival: A Population History since 1492.* Norman: University of Oklahoma Press, 1987.

Thornton, Russell, Gary D. Sendefur, and Harold G. Grasmick. *The Urbanization of American Indians: A Critical Bibliography.* Bloomington: Indiana University Press, 1982.

UTE

The Ute, along with the Southern Paiute, speak Southern Numic, which is a branch of Numic, the Uto-Aztecan language spoken by all Great Basin groups except the Hokan-speaking Washoe. Linguistic variation in the form of regional dialects and speech patterns were present among the several groups of Southern Numic speakers, although all were mutually intelligible.

Ute Bands

Identification of Ute bands from ethnographies varies depending upon the source, phonological scheme of the reporter, and time of attribution. At time of contact, Ute bands occupied most of Utah and Colorado and parts of southern Wyoming and northern New Mexico. Two of these bands, the Muache and Capote, ranged in southern Colorado and northern New Mexico (south to Santa Fe), and are now identified as the Southern Ute residing on the Southern Ute Reservation in southern Colorado. The Weeminuche (Wimonuch) band, whose historic territory extended west to the canyonlands of Utah, is now known as the Ute Mountain Ute and occupies a reservation by that name in the southeast corner of Colorado. The Uncompaghre (formerly Taviwach) of central and eastern Colorado were forced to sell their Colorado land in 1880 and move to the Ouray Reservation established for them in eastern Utah. The White River (formerly Parusanuch and Yampa bands) were forcibly relocated from Colorado to the already-established Uintah Reservation in northeastern Utah, after their participation in the "Meeker Massacre." Prior to the removal of the White River band, most of the bands in Utah (e.g., the Uintah, Pahvant, Timpanogots, Sanpits, and Moanunts) had been forcibly confined to the Uintah Reservation. The bands located on the consolidated Uintah-Ouray Reservation in Utah are today known as the Northern Ute.

Figure 1 provides a simplified concordance revealing the identity of a variety of Ute band names found in the ethnohistoric literature. For example, Schroeder (1965) details at least nine different historical references to the two Southern Ute bands that now occupy the Southern Ute Reservation. The Moache were also known as the Muache, Mouache, Mowatci, Muwach, Meuaches, Mohuache, Mowatsi, Muhuachis, and the Cimarron (after the agency they resided near in the 1870s). In some cases, phonetic similarity or geographical reference may not provide the necessary clues to identification, e.g., the Zaguaganas were also referred to as the Mowataviwatsiu.

Twentieth-Century History

Throughout the twentieth century, Utes have been confronted with the difficult challenges of exercising control over their land and resources, building viable reservation economies, improving living conditions for tribal populations, and maintaining their cultural and religious traditions. They have assumed some measure of self-sufficiency and self-determination, despite working within a reservation context and trust relationship with the federal government.

During the nineteenth century, Utes were displaced, forced to relocate, and had their land expropriated. Lands that Ute bands occupied aboriginally were reduced from around 79 million acres to original reservations of about 23 million acres. Only 4.5 million acres remained in tribal holdings by the beginning of the twentieth century due to additional land losses. Under provisions of the 1887 General Allotment Act, reservation lands were allotted in severalty to Southern Utes in 1895; and to Northern Utes in 1897 (the Uncompaghres) and in 1905 (the Uintahs and White Rivers), despite their resistance to the process. Most remaining lands were deposited into the public domain and opened to Anglo homesteading. The Ute Mountain Utes refused to cooperate with allotment and took the western end of the reservation formerly shared with Southern Utes, where they continued to hold land in common.

Allotment was part of the federal government's plan to turn Utes into farmers and promote agriculture as the basis of their reservation economies. Committed to extended kin, communitarian values of land ownership, and preference for traditional subsistence pursuits, Utes generally resisted farming as they had allotment (Southern Utes farmed more than Northern or Ute Mountain Utes). Utes preferred to raise cattle, sheep, and horses. Those who did farm raised horticultural crops and livestock feed. Utes' farms were not commercially viable, because they lacked access to capital to purchase technologically advanced farming equipment (the General Allotment Act only

		Figure 1			
		Abbreviated Concordance of Band Names in Ute Literature			
		Eastern Bands (Colorado) 1–6			

Band Name	Jefferson 1972	Stewart 1942	Jorgensen 1972	Schroeder 1965	Current Location
1. Muache	Mouache Muache	Mowatci	Muwach	Moache Mowatsi	Southern Ute Reservation
2. Capote	Capote	Kapota	Kapota	Capote Kapota Guaputa	Southern Ute Reservation
3. Weeminuche	Weeminuche	Wimonuntci	Winunch Wimonuch(1980)	Wemenuches Weminutc Womenuches Pa-Uches Pah-Utes	Ute Mountain Reservation
4. Uncompaghre	Tabeguache	Mowataviwatsiu[1]	Taviwach	Tabeguaches Tabehuachis Tabeguachis Taviwatsiu	Northern Ute Reservation
5. White River (Parusanuch)	Parianuc Grand River	Taviwatsiu[2]	Parusanuch	Zaguaganas Mowataviwatsiu	Northern Ute Reservation
6. White River (Yampa)	Yampa	Yamparkau	Yamparka	—	Northern Ute Reservation

| | | **Western Bands (Utah) 7–11** | | | |

Band Name	Jefferson 1972	Stewart 1942	Jorgensen 1972	Schroeder 1965	Current Location
7. Uintah	Uintah	—	Uintah	Uintah	Northern Ute Reservation
8. Timpanogots	Tumpanogots Timpanogos Timpanogotzi Timpanogs Timpannah Tenpenny	Tompanowatsnunts Uintahs Pagonunts Tompanowots	Timpananuuce	Tumpanuwach	Northern Ute Reservation
9. Pahvants	Pahvant Pavanduts	Pahvant	Pahvant	Pahvant	Northern Ute Reservation
10. Sanpits	Sampits	—	Sanpits	—	Northern Ute Reservation
11. Moanunts	Pavogogwunsin Fish Utes Red Lake Ute	Moanunts Pagonunts Uintahnunts	—	—	Northern Ute Reservation

[1]*Stewart said informants also called this group Uncompaghre, although his map on page 233 of the cited source would seem to identify them as White River.*

[2]*Stewart said informants commented that this group was also known among Indians as White River, however, Stewart's map on page 233 of the cited source would seem to identify them as Uncompaghre. This reversal (i.e., Mowataviwatsiu = White River, [not Uncompaghre]; and Taviwatsiu = Uncompaghre [not White River]) would make Stewart's designations comparable with the phonology of Jorgensen and Schroeder.*

Sources: See "Further Reading."

provided for hand implements), had little experience or training in small business and farm management, and contended with unfavorable soil, climate, terrain, and access to markets. Most Ute allotments were eventually leased to Anglos, tied up in complicated heirship status, or alienated. Allotment inequities among Northern Utes exacerbated tensions among the three bands forced to share that reservation. The opening of the Southern and Northern Ute reservations to white settlers resulted in a checkerboarded ownership pattern that has complicated tribal control and jurisdiction over reservation land and water.

The Indian Reorganization Act (IRA) of 1934 stemmed the alienation of allotments and provided a means for Utes to acquire and consolidate their lands. Even here, Utes found that scarce tribal capital provided by the IRA was used under the direction of non-Indian bureaucrats to pay debts incurred by individual allottees and to repurchase land from Anglos whose farms had failed during the Great Depression.

Figure 2, "Alienation of Ute Reservation Lands 1870–1966," provides a graphic display of Ute land losses. Clearly, the Southern Ute have recovered the least amount of acreage from their aboriginal range.

Land allotment on the Northern Ute and Southern Ute reservations was accompanied by the development of irrigation projects begun early in the twentieth century. Most construction costs were paid with tribal funds, while individual allottees incurred debts against their lands for operation and maintenance of these systems. Much of the land under these irrigation projects was leased or sold to Anglos under pressure to secure state water rights and to make the projects pay. Ute irrigation projects involved difficulties such as lawsuits with Anglos over water rights, monitoring water distribution to interspersed Ute and Anglo lands, and lack of storage reservoirs. Anglos

Figure 2
Alienation of Ute Reservation
Lands 1860–1966

Reservation Land	Southern Ute	Ute Mtn. Ute	Northern Ute
Original	9,500,000	9,500,000	3,972,500
1934	40,600	513,800	355,000
1950	309,500	533,900	1,061,700
1966	304,700	533,000	1,000,000
% Reduction	97%	95%	75%

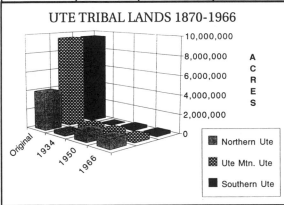

Source: Jorgensen (1972:94)

who homesteaded, purchased, or leased Ute lands were the primary beneficiaries of these projects.

Federal policies failed to produce viable agricultural economies on Ute reservations. For the first half of the twentieth century, Utes pieced together livelihoods through combinations of marginal agriculture, stockraising, some hunting and gathering, lease income, government rations, and some part-time employment. Few Utes migrated to urban areas to seek work, and those who were relocated under the Bureau of Indian Affairs' (BIA) Employment Assistance Program in the 1950s and early 1960s soon returned to their reservations. The common response to economic deprivation among Utes was to pool resources with

kin, which often increased the size of households and changed their compositions.

The 1950s brought accelerated economic change to Ute reservations when the tribes began receiving large sums of money from land claim settlements, mineral leases, and federal programs designed to ameliorate poverty and stimulate rural development. Some of this money was used to improve tribal members' dire economic circumstances through per capita distributions and service programs. Some of the money was used to promote reservation development through land purchases, loans to tribal members starting businesses, and investments in tribal enterprises. Soon after the receipt of these monies, a segment of the Northern Ute tribe, known as the Affiliated Ute Citizens, terminated their status with the tribe, taking their 27 percent portion of the divisible tribal assets.

Most of the Ute tribal enterprises were connected to tourism, such as motels, convention facilities, restaurants, cocktail lounges, gas stations, craft shops, and museums (the Southern Utes' tourist complex was named Pino Nuche Purasa, the Northern Utes' resort was named Bottle Hollow). The Northern Utes marketed big game hunting and fishing expeditions in the late 1950s and early 1960s. The Southern Utes operated an indoor rodeo rink, quarterhorse racetrack (Sky Ute Downs), and a bingo hall. In the spring of 1993, the Southern Utes have planned to renovate some of their tourist facilities into a casino and gaming complex. The Ute Mountain Ute were operating Ute Mountain Tribal Park, a 145,000-acre section of Mesa Verde featuring cliff dwellings, and the Ute Mountain Casino in Towaoc.

The Ute tribes also invested in agricultural and manufacturing enterprises. The Northern Utes still operate the Ute Tribal Livestock Enterprise, a farming operation, and used to operate a tannery, a cabinet and furniture shop, and an environmental research laboratory. Other tribal enterprises have provided services to tribal members, such as the Northern Ute culinary water system and coin-operated laundromats.

Ute tribal enterprises have met with limited success. Lack of infrastructure, including capital, skilled workers, and transportation systems linked to distant markets constrain the development of a manufacturing sector on Ute reservations. Most Ute employment remains in the government, service, and retail sectors. By and large, tribal enterprises (with the recent exception of gambling facilities) operate in the red. The reasons are complex and often misunderstood by non-Indians. One reason for tribal enterprise failures is inflexibility in federal bureaucracies. The Economic Development Administration (EDA), for instance, mandated the nature and form of many tribal economic developments (industrial parks and motel/restaurant complexes being two of their favorites), even when feasibility studies raised doubts about their probable success. The contradiction between a kin-based polity and enterprise management is another reason. Ute Tribal Council members are placed in the untenable position of being politicians responsible to the employment and service demands of their constituents, while at the same time being enterprise managers held accountable for the financial performance of tribal enterprises.

The increase in tribal funds during the 1950s had several consequences for Utes. It brought welcome cash and employment, but increased Utes' dependence on unearned income, much of it from nonrenewable resources. Decisions about expending these funds have been controversial and generally concerned whether to distribute this money to individuals or to invest in tribal enterprises. Distribution of these funds occasionally has exacerbated factionalism and caused conflict between tribal councils and membership. Additionally, the availability of these funds created expectations that Ute tribal council members are now pressured to fulfill.

Managing energy and mineral developments has been a major issue for Utes since the 1950s. Limited in their ownership and control over these developments, Utes have nonetheless become increasingly sophisticated in negotiating lease and royalty agreements, monitoring energy companies' activities, and exercising their regulatory and taxing authorities. Resource departments have been established by the tribes to actively manage energy and other resources. The Northern Utes have fought the State of Utah over oil severance taxes and over the distribution of federal mineral royalty and rental funds. In the early 1990s, the Southern Utes became the first tribe to buy and operate natural gas wells that traditionally were leased to major energy companies. Ute oil and gas revenues peaked during the mid-1980s, forcing the tribes to search for other means to sustain tribal revenues.

More recently, all three Ute tribes have been involved in negotiated water rights settlements. The Southern and Ute Mountain Utes' water settlement occurred in 1988, while a Northern Ute settlement is pending tribal and state votes in 1993. Each of these tribes had supported large, multipurpose Colorado River reclamation projects for years on the promise of water developments for their reservations. While the non-Indian portions of these projects proceeded, the economic feasibility and congressional support for completing these projects declined and environmental objections and cost-sharing stipulations increased. Confronted with usurpation of their water, financial inability to engage in water development on their own, and recent legal decisions on Indian water that left them wary of pressing their claims in court, the Ute tribes were forced to the negotiating table. The outline of the Ute water settlements is the same; in exchange for relinquishing legal claims to large amounts of water, the tribes are to receive assistance in developing smaller quantities of water and economic development funds. With declines in ranching and agriculture on Ute reservations, prohibitions against interstate water transfers, and new environmentalist concerns, the Ute tribes are challenged to secure the promised water developments and to find ways to utilize water they may receive.

Current Situation

Ute populations declined during the first half of the twentieth century but have grown since then, as detailed in figure 3, "Native American Population on Ute Reservations 1880–1990." Caution should be used in interpreting these figures as absolute numbers, since the sources of the population estimates vary widely. The 1990 figures are self-identified "American Indians" living on Ute reservations during the decennial 1990 census. Issues (often divisive) such as tribal or BIA measures of blood quantum are not considered in these figures. The decline in Ute Mountain populations may be an enumeration artifact and not indicative of processes such as migration or mortality. Since the 1950s, the Utes, and Native Americans in general, have had improved nutrition and health care, which has decreased infant and maternal mortality and controlled infectious diseases, once rampant in their populations.

The 1990 United States Census enumerates 7,273 self-identified Ute individuals living in the United States. About two-thirds live on reservations in the Rocky Mountain West, a quarter live off-reservation in the Rocky Mountain and Pacific states, and most of

Figure 3
Native American Population of
Ute Reservations 1880–1990

Year	Southern Ute	Ute Mtn. Ute	Northern Ute
1880	500	650	2,825
1890	428	530	1,854
1900	420	528	1,660
1910	353	463	1,150
1920	334	462	1,005
1930	369	485	917
1940	440	493	1,000
1950	479	570	1,150
1960	679	813	1,498
1970	711	1,099	1,611
1980	939	1,534	2,104
1990	1,044	1,264	2,650

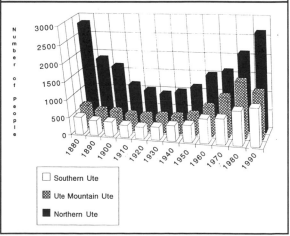

the rest live in the Northeast, the Midwest, and southern regions of the United States.

Figure 4
Age Distribution on
Ute Reservations 1980–1990

	Younger than 18		65+	
	1980	1990	1980	1990
Southern Ute	38%	39.4%	3.90%	5.40%
Ute Mountain Ute	40%	37.9%	2.40%	4.40%
Northern Ute	45%	47.6%	3.90%	4.50%

			Persons over 18:
	Median Age		Males/100 Females
	1980	1990	1990
Southern Ute	20.6	23.9	84.50%
Ute Mountain Ute	21.1	24.5	101.30%
Northern Ute	19.7	19.6	84.30%

As figure 4 demonstrates, a sizable portion of the Ute population is under the age of eighteen (nearly half the Northern Ute population!), indicating a high birth rate. This proportion is considerably larger than non-Native populations (e.g., Colorado with 27 percent) and has increased slightly during the last decade. An increasing proportion of individuals on all reservations are over the age of sixty-five. The low ratio of males over eighteen years of age to females on the Southern and Northern Ute reservations is probably indicative of selective migration for employment, and the high rates of mortality from accidents for young men. High proportions of young, old, and single female-headed households imply increasing demand for services (education, health, and child care) and employment, as well as increasing strains on families with limited financial resources.

Educational attainment for individuals over age twenty-five on all three reservations can be found in figure 5.

The proportion of non-Indians (whites) over age twenty-five without high-school diplomas living on the three Ute reservations has remained fairly constant between 1980 and 1990 (the national average is 23 percent). In contrast, as figure 6 demonstrates, there has been a significant increase in the proportion of Ute individuals over twenty-five who have received their high-school diplomas. Ute Mountain

Figure 6
Change in the Proportion
of Ute Individuals 25+ Without
a High School Diploma 1980–1990

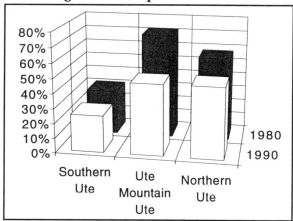

Figure 5
Educational Attainment by Ethnicity for Individuals 25+, 1990

Educational Attainment	Ute Mountain			Southern Ute			
	Native American		"White"*	Native American		"White"	
Before 9th Grade	120	23%	0	34	7%	236	6%
9th–12th Grade	132	25%	5	89	18%	421	10%
H.S. Graduate	183	35%	22	222	45%	1372	34%
Some College	68	13%	3	91	18%	907	23%
AA	10	2%	0	20	4%	207	5%
BA	13	2%	0	29	6%	582	14%
Grad/Professional	0	0%	0	10	2%	300	7%
	526	100%		495	100%	4025	100%

Educational Attainment	Northern Ute			
	Native American		"White"	
Before 9th Grade	97	9%	340	5%
9th–12th Grade	442	39%	1434	20%
H.S. Graduate	312	28%	2745	38%
Some College	188	17%	1538	21%
AA	45	4%	405	6%
BA	32	3%	622	9%
Grad/Professional	14	1%	216	3%
	1130	100%	7301	100%

*"White" is a census designation meaning individuals who are not Native American, Latino, or African American.

Figure 7
Bilingualism English/Ute
1990 Figures and 1980–1990 Comparisons

	Ute Mountain		Southern Ute		Northern Ute	
5–17 Years of Age **Other Language**						
Speak English "Very Well"	60	52%	48	79%	77	59%
Speak English "Well"	45	30%	8	13%	38	29%
Speak English "Not Well"	11	9%	5	8%	16	12%
	116	100%	61	100%	131	100%
18–64 Years of Age **Other Language**						
Speak English "Very Well"	247	55%	216	90%	525	79%
Speak English "Well"	158	35%	22	9%	109	16%
Speak English "Not Well"	46	10%	2	1%	31	5%
	451	100%	240	100%	665	100%
65+ Years of Age **Other Language**						
Speak English "Very Well"	12	29%	41	79%	63	71%
Speak English "Well"	12	29%	7	13%	15	17%
Speak English "Not Well"	18	43%	4	8%	11	12%
	42	100%	52	100%	89	100%
Proportion Population "Bilingual"	609	48%	353	34%	885	33%
% "Bilingual" Speak English "Not Well"	75	12%	11	3%	58	7%
	1980	1990	1980	1990	1980	1990
% "Bilingual" 5–17 Years of Age	69%	36%	43%	22%	56%	15%

Utes have experienced the most significant decrease in high school drop-outs during the last decade.

Figure 6a
Proportion of Individuals 25+
Without High School Diplomas

	% of Individuals 25+ Without High School Diploma			
	Native Americans		"White"	
	1980	1990	1980	1990
Southern Ute	30%	25%	16%	16%
Ute Mountain Ute	71%	48%	31%	NA
Northern Ute	57%	48%	26%	25%

About half the population of the Ute Mountain Ute Reservation and about one-third of the population of the other two reservations are bilingual to some degree (figure 7). The Ute language is still used in public forums and at cultural events, and translation often occurs. However, all reservations have exhibited a marked drop in bilingualism among youth five to seventeen years old during the last decade, especially among the Northern Ute, which experienced nearly a fourfold decrease. A high proportion

Figure 8
Characteristics of Ute
Households 1980–1990

		Average Household Size	Percent "Nuclear" Households	% of Female Headed HH's
Southern Ute	1980	4.47	56%	40%
	1990	3.25	56%	19%
Ute Mtn. Ute	1980	4.88	96%	4%
	1990	3.78	49%*	27%
Northern Ute	1980	5.00	71%	25%
	1990	3.91	59%	20%
Colorado/ US	1980	2.65	52%	10%
	1990	2.51	56%	9%

Current information does not allow us to explain this dramatic change.

of elders over sixty-five (especially on the Ute Mountain Ute Reservation) experience difficulty communicating in English, inhibiting conversations with their increasingly monolingual grandchildren. Loss of the language is an important concern, and the Ute tribes continue to support language programs.

Between 1980 and 1990, households on all three Ute reservations experienced a decline in size, most likely due to government housing programs (HUD). Historically Ute household size has fluctuated with the amount, source, and stability of household income. During poor economic times households increase in size as individuals with resources from part-time wage employment, social security, or supplemental security income (SSI) and aid to dependent children pool their incomes to cope with economic uncertainty. When income is high and predictable, household size decreases as extended and stem households fission to obtain greater privacy. While residence patterns have changed, economic and social support between kin is still reciprocated, albeit "between" rather than "within" households. Although average households on the Southern Ute and Ute Mountain Ute reservations have decreased in size, they are still significantly larger than average non-Indian households. A large decrease in the number of "nuclear" households among the Ute Mountain during the last decade has brought all three reservations in line with national averages. However, all three reservations experience two to three times the number of single female-headed households (with resident children) than one would expect given the United States average.

While national labor force participation rates increased slightly between 1980 and 1990, there has been a significant increase in labor force participation by Ute Mountain and Southern Utes (figure 9). Labor force participation among females increased much more dramatically than among males on all three reservations during the same period, accounting for nearly all of the total increases among Ute Mountain and Southern Utes. Still, Ute labor force participation rates were below national averages.

Official measures of unemployment often underestimate the true difficulties Utes experience in obtaining steady wage employment. In the case of Northern Utes, even official 1990 census data indicates an unemployment problem twice that of the national average. Occasional tribal and BIA surveys have indicated effective Ute unemployment rates as much higher than official statistics reveal. Decent measures on underemployment are also difficult to obtain, yet 1980 estimates showed that between 13 and 50 percent of the employed Ute work force (depending on gender) had worked less than six months during the previous reference year.

Off-reservation job opportunities for Utes remain limited by rural economic decline, lack of access to capital, and long-term problems in providing Utes with appropriate education and employment skills. This has left Utes dependent upon tribal and federal government employment. As figure 11 clearly indicates, about one-half to two-thirds of Utes employed in 1980 worked in government, with almost half or more of these jobs provided by tribal government. Many of these jobs are dependent on the vicissitudes

Figure 9
Labor Force Participation Ute Individuals 16+ 1980-1990

Labor Force Participation Rates 1980–1990

	Male 1980	Male 1990	Female 1980	Female 1990	Total 1980	Total 1990
Ute Mountain	61%	64%	43%	56%	52%	60%
Southern Ute	65%	70%	37%	57%	50%	63%
Northern Ute	65%	62%	37%	46%	55%	53%
United States	77%	77%	52%	57%	64%	67%

Figure 10
Native American Employment Status by Gender, 1990

Ute Mountain

	Male	Female	Total	% of Total
Civilian Employed	178	171	349	51%
Not in Labor Force	130	144	274	40%
Unemployed	52	13	65	9%
Total	360	328	688	100%

Northern Ute

	Male	Female	Total	% of Total
Civilian Employed	310	260	570	38%
Not in Labor Force	272	428	700	47%
Unemployed	124	104	228	15%
Total	706	792	1498	100%

Southern Ute

	Male	Female	Total	% of Total
Civilian Employed	179	181	360	53%
Not in Labor Force	94	159	253	37%
Unemployed	41	28	69	10%
Total	314	368	682	100%

Figure 11
Government Sector Employment for Ute Individuals 18+, 1980

Proportion and Source of Government Employment in Ute Work Force

	Southern Ute	Ute Mtn. Ute	Northern Ute	Non-Native
% Total Employment: Government	63%	56%	47%	21%
Source of Government Employment				
Federal	39%	52%	40%	N/A
State	3%	2%	5%	N/A
Tribal	58%	46%	55%	N/A

Figure 12
Distribution of Household Income by Ethnicity 1990

	Ute Mountain		Southern Ute			
	Native American		Native American		"White"	
<$5k	75	25%	32	11%	149	7%
$5k – $9,999	38	13%	57	19%	257	11%
$10k – $14,999	53	18%	45	15%	237	10%
$15k – $24,999	56	19%	77	25%	459	20%
$25k – $34,999	45	15%	42	14%	400	18%
$35k – $49,999	19	6%	28	9%	418	18%
$50k – $74,999	10	3%	20	7%	258	11%
$75k – $99,999	5	2%	2	1%	46	2%
>$100,000	0	0%	1	0%	56	2%
	301	100%	304	100%	2280	100%

	Northern Ute					
	Native American		"White"			
<$5k	167	25%	340	8%		
$5k – $9,999	87	13%	525	12%		
$10k – $14,999	94	14%	466	11%		
$15k – $24,999	140	21%	934	22%		
$25k – $34,999	69	10%	903	21%		
$35k – $49,999	88	13%	664	16%		
$50k – $74,999	9	1%	313	7%		
$75k – $99,999	3	0%	59	1%		
>$100,000	3	0%	48	1%		
	660	100%	4252	100%		

Distribution of Household Income by Ethnicity: Northern Ute Reservation

of congressional funding and the fluctuating royalties tribes receive from the depletion of their nonrenewable gas and oil resources. This employment profile contrasts sharply with non-Indians in surrounding communities, where about 20 percent of the work force is employed by various levels of government.

Figure 12 provides the distribution of income for Ute and "white" (i.e., non-Native, non-Latino, and non-African-American) households on the three reservations for 1990. Nearly half or more of Ute households have incomes under $15,000, with general income distributions significantly lower than their white neighbors.

The high proportion of Northern Ute households with incomes of less than $15,000 is in direct contrast to the small proportion of "white" households in this income range. There is a "crossover" point at $15,000 for Native and white households. Below this point the proportion of Native households is greater, while above this point the proportion of white households is greater.

Figure 13
Percent of Households (HH) Below Poverty Level 1980–1990

	Southern Ute		Ute Mountain		Northern Ute	
	1980	1990	1980	1990	1980	1990
% Native HH's below poverty level	37%	30%	37%	46%	30%	45%
% Non-Native HH's below poverty level	7%	16%	9%	N.A.	9%	17%

Figure 14
1990 Per Capita Income

	Ute Mountain	Southern Ute	Northern Ute
"White"	$2,665	$11,327	$8,184
Native American	$4,963	$6,124	$4,520

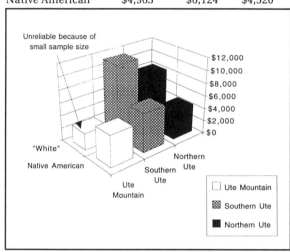

In general (Figure 13) two to three times as many Ute households are below the poverty line when compared with their non-Native neighbors. Moreover, with the exception of the Southern Ute, the proportion of Ute households below the poverty line has increased during the last decade, although the proportion of white households, reflecting worsening rural economic conditions, has also increased.

Reflective of the disparities between Utes and Anglos is the fact that individual Utes, on average, have about half the per capita income of their rural neighbors, as indicated in figure 14 (the low per capita income for "whites" on the Ute Mountain Ute Reservation is unreliable because of very low sample size).

Despite difficult economic conditions, Utes remain tied to their reservations as cultural homelands. Reservation life connects Utes to their past, enables them to sustain close ties with extended kin, and maintains continuity for their future. Reservations provide the setting for Utes to practice their religion, perform traditional ceremonies, and impart the Ute heritage to their children. *The Sun Dance Religion: Power for the Powerless*, Jorgensen's magisterial work on the Ute, contains a complete history and description of Ute ceremonial and religious activities. The Ute are still strongly committed to performing the Sun Dance, which employs elements of traditional, transformative, and Christian symbols. Fred Conetah, a Northern Ute and tribal historian, says that the dance is performed as a renewal of the spirit and group togetherness. He also notes that Ute participation in the Native American Church (Peyote Religion), like the Sun Dance, is an "expression of spiritual power in the face of lost political and economic control." The Native American Church has a significant proportion of adherents and it is not unusual for some Ute families to attend sweat lodges, the Native American Church, Sun Dance, and services of a Christian denomination. The Bear Dance continues to be the preeminent spring/early summer ceremonial and social event. Powwows are held on each of the Ute reservations.

Some Ute still work in buckskin, weave baskets, and do extensive beadwork. These items are often sold at gift shops associated with tribal enterprises, exchanged as presents, or worn at social and ceremonial occasions.

Donald G. Callaway

Joanna Endter-Wada

Further Reading

Aberle, David F., and Omer C. Stewart. *Navajo and Ute Peyotism: A Chronological and Distributional Study.* University of Colorado Series in Anthropology 6. Boulder: University of Colorado, 1957.

Callaway, Donald G., Joel Janetski, and Omer C. Stewart. "Ute." *Handbook of North American Indians.* Vol. 11. *Great Basin.* Ed. Warren L. d'Azevedo. Washington, DC: Smithsonian Institution, 1986.

Conetah, Fred. *A History of the Northern Ute People.* Salt Lake City, UT: Uintah-Ouray Ute Tribe, 1982.

Jefferson, James, Robert W. Delaney, and C. Gregory Thompson. *The Southern Utes: A Tribal History.* Ed. Floyd A. O'Neill. Ignacio, CO: The Southern Ute Tribe, 1972.

Jorgensen, Joseph G. *The Sun Dance Religion: Power for the Powerless.* IL: University of Chicago Press, 1972.

Schroeder, Albert H. "A Brief History of the Southern Ute." *Southwestern Lore* 30:4 (1965): 53–78.

Smith, Anne M. *Ethnography of the Northern Utes.* Museum of New Mexico Papers in Anthropology 17. Santa Fe: The Museum, 1974.

Stewart, Omer C. "Culture Element Distributions 18: Ute—Southern Paiute." *University of California Anthropological Records* 6 (1942): 231–355.

———. *Indians of the Great Basin, A Critical Bibliography.* Bloomington: Indiana University Press, 1982.

WACCAMAW-SIOUAN

The majority of the 1,500-member Waccamaw-Siouan Indian Tribe live in the three settlements of St. James, Rice Field, and Buckhead, on the border of Bladen and Columbus counties, North Carolina. The tribal members are believed to have descended from the Waccamaw tribe that inhabited the area in the early part of the eighteenth century. The Buckhead settlement can demonstrate continuous residence by tribal members from 1787.

As with other tribes in the Southeast, there is little documentation of tribal activities during most of the nineteenth century. Beginning in the 1890s and continuing until 1969, the Buckhead settlement had its own school known as the Wide Awake Indian School. Recognized as an Indian school by the State of North Carolina, it was financed by tribal members until 1941, when the state began providing funds. Its teachers were by and large Indians trained at the Pembroke Normal School. The school was closed under a desegregation order.

The efforts to initiate, maintain, finance, and accredit the school were led by a tribal organization, which by at least 1910 was known as the Council of Wide Awake Indians. This organization served as the tribe's governing body until the tribe received a state charter in the 1970s. The Council was made up of the principal Waccamaw-Siouan families.

Following World War II the tribal leaders made an effort to receive federal recognition. A local congressman introduced legislation in 1950, but unfortunately, the time was bad. Congress was in the mood to terminate tribes, not extend recognition, and so the effort failed. In 1971 the State of North Carolina extended recognition to the tribe, and since that time the tribe has been active in the development of the North Carolina State Indian policy.

Beginning in the 1960s the Tribal Council shifted its emphasis from the maintenance of its school to economic improvement. Tribal members formed the Waccamaw Indian Improvement Club to attract small industry to the community and assist tribal members in finding employment. Supported by their newly selected Chief Clifton Freeman and the Tribal Council, the continuing efforts met with modest success. By the 1970s the tribe was receiving assistance under a variety of federal poverty programs.

In 1972 the Tribal Council formed a nonprofit corporate body known as the Waccamaw-Siouan Development Association, Inc. This organization consists of a nine-member elected board of directors, which replaced the old tribal government. Under its aegis, the tribe operates an annual powwow, runs a commercial fish farm, a craft store, and programs.

With the development of a federal administrative policy for acknowledging tribes in 1978, the Waccamaw-Siouan Indian tribe began work on a petition for submission to the Bureau of Indian Affairs. However, a ruling in 1989 stopped the process; the tribe was found to be prohibited by a provision of the Lumbee Act of 1956. The tribe is presenting a review of that opinion.

Throughout its history, the tribe has had a number of effective, dedicated leaders. These include W.J. Freeman; the Reverend R.T. Freeman, and his nephew Clifton Freeman; Priscilla Jacobs, the present chief; and Darlene Graham, a lawyer with the state's attorney general. The tribe continues its struggle for federal recognition and its efforts to achieve economic and social improvements.

Jack Campisi

Further Reading

Blu, Karen L. *The Lumbee Problem: The Making of an Indian People.* New York, NY: Cambridge University Press, 1980.

Hudson, Charles. *The Southeastern Indians.* Knoxville: University of Tennessee Press, 1976.

Lerch, Patricia Barker. "State Recognized Indians of North Carolina, Including a History of the Waccamaw Sioux." *Indians of the Southeastern United States in the Late 20th Century.* Ed. Anthony Paredes. Tuscaloosa: University of Alabama (1992): 44–71.

Swanton, John R. *The Indians of the Southeastern United States.* Bureau of American Ethnology Bulletin 137 (1946). Reprint. Washington, DC: Smithsonian Institution, 1979.

Williams, Walter L., ed. *Southeastern Indians since the Removal Era.* Athens: The University of Georgia Press, 1979.

WAILAKI

The Wailaki (Wylacki), a southern Athabaskan-speaking people, are federally recognized as part of the Covelo Indian Community Council of the Round Valley Indian Reservation, in northwestern California. Authorized in 1864, enlarged in 1870, the 35,522.87-acre reservation located in present-day Mendocino and Trinity counties was established by executive order in 1875. The groups sharing the reservation, Wailaki, Yuki, Pit River, Achumawi, Pomo, Konkow,

Nomlaki, and Wintun, organized their tribal government under an Indian Reorganization Act Constitution and Bylaws, which were approved December 16, 1936.

The Wailaki are indigenous to the surrounding mountains and fiercely resisted being placed on the reservation. Most remained living in the hills working in the large cattle and sheep ranches of the white population. Others in the early 1900s homesteaded small parcels of land in their homeland. The widespread indenture of Indian children which accompanied the California Act for the Government and Protection of Indians (1850 and 1860 amendments) was particularly hard on the Wailaki, who began tattooing their young so they would always know of their ancestry. A particularly poignant account of this was narrated by Lucy Young in 1939; it has most recently been reprinted in 1992. The Wailaki resistance to being moved from their mountains into the reservation is reflected in today's small Wailaki population in the Round Valley. Total Wailaki population according to the 1990 census is 1,090.

The economic base of the Wailaki community both on and adjacent to the reservation has been primarily cattle and sheepranching; in the later twentieth century, the timber industry has been a major source of employment, but that is on the decline. Many people are forced to leave the reservation in order to find employment or to obtain higher education. Those living on the reservation share a common lifestyle, intertribal marriages, land base, and governmental responsibilities for the whole community. Concern for the preservation of traditional lifeways created a bond among the tribes which is reflected in the activities of the governing body. Development of a modern community with adequate resources to meet tribal needs has been and is a great challenge because of the remoteness of the community. The Tribal Council in 1974 developed a comprehensive development plan to address human services, land use, employment, economic development, culture, etc. One objective of the plan was to formalize a process and policy for the reacquisition of land in Round Valley, placing it in trust status in order to enlarge the land base of these groups. Towards this end, in the late 1980s they were able to purchase a large ranch which added about 16,000 acres of needed natural resources to the tribal land base. The tribal government continues to struggle with the social and economic issues which affect all the tribes on the reservation.

Wailaki were known for their healers and the manner in which they trained their young in the ways of medicine. They actually held a doctoring school that took place over a period of time with several doctors teaching their skills. Wailaki healers often work together or assist one another. Today, individuals continue to utilize the spiritual locations in their homeland. The healers who specialize in knowing plants continue to gather the healing herbs and to teach the simple living that goes with the understand-ing and use of plants. There are over ninety plants utilized in various types of healing. Subsistence gathering of such things as tan oak, black oak, and valley oak acorns, mushrooms, camas roots, berries, etc., still occurs for personal use and for the community ceremonies. There are also those who gather plant resources to continue traditional arts such as basketweaving, woodworking, and regalia making. Today's cultural struggle is around the issue of access to the aboriginal foods, plants, spiritual locations, etc., since all of the Wailaki aboriginal territory is either privately owned or in state or federal ownership, and is governed by land management methods which do not lend themselves to the cultural needs of the Wailaki community. This is extremely significant to the survival of traditional knowledges and uses. As part of the larger Indian community in northwestern California, the Wailaki are working with federal and state agencies to have their concerns heard and to affect the ways that these agencies can meet their needs. In 1991 a group of Wailaki formed the Wailaki Aboriginal Inter-Tribal Society in order to seek federal recognition as a distinct people.

Kathy Heffner-McClellan

See also **California Tribes**

Further Reading

Baumhoff, Martin. "California Athabascan Groups." *University of California Anthropological Records* 16:5 (1958): 157–238.

Elsasser, A.B. "Mattole, Nongatl, Sinkyone, Lassik, and Wailaki." *Handbook of North American Indians.* Vol. 8. *California.* Washington, DC: Smithsonian Institution (1978): 190–204.

Patterson, Victoria, et al., eds. *The Singing Feather.* Ukiah, CA: Mendocino County Library, 1990.

Sussman, Amelia. "The Round Valley Indians of California." *Contributions of the University of California Archaeological Research Facility* 31 (1976): 1–108.

Young, Lucy. "Out of the Past: Lucy's Story." *No Rooms of Their Own: Women Writers of Early California.* Ed. Ida Rae Egli. Berkeley, CA: Heyday Books (1992): 47–58.

WALAPAI

See Hualapai

WALLA WALLA

See Confederated Tribes of the Umatilla Indian Reservation

WAMPANOAG

The Wampanoag (known as the Pokanoket in early documents) have inhabited the southeastern portion of present-day Massachusetts—including Cape Cod—eastern Rhode Island, and Martha's Vineyard since at least the late fifteenth century. Best known in the literature for their relationship with the Plymouth Pilgrims, the Wampanoag have survived devastating

European-introduced epidemics, land loss, and the ill-fated attempt by Wampanoag sachem King Philip to rally the southern New England Indians against the colonists in the 1675 King Philip War. Despite these hardships, the Wampanoag survived the centuries and today they are fighting for both federal recognition and land. The Wampanoag currently number between 2,600 to 2,800.

Much of the ethnic pride the Wampanoag have today stems from the pan-Indian movement, which swept across the country during the first two decades of the twentieth century. Instrumental in this movement were the activities of two Mashpee men—Eben Queppish and Nelson Simons. Both men lived away from the Cape for a time: Queppish joined the Wild West shows of Buffalo Bill Cody, while Simons attended the Carlisle Indian School in Pennsylvania. They eventually returned home to Mashpee to galvanize Indian pride. They were instrumental in founding a confederacy known as the Wampanoag Nation in 1928.

The Wampanoag's current regional divisions are an outgrowth of the 1928 nation. The Wampanoag are divided into five regional autonomous groups or "bands." Gay Head on Martha's Vineyard and Mashpee on Cape Cod are the largest as well as the most politically and socially active subdivisions; followed by Assonet (from New Bedford to Rehoboth); Herring Pond (from Wareham to Middleboro); and Nemasket (the Middleboro region). Wampanoag Supreme Sachem Ellsworth Oakley, or Drifting Goose, appointed chiefs for the mainland groups during the mid-1970s and called Council of Chiefs meetings to discuss a variety of issues facing the Wampanoag. The Council still meets on occasion; however, the Wampanoag chiefs are likely to be joined by representatives from other Indian nations. The mainland groups also recognize a Supreme Medicine Man, John Peters, who is also the executive director for the Massachusetts State Commission on Indian Affairs.

Chiefs of the various groups in 1992 include: Earl Mills (Mashpee), Wind Song (Assonet), Alan Maxim (Herring Pond), and Donald Malonson (Gay Head). These leaders preside over a number of events, including the July Fourth Mashpee Powwow, Gay Head's Indian Day and Cranberry Day, and the Assonet's sacred New Year's ceremony and the Strawberry Festival.

The tribal councils of all of these groups manage political affairs, such as maintaining tribal rolls, managing finances, representing the group at both the state and federal levels, overseeing use of grants and various aid programs, filing landsuits, and "negotiating ethnicity." This latter task involves petitioning the United States government for federal recognition. Thus far, only Gay Head has received federal recognition (1987), while the Mashpee are responding to questions raised by the federal government about their petition. Tribal council positions are elected posts and are typically staggered so that

as one or two terms expire, other posts remain constant. The tribal councils operate according to written constitutions which specify terms of office, duties, and frequency of meetings.

Gay Head

The Gay Head count approximately 600 members, of whom 260 live scattered about the tiny island (100 square miles) of Martha's Vineyard. The Wampanoag here do not have a reservation per se; rather, the tribe owns certain lands in trust, such as the famous Cliffs of Gayhead, the cranberry bogs, a herring run, and some acreage near tribal offices. Tourism has become one of the major island businesses; individual families run some of the many snack bars and shops up at the Cliffs.

Economic necessity over the years has forced many Gay Headers to leave the island in pursuit of both education and jobs on the mainland. Most of those who leave, however, plan on returning one day. The Tribal Council chairwoman in 1992, Beverly Wright, is a case in point: she left the Vineyard after high school, coming back only in the summer to live with her people. Fifteen years ago she came back home for good.

The Gay Head successfully won federal recognition in 1987. That victory enabled them to receive a variety of federal monies (especially the "638" contracts that go to Native American communities) to provide health, educational, housing, and social services. The Gay Headers are in the midst of constructing thirty housing units and a multipurpose community building, which will house the tribal offices, a hall for special events, and a large kitchen. Many young Gay Headers have received scholarships to go to colleges on the mainland thanks to the 638 contracts. Educational monies are also spent to develop on-the-job training, and adult vocational training.

Gay Head celebrates Cranberry Day on the second Tuesday in October and Indian Day in August. Both events have sacred/private and secular/public components. Cranberry Day begins when Gay Headers go down to their bogs to give thanks to the Creator for the berries they are about to harvest. This private ritual is followed by a public display when the Indians return to the town hall, baskets filled with berries, for an afternoon of feasting, dancing, and drumming. On Indian Day, Gay Headers form the sacred circle—a symbol of all life—in the town hall, prior to feasting and dancing. Indian Day tends to be the more casual of the two events, and it is not uncommon for contemporary entertainers, like Arlo Guthrie, to perform. Gay Head hopes to bring back the pageants—Wright and other Gay Headers fondly recall these events from their youth, when the Wampanoag dressed in ceremonial regalia paraded on floats for the rest of the islanders to see.

Gay Head's priority in the twenty-first century is to provide a combination of educational, economic, and housing aid so that Indians can choose not to leave the island in pursuit of jobs.

Mashpee

The Mashpee Wampanaog number some 1,060, 600 of whom live in Mashpee. In 1976, the Mashpee filed a federal suit to recover the entire town of Mashpee or 16,000 acres of land, lakes, marshes, and tidewater areas. The Mashpees claimed that this land had been illegally taken from them in violation of the Trade and Intercourse Acts of the 1790s. Beginning in 1842 "the Commonwealth of Massachusetts divided ancestral lands that had been held in common by the Indians and parcelled them out to the Mashpees individually, and that culminated in 1870, when the legislature adopted laws changing the old Mashpee Indian District into an ordinary town and conveying the remaining tribal lands to the town," according to historian Paul Brodeur. The case went to court despite the Mashpees' efforts to resolve the issue. Tribal Council President Russell Peters says that Judge Walter J. Skinner—who presided over the long and controversial trial—made the recovery of land contingent upon the Indians' proving that they were indeed a tribe. On January 4, 1978, a landmark decision was reached: the court ruled that on certain key dates in Mashpee's history, the Indians did not constitute a "tribe."

Since losing this early battle, the Mashpee submitted their petition for federal recognition in 1989 and are anxiously awaiting the Branch of Acknowledgment and Research's decision. As for their land suit, Peters remains optimistic that "should we be successful in our fight for recognition, we will obtain some land somewhere."

Land and recognition are not the only issues at stake for the Mashpee as they move into the twenty-first century. Since the 1960s the Mashpees have watched as more and more tourists crowded into the Cape and began to buy up the lands in and around Mashpee. Whereas Mashpee used to be an "Indian town" governed by a combination of both Indian and non-Indian selectmen (in 1964 the first white selectman was elected), now it is a predominantly white town with no Indians serving as selectmen. The shooting of a Mashpee Indian by a policeman in 1988 threatened to further destroy an already deteriorating relationship between Indians and whites. However, the event has opened up a new dialogue between the two opposing groups—representatives from the Tribal Council and the town selectmen, along with representatives from the United States Department of Justice and the David Hendrix Committee on Civil Rights, are all meeting together to resolve this and other issues.

The Mashpee Tribal Council, incorporated in 1974 as the political arm of the tribe, is primarily responsible for both the petition and the former land suit. The Council is headed by a president, vice-president, secretary, and treasurer. An elected board of directors oversees the operations of the Council.

Best known of the Mashpee ceremonies is their powwow held over the July Fourth weekend. Wampanoag from all over the country "come home" to this event, because it is a time to renew friendships and family ties. The powwow is motivated by this familial incentive as well as by economic and educational incentives. The Mashpee Indians reap a profit from selling Native arts and foods to the public (the clambake is a big attraction), yet they also gain from educating the public about Native American culture and spirituality.

Laurie Weinstein

Further Reading

Brodeur, Paul. *Restitution: The Land Claims of the Mashpee, Passamaquoddy, and Penobscot Indians of New England.* Boston, MA: Northeastern University Press, 1985.

Campisi, Jack. *The Mashpee Indians: Tribe on Trial.* NY: Syracuse University Press, 1991.

Peters, Russell. *The Wampanoag of Mashpee.* Somerville, MA: Media Action, 1987.

Weinstein, Laurie. "We're Still Living on Our Traditional Homeland: The Wampanoag Legacy in New England." *Strategies for Survival.* Ed. Frank Porter, III. New York, NY: Greenwood Press (1986): 85–112.

———. *The Wampanoag.* New York, NY: Chelsea House, 1989.

WAPPO

The Wappo traditionally occupied the mountainous area in northern California from Cobb Mountain and The Geysers south to the Russian River valleys near Geyserville, and east into the Napa Valley just above the town of Napa, as well as a small area south of Clear Lake. Although geographically separated from the other Yukian-speaking peoples of northern Mendocino County, they are linguistically related to them. It is not clear whether their isolation from the other Yuki groups occurred through self-imposed migration or because of Pomo intrusion into their territory. The Wappo lived surrounded by Pomo, Lake Miwok, and Patwin people, and their language has been heavily influenced by them. The name Wappo is believed to be derived from the Spanish word *guapo*, because they were so brave and warrior-like in opposing the Spanish raids into their homelands. Wappo vocabulary was also greatly influenced by Spanish. They used Spanish loan words for most of the technology, food, and mission life they encountered outside their traditional world.

The Wappo territory included some of the richest mineral deposits and most prolific hot springs in northern California, and after the Spanish raids and missionization from San Rafael and Sonoma Missions, the American development of the area for both mining and resort trade occurred rapidly. Lytton Springs became well known for its cold seltzer water, while The Geysers became an international hot springs resort. All this activity affected Wappo life profoundly.

The former inhabitants of the Napa Valley were almost entirely gone by 1908. Some Wappo people eventually settled on the predominantly Pomo Dry Creek Rancheria, which was purchased, along with others, by C.E. Kelsey as part of the California homeless Indian appropriation program in 1914. Other Wappo had previously been given fifty-four acres in 1908 to form the Alexander Valley Rancheria. Wappo people also lived at Middletown and Big Valley rancherias in Lake County.

Most Wappo people during the 1930s and 1940s did seasonal agricultural wage work for others, primarily harvesting grapes, pears, and nuts. Wood-cutting provided some supplemental income during the winter. Racism was prevalent in surrounding white communities, and Indians rarely ventured into the towns except for occasional shopping.

In the 1990s a small number of Wappo people continue to live within their traditional territory in Sonoma and Lake counties. The most well-known Wappo person of recent times was Laura Fish Somersal, who worked with Jesse O. Sawyer on Wappo language, with the Army Corps of Engineers' Warm Springs sedge transplant project, with local dancers, and with many ethnographers. Laura received the first Woman of Achievement Award presented by the Sonoma County Commission on the Status of Women. She is most famous as a basketweaver and a photograph of her hands was featured on the 1983 National Women's History Week poster. She taught basketweaving to many and is fondly remembered for her great warmth and humor as well as her skill.

Victoria Patterson

See also **California Tribes**

Further Reading

Driver, Harold E. "Wappo Ethnography." *University of California Publications in American Archaeology and Ethnology* 36:3 (1936): 179–220.

Ortiz, Bev. "With Respect: Laura Fish Somersal, 1892–1992." *News from Native California* 5:1 (November/January 1990/91): 4–5.

Peri, David W., Scott M. Patterson, and Susan L. McMurray. *An Ethnographic and Historical Cultural Resources Study of the Aminoil, Little Geysers, Ford Flat, Cobb Mountain (Units 16, 18, 19, 20, 21) Geothermal Leaseholds, Sonoma and Lake Counties, California.* Rohnert Park, CA: Sonoma State University, Department of Anthropology, Ethnographic Laboratory, 1978.

Sawyer, Jesse O. "Wappo." *Handbook of North American Indians.* Vol. 8. *California.* Ed. Robert F. Heizer. Washington, DC: Smithsonian Institution (1978): 256–63.

WARM SPRINGS

See Confederated Tribes of the Warm Springs Reservation

WASHINGTON STATE TRIBES

See Chinook; Confederated Tribes of the Chehalis Reservation; Confederated Tribes of the Colville Reservation; Cowlitz; Duwamish; Hoh; Klallam; Lummi; Makah; Muckleshoot; Nisqually; Nooksack; Puyallup; Quileute; Quinault; Samish; Sauk-Suiattle; Shoalwater; Skokomish; Snohomish; Snoqualmie; Spokan; Squaxin Island; Steilacoom; Stillaguamish; Suquamish; Swinomish; Tulalip; Upper Skagit; Yakima Nation

See map on the following page.

WASHITA APACHE

See Plains Apache

WASHOE

The Washoe people today are members of the Washoe Tribe of Nevada and California. The name Washoe (obs. Washo) derives from the word *wá·šiw* or *wašt·šiw* in their own language.

Original Washoe territory comprised an area of more than 4,000 square miles from Honey Lake to the north, Antelope Valley to the south, and from the Sierra Nevada Mountains to the west and the Virginia and Pinenut ranges to the east. There were no dialectal or political divisions among subgroups, although the people often referred to themselves and others by terms indicating that they are southerners, northerners, westerners or valley-dwellers. The population at the time of white contact has been estimated at about 1,500 persons, but it may have been much larger. By the turn of the twentieth century various and unreliable census reports give population figures ranging from 150 to 800, indicating the effects of disease and starvation after white occupation. Their imminent extinction was predicted.

The Legacy of Conquest

The Washoe were never given a treaty or a reservation despite numerous petitions by Washoe leaders and some Indian agents urging the United States government to do so. They remained a virtually landless people under jurisdiction of the Carson Indian Agency until scattered allotments were awarded under the Dawes Severalty Act during the late nineteenth century, and until the establishment of Dresslerville and two other "colonies" on small parcels of land procured for them in 1917.

After the passage of the General Allotment Act of 1887, allotments were issued sporadically by agents assigning names arbitrarily upon township maps. The scattered plots were in the most desolate and waterless sections of the Pinenut Range or elsewhere. No lands around Lake Tahoe or in the fertile valleys were included. Whites trespassing for timber, mining, or sheep and cattlegrazing continued, despite the complaints raised by Washoe spokesmen such as Captain Jim, Captain Mayo, Captain Pete, Dick Bender, and others.

The opening of the Carson Indian School through federal legislation in 1891 was initiated by the forcible enrollment of hundreds of Washoe, Paiute, and Shoshone children over ensuing decades. Though

WASHINGTON STATE RESERVATIONS

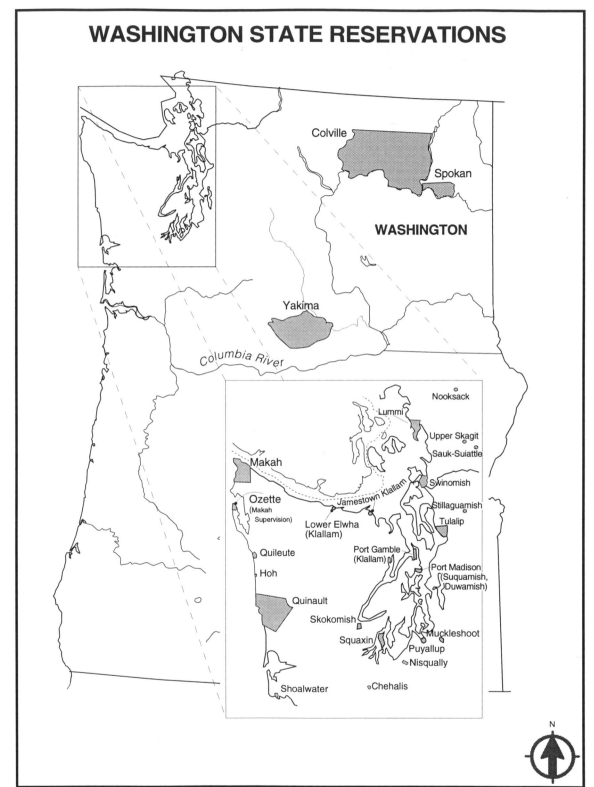

Source: *A Guide to the Indian Tribes of the Pacific Northwest* by Robert H. Ruby and John A. Brown.
Copyright © 1986, 1992 by the University of Oklahoma Press

Indian families resented the removal of their children to the boarding school where their language and culture were rigorously repressed, Indian students from surrounding states began to be admitted, and the quality of instruction markedly improved during the early twentieth century. A number of Washoe graduates were to become distinguished citizens. However, few Washoe children were able to attend Carson Indian School or the small government-funded day schools in the area. Segregated educational facilities were maintained until the 1950s, when all public schools were integrated.

Throughout this early period, the Washoe remained generally impoverished and disenfranchised. Housing was less than substandard, or nonexistent. Average family annual income (estimated at $640 in 1944) remained minimal even for families with a member employed on ranches or construction projects. A small supplemental income might be earned from the sale of pinenuts, firewood, or from grazing permits on allotment lands. A few women continued to make exceptionally fine baskets, and Louisa Kizer (known as Datsolalee) gained international recognition for her work. Yet she and the other Washoe weavers were able to sell the products of their remarkable artistry for only a mere fraction of the market value to traders.

Many Washoe families lived in camps on the ranches of white settlers where the women served as cooks and laundresses, and the men as low-paid laborers and cowboys. The Washoe population became increasingly concentrated in the ranching area of Carson Valley and around Carson City where there might be some opportunity for employment, and where the refuse of white towns often provided building materials and other items for their makeshift dwellings. The proximity of the Indian agency and the Carson Indian School improved access to sparse government patronage and also allowed them to be near any of their children who were enrolled. Yet a number of small Washoe groups continued to reside in their old habitation areas in Alpine County around Woodfords and Markleeville; in Washoe Valley; at Truckee and other towns along the headwaters of the Truckee River; around Reno in Truckee Meadows; and at Honey Lake and Sierra Valley to the north. Little was mentioned of these "scattered Indians" in official reports.

Transitions

In 1917 the federal government at last responded to petitioning from tribal leaders by the purchase of small tracts of land for the Washoe. Two ranches near Carson City consisting of 156 acres were to become the Carson Indian Colony. A forty-acre plot near Gardnerville in Carson Valley was placed in trust for the Washoe, and became the colony of Dresslerville. Reno-Sparks Indian Colony was established on the outskirts of Reno, with a small parcel purchased for the use of Washoe and Northern Paiute peoples in the area.

While citizenship was granted to the Washoe in 1924, segregated public facilities and schools were maintained in most areas until the 1950s. Minimal health care was provided by the Indian agency, which also administered police surveillance and courts. A Baptist mission was established at Dresslerville, which made its church available as a community center. Its ministers were respected for being among the few whites in the area to press state and local officials for improvements in the colony.

In the 1930s Ben Lancaster returned to Washoe country with the teachings of the Peyote Religion. Meetings of "The Tipi Way" were held throughout the area attended by hundreds of adherents attracted to the message of salvation from sickness, alcoholism, and oppression. The movement soon declined due in part to intense opposition from influential Indian doctors who perceived it as a threat to their profession, and from a disapproving white community. A few Washoe Peyotists continue as members of the Native American Church today, and are respected for their sober ways and maintenance of traditional values.

Under provisions of the Indian Reorganization Act of 1934, a Constitution was adopted in 1935 and a Corporate Charter was ratified in 1936. The language of the original Constitution seemed to delimit membership in "the Washoe Tribe" to those persons listed on the official census roles of the Carson Indian Agency and residing mainly in Dresslerville. Consequently, local councils were formed independently at Carson Indian Colony, at Reno-Sparks Colony, and at Woodfords in Alpine County, California. These eventually were incorporated with representation under a unified Washoe Tribal Council in the new Constitution of 1966. Recognition as a legally constituted entity made it possible for the tribe to acquire 794 acres of additional lands in trust. This parcel, adjacent to Dresslerville in Carson Valley, is known as the Washoe Ranch. Also, in 1970 the Washoe living in Alpine County, California, were able to establish a new "Woodfords Colony" on eighty acres of land in Diamond Valley granted by an act of Congress.

With the establishment of the Indian Claims Commission in 1946, the Washoe sought legal assistance and began to develop a comprehensive case. The prospect of tribal unity was enhanced by the inclusion of all identifiable Washoe groups regardless of state or local jurisdiction. Thus, in 1951 a claim was filed on behalf of "the Washoe Tribe of Nevada and California" requesting compensation of $42.8 million for an estimated 9,872 square miles of appropriated lands and resources. In 1970 they were awarded the token figure of about $5 million. Seventy percent of the funds were invested for expanded tribal development and for programs of education and general welfare. The remainder was distributed as per capita shares, mainly to elder members of the tribe who had waited so long for some restitution.

The Washoe Nation in the 1990s

Despite the dire predictions of their extinction in the early twentieth century, the Washoe Nation today comprises a population that exceeds estimates of their numbers prior to first intrusion of white settlers less than 150 years ago.

Moreover, the Washoe, who were never granted a treaty or a reservation, are in the process of recreating a land base from the remnants of their former territory, lands that they now refer to as the Washoe Reservation (see figure and map).

The Washoe Tribe of Nevada and California is governed by a fourteen-member Tribal Council with four-year terms of office. There are two representatives from each of the residential communities (the Colonies of Dresslerville, Carson, Woodfords, and Stewart), and three representatives of nonreservation groups (e.g., Reno-Sparks Colony, etc.). The tribal chairman is elected at large and serves as chief executive officer of the tribe, assisted by a vice-chairman and secretary-treasurer.

The former substandard housing has largely been replaced by almost 300 units of modern dwellings, of which most were provided by federal Housing and Urban Development grants. Extensive improvements have been made in community planning and public services assisted by the tribal operated Utility Authority. The long waiting list for new housing has required the implementation of an expanded residential program over the next few years.

A new tribal headquarters building on Highway 395 south of Gardnerville contains the offices of the chairman and a number of administrative operations including the tribal police force, judiciary court, planning department, and archives. The nearby Washoe Health Center provides a wide range of medical service and treatment programs. In Dresslerville, a new building of the Housing Authority contains a staff responsible for residential planning and assignment. The Senior Citizens Center, also in Dresslerville, has an enrollment of over 200 elders and provides a recreation hall, transportation, and daily lunches. A number of elders are involved in programs of oral history, the Washoe language, and demonstration of traditional crafts.

The tribe conducts a social services program that includes Head Start for youths from seven to fourteen years of age, as well as educational counseling in vocational training and job opportunities for public school graduates. A substance abuse program has been initiated to deliver information, treatment, and counseling to those with problems of alcoholism or drugs.

The Washoe Development Corporation manages the Washoe Ranch, a public campground, smokeshops and craft stores, and is also responsible for a forest resource fire management program. Efforts are underway to expand the economic base by promoting new commercial enterprises in tribal properties, such as recreational, residential, retail, and other facilities geared to the increasing tourism and local service economy. Special attention is being given to upgrading skills and vocational opportunities by employing tribal members in the new projects. In 1991, 20 percent of the tribal work force was seeking work, while 12 percent of those employed were earning less than $7,000 annual income. This problem is a major concern of the tribal government and is addressed as a major issue in all development programs.

In 1978 the Washoe established a Hunting and Fishing Commission, and in 1980 the tribe won jurisdiction in federal court over management of the deer herd as well as hunting and fishing activities in "Washoe Indian country." Through this program, the Washoe have asserted a significant role in the protection of an endangered habitat and the implementation of their traditional conservation practices.

A major concern confronting the Washoe in recent decades has been the erosion of cultural resources. Few remain who can speak the Washoe language fluently, or who can transmit the extended family values and religious and ceremonial traditions. There is an increasing concern among the youth to preserve the rich oral history and knowledge of the medicinal herbs and other gifts of the natural environment. The establishment of the Washoe Cultural Resource Program has been a large step forward in addressing these issues. Emphasis is placed upon senior citizens as the most cherished resource, and the elders are included as consultants and participants in all planning and implementation. Among the important initiatives of this program is the identification and documentation of historical and sacred sites increasingly endangered by the pressure of real estate development. Of special concern is the desecration of numerous isolated cemeteries and old burial places throughout the area, many of which are located on privately owned lands inaccessible to Washoe families who wish to visit them. The cultural program also sponsors classes in the Washoe language, in tribal history and custom, the procurement and preparation of Native foods and medicinal herbs, basketweaving, and other traditional crafts. Demonstrations and talks are presented at schools, public exhibits, and fairs.

From the nineteenth century to the present, the Washoe have never ceased to press for the recovery of some portion of their ancient holdings at Lake Tahoe. The formation of the Washoe Cultural Foundation almost a decade ago was for the purpose of soliciting funds and other support to establish a presence at the lake. At last, with the cooperation of the United States Forest Service, suitable sites have been made available for the development of a Washoe Cultural Center and campground at Taylor Creek on

WASHOE COLONIES AND RESERVATIONS

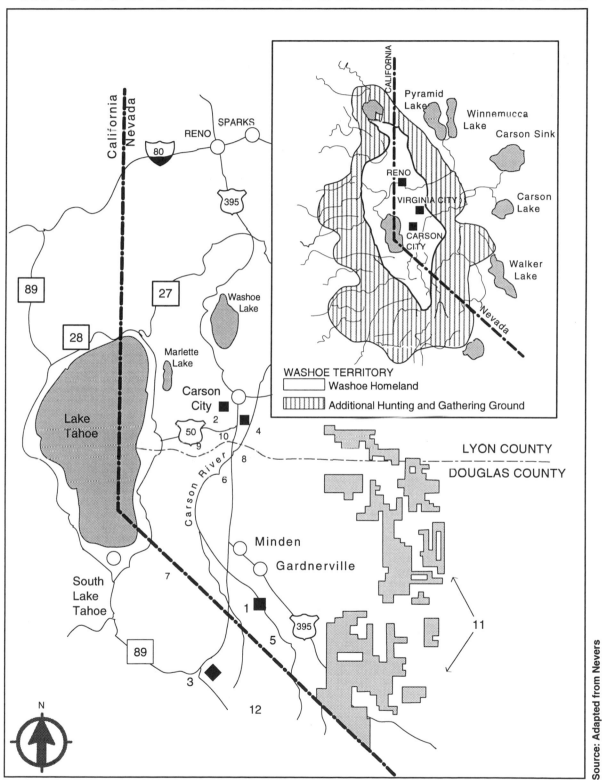

Numbers 1 to 12 refer to figure numbers on the following page.

Source: Adapted from Nevers

the western shore where a museum, amphitheater for ceremonial use, and areas for Washoe social gatherings are planned.

The Tribal Strategic Plan of 1991 places emphasis on a goal of self-governance, the development of a modern tribal society that is fully responsive to the needs of its members and increasingly effective in regional affairs. To achieve this goal, special attention must be directed to quality education, the creation of new tribal enterprises, and an increase in the level of Washoe influence over the Bureau of Indian Affairs and other agencies dealing with Indian policy. The aim is self-sufficiency and independence, while promoting cooperation and productive communication with local, state, and federal sectors of the larger society. Moreover, there is the expressed determination to preserve what is possible of a precious heritage and cultural identity.

Warren L. d'Azevedo

Washoe Communities and Lands, 1991

Reservation Lands	Acreage	Population	Resources
Residential Communities			
1. Dresslerville Colony	90	348	100 units
2. Carson Colony	160	275	74 units
3. Woodfords Colony	80	338	79 units
4. Stewart Community	329	90	30 units
["Off-Reservation" Washoe]		475	
Tribal Trust Lands			
5. Washoe Ranch	794	—	Agriculture
6. Stewart Ranch	2,960	—	Agriculture & Recreation
7. Wade Property	388	—	Development
8. Silverado Parcel	160	—	Development
9. Upper Clear Creek	157	—	Recreation
10. Lower Clear Creek	209	—	Development
Public Domain Allotments			
11. 435 in Nevada	65,000	—	Pinenut Harvest, Resource
12. 20 in California	2,500	—	Management & Conservation, Fish & Game
TOTAL	72,777	1,526	

See map on preceding page for locations

Further Reading

d'Azevedo, Warren L. "Washoe." *Handbook of North American Indians.* Vol. 11. *Great Basin.* Ed. Warren L. d'Azevedo. Washington, DC: Smithsonian Institution (1986): 466–98.

Downs, James F. *Two Worlds of the Washo, an Indian Tribe of California and Nevada.* New York, NY: Holt, Rinehart and Winston, 1966.

Nevers, Jo Ann. *Wa She Shu: A Washo Tribal History.* Reno: Intertribal Council of Nevada, 1976.

Price, John A. *The Washo Indians: History, Life Cycle, Religion, Technology, Economy and Modern Life.*

Nevada State Museum Occasional Paper 4. Carson City, NV: The Museum, 1980.

WATER RIGHTS

The water rights of American Indian tribes can only be understood in the greater context of nineteenth- and twentieth-century Native American history generally. Aboriginal claims, original treaty obligations, reservations allotment, assimilation, and the more recent trend toward tribal self-determination have all played a role in defining the status of tribal rights to water resources. In particular, the enduring three-way tension between tribal sovereignty, state government authority, and the federal trust responsibility has over the course of this century shaped water law and policy which is unique to American Indian tribes.

In the United States, authority over the allocation of rights to water resources is a matter which has most often been left to state governments, with the proviso that all surface water rights are held subject to the federal navigation servitude, and to the powers of Congress under the commerce, property, and supremacy clauses of the United States Constitution. Although Congress therefore has the power to overrule or modify state water doctrines in the national interest, it has generally avoided doing so—in no small part because of the influence of the western states congressional delegations, most of whom tend to hold private, state-regulated water rights somewhat sacrosanct. In its passage of the 1902 Reclamation Act, for instance, Congress agreed to abide by state water law doctrines in the acquisition and allocation of water from federally financed reclamation projects.

Thus, any discussion of tribal water rights must make reference to two important variables: the water rights allocation doctrine of the state of which the Indian reservation is a contiguous neighbor, and the doctrine(s) upon which the tribe bases its water rights claims. The two general state water rights doctrines are the "riparian" system—popular in the relatively damp climates of the northeastern and southeastern United States—in which all parties whose property adjoins a surface water supply share equal and common rights to the reasonable use of available supplies; and the "prior appropriation" system of the arid West, in which the first party to divert water out of a watercourse and devote it to a specified "beneficial use" (e.g., domestic, municipal, agricultural, or industrial) secures the use right—"first in time is first in right." Unlike the riparian system, in which all landowners sharing a waterway enjoy equal rights to it, prior appropriators stand in a hierarchical relationship, based on the seniority of the date of appropriation and the uses to which the water is devoted. In times of shortage, junior appropriators must forfeit some or all of their supplies to more senior water rights holders (i.e., those who historically began to withdraw water sooner). Another important feature of the prior appropriation doctrine is the "use it or lose it" principle; appropriators who do not use the full measure to which they are entitled may have that portion of their right reclaimed by the state and allocated to other users. While this aspect of the prior appropriation doctrine was intended to promote full use of water resources and discourage speculation in underdeveloped water rights, it has also encouraged the wasteful use of scarce western water, since water conserved may be forfeited to the state.

The two different principles on which tribal governments usually base their assertions of water rights are "aboriginal" or ancient use rights (founded on historic and prehistoric use, from "time immemorial"); and the "reserved rights" doctrine, based on judicial interpretation of the treaties and agreements creating the reservations, in which the federal courts have generally held that establishment of the reservation also by implication set aside for tribal use enough water to fulfill the purposes for which the reservation was created. Since by far the largest and greatest number of reservations, as well as the largest population of Native American peoples, are in the arid western states where water is scarcest, the most serious legal and political issues concerning tribal water rights have arisen from conflicts between the federal reserved rights doctrine and state prior appropriation principles (at the time of this writing, the only Native American water rights dispute implicating the riparian doctrine is part of a larger land use issue involving the Seminole tribe in Florida). The balance of this article therefore reviews the substance of reserved rights, the nature of their conflict with state law, dispute resolution efforts, and possible future developments in the definition of tribal rights. For brevity and simplicity's sake, attention is focused on the rights of tribes rather than individual allottees.

Reserved Rights
(the Winters Doctrine)

In 1908 the United States Supreme Court decided a case brought by the United States government against farmers in Montana, in which federal authorities had moved to enjoin them from diverting so much water from the Milk River that it left insufficient water for Indians at the downstream Fort Belknap Reservation to engage in even subsistence agriculture. In *Winters v. United States* (207 U.S. 564 [908]), the Court decided in favor of the United States and tribe, and also sought to establish a doctrine that would both set aside enough water to sustain Indian reservations *and* accommodate some features of the prior appropriation system. The high court held that: (1) whenever the federal government entered into an agreement for the creation of an Indian reservation, there was also by implication reserved for perpetual tribal use enough previously unappropriated water to fulfill the purposes for which the reservation was established; (2) to comport with the prior appropriation

doctrine, the date on which the reservation was created would be considered the date on which the tribe's water had been impliedly reserved; (3) tribes could devote the water to any use which fulfilled the reservation's purposes; but (4) unlike the prior appropriation system, the tribe's water rights could not be lost through nonuse. Since most Indian reservations were created in the latter half of the nineteenth century, this ruling retroactively recognized the tribes as among the most senior appropriators in every western state.

Although this decision represented a great legal victory for the tribes, the federal government did not vigorously assert tribal *Winters* rights on their behalf during the first half of the twentieth century, while it was distributing much of the West's remaining water to non-Indian farmers and ranchers (and indirectly, cities) under the auspices of the Reclamation Act. In the first fifty years after the *Winters* decision was handed down, Congress built most of the nation's reclamation projects to deliver what was in some measure rightfully tribal water to non-Indian customers; during that same time period, the federal government asserted tribal reserved rights in court only four times.

But in 1963, in *Arizona v. California* (273 U.S. 546 [1963]), the Supreme Court resoundingly reaffirmed the very senior and expansive rights held by the tribes, at least in theory. In this landmark decision, the Court ruled that the 3,500 Native Americans on reservations along the banks of the lower Colorado River were entitled to nearly a million acre-feet of water a year (1 acre-foot equals 326,000 gallons)—about three times the quantity awarded to the entire state of Nevada. The Court computed the tribe's share of the river by estimating how many acres of reservation land were irrigable, and multiplying that by the amount of water that would be needed per acre to grow a marketable crop. The Courts have since applied this "practiceably irrigable acreage" standard to many legal disputes over the quantification of tribal water rights.

In 1976 in *Cappaert v. United States* (426 U.S. 128 [1976]), the Supreme Court extended the principles of reserved rights to groundwater on and near federally created reservations, whenever a "hydrologic connection" between surface and groundwater can be shown. But also in that year—as well as in *Arizona v. San Carlos Apaches* (463 U.S. 545 [1983])—the high court ruled that under many circumstances the tribes may also be compelled to adjudicate their rights in assumedly more hostile state courts and water commissions instead of the federal courts, where the *Winters* doctrine originated. Historically the federal courts have also been much more sympathetic to indigenous American water rights claims than have state tribunals.

However, in the 1980s that situation began to change. During the eight years of the Reagan administration, nearly half the judges on the federal bench were replaced, including some members of the Supreme Court. On the whole, these relatively conservative jurists tend to be more deferential to states' rights than were their predecessors, with the result that in the 1980s the tribes lost five of the six water rights cases to come before the Supreme Court. Many tribes have of necessity become more interested in, if not enthusiastic over, the possible negotiated settlement of water rights disputes. Western tribal resource managers have also learned that simply securing a water rights entitlement legally is not the same as being able to put the water to use. In most of the West, any water use which involves taking it out of the water course and moving it somewhere else is expensive. For this reason, most of the negotiated settlements discussed below have involved convincing the tribes to accept less water than they are legally entitled to, in return for the promise of economic assistance in developing a lesser quantity of water.

Unresolved Issues and Dispute Resolution

In the early 1980s there were nearly fifty major indigenous American water rights disputes wending their way through court systems and commission hearings throughout the western states. Most of these cases involved some or all of the following issues: (1) *adjudicatory jurisdiction* (would the case be heard in state or federal court?); (2) *quantification* (how much water had been reserved for tribal use?); (3) *application* (to what uses could the water be put?); (4) *marketability* (should tribes be empowered to sell reserved waters to non-Indians?); and (5) *resource management and water quality* (should the tribes have the same comprehensive regulatory authority over water resource management as adjoining state governments, and should tribes be subject to any state water quality rules or only to federal agency rules and standards?)

Although most of these issues in the major cases were still being argued in court in the early 1990s, an increasing number of suits were also being settled through negotiation. In southern Arizona in 1982 federal legislation was adopted in which the Tohono O'odham agreed to withdraw a groundwater suit against the City of Tucson and other non-Indian neighbors in return for deliveries from the Central Arizona Project, similar to agreements involving the Ak Chin Community in 1984 and the Pimas in 1988. Also in 1988 the Mission Indians of southern California agreed to settle a suit in return for the water from a proposed conservation-based water project, while the Colorado Utes agreed to drop a reserved rights suit in return for water deliveries from the proposed Animas-La Plata reclamation project.

In most of these cases the tribes have agreed to withdraw their *Winters* doctrine suits (which had been slowing non-Indian water development because of the tribes' relatively powerful legal positions as theoretical senior appropriators) in return for congressional promises to build water projects to deliver water to reservation lands. Whether these agreements will

in the long run seem prudent depends heavily on whether Congress can and will continue to appropriate the funds to build the water projects promised to the tribes in these settlements. If Congress keeps its word, even in light of the unprecedented deficits facing the federal government in the last decade of the twentieth century, the western tribes may yet attain desperately needed water-related economic development on their reservations. But if Congress instead becomes forgetful of these promises, as it historically has regarding many nineteenth-century treaty obligations, the tribes will instead be litigating these rights well into the next millennium.

Furthermore, in addition to the major water rights conflicts between tribal and neighboring non-Indian governments in much of the West, many tribes are experiencing varying degrees of conflict within their own membership regarding the wisest and best use of the water resources they now are or soon will be controlling. Not unlike the value conflicts over natural resource management besetting American society generally, many western tribes are engaged in a searching internal dialogue between those urging the rapid and most remunerative development of water resources, and the generally more traditional advocates of instream uses (e.g., wildlife habitat maintenance) which entail less environmental disruption. And as with mineral resources, if history is a useful indicator, the more valuable water becomes in the future, the more actively western tribes will be urged to put their waters to classically Western utilitarian uses. The tribes, no less than other governmental entities with resource management rights and responsibilities, will inevitably be caught up in what is rapidly becoming a global debate over the prospects for genuinely sustainable environmental management.

Lloyd Burton

***See also* Economic Development; Fishing and Hunting Rights; Mining; Treaties**

Further Reading

Burton, Lloyd. *American Indian Water Rights and the Limits of Law.* Lawrence: University Press of Kansas, 1991, 1993.

Folk-Williams, John A. *What Indian Water Means to the West: A Sourcebook.* Santa Fe, NM: Western Network, 1982.

Fradkin, Phillip L. *A River No More: The Colorado River and the West.* New York, NY: Knopf, 1981.

Hundley, Norris. *Water and the West.* Berkeley: University of California Press, 1975.

McCool, Daniel. *Command of the Waters.* Berkeley: University of California Press, 1987.

Wilkinson, Charles. *American Indians, Time, and the Law.* New Haven, CT: Yale University Press, 1987.

———. *Crossing the Next Meridian.* Washington, DC: Island Press, 1992.

WEA

See Peoria; Miami

WEAVING

See Basketry; Textiles

WENDAT

See Wyandotte

WHALING

The Iñupiat, the aboriginal people of Alaska's Northwest and Arctic coasts, have a tradition of whaling dating back thousands of years. Wisdom, passed on from generation to generation, demonstrates that people have acquired and perpetuated intimate knowledge about the bowhead whale (*balaena mysticetus*), providing testimony that whaling has been, and continues to be, central to the existence of the Iñupiat.

As in days past, the act of whaling does not begin when the crews have prepared for the hunt and gone out to camp near the open leads, the openings in the ice through which the whales migrate on their way to summer feeding grounds, to wait for the right bowhead at the right time. Rather, it begins almost a year earlier in June and July when the men are out in their boats pursuing bearded seals. In addition to providing meat and seal oil for sustenance, the skins of the *ugruk* are used as a covering on the *umiaq*, the skin boat. Strips of blubber are placed in the skins before they are put into burlap bags and stored for use in the early spring when the skins of the boats are replaced.

Tradition dictates that the *umialik*, or captain, his wife, and crew, if they were successful in landing a bowhead in the spring are obligated to share the whale they caught three times during the year. Whale meat, *muktuk* (whale skin and blubber) and flipper are retrieved from the ice cellar to share in the joy of the catch with the community during *Nalukataq*, Thanksgiving and Christmas.

Preparations begin for the spring hunt with the cleaning of ice cellars upon the arrival of the "new sun." There is a belief that unless the cellar is clean and is lined with fresh new snow, that a whale will not give himself, as there is no home to which to go. Women undertake the task of sewing the *ugruk* skins for the new boat cover. Clothing must be made and mended. Men stretch the skins over the boat frame and organize the whaling gear and equipment. Once everything is ready, the wait for the ideal conditions begins. The east wind is needed to open the lead and the current must be right. People out on the ice must constantly utilize the knowledge that has been passed down to them about different ice conditions and wind and ocean currents.

Finally the long-awaited moment comes, when the Iñupiaq belief that a whale gives himself, comes to life. A bowhead has been landed; a whale has been successfully captured and brought to the edge of the shorefast ice. One of the crew members takes the captain's flag and races to shore to place it on the captain's house signifying the successful catch. Community members rush to participate in pulling the whale from the ocean onto the ice for butchering. All

the while preparations are being made at the captain's house for the feasting of all of the delicacies of the whale that will feed the whole community. It is indeed a time of great happiness, a time when what being Iñupiaq means comes to a peak.

The successful crews don't wait long to get the *mikigaq* (fermented whale) to begin being processed in preparation for *apuq*, the beaching of the boat, which marks the end of the season. Once again, the whole community partakes in the sharing of the whale by feasting on this delicacy. The season culminates in the *Nalukataq*, the Blanket Toss, where again the successful crews divide portions of the whale to the community. The skin of the boat that caught the whale is removed, made into a "blanket" and suspended from four posts with block and tackle. In celebration, people get on the blanket one at a time and are tossed into the air repeatedly until they lose their balance. The blanket is taken down at the end of the day for the traditional dance honoring the captains, their wives, and crews. Soon after the celebration is over, the cycle begins again.

These customs have persevered despite many odds. The continuation of traditions has been threatened numerous times by influences beyond the control of the Iñupiat. Nonetheless, they have continued their subsistence harvest of whales. Rosita Worl, in an extensive discussion of Iñupiat whaling in 1980, has concluded: "Communal participation in the traditional bowhead whaling complex, which forms the basis of the Iñupiat social and cultural system, remains the distinctive characteristic of these people."

In 1977 the International Whaling Commission (IWC) issued a total ban on the subsistence take of bowhead whales. The Iñupiat were stunned and angry that some distant foreign organization could issue such an order. The IWC Scientific Committee had concluded that " . . . any taking of bowhead whales could adversely affect the stock and contribute to preventing its eventual recovery, if in fact such recovery is still possible . . . on biological grounds exploitation of this species must cease." The IWC did not know very much about the bowhead and probably knew even less about the Iñupiat when they made their decision. At the time the ban was issued, IWC's biologists estimated the population at 600 to 2,000. These figures did not include an assessment of the population by the Iñupiat who, after many, many years of observation, were intimately familiar with the behavior and migration patterns of the whales.

The knowledge the Iñupiat had in relation to the health of the population was disregarded. There was no "valid scientific evidence" acceptable to the IWC that supported the claims the Iñupiat were making that the population was indeed healthy. The Iñupiat responded to the IWC whaling ban by forming the Alaska Eskimo Whaling Commission (AEWC) and, with the support of the North Slope Borough, sponsored research costing millions of dollars to substantiate what they had known all along. Then, however, they had to convince the IWC that the visual and acoustical census research was scientifically valid. Finally in 1992 the IWC accepted 7,500 as the "best estimate of the size of the Bering-Chukchi-Beaufort Seas stock of bowhead whales." Many Iñupiat consider this estimate to be low.

The Iñupiat continue to practice whaling, albeit under the purview of the IWC's quota system, which replaced the 1977 ban and which was developed as a result of AEWC pressure. They continually face scrutiny by IWC on various facets of whaling, including most recently the issue of "humane killing." If history is any indication, Iñupiat whaling will continue as it has for centuries to come, despite the constraints imposed by outside forces. It certainly is alive and well today.

Jana Harcharek

Further Reading

Blackman, Margaret B. *Sadie Brower Neakok: An Inupiaq Woman.* Seattle: University of Wahington Press, 1989.

O'Brien, Sharon. "Undercurrents in International Law: A Tale of Two Treaties." *Canada-United States Law Journal* 9:1 (1985): 1–57.

Worl, Rosita. "The North Slope Iñupiat Whaling Complex." *Alaska Native Culture and History.* Eds. Y. Kotani and W.B. Workman. Osaka, Japan: National Museum of Ethnology, Senri Ethnological Studies 4 (1980):305–32.

WHEELER-HOWARD ACT

See Indian Reorganization Act

WHITE EARTH CHIPPEWA

See Ojibwa: Ojibway in Minnesota

WICHITA

The Wichita or Kitikiti'sh are of Caddoan linguistic stock. Originally a number of affiliated tribal groups were confederated with the Wichita, and through the years these have become fully integrated into the tribe. Some of these associated groups are the Tayovayas, the Tawakoni, and the Waco.

Never a large group, estimates of the population in 1492 are around 3,800. By the 1890s, the Wichita numbered only 153. Numbers have increased steadily since then; in 1901 the population rebounded to 180; in 1976 it was 800; in 1983 about 1,000; and as of 1993 the Wichita population stands at 1,764.

In 1872 the Wichita, Caddo, and Affiliated Tribes agreed to accept a reservation of approximately 743,000 acres that is centered in present-day Caddo County, Oklahoma. However, Congress never ratified the agreement, clouding Wichita title to their original homeland. In 1901 Congress slated Wichita land for allotment, opening the "excess" to white settlement later that year and providing payment of $1.25 per acre to the tribe. Today the Wichita own only a ten-acre tract of land, but jointly own about 2,400 acres with the Caddo and Delaware tribes.

Originally an agricultural people who still live largely in rural areas, the Wichita today are employed in a variety of jobs. The tribal government, the Riverside Indian School, and the Anadarko Indian Health Center are major sources of employment.

As a small tribe, the Wichita have been buffeted by the whims of federal policies that have put great strains on maintaining traditional culture. Consequently, the Wichita language is spoken by only twenty or so fluent speakers. Efforts are underway to reverse this decline. Tribal, federal, and private support have funded the production of audio tapes to assist the Wichita in learning their language.

Most Wichita today are Baptists, although a number adhere to the Native American Church. Each August the tribe holds a dance on tribal grounds near Anadarko, and there is an annual get-together with the Pawnee Indians. Each tribe alternates from year to year as hosts to the other in an annual ceremony that includes visiting, camping, and dancing, and that culminates in gifts of money and food from the host tribe.

The Wichita adopted a governmental structure in accordance with the Oklahoma Indian Welfare Act of 1936, and are served by seven officers that include a chairman, vice-chairman, secretary, and treasurer. Gary McAdams is the tribal chairman in 1993. The tribe has recently established a tax commission to license and assess fees on vendors who deal with the tribe. Tribal offices are located near Anadarko, Oklahoma, where the tribal government actively seeks to rebuild the culture, attract jobs, provide for its elders, and protect the tribe's greatest asset—the children.

Ray Miles

See also **Allotment; Caddo; Economic Development; Oklahoma Tribes; Pawnee**

Further Reading

Chapman, Berlin B. "Establishment of the Wichita Reservation." *Chronicles of Oklahoma* 11:4 (1933): 1044–55.

———. "Dissolution of the Wichita Reservation." *Chronicles of Oklahoma* 22:2–3 (1944): 192–209; 300–14.

Curtis, Edward S. "The Wichita." *The North American Indian.* 20 vols. Norwood, MA: Plimpton Press, 1907–1930.

Newcomb, W.W., Jr. *The People Called Wichita.* Phoenix, AZ: Indian Tribal Series, 1976.

WINNEBAGO

The Winnebago were first encountered by Europeans in 1634 near what is now the Green Bay area of Wisconsin. The tribe was removed to Iowa in 1840, but by 1865 they had been relocated to Nebraska. However, half of the tribe returned to Wisconsin by the 1880s, resulting in the two separate political and cultural groups that exist in Nebraska and Wisconsin today.

WINNEBAGO IN NEBRASKA

The Winnebagos call themselves "Hochungra," meaning "People of the Parent Speech." The tribe was removed from their homeland in Wisconsin in 1840, and over the next twenty-six years they were moved to the Neutral Ground in northeast Iowa; the Long Prairie Reservation in central Minnesota; the Blue Earth Reservation in southern Minnesota, the Crow Creek Reservation in South Dakota, and finally to the Winnebago Nebraska Reservation in northeast Nebraska in 1863 to 1865. Half of the tribe had moved back to Wisconsin by the 1880s.

The land base of the reservation is composed of 40,000 acres, mostly crop land, woods, and pasture. The tribe lost two-thirds of their reservation due to the 1887 General Allotment Act. The population of the whole tribe, including those in Nebraska, Wisconsin, and urban centers, was 6,920 people according to the 1990 census. The Winnebago Nebraska Reservation is home to some 1,600 people.

The Winnebago Tribe of Nebraska is a federally recognized Indian tribe, organized under the 1934 Indian Reorganization Act. The Tribal Council is composed of a chairman, vice-chairman, secretary, and a treasurer. All officers serve a term of one year, but their term of office in the governing body is three years. The current tribal chairman is John Blackhawk. Past Winnebago leaders were Frank Beaver, Louis LaRose, Gordon Beaver, and Sam Tebo.

The tribe was awarded $4.6 million in 1975 by the Indian Claims Commission for the land lost in an 1837 land cession treaty with the Winnebago. The people voted to divide the money with 65 percent reserved for tribal programs and 35 percent for per capita payments. Three important programs were developed: credit, land acquisition, and a tribal wake and burial program.

In July of 1986 the tribe retroceded from the state, back to the federal government. All civil and criminal jurisdiction is now handled by the tribal court system, but under the plenary power of the Bureau of Indian Affairs (BIA).

The hub of Winnebago activity in Nebraska is the town of Winnebago. Here is located the Indian Health Service Hospital, the BIA agency office, tribal offices, schools, and businesses, such as the tribally owned grocery store, the Winnebago Company A Gas Station, and the new Winna-Vegas Casino, where a good portion of the tribe is employed. Most of the people live in three housing developments on the reservation. Winnebago children attend school beginning with the Native American Head Start program, and continuing on with education at the Winnebago Public Elementary and High School. Some students attend St. Augustine's Indian Mission Elementary School. After high school, the Winnebago students attend the Nebraska Indian Community College, Winnebago Campus. Others attend colleges and universities across the nation.

English is spoken in all homes, and the Winnebago language is used by only 10 percent of the people. Many Winnebago belong to various Christian churches and the Native American Church. The tribe holds its annual Homecoming Powwow the last week of July.

The main health problem on the reservation is diabetes. The tribe hopes to achieve economic and food self-sufficiency by the year 2000.

David Lee Smith

See also **Higher Education**

Further Reading

Jones, John Allen, Alice E. Smith, and Vernon Carterson. *Winnebago Indians: Winnebago Ethnology; Economic and Historical Background for the Winnebago Indian Claims.* New York, NY: Garland Publishing, 1974.

Lurie, Nancy Oestreich. "Winnebago." *Handbook of North American Indians.* Vol. 15. *Northeast.* Ed. Bruce G. Trigger. Washington, DC: Smithsonian Institution (1978): 690–707.

Mahan, Bruce E. "Moving the Winnebago." *The Palimpsest* (February 1922): 33–52.

Radin, Paul. "The Winnebago Tribe." *Bureau of American Ethnology 37th Annual Report* (1923). Lincoln: University of Nebraska Press, 1970.

WINNEBAGO IN WISCONSIN

The Winnebago call themselves "Wonkshieks," which means "First People of the Old Island" (North America). Their language belongs to the Chiwere Siouan family. Some Winnebago today call their "Hochungra," "People of the Big Voices," a name given them by the Iowa Indians after hearing Winnebago speeches at Prairie du Chien. The term "Winnebago" is an uncomplimentary Sac and Fox word that translates to "People of the Dirty Waters."

The major Winnebago town of Red Banks was located in their 2-million-acre homeland of the "Great Pinery," on the Red Banks peninsula of Wisconsin, near present-day Green Bay. Winnebago oral tradition claims the tribe took part in twenty-one treaties with the federal government, but only eleven treaties still exist. At the beginning of the treaty period (1816), Winnebago population was estimated at 5,000. By the end of the nineteenth century, after the trauma of removal and dispersal of the population, the Wisconsin Winnebago had been decimated to 1,500.

The Wisconsin Winnebago reluctantly formed a new government in 1963 based on the format laid out in the 1934 Indian Reorganization Act (IRA). However, they also retained their traditional chief-clan structure, with the two forming a matrix-like organization providing for two chains of command. The traditional chief-clan structure is culture-oriented, while the IRA government (the Wisconsin Winnebago Business Committee) favors assimilation.

The Winnebago in Wisconsin are organized into two moieties: Sky, consisting of four bird clans; and Earth, made up of five animal and three water creature clans. Chiefs are chosen from these clans, and tribal elders are highly venerated and looked to for guidance and wisdom. The traditional Winnebago religion still functions in the late twentieth century, featuring the vision quest and a ceremonial cycle based on a complex cosmology.

The Winnebago Nation in Wisconsin operates bingo games and casinos. Not all Winnebago are in favor of their participation in the gaming industry, and the elders and other traditionals fear that gaming will erode Winnebago culture, particularly among the young people. There is also state opposition to Indian gaming in Wisconsin. Anti-gaming legislation has been attempted in direct contradiction of Native sovereignty and treaty rights.

Military service is given great honor in Winnebago culture, and the tribe encourages young men and women to volunteer in one of the armed services. Clan ceremonies are conducted to reduce fear in warriors leaving to fight wars. Winnebago veterans have been among the most highly decorated in United States military history, earning awards from the Medal of Honor to the Purple Heart.

There were about 5,000 Winnebago in Wisconin in 1993, bringing the population back to its early nineteenth-century numbers. They no longer have a reservation in Wisconsin, but are concentrated in the communities of Black River Falls, Wisconsin Dells, Tomah-La Crosse, Wittenberg, and Wisconsin Rapids.

Walter Funmaker

Further Reading

Lurie, Nancy Oestreich. "Winnebago." *Handbook of North American Indians.* Vol. 15. *Northeast.* Ed. Bruce G. Trigger. Washington, DC: Smithsonian Institution (1978): 690–707.

Radin, Paul. "The Winnebago Tribe." *Bureau of American Ethnology 37th Annual Report* (1923). Lincoln: University of Nebraska Press, 1970.

WINTERS DOCTRINE

See Water Rights

WINTUN

The term "Wintun" is used to refer to the language group of Wintu, Nomlaki, and Patwin belonging to the Penutian family. The major divisions are related to the dominant geography and topography of each region. The Wintu are a mountain river people, the Nomlaki a prairie plains people, and the Patwin have two major areas of marshlands in the west and valleys and hills in the eastern part of their territory. While the Wintu inhabited parts of what are now Trinity, Shasta, Siskiyou, and Tehama counties in California, the Nomlaki were of two major divisions in what is now Tehama and Glenn counties, and the Patwin were located in the northern lands of the San Francisco Bay area. The Wintun could be characterized as situated in the greater Sacramento Valley, with the Sacramento River as a feature of all of these different geographical regions.

In the sixty years before the turn of the twentieth century, entire tribes in California were devastated;

at least 75 percent of the Patwin and Nomlaki were destroyed. The genocidal policies imposed on the Wintun, along with the pollution of the streams and the taking of their land, is reflected in the statistical information on their population. From a 12,500 estimated precontact population, the 1990 census shows 2,244 Wintu, 332 Nomlaki, and no Patwin.

The impact of white disruption was to destroy tribal unity by the taking of land and destroying traditional food and material gathering areas. The introduction of cattle, hogs, and sheep destroyed numerous plant and bulb areas. Damages to streams and vegetation from copper-processing plants in the 1880s and early 1900s and finally the inundation of lands by the construction of dams took their toll on the Wintun population. Not being able to practice some of their traditional activities due to the destruction of the land and habitat has been detrimental to the physical health of individuals.

The 25,000-acre Nome Lackee Reservation was established in 1854; however, white settlers found this land desirable and by 1863 the reservation was dissolved and the remaining Nomlaki were forcibly removed to the Round Valley Reservation. The settlements at Colusa, Cortina, Paskenta, and Grindstone were officially created under appropriation acts of 1906 to 1909, which is indicative of the need and vitality of these communities at the time. These reservations guaranteed a sanctuary for them. Reservations in this period did not have to deal with the raids and lawlessness that had characterized the earlier times. Reservations (or rancherias) created around the turn of the century helped to stabilize groups and even more importantly insured a safe place for the people, the sacred roundhouse, and the continuation of the ceremonies. In the 1970s the Stony-Elk Creek Dam, which would have inundated Grindstone, was successfully rebuffed by a coalition of local ranchers and the Grindstone Rancheria.

Several rancherias were terminated, but there are still Indian parcels of land in Wintun "ownership" in addition to the remaining rancherias. A special land issue is the Toyon-Wintu site. The Toyon Conservation Camp, located in Wintu tribal territory, was reacquired in 1973 and incorporated by the Wintu as the Toyon-Wintu Center. There was a seven-year agreement made between the government and Toyon-Wintu that recognized the tribe's right of "ownership" and the importance of keeping an updated enrollment. However, the United States government bulldozed all buildings and removed the people living on Toyon in 1984.

In the 1870s the Nomlaki adopted the Ghost Dance cult and in the early 1900s the Big Head; both rites continued to be performed as late as the 1930s and the Big Head has continued to the present time. One of the most important factors in maintaining cultural preservation of religions and ceremonial activities was the participation and dedication of the Maidu and the Wintun elders. Wallace Burrows was one of the most important singers and teachers of ceremonial information who kept the ceremony alive. In spite of much change, the Wintu still maintain an appreciation of their Indian history and traditional connection to the land. Florence Jones has been the most persistent elder in maintaining traditional religious activities and traditional involvement with the land. She is widely known by surrounding tribes as a spiritual leader, healer, and teacher of the youth. She has been a spokesperson in identifying and articulating traditional information on questions of a sacred nature.

Even though the turn of the century found most Wintun participating in mainstream society, they still valued their aboriginal culture. Traditional foods were used extensively in large gatherings of people and for "big times." Many people continue to use traditional foods, most significantly acorns. The importance of the Sacramento River was in its provision of salmon and as a meeting ground for exchange and trade.

The devout concern of the Wintun for the protection of burial grounds and other sacred places is continually being challenged by developers of new subdivisions, highways, and general construction; currently, the protection of Mt. Shasta as a viable sacred place is a major issue for the Wintun. Environmentalists have also joined them in this concern to protect the mountain from development. Other issues affecting most of the Wintun in the 1990s are the questions of reorganization and tribal recognition. Tribal organizations in Hayfork, Bald Hills, Winnemem, Toyon, and others are in the process of petitioning for federal acknowledgment and Paskenta is asking for recognition as they were removed in 1961. The Nomlaki are being forced to deal with the question of waste disposal dumping.

Because of the importance of maintaining the earth and the close connection the Wintun have with it, the violation of burials and sacred sites has a direct bearing on their emotional health because it affects religious concerns. Further destruction of the natural habitat, and the resulting negative impact on the traditional worldview, also affects the protection of traditional village and herb and basket gathering sites. The maintenance of traditional activity is very crucial to the preservation of the Wintun way of life. The Wintun would like to assume the responsibility of defining our own destiny, but it is very difficult under the present conditions to do this.

Frank LaPena

See also California Tribes

Further Reading

DuBois, Cora A. "Wintu Ethnography." *University of California Publications in American Archaeology and Ethnology* 36:1 (1935): 1–148.

Goldschmidt, Walter. "Nomlaki." *Handbook of North American Indians.* Vol. 8. *California.* Ed. Robert F. Heizer. Washington, DC: Smithsonian Institution (1978): 341–49.

Johnson, Patti J. "Patwin." *Handbook of North American Indians.* Vol. 8. *California.* Ed. Robert F. Heizer. Washington, DC: Smithsonian Institution (1978): 350–60.

LaPena, Frank R. "Wintu." *Handbook of North American Indians.* Vol. 8. *California.* Ed. Robert F. Heizer. Washington, DC: Smithsonian Institution (1978): 324–40.

WIYOT

The Wiyot (Weott) live in Northwestern California as part of the general population and on three rancherias: Rohnerville, Table Bluff, and Blue Lake. They are Algonquian speakers who historically lived primarily along the shores of Humboldt Bay and the mouths of the Mad and Eel rivers; they also utilized the forests and nearby prairies extensively. Living on the valuable waterways, the Wiyot were impacted extensively in the early 1850s when Americans began settling in this area. Not only were they pushed out, but they were killed in large numbers.

February 25, 1860, marks the event that lent a devastating blow to the population and culture of the Wiyot. The religious leaders of the tribe were conducting annual ceremonies on Indian Island, about one and a half miles off the shore in Humboldt Bay. Large numbers of people had gathered for this ceremony when in the early morning hours, while they slept, citizens of Eureka brutally attacked, killing all but a few. That night additional attacks took place at other locations simultaneously. Newspapers of the time indicated that as many as 250 Wiyot died that night. These atrocities were editorialized in the *New York Century* newspaper, where it was written: "In the Atlantic and Western States, the Indians have suffered wrongs and cruelties at the hands of the stronger race. But history has no parallel to the recent atrocities perpetrated in California." Damage to the Wiyots went far beyond the individuals who died during those early morning hours; it became a pervasive event in the lives of those who survived and still is embodied in the Wiyot of today.

On February 25, 1992, a group of Wiyots and others gathered to remember and honor those who lived and died some 122 years ago in the early morning hours during a time of religious celebration of life. These contemporaries wanted to bring to the attention of the local Eureka area residents the need and importance of the participation of the Wiyot community, both as individual citizens and as tribal governments, in the development and management of the Humboldt Bay area.

Wiyot individuals throughout the larger population do have a strong sense of cultural and tribal identity. In recent history, they have not held any of their traditional religious dances, but do attend and support the ceremonies of their neighboring tribes. Today, members of the three rancherias are working to establish viable tribal governments with an emphasis on community economic development. However, the larger Wiyot population does not live on the rancherias. The 1990 census gives a population figure of 450. Many Wiyot live in Eureka and other towns and cities in northern California, but they are not part of the federally recognized Wiyot community at this time.

Kathy Heffner-McClellan

See also **California Tribes**

Further Reading

Elsasser, A.B. "Wiyot." *Handbook of North American Indians*. Vol. 8. *California*. Ed. Robert F. Heizer. Washington, DC: Smithsonian Institution (1978): 155–63.

Loud, Llewellyn L. "Ethnography and Archaeology of the Wiyot Territory." *University of California Publications in American Archaeology and Ethnology* 14:3 (1918): 221–436.

Norton, Jack. *Genocide in Northwestern California: When Our Worlds Cried*. San Francisco, CA: Indian Historian Press, 1979.

WOUNDED KNEE II

During the spring of 1973, the nation's attention was captured by a spectacular seventy-one-day siege, conducted by federal authorities against traditional Oglala Lakotas and supporters from the American Indian Movement (AIM), at the tiny hamlet of Wounded Knee, on the Pine Ridge Reservation in South Dakota. "Wounded Knee II," as the historic standoff is known, was the largest and most sustained armed conflict in North America since the conclusion of the nineteenth-century Indian Wars. Its ramifications continue to be felt in federal/Indian relations through to the present day.

Background to Wounded Knee II

The context in which the fighting at Wounded Knee occurred concerned a top-secret plan undertaken by the Department of the Interior to effect an unratified transfer of the northwestern one-eighth of the Pine Ridge Reservation to the federal government, a contravention of the 1868 Fort Laramie Treaty. The area, known as the Sheep Mountain Gunnery Range, had been borrowed by the War Department at the outset of World War II for use as a training field for aerial gunners. Although the government promised the parcel would be returned to the Oglalas at the end of the war, it never was. By 1971, Indian efforts to recover this section of the reservation, a part of the larger Black Hills land claim struggle, had become increasingly vociferous and potentially embarassing to the United States.

Other things being equal, it is possible that federal officials might have responded favorably to Oglala demands in this regard. However, in 1970 a highly classified collaborative venture by the National Uranium Resource Evaluation Program, and the National Aeronautics and Space Administration, revealed rich uranium deposits near Sheep Mountain. From this point on federal planners intended to take the contested property permanently.

Dick Wilson and the GOON Squad

In 1972, Richard "Dick" Wilson was elected to the Pine Ridge tribal presidency by a narrow margin. He soon received a Bureau of Indian Affairs (BIA) grant of $67,000 with which to form a "Tribal Ranger Group." The group quickly started to refer to itself as the "GOON" Squad, an acronym allegedly standing for "Guardians of the Oglala Nation." It reported directly to the tribal president.

By mid-1972 it was general knowledge on the reservation that many of the Pine Ridge BIA police force were moonlighting on the GOON Squad. In addition to the local police, the GOONs consisted of up to a hundred other Indians retained periodically to serve in this capacity. While their official purpose was never clarified by Washington, they were soon accused of terrorizing the leaders of the land claims struggle and other members of the opposition in a series of beatings, shootings, vehicular assaults, and fire-bombings.

Bid for Wilson's Impeachment Fails

The initial response of those targeted by the GOON Squad was to form the Oglala Sioux Civil Rights Organization, which sought, to no avail, to compel the Justice Department to intervene in the pattern of political violence emerging on Pine Ridge. A second part of the group's strategy was to avail itself of its right under the tribal Constitution to impeach Dick Wilson. The organization gathered more signatures on a petition for Wilson's removal than had originally voted for him, forcing the BIA to schedule formal impeachment proceedings for mid-February 1973. The Bureau named Wilson to preside over his own impeachment process, which was held under the watchful eye of sixty armed United States Marshals from the Justice Department. Not surprisingly, when the vote on the tribal president's impeachment occurred on February 22, Wilson kept his office. He immediately proclaimed a reservation-wide ban on further meetings by his opponents.

AIM Caravan to Wounded Knee

In defiance of the ban, the Oglala Sioux Civil Rights Organization and the traditional Council of Elders held an extended emergency meeting at Calico Hall, near the reservation village of Oglala. On the afternoon of February 26, this group requested the assistance of AIM in attracting the attention of the general public to the conditions at Pine Ridge. After attempts by AIM leader Russell Means (Oglala) to meet with Dick Wilson were physically rebuffed, it was decided that a picked group should go to the symbolic location of Wounded Knee—site of the notorious massacre of more than 300 Lakotas by the United States Seventh Cavalry in 1890—to hold a press conference. A caravan of 54 cars set out for Wounded Knee on the night of February 27. A smaller group went to Rapid City to coordinate the desired media presence for the following morning.

At dawn on February 28 the Wounded Knee group discovered it had been sealed into the hamlet by a series of roadblocks erected overnight by the GOONs and BIA police. When FBI observers and United States Marshals began to arrive later in the morning, the "occupiers" expected the barricades to be dismantled and that they would be allowed to leave peacefully. Instead, the marshals began constructing their own positions.

By the end of the evening of the first day, Chief United States Marshal Wayne Colburn had assigned another 250 of his personnel to Pine Ridge, and had secured a number of BIA police SWAT teams from other reservations and fourteen tank-like armored personnel carriers from the South Dakota National Guard to back them up. FBI Special Agent in Charge Joseph Trimbach also arrived on the scene from Minneapolis to take personal charge of his agency's growing involvement. General Alexander Haig ordered two of his best irregular warfare specialists, Colonels Jack Potter and Volney Warner, to the reservation to coordinate direct military participation.

Inside the Hamlet

AIM members, most of whom had gone to Wounded Knee unarmed, finding themselves surrounded, broke into a trading post owned by the Gildersleeve family and armed themselves with the weapons for sale inside. By nightfall, they had begun constructing bunkers. AIM security coordinator Stan Holder (Wichita) organized a series of "fire teams" to man these strong points and to conduct patrols between them. The Gildersleeve Trading Post also provided initial food supplies for the approximately 200 people trapped inside the rapidly consolidated federal perimeter.

Wounded Knee Captures Nation's Attention

The Wounded Knee standoff immediately caught the nation's attention. Within the first few days, scores of people familiar with the local terrain began to backpack food, additional weapons, ammunition, and medical supplies through federal lines at night. This effort, augmented on two occasions by airdrops of food and medicine, allowed those inside Wounded Knee to continue. Federal authorities attempted to stem the flow of supplies to the defenders by imposing a five-state cordon around South Dakota. A nation-wide investigation of Wounded Knee support groups was initiated by the FBI. More than 2,500 people, most never prosecuted, were arrested for such activities as gathering canned goods and clothing to be shipped to Pine Ridge during the siege. During the next two months, two AIM members, Buddy Lamont (Oglala) and Frank Clearwater (Eastern Cherokee), were killed inside Wounded Knee by federal gunfire. Another fifteen people were seriously wounded. The federal forces suffered only one serious casualty during the same time, a marshal named Lloyd Grimm

who was hit in the back and paralyzed, probably from a bullet fired on his own side of the siege line. Altogether, more than a half-million rounds of military ball ammunition were fired into Wounded Knee during the course of the siege.

Negotiations

A government offer of amnesty to traditional Oglalas backfired on March 11, when authorities lifted their roadblocks, anticipating an immediate outflow of all non-AIM members from the hamlet. Instead, traditional people, among them the revered Oglala Head Chief Frank Fools Crow, poured into Wounded Knee. They ceremoniously reiterated their commonality with AIM, and declared themselves an "Independent Oglala Nation," wholly separate from the Wilson regime and its acceptance of United States domination.

A complicated sequence of negotiations began on March 13 between federal representatives and the coalition of AIM, the Independent Oglala Nation, and the Oglala Sioux Civil Rights Organization. On May 3, the government finally agreed to a formal meeting to discuss United States compliance with the terms of the 1868 Treaty and explore in good faith the possibility of reestablishing a federal treaty commission to serve as the medium through which United States relations with indigenous nations would be conducted. Authorities agreed to remove their roadblocks so that the funeral of Buddy Lamont might be conducted without interference. They also agreed to a seventy-two-hour moratorium marking the point when the Indians inside Wounded Knee laid down their arms, and the point when federal arrests were begun for crimes alleged to have occurred during the siege. Except for the funeral arrangements, the government ignored or refused to explore in good faith all of these agreements.

The Aftermath

When the siege ended, the government's campaign to neutralize Indian resistance was launched full-force. Of the 562 persons arrested, 185 were subsequently indicted by federal grand juries on the basis of evidence provided by the FBI. Only fifteen were ever convicted, all for offenses like "trespassing" and "interference with a postal inspector in performance of his lawful duty."

The government did succeed in tying up key leaders almost indefinitely. The classic illustration of this tactic is Russell Means, charged with thirty-seven felonies and three misdemeanors. At one point he faced an aggregate sentence of triple-life plus eighty-seven years. Freed from pretrial detention only after posting a $125,000 cash bond, Means was exonerated on all forty counts. This result required nearly three years of hearings, trials, and more than a million dollars in legal defense provided by the National Lawyers' Guild.

A much grimmer form of repression was manifested during this period on Pine Ridge itself. Between March of 1973 and March of 1976, there were a minimum of 342 serious physical assaults of AIM members and supporters on the reservation. Additionally, at least sixty-nine persons affiliated with the resistance were killed. Despite eyewitnesses who identified many assailants as known GOONs, not one of these homicides was solved by the FBI, the agency exercising preeminent jurisdiction over Indian country. By the spring of 1975, the supporters of the traditional community were presented with a clear choice: either abandon their oppositionist politics altogether, or adopt a posture of armed self-defense. On June 26, 1975, a firefight erupted between an AIM encampment and a large number of federal agents, BIA police, GOONs, and white vigilantes on the Jumping Bull property near the village of Oglala. Two FBI agents, Jack Coler and Ronald Williams, and an AIM member, Joe Stuntz Killsright, were killed during the fighting. Another AIM member, Leonard Peltier, was eventually sentenced to double-life imprisonment because of his alleged role in the deaths of the agents.

FBI Presence on Pine Ridge

The FBI quickly brought a massive military-style presence onto Pine Ridge. Throughout July and August of 1975, some 250 agents carried out an extended series of sweeps and air assaults across the reservation, conducting warrantless searches on a systematic basis and generally terrorizing the population.

By September 1975 the situation was finally considered to be sufficiently under control for Dick Wilson to sign the instrument transferring title for over 76,200 acres of the Sheep Mountain Gunnery Range to the Department of the Interior. The Interior Department assigned the parcel status as an annex to the adjoining Badlands National Monument, administered by the National Forest Service. In January 1976 Congress passed Public Law 90–468, codifying the transfer. In the face of mounting protests from the traditionals, and a potential lawsuit by the tribal government of Al Trimble, which had replaced the Wilson regime, the law was amended. While it now provides that the Oglalas may recover the surface area in question at any time by referendum, subsurface (mineral) rights are left permanently and exclusively in the hands of the federal government. The whole complex of conflict referred to as Wounded Knee II is part of what can be described as the continuing Indian wars of the United States.

Ward Churchill

See also **American Indian Movement; Red Power**

Further Reading

Burnette, Robert, with John Koster. *The Road to Wounded Knee.* New York, NY: Bantam Books, 1974.

Churchill, Ward, and Jim Vander Wall. *Agents of Repression: The FBI's Secret Wars Against the Black Panther Party and the American Indian Movement.* Boston: South End Press, 1988.

Ranck, Lee. "Siege at Wounded Knee." *Social Action* 1 (May 1973): 6–21.

Tilsen, Kenneth E. "U.S. Courts and Native Americans at Wounded Knee." *Guild Practicioner* 31 (Spring 1974): 61–69.

U.S. Congress. Senate. Committee on Interior and Insular Affairs. *Occupation of Wounded Knee: Hearings Before the Subcommittee on Indian Affairs, 93d Cong., 1st sess.* Washington, DC: U.S. Government Printing Office, 1973.

Voices from Wounded Knee, 1973. Mohawk Nation via Rooseveltown, NY: Akwesasne Notes, 1974.

Zimmerman, Bill. *Airlift to Wounded Knee.* Chicago, IL: Swallow Press, 1976.

WUKCHUMNI

See Yokuts

WYANDOTTE

During the twentieth century, most Wyandotte Indians lived in Oklahoma, Kansas, and Quebec. Disparagingly called "Huron" by the French, this term is in great use in historical documents and used by the members of this tribe still living in Quebec. The people call themselves "Wendat," meaning "Island People." Originally living along the northern banks of the St. Lawrence River, where contemporary Huron still reside, the Iroquois pushed many of them west to Ohio and Michigan. In 1843 the United States forcefully removed these people to Kansas. By 1857, they were driven out of Kansas and settled in northeastern Oklahoma near their old friends from Ohio, the Seneca-Cayuga.

To escape the fighting between the pro- and anti-slavery forces before the Civil War, many Wyandotte and Seneca-Cayuga moved south into Indian Territory. Both tribes remained on their lands in Indian Territory after the Civil War, while other Wyandotte stayed in Kansas. Allotment broke up the Oklahoma reservation in 1893, and the land was parceled out to the 241 Wyandotte living there. About seventy other Wyandottes arrived from Kansas too late to receive land; these people went back to Kansas or returned to Ohio, Michigan, or Quebec.

The Wyandotte Tribe of Oklahoma was established in 1937 following the passage of the Oklahoma Indian Welfare Act of 1936. Their Constitution provides for a tribal government comprised of a chief, elected representatives, and a Tribal Council that meets monthly. Leonard Cotter and Lawrence Zane each served as chief between 1937 and 1976. Mont Cotter and Philip Peacock followed them in office before the tribe elected Leaford Bearskin in 1983.

In 1956 the Wyandotte were one of the tribes singled out for termination during the Eisenhower administration. After twenty years of struggle, the tribe succeeded in regaining federal recognition in 1978. Today tribal enrollment stands at 3,617 members in Oklahoma. As of 1993 the Wyandotte own 192 acres in common, and individuals own their own allotments as well.

The tribe has made significant advances under the leadership of Chief Bearskin. The tribal government provides scholarships for students, daily meals for elders, new homes for tribal members, a health center, a tribal center and meeting hall, and a preschool facility. The Wyandotte are buying ten acres of land in Park City, Kansas, where they plan to build a gambling enterprise. They received a grant to fund the Wyandotte Museum and Cultural Center, as well as funds to locate, purchase, and catalogue the material culture of their people.

Another funded project seeks to conduct oral interviews of the elders to preserve the Wyandotte heritage and remnants of the language, and establish a library and archives. The historical committee of the tribe has a tradition of publishing, including a book by Robert E. Smith providing a brief history of the tribe, and a series of forthcoming paperbacks on tribal life, the most recent of which is *Our Great Chiefs*. Wyandottes are a diverse group with members who are farmers, ranchers, laborers, clerks, secretaries, nurses, artists, and teachers. Wyandottes in Okla-

homa and elsewhere treasure their Indian identity and rich heritage.

Clifford E. Trafzer

See also **Oklahoma Tribes; Seneca-Cayuga**

Further Reading

Smith, Robert E. *Wyandots: A Brief History*. Wyandotte, OK: Wyandotte Tribe of Oklahoma, 1974.

Trafzer, Clifford E. "The Wyandots: From Quebec to Indian Territory." *Oklahoma's Forgotten Indians*. Ed. Robert E. Smith. Oklahoma City: Oklahoma Historical Society, 1981.

Walsh, Martin W. "The 'Heathen Party': Methodist Observation of the Ohio Wyandot." *American Indian Quarterly* 16 (Spring 1992): 189–211.

Wright, Muriel H. *A Guide to the Indian Tribes of Oklahoma*. Civilization of the American Indian 33. 1951. Norman: University of Oklahoma Press, 1986.

YAKIMA NATION

The Yakima Indian Nation consists of formerly autonomous tribes, bands, and villages of indigenous peoples, who lived contiguously in the south central region of the present state of Washington. Their territories extended from the summit of the Cascade Mountains, across the Yakima River Valley and Great Columbia Plateau, to the Columbia River on the east and on the south. The people shared a common way of life and a general ethic of peaceful coexistence.

Major bands within this area were the Kittitas/ Upper Yakima, the Lower Yakima, the Klickitat (Klikitat), the Wanapam, the Wishham (Wishxam, Wishram), the Palus (Palouse), and the Wenatchi/Pisquose. South of the Lower Yakima, numerous independent villages were clustered along the Columbia River. The Dalles, a famous trading center on the plateau, was located in Wishham territory on the Columbia; upriver to the east was the great fishery of Celilo Falls. The Wenatchi and Yakima shared another noted fishery, Wenatshapam, later confiscated by the federal government. Most of the people spoke a Northwest Sahaptin dialect of the Sahaptian language. Wenatchi were Salish-speaking; Wishham spoke Upper Chinook. These are the people who were brought together by the Treaty of June 9, 1855, to become the "Consolidated Tribes and Bands of the Yakima Indian Nation."

People relied on fishing for salmon and other riverine resources, gathering wild plant foods, and hunting. Families came together in permanent winter villages and then dispersed to temporary camps from spring through fall. By the nineteenth century, villages consisted of extended family dwellings of rectangular mat-covered lodges, called longhouses, which persisted as both homes and places for religious worship into the twentieth century.

A major change in lifestyle occurred around 1730 with the acquisition of horses. With horses came greater mobility, more effective buffalo hunting, and increased contact with Plains tribes. Plains influences led to the selective adoption of a variety of Plains cultural traits, such as dancing apparel, still popular today for social ceremonies, powwow dancing, parades, and other occasions. And tipis, of canvas rather than skin, are still used to "camp."

Before extensive losses due to epidemics that spread into the Plateau by 1775, the Kittitas and Lower Yakima had a combined estimated population of around 7,000. By the time of first white contact in 1805, these bands had decreased to 3,500. The entire "New Yakima Nation" of the Treaty of 1855 was estimated to be only 2,000 to 2,500. The reservation count was only 1,362 in the census of 1910.

The New Yakima Nation

The Yakima Treaty Council, convened by Governor Isaac I. Stevens of Washington Territory in 1855, led to land cessions of 10.8 million acres and removal to a reservation, terms accepted under duress by Kamiakin, the great Lower Yakima chief, and other headmen representing the tribes, bands, and villages that formed the new political entity, the Yakima Indian Nation. A reservation of 1.2 million acres was set aside in Lower Yakima territory, a rough rectangle of about 58 kilometers from north to south, and 112.65 kilometers from east to west. To correct original survey errors, two disputed parcels of land were returned to the reservation in 1904 and in 1972. The reservation now covers approximately 1.4 million acres of land. The Wanapam were not named in the treaty, and some families remained in their village at Priest Rapids. They were finally designated as part of the Yakima Nation by the Indian Claims Commission in 1974. Most Wenatchi/Pisquose settled later on the Colville Reservation, choosing not to become part of the Yakima Nation.

According to treaty terms, the Yakima were to be permitted to continue to fish and to gather native plant foods at customary, off-reservation subsistence sites. No whites were to be allowed to homestead or traverse the reservation without permission. Within weeks, treaty terms were violated, leading to a series of armed conflicts. The Yakima and their allies were finally defeated in 1858, and Indian agents moved in, controlling reservation policies and activities.

In spite of attempts to enforce hair-cutting, and to eradicate the traditional Longhouse Religion, many families refused to comply. The Longhouse of Chief Kotiahkan became the center for Yakima *Wáashat* services. Smohalla, a Wanapam, led services at Priest Rapids. The Longhouse Religion is still followed, and its popularity has increased greatly during the latter half of the twentieth century.

Lands in the Yakima Valley were rapidly homesteaded by settlers. In 1884, when the Homestead Act was extended to Indians, some Yakima Nation individuals from the middle Columbia River established homesteads on original village sites off the reservation, where they have continued to live, despite loss of fisheries and litigation over land and fishing rights.

After the passage of the General Allotment Act of 1887 and allotment of lands to reservation Indians, young Chief Shawaway Kotiahkan, son of the Longhouse leader, led a successful fight to oppose the sale of "surplus" reservation acreage. These tribal lands, still held in trust, remain the basis for the extensive tribal holdings of the Yakima Nation today. When allotment rolls were closed on the reservation in 1914, 4,506 individuals (some non-Yakima) had received 440,000 acres. The Yakima Nation still communally held 780,000 acres.

Unfortunately, many of the individually allotted lands were quickly "alienated" due to sales to non-Indians, and titles to 26,953 acres of allotted land were transferred to non-Indian ownership. By 1913, most cultivated lands on the reservation were either leased or had been purchased by non-Indians. Valuable irrigated lands went quickly. By the 1980s, 80 percent of the reservation population was non-Indian. Many Indians became day laborers, picking hops and other crops, freighting, and \ king at other seasonal jobs. The reservation was irrevocably "opened."

Twentieth-Century History

By the twentieth century, both subsistence and commercial fishing were vital economic resources to the Yakima Indians. With the increase of the non-Indian population, Indians were often denied access to their traditional fisheries. Litigation was inevitable. In the first fishing rights case, *Taylor v. Yakima Tribe* (1887), a white settler's fence blocked access to a Yakima fishery. The Supreme Court judges of Washington Territory ruled in favor of the Indians' treaty right to fish at usual and accustomed places.

In *United States v. Winans* (1905), the right to fish at traditional Indian sites was again threatened. The United States Supreme Court upheld the Yakima Nation's right to use their "ancient and accustomed" fisheries, and that "the treaty was not a grant of rights *to* Indians but a grant of rights *from* them." By 1942, however, in *Tulee v. Washington State*, the court returned a mixed verdict: that Sampson Tulee did not need a state license to fish, but the state could regulate fishing for conservation.

In the 1960s, when the states of Washington and Oregon began to regulate off-reservation Indian fisheries, two federal court decisions upheld Indian treaty rights. In *Sohappy v. Smith* (1969), Judge Robert C. Belloni limited the states' powers to necessary conservation; and further, that Indians were entitled to a "fair and equitable" share of the catch. In *United States v. Washington* (1974), Judge George Boldt held that "fair and equitable" meant 50 percent of harvestable fish swimming to "usual and accustomed" places. Further, Boldt ruled that the authority to regulate tribal fishing on and off the reservations was reserved for tribes.

The construction of Bonneville Dam on the Columbia in 1938 flooded some of the Yakima's best fishing grounds, and construction of Grand Coulee Dam in 1941 blocked miles of spawning grounds, causing depletion of salmon runs. When the Dalles Dam on the Columbia was built in 1956, flooding the Celilo Falls fisheries, the Yakima Nation was paid $15,019,640 as compensation. However, benefits (money for education and per capita payments) were offset by loss of the fishery, a major subsistence resource, accounting for a 45 percent increase in unemployment. With the proliferation of dams, inadequate fish ladders further impeded adult salmon migrations and diverted critical water from spawning grounds.

Salmon runs on the Yakima and Columbia rivers were also affected by expanding irrigation projects throughout the Yakima River Basin from the early twentieth century onwards. Whereas 500,000 to 900,000 salmon and steelhead used to return annually to the Yakima River, by 1990 only 10,000 fish returned and only 50 natural egg nests (redds) remained in the Yakima Basin.

A new Yakima-Klickitat Fish Production Project, a joint effort by the Yakima Nation and Washington State's Fish and Wildlife Departments, has led to a major effort in the 1990s to rebuild endangered fish runs. The enhancement program has been targeted to become one of largest fishery conservation programs in the United States.

The use of water from the Yakima River and its tributaries for large-scale irrigation projects also threatened the Yakima Nation's primary right as "first user" of these waters. A lawsuit filed against the Yakima Nation in October 1977 to limit Yakima water rights, and several more recent ones, still remained in litigation in the 1990s.

The Reservation in the 1990s

About 50 percent of the reservation is mountain range and timbered slopes; 37 percent is open grazing in the dry foothills, used for 12,000 head of cattle and 14,000 sheep; and 13 percent, 154,000 acres, are under cultivation on the valley floor. Sugar beets, hops, fruit, and wheat are principal crops.

The tribe has spent over $54 million to buy back reservation land, in order to increase the tribal land base. Tribal holdings are principally in the dry foothills and mountain slopes. In 1977, the tribe communally held 866,445 acres, Indians owned 252,193 acres, and non-Indians owned 253,280 acres. Eighty percent of Indian irrigated lands were leased by non-Indians.

On the rich forested mountain slopes, 489,080 acres are covered with timber, the largest stand of commercial timber on any Indian reservation in the United States. In the 1990s, timber provided 90 percent of the annual income of the Yakima Nation.

Yakima Indian Agency headquarters are located just west of Toppenish. A General Council of voters eighteen years and older represents enrolled Yakima members. A Yakima Tribal Council of fourteen symbolically representing the fourteen original tribes, bands, and villages is empowered "to transact all business of the tribe." Since 1947 seven members of the Council are elected every two years to serve four-year terms. In 1992 four women served on the Tribal

Council, continuing a long-standing tradition of influence by women.

To be enrolled, a person is required to have one-quarter degree of Indian blood of one of the bands and tribes listed in the Yakima treaty. By the treaty centennial year of 1955, the Yakima Enrollment Office carried 4,316 people on the rolls. A steady increase continued, and by August, 1992, 8,315 were enrolled. About two-thirds of enrolled Yakima Indians live on the reservation; about 60 percent of these are full bloods; and over 50 percent of enrollees have three-quarters or more of Yakima blood.

The Yakima Nation Indian Health Center at the agency has provided medical, dental, and pharmacy services. A new, improved facility was opened in 1990; the original center now houses the Yakima Nation Comprehensive Alcohol Treatment Program. An elders' retirement center, built near the health center, opened in 1992.

Yakima children attend public schools on the reservation. Before the 1960s, Indians were seldom involved in public school education. In the 1970s, Yakima cultural and language teaching materials became part of elective school curricula. An accredited tribally run school, the Stanley Smartlowit Education Center, named for a leader in education, is located in Toppenish. It is headed by Dr. Martha B. Yallup, the first Yakima to receive a Ph.D. in education. Higher education is stressed and several Yakima have earned advanced degrees.

Tribally operated Head Start programs were available at Wapato, Toppenish, and White Swan. A private, accredited four-year liberal arts college, the Heritage College, opened on the reservation in the 1980s.

To further expand job opportunities for the Yakima people, an industrial park was established for light industry development, housing both tribally owned and private industries. The Yakima Land Enterprise Program develops fruit orchards, runs an outlet fruit stand, and operates an R-V park with spaces for ninety-five units.

As of 1992 some Yakima were employed by logging companies or sawmills, or in home or road construction. Six hundred were employed at the Yakima agency. Some leased their farming and grazing lands. Many supplemented their income by seasonal employment, picking fruit, working in hop fields, and fishing. Low income and unemployment remain a problem. In 1980, a good economic year, a median Yakima family income was $11,324; only 30 percent were unemployed, yet 38.7 percent lived at the poverty level. In 1988, due to a depressed lumber industry, unemployment was 61 percent and only 21 percent of workers made over $7,000.

Two tribal community centers have been built on the reservation in which to hold tribal functions. An All-Indian Rodeo and Indian National Basketball Tournament are also sponsored. The Yakima Nation Cultural Heritage Center opened in 1980. The Center features an imposing "Winter Lodge," which is used for meetings, banquets, and special tribal programs. Surrounding the Winter Lodge are the Yakima Nation Museum; a gift shop; a full-service library; the Heritage Inn Restaurant featuring Indian food; and a theater. The Yakima Museum is an outstanding showcase of Yakima life and values, attracting 22,000 visitors in 1988. The Center also houses the tribal newspaper offices, a media center with a radio station, and a media services division. The *Yakima Nation Review*, a biweekly newspaper edited by Ronn Washines, is one of the country's outstanding Indian newspapers.

Contemporary Yakima Culture

Yakima Indian children are still raised on cradleboards, and, as in the past, the close relationship between children and grandparents is maintained. Long hair for men and boys is still a traditional feature, but now it is usually braided rather than worn loose. Modern dress for men and women is usual, but women who are active Longhouse participants often wear a "wingdress," a cotton version of a traditional buckskin dress. The role of elders has changed little: they are expected to keep family ties strong and to act as repositories of Yakima beliefs and traditions. Many traditional men have not only been Longhouse leaders, but have maintained an active role on the Tribal Council. There is a remarkable continuity of service on the modern Tribal Council that follows the old "chiefly lines," passed along from father to son.

A formal network of close ties and family alliances through marriage links is also maintained, receiving formal social recognition by the continuing custom of "wedding trades." Since the 1950s, the necessity for a "legal" marriage instead of "Indian custom marriage" has led to a new Longhouse marriage rite, now an established custom. Traditional households of extended families are rare; nuclear family households represent a major change. People comment, "Now we live separate," adding that they miss the cooperation and sharing they used to have when "living together." Some young single families of siblings try to build their homes near to one another on a family allotment. The Yakima language is still spoken by many traditional people, and is being passed down to a younger generation at home and in the schools. Invocations before community events are recited in the Yakima language, and it remains the language of the Longhouse.

Skilled basketry has been kept alive by the basketmakers such as noted Mary Kiona and Sally Wahkiacus, and has undergone an extensive revival since the 1970s by teachers such as Nettie Kuneki Jackson. Beautiful hard coiled "Klickitat" baskets, soft rounded "Sally" bags, and flat-twined "cornhusk" bags are still given as gifts during giveaways and trades on special ceremonial occasions.

Some ancient spiritual traditions are still actively followed. A powerful guardian spirit, the sweat lodge, is still used by people to restore spiritual and physical well-being. Two sacred symbols hold special meaning for the people: Earth and Water, the nurturing foundations of Indian life. The earthen floor on which the people "dance" during *Wáashat* services brings sacred Earth into the Longhouse. Water, the source of all life, is symbolized in the snows on sacred Mt. Adams. It is sipped before every sacred meal and again at its conclusion, accompanied by prayers.

Four reservation Longhouses have remained the active centers for *Wáashat*, the Longhouse Religion, also known as the Seven Drum or Sunday Dance Religion, and another is maintained off-reservation by the Wanapam community at Priest Rapids. Longhouses are also maintained by off-reservation families at Rock Creek, Celilo, Alder Creek, and others. The religion is also active on the Warm Springs, Umatilla, Nez Perce, and Colville reservations. An extensive network of close ties and relationships, largely through marriage, exists among Longhouse families in all areas.

Longhouses still serve as the center of Yakima Indian identity, a place where the Indian language, foods, dress, customs, values, and beliefs are maintained and perpetuated. In addition to regular *Wáashat* Sunday services, large gatherings of people come for first foods feasts ("first roots" in early spring, "first salmon" later in the season, and "first berries" at the end of summer), and for other annually scheduled occasions. Many people also lend support at funerals and for memorial rites. Longhouses are the setting for family celebrations, such as namings, birthdays, wedding trades, and modern marriage ceremonies.

The Indian Shaker religion, a curing and purifying syncretic sect, spread from Puget Sound to the Columbia Plateau in 1889. Three Indian Shaker churches have remained active on the Yakima Reservation. A second curing sect, the Feather Dance Religion, is no longer active on the Yakima Reservation; its center is on the Warm Springs Reservation. Christianity coexists peacefully alongside the Indian Longhouse Religion.

A general philosophy of Yakima values was best expressed by Robert Jim, Tribal Council leader and Longhouse drummer, as he hosted a Longhouse ceremonial feast to honor his eldest son's shooting his first deer, a traditional contribution to the community's welfare: "These things we believe: cooperation, sharing, reciprocity, and conservation." That summarizes twentieth-century Yakima ideals.

Helen H. Schuster

See also Columbia River Indians; Fishing and Hunting Rights; Indian Shaker Church

Further Reading

Beavert, Virginia, Project Director. *The Way It Was: Anaku Iwacha, Yakima Indian Legends*. Olympia, WA: Franklin Press, 1974.

Daugherty, Richard D. *The Yakima People*. Phoenix, AZ: Indian Tribal Series, 1973.

Hunn, Eugene S. *Nch'i-Wana, The Big River: Mid-Columbia Indians and Their Land*. Seattle: University of Washington Press, 1990.

Schuster, Helen H. *The Yakimas: A Critical Bibliography*. Bloomington: Indiana University Press, 1982.

———. *The Yakima*. New York, NY: Chelsea House, 1990.

YANKTON AND YANKTONAI

Yankton, Yanktonai, and Assiniboine Indians (also called Stoneys or Hohes in Canada) appear in records as descendants from a single "council fire" of "Nakotas," who claimed territories at the center and northern perimeter of historic Sioux Country when non-Indians arrived. Yanktons ceded 2.2 million acres in 1830 and 11,155,890 acres in 1858 to the United States, and retained 430,000 acres as a reservation near Fort Randall. They also claimed the 648.2-acre Pipestone Reservation until 1929, then sold it for $328,588.90, plus federal assurance of Native American access.

Yanktonais settled in significant numbers on four reservations. After 1867 the Cut-Heads joined the Sisseton-Wahpeton peoples at Devil's Lake in North Dakota. In 1880 federal officials counted 5,208 Upper Yanktonais with 1,432 Assiniboines around Fort Peck Agency in Montana. In 1935, its last census to identify tribal affiliations reported 1,202 Sioux (Yanktonais and some Dakotas), 1,227 Assiniboines, and 234 Assiniboine-Sioux.

Other Upper Yanktonais settled beside Lower Yanktonais, also called Hunkpatinas, around Standing Rock Agency on the border of North and South Dakota. Its 1885 census included 1,976 Hunkpapas (Sitting Bull's tribe), 631 Upper and 1,347 Lower Yanktonais, 654 Blackfoot Sioux, and 113 of extraneous tribal heritage. Another contingent of Lower Yanktonais already had replaced Santee Dakotas at Crow Creek, Fort Thompson Agency in South Dakota, after Santees moved from Crow Creek to Nebraska in 1866.

Crow Creek

Only at Crow Creek have Yanktonais had a reservation of their own. As established in 1889, its boundaries contained 285,521 acres. By the 1920s, 1,599 members claimed 268,521 acres on allotments. By 1950 their acreage shrank to 154,872. Tribal members used only 34,539 acres, and families struggled with average annual incomes of only $1,167.

No "surplus land" sale fund generated income. New Deal programs brought relief, but records for 1942 indicate aggregate income of only $139,360 for nearly 1,000 people from hunting, trapping, fishing, arts and crafts, farming, business endeavors, wage labor, and public beneficence. After mid-century, they received $5,837,613.94 for 15,564.69 acres taken by the Fort Randall and Big Bend Dam projects on the Missouri River. Since then, temporary jobs at the Allsteel Muffler Plant, federal and tribal employment, work at Stephan Boarding School, or off-reservation jobs have sustained a marginal economic existence.

Resident census fell from 1,055 in 1895 to 846 by 1950, then gradually increased to approximately 1,200 (of 3,521 enrolled) in 1992. Plans for a casino in 1993 suggested the return of others.

A Business Committee under a General Council gave way to the Constitution and Bylaws of 1923. Members rejected revisions under the Indian Reorganization Act (IRA) in 1944, later accepted revision, yet have struggled with political connections to outsiders.

Offsetting economic and political disadvantages has been cultural integrity. Sun Dances were observed in 1883 and 1932. Sacred Pipe ceremonies and peyote meetings survived, and Yanktonai philosophies gained exquisite expression. John Saul portrayed them in images recently published as *Yanktonai Sioux Water Colors*. Artist Oscar Howe drew inspiration from Saul to profoundly express legacies representing the entire Sioux federation.

Standing Rock

Yanktonais with Hunkpapas and Blackfoot Sioux at Standing Rock became globally famous as "Sitting Bull people." This intertribal society resisted acculturation on a land base that shrank from 2,672,640 acres in 1889, to 1,064,000 by 1950, when residents reported the lowest annual family income in Lakota country, at $767. Residents accepted Indian New Deal rehabilitation, but long resisted IRA compliance or full-fledged federal funding. Their cultural integrity survives in isolation expressed through a curriculum at Standing Rock Community College (chartered in 1973).

Fort Peck

Similar retention of tribal ways at a community college, plus art forms by Roscoe White Eagle of Fort Peck in Montana, blend with success in tribal services to bespeak accommodation without submission. At a location reserved in 1874 for "hostile Indians," Yanktonais, Assiniboines, and some Dakotas occupied 2,094,144 acres, which shrank to 1,100,859 by 1935. Irrigated agriculture with mineral lease fees supplemented land sale proceeds. There were federal jobs in Fort Peck Dam construction and reservation programs during the 1930s and 1960s. But refusal to transform

a bingo hall at Wolf Point into a casino perpetuates an uncertain economic plight.

Fort Peck voters declined to organize their government for federal approval until 1960, but it has been effective. Some 5,000 members in 1874 shrank to 2,245 in residence by 1934, then increased to 10,474 in residence at five communities by 1960, and the number has grown steadily to the present.

Yankton Reservation

The Yankton Reservation in South Dakota also preserved cultural traditions through extraordinary leadership. In one family of Yanktons (enrolled at Standing Rock) Philip J. and Vine Deloria, Sr., worked between cultures as Episcopal clergymen. Ella Deloria bequeathed tribal knowledge in personal papers and publications. Vine Deloria, Jr., commands global fame as activist, academician, and writer.

The Yankton Charles Kills Enemy labored from his residence on Rosebud Reservation with other medicine men to bring Sacred Pipe ways from underground into open use, and to promote amalgamation of tribal with non-Indian ways. Joseph Rockboy demonstrated similar inclinations through personal success and instruction. His son, Clarence Rockboy, has expressed the teaching of forbears in exquisite beadwork. Asa Primeaux stands out in a network of spiritual and cultural leaders.

There was a price for cultural integrity. Acreage dwindled to 34,802 by 1980. One constitutional government approved in 1891 gave way to another in 1932, and Yanktons have yet to accept the terms of the IRA. New Dealers brought a full array of New Deal programs, featuring three communal colonies, but otherwise federal officials have slighted Yanktons for their cultural resistance. From 1931 to 1969 they had only a subagency under Rosebud, and like Minnesota Sioux received "left-over services."

Relentlessly, tribal leaders searched for the means of tribal livelihood. An electronic components manufacturing plant and a pork-processing plant collapsed because outside investors would not accommodate

YANKTON AND YANKTONAI

Reservation	Tribe	Enrolled	In Residence	Principal Industries
Devil's Lake	Sisseton, Wahpeton, Cuthead Yanktonai	4,420	2,900	Fort Totten Casino; Devil's Lake Sioux Manufacturing Co. (military camouflage)
Upper Sioux	Sisseton, Wahpeton, Flandreau Santee, Santee, Yankton	none	181	Fire Fly Casino
Yankton	Yankton	6,000	3,400	Fort Randall Casino
Crow Creek	Lower Yanktonai	3,521	1,200	Tribal Farm; Lode Star Casino (opened in 1993)
Fort Peck	Upper Yanktonai, Assiniboine, Sisseton-Wahpeton	10,500	6,700	Wolf Point Community Bingo Hall

cultural commitments with flexible hours. A tribal farm supported only a few families until "gaming" brought economic success. A bingo hall, changed into Fort Randall Casino in 1991, transformed 75 percent unemployment to full employment and produced $3 million in profit within eight months. In response came the expansion of population. From 2,200 tribal members in 1858, it rose to 4,500 in 1980, then burgeoned to some 6,000 members in 1992 (3,400 in residence).

Overall, people of Nakota culture represent a blend of traditionalism with acceptance of acculturation. Somewhat protected at the center and upper perimeter of Sioux Country, they have been less affected by outsiders than have been the Dakotas to their east. Yet they have been more prone to accommodate the ideas of non-Indians than have Lakotas to their west. Contemporary Nakota values are accessible in the contributions of Oscar Howe, John Saul, Roscoe White Eagle, Charles Kills Enemy, Joseph and Clarence Rockboy, Asa Primeaux, and the Delorias.

Herbert T. Hoover

See also Sioux Federation

Further Reading

Hoover, Herbert T. *The Yankton Sioux*. New York, NY: Chelsea House Publishers, 1988.

Brokenleg, Martin, and Herbert T. Hoover. *Yanktonai Sioux Water Colors*. Sioux Falls, SD: The Center for Western Studies, 1993.

Dockstader, Frederick J. *Oscar Howe: A Retrospective Exhibition*. Tulsa, OK: Thomas Gilcrease Museum, 1982.

Tape-recorded oral history collections are available for Yankton and all Yanktonai groups at the Oral History Center at the University of South Dakota in Vermillion.

YAQUI

The Yaqui (also known as Yoeme, Yueme, and Cahita) homeland is along the lower Yaqui River in southern Sonora, Mexico. Some 25,000 Yaquis live in the "Eight Towns" established by the Jesuits in the seventeenth century. Fighting tenaciously to preserve their rich agricultural territory, they suffered terribly during the rule of Porfirio Diaz (1884 to 1910) and most fled the Eight Towns. Returning after the Mexican Revolution, they reestablished their villages. In 1938 President Lázaro Cárdenas established the Yaqui Indigenous Community.

Many Yaquis, fleeing for their lives, crossed the border into Arizona as political refugees. Coming as individuals or in small groups, they slowly gathered into villages in southern Arizona.

Twentieth-Century History

On entering the United States these immigrants, at first fearful of revealing their identity due to the attempted genocide by the Mexicans in Sonora, soon after 1900 took courage and performed their all-important ceremonies, as they have continued to do to this day. They were treated as aliens, under surveillance by the Border Patrol. Now most are United States-born citizens. Juan "Pistola" Muñoz during the 1920s spoke for the people, calling himself "Commandante General" of all the Arizona Yaquis and was called "Chief" by the Anglos.

In 1964 by an act of Congress, the Bureau of Land Management transferred 202 acres to the newly formed Pascua Yaqui Association, Inc. (PYA). With grants from the Office of Economic Opportunity, the Department of Housing and Urban Development, the Ford Foundation, and donations from individuals, the residents from the cramped forty acres of (Old) Pascua began to build houses and a community in "New Pascua." The federal government's concern was for many years only through the Border Patrol, but on September 18, 1978, a bill sponsored by Congressman Morris Udall was signed by President Jimmy Carter, making New Pascua a federally recognized reservation under the Bureau of Indian Affairs (BIA). All Yaquis in the United States, no matter where they lived, were enabled to enroll in the Yaqui tribe and steps were taken toward tribal government.

Current Situation

The relationship between the Yaquis and the City of Tucson and Pima County, at first tenuous, has improved vastly over the years. The State of Arizona was largely uncooperative, officials saying that these poverty-stricken people should be shipped back to Mexico. They were indeed poor, and often in need.

After years of wrangling and factionalism, a BIA-approved Constitution was finally ratified on January 27, 1988. Elections for an interim Tribal Council had been held, but the election of June 4, 1988, was the first under the Constitution and the first run by the tribe. The Constitution provided for three branches of government: executive, legislative, and judicial. A court had been appointed earlier and had undergone various problems; after 1988 it functioned more effectively, as did the Tribal Council.

Jobs had always been a problem, particularly after 1948 when the cotton-picking machine became ubiquitous, replacing agricultural labor which had been the mainstay of these people. From the 1960s onward, much effort went into job training, particularly in construction; various enterprises were tried, such as a plant nursery and adobe-making, but what brought in the most cash for the tribe was bingo. However, branching-out into high-stakes gaming brought trouble with state and federal governments in 1991 and 1992. Negotiations allowed this venture to be restored in 1993.

In the early 1980s the Tucson City Council gave Housing and Community Development Block Grant funds for demolishing the decrepit housing in Old Pascua and completely rebuilding over fifty homes, working in cooperation with the San Ignacio Yaqui Council. At times unemployed homeowners have had difficulty paying the much-increased taxes; the tribe has been able to tide them over. The city also took over the religious plaza, which had been deeded to the Yaquis, and built an office, new kitchens, and an activity center. Guadalupe and Yoem Pueblo have also received funds for house repair.

Schooling for all Yaqui children has been the responsibility of the public schools, starting with the one-room schoolhouses in Old Pascua and Guadalupe. The dropout rate was and is a continual problem, although with creative encouragement, such as at Thamar Richey Elementary School in Old Pascua, the children have excelled. Some Yaquis have earned graduate degrees. For example, Octaviana Valenzuela Trujillo, vice-chairman of the tribe, is an educator, working with the public schools and the University of Arizona.

The founding of New Pascua and much of its development was due to the vision and constant effort of Anselmo Valencia, for many years the head of the Easter Ceremonial Society, called the *Kohtumbrem*. He was also the first director of the PYA, community manager, coordinator of bingo, and in his later years the spiritual leader and respected elder.

Had Ramón Ybarra (director of the PYA from 1975 to 1977) lived, the political course might have been smoother. From 1978 to 1988, a time of political discord, David Ramirez was tribal chairman, and Raul Silvas was leader of the opposing faction. Arcadio Gastelum was elected tribal chairman in 1988, followed by Albert Garcia in 1992. Their problems have been many: to solve the extremely high unemployment problem; to arrange transportation; to provide for adequate health care through the Indian Health Service and the establishment of clinics (the high incidence of diabetes is a threat; AIDS education is underway); to take care of the elderly; to furnish housing for a continually growing community; to satisfy the needs of widely spread enrolled members; to fight crime, and drug and alcohol abuse. These are common societal problems. However, overlying everything else is the age-old Yaqui tradition of cultural pride and independence, and their need to preserve the aboriginal language, culture, and religion.

Culture

Since Jesuit times, each of the Eight Towns of the Sonora Yaquis has its own governor and its own religious and ceremonial societies; all would come together on occasion. For the Arizona villages, this setup would be ideal but, in many respects, impossible to attain. Nevertheless, there is a desire for village autonomy and now for tribal autonomy—a nation within a state.

In the 1930s the people spoke Yaqui and Spanish; only a few of the young knew English. Now, English is spoken and there is a fear that Yaqui will die out. To counteract this, there are bilingual and trilingual programs in the schools. Yaqui scholars have developed a phonetic system with English orthography, and they are compiling a dictionary. Yaqui is a Cahitan language of the Uto-Aztecan linguistic stock.

Yaqui religious life and lore is rich and contains the identity symbols of the culture. When the Yaquis invited the Jesuits into their country in 1617, the fathers baptized thousands. The Jesuits taught elements of Catholicism, but over the years the Yaquis combined this Catholicism with their indigenous faith and practices, so that their current religion is a complex and inextricable mixture of both.

In the church and plaza of each village are held the well-known Easter Ceremonials, revived in Guadalupe in 1906, and in Tucson in 1909. The *Kohtumbrem* are those who manage these ceremonials throughout the Lenten Period. The deer dancer (*maso*) and the *pascola* dancers who act as ceremonial hosts are famous; they have their origins in aboriginal lore. The *matachines*, with European origins, are part of the hierarchy of the independent Yaqui church, which includes lay priests (*maestros*), sacristans, altar women, singers, and flag bearers. As head *maestros*, the religious leaders José Maria Garcia and Ignacio "Puri"

Yaqui Villages				
Name of Village	Date Settled	General Location	Land Area	Population 1992
Guadalupe	before 1900	SE of Phoenix	300+ acres	2,200
Eskatel, or Penjamo		near Scottsdale	A few blocks	175
Chandler High Town	1900s	SE of Phoenix	A block	200
Old Pascua	1922	NW Tucson	40 acres	386
Barrio Libre	1900–1910	South Tucson	Several blocks	130
New Pascua, or Pascua Pueblo (Yaqui Reservation)	1964	SW of Tucson	1,600 acres	2,737
Yoem Pueblo	ca. 1910	Marana	4 acres	100
Somerton		Near Yuma		?
Total living in villages			5,928	
Total enrolled tribal members as of September 9, 1992			7,891	
Enrollment pending			2,500	
Grand total, including those in six western states:			10,000–11,000	
All figures are approximate. Population figures are from the United States Census and special tribal study.				

Alvarez are remembered for their devotion and long service in Old Pascua.

Except for the *maso* and *pascola*, whose power comes from the forest, a ceremonial participant has made a solemn vow to a saint or deity to participate in one of the sodalities, and must do so on peril of the illness returning. The performance of the vows ensures the continuance of the culture. Each of life's crises has an accompanying ceremony, in which one or several of the sodalities must take part; they appear also on saints' days and at diverse celebrations. Also part of the social and religious structure is a complicated *compadrazgo* network, where individuals act as "coparents" or godparents.

The Yaquis have impressive talents in the arts, including music and dance, which are important in Yaqui culture. Anselmo Valencia and Felipe Molina know the deer songs and teach others. There are several self-taught painters, such as Daniel Leon, Jimmey Molina, Bernabé Tapia, and Julian Morillo, who are gaining wide recognition. In addition, the children produce remarkable artistic creations.

If one were to characterize Yaquis, they would have to be described as assertive, determined, creative, adaptive, and home-loving. A bumper sticker describes them best—"YAQUI and Proud."

Rosamond B. Spicer

See also Arizona Tribes

Further Reading

Evers, Larry, and Felipe S. Molina. *Yaqui Deer Songs, Maso Bwikam: A Native American Poetry*. Sun Tracks 14. Tucson: University of Arizona Press, 1987.

Painter, Muriel Thayer. *With Good Heart: Yaqui Beliefs and Ceremonies in Pascua Village*. Tucson: University of Arizona Press, 1987.

Spicer, Edward H. *The Yaquis: A Cultural History*. Tuscon: University of Arizona Press, 1980.

———. "Yaqui." *Handbook of North American Indians*. Vol. 10. *Southwest*. Ed. Alfonso Ortiz. Washington, DC: Smithsonian Institution (1983): 250–63.

YAVAPAI

The Yavapai Indians have three reservations in central Arizona governed by separate tribal governments, the Fort McDowell Mohave-Apache Indian Community, the Yavapai-Prescott Tribe, and the Camp Verde Yavapai-Apache Indian Community. The Yavapai (*Ba'ja*) are considered to be Upland Yumans by anthropologists, along with the Havasupai and Hualapai. The Upland Yumans speak a common language, although there are several dialects.

Culture

The Yavapai were hunter-gatherers and small-scale farmers during the pre-reservation era. Yavapai religion centered on curing by shamans, who are individuals of special, personal power. The Yavapai were heavily proselytized by Protestant religious organizations around the turn of the century. However, many traditional elements of Yavapai religion continue to be practiced.

Yavapai and Apache

At the time the first Anglos moved into Yavapai territory, the Yavapai and Western Apache shared a common border on the Yavapai's eastern range; the boundary line between the two groups was in transition. During this period, the lifestyle of the Western Apache and Yavapai had many similarities, both peoples being hunter-gatherers and part-time farmers. Some Yavapai and Apache married, and it is likely that there was some sharing of cultural traditions. As a result, Anglos were often unable to distinguish between Yavapai and Apache. This confusion led to the Yavapai being referred to, historically, as various types of Apache, including Mohave-Apache and Yuma-Apache.

History

After the Civil War, settlers began to enter central Arizona. Soon gold was discovered in the heart of Yavapai territory. Frontier posts became bases for military forays into Yavapai territory with the purpose of forcing them onto reservations. The pre-reservation era ended with the massacre of Yavapai by United States soldiers at Skeleton Cave in December of 1872. This devastating attack broke the resistance of the Yavapai, who were forced onto a reservation at Camp Verde in central Arizona.

In response to complaints by settlers, the United States government removed the Yavapai in 1875 to the San Carlos Apache Reservation, 180 miles to the east. However, the Yavapai continually requested to return to their homelands as a result of a longing for their ancestral lands, their minority status among Apache, and difficulties in maintaining irrigation systems. At the turn of the century, the Indian office finally allowed the Yavapai to return to central Arizona.

Establishment of the Reservations (1900 to 1935)

When the Yavapai left San Carlos, they settled onto the former military posts of Fort McDowell, Fort Whipple, and Camp Verde. They also settled in small communities near locations where they could obtain wage labor. Once settled, the Yavapai worked resolutely to obtain reservation status for their communities.

The Fort McDowell Reservation was established by executive order of Theodore Roosevelt in 1903. The Camp Verde Reservation was established in 1910, and several noncontiguous parcels, including Middle Verde, Clarkdale, and Rimrock, were added throughout the next sixty years. The Yavapai near Prescott, who settled on the former Fort Whipple, obtained reservation status in 1935.

Fort McDowell

The key variables that shaped the development of the community at Fort McDowell have been the significance of the water resources (the Verde River bisects the reservation), and the development of the Phoenix metropolitan area, which is only twenty-six miles away. Almost immediately after the establishment of the reservation in 1903, the Fort McDowell Yavapai had to respond to a series of attempts by local non-Indian interests to have them removed to the neighboring Salt River Pima-Maricopa Indian Reservation. During this time, they continually attempted to develop an irrigation system and to farm. Lack of federal funds to construct facilities to protect the irrigation structures forced many Yavapai to seek wage labor or to raise cattle.

Carlos Montezuma, a Yavapai who had been taken from his family in the late 1860s and raised by non-Indians, provided crucial political support to the efforts of the Yavapai at Fort McDowell to keep their reservation. Montezuma was one of the first American Indians to earn a medical degree (1889), and was a prominent Indian activist of the first two decades of the twentieth century. The Yavapai have continued to be politically active. In 1948, Frank Harrison, a veteran of World War II, and Harry Austin, a Fort McDowell community leader, both Yavapai, filed a lawsuit that led to Indian people in Arizona obtaining the right to vote in state and federal elections. Fort McDowell was organized as a tribal government under an Indian Reorganization Act constitution. Members vote for five council seats; the Tribal Council members select the chairman, vice-chairman, and treasurer.

In the early 1950s plans for Orme Dam, a component of the Central Arizona Project (CAP), began to have a serious, negative effect on Fort McDowell. Orme Dam was authorized as part of the federal CAP legislation and was to be built at the confluence of the Verde and the Salt rivers; the reservoir behind the dam would have flooded essentially all of the reservation. The legislation provided monetary compensation for the loss of land and 2,500 in lieu acres. The Fort McDowell Yavapai continually opposed the construction of Orme Dam over a thirty-year period. They worked with environmental, taxpayer, and religious organizations, as well as other tribes, tribal organizations, and concerned citizens to stop construction of the dam. Orme Dam became a national as well as international media and political issue. After preparation of two environmental impact statements, political opposition to Orme Dam had grown so strong that Secretary of Interior Cecil Andrus selected another alternative for CAP regulatory storage and flood control in 1983.

As a result of plans for Orme Dam, Fort McDowell had been unable to obtain most governmental funds or other capital for community development during the 1970s, a period of significant federal funding for Indian tribes. However, in the late 1980s, Fort McDowell undertook major community development activities, completing several housing and community infrastructure development programs. In addition, the tribe

has reclaimed farm land along the alluvial flood plain of the Verde River. The tribal farm, which will be expanded to 3,000 acres, is a major tribal enterprise. The tribe also operates a gas station and smoke-shop (retail store for selling cigarettes without state tax). In addition, the tribe operates a sand and gravel enterprise and a commercial nursery, largely for desert landscaping.

The other significant tribal effort in the 1980s was the settlement of the tribe's water rights claims through negotiation and legislative means. The Native American Rights Fund provided the legal support for the settlement. The Fort McDowell Indian Community Water Rights Settlement Act of 1990 established the tribe's rights to 36,350 acre feet of water, and included approximately $25 million of compensatory funds that the tribe will be using for community and economic development. The widening of a major transportation artery from the Phoenix area (State Route 87) that cuts through the southern end of the reservation will provide a commercial corridor for additional commercial development.

In 1984, the tribe opened a gaming center, which has provided a substantial, additional source of income. Following an attempt by the FBI to confiscate tribal gaming equipment, the tribe and the State of Arizona negotiated a compact, as required under the federal Indian Gaming Act.

Yavapai-Prescott

In 1935, the Yavapai who had settled near the former Fort Whipple near Prescott obtained reservation status. The community decided not to organize under the Indian Reorganization Act or through a treaty. Instead, in the 1950s the tribe organized through the "Articles of Association," which were approved by the secretary of the interior. Unique to this community was the continuation of traditional tribal leadership, initially through Chief Sam Jimulla. On his death, the tribe continued the leadership through his wife and subsequently through their two daughters. The Articles of Association include the chief/chieftess as a member of the board of directors. However, this system was discontinued in 1988.

The Yavapai-Prescott tribal land base is surrounded by the present-day Prescott city limits. The relationship between the tribe and the city is one of working cooperation. Approximately three generations of tribal members have been educated in the public school system. Although there are concerns from some city residents about the increased tribal economic development, the job opportunities from tribal developments have been beneficial to tribal residents, and for residents of Prescott and nearby communities. In the early 1980s, the tribe negotiated a lease with a developer who opened a Sheraton resort, providing job opportunities for 150 workers. The tribe also leased land for a shopping center called Frontier Village, which opened in 1990. Yavapai-Prescott also has a bingo operation and negotiated a

The Yavapai			
Reservation	Land Area (in acres)	Population	Economic Resources
Fort McDowell	24,967	640[1] 765[2]	6,000 acres of arable land High-quality water resources (Verde River) Sand and gravel deposits Proximity to Phoenix metro area
Camp Verde	1,092	650 618	Proximity to national park (Montezuma Castle) Proximity to major interstate highway (I-17) High-quality water resources
Prescott	1,399	130 159	Adjacent to the city of Prescott Proximity to state highway

[1]*Total enrollment, Bureau of Indian Affairs, 1992 Labor Force Reports.*
[2]*1990 Census, on-reservation population.*

compact with the state to expand their gaming enterprise. An important economic issue for the tribe in the 1990s is the potential congressional settlement of their water rights.

Camp Verde

A number of Apaches and Yavapai who left San Carlos around the turn of the century settled at Camp Verde. Unlike Prescott and Fort McDowell, the Apache ethnic identity predominates in the middle Verde Valley communities. The official tribal name, Yavapai-Apache, is an accurate description of the ethnic heritage of the tribal members at Camp Verde.

The reservation lands set aside for them were so limited that most community members had to work for wage labor in the copper mines and smelters in the Verde Valley area. The slowdown and closure of much of the mining operations in the Verde Valley in the 1930s and 1940s resulted in the return of many of the Yavapai to the comparatively small reservation parcels where economic opportunities were limited.

In the 1980s the tribe negotiated an agreement with the National Park Service and developed a visitor center associated with Montezuma Castle National Monument. The visitor center draws large numbers of tourists, and the tribe has made the area a development zone with a motel, gas station, RV park, and convenience market. Currently, the tribe has plans to cancel the Park Service lease and to convert the visitor center into a gaming hall. The tribe has attempted for the past eight years to expand its land base to include an additional 6,500 acres of the original Camp Verde. The tribe has obtained bipartisan, local support and S.1321, the Camp Verde Yavapai-Apache Land Transfer Act, was introduced in Congress in 1987. However, several key issues with the federal land management agencies still need to be resolved. These additional lands would provide a basis for sustained community and economic development for the Camp Verde Indian community.

Yavapai in the 1990s

In the late 1980s, the three Yavapai groups have joined together in a cultural renewal. The tribes co-sponsor *Ba'ja* days, which are joint cultural events; each tribe takes turns hosting the activities. In addition, Yavapai-Prescott has developed a cultural program and recently hired a full-time, tribal archeologist.

Patricia Mariella
Violet Mitchell-Enos

See also Apache; Arizona Tribes

Further Reading

Gifford, Edward W. *The Southeastern Yavapai.* University of California Publications in American Archaeology and Ethnology 29:3. Berkeley: University of California Press (1932): 177–252.
———. *Northeastern and Western Yavapai.* University of California Publications in American Archaeology and Ethnology 34:4. Berkeley: University of California Press (1936): 247–354.
Khera, Sigrid, and Patricia Mariella. "Long-Term Resistance to Relocation in an American Indian Community." *Involuntary Resettlement and Migration.* Eds. Art Hansen and Anthony Oliver-Smith. Denver, CO: Westview Press (1982): 159–178.
———."Yavapai." *Handbook of North American Indians.* Vol. 10. *Southwest.* Ed. Alfonso Ortiz. Washington, DC: Smithsonian Institution (1983): 38–54.
Schroeder, Albert H. "A Study of Yavapai History." *American Indian Ethnohistory: Indians of the Southwest.* New York, NY: Garland Publishing (1974): 23–354.

YOKUTS

"Yokuts" is a broad term applied to the Yokutsan speakers, a portion of the Penutian linguistic stock, who resided in California's San Joaquin Valley and foothills. Of the possible approximately sixty Yokuts tribes that once existed, only a few remain; the estimated aboriginal population is thought to have decreased by at least 75 percent as a result of disease and warfare following European contact. Present Yokuts descendants belong to the following tribes: Choinumni, Chukchansi, Tachi, and Wukchumni. There are a number of individuals who also claim other tribal affiliations, such as the Gashowu, Entimbich, Wuksachi, or Wowol; however, these people are small in number and presently do not constitute recognized groups.

There are currently three federally recognized rancherias and one reservation: the Picayune Rancheria is predominantly Chukchansi; Table Mountain Rancheria is a mixture of Chukchansi and Western Mono; and Santa Rosa Rancheria is Tachi. The Tule River Reservation is made up of several tribes: Wukchumni, Yawilmani, Wuksachi, Yaudanchi, Pankahlalchi, and Koyati. In the late 1800s through the early 1900s, many Indian families who were not members of rancherias or reservations received Indian allotment land under the terms of the General Allotment Act of 1887. Some families continue to live on allotment land, but many families have sold this land. Most Indian families do not live within their traditional tribal boundaries. The selection and placement of rancherias, the location of available jobs, and schooling have dispersed many people and/or displaced them from traditional tribal lands.

The main employment available for Indian people in the early twentieth century included logging, working for livestock ranchers as ranch hands, and working as farm laborers in the fruit, vegetable, and cotton fields of the San Joaquin Valley. While rancherias provide some employment, rancheria members often must find work elsewhere.

For many Yokuts, early twentieth century experiences included being sent to Indian boarding schools at Sherman Institute in Riverside, California, and Stewart Indian School in Stewart, Nevada. Local rancherias also had Indian schools. Some Yokuts were sent to the North Fork Mission, where they attended a public school in North Fork, California. By the 1950s most Indian people were attending local public schools. Socio-economic conditions of Yokuts peoples have contributed to academic achievement remaining below that of California in general; consequently, the rate of movement into professional fields is low.

Adaptation to white culture and the intrusion of schools and religious missions has altered or reduced many aspects of Native cultures. Traditions such as large ceremonial functions (especially funeral ceremonies), shamanistic healing, basketweaving, and the gathering of traditional plants and foods decreased and became more family oriented. Beginning in the early 1960s and continuing through the 1980s, revitalization of cultural practices occurred, particularly in the spiritual realm and various aspects of expressive culture (song, dance, oral traditions, craftsmanship). Larger ceremonial events such as annual tribal gatherings became sponsored by tribal groups. A modern approach among spiritual leaders (medicine people) is to belong to the Native American Culture Association, a local nonprofit organization. In addition, there are numerous intertribal (pan-tribal) functions and gatherings. Political activism was also seen in the 1960s by the formation of organizations such as the Sierra Indian Center. It involved people from many tribes and was pivotal in establishing other

organizations, both local and statewide, which exist up to the present. The Center also pushed to revitalize cultural practices.

The health care needs of residents of Fresno, Madera, and Kings counties are met by a centrally located Indian health center, Central Valley Indian Health. This largely federally funded comprehensive health center provides health care for approximately 80 percent of the local Indian population, regardless of whether or not they are members of federally recognized tribes. This center is also a hub for many Indian social, cultural, and political activities. Tule River Reservation has its own health center, which services Tulare County and has a satellite clinic in Visalia.

Important issues and concerns of the Yokuts today include health care, education, land rights, and the protection of sacred sites. Federal recognition is presently a major concern since it is increasingly becoming the basis for determining the legal rights of Indians in general. Currently there are many Indians residing within the central San Joaquin Valley and foothills, who belong to tribes that are not federally recognized. Rancherias were never established for the Choinumni or the Wukchumni tribes, and both are in the process of petitioning for federal recognition. Various members of both tribes have received allotment land, and both tribes have represented themselves as entities that work with federal, state, and local organizations in matters relating to tribal concerns. Rancherias and reservations continue to acknowledge the traditional geographical boundaries of tribes lacking federal recognition.

Members of the Choinumni Tribe have established the Choinumni Tribal Council and the Choinumni Cultural Association, a state nonprofit corporation. No formal census is available, but there are between 200 and 300 estimated members. Their traditional Harvest Gathering celebration occurs in the fall and is in celebration of a bountiful year. A recognized spokesperson is Angie Osborne, who acknowledges Julia Davis (her grandmother) and Eva Hammond as traditional elders who influenced Angie in carrying on the traditions of the Choinumni people.

The Wukchumni Tribe, estimated at about 250 to 300 members, has established the Wukchumni Tribal Council. The Council is intensely involved in the preservation of traditional village sacred sites and sees this as an ongoing battle. A recognized basketmaker and traditionalist, Beatrice Wilcox Arancis, was influential in instilling the need to continue cultural practices. Their traditional Spring Dance was revived in the late 1980s and is held in celebration of the renewal of all living things. While several elders stay active in matters concerning the tribe, they respect the teaching of Jenny "Grams" Franco and acknowledge her as an influential spiritual elder. Jenny Franco makes her home on the Tule River Reservation where her influence is also strongly felt.

Tule River Reservation was established in 1873 and encompasses 56,000 acres in Porterville, Tulare County. Tule represents several tribes who were forced together with the establishment of the reservation. The majority of the 750 members live on or within five miles of the reservation. Main economic endeavors include timber sales, public campgrounds, and firewood sales. The Tule River Economic Development Corporation is pursuing new development on tribally owned land, both on and off the reservation. The Tribal Council operates a variety of programs. The Tule River Housing Authority is responsible for housing needs and HUD projects. The education department provides job training and a variety of educational support services. Tule's yearly activities and ceremonies include the Elders' Gathering in August, and San Juan's Day in June.

Santa Rosa Rancheria was established in 1921 and includes 170 acres in Lemoore, Kings County. There are 400 enrolled Tachi members. Their sole economic endeavor and source of income for the tribe is a bingo enterprise, The Bingo Palace, which employs 80 percent of the members. Their main tribal activity is the March First Celebration, a time dedicated to spiritual renewal and future prosperity. This annual celebration is headed by the tribe's political and spiritual leader, Clarence Atwell, Jr. His political leadership includes twenty years as tribal chairman; his spiritual leadership position was inherited from his father.

Picayune Rancheria, with approximately 800 enrolled members, was established in 1912. Although it was officially functioning by the end of 1989 after reversal of their termination status in December 1984, it presently operates with no land base. While actively pursuing possible means of economic development, one of their main goals is to develop a land base. A respected elder and early political activist is Henry Jones. His personal involvement with issues of Indian rights, and the formation of the intertribal Sierra Indian Center in Fresno, helped heighten awareness of Indian needs in the valley. Fellow Chukchansi elders Margaret Hammond and Ruby Cordero work to encourage the younger generations to learn their culture.

Currently a small community of Chukchansi and Western Mono populates the Table Mountain Rancheria in Friant, Fresno County. It was originally established in 1916 and presently has about 100 tribal members on approximately 100 acres. The Table Mountain and Picayune rancherias operate as separate political entities despite their common ancestral history. Lewis Barnes is a recognized leader who has held the position of tribal chairman since 1957. The rancheria's main economic endeavor is the Table Mountain Bingo Enterprise.

Lorrie A. Planas

See also **California Tribes**

Further Reading

Gayton, Anna H. "Yokuts and Western Mono Ethnography." *University of California Anthropological Records* 10:1–2 (1948): 1–302.

Latta, Frank F. *Handbook of Yokuts Indians.* 2d ed. Santa Cruz, CA: Bear State Books, 1977.

Planas, Lorrie A. "The Dynamics of Cultural Change: A Study of the Indians of the Central San Joaquin Valley." Master's thesis, California State University, Sacramento, 1991.

YSLETA DEL SUR PUEBLO

The Ysleta del Sur Pueblo (Tigua Indian Tribe) is located within the city of El Paso, in the area known as Ysleta. Ysleta is the oldest settlement in Texas. It was founded by the Tigua Tribe in 1682 as an aftermath of the Great Pueblo Revolt of 1680. The original home of the tribe was Isleta, New Mexico. In Texas, the archaic spelling of Ysleta (little island) with a "Y" is observed; in New Mexico, they have adopted the modern spelling with an "I." The tribe is composed of descendants of Tigua, Piros, Manso, Apache, and Suma Indians. The predominate surviving culture and the tribal organization is distinctly Tigua and similar to the Tiwa culture found at the Pueblos of Isleta, Sandia, Picuris, and Taos, New Mexico. "Tigua" is the archaic Spanish spelling of "Tiwa."

The tribe was a latecomer to affiliation with the federal government, due to its geographical separation from the other Pueblos following the Pueblo Revolt and due to its residence in the state of Texas. The Treaty of Guadalupe Hildago and the Organic Act of 1850 established the present-day boundaries of Texas and resulted in the tribe being both physically and jurisdictionally separated from the other Pueblo groups. Since Texas retained its public lands, there was no land base for federal administration and the tribe dropped out of view from the federal perspective. Prior to 1850, the tribe was inventoried and treated the same as the other Pueblo tribes.

The tribe was recognized by the federal government in 1968, and trust responsibility was transferred to the State of Texas. The Indian leaders who testified before the House Interior and Insular Affairs Committee on the recognition bill were Jose Granillo, the *cacique*; Miguel Pedraza, the governor; and Trinidad Granillo, the war captain. After hearing the testimony of the chiefs, Wayne Aspinal, chairman of the committee, asked the *cacique* what he wanted the government to do for him. The chief's response in Spanish through an interpreter was: "There is nothing that the government can do for me, but you can help my people obtain water." Aspinal was so obviously struck with this simple request that he moved the bill onto the floor of Congress without further proceedings. The tribe today has ended its relationship with the State of Texas and has regained their federal status through a 1987 Restoration Act.

The tribe operates a cultural center on Old Pueblo Road in the suburb of Ysleta, which is recognized as an important economic factor in the El Paso area. The cultural center has a successful restaurant serving traditional foods and offers significant employment opportunities, but most people work in the larger community. In 1993 the tribe is entering into a management agreement with a professional gaming organization to start Class 2 and 3 gaming activities. Gaming is seen as the potential for the future. There are family-operated shops selling pottery, weavings, leather items, and "dream catchers" (feather-netted objects). Some art that is produced is nontraditional in form, but produced in a traditional manner. A vigorous reculturalization program is underway and young children are learning the Tigua language, which had all but disappeared by the time of recognition. While many other cultural activities such as clan organization has ceased to exist in the Pueblo, the traditional government has survived. The division of leadership between the *cacique*, who is a spiritual leader, the governor, who is a civil leader, and the war captain, who is in charge of the tribe during an emergency situation, is the same tribal political organization of the Pueblos encountered by Coronado in 1540.

The current reservation consists of less than 100 acres of land in El Paso County, Texas, but may be enhanced in the future by the settlement of pending land claims against the State of Texas and other parties. The rolls of the tribe today contain 1,425 names, and many of the tribal members live on the reservation in a work-equity project sponsored by the Department of Housing. Most of the children are finishing high school and many of them are going on to college.

The highest priority on the Tigua Indian's land claim agenda is the return of Hueco Tanks. Hueco Tanks is a dramatic extrusion of granite rock in the Hueco Bolson, east of El Paso. The formation is riddled with caves and water collects in natural basins. The tanks have been a gathering place for thirsty travelers through the arid lands of far west Texas for millennia.

The Tanks are of particular importance to the Ysleta del Sur Pueblo because of a deep religious association. The Tanks are frequently visited for ceremonial purposes, and, until this century, the Tiguas maintained summer homes in the various caves. The names of many of the old tribal leaders are inscribed in caves that their families used.

In 1968 the County of El Paso acquired title to Hueco Tanks, intending to make a gift of the property to the State of Texas for the use and benefit of the Tigua Indian Tribe. This gift was accepted by the state, but at the urging of legislators who doubted the Indian's abilities to administer the property, title was taken in the state without the trust relationship being established. As a compromise, there was an agreement that the Indians would maintain and operate the Tanks. For a short time, this agreement was respected by the State of Texas, and the Indians maintained the facility in excellent condition and were very proud of their stewardship.

In 1970 the Parks and Wildlife Commission of the State of Texas unilaterally terminated their arrangement with the Pueblo and took over administration of the facility. As a result of this breach of faith, many of the pictographs, which were national treasures, have been destroyed. The Indians are dismayed at the damage that has occurred and are very concerned about the use of their religious shrine for rock climbing events, vigorously protesting rock climbing as a sacrilegious activity.

One of the most significant pictographs at Hueco Tanks recounts a battle between the Kiowa and the Tigua in the early nineteenth century, and has almost been obliterated under Parks Department stewardship. This battle is memorialized in the Kiowa calendar. The Kiowa thought they were fighting against Apaches. The Tigua tradition is that the Indians who they had trapped in a cave were Apache. Ironically, the Apache were blamed by both sides as being the enemy, when they were nowhere near the place! The battle ended when the Tigua threw hot chili peppers on fires they started at the mouth of the cave where the Kiowa were holed up. The acrid chili smoke forced the Kiowa to discover a passage leading to an escape route high on a cliff, where they were able to reach safety by using scrub juniper trees growing out of cracks in the rock formation as hand holds.

A sequel to the battle between the Kiowa and the Tigua at Hueco Tanks occurred in 1985. A group of Kiowa elders were in El Paso attending an Indian health seminar. Through Vine Deloria, they asked the Tiguas to show them the battle site. A group of Tigua leaders met with the Kiowa at the Tanks and led them first to the pictograph memorializing the conflict, then to the mouth of the cave where the Kiowa were trapped. Few words were spoken as the former enemies paid respect to their forbearers. One Kiowa rolled a corn husk cigarette and wedged it into a crack in the rock, while a Tigua opened a pouch of cornmeal and cast meal in the cardinal directions.

There is a tradition in the Ysleta del Sur Pueblo that someday there will be a last Indian alive who cannot lay down and give up his burden of mortal care until he has taken the tribal drum back to the mother Pueblo in New Mexico, where he is obligated to break it and bury it in the soil from which it came.

Tom Diamond

Further Reading

"Chronology of the Pueblo de la Ysleta del Sur in Colorado, New Mexico and Texas, 10,000 B.C. to 1969." Diamond Rash, Leslie & Schwarts." Microfiche. *Expert Testimony before the Indian Claims Commission: The Written Reports.* New York, NY: Clearwater Pub., 1973. Docket 22-C.

"History and Administration of the Tigua Indians of Ysleta Del Sur in New Mexico, during the Spanish Colonial Period." Myra Ellen Jenkins. Microfiche. *Expert Testimony before the Indian Claims Commission: The Written Reports.* New York, NY: Clearwater Pub., 1973. Docket 22-C.

Houser, Nicholas P. "Tigua Pueblo." *Handbook of North American Indians*. Vol. 9. *Southwest*. Ed. Alfonso Ortiz. Washington, DC: Smithsonian Institution (1979): 336–42.

Martineau, LaVan. *The Rocks Begin to Speak*. Las Vegas, NV: KC Publication, 1973.

"The Tigua, Suma, and Manso Indians of Western Texas and New Mexico, from Aboriginal Times to the 1880's." Rex E. Gerald. Microfiche. *Expert Testimony Before the Indian Claims Commision: The Written Reports*. New York, NY: Clearwater Pub., 1973. Docket 22-C.

YUCHI

The Yuchi Nation (also known as the Euchees) first came into historical view in the documents of the DeSoto expedition of 1539. Living near the East Coast in Georgia, the Yuchis soon became involved in the warfare caused by the European invasion, and ultimately took refuge in the confederacy led by Mvskoke Creeks. The Yuchis are especially notable for having a language apparently unrelated to any other languages in the area, although with a possible distant relationship to the Siouan family. They were removed with the Creeks to Indian Territory in 1832, where they formed eleven rural communities in what is now Creek County.

During allotment in severalty in 1906, the Yuchis did not try to separate themselves legally from the Mvskoke Creeks, but maintained their own traditional stomp grounds and churches. When offered a separate political charter in 1938, they, like most of the Upper Creeks who were their political allies, refused, fearing entanglement with the federal government. Through the 1950s, under the leadership of their traditional chief, Samuel W. Brown, Jr., the Yuchis maintained their traditional language and culture and petitioned the Indian Claims Commission, although unsuccessfully, for compensation to land along the Savannah River. To stimulate interest in the suit, Brown led Yuchis in several pilgrimages to Georgia to visit religious sites and cemeteries.

Presently the Yuchis maintain three ceremonial grounds: Polecat (the mother ground), Sand Creek, and Duck Creek. Christian Yuchis are oriented toward a uniquely Indian Methodist Church, called Pickett Prairie Church, and the Yuchis also maintain a chapter of the Native American Church. From a low of about 500 persons at the turn of the century, the population has recovered to about 1,500, of whom about 50 speak the Native language fluently. The Yuchi Nation is currently petitioning the Branch of Acknowledgment and Research for recognition as a separate group under the Oklahoma Indian Welfare Act.

John H. Moore

See also **Creek; Oklahoma Tribes**

Further Reading

Ballard, W.L. *The Yuchi Green Corn Ceremonial*. Los Angeles: American Indian Studies Center, University of California, 1978.

Speck, Frank G. *Ethnology of the Yuchi Indian*. Anthropological Publications of the University of Pennsylvania Museum, Vol. 1, no. 1. 1909. Atlantic Highlands, NJ: Humanities Press, 1979.

YUKI

The history of the Yuki people during the twentieth century is difficult to separate from the history of the other northern California tribes (including the Wailaki, Maidu, Nomlaki, Achumawi, Pomo, Lassik, and Wintun), who were brought in the 1860s and 1870s to live on Round Valley Indian Reservation, located in traditional Yuki territory in northern Mendocino County.

In 1900, the Natives in Round Valley were farming and raising hogs and cattle. John Brown, the last strong Yuki chief, died in 1904. Native children attended boarding school on the reservation. For high school and vocational training, they were sent to boarding schools out of the valley. In 1914, the reservation school burned down and classes were held in the Methodist church until 1926, when the Office of Indian Affairs built a new elementary day school for Native students. Not until 1959 was an integrated Native-white high school system available in Round Valley.

After 1919 allottees began receiving patents-in-fee to their lands. At least 70 percent of Native-owned lands were quickly lost to unscrupulous non-Natives or lost for nonpayment of taxes; some Round Valley Natives sold their lands for ready cash. This has resulted in a checkerboard of Native-owned and non-Native-owned lands on the reservation in 1993. By the 1930s many Yuki and other Natives were spending about half of each year out of the valley working for non-Native ranchers and farmers.

Much of the Yuki's traditional culture was destroyed by non-Natives before 1900, and in 1993 no one speaks Yuki. The last Yuki dance house in Round Valley was demolished about 1945. One Yuki man, Ralph Moore, became well known as a Yuki consultant for anthropologists until his death about 1950. In 1929 the establishment of a Pentecostal church in Round Valley attracted many Yuki members. Still active in 1993, this church was responsible for eradicating the final traces of Yuki culture.

After the passage of the Indian Reorganization Act in 1934, the tribes in Round Valley voted to merge as "The Consolidated Tribes of Round Valley," and they elected a Yuki man, Arthur Anderson, as their first tribal chief. Women have served on the Tribal Council since the early 1950s and in 1978 Delores Bettega, a Yuki-Pomo woman, was elected as the first female tribal chief. In 1993 tribal affairs are administered by a Tribal Council headed by DeAnna Barney, a Wailaki-Concow woman.

After World War II, Louisiana Pacific took over the local lumber mill and provided employment for some Natives until 1992, when the mill closed. Other Natives found employment outside the valley and returned home periodically. In 1953, the Natives on Round Valley Reservation rejected termination. In the late 1960s, they joined with other Natives and non-Natives to successfully protest a proposed dam on the Eel River, which would have flooded their valley.

In 1974 the Tribal Council adopted a comprehensive plan to improve conditions on the reservation and to guide future planning. Since that time some land has been purchased to add to the reservation's land base; medical and dental centers have been constructed on the reservation; over 100 units of badly needed housing have been built; and a youth center and a senior center have begun. Career development counseling and assistance are available. As a result of an Indian Cultural Development Project begun in 1974, some Native culture has been recovered and instructional material on the Yuki and other groups has been incorporated into the local school curriculum. Since 1960, some Native students from Round Valley, including Yuki students, have graduated from major colleges and professional schools.

In recent years, the population of the Yuki and other reservation groups has increased, with about fifty Yuki people living on the reservation in 1993, among a total of 1,250 Natives. At least thirty more Yuki are on the tribal rolls, but live off the reservation. In Round Valley, Native families are held together by strong kinship ties and maintain traditional values of sharing food, money, and services. They lead a rural lifestyle, similar to that of their non-Native neighbors, but retain their Native identity. Discrimination against Natives in Round Valley has diminished through this century, but the Yuki and other Natives still face problems of substance abuse and a high drop-out rate from school. Welfare and unemployment rates remain high among reservation residents, while the Tribal Council works to improve employment opportunities for Natives in the valley.

Virginia P. Miller

See also California Tribes

Further Reading

Foster, George. "A Summary of Yuki Culture." *University of California Anthropological Records* 5:3 (1944): 155–244.

Miller, Virginia P. "Yuki, Huchnom, and Coast Yuki." *Handbook of North American Indians.* Vol. 8. *California.* Ed. Robert F. Heizer. Washington, DC: Smithsonian Institution (1978) 249–55.

Patterson, Victoria, et al., eds. *The Singing Feather.* Ukiah, CA: Mendocino County Library, 1990.

Susman, Amelia. "The Round Valley Indians of California." *Contributions of the University of California Archaeological Research Facility* 31 (1976): 1–108.

YUMA

See Quechan

YUP'IK

The Yup'ik, or the " Real People," are one of the Eskimo groups who make their home in Alaska. The Yup'ik live in the southwestern portion of the state, along the Bering Sea coast and the Yukon and Kuskokwim deltas between Bristol Bay and Norton Sound. The language is referred to as Central Yup'ik, which is one of three Yup'ik languages; the other two are Siberian Yup'ik and Alutiiq, or Pacific Gulf Yup'ik. The greatest number of Central Yup'ik Eskimos live in the Yukon and Kuskokwim deltas; there may have been as many as 15,000 Yup'ik Eskimos living in settlements and villages along the Kuskokwim River before contact with Russian explorers, traders, and clergy in the mid-1800s. By the early 1900s numbers were reduced by a third because of influenza epidemics brought by the Europeans. Current Yup'ik population is estimated at 18,000, with perhaps 13,000 speakers of Yup'ik as of 1982.

In the 1870s Presbyterian missionary and explorer Sheldon Jackson traveled up the Kuskokwim River and found a group of people living as they had for hundreds, if not thousands, of years. By the time Jackson arrived, however, these people had already experienced extensive contact with Russian traders. In 1885 the Moravian Church established itself on the Kuskokwim. The missionaries found the Yup'ik with beliefs and traditions very different from their own, and they immediately went to work to try and communicate with and convert the Natives. The Moravians were determined to learn the Yup'ik language to further their effort; they studied, practiced, wrote, and rewrote Yup'ik words as they heard and understood them. The missionaries learned quickly, for their teachers were friendly and very cooperative. As the Moravians began to understand and speak the language, they began the work of conversion in earnest. They told the Yup'ik people that their beliefs were "no good," and were derived from the devil. They said their Eskimo dancing was the practice of superstition, interjected with lewd and obscene puns and gestures. We Yup'ik largely acquiesced; that is, in Yup'ik culture, it is our custom to allow things to happen, to go their way.

The educational system was not kind to Yup'ik children, punishing them for speaking their native language in school. Since only English was allowed to be spoken in school, many children abandoned their native language. This continued until the early 1970s, when bilingual education programs began to be implemented as a result of the Bilingual Education Act passed by the state legislature in 1972.

Today, the Yup'ik face another kind of threat. We are losing our lives indirectly by losing our way of life, our lifestyle. We do not define ourselves to ourselves by how much money we make, how much we consume, how much we own, how much we can change nature, or how well we compete with our peers. Rather, we define ourselves by how well we cooperate with each other, avoid competition, live in harmony with nature, and adapt ourselves to it.

State legislation is currently being proposed to limit subsistence hunting and fishing rights by defining Native lifestyle in state law. The trouble with this approach is that state laws most often reflect a different lifestyle and a different set of values. Yup'ik have traditionally been a migratory, nomadic people. We hunt, fish, and gather wild plants as the seasons present them. Our instinct to survive has made us an integral part of nature. Our closeness to nature is religious, we call it spirituality. The Yup'ik believe that everything has a spirit. Animals, birds, and plants have an awareness, and we treat them with the same respect we have for ourselves. For instance, non-Natives refer to animals they hunt as "game"; hunting for them is a game. We do not play games with animals. When we bring animals into our homes, we treat them as guests. We talk to the fish and animals. We tell them we caught them because we need them to survive, and we will eat them with care. We thank them for having been caught and we believe their spirits will return to their makers and report on how they were cared for. If the animals were treated well, then their makers will provide more of the same. Yup'ik spirituality is being aware and conscious of everything around including animals, plants, and the environment.

Perhaps the most detrimental contribution of Western society to Yup'ik culture has been the introduction of the concept of individuality. Individuality is alien to Yup'ik culture. For thousands of years we have worked together hunting, gathering, and sharing, as evidenced by our customs of feasting and celebrating. Our ancestors placed the highest priority on the agreement of the group and gaining personal meaning from participation in the group; we have a sense of security when we belong to a group. This is exactly what is missing in the lives of so many people today. Somewhere along the line someone introduced the words "them" and "us." We feel security with all of "us" but threatened by all of "them." Today Yup'ik are being told to throw out thousands of years of belonging to "the group" for something totally alien. We were once a mighty people and still believe in our hearts that we are hunter-warriors. Today, as the Yup'ik move inexorably into the twenty-first century, we must become hunter-warriors again. This time we will not hunt and gather as in centuries past, but we will be warriors hunting for knowledge and self-determination.

On December 18, 1971, the Alaska Native Claims Settlement Act (ANCSA) was passed, settling the one-hundred-year-old question of the aboriginal land rights of Alaska Natives. With the enactment of ANCSA, significant changes in the control and use of Alaska land became law. Approximately 40 million acres of land was conveyed to Alaska Native corporations and, in addition to the land settlements, a cash settlement was awarded to the Native regional and village corporations which were to be organized in accordance with the settlement legislation. In order to select land or receive benefits, every Native village had to incorporate in a manner similar to the twelve regional corporations, except that the village corporations have a choice of becoming profit or nonprofit corporations, while the regional corporations were established as businesses for profit.

Calista, the largest of the three regional corporations serving Yup'ik territory, is the second largest regional corporation with 13,000 shareholders and land holdings totaling 6.5 million acres. The Yukon Kuskokwim Health Corporation (YKHC) is another organization located in the heart of Yup'ik Alaska, whose mission is to achieve the greatest possible improvement in the health status of the people of the region. YKHC is committed to the development of culturally relevant programs for primary care, prevention, and health promotion in a setting that fosters Native self-determination in the control and management of health delivery. 1991 was a memorable year for the YKHC, marking the culmination of a twenty year dream to consolidate the delivery of health care services under its umbrella. In the spring of 1991, the YKHC Board of Directors voted to authorize submission of a contract proposal to Indian Health Service for management of the Yukon-Kuskokwim Delta Regional Hospital, and in October of that year, YKHC signed a $24 million annual contract with the Alaska Area Native Health Service to manage the Bethel hospital.

The Association of Village Council Presidents (AVCP) is the regional nonprofit corporation of the Yukon-Kuskokwim deltas representing fifty-six villages. The right to subsistence hunting and fishing is still the main issue it is dealing with today, just as it has been since its formation as a Native association in 1964. AVCP also works very closely with the YKHC on health issues. It is pursuing the contracting of state and federal program services in the area, under the authority of the Indian Self-Determination and Education Assistance Act of 1975, since contracting will allow our people more involvement in how services should be provided, as well as make more funds available to do the work.

Ultimately AVCP's goal is to establish a regional tribal government, so that the Yup'ik people can have a stronger unified voice to respond to concerns and issues that affect them. It is the mission of AVCP to establish and maintain a close relationship with the fifty-six member villages and their people, to work closely with them to seek avenues of funding, programs, projects, and grants, and develop infrastructures which will allow this organization to help the villages improve the quality of life of all Native people of the region. The AVCP also advocates for the preservation of the diverse culture and traditions of the Yup'ik people. When this very way of life is threatened by both inside and outside interests, it is the charge of AVCP to bring these issues to the forefront and champion the causes of our Native people to protect that which makes us strong. It is only by working together, protecting ourselves, our families and children, our land and our environment, that we will prevail and survive as a people, proud and strong in both body and spirit.

John Active

See also Alaska Native Claims Settlement Act; Alaska Native Regional Corporations

Further Reading

Fienup-Riordan, Ann. *The Real People and the Children of Thunder: The Yup'ik Eskimo Encounter with the Moravian Missionaries John and Edith Kilbuck.* Norman: University of Oklahoma, 1991.

Henkelman, James W., and Kurt H. Vitt. *"Harmonious to Dwell": The History of the Alaska Moravian Church.* Bethel, AK: Tundra, 1985.

Oswalt, Wendell H. *Bashful No Longer: An Alaskan Eskimo Ethnohistory, 1778–1988.* Norman: University of Oklahoma, 1990.

VanStone, James W. "Mainland Southwest Alaska Eskimo." *Handbook of North American Indians.* Vol. 5. *Arctic.* Ed. David Damas. Washington, DC: Smithsonian Institution (1984): 224–42.

Vick, Ann, ed. *The Cama-i Book: Kayaks, Dogsleds, Bear Hunting, Bush Pilots, Smoked Fish, Mukluks, and Other Traditions of Southwestern Alaska.* Garden City, NY: Anchor Press/Doubleday, 1983.

YUROK

The Yurok Indians of northwestern California are indigenous to the lower Klamath River and the Pacific Coast adjacent to its mouth. Before contact, they were a cultural affiliation of about 2,500 people, living in approximately fifty-four hamlets united by a common (Algonquian) language, customary law, and a way of life supported primarily by salmon fishing, hunting, and acorn harvesting. Non-Indians first settled in Yurok territory during the Gold Rush of 1849. Varied white interests defeated ratification of an 1851 treaty that would have created a large reservation. The ensuing armed conflict between Yuroks and whites extended into the mid-1860s.

In 1855 President Pierce, by executive order, established the Klamath River Reservation in Yurok territory, a military zone along the lower twenty miles of the river. In 1864 Congress authorized a total of four reservations in the state of California. These included the twelve- by twelve-square-mile Hoopa Valley Reservation on the Trinity River, occupied by Hupa, Yurok, and other Indian people. In the 1880s and 1890s, the validity of the 1855 Klamath River Reservation came under attack. The conflict was resolved in 1891, when President Harrison issued an executive order enlarging the Hoopa Reservation by creating a "connecting strip" or "addition," joining the questionable Klamath River Reservation to the fully authorized Hoopa Valley Indian Reservation. The process resulted in the formation of an Extension to the Hoopa Square, forming a strip one mile wide on either side of the Klamath River, running downriver from the Square at the junction of the Klamath and the Trinity to the Pacific. The Square came to be popularly understood as a Hupa Indian reservation; the Extension was occupied primarily by Yuroks and is now called the Yurok Reservation. Three communal allotments have also been granted to pri-

marily Yurok residents on the coast, forming rancherias at Big Lagoon, Trinidad, and Klamath (Resighini).

In 1891 the Extension consisted of 58,168 acres. In 1892 and 1893, however, lands in the Extension were allotted to Yurok families and the putative "surplus" lands opened to whites. Timber companies and others bought up many allotments through questionable forced fee patents and eventually controlled 87 percent of the Extension. Today, only about 6,800 communal acres remain in the Yurok Reservation, although Yuroks hold an additional approximately 2,000 allotted acres.

From 1932 to 1933, Hupa Indians organized as the Hoopa Valley Indian Tribe, with a Tribal Council duly elected and a Constitution and Bylaws formally accepted by the federal government in 1952. Yuroks, however, while creating the Yurok Tribal Organization, failed in their efforts to have a Constitution approved. Timber companies anxious to log the Hoopa Square urged the Bureau of Indian Affairs (BIA) to exercise their authority to sell reservation timber. The BIA agreed to do so, but declined to distribute income from the sales until the Hoopa Valley Indian Tribe prepared a tribal roll and defined its membership in their Constitution. This was done between 1949 and 1955. Jessie Short filed suit on behalf of the Yuroks of the Square and the Extension, claiming that the Hoopa Valley Indian Tribe's membership definition was illegal, and that Yuroks had a right to a share in the timber revenues. *Jessie Short v. United States* was asserted in the United States Court of Claims in 1963, which was decided in the Yuroks' favor in 1973. The funds continued to be held in a trust, however, pending formal Yurok tribal organization, while a number of companion or collateral suits were also brought.

In 1988 the Hoopa-Yurok Settlement Act was passed, in part to resolve issues that arose in the *Short* case. The Square and its remaining timber went to the approximately 1,700 enrolled Hupa Indians, the far smaller Extension going to the more numerous Yuroks, together with exclusive Indian fishing rights in the lower Klamath. The timber trust funds (now called the Settlement Funds) were earmarked for per capita payments and for tribal use by the Yuroks when they organized. A Yurok Transition Team was appointed by the Department of the Interior, to oversee compilation of a Yurok roll, disbursement of the Settlement Funds, to set priorities for management of the Yurok Reservation, and to prepare for organization. More than 8,000 people applied for enrollment, subject to BIA approval and appeals. By the late summer of 1991, there were approximately 3,500 officially enrolled Yurok Indians. An Interim Council was elected later in that year to serve for two years. They were charged with drafting a tribal Constitution and overseeing the election of a Yurok Tribal Council in 1993. The Interim Council, however, has not waived Yurok rights to continue contesting the terms of the Settlement Act in court.

Yurok population reached a nadir of about 668 around 1910, a 73 percent decline from the estimated

1849 population. In the early years of this century, Yuroks began to seek relief from poverty and malnutrition through assured access to aboriginal subsistence sites alienated by the allotment process, an effort continued by the Yurok Tribal Organization from the 1930s on. Salmon canneries, beginning in 1877, provided some wage labor for Yuroks until the canneries were closed in 1934, when all Indian commercial fishing and subsistence gillnetting were also banned. These rights were not restored until 1977. Year-round Indian hunting rights in remaining Extension lands had been guaranteed in 1975.

Yuroks have long perceived the desecration of Indian gravesites on aboriginal lands now occupied by non-Indians as a pressing issue. In the 1930s the Tribal Organization, under the leadership of Robert Spott, began acting to protect them. This effort took on new energy in 1970 when Milton Marks founded the Northwest Indian Cemetery Protective Association (NICPA), which was to be central to a legal action of profound national significance.

Beginning in 1968 many Yuroks protested USDA Forest Service plans for a high-standard logging road—called the "GO-Road"—running across Six Rivers National Forest and connecting major highways at Gasquet, on the Smith River; and Orleans, on the Klamath. These protests culminated in the 1988 United States Supreme Court's hearing of *Lyng v. Northwest Indian Cemetery Protective Association*. The primary issue in the case was whether or not Native American sacred sites on public lands are protected by the First Amendment guarantee of the free exercise of religion. The Court's five to three decision in the Forest Service's favor was a stunning blow to Yuroks, as well as to their Karuk and Tolowa Indian neighbors. The federal government eventually set aside the GO-Road "high country" as a wilderness area legislatively, preserving its sacred sites, but avoiding setting a legal precedent regarding Native American religious freedom.

Yurok people at Requa were suing for the right of their children to attend public schools as early as the mid-1880s. Although some Yurok Indians were enrolled in BIA boarding schools on the Hoopa Valley Reservation and elsewhere, Yuroks did not attend public high schools in any numbers until after World War II. A very few Yurok men and women had begun seeking higher education in the San Francisco Bay area in the 1930s. In the 1960s, with the expansion of the California state higher education system, local opportunities for college and university education increased dramatically. The first book by a Yurok author, Lucy Thompson's *To the American Indian*, was published in 1916. English had become the primary language on the Klamath River by 1915, but the late 1960s also brought grassroots efforts, led by Yurok elders, to retain the rapidly disappearing Yurok language and traditional culture through elementary, high school, and college programs.

The number of traditional Yurok "Indian doctors" declined rapidly after 1849, although a very few

herbalists and modern Indian doctors continue to practice today. Affordable medical care, however, became absolutely necessary with the introduction of nonindigenous diseases. In the present century, a BIA hospital operated on the Hoopa Reservation until 1956 and was replaced briefly by a private hospital that opened in 1960. In 1974 the clinic that had grown out of that hospital came under Indian control, funded by the United Indian Health Services, Inc., which had also established the Tsurai Health Center on the Trinidad Rancheria in the late 1960s. The Tsurai Health Center now has over 5,000 active files. In addition to a variety of public health problems common on many reservations, Yurok Indians living along the Klamath today are particularly concerned about the effects of herbicides containing dioxin. These have been applied by the Forest Service and by timber companies since the 1970s to retard deciduous growth, increasing the yield of coniferous timber. The herbicides appear to pose a serious threat to human health and reproduction, as well as to anadromous fish stocks and to supplies of acorns and other vital subsistence, medicinal, and craft resources.

During this century, in addition to work related to fish packing, Yuroks have found seasonal employment in the hops fields of northern California and southern Oregon, and on the lily bulb farms of the coastal plain near the Smith River, on the California-Oregon border. Yurok men have enlisted in the armed services since World War I, many Yurok men and women have worked in the San Francisco Bay area since the years of the Great Depression, and Indian people continue to leave northwestern California, often only temporarily, in search of employment. Many Yuroks have entered the law and other professions. But above all throughout this century logging and commercial and subsistence fishing have been central to the economic welfare of the Yuroks.

By the 1970s careless corporate logging, causing silting in spawning beds, had proven detrimental to salmon fishing. Herbicides, over-fishing by foreign and domestic commercial offshore fleets, and river water levels lowered by upstream dams also contributed to the endangerment of the Klamath and Trinity River salmon stocks. In August of 1978, Indian gillnetting rights, restored the previous year, were unexpectedly placed under moratorium as a conservation measure and armed agents of the United States Fish and Wildlife Service moved in, instigating a "salmon war." The following year the federal government, attempting to restore peace, again allowed restricted gillnetting, assured Indian rights to subsistence fishing, and mandated salmon harvest allocations. The allocation system worked, however imperfectly, through the 1980s, and two small Yurok-managed salmon hatcheries were established in the Extension. Still, depletion of salmon stocks continues. Furthermore, with declining timber reserves and increasingly stringent environmental regulations, logging and milling industries in the region can no longer be depended upon as reliable sources of income.

A bingo parlor was established on the Trinidad Rancheria in the 1980s, and in 1991 Big Lagoon Rancheria invested in a major hotel in Arcata, California. However, greater economic strength is needed. For many Yuroks, building more plentiful and adequate housing, improving reservation roads and water systems, supplying electric service to the entire Extension, increasing the tribal land base through restoration of alienated portions of aboriginal territory, and securing a greater share in the sport fishing and tourism industries of the lower Klamath, are high priorities today.

Christian missionaries had little success on the lower Klamath until the 1920s, when Protestant sects began to gain converts. In addition, in 1926 Jimmy Jack started proselytizing for the syncretic Indian Shaker Church. Three Shaker churches were built in Yurok territory, introducing new traditions in healing as well as other religious practices. The ongoing Shaker congregation at Johnson's, on the Yurok Reservation, is perhaps the strongest in California today, and many Yuroks support other churches. Earlier traditional ways have continued as well.

In 1849 the Yuroks had six (or possibly seven) great regional renewal ceremonies, but by 1909 only three survived. The last of these, the Jump Dance at Pecwan, seemed to succumb in 1939, but in 1984 it was held again. The Jump Dance, whose purpose is to renew humanity spiritually and physically and to stamp out sickness, has been taking place at Pecwan every other year since 1984, following the traditional cycle, and now seems firmly reestablished. Brush Dances, three-day child-curing ceremonials, also still flourish as a major expression of Yurok spirituality. Former Brush Dance house-pits were rebuilt at Weitchpec and at Pecwan, following a disastrous flood in 1964. Another was reexcavated in 1976 and 1980 at the former site of a Yurok village, now in Redwood National Park, on the south side of the mouth of the Klamath. Men and women are making new Brush Dance songs today, in both Yurok and English, along with new men's gambling and Jump Dance songs. Such creativity has included a continuation of indigenous crafts. For example, excellent dance regalia, baskets, redwood canoes, and traditional cuisine are all being produced today.

Fine artists have emerged in recent years, some achieving national recognition for their modern improvisations rooted in local craft traditions and spirituality.

Many of these strands were woven together in Yurok craftsmen's painstaking recreation of a traditional redwood plank hamlet in Patrick's Point State Park, south of the mouth of the Klamath. The village, called Sumeg, was dedicated in September of 1990, with a three-day festival that included a new Brush Dance. At the same time, the solemn ten-day Jump Dance was getting underway upriver at Pecwan, and the Yurok Transition Team was moving into recently acquired tribal headquarters on the coast, north of the river's mouth. Taken together, these three occasions suggested both the diversity of the Yurok Indians' commitments, as well as their shared determination, to retain traditional ways in modern contexts, over which they exercise ever greater control.

Thomas Buckley, with the Yurok Transition Team

See also California Tribes; Sacred Sites

Further Reading

Berman, Joan. *Ethnography and Folklore of the Indians of Northwestern California: A Literature Review and Annotated Bibliography.* Salinas, CA: Coyote Press, 1986.

Falk, Donald. "Lyng v. Northwest Indian Cemetery Protective Association: Bulldozing First Amendment Protection of Indian Sacred Lands." *Ecology Law Quarterly* 16:2 (1989): 515–70.

Inouye, Daniel. Senate Report 100–564, Calendar No. 1025, September 30, 1988. *Report to Accompany S. 2723: Partitioning Certain Reservation Lands between the Hoopa Valley Tribe and the Yurok Indians, to Clarify the Use of Tribal Timber Proceeds, and for Other Purposes.* (SuDocs Y1.1/5:100–564)

Pilling, Arnold R. "Yurok." *Handbook of North American Indians.* Vol. 8. *California.* Ed. Robert F. Heizer. Washington, DC: Smithsonian Institution (1978): 137–54.

Spott, Robert. "Address." *The Commonwealth* 21:3 (1926): 133–35.

Thompson, Lucy. *To the American Indian.* Eureka, CA: 1916. Berkeley, CA: Heyday Books, 1991.

ZIA

See Pueblo of Zia

ZUNI

The Pueblo of Zuni is a federally recognized Indian tribe with a reservation consisting of four tracts of federal trust land in New Mexico and Arizona (see map). The main body of the reservation was established by an executive order in 1877. It borders the state line in west central New Mexico, and in 1992 included 636 square miles. In addition, the reservation includes a tract of land one square mile in size surrounding the Zuni Salt Lake, thirty miles south of the main reservation in New Mexico, and two tracts of land approximately eighteen square miles in size, near the confluence of the Zuni and Little Colorado rivers in east central Arizona.

In their own language, the Zuni people call themselves the A:shiwi. They and their ancestors have occupied the Zuni and Little Colorado River valleys for more than 2,000 years. Today all of the Zuni settlements are located on the main reservation. Zuni Pueblo, the principal town, was founded around 1350. Other settlements include outlying farming villages at Ojo Caliente, Pescado, Nutria, and Tekapo, and numerous "sheep camps" or ranches.

Twentieth-Century History

Population Growth. The Zuni population has significantly increased in the twentieth century (figure 1). Throughout the nineteenth and early twentieth centuries the Zuni people were subjected to recurring epidemics of smallpox and other diseases. As a result the population fluctuated between 1,000 and 2,000 people. Due to improved health care, the population began to increase exponentially in the 1930s, and today there are more than 9,000 Zunis.

Loss of Land. The taking of Zuni land by the United States created a fundamental economic problem the Zuni people are still working to overcome. Eighty-two percent of the aboriginal Zuni territory was taken before 1900, leaving the tribe with a land base inadequate to support its traditional agrarian lifestyle (figure 2). In the twentieth century, the United States took an additional 2,298,390 acres of Zuni land, leaving the tribe with a reservation that is less than 3 percent of the size of its original territory.

Economic Change. The dramatic increase in population and decrease in the land base have necessitated a major change in the Zuni economy in the twentieth century. The farming and ranching of sheep and cattle that were a significant part of the economy at the turn of the century have gradually decreased in importance. Since the 1930s the production of arts and crafts and wage labor have been the economic mainstays. Although many Zunis retain an interest in farming and grazing land, few tribal members are now totally dependent upon the land for their livelihood. Coal, oil and gas, and other minerals on the reservation have not attracted commercial development and play no role in the tribal economy.

Tribal Government. The traditional political structure of the Zuni tribe was theocratic; a Council of Priests installed and deposed a secular government consisting of a governor, lieutenant governor, and *Tenientes* (Tribal Council). In the 1890s the United States undermined this political system by jailing the Zuni Bow Priests and preventing them from exercising their traditional executive authority on behalf of the Priestly Council. Severe political turmoil and factionalism resulted, as the Council of Priests became directly involved in secular affairs in the early twentieth century. By 1934 the Zunis were no longer able to install a governor and Tribal Council by traditional means, and tribal members voted to elect their secular leaders through the democratic processes authorized by the Wheeler-Howard Act (Indian Reorganization Act). Completion of the transition from theocratic to democratic government took several decades. Zuni women gained the right to vote in 1965, and secret balloting was instituted the same year.

In 1970 the Zunis ratified the tribal Constitution authorized by the Wheeler-Howard Act. The tribal government was structured to include a legislative branch (governor, lieutenant governor, and six tribal councilmen with four-year terms), a judicial branch, and an executive branch (overseen by the governor, lieutenant governor, and tribal secretary). Significant funding for community and social services became available through grants and contracts during the Great Society programs of the 1960s, and the structure of the tribal government greatly increased in size. Under the policy of self-determination, the Zuni tribe now provides many basic community services under contract to the federal government. In 1980 the tribe employed 482 people in seventy-one tribal programs organized in nine divisions. Cuts in federal funding in the 1980s have caused attrition in the number of tribal programs and employees, but the tribal gov-

ZUNI INDIAN RESERVATION
IN NEW MEXICO AND ARIZONA (1992)

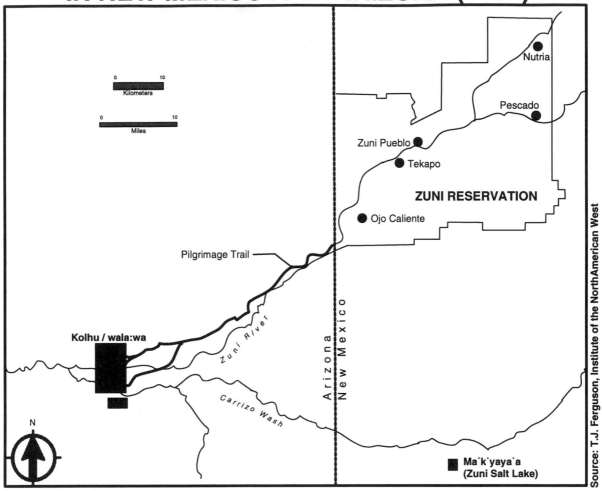

Source: T.J. Ferguson, Institute of the NorthAmerican West

An easement along a pilgrimage trail joins the main reservation in New Mexico with the new trust lands at Kolhu/wala:wa in Arizona.

ernment remains the largest employer on the reservation.

While many individual Zunis have held important positions in tribal government, there are several families that have provided successive generations of leaders to serve as governor. These families, with their members who served as governors listed in parentheses, include the Eriacho (Jesus, 1907; Leopoldo 1933, 1947 to 1951), Eustace (Usstisy 1924 to 1926; Calvin 1957 to 1960), Lewis (William F., 1912 to 1916, 1917; Robert E., 1965 to 1974, 1979 to 1982, 1987 to 1993), and Ondelacy (Mocko, 1923; Warren 1933, 1943, 1960 to 1962) lineages. Many additional families have provided community leaders who served as governors or tribal councilmen, including the Bowannie, Edaakie, Gaspar, Laselute, Mahooty, Nasheboo, Nastacio, Panteah, Simplicio, and Wyaco families. Robert E.

Lewis is the single most influential Zuni political leader in the twentieth century, serving for eight terms encompassing twenty-three years, during which time the Zuni Constitution was adopted and the Zuni land claims cases were initiated and concluded.

Interaction with Federal Government. The first Bureau of Indian Affairs (BIA) subagency was established in 1902, with offices at Black Rock five miles east of Zuni Pueblo. From 1904 to 1909, the BIA constructed the Black Rock Dam and Reservoir, which were intended to impound enough irrigation water to provide a small allotment of agricultural land for every Zuni man. This dam was the cornerstone of the BIA's attempt to implement the General Allotment Act at Zuni Pueblo. The dam failed immediately after construction, however, and even though it was repaired, the reservoir rapidly lost its storage capacity due to siltation. The Zuni people strongly opposed the allotment of their commonly held reservation into individually owned parcels, and the government failed to implement the General Allotment Act at Zuni Pueblo.

In 1907, the BIA established a boarding school at Black Rock, and this institution served as one of the means by which the federal government changed the Zuni's traditional agricultural technology. The BIA persuaded many Zunis to give up their long-standing agricultural strategy based on a mix of ditch irrigated and floodwater irrigated fields, cultivated with hand tools and communal labor, in favor of a "modern" technology, based on mechanical tools, draft animals, and individual farming of canal irrigated fields fed by large reservoirs. Canal irrigated farming could not be sustained, and the BIA's policies wreaked havoc on the communal labor organization that was the basis of traditional agriculture.

Further stress on Zuni agriculture in the late nineteenth and early twentieth centuries was caused by the degradation of Zuni land, primarily from erosion stemming from overgrazing and clear-cutting of the watershed upstream from the Zuni Reservation. As arroyo channels became deeply eroded, traditional techniques of diverting water from streams to spread it through farm fields were no longer effective. In the 1930s, the BIA constructed or enlarged additional reservoirs at Ojo Caliente, Nutria, and Pescado. These reservoirs also rapidly lost their storage capacity due to siltation, and the agricultural improvements they supported were short-lived. Zuni agriculture declined, and the acreage cultivated dropped from 10,000 acres in the nineteenth century, to less than 1,500 acres today.

In 1935, Black Rock became a subagency of the Albuquerque Area Office of the BIA, which governs all Pueblos in New Mexico. As an alternative to agriculture, the BIA promoted the Zuni livestock industry. Grazing regulations were instituted, and an open range was divided into individually assigned parcels. Ninety-five percent of the reservation was divided into approximately ninety-five family operated sheep ranches, and two cattle associations. Permanent ranch facilities and fencing became standard. About 14,000 sheep, 50 goats, and 550 cattle are grazed on the reservation.

More than 200 Zuni men entered the armed forces between 1941 and 1945 to serve their country during World War II. When these veterans returned, they became a catalyst for social and political change in the Pueblo. Zuni patriotism for the United States remains strong, and many Zunis continue to serve in the military.

In 1950, electricity was introduced in Zuni Pueblo using federal funds. By 1960, domestic water and sewer lines were installed to all homes desiring those facilities. Architectural change in the Pueblo has been dramatic, and the traditional multi-storied edifice of Zuni Pueblo has been reconstructed into single-storied houses. To alleviate a housing shortage, more than 800 single-family dwellings in suburban subdivisions have been constructed using Department of Housing and Urban Development funds.

Interaction with State Government. The State of New Mexico built and maintains sixty miles of state highways on the Zuni Reservation, which connect Zuni with surrounding communities. In the 1950s, the State of New Mexico replaced the BIA as the provider of educational services on the reservation, and the first high school was established at Zuni. In 1980, the Zunis became the first tribe in New Mexico to establish a state public school district whose boundaries coincide with their reservation. This has enabled the Zunis to gain local control over education, while retaining the benefits of New Mexico's commitment to funding Indian education.

Land Claims and Water Rights. Zuni leaders have continually protested that the executive order reservation was too small to support the tribe. In 1917, 1935, and 1949, petitions from Zuni leaders led to the expansion of the reservation. Even with these expansions, however, the size of the reservation was still inadequate, and successive Zuni Tribal Councils sought to redress this through litigation of land claims. Since the Zunis failed to file a land claim under the Indian Claims Commission, they had to obtain special legislation to enable them to sue the United States for compensation for lands taken without payment. This legislation was passed in 1978, in an act of Congress (P.L. 95–280), that also provided for the return of Salt Lake. The Zunis filed a claim for lands taken without payment in the Court of Claims (Docket 161–79L), and this case was litigated in 1981 in Salt Lake City,

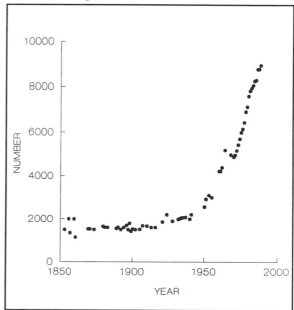

Figure 1
Zuni Population Growth since 1850

Source: E. Richard Hart, Institute of the NorthAmerican West.

Utah. At this time, the Zuni tribe filed a second land claim for damages to their remaining trust lands caused by the acts and omissions of the United States (Dockets 327–84L and 224–84L). The damages claimed by the Zunis included erosion, damage to archaeological sites, and takings of water, coal, salt, and other real property. Litigation to adjudicate the water rights within the Zuni River basin was also initiated in the 1980s, but this case was subsequently dismissed by the courts in New Mexico, and awaits reinstatement at some future date.

The Zuni tribe sought the return of one tract of land in Arizona surrounding *Kolhu/wala:wa*, a sacred area known as "Zuni Heaven," since this is where Zuni people reside after death. In 1984, Zunis were successful in obtaining an act of Congress (P.L. 98–408), which enabled the land transfers needed to add this area to the Zuni Reservation. A local rancher, however, tried to prevent the Zunis from crossing his land on their quadrennial pilgrimage to this sacred site. As a result, in 1985 the Zunis and the Department of Justice entered into litigation in the Federal District Court of Arizona, to obtain an easement to *Kolhu/wala:wa*. The Zunis established the elements needed for an easement in a trial held in Phoenix, in 1990, and the Court granted them the right to cross the private land separating the two parts of the reservation.

In 1987 the Court of Claims determined that all Zuni claims for land taken without payment were valid, and the case then entered the valuation phase to determine compensation. In 1990 a settlement of Zuni claims for land taken without payment was reached, awarding the Zuni tribe $25 million in compensation. In 1990 Congress also passed the Zuni Land Conservation Act (P. L. 101–486), as a legislative settlement of the claims for land damages. This Act authorized payment of an additional $25 million and established a permanent trust fund to be used for sustainable development and rehabilitation of degraded lands.

Current Situation. Since the 1960s the Zuni tribe has had three goals for development: increase individual income, enhance educational opportunity, and improve living conditions. To guide use of the $50 million obtained in the settlements of their land claims, the Zunis have started work on a plan for sustainable development to attain these goals and restore their landscape.

The rate of unemployment remains high on the reservation, but the tribe has established several successful businesses. These include Zuni Arts and Crafts, with stores in Zuni Pueblo and San Francisco, California, to market the tribal jewelry and crafts that have made the Zunis famous; and the Zuni Cultural Resources Enterprise, which provides archaeological services needed in regional development. Other tribally owned enterprises have been initiated with varying degrees of success. Several Zuni individuals have also established privately owned businesses.

Culture

Language. Although the culture of the Zuni people is closely related with other Pueblos (especially the neighboring Acoma and Hopi tribes), the Zuni language is a linguistic isolate unrelated to any other languages spoken in the Southwest. This language is the basis of Zuni culture, and it remains the primary language of most tribal members, although almost all Zunis also speak English. The Zuni tribe and the public school district have developed a literacy program designed to help preserve the Zuni language in written form.

Religion. The Zunis enjoy a rich and complex religion that reveres ancestors and brings rain, prosperity, and fertility to tribal members and their neighbors throughout the world. All males belong to one of six kiva groups, associated with kachinas. There are also twelve medicine societies that cure specific ills, and a number of priesthoods with responsibility for fetishes and other religious property. The ceremonial cycle includes an annual blessing during the *Shalako* ceremony, followed by new year rituals at the solstice, night dances in the winter and spring, and summer rain dances in the plazas of the Pueblo. Many religious practices are conducted in private and entail the use of shrines and sacred areas on and off the reservation. The Zuni religion integrates tribal society and provides the Zunis with a distinctive worldview.

While most Zunis continue to practice their tribal religion, some Zunis also engage in Christian worship. There are Catholic, Christian Reformed, Mormon, and Baptist churches on the reservation with small memberships.

Social Structure. Ties of kin and clan remain vitally important at Zuni. Large extended families provide economic and emotional support. An individual's clan membership is derived from the mother, but families also have important ties to their father's clan. Zuni clans are in a state of flux, as small clans die out or become incorporated into larger clans. Contemporary Zuni clans include Dogwood, Macaw, Crow, Eagle, Sun, Badger, Turkey, Corn, Frog, Crane, Coyote, Bear, Tobacco, Tansy Mustard, Deer, and Roadrunner.

Community Life. The Zunis have maintained a strong sense of community. The tribe sponsors a number of programs designed to enhance community life, including a Senior Citizens Center, a cultural and historic preservation program, and a tribal museum. The Zunis are proud of their fine silver and lapidary work, and the production of other arts. The tribe operates alcoholism and drug abuse programs to combat these social problems. The Indian Health Service maintains a hospital on the reservation, and sponsors a fitness program based on nutrition and running, which has led to a reduction of problems with obesity and adult onset diabetes. Zuni community life is so attractive that almost all tribal members continue to reside in the Pueblo, and those who leave to pursue careers off the reservation generally return there when their employment ends.

Prospects for the Twenty-First Century. During the twentieth century the Zuni population has finally reached or surpassed the size of the population before Europeans entered the area in the sixteenth century. The Zunis have successfully sought federal legislation to address long-standing inequities in land claims. The settlement of these claims has provided the tribe with the capital resources it needs for sustainable development, if these funds are wisely invested and used by tribal leaders. The tribe has embarked on a major project to restore degraded lands and implement sustainable development. Although some fundamental problems remain, i.e., unadjudicated water rights, the Zunis have taken control of their destiny and become responsible for how the tribe will develop in the twenty-first century.

T.J. Ferguson

Cal A. Seciwa

Further Reading

Bunzel, Ruth. "Introduction to Zuni Ceremonialism." *Bureau of American Ethnology 47th Annual Report* 1929–1930. Washington, DC: U.S. Government Printing Office (1932): 467–544.

Ferguson, T.J., and E. Richard Hart. *A Zuni Atlas.* Norman: University of Oklahoma Press, 1985.

Kroeber, A.L. " Zuni Kin and Clan." *Anthropological Papers of the American Museum of Natural History* 18: 2 (1917): 39–204.

Ladd, Edmund J. "Zuni Social and Political Organization." *Handbook of North American Indians.* Vol. 9. *Southwest.* Ed. Alfonso Ortiz. Washington, DC: Smithsonian Institution (1979): 482–91.

Stevenson, Matilda Coxe. "The Zuni Indians: Their Mythology, Esoteric Fraternities, and Ceremonies." *Bureau of American Ethnology 23rd Annual Report* 1901–1902. Washington, DC: U.S. Government Printing Office (1904): 3–634 .

Figure 2
Taking of Land by U.S. Government

Period	Acreage	Percent
Aboriginal	15,255,266	100.00
1846–1876	9,104,909	59.68
1877–1900	3,432,593	22.50
1901–1912	1,097,044	7.19
1913–1924	568,686	3.73
1925–1934	590,297	3.87
1935–1939	42,363	.28
TOTAL TAKEN	14,835,892	97.25
Remaining Trust Lands	419,374	2.75

Source: Institute of NorthAmerican West

INDEX

Page references for main entries are in boldface;
page numbers for illustrative and tabular material are in italic.

healing, traditional, 539, 642, 644. *See also* medicine, traditional
Health and Human Services, U.S. Department of, *214,* 658. *See also* Health, Education, and Welfare, U.S. Department of
health care, 77, **233–237**, 454. *See also* medical facilities; medicine, traditional
appropriations for, 223, 257
availability of, 258
and Bureau of Indian Affairs, 82, 257
clinics. *See individual tribal entries*
contracted to state or local non-Indian hospitals, 256
and education, 257, 284, 488, 508
for elders, 186. *See also* elders
eligibility for, 258
federal responsibility for, 216, 658
history of, 233–237
and Indian Health Service, *214,* **256–261**
for Indians and non-Indians, compared, 258
during Kennedy-Johnson administration, 83
legislation on, 224
mental health, **330–335**
and Meriam Commission, 335
surveys of, 256
Public Health Service. *See* Public Health Service
and self-governance, 236
tribal. *See individual tribes*
and tribal governments, 654
for urban Indians, 258, 671
Health, Education, and Welfare, U.S. Department of, 212, 223, 658, 669
health foods, 156
health records, used for genealogical research, 209
Heap-of-Birds, Edgar, 102
Heard Museum, 361
heart disease, 236, 260, 284
Heck, Peter, 266
Hedgepeth, Gordon, 230
Hedgepeth family (Haliwa-Saponi), 230
Hedushka. See War dances
Hedushka Society, 459
Heidelberg College, 138
Heiltsuk band, 526
The Heirs of Columbus, 318
heirship lands, 4, 5, 27, 29, 215, 393, 440, 673
heishi (shell beads), 597
Hell Gate Treaty of 1855, 129, 283
Helsinki Accords, 580
Helushka dance. *See* War dances
Hendricks, Namee, 581
Hendries, Little Crow, 391
Hendrix (David) Committee on Civil Rights, 684
Henry, Evelyn, 68
Henry, Gordon, 399
Henry, Jeannette, 34
Hensley, Willie, 275
Henson, Lance, 319
Hen-toh (Wyandotte poet), 318
herbalism, 642, 644, 720
herbicides, pollution from, 720
Hercules Aerospace Project, 596
hereditary chiefs. *See* chiefs, hereditary
hereditary council, 279

Heritage College, 705
Heritage Park, 452
Herrera, Joe H., 420, 492
Herrera, Joseph, 518
Herrera, Reyes, 518
Herrera, Velino, 417
Herring Pond group, 683
Hesperus Peak, 379
Hethu'shka. See songs: warrior
Hethuska Society, 461. *See also* Hedushka Society
Hewisedawi band, 455
Hewitt, John N.B., 316
Heye Foundation. *See* Museum of the American Indian
Hidatsa, 633, 634. *See also* Three Affiliated Tribes
high kick competition, 616
high-steel work, 94, 278. *See also* ironworkers
higher education. *See* education, higher
Higher Education Grant Program, 237
Hightower, Rosella, 169
Hilbert, Violet Anderson, 157, 316
Hill, Daniel C., 364
Hill, David Octavius, 449
Hill, Emily, 590
Hill, Joan, 420
Hill, Norbert, 407
Hill, Norbert S., Jr., 40
Hill, Rick, 407
Hill, Sarah, 581
Hill 57, 149, 150
Hillers, John K., 449
Hinman, Samuel, 162
Hinóno'éno', 48
hiring. *See* employment
hishe (turquoise beads), 71
Hispanics, 103, 531, 532
Histia, Ray A., 489
"historic areas," 554
Historic Period (1540–1880), 470
Historic Preservation Act of 1966, 51, *53*
Historic Sites Act of 1935, *53,* 543
History of the Ojibway People, 399
Hitchiti language, 150, 575
Hoag, Enoch, Sr., 89
Hoaina society, 519
hobbyists, non-Indian, 526, 559
Hochungra, 694. *See also* Winnebago in Nebraska
Hochunkra, 695
Hodenosaunee. See Iroquois Confederation
Hoffman, Dustin, *201*
hog raising, 716
Hogan, Linda, 105, 319, 320
hogans, 55, 649
Hoh, 108, **239–240,** 527, 528, 706
Hohokam, 452, 470
Hokan language, 284, 455
Hokeah, Jack, 289, 419
Holder, Stan, 36
Holikachuk, 18. *See also* Alaskan Athabaskans
Holkoma community, 357
Holland Land Company, 663
Holley, Glenn, 594
Hollow, Norman, 63
Hollywood, portrayal of Indians by, 197–202, 484

Hollywood Reservation, 575
Holm, Tom, 343
Holmes, David, 578
Holmes, Merle, 136
Holy Family Mission, 75
Holy Rosary Mission, 300
HOME Investment Partnership Program, 245
Home Missions Council, 347
home ownership, 244
homeless Indians, 325, 350, 639, 685
Homestead Act of 1862, 133, 703
homesteading, 28, 347. *See also* Indian Homestead Act
by tribes: Chehalis, 131; Confederated Tribes of Coos, Lower Umpqua, and Siuslaw, 133; Nooksack, 393; Sauk-Suiattle, 569; Ute, 672; Yakima, 703
homicide, 25, 481, 700
Homose Kohote (Mojave chief), 356
homosexuality, 208
honor songs, 300, 479
Honor the Earth Powwow, 404
Honwisioma, Randall, 599
Hood River band, 141
Hoodsport (Twana division), 600
Hoo-hoogam Ki Museum, 56, 453
Hoop Dance, 166, 365
Hoopa Square, 719
Hoopa Valley (tribe), **248–249**, 719. *See also* Hupa
Hoopa Valley Indian Reservation, 248, 639, 719, 720
Hoopa-Yurok Settlement Act, 248, 719
Hooshowhaw (Dakota chief), 162
Hoover, Herbert, 85–86, 146, 211, 216, 218, 285
Hoover, John, 574
Hoover Commission, 211, 221
hop fields, 458, 602
HOPE (Housing for People Everywhere), 245
Hopi, **240–243**
and agriculture, 3
architecture of, 55, 242
and arts and crafts, 68, 242, 361, 417, 473, 597, 599, 631
court cases concerning, 388
and dance, 165, 243
depicted in films, 198, 201
land claims, 305, 386–389
language of, 240, 311
mortuary customs of, 630
and Navajo-Hopi land controversy, 382, **386–389**
and Navajo Reservation, 544
photographs of, 451
and religion, 241, 386, 540, 541, 630
relocation to Colorado River Indian lands, 125, 241
repatriation of remains and artifacts, 543
ritual calendar of, 243
sacred sites of, 386, 565
and Sandia Pueblo, 509
and textiles, 631
traders, 386
and traditional medicine, 643
tribal government, 241, 386
Hopi Arts and Crafts Guild, 242
Hopi Craftsmen Show, 630
Hopi Cultural Center, 241

DATE DUE
